The Macmillan Dictionary of Political Quotations

The Macmillan Dictionary of Political Quotations

Lewis D. Eigen and Jonathan P. Siegel

Macmillan Publishing Company
New York

Maxwell Macmillan Canada
Toronto

Maxwell Macmillan International
New York • Oxford • Singapore • Sydney

Macmillan Publishing Company
866 Third Avenue
New York, NY 10022

Maxwell Macmillan Canada, Inc.
1200 Eglinton Avenue East, Suite 200
Don Mills, Ontario M3C 3N1

Macmillan Publishing Company is part of the Maxwell Communication Group of Companies.

Library of Congress Cataloging-in-Publication Data

Eigen, Lewis D.

The Macmillan dictionary of political quotations / Lewis D. Eigen and Jonathan P. Siegel

p. cm.

ISBN 0-02-610650-7

1. Political science—Quotations, maxims, etc. 2. Political science—Dictionaries.

I. Siegel, Jonathan P. (Jonathan Paul), 1944.
II. Title. III. Title: Dictionary of political quotations.
PN6084.P6E54 1992
082—dc20 91-40116

CIP

Macmillan books are available at special discounts for bulk purchases for sales promotions, premiums, fund-raising, or educational use. For details, contact:

Special Sales Director
Macmillan Publishing Company
866 Third Avenue
New York, NY 10022

10 9 8 7 6 5 4 3 2 1

Printed in the United States of America

Contents

Preface

This book is a practical tool for the politician, speechwriter, journalist, political scientist, historian, student of politics, or anyone interested in politics and its effect on our daily lives.

Organization

The quotations herein are organized by content areas such as Democracy; Freedom and Liberty; Congress; Voters, Voting, and Elections; Campaigns and Conventions, and so on. Within each chapter, the quotations appear alphabetically by author. Therefore, some quotees may be represented in more than one chapter.

Political quotations do not easily lend themselves to one-dimensional categorization. A quotation might deal with both "Freedom and Liberty" and "Democracy" or both "Congress" and "Corruption and Graft." In those instances where a quotation could easily fit into two or more different chapters, we have included it in only one. While some collections of quotations that are organized by subject matter repeat the same quotation in different chapters, we decided to keep this book to a more manageable printed size. Therefore, the reader should also consult the concept index for more material relating to chapter headings that might appear in other chapters.

Selection of Quotations

What makes an excellent political quotation? The answer to this question is subjective, and depends upon the personal taste and judgment of those performing the selection. Some readers will feel that we have missed important quotations. We invite our readers to contact us with suggestions for any future revisions and editions.

The criteria we used to select quotations were terseness, the character of the speaker or writer, the use of instructive or unusual analogies and metaphors, the persuasive impact of the quotation, the clear statement of an important principle, the classic framing of issues, controversy, humor, surprise, historical parallels, institutional insight, irony, emotion, and inspiration.

Authors

Some public figures are heavily cited in this book, while others are not. This in no way implies that certain individuals were less important than their more often quoted counterparts. Some people just have a knack for turning a phrase and providing us and the world with a good quotation. But most politicians are circumspect. The candor of U.S. Senate Minority Leader Robert J. Dole or President Harry S Truman gets them quoted more often than others. U.S. Secretary of the Interior Harold Ickes was a Republican in a solidly entrenched, successful Democratic administration. His secure position allowed him to be extremely outspoken, which in turn made him very quotable.

Politicians are usually serious or even dull, so a person of wit and humor like Senator Alan Simpson is heavily covered by the media and his views get more publicity than those of his less humorous colleagues. Radicals are often quoted because of the extremity of their views, villains as a result of their villainy, and racists and bigots because of their bigotry.

Some politicians had careers that spanned several decades. Others have been tireless in promoting themselves and their views. At one point in the creation of this work, we had more quotations from Eleanor Roosevelt than from her husband, President Franklin D. Roosevelt. A politician of the first order, Mrs. Roosevelt was also a writer and journalist who produced a nationally syndicated newspaper column almost every day for years.

Bias

In compiling this work we confronted systemic biases which are, perhaps, inevitable in a work of this kind. As a result, the people quoted herein are not necessarily representative of the society at large or members of a particular party or articulators of a political thought. We have attempted to overcome some of these biases, but we were not always successful. Some of the biases we encountered include gender, the written tradition, language, religion, and race.

Gender

The number of female politicians throughout history has been small indeed. Until recently women were denied participation in most political environments, and even in professions that relate to politics, such as journalism, history, diplomacy, and philosophy. Today the situation is much better, but males still predominate in the political arena. The relative paucity of political quotations from women clearly reflects the political gender discrimination of many centuries. We have endeavored to seek out and include quotations from women who have participated in and had an influence on politics, but we acknowledge our limited success in this area.

The Written Tradition

Prior to the modern era, someone had to write something somewhere in order for us to have a quotation today. Therefore, those cultures that had strong oral but weak written traditions are underrepresented in this book. Political traditions flourished in Africa: the leaders of the dominant Zulu clan, for example, and the sophisticated cultures of Benin must have been rich in political views and quotable expressions. Unfortunately, the lack of a written tradition makes it difficult for us to learn about them and almost impossible to transmit them accurately in the form of quotations, except for some proverbs. We look forward to the day when scholars will attempt to record the political legends and stories of the oral traditions of Africa.

Language

We have included many political quotations that originated in other languages, but those originally in English were more likely to reach our attention and be included in this work. We have tried nonetheless to represent a broad range of political views and styles in this work.

Religion

The bulk of this material comes from Judeo-Christian cultures, sources, and political traditions. There is still a paucity of politically relevant quotations reflecting many of the world's religious traditions, not because these cultures lack material on the subject, but because most of the material is not easily accessible in our libraries, and it is not quoted in our newspapers, journals, radio, or television.

Race

African-Americans did not enter the mainstream of American politics until relatively recent times, and even now are not proportionally represented as politicians, journalists, diplomats, or scholars. The strong African-American oral tradition is only available to us in relatively recent sound recordings and memoirs. To the extent that we have been able to include some of this material, we have.

Other ethnic minorities are also underrepresented, reflecting historical discrimination patterns and consequent political underrepresentation. We have tried to include quotations from American Indians, both early and modern. Hispanic material is also underrepresented, reflecting the language issue as well. But the reader will note many Canadian quotations, because Canadians are more frequently quoted in our newspapers and journals than are Mexican or Central American or South American politicians.

We invite all our readers to contact us with suggestions for political quotations from other countries and cultures to include in future editions of this book.

Balance

While we typically include quotations representing many different points of view, we have made no serious attempt to provide balance on issues. If, on a particular issue, one side was more witty, pithy, urbane, and widely published, that is the way it appears in this book. If you seek more knowledge of the personalities or the issues, please go beyond this volume and consult other publications.

Context

All quotations are, to a certain extent, taken out of context. Most politicians' views on any subject are far more complex and involved than can be expressed in a single quotation, or even many. Also, most politicians modify their political views and philosophy over time, and quotations from one point in a politician's career may contradict views held at another time. Further, political expediency often motivates politicians to say things that they do not necessarily believe and may repudiate at some later point in their careers. Many politicians have had genuine changes of heart and mind. Before the predominance of electronic media, and when newspaper coverage of campaigns was not as intense as in modern times, a politician could change or reverse a position within a matter of days to appeal to different and opposing constituencies. Although it is more difficult to get away with today, this practice still occurs.

We therefore urge the reader not to judge a particular politician's position and philosophy from a single quotation or even a group of quotations. Rather, consult biographies and studies of the politician, or the politician's own written work. We have made no effort whatsoever to select the quotations of a particular public figure to be a representative sample of his or her views. We simply attempted to get the best and most interesting quotations in the ninety-nine categories of this book. Of particular interest are quotations that seem to be out of character. This type of quotation was often chosen to demonstrate the inconsistency of politicians, the complexity of public leadership, the necessities and hypocrisies of politics, and the multi-faceted dimension of many figures whom popular condensed history has often characterized as unidimensional saints, sinners, or mediocrities.

Originality and Cross-References

Politicians often quote other politicians, frequently to associate themselves and their views with past popular and heroic leaders. When this occurs, the politician sometimes cites the originator. On other occasions he or she does not. Occasionally the use of an earlier quotation is not even conscious. The idea being expressed is in the mind of the politician (or speechwriter) in a form that has been used before.

Where we have observed politicians paraphrasing or using quotations from others, we have added a statement to that effect. When there was a paraphrase or an expression of the same idea in different language, we have attempted to cross-reference the quotations.

Originality is not something to which we can always attest. Our citation is to the earliest expression of the quotation that we have been able to find. While often the person cited did originate the material, there are doubtless many instances in which he or she did not. The person may have been the first to write it down or the first person using that phrase who was quoted by a journalist or another politician. We often have no practical way to establish the originality of a quotation; sometimes we know only that a particular person said it on a particular date. As we are constantly surprised to find even earlier versions and "original" quotations, we welcome readers informing us of such precedents.

We have followed the practice of attributing the quotation to the politician even in those instances where we know that the quotation originated with an assistant or a speechwriter. It is the politician who finally made the decision to speak or release the statement, whose political fortunes would stand or fall as a result, and who took the final "responsibility" for the material and the ideas. In some cases where a phrase became particularly meaningful, and the origin was known to us, we have added this information to the commentary.

Editorial Style

Citations and Sources

The New York Times is unquestionably the greatest American source and record of political writings and utterances. The breadth, depth, and accuracy of its coverage of American and world politics for more than a century, its availability on microfilm and computer in libraries throughout the country, make it the newspaper of American record. It has been one of our primary sources. Another is *The Washington Post*, in which national and international politics are local news. Frequently, we have cited *The New York Times* as the source for a quotation when the material appeared in other newspapers as well. The reason for this is the greater accessibility of back issues of *The New York Times*. For the reader who wants to obtain more of the context of the quotation, *The New York Times* is the most practical tool, and therefore we have selected it where there was a choice.

There are citations for all but a very few of the more than twelve thousand quotations in this book. Many are secondary sources. To those readers who require primary sources for their scholarship, we are pleased that we have put you on the right track by citing a secondary source. If you find a primary source that we have not indicated, please let us know. For the majority of readers, politicians, speechwriters, journalists, and political junkies, we trust that our sometimes secondary sources are adequate for your needs.

In some cases the only citation is a date, because we could not determine whether the person was giving a speech, engaging in debate, making a remark to an associate, or giving a statement to the press. We have followed the policy of providing the reader with whatever information we had, however thorough or sparse. The alternatives would have been to provide the reader with less information, in many cases, than we actually had, or to research every quotation back to its primary source. The former seemed senseless to us, and the latter was simply impractical.

Where the title of a book or article appears in the citation with no author, the quotee is the author of that work.

Accuracy

We have tried to present the quotations herein accurately. However, we are not always certain we have succeeded. First, there is the problem of secondary sources. These may or may not have correctly quoted an individual. This is particularly true where quotations have been attributed or where they originated in others' reminiscences. Occasionally, the quotation may have been through many iterations before we came across it. Further, we have taken much material from radio and television news reports, public affairs shows, and C-SPAN, and aural precision is not as accurate as written. Nonetheless, we have made a good-faith effort to reproduce the quotations as accurately as possible. We did not check the accuracy of the quotation by contacting the individual and verifying the wording of the quotation, but we were scrupulous in attempting to capture the sense of the quotation.

Sometimes politicians have denied saying what was attributed to them. This is not uncommon in politics, where it may serve another politician's interest to quote or misquote someone. Where we know that a quotee has denied the accuracy of the quotation, we have so stated in the commentary. However, there may be denials we are unaware of. We invite any who believe there are any inaccuracies in the material herein to contact us through the publisher so that we may consider this information for future editions.

Commentary

Throughout this work we have added our own brief commentary in brackets [ ], to provide a context for those quotations that do not stand on their own without some historical or factual background. In other cases we have added cross-references to other similar or contrasting quotations.

Titles

Most politicians have held different positions and offices during their careers. Listing all those roles would be impractical. Therefore, as a general rule, we cite only the highest political roles an individual has attained, and the party or parties with which they were affiliated during those terms. Presidents of the United States are cited only as President. Thus, John F. Kennedy is cited as 35th President of the United States (D-MA), but not as "U.S. Senator" or "U.S. Congressman." Most U.S. Senators have also been members of the House of Representatives, and many served in state legislatures as well. These latter are not given, but governorships and congressional positions are cited, along with political party or parties. Many of the quotations were made by the individual while he or she served in a capacity other than the one listed in the citation. When this is important to the context of the quotation, we mention this fact in the commentary.

Also, many of the best quotations from an individual were produced after he or she had retired from office. Then, politicians can afford to be more candid and less prudent. We still list the highest political titles with the quotation, and the reader should not necessarily infer that the quotation was made when the individual held that title.

Many of the best political quotations were never made by politicians, but by members of other professions. Journalists, writers, historians, political scientists, comedians, actors, and others have produced some of the most interesting political quotations. We have included many of these with the citation of the profession of the person quoted.

In some cases the person quoted is the leader of or representative of an important nongovernmental organization. In these cases, we cite the organization, such as American Civil Liberties Union, National Association for the Advancement of Colored People, John Birch Society.

Legislation, platforms, charters, and constitutions are almost always group processes. And these documents are often revised countless times, often by many different hands. When we have quoted from one of these, we usually cite the institutional source, such as "Massachusetts Colonial Legislature" or "South Carolina Constitution," with the date. Where a single individual is known to have drafted the quotation and was strongly associated with its passage in relatively unedited form, we have cited the document, such as in the case of the *Declaration of Independence*, and Thomas Jefferson. We have followed a similar practice with newspaper and magazine editorials from which we have drawn noteworthy quotations. In these cases we cite the publication as the quotee.

Disgrace, Scandal, and Criminality

Some politicians were involved in scandal and even criminal activity at some point in their careers. There are some who believe that this information should be included with the citation: "Evan Mecham, Impeached Governor of Arizona," "Richard M. Nixon, Resigned President, Pardoned for Criminal Activities," or "Mario Biaggi, Criminally Convicted U.S. Congressman." We decided not to include in our citations the foibles, disgraces, and convictions of quoted individuals. These are readily available to any serious student, biographer, and historian. However, where the particular quotation selected involved scandal or criminal activity or was ironic in the light of that activity, we have mentioned it in our commentary.

Dates of Birth and Death

We have provided the years of birth and death for all deceased quotees. In some cases one or both dates is approximate. In other cases we knew the quotee to be dead, but could not obtain the specific information. In a few cases only the century is provided. Life, after all, is transitory, and quotees who are alive today may be dead tomorrow. At any future time of reading, a quotee who was alive at the time of the publication of this book may have passed away since. Future editions of this work will note those passings.

Indexing

Author Index

The authors of the quotations are listed alphabetically by last name, and their quotations are referenced by chapter number and quotation number—not page number.

Concept Index

Each quotation is indexed by a set of conceptual terms by which the reader will be able to locate relevant material, regardless of the symbolic or metaphorical level of the quotation. There are more than ten thousand terms utilized. If you do not find the exact term you are looking for in the index, try a synonym.

Acknowledgments

This work could never have been produced without the help of many whose assistance is so gratefully acknowledged. To the many relatives, friends, colleagues and acquaintances who referred quotations for our consideration, we are grateful. To the quotees themselves, whose wit, perspicacity, and wisdom are herein reflected, we and civilization owe an abiding intellectual debt.

Mr. David McKinney of the University of Virginia was particularly helpful in researching many of the citations herein, and his thorough work is gratefully acknowledged.

To produce this material we had to consult thousands of books, and to the authors, editors, and compilers of these we are appreciative. But particular thanks must go to the libraries. Without access to these institutions this work would have been impossible. In this regard we are particularly grateful to:

- The Montgomery County, MD, Public Library System
- The University of California Library System
- The Toronto, Canada, Public Library System
- The University of Maryland Library System
- The Library of Congress
- The New York City Public Library System
- The Columbia University Library
- The University of Virginia Library

We would also like to express our appreciation to our research assistants and the Macmillan editorial staff, including Natalie Chapman, Nancy Cooperman, and Philip Turner.

L.D.E.
J.P.S.

Chapter 1

Abortion

1. ABORTION: THE ULTIMATE CHILD ABUSE
ABORTION IS MURDER
Signs at antiabortion rally, Washington, DC, Apr. 28, 1990.

2. Do all have the freedom of conscience except the King?
Baudouin I, King of Belgium. A Roman Catholic, on being required by the constitution to sign abortion legislation passed by his country's parliament. Quoted in *The New York Times*, Apr. 8, 1990.

3. This right of privacy, whether it be founded in the Fourteenth Amendment's concept of personal liberty and restrictions upon state action, as we feel it is, or, as the District Court determined, in the Ninth Amendment's reservation of rights to the people, is broad enough to encompass a woman's decision whether or not to terminate her pregnancy.
Harry A. Blackmun, U.S. Supreme Court Justice. *Roe* v. *Wade*, 1973.

4. Few decisions are more personal and intimate, more properly private, or more basic to individual dignity and autonomy than a woman's decision .... whether to end her pregnancy. A woman's right to make that choice freely is fundamental.
Harry A. Blackmun. *Thornburgh* v. *American College of Obstetricians and Gynecologists*, 1986.

5. Absolutely antichoice, antiabortion, except where the political life of the candidate may be in danger.
Herbert Block (Herblock), American political cartoonist. Cartoon caption, *The New York Times*, Dec. 31, 1989.

6. The main reason Italian women resort to abortion is the Catholic insistence that no birth control information be distributed.
Margherita Bonivar, Member of Parliament, Italy. Quoted in *The New York Times*, Feb. 19, 1989.

7. The entire matter of abortion is private and personal.
Barbara Boxer, U.S. Congresswoman (D-CA). Quoted in *The Washington Post*, Oct. 28, 1989.

8. The killing of the unborn is crazy.
Edmund G. (Jerry) Brown, Jr., Governor of California (D). Quoted in *Time*, Feb. 27, 1989.

9. He no play-a da game. He no make-a da rules.
Earl L. Butz, U.S. Secretary of Agriculture (R). Comment on the Pope's strictures against contraception, 1974.

10. I've always had both sides mad at me on this issue *[abortion]*.
Bill Clinton, 42nd President of the United States (D-AR). Remark, National Governors' Conference, Chicago, IL, July 30, 1989.

11. No one should tell a woman she has to bear an unwanted child.
Walter Cronkite, American TV journalist. Quoted in *Newsweek*, Dec. 5, 1988.

12. Whenever I hear people discussing birth control, I always remember that I was the fifth.
Clarence S. Darrow (1857-1937), American attorney and writer. Quoted in Fred Metcalf, *The Penguin Dictionary of Modern Humorous Quotations*, 1986.

13. I have set before you life and death, blessing and curse; therefore choose life, that you and your offspring may live.
(Verse often cited by antiabortion activists.)
Old Testament, *Deuteronomy* 30:19.

14. It is so very sad to see that political arguments can totally obscure the science of a drug. It's hard to see how to proceed if the release of such a vital drug *[RU 486]* can, and will, be held hostage to a minority of the American public.
Mark I. Evans, Director of Reproductive Genetics, Hutzel Hospital, Detroit, MI; Ethics Committee, American College of Obstetricians and Gynecologists. Quoted in *The Washington Post*, Oct. 30, 1988.

15. What is this life by which you, who exist still incomplete, count for more than I, who exist com-

plete already? What is this respect for you that removes respect for me? What is this right of yours to exist that takes no account of my right to exist?

Oriana Fallaci, Italian journalist. *Letter to a Child Never Born*, 1975.

16. Choice is a uniquely female issue. We don't share the same reproductive systems.

Dianne Feinstein, Mayor of San Francisco, CA (D). Interview, ABC, *This Week*, June 10, 1990.

17. Government should regulate the S&L's. Government should not regulate a woman's body.

Dianne Feinstein. Gubernatorial campaign speech, Oct. 1990.

18. We don't want a country populated by children feeding themselves from garbage dumps.

Alberto Fujimori, President of Peru. In support of birth control programs over church opposition. Statement to reporters, Nov. 1990.

19. It is not because woman is lacking in responsibility, but because she has too much of the latter that she demands to know how to prevent conception.

Emma Goldman (1869-1940), American anarchist. "The Social Aspects of Birth Control," *Mother Earth*, Apr. 1916.

20. I'm opposed to abortion because I happen to believe that life deserves the protection of society.

Ella Grasso (1919-1981), Governor of Connecticut and U.S. Congresswoman (R). Quoted in *Ms.*, Oct. 1974.

21. A statute making it a criminal offense for married couples to use contraceptives is an intolerable invasion of privacy in the conduct of the most intimate concerns of an individual's private life.

John Marshall Harlan (1899-1971), U.S. Supreme Court Justice. *Poe* v. *Ullman*, 1961.

22. I'm absolutely certain I'm right, and nobody's going to change my mind.

Jesse Helms, U.S. Senator (R-NC). On his opposition to abortion. Quoted in *Time*, May 30, 1988.

23. The issue has come to symbolize what role women are going to play in American society. It's about power as much as anything else.

Nancy Lee Johnson, U.S. Congresswoman (R-CT). Quoted in *The Chicago Tribune*, Nov. 19, 1989.

24. It would be a great tragedy if people decided who to vote for just on this issue *[abortion]*, because I think we'd be electing some very strange people.

Thomas H. Kean, Governor of New Jersey (R). Quoted in *The New York Times*, July 31, 1989.

25. If men could get pregnant, abortion would be a sacrament.

Florynce R. Kennedy, American feminist and TV talk-show host. "Institutionalized Oppression vs. the Female," *Sisterhood Is Powerful*, 1970.

26. I'm opposed to it *[abortion]*. But I also took an oath to uphold the law of the land.

C. Everett Koop, U.S. Surgeon General. Remark on abortion, Mar. 1989.

27. I regret, Mr. President, that in spite of a diligent review on the part of many in the Public Health Service and in the private sector, the scientific studies do not provide conclusive data about the health effects of abortion on women.

C. Everett Koop. Memorandum to Pres. George Bush, Mar. 1989.

28. Your body is a battleground.

Barbara Kruger, American artist. Photo montage for the 1989 abortion rights march, Washington, DC, Apr. 9, 1989.

29. It's not an issue you can waffle on.

Madeleine M. Kunin, Governor of Vermont (D). Quoted in *The New York Times*, July 31, 1989.

30. The difference between killing unborn children and killing your neighbor may only be a distinction in time.

Otto Lang, Minister of Justice, Canada. Quoted in *The Toronto Star*, Jan. 25, 1975.

31. Section 251 *[restricting abortion]* of the Criminal Code would be immediately repealed if we could magically turn on the light in the House of Commons to see how many Members of Parliament, in one way or another, have been personally connected with abortion – for their wives, their daughters, or mistresses.

Stuart Leggatt, Member of Parliament, Canada. Speech, Ottowa. Quoted in Pelrine, *Morgentaler: The Doctor Who Couldn't Turn Away*, 1979.

32. It is terrible to reduce such an important social issue to this, but the truth is that prenatal care delivery and the first year of life on welfare costs taxpayers $4,000 a year compared with $250 for an abortion.

Kate Michelman, Executive Director, National Abortion Rights Action League. Quoted in *The New York Times*, Nov. 27, 1988.

33. If you're out of touch with the pro-choice majority, you're out of office.

Kate Michelman. Quoted in *The Wall Street Journal*, June 27, 1990.

34. No public official, no congressman, has the right to tell a woman what decision she must make, and no congressman has the wisdom to dictate what is best for her.
James P. Moran, Jr., U.S. Congressman (D-VA). Quoted in *The Washington Times*, Aug. 23, 1990.

35. Every child a wanted child, every mother a willing mother.
Henry Morgentaler, Canadian physician and abortion pioneer. *Abortion and Contraception*, 1982.

36. It's a disservice to our political system if we allow it *[abortion]* to be the test of every candidate.
Kay Orr, Governor of Kansas (R). Remark, National Governors' Conference, Chicago, IL, July 30, 1989.

37. If we *[Republicans]* happen to be in the last week of Oct. ... in an election battle where abortion is the main issue, we will just get the bejabbers kicked out of us.
Robert W. Packwood, U.S. Senator (R-OR). Quoted in *The Chicago Tribune*, Nov. 22, 1989.

38. Women who have had an abortion need to speak up.
Joy Picus, City Councilwoman, Los Angeles, CA. Quoted in *Ms.*, Apr. 1989.

39. It is horrible to listen to men in black togas having discussions about your morals ... your feelings, your womb.
Gigliola Pierobon, Italian writer. *Ms.*, Oct. 1973.

40. Who we choose in the voting booth could determine whether we will be permitted to choose at home.
Anna Quindlen, American journalist and columnist. *The New York Times*, Jan. 28, 1990.

41. What we're doing is committing racial suicide.
Pat Robertson, American televangelist, and candidate for Republican presidential nomination. Quoted in *Newsweek*, Oct. 20, 1986.

42. Common sense, decency and a respect for women.
Charles E. Roemer III, U.S. Congressman and Governor of Louisiana (D). Response when asked why he had vetoed a bill outlawing abortion. Quoted in *Newsweek*, Aug. 6, 1990.

43. Women will vote these issues if you ask them. Why is it that gun owners are so politically powerful? There are more uterus owners than gun owners.
Polly Rothstein, Director, N.Y. Coalition for Legal Abortion. Quoted in *Newsweek*, July 17, 1989.

44. I am sick and tired of the government protecting my womb from underproduction and my brain from overproduction.
Laura Sabia, Canadian writer. Interview, Canadian radio, *Let's Discuss It*, Mar. 28, 1982.

45. Abortion is to the Republican party what race used to be to the Democrats. Every time the issue comes up it tears the party apart.
William Schneider, political analyst, American Enterprise Institute. ABC, *It's Your Business*, Nov. 19, 1989.

46. What is liberty if you can't control your own bedroom?
Patricia R. Schroeder, U.S. Congresswoman (D-CO). Interview, ABC, *This Week*, July 9, 1989.

47. We're not killing anyone. We're saving women's lives.
Eleanor Smeal, President, National Organization for Women. Speech, abortion rights march, Washington, DC, Apr. 9, 1989.

48. The government cannot control the abortion issue.
Arlen Spector, U.S. Senator (R-PA). Interview, CBS, *Face the Nation*, July 22, 1990.

49. Abortion is the most divisive issue since slavery.
Arlen Spector. Interview, PBS, *MacNeil-Lehrer News Hour*, Sept. 13, 1991.

50. There is simply no credible foundation for the proposition that abortion is a fundamental right.
Kenneth W. Starr, U.S. Solicitor General. Quoted in *The New York Times*, Nov. 24, 1989.

51. It is very little to me to have the right to vote, to own property, etc., if I may not keep my body, and its uses, in my absolute right.
Lucy Stone (1818-1893), founder, National American Woman Suffrage Association, and founder, *Women's Journal*. Letter to Antoinette Brown, 1855.

52. The practice of abortion is as old as pregnancy itself ... and in the matter of abortion the human rights of the mother with her family must take precedence over the survival of a few weeks' old foetus without sense or sensibility.
Edith Summerskill (1901-1980), Member of Parliament, Great Britain. *A Woman's World*, 1967.

53. The greatest destroyer of peace is abortion because if a mother can kill her own child, what is left for me to kill you and you to kill me? There is nothing between.

Mother Teresa, Nobel Laureate in Peace (India). Nobel address, 1979.

54. To give society – especially a male-dominated society – the power to sentence women to childbearing against their will is to delegate to some a sweeping and unaccountable authority over the lives of others.

Laurence Tribe, Tyler Professor of Constitutional Law, Harvard University, Cambridge, MA. *American Constitutional Law*, 1988.

Chapter 2

Agriculture and Farming

1. SOCIALISM – You have two cows, you give one to your neighbor
COMMUNISM – You have two cows, the government takes them both and gives you the milk
FASCISM – You have two cows, the government takes both and sells you the milk
NAZISM – You have two cows, the government takes both and shoots you
CAPITALISM – You have two cows, you sell one and buy a bull
TRADE UNIONISM – You have two cows, they take them from you, shoot one, milk the other, and throw the milk away
MORAL: Don't have anything to do with cows. They only bring you trouble.
Anonymous.

2. CRIME DOESN'T PAY, BUT NEITHER DOES FARMING
Bumper sticker in West Virginia, 1986.

3. We don't pay miners not to mine, and we shouldn't pay farmers not to farm.
Richard K. Armey, U.S. Congressman (R-TX). *The Washington Post*, July 24, 1990.

4. We all flourish or decline with the farmer.
Bernard M. Baruch (1870-1965), Chairman, War Industries Board, and U.S. Delegate to U. N. Atomic Energy Commission. Quoted in Davis, *On Agricultural Policy*, 1956.

5. The farmer may often have suffered from excessive interest and grasping creditors; but it was no less frequently the avarice of the lender that got him into trouble than the fact that he was too sanguine and too prone to believe that he could safely go into debt, on the assumption that crops and prices in the future would equal those in the present.
Arthur F. Bentley, American economist. *The Condition of the Western Farmer as Illustrated by the Economic History of a Nebraska Township*, 1893.

6. The great cities rest upon our broad and fertile prairies.... Burn down your cities and leave our farms, and your cities will spring up again as if by magic; but destroy our farms and the grass will grow in the streets of every city in the country.
William Jennings Bryan (1860-1925), U.S. Secretary of State (D). "Cross of Gold" speech, Democratic National Convention, Chicago, IL, July 8, 1896.

7. *[Food is a]* tool in the kit of American diplomacy.
Earl L. Butz, U.S. Secretary of Agriculture (R). Quoted in *The New York Times*, Nov. 17, 1974.

8. The only thing I'd like to see him *[Jimmy Carter]* do when he gets to the White House is appoint a working farmer as secretary of agriculture, that's all.
Billy Carter (1937-1988), President Jimmy Carter's brother. Rifkin and Howard, *Redneck Power: The Wit and Wisdom of Billy Carter*, 1977.

9. It has been attested by all experience that agriculture tends to discouragement and decadence whenever the predominant interests of the country turn to manufacture and trade.
Calvin Coolidge (1872-1933), 30th President of the United States (R-MA). 1925.

10. The only way to keep food prices down is to keep them *[farmers]* down on the farm after they've seen the parity.
Michael V. DiSalle (1908-1981), Governor of Ohio (D) and Director, U.S. Office of Price Stabilization. Statement, Apr. 21, 1973.

11. Marxism has not only failed to promote human freedom. It has failed to produce food.
John Dos Passos (1896-1970), American writer. *Occasions and Protests*, 1964.

12. Farming looks mighty easy when your plow is a pencil and you're a thousand miles from the corn field.

Dwight D. Eisenhower (1890-1969), 34th President of the United States (R-KS). Speech, Sept. 11, 1956.

13. The first farmer was the first man, and all historic nobility rests on possession and use of land.
Ralph Waldo Emerson (1803-1882), American writer. "Farming," *Society and Solitude*, 1870.

14. Pray for rain.
Marlin Fitzwater, White House spokesman (R). In response to reporters' queries regarding the administration's policy on dealing with the drought, June 1988.

15. The cultivation of the earth, as the primary and most certain source of national supply ... has intrinsically a strong claim to pre-eminence over every other kind of industry.
Alexander Hamilton (1755-1804), Member, Continental Congress and Constitutional Convention, and U.S. Secretary of the Treasury (Federalist-NY). *Report on Manufactures*, Dec. 5, 1791.

16. Middlemen are paying farmers less, charging consumers more and pocketing the difference.... For the first time in history consumers have gotten soaked by a drought.
Jim Hightower, Texas Agriculture Commissioner. Quoted on ABC, *Nightline*, July 26, 1988.

17. Whole towns, communities, and forms of agriculture with their homes, schools, and churches have been built up under this system of protection *[tariffs]*. The grass will grow in a hundred cities, a thousand towns; the weeds will overrun millions of farms if that protection is taken away.
Herbert Hoover (1874-1964), 31st President of the United States (R-IA). Speech, Madison Square Garden, New York City, Oct. 31, 1932.

18. The pen is *not* mightier than the sword; and mightier than either, and more necessary, is the hoe.
Edgar Watson Howe (1853-1937), American editor and writer. *Ventures in Common Sense*, 1919.

19. The earth is given as a common stock for man to labour and live on.... The small land holders are the most precious part of a state.
Thomas Jefferson (1743-1826), 3rd President of the United States (Democratic Republican-VA). Letter to the Rev. James Madison, Oct. 28, 1785.

20. Were we directed from Washington when to sow, and when to reap, we should soon want bread.
Thomas Jefferson. 1821.

21. The greatest service which can be rendered any country is to add a useful plant to its culture.
Thomas Jefferson. Quoted in Richard Hofstadter, *The American Political Tradition*, 1948.

22. Farmers are farmers in the first place because they have the deep-seated instinct to raise crops, not to cut them back, not to leave the land unproductive.
Lyndon B. Johnson (1908-1973), 36th President of the United States (D-TX). Campaign speech, Oct. 7, 1964.

23. We need fewer farmers.
David K. Karnes, U.S. Senator (R-NE). Quoted in *The Washington Post*, Oct. 23, 1988.

24. Farmers, they always talk about getting the government off their backs, but they feel pretty good when they get those *[government subsidy]* checks.
David K. Karnes. *Ibid.*

25. The American farmer is the only man in our economy who buys everything he buys at retail, sells everything he sells at wholesale, and pays the freight both ways.
John F. Kennedy (1917-1963), 35th President of the United States (D-MA). Campaign speech, Des Moines, IA, Sept. 22, 1960.

26. What you farmers need to do is raise less corn and more hell.
Mary Elisabeth Lease (1853-1933), American agrarian reformer and populist. Quoted in William E. Connelley, *History of Kansas: State and People*, 1928.

27. Because he was unorganized, the farmer has been made the financial shock absorber.... He fed the nation and he lost his home.
William Lemke (1878-1943), U.S. Congressman (R and Nonpartisan-ND). Letter to Ida Botz, Mar. 6, 1936.

28. Population must increase rapidly, more rapidly than in former times, and ere long the most valuable of all arts will be the art of deriving a comfortable subsistence from the smallest area of soil.
Abraham Lincoln (1809-1865), 16th President of the United States (R-IL). Speech, Milwaukee, WI, Sept. 30, 1859.

29. Agriculture, confessedly the largest interest in the nation, has not a department or a bureau, but a clerkship only, assigned to it in the government.... I venture the opinion that an agricultural and statistical bureau might profitably be organized.

Abraham Lincoln. 1st annual message to Congress, Dec. 3, 1861.

30. Man's true vocation is to cultivate the ground.
Napoléon I (1769-1821), military leader and Emperor of France. *Maxims*.

31. Let us change the merchant's yardstick and the Canaanitish scales for spade and plow!
Leo Pinsker (1821-1891), Russian physician and Zionist. Speech, Katowice, Poland, 1886.

32. Corn is the sinews of war.
François Rabelais (1495-1553), French writer. *Works*, I, xlvi.

33. We saw farms go on the auction block while we bought food from foreign countries. Well, that's wrong.
Ann Richards, Governor of Texas (D). Keynote address, Democratic National Convention, Atlanta, GA, July 18, 1988.

34. The chief problem of the low-income farmers is poverty.
Nelson A. Rockefeller (1908-1979), Governor of New York and Vice President of the United States (R). Speech, Minneapolis, MN, Jan. 7, 1960.

35. Private farmers will never be able to feed anyone.
Valery Romanov, Communist Party Agriculture Secretary, Sverdlovsk, U.S.S.R. Quoted in *The Washington Post*, Dec. 23, 1990.

36. If the farmer starves today we will all starve tomorrow.
Franklin D. Roosevelt (1882-1945), 32nd President of the United States (D-NY). Quoted in *The New York Times*, Dec. 11, 1929.

37. The American farmer, living on his own land, remains our ideal of self-reliance and spiritual balance – the source from which the reservoirs of the nation's strength are constantly renewed.
Franklin D. Roosevelt. Speech, 1933.

38. The most opulent nations, indeed, generally excel all their neighbors in agriculture as well as manufactures; but they are commonly more distinguished by their superiority in the latter than in the former.
Adam Smith (1723-1790), Scottish political economist. *The Wealth of Nations*, 1776.

39. You ask me to plow the ground. Shall I take a knife and tear my mother's skin?
Smohalla (1815?-1907), American Indian prophet and leader, Wanapum tribe. Statement to Indian agent, 1870's. Quoted in Ruby and Brown, *Half-Sun on the Columbia*, 1965.

40. And he gave it for his opinion, that whoever could make two ears of corn or two blades of grass to grow upon a spot of ground where only one grew before, would deserve better of mankind, and do more essential service to his country than the whole race of politicians put together.
Jonathan Swift (1667-1745), Irish clergyman and satirist. *Gulliver's Travels. Voyage to Brobdingnag*, 1726.

41. I wonder how many times you have to be hit on the head before you find out who's hitting you.
Harry S Truman (1884-1972), 33rd President of the United States (D-MO). Campaign speech to farmers about Republican policies, 1948.

42. This congress has already put a pitchfork in the back of the farmers.
Harry S Truman. Campaign speech, 1948.

43. Congress shall legislate that there will be assurance of production at a profit for the farmer.
Union Party Platform, 1936.

44. Let us never forget that the cultivation of the earth is the most important labor of man.... When tillage begins, other arts follow. The farmers, therefore, are the founders of human civilization.
Daniel Webster (1782-1852), U.S. Congressman (Federalist-NH and MA), U.S. Senator (Federalist and Whig-MA), and U.S. Secretary of State. Speech in Congress, Jan. 13, 1840.

45. Those agrarian movements too often appealed to the ne'er-do-wells, the misfits – farmers who had failed, lawyers and doctors who were not orthodox, teachers who could not make the grade, and neurotics full of hates and ebullient, evanescent enthusiasms.
William Allen White (1868-1944), American writer and editor. *Autobiography*, 1946.

46. The real issue with the ADC *[Federal Animal Damage Control]* program is public money used to kill public wildlife, often on public land, with no public input – all to benefit a handful of heavily subsidized ranchers and farmers.
Thomas Woods, Chairman, Arizona Game and Fish Commission. Quoted in *U.S. News & World Report*, Feb. 5, 1990.

Chapter 3

Alcohol, Tobacco, and Drugs

1. ALL NATIONS WELCOME EXCEPT CARRY

Sign in a saloon, Omaha, NE, referring to temperance agitator Carry Nation. 1900.

2. Who do we want? We want *[Al]* Smith.
What do we want? We want beer.

Chant at the Democratic National Convention, Chicago, IL, 1932.

3. Death for drug traffickers.

Stamped on entry permits in Malaysia, 1990.

4. *Plata o plomo.* (Silver or lead *[i.e. bribery or assassination]*).

Threat to local officials from Colombian drug dealers, to induce them into taking bribes. 1989.

5. It was when the upper middle class was threatened.... Until then nobody really cared about the war on drugs.

James G. Abourezk, U.S. Congressman and U.S. Senator (D-SD). Interview, WAMU-FM, *The Diane Rehm Show*, Nov. 20, 1989.

6. How many murders, suicides, robberies, criminal assaults, holdups, burglaries, and deeds of maniacal insanity it *[marijuana]* causes each year ... can only be conjectured.

Harry J. Anslinger (1892-1975), U.S. Commissioner of Narcotics. 1937.

7. Continuous use *[of marijuana]* leads directly to the insane asylum.

Harry J. Anslinger. 1938.

8. Liquor traffic is un-American, pro-German, crime-procuring, food-wasting, youth-corrupting, home-wrecking, treasonable.

Anti-Saloon League. Statement, 1918.

9. What could be more tragic than someone leaving a reception at the governor's mansion and killing someone while driving drunk?

John Ashcroft, Governor of Missouri (R). Explanation for allowing no alcohol to be served at official receptions. Speech, Dec. 4, 1990.

10. One reason I don't drink is that I want to know when I am having a good time.

Nancy Astor (1879-1964), American-born Mayor of Plymouth, England, and Member of Parliament (Liberal). Attributed.

11. We're becoming drug courts.

Edward R. Becker, Federal Judge. Quoted in *The New York Times*, Dec. 29, 1989.

12. I do not say a dollar a day is enough to support a working man, but it is enough to support a man. Not enough to support a man and five children if a man insists on smoking and drinking beer.

Henry Ward Beecher (1813-1887), American clergyman and writer. Quoted in *Harper's Weekly*, May 8, 1886.

13. We are very grateful for what Western society has brought us ... but we owe you no gratitude for the traffic of cocaine which is a foreign enterprise.... This problem is the responsibility of the consumer countries rather than the producing countries.

Fernando Belaunde, President of Peru. Quoted in Gabrial G. Nahas, *Cocaine: The Great White Plague*.

14. You've got to exact some cost from the people who are sending these drugs into our country.

William J. Bennett, Director, Office of National Drug Control Policy, and U.S. Secretary of Education (R). Defense of military or police drug interdiction action in foreign countries. Quoted on NBC, *Meet the Press*, Mar. 19, 1989.

15. Drugs are wrong. They burn out your brain and they sear your soul.

William J. Bennett. *Ibid.*

16. Professional sports has to be part of the solution *[to the drug problem]*. The question I put to the group *[of sports leaders]* is, "While we are pressing very hard on schools and others to have tough policies, it seems only right and reasonable that professional sports have these kind of standards."
William J. Bennett. Speech to professional sports leaders, Washington, DC, May 17, 1989.

17. It's hard to fight the war when you've got to debate the worthiness of fighting it.
William J. Bennett. On legalizing drugs. Interview, CNN, *Evans & Novak*, Dec. 16, 1989.

18. Having smoked a marijuana joint in 1968 is no big deal.
William J. Bennett. Quoted on PBS, *American Interests*, Apr. 28, 1990.

19. Drug education is the only vaccine we have against the danger of drug abuse of our children.
Joseph R. Biden, Jr., U.S. Senator (D-DE). Sept. 5, 1989.

20. The temperance movement must include all poisonous substances which create or excite unnatural appetite, and international prohibition is the goal.
Henry W. Blair (1834-1920), U.S. Congressman (R-NH), U.S. Senator, and U.S. Envoy Extraordinary to China. Letter to Wilber F. Crafts, 1905.

21. It gives a new meaning to the expression, "High Court."
James Brady, White House Press Secretary (R). On hearing that U.S. Supreme Court nominee Douglas Ginsburg admitted smoking marijuana while in school. *Newsweek*, Nov. 16, 1987.

22. Liquor drinking is not a wrong; but excessive drinking is.
Louis D. Brandeis (1856-1941), U.S. Supreme Court Justice. Quoted in Alpheus T. Mason, *Brandeis: A Free Man's Life*, 1946.

23. We know the war on drugs will not be won in Washington, DC. When the United States of America decides it wants to do something and the people pull together, amazing things can be done.
Terry Branstad, Governor of Iowa (R). Interview, C-SPAN, Sept. 4, 1989.

24. If you want to get high, meditate.
Edmund G. (Jerry) Brown, Jr., Governor of California (D). *Thoughts*, 1976.

25. Officers can't use drugs. The citizens of this city must have a feel – knowledge – that their police officers are drug free.
Lee Brown, Police Commissioner, New York City. Interview, NBC, Jan. 28, 1990.

26. Now that I'm gone, I tell you: Don't smoke! Whatever you do, just don't smoke!
Yul Brynner (1915-1986), American actor. TV commercial made just before his death from lung cancer, 1986.

27. Pints *[of liquor]* are very inconvenient in the house *[the White House]* as the article is not used in such small quantities.
James Buchanan (1791-1868), 15th President of the United States (D-PA). Instructions to the White House liquor merchant, 1857.

28. There isn't any way to keep drugs out of this country.
Dale Bumpers, U.S. Senator and Governor of Arkansas (D). Quoted in *The New York Times*, Oct. 2, 1988.

29. Turf battles won't win this war. Teamwork will.
George Bush, 41st President of the United States (R-TX). Speech, Sept. 5, 1989.

30. People say I lack political courage. But don't forget, I went right into the heart of Amish country and I told them: *Just say no*.
George Bush. Speech, Gridiron Club, Washington, DC, Apr. 1, 1989.

31. Drugs come to America, not by invasion, but by invitation.
Joseph A. Califano, Jr., U.S. Secretary of Health, Education and Welfare (D). *The New York Times*, Dec. 8, 1989.

32. Tolerance of public smoking promotes the addiction.
Richard Chapman, City Councilman, Albuquerque, NM. Quoted on National Public Radio, June 27, 1989.

33. In fighting the drug war, we are repeating all the mistakes of Vietnam, but on U.S. soil this time, with all U.S. casualties. The costs of winning far outweigh any possible benefits.
Craig M. Collins, assistant editor, *Reason*. "Face Off," *USA Today*, Oct. 11, 1988.

34. A degrading procedure that so detracts from human dignity and self-respect that it shocks the conscience and offends this court's sense of justice.
Robert Collins, Federal Judge. New Orleans, LA,

Federal District Court opinion on drug testing as carried out by the U.S. Customs Service. Nov. 1986.

35. We owe those people who live scared some immediate relief.... If this is really a war, let's declare war.
H. R. Crawford, City Councilman, Washington, DC (D). To urge use of the National Guard in drug-infested neighborhoods of the nation's capital. Quoted in *The Washington Post*, Feb. 26, 1989.

36. The problem of drugs is a national failure. We do not grow cocoa leaves in Albany.
Mario Cuomo, Governor of New York (D). Speech, June 1990.

37. The military is afraid to get into this war *[on drugs]* because it's a tough one.
Alfonse D'Amato, U.S. Senator (R-NY). Interview, PBS, *Ask Congress*, Dec. 25, 1988.

38. I'm going to defend to the death my glass of Chardonnay. This is going to be a holy war for us.
John De Luca, President, The Wine Institute. Reaction to a California proposal to raise taxes on alcoholic beverages. Quoted in *The Washington Post*, Oct. 30, 1990.

39. I can admit I tried coke *[cocaine]* as I have no intention to run for president.
Kirk Douglas, American actor. CBS, *The Phil Donahue Show*, Sept. 21, 1988.

40. The addict is under compulsion and not capable of management without outside help.... If addicts can be punished for their addiction, then the insane can also be punished for their insanity. Each has a disease and each must be treated as a sick person.
William O. Douglas (1898-1980), U.S. Supreme Court Justice. *Robinson* v. *California*, 1962.

41. Eat your bread with joy, drink your wine with a merry heart.
Old Testament, *Ecclesiastes* 9:7.

42. If it's not worth spending everything it takes, it's not a war *[on drugs]*.
Mickey Edwards, U.S. Congressman (R-OK). Quoted in *The New York Times*, Sept. 10, 1989.

43. Drunkenness excuses no vice.
English proverb, c. 1485.

44. If you call Escobar to trial, you can be sure that all the members of your family tree – ancestors and offspring – will be eliminated. We are capable of executing you anywhere on this planet. There is no place you can hide.
[Despite the threat, Judge Sanchez signed the indictment, then fled to the U.S. with her husband, under the protection of the Drug Enforcement Administration and the State Department.]
Pablo Escobar, chief enforcer, Medelin cocaine cartel. Letter to Colombia judge Consuelo Sanchez, 1988. Quoted by Jack Anderson and Dale Van Atta, *The Washington Post*, Mar. 20, 1989.

45. We can't offer young blacks a job at Wendy's or McDonald's as an alternative to selling crack.
Louis Farrakhan, Chief Minister, Nation of Islam. Interview with *The Washington Post* editors, Feb. 28, 1990.

46. The war on drugs has produced about ten thousand additional homicides a year.
Milton Friedman, Nobel Laureate in Economics (United States). Interview, PBS, *MacNeil-Lehrer News Hour*, Mar. 6, 1991.

47. We've been fighting this war on drugs for 60 or 70 years and haven't gotten anywhere yet.
Joseph Galiber, New York State Senator (D). ABC, *It's Your Business*, Sept. 16, 1990.

48. *[Casual drug users]* ought to be taken out and shot.... We're in a war and drug use is treason.
Daryl Gates, Chief of Police, Los Angeles, CA. Testimony, U.S. Senate Judiciary Committee. Quoted in *The Montgomery Journal*, Sept. 11, 1990.

49. Drug prohibition enriches criminals and creates an artificially inflated price that lures young people into the drug trade.... We have created a drug exception to the Constitution.
Ira Glasser, Executive Director, American Civil Liberties Union. Letter to *The New York Times*, Dec. 6, 1990.

50. The real drug "kingpin" is the user. It is the casual users who create the profits. But we can't put them all in prison; there isn't any room in the jails.
William P. Gramm, U.S. Congressman and U.S. Senator (R-TX). Quoted in *The New York Times*, Sept. 11, 1988.

51. For all our policing, we understand that law enforcement is not the solution to the problem of drugs in our society.
Charles A. Gruber, Chief of Police, Shreveport, LA. Quoted in *The New York Times*, Dec. 28, 1989.

52. Let's imagine for a minute that you could stop all drugs coming into the United States – all heroin, all cocaine. Synthetic drugs would take over within two months.

Francis C. Hall, Commander, Narcotics Division, New York City Police Department. Interview, *The New York Times*, Mar. 12, 1989.

53. I know of nothing you can sell where you can make a greater profit than drugs – if you survive.
Francis C. Hall. *Ibid.*

54. All federal employees should be subjected to drug tests.
Paula Hawkins, U.S. Senator (R-FL). *Congressional Digest*, May 1987.

55. People who need *[drug abuse]* treatment have got to get it. You don't have to be a humanitarian to believe addicts need treatment. The public is threatened every time a drug addict is told to come back next week.
Robert M. Hayes, Executive Director, Coalition for the Homeless. Quoted in *The New York Times*, Oct. 9, 1988.

56. No nation alone, however great its vigilance, can erect a barrier high enough to keep out narcotics when opium is grown or drugs are manufactured without limitation or restriction. The nations of the world must be aroused to cooperate.
William Randolph Hearst (1863-1951), U.S. Congressman (D-NY); founder, Independence League Party; journalist; and publisher. Quoted in Older, *William Randolph Hearst: American*, 1936.

57. They who drink beer will think beer.
Washington Irving (1783-1859), American writer and U.S. Diplomatic Attaché to Spain. *The Sketch-Book. Stratford-on-Avon*, 1820.

58. Up with hope, down with dope.
Jesse L. Jackson, Shadow Senator (D-DC). Slogan in his war against drugs, 1989.

59. Drugs are destroying more people than poverty ever did.
John E. Jacob, President, Urban League. Remark to William Bennett, 1989.

60. Crack has destroyed more families than poverty.
John E. Jacob. Quoted on *NBC News*, Sept. 16, 1989.

61. ... the sin of drunkenness which is the root of all sins.
James I (1566-1625), King of England. *A Counterblast to Tobacco*, 1604.

62. A custom loathsome to the eye, hateful to the nose, harmful to the brain, dangerous to the lungs, and in the black, stinking fume thereof, nearest resembling the horrible Stygian smoke of the pit that is bottomless.
James I. Description of smoking tobacco. *Ibid.*

63. No nation is drunken where wine is cheap; and none sober where the dearness of wine substitutes ardent spirits as the common beverage. It is, in truth, the only antidote to the bane of whiskey.
Thomas Jefferson (1743-1826), 3rd President of the United States (Democratic Republican-VA). Letter to M. de Neuville, Dec. 12, 1818.

64. There's no greater challenge to a parent or a school than to make children understand *why* they shouldn't take drugs.
Peter Jennings, American TV journalist. July 31, 1988.

65. Prevention is the best solution to drug use by young people, but it takes time, effort, and resources. Government can only do so much. Prevention has to begin in each community, in whatever ways make sense in that community. We want to support that.
Elaine M. Johnson, Director, Alcohol, Drug Addiction and Mental Health Administration, U.S. Public Health Service. Speech, October 15, 1991.

66. The alcoholic suffers from a disease.
Lyndon B. Johnson (1908-1973), 36th President of the United States (D-TX). 1966.

67. Wine cheers God and man.
Old Testament, *Judges* 9:13.

68. Every form of addiction is bad, no matter whether the narcotic be alcohol or morphine or idealism.
Carl Gustav Jung (1875-1961), Swiss psychiatrist. *Memories, Dreams, Reflections*.

69. We spend billions and billions to fight drugs but, comparatively, spend nothing against alcohol. And alcohol is a drug.
Joseph Kennedy III, U.S. Congressman (D-MA). To explain why he wants warnings in all alcohol ads. Quoted in *Advertising Age*, July 16, 1990.

70. They're trying to outdrug each other. Each one wants to seem tougher on drugs than the next one.
James J. Kilpatrick, American political columnist. In reference to the Congress. CBS, *Inside Washington*, Oct. 15, 1988.

71. If you want to use enforcement to control the cocaine problem, be ready to build another fifty thousand federal prison cells. Otherwise, you're bluffing.

Mark A. R. Kleiman, Director, Policy and Management Analysis, U.S. Department of Justice. Quoted in *The New York Times*, Oct. 16, 1988.

72. I don't care if they pay four penalties. I want them out.
Edward I. Koch, U.S. Congressman and Mayor of New York City (D). Reaction to criticism from civil libertarians for his position that foreigners selling drugs in the U.S. be jailed and deported. Interview, PBS, *Tony Brown's Journal*, Oct. 1, 1988.

73. Our nation has mobilized enormous resources to wage a war on drugs. We should also give priority to the one addiction – tobacco addiction – that is killing more than 300,000 Americans each year.
C. Everett Koop, U.S. Surgeon General. May 1988.

74. Nicotine is as addicting as heroin or cocaine.
C. Everett Koop. Quoted on ABC, *The Koppel Report*, Sept. 13, 1988.

75. The number of people who die every day from cigarette smoking is the same as if two jumbo jets crashed each day and not a single person walked away alive.
C. Everett Koop. Quoted on PBS, *Nova*, Oct. 10, 1989.

76. Am I a zealot? Probably about smoking I am.
C. Everett Koop. *Ibid.*

77. Politicians are ducking, candidates are hedging, the Anti-Saloon League is prospering, people are being poisoned, bootleggers are being enriched, and government officials are being corrupted.
Fiorello H. La Guardia (1882-1947), U.S. Congressman (R and Socialist-NY) and Mayor of New York City (R and Fusion Party). Description of Prohibition. House debate, 1928.

78. An era of chemical McCarthyism is at hand, and "guilty until proven innocent" is the new slogan.
George Lundberg, editor, *Journal of the American Medical Association*. On drug testing. Quoted in *U.S. News & World Report*, Dec. 15, 1986.

79. Drug addiction is the greatest threat to our civilization and government since the Civil War.
Stanley Lundine, Lieutenant Governor of New York (D). Quoted in *The New York Times*, Nov. 19, 1989.

80. Tobacco advertising has become the 2 Live Crew of commercial speech, and just as we shouldn't censor music, we shouldn't censor advertising.
Barry Lynn, Legislative Director, American Civil Liberties Union. Quoted in *Advertising Age*, June 25, 1990.

81. If the public realized the dangers that we are facing *[from drugs]*, they would be willing to put up with some inconvenience and accept the fact that we will enforce the laws and some persons may be innocently damaged.... I don't want anyone *[innocent]* hurt, but it may be part of the price we will have to pay.
Robert H. Macy, District Attorney, Oklahoma County, OK, and Chairman, National District Attorneys Association Drug Control Committee. Quoted in *The Washington Post*, Mar. 20, 1989.

82. There is no drug exception to the Constitution.
Thurgood Marshall, U.S. Supreme Court Justice. Quoted in *The New York Times*, Nov. 28, 1989.

83. The real victim of the war on drugs might be the constitutional rights of the American people.
Richard Matsch, Federal Judge. Quoted in *USA Today*, Nov. 15, 1989.

84. Too Orwellian to contemplate, they've gone way too far.
Walker Merryman, Vice President, Tobacco Institute. In reference to a voter initiative on the 1988 Oregon ballot to outlaw smoking in almost all public places. Quoted in *The New York Times*, Oct. 25, 1988.

85. Over himself, over his own body and mind, the individual is sovereign. In the part which merely concerns himself, his independence is of right, absolute.
John Stuart Mill (1806-1873), Member of Parliament, Great Britain, and political economist. A "natural right" view frequently used by opponents of government regulation of alcohol, tobacco, and other drugs. *On Liberty*, 1859.

86. To become a narcotic addict is an antisocial act, and the foundation of countermeasures against addiction is to treat and rehabilitate addicts.
Norbus Motohashi, Narcotics Chief, Ministry of Health, Japan. *Addiction in Japan*, 1973.

87. This vice brings in 100 million francs in taxes each year. I will certainly forbid it at once – as soon as you can name a virtue that brings in as much revenue.
Napoléon III (Louis Napoléon Bonaparte) (1808-1873), Emperor of France. Response when asked to forbid the vice of smoking tobacco. Quoted in *Conservative Digest*, Nov. 1987.

88. It's important to understand who the enemy is. It's the importers, the growers and the dealers, not the drug users.
Richard M. Nixon, 37th President of the United States (R-CA). Quoted in *USA Today*, Oct. 20, 1988.

89. You cannot solve the problem of drug violence through more violence *[police violence]*.
Ronald E. Paul, U.S. Congressman (R-TX). Speech, C-SPAN, Feb. 16, 1990.

90. Drunkenness ... spoils health, dismounts the mind, and unmans men.
William Penn (1644-1718), founder of Pennsylvania. *Some Fruits of Solitude, in Reflections and Maxims*, 1693.

91. There's no one in this country that believes that we're winning the war on drugs.
Carrie Saxon Perry, Mayor of Hartford, CT. Quoted on PBS, *MacNeil-Lehrer News Hour*, Dec. 18, 1989.

92. We're also in a war we shouldn't be in and can't win. The police are the victims of this war just as soldiers were the victims in Vietnam.
Wesley A. Pomeroy, Assistant Director, White House Office on Drug Abuse. Comparison of the war on drugs with Vietnam. Statement, Apr. 1, 1989.

93. You can't fight a war against drugs unless you have the kind of financial commitment that's necessary to put troops into the field.
Ernest D. Preate, Jr., Attorney General, Pennsylvania. Quoted in *The Washington Post*, Mar. 20, 1990.

94. Wine is a mocker, strong drink is raging; and whoever is deceived thereby is not wise.
Old Testament, *Proverbs* 23:20.

95. It is much easier to believe that it's *[the drug problem]* all a problem of crime and vice that can be resolved by the police. But it's more important that we understand the causes of drug trafficking and addiction.
Garcia Ramirez, Attorney General, Mexico. Quoted in *The New York Times*, July 31, 1988.

96. All drug use is related. Users of one drug are willing, if not eager, to try others.
Charles B. Rangel, U.S. Congressman (D-NY). 1990.

97. But what all of us have known in the back of our minds is becoming clearer with each passing day: that the harm done by our attempts to enforce antidrug laws is greater than the harm done by the drugs themselves.
William Raspberry, American columnist. *The Washington Post*, Oct. 9, 1989.

98. We must grow and sell opium to fight our holy war against the Russian nonbelievers.
Mohammad Rasul, American-backed Afghan rebel. Quoted in *Newsweek*, June 30, 1986.

99. Just say no!
Nancy Reagan, First Lady. Response when asked by a schoolgirl how youngsters should resist peer pressure to take drugs. 1986.

100. It is often easier to make strong speeches about foreign drug lords or drug smugglers than to arrest a pair of Wall Street investment bankers buying cocaine on their lunch break.
Nancy Reagan. Address to General Assembly of United Nations. Oct. 25, 1988.

101. This budget just says no.
Joseph P. Riley, Jr., Mayor of Charleston, SC, and President, U.S. Conference of Mayors. In reference to President Reagan's budgetary proposal to cut drug enforcement and education funds. Quoted in *Newsweek*, Jan. 19, 1987.

102. The South is dry and will vote dry. That is, everybody that is sober enough to stagger to the polls will.
Will Rogers (1879-1935), American humorist. Oct. 26, 1926.

103. *[Congress should]* impose such heavy duties upon distilled spirits as shall be effective to restrain their intemperate use in the country.
Benjamin Rush (1745-1813), American physician and Member, Continental Congress. Petition of Philadelphia College of Physicians to the U.S. Congress, 1790.

104. The prohibition law ... has divided the nation, like Gaul, into three parts – wets, drys, and hypocrites.
Florence Sabin (1871-1953), American physician and scientist. Speech, Feb. 9, 1931.

105. A kind of immolation of privacy and human dignity in symbolic opposition to drug use.
Antonin Scalia, U.S. Supreme Court Justice. Description of random drug testing. Quoted in *Newsweek*, June 26, 1989.

106. We should seriously debate whether the surgeon general should lead the war *[on drugs]* rather than the attorney general.
Kurt Schmoke, Mayor of Baltimore, MD (D). ABC, *The Koppel Report*, Sept. 13, 1988.

107. Depend upon it, of all vices drinking is the most incompatible with greatness.
Walter Scott (1771-1832), Scottish writer. Quoted in John Gibson Lockhart, *Life of Sir Walter Scott*, 1837.

108. Drunkenness is simply voluntary insanity.
Lucius Annaeus Seneca (The Younger) (4 B.C.-A.D. 65), Roman statesman, dramatist, and philosopher. *Epistolae ad Lucillum.*

109. There are other problems besides drug problems.
William Sessions, Director, Federal Bureau of Investigation. Interview, PBS, *John McLaughlin's One on One*, Sept. 17, 1989.

110. I disagree that we should first force the flow of U.S. cigarettes into *[foreign]* countries, get people addicted, and then expect public health anti-smoking campaigns to clean up the mess we've created.
Iris R. Shannon, President, American Public Health Association. Letter, *The New York Times*, Aug. 20, 1989.

111. We're not really going to get anywhere until we take the criminality out of drugs.
George P. Shultz, U.S. Secretary of State (R). Quoted on PBS, *MacNeil-Lehrer News Hour*, Dec. 18, 1989.

112. We're frying the brains of children.
Alan K. Simpson, U.S. Senator (R-WY). In reference to drug use. Interview, CNN, *Evans & Novak*, Sept. 17, 1989.

113. Most people don't like living in a police state – but they are willing for two weeks if there's a serious drug problem.
Leonard Sipes, President, National Crime Prevention Council. Quoted in *Governing the States and Localities*, Apr. 1988.

114. Didn't like it. Haven't touched it in 20 years. Don't smoke today.
James C. Slattery, U.S. Congressman (D-KS). Response to questions about his smoking marijuana earlier in his life. Remark to reporters, 1990.

115. Much has been said with respect to the effect my action on this bill may have on my own political future. I have no political future that I am willing to obtain by the sacrifice of any principles or convictions.
Alfred E. Smith (1873-1944), Governor of New York (D). Statement to press when signing a bill prohibiting the state from enforcing the federal prohibition laws, 1923.

116. Our involuntary slaves are set free, but our millions of voluntary slaves still clang their chains. The lot of the literal slave ... is a paradise compared to the lot of him who enslaves himself – especially of him who enslaved himself to alcohol.
Gerrit Smith (1797-1874), U.S. Congressman (Free Soil-NY). Speech, 1869.

117. This year *[1973]* we have spent $796.3 million *[on drug abuse]*. We will *[next year]* exceed the $1 billion mark. When we do so, we become, for want of a better term, a drug abuse industrial complex.
Michael R. Sonnenreich, Executive Director, National Commission on Marijuana and Drug Abuse. 1973.

118. The war on drugs has become a war on the Bill of Rights.
Nadine Strossen, President, American Civil Liberties Union. Speech, Libertarian Party National Convention, Chicago, IL, Aug. 29, 1991.

119. Smoking tobacco is one of the greatest sources of preventable disease and death in our population.
Louis W. Sullivan, U.S. Secretary of Health and Human Services. Quoted on ABC, *The Health Show*, Feb. 4, 1990.

120. It is immoral for civilized societies to condone the promotion and advertising of products which when used as they are intended cause disability and death.
Louis W. Sullivan. Speech, First International Conference on Smokeless Tobacco, Apr. 10, 1991.

121. No state, and no country, can long endure, half wet and half dry.
William Sulzer (1863-1941), U.S. Congressman and Governor of New York (D). Speech, Prohibition Party Convention, St. Paul, MN, July 20, 1916.

122. If we want to lose the war on drugs, just leave it to law enforcement.
Richard Thornburgh, U.S. Attorney General and Governor of Pennsylvania (R). Interview, ABC, *This Week*, Mar. 19, 1989.

123. The police alone cannot solve the drug problem. Any society whose appetite for illicit narcotics cannot be satisfied must suffer the consequences of eroding morality and deteriorating values which result in alarming increases in violent crime.
Maurice T. Turner, Jr., Chief of Police, Washington, DC. Quoted in *The Washington Post*, Oct. 27, 1988.

124. There's nothing in the Constitution that says you can't shoot down airplanes *[smuggling drugs]*.
William von Rabb, Director, U.S. Customs Service. Interview, National Public Radio, Aug. 2, 1989.

125. Some of my friends drink and some of my friends don't drink. And believe me, I'm for my friends.

James Eli Watson (1864-1948), U.S. Congressman and U.S. Senator (R-IN). Response when asked his position on Prohibition. Attributed.

126. All along the line, physically, mentally, morally, alcohol is a weakening and deadening force.
Beatrice Potter Webb (1858-1943), British Socialist, reformer, and cofounder, Fabian Society. *Health of Working Girls*, 1917.

127. Work is the curse of the drinking classes.
Oscar Wilde (1854-1900), Irish writer. In conversation.

Chapter 4

Appointments and Nominations

When voting on the confirmation of a presidential appointee, always vote no, because if he or she is confirmed, it won't be long before your vote is proved politically correct.

James G. Abourezk, U.S. Congressman and U.S. Senator (D-SD). *Advise and Dissent*, 1989.

This principle *[rotation-in-office]* is, indeed, more congenial to republicans out of than to those in office.

John Quincy Adams (1767-1848), 6th President of the United States (Ind.-MA). *Diary*, Feb. 21, 1821.

A man who can refuse no favor to any man. He would recommend ten persons for one and the same place rather than say no to any one of them.

John Quincy Adams. Reference to Richard M. Johnson, Vice President under Martin Van Buren. *Diary*, Feb. 18, 1820.

About one-half of the members of Congress are seekers for office at the nomination of the President. Of the remainder, at least one-half have some appointment or favor to ask for their relatives.

John Quincy Adams. *Diary*, 1821.

I have changed my ministers, but I have not changed my measures.

Anne (1665-1714), Queen of Great Britain and Ireland. Jan. 1711.

A wise man is better than a prophet.

Babylonian Talmud, *Baba Bathra* 12a.

We're a small office and I don't have any room for nice political people who don't know anything about drugs.

William J. Bennett, Director, Office of National Drug Control Policy, and U.S. Secretary of Education (R). Quoted on NBC, *Meet the Press*, Mar. 19, 1989.

8. He was among the first of the Secretaries to apply that system *[the spoils system]* to the dismission of clerks in his Department.... It is a detestable system, drawn from the worst periods of the Roman republic; and if it were to be perpetuated, if the offices, honors, and dignities of the people were to be put up to the scramble, to be decided by the result of every Presidential election, our Government and institutions, becoming intolerable, would finally end in a despotism as inexorable as that at Constantinople.

Henry Clay (1777-1852), U.S. Senator (National Republican and Whig-KY), Speaker of the House, and U.S. Secretary of State. Statement opposing Martin Van Buren's confirmation as U.S. Minister to Great Britain. Senate speech, Jan. 21, 1832.

9. The State, in choosing men to serve it, takes no notice of their opinions. If they be willing faithfully to serve it, that satisfies.

Oliver Cromwell (1599-1658), Lord Protector of England. Statement, July 2, 1644.

10. The last thing I would ever ask any man that I appoint to a high office is what are going to be his decisions in specific cases.

Dwight D. Eisenhower (1890-1969), 34th President of the United States (R-KS). Remark to reporters, 1955.

11. It will cost me some struggle to keep from despising the office-seeker.

James A. Garfield (1831-1881), 20th President of the United States (R-OH). *Journal*, Mar. 16, 1881.

12. The pay is low. The price in privacy invasion is high. The confirmation process is long.

David Gergen, American journalist and White House assistant (R). To explain the difficulty the Bush administration was having filling presidential appointments. PBS, *MacNeil-Lehrer News Hour* Apr. 6, 1990.

13. Every time I make one appointee I make nine disappointees.

Bibb Graves (1873-1942), Governor of Alabama (D). 1938.

14. The opposition to his appointment has only strengthened my conviction that I want him.... You can put that in block type and a box.

Warren G. Harding (1865-1923), 29th President of the United States (R-OH). Statement to reporters in reference to his nomination of Harry Daugherty as U.S. Attorney General. Quoted in *The New York Times*, Feb. 22, 1921.

15. When I came into power, I found that the party managers had taken it all to themselves. I could not name my own Cabinet. They had sold out every place to pay the election expenses.

Benjamin Harrison (1833-1901), 23rd President of the United States (R-IN). Remark to Theodore Roosevelt, quoted in Wallechinsky and Wallace, *The People's Almanac*, 1975.

16. All appointments hurt. Five friends are made cold or hostile for every appointment: no new friends are made.

Rutherford B. Hayes (1822-1893), 19th President of the United States (R-OH). Letter to Governor William McKinley (OH), Dec. 27, 1892.

17. I was driven years ago to the conclusion that political considerations had not hurt the character of appointments here *[the Supreme Court]*.

Oliver Wendell Holmes, Jr. (1841-1935), U.S. Supreme Court Justice. Letter to Harold J. Laski, 1925.

18. I am against government by crony.

Harold L. Ickes (1874-1952), U.S. Secretary of the Interior (R). 1946.

19. The public will never be made to believe that an appointment of a relative is ever made on the ground of merit alone, uninfluenced by family views; nor can they ever see with approbation offices, the disposal of which they entrust to their Presidents for public purposes, divided out as family property. Mr. *[John]* Adams degraded himself infinitely by his conduct on this subject, as General Washington had done himself the highest honor.

Thomas Jefferson (1743-1826), 3rd President of the United States (Democratic Republican-VA). Letter to George Jefferson, Mar. 27, 1801.

20. A very early recommendation had been given to the Postmaster General to employ no printer, foreigner, or Revolutionary Tory in any of his offices.

Thomas Jefferson. Letter to Nathaniel Macon, May 14, 1801.

21. Few die and none resign.
[Often attributed to Jefferson, it is actually a convenient shortening of the following communication:]
If a due participation of office is a matter of right, how are vacancies to be obtained? Those by death are few; those by resignation, none. Can any other mode than that of removal be proposed? This is a painful office, but it is my duty and I meet it as such.

Thomas Jefferson. On the removal of the federal tax collector at New Haven, CT. Letter to Elias Shipman and others, July 12, 1801.

22. The appointment of a woman to office is an innovation for which the public is not prepared, nor am I.

Thomas Jefferson. Letter to U.S. Secretary of the Treasury Albert Gallatin. Jan. 1807.

23. Is he honest? Is he capable? Is he faithful to the Constitution?

Thomas Jefferson. Response concerning questions a President should ask about a potential appointee. Quoted in Henry Adams, *History of the United States during the Administrations of Jefferson and Madison*, 1891.

24. It's probably better to have the son-of-a-bitch inside the tent pissing out than outside the tent pissing in.

Lyndon B. Johnson (1908-1973), 36th President of the United States (D-TX). Comment when considering not renewing the appointment of FBI Chief J. Edgar Hoover. Quoted in David Halberstam, *The Best and the Brightest*, 1969.

25. Assigning *[White House staff]* offices is more difficult than choosing the cabinet.

Hamilton Jordan, White House Chief of Staff (D). Remark to James Baker and Edwin Meese, Jan. 1981.

26. I can't see that it's wrong to give him a little legal experience before he goes out to practice law.

John F. Kennedy (1917-1963), 35th President of the United States (D-MA). Remark when appointing his brother Robert F. Kennedy as U.S. Attorney General. Quoted in *Time*, Feb. 3, 1961.

27. The practice of *[political]* appointments rejects completely the principle of collective work; it breeds irresponsibility.

Aleksandra Kollontai (1872-1952), Soviet diplomat and 1st Commissar of Public Welfare. *The Workers' Opposition in Russia*, c. 1921.

28. I don't think you should ever politicize a health appointment.

C. Everett Koop, U.S. Surgeon General. Interview, PBS, *MacNeil-Lehrer Report*, July 21, 1989.

29. The role of the nominee in the confirmation process is like that of the bridegroom. Stay out of the way and be on time.

Thomas Korologos, White House assistant (R). C-SPAN, *Lobbying and the Nomination Process*, July 4, 1990.

30. We cannot ask a man what he will do, and if we should, and he should answer us, we should despise him for it. Therefore, we must take a man whose opinions are known.

Abraham Lincoln (1809-1865), 16th President of the United States (R-IL). In reference to the process of appointing a Supreme Court Justice. Letter to W. B. Warren, Apr. 7, 1849.

31. The appointment of subordinates or the nominations for appointments are just as much a part of our *[Congress's]* responsibility as any other which we have, and a share in those appointments ... is one of the recognized rights of the people.

John Alexander Logan (1826-1886), U.S. Congressman and U.S. Senator (D-IL). Congressional debate, 1869.

32. Every time I fill a vacant office I make ten malcontents and one ingrate.

Louis XIV (1638-1715), King of France. Quoted in Molière, *Siècle de Louis Quatorze*.

33. Cabinet members aren't appointed to make easy decisions.

Manuel Lujan, Jr., U.S. Congressman (R-NM) and Secretary of the Interior. Speech, National Press Club, June 29, 1990.

34. The first impression that one gets of a ruler and his ability is from seeing the men that he has about him.

Niccolò Machiavelli (1469-1527), Florentine statesman and political philosopher. *The Prince*, 1513.

35. The President is responsible to the public for the conduct of the person he has nominated and appointed.

James Madison (1751-1836), 4th President of the United States (Democratic Republican-VA). Debate, First Congress, 1789-91.

36. Reward people who are bridge builders rather than bomb throwers.

William Maynes, editor, *Foreign Policy*. Comment on who should be appointed to the Cabinet. Quoted in *The Washington Post*, June 26, 1988.

37. People who are satisfied with a prospective *[presidential]* appointment do not make any particular noise about it, but those who do not like it clamor.

Charles Michelson, American journalist. *New York World*, Jan. 10, 1921.

38. I would rather have my fate in the hands of twenty-three representative citizens of the county *[the grand jury]* than in the hands of a politically appointed judge.

Robert Morganthau, District Attorney of New York City. Quoted in *Time*, Apr. 8, 1985.

39. No person who shall deny the being of God, or the truth of the Christian religion, shall be capable of holding any office or place of trust or profit.

North Carolina Constitution, 1836.

40. If I have got to be put away on the shelf, I suppose I might as well be on the top shelf.

Rufus Peckham (1838-1909), U.S. Supreme Court Justice. Comment upon his appointment to the Supreme Court. Quoted in William H. Rehnquist, *The Supreme Court: How It Was, How It Is*, 1987.

41. If Ministers are weak or ill Men, and so spoil their Places, it is the *Prince's* Fault that chose them: But if their Places spoil them, it is *their own Fault* to be made worse by them.

William Penn (1644-1718), founder of Pennsylvania. *Some Fruits of Solitude, in Reflections and Maxims*, 1693.

42. In every appointment which the President makes he disappoints half a dozen applicants and their friends, who, actuated by selfish and sordid motives, will prefer any other candidate in the next election, while the person appointed attributes the appointment to his own superior merit and does not even feel obliged by it.

James K. Polk (1795-1849), 11th President of the United States (D-TN). *Diary*, Jan. 7, 1847.

43. Every time a Congressman recommends a postmaster he makes one ingrate and eight enemies.

Thomas B. Reed (1839-1902), U.S. Congressman and Speaker of the House (R-ME). Attributed.

44. I have no Cabinet yet. I can't call in many people for advice and help without inviting speculation about whether I'm going to appoint them. That will embarrass them and me.

Franklin D. Roosevelt (1882-1945), 32nd President of the United States (D-NY). Statement during the interregnum between his presidential election in 1932 and his assuming office in Mar. 1933. Quoted in Raymond Moley, *After Seven Years*, 1939.

45. I was only one-half the appointing power. I nominated, but the Senate confirmed.
Theodore Roosevelt (1858-1919), 26th President of the United States (R-NY). *Autobiography*, 1919.

46. If I cannot find *[qualified]* Republicans, I am going to appoint Democrats.
Theodore Roosevelt. Quoted in Mark Sullivan, *Our Times*, 1927.

47. I don't think a life in politics trains you to pick staff.
Warren B. Rudman, U.S. Senator (R-NH). Interview, C-SPAN, *American Profile*, May 27, 1991.

48. If *Princes* would *Reflect* how much they are in the Power of their *Ministers*, they would be more circumspect in the *Choice* of them.
George Savile, 1st Marquess of Halifax (1633-1695), Lord Privy Seal of England. *Maxims of State*, 21.

49. ...being rewarded, as double-dealers frequently have been, with favour and preferment.
Walter Scott (1771-1832), Scottish writer. *The Heart of Midlothian*, 1818.

50. The wisest sovereigns err like private men,
And royal hand has sometimes laid the sword
Of chivalry upon a worthless shoulder,
Which better had been branded by the hangman.
What then? – Kings do their best – and they and we
Must answer for the intent, and not the event.
Walter Scott. *Kenilworth*, 1821.

51. Friendly counsel cuts off many foes.
William Shakespeare (1564-1616), English writer. I *King Henry VI*, iii.

52. Nobody ought to become Secretary of Education because they are out of a job.
Albert Shanker, President, American Federation of Teachers. Quoted in *Newsweek*, Dec. 24, 1990.

53. The position in which the President is now placed with regard to Congress is a constant source of irritation. Members of Congress ... claim the right to dictate local appointments, and if their wishes are not yielded to in every case, it creates at once a cause of quarrel, which finds its outlet in some legislation or other.
John Sherman (1823-1900), U.S. Congressman (R-OH), U.S. Senator, U.S. Secretary of the Treasury, and U.S. Secretary of State. Congressional debate, 1871.

54. ... a dropsical nepotism swollen to elephantiasis.
Charles Sumner (1811-1874), U.S. Senator (D, R, and Free Soil-MA). Senate speech describing the practice of Ulysses S. Grant in appointing old friends and cronies to political office.

55. The President is usually entitled to his judgment on these matters *[Cabinet members]*.
John G. Tower (1925-1991), U.S. Senator (R-TX). Quoted on ABC, *This Week*, Feb. 26, 1989.

56. Everyone is telling me who I should have on my staff and in my Cabinet. No S.O.B is going to dictate to me who I'm going to have.
Harry S Truman (1884-1972), 33rd President of the United States (D-MO). Speech, Washington, DC, 1945.

57. As the President has the right to nominate without assigning his reasons, so has the Senate a right to dissent without giving theirs.
George Washington (1732-1799), 1st President of the United States (VA). Comment, 1789. Quoted in *American Heritage*, Sept./Oct. 1989.

58. Virginia more than any other state in the Union has disavowed and condemned the doctrine of removals from office for opinion's sake.
Daniel Webster (1782-1852), U.S. Congressman (Federalist-NH and MA), U.S. Senator (Federalist and Whig-MA), and U.S. Secretary of State. Speech, Richmond, VA, 1840.

Chapter 5

Arts, Leisure, and Entertainment

1. I do think there is a clear distinction between freedom of expression as a concept, which is something I would defend forever, and the limit or license to use the taxpayer's money in a way that may be objectionable to a great many people.

    Livingston Biddle, Chairman, National Endowment for the Arts. Quoted in *The Washington Post*, June 25, 1989.

2. I don't know how you determine exactly what the American people approve of.

    Lynne Cheney, Chairman, National Endowment for the Humanities (R). Interview, PBS, *John M. McLaughlin's One on One*, Apr. 15, 1990.

3. Morals, not Art or Literature.

    Anthony Comstock (1844-1915), founder, New York Society for the Suppression of Vice, and official censor, U.S. Postal Service. Motto.

4. As long as federal dollars are used to finance art projects, Congress will have the responsibility to its constituents to determine what type of art taxpayer dollars will support.

    Philip M. Crane, U.S. Congressman (R-WI). Letter to *The New York Times*, May 21, 1990.

5. *Robert's Rules of Order* is the greatest book ever written.

    Richard J. Daley (1902-1976), Mayor of Chicago, IL (D). Remark at a City Council meeting. Quoted in *The Chicago Daily News*, Oct. 3, 1967.

6. No composer has yet caught this rhythm of America – it is too mighty for the ears of most.

    Isadora Duncan (1878-1927), American dancer and educator. *My Life*, 1927.

7. I am not going to be the decency czar.

    John Frohnmayer, Chairman, National Endowment for the Arts. Statement at NEA Advisory Council Meeting. Quoted in *The Washington Post*, Dec. 15, 1990.

8. Summoning artists to participate
In the august occasions of the state
Seems something artists ought to celebrate
A golden age of poetry and power
Of which this noonday's the beginning hour.

    Robert Frost (1874-1963), U.S. Poet Laureate. Poem written for the inauguration of John F. Kennedy, Jan. 20, 1961.

9. If a poet would influence politics he must join a party, and then he is lost as a poet: goodbye to his free spirit and his open mind.

    Johann Wolfgang von Goethe (1749-1832), German poet and dramatist. Quoted in Johann Peter Eckermann, *Conversations with Goethe*, 1848.

10. We are too easy a target in an election year when you have all those knights on white horses defending people from pornography.

    Roy M. Goodman, member, National Council on the Arts (R). Quoted in *The New York Times*, Mar. 3, 1990.

11. I only know two tunes. One of them is "Yankee Doodle." The other isn't.

    Ulysses S. Grant (1822-1885), 18th President of the United States (R-OH). Quoted in Paul F. Boller, Jr., *Presidential Anecdotes*, 1981.

12. This is just the old loyalty oath in new clothing.

    Loni Hancock, Mayor of Berkeley, CA. In reference to the 1989 National Foundation for the Arts regulations requiring grantees to sign an agreement regarding the content of their work. Quoted in *The New York Times*, Aug. 26, 1990.

13. That's the ugliest thing I ever saw.

    Lyndon B. Johnson (1908-1973), 36th President of the United States (D-TX). Comment to artist Peter Hurd, on seeing his official portrait for the first time. Quoted in *The New York Times*, Jan. 6, 1967.

14. I look forward to an America which will reward achievement in the arts as we reward achievement in business or statecraft.
[Inscribed on the Kennedy Center for the Performing Arts.]
John F. Kennedy (1917-1963), 35th President of the United States (D-MA). Speech, Amherst College, MA, Oct. 26, 1963.

15. When power corrupts, poetry cleanses.
John F. Kennedy. Quoted in *Forbes*, June 10, 1991.

16. If ten or twelve Hungarian writers had been shot at the right moment, there would have been no revolution.
Nikita S. Khrushchev (1894-1971), Premier of the U.S.S.R. Remark, 1957.

17. Soviet literature and art must be inseverably linked with the policy of the Communist Party.
Nikita S. Khrushchev. Quoted in *The New York Times Magazine*, Sept. 29, 1957.

18. The Parthenon without the marbles is like a smile with a tooth missing.
Neil Kinnock, Member of Parliament, Great Britain (Labour). To explain why, as Prime Minister, he would return the Elgin marbles to Greece. London, Jan. 4, 1984.

19. The artist is responsible only to himself.
Milan Knizak, Rector, Prague Academy of Fine Arts. Quoted in *Time*, Apr. 23, 1990.

20. It's not censorship. It's commonsense use of the taxpayer's money.
Martin H. Lancaster, U.S. Congressman (D-NC). In reference to the 1989 National Foundation for the Arts regulations requiring grantees to sign an agreement regarding the content of their work. Quoted in *The New York Times*, Aug. 26, 1990.

21. The world would be better off if more musicians were involved in politics.
Vyautas Landsbergis, President of Lithuania and musicologist. Interview, National Public Radio, May 10, 1991.

22. In deciding the ratings of the films, no consideration is given to artistic, technical, or dramatic values. Only moral content is weighed.
Legion of Decency, 1933.

23. The people are not satisfied with life alone but demand literature and art as well.
Mao Tse-tung (1893-1976), Chairman, Communist Party of China. Speech, Yenan, 1942.

24. There is in fact no such thing as art for art's sake, art that stands above classes, or art that is detached from or independent of politics.
Mao Tse-tung. Quoted in Engle and Engle, *Poems of Mao Tse-tung*, 1972.

25. One measure of the degree of civilization attained by a nation might fairly be the extent to which the nation's creative artists are supported, encouraged, and esteemed by the nation as a whole.
Vincent Massey (1887-1967), Governor General of Canada. 1951.

26. If an artist is going to take money from the taxpayers I guess he's got to be prepared to have the taxpayers dissatisfied with the product.
Charles McDowell, Jr., American journalist. Quoted on PBS, *Washington Week in Review*, Sept. 16, 1989.

27. The committee will be composed of open-minded people who agree with me.
Edward McKita, Mayor of Surrey, Canada. On forming a municipal art committee to censor art shows. Quoted in *Weekend Magazine*, Oct. 16, 1976.

28. When the guns boom, the arts die.
Arthur Miller, American playwright. Comment on declining an invitation to a White House arts function. Telegram to Pres. Lyndon B. Johnson, 1965.

29. Great artists have no fatherland.
Alfred de Musset (1810-1857), French poet. *Lorenzaccio*, I, 1834.

30. We demand legal prosecution of all tendencies in art and literature of a kind likely to disintegrate our life as a nation.
Nazi party program, Feb. 25, 1920.

31. Film producers are foreign born and are in a position of power to control what 80 million people a week see in our theaters.
Gerald P. Nye (1892-1971), U.S. Senator (R-ND). Quoted in David Brinkley, *Washington Goes to War*, 1988.

32. A great artist is answerable only to God.
Pablo Picasso (1881-1973), Spanish artist. Quoted in *Playboy*, Jan. 1964.

33. Where there's liberty art succeeds. In societies that are not free, art dies.
Ronald Reagan, 40th President of the United States (R-CA). Quoted in *The Washington Post*, Aug. 1, 1990.

34. Politics is the best show in America.
Will Rogers (1879-1935), American humorist. Remark, 1933.

35. I guess the only thing they can do is paint, and surely there must be some public place where paintings are wanted.
Franklin D. Roosevelt (1882-1945), 32nd President of the United States (D-NY). On providing work for artists under the Work Projects Administration. Speech, 1935.

36. The arts cannot thrive except where men are free to be themselves and to be in charge of the discipline of their own energies and ardors. The conditions for democracy and art are one.
Franklin D. Roosevelt. Speech at dedication of the Museum of Modern Art, New York City, May 10, 1939.

37. I say that our New World democracy, however great a success in uplifting the masses out of their sloughs, in materialistic development, products, and in a certain highly deceptive superficial popular intellectuality, is, so far, an almost complete failure in its social aspects, and in really grand, religious, moral, literary, and esthetic results.
Walt Whitman (1819-1902), American poet. *Democratic Vistas*, 1871.

38. Cultivated leisure is the aim of man.
Oscar Wilde (1854-1900), Irish writer. *The Soul of Man Under Socialism*, 1881.

39. Boycotts are as American as apple pie.
Donald E. Wildmon, founder, National Federation for Decency (American Family Association). Quoted in *The New York Times Magazine*, Sept. 2, 1990.

40. American taxpayers have a right to determine how their money should be used, but American citizens also understand that the federal government should not diminish the artist's right to offend.
Pat Williams, U.S. Congressman (D-MT). Quoted in *The New York Times*, Mar. 3, 1990.

41. Architecture has its political use; publick buildings being the ornament of a country; it establishes a nation; draws people and commerce; makes the people love their native country.
Christopher Wren (1632-1723), British architect. *Parentalia*.

Chapter 6

The Budget and Budgeting

1. There is no escape from the cost of public needs.
Jodi Allen, American economics journalist. ABC, *Money Politics*, Apr. 15, 1990.

2. How do you balance the budget, cut taxes and increase defense spending at the same time? It's very simple. You do it with mirrors.
John B. Anderson, U.S. Congressman (R-IL). Campaign speech attacking Ronald Reagan's campaign promises, 1980.

3. The federal government is currently operating on a budget passed in the dead of night just before Christmas. It comprised three massive documents, ran to a staggering 3,296 pages, weighed in at a hefty forty-three pounds, and had a price tag of $650 billion. Congress had about three hours to look at it before voting on it.
William L. Armstrong, U.S. Congressman and U.S. Senator (R-CO). Quoted in *Conservative Digest*, Apr. 1988.

4. Whatever pain we go through now, our suffering will provide for the future of the next generations.
Ibrahim Babangida, President of Nigeria. *Newsweek*, Aug. 27, 1990.

5. Our national leaders could learn some good habits and important lessons from city hall to take the place of the various gimmicks being used in Washington to duck federal budget responsibility.
Alan Beals, Director, National League of Cities. Quoted in *The Washington Post*, July 16, 1988.

6. There are two ways to reduce expenditures. There is the intelligent way ... going through each department and questioning each program. Then there is the stupid way: announcing how much you will cut and getting each department to cut that amount. I favor the stupid way.
Michel Bélanger, Chairman, Quebec National Bank. Quoted in *The Globe and Mail* (Toronto, Canada), May 7, 1982.

7. You know if you let me write $200 billion worth of hot checks, I could also give you the illusion of prosperity.
Lloyd M. Bentsen, Jr., U.S. Congressman and U.S. Senator (D-TX). Televised vice-presidential debate with Dan Quayle, Oct. 5, 1988.

8. The Social Security trust fund is not spare money; it is spoken for.
Alan S. Blinder, professr of economics, Princeton University, NJ. *Business Week*, July 4, 1988.

9. In peace and war it's always money.
David Brinkley, American TV journalist. ABC, *This Week*, Sept. 16, 1990.

10. Let us all be happy and live within our means, even if we have to borrow the money to do it with.
Charles Ferrar Browne (1834-1867), American journalist and lecturer. *Artemus Ward in London*, "Science and Natural History," 1872.

11. Not all spending initiatives were designed to be immortal.
George Bush, 41st President of the United States (R-TX). Address to Congress, Feb. 9, 1989.

12. All progress is based upon the universal innate desire on the part of every organism to live beyond its income.
Samuel Butler (1835-1902), British essayist and satirist. *The Note-Books of Samuel Butler*, 1912.

13. There is no belt to tighten anymore.
Cuauhtemoc Cardenas, leader, National Democratic Front, Mexico. Quoted in *Newsweek*, Aug. 1, 1988.

14. *[The]* up-and-down pattern of *[defense]* spending over the last eighteen years averages out to below zero percent real growth. In other words, if defense spending had followed a path of zero percent real growth, the U.S. probably could have

obtained more defense for its dollar.

Frank C. Carlucci, U.S. Secretary of Defense and National Security Advisor (D). Address, American Logistics Association, Oct. 1988.

15. There are but two ways of paying debt – increase of industry in raising income, increase of thrift in laying out.

Thomas Carlyle (1795-1881), Scottish essayist and historian. "Government," in *Past and Present*, 1843.

16. As Secretary of Defense my job would be much easier if I didn't have to put up with *[budget]* cuts.

Richard B. Cheney, U.S. Congressman (R-WY), White House Chief of Staff and U.S. Secretary of Defense. Interview, ABC, *This Week*, Nov. 19, 1989.

17. In Congress we face the possibility of radical cuts based on nothing save grand compromises over what parochial interests need to be satisfied.

Richard B. Cheney. Speech, National Newspaper Association, Washington, DC, Mar. 17, 1990.

18. We can't continue to spend where there isn't any money.

Lawton M. Chiles, Jr., U.S. Senator and Governor of Florida (D). Press conference, Apr. 1, 1991.

19. When it comes to budget cuts, everyone wants to go to heaven, but nobody wants to die.

Jean Chrétien, Minister of Finance, Canada. Nov. 2, 1978.

20. I'm sick of voting blank checks.

James B. (Champ) Clark (1850-1921), U.S. Congressman and Speaker of the House (D-MO). Reaction to the appropriations for the Work Projects Administration. Quoted in *Time*, Mar. 30, 1936.

21. Borrowed money, even when owing to a nation by another nation, should be repaid. They hired the money, didn't they? Let them pay it.

Calvin Coolidge (1872-1933), 30th President of the United States (R-MA). In response to a proposal that the United States help reduce the Allies' World War I debt. Remark, 1925.

22. I did not come into government to win an award as the great accountant in the sky and balance budgets.

Mario Cuomo, Governor of New York (D). *Inside Albany*, June 19, 1988.

23. You will succeed *[at negotiating a budget with Congress]* only if you first build trust. It's like wolves. They show each other their necks and don't bite.

Richard G. Darman, Director, U.S. Office of Management and Budget (R). Quoted in *The Washington Post*, May 14, 1989.

24. We have no choice but to make our local government fit the size of our local economy. We must all bear our share of the pain.

David Dinkins, Mayor of New York City (D). Statement announcing a 5 percent pay cut for himself and other top city administrators. Oct. 28, 1990.

25. You spend a billion here and a billion there. Sooner or later it adds up to real money.

Everett M. Dirksen (1896-1969), U.S. Congressman and U.S. Senator (R-IL). Attributed.

26. Only when the budget has been balanced and a substantial amount set aside for debt retirement, should we consider tax reduction.

Robert L. Doughton (1863-1954), U.S. Congressman (D-NC). Congressional debate, Mar. 26, 1947.

27. The good news is the Pentagon is going to make some significant budget cuts. The bad news is: They want to kill a plane that's built in your district.

Thomas J. Downey, U.S. Congressman (D-NY). Quoted in *New York Magazine*, Dec. 18, 1989.

28. Everyone is always in favour of general economy and particular expenditure.

Anthony Eden (1897-1977), Prime Minister of Great Britain (Conservative). Quoted in *The Observer*, June 17, 1956.

29. You just don't see people running through the streets to have the deficit cut.

Kathryn Eickhoff, chief economist, U.S. Office of Management and Budget. Quoted in *The New York Times*, Sept. 15, 1985.

30. The first order of business is the elimination of the annual deficit.

Dwight D. Eisenhower (1890-1969), 34th President of the United States (R-KS). Message to Congress, Feb. 3, 1953.

31. As quickly as you start spending federal money in large amounts, it looks like free money.

Dwight D. Eisenhower. Quoted in Susan Teltser-Schwartz, *Money Talks*, 1988.

32. Any crooked bookkeeper's books are balanced.

James E. Fergeson (1871-1944), Governor of Texas (D). Campaign speech, 1932.

33. Cost reduction and cost control are by their very nature sort of antisocial activities.

A. Ernest Fitzgerald, U.S. Deputy Assistant Secretary of the Air Force. Quoted in Rice, *The C-5A Scandal*, 1971.

34. The reason Congress hasn't balanced the budget is that the sky hasn't fallen lately.
William Frenzel, U.S. Congressman (R-MN). Speech, Economics Club, Sept. 18, 1990.

35. When the greatest part of the *[U.S.]* budget pays for our defense and the livelihood of retirees, it is pointless to pretend that public spending is an embarrassment consisting only of welfare and waste.
Benjamin Friedman, professor of economics, Harvard University. *Day of Reckoning*, 1988.

36. A nation's budget is full of moral implications; it tells what a society cares about and what it does not care about; it tells what its values are.
J. William Fulbright, U.S. Senator (D-AR). Quoted in Susan Teltser-Schwartz, *Money Talks*, 1988.

37. Budgets are not bottomless pits.
Isaac Fulwood, Jr., Chief of Police, Washington, DC. Quoted on WETA-TV, *Metro Week in Review*, Sept. 29, 1989.

38. Everybody's entitled to their own figures.
Eligio (Kika) de la Garza II, U.S. Congressman (D-TX). Speech, Commodity Club, Washington, DC, June 1990.

39. *[Federal deficits]* are like an athlete taking steroids. You get a short-term boost and long-term damage.
Albert A. Gore, Jr., U.S. Senator (D-TN) and Vice President of the United States. ABC, *This Week*, Oct. 16, 1988.

40. Balancing the budget is like going to heaven. Everybody wants to do it, but nobody wants to do what you have to do to get there.
Phil Gramm, U.S. Congressman and U.S. Senator (R-TX). Interview, ABC, *This Week*, Sept. 16, 1990.

41. Figures won't lie, but liars will figure.
Charles Henry Grosvenor (1833-1917), U.S. Congressman (R-OH). Favorite saying.

42. A national debt, if it is not excessive, will be to us a national blessing.
Alexander Hamilton (1755-1804), Member, Continental Congress and Constitutional Convention, and U.S. Secretary of the Treasury (Federalist-NY). Letter to Robert Morris, Apr. 30, 1781.

43. Financial markets will tolerate a Republican deficit but will run screaming in panic from a Democratic deficit a fraction its size.
Gary Hart, U.S. Senator (D-CO). July 1988.

44. It is a terribly hard job to spend a billion dollars and get your money's worth.
Anna Rosenberg Hoffman (1902-1983), U.S. Assistant Secretary of Defense. Quoted in *Look*, Feb. 23, 1954.

45. Blessed are the young, for they shall inherit the national debt.
Herbert Hoover (1874-1964), 31st President of the United States (R-IA). Remark, 1959.

46. There are only three ways to meet the unpaid bills of a nation. The first is taxation. The second is repudiation. The third is inflation.
Herbert Hoover. Quoted in *The Iowa City Press Citizen*, Dec. 31, 1990.

47. Every public official concerned with administering public funds owes it to all our citizens to be prepared at any time to account to the last penny of the public money placed in his hands.
Harry L. Hopkins (1890-1946), U.S. Secretary of Commerce; Director, Work Projects Administration; and Special Assistant to the President (D). Speech, Annual Conference of Mayors, Chicago, IL, Nov. 23, 1934.

48. A good budget is an oxymoron.
Amory Houghton, U.S. Congressman (D-NY). Quoted on C-SPAN, Oct. 7, 1990.

49. How does a government reduce expenditures? To be absolutely flat about it, 99 percent of it is accomplished by putting people out of work. Now that is a tough way to say it, but it is a fact.
George M. Humphrey (1890-1970), U.S. Secretary of the Treasury (R). Speech, Washington Conference of Governors, Apr. 1954.

50. Funding cuts translate into lives lost, not dreams deferred.
Charles J. Hynes, Jr., District Attorney, Brooklyn, NY (D). Meeting, New York City Council, May 21, 1991.

51. I am one of those who do not believe that a national debt is a national blessing, but rather a curse to a republic; inasmuch as it is calculated to raise around the administration a moneyed aristocracy dangerous to the liberties of the country.
Andrew Jackson (1767-1845), 7th President of the United States. Letter to T. H. Colman, Apr. 26, 1824.

52. It is incumbent on every generation to pay its own debts as it goes. A principle which, if acted on, would save one half the wars of the world.
Thomas Jefferson (1743-1826), 3rd President of

the United States (Democratic Republican-VA). Letter to Destutt de Tracy, 1820.

53. To preserve our independence, we must not let our rulers load us with perpetual debt.
Thomas Jefferson. Quoted in *Conservative Digest*, Apr. 1988.

54. How many more infants must die every day in Africa because resources are being swallowed up in debt repayment?
Pope John Paul II. Speech, Zambia, May 3, 1989.

55. One thousand dollars invested in salvaging an unemployable youth can return $40,000 or more in his lifetime.
Lyndon B. Johnson (1908-1973), 36th President of the United States (D-TX). First annual message to Congress, Jan. 8, 1964.

56. We are going to put "thrift" back in the dictionary.
Lyndon B. Johnson. Speech, Washington, DC, Dec. 4, 1964.

57. Like Ike *[President Eisenhower]* did. Talk economy and then spend away.
Lyndon B. Johnson. Instructions to U.S. Secretary of the Treasury Douglas Dillon on how to sell the proposed 1965 budget to Congress. Quoted in Merle Miller, *Lyndon: An Oral Biography*, 1980.

58. I've had a tough time learning how to act like a Congressman. Today, I actually spent some of my own money.
Joseph P. Kennedy III, U.S. Congressman (D-MA). Quoted in *Newsweek*, Feb. 9, 1987.

59. Let us act with our eyes open. We are going to have a deficit next fiscal year and the year after that.
Fiorello H. La Guardia (1882-1947), U.S. Congressman (R and Socialist) and Mayor of New York City (R and Fusion Party). Speech in Congress after the stock market crash, Dec. 5, 1929.

60. For heaven's sake, stop nickle-and-diming me to death.
Melvin R. Laird, U.S. Secretary of Defense (R). Remark to U.S. Office of Management and Budget Director Robert P. Mayo. Quoted in *The Washington Post*, Jan. 1, 1973.

61. The Republicans can't say no to military spending, and the Democrats can't say no to social spending.
Richard D. Lamm, Governor of Colorado (D). *Playboy*, Aug. 1984.

62. Christmas is a time when kids tell Santa what they want and adults pay for it. Deficits are when adults tell the government what they want – and their kids pay for it.
Richard D. Lamm. Speech, National League of Cities, Seattle, WA, Dec. 10, 1985.

63. No country can violate the laws of economic gravity too long.
Richard D. Lamm. Interview, PBS, *MacNeil-Lehrer News Hour*, Oct. 1990.

64. Can the amazing national debt *[of Great Britain]* be paid by a little trifling sum squeezed from year to year out of America?... Would it not be much superior wisdom, and sounder policy, for a distressed kingdom to retrench the vast unnecessary expenses continually incurred by its enormous vices?
Samuel Langdon (1723-1797), President, Harvard College, Cambridge, MA. Election sermon, Congress of the Massachusetts Bay Colony, Watertown, MA, May 31, 1775.

65. A behemoth budget does not mean there is much discretion in allocating it.
Kenneth Lipper, Deputy Mayor of New York City (D). *The New York Times Magazine*, Dec. 31, 1989.

66. International debts are like bills submitted to pay for the damage done on a wild party by one's grandfather. The payment seems to the debtor like pure loss, and when it is paid by one nation to another it seems the tribute by the conquered to the conqueror.
Walter Lippmann (1889-1974), American political writer. *The New York World*, 1926.

67. The House of Representatives cannot only refuse, but they alone can propose the supplies requisite for the support of the government. They, in a word, hold the purse: that powerful instrument by which we behold in the history of the British constitution an infant and humble representation of the people, gradually enlarging the sphere of its activity and importance, and finally reducing, as far as it seems to have wished, all the overgrown prerogatives of the other branches of the government.
James Madison (1751-1836), 4th President of the United States (Democratic Republican-VA). *The Federalist*, No. 58.

68. There are no uncontrollable outlays except for debt interest. Outlays are what they are due to legislation.
Paul W. McCracken, Chairman, Council of Economic Advisors. *The Wall Street Journal*, Dec. 6, 1988.

69. A nation is not in danger of financial disaster merely because it owes itself money.
Andrew William Mellon (1855-1937), U.S. Secretary of the Treasury (R). Attributed.

70. The budget is about day-to-day lives.
Barbara A. Mikulski, U.S. Congresswoman and U.S. Senator (D-MD). *The Washington Post*, Oct. 28, 1990.

71. When everybody is supposed to pay, nobody seems to get the bill.
Bruce Morrison, U.S. Congressman (D-CT). Letter, *The New York Times*, Sept. 3, 1990.

72. The deficit has had one very good effect. It has helped control spending.
John O'Sullivan, editor, *National Review*. PBS, *Firing Line*, Jan. 16, 1989.

73. No nation ought to be without a debt. A national debt is a national bond; and when it bears no interest, is in no case a grievance.
Thomas Paine (1737-1809), American political philosopher. *Common Sense*, Jan. 10, 1776.

74. The process of the budget has become basically a process of saying "no."
Leon E. Panetta, U.S. Congressman (D-CA). Quoted in *The New York Times*, Apr. 20, 1989.

75. Our country was founded by people who followed the simple ways of living. Those ways of living are safe and sound for us today.... I am fearful of unusual prosperity, it often leads us to overstep in speculation.
John C. Phillips (1870-1943), Governor of Arizona (R). Inaugural address, Jan. 7, 1929.

76. You have to put the money where the biggest need is.
Colin Powell, General, U.S. Army; National Security Advisor; and Chairman, Joint Chiefs of Staff. NBC, *Meet the Press*, Dec. 18, 1988.

77. We must be as candid as we can about how much things cost and how they are going to be paid for.
Robert Keith Rae, Premier of Ontario, Canada. Speech opening legislature, Nov. 20, 1990.

78. You start with the fact that the government has a sizable layer of fat, no matter how worthwhile the program. And I would include defense in that.
Ronald Reagan, 40th President of the United States (R-CA). Quoted in *Newsweek*, Mar. 24, 1975.

79. You and I, as individuals, can, by borrowing, live beyond our means, but only for a limited period of time. Why then should we think that collectively, as a nation, we're not bound by the same limitation?
Ronald Reagan. First inaugural address, January 20, 1980.

80. This administration is committed to a balanced budget, and we will fight to the last blow to achieve it in 1984.
Ronald Reagan. Sept. 21, 1981.

81. We do not face large deficits because American families are undertaxed; we face those deficits because the federal government overspends.... It's time we reduced the federal budget and left the family budget alone.
Ronald Reagan. Annual message to Congress, Feb. 2, 1986.

82. We're short of money – it's as simple as that.
Carl Reardon, Commissioner of Trust Funds, Swampscott, MA. Explanation of proposal to spend $100 of town funds to buy lottery tickets for the township. Quoted in *Newsweek*, May 19, 1986.

83. This is a billion-dollar country.
Thomas B. Reed (1839-1902), U.S. Congressman and Speaker of the House (R-ME). Explanation of the billion-dollar federal budget proposed by the Republican Harrison administration, 1889.

84. No single portion of the budget is capable of completely solving the budget deficit problem.
Robert D. Reischauer, Director, Congressional Budget Office. Quoted in *The Washington Post*, Nov. 22, 1989.

85. Whenever you get in a crash program, you can't help spending money.
L. Mendel Rivers (1905-1970), U.S. Congressman (D-SC). In defense of the C-5A overruns. House Armed Services Committee hearings, 1968.

86. There's been a lot of talk of sacrifice, but one just doesn't see it here.
Alice Rivlin, Director, Congressional Budget Office. Comment when reviewing Pres. Carter's budget. Quoted in *Time*, July 18, 1977.

87. If the nation is living within its income, its credit is good. If in some crisis it lives beyond its income for a year or two, it can usually borrow temporarily on reasonable terms. But if, like some spendthrift, it throws discretion to the winds, is willing to make no sacrifices at all in spending, extends its taxing up to the limit of the people's power to pay, and continues to pile up deficits, then it is on the road to bankruptcy.
Franklin D. Roosevelt (1882-1945), 32nd Presi-

dent of the United States. Speech, Pittsburgh, PA, Oct. 19, 1932.

88. Our national debt after all is an internal debt owed not only by the nation but to the nation. If our children have to pay interest on it, they will pay that interest to themselves.
Franklin D. Roosevelt. Speech, American Retail Foundation, May 22, 1939.

89. Our refusal to attack the deficit would be comic if it were not so irresponsible.
Daniel D. Rostenkowski, U.S. Congressman (D-IL). Quoted in *Time*, Oct. 23, 1989.

90. The only way to stop Congress from spending is to see that it gets less money. Less revenue, less spending.
William V. Roth, Jr., U.S. Congressman and U.S. Senator (D-DE). Remark to Adam Smith (George J. W. Goodman), 1981.

91. There are now over four hundred different accounting systems to be found in the federal government. They are not only incompatible, but the majority of them are ... substandard and inadequate.
William V. Roth, Jr. Senate committee hearing, May 13, 1986.

92. A bad idea whose time has come.
Warren B. Rudman, U.S. Senator (R-NH). Explanation of the Gramm-Rudman Budget Reduction Act. Quoted in *The Washington Post*, Oct. 8, 1989.

93. If you ask the Air Force what budget cuts they would suggest, they will always first suggest Air Force One, knowing you'll not cut it.
Donald Rumsfeld, U.S. Secretary of Defense (R). PBS, *Third Annual Report of the Secretaries of Defense*, Jan. 19, 1990.

94. The President says the defense budget is not sacrosanct. That means they are laying off six waiters at the Army-Navy club.
Mark Russell, American political comedian. Quoted in *Current Biography*, 1981.

95. This is a thousand points of light, but unfortunately the batteries aren't included.
James R. Sasser, U.S. Senator (D-TN). Comment on the proposed Bush administration budget for 1989. Quoted in *Newsweek*, Feb. 27, 1989.

96. The Pentagon will not provide the financial numbers to the Senate Budget Committee, so that must mean it's not good news.
James R. Sasser. Senate debate, Jan. 11, 1991.

97. The only way to judge *[government]* spending is as a percentage of gross national product.
Charles L. Schultze, Chairman, Council of Economic Advisors, and Director, U.S. Bureau of the Budget (D). PBS, *Wall Street Week*, Jan. 17, 1991.

98. Resources drive all of the agency's work.... There is not an agency ... that does not want more resources.
William Sessions, Director, Federal Bureau of Investigation. Interview, PBS, *John McLaughlin's One-on-One*, Sept. 17, 1989.

99. Every *[government]* budget I've ever known is phoney.
Hugh Sidey, American political columnist. CBS, *Inside Washington*, July 22, 1990.

100. Did the Pilgrims need subsidies?
William E. Simon, U.S. Secretary of the Treasury (R). Interview, *Playboy*, May 1975.

101. We've either got to get rid of the deficit or get rid of the notion that we've got to get rid of the deficit.
Herbert Stein, Chairman, Council of Economic Advisors. Quoted on National Public Radio, Oct. 2, 1990.

102. A veritable incubator of shortcuts, schemes, and devices to overcome the truth.
David A. Stockman, Director, Office of Management and Budget, and U.S. Congressman (R-MI). Description of the OMB. *The Triumph of Politics*, 1986.

103. After four years I am convinced that a large share of the problem is us. By that I mean Republicans.
David A. Stockman. In reference to the federal deficit. Interview, *Playboy*, 1986.

104. I am not concerned with what you are required to budget. I am concerned about what the taxpayers are required to pay.
Samuel Stratton, U.S. Congressman (D-NY). Explanation to an Air Force officer on the budgetary subtleties of the C-5A overrun. House Armed Services Committee hearing, 1969.

105. When it comes to dealing with the budget, the political process has become somewhere between timid and irrelevant.
Robert S. Strauss, Chairman, Democratic National Committee, and U.S. Ambassador to the U.S.S.R. Quoted in *The New York Times*, Mar. 18, 1990.

106. I would not want to skate on a flexibly frozen lake.
Lawrence Summers, economic advisor to Gov.

Michael Dukakis. Commenting on the concept of a "flexible freeze" as a budget reduction measure. Quoted in *Time*, Jan. 30, 1989.

107. Now when the army marches abroad, the treasury will be emptied at home. When the army engages in protracted campaigns, the resources of the State will not suffice.

Sun-tzu (c. 400 B.C.), Chinese writer of the Age of Warring States. *The Art of War*.

108. Budget drives strategy.

Maxwell D. Taylor (1901-1987), General, U.S. Army; Chairman, Joint Chiefs of Staff; and U.S. Ambassador to South Vietnam. Quoted on PBS, *MacNeil-Lehrer News Hour*, Feb. 13, 1989.

109. The only cut over there *[the Pentagon]* is when some general gets a vasectomy.

James A. Traficant, Jr., U.S. Congressman (D-OH). House debate, Oct. 8, 1990.

110. The federal government is far and away the nation's largest lender.

Paul S. Trible, Jr., U.S. Congressman and U.S. Senator (R-VA). Testimony, Senate Committee on Governmental Affairs, May 14, 1986.

111. Even when there's not enough money, choices still have to be made.

Reed V. Tucker, Commissioner of Public Health, Washington, DC. Interview, CNN, *Newsmaker*, Jan. 14, 1990.

112. No bankruptcy, no increase in taxation, no borrowing.

Anne Robert Jacques Turgot (1727-1781), Finance Minister of France, economist and statesman. Guiding maxim of his Finance Ministry (1774-1776) under Louis XVI.

113. African external debt, while it amounts to just small change in the overall Third World debt picture, is imposing intolerable burdens on the continent's people.

Tom Vraalsen, Norwegian Ambassador to the United Nations. *The Washington Post*, Nov. 14, 1989.

114. Every penny has to be voted. It's not as if the President has a big bag of money to hand out.

Vernon A. Walters, U.S. Ambassador to the United Nations and General, U.S. Army. Explanation as to why the U.S. administration could not provide funds to the U.N. without congressional action. Quoted in *The New York Times*, Aug. 9, 1988.

115. Good budgeting involves the even distribution of dissatisfaction.

Murray Weidenbaum, Chairman, Council of Economic Advisors. Interview, National Public Radio, Oct. 18, 1988.

116. It is always the "other fellow's" programs that should be cut. Unfortunately, there are not enough "other fellows" to go around.

Murray Weidenbaum. *CEO*, Mar.-Apr. 1989.

117. A trust fund without funds will not buy anything.

L. Douglas Wilder, Governor of Virginia (D). Campaign speech, Oct. 9, 1989.

118. Fiscal problems do a lot for moral uplift because sin takes a terrific shellacking from sin taxes.

George F. Will, American political columnist. *The Washington Post*, Feb. 26, 1989.

Chapter 7

Bureaucracy

1. A memorandum is written not to inform the reader but to protect the writer.
   Dean Acheson (1893-1971), U.S. Secretary of State (D). Quoted in Henry Metcalf, *The Penguin Dictionary of Modern Humorous Quotations*, 1986.

2. The Civil Service is a self-perpetuating oligarchy, and what better system is there?
   Robert Temple Armstrong, Civil Service Director, Great Britain. Remark, 1977.

3. No government under heaven could have prevented a people from ruin ... when they were exhausting their valuable resources in paying for superfluities, and running themselves in debt to foreigners, and to each other for articles of folly and dissipation.
   Benjamin Austin (1752-1820), publisher, *Boston Independent Chronicle*. Dec. 6, 1787.

4. Bureaucracy is a giant mechanism operated by pygmies.
   Honoré de Balzac (1799-1850), French writer. *Epigrams*.

5. These are the instructions you are getting today. It is only fair to tell you, however, that they may be changed tomorrow. And ten days later they may be changed back to the instructions you are getting now.
   Lemuel Boles, World War II Civil Defense Director, Washington DC. To his staff. Quoted in David Brinkley, *Washington Goes to War*, 1988.

6. I don't see anything wrong with overworking bureaucrats. I have yet to see the first one drop dead.
   Tony Bouza, Chief of Police, Minneapolis, MN, and Minnesota Gaming Commissioner. Quoted in *Newsweek*, Dec. 11, 1989.

7. If everyone in government would refuse to sign everything they couldn't read, everything would grind to a screeching halt.
   Edmund G. (Jerry) Brown, Jr., Governor of California (D). *Thoughts*, 1976.

8. When you come before us and tell us that we are to disturb your business interests, we reply that you have disturbed our business interests by your course. We say to you that you have made the definition of the businessman too limited in its application. The man who is employed for wages is as much a business man as his employer.
   William Jennings Bryan (1860-1925), U.S. Secretary of State (D). "Cross of Gold" speech, Democratic National Convention, Chicago, IL, July 8, 1896.

9. I'm surprised that a government organization could do it that quickly.
   Jimmy Carter, 39th President of the United States (D-GA). Response when told that the Great Pyramid had taken twenty years to complete. Quoted in Paul F. Boller, Jr., *Presidential Anecdotes*, 1981.

10. I confess to a prejudice against officialism and a dread of bureaucracy.
    Eugene V. Debs (1855-1926), American Socialist. *International Socialist Review*, Feb. 1912.

11. A government of statesmen or of clerks? Of Humbug or of Humdrum?
    Benjamin Disraeli, 1st Earl of Beaconsfield (1804-1881), Prime Minister of Great Britain (Conservative). *Coningsby*, 1844.

12. When we like our new rulers we call them public servants. When we are mad at them we call them bureaucrats; but it is the business of self-government to see that they remain servants of the public instead of becoming its masters.
    John Dos Passos (1896-1970), American writer. *Occasions and Protests*, 1964.

13. When they talk about belt-tightening in Washington, they are talking about tightening our belts.
    James J. Florio, U.S. Congressman and Governor of New Jersey (D). Quoted in *The New York Times*, Oct. 28, 1990.

14. A Royal Commission is a broody hen sitting on a china egg.

Michael Foot, Member of Parliament, Great Britain (Labour). Debate, House of Commons, 1964.

15. Red tape surrounded and almost smothered us; we as a nation were about to suffocate.
Gerald R. Ford, 38th President of the United States (R-MI). *A Time to Heal*, 1982.

16. One of the enduring truths of the nation's capital is that bureaucrats *survive*.
Gerald R. Ford. *Ibid.*

17. We have bureaucracy that doesn't really understand what the people want.
Gennadi I. Gerasimov, spokesman, Russian Foreign Ministry. Interview, CBS, *Face the Nation*, Feb. 4, 1990.

18. The moment responsibilities of any community, particularly in economic and social questions, are shifted from any part of the nation to Washington, then that community has subjected itself to a remote bureaucracy.... It has lost ... control of its own destiny.
Herbert Hoover (1874-1964), 31st President of the United States (R-IA). Statement, Feb. 1931.

19. To tell you the truth, we don't need ministries. We earn our own feed.... What can they give us? Nothing.
Vladimir P. Kabaidze, Russian industrial manager. Speech, Soviet Communist Party Conference, Moscow, U.S.S.R., June 29, 1988.

20. Government departments are like icebergs.
John F. Kennedy (1917-1963), 35th President of the United States (D-MA). Remark to Benjamin Bradlee, May 15, 1962.

21. You can't do anything in this department *[DOD]* without raising hackles. I was brought here to get things done, and you don't get things done without pissing people off.
Dennis Kloske, Pentagon analyst and Undersecretary for Export Administration, U.S. Department of Commerce. Quoted in *Regardie's*, May 1989.

22. Government is a hulk.
Edward I. Koch, U.S. Congressman and Mayor of New York City (D). 1987.

23. Bureaucracy ... is a direct negation of mass self-activity.
Aleksandra Kollontai (1872-1952), Soviet diplomat and 1st Commissar of Public Welfare. *The Workers' Opposition in Russia*, c. 1921.

24. No official yet born on this earth is wise enough or generous enough to separate good ideas from bad ideas, good beliefs from bad.
Walter Lippmann (1889-1974), American political columnist. *A Preface to Politics*, 1913.

25. Gobbledygook!
Maury Maverick (1895-1954), U.S. Congressman (D-TX). His self-coined term for bureaucratic double-talk. Quoted in David Brinkley, *Washington Goes to War*, 1988.

26. The only thing that saves us from the bureaucracy is inefficiency. An efficient bureaucracy is the greatest threat to liberty.
Eugene J. McCarthy, U.S. Congressman and U.S. Senator (D-WI). Quoted in *Time*, Feb. 12, 1979.

27. Bureaucracy, the rule of no one, has become the modern form of despotism.
Mary McCarthy (1912-1989), American writer. Quoted in *The New Yorker*, Oct. 18, 1958.

28. One thing about bureaucrats is that they never swallow their young. Leave them alone and you'll find them increasing every year.
Robert G. Menzies (1894-1978), Prime Minister of Australia (Liberal). 1946.

29. The needs of people are more important than the constraints of bureaucracy.
Eddie C. Moore, Director, Division of Developmental Disabilities, New Jersey. Explanation for spending $32 million without the authorization of his superiors. Quoted in *The New York Times*, Apr. 13, 1989.

30. Throughout the land people are repulsed by arrogant and unresponsive bureaucracies.
Ralph Nader, American consumer advocate. Congressional testimony, 1975.

31. I do not rule Russia; ten thousand clerks do.
Nicholas I (1796-1855), Czar of Russia. Attributed.

32. There is no Democratic or Republican way of delivering the mail. There is only the right way.
Richard M. Nixon, 37th President of the United States (R-CA). Message to Congress, May 27, 1969.

33. Bureaucracy defends the status quo long past the time when the quo has lost its status.
Laurence J. Peter, American educator and writer. *Peter's Quotations*, 1979.

34. Now so there will be no misunderstanding, it is not my intention to do away with the *[federal]* government. It is rather to make it work – work

with us, not over us; to stand by our side, not ride on our back.

Ronald Reagan, 40th President of the United States (R-CA). First inaugural address, Jan. 1981.

35. Most of the work in the Defense Department is writing reports.

Hyman G. Rickover (1900-1986), Admiral, U.S. Navy. Senate testimony, Jan. 28, 1982.

36. If you're going to sin, sin against God, not the bureaucracy. God will forgive you, but the bureaucracy won't.

Hyman G. Rickover. Quoted in *The New York Times*, Nov. 3, 1986.

37. The Treasury is so large and farflung and ingrained in its practices that I find it almost impossible to get the actions and results I want. But the Treasury is not to be compared to the State Department. You should go through the experience of trying to get any changes in the thinking, policy, and action of the career diplomats, and then you'd know what a real problem was.

Franklin D. Roosevelt (1882-1945), 32nd President of the United States (D-NY). Quoted in *American Heritage*, Feb. 1988.

38. A difficulty for every solution.

Herbert Louis Samuel, 1st Viscount Samuel (1870-1963), Home Secretary, Great Britain, and 1st High Commissioner to Palestine (Liberal). In reference to civil servants. Remark, 1922.

39. The working of great institutions is mainly the result of a vast mass of routine, petty malice, self-interest, carelessness, and sheer mistake.

George Santayana (1863-1952), American philosopher. *The Crime of Galileo*.

40. History shows that federal employees were cannon fodder in somebody else's political wars.

Patricia R. Schroeder, U.S. Congresswoman (D-CO). *Congressional Digest*, Jan. 1988.

41. They *[bureaucrats]* will answer the question you asked, but won't volunteer the answer to the question you should have asked.

Bruce Smart, U.S. Undersecretary of Commerce. *U.S. News & World Report*, June 20, 1988.

42. The next thing I view as being dangerous to national well-being is government by bureaucracy instead of government by law.

Alfred E. Smith (1873-1944), Governor of New York (D). Speech, 1936.

43. In place of the legitimist *[Bonaparte]* monarchy we will put the administrative monarchy.

Louis Adolphe Thiers (1797-1877), 1st President of the Third French Republic. Remark to Charles Cousin-Montauban during the Franco-Prussian War, 1870.

44. Any fool can make a rule.

Henry David Thoreau (1817-1862), American philosopher and naturalist. *Journal*, Feb. 3, 1860.

45. The leaden rump of bureaucracy outweighed the head of the revolution.

Leon Trotsky (1879-1940), Russian revolutionary theorist. *The Revolution Betrayed*, 1937.

46. In Washington if you wait long enough there will be another boss, with another set of priorities.

Marc Tucker, President, Center on Education and the Economy. Quoted in *The New York Times*, June 2, 1991.

47. Modern life does not run without bureaucracy.

Brian Urquhart, Undersecretary General of the United Nations. Interview, C-SPAN, Dec. 24, 1990.

48. You've got the best *[health]* research facility in the world held up by some functionaries *[the Office of Management and Budget]* who have no idea of what's needed.

James D. Watkins, Admiral, U.S. Navy, Chief of Naval Operations, and Chairman, Presidential AIDS Commission. Testimony, Senate Labor and Human Resources Committee, July 13, 1988.

49. Government organizations are especially risk averse because they are caught up in a web of constraints so complex that any change is likely to rouse the ire of some important constituency.

James Q. Wilson, American management consultant. *What Government Agencies Do and Why They Do It*, 1990.

50. I figured if the city is stupid enough to mail a one-cent bill, they're stupid enough to turn off the water for it.

Carol Wright. Explanation for paying a one-cent water bill promptly after the city of Columbus, OH, threatened to cut off her water. Quoted in *The Columbus Dispatch*, Oct. 20, 1988.

Chapter 8

Business and Commerce

1. Buy a hot dog from a poor Democrat!
Anonymous hot dog vendor outside the 1988 Republican National Convention. Quoted in *The Philadelphia Inquirer*, Aug. 15, 1988.

2. Big business does not want honest government.
James Truslow Adams (1878-1949), American historian. *The March of Democracy*, II, 1933.

3. A delusion and a sham, an empty menace to the great interests made to answer the clamor of the ignorant and unreasoning.
Nelson W. Aldrich (1841-1915), U.S. Congressman and U.S. Senator (R-RI). Comment on the Interstate Commerce Act, 1887.

4. We mean to make little business big, and all business honest, instead of striving to make Big Business little, and yet letting it remain dishonest.
Albert J. Beveridge (1862-1927), U.S. Senator (R-IN) and founder, Progressive League. Keynote address, Progressive (Bull Moose) Party Convention, Chicago, IL, Aug. 5, 1912.

5. *[Monopolies are]* ... the bane of our body politic at the present day.
Joseph P. Bradley (1813-1892), U.S. Supreme Court Justice. *Butchers' Union Co.* v. *Crescent City Co.*, 1884.

6. There must be reasonable restrictions upon competition else we shall see competition destroyed.
Louis D. Brandeis (1856-1941), U.S. Supreme Court Justice. Letter to Sen. Robert M. La Follette, May 27, 1913.

7. The goose that lays the golden egg has been considered a most valuable possession. But even more profitable is the privilege of taking the golden eggs laid by somebody else's goose. The investment bankers and their associates now enjoy that privilege. They control the people through the people's own money.
Louis D. Brandeis. "The Uses of Other People's Money," *Harper's Weekly*, 1914.

8. Surplus wealth is a sacred trust which its possessor is bound to administer in his lifetime for the good of the community.
Andrew Carnegie (1835-1919), American industrialist and philanthropist. "Wealth," *North American Review*, June 1889.

9. As we view the achievements of aggregated capital, we discover the existence of trusts, combinations, and monopolies, while the citizen is struggling far in the rear or is trampled to death beneath an iron heel. Corporations, which should be the restrained creatures of the law and the servants of the people, are fast becoming the nation's masters.
Grover Cleveland (1837-1908), 22nd and 24th President of the United States (D-NY). 4th annual message to Congress, Dec. 1888.

10. We discover that the fortunes realized by our manufacturers are no longer solely the reward of sturdy industry and enlightened foresight, but that they result from the discriminating favor of the government.
Grover Cleveland. *Ibid.*

11. Civilization and profits go hand in hand.
Calvin Coolidge (1872-1933), 30th President of the United States (R-MA). Speech, Nov. 27, 1920.

12. The business of America is business.
Calvin Coolidge. Speech, American Society of Newspaper Editors, Jan. 17, 1923.

13. As a class, merchants will always be opposed to the control of majorities.
James Fenimore Cooper (1789-1851), American writer. *The American Democrat*, 1838.

14. I ask every God-fearing citizen to save Boston from the banks and the railroads.
James M. Curley (1874-1958), U.S. Congressman and Mayor of Boston, MA (D). Campaign speech, 1913.

15. The war is on, knife to knife, hilt to hilt, foot to foot, knee to knee, between the corporations of Arkansas and the people.

Jeff Davis (1862-1913), U.S. Senator and Governor of Arkansas (D). Campaign speech. Quoted in Reinhard H. Luthin, *American Demagogues*, 1959.

16. Congress allowed America's savings and loans to be turned into casinos.

Millicent Fenwick (1910-1992), U.S. Congresswoman (R-NJ). PBS, *Mrs. Fenwick Goes to Washington*, June 26, 1991.

17. Among inalienable rights *[espoused in the Declaration of Independence]* was the right to pursue any lawful business or vocation.

Stephen J. Field (1816-1899), U.S. Supreme Court Justice. *Butchers' Union Co.* v. *Crescent City Co.*, 1884.

18. When things are going well, the companies *[defense contractors]* stress the idea of free enterprise, with no need for government regulation. But when things aren't going well, they suddenly become a "close partner" with the government, and want it to bail them out.

A. Ernest Fitzgerald, U.S. Deputy Assistant Secretary of the Air Force. Quoted in Rice, *The C-5A Scandal*, 1971.

19. An idealist is a person who helps other people to be prosperous.

Henry Ford (1863-1947), American industrialist and philanthropist. Testimony in his libel suit against the *Chicago Tribune*, Mt. Clemens, MI, July 1919.

20. There is something uniquely obscene about competition to promote weapons of mass destruction for purposes of improving the stock market position of a corporation.

John Kenneth Galbraith, American economist and U.S. Ambassador to India (D). Remark, 1969.

21. Politics is the reflex of the business and industrial world.

Emma Goldman (1869-1940), American anarchist. *The Tragedy of Women's Emancipation*, 1911.

22. It is the culture at the Fed *[Federal Reserve Board]* to seek consensus as distinct from merely recording one's vote.... Unless the chairman has everyone behind him, he can't go very far.

Alan Greenspan, Chairman, Federal Reserve Board. Quoted in *The New York Times Magazine*, Jan. 15, 1989.

23. The heart of America is small businesses.

Frank Guarini, U.S. Congressman (D-NY). Interview, C-SPAN, Jan. 30, 1991.

24. I stand with the people against the corporations.

Frank Hague (1876-1956), Mayor of Jersey City, NJ (D). Campaign speech, 1917.

25. An unrestrained intercourse between the States themselves will advance the trade of each.

Alexander Hamilton (1755-1804), Member, Continental Congress and Constitutional Convention, and U.S. Secretary of the Treasury (Federalist-NY). *The Federalist*, No. 11, Nov. 24, 1787.

26. The Republicans have received a clear mandate to govern the country in the interest of business expansion.

Mark A. Hanna (1837-1904), U.S. Senator and Chairman, Republican National Committee (R-OH). Speech following the election of William McKinley as President of the United States, Nov. 7, 1900.

27. The best thing that governments can do is get out of business. When governments interfere less, managers can do their jobs better.

Lord Hanson, Chairman, Hanson PLC, England. Quoted in *U.S. News & World Report*, June 20, 1988.

28. Less Government in Business and More Business in Government

Warren G. Harding (1865-1923), 29th President of the United States (R-OH). Title of campaign booklet and slogan, 1920.

29. American business is not a monster, but an expression of God-given impulse to create, and the savior of our happiness.

Warren G. Harding. Quoted in Wallechinsky and Wallace, *The People's Almanac*, 1975.

30. The prosperity of merchants depends on the purchasing power of the mass of the people.

William Randolph Hearst (1863-1951), U.S. Congressman (D-NY); founder, Independence League Party; journalist; and publisher. Interview, *Chicago Tribune*, Jan. 19, 1905.

31. The most enlightened judicial policy is to let people manage their own business in their own way.

Oliver Wendell Holmes, Jr. (1841-1935), U.S. Supreme Court Justice. *Miles* v. *Park*, 1911 (dissent).

32. The notion that a business is clothed with a public interest and has been devoted to the public use is little more than a fiction intended to beautify what is disagreeable to the sufferers.

Oliver Wendell Holmes, Jr. *Tyson* v. *Banton*, 1927.

33. It is just as important that business keep out of government as that government keep out of business.

Herbert Hoover (1874-1964), 31st President of the United States (R-CA). Campaign speech, Oct. 22, 1928.

34. Prosperity is just around the corner.

Herbert Hoover. Attributed, 1932.

35. Even if government conduct of business could give us more efficiency instead of less efficiency, the fundamental objection to it would remain unaltered and unabated. It would destroy political equality. It would increase rather than decrease abuse and corruption. It would stifle initiative and invention. It would undermine the development of leadership. It would cramp and cripple the mental and spiritual energies of our people. It would extinguish equality and opportunity. It would dry up the spirit of liberty and progress.

Herbert Hoover. Quoted in Foster Rhea Dulles, *The United States Since 1865*, 1959.

36. I believe our economic life based on a profit motive is the most effective economy known to assure the well being of all.

Harry L. Hopkins (1890-1946), U.S. Secretary of Commerce; Director, Federal Emergency Relief Administration; and Special Assistant to the President (D). Quoted in *Time*, July 18, 1938.

37. I do not dislike your bank any more than all banks.

Andrew Jackson (1767-1845), 7th President of the United States (D-TN). To Nicholas Biddle, head of the Bank of the United States, 1829.

38. You are a den of vipers and thieves. By the eternal God, I will rout you out.

Andrew Jackson. To bankers who advocated passage of the Bank Renewal Bill, 1832.

39. Every monopoly and all exclusive privileges are granted at the expense of the public.

Andrew Jackson. Veto message, Bank Renewal Bill, July 10, 1832.

40. I want to see a reasonable profit, a fair profit, but we can't tolerate obscene profits.

Henry M. Jackson (1912-1983), U.S. Congressman and U.S. Senator (D-WA). In reference to the oil companies, 1974.

41. It is certainly for the public good to keep all the banks competitors for our favors by a judicious distribution of them and thus to engage ... them in support of the reformed order of things or at least in an acquiescence under it.

Thomas Jefferson (1743-1826), 3rd President of the United States (Democratic Republican-VA). Letter to Treasury Secretary Albert Gallatin, 1801.

42. We must now place the manufacturer by the side of the agriculturist.

Thomas Jefferson. Letter to Dupont de Nemours, 1809.

43. Merchants have no country.

Thomas Jefferson. Letter to Horatio G. Spafford, Mar. 17, 1814.

44. I sincerely believe, with you, that banking establishments are more dangerous than standing armies.

Thomas Jefferson. Letter to John Taylor, May 28, 1816.

45. Institutions, both public and private, exist because the people want them, believe in them, or at least are willing to tolerate them. The day has passed when business was a private matter – if it ever really was. In a business society, every act of business has social consequences.

Robert Wood Johnson (1893-1968), founder, Johnson & Johnson Co. *Or Forfeit Freedom*, 1947.

46. The need for more government protections *[more stringent bank regulation]* became even more apparent after observing the risk-taking behavior of the banks in the marketplace.

Henry Kaufman, chief economist, Salomon Brothers Investment Bank. Speech, Natl. Press Club, Washington, DC, Mar. 10, 1983.

47. Our country and, for that matter, other industrialized nations have been unwilling to let full market discipline prevail *[and allow major economic entities to fail]*. The reason is simple: Millions of innocent bystanders would be hurt.

Henry Kaufman. *The New York Times Magazine*, Oct. 9, 1988.

48. They fucked us and we've got to try and fuck them.

John F. Kennedy (1917-1963), 35th President of the United States (D-MA). About the steel companies that reneged on their promises during the strike. Remark to Benjamin Bradlee, Apr. 13, 1962.

49. If they *[steel magnates]* don't do well, I don't do well.

John F. Kennedy. Quoted in *Time*, Nov. 7, 1988.

50. I want to talk to them *[industrialists]* because they stay in power and you change all the time.

Nikita S. Khrushchev (1894-1971), Premier of the

U.S.S.R. Remark to Italian politicians. Quoted in *Life*, Nov. 24, 1967.

51. International bankers ply their disloyal and nefarious practices.
Harold Knutson (1880-1953), U.S. Congressman (R-MN). Speech in Congress, June 29, 1939.

52. The consumer knows that his prices are made for him by those who control the avenues of trade and the highways of commerce.
Robert M. La Follette (1855-1925), Governor of Wisconsin and U.S. Senator (R). Senate speech, Apr. 23, 1906.

53. The time has come when the Executive branch of this Government must enforce the plain letter of the law and check monopoly, or it must turn the people over boldly into the hands of exploiters grown impudent and ruthlessly aggressive through long years of wanton violation of the law.
Robert M. La Follette. *La Follette's Magazine*, May 1922.

54. The people have been plundered by profiteers.... *[Saying]* that is not demagogy; it is democracy – the democracy of Jefferson. It is not radicalism; it is republicanism – the republicanism of Lincoln.
Fiorello H. La Guardia (1882-1947), U.S. Congressman (R and Socialist) and Mayor of New York City (R and Fusion Party). Quoted in *The Brooklyn Daily Eagle*, July 23, 1922.

55. Wars are directed by bankers.
Fiorello H. La Guardia. Quoted in Mann, *La Guardia: A Fighter Against His Times*, 1959.

56. The banks use rather surreal accounting practices.
James Madison Leach, U.S. Congressman (D-IA). Interview, PBS, *MacNeil-Lehrer Report*, Mar. 10, 1989.

57. Wall Street owns the country. It is no longer a government of the people, by the people, and for the people, but a government of Wall Street, by Wall Street, and for Wall Street.... Over 100,000 shopgirls are forced to sell their virtue for the bread their niggardly wages deny them.
Mary Elisabeth Lease (1853-1933), American agrarian reformer and populist. Speech, People's Party (Populist Party) Convention, Omaha, NE, July 2, 1892.

58. With the bank crash of 1931, the *[Third German]* Reich attained a position from which it dominates more than three-fourths of all German banking, and owns about 40 percent of their shares.... When this life-saving expedition was over, the Reich was the dictator of the whole German banking world.
Emil Lengyel (1895-1985), American political economist. *The New Deal in Europe*, 1937.

59. Capitalists are no more capable of self-sacrifice than a man is capable of lifting himself by his own bootstraps.
V. I. Lenin (1870-1924), Premier of the U.S.S.R. *Letters from Afar*, 1917.

60. Certain forms of property must be reserved to the state, since they carry with them an opportunity of domination too great to be left to private individuals without injury to the community at large.
Pope Leo XIII (1810-1903), Encyclical, *Rerum Novarum*, May 15, 1891.

61. Corporate welfare bums.
David Lewis, Member of Parliament, Canada (New Democratic Party). In reference to large corporations receiving substantial tax advantages and other subsidies. Speech, Glasgow, Nova Scotia, Aug. 3, 1972.

62. These capitalists generally act harmoniously and in concert, to fleece the people.
Abraham Lincoln (1809-1865), 16th President of the United States (R-IL). Speech, Illinois legislature, Jan. 1837.

63. Government has no other end but the preservation of property.
John Locke (1632-1704), English political philosopher. *Second Treatise on Civil Government*, 1690.

64. I say, Mr. President, and I say in all seriousness, that those packers in Chicago and those owners of the Standard Oil have done more to advance socialism and anarchism and unrest and agitation than all the socialistic agitators who stand today between the oceans.
Henry Cabot Lodge (1850-1924), U.S. Congressman and U.S. Senator (R-MA). Remark to Theodore Roosevelt, 1906.

65. Let's face it, people who work in the securities business are not people who care nothing for money.
Gary Lynch, Director of Enforcement, U.S. Securities and Exchange Commission. Comment on difficulties in regulating the securities business. Aug. 1987.

66. Capitalism will kill competition.
Karl Marx (1818-1883), German economist and Socialist. George Seldes, *The Great Quotations*, 1983.

67. Effective competition requires that traders have large freedom of action when conducting their own affairs.

James Clark McReynolds (1862-1946), U.S. Supreme Court Justice. *Federal Trade Commission* v. *Curtis Publishing Co.*, 1922.

68. If you steal from the American public, whether you use a gas pump or a gun, you ought to do hard time.

Barbara A. Mikulski, U.S. Congresswoman and U.S. Senator (D-MD). Quoted in *The Washington Post*, Sept. 16, 1990.

69. If we have done anything wrong, send your man to my man and they can fix it up.

J. Pierpont Morgan (1837-1913), American financier and industrialist. Remark to Pres. Theodore Roosevelt about antitrust actions being taken against his firm, Northern Securities Company, 1902.

70. Corporate taxpayers should pay for corporate scandals.

Ralph Nader, American consumer advocate. Criticism of the taxpayer bailout in the 1989 savings and loan crisis. Quoted on ABC, *Nightline*, Aug. 9, 1989.

71. We are gradually reaching a time, if we have not already reached that period, when the business of the country is controlled by men who can be named on the fingers of one hand.

George W. Norris (1861-1944), U.S. Senator (R and Independent Republican-NB). *Congressional Record*, Nov. 30, 1944.

72. Competition to a politician means greater efficiency – more goods are produced at cheaper prices for the benefit of all. To a business man it means somebody wins and somebody loses.

Lionel Olmer, U.S. Undersecretary of Commerce (R). Interview, NBC, *The McLaughlin Group*, July 18, 1989.

73. Socialized banking has not been denounced by those who fanatically advocate total freedom of private enterprise.

Major Owens, U.S. Congressman (D-NY). Comment on the massive government bailout in the 1989 savings and loan scandal. Quoted in *Roll Call*, May 21, 1990.

74. In the great commercial struggle between nations which is eventually to determine the welfare of all, national efficiency will be the deciding factor.

Gifford Pinchot (1865-1946), Governor of Pennsylvania (Progressive Republican), and Chief, U.S. Forest Service. 1912.

75. They have already plundered us. They will never plunder us again.

José Lopez Portillo, President of Mexico. Announcement of the nationalization of private banks in Mexico. Speech, Sept. 1, 1982.

76. Manufacturers fatten their already swollen purses with more ill-gotten gains wrung from the horny hands of the toiling masses.

Samuel T. Rayburn (1882-1961), U.S. Congressman and Speaker of the House (D-TX). First speech in Congress, May 6, 1913.

77. A tabby cat with soft gums, a plaintive mew, and an anemic appearance. It is a sort of legislative apology to the trusts, delivered hat in hand, and accompanied by assurances that no discourtesy is intended.

James A. Reed (1861-1944), U.S. Senator (D-MO). In reference to the Clayton Anti-Trust Act of 1914, which did little to control monopoly. Quoted in Link, *Woodrow Wilson and the Progressive Era*, 1954.

78. The merchants were the great men of the earth.

New Testament, *Revelation* 18:23.

79. There is a lot more to this life than just the struggle to make money.

Ann Richards, Governor of Texas (D). Interview, CBS, *Sunday Morning*, July 31, 1988.

80. The President *[Dwight D. Eisenhower]* is a good man and he would always try to do the right thing as he saw it, but he has a great admiration for the achievement of the successful businessman because he has never been a successful businessman and you always admire what you don't really understand.

Anna Eleanor Roosevelt (1884-1962), First Lady and U.S. Delegate to the United Nations. Interview, NBC, *Meet the Press*, Sept. 16, 1956.

81. One of my principal tasks is to prevent bankers and businessmen from committing suicide.

Franklin D. Roosevelt (1882-1945), 32nd President of the United States (D-NY). 1936.

82. We have always known that heedless self-interest was bad morals; we know now that it is bad economics.

Franklin D. Roosevelt. Second inaugural address, Jan. 20, 1937.

83. The individual must be encouraged ... to venture his own small savings, not in stock gambling, but in new enterprise investment.

Franklin D. Roosevelt. Message to Congress, Apr. 29, 1938.

84. They have raved against trusts, they have foamed at the mouth, prating of impossible remedies they would like to adopt.

Theodore Roosevelt (1858-1919), 26th President of the United States (R-NY). In reference to the Democrats' antitrust efforts. Campaign speech, 1900.

85. Web of corruption
Criminals of great wealth
Apologists for corrupt wealth
Powerful wrongdoers
Hypocritical baseness
Peculiarly flagrant iniquity
Flagrant dishonesty
Rottenness
Greed, trickery and cunning
Representatives of predatory wealth
Wealth accumulated by iniquity
Corrupt men of wealth
Law-defying wealth
Mammon of unrighteousness
Very wealthy criminals
Corruption of organized politics
Evil eminence of infamy
The death knell of the Republic
Wealthy malefactors

Theodore Roosevelt. Descriptions of big business in his annual message to Congress, Jan. 29, 1908.

86. There can be no effective control of corporations while their political activity remains.

Theodore Roosevelt. Speech, "The New Nationalism," Osawatomie, KS, Aug. 10, 1910.

87. I hold it to be our duty that the wage-worker, the small producer, the ordinary consumer, shall get their fair share of the benefit of business prosperity. But it ought to be evident to everyone that business has got to prosper before anybody can get any benefit from it.

Theodore Roosevelt. Speech, New York City. Feb. 1, 1912.

88. God, after all, created Switzerland for one purpose – to be the clearinghouse of the world.

Paul Rossy, Vice Chairman, Swiss Banking Commission. Quoted in *Time*, July 18, 1977.

89. We are reluctant to do stories that might tend to produce a run on the banks.... We tend to be more protective of institutions than we are of consumers.

Hobart Rowan, American economic journalist. C-SPAN, *The Media and The Savings and Loan Scandal*, Nov. 3, 1990.

90. Many other countries have made the mistake of mandating costly *[employment]* benefits, and they have mandated their citizens right out of jobs.

Phyllis Schlafly, President, Eagle Forum. Testimony, House Education and Labor Committee, Mar. 5, 1987.

91. Unless this dangerous tendency be checked *[toward monopolies and giant corporations being involved in politics]* ... our social life will be disastrously demoralized *[and]* our political contests mere wrangles between different bands of public robbers, legislation only a matter of purchase and sale and the whole government a festering mass of corruption.

Carl Schurz (1829-1906), U.S. Senator (R-MO). Speech opposing nomination of James G. Blaine for president. Republican National Convention, Chicago, IL, June 1884.

92. The present system for insuring bank deposits is a bad bet for society.

William Seidman, Chairman, Federal Deposit Insurance Corporation. Quoted on ABC, *Nightline*, July 29, 1990.

93. To prohibit a great people, however, from making all that they can of every part of their own produce, or from employing their stock and industry in the way they judge most advantageous to themselves, is a manifest violation of the most sacred rights of mankind.

Adam Smith (1723-1790), Scottish political economist. *The Wealth of Nations*, 1776.

94. People of the same trade seldom meet together but the conversation ends in a conspiracy against the public, or in some diversion to raise prices.

Adam Smith. *Ibid.*

95. The quicker you have monopoly in this country the quicker we will have socialism.

Charles Proteus Steinmetz (1865-1923), American electrical engineer and inventor. Quoted in *Congressional Record*, Jan. 27, 1989.

96. The truth is that Fascism is always and everywhere the instrument of ... the great capitalists using the *petit bourgeoisie* as its dupes.

Evelyn John St. Loe Strachey (1901-1963), Member of Parliament (Labour) and Secretary of War, Great Britain. *The Nature of the Capitalist Crisis*, 1935.

97. It is a fixed principle of our political institutions to guard against the unnecessary accumulation of power over persons and property in any hands. And no hands are to be less trusted with it than a moneyed corporation.

Roger B. Taney (1777-1864), Chief Justice, U.S. Supreme Court, and U.S. Secretary of the Treasury.

Quoted in Arthur M. Schlesinger, Jr., *The Age of Jackson,* 1945.

98. The love of money is the root of all evil.
New Testament, *Timothy* 6:10.

99. In democracies, nothing is more great or brilliant than commerce; it attracts the attention of the public, and fills the imagination of the multitude. All passions of energy are directed toward it.
Alexis de Tocqueville (1805-1859), French writer. *Democracy in America,* 1835.

100. The powerful force of competition ... will not disappear in a Socialist society, but ... will be sublimated.... The liberated passions will be channelized into techniques.
Leon Trotsky (1879-1940), Russian revolutionary theorist. *Literature and Revolution,* 1925.

101. Business will logically be required to disappear. This is not an overstatement for the sake of emphasis; it is literally meant.... National planning implies guidance of capital uses.... Capital allocation would depend on knowledge from some planning agency, of how much for a measured future period ought to be put to one use rather than another. The first step in control would be to limit self-allocation.
Rexford Guy Tugwell (1891-1979), U.S. Undersecretary of Agriculture; Chairman, New York City Planning Commission; and Governor of Puerto Rico (D). Statement, Dec. 1932.

102. There is sloth, there is waste and there is inefficiency in the insurance industry. The voters have clearly expressed their outrage.
John Van de Kamp, Attorney General of California. In reference to a 1988 voter initiative requiring insurance rate rollbacks in the state. Statement to California Supreme Court, Mar. 8, 1989.

103. The public be damned; you get out of here!
William H. Vanderbilt (1821-1885), President, New York Central Railroad. Remark to reporter who interrupted his dinner on his private railroad car, Chicago, IL, Oct. 8, 1882.

104. Society is full of excitement: competition comes in place of monopoly; and intelligence and industry ask only for fair play and an open field.
Daniel Webster (1782-1852), U.S. Congressman (Federalist-NH and MA), U.S. Senator (Federalist and Whig-MA), and U.S. Secretary of State. Speech in Congress, 1823-24 session (18th Congress).

105. It is not big business we have to fear. It is big government.
Wendell L. Willkie (1892-1944), Republican candidate for President (IN). Acceptance of his party's nomination, Philadelphia, PA, June 26, 1940.

106. The great monopoly in this country is the money monopoly.
Woodrow Wilson (1856-1924), 28th President of the United States (D-NJ). Campaign speech, 1911.

107. The masters of the government of the United States are the combined capitalists and manufacturers of the United States.
Woodrow Wilson. Campaign speech, 1912.

108. The welfare of the whole is not to be put to apparent hazard for the advantage of any particular members.
John Winthrop (1588-1649), Governor of Massachusetts Bay Colony. *A Declaration in Defense of an Order of Court,* May 1637.

109. Is it too expensive for the employee who loses his leg or eyesight? ... We are talking about people's lives, not the indifference of some cost accountants.
Ralph Yarborough, U.S. Senator (D-TX). In response to criticism that federal industrial safety regulations would be too expensive. Senate debate, 1970.

110. What people want in the world is not ideology; they want goods and services.
Andrew Young, U.S. Ambassador to the United Nations, U.S. Congressman (D), and Mayor of Atlanta, GA. Interview, *Newsweek,* Mar. 28, 1977.

Chapter 9

Campaigns and Conventions

1. BE THANKFUL ONLY ONE OF THEM CAN WIN!
Bumper sticker, Nixon v. Kennedy presidential campaign, 1960.

2. Blaine. James G. Blaine is a Know Nothing and persecutor of foreign-born citizens and Roman Catholics.
Democratic handbill headline during the 1884 presidential campaign.

3. Welcome home from the crow eaters
Sign on The Washington Post building as Harry S Truman returned to Washington after his reelection, Nov. 1948.

4. Don't make waves; don't back losers.
Political maxim, Chicago. Quoted in *The New York Times*, Oct. 16, 1988.

5. Bootleggers and harlots will dance on the White House lawn if Al Smith is elected President.
Leaflet derogating the campaign of Al Smith, Governor of New York (D), during his presidential campaign, 1928.

6. A little hypocrisy is better than losing.
Anonymous political consultant. Quoted on CBS, *Evening News*, Sept. 2, 1988.

7. So long as our politics are primarily concerned with men rather than measures, it will be men who will be attacked.
James Truslow Adams (1878-1949), American historian. 1932.

8. This day I learned that the caucus club meets at certain times in the garret of Tom Dawes, the adjutant of the Boston regiment.... There they smoke tobacco till you cannot see from one end of the room to another. There they drink flip, I suppose, and there they choose a moderator who puts questions to the vote regularly; and selectmen, assessors, collectors, firewards, and representatives are regularly chosen before they are chosen in the town *[of Boston]*.
John Adams (1735-1826), 2nd President of the United States (Federalist-MA). *Diary*, Feb. 1773.

9. This mode of electioneering suited neither my taste nor my principles. I thought it equally unsuitable to my personal character and to the station in which I am placed.
John Quincy Adams (1767-1848), 6th President of the United States (Ind-MA). Comment when urged to attend the opening of the Pennsylvania Canal and to speak to the German farmers. *Diary*, June 29, 1827.

10. A stranger would think that the people of the United States had no other occupation than electioneering.
John Quincy Adams. Remark after a visit to Baltimore, MD, in August of a campaign year. *Diary*, Aug. 5, 1828.

11. I never had asked, and never should ask, the vote of any person for any office.
John Quincy Adams. Comment when asked to run for President on the Anti-Mason ticket. Aug. 27, 1831.

12. These visits make me sick, and I really think they will make me crazy.
Louisa Catherine Johnson Adams (1775-1852), First Lady. Comment on her visits with the wives of Washington political notables. 1826.

13. We have to have campaign contributions to apprise the public about our qualifications.
Oscar Adams, Alabama State Supreme Court Justice. Reelection campaign speech. Quoted in *USA Today*, Oct. 20, 1988.

14. Every presidential election I've ever been involved with has been characterized as the dirtiest campaign in history.
Roger Ailes, American campaign media consul-

tant (R). Conference, "The Presidency in the 90's," Fordham University, Bronx, NY. C-SPAN, Sept. 4, 1989.

15. People lose their sense of humor in *[presidential]* campaigns.
Roger Ailes. *Ibid.*

16. Convention cities lie defenseless ... exposing their throats to the first impressions, superficial observations, and random episodes that occur to four-day visitors who spend most of their time in taxicabs, hotel lobbies, and convention halls.
Frederick Allen, American political analyst, CNN. *The Washington Post*, July 14, 1988.

17. All of you who were generals and had privates to stand guard over you, vote for my opponent. And all of you who were privates and stood guard over generals, vote for Johnny Allen.
John Mills Allen (1846-1917), U.S. Congressman (D-MS). Campaign speech, 1884.

18. The American people are not fools. They will sense it even if they cannot articulate it precisely when a candidate or party appears to be placing its political bets on continued bad news for the nation. And they will never forgive such a candidate or party.
Bernard Aronson, U.S. Assistant Secretary of State. Remark to Walter Mondale, 1980.

19. You don't win elections on Election Day. You win them by what you do all year round, by the day-to-day goodwill you generate in each precinct.
Jacob L. Arvey (1895-1977), Chicago, IL, politician (D). Quoted in Charles Henning, *The Wit and Wisdom of Politics*, 1989.

20. The welfare of the United States, and the happiness of our people, does not hang on the presence of Henry Fountain Ashurst in the Senate. When that realization first came to me, I was overwhelmed by the horror of it, but now it is a source of infinite comfort.
Henry Fountain Ashurst (1874-1962), U.S. Senator (D-AZ). Announcement of his decision not to seek reelection. Quoted in Morris K. Udall, *Too Funny to Be President*, 1988.

21. Candidates who went into an election with negatives higher than thirty or forty points just inevitably lost.... Drive up the opposition's negatives.
Lee Atwater (1950-1991), Chairman, Republican National Committee. Interview, 1985. Quoted in *The Washington Post*, Oct. 2, 1988.

22. You can never get your message across if you're always answering their *[reporters']* questions.
Lee Atwater. Interview, PBS, *John McLaughlin's One on One*, Oct. 9, 1988.

23. Republicans in the South could not win elections by talking about issues. You had to make the case that the other guy, the other candidate, was a bad guy.
Lee Atwater. Quoted in *The New York Times*, Mar. 31, 1989.

24. I am used to changing tactics to adapt to the climate.
Lee Atwater. Quoted in *The Washington Post*, June 18, 1989.

25. Every morning at seven o'clock you spend an hour and a half figuring out what you are going to do to get on the news that night.
Lee Atwater. Quoted in *The New York Times*, Mar. 18, 1990.

26. Political campaigns are only a slightly more polite form of ground battle.
Lee Atwater. Quoted on PBS, *Washington Week in Review*, Mar. 28, 1991.

27. I'm not the inventor of negative campaigning, but I'm an ardent practitioner.
Lee Atwater. *Ibid.*

28. I've heard one of the candidates' wives says she loves every minute of the race, and all I can say is, either she's lying or she's wacko.
Hattie Babbitt, wife of Bruce Babbitt, Governor of Arizona (D). To a reporter, 1988.

29. I don't think its particularly smart *[in a campaign]* to spend your time responding to the other candidate.
James A. Baker III, U.S. Secretary of State (R), U.S. Secretary of the Treasury, White House Chief of Staff, and presidential campaign manager. Interview, ABC, *This Week*, Sept. 25, 1988.

30. You simply cannot ever refuse to be on the attack in a campaign.
James A. Baker III. Interview, ABC, *This Week*, Nov. 6, 1988.

31. We have to deal in 30-second sound bites. It's not your fault. It's not our fault.
James A. Baker III. Response to reporters' criticism of the shallowness of the 1988 presidential campaign. Interview, ABC, *This Week*, Nov. 6, 1988.

32. You don't let the other side define the campaign.
Michael Barone, American political consultant. Interview, CNN, *Booknotes*, Apr. 22, 1990.

33. You can't win an election with money alone.
Marion Barry, Mayor of Washington, DC (D). Interview, WETA-TV, *Metro Week in Review*, Aug. 5, 1989.

34. I will not be a party to any attacks upon your personal integrity or personal life. We seem to have different views regarding the philosophy of government and on that alone am I willing to contend against you.
Bernard M. Baruch (1870-1965), Chairman, War Industries Board, and U.S. Delegate to the U.N. Atomic Energy Commission. Letter to Herbert Hoover, 1928.

35. We don't really have elections; we fight crusades. Each side usually believes that it, and it alone, represents the true faith.
Earl Behrens, American journalist. Quoted in Earl Katcher, *Earl Warren: A Political Biography*, 1967.

36. The election of the President and the Vice President of the United States has passed – not only from the college of electors to which the Constitution confided it, and from the people to which the practice under the Constitution gave it, and from the House of Representatives which the Constitution provided as ultimate arbiter – but has gone to an anomalous, irresponsible body *[the convention]*, unknown to law or constitution, unknown to the early ages of our government.
Thomas Hart Benton (1782-1858), U.S. Senator and U.S. Congressman (D-MO). *Thirty Years' View*, 1856.

37. Now that circumstances have blessed me in terms of my own financial security and sphere of influence, this is my opportunity to influence the direction of the country.
Jeffrey L. Berkowitz, American real estate developer and political contributor. Explanation of his political contributions. Quoted in *The New York Times*, Oct. 16, 1988.

38. State legislators are becoming more like congressmen in that incumbents nearly always win.
John F. Bibby, political scientist, University of Wisconsin. Quoted in *Governing the States and Localities*, May 1988.

39. Let him *[William Henry Harrison]* say not one single word about his principles, or his creed – let him say nothing – promise nothing. Let no committee or convention – no town meeting ever extract from him a single word, about what he thinks now, or what he will do hereafter. Let the use of pen and ink be wholly forbidden as if he were a mad poet in Bedlam.
Nicholas Biddle (1786-1844), President, Bank of the United States. Advice to Whig leaders, 1840.

40. The partisan strife in which the people of the country are permitted to periodically engage does not tend to the development of ugly traits of character, but merely discloses those that preexist.
Ambrose Bierce (1842-1914?), American journalist. In reference to election campaigns. *Wasp*, Nov. 8, 1884.

41. Gauge your public carefully, and be all things to all men.
Samuel G. Blythe (1868-1947), American political journalist. *The Fakers*, 1914.

42. Without bogeymen, it is hard to raise money and harder to grab at grass-roots America.
Gloria Borger, American journalist. *U.S. News & World Report*, Feb. 5, 1990.

43. Get an elbow, give an elbow.
William W. Bradley, U.S. Senator (D-NJ). Quoted in *U.S. News & World Report*, Nov. 26, 1990.

44. We have created our own monster. The three P's. Platforms, Primaries, and PAC's. The combination of all this reform *[allows]* the ideological activists of both parties to dominate the *[presidential]* nomination.
William Brock, U.S. Congressman (R-TN), U.S. Senator, and U.S. Secretary of Labor. Interview, *Newsweek*, Aug. 29, 1988.

45. It seems ironic that the same convention which thinks Will Rogers is a clown thinks Huey Long is a statesman.
Heywood C. Broun (1888-1939), American journalist. July 28, 1932.

46. If you're mean to a gentle man, it makes your meanness worse.
Edmund G. (Pat) Brown, Governor of California (D). In reference to Richard Nixon's tactics in first congressional campaign, against Jerry Voorhees. Quoted on PBS, *The Unauthorized Biography of Richard Nixon*, Mar. 9, 1989.

47. The trouble *[with modern political campaigns]* is that the technicians of the media and the professional campaign advisors believe that the negative commercials and the attack work better.
Edmund G. (Jerry) Brown, Jr., Governor of California (D). Quoted in *The New York Times*, Sept. 18, 1988.

48. As important as issues are, as important as money is ... you've got to have good candidates.

Ron Brown, Chairman, Democratic National Committee. Lecture, Harvard University, Cambridge, MA, Nov. 1989.

49. To win *[elections]* in this country these days you've got to campaign down to a thirteen-year old's level of mental development.

Willie Brown, Speaker of the California Assembly, (D). Quoted in *The New York Times*, Oct. 31, 1988.

50. In this crazy political business, at least in our times, a lie unanswered becomes truth within twenty-four hours.

Willie Brown. Quoted in *The New York Times*, Oct. 31, 1988.

51. We have submitted the issues to the American people, and their word is law.

William Jennings Bryan (1860-1925), U.S. Secretary of State (D). Concession telegram to William McKinley, Nov. 4, 1896.

52. Have you ever seen a candidate talking to a rich person on television?

Art Buchwald, American humorist. 1988.

53. There is no longer a value judgment on the need to tailor a message to television. It's now a matter of survival, not a matter of ethics or intellectual honesty.

John Buckley, Director of Communications, National Republican Congressional Committee, and press secretary to Congressman Jack Kemp (R-NY) during 1988 presidential race. Quoted in *The New York Times*, Oct. 2, 1988.

54. *[Thomas]* Dewey's view was that if he made no mistakes he would win *[the presidency against Harry Truman]*. So we sat around making sure he would make no mistakes. And I think we succeeded, but in fact that isn't the way it went.

McGeorge Bundy, presidential assistant for national security (D). Quoted in L. Mosley, *Dulles*, 1978.

55. If they can beat me, fine. But I'm not leaving until they beat me.

Quentin N. Burdick (1908-1992), U.S. Congressman and U.S. Senator (D-ND). On running for the Senate at age eighty. Quoted in *The New York Times*, Oct. 13, 1988.

56. My opponents can't get elected unless things get worse. And things aren't going to get worse unless they get elected.

George Bush, 41st President of the United States (R-TX). Campaign speech, Portland, OR, Nov. 1988.

57. Do not run a campaign that would embarrass your mother.

Robert C. Byrd, U.S. Congressman and U.S. Senator (D-WV). Quoted in *Newsweek*, Oct. 12, 1987.

58. The candidate who is successful in defining the election is usually the winner.

Patrick Caddell, American pollster and political advisor (D). Quoted by Hamilton Jordan in a memorandum to Pres. Carter, June 25, 1979.

59. In the end, members of the *[state]* legislature have to have their own organizations, raise their own money, and run their own campaigns if they are ... going to win.

Larry Campbell, Oregon State Representative (R). Quoted in *Governing the States and Localities*, May 1988.

60. You can't beat somebody with nobody.

Joseph G. Cannon (1836-1926), U.S. Congressman and Speaker of the House (R-IL). Attributed.

61. I certainly recognize that there will only be ten or twelve challengers *[for congressional seats]* in the whole country who win, but my job is to be one of them.

Glenn Carberry, Connecticut congressional candidate (R). Quoted in *The New York Times*, Oct. 27, 1988.

62. The people of the United States have made their choice, and of course I accept that decision – but I have to admit not with the same enthusiasm that I accepted the decision four years ago.

Jimmy Carter, 39th President of the United States (D-GA). Concession speech, Nov. 4, 1980.

63. We're always looking for candidates that have new approaches to problems.

Rosalyn Carter, First Lady. PBS, *America's Children: Who Should Care?*, Sept. 4, 1990.

64. I never like being hit without striking back.

Joseph Chamberlain (1836-1914), Colonial Secretary, Great Britian. Speech, London, Oct. 7, 1903.

65. Every now and then you dig a dry hole.

Albert B. (Happy) Chandler (1889-1991), Governor of Kentucky (D), U.S. Senator (R-KY), and U.S. Baseball Commissioner. Remark on his Senate primary defeat by Alben Barkley, 1938.

66. It's not a smear, if you please, if you point out the record of your opponent.

Murray Chotiner (1909-1974), American campaign strategist (R). Advice to Nixon campaign workers, 1958.

67. We had the election won. Debates couldn't help us and might hurt.

Murray Chotiner. Explanation of why his candidate, Earl Warren, refused to debate incumbent governor Olsen in the California gubernatorial campaign of 1942. In 1960, as Nixon presidential campaign advisor, he was opposed to Nixon debating John F. Kennedy. Quoted in Earl Katcher, *Earl Warren: A Political Biography*, 1967.

68. An attack is always a smear when it is directed against you.

Murray Chotiner. Quoted in Leonard Lurie, *The Running of Richard Nixon*, 1972.

69. Deny what they didn't charge and charge what they can't deny.... If it's our charge, we're revealing the facts; if it's theirs, it's a smear.

Murray Chotiner. Quoted in *Playboy*, Feb. 1974.

70. This office seeking is a disease. It is even catching.

Grover Cleveland (1837-1908), 22nd and 24th President of the United States (D-NY). Interview, 1885.

71. *[The 1948 Truman presidential campaign]* was probably the last campaign where the candidate went out personally to the people.

Clark P. Clifford, U.S. Secretary of Defense (D) and Special Counsel to the President. Quoted on PBS, *The Great Upset of '48*, Nov. 2, 1988.

72. I would walk over my grandmother if necessary to get Nixon reelected!

Charles W. Colson, presidential assistant (R). Quoted in Barbara Rowes, *The Book of Quotes*, 1979.

73. No thank you, I don't engage in criminal practice.

Roscoe Conkling (1829-1888), U.S. Congressman and U.S. Senator (R-NY). Response when asked to campaign for the presidency of his rival, James G. Blaine. 1884.

74. Negative advertising is the only way voters can find out that a candidate may be unfit for public office.

Charles Cook, American political columnist. Interview, C-SPAN, Sept. 17, 1990.

75. I do not choose to run for President in 1928.

Calvin Coolidge (1872-1933), 30th President of the United States (R-MA). Written statement, Aug. 2, 1927.

76. With the exception of the occasion of my notification, I did not attend any partisan meetings or make any purely political speeches during the campaign. I spoke several times at the dedication of a monument, the observance of the anniversary of an historic event, at a meeting of some commercial body, or before some religious gathering.

Calvin Coolidge. *Autobiography*, 1929.

77. Ticket balancing, or United Nations politics, as it is sometimes called, is perhaps symbolic of the ultimate step in the process of granting group recognition and confirming the fact that something approaching intergroup equality has been achieved.

Elmer E. Cornwell, Jr., American political scientist. *Annals of the American Academy of Political and Social Science*, May 1964.

78. Promise all that is asked and more if you can think of anything. Offer to build a bridge or a church, to divide a county, create a batch of new offices, make a turnpike, or anything they like. Promises cost nothing, therefore deny nobody who has a vote.

David Crockett (1786-1836), U.S. Congressman (Anti-Jacksonian-TN). *The Life of Davy Crockett*, 1889.

79. Do all you can to appear to advantage in the eyes of the women. That's easily done – you have but to kiss and slabber their children.

David Crockett. *Ibid.*

80. You campaign in poetry. You govern in prose.

Mario Cuomo, Governor of New York (D). Quoted in *The New Republic*, Apr. 8, 1985.

81. No! I won't rule out center field for the Yankees, either.

Mario Cuomo. Response when asked if he would rule out a run for the presidency. Quoted in *Newsweek*, June 2, 1986.

82. I endorse him! I endorse him! I endorse him! There, three times I endorsed him.

Mario Cuomo. Response when asked why he was being coy about endorsing Michael Dukakis for the presidency. Quoted in *Newsweek*, June 29, 1988.

83. I propose to be mayor for the Republicans, Progressives, Socialists, and independent voters as well as the Democrats.

James M. Curley (1874-1958), Governor of Massachusetts (D), U.S. Congressman, and Mayor of Boston, MA. Campaign speech, 1913.

84. You look for people who want to touch history and then go back to their careers.

Peter H. Daley, American political consultant. On recruiting presidential campaign workers. Quoted in *The New York Times*, May 8, 1988.

85. It *[television]* has locked candidates into ridiculous positions because only ridiculous positions can be compacted into thirty-second commercials.

John C. Danforth, U.S. Senator (R-MO). Quoted in *The New York Times*, Mar. 18, 1990.

86. The convention will be deadlocked, and after the other candidates have gone their limit, some twelve or fifteen men, worn-out and bleary-eyed for lack of sleep, will sit down about two in the morning around a table in a smoke-filled room in some hotel and decide the nomination. When that time comes *[Warren G.]* Harding will be selected.

Harry M. Daughtery (1860-1941), U.S. Attorney General (R). Statement to reporters during the Republican National Convention, Chicago, IL, June 10, 1920.

87. The media, while they won't admit it, are not in the news business; they're in entertainment. We tried to create the most entertaining, visually attractive scenes ... so that the networks would have to use it.

Michael Deaver, presidential media advisor (R). Quoted in *The New York Times*, Mar. 4, 1990.

88. The people want a blood-and-thunder campaign.

Thomas E. Dewey (1902-1971), Governor of New York (R). Remark after losing the presidential election to Harry S Truman, Nov. 6, 1948.

89. It sounds good to say you're going to campaign everywhere, but ultimately you have to make choices.

Linda Divall, American political pollster (R). Quoted in *The Washington Post*, July 23, 1988.

90. Politics ... is going to be diluted down into a ten-second window, where you whack the guy as hard as you can and then get out of there.

Alan Dixon, U.S. Senator (D-IL). Quoted in *The San Francisco Examiner*, Dec. 29, 1990.

91. Contrary to reports that I took the loss badly, I want to say that I went home last night and slept like a baby – every two hours I woke up and cried.

Robert J. Dole, U.S. Senator (R-KS). Comment affter losing the election in which he was the vice-presidential candidate, 1976.

92. When you lose *[a primary election]*, you either sit and pout somewhere or you go out and help the winner.

Robert J. Dole. ABC, *This Week*, Aug. 14, 1988.

93. Stop lying about my record.

Robert J. Dole. Said to opponent George Bush during the 1988 Republican presidential primary campaign.

94. I was told that people did not like negative ads. So I didn't run any. I lost.

Robert J. Dole. Description of his race for the Republican presidential nomination against George Bush. Quoted on ABC, *Nightline*, Nov. 10, 1988.

95. You never know whether you're elected because people know who you are or people don't know who you are.

Robert J. Dole. Quoted on C-SPAN, *Booknotes*, Sept. 9, 1990.

96. Any time you put your name on a ballot, there is a risk of election.

Curt Donaldson, unsuccessful Democratic nominee for Congress in 1982, and columnist, the *Lincoln* (NB) *Star*. *USA Today*, Oct. 20, 1988.

97. When the candidate must seek support from all levels of his community, his political creed will be tolerance, not hatred; equal protection for every minority, not discrimination.

William O. Douglas (1898-1980), U.S. Supreme Court Justice. *We the Judges*, 1956.

98. Am deeply disappointed. Your campaign had dignity and elevation and was in the best American tradition. I am rather frightened by the influences which prevented it from succeeding.

John Foster Dulles (1888-1959), U.S. Secretary of State and U.S. Senator (R-NY). Consolation telegram to Thomas E. Dewey, Nov. 1948.

99. I don't think politics has gotten too negative. I ... believe in going after the opposition on the issues.

Jennifer Dunn, Chairman, Washington State Republican Committee. Quoted in *The Washington Post*, June 18, 1989.

100. The Bible would be cast into a bonfire, our holy worship changed into a dance of *[French]* Jacobin phrensy, our wives and daughters dishonored, and our sons converted into the disciples of Voltaire and the dragoons of Marat.

Timothy Dwight (1752-1817), President, Yale College, New Haven, CT. Sermon predicting what would happen if Thomas Jefferson were elected President, 1800.

101. I could not lose *[the gubernatorial race]* unless I was caught in bed with a dead girl or a live boy.

Edwin W. Edwards, Governor of Louisiana (D). Quoted in *Time*, Mar., 11, 1985.

102. To think that an old soldier should come to this.
Dwight D. Eisenhower (1890-1969), 34th President of the United States (R-KS). Remark to Rosser Reaves after making the first TV political commercials ever used in a presidential election, 1952.

103. There is a certain satisfaction in coming down to the lowest ground of politics, for we get rid of cant and hypocrisy.
Ralph Waldo Emerson (1803-1882), American writer. "Napoleon," *Representative Men*, 1876.

104. When you strike at a king, you must kill him.
Ralph Waldo Emerson. Recollected by Oliver Wendell Holmes, Jr. Quoted in Max Lerner, *The Mind and Faith of Justice Holmes*, 1943.

105. I generally send my signals on the telephone, not on national television.
Susan Estrich, Director, Michael Dukakis' 1988 presidential campaign, and professor, Harvard Law School. CBS, *Face the Nation*, Aug. 20, 1988.

106. The politics of crime is not about a party's record or a candidate's proposals, but about perceived character and values.
Susan Estrich. "The Hidden Politics of Race," *The Washington Post Magazine*, Apr. 20, 1989.

107. No matter what was written or what was charged, the harmful effect was largely washed away as soon as the reassuring voice of the President of the United States started coming through the ether into the family living room.
James A. Farley (1888-1976), Chairman, Democratic National Committee, and U.S. Postmaster General. *Behind the Ballots*, 1938.

108. A rigged convention is one with the other man's delegates in control. An open convention is when your delegates are in control.
James A. Farley. Quoted on NBC, *Convention and Election Almanac*, 1964.

109. Women are getting a lot smarter. Before they were very adventuresome. Today, women are not going to take chances on higher office unless there's a good chance of winning.
Geraldine A. Ferraro, U.S. Congresswoman (D-NY). Quoted in *The New York Times*, June 26, 1989.

110. I learned I can't make promises I can't keep. I owe the people ... honesty.
Ray Flynn, Mayor of Boston, MA (D). Quoted in *Time*, Apr. 4, 1988.

111. Trust is leveling with people before the election about what you're going to do after the election.
Gerald R. Ford, 38th President of the United States (R-MI). Quoted in *The New York Times*, Nov. 1, 1976.

112. The paid political campaign managers are the problem *[with modern campaigns]*. They are overpaid for doing the wrong things.
Gerald R. Ford. PBS, *MacNeil-Lehrer Report*, Nov. 21, 1988.

113. We're all candidates all the time. Claude Pepper is eighty-seven, and he's worried about redistricting in 1992.
Barney Frank, U.S. Congressman (D-MA). PBS, *The Politics of Privacy*, Sept. 26, 1988.

114. Odious campaigns are a national tradition, and so is complaining about them.
Charles Freund, American journalist. "What's New? Mud-Slinging Is an American Tradition," *The Washington Post*, Oct. 30, 1988.

115. It is never the case that a surrogate can deliver *[votes]* like a principal can.
Curtis Gans, Director, Committee for the Study of the American Electorate. Interview, National Public Radio, *The Fred Fisk Show*, Nov. 12, 1988.

116. It works. People respond to it.
Robert K. Gardner, media producer for Gerald Ford's presidential 1976 campaign. Remark on negative campaigning. *Business Week*, June 20, 1988.

117. WARNING: POLITICAL ADVERTISING CAN LEGALLY DISTORT THE TRUTH.
Bob Garfield, editor-at-large, *Advertising Age*. Suggested warning label for political advertising. *Advertising Age*, Nov. 5, 1990.

118. It now appears we are defeated by the combined power of rebellion, Catholicism, and whiskey, a trinity very hard to conquer.
James A. Garfield (1831-1881), 20th President of the United States (R-OH). Comment after the erroneous announcement that Democrat Samuel J. Tilden had won the presidency. Nov. 9, 1876.

119. It's hard to make corruption a partisan issue because voters are cynical about everybody in politics.
Geoffrey Garin, American political pollster (D). Quoted in *The New York Times*, Apr. 16, 1989.

120. For the presidency, you run on a record and not on your legs.
John Nance Garner (1868-1967), Vice President of the United States, U.S. Congressman, and Speaker of the House (D-TX). Response when asked if Franklin D.

Roosevelt's paralysis would preclude his presidential candidacy. Quoted in Ralph G. Martin, *Ballots and Bandwagons*, 1964.

121. I have against me the bourgeois, the military, and the diplomats, and for me, only the people who take the Métro.
Charles de Gaulle (1890-1970), President of France. Quoted in *The New York Times*, May 12, 1968.

122. Americans want their political candidates to want the job. They don't like what many of them do to get it, but they want them to want it.
Jack Germond, American political columnist. Interview, PBS, June 25, 1988.

123. No deals for jobs, no deals for contributions. What you see is what you get.
Rudolph W. Giuliani, U.S. Attorney, New York. Announcement of his candidacy for Mayor of New York City. Quoted in *The New York Times*, May 21, 1989.

124. We're not going to get the Negro vote as a bloc in 1964 or 1968, so we ought to go hunting where the ducks are.
Barry M. Goldwater, U.S. Senator (R-AZ). Speech, Atlanta, GA, Nov. 18, 1961.

125. You could have whipped my butt in 1964, but I went out and worked a helluva lot harder than you did over the years. As a result, a lot of people worked for me.
Barry M. Goldwater. Remark to Gov. Nelson A. Rockefeller, 1966.

126. Three weeks is a lifetime in presidential politics. The conventional wisdom changes so suddenly.
Albert A. Gore, Jr., U.S. Senator (D-TN) and Vice President of the United States. Quoted in *USA Today*, Oct. 20, 1988.

127. Whatever is happening between two people is greatly intensified during the campaign. If the wife is unhappy with politics, it can seriously stress the marriage.
Tipper Gore, wife of Sen. Albert Gore, Jr. Quoted in *The Washington Post*, Nov. 19, 1989.

128. I keep my campaign promises, but I never promised to wear stockings.
Ella Grasso (1919-1981), U.S. Congresswoman and Governor of Connecticut (R). Quoted in *Time*, Nov. 18, 1974.

129. When you have incumbents funded at a rate of 30 to 1 over challengers, it really makes elections meaningless ... a sicko system.
C. Boyden Gray, White House counsel (R). Quoted in *The Washington Post*, Nov. 11, 1990.

130. Mr. Lincoln is already beaten. He cannot be elected.
Horace Greeley (1811-1872), American newspaper editor and U.S. Congressman (Whig-NY). Editorial, *New York Tribune*, Aug. 1864.

131. Political candidates are always looking to capture the future.
Jeff Greenfield, American political journalist. Conference, "The Presidency in the 90's," Fordham University, Bronx, NY. C-SPAN, Sept. 4, 1989.

132. In politics, demonstration not description is the name of the game.
Meg Greenfield, American political columnist. *Newsweek*, Aug. 15, 1988.

133. Politicians have always said what has proven to win.
Alexander M. Haig, General, U.S. Army; U.S. Secretary of State; and White House Chief of Staff (R). Interview, CBS, *20:26*, Feb. 4, 1990.

134. If I am nominated *[for the presidency]*, I will not run. If I am elected, I will not serve. But if you beg me, I just might reconsider.
Alexander M. Haig. Speech, Northeast Missouri State University, Trenton, MO. Mar. 1987.

135. You sell your candidates and your programs the way a business sells its products.
Leonard Hall, Chairman, Republican National Committee. Quoted in Leonard Lurie, *The Running of Richard Nixon*, 1972.

136. To stabilize America first
To safeguard America first
To prosper America first
To think of America first
To exalt America first
To live for and revere America first.
Warren G. Harding (1865-1923), 29th President of the United States (R-OH). Speech outlining his six-point program for America. Ohio Society, New York City, 1920.

137. I don't know much about Americanism, but it's a damn good word with which to carry an election.
Warren G. Harding. Quoted in Henry Metcalf, *The Penguin Dictionary of Modern Humorous Quotations*, 1987.

138. Never defend and always attack.
Thomas R. Harkin, U.S. Senator (D-IA). Quoted in *Newsweek*, Aug. 26, 1991.

139. I have a great risk of meeting a fool at home, but the candidate who travels cannot escape him.

Benjamin Harrison (1833-1901), 23rd President of the United States (R-IN). Comment on why he refused to leave his home during the presidential campaign. Sept. 1888.

140. I knew that my staying up would not change the result if I were defeated, while if elected I had a hard day ahead of me.

Benjamin Harrison. Explanation for going to bed early on election night. Quoted in Paul F. Boller, Jr., *Presidential Anecdotes*, 1981.

141. This cassette *[of Walt Disney's Dumbo]* was a documentary of my campaign.

Gary Hart, U.S. Senator (D-CO). Remark in a video store, NH, Mar. 1988.

142. Yes, we always do that. In the state of New York, where the Democratic majority is 40,000 and 50,000 we throw their way. In the state of Massachusetts, where the Republican party is dominant, they probably have the call. Wherever there is a dominant party it gets the contribution.

Henry O. Havemeyer (1847-1907), President, American Sugar Refining Company. Response when asked why his company made political contributions to both major parties. Senate testimony, 1894.

143. Returned last night from Ohio Day at the Centennial. It was an enthusiastic and prodigious crowd which greeted me. I managed to shake some four thousand people by the hand and to make half a dozen speeches from steps, windows, and the roof of the Ohio Building, without saying anything I regret – without "slopping over."

Rutherford B. Hayes (1822-1893), 19th President of the United States (R-OH). *Diary*, Oct. 29, 1876.

144. *[McKinley]* is on a stumping tour ... I criticized the bloody-shirt course of the canvass *[campaign]*. It seems to be bad "politics," and of no use.

Rutherford B. Hayes. *Diary*, Sept. 11, 1885.

145. I have supported a great many who promised to do things that I thought ought to be done, who proved faithless to their promises.

William Randolph Hearst (1863-1951), U.S. Congressman (D-NY); founder, Independence League Party; journalist; and publisher. Debate with Elihu Root, Elmira, NY, 1906.

146. Seeing we also are compassed about with so great a cloud of witnesses ... let us run with patience the race that is set before us.

New Testament, *Hebrews* 12:1.

147. Unpack.

Bob Hope, American actor and comedian. Telegram to Thomas E. Dewey after his presidential defeat. Nov. 8, 1948.

148. Part of the game in the first three years *[of a four-year term]* is to make sure that during the year the Mayor runs there is an unusually large expansion of services.

Raymond D. Horton, member, Citizens' Budget Committee, New York City. Quoted in *The New York Times*, July 10, 1988.

149. It's not what they take away from you that counts. It's what you do with what you have left. Never give up and never give in.

Hubert H. Humphrey (1911-1978), Vice President of the United States and U.S. Senator (D-MN). Remark to reporters after losing the presidential election, Nov. 10, 1968.

150. I think it's going to be a doosey. I mean, talk about a fistfight in a whorehouse.

Molly Ivins, American political columnist. In reference to the upcoming presidential campaign battle in Texas. CBS, *Evening News*, Aug. 3, 1988.

151. We must not just change presidents. We must change direction.

Jesse L. Jackson, Shadow Senator (D-DC). Interview, PBS, *MacNeil-Lehrer News Hour*, June 16, 1988.

152. If you have run with footmen and they have wearied you, then how can you contend with horses?

Old Testament, *Jeremiah* 12:5.

153. I just go along ... and sit on the platform to show that I don't have a club foot.

Claudia (Lady Bird) Johnson, First Lady. Quoted in exhibit, "The First Ladies," The Hoover Museum, Iowa City, IA, 1990.

154. No, I don't have any favorite opponent. It is not my duty to select my opposition.

Lyndon B. Johnson (1908-1973), 36th President of the United States (D-TX). Remark to reporters, Feb. 1, 1964.

155. Alexandria has been chosen as the first stop for one of the greatest campaigners in America, and I am very proud to announce that I am her husband.

Lyndon B. Johnson. In reference to Lady Bird Johnson's role in his campaigns. Campaign speech, Alexandria, VA, Oct. 6, 1964.

156. I shall not seek and I will not accept the nomination of my party for another term as president.
Lyndon B. Johnson. TV address, Mar. 31, 1968.

157. We're going through an era of feel-good politics in which talking about tough issues and making tough decisions are not the way to get elected.
James R. Jones, U.S. Congressman (D-OK). Quoted in *The New York Times*, Jan. 15, 1989.

158. Southern regional pride can be used to great advantage without unnecessarily alienating potential anti-Southern votes.
Hamilton Jordan, White House Chief of Staff (D). Memorandum to Jimmy Carter, 1972.

159. Mr. Truman is still ahead, but these are returns from a few cities. When the returns come in from the country, the results will show Dewey winning overwhelmingly.
Hans Von Kaltenborn (1878-1965), American radio journalist. Nationwide report, election night, Nov. 2, 1948.

160. The campaign never stops. I'm an old football quarterback. We used to play in this stuff.
Jack F. Kemp, U.S. Congressman and U.S. Secretary of Housing and Urban Development (R-NY). Statement to reporters during a blizzard, Sioux City, IA, Jan. 1988.

161. We can't win with an issueless, themeless, idealess campaign.
Jack F. Kemp. Quoted in *The Washington Post*, June 25, 1988.

162. Speak of a vision, work hard, and get a good road map of Iowa.
Edward M. Kennedy, U.S. Senator (D-MA). Advice to presidential primary candidates. Quoted in *Newsweek*, July 13, 1987.

163. So young and so wrong.
John F. Kennedy (1917-1963), 35th President of the United States (D-MA). In response to seeing a young girl with a Nixon sign. Remark, Mt. Prospect, IL, 1960.

164. If you tell everybody that you like me better than *[Richard M.]* Nixon, I'll be ruined at home.
John F. Kennedy. Remark to Soviet Premier Nikita Krushchev, Vienna, Austria, June 1961.

165. It would be premature to ask your support in the next election, and it would be inaccurate to thank you for it in the past.
John F. Kennedy. Remark to a group of businessmen soon after his election, 1961.

166. I ask for your help. I think that we can make a difference.
Robert F. Kennedy (1925-1968), U.S. Attorney General and U.S. Senator (D-NY). Senate campaign speech, 1968.

167. It's our own money, and we're free to spend it any way we choose. It's part of this campaign business. If you have money, you spend it to win. And the more you can afford, the more you'll spend.
Rose Kennedy, mother of John, Robert, and Edward Kennedy. Remark on campaign financing. Quoted in Ralph G. Martin, *A Hero for Our Time*, 1983.

168. If you are going to run for national office, you'd better understand that optimism is something Americans expect.
Tom Kiley, media advisor to Gov. Michael Dukakis' presidential campaign (D). *U.S. News & World Report*, June 20, 1988.

169. There's only one problem with this year's upcoming presidential election – one of the candidates has to win.
Alan King, American comedian. Oct. 1988.

170. I'll never run again. It is a filthy business.
Edward I. Koch, U.S. Congressman and Mayor of New York City (D). After his congressional election loss, 1962.

171. If you've been in office for many years, you accumulate opponents.
Edward I. Koch. Explanation for his declining margins of victory in successive election. Interview, PBS, *Tony Brown's Journal*, Oct. 1, 1988.

172. Believe me, there is life after the mayoralty.
Edward I. Koch. Comment following his defeat in the primaries after serving three terms as mayor. Quoted on *NBC News*, Sept. 15, 1989.

173. I've never been a politician *[before]*. I've got to spend money so people will know who I am.
Herbert Kohl, Wisconsin Democratic senatorial candidate. Quoted in *The New York Times*, Oct. 31, 1988.

174. A three-year diet of rubber chicken and occasional crow.
Charles Krauthammer, American political columnist. Description of a presidential campaign. Quoted in *Time*, May 14, 1982.

175. When you run a campaign, the idea is not to appeal to pundits but to appeal to people.
Charles Krauthammer. Quoted on CBS, *Inside Washington*, Oct. 28, 1988.

176. Do after election as before election you said you would.

Fiorello H. La Guardia (1882-1947), U.S. Congressman (R and Socialist) and Mayor of New York City (R and Fusion Party). Quoted in the *New York Evening Journal*, July 22, 1922.

177. We're starting to see *[gender voting]* gaps right down to races for dog catcher.

Celinda Lake, American political pollster. Quoted in *The Washington Post*, June 26, 1988.

178. I ring eight thousand to ten thousand doorbells every time I run.

Louis LaPolla, Mayor of Utica, NY (D). Quoted in Alan Ehrenhalt, *The United States of Ambition*, 1991.

179. We promise according to our hopes, and perform according to our fears.

François de La Rochefoucauld (1613-1680), French nobleman and writer. *Reflexions ou Sentences et Maximes Morales*, 1665.

180. Issue definition implies the possibility of offending various constituency or interest groups – but if you don't offend them, you'll offend the body politic.

James Madison Leach, U.S. Congressman (D-IA). Quoted in *The Washington Post*, June 25, 1988.

181. Campaigning is uncomfortable when you start.

James Madison Leach. Interview, CNN, *An American Profile*, Sept. 3, 1990.

182. First, he demands votes; second, he asks for votes; third, he begs for them; fourth, he weeps for them.

Sol Levitan (1862-1940), Treasurer of Wisconsin (Progressive). Explanation of how a politician gets votes.

183. The politics of character tend to drive out the politics of substance.

Judith Lichtenberg, American political scientist. Quoted in *The New York Times*, Mar. 18, 1990.

184. I refuse to lose this race because I didn't have enough money.

Joseph I. Lieberman, Attorney General of Connecticut (D). Quoted in *The New York Times*, Sept. 30, 1988.

185. If elected I shall be thankful; if not, it will be all the same.

Abraham Lincoln (1809-1865), 16th President of the United States (R-IL). Frequent campaign statement, 1830's and 1840's.

186. I am not a candidate for renomination or election.

Abraham Lincoln. Letter to Richard Thomas, Mar. 1, 1848.

187. I think too much reliance is placed in noisy demonstrations, importing speakers from a distance and the like. They excite prejudice and close the avenues to sober reason. The "home production" principle in my judgment is the best.

Abraham Lincoln. Letter to Andrew McCollen, June 19, 1858.

188. We *[Republicans]* have to fight this battle *[against slavery]* upon principle alone, so I hope those with whom I am surrounded have principle enough to nerve themselves for the task, and leave nothing undone that can fairly be done to bring about the right result.

Abraham Lincoln. Campaign speech, Springfield, IL, July 17, 1858.

189. I would despise myself if I thought that I was procuring your votes by concealing my opinions, and by avowing one set of principles in one part of the state and a different set in another.

Abraham Lincoln. Campaign debate with Sen. Stephen A. Douglas, Galesburg, IL, Oct. 7, 1858.

190. In the absence of formal written platforms, the antecedents of candidates become their platforms. On just such platforms all our earlier and better Presidents were elected.

Abraham Lincoln. Speech, Wichita, KS, Dec. 2, 1859.

191. My name is new in the field, and I suppose I am not the first choice of a very great many. Our policy then is to give no offense to others – leave them in a mood to come to us if they shall be compelled to give up their first love.

Abraham Lincoln. Letter to Ohio Republicans outlining his strategy for winning the nomination, 1860.

192. You suggest that a visit to the place of my nativity *[Kentucky]* might be pleasant to me. Indeed it would. But would it be safe? Would not the people lynch me?

Abraham Lincoln. Letter to Samuel Haycroft, June 4, 1860.

193. I do not allow myself to suppose that either the *[Republican]* convention or the League have concluded to decide that I am either the greatest or the best man in America, but rather they have concluded it is not best to swap horses while crossing the river, and have further concluded that I am not so poor a horse that they might not make a botch of it in trying to swap.

Abraham Lincoln. Statement to National Union League delegation after his nomination for a second term, June 9, 1864.

194. It seems exceedingly probable that this administration will not be reelected. Then it will be my duty to cooperate with the President-elect, as to save the Union between the election and the inauguration, as he will have secured his election on such ground that he cannot possibly save it afterward.

Abraham Lincoln. Sealed message to the Cabinet, Aug. 1864.

195. We offer more than a program; we offer a man *[Richard M. Nixon]* to carry it out.

Henry Cabot Lodge, Jr. (1902-1986), U.S. Senator (R-MA), U.S. Ambassador to the United Nations, head of the American delegation to the Paris Peace Conference for Vietnam peace negotiations. Address, Republican National Convention, July 28, 1960.

196. What I've had to do is divide my time between black churches and white garden clubs. I want to be Atlanta's mayor, but I would also like to be Georgia's governor or senator. I can't be that without white support.

Michael Lomax, Chairman, Fulton County, GA Commission (D). Quoted in *The New York Times*, July 16, 1988.

197. It's personalities, not party, that settles the vote.

Pyotr K. Luchinisky, Communist Party leader, Moldavian Republic, U.S.S.R. Quoted in *The New York Times*, Feb. 25, 1990.

198. An election is like a horse race in that you can tell more about it the next day.

John A. MacDonald (1815-1891), 1st Prime Minister of Canada. Quoted by John G. Diefenbaker, *The Years of Achievement*, 1976.

199. If you have sacred principles which you must defend, or certain credos which are sacred, please leave their defense until after the election.

F. R. MacKinnon, Nova Scotia, Canada, politician. Quoted in *The Globe and Mail*, Sept. 18, 1978.

200. Teflon breaks if you keep hitting hard enough.

M. Boyd Marcus, Jr., Virginia Republican gubernatorial campaign manager. Quoted in *The Washington Post*, Oct. 12, 1989.

201. If they *[political opponents]* go around lying about your record, insulting your job performance, your wife, and your patriotism, you ought to double up your fist and knock the crap out of them.

Ed Martin, Executive Director, Texas Democratic Party. Quoted in *The New York Times Magazine*, Oct. 30, 1988.

202. There's nothing more exhilarating than being out on the campaign trail.

Lynn M. Martin, U.S. Congresswoman and U.S. Secretary of Labor (R-IL). Seminar, National Press Club, Washington, DC, Mar. 29, 1990.

203. Men are uncomfortable running against women because they've had so little experience doing it.

Lynn M. Martin. Interview, ABC, *This Week*, June 10, 1990.

204. If you constantly cross your own centers of power, you lose the energy that wins elections.

Bob Martinez, Director, Office of National Drug Control Policy, and Governor of Florida (R). Explanation of why he led an unsuccessful fight to restrict abortions in Florida, pleasing some of his core constituency but alienating many other voters. Speech, Southern Republican Exchange, Baton Rouge, LA, Oct. 28, 1989.

205. It's not that people voted for me because I was an athlete, but what did help was that people knew my name.... The two Olympic gold medals were the most important contributions to my campaign fund.

Bob Mathias, U.S. Congressman (R-CA). Quoted in *Playboy*, Nov. 1967.

206. *[Campaign life]* demands a wife and family, ever faithful, ever admiring, ever at the side of the ideal husband and father.

Abigail McCarthy, wife of Sen. Eugene J. McCarthy. *Private Faces/Public Places*, 1972.

207. The first law of politics: Never say anything in a national campaign that anyone might remember.

Eugene J. McCarthy, U.S. Congressman and U.S. Senator (D-WI). Quoted in *U.S. News & World Report*, Nov. 26, 1990.

208. Conventions don't nominate people anymore. Primaries do.

Charles McDowell, Jr., American political journalist. PBS, *Convention Week in Review*, July 20, 1988.

209. Never attack a politician through his children.

Mary McGrory, American political columnist. *The Washington Post*, July 22, 1990.

210. I might as well put up a trapeze on my front lawn and compete with some professional athlete, as go out speaking against *[William Jennings]* Bryan.

William McKinley (1843-1901), 25th President of the United States (R-OH). Remark, 1896.

211. A national campaign is better than the best circus ever heard of, with a mass baptism *[the convention]* and a couple of hangings thrown in. It is better, even, than war.
H. L. Mencken (1880-1956), American journalist. *Generally Political*, 1944.

212. If politicians throwing mud begin to slip in it, perhaps they will head for higher ground.
Jean Meserve, American journalist. *ABC News*, Nov. 5, 1989.

213. Before you can save the world, you have to save your seat.
George Miller, U.S. Congressman (R-CA). Quoted on PBS, *The Power Game*, Jan. 2, 1989.

214. Unless you are a prohibitive front-runner, an unanswered smear is believed.
Richard Moe, American political consultant. Quoted in *The Washington Post*, Oct. 28, 1988.

215. I work every day like I was running for reelection and the race was tight. That's the only way I know how. That's what my mother taught me.
Rose Mofford, Governor of Arizona (D). Quoted in John L. Myers, ed., *The Arizona Governors, 1912-1990*, 1989.

216. In politics where immediate success is attained by saying what people can be made to believe, rather than what is demonstrably true, accent is generally placed on the desirable rather than on the possible.
Raymond Moley (1886-1975), U.S. Assistant Secretary of State and presidential assistant (D). Quoted in *The New Dictionary of American Thoughts*, 1957.

217. Anybody who says negative commercials are wrong and shouldn't be used doesn't know anything about politics. The fact is people respond to those commercials.
Guy V. Molinari, U.S. Congressman (R-NY). Quoted in *The Washington Post*, Oct. 29, 1989.

218. *[Jimmy]* Carter's campaign strategy was to remain unclear on all the issues.
Walter F. Mondale, Vice President of the United States and U.S. Senator (D-MN). Quoted in Celebrity Research Group, *The Bedside Book of Celebrity Gossip*, 1984.

219. Doing my job well is the best way to campaign.
Constance A. Morella, U.S. Congresswoman (R-MD). Quoted on C-SPAN, Oct. 7, 1990.

220. It's been proven with consistency. The only way to win is to walk. You have to like going out and pressing the flesh and placing yourself at risk.
Ron Mullin, Mayor of Concord, CA. Quoted in *Governing*, Mar. 1988.

221. People vote their resentment, not their appreciation.
William Bennett Munro (1875-1957), American political scientist. Quoted in *The New Dictionary of American Thoughts*, 1957.

222. While splendidly progressive it is at the same time amply conservative and sound.
Frank Andrew Munsey (1854-1925), American newspaper publisher. In reference to Theodore Roosevelt's views presented to the Progressive (Bull Moose) Party convention in 1912. Quoted in Richard Hofstadter, *The American Political Tradition*, 1948.

223. In these elections of 1970, something has gone wrong. There has been name-calling and deception of almost unprecedented volume. Honorable men have been slandered. Faithful servants of the country have had their motives questioned and their patriotism doubted.... The danger from this assault is not that a few more Democrats might be defeated – the country can survive that. The true danger is that the American people will have been deprived of that public debate, that opportunity for fair judgment, which is the heartbeat of the democratic process. And that is something the country cannot afford.
Edmund S. Muskie, Governor of Maine (D), U.S. Senator, and U.S. Secretary of State. In reference to attacks on him by Richard Nixon and Spiro Agnew. Televised speech, Nov. 2, 1970.

224. The best way to keep one's word is not to give it.
Napoléon I (1769-1821), military leader and Emperor of France. *Maxims*.

225. We need accessible candidates and accountable candidates.
Nancy Neuman, President, League of Women Voters. Interview, ABC, *20:20*, Nov. 6, 1988.

226. Radio "hook-up" has destroyed the old-time politicians' game of promising in each locality the things which that locality wishes.
Editorial, *The New York Times*, Nov. 4, 1928.

227. It enlarges democracy when nominees are chosen by the people instead of by bosses.
Editorial, *The New York Times*, June 12, 1988.

228. The New Politics should be more activist, more radically concerned with institutions, more concerned with cultural issues, more like a social movement than a political campaign.

Jack Newfield, American political columnist. *The Nation*, July 28, 1969.

229. You don't win campaigns with a diet of dishwater and milktoast.
Richard M. Nixon, 37th President of the United States (R-CA). Remark to Murray Chotiner, 1960.

230. Whatever the political consequences we are not going to outpromise our opponents in this campaign.... We are not going to buy people's votes with their own money.
Richard M. Nixon. Presidential nomination acceptance speech. Republican National Convention, Chicago, IL, July 27, 1960.

231. Campaigning is not easy; it's particularly hard on the wives. They have to hear you make that same speech all the time and look as if it is new.
Richard M. Nixon. Press conference, Kansas City, KS, Sept. 24, 1960.

232. Nobody knows better than I that anyone who enters the arena will subject himself to the most vicious and unprincipled attacks.
Richard M. Nixon. Speech to Republican women, Sun Valley, ID, Sept. 30, 1961.

233. I am overnominated and underelected.
Richard M. Nixon. Quoted in *The New York Times*, Apr. 25, 1965.

234. There's an old saying: Never strike a king unless you kill him. In politics you don't hit your opponent unless you knock him out.
Richard M. Nixon. Quoted in *The Saturday Evening Post*, Feb. 25, 1967.

235. I have never campaigned against another Republican, and I'm not going to start it now. The way for a Republican to win is not to show how he can take on other Republicans, but to show how he can take on Lyndon Johnson.
Richard M. Nixon. Quoted in *Esquire*, May 1968.

236. I'll speak for the man, or against him, whichever will do him the most good.
Richard M. Nixon. Quoted in *The Macmillan Dictionary of Quotations*, 1987.

237. I have no regrets because I'm convinced that the strength of these elections is that the people taking part in them really made a choice rather than just "voting." My conclusion is that one cannot rely on old methods of political work under the new conditions. As a candidate I should have met with more people, reached every voter, and set out my election program better.
V. I. Novozhilov, General, Soviet Army, and Communist Party leader. Comment after losing his first contested election. Quoted in *The Washington Post*, Apr. 7, 1989.

238. If more politicians in this country were thinking about the next generation instead of the next election, it might be better for the United States and the world.
Claude D. Pepper (1901-1989), U.S. Senator and U.S. Congressman (D-FL). Quoted in *The Orlando Sentinel-Star*, Dec. 29, 1946.

239. We should limit the time of election campaigns and limit the amount of money that can be spent.
Claude D. Pepper. Interview, Aug. 20, 1988.

240. I have not run in vain, nor labored in vain.
New Testament, *Philippians* 2:16.

241. The moment a man becomes valuable or terrible to the politician, his rights will be respected. Give the Negro a vote in his hand, and there is not a politician from Abraham Lincoln down to the laziest loafer in the lowest ward of this city who would not do him honor.
Wendell Phillips (1811-1884), American orator and reformer. Quoted in Richard Hofstadter, *The American Political Tradition*, 1948.

242. I have only one letter of recommendation and that is from His Holiness, the Pope. I have it here in my hand. I did not hear my opponent read from His Holiness.
Jean-François Pouliot, French-Canadian politician. Campaign speech, Quebec, Canada, 1924.

243. No, siree. I'd make the Republicans mad and I'd make the Democrats mad. And they're both my customers.
Frederick C. Proehl, merchant and Greenback Party presidential nominee. Response when asked if he campaigned in his store. Quoted in *The Washington Times*, Oct. 18, 1956.

244. The people who are giving the money *[PAC's and large campaign contributions]* are just trying to buy a vote.
William Proxmire, U.S. Senator (D-WI). Oct. 1990.

245. If you have a weak candidate and a weak platform, wrap yourself in the American flag and talk about the Constitution.
Matthew S. Quay (1833-1904), U.S. Senator (R-PA). 1886.

246. You can bet your spring petunias that *this* congressman will vote to override *[the veto of his party's President]*.... He *[the President]* ain't gonna be running in '88, but I am.

Arthur Ravenal, Jr., U.S. Congressman (R-SC). Quoted in *Newsweek*, Apr. 13, 1987.

247. The perceived need to get reelected hampers one's better judgment.

Dixy Lee Ray, Governor of Washington and Chairman, U.S. Atomic Energy Commission (D). Interview, C-SPAN, *Booknotes*, June 16, 1991.

248. I will not deny that there are men in this district better qualified than I to go to Congress, but, gentlemen, these men are not in the race.

Samuel T. Rayburn (1882-1961), U.S. Congressman and Speaker of the House (D-TX). Campaign speech, 1912.

249. Anyone can be elected once by accident. Beginning with the second term, it's worth paying attention.

Samuel T. Rayburn. Quoted in Charles Henning, *The Wit and Wisdom of Politics*, 1989.

250. A candidate doesn't make the decision whether to run for President; the people make it for him.

Ronald Reagan, 40th President of the United States (R-CA). *An American Life*, 1990.

251. If you're not big enough to lose, you're not big enough to win.

Walter P. Reuther (1907-1970), President, United Auto Workers of America. Comment on running for union office.

252. July does not a November election make.

Ann Richards, Governor of Texas (D). In reference to early poll results. CBS, *Face the Nation*, July 3, 1988.

253. I'm not enormously skilled at sound bites.

John D. Rockefeller IV, U.S. Senator and Governor of West Virginia (D). Quoted in *The Washington Post*, May 21, 1991.

254. Campaign platforms are like train platforms. They're for getting in on, not for standing on.

Will Rogers (1879-1934), American humorist. Quoted on CBS campaign coverage, July 19, 1988.

255. I think TV has completely revolutionized what should go on at a political convention. I was bored to death by the parades and floor demonstrations. If we can possibly prevent any such goings-on at our convention, it would gain in dignity and interest and in educational value to the TV audience.

Anna Eleanor Roosevelt (1884-1962), First Lady and U.S. Delegate to the United Nations. Letter to Democratic National Chairman Frank E. McKinney, July 13, 1952.

256. This is more than a political campaign; it is a call to arms.

Franklin D. Roosevelt (1882-1945), 32nd President of the United States (D-NY). Presidential nomination acceptance speech, Democratic National Convention, Chicago, IL, July 2, 1932.

257. The largest single item in our *[presidential campaign]* budget is to buy *[radio]* time over the air.

Franklin D. Roosevelt. Remark, 1932.

258. In the olden days campaigns were conducted amid surroundings of brass bands and red lights.... With the spread of education, and the wider reading of newspapers and especially with the advent of radio, mere oratory and mere emotion are having less to do with the determination of public questions.... Today, common sense plays the greater part and final opinions are arrived at in the quiet of the home.

Franklin D. Roosevelt. Radio address, July 30, 1932.

259. He's still a son of a bitch.

Franklin D. Roosevelt. Remark after Thomas E. Dewey refused to congratulate him. Election night, 1944.

260. My hat is in the ring.

Theodore Roosevelt (1858-1919), 26th President of the United States (R-NY). Announcement that he would contest Pres. Taft for the Republican presidential nomination. Cleveland, OH, Feb. 21, 1912.

261. To you men who have come together to spend and be spent in the endless crusade against wrong, to you who face the future resolute and confident, to you who strive in a spirit of brotherhood for the betterment of our nation I say now as I said here six weeks ago, we stand at Armageddon and we battle for the Lord.

Theodore Roosevelt. Presidential nomination acceptance speech, Progressive Party (Bull Moose) Convention, Chicago, IL, Aug. 5, 1912.

262. A President of the United States can, if he knows how to use the machinery at his disposal, renominate himself, even though the majority of his party is against him.

Theodore Roosevelt. Remark, 1912.

263. I have a safe seat because I work hard.
Benjamin S. Rosenthal (1923-1983), U.S. Congressman (D-NY). Quoted in Daniel Rapoport, *Inside the House*, 1975.

264. Candidates *[for Congress]* should mesh with local interests and local concerns.
Marge Roukema, U.S. Congresswoman (R-NJ). Interview, ABC, *20:20*, Feb. 4, 1990.

265. How can I explain a plan *[for the country]* when I don't have one?
Silvio Santos, Brazilian TV star and presidential candidate. Press conference, Rio de Janeiro, Nov. 3, 1989.

266. You're the soldiers that make democracy work.
Paul S. Sarbanes, U.S. Congressman and U.S. Senator (D-MD). Speech thanking his campaign workers after his reelection to the Senate, Nov. 8, 1988.

267. Campaigns go on for so long that they've become like elevator music. You know it's there, but you don't really hear it.
Robert Scheifer, American TV journalist. CBS, *Sunday Morning*, Nov. 6, 1988.

268. Governing has become the brief interval between campaigns.
Robert Scheifer. *Ibid.*

269. I wonder who the people are who vote for the *[presidential]* ticket because of the Vice President rather than the President?
Arthur M. Schlesinger, Jr., American historian and presidential advisor (D). Interview, PBS, *MacNeil-Lehrer News Hour*, June 16, 1988.

270. When the big issues matter less, the small issues matter more. So small things, like one-liners and gaffes, can make a difference.
William Schneider, political analyst, American Enterprise Institute. Comment on political debates. Quoted in *The New York Times*, Sept. 25, 1988.

271. The American people can deal intelligently with issues when they are painted in hues more subtle than black and white.
Charles L. Schultze, Chairman, Council of Economic Advisors, and Director, U.S. Bureau of the Budget (D). *The Public Use of Private Interest*, 1977.

272. You can't tell people something when they know the opposite.
Tony Schwartz, American political TV ad producer (D). Quoted in Kathleen Hall Jamieson, *Packaging the Presidency*, 1984.

273. I think George Bush is going to win the election. Some people think he's going to win by a landslide. I don't think so. I think he's going to win by a mudslide.
Tony Schwartz. Quoted on CBS, *West 57th Street*, Nov. 5, 1988.

274. The campaign takes place in the living room.
Tony Schwartz. Interview, PBS, *A Walk Through the 20th Century: The 30 Second President*, July 23, 1990.

275. To doubt is to lose.
Walter Scott (1771-1832), Scottish writer. Quoted in John Gibson Lockhart, *Life of Sir Walter Scott*, 1837.

276. The power of hope to sway voters fits with what we know about people's tendency to like more positive people.
David Sears, editor, *Journal of Political Psychology*. Quoted in *The New York Times*, May 8, 1988.

277. Inherited wealth might be an advantage in politics. The voters know he *[Dan Quayle]* didn't steal it.
Eric A. Sevareid (1913-1992), American broadcast journalist and writer. *CBS News*, Aug. 17, 1988.

278. A crawling reptile, whose only claim *[to the presidency]* was that he *[Martin Van Buren]* has inveigled the confidence of a credulous, blind, dotard, old man *[Andrew Jackson]*.
William H. Seward (1801-1872), Governor of New York (Whig), U.S. Senator (Whig and R), and U.S. Secretary of State.

279. No age or condition is without its heroes. The least incapable general in a nation is its Caesar, the least imbecile statesman its Solon, the least confused thinker its Socrates, the least commonplace poet its Shakespeare.
George Bernard Shaw (1856-1950), Nobel Laureate in Literature (England). *Maxims for Revolutionists*, 1903.

280. If nominated, I will not accept. If elected, I will not serve.
William Tecumseh Sherman (1820-1891), General, U.S. Army. Telegram to Sen. John B. Henderson, presiding officer of the Republican National Convention, Chicago, IL, June 5, 1884.

281. He touched all the erogenous zones of the body politic.
Mark Shields, American political columnist. In reference to presidential candidate George Bush's campaign tactics. PBS, *Washington Week in Review*, July 29, 1988.

282. Most women have some *pro bono* experience that propels them into politics. Men go to law school.

Claire Shulman, Borough President of Queens (New York City) (D). Quoted in *The New York Times*, June 26, 1989.

283. No man should win or deserve to win who depends on the rabble rather than upon the conservative men of affairs.

Joseph C. Sibley (1850-1926), U.S. Congressman (R-PA). Remark to Theodore Roosevelt, 1912.

284. If the candidate makes any effort to enlarge upon that sound bite, he is then accused of having changed his position.

John Silber, President, Boston University, and Democratic candidate for Governor of Massachusetts. Quoted in *The Washington Post*, Sept. 23, 1990.

285. An attack unanswered is an attack believed.

Alan K. Simpson, U.S. Senator (R-WY). Seminar, The National Press Club, Mar. 29, 1990.

286. It *[the negative campaign commercial]* will disappear from the American political scene when it doesn't work any more.

Don Sipple, American political TV ad producer (R). Quoted in *The New York Times*, Sept. 9, 1990.

287. I like it *[campaigning]*.... It gets into your blood.

Alfred E. Smith, Governor of New York (D). Quoted in M. and H. Josephson, *Al Smith: Hero of the Cities*, 1969.

288. A man gets his first idea of real campaigning when he begins to spread out from the locality in which he is known to search for votes in a new region.

Alfred E. Smith. *Ibid.*

289. The people want a winner.

Alfred E. Smith. Remark, 1924.

290. They tell me I mustn't refer to our sacred flag. That would make me a rabble-rouser. They say I must not speak of our glorious Constitution. That would be rabble-rousing. They tell me that I cannot quote from my beloved Bible, which I hold here in my hand. Let me tell you, my friends, that if it is rabble-rousing to praise the flag and the Constitution and to love and revere the Holy Bible, then I pray to God that He in His wisdom will make me the greatest rabble-rouser in the land.

Gerald L. K. Smith (1898-1976), American clergyman and cofounder, Union Party. Speech, 1936.

291. WHITE PEOPLE, WAKE UP BEFORE IT'S TOO LATE.

Willis Smith (1897-1953), U.S. Senator (D-NC). Campaign sign, 1950.

292. I might one day be opposed by a multimillionaire who might be prepared to spend millions of dollars.

Stephen J. Solarz, U.S. Congressman (D-NY). Explanation for accumulating a million-dollar campaign war chest. Quoted on PBS, *The Power Game*, Jan. 2, 1989.

293. *[Presidential]* debates, like campaigns, are having less and less to do with what goes on in the Oval Office.

Theodore Sorensen, presidential assistant and speech writer (D). Interview, CBS, *This Week*, Sept. 25, 1988.

294. If he *[Ronald Reagan]* got a bullet in the toe, it would help the election.

Stuart Spencer, American political consultant (R). Quoted in Mayer and McManus, *Landslide: The Unmasking of the President, 1984-1988*, 1988.

295. You see, in elections for members to sit in Parliament, how far saluting rows of old women, drinking with clowns, and being upon a level with the lower part of mankind in that wherein they themselves are lowest, their diversions, will carry a candidate.

Richard Steele (1672-1729), English writer. *The Spectator*, No. 336, Apr. 4, 1712.

296. If the Republicans stop telling lies about us, we will stop telling the truth about them.

Adlai E. Stevenson (1900-1964), Governor of Illinois (D), and U.S. Ambassador to the United Nations. Campaign speech, Bakersfield, CA, Sept. 6, 1952.

297. The people might be better served if a party purchased a half hour of radio and TV silence during which the audience would be asked to think quietly for themselves.

Adlai E. Stevenson. Remark, 1952.

298. Better we lose the election than mislead the people.

Adlai E. Stevenson. Presidential nomination acceptance speech, Democratic National Convention, Chicago, IL, July 26, 1952.

299. The idea that you can merchandise candidates for high office like breakfast cereal is the ultimate indignity for the democratic process.

Adlai E. Stevenson. Comment after accepting the Democratic nomination for the presidency. Chicago, IL, Aug. 18, 1956.

300. The hardest thing about any political campaign is how to win without proving that you are unworthy of winning.
Adlai E. Stevenson. Speech, Fresno, CA, Oct. 11, 1956.

301. There have been a couple of times when I yearned for the serenity I knew as a Marine Corps tank commander in Korea.
Adlai Stevenson III, Treasurer of Illinois and U.S. Senator (D-IL). Comment on his campaign for governor. Quoted in *Newsweek*, Aug. 25, 1986.

302. It takes a lot of guts to stick your neck out and run for any public office. But the only thing that's tougher than announcing for office is withdrawing from a race, because when you drop out you are saying that you are quitting and that you're beaten.
Robert S. Strauss, Chairman, Democratic National Committee, and U.S. Ambassador to the U.S.S.R. Remark to Hamilton Jordan, Mar. 19, 1980.

303. Campaigns are a form of bloodless warfare.
Raymond D. Strother, American political consultant (D). *Newsweek*, Feb. 24, 1986.

304. If you squeeze the flesh, you are close to your constituency ... this is a very human thing. It is a good new thing.
Milos Sturlar, Russian journalist, *Isvestia*. Comment on American political techniques. PBS, *Campaign: A View from Abroad*, Oct. 17, 1988.

305. We spend an exorbitant amount of time raising money while we should spend the time working for the people.
Michael L. Synar, U.S. Congressman (D-OK). C-SPAN, *Close-Up*, Feb. 24, 1990.

306. Even a rat will fight when driven in a corner.
[At first Taft refused to go out "stumping" for the presidency, but Theodore Roosevelt's active Bull Moose campaign caused him to yield to necessity.]
William H. Taft (1857-1930), 27th President of the United States (R-OH) and Chief Justice, U.S. Supreme Court. 1912.

307. I have one consolation. No candidate was elected ex-President by such a large majority.
William H. Taft. Comment on his overwhelming presidential reelection loss to Woodrow Wilson. 1912.

308. Throw mud, throw mud. Some of it may stick.
Charles-Maurice de Talleyrand-Périgord (Prince de Bénévent) (1754-1838), French diplomat and statesman. Quoted by William Randolph Hearst, congressional campaign speech, 1906.

309. Elections are not won by prayers alone.
Joseph Israel Tarte (1848-1907), Member of Parliament, Canada. Remark after winning an election, 1896.

310. Your remarks in relation to my being a candidate for the presidency are very flattering, but I think you will know without the necessity of saying so to you, that I am not and shall never be an aspirant for that honor. My opinion has always been against the elevation of a military chief to that position.
Zachary Taylor (1784-1850), 12th President of the United States (Whig-VA). Letter to Gen. Thomas Young, Newcastle, DE, July 18, 1846.

311. An honest day's work for an honest day's pay, live within your means, put a nest egg by for a rainy day, pay your bills on time and support the police.
Margaret Thatcher, Prime Minister of Great Britain (Conservative). Campaign speech, 1983.

312. We were told our campaign wasn't sufficiently slick. We regard that as a compliment.
Margaret Thatcher. Comment after winning an unprecedented third term. Quoted in *The New York Times*, June 12, 1987.

313. The other side *[the Labour party]* have got an ideology. We must have one as well.
Margaret Thatcher. Comment made shortly after being elected Prime Minister. Quoted in Hugo Young, *The Iron Lady*, 1989.

314. Send me to Washington and I'll stick my pitchfork into his *[President Cleveland's]* ribs!
Benjamin Ryan Tillman (1847-1918), Governor of South Carolina (D) and U.S. Senator. Senate campaign promise, 1894.

315. In military battle and political battle, always attack ... even when you are low on ammunition.
Omar Torrijos (1926-1981), President of Panama. Remark to Hamilton Jordan, Mar. 21, 1980.

316. I'm going to give 'em hell!
Harry S Truman (1884-1972), 33rd President of the United States (D-MO). Remark to Alben Barkley on his campaign strategy, 1948.

317. It's plain hokum. If you can't convince 'em, confuse 'em. It's an old political trick. But this time it won't work.
Harry S Truman. In reference to Republican attacks on him and his administration. Campaign speech, 1948.

318. I do not want and will not accept the political support of Henry Wallace and his communists.
Harry S Truman. Campaign speech, 1948.

319. In most of my campaigns, I find it best not to mention my opponent by name because, by doing so, it just gives him a chance to get into the headlines.
Harry S Truman. Remark, 1948.

320. We have told the people the truth and the people are with us. The people are going to win this election.
Harry S Truman. Statement to reporters, Nov. 1, 1948.

321. The experts get more wrong all the time.
Harry S Truman. On public opinion polls. Remark to Clark Clifford, Oct. 1948.

322. The people could be convinced.
Harry S Truman. His explanation of his 1948 upset victory over Thomas E. Dewey. November 1948.

323. If you want to get elected, shake hands with 25,000 people between now and November 7.
Harry S Truman. Advice to William Benton, Sept. 11, 1950.

324. When you're in politics, you've got to be elected. You can't be unless the people who control the votes are for you. But when you have a good reputation and are a good vote getter, the people who control the votes are more likely to be for you.
Harry S Truman. Reaction to criticism that he was too close to the graft-ridden Pendergast machine in Missouri. Quoted in Paul F. Boller, Jr., *Presidential Anecdotes*, 1981.

325. The people have spoken – the bastards!
Dick Tuck, American political operative (D, R). Comment after losing the election for a California state legislative seat. *Playboy*, Feb. 1974.

326. It is difference of opinion that makes horse races.
Mark Twain (Samuel Langhorne Clemens) (1835-1910), American writer. *Pudd'nhead Wilson's Calendar*, 1894.

327. It is easier to stay out than to get out.
Mark Twain. *The Tragedy of Pudd'nhead Wilson*, 1894.

328. I don't care who does the electing so long as I do the nominating.
William Marcy Tweed (1823-1878), U.S. Congressman (D-NY) and Tammany Hall leader, New York City. Quoted in *Modern Maturity*, July 30, 1988.

329. Few candidates ever make a *[campaign]* budget and stick to it. Each candidate's budget is made by his opponent.
Morris K. Udall, U.S. Congressman (D-AZ). *Playboy*, Nov. 1967.

330. The people will never make a man President who is so importunate as to show ... that he ... is in active pursuit of the office.
Martin Van Buren (1782-1862), 8th President of the United States (D-NY). Letter of political advice to his son, John, Mar. 16, 1858.

331. We have assembled a Gideon's army – small in number, powerful in conviction, ready for action ... unfettered by any principle but the general welfare. By God's grace, the people's peace will usher in the century of the common man.
Henry A. Wallace (1888-1965), U.S. Secretary of Agriculture, U.S. Secretary of Commerce, and Vice President of the United States (D-IA). Radio address announcing his independent candidacy for the presidency, Dec. 29, 1947.

332. I think he thinks I'm important, and that may be as important as being important.
Benjamin Ward, Police Commissioner, New York City. Response when asked if he was important to Mayor Edward Koch's reelection bid. Quoted in *The New York Times*, Oct. 27, 1988.

333. They didn't contribute to me. They contributed to good government. And if they didn't know that good government meant no special treatment for anyone, they know it now.
Earl Warren (1891-1974), Chief Justice, U.S. Supreme Court, and Governor of California (R). Comment on how he could accept campaign contributions from people and then attack them. Remark to Lt. Governor Goodwin J. Knight, 1943.

334. You bet your life they *[the Republicans]* can lose. They can lick themselves. In my opinion, the Republican Congress *[the 80th]* is on probation before the people, and the final outcome will be determined by the manner in which the Congress acquits itself before the American people.
Earl Warren. Statement, Mexico City, Dec. 1947.

335. A chief justice cannot be a candidate for the presidency without damaging the office he holds and himself too.
Earl Warren. Statement, 1956.

336. When you search the history books for some golden age of positive campaigning, you have a hard time finding it.
Editorial, *The Washington Post*, Oct. 22, 1988.

337. Anyone who does not vote for this ticket is not my friend.
Harold Washington (1922-1987), Mayor of Chicago, IL, and U.S. Congressman (D). Statement, Nov. 1987.

338. All I have to offer you is me.
Dorothy Wayatt, Mayor of St. John's, Newfoundland, Canada. Campaign statement quoted in *The Toronto Star*, Nov. 8, 1981.

339. *[James]* Buchanan's margin of victory *[in the election]* was $50,000.
Thurlow Weed (1797-1882), American editor and leader of Whig and Republican parties. Remark, 1856.

340. I was not long in discovering that it was easy to enlist the laboring classes against a "monster bank" or "monied aristocracy."
Thurlow Weed. Quoted in Richard Hofstadter, *The American Political Tradition*, 1948.

341. I don't have $6 million to spend, so I'm going to have to talk fast.
Paul Wellstone, U.S. Senator (D-MN). TV campaign ad, Oct. 1990.

342. If the deck is stacked so that incumbents can't lose and challengers can't win, then there is no accountability.
Fred Wertheimer, President, Common Cause. In reference to congressional elections. Interview, ABC, *This Week*, Oct. 9, 1988.

343. Unless you have your own personal wealth or access to large sums of special interest money, you face an extraordinarily difficult chance of winning *[congressional elections]*.
Fred Wertheimer. Quoted in *The New York Times*, Oct. 31, 1988.

344. I have daily issued a challenge to the men of all parties in my audience to name a single national administration in American history that was as venal, as corrupt, and as careless of the rights of American citizens as that of the past three and one-half years.
Burton K. Wheeler (1882-1975), U.S. Senator (D-MT). Comment when campaigning against Calvin Coolidge and his administration. Press release, Oct. 22, 1924.

345. Run for president? I should say not. The truth alone would beat me ... not to mention what the opposition would dig up.
William A. Wheeler (1819-1887), U.S. Congressman and Vice President of the United States (R-NY). Quoted in *Conservative Digest*, Mar. 1988.

346. It's a once-in-a-lifetime deal. They burn out. Advance men have to be over twenty-five and under thirty-eight.
John Whitaker, advance man in Richard Nixon's presidential campaigns. Quoted in Theodore H. White, *Breach of Faith*, 1975.

347. If I can control the dialogue of a campaign, I can win. If I can control what my opponent is saying and having to react to, I can win. If he controls it, I'm in danger of losing.
Joe White, American political TV ad producer. Quoted on CBS, *West 57th Street*, Nov. 5, 1988.

348. Every political campaign that this writer has ever covered has had a budget item, under whatever rubric used for decency, which was devoted to campaign intelligence.
Theodore H. White (1915-1986), American political analyst and writer. *Breach of Faith*, 1975.

349. The flood of money that gushes into politics today is a pollution of democracy.
Theodore H. White. Quoted in *Time*, Nov. 19, 1984.

350. With the end of the nominating process, American politics leaves logic behind.
Theodore H. White. Quoted in *Newsweek*, May 26, 1986.

351. The higher the office, the more important the candidate is.
Theodore H. White. Quoted in *The Washington Post*, Oct. 24, 1988.

352. There is no excitement anywhere in the world – short of war – to match the excitement of an American presidential campaign.
Theodore H. White. Attributed.

353. Express your outrage on Tuesday at the polls.
L. Douglas Wilder, Governor of Virginia (D). Statement to hecklers at the College of William and Mary, Williamsburg, VA, Nov. 2, 1989.

354. If you just keep the lies coming fast enough, then they *[the opponent]* just cannot keep up.
George F. Will, American political columnist. ABC, *This Week*, Oct. 30, 1988.

355. The biggest bang for the buck comes from negative campaigning.
George F. Will. Quoted on ABC, *This Week*, Oct. 28, 1989.

356. I'd rather be out of a job for doing something than for doing nothing.
John Wilson, President, Washington DC City Council (D). Comment after losing the mayorality election, Nov. 1990.

357. Concept spots are not representative of the candidate or the campaign but an abstract thought about what some outsider thinks the campaign is about.
William Wilson, American presidential campaign media advisor (D). Quoted in Kathleen Hall Jamieson, *Packaging the Presidency*, 1984.

358. Would that we could do something at once dignified and effective to knock Mr. *[William Jennings]* Bryan once for all into a cocked hat.
Woodrow Wilson (1856-1924), 28th President of the United States (D-NJ). Letter, 1907.

359. A presidential campaign may easily degenerate into a mere personal contest, and so lose its real dignity. There is no indispensable man.
Woodrow Wilson. Presidential nomination acceptance speech, June 29, 1912.

360. I don't want politics to be too exciting. I just want to win.
Andrew Young, U.S. Ambassador to the United Nations, U.S. Congressman, and Mayor of Atlanta, GA (D). Quoted in *The Washington Post*, July 13, 1988.

361. More candidates lose elections through fatigue than by not working hard enough.
Andrew Young. *Ibid.*

362. Personality can prevail over ideology in elections. Whether it can prevail over race, though, has yet to be proven.
Andrew Young. Quoted in *The New York Times*, Feb. 26, 1989.

Chapter 10

Capital Punishment

1. For God's sake, if you acknowledge that you should not put children to death, acknowledge that you should not put to death the mentally retarded.
Joseph R. Biden, Jr., U.S. Senator (D-DE). Senate debate, May 25, 1990.

2. The death penalty has been a gross failure. Beyond its horror and incivility, it has neither protected the innocent nor deterred the wicked. The recurrent spectacle of publicly sanctioned killing has cheapened human life and dignity without the grace which comes from justice meted out swiftly, evenly, humanely.
Edmund G. (Pat) Brown, Governor of California (D). Message to California legislature, 1960.

3. Drug dealers need to understand a simple fact. You shoot a cop and you're going to be severely punished – fast. And if I had my way, I'd say with your life.
George Bush, 41st President of the United States (R-TX). Quoted in *The Washington Post*, Mar. 10, 1989.

4. People want to kill people because they don't want them out on the street again.
Patrick Caddell, American political pollster (D). Quoted in *The New York Times Magazine*, Sept. 30, 1990.

5. The death penalty will seem to the next generation, as it seems to many even now, an anachronism too discordant to be suffered, mocking with grim reproach all our clamorous professions of the sanctity of life.
Benjamin N. Cardozo (1870-1938), U.S. Supreme Court Justice. *Law and Literature*, 1931.

6. The thirst for vengeance is a very real, even if a hideous, thing; and states may not ignore it till humanity has been raised to greater heights than any that have yet been scaled in all the long ages of struggle and ascent.
Benjamin N. Cardozo. *Ibid*.

7. You know, there is a certain perception of wimpishness about being against the death penalty. I mean, some of my colleagues say to me, "Fry these vermin, John. What's the problem, man?"
John Conyers, Jr., U.S. Congressman (D-MI). Quoted in *The Washington Post*, Dec. 15, 1990.

8. I believe the death penalty demeans the values that form the core of American life.... Capital punishment is a terrible concession, a desperate response that substitutes one evil for another.... There is a better response to killing than killing.
Mario Cuomo, Governor of New York (D). Message concerning his veto of a capital punishment bill passed by the state legislature, 1984.

9. I'm pro-death. I believe in the death penalty. Let's get on with it.
Richard M. Daley, Mayor of Chicago, IL (D). 1990.

10. Do you think you can cure the hatreds and maladjustments of the world by hanging them?
Clarence S. Darrow (1857-1938), American attorney and writer. Closing statement, Leopold and Loeb murder trial, 1924.

11. Are we deluding ourselves that by snuffing out the lives of our misfits, our nitwits, and our psychopathic personalities, we are creating a better world for ourselves?
Michael V. DiSalle (1908-1981), Governor of Ohio (D) and Director, U.S. Office of Price Stabilization. *Playboy*, May 1966.

12. And if men strive together and hurt a woman with child, so that her fruit depart from her, and yet no harm *[to her]* follows, he shall surely be fined, according as the woman's husband shall lay upon him, and he shall pay as the judges determine. But if any harm follows *[the woman]*, then thou shall give a life for a life, an eye for an eye, a tooth for a tooth, a hand for a hand, a foot for a foot, burning for burning, a wound for wounding, a stripe for a stripe.
Old Testament, *Exodus* 21:22-24.

13. As I live, says the Lord God, I have no pleasure in the death of the wicked, but that the wicked shall

turn from his way and live.
Old Testament, *Ezekiel* 33:11.

14. It's a terrible commentary on society, but I'm afraid we have reached the point where some people, by their acts, do give up their right to survive.
Dianne Feinstein, Mayor of San Francisco, CA (D). *Los Angeles Times*, Feb. 17, 1990.

15. Whoso sheds man's blood, by man shall his blood be shed.
Old Testament, *Genesis* 9:5-6.

16. It *[the death penalty]* is a phony issue. To pretend the death penalty is going to end crime in the United States is to fool people, to promote public ignorance.
Rudolph Giuliani, U.S. Attorney, NY. Quoted in *The Washington Post*, June 27, 1989.

17. Having fully expressed our conviction that the punishment of death is one which should sometimes be inflicted, we may add that we would have it resorted to as unfrequently as possible.
Horace Greeley (1811-1872), American editor and U.S. Congressman (Whig-NY). *The New Yorker*, June 1836.

18. My machine *[the guillotine]* will take off a head in a twinkling and the victim will feel nothing but a refreshing coolness. We cannot make too much haste, gentlemen, to allow the nation to enjoy this advantage.
Joseph Guillotin (1738-1814), French physician, inventor, and politician. Speech, National Assembly, 1789.

19. What is murder in the first degree? It is the cruel, calculated, cold-blooded killing of a fellow human man. It is the most wicked of crimes and the State is guilty of it every time it executes a human being.
William Randolph Hearst (1863-1951), U.S. Congressman (D-NY); founder, Independence League Party; journalist; and publisher. *The New York American*, 1925.

20. I am opposed to the antilynching bill because the federal government has no more business enacting a law against one kind of murder than another.
Lyndon B. Johnson (1908-1973), 36th President of the United States (D-TX). Speech, Austin, TX, May 22, 1948.

21. I even opposed the death penalty for the man who killed my brother *[Robert F. Kennedy, in 1968]*.
Edward M. Kennedy, U.S. Senator (D-MA). Quoted in *The Washington Post Magazine*, Apr. 29, 1990.

22. This *[debate]* is about the only democracy in the world that has the death penalty, and we're arguing about whether we're going to execute the mentally retarded – that says something about our society.
Edward M. Kennedy. Senate debate, May 25, 1990.

23. The author of the *Satanic Verses* book *[Salman Rushdie]*, which is against Islam, the Prophet, and the Koran, and all those involved in its publication who were aware of its content, are sentenced to death.
Ruhollah Khomeini (1900-1989), Iranian ayatollah (cleric) and revolutionary leader. Fatwa (theological ruling), Feb. 14, 1989.

24. Capital punishment may not be much of a deterrent against murder, but the sight of a few corpses swinging from a scaffold might work with drug dealers.
James J. Kilpatrick, American political columnist. Quoted in *Newsweek*, June 30, 1986.

25. We cheapen the value of human life when we fail to impose the most severe penalty upon criminals who violently take the lives of others.
Edward I. Koch, U.S. Congressman and Mayor of New York City (D). 1986.

26. I am a proponent of capital punishment. I am not a proponent of capital torture.
Fred A. Leuchter, Jr., American execution consultant. Quoted in *The New York Times*, Oct. 13, 1990.

27. There is certainly nothing anomalous in punishing the crime of murder differently in different jurisdictions.
Joseph McKenna (1843-1926), U.S. Supreme Court Justice. *Johnson* v. *United States*, 1911.

28. Let no one hurt him.
William McKinley (1843-1901), 25th President of the United States (R-OH). Remark after he was shot by anarchist Leon Czolgosz, Buffalo, NY, Sept. 6, 1901.

29. Capital punishment is one of the must flagrant examples of human rights abuses in the world today.... A gruesome example of governments killing their citizens.
Winston Nagen, spokesman, Amnesty International. Interview, C-SPAN, *Current Issues*, Feb. 21, 1990.

30. The day may come when there is such general legislative rejection of the execution of 16- or 17-

year-old capital murderers that a clear national consensus can be said to have developed.... I do not believe that day has yet arrived.

Sandra Day O'Connor, U.S. Supreme Court Justice. Statement made when concurring with the majority opinion of Justice Scalia in *Stanford* v. *Kentucky* and *Wilkins* v. *Missouri*, June 26, 1989.

31. The sight of it gave me infinite pleasure, as it proved that I was in civilized society.

Mungo Park (1771-1806), Scottish explorer. Comment on finding a gallows in an unexplored part of Africa. Quoted in *The Macmillan Dictionary of Quotations*, 1989.

32. When you're running *[for political office]* in the 90's, you not only have to be for the death penalty, you have to enjoy it.

Mark Russell, American political comedian. PBS, *The Mark Russell Comedy Hour*, Apr. 24, 1990.

33. Stupid men – you would believe in laws which punish murder by murder.

George Sand (Amandine-Aurore-Lucie Dudevant) (1804-1876), French writer. *Intimate Journal*, June 13, 1837.

34. Men are not hanged for stealing horses, but that horses may not be stolen.

George Savile, 1st Marquess of Halifax (1633-1695), Lord Privy Seal of England. *Political Thoughts and Reflections*, 1750.

35. I always look forward to the opportunity to chop off more heads so that I can earn more money.

Saeed Al Sayyaf, state executioner, Saudi Arabia. Quoted in *Newsweek*, July 3, 1989.

36. Criminals do not die by the hands of the law. They die by the hands of other men.

George Bernard Shaw (1856-1950), Nobel Laureate in Literature (Great Britain). *Maxims for Revolutionists*, 1903.

37. Assassination on the scaffold is the worst form of assassination, because there it is invested with the approval of society.

George Bernard Shaw. *Ibid.*

38. Murder and capital punishment are not opposites that cancel one another, but similars that breed their kind.

George Bernard Shaw. *Ibid.*

39. Hangmen are a dying breed.

Fred S. Silverman, Deputy Attorney General, DE. On the difficulty in hiring an executioner. Quoted in *The New York Times*, Oct. 13, 1990.

40. If I had engaged in politics, O men of Athens, I should have perished long ago, and done no good either to you or to myself.

Socrates (c.470-399 B.C.), Greek philosopher. Quoted by Plato, *Apology*.

41. The existence of the soldier is (next to the death penalty) the most painful vestige of barbarism surviving among men.

Alfred de Vigny (1797-1863), French writer and soldier. *Servitude et grandeur militaires*, 1835.

42. In this country *[England]* it is good to kill an admiral from time to time, to encourage the others.

Voltaire (François-Marie Arouet) (1694-1778), French historian and dramatist. *Candide*, 1759.

43. If any man shall Blaspheme the name of god, the father, Sonne or Holie ghost, with direct, espresse, presumptious or high handed blasphemie, or shall curse god ... he shall be put to death.

Nathaniel Ward (c.1578-1652), Puritan leader and codifier. *The Massachusetts Body of Liberties*, 1641.

44. The death penalty has been employed throughout our history, and, in a day when it is still widely accepted, it cannot be said to violate the constitutional concept of cruelty *[the Eighth Amendment]*.

Earl Warren (1891-1974), Chief Justice, U.S. Supreme Court, and Governor of California (R). *Trop* v. *Dulles*, 1957.

45. These hardened criminals will never again murder, rape, or deal drugs. As governor, I made sure they received the ultimate punishment – death – and Texas is a safer place for it.

Mark White, Governor of Texas (D). TV campaign ad, 1990.

46. The case for capital punishment stands or falls on the issue of proportionality, on the intuition that it is disrespectful of human dignity not to take a life as punishment for especially cruel, wanton or cold-blooded killing. Today, capital punishment is essentially restricted to the function of expressing society's horror of such crimes.

George F. Will, American political columnist. *The Washington Post*, Apr. 30, 1987.

47. The death penalty is 100 percent effective in preventing recidivism.

George F. Will. ABC, *This Week*, Apr. 8, 1990.

48. The death penalty has become a small symbolic event, and all the arguing is about that symbolism.

Franklin Zimring, Director, Earl Warren Legal Institute. Quoted in *The New York Times*, Sept. 10, 1989.

Chapter 11

Citizens and Citizenship

1. I am a Canadian, a man, and a black man in that order.
   Lincoln Alexander, Member of Parliament and Lieutenant Governor of Ontario, Canada. Quoted in *The Globe and Mail*, Feb. 17, 1973.

2. It was we, the people; not we, the white male citizens; nor yet we, the male citizens; but we, the whole people who formed the Union. And we formed it, not to give the blessings of liberty, but to secure them; not to the half of ourselves and the half of our posterity, but to the whole people – women as well as men.
   Susan B. Anthony (1820-1906), American suffragist. Speech, 1873.

3. It is not always the same thing to be a good man and a good citizen.
   Aristotle (384-322 B.C.), Greek philosopher and teacher. *Nicomachean Ethics.*

4. He who has the power to take part in the deliberative or judicial administration of any state is said by us to be a citizen of that state.
   Aristotle. *Politics.*

5. Mr. President, this great new baby state *[Arizona]* is magnificent, this great new baby is ready to join the pantheon of other splendid states in our fair union, this great new baby state is poised to become a veritable paradise. We need only two things: water and lots of people.
   [An anonymous senator called out: That's all they need in hell.]
   Henry Fountain Ashurst (1874-1962), U.S. Senator (D-AZ). Maiden speech in the Senate, 1912.

6. We will never bring disgrace to this, our country, by any act of cowardice. We will fight for the ideals of this, our country. We will revere and obey the laws. We will strive to quicken our sense of civic duty. Thus, in all these ways, we will transmit this country greater, better, stronger, prouder, and more beautiful than it was transmitted to us.
   Ancient Athenian pledge. Quoted by Michael Dukakis, accepting the Democratic Party presidential nomination, Atlanta, GA, July 21, 1988.

7. Take care always to remember that you are a Roman.... Have a care you are not too much of a Caesar!
   Marcus Aurelius (A.D. 121-180), Emperor of Rome and Stoic philosopher. Passage marked in Cecil Rhodes's personal copy of *Meditations*.

8. The making of an American begins at that point where he himself rejects all other ties, any other history, and adopts the vesture of his adopted land.
   James Baldwin (1924-1987), American writer. *Notes of a Native Son*, 1955.

9. Government is not a substitute for people, but simply the instrument through which they act. And if the individual fails to do his duty as a citizen, government becomes a very deadly instrument indeed.
   Bernard M. Baruch (1870-1965), Chairman, War Industries Board, and U.S. Delegate to the U.N. Atomic Energy Commission. Quoted in Edward F. Murphy, *2,715 One-Line Quotations*, 1981.

10. I am a citizen of the world: I serve neither the emperor nor the king of France; I am at the service of Truth; she is my only Queen.
    Pierre Bayle (1647-1706), French philosopher and writer. *Dictionnaire historique et critique*, s.v. *Usson*, 1697.

11. I pledge allegiance to the flag of the United States of America, and to the republic for which it stands, one nation, indivisible, with liberty and justice for all.
    (The words "under God" were added in 1952 by an Act of Congress.)
    Francis Bellamy (1855-1931), Vice President, Society of Christian Socialists. "The Pledge of Allegiance," *Youth's Companion*, Sept. 8, 1892.

12. The State of Israel represents and speaks only on behalf of its own citizens, and in no way presumes to represent or speak in the name of the Jews who are citizens of any other country.

David Ben-Gurion (1886-1973), 1st Prime Minister of Israel (Labour). Speech, Jerusalem, Aug. 23, 1950.

13. There shall be no differences save by merit of character, by merit of ability, by merit of service to country. Those are the true tests of the value of any man or woman, white or coloured.
Annie Wood Besant (1847-1933), President, Indian National Congress. *Wake Up, India*, 1913.

14. The most important office ... that of private citizen.
Louis D. Brandeis (1856-1941), U.S. Supreme Court Justice. Letter, *The Boston Record*, Apr. 14, 1903.

15. The right to speak freely concerning functions of the federal government is a privilege of immunity of every citizen of the United States which, even before the adoption of the Fourteenth Amendment, a state was powerless to curtail.
Louis D. Brandeis. Quoted by Alfred Lief, *The Social and Economic Views of Mr. Justice Brandeis*, 1934.

16. I have never been in harmony with the proposition to apply the educational test *[to immigrants]*. If that test had been applied two hundred years ago, I have ancestors who never would have gotten in.
Joseph G. Cannon (1836-1926), U.S. Congressman and Speaker of the House (R-IL). Address, General Convention, International Order of B'nai B'rith, Washington, DC, Apr. 6, 1910.

17. Whatever is a privilege rather than a right, may be made dependent upon citizenship.
Benjamin N. Cardozo (1870-1938), U.S. Supreme Court Justice. *People* v. *Crane*, 1915.

18. If the Germans want to put the yellow Jewish star in Denmark, I and my whole family will wear it as a sign of the highest distinction.
(The day after these words were spoken, the king rode his horse in public, wearing the yellow star prominently on his tunic.)
Christian X (1870-1947), King of Denmark. Oct. 11, 1943.

19. I have no country to fight for; my country is the earth, and I am a citizen of the world.
Eugene V. Debs (1855-1926), American Socialist. Speech, 1914.

20. We Europeans will always have two fatherlands. One is Europe, and the other is our own country. It is unified in its diversity – this Europe.
Jacques Delors, President, European Community Commission. Quoted in *The New York Times*, July 28, 1988.

21. Asked from what country he came, Diogenes the Cynic replied, "I am a citizen of the world."
Diogenes the Cynic (412-322 B.C.), Greek philosopher. Quoted by Diogenes Laertius, *Diogenes*, 6.

22. Once let the black man get upon his person the brass letters, U.S. – let him get an eagle on his button, and a musket on his shoulder, and bullets in his pocket, and there is no power on earth which can deny that he has earned the right to citizenship.
Frederick Douglass (c.1817-1895), Recorder of Deeds, District of Columbia, and U.S. Minister to Haiti. Quoted in Henry Steele Commager, *An Illustrated History of the Civil War*, 1976.

23. Nobody from the CIA is going to account for their loyalty to *[Sen. Joseph]* McCarthy.
Allen W. Dulles (1893-1969), Director, Central Intelligence Agency. Remark to William Bundy, ordering him not to testify before McCarthy's subcommittee.

24. They *[the Founding Fathers]* proclaimed to all the world the revolutionary doctrine of the divine rights of the common man. That doctrine has ever since been the heart of the American faith.
Dwight D. Eisenhower (1890-1969), 34th President of the United States (R-KS). Bicentennial address, Columbia University, New York City, May 1954.

25. The true test of civilization is not the census, nor the size of cities, nor the crops – no, but the kind of man the country turns out.
Ralph Waldo Emerson (1803-1882), American writer. "Civilization," in *Society and Solitude*, 1870.

26. A patriotic native-born Japanese, if he wants to make his contribution, will submit himself to a concentration camp.
Leland Ford (1893-1965), U.S. Congressman (R-CA). Quoted in Melvin I. Urofsky, *A March of Liberty*, 1988.

27. The citizen who criticizes his country is paying it an implied tribute.... It means that he has not given up hope for his country, that he still has hope for it ... I do not think it is "selling America short" when we ask a great deal of her; on the contrary, it is those who ask nothing, those who see no fault, who are really selling America short!
J. William Fulbright, U.S. Senator (D-AR). Senate speech, 1966.

28. Unlike many other peoples less happy, we give our devotion to a government, to its Constitution, to its flag, and not to men.

Benjamin Harrison (1833-1901), 23rd President of the United States (R-IN). Speech, Monterey, CA, Apr. 30, 1891.

29. The distinctions between Virginians, Pennsylvanians, New Yorkers, and New Englanders are no more. I am not a Virginian; I am an American.... All distinctions are thrown down; all America is one mass.

Patrick Henry (1736-1799), Member, Virginia House of Burgesses and Continental Congress, and Governor of Virginia. Speech, First Continental Congress, Oct. 14, 1774.

30. The Union has become not merely a physical union of states, but rather a spiritual union in common ideals of our people. Within it is room for every variety of opinion, every possible experiment in social progress. Out of such variety comes growth, but only if we preserve and maintain our spiritual solidarity.

Herbert Hoover (1874-1964), 31st President of the United States (R-IA). Memorial Day address, Gettysburg National Cemetery, PA, 1929.

31. The man who first called us the Common People was nearly right.

Edgar Watson Howe (1853-1937), American newspaper editor. *Ventures in Common Sense*, 1919.

32. Our Christian civilization will have to christianize itself in a hurry. It will have to dedicate itself to the proposition that men are men before they are Englishmen, businessmen, workingmen, or Americans, and that all men are brothers.... This proposition, always popular on Sundays, requires the subordination of Americanism to Humanity.

Robert M. Hutchins (1899-1977), President, University of Chicago, and President, Center for the Study of Democratic Institutions. Quoted in Lawrence Wittner, *Rebels Against War*, 1969.

33. No encouragement must be given to social and political organizations or methods which perpetuate in this country foreign ideas and customs. An Irish-American, a German-American, or a French-American vote is an intolerable anomaly.

John Ireland (1838-1918), American Roman Catholic archbishop. Lincoln Day speech, Chicago, IL, Feb. 22, 1895.

34. A man's mere property status, without more, cannot be used by a state to test, qualify, or limit his rights as a citizen of the United States.

Robert H. Jackson (1892-1954), U.S. Attorney General (D) and U.S. Supreme Court Justice. *Edwards* v. *California*, 1941.

35. The power of citizenship as a shield against oppression was widely known from the example of Paul's Roman citizenship, which sent the centurion scurrying to his higher-ups with the message: "Take heed what thou doest; for this man is a Roman."

Robert H. Jackson. *Ibid.*

36. Political action is the highest responsibility of a citizen.

John F. Kennedy (1917-1963), 35th President of the United States (D-MA). Campaign speech, Oct. 20, 1960.

37. Ask not what your country can do for you – ask what you can do for your country.

John F. Kennedy. Inaugural address, Jan. 20, 1961.

38. There will be neither rest nor tranquility in America until the Negro is granted his citizenship rights.

Martin Luther King, Jr. (1929-1968), American clergyman and civil rights leader. Speech, Washington, DC, Aug. 28, 1963.

39. George Washington would be very proud to know that we celebrate his birthday each year with a mattress sale.

Robert Klein, American comedian. Symposium, "Humor and the Presidency," Grand Rapids, MI, Sept. 1986.

40. What most charms me *[in America]* is that all the citizens are brethren.

Marquis de Lafayette (1757-1834), French statesman and Major General, Continental Army. Letter to his wife, June 20, 1777.

41. The Jews are a grave misfortune to every European people. It follows for Germany that the Jews must either emigrate from Germany or become Germans within it.

Paul de Lagarde (1827-1891), German orientalist. *Schriften*, I, 1884.

42. I am the fellow citizen of every thinking man: Truth is my native land.

Alphonse de Lamartine (1792-1869), French historian and politician. *La Marseillaise de la Paix*, 1841.

43. I am as much a citizen of the world as I am of my country.

Mickey Leland (1944-1989), U.S. Congressman (D-TX). Quoted in *The New York Times*, Aug. 14, 1989.

44. Let us at all times remember that all American citizens are brothers of a common country, and

should dwell together in the bonds of fraternal feeling.

Abraham Lincoln (1809-1865), 16th President of the United States (R-IL). Speech, Springfield, IL, Nov. 20, 1860.

45. We must be now and forever for Americanism and Nationalism and against Internationalism.

Henry Cabot Lodge (1850-1924), U.S. Congressman and U.S. Senator (R-MA). Keynote speech, Republican National Convention, Chicago, IL, June 8, 1920.

46. Individuals do not derive from government their right to contract, but bring that right with them into society.... Every man retains the right to acquire property, to dispose of that property according to his own judgment, and to pledge himself for a future act.

John Marshall (1755-1835), Chief Justice, U.S. Supreme Court. *Ogden* v. *Saunders*, 1827.

47. If you don't like what's going on, you have to get involved.

Mary Moran, Mayor of Bridgeport, CT (R). CBS, *60 Minutes*, June 16, 1991.

48. Though I have become Emperor, I have not ceased to be a citizen.

Napoléon I (1769-1821), military leader and Emperor of France. Remark to officers, 1813.

49. The *[American]* colonists are by the law of nature free-born, as indeed all men are, white or black.

James Otis (1725-1783), American attorney and Member, Colonial Massachusetts legislature. *The Rights of the British Colonies Asserted and Proved*, 1764.

50. I am myself an American and I love to preach my doctrine before undiluted 100 percent Americans, because my platform is, in a word, undiluted Americanism and undying loyalty to the republic.

A. Mitchell Palmer (1872-1936), U.S. Congressman (D-PA) and U.S. Attorney General. Speech, Philadelphia, PA, 1919.

51. A citizen already has a calling which will make full demands on him, in view of the constant practice and wide study it involves, in the preservation and enjoyment of the public social order – a task which permits of no relegation to second place.

Plato (427-347 B.C.), Greek philosopher. *Laws*, VIII.

52. Your countrymen are right in admitting the tinker and cobbler to advise about politics.

Plato. *Protagoras*.

53. Socrates said he was not an Athenian or a Greek, but a citizen of the world.

Plutarch (c.46-c.120), Greek biographer. *On Banishment*.

54. As we have recaptured and rekindled our pioneering spirit, we have insisted that it shall always be a spirit of justice, a spirit of teamwork, a spirit of sacrifice, and above all, a spirit of neighborliness.

Franklin D. Roosevelt (1882-1945), 32nd President of the United States (D-NY). Oct. 4, 1933.

55. The first requisite of a good citizen in this republic of ours is that he shall be able and willing to pull his weight.

Theodore Roosevelt (1858-1919), 26th President of the United States (R-NY). Speech, New York City, Nov. 11, 1902.

56. There is no room in this country for hyphenated Americanism.

Theodore Roosevelt. 1915.

57. There can be no fifty-fifty Americanism in this country. There is room here for only 100 percent Americanism.

Theodore Roosevelt. Speech, Sarasota, NY, July 19, 1918.

58. Money buys everything, except morality and citizens.

Jean Jacques Rousseau (1712-1778), French philosopher. *Discourse on the Sciences and the Arts*, 1750.

59. Civilization is the making of civil persons.

John Ruskin (1819-1900), English art historian. *The Crown of Wild Olive*, 1866.

60. In this colony of free humanity, they *[the Founding Fathers]* established the Republic of Equal Rights, where the title of manhood is the title of citizenship.

Carl Schurz (1829-1906), U.S. Senator (R-MO). Speech, Faneuil Hall, Boston, MA, Apr. 1859.

61. Deprived as we *[Jews]* heretofore have been of the invaluable rights of free citizens, we now behold a Government which to bigotry gives no sanction, to persecution no assistance, but generously affording to all, liberty of conscience, and immunities of citizenship, deeming every one, of whatever Nation, tongue, or language, equal parts of the great Government Machine whose basis is Mutual Confidence and Public Virtue.

Moses Mendez Seixas (1744-1809), American banker, merchant, and philanthropist. Letter to George

Washington on behalf of the Hebrew Congregation of Newport, RI, Aug. 17, 1790.

62. We hold these truths to be self-evident: that all men and women are created equal.... We insist that *[women]* have immediate admission to all the rights and privileges which belong to them as citizens of the United States.
Elizabeth Cady Stanton (1815-1902), 1st President, National Woman Suffrage Association. *Declaration of Independence for Women*, Seneca Falls, NY, July 1848.

63. No citizen of the United States is an alien in any state of the Union.
George Sutherland (1862-1942), U.S. Supreme Court Justice. *Colgate* v. *Harvey*, 1935.

64. If you think you're a second-class citizen, you are.
Ted Turner, American TV network owner. 1977.

65. I hereby declare, on oath, that I (name) absolutely and entirely renounce and abjure all allegiance and fidelity to any foreign prince, potentate, state, or sovereignty of whom or which I have heretofore become a subject or citizen; that I will support and defend the Constitution and laws of the United States of America against all enemies, foreign and domestic; that I will bear true faith and allegiance to the same; and that I take this obligation freely without any mental reservation and purpose of evasion; so help me God.
Oath of American Citizenship.

66. I doubted that the coconut-headed, chocolate-colored, typical coon who blacks my shoes every morning was fit for citizenship.
James K. Vardaman (1861-1930), Governor of Mississippi (D) and U.S. Senator. Quoted in G. Franklin Frazier, *The Negro in the United States*, 1949.

67. Whoever serves his country well has no need of ancestors.
Voltaire (François-Marie Arouet) (1694-1778), French historian and dramatist. *Essays*.

68. Use of denationalization as a punishment is barred by the Eighth Amendment *["excessive bail ... cruel and unusual punishment"]*. There may be involved no physical mistreatment, no primitive torture. There is instead the total destruction of the individual's status in organized society. It is a form of punishment more primitive than torture, for it destroys for the individual the political existence that was centuries in the development.
Earl Warren (1891-1974), Chief Justice, U.S. Supreme Court, and Governor of California (R). *Trop* v. *Dulles*, 1957.

69. When we assumed the soldier we did not lay aside the citizen.
George Washington (1732-1799), 1st President of the United States (VA). Speech to the New York Provincial Congress, before taking command of the Continental Army. Albany, NY, June 26, 1775.

70. May the children of the Stock of Abraham, who dwell in this land, continue to merit and enjoy the good will of the other inhabitants, while every one shall sit in safety under his own vine and fig-tree, and there shall be none to make them afraid.
George Washington. Reply to the Jews of Newport, RI, 1790 (see Moses Mendez Seixas above; for "dwell in safety under his own vine," see *1 Kings* 4:25, *Micah* 4:4).

71. Citizens by birth or choice, of a common country, that country has a right to concentrate your affections. The name of AMERICAN, which belongs to you, in your national capacity, must always exalt the just pride of Patriotism, more than any appellation derived from local discriminations. With slight shades of difference, you have the same Religion, Manners, Habits, and political Principles. You have in a common cause fought and triumphed together. The independence and liberty you possess are the work of joint councils, and joint efforts; of common dangers, sufferings, and successes.
George Washington. Farewell address, Sept. 17, 1796.

72. Whatever makes good Christians, makes them good citizens.
Daniel Webster (1782-1852), U.S. Congressman (Federalist-NH and MA), U.S. Senator (Federalist and Whig-MA), and U.S. Secretary of State. Speech, Plymouth, MA, Dec. 22, 1820.

73. One Country, One Constitution, and One Destiny.
Daniel Webster. Whig Party speech, Niblo's Saloon, New York City, Mar. 15, 1837.

74. I was born an American; I live an American; I shall die an American.
Daniel Webster. Speech, July 17, 1850.

75. The Constitution does not provide for first and second class citizens.
Wendell L. Willkie (1892-1944), Republican candidate for President (IN). *An American Program*, 1940.

76. Under that constitution *[of the United States]* there are citizens, but no subjects.
James Wilson (1742-1798), U.S. Supreme Court Justice. *Chisholm* v. *Georgia*, 1793.

77. Would man but generously snap our chains, and be content with rational fellowship instead of slavish obedience, they would find us more observant daughters, more affectionate sisters, more faithful wives, more reasonable mothers – in a word, better citizens.

Mary Wollstonecraft (1759-1797), British writer and feminist. *A Vindication of the Rights of Women*, 1792.

Chapter 12

Civil Disorder, Protests, and Demonstrations

1. From hence, let fierce contending nations know
What dire effects from civil discord flow.
Joseph Addison (1672-1719), Secretary of State, Great Britain (Whig). *Cato,* IV, 1713.

2. In the United States today, we have more than our share of the nattering nabobs of negativism.
Spiro T. Agnew, Governor of Maryland and Vice President of the United States (R). Speech, San Diego, CA, Sept. 11, 1970.

3. Generally, an agitator is a rough man of the *[Irish nationalist Daniel]* O'Connell type, who says anything himself and lets others say anything. "You peg into me and I will peg into you, and let us see which one will win," is his motto.
Walter Bagehot (1826-1877), British economist and writer. *Biographical Studies,* 1889.

4. Government is the common enemy. All weapons are justifiable in the noble struggle against this terrible curse.
Alexander Berkman (1870-1936), American anarchist. *Prison Memoirs of an Anarchist,* 1912.

5. Our apologies, good friends, for the fracture of good order, the burning of paper instead of children, the angering of the orderlies in the front parlor of the charnel house.
Daniel Berrigan, American Roman Catholic priest and anti-war activist. Comment after entering a draft board office in Catonsville, MD, and burning the records in front of reporters and onlookers. *Meditation,* 1967.

6. You don't change the course of the country in twenty-four hours.
Barbara Boxer, U.S. Congresswoman (D-CA). Interview, CNN, *Crossfire,* Mar. 14, 1990.

7. Violence is as American as cherry pie.
H. Rap Brown, Director, Student Nonviolent Coordinating Committee. *Die Nigger Die!,* 1969.

8. You better go get yourself some guns. The only thing honkies respect is guns.
H. Rap Brown. Speech, Cambridge, MD, 1967.

9. Advocacy is in the courtroom – not out in the streets.
Warren E. Burger, Chief Justice, U.S. Supreme Court. In defense of banning demonstrations at the Supreme Court building. Interview, PBS, *MacNeil-Lehrer News Hour,* Sept. 13, 1990.

10. He that wrestles with us strengthens our nerves, and sharpens our skill. Our antagonist is our helper.
Edmund Burke (1729-1797), British statesman. *Reflections on the Revolution in France,* 1790.

11. The tyranny of a multitude *[mob]* is a multiplied tyranny.
Edmund Burke. Letter to Thomas Mercer, Feb. 26, 1790.

12. This nation openly endorses, tolerates, and legalizes the very abuses against which she originally waged a bloody revolution.
Nannie Helen Burroughs (1883-1961), American journalist. Writing about the Harlem riots of the day. "Declaration of 1776 Is Cause of Harlem Riot," *The Afro-American,* Apr. 13, 1935.

13. The anarchist is not at liberty to break the law because he reasons that all government is wrong.
Benjamin N. Cardozo (1870-1938), U.S. Supreme Court Justice. *People* v. *Schmidt,* 1926.

14. As the first man from the Deep South in 130 years to be President of this nation, I say that these people in white sheets do not understand our region and what it's been through. They do not understand what our country stands for.
Jimmy Carter, 39th President of the United States (D-GA). Comment after his speech was interrupted several

times by Ku Klux Klansmen. Labor Day address, Tuscumbia, AL, Sept. 1, 1980.

15. Recent events in Alabama, involving murder, savage brutality, and violence by local police *[against civil rights protesters]* ... have so aroused the nation as to make action by this Congress necessary and speedy.

Emmanuel Cellar (1888-1981), U.S. Congressman (D-NY). Debate on the Voting Rights Act, House of Representatives, Mar. 1965.

16. We will send a petition to Washington with boots on.

Jacob S. Coxey (1854-1951), organizer, march on Washington, DC, to protest unemployment. Speech, Massilon, OH, 1894.

17. Shoot to maim or cripple anyone looting any stores in our city.

Richard J. Daley (1902-1976), Mayor of Chicago, IL (D). Televised order to police following the assassination of Martin Luther King, Jr., Apr. 16, 1968.

18. This administration and the people of Chicago have never condoned brutality at any time, but they will never permit a lawless violent group of terrorists to menace the lives of millions of people, destroy the purpose of this national political convention, and take over the streets of Chicago.

Richard J. Daley. Statement to Democratic National Convention delegates defending his administration and the Chicago police against the charge that they used excessive force and caused a police riot, Sept. 8, 1968.

19. We can afford to spill a little blood.

Deng Xiaoping, Premier of China. Speech to Communist party leaders after the Tiananmen Square massacre, 1989.

20. This disturbance was something beyond anyone's control.

Deng Xiaoping. Statement after Chinese troops massacred hundreds of unarmed protesters in Tiananmen Square, Beijing. June 9, 1989.

21. In the 1960's and 1970's there were many student movements and turmoils in the United States. Did they have any other recourse but to mobilize the police and troops, arrest people, and shed blood?

Deng Xiaoping. Justification of China's massacre of protesting students in Tianennmen Square. Quoted in *Newsweek*, July 3, 1989.

22. I do not know of any salvation for society except through eccentrics, misfits, dissenters, people who protest.

William O. Douglas (1898-1980), U.S. Supreme Court Justice. Quoted in Robert M. Hutchins, *The Power of Reason*, 1964.

23. Political or religious dissenters are the plague of every totalitarian regime.

William O. Douglas. *We the Judges*, 1956.

24. Mob rule cannot be allowed to override the decisions of our courts.

Dwight D. Eisenhower (1890-1969), 34th President of the United States (R-KS). Comment on reactions to Supreme Court desegregation decisions. Address, Sept. 23, 1957.

25. This filthy enactment *[the Fugitive Slave Law]* was made in the nineteenth century, by people who could read and write. I will not obey it, by God.

Ralph Waldo Emerson (1803-1882), American writer. *Journals*, July 1851.

26. Do not follow a multitude to do evil.

Old Testament, *Exodus* 23:2.

27. How long are we going to abdicate law and order – the backbone of civilization – in favor of a soft social theory that the man who heaves a brick through your window or tosses a fire bomb into your car is simply the misunderstood and underprivileged product of a broken home?

Gerald R. Ford, 38th President of the United States (R-MI). Reaction to urban riots and disorders. Speech, 1966.

28. The Boston Mob, raised first by the Instigation of Many of the Principle Inhabitants, Allured by Plunder, rose shortly after of their own accord.

Thomas Gage (1721-1787), Royal Governor of Massachusetts, and Military Commander in North America. Comment on the Stamp Act riots in Boston, 1767.

29. Noncooperation with evil is as much a duty as is cooperation with good.

Mohandas K. Gandhi (1869-1948), Indian political and spiritual leader. Speech, Mar. 23, 1922.

30. Disobedience to be "civil" must be sincere, respectful, restrained, never defiant, and it must have no ill-will or hatred behind it.

Mohandas K. Gandhi. Quoted in Hobhouse, *True Patriotism: Some Sayings of Mahatma Gandhi*, 1939.

31. Nonviolence is not a garment to be put on and off at will. Its seat is in the heart, and it must be an inseparable part of our very being.

Mohandas K. Gandhi. *Non-Violence in Peace and War*, 1948.

32. It is my lot to be branded as an agitator, a fanatic, an incendiary, and a madman.

William Lloyd Garrison (1805-1879), American editor and abolitionist. Quoted in Garrison and Garrison *William Lloyd Garrison: The Story of His Life Told by His Children*, I, 1885.

33. It is organized violence on top which creates individual violence at the bottom.
Emma Goldman (1869-1940), American anarchist. Statement at her trial, June 15, 1917.

34. Pluralism of opinions is not dissent but democratic centralism understood in a new way.
Mikhail Gorbachev, President of the U.S.S.R. Speech, Communist Party Central Committee, Moscow, Feb. 7, 1990.

35. If every Negro said "I'm nonviolent," white folks would love it. But if we had to fight Russia and we said we're nonviolent and don't believe in killing nobody, we'd be hauled off to a concentration camp.
Dick Gregory, American comedian and writer. Interview, *Playboy*, Aug. 1964.

36. People never improve by contradiction, but by *agreeing to differ*.
William Hazlitt (1778-1830), English writer and critic. *Characteristics*, 1823.

37. He that is taken and put into prisoner chains is not conquered, though overcome; for he is still an enemy.
Thomas Hobbes (1588-1679), English political philosopher. *Leviathan*, 1651.

The diabolical influence of Communism on youth was manifested in the ... Communist-inspired riots in San Francisco, where students were duped into disgraceful demonstrations against a congressional committee.
J. Edgar Hoover (1895-1972), Director, Federal Bureau of Investigation. Speech, American Legion Convention, Miami, FL, Oct. 18, 1960.

39. What happens to a dream deferred? Does it dry up like a raisin in the sun? Or fester like a sore? ... Maybe it just sags like a heavy load. Or does it explode?
Langston Hughes (1902-1967), American poet. *Lenox Avenue Mural*.

40. Better one hundred years of tyranny than one day of anarchy.
Islamic proverb.

41. Gentlemen, I shall be glad to see this mob on Capitol Hill. I will fix their heads on the iron palisades around the square to assist your deliberations. The leaders I will hang as high as Haman to deter forever all attempts to control the legislature of the Congress by intimidation and design.
Andrew Jackson (1767-1845), 7th President of the United States (D-TN). Statement to congressional delegation during the rancorous debate on the Bank of the United States, 1832.

42. Violence is a great breeder of violence.
Roy Jenkens, Home Secretary and Chancellor of the Exchequer, Great Britain (Conservative). PBS, *Worlds Without Walls*, University of Pennsylvania, Philadelphia, PA, May 17, 1990.

43. A rioter with a Molotov cocktail in his hands is not fighting for civil rights any more than a Klansman with a sheet on his back and mask on his face. They are lawbreakers, destroyers of constitutional rights and liberties and ultimately destroyers of a free America.
Lyndon B. Johnson (1908-1973), 36th President of the United States (D-TX). In reference to riots in the Watts section of Los Angeles, CA. Speech, Aug. 20, 1965.

44. Mr. Mayor. I've decided the best place for the '68 *[Democratic]* convention is Chicago! You are the one who can handle it!
Lyndon B. Johnson. Remark to Chicago Mayor Richard J. Daley, Oct. 7, 1967.

45. We cannot, we just must not, tolerate the sway of violent men among us. We must not permit men who are filled with hatred, and careless of innocent lives, to dominate our streets and fill our homes with fear.
Lyndon B. Johnson. National TV address after the assasination of Sen. Robert F. Kennedy, June 4, 1968.

46. A riot is somebody talking. A riot is a man crying out, "Listen to me, mister. There's something I've been trying to tell you, and you're not listening."
Nicholas Johnson, Federal Communications Commissioner. Quoted in George Leinwand, *Riots*, 1970.

47. What you see *[in Northern Ireland]* is a social conflict between the descendants of Protestant settlers of the seventeenth century and the Catholic dispossessed. They may seem to be wearing the badges of religion, but they are actually the badges of caste. If we were really arguing about religion, it wouldn't be much hope; but if we are arguing about social and economic conditions, we can do something about it.
Eamon Kennedy, Irish Ambassador to the United States. Speech, Overseas Press Club, New York City, Mar. 19, 1975.

48. Don't agonize. Organize.
Florynce R. Kennedy, American writer, feminist, and TV talk-show host. *Ms.*, Mar. 1973.

49. Let us not be afraid of debate or discussion – let us encourage it. For if we should ever abandon these basic American traditions in the name of fighting Communism, what would it profit us to win the whole world when we have lost our soul?
John F. Kennedy (1917-1963), 35th President of the United States (D-MA). Address, National Civil Liberties Conference, Washington, DC, Apr. 16, 1959.

50. I want every American to stand up for his rights, even if he has to sit down for them.
John F. Kennedy. In reference to sit-ins at southern lunch counters. Campaign speech, Aug. 3, 1960.

51. The fires of discord are busy in every city. Redress is sought in the street, in demonstrations, parades, and protests which create tensions and threaten violence. We face, therefore, a moral crisis as a country and as a people.
John F. Kennedy. National television address, June 11, 1963.

52. A riot is at bottom the language of the unheard.
Martin Luther King, Jr. (1929-1968), American clergyman and civil rights leader. *Where Do We Go From Here – Chaos Or Community?*, 1967.

53. Nonviolent direct action seeks to create such a crisis and foster such a tension that a community which has constantly refused to negotiate is forced to confront the issue.
Martin Luther King, Jr. *Letter from A Birmingham Jail*, Apr. 16, 1963.

54. Urban riots must now be recognized as a durable social phenomenon. They are a special form of violence ... mainly intended to shock the white community.
Martin Luther King, Jr. *American Psychologist*, 1968.

55. China remains too important for America's national security to risk the relationship on the emotions of the moment.... No government in the world would have tolerated having the main square of its capital occupied by tens of thousands of demonstrators.
Henry M. Kissinger, U.S. Secretary of State and National Security Advisor (R). Comment after the Tiananmen Square massacre, when Congress voted economic sanctions against China. Quoted in *The New York Times*, Aug. 20, 1989.

56. If people demonstrate in a manner to interfere with others, they should be rounded up and put in a concentration camp.
Richard G. Kleindienst, U.S. Attorney General (R). Statement to reporters, 1972.

57. We *[the British]* are a government of opposition, no matter who is in power.
Andrew Knight, editor, *The Economist*. Sept. 1975.

58. I took the bastard to court and he's going to do some time in jail. That's what he deserves. I won't take that from anybody.
Edward I. Koch, U.S. Congressman and Mayor of New York City (D). Comment after being pelted with eggs by a demonstrator, 1979.

59. We must accept the possibility of bloodshed if we are to bring about order.
Vladimir Kryuchkov, Director, Soviet KGB. Speech, Congress of People's Deputies, Moscow, Dec. 22, 1990.

60. Former good legislators have erred, and those of the best polity may err again, and enact laws which ought to be disobeyed and resisted.
Samuel Langdon (1723-1797), President, Harvard College, Cambridge, MA. Election sermon, Massachusetts Bay Colony Congress, Watertown, MA, May 31, 1775.

61. You should not neglect agitation; each of you should make it his task.
Ferdinand Lassalle (1825-1864), German labor leader. Speech, General Union of German Workers, Barmen, Sept. 26, 1863.

62. As soon as a certain number of living beings are gathered together ... they place themselves instinctively under the authority of a chief. In the case of human crowds the chief is often nothing more than a ringleader or agitator, but as such he plays a considerable part.
Gustave Le Bon (1841-1931), French physician and sociologist. *The Crowd*, 1895.

63. If the laws of the state are openly at variance with the laws of God – if they inflict injury upon the Church – ... then indeed it becomes a duty to resist them, a sin to render obedience.
Pope Leo XIII (1810-1903), Encyclical, *Catholicae Ecclesiae*, Nov. 20, 1890.

64. This group of people got what they deserved.
Li Zhiyun, Commander, Chinese Army troops clearing Tiananmen Square. Statement, Beijing, June 26, 1989.

65. It was a bad looking mob. It was animated by the essence of revolution.
Douglas MacArthur (1880-1964), General, U.S. Army. Remark on his dispersal of the Bonus Army march on Washington, DC, July 1932.

66. They *[the Jews]* stand alone among nations in their stiff-necked resistance to kings.
Apocrypha, *3 Maccabees* 3:19.

67. The protest is part of the American way of life.
Thurgood Marshall, U.S. Supreme Court Justice. Interview, ABC, *Nightline*, June 27, 1991.

68. The only way to get respect is to be willing to use violence.
Michael McGee, Milwaukee City Alderman. Quoted in *The New York Times*, Apr. 8, 1990.

69. Black people don't own Harlem, so why should Black people care whether it burns down or not?
Floyd B. McKissick (1922-1991), Director, Congress of Racial Equality. Quoted on PBS, *Making Sense of the Sixties*, Jan. 22, 1991.

70. The purpose of Earth Day was a demonstration so big that the political establishment would have to pay attention.
Gaylord Nelson, Governor of Wisconsin and U.S. Senator (D). Speech, National Press Club, C-SPAN, Apr. 16, 1990.

71. You ask me, brother, why am I in here. Brother, why are you not in here?
Martin Niemöller (1892-1984), German Protestant pastor. Response when asked by a colleague what he was doing in prison, after being jailed by the Nazis for resistance, July 1937.

72. My concern today is not with the length of a person's hair but with his conduct.
Richard M. Nixon, 37th President of the United States (R-CA). Commencement address, General Beadle State College, Madison, SD, June 3, 1969.

73. When students on university campuses burn buildings, when they engage in violence, when they break up furniture, when they terrorize their fellow students and terrorize the faculty, then I think "bums" is perhaps too kind a word to apply to that kind of person.
Richard M. Nixon. Press conference, May 1970.

74. Hungry people with no jobs will not continue to go hungry without reacting. They will soon take action and follow anyone who can give them ... or even promises to do so.
Kwame Nkrumah (1909-1972), President of Ghana. Letter to Prime Minister Patrice Lumumba of the Congo, Sept. 12, 1960.

75. The reason people riot is for fun and profit.
Robert Novak, American political columnist. CNN, *Capital Gang*, May 11, 1991.

76. I can drive a coach and six through any act of Parliament.
Daniel O'Connell (1775-1847), Irish nationalist leader and Lord Mayor of Dublin. Attributed.

77. We have been blamed for being agitators. I thank God for being one. Whatever little we have gained, we have gained by agitation, while we have uniformly lost by moderation.
Daniel O'Connell. Speech, Dublin, Feb. 24, 1824.

78. Civilization is nothing else than the attempt to reduce force to being the last resort. "Direct action" *[a Fascist term]* consists in inverting the order and proclaiming violence as the first resort, or strictly as the sole resort. It is the norm which proposes the annulment of all norms.... It is the Magna Charta of barbarianism.
José Ortega y Gasset (1883-1955), Spanish philosopher and statesman. *The Revolt of the Masses*, 1930.

79. Fully 90 percent of the Communist and anarchist agitation is traceable to aliens.
A. Mitchell Palmer (1872-1936), U.S. Attorney General and U.S. Congressman (D-PA). *Attorney General's Report*, 1918.

80. We are driven to do this. We are determined to go on with the agitation. We are in honor bound to do so until we win. Just as it was the duty of our forefathers to do it for you.
Emmeline Pankhurst (1858-1928), British suffragist. Speech, 1908.

81. The condition of our sex is so deplorable that it is our duty even to break the law in order to call attention to the reasons why we do so.
Emmeline Pankhurst. Speech at her trial, Oct. 21, 1908.

82. My only concern was to get home after a hard day's work.
Rosa Parks, Montgomery, AL, citizen who on Dec. 1, 1955 refused to give up her bus seat to a white man, inspiring a bus boycott that led to the civil rights movement of the 1960's. Quoted in *Time*, Dec. 15, 1975.

83. For the people is the Politick Wife of the Prince, that may be better managed by Wisdom than ruled by force.
William Penn (1644-1718), founder of Pennsylvania. *Some Fruits of Solitude, in Reflections and Maxims*, 1693.

84. The order of the day for every Peronist is to answer a violent action with another action even more violent. When one of our people falls, five of them will fall.
Juan Domingo Perón (1895-1974), President of Argentina. Quoted in *The Nation*, Sept. 10, 1955.

85. Immoral laws are doubtless void, and should not be obeyed.
Wendell Phillips (1811-1884), American orator and reformer. Quoted in Richard Hofstadter, *The American Political Tradition*, 1948.

86. Republics exist only on the tenure of being constantly agitated.
Wendell Phillips. *Ibid.*

87. We cannot live like this anymore. Go out on the streets tomorrow to help change the situation.
Gavrill K. Popov, Mayor of Moscow, Russia. Television address, *Vremya*, Sept. 1990.

88. It was not a riot *[in Harlem]*. It was an open, unorganized protest against empty stomachs, overcrowded tenements, filthy sanitation, rotten foodstuffs, and chiseling landlords. It was not caused by Communists.
Adam Clayton Powell (1908-1972), U.S. Congressman (D-NY). Letter to the editor, *The New York Post*, 1935.

89. We are gathered here in the largest demonstration in the history of this nation. Let the nation and the world know the meaning of our numbers. We are not a pressure group, we are not an organization or a group of organizations, we are not a mob. We are the advance guard of a massive moral revolution for jobs and freedom.
A. Philip Randolph (1889-1979), President, Brotherhood of Sleeping Car Porters. Speech, march on Washington, DC, Aug. 28, 1963.

90. Weak minds are commonly overpowered by clamour.
Cardinal de Retz (1614-1679), French cleric and politician. *Political Maxims*.

91. Those who head factions have no way of maintaining their authority but by preventing or quieting discontent.
Cardinal de Retz. *Ibid.*

92. We can take very little comfort and it does us no good to be the first city in America to achieve integrated looting.
Walter Reuther (1907-1970), President, United Auto Workers of America. Remark on the Detroit riots, 1967.

93. We shall guard as zealously the rights of the striker as those of the employer. But when riot is menaced it is different. The mob takes its own chance. Order will be kept at whatever cost. If it comes to shooting we shall shoot to hit. No blank cartridges or firing over the head.
Theodore Roosevelt (1858-1919), 26th President of the United States (R-NY). Quoted in *The Evening Post*, 1895.

94. Dissenters have no greater moral or political rights than nondissenters. Complaint contains no carte blanche security; if it did, hypochondriacs should be kings.
Leo Rosten, American writer and Deputy Director, War Information Office. *A Trumpet for Reason*, 1970.

95. Government and cooperation are in all things the law of life; anarchy and competition the laws of death.
John Ruskin (1819-1900), British art historian. "Unto This Last," *Cornhill Magazine*, 1860.

96. The people can seldom agree to move together against a government, but they can to sit still and let it be undone.
George Savile, 1st Marquess of Halifax (1633-1695), Lord Privy Seal of England. *Political Thoughts and Reflections*, 1750.

97. Civil war is a species of misery which introduces men to strange bedfellows.
Walter Scott (1771-1832), Scottish writer. Appendix, *Rob Roy*, 1817.

98. Assassination is the extreme form of censorship.
George Bernard Shaw (1856-1950), Nobel Laureate in Literature (Great Britian). *The Rejected Statement*, 1916.

99. The Communist loves nothing better than to be arrested. But he is not like the martyr for the faith. St. Joan of Arc did not like being tied to a stake; a Communist does.
Fulton J. Sheen (1895-1979), American Roman Catholic archbishop and television personality. 1955.

100. It is a confession of the weakness of our own faith in the righteousness of our cause when we attempt to suppress by law those who do not agree with us.
Alfred E. Smith (1873-1944), Governor of New York (D). 1920.

101. We here and now join hands in what shall result in a nationwide protest against this Communist dictatorship *[the Roosevelt Administration]* in Washington.
Gerald L. K. Smith (1898-1976), American clergyman and cofounder, Union Party. Quoted in *Newsweek*, June 13, 1936.

102. Extremism ... is increasingly forcing upon the American people the narrow choice between anarchy and repression. And make no mistake about it, if that narrow choice has to be made, the American people, even if with reluctance and misgiving, will choose repression.
Margaret Chase Smith, U.S. Congresswoman and U.S. Senator (R-ME). Quoted in *The New York Times*, June 2, 1970.

103. If you kill me you will not easily find a successor to me who will be, if I may use such a ridiculous figure of speech, a sort of gadfly, attached to the state by God, for the state is a great and noble horse who is rather sluggish, owing to his very size, and requires to be stirred into life.
Socrates (c.470-399 B.C.), Greek philosopher. Speech to the Athenians. Quoted by Plato, *Apology*.

104. I have come to commit civil disobedience.
Benjamin Spock, American pediatrician. Statement at a rally protesting the Vietnam War, New York City, Dec. 5, 1967.

105. We can no longer depend on the electoral system. The street is the only place for our movement.
Gloria Steinem, American editor and feminist. Statement after U.S. Congresswoman Bella Abzug (D-NY) lost her reelection bid, Nov. 1978.

106. We must mark him now, if we have not done so before, as the most dangerous Negro of the future in this nation from the standpoint of Communism, the Negro, and national security.
William C. Sullivan, Director, FBI Domestic Intelligence Division, and Assistant Director, Federal Bureau of Investigation. Memorandum written after Martin Luther King, Jr.'s "I have a dream" speech, Aug. 30, 1963.

107. The more you mow us down, the more we grow; the blood of the martyrs is the seed of the Church. (*Plures efficimus quoties metimur a vobis; semen est sanguis Christianorum.*)
Tertullian (c.150-c.225), early Christian writer. *Apologeticus.*

108. How does it become a man to behave toward the American government today? I answer, that he cannot without disgrace be associated with it.
Henry David Thoreau (1817-1862), American naturalist and philosopher. *On the Duty of Civil Disobedience,* 1849.

109. I was confronted with a group of trigger-happy, nervous soldiers in the National Guard. I had no intention of having any of those soldiers shoot innocent people or small children.
John L. Throckmorton, General, U.S. Army. Comment on why he ordered National Guardsmen to unload their weapons during urban riots in Detroit, MI. Testimony, House Armed Services Committee, 1967.

110. We were overtaken by events because our ears were not tuned sharply enough.
Josip Broz Tito (1892-1980), President of Yugoslavia. Television address after student riots, June 9, 1968.

111. I want to agitate, even as I am agitated.
Laura M. Towne (1825-1901), American educator and reformer. *Diary,* 1862.

112. I think there have been two battlefields in the war. One in Vietnam, and the other on our university campuses. And they are not good places for battlefields.
David Truman, Vice President, Columbia University, New York City. Quoted in *The Cox Commission Report,* 1968.

113. The demagogues, crackpots, and professional patriots had a field day pumping fear into the American people *[during the late 1940's and early 1950's]*.... Many good people actually believed that we were in imminent danger of being taken over by the Communists and that our government in Washington was Communist-riddled. So widespread was this campaign that it seemed no one would be safe from attack. This was the tragedy and shame of our time.
Harry S Truman (1884-1972), 33rd President of the United States (D-MO). *Memoirs,* II, 1956.

114. As for their policy, that will come to an end. It was necessary for this socialism movement to take place. Well, now it is over, it will be defeated; and if the government of the Republic, as is its duty and its right, employs terrible means of repression, republican France will have fifty years of internal peace.
Jules Verne (1828-1905), French writer and politician. In reference to Socialist partisans of the *Commune.* Letter to his publisher, Pierre Jules Hetzel, 1871.

115. It is better, infinitely better, that blood should flow to the horses' bridles than our national liberties should be destroyed.
Davis H. Waite (1825-1901), Governor of Colorado. Statement condoning riots over the Sherman Silver Purchase Act, 1893.

116. When both national parties kowtow to a bunch of anarchists, then neither of those parties is fit to govern.
George C. Wallace, Governor of Alabama (D). In reference to campus protests and disorders. Campaign speech, 1968.

117. You must build your House of Parliament upon the river: the populace cannot exact their demands by sitting down round you.
Arthur Wellesley, 1st Duke of Wellington (1769-1852), Chief General at Waterloo, Ambassador to France, and Prime Minister of Great Britain (Tory). Quoted in William Fraser, *Words on Wellington.*

118. The first excuse given to the civilized world for the murder of unoffending Negroes was the necessity of the white man to repress and stamp out "race riots."... It was always a remarkable feature of these insurrections and riots that only Negroes were killed during the rioting, and that all the white men escaped unharmed.
Ida B. Wells (1862-1931), American educator and cofounder, National Association for the Advancement of Colored People. *A Red Record,* 1895.

119. Wherever there is a man who exercises authority, there is a man who resists authority!
Oscar Wilde (1854-1900), Irish writer. *The Soul of Man Under Socialism,* 1891.

120. *[Protesting]* is all we know how to do any more, except fight with sticks and stones and ball bats.

William Wimpsinger, President, International Brotherhood of Machinists. Quoted in *Rolling Stone,* Oct. 17, 1991.

121. We understand the state to be that body which claims the right to a monopoly on the use and control of force. Because it has misused that right so extensively, individuals, groups, and populations in the United States are challenging that right. In the resulting clash there has been an explosion of violence.

Statement, World Council of Churches, July 1966. Quoted in *Current,* May 1968.

Chapter 13

Congress

1. Congress is a middle-aged, middle-class, white male power structure. No wonder it has been so totally unresponsive to the needs of this country.
   Bella Abzug, U.S. Congresswoman (D-NY). Speech, Washington DC, July 10, 1971.

2. No person could be degraded by serving the people as a Representative to Congress. Nor in my opinion would an ex-President of the United States be degraded by serving as a selectman of his town, if elected thereto by the people.
   John Quincy Adams (1767-1848), 6th President of the United States (Ind.-MA). Statement on why he sought a congressional seat after serving as President. Plymouth, MA, Sept. 1830.

3. I passed an entirely sleepless night. The iniquity of the bill and the disreputable means by which so partial and unjust a distribution had been effected, agitated me so that I could not close my eyes.
   John Quincy Adams. On a redistricting bill that passed in the House of Representatives. *Diary*, 1832.

4. Either impeach him *[Richard Nixon]* or get off his back.
   George D. Aiken (1892-1984), Governor of Vermont and U.S. Senator (R). Remark in the Senate, Nov. 7, 1973.

5. The wisdom of silence is a great asset.
   De Alva Stanwood Alexander (1846-1925), U.S. Congressman (R-NY). On the power of the Speaker of the House. *History and Procedure of the House of Representatives*, 1916.

6. If you want to do something for your country or your district and you're not a chairman, you run into a brick wall.
   William V. Alexander, Jr., U.S. Congressman (D-AR). Quoted by Daniel Rapoport, *Inside the House*, 1975.

7. The House *[of Representatives]* is composed of sober, solid, old-charter folks.... There are few shining geniuses; there are many who have experience, the virtues of the heart, and the habits of business. It will be quite a republican assembly.
   Fisher Ames (1758-1808), U.S. Congressman (Federalist-MA). *Observations on the First Congress*, Mar. 1789.

8. The public will forget the government before it is born.
   Fisher Ames. Remark when only 21 members of the 1st Congress showed up, not even a quorum. Mar. 4, 1789.

9. As we manage our time *[in the House of Representatives]* I think we shall never get out of employment.
   Fisher Ames. *Works*, 1854.

10. I don't care what my district thinks of Congress as long as 51 percent of it likes me.
    Leslie Aspin, U.S. Congressman (D-WI). Quoted in *The Washington Post*, June 22, 1975.

11. You've got to have a theme if you're going to get Congress to do something difficult.
    Leslie Aspin. Interview, ABC, *This Week*, Apr. 29, 1990.

12. Something is systemically wrong with Congress today, and it's money, the pursuit of money, the endless pursuit of money, the virtual hourly pursuit of money, either to finance the perpetual campaign or to maintain a certain standard of living.
    Les AuCoin, U.S. Congressman (D-OR). Quoted in *The New York Times*, June 4, 1989.

13. Who ever heard of a charismatic Congress?
    Lloyd M. Bentsen, Jr., U.S. Congressman and U.S. Senator (D-TX). Quoted by Daniel Rapoport, *Inside the House*, 1975.

14. I'm always impressed by your disdain for Congress. That's one of the reasons you have such good relations with us.
    Joseph R. Biden, Jr., U.S. Senator (D-DE). To Attorney General Edwin Meese III. Quoted in *Newsweek*, May 18, 1987.

15. To the extent that congressional powers have ebbed as a result of failure to develop timely and coherent responses to public problems, Congress has only itself to blame for its own predicament.
Richard W. Bolling (1916-1991), U.S. Congressman (D-MO). Report, House Select Committee on Committees, Mar. 21, 1974.

16. Special interests and Congress are too closely connected, and the ties that bind are the millions spent on campaigns.
David L. Boren, Governor of Oklahoma and U.S. Senator (D). *The New York Times*, May 29, 1989.

17. There are too many cowardly lions walking the halls of Congress.
James Brady, White House press secretary (R). Quoted on CBS News, Nov. 25, 1989.

18. Open each session *[of Congress]* with a prayer and close it with a probe.
Clarence J. Brown (1893-1965), U.S. Congressman (R-OH). Quoted in *Time*, Aug. 4, 1947.

19. Without the authority of Congress, the President cannot fire a hostile gun in any case except to repel the attacks of the enemy.
James Buchanan (1791-1868), 15th President of the United States (D-PA). Quoted in J. D. Richardson, *Messages and Papers of the Presidents*, 1897.

20. You don't know what the *[ethical]* rules are until the gallows pull up in front of your door and they drag you out to hang you.
John Buckley, Director of Communications, National Republican Congressional Committee, and press secretary to Cong. Jack Kemp during the 1988 presidential campaign. Quoted in *The Washington Post*, June 4, 1989.

21. You can always depend on Congress to overreact.
Dale Bumpers, U.S. Senator and Governor of Arkansas (D). Quoted in Tolchin and Tolchin, *Dismantling America: The Rush to Deregulate*, 1983.

22. I've seen senators, whose character and intelligence I know reasonably well, vote a certain way just because staff tells them to.
Dale Bumpers. Quoted in James Miller, *Running in Place*, 1986.

23. Parliament is not a congress of ambassadors from different and hostile interests.... Parliament is a deliberative assembly of one nation, with one interest, that of the whole – where not local purpose, not local prejudices, ought to guide, but the general good, resulting from the general reason of the whole.
Edmund Burke (1729-1797), British statesman. Speech to the Electors of Bristol, Nov. 3, 1774.

24. We enjoy bashing Congress because they are us.
James MacGregor Burns, American political historian. Quoted on PBS, *The Congress*, 1990.

25. I have found a reality in life, and that reality is the United States Congress.
George Bush, 41st President of the United States (R-TX). PBS, Interview with Robert Frost, Sept. 5, 1989.

26. I haven't the heart to take a minute away from the men. The poor dears love it so.
Hattie W. Caraway (1878-1950), U.S. Senator (D-AR). Quoted in David Brinkley, *Washington Goes to War*, 1988.

27. Farmers, traders, and mechanics ... all ought to have a competent number of their best informed members in the legislature.
Samuel Chase (1741-1811), American revolutionary leader and U.S. Supreme Court Justice. Quoted in Crowl, *William and Mary Quarterly*, 1947.

28. *[Warren]* Harding didn't like being a Senator; he liked being in the Senate.
George B. Christian, Jr. (1873-1951), personal secretary to President Harding. Quoted in Ralph G. Martin, *Ballots & Bandwagons*, 1964.

29. People don't give a damn what the average Senator or Congressman says. The reason they don't care is that they know that what you hear in Congress is 99 per cent tripe, ignorance, and demagoguery and not to be relied on.
Raymond Clapper (1892-1944), American political columnist. Quoted in David Brinkley, *Washington Goes to War*, 1988.

30. The Senate establishment is almost the antithesis of democracy. It is what might be called a self-perpetuating oligarchy with only mild overtones of a plutocracy.
Joseph S. Clark (1902-1990), Mayor of Philadelphia, PA, and U.S. Senator (D). Senate speech, 1963.

31. It's better to be in session than go home and face the voters.
Daniel R. Coates, U.S. Congressman (R-IN). Quoted in *The New York Times*, Oct. 27, 1990.

32. Congress ... is far more than the simple, limited advisory council that most Presidents would like to maintain.
William S. Cohen, U.S. Senator (R-ME). Senate speech, Mar. 3, 1988.

33. It's lonely up here.
Cardiss Collins, U.S. Congresswoman (D-IL). Fundraising letter, 1990.

34. *[Congress functions]* the way the Founding Fathers intended – not very well. They understood that if you move too quickly, our democracy will be less responsible to the majority.
Barber D. Conable, U.S. Congressman (R-NY) and Chairman, World Bank. Quoted in *Time,* Oct. 22, 1984.

35. The Congress has sometimes been a sore trial to Presidents.
Calvin Coolidge (1872-1933), 30th President of the United States (R-MA). *Autobiography,* 1929.

36. We generally lounge or squabble the greater part of the session, and crowd into a few days of the last of the term three or four times the business done during as many preceding months.
David Crockett (1786-1836), U.S. Congressman (Anti-Jacksonian-TN). *The Life of Davy Crockett,* 1889.

37. Term limitation is the latest manifestation of public irresponsibility.
John C. Culver, U.S. Congressman and U.S. Senator (D-IA). Quoted in *The Washington Post,* Jan. 6, 1991.

38. Honorariums are really dishonorariums. So long as they continue, public trust in Congress will sink even below its minimal level today.... Public officials should have only one paymaster: the government. When the government pays too little, the temptation to find other paymasters becomes far harder to resist.
Lloyd N. Cutler, counsel to the President and member, President's Commission on Federal Ethics Law Reform (D). *The New York Times,* Apr. 20, 1989.

39. It is in the committee that the dirty work is done ... away from the many-eyed scrutiny of the rest of Congress and the public.... Special interest legislation usually originates in the committee room.
James Deakin, American political journalist. *The Lobbyists,* 1966.

40. The government of the United States is, and always has been, a lawyer's government.
Chauncey M. Depew (1834-1928), Secretary of State of New York and U.S. Senator (R). Speech, New York City, Nov. 5, 1898.

41. When it comes to legislative inquiry there are no rules and actually the sky is the limit. I can ask a witness almost any question under the canopy of heaven, and if one of my colleagues should intrude, I can say, "You mind your own business and I'll mind mine."
Everett M. Dirksen (1896-1969), U.S. Congressman and U.S. Senator (R-IL). Interview, ABC, June 1959.

42. We are not being invited to speak *[and be paid honoraria]* because of our forensic abilities ... or because we have some fantastical insights to offer. We are being invited because we sit on a committee that involves legislation that affects those interests.
Christopher J. Dodd, U.S. Senator (D-CT). Quoted in *The Washington Post,* Aug. 6, 1990.

43. If you're hanging around with nothing to do and the zoo is closed, come over to the Senate. You'll get the same kind of feeling and you won't have to pay.
Robert J. Dole, U.S. Senator (R-KS). Quoted in *The New York Times,* May 9, 1985.

44. Congress is constantly engaged in a struggle for the respect of the people.
Herman P. Eberharter (1892-1958), U.S. Congressman (D-PA). Letter to Congressmen regarding introduction of the "21-day rule" in the House Rules Committee, Dec. 1948.

45. The people never have and never will be able to understand how the will of a majority of the House of Representatives can be set aside by the judgment of a few men on a powerful committee.
Herman P. Eberharter. *Ibid.*

46. We admire the President. We support the President. But we don't work for the President.
Mickey Edwards, U.S. Congressman (D-OK). Quoted on PBS, *MacNeil-Lehrer News Hour,* July 18, 1990.

47. Our people are slow to learn the wisdom of sending character instead of talent to Congress. Again and again they have sent a man of great acuteness, a fine scholar, a fine forensic orator, and some master of the brawls has crunched him up in his hands like a bit of paper.
Ralph Waldo Emerson (1803-1882), American writer. *Journals,* May 8, 1844.

48. Congress is the chief aggrandizer of the Executive.
Samuel J. Ervin, Jr. (1896-1985), U.S. Congressman and U.S. Senator (D-NC). *Congressional Record,* Mar. 8, 1973.

49. I want us to war over principles, policies, programs and alternative visions of the future ... but I want us to be able to do that without turning the place *[the Congress]* into a political Beirut.

Thomas S. Foley, U.S. Congressman and Speaker of the House (D-WA). Quoted in *Newsweek*, June 19, 1989.

50. The speakership isn't a dictatorship.
Thomas S. Foley. Quoted in Michael Oreskes, "Foley's Law," *The New York Times Magazine*, Nov. 11, 1990.

51. Congress no longer exercises its lawful function of lawmaking; that has gone to the committees.
Mary P. Follett (1868-1933), American political scientist. *The Speaker of the House of Representatives*, 1896.

52. Joint hearings ... destroy the check and balance that we have by having a House and Senate act independently.
Gerald R. Ford, 38th President of the United States (R-MI). 1973.

53. This *[Washington and Congress]* is a miserable place, but the elect of all the states are assembled in it, and really such a gang to have the affairs of an empire ... entrusted to them, makes one shudder. Imagination is dead in this country. Wit is neither to be found nor is it understood among them.... There are about five persons who look like gentlemen. All the rest come in the filthiest dresses and are well indeed if they look like farmers – but most seem to be apothecaries and attorneys.
Augustus Foster (1780-1848), Secretary of the English Legation to the United States. Letter to the Duchess of Devonshire, Feb. 8, 1805.

54. Joint committees *[of the two houses of Congress]* are heat generators rather than light producers.
William Frenzel, U.S. Congressman (R-MN). Hearing, House Select Committee on Committees, 1973.

55. I can't vote my own convictions on civil rights. If I did, I wouldn't be returned to the Senate. It's as simple as that.
J. William Fulbright, U.S. Senator (D-AR). Explanation of his opposition to civil rights legislation. Quoted in Jules Archer, *The Unpopular Ones*, 1968.

56. The collective judgment of the Congress, with all its faults, could be superior to that of one man who makes the final decision, in the Executive.
J. William Fulbright. Senate Foreign Relations Committee, Report, *War Powers Legislation*, 1971.

57. It is a terrible thing to live in fear of their constituents to the extent which many members *[of Congress]* do. I would rather be defeated every day in the year than suffer such fear.
James A. Garfield (1831-1881), 20th President of the United States (R-OH). *Diary*, Feb. 19, 1872.

58. The only way to get anywhere in Congress is to stay there and let seniority take its course.
John Nance Garner (1868-1967), U.S. Congressman, Speaker of the House, and Vice President of the United States (D-TX). Quoted in Alfred Steinberg, *Sam Rayburn*, 1975.

59. We're *[Congress is]* a little like Sears Roebuck or any other consumer-oriented company. We have a wide range of people who want our help, and we have a steady increase in customer service.
Newton L. Gingrich, U.S. Congressman (R-GA). PBS, *Congress: We the People*, 1989.

60. The Congress is getting too powerful.
Barry M. Goldwater, U.S. Senator (R-AZ). Interview, PBS, *Firing Line*, Nov. 18, 1989.

61. Are there two sets of laws in this country – one that applies to Congress and one for the rest of America? At a minimum, it goes to a lack of public accountability. At its worst, it's raw hypocrisy. The practice ought to stop, and today is as good a time as any to start.
Charles E. Grassley, U.S. Congressman and U.S. Senator (R-IA). Senate speech noting that Congress routinely exempts itself from civil rights, labor, and handicapped-access legislation, Sept. 7, 1989.

62. If you vote no, you don't go.
William H. Grey III, U.S. Congressman (D-PA). Remark on savings and loan bailout legislation before the Congress just before the Labor Day recess, Aug. 1989.

63. A ruling class has emerged. We no longer have government of, by, and for the people but rather by professional legislators.
Thomas F. Hartnett, U.S. Congressman (R-SC). Quoted in *Reader's Digest*, June 1989.

64. Members *[of Congress]* never make mistakes. Only the staff make mistakes.
Mark O. Hatfield, Governor of Oregon and U.S. Senator (R). PBS, *Congress: We the People*, 1989.

65. The traditions and courtesies of the Senators and Representatives stand in the way of the Executive, however, as defined by the Constitution, and no man who is trained in the congressional school fails to suffer by them in a way that men of merely executive experience know nothing of.
Rutherford B. Hayes (1822-1893), 19th President of the United States (R-OH). *Diary*, Apr. 25, 1881.

66. To be objective you don't have to be an adversary. You don't have to be a bulldog tearing down everything. To make the system of checks and balances and separation of powers work, you don't have to be on their ass all the time.
   Felix E. Hébert (1901-1979), U.S. Congressman (D-LA). Interview with Daniel Rapoport, 1974.

67. We have a Congress to serve the people who provide the money.
   Cecil Heftel, U.S. Congressman (D-HI). Speech, Coalition to Prevent a Permanent Congress, C-SPAN, Mar. 22, 1991.

68. Mere law cannot reform Congress.... We must amend the Constitution to limit terms. Imagine the intellectual honesty and political courage that would be brought to bear on national problems when men and women entering Congress knew with certainty they could not build a career in that place by currying favor with special interest groups.
   Gordon J. Humphrey, U.S. Senator (R-NH). Letter to the Editor, *The Wall Street Journal*, Dec. 19, 1989.

69. They *[Congressmen]* may ... consult and prefer the interests of their particular constituents when they come in conflict with any other particular or local interest, yet it is their first or highest duty, as representatives of the United States, to promote the general good.
   Andrew Jackson (1767-1845), 7th President of the United States (D-TN). In reference to nullification of the Tariff Act of 1832. *Proclamation to the People of South Carolina*, Dec. 10, 1832.

70. We *[the Supreme Court]* may say that power to legislate for emergencies belongs in the hands of Congress, but only Congress itself can prevent power from slipping through its fingers.
   Robert H. Jackson (1892-1954), U.S. Attorney General (D) and U.S. Supreme Court Justice. *Youngstown Sheet & Tube Co.* v. *Sawyer*, 1952.

71. It is a breach of order in debate to notice what has been said on the same subject in the other House, or the particular votes or majorities on it there, because the opinion of each house should be left to its own independency, not to be influenced by the proceedings of the other; and the quoting them might beget reflections leading to a misunderstanding between the two Houses.
   Thomas Jefferson (1743-1826), 3rd President of the United States (Democratic Republican-VA). *Jefferson's Manual of Parliamentary Practice*, XVII.

72. The tyranny of the legislature is really the danger most to be feared.... The tyranny of the executive power will come in its turn, but at a more distant period.
   Thomas Jefferson. Letter to James Madison, Mar. 15, 1787.

73. Congress is the great commanding theater of this nation, and the threshold to whatever department of office a man is qualified to enter.
   Thomas Jefferson. Letter to William Wirt, 1808.

74. That 150 lawyers should do business together *[in the U.S. Congress]* ought not to be expected.
   Thomas Jefferson. *Notes for an Autobiography*, Jan. 6, 1821.

75. A good Congress is measured by laws that mean something to people – p-e-e-p-u-l, p-e-e-p-l-e, p-e-e-p-u-l – you know what I'm talkin' about, just plain folks.
   Lyndon B. Johnson (1908-1973), 36th President of the United States (D-TX). Speech, Newark, NJ, Oct. 7, 1966.

76. The difference between being a member of the House and being a member of the Senate is the difference between chicken salad and chicken shit.
   Lyndon B. Johnson. Remark to freshman congressman George Bush, 1970.

77. It is much easier in many ways for me ... when Congress is not in town.
   John F. Kennedy (1917-1963), 35th President of the United States (D-MA). Press conference, Washington, DC, June 28, 1962.

78. It would be unrealistic to base actions on a numerical average of opinion-letters on various measures. These do not necessarily reflect cross-section opinion as there are many people who never write letters to their representatives.
   Coya G. Knutson, U.S. Congresswoman (D-Farmer-Labor-MN). *Congressional Record*, June 28, 1958.

79. Once you're in the House for a few terms, it's hard to leave.
   James Madison Leach, U.S. Congressman (R-IA). Interview, CNN, *An American Profile*, Sept. 3, 1990.

80. You don't want Congress peopled by millionaires.
   Mel Levine, U.S. Congressman (D-CA). Quoted in *The Washington Post*, June 4, 1989.

81. Members of Congress are the human connection between the citizen and his government.
   Elliott H. Levitas, U.S. Congressman (D-GA). Hearings, Senate Judiciary Committee, 1979.

82. The American House of Representatives today is a complete travesty upon representative government, upon popular government, and upon government by the majority.

Henry Cabot Lodge (1850-1924), U.S. Congressman and U.S. Senator (R-MA). Complaint about unwieldy House rules. *North American Review*, Sept. 1889.

83. I believe it to be the duty of the Speaker *[of the House]*, standing squarely on the platform of his party, to assist insofar as he properly can, the enactment of legislation in accordance with the declared principles and policies of his party and by the same token to resist the enactment of legislation in violation thereof.

Nicholas Longworth (1869-1931), U.S. Congressman and Speaker of the House (R-OH). 1925.

84. The *[congressional]* lawmaker is not to be purely an agent, vainly trying to decide what the majority of his principles desire. He is not to be purely a trustee, making wholly independent decisions, self-conceived and self-sustained. He is to be both agent and trustee as far as may be.

Robert Luce (1862-1946), U.S. Congressman (R-MA). *Congress: An Explanation*, 1926.

85. To declare war is the highest act of sovereignty ... and should not be delegated to any man or body of men.

Louis L. Ludlow (1873-1950), U.S. Congressman (D-IN). Comment after introducing a constitutional amendment to require a national referendum for a declaration of war, 1935.

86. It is against the enterprising ambition of this department *[the legislature]* that the people ought to indulge all their jealousy and exhaust all their precautions.

James Madison (1751-1836), 4th President of the United States (Democratic Republican-VA). *The Federalist*, No. 48, Feb. 1, 1788.

87. The people can never err more in supposing that by multiplying their representatives beyond a certain limit they strengthen the barrier against the government of a few.

James Madison. *The Federalist*, No. 58, Feb. 22, 1788.

88. Congress ... ought to work five days a week to keep legislation from piling up.

Mike Mansfield, U.S. Ambassador to Japan and U.S. Senator (D-MT). Quoted in *The Washington Post*, Jan. 6, 1991.

89. I almost felt that I should offer to serve coffee.

Lynn M. Martin, U.S. Congresswoman and U.S. Secretary of Labor (R-IL). Description of her feeling as the only woman in a party congressional leadership meeting. Interview, ABC *This Week*, June 10, 1990.

90. The Senate is, in a way, the last primitive society in the world. As civilization progresses we honor all the ancient principles of seniority and respect for our elders and occupancy. Territorial imperative runs very strongly in the Senate. And our ultimate test is a trial by ordeal – which we practice in the filibuster.

Eugene J. McCarthy, U.S. Congressman and U.S. Senator (D-WI). Campaign speech, Feb. 1968.

91. If you purify the pond, the water lilies die.

Eugene J. McCarthy. On congressional reform. Quoted in *U.S. News & World Report*, Nov. 26, 1990.

92. Twenty years ago, outside income was a means of keeping the Congress a citizen legislature. Today, outside income is a corrupting influence.

Robert H. Michel, U.S. Congressman (R-IL). *The New York Times*, June 18, 1989.

93. When a Speaker of the House can wield such power that he can "create" a new legislative day with the flick of his gavel ... something is wrong.

Robert H. Michel. *Ibid.*

94. Franking junkies.

Robert H. Michel. Description of his congressional colleagues' use of free mail privilege. Quoted in *Roll Call*, May 28, 1990.

95. The public has been much abused, the time of legislative bodies uselessly consumed, and the rights of citizens ruthlessly invaded under the now familiar pretext of legislative investigation.

Samuel Freeman Miller (1816-1890), U.S. Supreme Court Justice. 1880.

96. One advantage to covering the Congress rather than the White House is that no one is controlling the agenda.

Andrea Mitchell, American journalist. Symposium, "The Press and a Divided Government," National Press Foundation, Washington, DC, Dec. 6, 1989.

97. Anyone who works in the Senate is often in doubt as to the will of the Senate.

George J. Mitchell, U.S. Senator (D-ME). Senate debate, Jan. 10, 1990.

98. Since 1920 ... there have been four additional members of Congress established. We have built an office building for each one of them.

Daniel P. Moynihan, Chief American Delegate to the United Nations and U.S. Senator (D-NY). In reference to four congressional office buildings constructed in the past sixty years. PBS, *Congress: We the People,* 1989.

99. It is necessary to investigate before legislating. But the line between investigation and persecution is a fine one.
Edward R. Murrow (1908-1965), American broadcast journalist and Director, United States Information Agency. In reference to Sen. Joseph R. McCarthy. CBS, *See It Now*, Mar. 7, 1954.

100. I wish to make a unanimous-consent request, the necessity of which I find incredible. I ask unanimous consent to use hand calculators on the Senate floor.... I understand that the rules are so ancient that the ability to use these calculators except by unanimous consent seems to be in doubt.
Edmund S. Muskie, Governor of Maine (D), U.S. Senator, and U.S. Secretary of State. Senate debate, Apr. 29, 1975.

101. The Senate never wanted a leader, and it has seldom had one.
Edmund S. Muskie. Quoted in Jack Germond, *Congress and Carter*, 1980.

102. The worst problem is that by the time we attend hearings, meet with every group in sight who wants to talk with us about legislation, and meet with every group at home ranging from mayors and county boards, to private citizens, we have precious little time to do what is most important – to read and think about problems that we have been sent here to deal with in the first place.
David R. Obey, U.S. Congressman (D-WI). Letter to a constituent, May 19, 1975.

103. The only people who will be able to get to Congress will be the half-witted sons of the rich. The bright sons of the rich are needed to run the businesses, and the poor cannot afford to run.
Thomas P. (Tip) O'Neill, Jr., U.S. Congressman and Speaker of the House (D-MA). Interview, ABC, *Nightline*, May 31, 1989.

104. Any gentlemen of any party who could command a majority of the votes for Speaker *[of the House]* was bound, in deference to the public exigencies, to accept the responsibility as an act of patriotic duty.
William Pennington (1796-1862), Governor of New Jersey (R), U.S. Congressman, and Speaker of the House. Acceptance speech, Feb. 1, 1860.

105. I loved the Senate. I dearly loved the House.
Claude D. Pepper (1901-1989), U.S. Senator and U.S. Congressman (D-FL). *Eyewitness to a Century*, 1987.

106. I'd like to stay on in the Congress until I'm one hundred. I might want to retire then.
Claude D. Pepper. Interview, *Ask Congress*, Aug. 20, 1988.

107. A United States Senator has the best elective job in the world.
Charles H. Percy, U.S. Senator (R-IL). Interview, *Playboy*, Apr. 1968.

108. To hear some men talk of the government, you would suppose that Congress was the law of gravitation, and kept the planets in their places.
Wendell Phillips (1811-1884), American orator and reformer. *Orations, Speeches, Lectures and Letters*, 1863.

109. There is more selfishness and less principle among members of Congress ... than I had any conception of, before I became President of the U.S.
James K. Polk (1795-1849), 11th President of the United States (D-TN). *Diary*, Dec. 16, 1846.

110. I am the first bad nigger in Congress.
Adam Clayton Powell (1908-1972), U.S. Congressman (D-NY). Quoted on PBS, *The American Experience*, Nov. 28, 1989.

111. Resolved, That it is the sense of the Senate that there be no more "sense of the Senate" resolutions.
David H. Pryor, U.S. Congressman and U.S. Senator (D-AK). Senate Resolution No. 194, July 23, 1981.

112. To my mind it *[the House of Representatives]* is a political non-descript. It acts, and reasons, and votes, and performs all the operations of an animated being, and yet ... I cannot refrain from concluding that all great political questions are settled somewhere else than on this floor.
Josiah Quincy (1772-1864), President, Harvard College, Cambridge, MA, and U.S. Congressman (Federalist-MA). House debate, 1809.

113. We *[women]* are half the people; we should be half the Congress.
Jeanette Rankin (1880-1973), U.S. Congresswoman (R-MT). Quoted in *Newsweek*, Feb. 14, 1966.

114. In Congress you get along by going along.
Samuel T. Rayburn (1882-1961), U.S. Congressman and Speaker of the House (D-TX). Advice to freshman Congressman Lyndon B. Johnson, 1937.

115. If you can't feel things that you can't see or hear, you don't belong here *[in Congress.]*
Samuel T. Rayburn. Quoted in Robert A. Caro, *Lyndon B. Johnson*, 1982.

116. Dick, you've got to be popular in this place.
Samuel T. Rayburn. Advice to Congressman Richard W. Bolling (MO), who wanted to be Speaker but was known for stepping on colleagues' toes. Quoted in *The Washington Post*, Apr. 22, 1991.

117. A Congressman's first duty is to get elected. Always vote your district.
Samuel T. Rayburn. Advice to all Congressmen.

118. The only way to do business inside the *[House]* rules is to suspend the rules.
Thomas B. Reed (1839-1902), U.S. Congressman and Speaker of the House (R-ME). Quoted in George B. Galloway, *History of the House of Representatives*, 1976.

119. Every numerous assembly is a mob; consequently everything there depends upon instantaneous turns.
Cardinal de Retz (1614-1679), French priest and politician. *Political Maxims*.

120. With Congress, every time they make a joke it's a law, and every time they make a law it's a joke.
Will Rogers (1879-1935), American humorist. Quoted in Fred Metcalf, *The Penguin Dictionary of Modern Humorous Quotations*, 1986.

121. It is the duty of the President to propose and it is the privilege of the Congress to dispose.
Franklin D. Roosevelt (1882-1945), 32nd President of the United States (D-NY). Remark to reporters, July 23, 1937.

122. When a country is at war we want Congressmen, regardless of party, to back up the government of the United States.
Franklin D. Roosevelt. Remark, 1942.

123. Congress does from a third to a half of what I think is the minimum that it ought to do, and I am profoundly grateful that I get as much.
Theodore Roosevelt (1858-1919), 26th President of the United States (R-NY). Remark to Leonard Wood, 1904.

124. You can't be up there every day on everything, in every battle. You've got to pick and choose.
Benjamin S. Rosenthal (1923-1983), U.S. Congressman (D-NY). Quoted in Daniel Rapoport, *Inside the House*, 1975.

125. About a third of the people here *[the Senate]* really want to get something done and know how to do it. Another third want to get something done but don't know how to do it. And the remaining third, well, I'm not sure why they're here.
Warren B. Rudman, U.S. Senator (R-NH). Quoted in James Miller, *Running in Place*, 1986.

126. Give a member of Congress a junket and a mimeograph machine and he thinks he is Secretary of State.
Dean Rusk, U.S. Secretary of State (D). Quoted in *Time*, May 6, 1985.

127. Being eyeball-to-eyeball is a hundred times more effective than writing a letter.
Claudine Schneider, U.S. Congresswoman (R-RI). On influencing members of Congress. Quoted in *Ms.*, Apr. 1989.

128. I believe, Mr. Chairman, that the day has passed when the power of a position such as you hold can be used to compel uniformity of vote or view. Members of Congress are responsible to their constituents and to their consciences – not to their committee chairmen.
Patricia R. Schroeder, U.S. Congresswoman (D-CO). Letter to Felix E. Hébert (unsent), 1973.

129. Spine transplants are what we *[in Congress]* really need.
Patricia R. Schroeder. Quoted in *The New York Times*, Jan. 14, 1985.

130. I not only defend his *[Sen. J. William Fulbright's]* right to express his deeply felt views and his sharp dissent; I admire him for speaking his mind and his conscience. I admire him for his courage to run counter to conformity and the overwhelming majority.
Margaret Chase Smith, U.S. Congresswoman and U.S. Senator (R-ME). Quoted in Jules Archer, *The Unpopular Ones*, 1968.

131. Congress can't do its work with the amount of absenteeism there is.
Margaret Chase Smith. Quoted in *The Washington Post*, Jan. 6, 1991.

132. Members of Congress are basically solid and sound, but every two years they spend all their time telling the public what boobs their colleagues are at best, and what crooks at worst.
Robert T. Stafford, U.S. Congressman and U.S. Senator (R-VT). Quoted in *The Washington Post*, Jan. 6, 1991.

133. If you want to get a fifteen- or thirty-second bite, you have to have a prominent witness and a zinger of a question.
Peter Stark, U.S. Congressman (D-CA). On congressional hearings. Quoted in *The New York Times*, Feb. 10, 1990.

134. As Congress shall order, he *[the President]* must obey.

Thaddeus Stevens (1792-1868), U.S. Congressman (Whig and R-PA). Quoted in Arthur M. Schlesinger, Jr., *The Imperial Presidency*, 1973.

135. Often there is not a distinguished man in the whole number *[Congress]*. Its members are almost all obscure individuals ... village lawyers, men in trade, or even persons belonging to the lower classes of society.

Alexis de Tocqueville (1805-1859), French writer. *Democracy in America*, 1835.

136. It can be a terrible burden for a congressional leader to have a President of his own party.

Martin Tolchin, American journalist. Symposium, "The Press and a Divided Government," National Press Foundation, Washington, DC, Dec. 6, 1989.

137. Let's take a look at the record of the 80th Congress they're so proud of. I call it the "notorious, do-nothing Republican 80th Congress." Maybe I ought to leave out the "do-nothing" part of it, because it did some things – most of them bad.

Harry S Truman (1884-1972), 33rd President of the United States (D-MO). Campaign speech, Philadelphia, PA. Oct. 6, 1948.

138. If you tell Congress everything about the world situation, they get hysterical. If you tell them nothing, they go fishing.

Harry S Truman. Remark, July 17, 1950.

139. It could probably be shown by facts and figures that there is no distinctly native American criminal class except Congress.

Mark Twain (Samuel Langhorne Clemens) (1835-1910), American writer. *Following the Equator*, 1897.

140. Fleas can be taught nearly everything that a Congressman can.

Mark Twain, *What is Man?*, 1906.

141. The member of Congress soon has to decide whether he is going to be a glorified office boy, attending with great punctiliousness to his mail, calling on departments for little favors for his constituents, or whether he is going to be a legislator. He cannot be both.

Millard E. Tydings (1890-1961), U.S. Congressman and U.S. Senator (D-MD). Quoted in J. T. Salter, ed., *The American Politician*, 1938.

142. If I can't vote my sentiments here – to hell with the job.

Millard E. Tydings. Remark in the Senate, 1938.

143. Congressmen and Senators are expendable rather than indispensable, and no Congressman or Senator should cast a vote he knows is wrong in order to be reelected.

John M. Vorys (1896-1968), U.S. Congressman (R-OH). Quoted in *The New York Times Magazine*, Jan. 25, 1948.

144. The good nature of members *[of the House of Representatives]* in granting unanimous consent breeds ignorance.

Israel Washburn, Jr. (1813-1883), U.S. Congressman (R-ME). Quoted in *The Congressional Globe*, 36th Congress (1859-61).

145. We have been taught to regard a representative of the people as a sentinel on the watchtower of liberty.

Daniel Webster (1782-1852), U.S. Congressman (Federalist-NH and MA), U.S. Senator (Federalist and Whig-MA), and U.S. Secretary of State. Senate speech, May 7, 1834.

146. People feel closer to the planet Pluto than to the U.S. Senate.

Paul Wellstone, U.S. Senator (D-MN). Quoted in *The Washington Post*, July 1, 1990.

147. I have several votes that I would like to have back.

Charles W. Whalen, Jr., U.S. Congressman (R-OH). Quoted in Daniel Rapoport, *Inside the House*, 1975.

148. The rules *[of the House of Representatives]* must conform to the will of the majority.

John White (1802-1845), U.S. Congressman and Speaker of the House (Whig-KY). 1841.

149. I've got two very good friends in the race and I've promised *[my support and vote]* to both of them, so I'd rather not say.

Charles Wilson, U.S. Congressman (D-TX). Response when asked whom he favored in an upcoming party contest for Majority Whip. Interview, PBS, *John McLaughlin's One on One*, June 4, 1989.

150. I know not how better to describe our form of government than by calling it a government by the chairmen of the Standing Committees of Congress.

Woodrow Wilson (1854-1924), 28th President of the United States (D-NJ). *Congressional Government, A Study in American Politics*, 1885.

151. Congress in session is Congress on public exhibition, whilst Congress in its committee rooms is Congress at work.

Woodrow Wilson. *Ibid.*

152. The chairmen of the standing committees *[of Congress]* do not constitute a cooperative body like a ministry. They do not consult and concur in the adoption of homogeneous and mutually helpful measures; there is no thought of acting in concert. Each committee goes its own way at its own pace.

Woodrow Wilson. *Ibid.*

153. The first of Thomas Edison's three thousand patented inventions was an electronic vote recorder, which would have helped Congress speed up its work by eliminating lengthy roll call votes. But Congress refused to use it, fearing the machine would not permit members to change their votes during the roll call.

S. B. Woo, Lieutenant Governor of Delaware. *Governing*, Sept. 1988.

154. Congress is a collection of ordinary men and women grappling with extraordinary problems.

James C. Wright, Jr., U.S. Congressman and Speaker of the House (D-TX). Interview, PBS, *MacNeil-Lehrer Report*, June 1, 1989.

Chapter 14

The Constitution and the Bill of Rights

1. Our Constitution professedly rests upon the good sense and attachment of the people. This basis, weak as it may appear, has not yet been found to fail.

   John Quincy Adams (1767-1848), 6th President of the United States (Ind-MA). Letter to William Vans Murray, Jan. 27, 1801.

2. Constitutions are but paper; society is the substratum of government.

   Fisher Ames (1758-1808), U.S. Congressman (Federalist-MA). Remark to members of the Governor's Council, 1800.

3. The Constitution protects people from the federal government and in some cases from the states, but it doesn't apply to private companies unless there is a specific statute dealing with the issue.

   Lori B. Andrews, Director of Communications, American Bar Foundation. Quoted in *The Washington Post*, Feb. 19, 1989.

4. The English constitution is founded on the principle of choosing a single sovereign authority and making it good.

   Walter Bagehot (1826-1877), British economist and writer. *The English Constitution*, 1867.

5. Among the many defects that have been pointed out in the federal Constitution ... is an office for promoting and preserving perpetual peace in our country.... Let a Secretary of Peace be established.

   Benjamin Banneker (1731-1806), American publisher and scientist. *Banneker's Almanac*, 1792.

6. The Constitution was essentially an economic document based upon the concept that the fundamental rights of private property are anterior to government and morally beyond the reach of popular majorities.

   Charles A. Beard (1874-1948), American historian. *The Economic Interpretation of the United States*, 1935.

7. The Constitution has never greatly bothered any wartime President.

   Francis B. Biddle (1886-1968), U.S. Attorney General (D). *In Brief Authority*, 1962.

8. We have a right to know and a duty to discover what you think of the great constitutional issues of our time.

   Joseph R. Biden, Jr., U.S. Senator (D-DE). Statement to Supreme Court nominee David Souter. Senate Judiciary Committee confirmation hearings. Sept. 13, 1990.

9. Our Constitution was not written in the sands to be washed away by each successive wave of new judges blown in by each successive political wind.

   Hugo L. Black (1886-1971), U.S. Senator (D-AL) and U.S. Supreme Court Justice. Speech, Jan. 20, 1970.

10. Whenever the Constitution comes between me and the virtue of the white women of South Carolina, I say to hell with the Constitution.

    Coleman L. Blease (1868-1942), Governor of South Carolina and U.S. Senator (D). Campaign speech defending lynching. Quoted in *The New York Telegram*, July 12, 1930.

11. It is necessary to establish the proposition that the framers' intentions with respect to freedoms are the sole legitimate premise from which constitutional analysis may proceed.

    Robert H. Bork, U.S. Solicitor General and Judge, U.S. Court of Appeals, Washington, DC. *Tradition and Morality in Constitutional Law*, 1984.

12. The original Constitution was devoted primarily to the mechanisms of democratic choice.... *[It]* provided wide powers to the representative assemblies and ruled only a few subjects off limits by the Constitution.

    Robert H. Bork. *Ibid.*

13. The Constitution is ... power. That is why we see political struggle over the selection of judges who will wield that power.
    Robert H. Bork. *The Tempting of America*, 1991.

14. The federal Constitution is perhaps the greatest of human experiments.
    Louis D. Brandeis (1856-1941), U.S. Supreme Court Justice. Quoted in Solomon Goldman, *The Words of Justice Brandeis*, 1953.

15. The genius of the Constitution rests not in any static meaning it might have had in a world that is dead and gone, but in the adaptability of its great principles to cope with current problems and current needs.... It is arrogant to pretend that ... we can gauge accurately the intent of the framers on application of principle to specific, contemporary questions.
    William J. Brennan, Jr., U.S. Supreme Court Justice. Speech, Georgetown University, Washington, DC, 1985.

16. Our Constitution is a conservative document. It's a document which is established to maintain the status quo unless an overwhelming majority to change that status quo can be martialed.
    Tyrone Brown, American civil rights attorney. "Blacks and the Constitution," WHMM-TV, Ohio State University, Oct. 25, 1988.

17. What's the Constitution between friends?
    Timothy J. Campbell (1840-1904), U.S. Congressman (D-NY). Reply to President Cleveland, who balked at introducing legislation that might be unconstitutional, 1898.

18. I thought that we would wake up this morning and have the same rights as our husbands, grandsons, and garbagemen – but we are still begging to be let into our country's Constitution.
    Liz Carpenter, presidential assistant (D) and founder, National Women's Political Caucus. Speech, New York City, Mar. 22, 1979.

19. What is constitutional may still be unwise.
    Zechariah Chafee, Jr. (1885-1957), professor of law, Harvard University. *The Nation*, July 28, 1952.

20. If the Federal Legislature should, at any time, pass a Law contrary to the Constitution of the United States, such Law would be void.
    Samuel Chase (1741-1811), American revolutionary leader and U.S. Supreme Court Justice. Instructions to Pennsylvania grand jury, Apr. 12, 1800.

21. The Constitution of the United States was made not merely for the generation that then existed, but for posterity – unlimited, undefined, endless, perpetual posterity.
    Henry Clay (1777-1852), U.S. Congressman, U.S. Senator (R and Whig-KY), Speaker of the House, and U.S. Secretary of State. Senate speech, 1850.

22. People seem to be concerned about the Constitution of the United States only when it pertains to something that is of concern to them.
    Thomas B. Curtis, U.S. Congressman (R-MO). Congressional debate, Aug. 18, 1964.

23. The Constitution of the United States is a law for rulers and people, equally in war and peace.
    David Davis (1815-1886), U.S. Supreme Court Justice. *Ex Parte Mulligan*, 1866.

24. The language is, "We the people"; not we the white people, not even we the citizens, not we the privileged class, not we the high, not we the low, but *we the people*; not we the horses, sheep, and swine, and wheelbarrows, but we the people, we the inhabitants of America; and if Negroes are people, they are included in the benefits for which the Constitution of America was ordained and established.
    Frederick Douglass (c.1817-1895), Recorder of Deeds, District of Columbia, and U.S. Minister to Haiti. Lecture, Rochester, NY, 1885.

25. I think the great thing about the First Amendment is that it extends its rights to everyone. The wise and the foolish.
    Samuel J. Ervin, Jr. (1896-1985), U.S. Congressman and U.S. Senator (D-NC). Quoted on PBS, *Senator Sam*, Oct. 25, 1988.

26. God knows that I detest slavery, but it is an existing evil, for which we are not responsible, and we must endure it, and give it such protection as is guaranteed by the Constitution, till we can get rid of it without destroying the last hope of free government in the world.
    Millard Fillmore (1800-1874), 13th President of the United States (Whig-NY). Severance, *Millard Fillmore Papers*, 1959.

27. Our long national nightmare is over. Our Constitution works.
    Gerald R. Ford, 38th President of the United States (R-MI). Speech when sworn in as President after the resignation of Richard M. Nixon. Aug. 9, 1974.

28. I confess that there are several parts of this Constitution of which I do not at present approve, but I am not sure I shall never approve of them; for having lived long, I have experienced many instances of being obliged by better information or

fuller consideration to change opinions, even on important subjects, which I once thought right but found to be otherwise.... In these sentiments, Sir, I agree to this Constitution with all its faults, if they are such.... I doubt too whether any other convention we can obtain may be able to make a better Constitution.

Benjamin Franklin (1706-1790), Member, Continental Congress and Constitutional Convention, Governor of Pennsylvania, and U.S. Minister to France. Speech, Constitutional Convention, Philadelphia, PA, Sept. 17, 1787.

29. If our Constitution does not guarantee freedom for all, it is not a Constitution I can subscribe to. And now let me give the sentiment which has been, and ever will be, the governing passion of my soul: *Liberty for each, for all, for ever.*

William Lloyd Garrison (1805-1879), American editor and abolitionist. Speech, Fort Sumter, SC. Apr. 15, 1865.

30. If there should happen to be an irreconcilable variance between the two *[the Constitution and legislation]*, that which has superior obligation and validity ought, of course, to be preferred; or, in other words, the Constitution ought to be preferred to the statute, the intention of the people to the intention of their agents.

Alexander Hamilton (1755-1804), Member, Continental Congress and Constitutional Convention, and U.S. Secretary of the Treasury (Federalist-NY). *The Federalist*, No. 78.

31. The Constitution is itself in every rational sense, and to every useful purpose, A BILL OF RIGHTS.

Alexander Hamilton. *The Federalist*, No. 84.

32. The Constitution only works when branches of government trust one another and cooperate.

Lee Hamilton, U.S. Congressman (D-IN). Quoted in Nathan Miller, *Spying for America*, 1989.

33. We raised our right hands ... and swore to uphold and defend the Constitution. We didn't swear to support and defend the President.

Thomas R. Harkin, U.S. Senator (D-IA). Interview, NBC, *Meet the Press*, Jan. 6, 1991.

34. Tinkers may work, quacks may prescribe, and demagogues may deceive, but I declare to you that there is no remedy for us ... but in adhering to the Constitution.

Benjamin H. Hill (1823-1882), U.S. Congressman (D-GA), U.S. Senator, and Senator in the Confederate Congress. Quoted in Benjamin Hill, Jr., *Senator Benjamin H. Hill: His Life, Speeches and Writings*, 1893.

35. We are under a Constitution, but the Constitution is what the judges say it is.

Charles Evans Hughes (1862-1948), Chief Justice, U.S. Supreme Court, and U.S. Secretary of State (R). Speech, Elmira, NY, May 3, 1907.

36. The Constitution is a list of things the government may not do.

Gordon J. Humphrey, U.S. Senator (R-NH). Quoted in *The Washington Post*, June 13, 1990.

37. The opinion of the Supreme Court ... ought not to control the coordinate authorities of this government. The Congress, the Executive, and the Court must each be guided by its own opinion of the Constitution.

Andrew Jackson (1767-1845), 7th President of the United States (D-TN). Veto, Bank Renewal Bill, July 10, 1832.

38. Our Constitution does not contain the absurdity of giving power to make laws and another to resist them.... The Father of His Country *[George Washington]* did not affix his revered name to so palpable an absurdity. Nor did the states, when they severally ratified it, do so under the impression that a veto on the laws of the United States was reserved to them or that they could exercise it by implication.

Andrew Jackson. Response to South Carolina's nullification of the Tariff Act. *Proclamation to the People of South Carolina*, Dec. 10, 1832.

39. The mere state of being without funds is a neutral fact – constitutionally an irrelevance, like race, creed, or color.

Robert H. Jackson (1892-1954), U.S. Attorney General (D) and U.S. Supreme Court Justice. *Edwards* v. *California*, 1941.

40. If there is any fixed star in our constitutional constellation, it is that no official, high or petty, can prescribe what shall be orthodox in politics, nationalism, religion, or other matters of opinion.

Robert H. Jackson. *West Virginia State Board of Education* v. *Barnette*, 1943.

41. Just what our forefathers did envision or would have envisioned had they foreseen modern conditions, must be divined from materials almost as enigmatic as the dreams Joseph was called upon to interpret for the Pharaoh.

Robert H. Jackson. Quoted in *The Washington Post*, Nov. 6, 1988.

42. The President may be right in how he reads the Constitution. But he also may be wrong. And if he is wrong, who is there to tell him so? And if

there is no one, the President, of course, is free to pursue his course of erroneous interpretations. What then becomes of our constitutional form of government?
Leon Jaworski (1905-1982), Watergate special prosecutor. Oral argument before the U.S. Supreme Court, July 8, 1974.

43. I have a right to nothing, which another has a right to take away; and Congress will have a right to take away trials by jury in civil cases. Let me add that a bill of rights is what the people are entitled to against every government on earth ... and what no just government should refuse, or rest upon inferences.
Thomas Jefferson (1743-1826), 3rd President of the United States (Democratic Republican-VA). Letter to James Madison, Sept. 6, 1787.

44. No society can make a perpetual constitution or even a perpetual law.
Thomas Jefferson. Letter to James Madison, 1789.

45. The Constitution of the United States is the result of the collected wisdom of our country.
Thomas Jefferson. Letter to A. Marsh, 1801.

46. Honest conviction is my courage, the Constitution is my guide.
Andrew Johnson (1808-1875), 17th President of the United States (War D-TN). Quoted in "39 Men" exhibit.

47. The Bill of Rights was not ordained by nature or God. It's very human, very fragile.
Barbara Jordan, U.S. Congresswoman (D-TX). Quoted in *The New York Times Magazine*, Oct. 21, 1990.

48. The hard fact is that sometimes we must make decisions that we do not like. We make them because they are right, right in the sense that the law and the Constitution, as we see them, compel the result.
Anthony M. Kennedy, U.S. Supreme Court Justice. Quoted in *The New York Times*, June 25, 1989.

49. Rights that depend on the sufferance of the state are of uncertain tenure.
Suzanne La Follette (1893-1983), American politician and writer. *Concerning Women*, 1926.

50. All free constitutions are formed with two views – to deter the governed from crime, and the governors from tyranny.
John Lansing, Jr. (1754-1829), Member, Continental Congress, Mayor of Albany, NY, and Chief Justice, New York State Supreme Court. Debate, Constitutional Convention, Philadelphia, PA, July 1787.

51. All Catholics should do all in their power to cause the constitutions of states and legislation to be modeled on the principles of the true Church.
Pope Leo XIII (1810-1903). Encyclical, *Immortale Dei*, Nov. 1, 1885.

52. A constitution would weaken authority in Russia, would not have the time to inculcate the devotion the English have for legislation.
Konstantin Nikolaevich Leontiev (1831-1891), Russian socialist philosopher. Letter, 1890.

53. The framers intended the Senate to be the principal architect of foreign policy. Had original intent prevailed, we would speak of the imperial Senate, not the imperial presidency.
Leonard W. Levy, American constitutional historian, Claremont College, CA. *Original Intent and the Framers' Constitution*, 1988.

54. All government and all private institutions must be designed to promote and protect and defend the integrity and the dignity of the individual. And that is the essential meaning of the Constitution and the Bill of Rights.
David E. Lilienthal (1899-1981), Chairman, Tennessee Valley Authority, and Chairman, U.S. Atomic Energy Commission. Congressional testimony, Feb. 4, 1947.

55. Don't interfere with anything in the Constitution. That must be maintained, for it is the only safeguard of our liberties.
Abraham Lincoln (1809-1865), 16th President of the United States (R-IL). Speech, Kalamazoo, MI, Aug. 27, 1856.

56. I think the Negro is included in the word "men" used in the Declaration of Independence.
Abraham Lincoln. Letter to J. N. Brown, Oct. 18, 1858.

57. The right of peaceable assembly and of petition ... is the constitutional substitute for revolution.
Abraham Lincoln. Letter to Alexander Stephens, Jan. 19, 1859.

58. Our adversaries *[the Confederate States of America]* have adopted some declarations of independence, in which, unlike our good old one penned by Jefferson, they omit the words "all men are created equal." Why? They have adopted a temporary national constitution, in the preamble of which, unlike our good old one signed by Washington, they omit "We, the people," and substitute: "We,

the deputies of the sovereign and independent states." Why? Why this deliberate pressing out of view the rights of men and the authority of the people?

Abraham Lincoln. Message to Congress, July 4, 1861.

59. Your Constitution is all sail and no anchor.

Thomas Babington Macaulay, 1st Baron Macaulay (1800-1859), British historian and Secretary of War (Liberal). Letter to Henry S. Randall, May 23, 1857.

60. Whatever may have been the intention of the framers of a constitution, or of a law, that intention is to be sought for in the instrument itself, according to the usual and established rules of construction.

James Madison (1751-1836), 4th President of the United States (Democratic Republican-VA). *Opinion on the Constitutionality of an Act to Establish a Bank*, 1791.

61. We must never forget that it is a *constitution* we are expounding ... a constitution intended to endure for ages to come, and consequently, to be adopted to the various *crises* of human affairs.

John Marshall (1755-1835), Chief Justice, U.S. Supreme Court. *McCulloch* v. *Maryland*, 1819.

62. If there be any who deny its *[the Constitution's]* necessity, none can deny its authority.

John Marshall. *Cohens* v. *Virginia*, 1821.

63. This *[the Constitution]* is the authoritative language of the American people; and, if gentlemen please, of the American States.

John Marshall. *Ibid.*

64. The government they devised was defective from the start.

Thurgood Marshall, U.S. Supreme Court Justice. In reference to the fact that the framers of the Constitution did not deal with slavery or women's suffrage. Quoted in *Newsweek*, May 18, 1987.

65. We, whose names are underwritten ... doe, by these presents solemnly and mutually in the presence of God, and of one another, covenant and combine ourselves together into a civill body politick for our better ordering and preservation and furtherance of the ends aforesaid; and by virtue hereof to enacte, constitute and frame such just and equall laws, ordinances, acts, constitutions, and offices, from time to time, as shall be thought most meete and convenient for the general good of the Colonie, unto which we promise all due submission and obedience.

Mayflower Compact. Signed at Cape Cod, MA, Nov. 20, 1620.

66. What, then, should a constitutional jurisprudence actually be? It should be a jurisprudence of Original Intention.... The original meaning of constitutional provisions and statutes *[is]* the only reliable guide for judgment.

Edwin Meese III, U.S. Attorney General (R). Address, American Bar Association, July 19, 1985.

67. What is called a constitution today is nothing but "get out so I can get in."

Klemens von Metternich (1773-1859), Austrian statesman. Letter from Vienna, Sept. 15, 1821.

68. Constitutions are good only as we make progress under them.

Napoléon I (1769-1821), military leader and Emperor of France. *Maxims*.

69. We *[the American Civil Liberties Union]* like to think of ourselves as the enforcement arm of the Constitution.

Bert Neuborn, advisor, American Civil Liberties Union. Quoted on PBS, *MacNeil-Lehrer News Hour*, Oct. 10, 1988.

70. A Constitution is not the Act of a Government, but of a people constituting a Government; and Government without a Constitution is Power without a Right.

Thomas Paine (1737-1809), American political philosopher. *The Rights of Man*, 1795.

71. The "separate" powers are now too separate. Government in Washington all too often resembles a series of bunkers held by mutually suspicious troops, and nothing in the Constitution provides for issuing orders to demobilize.

Kevin Phillips, American political consultant (R). *Post-Conservative America*, 1983.

72. The people, by the Constitution, have commanded the President, as much as they have commanded the legislative branch of the government, to execute their will.

James K. Polk (1795-1849), 11th President of the United States (D-TN). Annual message to Congress, Dec. 5, 1848.

73. The adoption of the constitution was a triumph of virtue and good sense, over the vices and follies of human nature.

David Ramsay (1749-1815), Member, Continental Congress (PA). 1808.

74. The popular thing to do when the flag goes up and the marines land is not to knock it.... Being popular is less important to me than protecting that Constitution.... The prerogatives of the

Congress have been invaded by the President as he invaded Panama.
Charles B. Rangel, U.S. Congressman (D-NY). To oppose the 1989 invasion of Panama on constitutional grounds. CNN, *Evans & Novak*, Dec. 24, 1989.

75. Our Constitution is to be celebrated not for being old, but for being young.
Ronald Reagan, 40th President of the United States (R-CA). Annual message to Congress, Jan. 27, 1987.

76. There is a tendency, and in my mind a dangerous tendency, on the part of our national government, to encroach, on one excuse or another, more and more upon state supremacy. The elastic theory of interstate commerce ... has been stretched almost to the breaking point to cover certain regulatory powers desired by Washington.
Franklin D. Roosevelt (1882-1945), 32nd President of the United States (D-NY). Speech, National Governors' Conference, 1929.

77. Our Constitution is so simple and practical that it is possible always to meet extraordinary needs by changes in emphasis and arrangement without loss of essential form.
Franklin D. Roosevelt. First inaugural address, Mar. 4, 1933.

78. It is hard to organize a constitutional society of free men; it is easy to impose a reign of terror.
Dean Rusk, U.S. Secretary of State (D). Speech, Nov. 1951.

79. A true test of one's commitment to constitutional principles is the extent to which recognition is given to the rights of those in our midst who are the least affluent, least powerful, and least welcome.
Leonard B. Sand, Federal Judge. Quoted in *The New York Times*, Jan. 28, 1990.

80. There is a higher law than the Constitution which regulates our authority over the domain.
William H. Seward (1801-1872), Governor of New York (Whig), U.S. Senator (Whig and R), and U.S. Secretary of State. Senate speech opposing the Compromise of 1850, Mar. 11, 1850.

81. It is the right of our people to organize to oppose any law and any part of the Constitution with which they are not in sympathy.
Alfred E. Smith (1873-1944), Governor of New York (D). Speech, League of Women Voters, Dec. 2, 1927.

82. I am gratified that the Bill of Rights has not become the first casualty of the war on drugs.
Arthur B. Spitzer, Legal Director, Washington, DC, American Civil Liberties Union. Response when a Federal judge ruled that the Justice Department could not implement a random drug testing program of its employees. Quoted in *The New York Times*, July 30, 1988.

83. The promise of the Fourteenth Amendment was not kept by the Congress.
Potter Stewart (1915-1985), U.S. Supreme Court Justice. To explain necessity of action by the Supreme Court in the civil rights field. Debate, PBS, *The Constitution: That Delicate Balance*, Apr. 1982.

84. The privilege of bringing every law to the test of the Constitution belongs to the humblest citizen, who owes no obedience, to any legislative act which transcends the constitutional limits.
Joseph Story (1779-1845), U.S. Supreme Court Justice. *Miscellaneous Writings*, 1835.

85. Upon constitutional questions, the public have a right to know the opinion of every judge who dissents from the opinion of the court, and the reasons of his dissent.
Joseph Story. *Briscoe* v. *Bank of Kentucky*, 1837.

86. The Union existed before the Constitution, which was ordained and established among other things to form "a more perfect union."
George Sutherland (1862-1942), U.S. Supreme Court Justice. *United States* v. *Curtiss Wright Corp.*, 1936.

87. Constitutions are checks upon the hasty action of the majority. They are the self-imposed restraints of a whole people upon a majority of them to secure sober action and a respect for the rights of the minority.
William Howard Taft (1857-1930), 27th President of the United States (R-OH), and Chief Justice, U.S. Supreme Court. Veto, Arizona Enabling Act, Aug. 22, 1911.

88. No doctrine involving more pernicious consequences was ever invented by the wit of man than that any *[constitutional]* provisions can be suspended during any of the great exigencies of government.
Roger B. Taney (1777-1864), Chief Justice, U.S. Supreme Court. *Ex parte Milligan*, June 1, 1866.

89. *[The Twenty-second Amendment makes]* a "lame duck" out of every second-term President for all time in the future.

Harry S Truman (1884-1972), 33rd President of the United States (D-MO). Quoted in Melvin I. Urofsky, *A March of Liberty*, 1988.

90. Every exercise of governmental power must find its source in the Constitution.

Earl Warren (1891-1974), Chief Justice, U.S. Supreme Court, and Governor of California (R). *Perez* v. *Brownell*, 1957.

91. I wish the Constitution, which is offered, had been made more perfect; but I sincerely believe it is the best that could be obtained at this time.

George Washington (1732-1799), 1st President of the United States (VA). Letter to Patrick Henry, Sept. 24, 1787.

92. The basis of our political systems is the right of the people to make and alter their constitutions of government.

George Washington. Farewell address, Sept. 17, 1796.

93. The Declaration of Independence ... is an eminently practical document, meant for the use of practical men; not a thesis for philosophers, but a whip for tyrants; not a theory of government, but a program of action.

Woodrow Wilson (1856-1924), 28th President of the United States (D-NJ). *The New Freedom*, 1913.

Chapter 15

Corruption and Graft

1. Turn the rascals out!

   Liberal Republican slogan supporting Horace Greeley against incumbent President Ulysses S. Grant, 1872.

2. Both parties are impossibly corrupt and the public thoroughly indifferent.

   Henry Adams (1838-1918), American historian. Letter to Charles Milnes Gaskell, Sept. 8, 1876.

3. Every link in the chain that runs from the corporation desiring political favors down to the policeman on the beat levying his toll on the prostitute or the apple seller is too strong to have been broken yet.

   James Truslow Adams (1878-1949), American historian. *The March of Democracy*, II, 1933.

4. When vice prevails, and impious men bear sway, The post of honour is a private station.

   Joseph Addison (1672-1719), Undersecretary of State, Britain (Whig). *Cato*, ii.

5. The grocer, the butcher, the baker, the merchant, the landlord, the druggist, the liquor dealer, the policeman, the doctor, the city father, and the politicians – these are the people who make money out of prostitution.

   Polly Adler (1900-1962), American madam. *A House Is Not a Home*, 1953.

6. I have nothing to hide.

   Spiro T. Agnew, Governor of Maryland and Vice President of the United States (R). Consent to federal prosecutor's request to turn over personal records with regard to bribery, extortion, conspiracy, and tax fraud; he resigned soon thereafter. Aug. 14, 1972.

7. I have found there is no difficulty in inducing men to look after their own property.

   (As a lobbyist for the Union Pacific Railroad, Ames "distributed" railroad stock to Congressmen voting on railroad subsidies in connection with the Crédit Mobilier.)

   Oakes Ames (1804-1873), U.S. Congressman (R-MA). 1868.

8. Dear Senator: In accordance with our understanding I now beg to enclose your certificate of deposit to your favor for $15,000. Kindly acknowledge receipt and oblige.

   John D. Archbold (1848-1916), chief agent and lobbyist, Standard Oil Company. Letter to Sen. Bensen Foraker, Mar. 26, 1900.

9. When a public official accepts a gift, he dissolves the pearl of independence in the vinegar of obligation.

   Henry Fountain Ashurst (1874-1962), U.S. Senator (D-AZ). Quoted in Morris K. Udall, *Too Funny to Be President*, 1988.

10. For there is nothing so social by nature, *[and]* so unsocial by its corruption, as this race.

    Saint Augustine (354-430), Church father and philosopher. *The City of God*, XII.

11. If $50 will purchase the vote of one supervisor, the votes of how many supervisors will $350 purchase?

    Ambrose Bierce (1842-1914?), American journalist. Suggestion that this arithmetic problem be included in California textbooks. *News Letter*, May 8, 1869.

12. Getting an advantage at the expense of somebody else – that really is what graft is.

    Louis D. Brandeis (1856-1941), U.S. Supreme Court Justice. Quoted in *The Boston American*, July 22, 1905.

13. No, but it can be rented.

    John B. Breaux, U.S. Congressman and U.S. Senator (D-LA). Response when asked if his vote could be bought. Quoted in *The Washington Post*, Jan. 14, 1983.

14. That's garbage. Why can't they catch me in a sex scandal? I could use some good publicity.

    Willie Brown, Speaker of the California Assembly (D). On reports that the FBI was investigating his alleged involvement with a garbage company. Quoted in *Newsweek*, Dec. 31, 1990.

15. Next in importance to the maintenance of the Constitution and the Union is the duty of preserving the government free from the taint or even the suspicion of corruption.
James Buchanan (1791-1868), 15th President of the United States (D-PA). Inaugural address, Mar. 4, 1857.

16. Among a people generally corrupt, liberty cannot last long.
Edmund Burke (1729-1797), British statesman. Letter to the sheriffs of Bristol, 1777.

17. Alas, what is terrible is not the skeletons, but the fact that I am no longer terrified by them.
Anton Chekhov (1860-1904), Russian writer. *Notebooks.*

18. If a large city can, after intense intellectual efforts, choose for its mayor a man who merely will not steal from it, we consider it a triumph of the suffrage.
Frank Moore Colby (1865-1925), American writer and editor. *The Colby Essays,* I, 1926.

19. We did not wage the civil rights struggle merely to replace one form of judicial corruption with another.... It would be disloyal to ... my oath of office to attempt ... to set up a double standard for those who share my principles and those who oppose them. In order to be true to our principles we must demand that all persons live up to the same high standards.
John Conyers, Jr., U.S. Congressman (D-MI). Comment on voting for impeachment of the first black federal judge, Alcee L. Hastings, for corruption. Quoted in *The New York Times,* July 8, 1988.

20. Some governments are corrupt but are known for their competency in running the city. Others are incompetent but are considered "clean." *[Washington,]* DC's government is scandalously corrupt and hopelessly incompetent.
John C. Danforth, U.S. Senator (R-MO). Quoted in *Regardie's,* May 1989.

21. Debt is a prolific mother of folly and of crime.
Benjamin Disraeli, 1st Earl of Beaconsfield (1804-1881), Prime Minister of Great Britian (Conservative). *Henrietta Temple,* 1837.

22. The story in its facts and in its inferences is totally inaccurate. Gary Hart will not dignify it with a comment because it's character assassination. It's harassment. He's offended and he's outraged. He's furious. He's a victim. Someone has got to say at some point that enough is enough.
William Dixon, campaign manager, Hart for President. On reports that the Senator spent the night with a young woman while his wife was out of town. Quoted in *The Washington Post,* May 4, 1987.

23. When corruption enters, the election is no longer free, the choice of the people is affected.
William O. Douglas (1898-1980), U.S. Supreme Court Justice. *United States* v. *Classic,* 1940.

24. Dead flies cause the ointment of the apothecary to send forth a stinking savor; so too does a little folly for a person of wisdom and honor.
Old Testament, *Ecclesiastes* 10:1.

25. Gifts can incline great hearts.
English proverb, 1420.

26. Do not take bribes, for they blind the clear-eyed and upset the pleas of the just.
Old Testament, *Exodus* 23:8.

27. Little sins are great when great men commit them.
Abraham ibn Ezra (1097-1167), Spanish poet and grammarian. Commentary to *Genesis* 32:9.

28. Some statesmen go to Congress and some go to jail. It is the same thing, after all.
Eugene Field (1850-1895), American journalist and poet. *The Tribune Primer,* 1882.

29. We bought the son of a bitch, but he didn't stay bought.
Henry Clay Frick (1849-1919), American industrialist. Remark about Theodore Roosevelt, who accepted campaign contributions from big business in the presidential race of 1904 but later crusaded to reform monopolistic excesses of Frick and others.

30. Whatsoever a man soweth, that shall he also reap.
New Testament, *Galatians* 6:7.

31. We've passed from the age of the common man to the common crook.
John Kenneth Galbraith, American economist and U.S. Ambassador to India (D). Comment on Richard M. Nixon's administration. 1973.

32. Corruption, the most infallible symptom of constitutional liberty.
Edward Gibbon (1737-1794), British historian. *Decline and Fall of the Roman Empire,* V, 1788.

33. On 106 occasions, bribes were offered or discussed. On 105 of those occasions, the public official involved accepted the bribe. And on the other occasion, he turned it down because he didn't think the amount was large enough.

Rudolph Giuliani, U.S. Attorney, NY. Comment on an FBI sting operation to uncover government corruption. Quoted in *Newsweek*, Aug. 24, 1987.

34. There is no hope even that woman, with her right to vote, will purify politics.
Emma Goldman (1869-1940), American anarchist. *The Tragedy of Women's Emancipation*, 1911.

35. Most members of Congress were simply on the take from the savings and loan industry.
Edwin J. Gray, Chairman, Federal Home Loan Bank Board (R)). C-SPAN, *The Media and the Savings and Loan Scandal*, Nov. 3, 1990.

36. It is money that achieves success nowadays. Thank God, my political career ended with the beginning of this corrupt political era.
James W. Grimes (1816-1872), U.S. Senator and Governor of Iowa (R). Remark, Aug. 1869.

37. When the *[political]* clubhouse gets control of the seat of government, invariably the private interest outweighs the public interest, and corruption sets in.
Raymond B. Harding, Chairman, New York State Liberal Party. Quoted in *The New York Times*, Oct. 10, 1989.

38. Follow me around.... I'm serious. If anybody wants to put a tail on me, go ahead. They'd be very bored.
Gary Hart, U.S. Senator (D-CO). Quoted in *The New York Times Magazine*, May 3, 1987.

39. Both Republicans and Democrats are corrupt. The motto of the Democratic Party is, "Anything to get in." The motto of the Republican Party is "Anything to stay in."
William Randolph Hearst (1863-1951), U.S. Congressman (D-NY); founder, Independence League Party; journalist; and publisher. Speech, Independence League dinner, Apr. 13, 1907.

40. *[Milwaukee]* was in the grasp of the sinister and slimy hand of special interests, dive-keepers, crooked contractors, petty racketeers, and political bosses. The city was then as graft-ridden as any other.
Daniel Webster Hoan (1881-1961), Mayor of Milwaukee, WI (Socialist). Description of the city in 1912, when he took office. *City Government*, 1936.

41. If you have to pay money to have the right thing done, it is only just and fair to do it.
Collis P. Huntington (1821-1900), President, Southern Pacific Railroad. Letter to his agent and lobbyist, 1893.

42. The wonder of this month's military procurement scandal is that it can still scandalize us. The practices that are being exposed – the revolving door between government and industry, the mutual backscratching between the military and the companies that build the weapons – aren't abuses of the system. They are the system.
David Ignatius, American journalist and editor. *The Washington Post*, June 26, 1988.

43. The purification of politics is an iridescent dream. Government is force.... The Decalogue and the Golden Rule have no place in a political campaign. The commander who lost the battle through the activity of his moral nature would be the derision and jest of history.
John James Ingalls (1833-1900), U.S. Senator (R-KS). *New York World*, 1890.

44. Fire shall consume the tabernacles of bribery.
Old Testament, *Job* 15:34.

45. He that is without sin among you, let him cast the first stone.
New Testament, *John* 8:7.

46. When a gas and oil bill comes in here, everybody says it's crooked, for the same reason they think a girl on the street after midnight is probably up to something. But for me, I don't accuse a girl until I see her doing more than walking.
Lyndon B. Johnson (1908-1973), 36th President of the United States (D-TX). Quoted in Merle Miller, *Lyndon: An Oral Biography*, 1980.

47. One question, among the many others raised in recent weeks, had to do with whether my financial support in any way influenced several political figures to take up my cause. I want to say in the most forceful way that I can: I certainly hope so.
Charles H. Keating, Jr., owner and CEO, Lincoln Savings and Loan. Quoted in *The Washington Post*, Nov. 10, 1989.

48. Private profit by public servants at the expense of the general welfare is corrupt – period.
Estes Kefauver (1903-1963), U.S. Senator (D-TN). 1958.

49. I knew it was a swamp. I just didn't know that it was at the level it is.
Jack F. Kemp, U.S. Congressman and U.S. Secretary of Housing and Urban Development (R-NY). In reference to corruption in the department he had taken over. Quoted in *Newsweek*, June 26, 1989.

50. Corruption is not a party liability.
Frank R. Kent (1877-1958), American journalist. *Political Behavior*, 1928.

51. The Court is corrupt:
The fields are overgrown with weeds;
The granaries are empty.
Yet there are those dressed in fineries,
With swords at their sides:
Filled with food and drink,
Possessed of too much wealth.
This is called "Taking the lead in robbery."
Lao-tzu (c.604-531 B.C.), Chinese philosopher and founder of Taoism. *Tao Te Ching*.

52. For Louisiana politicians, bribery is an occupational hazard. When I took the oath of office, I didn't take an oath of poverty.
Richard Leche (1898-1965), Governor of Louisiana (D). Comment on his conviction for accepting bribes while in office. 1940.

53. While the people retain their virtue and vigilance, no administration, by any extreme of wickedness or folly, can very seriously injure the government in the short space of four years.
Abraham Lincoln (1809-1865), 16th President of the United States (R-IL). First inaugural address, Mar. 4, 1861.

54. A thug in a Congressman's suit.
Edward J. M. Little, U.S. Attorney, NY. In referring to U.S. Congressman Mario Biaggi (D-NY), defendant in the Wedtech corruption trial. Federal District Court, NY, July 20, 1988.

55. I have sat at the sumptuous table of power, but I have not run away with the silverware.
Diosdado Macapagal, President of the Philippines. Quoted in *Time*, Nov. 24, 1961.

56. If the chief party ... be corrupt, you must follow their humor and indulge them, and in that case honesty and virtue are pernicious.
Niccolò Machiavelli (1469-1527), Florentine statesman and political philosopher. *The Prince*, 1513.

57. Some degree of abuse is inseparable from the proper use of everything.
James Madison (1751-1836), 4th President of the United States (Democratic Republican-VA). Quoted in *Forbes*, Apr. 3, 1989.

58. I knew I took a risk, to confront people who were engaged in corrupt activities.
Leslie F. Manigat, President of Haiti. Reflection on the coup that ousted him from office. Quoted in *The New York Times*, June 26, 1988.

59. In any single "first-class" hotel in Washington, at any time during midsession, at least half a dozen of these lobbyesses are thus at work at once, each one roping in her dozen or ten of wild-cat Congressmen. The lever of lust is used to pry up more legislators to the sticking point than money itself avails to seduce.
Edward Winslow Martin (James D. McCabe) (1842-1883), American historian. *Behind the Scenes in Washington*, 1873.

60. There is always some basic principle that will ultimately get the Republican party together. If my observations are worth anything, that basic principle is the cohesive power of public plunder.
Anselm Joseph McLaurin (1848-1909), Governor of Mississippi and U.S. Senator (D). 1906.

61. Find the corrupt officials and then prosecute them and send them to prison!
John N. Mitchell (1913-1988), U.S. Attorney General (R). Speech, Republican Governors' Conference, Dec. 13, 1969.

62. I bought two baseballs and two bats for each playground in the city, and they say I ought to be sent to jail for giving the kids a ball to play with.
A. Harry Moore (1879-1952), Governor of New Jersey (D). Campaign speech, 1921.

63. *To* place and power all public spirit tends,
In place and power all public spirit ends;
Like hardy plants, that love the air and sky,
When out, 'twill thrive – but taken *in*, 'twill die!
Thomas Moore (1779-1852), Irish poet. *Corruption*.

64. A bastard who will stay bought.
Sydney E. Mudd (1858-1911), U.S. Congressman (R-MD). Definition of an honest politician.

65. The accomplice to the crime of corruption is frequently our own indifference.
Bess Myerson, Consumer Affairs Commissioner, New York City (D). Quoted in *Redbook*, Apr. 1974.

66. I apologize for causing public distrust in politics.
Yasuhiro Nakasone, Prime Minister of Japan. Statement to Japanese Parliament after a bribery scandal caused him to resign, May 25, 1989.

67. Old and corrupted nations cannot be governed on the same principles with those *[young nations]* which are simple and virtuous.
Napoléon I (1769-1821), military leader and Emperor of France. *Maxims*.

68. We find embezzlement, thievery, knavery, and criminal carelessness rife in American government under the Truman administration, yet Mr. *[Adlai]* Stevenson claims he can unscramble this odious egg. I say when an egg goes bad you throw it out.

Richard M. Nixon, 37th President of the United States (R-CA). Campaign speech, Oct. 3, 1952.

69. Cashing in. That's what we all do. It's called experience.

Lynn Nofziger, White House political director (R). To explain his conviction for corruption. ABC, *This Week*, July 31, 1988.

70. The entire state of California was controlled by the Southern Pacific Railroad. Not only did this political organization dominate the legislature, the courts, the municipal governments ... but it also had complete control of the newspapers of the state ... and through them controlled public opinion.... The Southern Pacific was openly the Republican party.

Fremont Older (1856-1935), American reformer and journalist. *My Own Story*, 1919.

71. *[Before the revolution]* the only *habeas corpus* of the Russian citizen was the institution of bribery.

Moissave Joseph Olgin (1878-1939), Russian writer and editor. *The Soul of the Russian Revolution*, 1917.

72. Corruption is like the garbage. It has to be removed daily.

Ignacio Pichardo Pagaza, Controller-General of Mexico. Quoted in *The New York Times*, Apr. 17, 1987.

73. We have a high tolerance for corruption here *[Chicago]* for officials who serve the public well in other ways.

Clarence Page, American political columnist. Quoted on PBS, *MacNeil-Lehrer News Hour*, Apr. 20, 1989.

74. Better a hundred times an honest and capable administration of an erroneous policy than a corrupt and incapable administration of a good one.

Edward John Phelps (1822-1900), U.S. Controller of the Treasury and founder, American Bar Association. Speech, New York City Chamber of Commerce, Nov. 19, 1889.

75. Every government is always growing corrupt.

Wendell Phillips (1811-1884), American orator and reformer. Quoted in Richard Hofstadter, *The American Political Tradition*, 1948.

76. When the Pentagon makes crooks rich and doesn't make America strong, it's a bum deal.

Ann Richards, Governor of Texas (D). Keynote address, Democratic National Convention, Atlanta, GA, July 18, 1988.

77. Like other states we've had our share of political corruption. Unlike other states we seem to be proud of it. We've had our bad moments, and we seem to have enjoyed them too much.

Charles E. Roemer III, U.S. Congressman and Governor of Louisiana (D). Interview, C-SPAN, Sept. 4, 1989.

78. France fell *[in World War II]* because there was corruption without indignation.

Romain Rolland (1866-1944), French writer. 1940.

79. Whenever the federal government puts up a lot of money for a program, there are people in this country who are going to find devious ways of getting it.

George Romney, U.S. Secretary of Housing and Urban Affairs and Governor of Michigan (R). Quoted in *The New York Times*, Aug. 13, 1989.

80. We must especially beware of that small group of selfish men who would clip the wings of the American eagle in order to feather their own nests.

Franklin D. Roosevelt (1882-1945), 32nd President of the United States (D-NY). Message to Congress, Jan. 6, 1941.

81. In corrupted Governments the Place is given for the sake of the Man; in good ones the Man is chosen for the sake of the Place.

George Savile, 1st Marquess of Halifax (1633-1695), Lord Privy Seal of England. *Political Thoughts and Reflections*, 1750.

82. In a corrupted Age the putting the World in order would breed Confusion.

George Savile. *Miscellaneous Thoughts and Reflections*, 1750.

83. Every time you turn over a new rock at HUD *[Department of Housing and Urban Affairs]*, you find more worms and slime underneath.

Charles E. Schumer, U.S. Congressman (D-NY). Comment on scandals at the U.S. Department of Housing and Urban Affairs, June 12, 1989.

84. Danger to the party lies with the sycophants who, by covering up every abuse ... defending every violation of the law ... have produced ... an atmosphere in which corruption can grow and thrive.

Carl Schurz (1829-1906), U.S. Senator (R-MO). Senate debate, 1872.

85. Bitterly experiencing the truth of the political maxim, that if the great have frequent need of base tools, they make amends to society by abandoning them to their fate, so soon as they find them no longer useful.

Walter Scott (1771-1832), Scottish writer. *Quentin Durward*, 1823.

86. The corruption of every government begins nearly always with that of principles.

Charles-Louis de Secondat, Baron de La Brède et de Montesquieu (1689-1755), French writer. *The Spirit of the Laws*, VIII, 1, 1748.

87. He who profits by crime is guilty of it.

Lucius Annaeus Seneca (The Younger) (4. B.C.-A.D. 65), Roman statesman, dramatist, and philosopher. *Medea*.

88. Something is rotten in the state of Denmark.

William Shakespeare (1564-1616), English writer. *Hamlet*, I, iv.

89. One corrupt official is one too many.

Adlai E. Stevenson (1900-1965), Governor of Illinois (D) and U.S. Ambassador to the United Nations. Speech, Democratic National Committee, Chicago, IL, Dec. 13, 1951.

90. Corruption in public office is treason.

Adlai E. Stevenson. Speech, Colorado Volunteers for Stevenson, Sept. 5, 1952.

91. Governments are not always overthrown by direct and open assaults.... The continual drippings of corruption may wear away the solid rock, when the tempest has failed to overturn it.

Joseph Story (1779-1845), U.S. Supreme Court Justice. *Miscellaneous Writings*, 1835.

92. Politics, as the word is commonly understood, are nothing but corruptions.

Jonathan Swift (1667-1745), Irish clergyman and satirist. *Thoughts on Various Subjects*, 1706.

93. First in war, first in peace, first in the pockets of its countrymen.

Time magazine. Description of New York City's Tammany Hall in the early 1930's.

94. Three things ruin a man – power, money, and women. I never wanted power, I never had any money, and the only woman in my life is up at the house right now.

Harry S Truman (1884-1972), 33rd President of the United States (D-MO). Statement to reporters on his 75th birthday, Independence, MO, May 8, 1959.

95. When I want to buy up any politicians, I always find the antimonopolists the most purchasable. They don't come so high.

William H. Vanderbilt (1821-1885), President, New York Central Railroad. Quoted in *The Chicago Daily News*, Oct. 9, 1882.

96. Chimney corner patriots abound; venality, corruption, prostitution of office for selfish ends, abuse of trust, perversion of funds from a national to a private use, and speculations upon the necessities of the times pervade all interests.

George Washington (1732-1799), 1st President of the United States (VA). 1776.

97. Few men have virtue to withstand the highest bidder.

George Washington. *Moral Maxims*.

98. The officer who accepts a bribe or neglects his duty must be fully aware that he is not simply an indifferently honest man, like many of his fellows in private trade, but the deliberate betrayer of the means of salvation to thousands of his fellow countrymen of this and all future generations.

Beatrice Potter Webb (1858-1943), British Socialist, reformer, and cofounder, Fabian Society. *The Co-operative Movement in Great Britain*, 1891.

99. Since I arrived here *[Congress]*, I have had an application to be concerned, professionally, against the bank, which I have declined, of course, although I believe my retainer has not been renewed, or refreshed as usual. If it is wished that my relation to the bank be continued, it may be well to send me the usual retainers.

Daniel Webster (1782-1852), U.S. Congressman (Federalist-NH and MA), U.S. Senator (Federalist and Whig-MA), and U.S. Secretary of State. Letter to Nicholas Biddle, Dec. 21, 1833.

100. With very few exceptions the city governments of the United States are the worst in Christendom – the most expensive, the most inefficient, and the most corrupt.

Andrew D. White (1832-1918), U.S. Ambassador to Germany. *Forum*, Dec. 1890.

101. We were as blind to real civil morals as the Spanish of the Inquisition must have been to the morality of Christ.

William Allen White (1868-1944), American writer and editor. *McClure's*, Jan. 1907.

Chapter 16

Defense and National Security

1. Only in time of fear is government thrown back to its primitive and sole function of self-defense, and the many interests of which it is the guardian become subordinated to that.

   Jane Addams (1860-1935), American social settlement worker, peace advocate, and Nobel Laureate in Peace. "Women, War and Suffrage," *Survey*, Nov. 6, 1915.

2. We have to rearrange in our minds what defense actually means. Does it mean you're going to try to protect the boundaries of a piece of land, or does it mean you're going to try to help the people on that piece of land to live a better life?

   Joan Baez, American folk singer and pacifist. Interview, *Playboy*, July 1970.

3. The control of prices is essential for the successful conduct of our national defense, for avoiding social and economic aftermaths of war, for taking the profits out of war, for the maintenance of morale, the stoppage of inflation, and the placing of America in the dominating place at the peace table.

   Bernard M. Baruch (1870-1965), Chairman, War Industries Board, and U.S. Delegate to the U.N. Atomic Energy Commission. Testimony, House Banking and Currency Committee, Sept. 19, 1941.

4. There will never be another Holocaust in the history of the Jewish people. Never again, never again!

   Menachem Begin (1913-1992), Prime Minister of Israel (Likud), and Nobel Laureate in Peace. Comment after Israel bombed a nuclear reactor in Iraq, June 1981.

5. The royal navy of England hath ever been its greatest defence and ornament; it is its ancient and natural strength – the floating bulwark of the island.

   William Blackstone (1723-1780), British jurist. *Commentaries on the Laws of England*, I, 1765.

6. It is essential that we maintain the capability at all times to inflict an unacceptable level of damage on the Soviet Union, including the destruction of two hundred major Soviet cities.

   Harold Brown, U.S. Secretary of Defense (D). 1978.

7. The notion that our only strategic choice is MAD *[mutually assured destruction]* – which means nothing less than an unstable pact to commit instant and total mutual suicide in the event of war – is irrational, immoral, and unnecessary.

   Zbigniew Brzezinski, U.S. Secretary of State and National Security Advisor (D). "Entering the Age of Defense," *The Washington Post*, Oct. 2, 1988.

8. When America is stronger, the world is safer.

   George Bush, 41st President of the United States (R-TX). Congressional address, Feb. 9, 1989.

9. We are a strong nation and we do not have to prove it, but our patience is beginning to look like a demonstration of cowardice of which we cannot be proud and which I will not allow to become a way of life.

   Jimmy Carter, 39th President of the United States (D-GA). Statement to French intermediaries during Iran hostage crisis, Mar. 25, 1980.

10. An armed Communist advances against you and you react against him. Therefore, you are a reactionary!

    Winston Churchill (1874-1965), Prime Minister of Great Britain (Conservative). Comment when accused of being a reactionary for supporting the Greek royalists with the U.S., against the Communists. Debate, House of Commons, 1946.

11. An army abroad is of little use unless there are prudent counsels at home. *(Parvi enim sunt foris arma, nisi est consilium domi.)*

    Marcus Tullius Cicero (106-43 B.C.), Roman statesman and writer. *De Officiis*, I.

12. If anyone were to suggest that we should be prepared to burn a woman at the stake in the name of national security, he would be taken to a mental ward. But if someone were to be prepared to burn millions of women in the name of national security, he is highly electable to the highest office of the land.
William Sloane Coffin, Jr., American clergyman and President, SANE/Freeze. PBS, *To What End?*, Oct. 10, 1988.

13. Everything belongs to the fatherland when the fatherland is in danger.
Georges-Jacques Danton (1759-1794), French revolutionary and Jacobin. Speech, National Assembly, Paris, Aug. 28, 1792.

14. Assure personal survival in any kind of disaster.
John E. Davis, Governor of North Dakota (R) and U.S. Civil Defense Director. Quoted in *The Washington Post*, Jan. 15, 1973.

15. Defend yourselves instantly, and I say you will be wise; delay it, and you may wish in vain to do so hereafter.
Demosthenes (385?-322 B.C.), Athenian statesman. Speech urging resistance to Philip of Macedon, 341 B.C.

16. There is one safeguard known generally to the wise, which is an advantage and security to all, but especially to democracies as against despots. What is it? Distrust.
Demosthenes. *Philippic*.

17. In an age of bullies, we cannot afford to be a sissy.
William J. Donovan (1883-1959), Director, Office of Strategic Services (precursor to CIA), and U.S. Assistant Attorney General. Quoted in Nathan Miller, *Spying for America*, 1989.

18. If the national security is involved, anything goes. There are no rules.
Helen Gahagan Douglas (1900-1980), U.S. Congresswoman (D-CA). Quoted in *Ms.*, Oct. 1973.

19. Even in matters of defense – the purpose for which government was instituted among men – no government can promise any longer that it can protect civilians and that they are not going to be harmed by war.
Peter F. Drucker, American management writer. Quoted in *U.S. News & World Report*, Dec. 21, 1981.

20. Local defenses must be reinforced by the further deterrent of massive retaliatory power.
John Foster Dulles (1888-1959), U.S. Secretary of State and U.S. Senator (R-NY). Speech, New York City, 1954.

21. In the last resort nations can only find security in doing what their material interests dictate.
Abba Eban, Foreign Secretary, Israel (Labour) and Israeli Ambassador to the United Nations. Speech, Washington, DC, May 18, 1989.

22. If all that Americans want is security, they can go to prison.
Dwight D. Eisenhower (1890-1969), 34th President of the United States (R-KS). Remark when president of Columbia University, 1949.

23. A man's own safety is a god that sometimes makes very grim demands.
George Eliot (Mary Ann Evans) (1819-1880), British writer. *Romola*, 1863.

24. Our neutrality is our security.
Guillermo Endara, President of Panama. Interview, ABC, *This Week*, Jan. 28, 1990.

25. To deploy this *[antiballistic missile system]* would jeopardize our security rather than improve it.
J. William Fulbright, U.S. Senator (D-AR). Remark, Senate debate on the ABM treaty. Quoted on PBS, *War and Peace in the Nuclear Age*, Mar. 6, 1989.

26. No government, no head of government can last if the people feel that this government is not going to defend the security of the country.
Indira Gandhi (1917-1984), Prime Minister of India. Speech, Columbia University, New York City, Nov. 7, 1971.

27. Wake up, America.
Augustus P. Gardner (1865-1881), U.S. Congressman (R-MA). Speech, House of Representatives, Oct. 16, 1916.

28. For mere revenge I would do nothing. This nation is too great to look for mere revenge. But for the security of the future I would do everything.
James A. Garfield (1831-1881), 20th President of the United States (R-OH). Speech after Abraham Lincoln's assassination, New York City, Apr. 15, 1865.

29. There is no safety where there is no strength.
William Lloyd Garrison (1805-1879), American editor and abolitionist. Quoted in Garrison and Garrison, *William Lloyd Garrison: The Story of His Life Told by His Children*, 1885-1889.

30. No man can rely upon any permanent security for his own rights unless he respects the rights of his neighbours.
William E. Gladstone (1809-1898), Prime Minister of Great Britain (Liberal). Speech, Dec. 9, 1879.

31. The basic reason Russia has not attacked us is that we can outproduce her.
Barry M. Goldwater, U.S. Senator (R-AZ). Quoted in *The Phoenix Gazette*, Aug. 9, 1956.

32. *[In a nuclear era]* it is necessary for all *[nations]* to feel they are equally secure.
Mikhail Gorbachev, President of the U.S.S.R. Quoted in Alan Sherr, *The Other Side of Arms Control*, 1988.

33. Safety from external danger is the most powerful director of national conduct.
Alexander Hamilton (1755-1804), Member, Continental Congress and Constitutional Convention, and U.S. Secretary of the Treasury (Federalist-NY). *The Federalist*, No. 8, Nov. 20, 1787.

34. The rights of neutrality will only be respected when they are defended by an adequate power. A nation, despicable by its weakness, forfeits even the privilege of being neutral.
Alexander Hamilton. *The Federalist*, No. 11, 1787.

35. I wish for an America no less alert in guarding against dangers from within than it is watchful against enemies from without.
Warren G. Harding (1865-1923), 29th President of the United States (R-OH). Quoted in *The New York Times*, Mar. 5, 1921.

36. I could not conceive of any President engaging in all-out nuclear war unless we were in danger of all-out devastation ourselves.
Christian A. Herter (1895-1966), U.S. Secretary of State (R). Senate confirmation hearings, Apr. 21, 1959.

37. A man without a stick will be bitten even by a sheep.
Hindu proverb.

38. A "soft" approach toward the menace of Communism can only lead to national disaster. We cannot defeat Communism with Socialism, nor with secularism, nor with pacifism, nor with appeasement or accommodation. The fight against crime and Communism can be won, and it will be won, but only with the help of every decent American citizen.
J. Edgar Hoover (1895-1972), Director, Federal Bureau of Investigation. Speech, American Legion national convention, Washington, DC, Oct. 9, 1962.

39. The only foes that threaten America are the enemies at home, and these are ignorance, superstition, and incompetence.
Elbert Hubbard (1856-1915), American writer and publisher. *The Philistine*, 1912.

40. I believe that a navy is the greatest insurer of peace that we could possibly have – a navy commensurate with our resources and commensurate with the number of dependencies we have and commensurate with our population and commensurate with our influence as a world power.
Charles Evans Hughes (1862-1948), Chief Justice, U.S. Supreme Court and U.S. Secretary of State (R). Speech, Tippecanoe Club, Cleveland, OH, Jan. 29, 1908.

41. Drugs are the greatest threat to our national security.
Jesse L. Jackson, Shadow Senator (D-DC). ABC, *The Koppel Report*, Sept. 13, 1988.

42. If the *[present]* deterrent is the mutual annihilation of each other, what else do we need and why?
Jacob K. Javits (1904-1986), U.S. Congressman and U.S. Senator (R-NY). Quoted on PBS, *War and Peace in the Nuclear Age*, May 1989.

43. The only safety of the nation lies in a generous and expansive plan of conciliation *[after the Civil War]*.
Andrew Johnson (1808-1875), 17th President of the United States (War Democrat). Quoted in Howard K. Beale, *The Critical Year: A Study of Andrew Johnson*, 1930.

44. I want Joe Stalin to know that if he starts something at four o'clock in the morning, the fighting power and strength of America will be on the job at five o'clock in the morning.
Louis A. Johnson (1891-1956), U.S. Secretary of Defense (D). Speech, University of Virginia, Charlottesville, VA, 1950.

45. We don't propose to sit here in our rocking chair with our hands folded and let the Communists set up any government in the Western Hemisphere.
Lyndon B. Johnson (1908-1973), 36th President of the United States (D-TX). Statement on sending troops to the Dominican Republic, 1965.

46. The safety of the state is the highest law.
Justinian I (483-565), Emperor of Byzantium. *The Twelve Tables*.

47. My male colleagues sometimes wonder if I understand as much about defense as I ought to. Of course if I agree with them, they think that I do.
Nancy Landon Kassebaum, U.S. Senator (R-KS). Interview, C-SPAN, Oct. 9, 1989.

48. In times of clear and present danger, the courts have held that even the privileged rights of the First Amendment must yield to the public's need for national security.

John F. Kennedy (1917-1963), 35th President of the United States (D-MA). Comment made ten days after the Bay of Pigs invasion, Apr. 27, 1961.

49. Preparing for suicide is not a very intelligent means of defense.
Bruce Kent, British nuclear disarmament movement leader. Quoted in *The Observer*, Aug. 10, 1986.

50. When the guns of war become a national obsession, social needs inevitably suffer.
Martin Luther King, Jr. (1929-1968), American clergyman and civil rights leader. 1968.

51. Communism will never be defeated by atomic bombs or nuclear weapons.... Our greatest defense against Communism is to take offensive action in behalf of justice and righteousness.... We must ... seek to remove ... conditions of poverty, insecurity, injustice, and racial discrimination.
Martin Luther King, Jr. Quoted in Lawrence Wittner, *Rebels Against War*, 1969.

52. The art of government is to deal with threats before they become overwhelming.
Henry M. Kissinger, U.S. Secretary of State and National Security Advisor (R). NBC, *Meet the Press*, July 31, 1988.

53. The new technique of war has created the necessity of developing a new technique of civil defense. It is not just community singing, sweater knitting, and basket weaving that is needed.
Fiorello H. La Guardia (1882-1947), U.S. Congressman (R and Socialist) and Mayor of New York City (R and Fusion Party). Letter to Pres. Franklin D. Roosevelt, 1942.

54. When are we defending something that isn't worth defending anymore?
John Le Carré (John Moore Cornwell), British spy novelist. Interview, PBS, *MacNeil-Lehrer News Hour*, June 13, 1989.

55. A certain degree of preparation for war ... affords also the best security for the continuance of peace.
James Madison (1751-1836), 4th President of the United States (Democratic Republican-VA). Quoted in *Smithsonian*, Sept. 1987.

56. A defenseless country cannot be secure.
John Marshall (1755-1835), Chief Justice, U.S. Supreme Court. Quoted in John E. Oster, *The Political and Economic Doctrines of John Marshall*, 1914.

57. The dangers of atomic war are overrated. It would be hard on little, concentrated countries like England. In America we have lots of space.
Robert R. McCormick (1880-1955), American editor and publisher, *Chicago Tribune*. Feb. 23, 1950.

58. How is it possible for free institutions to flourish, or even maintain themselves, in a situation where defenses, civil and military, must be ceaselessly poised to meet an attack that might incinerate 50 million Americans – not in the space of an evening, but in the space of moments.
Brien McMahon (1903-1952), U.S. Senator (D-CT). Senate speech, 1950.

59. We will use nuclear weapons whenever it serves our vital interests.
Robert S. McNamara, U.S. Secretary of Defense (D). Speech, 1961.

60. How much do we really need for the defense of the United States of America? Only the defense to defend its shores? Well I suppose that the maximum for the defense of our shores is $1 billion. So the rest of our defense budget relates to what we regard as our responsibilities as a world power.
John McNaughton, U.S. Assistant Secretary of Defense. Quoted in David Halberstam, *The Best and the Brightest*, 1969.

61. To be or not to be is not a question of compromise. Either you be or you don't be.
Golda Meir (1898-1978), Prime Minister of Israel (Labour). On compromise with Israel's enemies. Remark at the White House, Dec. 12, 1974.

62. National security is not only building war machines to kill. National security is as much a policy of the living who prefer life over death, wellness over sickness, work over idleness, education over illiteracy, and food over hunger.
Patsy Takemoto Mink, U.S. Congresswoman (D-HI). Quoted in *Ms.*, Oct. 1981.

63. Deterrence is to prevent war, not to win a war.
François Mitterrand, President of France (Socialist). Quoted in *The Washington Post*, July 7, 1990.

64. For the welfare of the state, the one of my sons to whom God grants the sultanate may lawfully put his brothers to death.
Mohammed II (1429-1481), Ottoman (Turkish) sultan. Pronouncement before his death.

65. Preparation for war is a constant stimulus to suspicion and ill will.
James Monroe (1758-1831), 5th President of the United States (Democratic Republican-VA). Statement, Apr. 28, 1818.

66. When the enemy is right next door, no one from a distance has a right to dismiss the threat.
Bill Moyers, American journalist, Special Assistant to Pres. Lyndon B. Johnson, and White House Press Secretary. CNN, *Commentary*, Jan. 22, 1991.

67. The national security state controls the President. It controls most of the executive departments.
Daniel P. Moynihan, Chief American Delegate to the United Nations and U.S. Senator (D-NY). Quoted in *The New York Times Magazine*, Sept. 16, 1990.

68. The new test of classifying secret documents now seems to be not whether the publication of a document would affect the security of the nation, but whether it will affect the political security of the administration.
Richard M. Nixon, 37th President of the United States (R-CA). Statement, 1951.

69. The core of our defense is the faith we have in the institutions we defend.
Franklin D. Roosevelt (1882-1945), 32nd President of the United States (D-NY). Speech, Dayton, OH, Oct. 12, 1940.

70. When you see a rattlesnake poised to strike, you do not wait until he has struck before you crush him.
Franklin D. Roosevelt. Announcement that U.S. naval forces would attack German war vessels that entered "American-protected waters" despite our not being at war. Speech, Sept. 11, 1941.

71. We must be the great arsenal of democracy.
Franklin D. Roosevelt. Fireside Chat, Dec. 29, 1941.

72. It is my resolve and yours to build up our armed defenses. We shall build them to whatever heights the future may require. We shall build them swiftly, as the methods of warfare quickly change.
Franklin D. Roosevelt. Message to Congress, Feb. 1942.

73. Preparation for defense is an inalienable prerogative of a sovereign state.
Franklin D. Roosevelt. Quoted in Arthur M. Schlesinger, Jr., *The Imperial Presidency*, 1973.

74. The voters must choose: War from weakness, or peace through strength; suicide through surrendering our arms, or survival in freedom.
Phyllis Schlafly, President, Eagle Forum. In support of Barry Goldwater for President. *The Gravediggers* (with Adm. Chester Ward), 1964.

75. The notion of a defense that will protect American cities is one that will not be achieved, but it is that goal that supplies the political magic.
James R. Schlesinger, U.S. Secretary of Defense (R), U.S. Secretary of Energy, and Director, Central Intelligence Agency. Testimony, Senate Foreign Relations Committee, Feb. 1987.

76. Governments cannot be denied the right to legitimate self-defense once every means of peaceful settlement has been exhausted.
Second Vatican Council, *The Church in the Modern World*, Dec. 1965.

77. One cannot defend a state with mere words.
Caterina Sforza (1462-1509), Italian military and political ruler. Letter, Nov. 14, 1498.

78. Truth telling is not compatible with defence of the realm.
George Bernard Shaw (1856-1950), Nobel Laureate in Literature (Great Britain). *Heartbreak House*, 1917.

79. If any particular manufacture was necessary for national power and for the defense of society, it might not always be prudent to depend on our neighbor for supply. And if such manufacturers could not otherwise be supported at home, it might not be unreasonable that all other branches of industry be taxed to support it.
Adam Smith (1723-1790), Scottish political economist. Quoted in *The Washington Post*, July 22, 1990.

80. The key to security is public information.
Margaret Chase Smith, U.S. Congresswoman and U.S. Senator (R-ME). *Reader's Digest*, Mar. 1972.

81. War is like unto fire; and those who will not put aside weapons are themselves consumed by them. Thus, those who are unable to understand the dangers inherent in employing troops are equally unable to understand the advantageous ways of doing so.
Sun-tzu (c.400 B.C.), Chinese writer of the Age of Warring States. *The Art of War*.

82. We should provide in peace what we need in war.
Publilius Syrus (c.43 B.C.), Syrian writer. *Maxims*.

83. The next war is going to be a "come as you are" party. You go with what you've got.
John G. Tower (1925-1991), U.S. Senator (R-TX). Statement, Dec. 25, 1988.

84. If we can make it sufficiently clear ... that any armed attack affecting our national security would be met with overwhelming force, the armed attack might never occur.

Harry S Truman (1884-1972), 33rd President of the United States (D-MO). Inaugural address, Jan. 20, 1949.

85. It is a lot better to have a strong national defense than a balanced budget.

Harry S Truman. Statement, Feb. 17, 1957.

86. To be prepared for war is one of the most effectual means of preserving peace.

George Washington (1732-1799), 1st President of the United States (VA). Address to Congress, Jan. 8, 1790.

87. God grants liberty only to those who love it, and are always ready to guard and defend it.

Daniel Webster (1782-1852), U.S. Congressman (Federalist-NH and MA), U.S. Senator (Federalist and Whig-MA), and U.S. Secretary of State. Speech, June 3, 1834.

88. Defense expenditures in democracies have always been unpopular.

Caspar Weinberger, U.S. Secretary of Defense and U.S. Secretary of Health, Education and Welfare (R). Interview, PBS, *Adam Smith's Money World*, Jan. 14, 1989.

89. Cutting the heart out of our defenses for the next several years is roughly like canceling all your fire insurance because you did not have a fire last year.

Caspar Weinberger. Reaction to proposals to reduce defense expenditures in a time of international tranquility. *The New York Times*, Nov. 28, 1989.

90. Ten men in the basement of City Hall will not save us from an atomic holocaust.

Kevin White, Mayor of Boston, MA (D). On why he abolished Boston's civil defense agency. Quoted in *The Washington Post*, Jan. 15, 1973.

91. Faith and confidence are the bedrock of all states, free and tyrannical. Without faith no state can survive.

Theodore H. White (1915-1986), American political analyst and writer. *Breach of Faith*, 1975.

92. What we demand is that the world be made fit and safe to live in.

Woodrow Wilson (1856-1924), 28th President of the United States (D-NJ). 1918.

Chapter 17

Democracy

1. Democracy is like sex. When it is good, it is very, very good. And when it is bad, it is still pretty good.
Anonymous.

2. She had got to the bottom of this business of democratic government and found out that it was nothing more than government of any other kind.
Henry Adams (1838-1918), American historian. *Democracy*, 1880.

3. As the happiness of the people is the sole end of government, so the consent of the people is the only foundation of it.
John Adams (1735-1826), 2nd President of the United States (Federalist-MA). Proclamation, 1774.

4. Democracy never lasts long. It soon wastes, exhausts, and murders itself. There never was a democracy that did not commit suicide.
John Adams. Letter to John Taylor.

5. I've never known a country to be starved into democracy.
George D. Aiken (1892-1984), Governor of Vermont and U.S. Senator (R). Favoring an end to the U.S. economic boycott of Cuba. Press statement, Mar. 27, 1964.

6. The people's government has come to be less and less the people's business.
Joseph Alsop (1910-1989), American political columnist. *The Reporters's Trade*, 1958.

7. A government by the passions of the multitude, or, no less correctly, according to the vices and ambitions of their leaders, is a democracy.
Fisher Ames (1758-1808), U.S. Congressman (Federalist-MA). *The Dangers of American Liberty*, 1805.

8. Democracy is the only form of government which dislikes itself.
Maurice Sheldon Amos (1872-1940), British jurist. Quoted by E. S. P. Haynes, *Life, Law and Letters*, 1936.

9. Democracy takes time. Dictatorship is quicker, but too many people get shot.
Jeffrey Archer, Member of Parliament, Great Britain, and mystery writer. *A Very British Coup*, 1980.

10. A democracy is a government in the hands of men of low birth, no property, and vulgar employments.
Aristotle (384-322 B.C.), Greek philosopher and teacher. *Politics*.

11. Democracy is the form of government in which the free are rulers.
Aristotle. *Ibid.*

12. A democracy, when put to the strain, grows weak; and it is supplanted by oligarchy *[rule by the few]*.
Aristotle. *Rhetoric*, I.

13. Democracy means government by discussion but it is only effective if you stop people talking.
Clement R. Attlee, Viscount Prestwood (1883-1967), Prime Minister of Great Britain (Labour). Quoted in Anthony Sampson, *Anatomy of Britain*, 1962.

14. We must remember that the people do not belong to the government but that government belongs to the people.
Bernard M. Baruch (1870-1965), Chairman, War Industries Board, and U.S. Delegate to the U.N. Atomic Energy Commission. Speech, U.N. Atomic Energy Commission, June 14, 1946.

15. The real democratic idea is not that every man shall be on a level with every other, but that everyone shall have liberty, without hindrance, to be what God made him.
Henry Ward Beecher (1813-1887), American clergyman and writer. *The Dishonest Politician*.

16. The primal principle of democracy is the worth and dignity of the individual.
Edward Bellamy (1850-1898), American Utopian and writer. *Looking Backward*, 1888.

17. The test of democracy is freedom of criticism.
David Ben-Gurion (1886-1973), 1st Prime Minister of Israel. Quoted in James G. McDonald, *My Mission in Israel*, 1951.

18. The function of a parliamentary democracy, under universal suffrage, historically considered, is to expose wealth-privilege to the attacks of the people.
Aneurin Bevan (1897-1960), Minister of Health, Great Britian (Socialist). Quoted in *The New York Times Magazine*, Oct. 27, 1957.

19. The rule of liberty that all government derives its authority from the consent of the governed applies only to those who are capable of self government. We govern the Indians without their consent, we govern our territories without their consent, we govern our children without their consent.
Albert J. Beveridge (1862-1927), U.S. Senator (R-IN) and founder, Progressive League. Speech, Indianapolis, IN, Sept. 16, 1898.

20. Democracy is the best revenge.
Benazir Bhutto, Prime Minister of Pakistan. Speech, joint session of Congress, June 7, 1989.

21. One of the distinctions between democracy and other forms of government is that while democracy is messy on the surface, other forms of government are messy underneath.
Daniel Boorstin, American historian and Librarian of Congress. Testimony, U.S. Senate Select Committee on Watergate, July 7, 1973.

22. An article of the democratic faith is that greatness lies in each person.
William W. Bradley, U.S. Senator (D-NJ). Commencement address, Middlebury College, CT, May 1989.

23. Democracy is moral before it is political.
Louis D. Brandeis (1856-1941), U.S. Supreme Court Justice. 1901.

24. The wastes of democracy are among the greatest obvious wastes, but we have compensations in democracy which far outweigh that waste and make it more efficient than absolutism.
Louis D. Brandeis. *Other People's Money*, 1914.

25. Democracy substitutes self-restraint for external restraint. It is more difficult to maintain than to achieve.
Louis D. Brandeis. Letter to R. W. Bruere, Feb. 25, 1922.

26. Democracy means not merely, I had almost said not so much, the rights of the whole people, as the duties of the whole people.
Louis D. Brandeis. Quoted by Solomon Goldman, *The Words of Justice Brandeis*, 1953.

27. Well, will anybody deny now that the government at Washington, as regards its own people, is the strongest government in the world at this hour? And for this simple reason, that it is based on the will, and the good will, of an instructed people.
John Bright (1811-1889), Member of Parliament, Great Britain (Liberal). Speech at Rochdale, England, Nov. 24, 1863.

28. Whatever faults modern democracies may have committed ... the faults chargeable on monarchs and oligarchies have been less pardonable and more harmful to the peace and progress of mankind.
James Bryce (1838-1922), British Ambassador to the United States. *Modern Democracies*, 1921.

29. The people are the masters.
Edmund Burke (1729-1797), British statesman. Feb. 11, 1780.

30. We love your adherence to democratic principles and democratic processes.
George Bush, 41st President of the United States (R-TX). Toast to Ferdinand Marcos, President of the Philippines, 1981 (Bush was then Vice President).

31. Legitimacy *[of governments]* is not bought by force; it is earned by the consensus of the people.
George Bush. Press conference, Jan. 13, 1991.

32. Which is better, to be ruled by one tyrant three thousand miles away, or by three thousand tyrants not a mile away?
Mather Byles (1706-1788), Massachusetts clergyman and British loyalist. Sermon, Boston, MA, 1776.

33. The experience of democracy is like the experience of life itself – always changing, infinite in its variety, sometimes turbulent and all the more valuable for having been tested by adversity.
Jimmy Carter, 39th President of the United States (D-GA). Speech to Parliament of India, New Delhi, Jan. 2, 1978.

34. Democracy means government by the uneducated, while aristocracy means government by the badly educated.
G. K. Chesterton (1874-1936), British writer. Quoted in *The New York Times*, Feb. 1, 1931.

35. Democracy is the worst form of government except all those other forms that have been tried from time to time.

Winston Churchill (1874-1965), Prime Minister of Great Britain (Conservative). Speech, House of Commons, Nov. 1947.

36. We live in a moment of change, the winds of democracy are blowing across a good part of the world.

Luis Donaldo Colosio, National Chairman, Institutional Revolutionary Party (PRI) of Mexico. Quoted in *The Los Angeles Times*, July 5, 1989.

37. If our democracy is to flourish, it must have criticism; if our government is to function, it must have dissent.

Henry Steele Commager, American historian. *Freedom, Loyalty, Dissent*, 1954.

38. If the people be governors, who shall be governed?

John Cotton (1585-1652), New England clergyman. Letter, 1633.

39. The one pervading evil of democracy is the tyranny of the majority.

John Dahlberg, 1st Baron Acton (1834-1902), British historian. *The History of Freedom*, 1907.

40. Neither current events nor history shows that the majority rules, or ever did rule.

Jefferson Davis (1808-1889), U.S. Congressman (D-MS), U.S. Senator, U.S. Secretary of War, and President of the Confederate States of America. Letter, July 17, 1864.

41. We cannot do without dictatorship. We must use it when necessary.

Deng Xiaoping, Premier of China. May 25, 1989.

42. Democracy doesn't mean electing a dictator every five years.

Hernando De Soto, Central Bank Director and economist, Peru. Interview, PBS, *American Interests*, Jan. 6, 1990.

43. A democracy is more than a form of government; it is primarily a mode of associated living, of conjoint communicated experience.

John Dewey (1859-1952), American philosopher and educator. *Democracy and Education*, 1916.

44. The method of democracy is to bring ... conflicts out into the open where their special claims can be seen and appraised, where they can be discussed and judged.

John Dewey. Quoted in *Columbia Journalism Review*, Sept.-Oct. 1990.

45. The great postulate of our democracy is confidence in the common sense of the people and in their maturity of judgment, even on great issues – once they know the facts.

William O. Douglas (1898-1980), U.S. Supreme Court Justice. *We the Judges*, 1956.

46. American democracy is at its best in its talent for the transfer of power.

Abba Eban, Foreign Secretary, Israel (Labour) and Israeli Ambassador to the United Nations. *An Autobiography*, 1977.

47. Democracy becomes a government of bullies tempered by editors.

Ralph Waldo Emerson (1803-1882), American writer. *Journals*, 1847.

48. Give me a bad democracy, a sick democracy, but democracy!

Oriana Fallaci, Italian journalist. Interview, *Playboy*, Nov. 1981.

49. Two cheers for democracy: one because it admits variety and two because it permits criticism.

E. M. Forster (1879-1970), British novelist. *Two Cheers for Democracy*, 1951.

50. In a democracy we assume that people can define their own interest and vote that way.

Donald Fowler, Chairman, South Carolina Democratic Party. PBS, *Firing Line*, Oct. 1, 1988.

51. A constitutional democracy like ours is perhaps the most difficult of man's social arrangements to manage successfully. Our scheme of society is more dependent than any other form of government on knowledge and wisdom and self-discipline for the achievement of its aims. For our democracy implies the reign of reason on the most extensive scale.

Felix Frankfurter (1882-1965), U.S. Supreme Court Justice. *Youngstown Sheet & Tube Co.* v. *Sawyer*, 1951.

52. Democratic government may indeed be defined as the government which accepts in the fullest sense responsibility to explain itself.

Felix Frankfurter. Quoted in Arthur M. Schlesinger, Jr., *The Imperial Presidency*, 1973.

53. Democracy is not a state in which people act like sheep. Under democracy individual liberty of opinion and action is jealously guarded.

Mohandas K. Gandhi (1869-1948), Indian political and spiritual leader. *Young India*, Mar. 22, 1922.

54. On the eve of the first Tuesday in November, once again we are faced with the ugly paradox of thirty-second-spot democracy: To prove they are worthy of governing us in all that we hold dear, America's politicians must behave in a way that proves they aren't.

Bob Garfield, editor-at-large, *Advertising Age*. Comment on negative campaigning. *Advertising Age*, Nov. 5, 1990.

55. All free governments are managed by the combined wisdom and folly of the people.

James A. Garfield (1831-1881), 20th President of the United States (R-OH). Attributed.

56. The great thing about democracy is we're free to take in all this information and make up our own minds about what is truth.

Michael Gartner, President, NBC News. Quoted in *Brown Alumni Monthly*, May 1991.

57. The evils we experience flow from an excess of democracy.

Elbridge Gerry (1744-1814), U.S. Congressman (Anti-Federalist-MA) and Vice President of the United States (D). Debate, Constitutional Convention, Philadelphia, PA, 1787.

58. In this situation *[perestroika]* problems and difficulties are unavoidable. For it involves far-reaching changes in everything – in the way of life, the attitude toward work and civic duty. We have chosen, definitively and irrevocably, the route leading to new forms of life: democratizing our society in all spheres.

Mikhail Gorbachev, President of the U.S.S.R. To reporters, London, Apr. 1989.

59. Democracies have been, and governments called, free; but the spirit of independence and the consciousness of inalienable rights were never before transfused into the minds of a whole people.

Sarah J. Hale (1788-1879), American magazine editor. *Sketches of American Character*, 1829.

60. The only legitimate right to govern is an express grant of power from the governed.

William Henry Harrison (1773-1841), 9th President of the United States (Whig-OH). Inaugural address, Mar. 4, 1841.

61. We are in a bad way. That herd of wild asses' colts *[see Job 11:12]*, braying and kicking up their heels, is an unsatisfactory result of a hundred years of democracy.

John Milton Hay (1838-1905), U.S. Ambassador to Great Britain and U.S. Secretary of State (R). Letter to William D. Howells, Feb. 20, 1877.

62. You would be wrong to assume democracy would be the only alternative if the old regimes *[in the Middle East]* fell. There is a much better organized alternative already waiting, and that is ... fundamentalism.

Muhammad Heikal, Egyptian journalist. Quoted in *Newsweek*, Jan. 7, 1991.

63. The democracy of the Western countries is the predecessor of Marxism, which would be unthinkable without democracy.

Adolf Hitler (1889-1945), Führer of the Third German Reich. *Mein Kampf*, 1933.

64. In contrast to totalitarianism, democracy can face and live with the truth about itself.

Sidney Hook (1902-1989), American philosopher. *The New York Times Magazine*, Sept. 30, 1951.

65. Democracy is a fickle employer.

Herbert Hoover (1874-1964), 31st President of the United States (R-IA). Quoted in "39 Men" exhibit.

66. I swear to the Lord
I still can't see
Why Democracy means
Everybody but me.

Langston Hughes (1902-1967), American poet. *The Black Man Speaks*, 1943.

67. Democratic government consists of listening, deciding, persuading.

Douglas Hurd, Foreign Minister, Great Britain (Conservative). Quoted in *The Washington Post*, Nov. 24, 1990.

68. The death of democracy is not likely to be an assassination from ambush. It will be a slow extinction from apathy, indifference, and undernourishment.

Robert M. Hutchins (1899-1977), President, University of Chicago, and President, Center for the Study of Democratic Institutions. *The Great Books*, 1932.

69. America's experiment with government of the people, by the people, and for the people depends not only on constitutional structure and organization, but also on the commitment, person to person, that we make to each other.

Robert M. Hutchins. *The Power of Reason*, 1964.

70. Democracy is only an experiment in government, and it has the obvious disadvantage of counting votes instead of weighing them.

William Ralph Inge (1860-1965), Anglican prelate and dean of St. Paul's, London. *Possible Recovery?*

71. I will govern according to the common weal, but not according to the common will.

James I (1566-1625), King of England. Quoted in J. R. Green, *The History of the English People*, 1880.

72. Every government degenerates when trusted to the rulers of the people alone. The people themselves therefore are its only safe depositories.

Thomas Jefferson (1743-1826), 3rd President of the United States (Democratic Republican-VA). *Notes on the State of Virginia*, 1784.

73. Public participation in the process of government is the essence of democracy.

Lyndon B. Johnson (1908-1973), 36th President of the United States (D-TX). Message to Congress, May 25, 1967.

74. It is a common failing of totalitarian regimes that they cannot really understand the nature of our democracy. They mistake dissent for disloyalty. They mistake restlessness for a rejection of policy. They mistake a few committees for a country. They mistake individual speeches for public policy.

Lyndon B. Johnson. Speech, San Antonio, TX, Sept. 29, 1967.

75. The deadliest foe of democracy is not autocracy but liberty frenzied.

Otto H. Kahn (1867-1934), American banker and publicist. Speech, University of Wisconsin, Madison, WI, Jan. 14, 1918.

76. Racism is the unfinished business of American democracy.

Marvin I. Kalb, American journalist. Speech, John F. Kennedy School for Government, Harvard University, Cambridge, MA, May 1990.

77. Democracy is the superior form of government, because it is based on a respect for man as a reasonable being.

John F. Kennedy (1917-1963), 35th President of the United States (D-MA). *Why England Slept*, 1940.

78. Freedom has many flaws and our democracy is imperfect, but we have never had to put up a wall to keep our people in.

John F. Kennedy. Speech at City Hall, West Berlin, June 26, 1963.

79. Democracy is a difficult kind of government. It requires the highest qualities of self-discipline, restraint, a willingness to make commitments and sacrifices for the general interest, and it also requires knowledge.

John F. Kennedy. Speech, Dublin Castle, Ireland, June 28, 1963.

80. Democracy is finished in England.

Joseph P. Kennedy (1888-1969), American businessman and U.S. Ambassador to Great Britain (D). Interview, *The Boston Globe*, Nov. 1940.

81. If you stand before the people ... and tell them that anything goes so long as they give government the power to deal with the consequences, then you end up with a weak people, a strong government, and no democracy.

Alan L. Keys, Maryland Republican senatorial candidate. Quoted in *The Washington Post*, June 26, 1988.

82. If the people want a government of their own, they must do the work of making it their own.

Robert M. La Follette (1855-1925), Governor of Wisconsin and U.S. Senator (R). Senate speech, Jan. 16, 1919.

83. Democracy is of great importance for the working class in its struggle for freedom against the capitalists. But ... it is only one of the stages in the course of development from feudalism to capitalism, and from capitalism to Communism.

V. I. Lenin (1870-1924), Premier of the U.S.S.R. *The State and Revolution*, 1917.

84. A democracy is a state which recognizes the subjection of the minority to the majority, that is, an organization for the systematic use of violence by one class against the other, by one part of the population against another.

V. I. Lenin. *Ibid.*

85. Of the many things we have done to democracy in the past, the worst has been the indignity of taking it for granted.

Max Lerner, American journalist and historian. Quoted in George Seldes, *The Great Quotations*, 1983.

86. On the whole, with scandalous exceptions, democracy has given the ordinary worker more dignity than he ever had.

Sinclair Lewis (1885-1951), Nobel Laureate in Literature (United States). *It Can't Happen Here*, 1935.

87. It is citizen participation that nourishes the strength of a democracy.

David E. Lilienthal (1899-1981), Chairman, Tennessee Valley Authority, and Chairman, U.S. Atomic Energy Commission. *This I Do Believe*, 1949.

88. As I would not be a slave, so I would not be a master. Whatever differs from this, to the extent

of the difference, is no democracy.

Abraham Lincoln (1809-1865), 16th President of the United States (R-IL). Fragment, "On Slavery," Aug. 1, 1858.

89. I am a firm believer in the people. If given the truth, they can be depended upon to meet any national crisis. The great point is to bring them the real facts.

Abraham Lincoln. Quoted in George Seldes, *The Great Quotations*, 1983.

90. "The consent of the governed" is more than a safeguard against ignorant tyrants: it is an insurance against benevolent despots as well.

Walter Lippmann (1889-1974), American political columnist. *A Preface to Politics*, 1914.

91. Democracy does not mean perfection. It means a chance to fight for improvement.

Meyer London (1871-1926), U.S. Congressman (Socialist-NY). Labor Day speech, Brooklyn, NY, 1915.

92. Democracy is like a raft. You won't sink, but you'll always have your feet wet.

Russell B. Long, U.S. Senator (D-LA). Quoted in *Reader's Digest*, Jan. 1988.

93. Democracy gives every man a right to be his own oppressor.

James Russell Lowell (1819-1891), U.S. Ambassador to Spain and England. *The Bigelow Papers*, II, 1867.

94. Anyone who attacks the authority of the government is against democracy, against the nation.

Patrice Lumumba (1925-1961), 1st Prime Minister of the Congo (Zaire). Quoted in Jean Van Lierde, *Lumumba Speaks*, 1972.

95. Thus our *[British]* democracy was from an early period the most aristocratic, and our aristocracy the most democratic.

Thomas Babington Macaulay, 1st Baron Macaulay (1800-1859), British historian and Secretary of War (Liberal). *History of England*, I, 1848.

96. American democracy must be a failure because it places the supreme authority in the hands of the most ignorant part of society.

Thomas Babington Macaulay. Quoted by Pres. Franklin D. Roosevelt, 1937.

97. Democracies have ever been spectacles of turbulence and contention, have ever been found incompatible with personal security or the rights of property, and have in general been as short in their lives as they have been violent in their deaths.

James Madison (1751-1836), 4th President of the United States (Democratic Republican-VA). *The Federalist*, No. 10, Nov. 23, 1787.

98. What right has the West, what right have the whites anywhere, to teach us about democracy when they executed those who asked for democracy during the time of the colonial era?

Nelson Mandela, Deputy President, African National Congress, South Africa. Speech, Nairobi, Kenya, July 13, 1990.

99. Free and open communication is the best guarantee of democracy.

Edward Markey, U.S. Senator (D-MA). *The New York Times*, June 13, 1990.

100. What are the maxims of democracy?... A strict observance of justice and public faith, and a steady adherence to virtue.

John Marshall (1755-1835), Chief Justice, U.S. Supreme Court. Quoted in Albert J. Beveridge, *The Life of John Marshall*, I, 1916.

101. A democratic government must always be left free to be operated upon by the will of the majority of the time being. All that the government of the day can do is to ascertain what now appears to be the best principle.

Harriet Martineau (1802-1876), British reformer. *Society in America*, 1837.

102. Resistance to absolutism is characteristic of democratic progress.

Tomas G. Masaryk (1850-1937), 1st President of Czechoslovakia. *The Making of a State, 1914-1918*, 1927.

103. The most profound argument for democracy is its faith in man.

Tomas G. Masaryk. Attributed.

104. Democracy is not only a form of government, it is not only what is written in constitutions. Democracy is a view of life, it rests on faith in men, in humanity, and in human nature.

Tomas G. Masaryk. Quoted in Karel Capek, *Masaryk on Thought and Life*, 1938.

105. Notwithstanding the oppression and injustice experienced among us from democracy, the genius of the people is in favor of it, and the genius of the people must be consulted.

George Mason (1725-1792), Member, Virginia and Federal Constitutional Conventions. 1789.

106. Democracy is liberty plus economic security. We Americans want to pray, think as we please – and eat regular.

Maury Maverick (1895-1954), U.S. Congressman (D-TX). Attributed.

107. Democracy without a free press is inconceivable.
Ian Robert Maxwell (1923-1991), Member of Parliament, Great Britain (Conservative) and newspaper publisher. Speech, National Press Club, Washington, DC, June 1, 1991.

108. Democracy is ... a form of religion; it is the worship of jackals by jackasses.
H. L. Mencken (1880-1956), American journalist. *Sententiae*, 1920.

109. Democracy is the theory that the common people know what they want and deserve to get it good and hard.
H. L. Mencken. *A Book of Burlesques*, 1920.

110. Democracy is hypocrisy without limitation.
Iskander Mirza (1899-1969), President of Pakistan. Quoted in *Time*, Oct. 20, 1958.

111. American democracy is a unique form of government which at the same time requires *[political]* competition and cooperation.
George J. Mitchell, U.S. Senator (D-ME). PBS, *MacNeil-Lehrer News Hour*, Aug. 4, 1989.

112. Tell me if ever in history there was a government which was based exclusively upon the consent of the people, and which was ready to dispense altogether with the use of force. There has never been and never will be such a government.
Benito Mussolini (1883-1945), dictator of Italy (Fascist). *Gerarchia*, Mar. 1923.

113. Politically, we are currently in the process of a massive shift from a representative to a participatory democracy.
John Naisbitt, American futurist and writer. *Megatrends*, 1982.

114. In a dictatorship the people are afraid to tell the truth to their leaders; in a democracy the leaders are afraid to tell the truth to the people.
Richard J. Needham, Canadian columnist. *The Globe and Mail*, Dec. 14, 1976.

115. Democracy is good. I say this because other systems are worse.
Jawaharlal Nehru (1889-1964), 1st Prime Minister of India. Quoted in *The New York Times*, Jan. 25, 1961.

116. Man's capacity for justice makes democracy possible; but man's inclination to injustice makes democracy necessary.
Reinhold Niebuhr (1892-1971), American Protestant theologian. *The Children of Light and the Children of Darkness*, 1944.

117. Democracy represents the disbelief in all great men and in all elite societies: Everybody is everybody's equal.
Friedrich Wilhelm Nietzsche (1844-1900), German philosopher. *The Will to Power*, 1888.

118. For democracy to survive in any country it must evolve from within and not be the one imposed from without.
Peter Maragia Nyamweya, Kenyan High Commissioner in Canada. Letter to *The Globe and Mail*, Nov. 28, 1990.

119. The boycott is a splendid example of consumer democracy at its best.
Anthony O'Reilly, Chairman, H. J. Heinz Co. In reference to environmentalists' boycott of Heinz's tunafish products because the methods used to catch tuna also destroyed dolphins. Quoted in *The Washington Post*, Apr. 17, 1990.

120. Every government is a parliament of whores. The trouble is, in a democracy the whores are us.
P. J. O'Rourke, Washington, DC, correspondent, *Rolling Stone*. *Parliament of Whores*, 1991.

121. There is one thing better than good government, and that is government in which all the people have a part.
Walter Hines Page (1855-1918), U.S. Ambassador to Great Britain. Quoted in Burton J. Hendrick, *The Life and Letters of Walter H. Page*, 1925.

122. Thought is to be free, speech is to be free, and worship is to be free. Such is the democratic idea.
Theodore Parker (1810-1860), American clergyman and abolitionist. Sermon, Nov. 28, 1850.

123. Let the People think they Govern and they will be Govern'd.
William Penn (1644-1718), founder of Pennsylvania. *Some Fruits of Solitude, in Reflections and Maxims*, 1693.

124. Socialist democracy is one million times better than bourgeois democracy.
Editorial, *People's Daily*, Chinese Communist Party newspaper. Nov. 1990.

125. One has the right to be wrong in a democracy.
Claude D. Pepper (1901-1989), U.S. Senator and U.S. Congressman (D-FL). House debate, May 27, 1946.

126. It is a pleasant change to be in a country not ruled by its people.

Philip, Duke of Edinburgh (Prince Consort of Queen Elizabeth II). Remark to dictator Alfredo Stroessner of Paraguay.

127. Of cities there are two kinds: The better enjoys a democratic government which honors equality, and has law and justice for its rulers – such a constitution is a hymn to God. The worst is an ochlocracy, mob-rule.

Philo Judaeus (c.20 B.C.-c.A.D. 40), Alexandrian philosopher and diplomat. *Of the Confusion of Tongues*, XXIII.

128. Democracy passes into despotism.

Plato (427-347 B.C.), Greek philosopher. *The Republic*, IV.

129. Democracy is a charming form of government, full of variety and disorder, and dispensing a sort of equality to equals and unequals alike.

Plato. *The Republic*.

130. Either let us practice the democracy we are preaching or shut up.

Adam Clayton Powell (1908-1972), U.S. Congressman (D-NY). Quoted on PBS, *The American Experience*, Nov. 28, 1989.

131. Where there is no counsel, the people fall; but in the multitude of councilors there is safety.

Old Testament, *Proverbs* 11:14.

132. Establish democracy ... based on human rights as superior to property rights.

Jeanette Rankin (1880-1973), U.S. Congresswoman (R-MT). Quoted in Hannah Geffen Josephson, *Jeannette Rankin: First Lady in Congress*, 1974.

133. Democracy faces many enemies: poverty, illiteracy, hunger, and despair.

Ronald Reagan, 40th President of the United States (R-CA). Speech, 1986.

134. Democracy is that state in which the people, guided by laws that are its own work, executes for itself all that it can well do, and, by its delegates, all that it cannot do itself.

Maximilien-François-Marie de Robespierre (1758-1794), French revolutionist and Jacobin. Speech, Paris, Feb. 5, 1794.

135. Politics is the life blood of democracy. To call politics "dirty" is to call democracy "dirty."

Nelson A. Rockefeller (1908-1979), Governor of New York and Vice President of the United States (R). *The Future of Federalism*, 1962.

136. Democracy cannot be static. Whatever is static is dead.

Anna Eleanor Roosevelt (1884-1962), First Lady and U.S. Delegate to the United Nations. Jan. 1942.

137. Democracy has disappeared in several other great nations, not because those nations disliked democracy, but because they had grown tired of unemployment and insecurity, of seeing their children hungry.... The people of America are in agreement in defending their liberties at any cost, and the first line of that defense lies in the protection of economic security.

Franklin D. Roosevelt (1882-1945), 32nd President of the United States (D-NY). 1937.

138. We *[Cuban Americans]* probably take democracy a lot more seriously than others because we lost our homeland.

Ileana Ros-Lehtinen, U.S. Congresswoman (R-FL). Quoted in *The Boston Globe*, Aug. 31, 1989.

139. I went to Russia, had long talks with Lenin and other prominent men, and saw as much as I could of what was going on. I came to the conclusion that everything that was being done and intended was totally contrary to what any person of liberal outlook would desire. I thought the regime already hateful and certain to become more so. I found the source of evil in a contempt for liberty and democracy which was a natural outcome of fanaticism.

Bertrand Russell, 3rd Earl Russell of Kingston (1872-1970), British philosopher and reformer. *Portraits from Memory*, 1969.

140. Electoral democracy cannot be attained by engaging in practices that jeopardize the country's stability or the continuity of its institutions.

Carlos Salinas de Gortarì, President of Mexico. Speech to Mexican Congress. Quoted in *The New York Times*, Nov. 25, 1990.

141. Democracy offers opportunity, not a sure thing.

Howard D. Samuel, President, Industrial Union Department, AFL-CIO. Letter to the Editor, *The Washington Post*, Sept. 2, 1990.

142. In democracies the people seem to act as they please.

Charles-Louis de Secondat, Baron de La Brède et de Montesquieu (1689-1755), French writer. *The Spirit of the Laws*, 1748.

143. Democracies are prone to war, and war consumes them.

William H. Seward (1801-1872), Governor of New York (Whig), U.S. Senator (Whig and R) and U.S. Secretary of State. Eulogy for John Quincy Adams, 1848.

144. Democracy substitutes election by the incompetent many for appointment by the corrupt few.
George Bernard Shaw (1856-1950), Nobel Laureate in Literature (Great Britain). *Maxims for Revolutionists*, 1903.

145. The more democratic a government is the more authoritative it is, for with the people behind it, it can push its authority further than any Tsar or foreign despot dare do.
George Bernard Shaw. Letter to the Editor, *The New Republic*, Apr. 14, 1937.

146. The voice of the people is the voice of humbug.
William Tecumseh Sherman (1820-1891), General, U.S. Army. Letter to his wife, June 2, 1863.

147. All the ills of democracy can be cured by more democracy.
Alfred E. Smith (1873-1944), Governor of New York (D). Speech, Albany, NY, June 27, 1933.

148. The democratic method ... is a lot of baloney; it doesn't really mean anything. We can tell what they're thinking without taking a vote.
Gerald L. K. Smith (1898-1976), American clergyman and cofounder, Union Party. Quoted in *New Masses*, XX, No. 5.

149. Democracy is a way of getting ahead without leaving any of us behind.
Thomas V. Smith (1890-1964), U.S. Congressman (D-IL). Quoted in *Dwight D. Eisenhower's Favorite Poetry, Prose and Prayers*, 1957.

150. It would serve no purpose to explain to the poor that they ought not to feel sentiments of jealousy and vengeance against their masters; these feelings are too powerful to be suppressed by exhortations; it is on the prevalence of these feelings that democracy chiefly founds its strength.
Georges Sorel (1847-1922), French journalist and political philosopher. *Reflections on Violence*, 1908.

151. I believe democracy to be of all forms of government the most natural, and the most consonant with individual liberty. In it no one transfers his natural rights so absolutely that he has no further voice in affairs.
Benedict Spinoza (1632-1677), Dutch philosopher. *Theological-Political Treatise*, 1670.

152. The revolutionary dictatorship of the proletariat ... *[is]* a proletarian democracy – the democracy of the exploited majority based upon the limitation of the rights of an exploiting minority and directed against this minority.
Joseph Stalin (1879-1953), Premier of the U.S.S.R. *Foundations of Leninism*, 1933.

153. Self-criticism is the secret weapon of democracy.
Adlai E. Stevenson (1900-1965), Governor of Illinois (D) and U.S. Ambassador to the United Nations. Presidential nomination acceptance speech, Chicago, IL, July 21, 1952.

154. Government in a democracy cannot be stronger or more tough-minded than its people. It cannot be more inflexibly committed to the task than they. It cannot be wiser than the people.
Adlai E. Stevenson. Speech, Chicago, IL, Sept. 29, 1952.

155. Criticism in time of war is essential to the maintenance of any kind of democratic government.
Robert A. Taft (1889-1953), U.S. Senator (R-OH). Senate speech, 1942.

156. We are called a democracy, for the administration is in the hands of the many and not of the few.
Thucydides (c.460-c.400 B.C.), Greek historian. *History of the Peloponnesian War*.

157. Democratic institutions generally give men a lofty notion of their country and themselves.
Alexis de Tocqueville (1805-1859), French writer. *Democracy in America*, 1835.

158. One of the chief virtues of a democracy is that its defects are always visible.
Harry S Truman (1884-1972), 33rd President of the United States (D-MO). Congressional address, Mar. 12, 1947.

159. Democracy is based on the conviction that man has the moral and intellectual capacity, as well as the inalienable right, to govern himself with reason and justice.
Harry S Truman. Inaugural address, Jan. 20, 1949.

160. Democracy is a war of all against all.
Lech Walesa, President of Poland, trade unionist, and founder, Solidarity. Quoted in *The Washington Post*, Aug. 14, 1990.

161. It is a mistake to expect all to practice democracy as we do. There are as many democratic ways of getting things done as there are uses of the imagination and vision. Free government is not so

much a question of the form of the institution as it is a way of life of the people.

Earl Warren (1891-1974), Chief Justice, U.S. Supreme Court, and Governor of California (R). Interview, *Saturday Evening Post*, 1965.

162. People should have democracy. If they ask for democracy, they are only asking for something they rightfully own. Anyone refusing to give them democracy is a shameless bandit no better than the capitalist who robs workers of their money earned with their sweat and blood.

Wei Jingsheng, Chinese dissident. *The Fifth Modernization*, 1978.

163. Democracy means simply the bludgeoning of the people by the people for the people.

Oscar Wilde (1854-1900), Irish writer. *The Soul of Man Under Socialism*, 1881.

164. Socialism must be connected to democracy.

Hans-Jochim Willerding, member, East German Politburo. Interview, ABC, *This Week*, Nov. 19, 1989.

165. Sovereigne, originall and foundation of civill power lies in the people.

Roger Williams (c.1603-1683), English clergyman and founder, Rhode Island. Quoted in William O. Douglas, *An Almanac of Liberty*, 1954.

166. I believe in democracy because it releases the energies of every human being.

Woodrow Wilson (1856-1924), 28th President of the United States (D-NJ). Speech, Workingman's Dinner, Sept. 4, 1912.

167. The whole purpose of democracy is that we may hold counsel with one another, so as not to depend upon the understanding of one man, but to depend upon the counsel of all.

Woodrow Wilson. *The New Freedom*, 1913.

168. Authoritarian leadership and therefore a lack of democracy have led to a certain apathy among the people, to a sort of civil nihilism, a skepticism.

Boris Yeltsin, Premier of the U.S.S.R. Interview, *Time*, Mar. 20, 1989.

Chapter 18

Diplomacy and Diplomats

1. Czechoslovakia is the most neutral country in the world. It never interferes in any country's internal affairs, even its own.
   Popular joke in Czechoslovakia following the Russian invasion. Aug. 1968.

2. Can two walk together, except they be agreed?
   Old Testament, *Amos* 3:3.

3. Normalization of relations with the United States should not be a reward for good behavior.... It should depend on America's interests.
   Chester A. Atkins, U.S. Congressman (D-MA). Interview, PBS, *American Interests*, Nov. 25, 1989.

4. It is better for aged diplomats to be bored *[negotiating and debating]* than for young men to die.
   Warren Austin (1877-1962), U.S. Delegate to the United Nations. Remark, 1958.

5. There will be not only peace between us and the Arabs ... but close friendship and cooperation.
   David Ben-Gurion (1886-1973), 1st Prime Minister of Israel (Labour). Testimony before the Anglo-American Committee, Mar. 8, 1946.

6. Pakistan was once called the most allied ally of the United States. We are now the most nonallied.
   Zulfikar Ali Bhutto (1928-1979), President of Pakistan. Quoted in *The New York Times*, July 6, 1973.

7. Be polite. Write diplomatically. Even in a declaration of war one observes the rules of politeness.
   Otto von Bismarck-Schoenhausen (1815-1898), Chancellor of Germany. 1872.

8. A pupil of diplomacy has to learn three things: to speak French, to speak nothing, and to speak falsehood.
   Ludwig Boerne (1786-1837), German journalist. *Fragments & Aphorisms*, No. 46.

9. The function of a briefing paper is to prevent the ambassador from saying something dreadfully indiscreet. I sometimes think its true object is to prevent the ambassador from saying anything at all.
   Kingman Brewster, Jr., U.S. Ambassador to Great Britain and President, Yale University, New Haven, CT. Speech, Edinburgh, Scotland, Sept. 8, 1977.

10. Force is not a remedy.
    John Bright (1811-1889), Member of Parliament, Great Britain (Liberal). Speech, Nov. 16, 1880.

11. I don't like hypocrisy – even in international relations.
    Kofi Busia, Prime Minister of Ghana. Feb. 2, 1970.

12. Guns and blockades are not conducive to meaningful dialogue.
    Pierre Cadieux, Solicitor General, Canada. Statement, July 19, 1990.

13. If the distinction must be taken, men are everything, measures comparatively nothing.
    George Canning (1770-1827), Undersecretary for Foreign Affairs, Great Britain. Speech, 1801.

14. Councilors of state sit plotting their high chess-game whereof the pawns are men.
    Thomas Carlyle (1795-1881), Scottish essayist and historian. *Sartor Resartus*, 1834.

15. *[Menachem Begin, Prime Minister of Israel]* has a tendency to treat the Palestinians with scorn, to look down on them almost as subhumans, and to rationalize his abusive attitude toward them by categorizing all Palestinians as terrorists.
    Jimmy Carter, 39th President of the United States (D-GA). Quoted in Celebrity Research Group, *The Bedside Book of Celebrity Gossip*, 1984.

16. I have discovered the art of deceiving diplomats. I speak the truth, and they never believe me.
    Camillo Benso di Cavour (1810-1861), Italian statesman. Attributed.

17. All diplomacy is a continuation of war by other means.
    (A reversal of Clausewitz's famous dictum.)

Chou En-lai (1898-1976), Premier of China. Quoted in *The Saturday Evening Post*, Mar. 27, 1954.

18. An appeaser is one who feeds a crocodile, hoping it will eat him last.

Winston Churchill (1874-1965), Prime Minister of Great Britain (Conservative). On Neville Chamberlain's negotiations with Hitler that led to the Munich Pact. Speech, House of Commons, Oct. 2, 1938.

19. We have sustained a defeat without a war.

Winston Churchill. Description of the Munich Pact. Speech, House of Commons, Oct. 5, 1938.

20. Sacagewea *[a Shoshone Indian woman who accompanied Lewis and Clark in exploring the Louisiana Territory]* reconciles all the Indians to our friendly intentions. A woman with a party of men is a token of peace.

George Rogers Clark (1752-1818), Revolutionary War leader and explorer. *History of the Expedition of Capts. Lewis and Clark, 1804-5-6*, 1814.

21. Honor and good faith and justice are equally due from this country toward the weak as toward the strong.

Henry Clay (1777-1852), U.S. Senator (National Republican and Whig-KY), Speaker of the House, and U.S. Secretary of State. Letter, 1843.

22. We cannot recognize, hold official relations with, or give friendly reception to the agents of a government which is determined and bound to conspire against our institutions.

Bainbridge Colby (1869-1950), U.S. Secretary of State (D) and founder, Progressive Party. To explain refusal of U.S. to have diplomatic relations with Soviet Russia. Communiqué to Italian government, Aug. 1920.

23. American diplomacy is easy on the brain but hard on the feet.

Charles G. Dawes (1865-1951), U.S. Comptroller of the Currency; Director, U.S. Bureau of the Budget; Brigadier General, Allied Expeditionary Forces; Vice President of the United States (R); U.S. Ambassador to Great Britian; and Nobel Laureate in Peace. Remark to Henry P. Fletcher, 1930.

24. In addition to impartiality and honesty, people engaged in good offices must have the gift of good timing and a flawless sense of balance.

Alvaro De Soto, assistant to the U.N. Secretary General. *The New York Times Magazine*, Sept. 10, 1989.

25. I never refuse. I never contradict. I sometimes forget.

Benjamin Disraeli, 1st Earl of Beaconsfield (1804-1881), Prime Minister of Great Britain (Conservative). To explain his successful relationship with Queen Victoria. 1877.

26. Why employ intelligent and highly paid ambassadors and then go and do their work for them? You don't buy a canary and sing yourself.

Alexander F. Douglas-Home, Prime Minister of Great Britain (Conservative). Quoted in *The New York Times*, Apr. 21, 1961.

27. Nothing to bother about, the man was a Bolshevik.

Ellis Loring Dresel (1865-1925), Chief, American Diplomatic Mission to Germany. Statement to press when Paul E. De Mott, an American Quaker famine relief worker in Germany, was arrested as a Bolshevik and murdered without trial, 1921.

28. There isn't any rule in diplomacy that can't be broken.... There are times when diplomatic principles should be violated, but when you violate them you ought to know you're violating them.

John Foster Dulles (1888-1959), U.S. Secretary of State and U.S. Senator (R-NY). Remark to William Macomber.

29. Surely diplomacy is needed when there is conflict, not when there is harmony.

Abba Eban, Foreign Secretary of Israel and Israeli Ambassador to the United Nations (Labour). Remark to Soviet Ambassador Dmitri Chuvakhin when Russia was breaking diplomatic relations with Israel. July 1967.

30. Since war is everybody's tragedy, diplomacy is everybody's business.

Abba Eban. *An Autobiography*, 1977.

31. For Christ sake, why do you make an appointment with a guy that's gonna kiss me?

Dwight D. Eisenhower (1890-1969), 34th President of the United States (R-KS). On learning that an appointment had been made for Greek Orthodox Archbishop H. G. Athenagoras, who, as was his custom, had kissed President Truman on a previous visit. Quoted in Robert J. Donavan, *Confidential Secretary*, 1988.

32. I wish to see the discovery of a plan that would induce and oblige nations to settle their disputes without cutting one another's throats.

Benjamin Franklin (1706-1790), Member, Continental Congress and Constitutional Convention, Governor of Pennsylvania, and U.S. Minister to France. 1780.

33. Diplomacy without arms is music without instruments.

Frederick II (The Great) (1712-1786), King of Prussia. Remark, 1870.

34. There is something about the Foreign Service that takes the guts out of people.
Evan G. Galbraith, U.S. Ambassador to France. Quoted in *The New York Times*, Feb. 13, 1985.

35. Diplomats are only useful in fair weather. As soon as it rains they drown in every drop.
Charles de Gaulle (1890-1970), President of France. Quoted in *Newsweek*, Oct. 1, 1962.

36. Diplomacy is to do and say
The nastiest things in the nicest way.
Isaac Goldberg (1887-1938), American writer. *Reflex*, Oct. 1927.

37. There is little incentive for initiative just now: the *[State]* Department seems to take no interest; we never receive comments on our work and many of our questions go unanswered.
Joseph C. Grew (1880-1965), U.S. Undersecretary of State and U.S. Minister to Denmark, Turkey, and Japan. Dec. 1920.

38. The British courtiers are ridiculing our situation very much and tell *[Secretary of State]* Mr. *[John]* Adams, in a sneering manner, when America shall assume some kind of government, then England will speak to her.
Cyrus Griffin (1748-1810), President of the Continental Congress (VA). 1788.

39. The most fatal of all neutralities is that which results not from choice, but from irresolution.
Francesco Guicciardini (1483-1540), Florentine historian and statesman. *Storia d'Italia*, 1561.

40. Ambassadors are the eyes and ears of states.
Francesco Guicciardini. *Ibid*.

41. Do you know why everybody wants to be an ambassador? It's because when an ambassador walks down the corridor of his embassy, everybody kisses his ass.
Philip Habib, U.S. Undersecretary of State and Special Envoy to the Middle East. Quoted in Martin Mayer, *The Diplomats*, 1983.

42. At any rate, your contempt for your fellow human beings does not prevent you ... from trying to win their respect.
Dag Hammerskjöld (1905-1961), Secretary-General of the United Nations (Sweden). *Markings*, 1965.

43. *[American diplomats in England are]* more snobbish than their English butlers.
William Randolph Hearst (1863-1951), U.S. Congressman (D-NY); founder, Independence League Party; journalist; and publisher. Quoted in *The New York Times*, Nov. 2, 1907.

44. You can't get a diplomatic solution unless behind that is the threat of force.
Henry J. Hyde, U.S. Congressman (R-IL). Interview, CNN, *Newsmaker Saturday*, Sept. 1, 1990.

45. It was as far as I could send him ... where he could do the least harm. I would have sent him to the North Pole if we had kept a minister there.
Andrew Jackson (1767-1845), 7th President of the United States (D-TN). To explain why he appointed James Buchanan U.S. Ambassador to Russia. Quoted in *Conservative Digest*, May 1987.

46. If talk is impossible, then war is inevitable.
Jesse L. Jackson, Shadow Senator (D-DC). Interview, CNN News, Sept. 3, 1990.

47. I succeed him. No one can replace him.
Thomas Jefferson (1743-1826), 3rd President of the United States (Democratic Republican-VA). Remark when appointed Minister to France and presenting himself to the French Minister of Foreign Affairs, who asked if he was replacing Benjamin Franklin, 1785.

48. The Four Great Powers? Who the hell are the other two?
Lyndon B. Johnson (1908-1973), 36th President of the United States (D-TX). Remark to Abba Eban, May 26, 1967.

49. If you let a bully come into your front yard, he'll be on your porch the next day, and the day after that he'll rape your wife in your own bed.
Lyndon B. Johnson. On appeasement. Quoted in Isaacson and Thomas, *The Wise Men*, 1986.

50. The best way to influence our enemies is to stand steadfastly by our friends.
Walter H. Judd, U.S. Congressman (R-MN). Speech, Taft School, Watertown, CT, 1953.

51. The difference between diplomatic contact and diplomatic exchange is diplomatic gibberish.
Bernard Kalb, American journalist and spokesperson, U.S. State Department. Quoted in *The New York Times Magazine*, Jan. 7, 1990.

52. As a diplomat I can neither be honest with myself nor with other people.
George F. Kennan, U.S. Ambassador to Russia and Yugoslavia. Letter to his cousin.

53. The State Department is a bowl of jelly.
John F. Kennedy (1917-1963), 35th President of

the United States (D-MA). Quoted in *Newsweek*, Oct. 30, 1989.

54. Diplomacy is the art of restraining power.
Henry M. Kissinger, U.S. Secretary of State and National Security Advisor (R). 1973.

55. One has to be careful when listening to diplomats to hear exactly what is being said.
Ted Koppel, American TV journalist. Remark to Iraqi Foreign Minister Tariq Aziz, ABC, *Nightline*, Aug. 15, 1990.

56. I speak not in official character, imparted by diplomacy, whose secrecy is the curse of the world, but I am the harbinger of the public spirit of the people.
Lajos Kossuth (1802-1894), Member of Parliament, Hungary. Speech, New York City, Dec. 6, 1851.

57. If any good reason exists why we should persevere longer in withholding our recognition of the independence and sovereignty of Hayti and Liberia, I am unable to discern it.... I submit for your consideration the expediency of an appropriation for maintaining a *chargé d'affaire* near each of these new states.
Abraham Lincoln (1809-1865), 16th President of the United States (R-IL). First annual message to Congress, Dec. 3, 1861.

58. Diplomacy: the art of jumping into troubled waters without making a splash.
Art Linkletter, American comedian. 1978.

59. The politician says: "I will give you what you want." The statesman says: "What you think you want is this. What it is possible for you to get is that. What you really want, therefore, is the following."
Walter Lippmann (1889-1974), American political columnist. *A Preface to Morals*, 1929.

60. The history of diplomacy is the history of relations among rival powers which did not enjoy political intimacy and did not respond to appeals to common purposes. Nevertheless ... to think that rival and unfriendly powers cannot be brought to a settlement is to forget what diplomacy is about.
Walter Lippmann. *The Cold War*, 1947.

61. The fact that talk may be boring or turgid or uninspiring should not cause us to forget the fact that it is preferable to war.
Henry Cabot Lodge, Jr. (1902-1986), U.S. Senator (R-MA), U.S. Ambassador to Vietnam and Germany, and Head of American delegation to Paris Peace Conference for Vietnam peace negotiations. Jan. 1954.

62. In coalitions of bitter enemies the thugs usually prevail.
Winston Lord, U.S. Ambassador to China. *The New York Times*, Dec. 10, 1989.

63. If war is so easily averted as all this it does seem a pity no P*[rime]* M*[inister]* except Neville *[Chamberlain]* has thought of it before. Peace without Honour seems to be what we have got. I'm glad. One can't expect both.
Rose Macaulay (1889-1958), British writer. In reference to the signing of the Munich Pact. Letter to Daniel George Bunting, Oct. 14, 1938.

64. I have treated Japan as I would like to be treated, and they have responded in kind.
Mike Mansfield, U.S. Senator (D-MT) and U.S. Ambassador to Japan. Resignation speech, Tokyo, Nov. 14, 1988.

65. Your governor is but a subject of King Charles of England. I shall not treat with a subject. I shall treat of peace only with the King, my brother. When he comes, I am ready.
Massasoit (?-1661), Chief, Wampanoag Indians. Message to Edward Winslow, Governor of Plymouth Colony, who wanted to know why the Indian chief planned a war against England.

66. Diplomacy is an activity between two sovereign entities, neither of which can control the activities of the other.
Martin Mayer, American journalist and writer. *The Diplomats*, 1983.

67. We're not trying to start a war; we're trying to send a political message.
Robert S. McNamara, U.S. Secretary of Defense (D). Instructions to the Chief of Naval Operations during the Cuban missile crisis, Oct. 1962.

68. Iran explains nothing to anyone but God.
Mir Hussein Moussavi, Prime Minister of Iran. Explanation of Iran's refusal to extradite the hijackers of an American aircraft. Quoted in *The New York Times*, Dec. 13, 1984.

69. There's always a way to talk.
Edmund S. Muskie, Governor of Maine (D), U.S. Senator, and U.S. Secretary of State. Congressional testimony, July 29, 1990.

70. In diplomacy, tact and good management are better than cunning.... Dissimulation is always a mark of weakness.

Napoléon I (1769-1821), military leader and Emperor of France. *Maxims.*

71. Diplomacy is the police in grand costume.
Napoléon I. *Ibid.*

72. He who is audacious wins.
Alan García Pérez, President of Peru. Remark on international diplomacy. Quoted in *The New York Times,* Aug. 20, 1989.

73. A bad messenger falls into mischief, but a faithful envoy brings healing.
Old Testament, *Proverbs* 13:17.

74. Dollar diplomacy involves a lot of dollars and very little diplomacy.
Will Rogers (1879-1935), American humorist. Quoted on PBS, *Will Rogers U.S.A.*, Oct. 3, 1988.

75. We have to face the fact that either all of us are going to die together or we are going to learn to live together, and if we are to live together, we have to learn to talk.
Anna Eleanor Roosevelt (1884-1962), First Lady and U.S. Delegate to the United Nations. 1960.

76. My advice to any diplomat who wants to have good press is to have two or three kids and a dog.
Carl T. Rowan, Jr., U.S. Ambassador to Finland and political columnist. Quoted in *The New Yorker*, Dec. 7, 1963.

77. The barrier of distrust that has been between us during the last thirty-five years has been broken down in thirty-five hours.
Anwar Sadat (1918-1981), President of Egypt. Remark after his trip to Israel. Nov. 22, 1977.

78. Diplolingo: the creative use of synonymy to put a peaceful spin on a warlike act.
William Safire, American political columnist and presidential speech writer (R). *The New York Times Magazine*, Sept. 2, 1990.

79. Could we know what men are most apt to remember, we might know what they are most apt to do.
George Savile, 1st Marquess of Halifax (1633-1695), Lord Privy Seal of England. *Moral Thoughts and Reflections*, 1750.

80. One must deprecate whatever keeps up ill-will betwixt America and the mother country; and *we* in particular should avoid awakening painful recollections. Our high situation allows us to contemn petty insults, and to make advances toward cordiality.
Walter Scott (1771-1832), Scottish writer. Quoted in John Gibson Lockhart, *Life of Scott*, 1837.

81. As a diplomat you learn to develop certain reflexes. You learn to be proper and sober and show no emotion, and of course that's fatal for a politician.
Leticia Ramos Shahani, Ambassador and Senator, the Philippines. Quoted in *The New York Times*, Nov. 9, 1989.

82. All day long at the State Department we're deciding things. It's a very operational department. Very real time. That's one of the reasons why people enjoy it so much. It's fun.
George P. Shultz, U.S. Secretary of State (R). Quoted in *The Washington Post*, Mar. 19, 1989.

83. America's diplomats – unlike her intelligence and military services – have no domestic constituency.
Richard Spiers, Undersecretary of the United Nations and U.S. Assistant Secretary of State. *The Washington Post*, July 23, 1989.

84. Statesmen ... are suspected of plotting against mankind, rather than consulting their interests, and are esteemed more crafty than learned.
Benedict Spinoza (1632-1677), Dutch philosopher. *Theological-Political Treatise*, 1670.

85. Sincere diplomacy is no more possible than dry water or wooden iron.
Joseph Stalin (1879-1953), Premier of the U.S.S.R. Remark.

86. I am willing to let him *[Saddam Hussein]* have his way with me if in exchange he frees the hostages.
Illona Staller, Member of Parliament, Italy, and porn star. Quoted in *Time*, Sept. 3, 1990.

87. We must try if we can to bring the world back to peaceful habits.
Robert Stewart, 2nd Marquis of Londonderry and Viscount Castlereagh (1769-1822), Foreign Secretary, Great Britain, and leader of the House of Commons. Statement at the Congress of Vienna, 1815.

88. Do not allow your enemies to get together. Look into the matter of his alliances and cause them to be severed and dissolved.
Sun-tzu (c.400 B.C.), Chinese writer of the Age of Warring States. *The Art of War*.

89. The two maxims of any great man at court are, always to keep his countenance, and never to keep his word.
Jonathan Swift (1667-1745), Irish clergyman and satirist. *Thoughts on Various Subjects*, 1706.

90. We didn't have time to do the minuets of diplomacy. We got down to business.

Margaret Thatcher, Prime Minister of Great Britain (Conservative). Description of a meeting with Soviet Pres. Mikhail Gorbachev. *CBS News*, Mar. 11, 1985.

91. Striped pants boys

Harry S Truman (1884-1972), 33rd President of the United States (D-MO). Phrase often used to describe State Department officials.

92. If we see that Germany is winning, we ought to help Russia, and if we see Russia is winning, we ought to help Germany, and that way let them kill as many as possible.

Harry S Truman. 1941.

93. I felt that Israel deserved to be recognized, and I didn't give a damn whether the Arabs liked it or not.

Harry S Truman. *Where the Buck Stops: The Personal and Private Writings of Harry S Truman*, 1989.

94. Ambassadorships are still too important to be available to the highest bidder.

Cyrus R. Vance, U.S. Secretary of State (D). *The New York Times*, Nov. 10, 1989.

95. The civilian once under the mantle of officialdom, whatever it may be, is subject to the rules governing civilian behavior under official circumstances.

Amy Vanderbilt (1908-1974), American hostess and writer. *New Complete Book of Etiquette*, 1963.

96. The ambassador to a foreign country in a couple of years gets more British than a Britisher, more Spanish than a Spaniard, more French than a Frenchman. They seem to be ashamed of their Americanism when they come into the courts of Europe.

James J. Walker (1881-1946), Mayor of New York City (D). Quoted in George Seldes, *You Can't Print That*, 1929.

97. What is the difference between the diplomat and the military man? They both do nothing, but the military get up very early in the morning to do it with great discipline, while the diplomats do it late in the afternoon, in utter confusion.

Vernon A. Walters, General, U.S. Army, and U.S. Ambassador to the United Nations. Quoted in *M*, 1986.

98. Diplomacy is the lowest form of politeness because it misquotes the greatest number of people.

E. B. White (1899-1986), American writer. *One Man's Meat*, 1944.

99. The only use of our attachés is that they supply their friends with excellent tobacco.

Oscar Wilde (1854-1900), Irish writer. *The Critic as Artist*, 1890.

100. In matters of grave importance, style, not sincerity, is the vital thing.

Oscar Wilde. *The Importance of Being Earnest*, 1895.

101. You diplomats are full of shit and the whole Wilhelmstrasse stinks.

Wilhelm II (1859-1941), Emperor of Germany and King of Prussia. Remark to a German diplomat, 1918.

102. We find that those who have been occupying the legations and embassies have been habituated to a point of view which is very different, indeed, from the point of view of the present administration.... They have been so bred in a different school that we have found ... that it was difficult for them to comprehend our point of view.

Woodrow Wilson (1856-1924), 28th President of the United States (D-NJ). Letter to Charles W. Eliot, Sept. 17, 1913.

103. An ambassador is an honest man, sent to lie abroad for the good of his country.

Henry Wotton (1568-1639), English diplomat and poet. Attributed.

Chapter 19

Disarmament and Arms Control

1. WAR IS NOT HEALTHY FOR CHILDREN AND OTHER LIVING THINGS
   Pacifist poster, 1960's.

2. Better red than dead.
   Slogan of nuclear disarmament movement, 1970's.

3. Trust but verify. (*Doveryai no proveryai.*)
   Russian proverb frequently quoted by Ronald Reagan regarding disarmament negotiations, 1980's.

4. Let no one expect us to disarm unilaterally. We are not a naive people.
   Yuri Andropov (1914-1983), Director, KGB, and President of the U.S.S.R. Speech, Communist Party Central Committee, Moscow, Nov. 22, 1982.

5. The way to win an atomic war is to make sure it never starts.
   Omar N. Bradley (1893-1981), General, U.S. Army, and Permanent Chairman, Joint Chiefs of Staff. Quoted in *The Observer*, Apr. 20, 1952.

6. The pens which write against disarmament are made with the same steel from which guns are made.
   Aristide Briand (1862-1932), Nobel Laureate in Peace (France). Speech, Geneva, Switzerland, Sept. 23, 1930.

7. It is the ultimate end of absurdity for the arms race to go on.
   Clark P. Clifford, U.S. Secretary of Defense and Special Counsel to the President (D). PBS, Interview with Bill Moyers, 1981.

8. Advances in weaponry go much faster than arms control.
   William Sloane Coffin, American clergyman and President, SANE/Freeze. Interview, *Time*, June 5, 1989.

9. Talking to the superpowers about disarmament is like talking to drug dealers about stopping drug deliveries.
   Volkmar Deile, Secretary, Action for Reconciliation, West Germany. Quoted in *The New Yorker*, Oct. 17, 1983.

10. One of my age thinks about his destiny a little. I should not like to have written on my tombstone, "He knew what happened at Hiroshima, but he did not take a first step."
    Everett M. Dirksen (1896-1969), U.S. Congressman and U.S. Senator (R-IL). On his support of the Nuclear Test Ban Treaty, a position not encouraged by the Republican Party. Tribute to Everett Dirksen; quoted by John Dellenback (R-OR), Washington, DC, Sept. 8, 1969.

11. It is not enough just to take this weapon *[nuclear bombs]* out of the hands of the soldiers. It must be put into the hands of those who will know how to strip its military casing and adapt it to the arts of peace.
    Dwight D. Eisenhower (1890-1969), 34th President of the United States (R-KS). Speech, United Nations General Assembly, Dec. 8, 1953.

12. We should, I believe, announce in no uncertain terms that we are against disarmament.
    Barry M. Goldwater, U.S. Senator (R-AZ). *Why Not Victory?*, 1963.

13. Great armaments lead inevitably to war.
    Edward Grey, Viscount Grey of Fallodon (1862-1933), Foreign Secretary, Great Britain (Liberal). *Twenty-Five Years, 1892-1916*, 1925.

14. I would be reluctant to suspend our capital ship building program until we have entered into an agreement for disarmament with other nations.
    Warren G. Harding (1865-1923), 29th President of the United States (R-OH). Remark to Sen. Henry Cabot Lodge, Feb. 1921.

15. Shall we be defenseless America, a weak and harmless nation, or shall we be defensive America, the fear and dread of all nations?
Felix E. Hébert (1901-1979), U.S. Congressman (D-LA). Quoted in Daniel Rapoport, *Inside the House*, 1975.

16. Arms control has to have a future, or none of us does.
Stanley Hoffmann, Director, Harvard Center for European Studies. Quoted in *Newsweek*, Oct. 1, 1984.

17. Preparedness never caused a war and unpreparedness never prevented one.
Florence Prag Kahn (1868-1948), U.S. Congresswoman (D-CA). Quoted in Esther Stineman, *American Political Women*, 1980.

18. The more bombers, the less room for doves of peace.
Nikita S. Khrushchev (1874-1971), Premier of the U.S.S.R. Radio Moscow, Mar. 14, 1958.

19. I would die for my country ... but I would not let my country die for me.
Neil Kinnock, Member of Parliament, Great Britain (Labour). Nuclear disarmament speech, 1987.

20. It is a mistake to isolate arms control from other areas of policy.... There is a danger that arms control will be a safety valve for an otherwise overly aggressive foreign policy.
Henry M. Kissinger, U.S. Secretary of State and National Security Advisor (R). Quoted on PBS, *War and Peace in the Nuclear Age*, May 1989.

21. We women have the power to compel disarmament. We need not plead or beg. We have the ballot. On this issue of militarism we hold the balance of power.
Belle Case La Follette (1859-1931), President, Women's Committee for World Disarmament. Speech, Washington, DC, 1920.

22. Armament firms have been active in fomenting war scares and in persuading their own countries to increase their armaments.
League of Nations, Commission report, 1921.

23. Wars occur because people prepare for conflict, rather than for peace.
Trygve Lie (1896-1968), Secretary General of the United Nations (Norway). Sept. 6, 1947.

24. Among other evils which being unarmed brings you, it causes you to be despised.
Niccolò Machiavelli (1469-1527), Florentine statesman and political philosopher. *The Prince*, 1513.

25. All armed prophets have been victorious and all unarmed prophets have been destroyed.
Niccolò Machiavelli. *Ibid.*

26. Don't bother about the complicated details. The issue is hot.
Edward Markey, U.S. Senator (D-MA). To urge his congressional colleagues to campaign on the nuclear freeze issue. 1984.

27. Blessed are the peacemakers, for they shall be called the children of God.
New Testament, *Matthew* 5:9.

28. It is at least inconsistent to declare that there can be no doubt as to the defensive nature of American preparations, while seizing upon every similar step by the Soviet Union as incontrovertible evidence of its insatiable imperialism.
Cord Meyer, Jr., President, United World Federalists. *Peace or Anarchy?*, 1947.

29. Both say to the other "I don't trust you and will not take any chances, but I ask you to trust me and take the chances which that involves."
A. J. Muste (1885-1967), American clergyman and pacifist. An observation of the similarity between the American and Russian disarmament proposals. Letter to Henry A. Wallace, Sept. 26, 1945.

30. Jobs are always at stake.
Samuel A. Nunn, U.S. Senator (D-GA). In reference to disarmament and weapons systems reductions. Interview, NBC, *Meet the Press*, July 23, 1989.

31. If you wish to be brothers, drop your weapons.
Pope Paul VI (1897-1978). Speech, United Nations General Assembly, Oct. 4, 1965.

32. Any lawyer would indict disarmament as the arch villain of history. It has been tried again and again since centuries before Christ, and it has *always* led to war, *never* to peace. Sure we are in an arms race, and we had better win it. It's a lot better than having to win a shooting war.
Thomas S. Power, Commander, U.S. Strategic Air Command. *Reader's Digest*, May 1964.

33. We don't mistrust each other because we're armed. We're armed because we mistrust each other.
Ronald Reagan, 40th President of the United States (R-CA). Remark to Soviet Pres. Mikhail Gorbachev, quoted on CBS, *60 Minutes*, Jan. 15, 1989.

34. The military likes arms control because they can get their weapons produced so they can be used as bargaining chips. If an agreement is reached,

new weapons are needed to see that the Russians live up to their commitments.

Gerard Smith, U.S. arms control negotiator. Quoted on PBS, *War and Peace in the Nuclear Age*, May 1989.

35. Nobody can escape the logical conclusion that if our best hope *[for defense]* is fear of retaliation, then our best defense is not disarmament, but scientific armament.

Norman Thomas (1884-1968), American Socialist and Director, League for Industrial Democracy. *Appeal to the Nations*, 1947.

36. We must delegitimize the development of nuclear arms by moving toward a ban on testing them, rather than continuing by our own example to promote the glory of nuclear power status.

Paul Warnke, Director, U.S. Arms Control and Disarmament Agency, and chief negotiator, SALT II. *The Washington Post*, Dec. 9, 1990.

Chapter 20

Discrimination and Human Rights

1. DON'T BUY WHERE YOU CAN'T WORK
Boycott sign, Harlem, NY, 1939.

2. Favors granted always become defined as rights.
Saul D. Alinsky (1909-1972), American community organizer. Dictum.

3. If you love your children, if you love your country, if you love the God of love, clear your lands from slaves, burden not your children or country with them.
Richard Allen (1760-1831), Founder, African Methodist Episcopal Church. Quoted in Lerone Bennett, Jr., *Pioneers of Protest*, 1968.

4. Race is, politically speaking, not the beginning of humanity but its end, not the origin of peoples but their decay, not the natural birth of man but his unnatural death.
Hannah Arendt (1906-1975), American political philosopher. *The Origins of Totalitarianism*, 1951.

5. The world is white no longer, and it will never be again.
James Baldwin (1924-1987), American writer. *Notes of a Native Son*, 1955.

6. There is no birthright in the white skin that it shall say that wherever it goes, to any nation, amongst any people, there the people of the country shall give way before it, and those to whom the land belongs shall bow down and become its servants.
Annie Wood Besant (1847-1933), President, Indian National Congress. *Wake Up, India*, 1913.

7. The drums of Africa still beat in my heart. They will not rest while there is a single Negro boy or girl without a chance to prove his worth.
Mary McLeod Bethune (1875-1955), American educator. Quoted in *Who*, June 1941.

8. The natural and proper timidity and delicacy which belongs to the female sex evidently unfits it for many of the occupations of civil life.... The paramount destiny and mission of women are to fulfill the noble and benign offices of wife and mother. This is the law of the Creator.
Joseph P. Bradley (1813-1892), U.S. Supreme Court Justice. *Bradwell* v. *Illinois*, 1873.

9. Experience has shown that no civil right has ever been secured without legislation.
James Brady, White House press secretary (R). *The New York Times*, August 29, 1989.

10. Discrimination is the act of treating differently two persons or things, under like circumstances.
Louis D. Brandeis (1856-1941), U.S. Supreme Court Justice. *National Life Insurance Co.* v. *United States*, 1927.

11. To have the same commander in chief demand that our soldiers die for their country when he does not guarantee the protection of their civil rights at home is extraordinarily disappointing.
H. H. Brookins, Bishop, African Methodist Episcopal Church, Washington, DC. Quoted in *Newsweek*, November 26, 1990.

12. Civil rights are meaningless without economic rights.
Tony Brown, American TV journalist. PBS, *Tony Brown's Journal*, December 16, 1990.

13. No, I don't believe it's prejudice. I truly believe they *[blacks]* may not have some of the necessities to be, let's say, a field manager or perhaps a general manager.
Al Campanis, Vice President, Los Angeles Dodgers. Comment when asked if there was racial prejudice in major league baseball. Interview, ABC, *Nightline*, 1987.

14. The term person means an individual other than an Indian.
Canadian Indian Act of 1880.

15. No self-respecting white man can ally himself with the President after what has occurred.
Allen D. Candler (1834-1910), U.S. Congressman and Governor of Georgia (D). Statement when Pres. Theodore Roosevelt invited Booker T. Washington to dine at the White House, 1901.

16. The only good Zionist is a dead Zionist.... We must take a lesson from Hitler.... Zionism will be crushed in the name of humanity.
Stokley Carmichael (Kwame Toure). Chairman, Student Non-Violent Coordinating Committee. Speech, University of Maryland, College Park, MD, 1986.

17. I am a candidate for the presidency of the United States. I make that statement proudly in the full knowledge that, as a black person and as a female person, I do not have a chance of actually gaining that office in this election year.
Shirley A. Chisholm, U.S. Congresswoman (D-NY). Presidential candidacy announcement, June 4, 1972.

18. Let's not kid ourselves. Passing an *[anti-discrimination]* law does not mean an end to homophobia.
David Clarenbach, Wisconsin State Representative. Quoted in *USA Today*, November 15, 1989.

19. I do not believe in the law of hate.
Clarence S. Darrow (1857-1938), American attorney and writer. Statement after his successful defense of blacks who used guns to defend themselves against a white mob attacking their homes. May 19, 1926.

20. No one will treat with indifference the principle of race. It is the key of history.
Benjamin Disraeli, 1st Earl of Beaconsfield (1804-1881), Prime Minister of Great Britain (Conservative). *Endymion*, 1880.

21. We want no black Ireland in America. We want no aggrieved class in America.
Frederick Douglass (c.1817-1895), Recorder of Deeds, District of Columbia, and U.S. Minister to Haiti. Speech, Washington DC, 1883.

22. Though the colored man is no longer subject to be bought and sold, he is still surrounded by an adverse sentiment which fetters all his movements. In his downward course he meets with no resistance, but his course upward is resisted at every step of his progress.
Frederick Douglass. Speech, September 24, 1883.

23. The work does not end with the abolition of slavery but only begins.
Frederick Douglass. Quoted on PBS, *The Civil War*, September 23, 1990.

24. I want to allay fears that I will be divisive or a problem in this great body. I truly believe when we took the pledge of allegiance this morning and we said justice for all, I believe in that for America. And I believe that discrimination is wrong and reprehensible when it is waged against anyone, black or white, in this country.
David Duke, Grand Wizard of the Ku Klux Klan and Louisiana State Legislator (R). First statement to the Louisiana House, Baton Rouge, LA, Feb. 22, 1989.

25. We have a full right, by our own best wisdom, and then even by compulsion to dictate terms and conditions to them *[Native Americans]*.... The Indian must be made to feel he is in the grasp of a superior.
George E. Ellis (1814-1894), American clergymen and Indian expert. 1882.

26. You complain that Negroes are a base class. Who makes and keeps the Jew or the Negro base, who but you, who exclude them from the rights which others enjoy?
Ralph Waldo Emerson (1803-1882), American writer. *Journal*, Apr. 1867.

27. Fear always springs from ignorance.
Ralph Waldo Emerson. "The American Scholar," in *Nature, Addresses, and Lectures*, 1855.

28. Whenever Americans are free to select their own associates they almost always select associates of their own race.
Samuel J. Ervin, Jr. (1896-1985), U.S. Congressman and U.S. Senator (D-NC). Quoted on PBS, *Senator Sam*, Oct. 25, 1988.

29. If this boy passes the examination, he will be admitted; and if the white students choose to withdraw, all of the income of the college will be devoted to his education.
Edward Everett (1794-1865), President, Harvard College, Cambridge, MA; U.S. Secretary of State (National Republican), U.S. Congressman, U.S. Senator, and Governor of Massachusetts. Statement when a free black applied for admission to Harvard, amid protests from white students and alumni, 1848.

30. Blood will run in the streets if Negro pupils should attempt to enter Central High School.
Orval E. Faubus, Governor of Arkansas (D). Statement, Sept. 1957.

31. You cannot shake hands with a clenched fist.
Indira Gandhi (1917-1984), Prime Minister of India. Press conference, New Delhi, Oct. 19, 1971.

32. Don't knock a man down and then ask him why he lives in the dirt. Don't filch a man of his authority, his right to rule his home, his dignity as a man, and then ask him why his culture is substandard.
Dan George (1899-1982), Canadian Indian chief. Speech, Williams Lake, British Columbia, 1975.

33. One of these days every person in Canada will be a Canadian.
Dan George. Quoted in Cowan, *My Canada*, 1984.

34. Are you running an airline or a whorehouse?
Martha Griffiths, U.S. Congresswoman and Lieutenant Governor of Michigan (D). Letter to United Airlines asking why all stewardesses had to be young and attractive. 1961.

35. I put sex in the Civil Rights Act.
Martha Griffiths. Statement after adding a floor amendment to include gender as a prohibited type of discrimination in the Civil Rights Act of 1964. Quoted in Daniel Rapoport, *Inside the House*, 1975.

36. You've got to be qualified. The problem with all the affirmative action laws is that if you have been sufficiently discriminated against in education and training, then you can't take advantage of the law because you're not qualified to hold the job. If you can't show that you're qualified, the employer doesn't have to hire you.
Augustus Hawkins, U.S. Congressman (D-CA). Quoted in *The Washington Post*, Dec. 9, 1990.

37. The failure of the South to faithfully observe the Fifteenth Amendment is the cause of the failure of all efforts toward complete pacification. It is on this hook that the bloody shirt now hangs.
Rutherford B. Hayes (1822-1893), 19th President of the United States (R-OH). *Diary*, July 21, 1880.

38. The only job for which no woman is or can be qualified is sperm donor.
Wilma Scott Heide, President, National Organization for Women. 1971.

39. There is a tendency to judge a race, a nation, or a distinct group by its least worthy members.
Eric Hoffer (1902-1983), American philosopher and longshoreman. *The True Believer*, 1951.

40. The present Supreme Court is more dangerous to the legitimate hopes and aspirations of black people in this nation than any Bull Connor with a firehose.
Benjamin Hooks, Executive Director, National Association for the Advancement of Colored People. Speech, Detroit, MI, July 9, 1989.

41. The American civil rights movement is not and never has been dominated by the Communists – because the overwhelming majority of civil rights leaders in this country, both Negro and white, have recognized and rejected Communism as a menace to the freedom of all.
J. Edgar Hoover (1895-1972), Director, Federal Bureau of Investigation. Quoted in *National Review*, Oct. 19, 1965.

42. If you object that I discriminate, then I say to you, "You can organize your own club."
Alfred Hopkins, Mayor of Annapolis, MD. Quoted in *Regardie's*, Dec. 1990.

43. I am the poor white, fooled and pushed apart,
I am the Negro bearing slaver's scars,
I am the Red man driven from the land,
I am the immigrant clutching the hope I seek –
And finding only the same ole stupid plan
Of dog eat dog, of mighty crush the weak.
Langston Hughes (1902-1967), American poet. *Let America Be America Again*, 1938.

44. The time has come for the Democratic Party of America to get out of the shadow of states' rights and forthrightly into the sunshine of civil rights.
Hubert H. Humphrey (1911-1978), Vice President of the United States and U.S. Senator (D-MN). Speech, Democratic National Convention, Philadelphia, PA, July 15, 1948.

45. Until racial justice and freedom is a reality in this land, our union will remain profoundly imperfect.... The Negro is going to get justice or this society will be ripped apart.
Hubert H. Humphrey. Senate debate, Mar. 30, 1964.

46. Winning the presidency, for me, is not worth the price of silence on the issue of human *[civil]* rights.
Hubert H. Humphrey. Presidential nomination acceptance speech, Chicago, IL, Aug. 1968.

47. The opposite of segregation is not integration. Martin Luther King didn't dream about a completely integrated world. He knew this was a pluralistic society and that ethnics tend to keep an identity. It's not a contradiction.
Jesse L. Jackson, Shadow Senator (D-DC). Quoted in *The Los Angeles Times*, Jan. 20, 1975.

48. Nature has given to our black brethren talents equal to those of any other color of men; and that the appearance of the want of them is owing merely to the degraded condition of their existence.

Thomas Jefferson (1743-1826), 3rd President of the United States (Democratic Republican-VA). Letter to Benjamin Banneker, Aug. 30, 1791.

49. Government, as well as religion, has furnished its schisms, its persecutions, and its devices for fattening idleness on the earnings of the people. It has its hierarchy of emperors, kings, princes, and nobles, as that has of popes, cardinals, archbishops, bishops, and priests. In short, cannibals are not to be found in the wilds of America only, but are reveling on the blood of every living people.

Thomas Jefferson. Letter to Charles Clay, Jan. 29, 1815.

50. This civil rights program about which you have heard so much is a farce and a sham – an effort to set up a police state in the guise of liberty. I am opposed to that program. I fought it in Congress. It is the province of the state to run its own elections.

Lyndon B. Johnson (1908-1973), 36th President of the United States (D-TX). Speech, Austin, TX, May 22, 1948.

51. As long as I am your president, I am going to be president of all the people.

Lyndon B. Johnson. Campaign speech to a black audience, New Orleans, LA, 1964.

52. We have talked long enough in this country about equal rights. We have talked for one hundred years or more. It is time now to write the next chapter, and to write it in the books of law.

Lyndon B. Johnson. Address to Congress, Nov. 27, 1963.

53. The right to vote with no ifs, ands, or buts, that's the key. When the Negroes get that, they'll have every politician, north and south, east and west, kissing their ass, begging for their support.

Lyndon B. Johnson. Remark to Hubert H. Humphrey, 1964. Quoted in Merle Miller, *Lyndon: An Oral Biography*, 1980.

54. *[Mississippi Senator]* Jim Eastland could be standing right in the middle of the worst Mississippi flood ever known, and he'd say the niggers caused it, helped out by some Communists.

Lyndon B. Johnson. Quoted in Merle Miller, *Lyndon: An Oral Biography*, 1980.

55. I am willing to love all mankind, except an American.

Samuel Johnson (1709-1784), British writer and lexicographer. Quoted in James Boswell, *The Life of Samuel Johnson*, Apr. 15, 1778.

56. *[The Emperor]* Vespasian's friends overcame his scruples by telling him that against Jews there could be no question of impiety, and that he ought to prefer expediency to decency when the two were incompatible.

Flavius Josephus (37-105), Roman-Jewish general and historian. *Wars*, III.

57. There can be no really pervasive system of oppression *[discrimination against women]*, such as that in the United States, without the consent of the oppressed.

Florynce R. Kennedy, American writer, feminist, and TV talk-show host. "Institutionalized Oppression vs. the Female," *Sisterhood Is Powerful*, 1970.

58. The rights of all men are diminished when the rights of any man is threatened.

John F. Kennedy (1917-1963), 35th President of the United States (D-MA). 1961.

59. I want to be the white man's brother, not his brother-in-law.

Martin Luther King, Jr. (1929-1968), American clergyman and civil rights leader. Quoted in *The New York Journal-American*, Sept. 10, 1962.

60. We are not satisfied and we will not be satisfied until justice rolls down like water and righteousness like a mighty stream.

Martin Luther King, Jr.. Speech, Washington, DC, Aug. 28, 1963 (quoting *Amos* 5:24).

61. I would rather die on a highway in Alabama than make a butchery of conscience by compromising with evil.

Martin Luther King, Jr., Remark to LeRoy Collins of the U.S. Justice Department, who tried to persuade King that a civil rights march in Selma, AL, would be dangerous. 1965.

62. You can legislate against discrimination, but you can't legislate compassion, understanding, and good will.

David Lam, Lieutenant Governor, British Columbia, Canada. Quoted in *The New York Times*, Mar. 17, 1990.

63. Racism in our society is a motion for cloture. Accuse anybody of racism and it almost stops the debate.

Richard D. Lamm, Governor of Colorado (D). Quoted in *The Washington Post*, Oct. 24, 1988.

64. The fight must go on. The cause of civil liberty must not be surrendered at the end of one or even one hundred defeats.

Abraham Lincoln (1809-1865), 16th President of the United States (R-IL). Letter to Henry Asbury, Nov. 19, 1858.

65. I have no purpose, directly or indirectly, to interfere with the institution of slavery in the states where it exists. I believe I have no lawful right to do so, and I have no inclination to do so.

Abraham Lincoln. First inaugural address, Mar. 4, 1861.

66. My paramount object in this struggle is to save the Union, and is not either to save or destroy slavery.

Abraham Lincoln. Letter to Horace Greeley, Aug. 22, 1862.

67. Of all the bigotries that ravage the human temper there is none so stupid as the anti-Semitic. It has no basis in reason, it is not rooted in faith, it aspires to no ideal.

David Lloyd George, 1st Earl of Dwyfor (1863-1945), Prime Minister of Great Britain (Liberal). July 22, 1923.

68. Neither Pagan nor Mahometan nor Jew ought to be excluded from the civil rights of the Commonwealth because of his religion.

John Locke (1632-1704), English political philosopher. *Letter Concerning Toleration*, 1689.

69. That's part of American greatness ... discrimination. Yes, sir. Inequality ... breeds freedom and gives a man opportunity.

Lester Maddox, Governor of Georgia (D). Quoted in *The New York Times Magazine*, Nov. 6, 1966.

70. The very essence of civil liberty, is the right of every individual to claim the protection of the laws, whenever he receives an injury.

John Marshall (1755-1835), Chief Justice, U.S. Supreme Court. *Marbury* v. *Madison*, 1803.

71. In the nineteenth century exceptional *[discriminatory]* laws for the Jews can be nothing more than a blunder and an absurdity.

Giuseppe Mazzini (1805-1872), Italian statesman. Letter to his mother, Nov. 9, 1835.

72. We do not discriminate concerning marriage in the South; we simply do not let the whites and Negroes intermarry. We treat the white the same as the Negro.

John L. McClellan (1896-1977), U.S. Congressman and U.S. Senator (D-AR). Senate debate, 1944.

73. If you wish the Jews to become better men and useful citizens, then banish every humiliating restriction, open to them every avenue of gaining a livelihood.

Honoré de Mirabeau (1749-1791), French revolutionary and President, National Assembly. *On Political Reform of Jews*, 1787.

74. Race must never be a partisan issue.

Daniel P. Moynihan, Chief American Delegate to the United Nations and U.S. Senator (D-NY). Interview, CNN, *Evans & Novak*, May 12, 1991.

75. Everyone is a prisoner of his own experience. No one can eliminate prejudices – just recognize them.

Edward R. Murrow (1908-1965), American broadcast journalist and Director, United States Information Agency. Dec. 31, 1955.

76. In Germany the Nazis came for the Communists, and I didn't speak up because I was not a Communist. Then they came for the Jews and I didn't speak up because I was not a Jew. Then they came for the trade unionists and I didn't speak up because I was not a trade unionist. Then they came for the Catholics and I was a Protestant so I didn't speak up. Then they came for me. By that time there was no one to speak up for anyone.

Martin Niemöller (1892-1984), German Protestant pastor. Attributed.

77. Black-white relations between average Americans are not hostile – they are simply not close enough.

Eleanor Holmes Norton, Delegate, U.S. Congress (D-DC) and Chair, Equal Employment Opportunity Commission. *USA Today*, Sept. 11, 1989.

78. The remedy for bigotry is to surround the bigots and make sure that they are outnumbered.

Eleanor Holmes Norton. C-SPAN, June 24, 1990.

79. The people of this country are so goddamned tired of the mamby-pamby that's in Washington, it's a disgrace. There's nobody in the whole country that's got the spine to stand up to the goddamned niggers except me.

John Malcolm Patterson, Governor of Alabama (D). Statement to John Seigenthaler, May 1961.

80. There is nothing stronger than human prejudice.

Wendell Phillips (1811-1884), American orator and reformer. Jan. 28, 1852.

81. America's view of apartheid is simple and straightforward: We believe it is wrong. We condemn it. And we are united in hoping for the day when apartheid will be no more.

Ronald Reagan, 40th President of the United States (R-CA). Statement on on ordering economic sanctions against South Africa, Sept. 9, 1985.

82. I convinced *[Lyndon]* Johnson that it would be possible to pass a civil rights bill if you limited it to voting rights. Because I had a sense that southerners felt guilty about depriving the Negroes of voting. They didn't feel at all guilty of depriving them of jobs, they didn't feel sensitive about housing, but they were defensive about the vote thing. That they couldn't justify.

George E. Reedy, White House press secretary (D). Quoted in Merle Miller, *Lyndon: An Oral Biography*, 1980.

83. I don't think a Jew should be putting Negro children in white Protestant schools in the South ... at the instructions of a Catholic.

Abraham A. Ribicoff, Governor of Connecticut (D), U.S. Congressman, U.S. Senator, and U.S. Secretary of Health, Education and Welfare (D). On turning down Pres. Kennedy's offer to appoint him U.S. Attorney General. Quoted in Guthman and Shulman, *Robert Kennedy in His Own Words*, 1988.

84. I belong to an organization *[the DAR]* in which I can do no active work. They have taken an action which has been widely talked of in the press. To remain as a member implies approval of that action, and therefore I am resigning.

Anna Eleanor Roosevelt (1884-1962), First Lady and U.S. Delegate to the United Nations. Statement after the Daughters of the American Revolution barred black contralto Marian Anderson from singing in Constitution Hall, Washington, DC. "My Day," Feb. 7, 1939.

85. About as aggressive as a meek little rabbit.

Anna Eleanor Roosevelt. Description of Pres. Eisenhower's stand on civil rights. Quoted in Joseph P. Lash, *Eleanor: The Years Alone*, 1972.

86. No discrimination on grounds of race, color, creed, or national origin.

Franklin D. Roosevelt (1882-1945), 32nd President of the United States (D-NY). *Executive Order 8892*, 1941, drafted by Joseph L. Rauh, Jr..

87. It was my good fortune at Santiago to serve beside colored troops. A man who is good enough to shed his blood for the country is good enough to be given a square deal afterward. More than that no man is entitled to, and less than that no man shall have.

Theodore Roosevelt (1858-1918), 26th President of the United States (R-NY). Speech, Springfield, IL, June 4, 1903.

88. We repudiate the efforts of extremist groups such as the Communist Party, the Ku Klux Klan, the John Birch Society and others.

Hugh D. Scott, Jr., U.S. Congressman and U.S. Senator (R-PA). Resolution proposed and rejected at the Republican National Convention, 1964.

89. Every type of discrimination whether social or cultural, whether based on sex, race, social condition, language, or religion, is to be overcome and eradicated as contrary to God's intent.

Second Vatican Council, *The Church in the Modern World*, Dec. 1965.

90. Please note that long-haired persons will be served last at all Government departments and offices.

Singapore government tourist brochure, 1981.

91. The world knows no greater mockery than the use of the blazing cross *[by the KKK]*, the cross upon which Christ died – as a symbol to instill in the hearts of men a hatred for their brethren.

Alfred E. Smith (1873-1944), Governor of New York (D). Campaign speech, Oklahoma City, OK, 1928.

92. It *[the Ku Klux Klan]* must in time fall to the ground of its own weight. The Catholics of the country can stand it. The Jews can stand it. But the United States cannot stand it.

Alfred E. Smith. 1928.

93. At a time like this *[the depression]*, when millions of men, women, and children are starving throughout the land, there is always the temptation to some men to stir up class prejudice, to stir up the bitterness of the rich against the poor, and the poor against the rich. Against that effort I set myself uncompromisingly.

Alfred E. Smith. Speech, Washington, DC, Apr. 1932.

94. If we herd all Reds and Communists into concentration camps and outlaw about half the movies and then turn to Christian statesmanship, our problems would be solved.

Gerald L. K. Smith (1898-1976), American clergyman and cofounder, Union Party. Presidential campaign speech, 1944. House Un-American Activities Committee, *Investigation of Gerald L. K. Smith*, 1946.

95. It is useless to try and govern black and white in the same way and subject them to the same forms of legislation.

Jan Christiaan Smuts (1870-1950), Prime Minister of South Africa. 1917.

96. Live people are being sacrificed because of what dead people did.

Thomas Sowell, Fellow, Hoover Institution. On reverse discrimination in affirmative action programs. Quoted in *The New York Times,* July 1, 1990.

97. Everyone has as much right as he has might.

Benedict Spinoza (1632-1677), Dutch philosopher. *Theological-Political Treatise,* 1670.

98. It is impossible for one class to appreciate the wrongs of another.

Elizabeth Cady Stanton (1815-1902), 1st President, National Woman Suffrage Association. *History of Woman Suffrage,* 1881.

99. The average age of a woman in the state legislature is much higher than that of a man. The legislature is a woman's ultimate reward for years of civic work, while the male politician normally starts out on his career in this job.

Gloria Steinem, American editor and feminist. Quoted in O'Neil and Brink, *The World According to Breslin,* 1984.

100. Ignorance is stubborn and prejudice dies hard.

Adlai E. Stevenson (1900-1965), Governor of Illinois (D) and U.S. Ambassador to the United Nations. Speech, Oct. 1, 1963.

101. Civil wrongs don't make civil rights. Civil wrongs probably only beget civil wrongs.

Adlai E. Stevenson. Interview, ABC, *Issues and Answers,* Apr. 19, 1964.

102. It will be helpful ... to allow every man in America to look his neighbor in the face and see a man – not a color.

Adlai E. Stevenson. Quoted in *The New York Times,* June 22, 1964.

103. A fundamental interdependence exists between the personal right to liberty and the personal right in property. Neither could have any meaning without the other. That rights in property are basic civil rights has long been recognized.

Potter Stewart (1915-1985), U.S. Supreme Court Justice. *Lynch* v. *Household Finance Corporation,* 1972.

104. Take care of my civil rights bill.

Charles Sumner (1811-1874), U.S. Senator (D, R, and Free Soil-MA). Last words to Frederick Douglass and other civil rights leaders. Mar. 11, 1874.

105. The battle for women's rights has been largely won.

Margaret Thatcher, Prime Minister of Great Britain (Conservative). Quoted in *The Guardian,* 1962.

106. It is never too late to give up our prejudices.

Henry David Thoreau (1817-1862), American philosopher and naturalist. *Walden, or Life in the Woods,* 1854.

107. The ultimate aim of the Zionists is to liberate the Jewish people from the peculiar psychological complex induced by the penalization to which they have been subject for centuries in the gentile world.

Arnold J. Toynbee (1899-1975), British historian. *A Study of History,* II, 1934.

108. I am not interested in picking up crumbs of compassion thrown from the table of someone who considers himself my master. I want the full menu of rights.

Desmond M. Tutu, Anglican archbishop of South Africa and Nobel Laureate in Peace. Quoted on NBC, *Today,* Jan. 9, 1985.

109. Prejudices are what fools use for reasons.

Voltaire (François-Marie Arouet) (1694-1778), French historian and dramatist. *Poème sur la loi naturelle,* IV, 1756.

110. Here in Alabama no Negro is ever embarrassed. He knows what cafes he goes to and which ones the whites go to.

George C. Wallace, Governor of Alabama (D). Statement to reporters, 1961.

111. Our task must be simply to make clear that the movement known as "civil rights" is Communist-plotted, Communist controlled, and ... serves only Communist purposes.

Robert Welch, founder, John Birch Society. *John Birch Society Bulletin,* June 1965.

112. It is rather hard to be accused of shiftlessness and idleness when the accuser closes the avenue of labor and industrial pursuits to us.

George H. White (1852-1918), U.S. Congressman (R-NC). Farewell speech, House of Representatives, Feb. 23, 1900.

113. I'm not going to waste my time trying to eliminate racism. I'm just trying to make sure that racism doesn't eliminate me.

Polly Williams, Wisconsin State Legislator (D). CBS, *60 Minutes,* Dec. 9, 1990.

114. Segregation is not humiliating but a benefit, and ought to be so regarded by you gentlemen.

Woodrow Wilson (1856-1924), 28th President of the United States (D-NJ). Statement to black leaders, Washington, D.C., Nov. 1913.

115. No nation is fit to sit in judgement upon any other nation.

Woodrow Wilson. Speech, Philadelphia, PA, Oct. 1915.

116. Take away natural rights and duties become null.

Mary Wollstonecraft (1759-1797), British writer and feminist. *A Vindication of the Rights of Women*, 1792.

Chapter 21

Disinformation, Propaganda, and Rumors

1. Any excuse will serve a tyrant.
   Aesop (620-560 B.C.), Greek fabulist. *The Wolf and the Lamb.*

2. I run the *Daily Express* purely for propaganda and for no other purpose.
   William Maxwell Aitkin, 1st Baron Beaverbrook (1879-1964), British publisher. Statement to the Royal Commission on the Press, 1948.

3. Calumniate, Calumniate! Something will always stick!
   Pierre Beaumarchais (1732-1799), French playwright. *The Barber of Seville*, III, 1775.

4. A hit-and-run propagandist on the Kremlin model.
   William Benton (1900-1973), U.S. Senator (D-CT). In reference to Sen. Joseph R. McCarthy. Letter to John Howe, Feb. 21, 1955.

5. What's public is propaganda, what's secret is serious.
   Charles E. Bohlen (1904-1974), U.S. Ambassador to the U.S.S.R. 1969.

6. I don't want to defend rumors. It's certainly nothing new. The only development in recent years is the *[lower]* threshold at which news organizations will print rumors.
   John Buckley, Director of Communications, National Republican Congressional Committee, and press secretary to Congressman Jack Kemp (R-NY) during the 1988 presidential nomination race. Quoted in *The Washington Post*, June 8, 1989.

7. Propaganda is that branch of the art of lying which consists in nearly deceiving your friends without quite deceiving your enemies.
   Francis M. Cornford (1874-1943), British philosopher. Quoted in *The New Statesman*, Sept. 15, 1978.

8. When you're in the middle of a rumor storm, your two choices *[ignoring them and letting the pressure build, or denying them and taking the hit]* are not very good.... And there are some Americans who will believe that where there's smoke there's fire.
   Susan Estrich, professor, Harvard Law School, and director of Michael Dukakis's 1988 presidential campaign. Quoted in *The Washington Post*, June 8, 1989.

9. Manipulation is persuading people to make up their minds while withholding some of the facts from them.
   Harold Evans, British journalist. *The Sunday Times*, 1971.

10. Even intelligent people succumb to their own propaganda.
    Nicholas Freeling, British novelist. Foreword to *The Dresden Green*, 1966.

11. The secret to modern propaganda is to simplify and repeat.
    Fritz Hippler, German Nazi propagandist. Quoted on PBS, *Walk Through the 20th Century*, July 16, 1990.

12. If we don't like the information, it's propaganda. If we like the information, it's information.
    Marvin I. Kalb, American journalist. Interview, PBS, *MacNeil-Lehrer News Hour*, Aug. 29, 1990.

13. The great enemy of truth is very often not the lie – deliberate, contrived, and dishonest – but the myth, persistent, persuasive, and realistic.
    John F. Kennedy (1917-1963), 35th President of the United States (D-MA). Quoted in *The Washington Post*, Aug. 19, 1990.

14. The press is our chief ideological weapon.
    Nikita S. Khrushchev (1894-1971), Premier of the U.S.S.R. Quoted in *The New York Times*, Sept. 29, 1957.

15. I've known the last half-dozen budget directors, and not one of them ever leveled with me.
James J. Kilpatrick, American political columnist. CBS, *Inside Washington*, July 22, 1990.

16. The press should be not only a collective propagandist and a collective agitator, but also a collective organizer of the masses.
V. I. Lenin (1870-1924), Premier of the U.S.S.R. Quoted in *The New York Times*, Dec. 26, 1955.

17. Lies written in ink cannot obscure a truth written in blood.
Lu Xun (1881-1936), Chinese writer. Written after Chinese government security forces killed forty student protestors in Beijing, Mar. 18, 1926.

18. In every age the vilest specimens of human nature are to be found among demagogues.
Thomas Babington Macaulay, 1st Baron Macaulay (1800-1859), historian and Secretary of War, Great Britain (Liberal). *History of England*, V, 1861.

19. I'll bet each of these conflicting allegations comes from an "unimpeachable source."
Robert G. Menzies (1894-1978), Prime Minister of Australia (Liberal). Quoted in *The Wit of Sir Robert Menzies*, 1966.

20. The measure of our *[the Voice of America's]* success will be the degree to which we are believed.
Edward R. Murrow (1908-1965), American broadcast journalist and Director, United States Information Agency. Senate testimony.

21. When war is declared, truth is the first casualty.
Arthur Ponsonby, 1st Baron Ponsonby of Shulbrede (1871-1946), Undersecretary for Foreign Affairs, Great Britain (Labour). *Falsehood in Wartime*, 1928.

22. Washington is the only city where sound travels faster than light.
Ronald Reagan, 40th President of the United States (R-CA). 1983.

23. Promote our way of thinking.
John J. Rooney (1903-1975), U.S. Congressman (D-NY). View of the mission of Voice of America. Quoted in Thomas C. Sorensen, *The Word War: The Story of American Propaganda*, 1968.

24. Why is propaganda so much more successful when it stirs up hatred than when it tries to stir up friendly feeling?
Bertrand Russell, 3rd Earl Russell of Kingston (1872-1970), British philosopher and reformer. *The Conquest of Happiness*, 1930.

25. There is no nonsense so arrant that it cannot be made the creed of the vast majority by adequate governmental action.
Bertrand Russell. *Unpopular Essays*, 1950.

26. Men are so unwilling to displease a Prince, that it is as dangerous to inform him right, as to serve him wrong.
George Savile, 1st Marquess of Halifax (1633-1695), Lord Privy Seal of England. *Political Thoughts and Reflections*, 1750.

27. I hate deception, even where the imagination only is concerned.
George Washington (1732-1799), 1st President of the United States (VA). Letter to Dr. Cochran, Aug. 16, 1779.

28. Credibility gap
David Wise, American journalist. First used in reference to the Johnson administration's reporting of the Vietnam War. *New York Herald Tribune*, May 1965.

Chapter 22

The Economy and Fiscal Affairs

1. Prosperity is just around the corner.
Slogan during the Hoover administration (1929-1933), based on a variety of statements made by the President during the Depression.

2. IT IS GLORIOUS TO BE RICH
Common billboard message, post-Mao China.

3. The capitalist system of production and distribution is doomed. It threatens to engulf humanity in chaos.
American Labor Party (Socialist) platform, 1924.

4. The social order we have built recognizes no exploitation of man by man. In our country there are no rich people to live at the expense of the workers and peasants. Just as there are no poor people living on the charity of others.
Ramiz Alia, President of Albania. Quoted in *The New York Times*, Feb. 9, 1990.

5. The bottom line of a successful economic policy is jobs.
Martin Anderson, domestic policy advisor to Ronald Reagan (R). Quoted in *The New York Times*, July 22, 1988.

6. War can be done by arms. War can be done by economic means.
Tariq Aziz, Foreign Minister, Iraq. Interview, ABC, *Nightline*, Aug. 15, 1990.

7. Money is like muck, not good except it be spread.
Francis Bacon, 1st Baron Verulam and Viscount St. Albans (1561-1626), Lord Chancellor of England. *Essays*. "Of Seditions and Troubles," 1625.

8. Bend everything toward improving the standard of living of the people.
Bernard M. Baruch (1870-1965), Chairman, War Industries Board, and U.S. Delegate to the U.N. Atomic Energy Commission. Advice to Soviet Commissar Leonid Krassin, 1925.

9. Capitalism robs you and makes a wage slave of you. The law upholds and protects that robbery. The government fools you into believing that you are independent and free. In this way you are fooled and duped every day of your life.
Alexander Berkman (1870-1936), American anarchist. *What Is Communist Anarchism?*, 1920.

10. Our prosperity comes from something that is really marvelous – that is, unlimited freedom.
Daniel Boorstin, American historian and Librarian of Congress. Interview, ABC, *This Week*, Dec. 31, 1989.

11. We have learned that the various schools of *[economic]* thought all have important elements of truth in them. But none of them is by itself a sufficient explanation of what goes on in the economy.
Michael Boskin, Chairman, President's Council of Economic Advisors. Quoted in *Time*, Jan. 30, 1989.

12. I don't think it's the end of the world even if we have a recession. We'll pull back out of it again. No big deal.
Nicholas Brady, U.S. Secretary of the Treasury (R). Interview, NBC, *Meet the Press*, 1990.

13. It is the unvarying law that the wealth of the community will be in the hands of the few.
David J. Brewer (1837-1910), U.S. Supreme Court Justice. Speech, New York City Bar Association, 1893.

14. A dollar approaches honesty as its purchasing power approaches stability.
William Jennings Bryan (1860-1925), U.S. Secretary of State (D). Election debate, 1896.

15. You shall not press down upon the brow of labor this crown of thorns, you shall not crucify mankind upon a cross of gold.
William Jennings Bryan. "Cross of Gold"

speech, Democratic National Convention, Chicago, IL, July 8, 1896.

16. Communism has ... made people *[Russian workers]* very lazy.

Zbigniew Brzezinski, U.S. Secretary of State and National Security Advisor (D). Quoted on NBC, *John McLaughlin's One on One*, Apr. 30, 1989.

17. Nothing beats Reaganomics – though herpes can run it pretty close.

Art Buchwald, American humorist. 1983.

18. Government is a contrivance of human wisdom to provide for human wants. Men have a right that these wants should be provided for by this wisdom.

Edmund Burke (1729-1797), British statesman. *Reflections on the Revolution in France*, 1790.

19. It is no longer a matter of serious controversy whether the government should play a positive role in helping to maintain a high level of economic activity. What we debate nowadays is not the need for controlling business cycles but rather the nature of governmental action, its timing and its extent.

Arthur F. Burns, Chairman, President's Council of Economic Advisors (D). 1954.

20. Voodoo economics.

George Bush, 41st President of the United States (R-TX). Characterization of Ronald Reagan's economic views. Presidential campaign, 1980.

21. I don't know of any President, now or in the past, who does not favor lower interest rates. That's the American way.

George Bush. Statement, Aug. 1989.

22. It's not our business for the United States to sort out the other fellow's economic problems. We've got enough of our own.

George Bush. Quoted on CNN, May 28, 1990.

23. Without economic security, we cannot have national security.

Robert C. Byrd, U.S. Congressman and U.S. Senator (D-WV). Quoted in *The Washington Post*, Aug. 4, 1988.

24. A power has risen up in the government greater than the people themselves, consisting of many and various and powerful interests, combined into one mass, and held together by the cohesive power of the vast surplus in the banks.

John C. Calhoun (1782-1850), U.S. Congressman (D-SC), U.S. Senator, U.S. Secretary of War, U.S. Secretary of State, and Vice President of the United States. Senate speech, May 28, 1836.

25. Every time we hear some capitalist fool brag about the glories of this system, let's just remember, "This is as good as it gets under capitalism." Only a lucky few will do better.

Editorial, *Challenge* (weekly newspaper of the Progressive Labor Party), Mar. 14, 1990.

26. I don't think we should be in the business of proliferating arms sales just to protect our industrial base.

Richard B. Cheney, U.S. Congressman (R-WY), White House Chief of Staff, and U.S. Secretary of Defense. Interview, CNN, *Evans & Novak*, May 20, 1990.

27. The goal of economic progress is the extension of human liberty, not ... the open-ended servicing of human greed.

Joe Clark, Prime Minister of Canada (Conservative). Speech, London, England, Sept. 21, 1976.

28. Our progress toward a wise conclusion will not be improved by dwelling upon the theories.... It is a condition which confronts us – not a theory!

Grover Cleveland (1837-1908), 22nd and 24th President of the United States (D-NY). Annual message to Congress, declaring for tariff reductions, contrary to the prevailing economic wisdom. Dec. 6, 1887.

29. You can't just shut off the borders of a community.

Janis Cohen, Mayor of San Gabriel, CA. Statement after her ouster for opposing growth limitation proposals. Quoted in *The New York Times*, June 12, 1988.

30. When wealth is centralized, the people are dispersed. When wealth is distributed, the people are united.

Confucius (551-479 B.C.), Chinese philosopher. *Analects*.

31. Since ours is an economy based on growth through risk-taking, we should provide encouragement not only for saving but for prudent investment of those savings.

Philip M. Crane, U.S. Congressman (R-WI). *Conservative Digest*, October 1987.

32. It is but right that the men of brains and brawn who produce shall be recognized in the distribution. We simply ask a just proportion of the proceeds.

Eugene V. Debs (1855-1926), American Socialist. "A Grand Brotherhood," Sept. 22, 1885.

33. Capitalists personally are often the mildest-mannered men that ever shattered a family or drained a workingman of his marrow.
Daniel De Leon (1852-1914), American Socialist. Quoted in *The People*, Mar. 9, 1991.

34. We don't want to saw off the first rung of the economic ladder.
Elizabeth H. Dole, U.S. Secretary of Labor and U.S. Secretary of Transportation (R). Argument for a smaller increase in the minimum wage. Quoted on CBS, *Inside Washington*, Mar. 21, 1989.

35. Well, this is the end of Western civilization.
Lewis W. Douglas (1894-1974), U.S. Congressman (D-AZ), Director, U.S. Bureau of the Budget, and U.S. Ambassador to Great Britain. Reaction to Franklin Roosevelt's taking America off the gold standard. 1933.

36. There are two problems in my life. The political ones are insoluble and the economic ones are incomprehensible.
Alexander F. Douglas-Home, Prime Minister of Great Britain (Conservative). Quoted in *The New York Times*, Jan. 9, 1964.

37. It is not the federal government that makes prosperity in this country.
Dwight D. Eisenhower (1890-1969), 34th President of the United States (R-KS). Press conference, 1955.

38. A creative economy is the fuel of magnificence.
Ralph Waldo Emerson (1803-1882), American writer. "Aristocracy," in *English Traits*, 1876.

39. I spent half my life on economic relations and building relationships with allies and friends; I spent the other half of it on warfare and the Third World. Some people tell me that the mixture of economic analysis and warfare is ideal training for Wall Street.
Thomas Enders, U.S. Assistant Secretary of State. Mar. 1987.

40. If ... the taking over the tobacco trade by the state was socialistic, Napoléon and Metternich would rank among the founders of Socialism.
Friedrich Engels (1820-1895), German Socialist and revolutionary theorist. *Anti-Duering*.

41. The prince should try to prevent too great an inequality of wealth .... prevent the wealth of the multitude from being hoarded by a few.
Desiderius Erasmus (c. 1466-1536), Dutch scholar and theologian. *The Praise of Folly*, 1509.

42. We can wreck the economy in the process of trying to fight the cold war.
James V. Forrestal (1892-1949), U.S. Secretary of the Navy and U.S. Secretary of Defense. 1948.

43. Our whole evolutionary thinking leads us to the conclusion that economic independence lies at the very foundation of social and moral well-being.
Felix Frankfurter (1882-1965), U.S. Supreme Court Justice. *Law and Politics*, 1936.

44. Nothing so weakens governments as persistent inflation.
John Kenneth Galbraith, American economist and U.S. Ambassador to India (D). *The Affluent Society*, 1968.

45. In considering economic behavior, humor is especially important for, needless to say, much of that behavior is infinitely ridiculous.
John Kenneth Galbraith. *A Contemporary Guide to Economics, Peace and Laughter*, 1971.

46. There are two kinds of economists in the world. Those who don't know the future and those who don't know that they don't know the future.
John Kenneth Galbraith. Quoted on PBS, *MacNeil-Lehrer News Hour*, Aug. 6, 1990.

47. All amassing of wealth or hoarding of wealth above and beyond one's legitimate needs is theft.
Mohandas K. Gandhi (1869-1948), Indian political and spiritual leader. Quoted in Edgar Snow, *Journey to the Beginning*, 1958.

48. Capital is good; the capitalist is a helper if he is not also a monopolist. We can safely let anyone get as rich as he can if he will not despoil others in doing so.
Henry George (1839-1897), American political economist. *Social Problems*, 1884.

49. There are three ways by which an individual can get wealth – by work, by gift, and by theft. And, clearly, the reason why the workers get so little is that the beggars and thieves get so much.
Henry George. *Ibid.*

50. When the economy is bad, the party in power is blamed. When the economy is good, people look at other issues.
Jack Germond, American political columnist. NBC, *The McLaughlin Group*, July 30, 1988.

51. Is supply-side economics finished? Only in the sense that Gen. George S. Patton's army was finished in Germany in May, 1945.
Newton L. Gingrich, U.S. Congressman (R-GA). Quoted in *The 1989 Conservative Calendar*.

52. The notion that free enterprise exists has got to be acknowledged as being a myth. If I had a choice between believing in free enterprise and Santa Claus, I'd tell you I believe in Santa Claus.
Richard Hatfield, Premier of New Brunswick, Canada. Speech, Dec. 2, 1983.

53. The distribution of wealth is just as important as its creation.
William Randolph Hearst (1863-1951), U.S. Congressman (D-NY); founder, Independence League Party; journalist; and publisher. Interview, *Chicago Tribune*, Jan. 19, 1905.

54. There are three things not worth running for – a bus, a woman, or a new economic panacea; if you wait a bit, another one will come along.
Derick Heathcoat-Amory, Chancellor of the Exchequer, Great Britain. Quoted in Fred Metcalf, *The Penguin Dictionary of Modern Humorous Quotations*, 1986.

55. Prosperity seldom chooses the side of the virtuous.
Héloise (1098-1164), French abbess. Letter to Peter Abelard, c.1122.

56. I'll see to it that prices remain stable. That's what I have my storm troopers for.
Adolf Hitler (1889-1945), Führer of the Third German Reich. 1934.

57. During the twenty-six years I have spent in the public service I have been guided wholly by these economic formulas *[of Marxist Socialism]* as a foundation in effectuating policies and in promoting governmental measures.
Daniel Webster Hoan (1881-1961), Mayor of Milwaukee, WI (Socialist). *City Government*, 1936.

58. If ignorance paid dividends, most Americans could make a fortune out of what they don't know about economics.
Luther H. Hodges (1898-1974), U.S. Secretary of Commerce and Governor of North Carolina (D). Quoted in *The Wall Street Journal*, Mar. 14, 1962.

59. A constitution is not intended to embody a particular economic theory.
Oliver Wendell Holmes, Jr. (1841-1935), U.S. Supreme Court Justice. *Lochner* v. *New York*, 1906.

60. When the war *[World War I]* closed ... we were challenged with a peacetime choice between the American system of rugged individualism and a European philosophy of ... paternalism and state socialism.
Herbert Hoover (1874-1964), 31st President of the United States (R). Campaign speech, New York City, October 22, 1928.

61. I am firmly opposed to the government entering any business the major purpose of which is competition with our citizens.
Herbert Hoover. Message to the Senate vetoing the Muscle Shoals Bill, Mar. 3, 1931.

62. The fundamental business of the country, that is, production and distribution of commodities, is on a sound and prosperous basis.
Herbert Hoover. Campaign speech, Sept. 1932.

63. The test of the rightfulness of our decisions must be whether we have sustained and advanced ... prosperity.
Herbert Hoover. Quoted in Richard Hofstadter, *The American Political Tradition*, 1948.

64. The stock boom was blowing great guns when I came into office.
Herbert Hoover. *Memoirs*, 1952.

65. The new frontier is idle men, money, and machines, and all the resourcefulness, ingenuity, and courage that reside in twelve or thirteen million unemployed men is helpless to take up this new frontier without tremendous organization of productive forces such as only government can supply when business is in the doldrums.
Harry L. Hopkins (1890-1946), U.S. Secretary of Commerce; Director, Work Projects Administration; Director, Federal Emergency Relief Administration; and Special Assistant to the President (D). Quoted in *Time*, July 18, 1938.

66. The law of supply and demand holds eternal.
Louis McHenry Howe (1871-1935), presidential assistant (D). *Life More Abundant*, 1934.

67. I learned more about economics from one South Dakota dust storm than I did in all my years in college.
Hubert H. Humphrey (1911-1978), Vice President of the United States and U.S. Senator (D-MN). To hecklers during a speech at the University of Wisconsin, Madison, WI. Aug. 23, 1965.

68. Cutting necks is better than cutting the means of living.
Saddam Hussein, President of Iraq. Speech, 1990.

69. High interest rates are the cruelest taxes of all.
Lee Iacocca, Chairman, Chrysler Corp., and member, National Economic Commission. *The Washington Post*, Mar. 12, 1989.

70. No man should be allowed to own any land he does not use.

Robert Green Ingersoll (1833-1899), Attorney General of Illinois (R). Quoted in George Seldes, *The Great Quotations*, 1983.

71. I would like to see a fair division of profits between capital and labor, so that the toiler could save enough to mingle a little June with the December of his life.

Robert Green Ingersoll. *What I Want for Christmas*.

72. Agriculture, manufactures, commerce, and navigation, the four pillars of our prosperity, are the most thriving when left most free to individual enterprise.

Thomas Jefferson (1743-1826), 3rd President of the United States (Democratic Republican-VA). First inaugural address, Mar. 4, 1801.

73. The free market is the most efficient for utilizing resources and responding to needs, but there are many human needs which find no place on the market.

Pope John Paul II. *Centesimus Annus*, May 3, 1991.

74. *[Gerald]* Ford's economics is the worst thing that's happened to this country since pantyhose ruined finger-fucking.

Lyndon B. Johnson (1908-1973), 36th President of the United States (D-TX). Quoted in Merle Miller, *Lyndon: An Oral Biography*, 1980.

75. I believe in municipal ownership of all public service monopolies for the same reason that I believe in the municipal ownership of waterworks, of parks, of schools. I believe in the municipal ownership of these monopolies because if you do not own them, they will own you. They will rule your politics, corrupt your institutions, and finally destroy your liberties.

Tom L. Johnson (1854-1911), U.S. Congressman and Mayor of Cleveland, OH (D). Quoted in William O. Douglas, *An Almanac of Liberty*, 1956.

76. Admittedly, the task of orchestrating monetary and fiscal policies so that they are in tune with the business cycle is little short of awesome.

Henry Kaufman, chief economist, Salomon Brothers Investment Bank. *The New York Times Magazine*, October 9, 1988.

77. The real wealth of a nation resides in its farms and factories and the people who man them.

John F. Kennedy (1917-1963), 35th President of the United States (D-MA). Quoted in Susan Teltser-Schwartz, *Money Talks*, 1988.

78. If Enterprise is afoot, wealth accumulates whatever may be happening to Thrift; and if Enterprise is asleep, wealth decays whatever Thrift may be doing.

John Maynard Keynes (1883-1946), British economist and diplomat. *A Treatise on Money*, 1930.

79. The ideas of economists and political philosophers, both when they are right and when they are wrong, are more powerful than is commonly understood.... Practical men, who believe themselves to be quite exempt from any intellectual influences, are usually the slaves of some defunct economist. Madmen in authority, who hear voices in the air, are distilling their frenzy from some academic scribbler of a few years back.

John Maynard Keynes. *The General Theory of Employment, Interest, and Money*, 1936.

80. We cannot remove the evils of capitalism without taking its source of power: ownership.

Neil Kinnock, Member of Parliament, Great Britain (Labour). 1975.

81. The job of city government is to provide a climate for the creation of jobs and profits in the private sector.

Edward I. Koch, U.S. Congressman and Mayor of New York City (D). 1980.

82. If people have jobs they can solve 90 percent of their problems themselves, and we can work on the other 10 percent.

Edward I. Koch. Quoted in *Governing the States and Localities*, May 1988.

83. Politics is economics in action.

Robert M. La Follette (1855-1925), Governor of Wisconsin and U.S. Senator (R). Recalled on his death.

84. An industry that cannot pay its workers a decent living wage has no right to exist.

Fiorello H. La Guardia (1882-1947), U.S. Congressman (R and Socialist) and Mayor of New York City (R and Fusion Party). Speech, House of Representatives, Feb. 8, 1928.

85. That industries like coal and electric power, transport and banking, the supply of meat and the provision of houses, should be left to the hazards of private enterprise will appear as unthinkable to a future generation as it is unthinkable to our own that the army of the State should be left to private hands.... That does not mean direct operation by government.... It means the planning of

constitutions for essential industries.

Harold J. Laski (1893-1950), British political scientist. *A Grammar of Politics*, 1925.

86. A recession is a period in which you tighten your belt. In a depression you have no belt to tighten. In a panic you have no pants left to hold up.

Stephen Leacock (1869-1944), Canadian humorist and economist. Quoted in Allan Anderson, *Remembering Leacock*, 1984.

87. The question today is whether we should be creating millions of new jobs at present wages or fewer new jobs at better wages.

Frank Levy, professor of labor economics, University of Maryland, College Park, MD. Quoted in *The New York Times*, Sept. 4, 1988.

88. The basic law of capitalism is you or I, not both you and I.

Karl Liebknecht (1871-1919), German Socialist. Speech, Socialist Young People's Conference, Stuttgart, Germany, 1907.

89. That some should be rich shows that others may become rich, and hence is just encouragement to industry and enterprise.

Abraham Lincoln (1809-1865), 16th President of the United States (R-IL). Reply to committee of the Workingman's Association of New York. Mar. 21, 1864.

90. The emancipation of the masses can become a reality only with the abolition of the competitive system of society.

Meyer London (1871-1926), U.S. Congressman (Socialist-NY). Congressional speech, 1916.

91. Unless you redistribute the wealth of a country into the hands of the people every fifty years, your country's got to go to ruination.

Huey P. Long (1893-1935), Governor of Louisiana and U.S. Senator (D). Campaign speech, 1932.

92. We need to share the wealth. Let's put the jam jar on the lower shelf where the little man can reach it.

Huey P. Long. Quoted on CBS, *Sunday Morning*, Aug. 14, 1988.

93. You can strike an emotional chord, but it's very difficult to strike an economic chord.

Flora MacDonald, Member of Parliament, Canada. Quoted in *The Canadian*, May 3, 1975.

94. You don't have to kill the economy to regulate it.

Ronald Machtley, U.S. Congressman (R-RI). Quoted in *The Wall Street Journal*, May 4, 1990.

95. Selling the family silver.

Harold Macmillan (1894-1986), Prime Minister of Great Britain (Conservative). Description of privatization and the selling of profitable state-owned enterprises. Speech, House of Lords, 1986.

96. No sheriff or bailiff of ours, or any other, shall take horses or carts of any freeman for transportation, unless with the consent of that freeman.

Magna Carta, sealed by John Lackland (c.1167-1216), King of England, June 15, 1215, under duress. Later repudiated with Papal assistance.

97. There is a serious tendency toward capitalism among the well-to-do peasants.

Mao Tse-tung (1893-1976), Chairman, Communist Party of China. 1966.

98. In a morally adjusted economy ... the rich should not get richer if the poor get poorer.

Malachi Martin, American Roman Catholic theologian and writer. Explanation of the position of Pope John Paul II. *The Keys of This Blood*, 1990.

99. Capital is dead labor that, vampirelike, only lives by sucking living labor.

Karl Marx (1818-1883), German economist and Socialist. *Das Kapital*, 1867.

100. Democratic capitalism, combined with industrial democracy, is unquestionably the best way of life for mankind.

David J. McDonald (1902-1979), President, United Steelworkers of America. Quoted in *The New York Post*, October 30, 1957.

101. The middle class is the group in this country that has been taken for a ride.

George S. McGovern, U.S. Congressman and U.S. Senator (D-SD). PBS, *Firing Line*, Sept. 14, 1990.

102. The question is not whether the nation should reduce current consumption. It should. The question is, Whose consumption should be reduced?

Robert S. McIntyre, Director, Citizens for Tax Justice. *The New York Times*, May 14, 1990.

103. Liquidate labor, liquidate stocks, liquidate farmers.

Andrew W. Mellon (1855-1937), U.S. Secretary of the Treasury (R). Advice to President Hoover on the depression. 1931.

104. We must be careful that the people who make $5,000 a year are not pitted against those that make $25,000 a year by those who make $900,000.

Barbara A. Mikulski, U.S. Congresswoman and U.S. Senator (D-MD). Campaign speech, 1974.

105. The distribution of wealth ... depends on the laws and customs of society ... what the opinions and feelings of the ruling class make them, and are very different in different ages and countries; and might be still more different, if mankind so chose.
John Stuart Mill (1806-1873), Member of Parliament, Great Britain, and political economist. *Principles of Political Economy*, 1848.

106. The future of a nation will be shaped by its ability to produce planes, cars, electronics ... not by how slick its financial markets can shuffle paper assets around.
Akio Morita, Founder and Chairman, Sony Corp. Speech, Yale University, New Haven, CT, Oct. 1990.

107. Those who are seeking miraculous remedies for the depression are mistaken. Either the present depression is a periodic depression with the economic system, in which case it will be overcome, or it represents a transition from one stage of civilization to another.
Benito Mussolini (1883-1945), dictator of Italy (Fascist). Speech, October 16, 1932.

108. I want to establish the corporate regime.... The corporations will be called upon to regulate all problems of production. A policy of unregulated production is folly and generally catastrophic.
Benito Mussolini. October 7, 1933.

109. Corporative economy introduces order even into economy. If there is a phenomenon which ought to be well ordered, which ought to be directed toward certain definite aims, it is precisely the economic phenomenon, which interests the whole of the citizens. Not only industrial economy ought to be disciplined, but also agricultural economy, commercial economy, banking economy, and even the work of artisans.
Benito Mussolini. Speech, Italian Senate, Jan. 13, 1934.

110. They *[the English]* are nothing but shopkeepers; their glory is in their wealth.
Napoléon I (1769-1821), Military leader and Emperor of France. *Maxims*.

111. In the unplanned economy it's dog eat dog; in the planned one, both starve to death.
Richard J. Needham, Canadian columnist. *The Globe and Mail*, October 27, 1980.

112. The forces of a capitalistic society, if left unchecked, tend to make the rich richer and the poor poorer.
Jawaharlal Nehru (1889-1964), 1st Prime Minister of India. *Credo*.

113. I will not take the nation down the road of wage and price controls however politically expedient they may seem.
Richard M. Nixon, 37th President of the United States (R-CA). Statement, 1971.

114. I am today ordering a freeze on all prices and wages throughout the United States.
Richard M. Nixon. Address to the nation, 1971.

115. Capitalism is too complicated a system for a newly independent nation.
Kwame Nkrumah (1909-1972), President of Ghana. Quoted in *The New York Times Magazine*, July 2, 1958.

116. If we let inflation get out of control, we're going to get blown out of the game before we have a chance to move the ball.
Robert Ortner, U.S. Undersecretary of Commerce. Quoted in *The Washington Post*, Mar. 5, 1989.

117. Man is the only creature that consumes without producing.
George Orwell (Eric Blair) (1903-1950), British writer. *Animal Farm*, 1945.

118. Perhaps our going to war is the only way in which our preeminent trade position can be maintained and a *[financial]* panic averted. The submarine has added the last item to the danger of a financial world crash.
Walter Hines Page (1855-1918), U.S. Ambassador to Great Britain. Cable to Pres. Wilson, Mar. 5, 1917.

119. Wealth makes many friends.
Old Testament, *Proverbs* 19:4.

120. The rich rule over the poor, and the borrower is servant to the lender.
Old Testament, *Proverbs* 22:7.

121. This is a capitalist society. Capital is what moves our society.
William Proxmire, U.S. Senator (D-WI). Interview, NBC, *John McLaughlin's One on One*, Dec. 25, 1988.

122. Creation comes before distribution – or there will be nothing to distribute.
Ayn Rand (1905-1982), American philosopher. *The Fountainhead*, 1943.

123. Inflation is as violent as a mugger, as frightening as an armed robber, and as deadly as a hit-man.
Ronald Reagan, 40th President of the United States (R-CA). October, 1978.

124. Can we solve the *[economic]* problems facing us? The answer is an unequivocal and emphatic yes. To paraphrase Winston Churchill, I did not take the oath I have just taken with the intention of presiding over the dissolution of the world's strongest economy.

Ronald Reagan. First inaugural address, Jan. 1981.

125. One thing that has happened ... is a rise in the expectations held of life by many Americans who have risen above subsistence. This is the American form of "the revolution of rising expectations," of which the motto is "If things are good, why aren't they better still?"

David Reisman, professor of sociology, Harvard University, Cambridge, MA. *The Lonely Crowd*, 1951.

126. We have learned to create economic abundance ... but we have not created the economic and social mechanisms within the framework of our free society that will allow us to manage abundance by learning to share it.

Walter P. Reuther (1907-1970), President, United Auto Workers of America. *First Things First*, 1964.

127. The conflict in America is between two kinds of planning. It is privately planned economic scarcity by companies for profits or publicly planned economic abundance for people.

Walter P. Reuther. Quoted in George Seldes, *The Great Quotations*, 1983.

128. The interest of the landlords is always opposed to the interest of every other class in the community.

David Ricardo (1772-1823), British political economist. *Principles of Political Economy and Taxation*, 1817.

129. There is no way of keeping profits up but by keeping wages down.

David Ricardo. *On Protection to Agriculture*, 1820.

130. The President *[Gerald Ford]* said he intended to assign me important responsibilities. In fact, he said he was willing to make me responsible for inflation and recession.

Nelson A. Rockefeller (1908-1979), Governor of New York and Vice President of the United States (R). Quoted in Skubik and Short, *Republican Humor*, 1976.

131. The power of the few to manage the economic life of the nation must be diffused among the many or be transferred to the public and its democratically responsible government.

Franklin D. Roosevelt (1882-1945), 32nd President of the United States (D-NY), 1945). First message to Congress, March 9, 1933.

132. I want to emphasize to you that the domestic situation is inevitably and deeply tied in with the conditions in all the other nations of the world.

Franklin D. Roosevelt. Fireside Chat, May 7, 1933.

133. The royalists of the economic order have conceded that political freedom was the business of the government, but they have maintained that economic slavery was nobody's business.

Franklin D. Roosevelt. Presidential nomination acceptance speech, Democratic National Convention, Philadelphia, PA, June 27, 1936.

134. Economic freedom for the average man ... will give his political freedom reality.

Franklin D. Roosevelt. Labor Day radio address, Sept. 6, 1936.

135. The commercial classes are only too likely to regard everything merely from the standpoint of "Does it pay?" and many a merchant does not take any part in politics because he is short-sighted enough to think that it will pay him better to attend purely to making money, and too selfish to be willing to undergo any trouble for the sake of abstract duty.

Theodore Roosevelt (1858-1919), 26th President of the United States (R-NY). *Century*, 1886.

136. Economic progress, in capitalist society, means turmoil.

Joseph A. Schumpeter (1883-1950), American economist. *Capitalism, Socialism and Democracy*, 1942.

137. Republics come to an end by luxurious habits; monarchies by poverty.

Charles-Louis de Secondat, Baron de La Brède et de Montesquieu (1689-1755), French writer. *The Spirit of the Laws*, VII, 4, 1748.

138. If all economists were laid end to end, they would not reach a conclusion.

George Bernard Shaw (1856-1950), Nobel Laureate in Literature (Great Britain). *Caesar and Cleopatra*, 1898.

139. An economist's lag can be a politician's nightmare.

George P. Shultz, U.S. Secretary of State (R). Quoted in *The Economist*, Oct. 6-12, 1990.

140. An optimist is someone who believes in Reaganomics. A pessimist is someone who understands Reaganomics.

Paul Simon, U.S. Senator (D-IL). Remark, 1982.

141. It is not from the benevolence of the butcher, the brewer, or the baker that we expect our dinner, but from their regard of their own self-interest.
Adam Smith (1723-1790), Scottish political economist. *The Wealth of Nations*, 1776.

142. Socialism is nothing but the capitalism of the lower classes.
Oswald Spengler (1880-1936), German philosopher. *The Hour of Decision*, Part I: *Germany and the World Historical Evolution*, 1934.

143. Industrial crisis, unemployment, waste, widespread poverty, these are the incurable diseases of capitalism.
Joseph Stalin (1879-1953), Premier of the U.S.S.R. Speech to Soviet industrial managers, Leningrad, Feb. 4, 1931.

144. The government must be the trustee for the little man, because no one else will be. The powerful can usually help themselves – and frequently do!
Adlai E. Stevenson (1900-1965), Governor of Illinois (D) and U.S. Ambassador to the United Nations. Speech, Democratic rally, Duluth, MN, October 29, 1955.

145. There is nothing fundamentally wrong with America's cities that money can't cure.
Carl B. Stokes, Mayor of Cleveland, OH (D). *Playboy*, Jan. 1971.

146. Free competition means a free and open market among both buyers and sellers for the sale and distribution of commodities.
Harlan Fiske Stone (1872-1946), Chief Justice, U.S. Supreme Court, and U.S. Attorney General. *Maple Floor Manufacturers Association* v. *United States*, 1924.

147. Capital has got possession of the government.
Alexander H. H. Stuart (1807-1891), U.S. Congressman and U.S. Secretary of the Interior (Whig-VA). Quoted in *The New York World*, October 14, 1872.

148. Today's family needs at least two paychecks just to maintain yesterday's standard of living.
John J. Sweeney, President, Service Employees International Union. Testimony, House Education and Labor Committee, Feb. 25, 1987.

149. Our national strength also depends on a strong economy.
Maxwell D. Taylor (1901-1987), General, U.S. Army, Chairman, Joint Chiefs of Staff, and U.S. Ambassador to South Vietnam. Quoted by Gov. Richard Lamm, *Playboy*, Aug. 1984.

150. No one would remember the Good Samaritan if he only had good intentions. He had money as well.
Margaret Thatcher, Prime Minister of Great Britain (Conservative). Attributed.

151. Free enterprise and competition are the engines of prosperity.
Margaret Thatcher. 1980.

152. State socialism is totally alien to the British character.
Margaret Thatcher. Quoted in *The London Times*, 1983.

153. If you let the Republicans get control of the government, you will be making America an economic colony of Wall Street.
Harry S Truman (1884-1972), 33rd President of the United States (D-MO). Campaign speech, 1948.

154. It's a recession when your neighbor loses his job. It's a depression when you lose your own.
Harry S Truman. Quoted in *The Observer*, Apr. 6, 1958.

155. I was in search of a one-armed economist so that the guy could never make a statement and then say, "On the other hand."
Harry S Truman. Quoted in *Time*, Jan. 30, 1989.

156. There is no way we can avoid a clash between monetary restraint ... and the growth of economic activity.
Paul A. Volcker, Chairman, Federal Reserve Board. Speech, Milwaukee, WI, 1980.

157. There are persons who constantly clamor. They complain of oppression, speculation, and pernicious influence of wealth. They cry out against all banks and corporations.... They carry on mad hostility against all established institutions. They would choke the fountain of industry and dry up all streams.
Daniel Webster (1782-1852), U.S. Congressman (Federalist-NH and MA), U.S. Senator (Federalist and Whig-MA), and U.S. Secretary of State. Senate debate, Mar. 12, 1838.

158. The American economy is not going to prosper unless Americans regard as necessities what other people look on as luxuries.
Wendell L. Willkie (1892-1944), Republican candidate for President (IN). *One World*, 1943.

159. All political history shows that the standing of a government and its ability to hold the confidence of the electorate ... depend on the success of its economic policy.

Harold Wilson, Prime Minister of Great Britain (Labour). 1968.

160. One man's pay increase is another's price increase.
Harold Wilson. Quoted in *The Observer*, Jan. 11, 1970.

161. The truth is, we are all caught in a great economic system which is heartless.
Woodrow Wilson (1856-1924), 28th President of the United States (D-NJ). Quoted in Richard Hofstadter, *The American Political Tradition*, 1948.

162. In order to invest it is necessary to have money, and we have neither money nor pockets.
Grigory Yavlinsky, Russian economist and Finance Minister, U.S.S.R. Response when asked about his country's investment policy. Quoted in *The New York Times*, June 2, 1991.

163. A market can be a capitalist or a socialist one, but it is still a market.
Boris Yeltsin, President of the U.S.S.R. Quoted in *Time*, Mar. 20, 1989.

Chapter 23

Education

1. If you think education's expensive, try ignorance.
Advertisement, *The New York Times*, Oct. 25 1988.

2. WE WANT TO GO TO SCHOOL
55 HOURS OR NOTHING
Slogans of striking children, Philadelphia, PA, 1903.

3. Public television is the world's largest classroom.
Public television ad, *Roll Call*, May 21, 1990.

4. READING ZONE
BALTIMORE: THE CITY THAT READS
Signs on park benches in Baltimore, MD. Introduced by Mayor Kurt Schmoke (D), 1988.

5. To be literate is to be liberated.
Slogan of Cuban Communist revolutionaries, 1960's.

6. A teacher affects eternity; he can never tell where his influence stops.
Henry Adams (1838-1918), American historian. *The Education of Henry Adams*, 1907.

7. Ours has become a culture more concerned with developing personal relationships than wrestling with ideas and innovations that shape the future.... Opportunities will arise from control of knowledge.
Clifford Adelman, researcher, U.S. Department of Education. *The New York Times*, July 22, 1989.

8. Choice *[in education]* is an American value.
Lamar Alexander, Governor of Tennessee and U.S. Secretary of Education (R). Interview, CNN, *Evans & Novak*, Apr. 21, 1991.

9. The world has changed but our school systems haven't.
Lamar Alexander. *Ibid.*

10. All the youth ... who are rich enough to be able to devote themselves to it be set to learn ... until they are able to read English writing well.
Alfred (The Great) (849-901), King of the West Saxons. *Cura Pastoralis*.

11. The declaration that any legal issue is "not an open question in a law school" is a declaration of war upon everything that a law school is. Most fundamentally, a law school is a place of intellectual inquiry, where the acceptability of ideas can only be determined by examining them.
Anthony Amsterdam, dean, New York University Law School. In response to students who refused to argue a moot court case involving a lesbian mother's custody of her five-year old daughter because arguments about the mother's unfitness were "hurtful to a group of people and therefore hurtful to all of us," 1990.

12. We are elitist, but not exclusive. And I'm not ashamed in the least of being elitist. All that means is aiming at the highest standards you can achieve.
Eric Anderson, headmaster, Eton College, London, England. Quoted in *Time*, Dec. 10, 1990.

13. The legislator should direct his attention above all to the education of youth.
Aristotle (384-322 B.C.), Greek philosopher and teacher. *Politics*.

14. There are only two positions; either you support multiculturalism in American education, or you support the maintenance of white supremacy.
Molefi Asante, chairperson, African American Studies Department, Temple University, Philadelphia, PA. Quoted in *Newsweek*, Dec. 24, 1990.

15. A Harvard professor is an educator who thinks the American Eagle has two left wings.
John M. Ashbrook (1928-1982), U.S. Congressman (R-OH). Quoted in *Conservative Digest*, Aug. 1988.

16. The government's most creative and significant duty is education.
Kemal Atatürk (1881-1938), founder and 1st President of the Turkish Republic. Quoted in *Ataturk: Creator of Modern Turkey*, 1981.

17. We can't go on appropriating more and more money to state universities without knowing that we're getting an excellent product back out of them.

Donald Avenson, Speaker, Iowa House of Representatives. Quoted in *Des Moines Register*, July 3, 1988.

18. Keep schools open from sunset to sundown.
Bruce Babbitt, Governor of Arizona (D). PBS, *America's Children: Who Should Care?*, Sept. 4, 1990.

19. Knowledge itself is power.
Francis Bacon, 1st Baron Verulam and Viscount St. Albans (1561-1626), Lord Chancellor of England. *Religious Meditations*, "Of Heresies."

20. You've got close to educational meltdown here *[in Chicago]*.
William J. Bennett, Director, Office of National Drug Control Policy, and U.S. Secretary of Education (R). Quoted in *The New York Times*, July 13, 1988.

21. They *[educators]* don't want to hear my views on education. They just want the *[federal]* money.
William J. Bennett. PBS, *MacNeil-Lehrer Report*, Sept. 20, 1988.

22. I thank God we have no free schools nor printing .... for learning has brought disobedience and heresy and sects into the world; and printing has divulged them and libels against the government. God keep us from both.
William Berkeley (1606-1677), Colonial Governor of Virginia. 1671.

23. Liberal democracies exist only where there are free universities.
Alan Bloom (1930-1962), philosophy professor, University of Chicago. *The Closing of the American Mind*, 1989.

24. It is hard to be an island of excellence in a sea of indifference.
Ernest Boyer, U.S. Commissioner of Education. Interview, PBS, *MacNeil-Lehrer News Hour*, Sept. 28, 1989.

25. Students now see college more as a credentialing institution rather than an academic institution.
Ernest Boyer. Interview, ABC, *Nightline*, Apr. 16, 1990.

26. If we are going to lead the world, we have to know where it is.
William W. Bradley, U.S. Senator (D-NJ). Reaction to a study showing that American' knowledge of geography was less than that of other nations. Interview, ABC, *Nightline*, July 27, 1988.

27. "Relevance" may not be best.... Impetuous action, conscious oversimplification, refusal to doubt, rejection of reason, are enemies of the university.
Kingman Brewster, Jr., U.S. Ambassador to Great Britain and President, Yale University, New Haven, CT. In response to student demands for "relevant" courses and studies. *The American Scholar*, Spring 1970.

28. It's an insane tragedy that 700,000 people get a diploma each year and can't read the damned diploma.
William Brock, U.S. Congressman (R-TN), U.S. Senator, and U.S. Secretary of Labor. Quoted in *Newsweek*, Jan. 26, 1987.

29. Education makes a people easy to lead, but difficult to drive; easy to govern, but impossible to enslave.
Henry Peter Brougham, Baron Brougham and Vaux (1798-1868), Scottish jurist and Member of Parliament, Great Britain (Whig). *The Present State of the Law*.

30. Has America become a country where classroom discussion of the Ten Commandments is impermissible, but teacher instructions in safe sodomy are to be mandatory?
Patrick Buchanan, White House speech writer and political columnist (R). In reference to AIDS health instruction in schools. Quoted in *Conservative Digest*, Aug. 1988.

31. Education is the first step on the ladder to economic empowerment.
George Bush, 41st President of the United States (R-TX). Sept. 27, 1989.

32. If you're someone who reads, find someone who can't.... Join the community of conscience.
George Bush. Annual message to Congress, Jan. 29, 1990.

33. As a matter of principle, science teachers are professionally bound to limit their teaching to science and should resist pressure *[from religious fundamentalists]* to do otherwise.
Policy statement, California Board of Education, Jan. 13, 1989.

34. Please, children, do not leave school.
Lauro F. Calvazos, U.S. Secretary of Education (R). Remark (originally in Spanish) upon his assumption of office, Sept. 1988.

35. This nation suffers from three deficits – a trade deficit, a budget deficit, and an education deficit. I submit, that the trade and budget deficits will not be resolved until we overcome the education deficit.
Lauro Calvazos. Speech, Education Press Association, 1989.

36. The sheltering of upper income children in private schools not only accelerates the deterioration of public education, it hides its consequences from precisely those people who could do something about it.

Hodding Carter, presidential assistant (D). "In Public Schools, Class Will Tell," *The New York Times*, June 13, 1990.

37. The state has a right to insist that its citizens shall be educated.

Catholic Church, *Pastoral Letter of the Roman Catholic Hierarchy*, Feb. 1920.

38. Forget they are white children. Forget they are black children. Just remember one thing. They are America's children.

Shirley A. Chisholm, U.S. Congresswoman (D-NY). Comment when an antibusing amendment was debated in the House, Nov. 4, 1971.

39. Headmasters have powers at their disposal with which Prime Ministers have never yet been invested.

Winston Churchill (1874-1965), Prime Minister of Great Britain (Conservative). *My Early Life*, 1930.

40. A government can be expected to be enjoyed no longer than while its Citizens continue virtuous and while the majority of the People, through the advantage of a proper, early education possess sufficient knowledge to enable them to understand and pursue their best interests.

De Witt Clinton (1769-1828), U.S. Senator (Anti-Federalist Republican), Mayor of New York City, Governor of New York, and "Father of Free Public Schools." Speech, New York City, Feb. 25, 1805.

41. Most governors know more about education than other elected officials because education is our major job.

Bill Clinton, 42nd President of the United States (D-AR). Interview, National Public Radio, Sept. 25, 1989.

42. This College system went into practice to draw a line of demarcation between the two classes of society – it separated the children of the rich from the children of the poor.

David Crockett (1786-1836), U.S. Congressman (D-TN). Congressional debate, Jan. 5, 1829.

43. The slave must be made fit for his freedom by education and discipline and thus made unfit for slavery.

Jefferson Davis (1808-1889), U.S. Congressman and U.S. Senator (D-MS), U.S. Secretary of War, and President, Confederate States of America. Senate speech, July 12, 1848.

44. For the first time the storm troops of Adolf Hitler could appear freely *[on a campus]*, and the brown ceremonial uniform *[of the Nazi party]* gave new luster to the impressive scene.

Editorial, *Der Alemanne*, May 28, 1933, On Martin Heidegger's elevation to rector of the University of Freiburg, Germany.

45. Education is not preparation for life; education is life itself.

John Dewey (1859-1952), American philosopher and educator. Motto.

46. Upon the education of the people of this country the fate of this country depends.

Benjamin Disraeli, 1st Earl of Beaconsfield (1804-1881), Prime Minister of Great Britain (Conservative). Debate, House of Commons, June 15, 1874.

47. I do not believe that the State Education Department should tell the people how they must spell.

Andrew S. Draper (1848-1913), Superintendent of Public Instruction, New York, and President, University of Illinois. Statement to reporters, disapproving of Pres. Theodore Roosevelt's attempts to simplify American spelling, 1906.

48. Only the educated are free.

Epictetus (55-135), Phrygian Stoic philosopher. *Discourses*.

49. Courses whose primary purposes are political or racial indoctrination have no place in our educational system – no matter who demands them or what noble purposes they seem to serve.

Bergen Evans (1904-1978), American linguist and editor. Commencement address, Northwestern University, Evanston, IL, June 14, 1968.

50. As a society we're not squeamish about suggesting norms for what individuals should weigh, how much money they must earn in order not be judged impoverished, and how much cholesterol is okay in their blood.... In education we have lots of tests, but we don't really have any norms.

Chester E. Finn, Jr., U.S. Assistant Secretary of Education. *The Washington Post*, July 16, 1989.

51. Education policy ... has not been driven by sound educational considerations. It has been driven by the budget process.

William D. Ford, U.S. Congressman (D-MI). Quoted in *The Washington Post*, Jan. 4, 1991.

52. I have no need of learned men. I want faithful subjects. Be such: that is your duty.
Francis I (1768-1835), Emperor of Austria. Address to professors, 1821.

53. A Bible and a newspaper in every house, a good school in every district ... are the principal support of virtue, morality, and civil liberty.
Benjamin Franklin (1706-1790), Member, Continental Congress and Constitutional Convention, Governor of Pennsylvania, and U.S. Minister to France. *Autobiography*, 1791.

54. The mob does not deserve to be enlightened.
Frederick II (The Great) (1712-1786), King of Prussia. Letter to Voltaire, Aug. 7, 1766.

55. I'm sure that President *[Lyndon]* Johnson would never have pursued the war in Vietnam if he'd ever had a Fulbright *[scholarship]* to Japan, or say Bangkok, or had any feeling for what these people are like and why they acted the way they did. He was completely ignorant.
J. William Fulbright, U.S. Senator (D-AR). Quoted in *The New York Times*, June 26, 1986.

56. Education is not just another consumer item. It is the bedrock of our democracy.
Mary Hatwood Futrell, President, National Education Association. "Real Parental Choice," *The Washington Post*, Jan. 15, 1989.

57. The ultimate goal of the educational system is to shift to the individual the burden of pursuing his own education.
John W. Gardner, U.S. Secretary of Health, Education and Welfare and Chairman, Common Cause. Quoted in *Forbes*, July 24, 1989.

58. Next in importance to freedom and justice is popular education, without which neither freedom nor justice can be permanently maintained.
James A. Garfield (1831-1881), 20th President of the United States (R-OH). Letter accepting his party's nomination for the presidency, July 12, 1880.

59. Dictators are as scared of books as they are of cannon.
Harry Golden (1902-1981), American editor and humorist. *Only in America*, 1958.

60. Federal oversight has focused primarily on fiscal accountability and not on educational accountability.
William Goodling, U.S. Congressman (R-PA). "Quality Education: How to Get There?" *Roll Call*, May 21, 1990.

61. No sectarian tenets shall ever be taught in any school supported in whole or in part by the State, nations, or by the proceeds of any tax levied upon any community.
Ulysses S. Grant (1822-1885), 18th President of the United States (R-OH). Message to Congress, Dec. 7, 1875.

62. It is necessary that all our people be instructed, as universal education is the main pillar that must eventually support the temple of liberty.
Sarah Josepha Hale (1788-1879), American magazine editor. *Sketches of American Character*, 1829.

63. Some people believe that school cannot really be changed until the whole of society is changed. They are right.
Soren Hansen and Jesper Jensen, Danish educators. *the little red schoolbook*, 1971.

64. Sit down and read. Educate yourself for the coming conflicts.
Mary Harris (Mother Jones) (1830-1930), American labor organizer. Quoted in *Ms.*, Nov. 1981.

65. Knowledge and German destiny must come to power above all in the adherence to tradition, and will do so only when teachers and students alike suspend knowledge as their innermost need, and participate in the destiny of Germany in its most extreme need.
Martin Heidegger (1899-1976), German philosopher. Speech on becoming rector of the University of Freiburg, Germany, May 28, 1933.

66. There is a revolution in Germany, and we must ask ourselves, "Is there a revolution in the university?" No. The fighting is still in the skirmishing stage.
Martin Heidegger. Address to students and faculty of the University of Heidelberg, Germany, June 30, 1933.

67. Your tax dollars are being used to pay for grade school classes that teach our children that cannibalism, wife-swapping, and the murder of infants and the elderly are acceptable behavior.
Jesse Helms, U.S. Senator (R-NC). Fund raising letter, National Conservative Political Action Committee, 1981.

68. America shortchanges half its youth, the half that doesn't go to college.
Harold Howe II, U.S. Commissioner of Education and Chairman, Commission on Work, Family and Citizenship. Quoted in *The Washington Post*, Nov. 18, 1988.

69. This will never be a civilized country until we spend more money for books than we do for chewing gum.

Elbert Hubbard (1856-1915), American writer and publisher. *The Philistine*, 1911.

70. It was a shock to visit a Job Corps camp and see adults who had been through some years of our public education system stare at a blackboard where a teacher was writing CAT or helping them write their own names. In another room men were learning to tell time.

Hubert H. Humphrey (1911-1978), Vice President of the United States and U.S. Senator (D-MN). *The Education of a Public Man*, 1977.

71. Academic freedom is simply a way of saying that we get the best results in education and research if we leave their management to people who know something about them.

Robert M. Hutchins (1899-1977), President, University of Chicago, and President, Center for the Study of Democratic Institutions. *The Higher Learning in America*, 1936.

72. My people are gone into captivity for want of knowledge.

Old Testament, *Isaiah* 5:13.

73. It's a damn poor mind indeed which can't think of at least two ways to spell any word.

Andrew Jackson (1767-1845), 7th President of the United States (D-TN). Remark, 1833.

74. Said Aldermen shall forwith proceed to have a schoolhouse built ... and shall see that the same be kept in repair.... At everyone of these schools shall be taught reading, writing, and common arithmetic, and the books which shall be used herein for instructing the children to read shall be such as will at the same time make them acquainted with Grecian, Roman, English, and American history.

Thomas Jefferson (1743-1826), 3rd President of the United States (Democratic Republican-VA). *Bill for the More General Diffusion of Knowledge*, Dec. 1778; adopted by the Virginia Assembly in 1779.

75. If a nation expects to be ignorant and free, in a state of civilization, it expects what never was and never will be.

Thomas Jefferson. Letter to Col. Yancey, 1816.

76. I know of no safe depository of the ultimate powers of the society but the people themselves; and if we think them not enlightened enough to exercise their control with a wholesome discretion, the remedy is not to take it from them, but to inform their discretion by education.

Thomas Jefferson. Letter to William C. Jarvis, Sept. 28, 1820.

77. I am going to use every rostrum and every forum and every searchlight that I can to tell the people of the country and their elected representatives that we can no longer afford overcrowded classrooms and half-day sessions. We just must not, we just cannot afford the great waste that comes from the neglect of a single child.

Lyndon B. Johnson (1908-1973), 36th President of the United States (D-TX). Speech, National Conference on Educational Legislation, Mar. 1, 1965.

78. I don't believe I'll ever get credit for anything I do in foreign affairs, no matter how successful it is, because I didn't go to Harvard.

Lyndon B. Johnson. Quoted in Isaacson and Thomas, *The Wise Men*, 1986.

79. One of the really painful things we have found out about weapons carried by our kids is that they think they have to bring in the weapons to protect themselves.

Henry Joubert, information officer, New Orleans, LA, School District. Quoted in *The New York Times*, July 27, 1988.

80. Teachers cannot stand alone.... They cannot be expected to address every conceivable problem which finds its way into the classroom.

Nancy Landon Kassebaum, U.S. Senator (R-KS). *Roll Call*, May 21, 1990.

81. We all know that money alone will not solve the problems faced by our schools. However, to imply that increased spending is counterproductive is itself counterproductive.

J. Robert Kerrey, Governor of Nebraska and U.S. Senator (D). *The Washington Post*, June 27, 1989.

82. The function of education is to teach one to think intensively and to think critically.... Intelligence plus character – that is the goal of true education.

Martin Luther King, Jr. (1929-1968), American clergyman and civil rights leader. Speech, Washington, DC, Mar. 26, 1964.

83. The threat of AIDS should be sufficient to permit a sex-education curriculum.

C. Everett Koop, U.S. Surgeon General. Oct. 1986.

84. Our university is a state university. It belongs to the people of Wisconsin. The state was not made for the university. The university was established to serve the state.

Robert M. La Follette (1855-1925), Governor of

Wisconsin and U.S. Senator (R). Letter to John C. Schmidtmann, Jan. 13, 1925.

85. Exterminate learning and there will be no more worries.

Lao-tzu (c.604-531 B.C.), Chinese philosopher and founder of Taoism. *Tao Te Ching*.

86. Give me four years to teach the children, and the seed I have sown will never be uprooted.

V. I. Lenin (1870-1924), Premier of the U.S.S.R. Attributed.

87. Upon the subject of education, not presuming to dictate and plan or system respecting it, I can only say that I view it as the most important subject which we as a people can be most engaged in.

Abraham Lincoln (1809-1865), 16th President of the United States (R-IL). First public speech, Mar. 9, 1832.

88. No amount of charters, direct primaries, or short ballots will make a democracy out of an illiterate people.

Walter Lippmann (1889-1974), American political columnist. *A Preface to Politics*, 1913.

89. The American idea is a free church in a free state, and a free and unsectarian public school in every ward and every village with its door wide open to children of all races and every creed.

Henry Cabot Lodge (1850-1924), U.S. Senator (R-MA). 1888.

90. But it was in making education not only common to all, but in some sense compulsory on all, that the destiny of the free republics of America was practically settled.

James Russell Lowell (1819-1891), U.S. Ambassador to Spain and England. "New England Two Centuries Ago," in *Among My Books*, 1870.

91. If you educate a man you educate a person. If you educate a woman you educate a family.

Ruby Manikan, Indian religious leader. Quoted in *The Observer*, Mar. 30, 1947.

92. If we do not prepare children to be good citizens; if we do not develop their capacities, if we do not enrich their minds with knowledge, imbue their hearts with love of truth and duty, and a reverence for all things sacred and holy, then our republic must go down to destruction , as others have gone before it.

Horace Mann (1796-1859), American educator, founder and 1st President, Antioch College, Yellow Springs, OH. Quoted in *The New York Times*, Sept. 15, 1953.

93. What is the purpose of education if not, at a minimum, to prepare people for work?

Ann McLaughlin, U.S. Secretary of Labor (R). *The New York Times*, Sept. 25, 1989.

94. The draft is the largest educational institutional in the world.

Robert S. McNamara, U.S. Secretary of Defense (D). Statement to the press, 1966.

95. The fundamental theory of liberty upon which all governments in this Union repose excludes any general power of the state to standardize its children by forcing them to accept instruction from public teachers only.

James Clark McReynolds (1862-1946), U.S. Supreme Court Justice. *Pierce* v. *Society of Sisters*, 1924.

96. What is the first part of politics? Education. What is the second? Education. And the third? Education.

Jules Michelet (1798-1874), French historian. Introduction, *The People*, 1846.

97. I went to nine different universities and never paid a nickel of my own money. My wife got many scholarships. We are children of the United States.

James A. Michener, American writer. Interview, CBS, *Sunday Morning*, Sept. 25, 1988.

98. Public education is not suitable for them *[women]*, because they are never called upon to act in public.

Napoléon I (1769-1821), military leader and Emperor of France. *Maxims*.

99. One of my grand objects was to render education accessible to everybody. I caused every institution *[to offer]* ... instruction to the public either gratis, or at a rate so moderate as not to be beyond the means of the peasant. The museums were thrown open to the whole people. All my efforts were directed to illuminate the mass of the nation, instead of brutifying them by ignorance and superstition.

Napoléon I. *Ibid*.

100. Ignorance is not innocence, but is the promoter of crime.

Carry A. Nation (1846-1911), American temperance agitator. To argue for frank, straightforward sex education of young people by parents. *The Use and Need of the Life of Carry A. Nation*, 1908.

101. No school in which any religious sectarian doctrine shall be taught shall receive *[state]* moneys.

New York State law, passed Apr. 11, 1842.

102. Religion, morality, and knowledge being necessary to good government and the happiness of mankind schools and the means of education shall forever be encouraged.
Northwest Ordinance, 1787.

103. We cannot allow *[college]* campuses to become breeding grounds for racism which will then spread to the society at large.
Eleanor Holmes Norton, Delegate to U.S. Congress (D-DC) and Chair, Equal Employment Opportunity Commission. C-SPAN, June 24, 1990.

104. No school district can please all students all the time, but without *[parental]* choice, school districts have little incentive to change.
Rudy Perpich, Governor of Minnesota (R). Quoted in *Time*, Mar. 13, 1989.

105. When the military is having problems, we allocate money. When the savings and loan industry is having problems, we allocate money. When education is having problems, we say we could possibly allocate a few dollars.
Robert S. Peterkind, Superintendent of Schools, Milwaukee, WI. Quoted in *The New York Times*, Dec. 6, 1989.

106. The direction in which education starts a man will determine his future life.
Plato (427-347 B.C.), Greek philosopher. *The Republic.*

107. 'Tis education forms the common mind,
Just as the twig is bent, the tree's inclined.
Alexander Pope (1688-1744), British poet and Tory activist. *Moral Essays*, Epistle 1.

108. God should never have been expelled from America's classrooms in the first place.
Ronald Reagan, 40th President of the United States (R-CA). To call for a constitutional amendment permitting school prayer. Annual message to Congress, Jan. 25, 1983.

109. Beneath the "affirmative action" bandage there has been festering a public education cancer receiving neither attention nor treatment.
William Bradford Reynolds, U.S. Assistant Attorney General for Civil Rights. *The Washington Post*, Dec. 18, 1990.

110. Educational relations make the strongest tie.
Cecil Rhodes (1853-1902), Prime Minister of Cape Colony, South Africa, industrialist, and philanthropist. Last will and testament, bequeathing £6 million to endow 170 scholarships at Oxford University for American, English, and German youth.

111. *[Sen. Benjamin R. Tillman of South Carolina is]* an embodied retribution on the South for having failed to educate the cracker, the poor white.
Theodore Roosevelt (1858-1919), 26th President of the United States (R-NY). 1896.

112. Anything I can do to get people to read I try to do.
Warren B. Rudman, U.S. Senator (R-NH)). Interview, C-SPAN, *American Profile*, May 27, 1991.

113. If all governments taught the same nonsense, the harm would not be so great. Unfortunately each has its own brand, and the diversity serves to produce hostility between the devotees of different creeds. If there is ever to be peace in the world, governments will have to agree either to inculcate no dogmas, or all to inculcate the same.
Bertrand Russell, 3rd Earl Russell of Kingston (1872-1970), British philosopher and reformer. *Unpopular Essays*, 1950.

114. I thought that it would be like catching a wild animal and taming it.
Sequoyah (1770-1843), Cherokee Indian who created a written version of his language and taught it to his tribe.

115. How can we reform education while preoccupied with fighting off disastrous budget cuts?
Albert Shanker, President, American Federation of Teachers. Apr. 1971.

116. He who can, does. He who cannot, teaches.
George Bernard Shaw (1856-1950), Nobel Laureate in Literature (Great Britain). *Maxims for Revolutionists*, 1903.

117. All our children must come to know more about the rest of our children.
Thomas Sobol, Commissioner of Education, New York. Quoted in *The New York Times*, Feb. 11, 1990.

118. Education has for its object the formation of character.
Herbert Spencer (1820-1903), English social philosopher. *Social Statics*, 1850.

119. Education is a weapon, whose effect depends on who holds it in his hands and at whom it is aimed.
Joseph Stalin (1879-1953), Premier of the U.S.S.R. Interview with H. G. Wells, July 23, 1934.

120. A government's responsibility to its young citizens does not magically begin at the age of six. It makes more sense to extend the free universal school system downward.

Gloria Steinem, American editor and feminist. *Ms.*, Apr. 1974.

121. The blessings of education shall be conferred on every son of Pennsylvania, shall be carried home to the poorest child of the poorest inhabitant of the meanest hut of your mountains.

Thaddeus Stevens (1792-1868), U.S. Congressman (Whig and R-PA). Quoted in J. Woodburn, *Life of Thaddeus Stevens*, 1913.

122. The truest glory of our forefathers is in that system of public instruction, which they instituted by law, and to which New England owes more of its character, its distinction, and its prosperity, than to all other causes.

Joseph Story (1779-1845), U.S. Supreme Court Justice. *Miscellaneous Writings*, 1835.

123. By making the science of government *[political science or civics]* an indispensable branch of popular education, we may gradually prepare the way for such a mastery of its principles, by the people at large, as shall confound the sophist, repress the corrupt, disarm the cunning, animate the patriotic, and sustain the moral and religious.

Joseph Story. *Ibid.*

124. Every successive generation becomes a living memorial of our public schools, and a living example of their excellence. Never, never may this glorious institution be abandoned or betrayed by the weakness of its friends, or the power of its adversaries.

Joseph Story. *Ibid.*

125. I would not want our cities to have the schools of last resort.

Gerald N. Tirozzi, Commissioner of Education, Connecticut. On free choice of public schools. Quoted in *The New York Times*, Feb. 19, 1989.

126. Knowledge diffused among all ranks checks the oppression of aspiring governments.

Daniel D. Tompkins (1774-1825), Governor of New York (Democratic Republican), U.S. Congressman, and Vice President of the United States. Written while a student at Columbia College, 1793.

127. Without a strong educational system – free of government control – democracy is crippled.

Harry S Truman (1884-1972), 33rd President of the United States (D-MO). Speech, Indianapolis, IN, Oct. 15, 1948.

128. It's what you learn after you know it all that counts.

Harry S Truman. 1950.

129. People who call themselves *[educational]* radicals have adopted the slogan that "the customer is always right" – in a strange kind of long-hair capitalism. The result is turmoil.

Joseph Tussman. Provost, University of California at Berkley. Quoted in *The New York Times Magazine*, Jan. 11, 1970.

130. Soap and education are not as sudden as a massacre, but they are more deadly in the long run.

Mark Twain (Samuel Langhorne Clemens) (1835-1910), American writer. "The Facts Concerning the Recent Resignation," in *Sketches New and Old*, 1900.

131. The GI Bill of Rights was the greatest piece of legislating ever passed in this country. It educated an entire group of Americans.

Jack Valenti, Special Assistant to the President (D). Interview, C-SPAN, *An American Profile*, Feb. 19, 1990.

132. No girl was ever ruined by reading a book.

James J. Walker (1881-1946), Mayor of New York City (D). Attributed.

133. In the field of public education, the doctrine of "separate but equal" has no place. Separate educational facilities are inherently unequal.

Earl Warren (1891-1974), Chief Justice, U.S. Supreme Court, and Governor of California (R). *Brown* v. *Board of Education of Topeka, KS*, 1954.

134. On the diffusion of education among the people rest the preservation and perpetuation of our free institutions.

Daniel Webster (1782-1852), U.S. Congressman (Federalist-NH and MA), U.S. Senator (Federalist and Whig-MA), and U.S. Secretary of State. Speech, Madison, IN, June 1, 1837.

135. The Battle of Waterloo was won on the playing fields of Eton.

Arthur Wellesley, 1st Duke of Wellington (1769-1852), Chief General at Waterloo, Ambassador to France, and Prime Minister of Great Britain (Tory). Attributed.

136. The taste of men, whatever it happens to be, has been made into a standard for the formation of the female character.

Emma Willard (1787-1870), American reformer, educator, and founder, Troy Female Seminary. Speech to the New York State Legislature, 1819.

Chapter 24

The Elderly, Social Security, and Pensions

1. To me, old age is always fifteen years older than I am.
   Bernard M. Baruch (1870-1965), Chairman, War Industries Board and U S. Delegate to the U.N. Atomic Energy Commission. Remark to reporters, 1958.

2. Politics is, like croquet, a sport for the old. The males who dominate it are either white haired or bald. The bellies protrude, the eyes weaken, the faces grow flush from even a flight of stairs. A touch of emphysema is the badge of a great political hero.
   Jimmy Breslin, American journalist. Quoted in O'Neil and Brink, *The World According to Breslin*, 1984.

3. I have been asked how I grow old so easily. The answer is: I give all my time to it.
   Emanuel Celler (1888-1981), U.S. Congressman (D-NY). Remark on his 83rd birthday, May 6, 1971.

4. For in all the world there are no people so piteous and forlorn as those who are forced to eat the bitter bread of dependency in their old age.
   Dorothy Dix (1861-1951), American columnist. *Dorothy Dix, Her Book*, 1926.

5. America is a country of young men.
   Ralph Waldo Emerson (1803-1882), American writer. "Old Age," in *Society and Solitude*, 1870.

6. It's a great job for a retired person. They feel a little important, get out of the house.
   Gary Gilmore, New Hampshire State Representative (D). On being a state legislator. Quoted in *The Washington Post*, Apr. 30, 1989.

7. Why not dream? It keeps you young. The only difference between me and a child is sixty-five years.
   Walter J. Hickel, Governor of Alaska and U.S. Secretary of the Interior (R). Quoted in *Newsweek*, Dec. 24, 1990.

8. It is extraordinary how reluctant aged judges are to retire and to give up their accustomed work. They seem to be tenacious in the appearance of adequacy.
   Charles Evans Hughes (1862-1948), Chief Justice, U.S. Supreme Court, and U.S. Secretary of State (R). *The Supreme Court of the United States*, 1928.

9. With the ancient *[person]* is wisdom, and in length of days understanding.
   Old Testament, *Job* 12:12.

10. We treat old people like we treat animals – just put them in a cage somewhere until they die.
    Lyndon B. Johnson (1908-1973), 36th President of the United States (D-TX). Remark to Larry Temple about many nursing homes. 1962.

11. Our nation's long neglect of minorities whose skin is dark is perhaps only a little worse than our neglect of another minority whose hair is white.
    Lyndon B. Johnson. Message to Congress, Sept. 5, 1966.

12. The myth is that people get their money back from Social Security. Not true. You get somebody else's money back. This is an intergenerational transfer.
    Richard D. Lamm, Governor of Colorado (D). Interview, *USA Today*, Oct. 20, 1988.

13. Handling the people's money is not a job for a politician. There's too much temptation. It might be good to let an elderly man handle your money. He's looking for the Golden Gate, not the Golden Calf.
    Sol Levitan (1862-1940), Treasurer of Wisconsin (Progressive). Remark when told that he was too old to run again for such a high office. 1936.

14. The old people we respect most are the ones who will fight for their independence, who would sooner starve to death than ask for help. We in

America have very little sense of interdependence.

Margaret Mead (1901-1978), American anthropologist. Quoted in *Family Circle*, July 26, 1977.

15. I don't think I should become senile as a matter of law.

Louis Peck, Vermont Supreme Court Justice. Statement on refusing to retire at age 65, as required by Vermont's constitution. Quoted in *The New York Times*, Apr. 20, 1989.

16. The *[Reagan]* administration is trying to make Social Security a no-frills program. The problem is that their idea of a frill is eating.

Claude D. Pepper (1901-1989), U.S. Senator and U.S. Congressman (D-FL). Statement, 1984.

17. It is becoming more or less a common criticism that we are already giving a little too much to the elderly. We are not giving them too much, and they need even more than they are getting ... but they are no different in that respect than the rest of the population including the children of the country who are chronically ill.

Claude D. Pepper. Remark during congressional hearings on long-term care insurance. Aug. 2, 1988.

18. I have so much to do every morning that I don't have any time to think about getting old.

Claude D. Pepper. Statement at age 88. Interview, CBS, *Ask Congress*, Aug. 20, 1988.

19. This country will not be remembered for how we put a man on the moon but how we treated a generation that could not treat itself.

David H. Pryor, U.S. Congressman and U.S. Senator (D-AK). Interview, CBS, *Sunday Morning*, Jan. 21, 1990.

20. I will not make age an issue in this campaign. I am not going to exploit for political purposes my opponent's youth and inexperience.

Ronald Reagan, 40th President of the United States (R-CA). Response when Walter Mondale alluded to his age. Televised presidential debate, Oct. 21, 1984.

21. For too long many of our senior citizens have been faced with making an intolerable choice, a choice between bankruptcy and death.

Ronald Reagan. Message to Congress, Feb. 1987.

22. I don't care. I'll be dead by then.

Donald T. Regan, U.S. Secretary of the Treasury (R). Response when asked how Social Security will be funded in fifty years. Quoted in *The Washington Star*, Apr. 18, 1981.

23. Now this is a pension program. It isn't welfare, is it?

Franklin D. Roosevelt (1882-1945), 32nd President of the United States (D-NY). Remark on signing the Social Security bill into law, 1935.

24. We have to have it *[Social Security]*. The Congress can't stand the pressure of the Townsend Plan unless we have a real old-age insurance system.

Franklin D. Roosevelt. Comment, 1935. Quoted in Frances Perkins, *The Roosevelt I Knew*, 1946.

25. Old Men have in some degree their Reprisals upon younger, by making nicer Observations upon them, by virtue of their Experience.

George Savile, 1st Marquess of Halifax (1633-1695), Lord Privy Seal of England. *Miscellaneous Thoughts and Reflections*, 1750.

26. Doesn't a boy always put his mother first? We do it socially, why not economically? You take your hat off to her when she gets out of the elevator, but you let her starve when she gets old.

Gerald L. K. Smith (1898-1976), American clergyman and cofounder, Union Party. Quoted in *Literary Digest*, Aug. 1, 1936.

27. I shall not grow conservative with age.

Elizabeth Cady Stanton (1815-1902), 1st President, National Woman Suffrage Association. Letter to Susan B. Anthony, 1860.

28. Elderly people, trained and experienced by life's activities, can be made the greatest asset humanity possesses if they are liberated from the slavery of poverty and are permitted to exercise their talents as circulators of money.

Francis E. Townsend (1867-1960), American physician and cofounder, Union Party. 1935.

29. My favorite animal is the mule. He has a lot more horse sense than a horse. He knows when to stop eating. And he knows when to stop working.

Harry S Truman (1884-1972), 33rd President of the United States (D-MO). Announcement of his retirement, Jan. 1952.

30. We have a contract between the generations, and it roughly is, "Hey, parents, you take care of me as a youngster. When you retire, I will continue to pay into your Social Security fund on the basis that I'm going to have a contract with my own children – your grandchildren." And that's what generational equity is all about.

J. J. Wuerthner, Executive Director, Americans for Generational Equity. Interview, *USA Today*, Oct. 20, 1988.

Chapter 25

Energy

1. As nations continue to develop they will require more, not less, total energy; their industrialization and rapidly growing populations will depend on it.
   Gro Harlem Brundtland, Prime Minister of Norway. *Scientific American*, Sept. 1989.

2. A drop of oil is worth a drop of blood.
   Georges Clemenceau (1841-1929), Premier of France and journalist. Remark, 1922.

3. We have a military policy instead of an energy policy.
   Barry Commoner, American environmentalist and founder, Common Cause. Comment after American troops were deployed to Saudi Arabia following Iraq's invasion of Kuwait. Quoted in *The Washington Post*, August 25, 1990.

4. Without oil our Navy would be like painted ships upon a painted ocean.
   Josephus Daniels (1862-1948), U.S. Secretary of the Navy and U.S. Ambassador to Mexico (D). Speech, American Society of Engineers, Dec. 18, 1920.

5. The most egregious form of corporate welfare imaginable.
   Dennis E. Eckart, U.S. Congressman (D-OH). In reference to the Price-Anderson Act, limiting the liability of corporations in nuclear accidents regardless of negligence. United Press International, August 2, 1988.

6. Not only will atomic power be released, but someday we will harness the rise and fall of the tides and imprison the rays of the sun.
   Thomas Alva Edison (1847-1931), American inventor. Interview, August 22, 1921.

7. The growth in our electricity use is outpacing our electrical capacity additions. I hate to think the country has reached the point where only a recession can guarantee that our electrical supplies are adequate.
   Harold B. Finger, President, U.S. Council for Energy Awareness. Quoted in *The New York Times*, Oct. 2, 1988.

8. You know, I think we ought to sell TVA.
   Barry M. Goldwater, U.S. Senator (R-AZ). Quoted in *The Saturday Evening Post*, Aug. 31, 1963.

9. We are ready to kill to keep our automobiles running. We're ready to kill to keep up our materialistic, wasteful economy.... I am sick and tired of eighteen-year-olds being coerced into bearing the burden of the failures of politicians to face the tough economic choices needed to end our dependency on foreign oil.
   Mark O. Hatfield, Governor of Oregon and U.S. Senator (D). 1974.

10. Those who say "not in my backyard" are saying "rape someone else's backyard.
    Walter J. Hickel, Governor of Alaska and U.S. Secretary of Interior (R). Comment on demands for restrictions on oil drilling. Speech, National Press Club, Feb. 5, 1991.

11. Free trade in energy with the Americans is like wife-swapping with a bachelor.
    Ramon Hnatyshyn, Minister of Energy, Canada. Quoted in *The Toronto Star*, August 4, 1979.

12. The negation of the ideals upon which our civilization has been based.
    Herbert Hoover (1874-1964), 31st President of the United States (R-IA). Comment on government ownership of hydro-electric power. 1931.

13. The country needs a gas tax.... That's good for the country.... What's good for the country is good for Chrysler.
    Lee Iacocca, Chairman, Chrysler Corp., and member, National Economic Commission. Letter to *The New York Times*, Dec. 14, 1988.

14. Communism is Soviet power plus the electrification of the whole country.
    V. I. Lenin (1870-1924), Premier of the U.S.S.R. 1920.

15. When we turn to foreign lands to supply our energy needs, then I can't help but feeling that

somewhere along the way we've surrendered something of our freedom.

Manuel Lujan, Jr., U.S. Congressman and U.S. Secretary of the Interior (R-NM). Speech, Midland, TX, Nov. 10, 1989.

16. Fission is like kissing your wife. Fusion is like kissing your mistress.

Robert B. Macaulay, Minister of Energy Resources, Ontario, Canada. Quoted in *The Globe and Mail,* June 8, 1983.

17. "Energy patriotism" – we could all stick it to *[Iraqi Pres.]* Saddam Hussein today if we all drove fifty-five miles an hour around our Capital Beltway.

Barbara A. Mikulski, U.S. Congresswoman and U.S. Senator (D-MD). Speech, Bethesda, MD, Dec. 18, 1990.

18. We are a nation that is totally dependent on one resource only – oil. And that's a mistake.

Leon E. Panetta, U.S. Congressman (D-CA). Debate, ABC, *It's Your Business,* Sept. 17, 1989.

19. The era of low-cost energy is almost dead. Popeye is running out of spinach.

Peter G. Peterson, U.S. Secretary of Commerce (R). Testimony, Senate confirmation hearings, 1972.

20. If sunbeams were weapons of war, we would have had solar energy long ago.

George Porter, British scientist. Quoted in *The Observer,* August 26, 1973.

21. There is no organized *[energy]* conservation industry.... The oil companies and utilities are busy talking up how much they need to produce. But no one's out there wholesaling conservation by the ton and barrel.

Roger Sant, Assistant Administrator, Federal Energy Administration. Speech, The Conference Board, Sept. 30, 1975.

22. It's too bad it *[Chernobyl]* didn't happen closer to the Kremlin.

Steven D. Symms, U.S. Congressman and U.S. Senator (R-ID). Quoted in *Spy,* Feb. 1989.

23. I understand that your *[energy]* policy is no policy. And this in itself is supposed to be a policy, according to some people in the administration.

Ahmed Zaki Yamani, Minister of Petroleum and Mineral Resources, Saudi Arabia. Interview, *Time,* Dec. 3, 1990.

Chapter 26

English and Bilingualism

1. It is a dangerous thing for the educated classes of important countries not to speak foreign languages. We are heading into an era of greater mutual incomprehension among peoples, when demographic trends are destabilizing many countries, when Latin America is economically unstable, when communist societies are unstable, when we may be on the edge of chaos.
   Maurice Allais, Nobel Laureate in Economics (France). Quoted in *The Washington Post,* Aug. 28, 1989.

2. We quarrel with no man for being a foreigner, but we recognize the moral right in no class of American citizens to train up their children to be foreigners, and then to claim for them all the rights, franchises, and immunities of American citizens.
   Orestes Augustus Brownson (1803-1876), American clergyman, writer, and founder, Working-men's Party. *Public and Parochial Schools,* 1859.

3. Unless you speak English and read well, you'll never be a first-class citizen ... but when you say "official," that becomes a racial slur.
   Barbara Bush, First Lady. Quoted in *USA Today,* Oct. 15, 1990.

4. English is the lingua franca of world business, the key to clinching deals from Hong Kong to Toronto.
   George Bush, 41st President of the United States (R-TX). Speech in Budapest, Roumania, announcing that Peace Corps English teachers were going to Eastern Europe for the first time, July 1990.

5. If a child cannot speak English the first day at school, that child is not ready to learn.
   Lauro F. Calvazos, U.S. Secretary of Education (R). Speech, Laredo, TX, Aug. 17, 1990.

6. We deny in the most positive language that this is an Anglo-Saxon nation. We deny that England is the mother country, and we deny that the great progress and achievements of this country have been brought about solely through the efforts and influence of the Puritans.... All Europe is our mother, not England.
   Mathew Cummins, President, Ancient Order of Hibernians. Speech, German Day, New York City, Oct. 6, 1908.

7. For the benefit of those who are not bilingual, I will now continue in English.
   John G. Diefenbaker (1895-1975), Prime Minister of Canada (Conservative). Quoted in Tom Van Dusen, *The Chief,* 1968.

8. I'm against the idea of force-feeding all of Canada on two languages.
   Joe Fratesi, Mayor of Sault Sainte Marie, Quebec, Canada. Explanation of the English-only law of his city. Quoted in *Time,* June 25, 1990.

9. The whole earth was of one language and one speech.
   Old Testament, *Genesis* 11:1.

10. The English language is the law of the people of the United States.
    Charles Henry Grosvenor (1833-1917), U.S. Congressman (R-OH). Speech, House of Representatives, 1906.

11. A command of English is the fastest way out of the ghetto.
    S. I. Hayakawa (1906-1992), U.S. Senator (R-CA). Explanation of his support for a constitutional amendment to make English the official language of the United States. 1989.

12. I think we should have a President who is fluent in at least one language.
    Bob Hope, American actor and comedian. In reference to George Bush's propensity to mangle the English language. 1988.

13. Be it enacted by the People of the State of Illinois, represented in the General Assembly: The official language of the state of Illinois shall hereafter be known as the "American" language and not as the "English" language.
    Act of the Illinois Legislature, 1923.

14. I didn't move to Miami to live in a Spanish-speaking province.

Mark A. LaPorta, President, Official English. Quoted in *The New York Times*, Oct. 26, 1988.

15. The United States of America has been enriched by the cultural contributions of immigrants with many traditions, but blessed with one common language that has united a diverse nation and fostered harmony among its people.
Lowell, MA, voter resolution. Passed, Nov. 1989.

16. If any English is to be considered proper for classroom instruction, it should be the English of the upper classes, since it is the English most likely to help you get a job.
Clarence Page, American political columnist. *The Chicago Tribune*, Sept. 30, 1989.

17. We have room for but one language here, and that is the English language, and we intend to see that the crucible turns our people out as Americans, and not as dwellers of a polyglot boarding-house.
Theodore Roosevelt (1858-1919), 26th President of the United States (R-NY). 1905.

18. Every immigrant who comes here should be required within five years to learn English or leave the country.
Theodore Roosevelt. Quoted in *The Kansas City Star*, Apr. 27, 1918.

19. It's a put-down message on recent immigrants.
Ileana Ros-Lehtinen, U.S. Congresswoman (R-FL). On efforts to make English the official language of the United States. Interview, *USA Today*, Sept. 11, 1989.

20. Should it not be our aim to build on the foundations of our own accumulated lore and inherited stock of capacities and temperament, a stately and enduring structure with the full aid of Western learning and science and thus to develop our own soul?
Raja Ram Mohan Roy (1772-1833), Indian Hindu leader and English-language advocate. 1817.

21. The doors to educational, economic, and political opportunity will remain closed to those without the key of common language. This bill isn't about discrimination; it's about fuller participation.
Richard Shelby, U.S. Congressman and U.S. Senator (D-AL). Explanation for his sponsship of a bill making English the official language of the United States and requiring that all official acts of government be performed in English. Quoted in *USA Today*, Oct. 15, 1990.

22. America rests upon four cornerstones: the English Bible, the English language, the common law, and the tradition of liberty.
Odell Shepard (1884-1967), American writer. *Southern Workman*, Nov. 1935.

23. If foreign races learn our language, they are more easily assimilated by us.... On the other hand, if we know the language of foreign countries, then we are more easily assimilated by foreigners.
Sun Yat-sen (1866-1925), Chinese political leader. Lecture, "The Three Principles of the People," 1924.

24. I will not leave Ottawa until the country and the government are irreversibly bilingual.
Pierre Elliott Trudeau, Prime Minister of Canada (Liberal). Speech, Montreal, Jan. 31, 1975.

25. Canada has two official languages and I don't speak none of them.
Eugene Whelan, Member of Parliament and Minister of Agriculture, Canada. *Whelan*, 1986.

26. We have really everything in common with America nowadays, except, of course, language.
Oscar Wilde (1854-1900), Irish writer. *The Canterville Ghost*, 1887.

Chapter 27

The Environment and Natural Resources

1. Everyone lives downstream from someone else.
   Northwest American saying. Quoted in *The New York Times*, Nov. 27, 1990.

2. The real owners of the land are not yet born.
   Canadian Indian saying.

3. STOP POLLUTION OR THE FUTURE WILL BE A THING OF THE PAST.
   Bumper sticker, Ann Arbor, MI, 1973.

4. Doing everything the scientists wanted us to do *[to protect the environment]* would be ruinous.
   Richard Allen, National Security Advisor (R). PBS, *Great Decisions, 1990*, Mar. 3, 1990.

5. If they *[the federal government]* can't handle the *[toxic]* waste, they shouldn't generate it.
   Cecil D. Andrus, Governor of Idaho and U.S. Secretary of the Interior (D). Interview, CBS, *Morning News*, Oct. 24, 1988.

6. Canada was built on dead beavers.
   Margaret Atwood, Canadian poet. Quoted on National Public Radio, *Canada: True North*, Sept. 19, 1988.

7. Man was not made for the world, but the world for man.
   Apocrypha, *2 Baruch* 14:18.

8. Half of Americans breathe air that is unhealthy.
   Max S. Baucus, U.S. Congressman and U.S. Senator (D-MT). Quoted on ABC, *This Week*, June 18, 1989.

9. Pollution doesn't respect state boundaries, and it is difficult if not impossible to solve these problems on a state-by-state basis.
   S. William Becker, Executive Director, State Air Pollution Program Administrators. Quoted in *The New York Times*, Jan. 22, 1989.

10. The only thing to do is say, "If you generate it in your country, you take care of it."
    Uta Bellion, toxic waste specialist, Greenpeace. Quoted in *The New York Times*, Oct. 16, 1988.

11. The problems of the Third World--its poverty, its ignorance, its debt--never really seemed to affect Europeans and Americans. No longer. It's a little warmer than it used to be. The water is rising.
    Henry R. Breck, trustee, Natural Resources Defense Council. *Newsweek*, Dec. 5, 1988.

12. The landscape has been so transformed by ignorance, arrogance, and greed that those who must prove their case are not those who call for forest protection, but those who call for business as usual.
    Richard Brown, spokesman, National Wildlife Federation. Quoted in *Time*, June 25, 1990.

13. It is futile to seek solutions to environmental disturbances without considering them from a broad perspective that encompasses the factors underlying world poverty and the inequities within and among nations.
    Gro Harlem Brundtland, Prime Minister of Norway. *Scientific American*, Sept. 1989.

14. Our beaches should not be garbage dumps. Our oceans must not be cesspools.
    George Bush, 41st President of the United States (R-TX). Presidential nomination acceptance speech, Republican National Convention, New Orleans, LA, Aug. 18, 1988.

15. Every American deserves to breathe clean air.
    George Bush. June 1989.

16. We can no longer throw our waste away because there is no "away."
    William T. Cahill, Governor of New Jersey (R). 1971.

17. As cruel a weapon as the cave man's club, the chemical barrage has been hurled against the fabric of life.
Rachel Carson (1907-1964), American biologist and writer. *The Silent Spring*, 1962.

18. There are real and growing dangers to our simple and most precious possessions: the air we breathe, the water we drink, and the land which sustains us.... If we do not act, the world of the year 2000 will be much less able to sustain life than it is now.
Jimmy Carter, 39th President of the United States (D-GA). Farewell address, Jan. 14, 1989.

19. To protect the environment, you have to work from the outside, not the inside.
Jacques Cousteau, French marine scientist. Quoted in *The Washington Post*, July 10, 1990.

20. The very survival of the human species depends upon the maintenance of an ocean clean and alive. The ocean is our planet's life belt.
Jacques-Yves Costeau, French marine explorer. 1980.

21. I've never seen such a goddamned mess in my life.
Steve Cowper, Governor of Alaska (D). Statement while standing on the deck of the Exxon *Valdez* watching the oil leak out. Quoted in Art Davidson, *In the Wake of the Exxon* Valdez, 1990.

22. It's nice to think about having everything natural and similar to pre-Columbian times.... In fact, man himself has long been part of that environment, and there is no way to separate him from that environment.
Frank Craighead, American ecologist. Quoted in *The New York Times*, Oct. 30, 1988.

23. It'll go away only if we make it go away – by not using water.
Mario Cuomo, Governor of New York (D). Comment on a drought that threatened New York's water supply. Quoted in *The New York Times*, Mar. 18, 1989.

24. They are not valuable wetlands. They are degraded industrial wastelands.
Richard M. Daley, Mayor of Chicago, IL (D). Letter to CBS, *Sunday Morning*, June 16, 1991.

25. When you have to besiege a city for a long time, you must not destroy its trees, wielding an ax against them. You may eat of them, but you must not cut them down. Are the trees human, to withdraw before your siege?
Old Testament, *Deuteronomy* 20:19.

26. No compromise in defense of Mother Earth.
Slogan of Earth First, 1980.

27. What covers 13 million acres, sleeps 60 million people, and desperately needs money? America's state parks.
Hoyt Gimlin, American writer. Quoted in *Governing*, Sept. 1988.

28. If you don't look for a problem, you won't find it.
Eric Goldstein, Director, Natural Resources Defense Council. On using sophisticated technology and instruments to measure air quality. Quoted in *The New York Times*, July 23, 1989.

29. The world's forests are being destroyed at the rate of one football field's worth every second. One Tennessee's worth every year.
Albert A. Gore, Jr., U.S. Senator (D-TN) and Vice President of the United States. "An Ecological Kristallnacht. Listen," *The New York Times*, Mar. 19, 1989.

30. L.A.'s air pollution has turned an environmental issue into everybody's issue.
Tom Hayden, California State Senator (D) and founder, Students for a Democratic Society. Quoted in *Newsweek*, Aug. 29, 1988.

31. We have done extraordinary things to destroy our waters. We can never do enough to research and coordinate cleaning these waters up.
George J. Hochbrueckner, U.S. Congressman (D-NY). *The New York Times*, Aug. 7, 1988.

32. The cheap and easy days of waste disposal are over.
Anne Hoey, Public Space Administrator, District of Columbia. Quoted in *The Washington Post*, Sept. 4, 1988.

33. Industrialism is the systematic exploitation of wasting assets. Progress is merely an acceleration in the rate of that exploitation. Such prosperity as we have known up to the present is the consequence of rapidly spending the planet's irreplaceable capital.
Aldous Huxley (1894-1963), British writer. *Themes and Variations*, 1950.

34. In nature there are neither rewards nor punishments; there are consequences.
Robert Green Ingersoll (1833-1899), Attorney General of Illinois (R). Quoted in *Isaac Asimov's Book of Science and Nature Quotations*, 1988.

35. The common people who marched for the right to vote must now march for the right to breathe.

Jesse L. Jackson, Shadow Senator (D-DC). Speech, Mar. 29, 1990.

36. I do believe this period of the 1980's will be remembered as the time the planet struck back. The planet is telling us we can't treat it this way anymore.

Stephen C. Joseph, Health Commissioner, New York City. Comment on pollution that kept New York City beaches closed. Quoted in *The New York Times*, July 17, 1988.

37. Why did they have to build the damn lake *[Lake Michigan]* so close to the city?

Michael (Hinky Dink) Kenna (1858-1946), Chicago, IL, politician (D). Attributed.

38. The supreme reality of our time is the vulnerability of this planet.

John F. Kennedy (1917-1963), 35th President of the United States (D-MA). Speech, Dublin, Ireland, June 28, 1963.

39. Asking the Oregon congressional delegation in 1990 to deal rationally with the end of ancient-forest cutting is like asking the Mississippi delegation in 1960 to deal rationally with the end of segregation.

Andrew Kerr, Oregon environmentalist. Quoted in *Time*, June 25, 1990.

40. Drink seltzer.

Edward I. Koch, U.S. Congressman and Mayor of New York City (D). Comment when told by a woman caller that the water in her sink was coming out brown. *How'm I Doing?*, 1981.

41. There can't be an entirely painless transition from this throw-away society to a conservation-minded society.

Madeleine M. Kunin, Governor of Vermont (D). Quoted in *The New York Times*, Dec. 31, 1989.

42. If you want the light *[electricity]*, you will have to pay for it every month.

Amakuade Wyete Ajeman Labie II, Paramount Chief, Awutu tribe, Ghana. Message to his tribesmen. Quoted in *The Washington Post*, July 21, 1990.

43. We're trying to let people see what their grandfather told them about.

Larry Larson, park naturalist, Prairie State Park, MT. Quoted in *Governing*, Sept. 1988.

44. We have to litigate to maintain our credibility. Otherwise industry would never take us seriously.

Jonathan Lash, attorney, Natural Resources Defense Council. Quoted in Tolchin and Tolchin, *Dismantling America: The Rush to Deregulate*, 1983.

45. Atomic energy bears that same duality ... expressed in the Book of Books thousands of years ago: "See, I have set before thee life and good, and death and evil ... therefore choose life."

David E. Lilienthal (1899-1981), Chairman, Tennessee Valley Authority and Chairman, U.S. Atomic Energy Commission. *This I Do Believe*, 1949; reference is to *Deuteronomy* 30:15, 19.

46. Real estate interests are wiping out habitat all over the world.

Michael Lowry, U.S. Congressman (D-WA). House hearings, Mar. 14, 1985.

47. It really depends on how thirsty I was.

Ian Macdonald, U.S. Assistant Secretary for Health. Response when asked if he would drink West Coast rainwater after Chernobyl. Quoted in *Newsweek*, May 19, 1986.

48. Land is not something you inherit from your parents. It is something you borrow from your children.

Elmer H. MacKay, Member of Parliament, Canada. Quoted in *The Vancouver Sun*, Mar. 11, 1978.

49. Man is everywhere a disturbing agent. Wherever he plants his foot, the harmonies of nature are turned to discords.

George Perkins Marsh (1801-1882), U.S. Congressman (Whig-VT). *Man and Nature*, 1864.

50. This is not a disposable planet. It is the only one we have.

Robert Maynard, American editor and journalist. Quoted on PBS, *MacNeil-Lehrer News Hour*, Sept. 14, 1988.

51. Conservation is not without a cost.

James A. McClure, U.S. Congressman and U.S. Senator (R-ID). Interview, CNN, Feb. 3, 1991.

52. Americans love their billboards. Visual pollution? Billboards reflect visual vitality.

B. Roland McElroy, President, Outdoor Advertising Association of America. Quoted in *Audubon Magazine*, July 1991.

53. The free market should not include the right to pollute our environment.

George S. McGovern, U.S. Congressman and U.S. Senator (D-SD). PBS, *Firing Line*, Sept. 13, 1989.

54. It is a crime now in my country to talk about the government's crimes.

David McTaggart, Canadian cofounder of Greenpeace. In reference to an Order-in-Council forbidding any discussions of the Canadian Cabinet's secret uranium deals. *Greenpeace III*, 1978.

55. If you feel so strongly about it, why don't you make it an issue and run against me?

Harvey Milk (1930-1978), San Francisco City Supervisor. Remark to a citizen who denounced a recently passed ordinance requiring curbing of dogs. Quoted in Edward Shilts, *The Mayor of Castro Street*, 1982.

56. Everyone realizes that we have to clean up the environment, but no one likes the cost.

Carlos J. Moorhead, U.S. Congressman (R-CA). Quoted in *USA Today*, Nov. 15, 1989.

57. We ought to move toward the objective of allowing our state to become number one, not in the protection of toxic substances, but in the prosecution of those who are polluting our environment.

Dan Morales, Texas State Legislator (D). Quoted in *Hispanic*, Oct. 1990.

58. Toxins of bad politics have paralyzed stewardship of public land.

James P. Moran, Jr., U.S. Congressman (D-VA). Quoted in *Outdoor Life*, Feb. 1992.

59. Free the rivers

John Muir (1838-1914), founder, Sierra Club. Statement opposing dams; painted on Hetch Hetchy Dam, Yosemite National Park, by protesters, 1987.

60. I think that I shall never see
A billboard lovely as a tree
Indeed, unless the billboards fall
I'll never see a tree at all.

Ogden Nash (1902-1971), American poet and humorist. 1937.

61. Every place you turn we are degrading, compromising, destroying the capital resources of this country.

Gaylord Nelson, U.S. Senator and Governor of Wisconsin (D). Speech, National Press Club. C-SPAN, April 16, 1990.

62. Some people are going to die from radon even if they don't smoke.

Margo Oge, Director, Radon Office, Environmental Protection Agency. Quoted in *The New York Times*, Sept. 18, 1988.

63. Man is complex – he makes deserts bloom and lakes die.

Laurence J. Peter, American educator and writer. Quoted in *The Los Angeles Times*, Mar. 8, 1983.

64. Since it is the poor and disadvantaged who are most directly affected by the degradation of the natural environment, as resources become scarce and the quality of the environment declines still further, even more people are bound to become poor and disadvantaged. The best hope of limiting the increase in the number of such people would be if the world population could be stabilized.

Philip, Duke of Edinburgh (Prince Consort of Queen Elizabeth II), President, World Wide Fund for Nature. Speech, United Nations, Mar. 30, 1990.

65. Unless we practice conservation, those who come after us will have to pay the price of misery, degradation and failure for the progress and prosperity of our day.

Gifford Pinchot (1865-1946), Governor of Pennsylvania (D) and Chief, U.S. Forest Service. 1902.

66. The parks are the lungs of London.

William Pitt, 1st Earl of Chatham (1708-1778), Secretary of State, Great Britain, Lord Privy Seal, and leader of the House of Commons. Quoted by William Windham, Speech, House of Commons, June 30, 1808.

67. Wildlife should not have to pay its own way nor should its right to exist depend solely on the degree to which it profits or amuses man.

Robert Poole, Director, African Wildlife Leadership Foundation, Kenya. 1974.

68. The public may not want to hear how much it will cost or how long it will take, but in the land of hazardous waste there is no magic wand.

John Quarles, Deputy Administrator, U.S. Environmental Protection Agency. Quoted in *The New York Times*, July 16, 1988.

69. The people who have to bear the burden *[of eliminating acid rain]* will not get the benefits.

William K. Reilly, Administrator, U.S. Environmental Protection Agency. Interview, PBS, *MacNeil-Lehrer News Hour*, June 12, 1989.

70. There are always court suits. Four out of every five decisions we make involve court suits. We are an extremely litigious society.

William K. Reilly. Interview, ABC, *This Week*, April 15, 1990.

71. The notion that man can subjugate and control the forces of nature ... has led the whole planet to where it's reeling.

Jeremy Rifkin, President, Foundation on Economic Trends. Quoted in *The New York Times Magazine*, Oct. 16, 1988.

72. They *[business]* will have to meet our *[environmental]* standards. If they can't, they can go to Kentucky, Tennessee, or God cares where.
Charles E. Roemer III, Governor of Louisiana and U.S. Congressman (D). Quoted in *The New York Times*, Nov. 18, 1989.

73. Men and Nature must work hand in hand. The throwing out of balance of the resources of Nature throws out of balance also the lives of men.
Franklin D. Roosevelt (1882-1945), 32nd President of the United States (D-NY). Jan. 24, 1935.

74. The forest and water problem are perhaps the most vital internal problems of the United States.
Theodore Roosevelt (1858-1919), 26th President of the United States (R-NY). Message to Congress, Dec. 3, 1901.

75. Leave it as it is. You cannot improve upon it. The ages have been at work on it and man can only mar it. What you can do is keep it for your children, your children's children, and for all those who come after you.
Theodore Roosevelt. Speech, Grand Canyon, 1903.

76. We are prone to speak of the resources of this country as inexhaustible; this is not so. The mineral wealth of the country, the coal, iron, oil, gas, and the like, does not reproduce itself, and therefore is certain to be exhausted ultimately; and wastefulness in dealing with it today means that our descendants will feel the exhaustion a generation or two before they otherwise would.
Theodore Roosevelt. Annual message to Congress, Mar. 4, 1907.

77. The conservation of our natural resources and their proper use constitute the fundamental problem which underlies almost every other problem of our national life.
Theodore Roosevelt. Message to Congress, Dec. 3, 1907.

78. Conservation is a great moral issue, for it involves the patriotic duty of insuring the safety and continuance of the nation.
Theodore Roosevelt. Speech, "The New Nationalism," Osawatomie, KS, Aug. 31, 1910.

79. The relationship of conservation of natural resources to the problems of national welfare and national efficiency had not yet dawned on the public mind.
Theodore Roosevelt. *Autobiography*, 1919.

80. The nation behaves well if it treats its natural resources as assets which it must turn over to the next generation increased and not impaired in value.
Theodore Roosevelt. Quoted in Endangered Species Act Hearings, U.S. House of Representatives, Mar. 14, 1985.

81. It is shocking to smite down trees for mere decorations.
Theodore Roosevelt. Explanation of his refusal to have a cut Christmas tree in the White House. Quoted in *Where Washington?*, Dec. 1989.

82. Everything is good when it leaves the hands of the Creator; everything degenerates in the hands of man.
Jean-Jacques Rousseau (1712-1778), French philosopher. *Emile*, 1762.

83. Everybody wants everything picked up, and nobody wants anything put down.
William Ruckelshaus, Administrator, Environmental Protection Agency (R), and U.S. Deputy Attorney General. In reference to waste disposal. Quoted on PBS, *Adam Smith's Money World*, May 6, 1989.

84. Congress mandated that we do the impossible – create a permanently perfect environment.
William Ruckelshaus, Quoted in *Smithsonian*, April 1990.

85. Has the white man become a child that he should slay and not eat?
Satana (1830-1878), Chief, Kiowa Indians. Observation on whites hunting for sport. Statement to the Medicine Lodge Grand Council, Oct. 1867.

86. American industry has been into excessive reliance on virgin materials and doesn't know how to use scrap.
Brendon Sexton, Sanitation Commissioner, New York City. Quoted in *The New York Times*, Dec. 10, 1989.

87. I don't know anybody who really believes in dirty air or dirty water.... Water that comes out of our plants ... in many cases ... is purer than the water that came from the river before we used it.
Irving Shapiro, Chairman, DuPont Corporation. Quoted in *The Washington Post*, Feb. 8, 1981.

88. We're not dealing with an exact science here. Estimates of *[global]* warming are going to continue to go up and down like yo-yos for the next couple of years.
Tony Slingo, Director, National Center for Atmospheric Research, Boulder, CO. Response when asked to explain why scientists halved their earlier predictions

of how much global temperatures will rise. Quoted in *The Washington Post*, Sept. 14, 1989.

89. The only way to protect areas that are economically and ecologically valuable is to keep oil out.
Lisa Speer, spokesperson, National Resources Defense Council. Comment on the danger of oil spills at sea and the difficulty oil companies face in mounting emergency cleanups. Quoted in *The New York Times*, April 2, 1989.

90. Something other than leaving the land to look nice has to be done, because that generates no dollars.
Patrick D. Spurgin, Director, Utah State Lands and Forestry. Quoted in *The New York Times*, Oct. 10, 1989.

91. Men as a general rule have very little reverence for trees.
Elizabeth Cady Stanton (1815-1902), 1st President, National Woman Suffrage Association. *Diary*, 1900.

92. In the United States there is more space where nobody is than where anybody is. That is what makes America what it is.
Gertrude Stein (1874-1946), American writer. *The Geographical History of America*, 1936.

93. We forsake common sense and blindly enforce regulations that fail to consider the impact on the human environment.... How would you like to tell 400,000 of your citizens that they don't have drinking water because we are protecting a dwindling population of snakes *[Concho River water snakes]* whose future is in jeopardy regardless of the measures taken to protect it?
Charles W. Stenholm, U.S. Congressman (D-TX). Hearing, House Subcommittee on Fisheries and Wildlife Conservation and the Environment, Mar. 17, 1987.

94. To kill a man for shooting an animal is a very delicate matter.
Glen Tatham, park warden, Zimbabwe, Rhodesia. Comment on the execution of game poachers. Quoted in *The New York Times*, May 6, 1986.

95. I don't think you can put a dollar-and-cents value on species of animals, and particularly when they reach the point of being threatened or endangered.
Robert Lindsay Thomas, U.S. Congressman (D-GA). Hearing, House Subcommittee on Fisheries and Wildlife Conservation and the Environment, Mar. 17, 1987.

96. What is the use of a house if you haven't got a tolerable planet to put it on?
Henry David Thoreau (1817-1862), American philosopher and naturalist. Quoted in *Omni*, July 1987.

97. If you eliminate this constituency *[hunters]*, you lose the greatest source of conservation revenue.
John Turner, Director, Fish and Wildlife Service, U.S. Department of the Interior. Quoted in *U.S. News & World Report*, Feb. 5, 1990.

98. The best qualities in man must atrophy in a standing-room-only environment.
Stewart L. Udall, U.S. Congressman and U.S. Secretary of the Interior (D). *The Quiet Crisis*, 1963.

99. Environmental issues and health care issues merge.
Paul Wellstone, U.S. Senator (D-MN). Speech, State Alliance for Universal Health Care. C-SPAN, Dec. 25, 1990.

100. We have to make environmental choices not based on possibilities but on probabilities.
George F. Will, American political columnist. Quoted on ABC, *This Week*, April 2, 1989.

101. The American public's view is very clear. They want clean air and water, and they want everybody else to pay for it.
George F. Will. Quoted on ABC, *This Week*, June 18, 1989.

102. Tough fish or wildlife management decisions are difficult to carry out in a democratic society. Wild things sometimes suffer because federal, state, or local authorities are reluctant to act in the face of controversy.
Lonnie Williamson, American writer and editor. *Outdoor Life*, Sept. 1984.

Chapter 28

Equality

1. If you think equality is the goal your standards are too low.
   Saying on a feminist T-shirt, Ann Arbor, MI, 1974.

2. Equal rights for all, special privileges for none.
   Jacksonian campaign slogan, 1836; revived by Populists, 1896.

3. Inequality of Mind and Body are so established by God Almighty in his Constitution of Human Nature that no art or policy can ever plane them down to a level.
   John Adams (1735-1826), 2nd President of the United States (Federalist-MA). 1813.

4. If the spirit of equality means anything, it means like opportunity, and if we once lose like opportunity, we lose the only chance we have toward equality throughout the nation.
   Jane Addams (1860-1935), American social settlement worker and Nobel Laureate in Peace. Washington's Birthday address, Union League, Chicago, IL, Feb. 22, 1903.

5. There never will be complete equality until women themselves help to make laws and elect lawmakers.
   Susan B. Anthony (1820-1906), American woman's suffrage leader. *The Arena*, May 1897.

6. Equality ... is the result of human organization.... We are not born equal.
   Hannah Arendt (1906-1975), American political philosopher. *The Origins of Totalitarianism*, 1951.

7. Ours has not been a racially democratic society for 300 years.
   Frank Askin, general counsel, American Civil Liberties Union. Quoted in *U.S. News & World Report*, Oct. 3, 1977.

8. Equality may perhaps be a right, but no power on earth can ever turn it into a fact.
   Honoré de Balzac (1799-1850), French writer. *La Duchesse de Langeais*.

9. There is no case in history where the Caucasian race has survived social integration.... We must either submit to the unlawful dictate of the federal government or stand up like men and tell them, "Never."
   Ross Barnett (1898-1987), Governor of Mississippi (D). Speech, Sept. 1962.

10. The dogma of woman's complete historical subjection to men must be rated as one of the most fantastic myths ever created in the human mind.
    Mary R. Beard (1876-1958), American historian. *Woman as a Force in History*, 1946.

11. Society, being codified by man, decrees that woman is inferior: She can do away with this inferiority only by destroying the male's superiority.
    Simone de Beauvoir, French writer. *The Second Sex*, 1953.

12. What makes equality such a difficult business is that we only want it with our superiors.
    Henry Becque (1837-1899), French dramatist. *Querelles littéraires*, 1890.

13. Is the great working class oppressed? Yes, undoubtedly it is. God has intended the great to be great and the little to be little.
    Henry Ward Beecher (1813-1887), American clergyman and writer. Quoted in *The New York Times*, July 30, 1877.

14. As a representative of women let my message be: Yes you can.
    Benazir Bhutto, Prime Minister of Pakistan. Address to Congress, June 5, 1989.

15. My opinion, Legislators, is that the fundamental basis of our political system hinges directly and exclusively upon the establishment and practice of equality in Venezuela.
    Simón Bolívar (1783-1830), Supreme Chief of Colombia, President of Peru, and founder of Bolivia. Address, Congress of Angostura, Feb. 1819.

16. When a man has emerged from slavery, and by the aid of beneficent legislation has shaken off the inseparable concomitants of the state, there must be some stage in the progress of the elevation when he takes the rank of a mere citizen, and ceases to be the special favorite of the law.

Joseph P. Bradley (1813-1892), U.S. Supreme Court Justice. 1883.

17. The middle class is always a firm champion of equality when it concerns a class above it; but it is its inveterate foe when it concerns elevating a class below it.

Orestes Augustus Brownson (1803-1876), American clergyman, writer, and founder, Workingmen's Party. *The Laboring Classes*, 1840.

18. It is not healthy when a nation lives within a nation.... A nation cannot be confident of its tomorrow if its refugees are among its own citizens.

Pearl S. Buck (1892-1973), Nobel Laureate in Literature (United States). *What America Means to Me*, 1943.

19. It's very easy for liberals and conservatives to agree upon liberty, but it is harder for them to agree upon equality.

James MacGregor Burns, American political historian. Interview, PBS, *MacNeil-Lehrer Report*, July 4, 1989.

20. The government of the United States is a device for maintaining in perpetuity the rights of the people, with the ultimate extinction of all privileged classes.

Calvin Coolidge (1872-1933), 30th President of the United States (R-MA). Speech, Philadelphia, PA, Sept. 25, 1924.

21. The very existence of government implies inequality. The citizen who is preferred to office becomes the superior of those who are not, as long as he is the repository of power.

James Fenimore Cooper (1789-1851), American writer. *The American Democrat*, 1838.

22. All good Americans, while verbally asking for nothing but equal rights, interpret the phrase so that equal rights become equivalent to special rights.

Herbert David Croly (1869-1930), American writer and founder, *The New Republic*. *The Promise of American Life*, 1909.

23. America is preeminently the land of great possibilities, of great opportunities, and of no less great probabilities.... We all stand on the great field of renown, with a free and equal chance.... We all have a fair chance and an open field. Long may it so remain.

Eugene V. Debs (1855-1926), American Socialist. *Locomotive Fireman's Magazine*, Mar. 1878.

24. In order to have economic democracy you have to have equal access to property.

Hernando De Soto, economist and Director, Central Bank of Peru. Interview, PBS *American Interests*, Jan. 6, 1990.

25. It is the policy of the state *[New York]* that the American ideal of equality of opportunity requires that students be admitted to educational institutions without regard to race, color, religion, creed, or national origin.

Thomas E. Dewey (1902-1971), Governor of New York (R). Proclamation, Albany, NY, Apr. 3, 1948.

26. I am involved in mankind, and whatever the skin, we are all involved in mankind. Equality of opportunity must prevail if we are to complete the covenant that we have made with the people, and when we held up our hands to take an oath to defend the laws and to carry out the Constitution of the United States.

Everett M. Dirksen (1896-1969), U.S. Congressman and U.S. Senator (R-IL). Senate speech supporting the Civil Rights Act, June 19, 1964.

27. I am no leveller; I look upon an artificial equality as equally pernicious with a factitious aristocracy; both depressing the energies and checking the enterprise of a nation.

Benjamin Disraeli, 1st Earl of Beaconsfield (1804-1881), Prime Minister of Great Britain (Conservative). *Coningsby*, 1844.

28. The difference of race is one of the reasons why I fear war may always exist. Because race implies difference, difference implies superiority, and superiority leads to predominance.

Benjamin Disraeli. Debate, House of Commons, Feb. 1, 1849.

29. When a great truth once gets abroad in the world, no power on earth can imprison it, or prescribe its limits, or suppress it. It is bound to go on till it becomes the thought of the world. Such a truth is woman's right to equal liberty with man. She was born with it. It was hers before she comprehended it. It is prescribed upon all the powers and faculties of her soul, and no custom, law nor usage can ever destroy it.

Frederick Douglass (c.1817-1895), Recorder of Deeds, District of Columbia, and U.S. Minister to Haiti. Speech, International Council of Women, Washington, DC, Mar. 1888.

30. Equal doesn't mean identical.
Hugh Downs, American TV journalist. ABC, *20/20*, Sept. 14, 1990.

31. Do equall Law and right to all the King's Subjects rich and poor.
Daniel Dulany (1687-1753), Attorney General, Colony of Maryland. Resolution to judges, 1722.

32. The only way you get to the goal of color blindness is to be color conscious along the way.
Harry Edwards, Federal Judge. PBS, *The Constitution: That Delicate Balance*, Apr. 1982.

33. As to what we call the masses and the common men – there are no common men. All men are at last of a size.
Ralph Waldo Emerson (1803-1882), American writer. "Uses of Great Men," in *Representative Men*, 1876.

34. The Spartan principle of "calling that which is just, equal"; not that which is equal, just.
Ralph Waldo Emerson. "Politics," in *Essays*, second series, 1876.

35. Tonight the Negro knows from his radio and television that a Congo native can be a locomotive engineer, but in Jackson *[MS]* he cannot even drive a garbage truck.
Medgar W. Evers (1926-1963), American civil rights leader. Speech, Jackson, MS, May 1963.

36. Only as an egg in the womb are we all equal.
Oriana Fallaci, Italian journalist. *Letter to a Child Never Born*, 1975.

37. Men are made by nature unequal. It is vain, therefore, to treat them as if they were equal.
James Anthony Froude (1818-1894), British historian. *Party Politics*.

38. Personally I prefer that men shall attend to all public matters.
Miriam Amanda Furguson (1875-1961), Governor of Texas (D). Comment made when she was the governor's wife; a few years later she was elected governor as a surrogate for her husband, who had been impeached for corruption. Interview, *Dallas Morning News*, 1916.

39. As for Western women, it seems to me that they have often had to struggle to obtain their own rights. That did not leave them much time to prove their abilities. The time will come.
Indira Gandhi (1917-1984), Prime Minister of India. Quoted in *Oui*, 1975.

40. To bear and rear the majestic race to which they can never fully belong! To live vicariously forever, through their sons, the daughters being just another vicarious link! What a supreme and magnificent martyrdom!
Charlotte Perkins Gilman (1860-1935), American writer, social critic, and reformer. *Women and Economics*, 1898.

41. The soldier's business is to take life. For that he is paid by the State, eulogized by political charlatans and upheld by public hysteria. But woman's function is to give life, yet neither the State nor politicians nor public opinion have ever made the slightest provision in return for the life woman has given.
Emma Goldman (1869-1940), American anarchist. "The Social Aspects of Birth Control," *Mother Earth*, Apr. 1916.

42. Apart from undeniable gains, there are still daily cares largely preventing women from enjoying their rights fully.
Mikhail Gorbachev, President of the U.S.S.R. Keynote address, 19th All-Union Communist Party Conference, Moscow, July 1988.

43. A man does not have to like me to work by my side, or in my employ or to be my next-door neighbor. But he does *not* have the right to limit my opportunities for employment or my choice of housing.
Dick Gregory, American comedian and writer. *Write Me In*, 1968.

44. I recognize no rights but human rights – I know nothing of men's rights and women's rights.
Angelina Grimké (1805-1879), American abolitionist and suffragist. *Letters to Catherine Beecher*, No. 12, 1836.

45. For almost all of this nation's history the major decisions have been made by white Christian men.
Andrew Hacker, American political scientist. Quoted in *The New York Times*, Feb. 11, 1990.

46. The feeling of equality which they *[Americans]* proudly cherish does not proceed from an ignorance of their station, but from the knowledge of their rights; and it is this knowledge which will render it so exceedingly difficult for any tyrant ever to triumph over the liberties of our country.
Sarah J. Hale (1788-1879), American magazine editor. *Sketches of American Character*, 1829.

47. I consider every attempt to induce women to think they have a just right to participate in the

public duties of government as injurious to their best interests and derogatory to their character.

Sarah J. Hale. Editorial, *The Ladies' Magazine and Literary Gazette*, Feb. 1832.

48. Our Constitution is colorblind and neither knows nor tolerates classes among citizens. The arbitrary separation of citizens, on the basis of race ... is a badge of servitude wholly inconsistent with civil freedom.

John Marshall Harlan (1833-1911), U.S. Supreme Court Justice. *Plessy* v. *Furgeson*, 1896 (sole dissent).

49. All men are created equal in one respect, at least, and that is their desire to be unequal.

William Randolph Hearst (1863-1951), U.S. Congressman (D-NY); founder, Independence League Party; journalist; and publisher. 1930.

50. Honor to the French! They have taken good care of the two greatest human needs – good eating and civic equality.

Heinrich Heine (1797-1856), German writer. *Journey from Munich to Genoa*, No. 29.

51. Give men opportunity and opportunity will give you men.

George D. Herron (1862-1925), American clergyman. Quoted in Upton Sinclair, *The Cry for Justice*, 1920.

52. Nature hath made men so equal in the faculties of the body and mind, as that, though there be found one man sometimes manifestly stronger in body or of quicker mind than another, yet when all is reckoned together the difference between man and man is not so considerable as that one man can thereupon claim to himself any benefit to which another may not pretend as well as he.

Thomas Hobbes (1588-1679), English political philosopher. *Leviathan*, 1651.

53. Our country has become the land of opportunity to those born without inheritance.

Herbert Hoover (1874-1964), 31st President of the United States (R-CA). Campaign speech, Oct. 22, 1928.

54. O, let my land be a land where Liberty
Is crowned with no false patriotic wreath,
But opportunity is real, and life is free,
Equality is in the air we breathe.

Langston Hughes (1902-1967), American poet. *The Black Man Speaks*, 1943.

55. Unless the woman is liberated, there is no freedom in Iraqi land.

Saddam Hussein, President of Iraq. Quoted in *Arab American Affairs*, Summer 1989.

56. That all men are equal is a proposition to which, at ordinary times, no sane individual has ever given his assent.

Aldous Huxley (1894-1963), British writer. *Proper Studies*.

57. Distinction in society will always exist under every just government. Equality of talents, of education, or of wealth cannot be produced by human institutions.

Andrew Jackson (1767-1845), 7th President of the United States (D-TN). Message to Congress vetoing the Bank Renewal Bill, July 10, 1832.

58. In the last era of the *[civil rights]* movement, the disenfranchised were the blacks, the colored. Now the disenfranchised are the have-nots, the unemployed, the hungry.

Jesse L. Jackson, Shadow Senator (D-DC). Interview, *San Francisco Examiner & Chronicle*, Feb. 16, 1975.

59. We hold these truths to be self-evident: that all men are created equal; that they are endowed by their Creator with certain unalienable rights; that among these are life, liberty, and the pursuit of happiness.

Thomas Jefferson (1743-1826), 3rd President of the United States (Democratic Republican-VA). *Declaration of Independence*, July 4, 1776.

60. I believe the Indian then to be in body and mind equal to the white man.

Thomas Jefferson. Letter to Gen. Chastellux, June 7, 1785.

61. There is a natural aristocracy among men. The grounds of this are virtue and talent.

Thomas Jefferson. Letter to John Adams, Oct. 28, 1813.

62. No man has a natural right to commit aggression on the equal rights of another.

Thomas Jefferson. Letter to Francis W. Gilmer, 1816.

63. The mass of mankind has not been born with saddles on their backs, nor a favored few booted and spurred, ready to ride them legitimately, by the grace of God.

Thomas Jefferson. Letter to Roger C. Weightman, June 24, 1826.

64. Until justice is blind to color, until education is unaware of race, until opportunity is unconcerned with the color of men's skins, emancipation will be a proclamation but not a fact.

Lyndon B. Johnson (1908-1973), 36th President of the United States (D-TX). Speech, Gettysburg, PA, May 30, 1963.

65. To conclude that women are unfitted to the task of our historic society seems to me the equivalent of closing male ideas to female facts.
Lyndon B. Johnson. Apr. 13, 1964.

66. Your levellers wish to level *down* as far as themselves; but they cannot bear levelling *up* to themselves.
Samuel Johnson (1709-1784), English writer and lexicographer. James Boswell, *The Life of Samuel Johnson*, July 21, 1763.

67. It is better that some should be unhappy than that none should be happy, which would be the case in a general state of equality.
Samuel Johnson. *Ibid.*, Apr. 7, 1776.

68. Republicans many times can't get the words "equality of opportunity" out of their mouths. Their lips do not form that way.
Jack F. Kemp, U.S. Congressman and U.S. Secretary of Housing and Urban Development (R-NY). Quoted in *Newsweek*, July 18, 1988.

69. There are very few jobs that actually require a penis or vagina. All other jobs should be open to everybody.
Florynce R. Kennedy, American writer, feminist, and TV talk-show host. "Institutionalized Oppression vs. the Female," *Sisterhood Is Powerful*, 1970.

70. There is always inequality in life. Some men are killed in war and some men are wounded and some men never leave the country. Life is unfair.
John F. Kennedy (1917-1963), 35th President of the United States (D-MA). Speech, Mar. 21, 1962.

71. We are confronted primarily with a moral issue. It is as old as the Scriptures and as plain and as clear as the American Constitution. The heart of the question is whether all Americans are to be afforded equal rights and equal opportunities.
John F. Kennedy. National television address on civil rights, June 1963.

72. Lamentably, it is a historical fact that privileged groups seldom give up their privileges voluntarily.
Martin Luther King, Jr. (1929-1968), American clergyman and civil rights leader. *Letter from a Birmingham Jail*, Apr. 16, 1963.

73. I have a dream that one day on the red hills of Georgia, sons of former slaves and sons of former slave owners will be able to sit down together at the table of brotherhood.
Martin Luther King, Jr.. Speech, Washington, DC, Aug. 28, 1963.

74. I am not satisfied as long as the Negro sees life as a long and empty corridor with a "No Exit" sign at the end. The cup of endurance has run over.
Martin Luther King, Jr.. Speech, Montgomery, AL, Mar. 1965.

75. I'd like to get to the point where I can be just as mediocre as a man.
Juanita Kreps, U.S. Secretary of Commerce (R). Quoted in Stineman, *American Political Women*, 1980.

76. We *[in France]* have made an admirable and almost incredible destruction of all abuses and prejudices; that everything not directly useful to, or coming from, the people has been levelled.
Marquis de Lafayette (1757-1834), French statesman and Major General, Continental Army. Letter to George Washington, Mar. 17, 1790.

77. The function of government is to establish and maintain equal opportunity and industrial justice.
Fiorello H. La Guardia (1882-1947), U.S. Congressman (Republican and Socialist-NY) and Mayor of New York City (Republican and Fusion Party). Quoted in Arthur Mann, *La Guardia: A Fighter Against His Times*, 1959.

78. Those who desire the good of all begin by the abolition of special privilege.
Harold J. Laski (1893-1950), British political scientist. *A Grammar of Politics*, 1925.

79. Inequality of rights and power proceeds from the very Author of nature, from whom all paternity in heaven and earth is named.
Pope Leo XIII (1810-1903). Encyclical, *Quod Apostolici Muneris*, Dec. 28, 1878.

80. By the force of our demands, our determination, and our numbers, we shall splinter the segregated South into a thousand pieces, and put them back in the image of God and democracy.
John R. Lewis, Chairman, Student Non-Violent Coordinating Committee, and U.S. Congressman (D-GA). Speech, Washington, DC, Aug. 28, 1963.

81. Equal justice to the South, it is said, requires us to consent to the extension of slavery to new countries *[states]*. That is to say, inasmuch as you do not object to my taking my hog to Nebraska, therefore I must not object to your taking your slave. Now, I admit this is perfectly logical, if there is no difference between hogs and Negroes.

Abraham Lincoln (1809-1865), 16th President of the United States (R-IL). Speech, Peoria, IL, Oct. 16, 1854.

82. I have said that in their right to "life, liberty and pursuit of happiness," as proclaimed in that old Declaration, the inferior races are our equals.

Abraham Lincoln. Debate with Stephen Douglas, Galesburg, IL, Oct. 1, 1858.

83. Fourscore and seven years ago, our fathers brought forth on this continent a new nation, conceived in liberty and dedicated to the proposition that all men are created equal.

Abraham Lincoln. Dedication speech, Gettysburg National Cemetery, Gettysburg, PA, Nov. 19, 1863.

84. Equal and exact justice to every class of our citizens without distinction of color, sex, or nationality.

Belva Ann Lockwood (1830-1917), American attorney and cofounder, Equal Rights Party. Platform, Equal Rights Party, 1884 presidential election.

85. If women are given equal pay for Civil Service jobs, maybe other employers will do the same.

Belva Ann Lockwood. Quoted in Mary Virginia Fox, *Lady for the Defense*, 1975.

86. I am for lifting everyone off the social bottom. In fact, I am for doing away with the social bottom altogether.

Clare Boothe Luce (1903-1987), U.S. Congresswoman (R-CT) and U.S. Ambassador to Italy and Brazil. Quoted in *Time*, Feb. 14, 1964.

87. An earthly kingdom cannot exist without inequality of persons. Some must be free, some serfs, some rulers, some subjects.

Martin Luther (1483-1546), German Protestant theologian. *Works*, Vol. XVIII.

88. Let us no longer be deceived by the cry of those who produce nothing and who enjoy all, and who insultingly call us the lower orders, and claim our homage for themselves, as the higher orders; while the Declaration of Independence asserts that all men are created equal.

Seth Luther (1795-1846), American labor leader. Speech, Boston, MA, 1832.

89. Mississippi is now the South's most progressive environment. Because of our history, we went through a crucible others didn't. And that has enabled us to move on in ways that others haven't.

Ray Mabus, Governor of Mississippi (D). Quoted in *The New York Times Magazine*, July 23, 1989.

90. Let us do justice to them *[the Jews]*.... Let us open to them every career in which ability and energy can be displayed. Till we have done this, let us not presume to say that there is no genius among the countrymen of Isaiah, no heroism among the descendants of the Maccabees.

Thomas Babington Macaulay, 1st Baron Macaulay (1800-1859), historian and Secretary of War, Great Britain (Liberal). Speech, House of Commons, on a bill to allow Jews the vote, Apr. 17, 1833.

91. If a test of civilization be sought, none can be so sure as the condition of the half of society over which the other half has power – from the exercises of the right of the strongest.

Harriet Martineau (1802-1876), British reformer. *Society in America*, 1837.

92. I know that men are not equal; nowhere on the earth or in Nature is there equality – there is variety.... The natural variety must be organized through the division and gradation of functions and work; no organization of men is possible without superiors and subordinates, but it must just be an organization, and not a privilege, not aristocratic coercion but mutual service.

Tomas G. Masaryk (1850-1937), 1st President of Czechoslovakia. Quoted in Karyl Capek, *Masaryk on Thought and Life*, 1938.

93. A woman is a citizen who works for Mexico. We must not treat her differently from a man, except to honor her more.

Adolfo Lopez Mateos (1910-1969), President of Mexico. Quoted in *Time*, Oct. 12, 1959.

94. Your Country should be your Temple, God at the summit, a People of equals at the base.

Guiseppe Mazzini (1805-1872), Italian statesman. *The Duties of Man*, 1858.

95. I already belong to a very exclusive club. It's called the U.S. Senate.

Barbara A. Mikulski, U.S. Congresswoman and U.S. Senator (D-MD). Response when asked if she would join an exclusive club that had just changed its policies to accept women. Quoted in *The Washington Post*, July 17, 1988.

96. We *[women]* seek equality. We don't seek sameness.

Barbara A. Mikulski. Interview, ABC, *This Week*, June 10, 1990.

97. There should be an equality among all men.

Book of Mormon, *Mosiah* 27:3.

98. Universal tolerance is the very soul of happiness to a populous and enlightened nation.
Napoléon I (1769-1821), military leader and Emperor of France. *Maxims.*

99. Reasonable democracy will never aspire to anything more than obtaining an equal power of elevation to all.
Napoléon I. *Ibid.*

100. Wrong never lies in unequal rights; it lies in the pretension of equal rights.
Friedrich Wilhelm Nietzsche (1844-1900), German philosopher. *The Antichrist*, 1888.

101. This isn't going to be a good country for any of us to live in until it's a good country for all of us to live in.
Richard M. Nixon, 37th President of the United States (R-CA). Quoted in *The Observer*, Sept. 29, 1968.

102. A woman can and should be able to do any political job a man can do.
Richard M. Nixon. Speech, League of Women Voters, Washington, DC, Apr. 16, 1969.

103. The class struggle has become the race struggle.... Race forms the class struggle of the modern world.
Kwame Nkrumah (1909-1972), President of Ghana. 1967.

104. Government ought to be based on fairness.
David R. Obey, U.S. Congressman (D-WI). Interview, PBS, *MacNeil-Lehrer News Hour*, Oct. 5, 1990.

105. All animals are equal but some animals are more equal than others.
George Orwell (Eric Blair) (1903-1950), British writer. *Animal Farm*, 1945.

106. It is time that the women took their place in Imperial politics.
Emmeline Pankhurst (1858-1928), English suffragist. Quoted in *The London Standard*, Oct. 5, 1911.

107. Democracy means not "I am as good as you are" but "You are as good as I am."
Theodore Parker (1810-1860), American clergyman and abolitionist. *Thoughts on Labor*, 1841.

108. *[Comparable worth is]* the looniest idea since *Looney Tunes.*
Clarence Pendleton, Chairman, U.S. Civil Rights Commission (R). Quoted in *The New York Times*. Nov. 17, 1984.

109. Equality is the mother of Justice, queen of all virtues.
Philo Judaeus (c. 20 B.C.-c. A.D. 40), Alexandrian philosopher and diplomat. *Noah's Work as a Planter*, XXVIII.

110. Human society, as established by God, is composed of unequal elements.... To make them all equal is impossible, and would mean the destruction of human society itself.
Pope Pius X (1835-1914). *Apostolic Letter on Catholic Action*, 1903.

111. The guarantee of equal protection cannot mean one thing when applied to one individual and something else when applied to a person of another color. If both are not accorded the same protection, then it is not equal.
Lewis F. Powell, Jr., U.S. Supreme Court Justice. *University of California* v. *Bakke*, 1978.

112. I am an aristocrat. I love liberty. I hate equality.
John Randolph (1773-1833), U.S. Congressman (States Rights Democrat-VA), U.S. Senator, and U.S. Minister to Russia. Quoted in W. C. Bruce, *Randolph of Roanoke*, 1922.

113. Equal rights for every civilized man.
Cecil Rhodes (1853-1902), Prime Minister of Cape Colony, South Africa, industrialist, and philanthropist. Quoted in Lewis Mitchell, *The Life and Times of the Right Honourable Cecil John Rhodes*, 1910.

114. No one can make you feel inferior without your consent.
Anna Eleanor Roosevelt (1884-1962), First Lady and U.S. Delegate to the United Nations. *This Is My Story*, 1937.

115. We must make American individualism what it was intended to be – equality of opportunity for all, the right of exploitation for none.
Franklin D. Roosevelt (1882-1945), 32nd President of the United States (D-NY). Campaign speech, Columbus, OH, 1932.

116. When I say I believe in a square deal I do not mean, and nobody who speaks the truth can mean, that he believes it possible to give every man the best hand. If the cards do not come to any man, or if they do come, and he has not got the power to play them, that is his affair. All I mean is that there shall not be any crookedness in the dealing.
Theodore Roosevelt (1858-1919), 26th President of the United States (R-NY). Speech, Dallas, TX, Apr. 5, 1905.

117. At every stage, and under all circumstances, the essence of the struggle is to equalize opportunity, destroy privilege, and give to the life and citizenship of every individual the highest possible value both to himself and to the commonwealth.
Theodore Roosevelt. Speech, "The New Nationalism," Osawatomie, KS, Aug. 31, 1910.

118. I stand for the square deal.... I mean not merely that I stand for fair play under the present rules of the game, but I stand for having those rules changed so as to work for a more substantial equality of opportunity and reward.
Theodore Roosevelt. *Ibid.*

119. The nature of things continually tends to the destruction of equality.
Jean-Jacques Rousseau (1712-1778), French philosopher. *The Social Contract*, 1762.

120. Demagogy enters at the moment when for want of a common denominator, the principle of equality degenerates into a principle of identity.
Antoine de Saint-Exupéry (1900-1944), French writer and aviator. *Flight to Arras*, 1942.

121. We do not all start out in life on an even playing field.
Antonin Scalia, U.S. Supreme Court Justice. PBS, *Ethics in America*, Feb. 14, 1989.

122. My dream is that 1989 will be the last time they swear in a President of the United States under a Constitution that does not treat women as equals.
Patricia R. Schroeder, U.S. Congresswoman (D-CO). In reference to the Equal Right Amendment. Quoted in *Des Moines Register*, July 1, 1988.

123. Equality of rights, embodied in general self-government, is the great moral element in modern democracy.... There is the solid foundation of our system of government. There is our greatness. There is our safety. There, and nowhere else!
Carl Schurz (1829-1906), U.S. Senator (R and Ind.-MO). Speech, Faneuil Hall, Boston, MA, Apr. 1859.

124. Democracy has two extremes to avoid: the spirit of inequality, which leads to an aristocracy, or to the government of a single individual; and the spirit of extreme equality, which conducts it to despotism, as the despotism of a single individual finishes it by conquest.
Charles-Louis de Secondat, Baron de La Brède et de Montesquieu (1689-1755), French writer. *The Spirit of the Laws*, VIII, 2, 1748.

125. This is the Juggling trick of the Parity, they would have nobody above them, but they do not tell you that they would have nobody under them.
John Selden (1584-1654), jurist and Member of Long Parliament, England. *Table-Talk: Parity*, 1689.

126. Socialism means equality of income or nothing.
George Bernard Shaw (1856-1950), Nobel Laureate in Literature (Great Britain). *The Intelligent Woman's Guide to Socialism, Capitalism, Sovietism and Fascism*, 1928.

127. The French Revolution made all men equal before the law; the Communist revolution makes all equal before the dictator.
Fulton J. Sheen (1895-1979), American Catholic archbishop and television personality. *Freedom Under God*, 1940.

128. People with handicaps are no longer interested in hearing statements about their rights; they want everyday access to movie theaters, schools, public transportation; they are entitled to active work and social lives.
Eunice Kennedy Shriver, founder and Chair, Special Olympics. "Letter to the Next Generation," *Newsweek* and *Time*, Nov. 6, 1989.

129. Compensations given without incentives do nothing to help the disadvantaged.
Thomas Sowell, Senior Fellow, Hoover Institution. *Preferential Policies: An International Perspective*, 1990.

130. Woman's degradation is in man's idea of his sexual rights.
Elizabeth Cady Stanton (1815-1902), 1st President, National Woman Suffrage Association. Letter to Susan B. Anthony, 1860.

131. Whoever kindles the flame of intolerance in America is lighting a fire underneath his own home.
Harold E. Stassen, Governor of Minnesota (R). *Where I Stand*, 1947.

132. I repose in this quiet and secluded spot, not from any natural preference for solitude, but, finding other cemeteries limited by charter rules as to race, I have chosen this that I might illustrate in my death the principles which I have advocated through a long life, Equality of Man before his Creator
Thaddeus Stevens (1792-1868), U.S. Congressman (Whig and R-PA). Self-written epitaph on his tombstone in a Negro cemetery.

133. The great are great only because we are on our knees. Let us rise!
Max Stirner (Johann Kaspar Schmidt) (1806-1856), German anarchist. *The Ego and His Own*, 1845.

134. By the same title that we claim Liberty do we claim Equality also. One is the complement of the other.
Charles Sumner (1811-1874), U.S. Senator (D, R, and Free Soil-MA). Congressional address, "The Equal Rights of All," Feb. 6, 1866.

135. Equality of rights is the standing promise of nature to man.
Charles Sumner. Quoted in Lerone Bennett, Jr., *Pioneers in Protest*, 1968.

136. Elect me and I'll put inspectors at the state line to look into every *[railroad]* sleeping car and see that there is no mixing of the races.
Eugene Talmadge (1884-1946), Governor of Georgia (D). Campaign speech, 1946.

137. No woman in my time will be prime minister or chancellor or foreign secretary – not the top jobs.
Margaret Thatcher, Prime Minister of Great Britain (Conservative). Comment when she was selected for a minor government post. Quoted in *London Sunday Telegraph*, Oct. 26, 1969.

138. Let our children grow tall, and some taller than others if they have it in them to do so.
Margaret Thatcher. Speech, 1975.

139. One does wish that there were a few more women in parliament. Then one could be less conspicuous oneself.
Margaret Thatcher. Quoted in *The Observer*, May 6, 1979.

140. Since the days when the great fleet of Columbus sailed into the waters of the New World, American has been another name for opportunity.
Frederick Jackson Turner (1861-1932), American historian. *The Significance of the Frontier in American History*, 1893.

141. No man should be a serf, not do homage, or any manner of service to any lord.
Wat Tyler (d. 1381), leader, English peasant's revolt. Quoted in *Anonimalle Chronicle*.

142. All children, whether born in or out of wedlock, shall enjoy the same social protection.
United Nations, *Universal Declaration of Human Rights*, approved by the General Assembly in 1948.

143. It is untrue that equality is a law of nature. Nature has made nothing equal. Her law is subordination and dependency. Law has no power to equalize men in defiance of nature.
Marquis de Vauvenargues (1715-1747), French soldier and moralist. *Réflexions et Maximes*.

144. Segregation now, segregation tomorrow, segregation forever.
George C. Wallace, Governor of Alabama (D). First inauguration address, Jan. 14, 1963.

145. Segregation *[of black schoolchildren]* from others of their age and qualifications solely because of their race generates a feeling of inferiority as to their status in the community that may affect their hearts and minds in a way unlikely ever to be undone.... Segregation, with the sanction of the law, therefore has a tendency to retard the educational and mental development of Negro children.
Earl Warren (1891-1974), Chief Justice, U.S. Supreme Court, and Governor of California (R). *Brown* v. *Board of Education of Topeka, KS*, 1954.

146. In all things that are purely social we can be as separate as the fingers, yet one as the hand in all things essential to our mutual progress.
Booker T. Washington (1856-1915), American educator and President, Tuskegee Institute. *Up from Slavery*, 1901.

147. We have every kind of mix you can have. I have a black, I have a woman, two Jews and a cripple. And we have talent.
James G. Watt, U.S. Secretary of the Interior (R). Description of his staff to visitors from the U.S. Chamber of Commerce. Sept. 21, 1983.

148. The so-called Moslems who preach black supremacy and hatred of all white people have gained a following only because America has been so slow in granting equality opportunities and has permitted the abuse and persecution of Negro citizens.
Roy Wilkins, Executive Director, National Association for the Advancement of Colored People. Quoted in *The Chicago Defender*, Aug. 8, 1959.

149. Neither slavery nor involuntary servitude shall exist ... except for crime, whereof the party shall first be duly convicted.
David Wilmot (1815-1868), U.S. Congressman (D-PA) and U.S. Senator (R-PA). Rejected amendment offered to House appropriations bill, Aug. 8, 1846.

150. Let every man and woman, without distinction of sect or party ... bear testimony against the system which fills the prisons of a free republic with men whose only crime is a love of freedom – which strikes down the habeas corpus and trial by jury, and converts the free soil of Massachusetts into hunting ground for the Southern kidnappers.
Henry Wilson (1812-1875), U.S. Senator (Free Soil, American, D, and R-MA), and Vice President of the Uni-

ted States (R-MA). Handbill for political rally opposing the Fugitive Slave Act, Apr. 3, 1851.

151. The government of our country cannot be lodged in any special class.

Woodrow Wilson (1856-1924), 28th President of the United States (D-NJ). Presidential campaign speech, 1912.

152. Woman suffrage, madam, is not a question that is dealt with by the national government at all, and I am here only as a representative of the national party.

Woodrow Wilson. Remark to a female heckler during a campaign speech, Brooklyn Academy of Music, 1912.

153. I intend to do all in my small power toward the overthrow of that other slavery, more deeply rooted, more subtle, more obscure and tenacious, and more demoralizing than ever the slavery of the black man was.

Victoria Woodhull (1838-1927), American suffragist, publisher, and Equal Rights Party Candidate for President. *Woodhull & Clafin's Weekly*, Oct. 1, 1870.

154. Yes! I am a free lover! I have an inalienable, constitutional, and natural right to love whom I may, to love as long or as short a period as I can, to change that love every day if I please.

Victoria Woodhull. In response to a heckler who accused her, a divorcee, of being a free lover. Speech, Steinway Hall, New York City, Jan. 2, 1875.

Chapter 29

Espionage and Intelligence

1. We shouldn't send CIA spooks to overthrow governments.
   James G. Abourezk, U.S. Congressman and U.S. Senator (D-SD). Interview, WAMU-FM, *The Diane Rehm Show*, Nov. 20, 1989.

2. Only enemies of the Soviet Union can think of the KGB as some kind of secret police.
   Yuri Andropov (1914-1983), Director, KGB, and President of the U.S.S.R. Remark, 1967.

3. It's inconceivable that a secret intelligence arm of the government has to comply with all the overt orders of the government.
   James Angleton (1919-1987), Counterintelligence Chief, Central Intelligence Agency. Congressional testimony, 1975.

4. Are you now or have you ever been a member of a godless conspiracy controlled by a foreign power?
   Richard Arens (1913-1969), staff member, House Un-American Activities Committee. Frequent question of witnesses, early 1950's.

5. It's impossible for somebody to defect from the United States. Edward Lee Howard is not a defector. He's a traitor.
   Michael Armacost, U.S. Undersecretary of State. Comment on a Central Intelligence Agency agent's defection to the U.S.S.R. Quoted in *Newsweek*, Nov. 17, 1986.

6. Now that you have the Xerox machine, you can't keep many secrets.
   Lloyd M. Bentsen, Jr., U.S. Congressman and U.S. Senator (D-TX). PBS, *MacNeil-Lehrer Report*, Aug. 17, 1988.

7. An increasing share of the espionage directed against the United States comes from spying by foreign governments against private American companies aimed at stealing commercial secrets to gain a national economic advantage.
   David L. Boren, Governor of Oklahoma and U.S. Senator (D). Quoted in *The Washington Post*, June 26, 1990.

8. I am very much interested in seeing the United States have as fine a foreign military and naval intelligence as they can possibly have, but I am not interested in setting up here in the United States any particular agency under any President ... and just allow him to have a Gestapo of his own if he wants to have it.
   Clarence J. Brown (1893-1965), U.S. Congressman (R-OH). Congressional hearings, Apr. 25, 1947.

9. No amount of congressional supervision will render our nation's intelligence efforts effective if the people who are managing these efforts ... are ineffective.
   Frank C. Carlucci, U.S. Secretary of Defense and National Security Advisor (D). Testimony, Senate Select Committee on Intelligence, Dec. 16, 1987.

10. I am not satisfied with the quality of our political intelligence.
    Jimmy Carter, 39th President of the United States (D-GA). Handwritten note to Central Intelligence Agency Director Stansfield Turner, 1988.

11. You have to put together bits and pieces of information before you can draw overall conclusions.
    Richard B. Cheney, U.S. Congressman (R-WY), White House Chief of Staff, and U.S. Secretary of Defense. Quoted on CNN, *Evans & Novak*, Nov. 19, 1989.

12. The intelligence community is intended to base its intelligence estimates on facts and analysis – not philosophy and conviction.
    Ray Cline, U.S. Assistant Secretary of State. Quoted on PBS, *Frontline*, Oct. 24, 1988.

13. Congress has chosen to recognize that a President may be forced to pursue legitimate foreign policy objectives by covert means. Such recognition, however, does not mean it surrenders the right to be informed of covert measures so that it can express its views as to the legitimacy of the goals or the wisdom of seeking to achieve them.
    William S. Cohen, U.S. Congressman and U.S. Senator (R-ME). *The Washington Post*, Sept. 18, 1988.

14. CIA will not develop operations to penetrate another government agency, even with the approval of its leadership.
William Colby, Director, Central Intelligence Agency. Memorandum, July 1973.

15. The United States Intelligence community collects too much information.
Hugh Cunningham, Central Intelligence Agency Study Director, Board of National Estimates. Quoted in Marchetti and Marks, *The CIA and the Cult of Intelligence,* 1974.

16. If communism in Hollywood is now mythical, it is only because this committee conducted three investigations to bring it about. The industry itself did certainly not accomplish this.
Martin Dies (1901-1972), U.S. Congressman (D-TX). H. R. *Report* No. 2431, 82d Congress, 2d Session, 1951.

17. Plots, true or false, are necessary things,
To raise up commonwealths, and ruin kings.
John Dryden (1631-1700), English poet and dramatist. *Absalom and Achitophel,* I.

18. Obviously you cannot tell of operations that go along well. Those that go badly generally speak for themselves.
Allen W. Dulles (1893-1969), Director, Central Intelligence Agency. Remark, 1965.

19. I have to send people out to get killed.
Allen W. Dulles. Remark to his sister. Quoted in Leonard Mosley, *Dulles,* 1978.

20. There are few archbishops in espionage. He's on our side and that's all that matters. Besides, one needn't ask him to one's club.
Allen W. Dulles. On working with Reinhard Gehlen, a vicious and fanatical Nazi intelligence officer, at the end of World War II. *Ibid.*

21. From little involvements – little CIA wars – big wars grow.
Thomas F. Eagleton, U.S. Senator (D-MO). Senate debate, July 20, 1973.

22. There can be no greater folly than fearing that which is not.
Elizabeth I (1533-1603), Queen of England. Letter, Nov. 5, 1595.

23. There is not a syllable in the Constitution that gives the federal government the right to spy on civilians.
Samuel J. Ervin, Jr. (1896-1985), U.S. Congressman and U.S. Senator (D-NC). Oct. 18, 1966.

24. Fewer than a dozen members of Congress have any idea how much money the CIA spends each year, and probably none of them has much of an idea what the agency actually does with that money.
Paul Findley, U.S. Congressman (R-IL). House debate, May 8, 1973.

25. The Pentagon suffers from too much Intelligence. They can't use what they get because there is too much collected. It would almost be better if they didn't have it because it's difficult to find out what's important.
Gilbert W. Fitzhugh, Chairman, Metropolitan Life Insurance Company; appointed by President Nixon to head a blue ribbon panel to review the U.S. Department of Defense. Press conference, July 1970.

26. No person employed by or acting on behalf of the United States government shall engage in, or conspire to engage in, assassination.
Gerald R. Ford, 38th President of the United States (R-MI). Executive Order No. 12333, Feb. 18, 1976.

27. It was given for all purposes to which a secret service fund should or could be applied to the public benefit – for spies, if the gentleman pleases.
John Forsyth (1780-1841), Governor of Georgia (D), U.S. Congressman, U.S. Senator, and U.S. Secretary of State. Defense of the administration's use of an unvouchered Secret Service fund. Senate debate, 1831.

28. I have long observed one Rule.... It is simply this, to be concern'd in no Affairs that I should blush to have made publick, and to do nothing but what spies may see.
Benjamin Franklin (1706-1790), Member, Continental Congress and Constitutional Convention, Governor of Pennsylvania, and U.S. Minister to France. Quoted in Nathan Miller, *Spying for America,* 1989.

29. The people who classify *[government]* documents tend to be excessive.
Erwin N. Griswold, Dean, Harvard Law School, and U.S. Solicitor General. Quoted on ABC, *This Week,* Feb. 18, 1989.

30. Every kind of service necessary to the public good becomes honorable by becoming necessary.
Nathan Hale (1755-1776), Captain, Continental Army. Remark to William Hull before leaving on an intelligence mission behind English lines. Sept. 1776.

31. I am not working for the U.S. government that I know of.
Sam Hall, American pilot captured on a "reconnaissance mission" for a private organization in Nicaragua. Jan. 1987.

32. It is the nature of covert activities to be controversial.
Orrin G. Hatch, U.S. Senator (R-UT). Senate speech, Mar. 4, 1988.

33. We do not target on American citizens.
Richard Helms, Director, Central Intelligence Agency, and U.S. Ambassador to Iran (R). Statement, Apr. 14, 1971.

34. The nation must to a degree take it on faith that we *[the CIA]* too are honorable men devoted to her service.
Richard Helms. Speech, Aug. 14, 1971.

35. Why should you care? Your side won.
Richard Helms. Response when asked if the Central Intelligence Agency had influenced the 1970 Chilean election through covert activities. Lecture, The Johns Hopkins University, Baltimore, MD, 1972.

36. It is incontestable that even under the best of circumstances and when dealing with the friendliest and most stable of allies that intelligence organizations of foreign powers must not be permitted to become established on American soil and should be discouraged wherever possible from taking root any place in this hemisphere.
J. Edgar Hoover (1895-1972), Director, Federal Bureau of Investigation. Memorandum to Attorney General Francis Biddle on the possibility of France establishing an intelligence force in U.S. Dec. 1944.

37. Use of this technique is clearly illegal: it amounts to burglary. It is also highly risky and could result in great embarrassment if exposed. However, it is also the most fruitful tool and can produce the kind of intelligence which cannot be obtained in any other fashion.
Tom C. Houston, presidential assistant (R). Memorandum to H. R. Haldeman recommending that President Nixon lift restrictions on "black bag" jobs against foreign embassies and suspected domestic subversives, July 23, 1970.

38. Go ahead and investigate the bastards.
Cordell Hull (1871-1955), U.S. Congressman (D-TN), U.S. Senator, U.S. Secretary of State, and Nobel Laureate in Peace. Agreeing that the FBI should investigate American Communist and Fascist groups. 1936.

39. I had been given some training in my past CIA career to do just this sort of thing ... floating forged newspaper accounts, telegrams, that sort of thing.
E. Howard Hunt, Central Intelligence Agency agent, Watergate burglar, and spy novelist. Statement to prosecutor, when questioned about his forgery of a State Department cable linking the Kennedy administration to the 1963 assassination of Pres. Ngo Dinh Diem of South Vietnam, 1973.

40. Communicate no other intelligence to Congress at large than what may be necessary to promote the common weal, not to gratify the curiosity of individuals.
[Information had been leaked by members of the Congress when Jay was engaged in secret counterintelligence operations in upstate New York during the Revolutionary War.]
John Jay (1745-1829), President of the Continental Congress, Governor of New York (Federalist), U.S. Foreign Secretary, and 1st Chief Justice of the U.S. Supreme Court. Dispatch to Robert Morris, 1778.

41. I am dogged and watched in the most extraordinary manner.
Thomas Jefferson (1743-1826), 3rd President of the United States (Democratic Republican-VA). Apology to hostess for arriving late to a party. Quoted in John C. Miller, *The Federalist Era*, 1960.

42. No more of this coup shit.
Lyndon B. Johnson (1908-1973), 36th President of the United States (D-TX). Instructions to staff after an American-engineered coup toppled the government of President Ngo Dinh Diem of South Vietnam, and replaced it with one thought to be more reliable. 1963.

43. I thought that you guys *[the CIA]* had people everywhere, that you knew about everything, and now you don't even know anything about a raggedy-ass, little fourth-rate country. All you have to do is get some Chinese coolies from a San Francisco laundry shop and drop them over there and use them.
Lyndon B. Johnson. Remark to CIA Director John F. A. McCone about the lack of reliable intelligence on North Vietnam, 1963.

44. I consider your crime worse than murder.
Irving R. Kaufman, Federal Appeals Court Judge and Chairman, Commission on Organized Crime. Statement when sentencing Julius and Ethel Rosenberg to death for stealing atomic bomb secrets. Apr. 5, 1951.

45. The officials most responsible for covert actions are those who are the least accountable.
John Keker, Special Prosecutor at Oliver North's "Contragate" trial. Speech, Commonwealth Club of California, Dec. 2, 1989.

46. Success in covert actions is always a matter of opinion.
John Keker. *Ibid.*

47. The toughest things to estimate are intentions.
John Kelly, U.S. Assistant Secretary of State for Near Eastern and South Asian Affairs. House hearings on espionage, Sept. 18, 1990.

48. I don't think the intelligence reports *[from the CIA, NSA, and other government agencies]* are all that hot. Some days I get more out of *The New York Times*.
John F. Kennedy (1917-1963), 35th President of the United States (D-MA). Attributed.

49. Did the CIA kill my brother?
Robert F. Kennedy (1925-1968), U.S. Senator (D-NY) and U.S. Attorney General. Question of CIA Dir. John F. A. McCone. Quoted in Collier and Horowitz, *The Kennedys*, 1984.

50. I believe we get the same reports, and probably from the same people.
Nikita S. Khrushchev (1894-1971), Premier of the U.S.S.R. Remark to CIA Dir. Allen W. Dulles, 1959.

51. I don't see that we need to stand by and watch a country go Communist due to the irresponsibility of its own people.
Henry M. Kissinger, U.S. Secretary of State and National Security Advisor (R). Justification of "destabilization" of Salvador Allende's democratically elected government in Chile. 1970.

52. We coexist. They work, and we work.
Vladimir Kryuchkov, Director, KGB. In reference to the CIA. Quoted in *Time*, Apr. 23, 1990.

53. Intelligence is both critical and costly.
Melvin R. Laird, U.S. Secretary of Defense (R). Defense budget statement, 1970.

54. Intelligence work has one moral law – it is justified by results.
John Le Carré (John Moore Cornwell), British espionage novelist. *The Spy Who Came In from the Cold*, 1963.

55. We cannot afford methods less ruthless than those of our opposition.
John Le Carré. *Ibid.*

56. The vast industry of mutual surveillance that grew up alongside the industry of mutual destruction is not about to disappear. The spies, like the weapons, are here to stay. And proliferate, sooner or later, whether we like it or not.
John Le Carré. Response to suggestions that with the demise of the Berlin wall the spying business will come to a halt. Speech, Tulsa, OK, Dec. 1990.

57. Secrecy now beclouds everything about the CIA – its cost, its efficiency, its successes, and its failures.
Mike Mansfield, U.S. Congressman (D-MT), U.S. Senator, and U.S. Ambassador to Japan. Senate statement, 1953.

58. While the interests of the Intelligence community should not be taken lightly, we must remember that they exist to serve, not dictate.
Edward Markey, U.S. Senator (D-MA). *The New York Times*, June 13, 1990.

59. One way or another ... the CIA is making a lot of extra money the citizen's aren't supplying, and that money gives the agency an undesirable, possibly dangerous independence of congressional control.
John Marks, intelligence officer, U.S. State Department. *Playboy*, Aug. 1975.

60. There will always be men who from malice or for money will betray their kith and kin, and there will always be men who, from love of adventure or a sense of duty, will risk a shameful death to secure information valuable to their country.
W. Somerset Maugham (1874-1965), British writer. Preface to *Ashendon; or, The British Agent*, 1928.

61. We cannot be in a position of stimulating, approving, or supporting assassination.
John F. A. McCone (1902-1991), Director, Central Intelligence Agency. Statement regarding the possible overthrow of President Ngo Dinh Diem of South Vietnam, who was murdered during the coup. 1963.

62. Do the American people really want their President ... to have no other option than to go to war or do nothing?
Robert C. McFarlane, National Security Advisor (R). On the importance of covert operations. Quoted in Nathan Miller, *Spying for America*, 1989.

63. Spies are great, and when you need 'em, you need 'em. But they are no substitute for insight.
Herbert Meyer, agent, Central Intelligence Agency. Speech, Intelligence and Free Society Conference, National Forum Foundation, Washington, DC, May 30, 1989.

64. Accurate intelligence is not always popular intelligence.
Nathan Miller, American writer. *Spying for America*, 1989.

65. It's very difficult for those who gather intelligence to totally divorce themselves from the policies of their superiors.

George J. Mitchell, U.S. Senator (D-ME). Interview, ABC, *This Week*, Jan. 12, 1990.

66. The Fifth Column.

Emilio Mola (1887-1937), Spanish Nationalist General. Reply when asked which of four nationalist army columns would take Madrid; he referred to Communist sympathizers inside the city. Oct. 1937.

67. For twenty-five years the CIA told the President everything there was to know about the Russians except that they were about to collapse.

Daniel P. Moynihan, Chief American Delegate to the United Nations and U.S. Senator (D-NY). Interview, PBS, *MacNeil-Lehrer News Hour*, Sept. 12, 1991.

68. They *[the CIA]* have got forty thousand people out there reading newspapers.

Richard M. Nixon, 37th President of the United States (R-CA). Remark, 1969.

69. It is time in this country to quit making national heroes out of those who steal secrets and publish them in the newspapers.

Richard M. Nixon. In reference to Daniel Ellsberg's leaking of secret Pentagon papers to *The New York Times* in 1971. Speech to Vietnam veterans, Washington, DC, May 24, 1973.

70. A covert operation is, in its nature, a lie.

Oliver L. North, Lt. Col., U.S. Marine Corps, and staff member, National Security Council. Testimony, Iran-Contra congressional hearings, July 7, 1987.

71. I owe my throne to God, my people, my army, and to you.

Mohammed Reza Pahlavi (1919-1980), Shah of Iran. Remark to Amb. Kermit Roosevelt, who had organized the CIA coup that overthrew Iranian Premier Mohammed Mossadegh. 1953.

72. Three Things contribute much to ruin Government: *Looseness*, *Oppression*, and *Envy*.

William Penn (1644-1718), founder of Pennsylvania. *Some Fruits of Solitude, in Reflections and Maxims*, 1693.

73. To betray you must first belong. I never belonged.

Kim Philby (1912-1988), British journalist and Soviet spy. Remark, 1967.

74. To tell the truth about men and movements, without passion and without resentment, even though I differed from men and movements. I think that is the essential thing.... When we understand what it *[the Russian Revolution]* is, when we know the facts behind it, when we do not libel or slander it or do not lose our heads and become its advocates and defenders, and really know what the thing is, and then move forward to it, then we will serve our country and our time.

Raymond Robins (1873-1954), Director, American Red Cross in revolutionary Russia. Senate hearings, 1918.

75. We have somehow got to get the State Department to take espionage seriously.

William V. Roth, Jr., U.S. Congressman and U.S. Senator (D-DE). Reaction to Soviet bugging of the U.S. embassy in Moscow. Quoted in *Newsweek*, Apr. 13, 1987.

76. It is not a reluctance on the part of CIA officials to speak to us. Instead it is a reluctance ... to seek information and knowledge of subjects which I ... would rather not have.

Leverett Saltonstall (1892-1979), Governor of Massachusetts (R) and U.S. Senator. Quoted in Nathan Miller, *Spying for America*, 1989.

77. When a Prince trusteth a Man with a dangerous Secret, he would not be sorry to hear the Bell toll for him.

George Savile, 1st Marquess of Halifax (1633-1695), Lord Privy Seal of England. *Political Thoughts and Reflections*, 1750.

78. All intelligence agencies, protected from oversight long enough, begin to take the law into their own hands.

Arthur M. Schlesinger, Jr., American historian and presidential advisor (D). Interview, PBS, *Secret Intelligence*, Feb., 1989.

79. We have a problem ... we just have too many people.

James R. Schlesinger, U.S. Secretary of Defense, U.S. Secretary of Energy, and Director, Central Intelligence Agency. On security problems, when he headed the CIA. Testimony, Senate Armed Forces Committee, Apr. 5, 1973.

80. I regard newspaper correspondents as spies.

William Tecumseh Sherman (1820-1891), General, U.S. Army. Letter from Vicksburg, MS, Feb. 17, 1863.

81. The Committee appointed to investigate Bolshevism may be creating something for it to investigate.

Alfred E. Smith (1873-1944), Governor of New York (D). On overzealous "red scare" investigations. Jefferson Day dinner speech, Apr. 13, 1919.

82. A foreign Minister, who is concerned in great affairs, must necessarily have spies in his pay: but he must not too easily credit their informations, which are never exactly true, often very false. His best spies will always be those whom he does not pay, but whom he has engaged in his service by his dexterity and address, and who think themselves nothing but spies.

Philip Dormer Stanhope, 4th Earl of Chesterfield (1694-1773), Member of Parliament, Great Britian (Whig), and Lord-Lieutenant of Ireland. *Maxims.*

83. Spying is spying. You have to ... protect it as such, and shut your eyes some and take what is coming.

John C. Stennis, U.S. Senator (D-MS). 1971.

84. I'm ashamed of what the CIA has done at home.

John C. Stennis. 1975.

85. Gentlemen do not read other people's mail.

Henry L. Stimson (1867-1950), U.S. Secretary of State (R), U.S. Secretary of War, and Governor General, Philippine Islands. 1929.

86. The intelligence books have been juggled so that the budget books could be balanced.

Stuart Symington, U.S. Senator (D-MO) and U.S. Secretary of the Air Force. Comment accusing the Eisenhower administration of suppressing conclusions that the Soviets had a missile lead over the United States. Jan. 1960.

87. There is no federal agency of our government whose activities receive less scrutiny and control *[than the CIA]*.

Stuart Symington. Senate debate, Nov. 23, 1971.

88. It has become ... at times a policy-making arm of the government.... I never had any thought when I set up the CIA that it would be injected into peacetime cloak-and-dagger operations.

Harry S Truman (1884-1972), 33rd President of the United States (D-MO). 1963.

89. The technical systems for collecting data had overwhelmed the old spy systems.

Stansfield Turner, Admiral, U.S. Navy, and Director, Central Intelligence Agency. Quoted on PBS, *Secret Intelligence*, Feb. 13, 1989.

90. The sums made available to the agency *[CIA]* may be expended without regard to the provisions of law and regulations relating to the expenditure of government funds.

U.S. Congress, Central Intelligence Act, 1949.

91. The most necessary and essential kind of information, without which no war plan can be made that is worth the paper it is written on, does not come of its own accord or as a matter of routine. It must be actively sought, traced out, and proved out.

Ralph H. Van Deman (1865-1952), Director of U.S. Military Intelligence. Quoted in William R. Corson, *Armies of Ignorance*, 1977.

92. K mart protects its toothpaste better than the Navy protects its secrets.

J. Anthony Walker, Jr., convicted American spy for the Soviets. Interview, PBS, *Frontline: The Spy Who Broke the Code*, Jan. 24, 1989.

93. Intelligence agencies ... frustrate investigations of their own misconduct by professing exaggerated concerns for the preservation of national security.

Lawrence E. Walsh, Special Prosecutor, Iran-Contra hearings. Quoted in *The Washington Post*, Oct. 25, 1990.

94. Americans have always had an ambivalent attitude toward intelligence. When they feel threatened, they want a lot of it, and when they don't, they regard the whole thing as somewhat immoral.

Vernon A. Walters, General, U.S. Army, and U.S. Ambassador to the United Nations. *Silent Missions*, 1978.

95. Even minutae should have a place in our *[intelligence]* collection, for things of a seemingly trifling nature when enjoined with others of a more serious cast may lead to valuable conclusions.

George Washington (1732-1799), 1st President of the United States (VA). Directive to army commanders, 1777.

96. Our job is not to be part of a plan to cause the death of a political figure.

William H. Webster, Director, Central Intelligence Agency. Quoted in *The Washington Post*, Nov. 4, 1989.

97. I can tell you a lot about him, but I don't know whether any of it is true.

William H. Webster. Response when asked about Palestinian terrorist Abu Nidal. Quoted in *Newsweek*, Dec. 11, 1989.

98. Spying is forever.

Marcus F. Wolf, Director of East German Intelligence. Quoted on ABC, *Prime Time*, May 31, 1990.

99. In no other manner could the United States obtain an intimate knowledge of the true sentiments and intentions of other nations.... If we were caught, it would be just too bad.

Herbert O. Yardley (1889-1958), Director, U.S. Cryptographic Bureau. Comment on the need to intercept and decode international cables during World War I. *The American Black Chamber*, 1931.

Chapter 30

Ethics and Conflict of Interest

1. ONLY LIE ABOUT THE FUTURE.
   Desk sign, "Politician's motto."

2. MORAL VICTORIES DON'T COUNT.
   Sign on a Pentagon office door, 1988.

3. A contribution of $2,500 is not going to buy the reputation and decisions of an elected official.
   Robert Abrams, Attorney General of New York. Testimony, N.Y. State Commission on Government Integrity, Mar. 10, 1989.

4. Government of the people, by the people, for the benefit of the Senators.
   Henry Adams (1838-1918), American historian. Description of American government in the 1880's. *Democracy*, 1880.

5. In politics as in private life, *[Henry]* Clay is essentially a gamester, and, with a vigorous intellect, an ardent spirit, a handsome elocution, though with a mind very defective in elementary knowledge, and a very undigested system of ethics, he has all the qualities which belong to that class of human characters.
   John Quincy Adams (1767-1848), 6th President of the United States (Ind.-MA). *Diary*, Apr. 6, 1820.

6. He rather turns his eye from misconduct, and betrays a sensation of pain when it is presented directly to him.
   John Quincy Adams. On President Monroe's reluctance to deal with corruption. *Diary*, June 23, 1820.

7. *[Thomas Jefferson is]* a slur upon the moral government of the world.
   John Quincy Adams. Quoted in Nancy McPhee, *The Book of Insults*, 1978.

8. One's concern with the ethics of means and ends varies inversely with one's personal interest in the issue. Any effective means is automatically judged by the opposition as being unethical.
   Saul D. Alinsky (1909-1972), American community organizer. *Rules for Radicals*, 1971.

9. Law-makers should not be law-breakers.
   American proverb.

10. *[It was]* the same thing as going into a business community and interesting the leading businessmen by giving them shares.
    Oakes Ames (1804-1873), U.S. Congressman (R-MA). In reference to his practice of distributing shares of stock to other Congressmen on behalf of Crédit Moblier and Union Pacific Railroad. Quoted in Richard Hofstadter, *The American Political Tradition*, 1948.

11. A man should be upright, not be kept upright.
    Marcus Aurelius Antonius (121-180), Emperor of Rome and Stoic philosopher. *Meditations*.

12. The sad truth is that most evil is done by people who never made up their minds to be either good or evil.
    Hannah Arendt (1906-1975), American political philosopher. Quoted in *The New Yorker*, Dec. 5, 1977.

13. I suppose we should all sing "Bail to the Chief."
    Howard H. Baker, Jr., U.S. Senator and White House Chief of Staff (R-TN). Remark during the last days of Richard Nixon's presidency.

14. It has always been desirable to tell the truth, but seldom if ever necessary.
    Arthur James Balfour, 1st Earl of Balfour (1848-1930), Prime Minister of Great Britain (Conservative). Attributed.

15. I am not one of those Senators who feel it is necessary for the Senate to pass a resolution binding the membership to be honorable men. If I thought it was necessary to pass a resolution to make us honorable, I would not want to be a member of this body.
    Alben W. Barkley (1877-1956), U.S. Congressman

(D-KY), U.S. Senator, and Vice President of the United States. Response when Sen. Sheridan Downey introduced a resolution calling on Senators to accept World War II rationing restrictions and not use their position to evade the restrictions. Senate debate, 1942.

16. I didn't run to be pope. I ran to be mayor.
Marion Barry, Mayor of Washington, DC (D). Response to criticism of his flamboyant personal lifestyle. Interview, PBS, *MacNeil-Lehrer Report*, Feb. 9, 1989.

17. We are now facing a problem more of ethics than of physics.
Bernard M. Baruch (1870-1965), Chairman, War Industries Board, and U.S. Delegate to the U.N. Atomic Energy Commission. Speech, U.N. Atomic Energy Commission, June 14, 1946.

18. A very foolish lapse of judgment on my part.
Stanley G. Bedford, Chairman, NJ State Election Law Enforcement Commission (R). Comment when found guilty of making improper political contributions. Quoted in *The New York Times*, Nov. 24, 1988.

19. You're either in a conflict or you're not in a conflict.
Griffin Bell, U.S. Attorney General and member, President's Commission on Ethics (D). Argument against rules limiting the appearance of conflict of interest. Quoted in *The Washington Post*, Feb. 26, 1989.

20. It is our character that supports the promise of our future – far more than particular government programs or policies.
William J. Bennett, Director, Office of National Drug Control Policy, and U.S. Secretary of Education (R). Quoted in *The 1989 Conservative Calendar*.

21. It is the greatest good to the greatest number which is the measure of right and wrong.
Jeremy Bentham (1748-1832), British jurist and philosopher. *The Commonplace Book*.

22. I have never regarded politics as an arena of morals. It is the arena of interests.
Aneurin Bevan (1897-1960), Minister of Health, Great Britain (Socialist). 1951.

23. Anything done *[in politics]* is all right unless you get caught.
Theodore G. Bilbo (1877-1947), Governor of Mississippi and U.S. Senator (D). Quoted in Reinhard H. Luthin, *American Demagogues*, 1959.

24. It's easy to get into the gray zone *[of ethics]*.
Sherwood L. Boehlert, U.S. Congressman (R-NY). Quoted in *The New York Times*, June 4, 1989.

25. Truth has a way of shifting under pressure.
Curtis Bok (1897-1962), Federal Judge. Speech, Feb. 13, 1954.

26. Ours is a world of nuclear giants and ethical infants.
Omar N. Bradley (1893-1981), General, U.S. Army, and Permanent Chairman, Joint Chiefs of Staff. Armistice Day speech, 1948.

27. Despotism, be it financial or political, is vulnerable, unless it is believed to rest upon a moral sanction.
Louis D. Brandeis (1856-1941), U.S. Supreme Court Justice. *Other People's Money*, 1914.

28. I have not much faith in "good government." What we need is the development of the individual.
Louis D. Brandeis. Letter to Alfred Lief, Apr. 16, 1934.

29. Self-respect and prosperity are the most effective guardian of morals.
Louis D. Brandeis. Quoted in Alpheus T. Mason, *Brandeis: A Free Man's Life*, 1946.

30. A government job is an occasion for public service, not special privilege. The undivided loyalty to the public interest required of the governorship makes it inappropriate to keep the profusion of gifts that arrive every day at this office.
Edmund G. (Jerry) Brown, Jr., Governor of California (D). Note with returned gifts. *Thoughts*, 1976.

31. The great political questions are in their final analysis great moral questions.
William Jennings Bryan (1860-1925), U.S. Secretary of State (D). Quoted in Richard Hofstadter, *The American Political Tradition*, 1948.

32. In no other country is the ideal side of public life so ignored by the mass and repudiated by its leaders.
James Bryce (1838-1922), British Ambassador to the United States. *The American Commonwealth*, 1888.

33. Public virtue is the vital spirit of republics, and history proves that when this has decayed and the love of money has usurped its place, although the forms of the free government may remain for a season, the substance has departed forever.
James Buchanan (1791-1868), 15th President of the United States (D-PA). Inaugural address, Mar. 4, 1857.

34. When hope is taken away from the people, moral degeneration follows swiftly after.

Pearl S. Buck (1892-1973), Nobel Laureate in Literature (United States). Letter to *The New York Times*, Nov. 14, 1941.

35. A man's virtue is best secured by shame, and best improved by emulation in the society of virtuous men.
Edmund Burke (1729-1797), British statesman. Letter to Bishop Markham, 1771.

36. When government tries to serve as a parent or teacher or a moral guide, individuals may be tempted to discard their own sense of responsibility, to argue that only government must help people in need. If we've learned anything in the past quarter century, it is that we cannot federalize virtue.
George Bush, 41st President of the United States (R-TX). Commencement address, University of Michigan, Ann Arbor, MI, May 4, 1991.

37. You, too, Brutus! (*Et tu, Brute.*)
Julius Caesar (100-44 B.C.), Emperor of Rome. On being stabbed by Brutus, Mar. 15 (the Ides of March), 44 B.C. Quoted in Shakespeare, *Julius Caesar*, III, i.

38. If the moral and physical fiber of its manhood and its womanhood is not a state concern, the question is, what is?
Benjamin N. Cardozo (1870-1938), U.S. Supreme Court Justice. *Adler* v. *Deegan*, 1919 (NY).

39. A trustee *[of a public corporation or organization]* is held to something stricter than the morals of the marketplace. Not honesty alone, but the *punctilio* of an honor the most sensitive, is then the standard.
Benjamin N. Cardozo. *Meinhard* v. *Salmon*, 1928.

40. I'll never tell a lie. I'll never make a misleading statement.
Jimmy Carter, 39th President of the United States (D-GA). Campaign speech, 1972.

41. I have looked on a lot of women with lust. I've committed adultery in my heart many times. God recognizes I will do this and forgives me.
Jimmy Carter. Interview in *Playboy* during the 1976 campaign.

42. Since the state is a community of human beings it is as truly subject to the moral law as any private society.
Catholic Association for International Peace, *International Ethics*, 1942.

43. The courage of New England was the courage of conscience.
Rufus Choate (1779-1859), U.S. Congressman and U.S. Senator (Whig-MA). Speech, Ipswich, MA, 1834.

44. The flame of Christian ethics is still our highest guide.
Winston Churchill (1874-1965), Prime Minister of Great Britain (Conservative). Speech, Mar. 31, 1949.

45. The assumption *[implicit in the weak ethics rules of the U.S. House of Representatives]* has to be that members of Congress are, like eunuchs in a harem, physically incapable of a conflict of interest.
Richard Cohen, American columnist. *The Washington Post*, June 14, 1988.

46. They *[corporations]* cannot commit treason, nor be outlawed, nor excommunicated, for they have no souls.
Edward Coke (1552-1634), Solicitor General, Attorney General, England, and Speaker of the House of Commons. *Case of Sutton's Hospital*, 1612.

47. If the official is himself upright, the people will play their roles without orders. If he is not upright, even under orders the people will be disobedient.
Confucius (551-479 B.C.), Chinese philosopher. *Analects*.

48. Character is the only secure foundation of the state.
Calvin Coolidge (1872-1933), 30th President of the United States (R-MA). Lincoln's Birthday speech, New York City, Feb. 12, 1924.

49. It has been my philosophy all my life that good government is good politics.
Richard J. Daley (1902-1976), Mayor of Chicago, IL (D). Inaugural address, Apr. 20, 1955.

50. I give special consideration to everybody.
Alfonse D'Amato, U.S. Senator (R-NY). On his support of U.S. Department of Housing and Urban Development applications from campaign contributors. Quoted in *The Washington Post*, Apr. 22, 1990.

51. In politics nothing is contemptible.
Benjamin Disraeli, 1st Earl of Beaconsfield (1804-1881), Prime Minister of Great Britain (Conservative). *Vivian Grey*, 1824.

52. Circumstances are beyond the control of man; but his conduct is in his own power.
Benjamin Disraeli. *Contarini Fleming*, 1832.

53. A first principle of Anglo-American jurisprudence is that the ends do not justify the means.

William O. Douglas (1898-1980), U.S. Supreme Court Justice. *We the Judges*, 1956.

54. It is not morality that makes Jews bad, but the Jews make bad morality.... Morals and religion are the products of race.

Karl Eugen Dühring (1833-1921), German philosopher and economist. *Der Antisemitismus und die ethische Bewegung*, 1893.

55. I have learned that a clear conscience, or a legal opinion, does not make you ethically bulletproof.

David Durenburger, U.S. Senator (R-MN). Statement to Senate Ethics Committee, June 1988.

56. What man's mind can create, man's character can control.

Thomas A. Edison (1847-1931), American inventor. Attributed.

57. People say I've had brushes with the law *[a dozen grand jury probes]*. That's not true. I've had brushes with overzealous prosecutors.

Edwin W. Edwards, Governor of Louisiana (D). Quoted in *The New York Times*, Oct. 24, 1983.

58. And I think after the history of this first term is written and you look back, you're going to see that compared to other administrations or by any other standard you'd want to apply, that it has been an extraordinarily clean, corruption-free administration because the President insists on that.

John D. Ehrlichman, Domestic Advisor to President Nixon. PBS, *Thirty Minutes with ...*, Sept. 7, 1972.

59. Whosoever fails to take small matters seriously in the spirit of truth cannot be trusted in greater affairs.

Albert Einstein (1879-1955), Nobel Laureate in Physics (Switzerland). Undelivered speech, Apr. 1955.

60. Union is a delectable thing, and so is wealth, and so is life, but they may all cost too much, if they cost honor.

Ralph Waldo Emerson (1803-1882), American writer. In reference to the Fugitive Slave Law. *Journals*, May 1851.

61. Our citizens do not know whom to believe, and many of them have concluded that all the processes of government have become so compromised that honest government has been rendered impossible.

Samuel J. Ervin, Jr. (1896-1985), U.S. Congressman and U.S. Senator (D-NC). Remark during the Senate Watergate hearings. May 17, 1973.

62. Evil societies always try to kill their consciences.

James Farmer, National Director, Congress of Racial Equality. Funeral address for slain civil rights worker Michael Schwerner, Aug. 1964.

63. Lying *[to cover up military procurement scandals]* was a way of life. The solution to the problem is ultrasimple: tell the truth, no matter how painful.

A. Ernest Fitzgerald, U.S. Deputy Assistant Secretary of the Air Force. Letter to his supervisors, 1967.

64. Let's face it, the thing was a fund-raising appeal and with a fund-raising appeal, you always fire for effect. You always exaggerate a bit.

Daniel E. Flemming, Chairman, Maryland Republican Party. Comment on a vicious, racist, and inaccurate campaign letter. Quoted in *The New York Times*, Oct. 31, 1988.

65. Gentlemen, in light of this discussion, I must really leave the room. I can't stay any longer. It wouldn't be proper for me to remain.

Gerald R. Ford, 38th President of the United States (R-MI). Statement when Republican Senators began discussing the possibility of sending a delegation to President Nixon, advising him to resign. Quoted in Woodward and Bernstein, *The Final Days*, 1976.

66. Nature has no principles. She furnishes us with no reason to believe that human life is to be respected. Nature, in her indifference, makes no distinction between good and evil.

Anatole France (Jacques Anatole François Thibault) (1844-1924), Nobel Laureate in Literature (France). Speech, Tours, France, Aug. 1919.

67. If we're not careful, to be in public life you're going to have to be the product of a virgin birth.

Martin Franks, Executive Director, Democratic Congressional Campaign Committee. Quoted in *The Washington Post*, May 28, 1989.

68. I begin by taking. I shall find scholars afterwards to demonstrate my perfect right.

Frederick II (The Great) (1712-1786), King of Prussia. Remark to his ministers, 1756.

69. If you want to ... make money in the private sector, you should stay out of the political arena. If you want to go into the political arena, then you should stay out of doing business with the government.

Stanley M. Friedman, Democratic Party leader, Bronx, NY. Sentiments expressed after he began serving a jail sentence for conflict of interest. Quoted in *The New York Times*, July 7, 1988.

70. Men say that I am a saint losing myself in politics. The fact is that I am a politician trying my hardest to be a saint.

Mohandas K. Gandhi (1869-1948), Indian political and spiritual leader. Quoted in Louis Fischer, *The Life of Mahatma Gandhi*, 1950.

71. I am not worth it *[the high salary]* as John Garner, and any value I have attained as Vice President of the United States is not for sale.

John Nance Garner (1868-1967), U.S. Congressman (D-TX), Speaker of the House, and Vice President of the United States. Response to a radio station that offered him substantial remuneration for broadcasting. Quoted in Bascomb Timmons, *Garner of Texas*, 1948.

72. I would rather risk my Crown than do what I think personally disgraceful.... It is impossible that the nation shall not stand by me; if they will not, they shall have another King.

George III (1738-1820), King of England. Letter to Lord North, Mar. 17, 1778.

73. In this cold and ruthless city *[Washington, DC]* the center of hypocrisy is Capitol Hill.

Newton L. Gingrich, U.S. Congressman (R-GA). PBS, *Ethics in America*, Feb. 14, 1989.

74. The history of governments is one of the most immoral parts of human history.

William E. Gladstone (1809-1898), Prime Minister of Great Britain (Liberal). Quoted in Brand, *Gladstone*.

75. Important is not what is right but what wins.

Joseph Goebbels (1897-1945), Minister for Propaganda and National Enlightenment, Third German Reich. Quoted in *The Atlantic Monthly*, June 1940.

76. We are not far from the kind of moral decay that has brought on the fall of other nations and peoples.

Barry M. Goldwater, U.S. Senator (R-AZ). TV presidential ad, 1964.

77. We can be lied to only so many times. The best thing that he *[President Nixon]* can do for the country is to get the hell out of the White House and get out this afternoon.

Barry M. Goldwater. Remark, Senate Republican policy luncheon, Aug. 6, 1974.

78. No matter what you do, be honest. That sticks out in Washington.

Barry M. Goldwater. Quoted in *The New York Times*, Oct. 4, 1988.

79. If you will keep clean and work hard and stay honest, like your mayor, you can grow up like him and be respected as the first citizen of your city.

Frank Hague (1876-1956), Mayor of Jersey City, NJ (D). Advice to schoolchildren.

80. What would Jesus have done in precisely similar situations?

John P. Hale (1806-1873), U.S. Congressman, U.S. Senator (D-NH), and U.S. Minister to Spain. Quoted in Richard H. Sewell, *John P. Hale and the Politics of Abolition*, 1965.

81. We suppose mankind more honest than they are.

Alexander Hamilton (1755-1804), Member, Continental Congress and Constitutional Convention, and U.S. Secretary of the Treasury (Federalist-NY). 1783.

82. In place of a pay raise, we're going to enact legislation that will provide every senator and member of Congress at all times with an accountant and a clergyman.

Thomas R. Harkin, U.S. Congressman and U.S. Senator (D-IA). Quoted in *The Washington Post*, June 19, 1989.

83. I made a serious mistake. I should not have been in the company of any woman not my wife.

Gary Hart, U.S. Senator (D-CO). Interview, ABC, *Nightline*, May 10, 1987.

84. Abhorrence of apartheid is a moral attitude, not a policy.

Edward Heath, Prime Minister of Great Britain (Conservative). Speech at the Lord Mayor's banquet, London, Nov. 16, 1970.

85. I cannot and will not cut my conscience to fit this year's fashions.

Lillian Hellman (1905-1984), American writer. Letter to House Un-American Activities Committee refusing to testify against her associates, May 19, 1952.

86. It may well be true that, as a former Cabinet member, I had better access than some.

Carla Hills, U.S. Secretary of Housing and Urban Development (R). Comment on becoming a lobbyist after her tenure in office. House testimony, July 17, 1989.

87. Propaganda must not serve the truth, especially insofar as it might bring out something favorable to the opponent.... The victor will never be asked if he told the truth.

Adolf Hitler (1889-1945), Führer of the Third German Reich. *Mein Kampf*, 1933.

88. Men must turn square corners when they deal with the government.

Oliver Wendell Holmes, Jr. (1841-1935), U.S. Supreme Court Justice. *Rock Island Railroad* v. *United States*, 1919.

89. Our system of morals is a body of imperfect social generalizations expressed in terms of emotion.

Oliver Wendell Holmes, Jr. *Collected Legal Papers*, 1920.

90. When there is a lack of honor in government, the morals of the whole people are poisoned.

Herbert Hoover (1874-1964), 31st President of the United States (R-IA). Quoted in *The New York Times*, Aug. 9, 1964.

91. Ronald Reagan is not a typical politician because he doesn't know how to lie, cheat, and steal. He's always had an agent for that.

Bob Hope, American actor and comedian. Remark during the Iran-Contra congressional hearings, July 1987.

92. You can't adopt politics as a profession and remain honest.

Louis McHenry Howe (1871-1935), presidential assistant (D). Address, Columbia University, New York City, Jan. 17, 1933.

93. Conscience is the highest of all courts.

Victor Hugo (1802-1885), French writer and Member, Constituent Assembly and National Assembly at Bordeaux. *Les Misérables*, 1862.

94. The Decalogue and the Golden Rule have no place in a political campaign. The commander who lost the battle through the activity of his moral nature would be the derision and jest of history.

John James Ingalls (1833-1900), U.S. Senator (R-KS). Quoted in *New York World*, Sept. 5, 1890.

95. ... having myself made it a rule never to engage in a lottery or any other adventure of mere chance, I can, with less candor or effect, urge it on others, however laudable or desirable its object may be.

Thomas Jefferson (1743-1826), 3rd President of the United States (Democratic Republican-VA). Reply to Hugh Lawson White and others who asked for his support of a lottery to benefit East Tennessee College, May 6, 1810.

96. He who thinks that anything can be accomplished with money will himself likely do anything for money.

Jewish proverb.

97. Evil does not grow out of the soil, nor does mischief spring from the ground. Only man is born to do mischief, just as sparks fly upward.

Old Testament, *Job* 5:6-7.

98. One cannot but regret the deliberate absence of every transcendental moral reference in governing the so-called developed society.

Pope John Paul II. State of the World address, Jan. 1990.

99. You try to force me to do a dishonorable act, contrary to the law as I see it, and against my conscience, and rather than do your bidding I'll suffer my right arm torn from the socket.... I regard you as a damn villain, and get out of my office, or, damn you, I'll kick you out.

Andrew Johnson (1808-1875), 17th President of the United States (War Democrat-TN). To his attorney, Jeremiah S. Black, who suggested a government financial scheme that would enrich a small group of House members who were leaning toward impeachment. Quoted in Claude Bowers, *The Tragic Era*, 1929.

100. Evil acts of the past are never rectified by evil acts of the present.

Lyndon B. Johnson (1908-1973), 36th President of the United States (D-TX). Quoted in *Forbes*, Apr. 2, 1990.

101. In those days *[after Samson's death]* there was no king in Israel, but every man did what was right in his own eyes.

Old Testament, *Judges* 17:6.

102. There are things a man must not do to save a nation.

Murray Kempton. American journalist. *America Comes of Middle Age*, 1963.

103. The basis of effective government is public confidence.

John F. Kennedy (1917-1963), 35th President of the United States (D-MA). Message to Congress, Apr. 27, 1961.

104. It is not my habit to employ duplicity or artifice. But I want to make it clear that I am not Billy Budd. Billy Budd was a schmuck.

Edward I. Koch, U.S. Congressman and Mayor of New York City (D). 1983.

105. If we insist that public life be reserved for those whose personal history is pristine, we are not going to get paragons of virtue running our affairs. We will get the very rich, who will contract out the messy things in life; the very dull, who have nothing to hide and nothing to show; and the very devious, expert at covering their tracks

and ambitious enough to risk their discovery.
Charles Krauthammer, American political columnist. *Time*, Sept. 10, 1984.

106. I did not wish to bribe myself.
William Lamb, 2nd Viscount Melbourne (1779-1848), Prime Minister of Great Britain (Tory). Response when asked why he did not accept the Royal Order of the Garter, 1839.

107. If you are a model to the Empire, then constant virtue will not be wanting.
Lao-tzu (c.604-531 B.C.), Chinese philosopher and founder of Taoism. *Tao Te Ching*.

108. I cannot consent to receive pay for services I do not render.
Robert E. Lee (1807-1870), General-in-Chief, Confederate Army. Response when offered $50,000 by an insurance company for the use of his name after the war. Quoted on PBS, *The Civil War*, Sept. 23, 1990.

109. Truth is on the scaffold, wrong is on the throne.
William Lemke (1878-1943), U.S. Congressman (R and Non-partisan-ND). Objection to Pres. Franklin D. Roosevelt's administration policies. Address, Feb. 14, 1936.

110. There are no morals in politics; there is only expedience. A scoundrel may be of use to us just because he is a scoundrel.
V. I. Lenin (1870-1924), Premier of the U.S.S.R. Speech, Sept. 1915.

111. You cannot institute any equality between right and wrong.
Abraham Lincoln (1809-1865), 16th President of the United States (R-IL). Debate with Stephen Douglas, Galesburg, IL, Oct. 1, 1858.

112. If the national government falls into the hands of sufficiently unprincipled men, they can do terrible things before anyone can stop them.
Walter Lippmann (1889-1974), American political columnist. Remark during Watergate, June 21, 1973.

113. Meese was a sleaze.
Edward J. M. Little, U.S. Attorney. In reference to U.S. Attorney General Edwin M. Meese III in the Wedtech case. Address to the jury, Federal District Court, NY, July 21, 1988.

114. We know of no spectacle so ridiculous as the British public in one of its periodical fits of morality.
Thomas Babington Macaulay, 1st Baron Macaulay (1800-1859), historian and Secretary of War, Great Britain (Liberal). "Moore's Life of Byron," in *Edinburgh Review*, June 1830.

115. Politics have no relation to morals.
Niccolò Machiavelli (1469-1527), Florentine statesman and political philosopher. *The Prince*, 1513.

116. No government any more than an individual will long be respected without being truly respectable.
James Madison (1751-1836), 4th President of the United States (Democratic Republican-VA). *The Federalist*, No. 63, Mar. 1, 1788.

117. I had believed it *[organizing the Watergate break-in]* was wrong but believed that the greater good was in serving the President.
Jeb Stuart Magruder, presidential assistant (R). Quoted on ABC, *Lying, Cheating, Stealing in America*, June 1, 1989.

118. A harmful truth is better than a useful lie.
Horace Mann (1796-1859), American educator, founder and 1st President, Antioch College, Yellow Springs, OH. Attributed.

119. In friendships you expect total trust; in business you expect some dishonesty. But in politics you not only expect distortion as a way of life but accept it with pleasure.
Jackie Mason, American comedian. Quoted in *The New York Times*, Aug. 14, 1988.

120. What has a man profited if he shall gain the whole world, and lose his own soul?
New Testament, *Matthew* 16:26.

121. If you've been around for thirty years posing moral judgments on politics and society, you've got to take a stand. You can't go waving your wooden sword forever.
Eugene J. McCarthy, U.S. Congressman and U.S. Senator (D-WI). To explain why he would run for President. Feb. 1968.

122. Richard Nixon was the greatest moral leader of the last third of this century.
John McLaughlin, American TV journalist. NBC, *The McLaughlin Report*, 1974.

123. Time is a great legalizer, even in the field of morals.
H. L. Mencken (1880-1956), American journalist. *Prejudices, First Series*, 1919.

124. Conscience is the inner voice that warns us that someone may be looking.
H. L. Mencken. *Sententiae*, 1920.

125. The public weal requires that men should betray, and lie, and massacre.
Michel Eyquem de Montaigne (1533-1592), French philosopher, writer, and Mayor of Bordeaux. *Essays: Of Profit and Honesty*, 1580-1588.

126. When I became press secretary my father sent me a telegram and said, "Tell the truth if you can, and if you can't tell the truth, don't tell a lie." That became very difficult to do.
Bill Moyers, Special Assistant to Pres. Lyndon B. Johnson and White House Press Secretary. Quoted on ABC, *It's Your Business*, Apr. 8, 1990.

127. It shows the pettiness and corruption of these people *[members of Congress]*. Do they have to be bribed into cleaning up their own shop?
Ralph Nader, American consumer advocate. Statement when a 50 percent congressional pay raise bill was defeated after a huge public outcry, and congressional efforts at campaign finance reform were put on hold. Quoted in *The New York Times*, Feb. 19, 1989.

128. Deceit has a very short reign.
Napoléon I (1769-1821), military leader and Emperor of France. *Maxims*.

129. With politics, a man must have a conventional conscience.
Napoléon I. *Ibid.*

130. Our record as a righteous nation has proved so filled with error that, obviously, we must stop thanking God that we are not like other nations.
Reinhold Niebuhr (1892-1971), American Protestant theologian. Statement, 1971.

131. You must pursue this investigation even if it leads to the President. I'm innocent. You've got to believe I'm innocent. If you don't, don't take the job.
Richard M. Nixon, 37th President of the United States (R-CA). Statement to Elliot L. Richardson during the Watergate crisis, to persuade him to take the vacant post of U.S. Attorney General. Camp David, MD, Apr. 29, 1973.

132. I am not a crook.
Richard M. Nixon. Nov. 17, 1973.

133. Lying does not come easy to me.... I had to decide between lying and lives.
Oliver L. North, Lt. Col., U.S. Marine Corps and staff member, National Security Council. Testimony, Iran-Contra congressional hearings, July 7, 1987.

134. It's the end of civilization as we know it.
Robert Novak, American political columnist. On new ethics regulations prohibiting government employees from accepting drinks or meals from journalists. *Newsweek*, Nov. 9, 1987.

135. Elevation in office, and wealth and titles, and political rank and dignity have no influence at all in making men good and honest.
William Paca (1740-1799), Governor of Maryland and Delegate to Continental Congress. Quoted in *Baltimore Journal*, Feb. 20, 1787.

136. The guilt of a government is the crime of a whole country.
Thomas Paine (1737-1809), American political philosopher. *The American Crisis*, Dec. 23, 1776.

137. It is not permitted for the most equitable of men to be a judge in his own cause.
Blaise Pascal (1623-1662), French mathematician and philosopher. *Pensées*.

138. If men be good, then government cannot be bad.
William Penn (1644-1718), founder of Pennsylvania. *Some Fruits of Solitude, in Reflections and Maxims*, 1693.

139. Governments can never be well administered, but where those entrusted make *Conscience* of well discharging their Place.
William Penn. *Ibid.*

140. People in public life have a responsibility to behave in a certain way that can be respected and emulated by children and ordinary citizens.
Howard Phillips, Chairman, Conservative Caucus. Quoted in *The Washington Post Magazine*, Apr. 29, 1990.

141. Ethics is not as great a problem with Congress as is courage. Your ethics rules have emasculated you.... This nation was built by men who couldn't and wouldn't have lived by your rules.
Otis Pike, U.S. Congressman (D-NY). Quoted in *The Washington Post*, May 28, 1989.

142. Lying is an occupation
Used by all who mean to rise;
Politicians owe their station
But to well-concerted lies.
Laetitia Pilkington (1712-c.1751), British poet and playwright. *Song*, 1748.

143. George Washington Plunkitt: He seen his opportunities, and he took 'em.
George Washington Plunkitt (1842-1924), Tammany Hall leader, New York City (D). Self-written epitaph.

144. The papers and some people are always ready to find wrong motives in what us statesmen do. If we bring about some big improvement that benefits the city and it just happens, as a sort of coincidence, that we make a few dollars out of the improvement, they say we are grafters. But we are used to this kind of ingratitude. It falls to the lot of all statesmen.

George Washington Plunkitt. Quoted in M. R. Werner, *Tammany Hall*, 1928.

145. I cannot express the contempt I feel for Mr. *[John C.]* Calhoun for such profligate political inconsistency. If I had retained him in my Cabinet and consented to yield myself up to his control, I might have secured his support, but not by the support of principle.

James K. Polk (1795-1849), 11th President of the United States (D-TN). *Diary*, Apr. 12, 1847.

146. What we need and what we want is to moralize politics, and not to politicize morals.

Karl Popper, British political philosopher. *The Open Society and Its Enemies*, 1945.

147. As long as one hundred plus members of Congress do it ... then I'll do it.

Adam Clayton Powell (1908-1972), U.S. Congressman (D-NY). Response when asked if he saw anything wrong with putting relatives on his congressional payroll. Testimony, House Ethics Committee hearings, 1966.

148. I lied, and worse than that, I don't have any regrets about it.

Jody Powell, White House Press Secretary (D). PBS, *Presidency, the Press and the People*, Apr. 2, 1990.

149. There's nothing illegal about it. It's just wrong.

William Proxmire, U.S. Senator (D-WI). In reference to charge that he was one of five Senators who took large campaign contributions from a bank and then intervened in the regulatory process involving that bank in the savings and loan scandals. Quoted in *The Chicago Tribune*, Dec. 18, 1989.

150. If you can't trust the federal government, who can you trust?

James Quillen, U.S. Congressman (R-TN). Quoted in *The Washington Post*, June 13, 1989.

151. A man must sometimes rise above principle.

Percy Edwards Quin (1872-1932), U.S. Congressman (D-MS). 1921.

152. There are no degrees in honorableness. You either are or you aren't.

Samuel T. Rayburn (1882-1961), U.S. Congressman and Speaker of the House (D-TX). Quoted in *Life*, Dec. 1, 1961.

153. We do many things at the federal level that would be considered dishonest and illegal if done in the private sector.

Donald T. Regan, U.S. Secretary of the Treasury and White House Chief of Staff (R). Quoted in *The New York Times*, Aug. 25, 1986.

154. That was not soliciting. It was looking for help.

Edward V. Regan, Comptroller of New York (R). Statement when accused of soliciting campaign contributions from the financial institutions to which his office gave the state's bond and pension business. Quoted in *The New York Times*, Oct. 2, 1988.

155. Conscience is the voice of values long and deeply infused into one's sinew and blood.

Elliot L. Richardson, U.S. Attorney General (R), U.S. Secretary of Health, Education and Welfare, and U.S. Secretary of Defense. Response when told by President Nixon to fire Watergate Special Prosecutor Archibald Cox; he resigned instead. 1973.

156. No man is justified in doing evil on the ground of expedience.

Theodore Roosevelt (1858-1919), 26th President of the United States (R-NY). Speech, Chicago, IL, 1899.

157. We draw the line against misconduct, not against wealth.

Theodore Roosevelt. Congressional address, Dec. 2, 1902.

158. I've been on the Ethics Committee for six years now. There are a few bad apples around here, but in the main, people are pretty ethical. This is a far different Congress than it was even thirty years ago. That may not be the public perception, but it's a fact.

Warren B. Rudman, U.S. Senator (R-NH). Interview, *Time*, Sept. 3, 1990.

159. This war has been marked by so many lies, let's not end the war on a lie.

Donald Rumsfeld, U.S. Secretary of Defense (R). Response upon hearing that not all American troops had been pulled out of Vietnam, as had been announced. Remark to White House Press Secretary Ron Nessen, 1972.

160. Nothing can be politically right that is morally wrong; and no necessity can ever sanctify a law that is contrary to equity.

Benjamin Rush (1745-1813), American physician and member, Continental Congress. Statement to students at the Philadelphia Academy (later the University of Pennsylvania), 1786.

161. If you begin by saying "Thou shalt not lie," there is no longer any possibility of political action.

Jean-Paul Sartre (1905-1980), French philosopher. Quoted on his death, *Time*, Apr. 28, 1980.

162. It is a gross mistake to think, That a *Knave* between Man and Man, can be honest to a *King*, whom, of all others, Men generally make the least Scruple to deceive.

George Savile, 1st Marquess of Halifax (1633-1695), Lord Privy Seal of England. *Maxims of State*, No. 14.

163. Too much loose money and too little concern in Washington about ethics in government.

Whitney North Seymour, Special Prosecutor appointed to investigate former White House Chief of Staff Michael Deaver. Comment on why scandal seems to surface regularly in Washington. Quoted on ABC, *This Week*, July 31, 1988.

164. A dishonest politician will invariably accuse all politicians of being dishonest.

Fulton J. Sheen (1895-1979), American Roman Catholic archbishop and television personality. *Love One Another*, 1944.

165. The Senate has been debased to the level of a forum of hate and character assassination sheltered by the shield of congressional immunity.

Margaret Chase Smith, U.S. Congresswoman and U.S. Senator (R-ME). In reference to Sen. Joseph R. McCarthy. Quoted in *The New York Times*, June 2, 1950.

166. Greatness is not manifested by unlimited pragmatism, which places such a high premium on the end justifying any means and any methods.

Margaret Chase Smith. Speech, National Republican Women's Conference, Apr. 16, 1961.

167. It is safest to be moderately base – to be flexible in shame, and to be always ready for what is generous, good, and just, when anything is to be gained by virtue.

Sydney Smith (1771-1845), British clergyman and essayist. Letter to the Electors on the Catholic Question, 1826.

168. No man, I fear, can effect great benefits for his country without some sacrifice of the minor virtues.

Sydney Smith. Quoted in Burton Stevenson, *The Home Book of Quotations*, 1967.

169. Any society that fails to distinguish between those who build it up and those who tear it down has the moral equivalent of AIDS.

Thomas Sowell, Fellow, Hoover Institution, Stanford University, Palo Alto, CA. Scripps-Howard News Service, May 27, 1986.

170. Both simulation and dissimulation are absolutely necessary for a foreign Minister; and yet they must stop short of falsehood and perfidy: that middle point is the difficult one; there ability consists. He must often seem pleased, when he is vexed; and grave when he is pleased; but he must never say either; that would be falsehood, an indelible stain to character.

Philip Dormer Stanhope, 4th Earl of Chesterfield (1694-1773), Member of Parliament, Great Britain (Whig), diplomat, and Lord-Lieutenant of Ireland. *Maxims*.

171. Cannot an honest man do dishonest things and remain honest?

Joseph Lincoln Steffens (1866-1936), American journalist and reformer. Regarding campaign practices. *Autobiography*, 1931.

172. It is often easier to fight for principles than to live up to them.

Adlai E. Stevenson (1900-1965), Governor of Illinois (D) and U.S. Ambassador to the United Nations. Campaign speech, New York City, Aug. 27, 1952.

173. You *[journalists]* are all mixed up about what you have a right to do under the first amendment and what is the right thing to do.

Potter Stewart (1915-1985), U.S. Supreme Court Justice. Quoted on PBS, *The Other Side of the News*, Apr. 12, 1989.

174. This is not a good society and it is not led by honest men.

I. F. Stone (1908-1989), American investigative journalist. Comment after visiting the Soviet Union, 1956.

175. In politics ... it is a ... maxim that some men should be ruined for the good of others.

Jonathan Swift (1667-1745), Irish clergyman and satirist. *Essay on English Bubbles*.

176. I never wonder to see men so wicked, but I often wonder to see them not ashamed.

Jonathan Swift. *Thoughts on Various Subjects*, 1706.

177. It's an inherent government right, if necessary, to lie to save itself.

Arthur Sylvester, U.S. Assistant Secretary of Defense for Public Information. Press statement, Dec. 6, 1962.

178. The standard I have for myself and my office is whether or not I want to see it on the front page of the newspaper in my hometown.

Michael L. Synar, U.S. Congressman (D-OK). C-SPAN, *Close-Up*, Feb. 24, 1990.

179. Many *[Japanese]* businessmen do this kind of thing for Liberal Democratic Party and even opposition party politicians.

Seiichi Tagawa, Member of Parliament, Japan (Liberal Democratic). In reference to the practice of businessmen giving company stock to politicians. Quoted in *The New York Times*, July 7, 1988.

180. Sure I stole, but I stole it for you.

Eugene Talmadge (1884-1946), Governor of Georgia (D). Remark after illegally spending $10,000 of state funds to demonstrate the quality of Georgia peanut-fed hogs. Campaign speech, 1930.

181. You don't tell deliberate lies, but sometimes you have to be evasive.

Margaret Thatcher, Prime Minister of Great Britain (Conservative). Remark, 1976.

182. Abstain from all appearance of evil.

New Testament, *1 Thessalonians* 5:22.

183. One has to be hypersensitive to appearances of impropriety as well as impropriety itself. And believe me, after over twenty years in public life, I think I have learned to be hypersensitive.

Richard Thornburgh, U.S. Attorney General and Governor of Pennsylvania (R). Quoted in *The New York Times*, Aug. 6, 1988.

184. As guardian of his Majesty's conscience ...

Edward Thurlow, 1st Baron Thurlow (1731-1806), Lord Chancellor of England. Speech in the House of Lords explaining the Courts of Equity, 1779.

185. In order to obtain and hold power a man must love it. Thus the effort to get it is not likely to be coupled with goodness, but with the opposite qualities of pride, craft, and cruelty.

Leo Tolstoy (1828-1910), Russian writer and philosopher. *The Kingdom of God Is Within You*, 1893.

186. I suppose there is a certain amount of amorality that almost all politicians will tolerate, but there is also a threshold.

John G. Tower (1925-1991), U.S. Senator (R-TX). Quoted in Woodward and Bernstein, *The Final Days*, 1976.

187. A person who is fundamentally honest doesn't need a code of ethics. The Ten Commandments and the Sermon on the Mount are all the ethical codes anybody needs.

Harry S Truman (1884-1972), 33rd President of the United States (D-MO). Remark to reporters, July 10, 1958.

188. Scrupulous people are not suited to great affairs.

Anne Robert Jacques Turgot (1727-1781), Minister of Finance, France. Attributed.

189. A jay hasn't got any more principle than a Congressman. A jay will lie, a jay will steal, a jay will deceive, a jay will betray; and four times out of five, a jay will go back on his solemnest promise.

Mark Twain (Samuel Langhorne Clemens) (1835-1910), American writer. *A Tramp Abroad*, 1880.

190. Always do right. This will gratify some people and astonish the rest.

Mark Twain. Quotation kept on the desk of Pres. Harry S Truman.

191. *[Jimmy]* Carter was the first politician in memory to come complete with halo.

Morris K. Udall, U.S. Congressman (D-AZ). 1981.

192. A cadet will not lie, cheat, or steal, or tolerate those who do.

U.S. Military Academy at West Point, Honor Code.

193. The nation, being in effect a licensed predatory concern, is not bound by the decencies of that code of laws and morals that governs private conduct.

Thorstein Veblen (1857-1929), American political economist. *Absentee Ownership*, 1923.

194. Everybody uses everybody.

Lech Walesa, President of Poland, trade unionist, and founder, Solidarity. Quoted in *The Washington Post*, Nov. 13, 1989.

195. Every man has his price.

Robert Walpole, 1st Earl of Oxford (1676-1745), Prime Minister of Great Britain (Whig). Speech, Nov. or Dec. 1734.

196. A man should never be in a hurry for a political job; when he starts pushing, he thinks and does things he would never do under normal circumstances.

Earl Warren (1891-1974), Chief Justice, U.S. Supreme Court, and Governor of California (R). Quoted in Earl Katcher, *Earl Warren: A Political Biography*, 1967.

197. Let us raise a standard to which the wise and honest can repair; the rest is in the hands of God.
George Washington (1732-1799), 1st President of the United States (VA). Speech to the Constitutional Convention, Philadelphia, PA, 1787.

198. I hope I shall always possess firmness and virtue enough to maintain what I consider the most enviable of all titles, the character of an "Honest Man."
George Washington. *Moral Maxims*.

199. They think they can tell right from wrong with the precision of an algebraic equation. It cannot be done.
Daniel Webster (1782-1852), U.S. Congressman (Federalist-NH and MA), U.S. Senator (Federalist and Whig-MA), and U.S. Secretary of State. Senate debate on the Compromise of 1850.

200. Until this moment I think I never really gauged your cruelty or your recklessness.... Little did I dream you could be so reckless and so cruel as to do injury to that lad.... If it were in my power to forgive you for your reckless cruelty, I would do so. I like to think that I am a gentleman, but your forgiveness will have to come from someone other than me.... Have you no sense of decency, sir, at long last? Have you no sense of decency?
Joseph N. Welch (1890-1960), counsel, U.S. Army. Remark when Sen. Joseph McCarthy made a series of personal attacks on a young associate of Welch's law firm. Army-McCarthy hearings, 1954.

201. Members of Congress simply cannot fully meet their public responsibility when they are indebted to private interest groups who are paying them large honoraria fees, ostensibly for giving speeches.... Honoraria fees are undermining the integrity of Congress and should be banned outright.
Fred Wertheimer, President, Common Cause. Quoted in *The New York Times*, Aug. 4, 1988.

202. You can't make people good by Act of Parliament.
Oscar Wilde (1854-1900), Irish writer. In conversation.

203. The practice of honoraria has become evil.
Malcolm Wilkey, Chairman, President's Commission on Ethics. Quoted in *The Washington Post*, Feb. 26, 1989.

204. If people behaved in the way nations do, they would all be put in straitjackets.
Tennessee Williams (1911-1983), American playwright. Interview, BBC, 1980.

205. The moral losses of expediency always far outweigh the temporary gains.
Wendell L. Willkie (1892-1944), Republican candidate for President (IN). *One World*, 1943.

206. I thought what was good for the country was good for General Motors, and vice versa.
Charles E. Wilson (1890-1961), U.S. Secretary of Defense (R) and CEO, General Motors Corporation. Explanation of why he did not want to sell his General Motors stock when he became Secretary of Defense. 1953.

207. They *[the diplomatic corps]* have had the material interests of individuals in the United States very much more in mind than the moral and public considerations which it seems to us they ought to control.
Woodrow Wilson (1856-1924), 28th President of the United States (D-NJ). Letter to Charles W. Eliot, Sept. 17, 1913.

208. Once lead this people into war, and they'll forget there ever was such a thing as tolerance. To fight you must be brutal and ruthless, and the spirit of ruthless brutality will enter into the very fiber of our national life, infecting Congress, the courts, the policeman on the beat, the man in the street.
Woodrow Wilson. Remark to Frank Cobb of the *New York World*. Apr. 1, 1917.

209. Make values the center of political life – not money.
Harriett Woods, Lieutenant Governor of Missouri (D). Speech, Coalition for Democratic Values, Jan. 1991.

210. I spent thirty-five years being a Congressman and that's all I ever wanted to do.... If the members really ought to have a standard that's a higher standard than the rest of the members, maybe that's fair game.
James C. Wright, Jr., U.S. Congressman and Speaker of the House (D-TX). Statement to House Ethics Committee investigating of his finances. Quoted in *The Washington Post*, Mar. 15, 1989.

Chapter 31

Expansionism and Imperialism

1. The winds and seas are Britain's wide domain,
And not a sail, but by permission, spreads.

Motto of British Naval Register.

2. Fifty-four Forty or Fight!

Political slogan of Polk supporters, In reference to western land that had been held by Russia, England, and Spain up to the 54°40' parallel. 1844.

3. Seward's Folly
Seward's Icebox

Nicknames for the purchase of Alaska from Russia by U.S. Secretary of State William Seward in 1867.

4. The 1947 assumption of responsibility in the Eastern Mediterranean, the 1948 grandeur of the Marshall Plan, the response to the blockade of Berlin, the NATO defense of Europe in 1949, and the intervention in Korea in 1950 – all those constituted expanded action in truly heroic mold. All of them required rare capacity to decide and act.

Dean Acheson (1893-1971), U.S. Secretary of State (D). Comment about Harry S Truman. *Present at the Creation*, 1969.

5. Count Romanzoff *[of Russia]* had appointed me to call upon him this morning at eleven o'clock, which I accordingly did. I found an officer with him, who immediately retired. The Count told me that the officer had been at their settlement on the northwest coast of America *[the Kodiak Islands]*, and gave him an indifferent account of it. He was afraid they would never be able to make much of it.

John Adams (1735-1826), 2nd President of the United States (Federalist-MA). *Diary*, Jan. 3, 1811.

6. *[England wanted to keep Oregon]* ... for the benefit of the wild beasts as well as the savage nations.... *[The United States claim to 54° 40' was]* to make the wilderness blossom as the rose, to establish laws, to increase, multiply, and subdue the earth *[see Genesis 1:28]*.

John Quincy Adams (1767-1848), 6th President of the United States (Ind-MA). Speech to Congress, Feb. 9, 1846.

7. It would certainly be for the good of mankind to have all the mighty empires and monarchies of the world cantoned out into petty states and principalities.

Joseph Addison (1672-1719), Secretary of State, Great Britain (Whig). *On Italy*.

8. Everybody is getting a little bigger nowadays.

Alexander I (1777-1825), Czar of Russia. Remark after Adams explained why the United States had virtually annexed portions of Spanish West Florida in contravention of then international standards of conduct. Statement to John Quincy Adams, 1810.

9. The end and perfection of our victories is to avoid the vices and infirmities of those whom we subdue.

Alexander III (The Great) (356-323 B.C.), King of Macedonia. Quoted by Plutarch, *The Parallel Lives: Alexander*.

10. ... nor do I believe we have a right to use military force to compel the reception of our relief agencies.

Newton D. Baker, U.S. Secretary of War. Objection to seven thousand American troops remaining in Russian Siberia after World War I ostensibly to protect our relief efforts there. Memorandum to President Wilson, Nov. 1918.

11. We have loosened the formal bonds of unity with the great dominions. The destinies of their peoples are guided by their own governments. No rigid framework cramps our conversations with one another or with the world outside the family circle. When we meet together in equal freedom we are united by common allegiance to the Crown. In that model unity lies our strength.

Stanley Baldwin, 1st Earl Baldwin of Bewdley (1867-1947), Prime Minister of Great Britain (Conservative). Explanation of British Commonwealth. Speech, Hyde Park, London, Empire Day (Queen Victoria's birthday), May 24, 1929.

12. His Majesty's Government view with favour the establishment in Palestine of a national home for the Jewish people, and will use their best endeavours to facilitate the achievement of this object, it being clearly understood that nothing shall be done which may prejudice the civil and religious rights of existing non-Jewish communities in Palestine, or the rights and political status enjoyed by the Jews in any other country.

Arthur James Balfour, 1st Earl of Balfour (1848-1930), Prime Minister of Great Britain (Conservative). Memorandum to Baron Edmund de Rothschild, Nov. 2, 1917 (the Balfour Declaration).

13. At first we had the land and the white man had the Bible. Now we have the Bible and the white man has the land.

Bantu saying.

14. Sirs, our natural boundary is the Pacific Ocean. The swelling tide of our population must and will roll on until that mighty ocean interposes its waters, and limits our territorial empire.

Francis Baylies (1784-1852), U.S. Congressman and *Chargé d'Affaires* to Argentina (Federalist-MA). Speech in Congress, Jan. 24, 1823.

15. We don't use the word annexation. You annex foreign land, not your own country.

Menachem Begin (1913-1992), Prime Minister of Israel (Likud) and Nobel Laureate in Peace. Remark to reporters, 1977.

16. It is our manifest destiny to lead and rule all nations.

James Gordon Bennett (1841-1918), American journalist and editor. Editorial, *New York Herald*, Apr. 3, 1865.

17. The white race were a land-loving people, and had a right to possess it because they used it according to the intentions of the CREATOR.

Thomas Hart Benton (1782-1858), U.S. Senator and U.S. Congressman (D-MO). Senate speech, Jan. 12, 1843.

18. The times call for candor. The Philippines are ours forever – "country belonging to the United States" – as the Constitution calls them, and just beyond the Philippines are China's illimitable markets. We will not retreat from either. We will not repudiate our duty in the archipelago. We will not renounce our part in the mission of our race, trustee under God, of the civilization of the world. And we will move forward to our work, not howling out our regrets, like slaves whipped to their burdens, but with gratitude for a task worthy of our strength and thanksgiving to Almighty God that He has marked us as His chosen people to lead in the regeneration of the world.

Albert J. Beveridge (1862-1927), U.S. Senator (R-IN) and founder, Progressive League. Senate speech, Jan. 9, 1900.

19. The power that rules the Pacific ... is the power that rules the world. And, with the Philippines, that power is and will forever be the American Republic.

Albert J. Beveridge. Campaign speech, 1900.

20. The interests, commercial and political, of the U.S., on this continent, transcend in extent and importance those of any other power.

James G. Blaine (1830-1893), U.S. Congressman and U.S. Senator (R-ME). Sept. 5, 1881.

21. A people that patiently lets itself be trampled deserves to be trampled and crushed.

Ludwig Boerne (1786-1837), German journalist. *Letters from Paris*, Feb. 11, 1831.

22. United, France and Germany can accomplish and prevent anything. On their union depends, therefore, not only their own welfare but also the destiny of all of Europe.

Ludwig Boerne. *Introduction à la Balance*, 1836.

23. Destiny beckons us to hold and civilize Mexico.

James Buchanan (1791-1868), 15th President of the United States (D-PA). 1848.

24. Our democracy has been marred by imperialism.

Pearl S. Buck (1892-1973), Nobel Laureate in Literature (United States). Speech, "Freedom for All," New York City, Mar. 14, 1942.

25. One conquered nation is one too many.

George Bush, 41st President of the United States (R-TX). Pentagon speech, Aug. 15, 1990.

26. The world must not reward aggression.

George Bush. "Why We Are in the Gulf," *Newsweek*, Nov. 26, 1990.

27. I spent thirty-three years ... most of my time being a high class muscle man for Big Business, for Wall Street and the bankers. In short I was a racketeer for capitalism.

Smedley Butler (1881-1940), Major General, U.S.

Marine Corps. Quoted in *The New York Times*, Aug. 21, 1931.

28. For Carolina once ruined and destroyed, the extermination of her *[England's]* colonial dependencies will follow.
José del Campillo y Cosio (1693-1743), Minister to King Philip V of Spain. Letter to the king, 1742.

29. If there was in the history of humanity an enemy who was truly universal, an enemy whose acts and moves trouble the entire world, threaten the entire world ... that real and universal enemy is precisely Yankee imperialism.
Fidel Castro, Premier of Cuba. Speech, International Cultural Congress, Havana, Jan. 12, 1968.

30. The day of the small nations has passed away; the day of Empires has come.
Joseph Chamberlain (1836-1914), Colonial Secretary, Great Britain (Liberal). Speech, Birmingham, England, May 13, 1904.

31. I have not become the King's First Minister in order to preside over the liquidation of the British Empire.
Winston Churchill (1874-1965), Prime Minister of Great Britain (Conservative). Speech, House of Commons, Nov. 10, 1942.

32. I certainly am not willing to involve the country in a foreign war for the object of acquiring Texas.
Henry Clay (1777-1852), U.S. Senator (National Republican and Whig-KY), Speaker of the House, and U.S. Secretary of State. 1843.

33. Hawaii is ours. As I look back upon the first steps in this miserable business and as I contemplate the outrage, I am ashamed of the whole affair.
Grover Cleveland (1837-1908), 22nd and 24th President of the United States (D-NY). Letter to Richard Olney after the United States annexed Hawaii, July 7, 1898.

34. They would make fine servants.... With fifty men we could subjugate them all and make them do whatever we want.
Christopher Columbus (1451-1506), Italian explorer. In reference to the Arawak natives he found when he landed in the "new world." Ship's log, 1492.

35. We are not making war on Nicaragua any more than a policeman on the street is making war on passers-by.
Calvin Coolidge (1872-1933), 29th President of the United States (R-VT). In reference to U.S. Marines who were periodically sent to Nicaragua to prevent the fiscal protectorate from revolution. 1926.

36. This uneasy desire to augment our territory has depraved the moral sense and blighted the otherwise keen sagacity of our people.
Thomas Corwin (1794-1865), Governor of Ohio (Whig), U.S. Congressman, U.S. Senator, U.S. Secretary of the Treasury, and U.S. Minister to Mexico. Senate speech during the Mexican War, Feb. 11, 1847.

37. Once Catholics and Protestants *[in Northern Ireland]* get used to our presence they will hate us more than they hate each other.
Richard Crossman (1907-1974), Member of Parliament, Great Britain (Socialist). *Diary*, Aug. 17, 1969.

38. Empire can only be achieved with satisfaction, or maintained with advantage, provided it has a moral basis.
George Nathaniel Curzon, 1st Baron and 1st Marquis Curzon of Kedleston (1859-1925), Secretary of State for Foreign Affairs and leader of House of Lords, Great Britain (Conservative). Speech, Birmingham, England, Dec. 11, 1907.

39. *[Cyrus the Great, King of Persia]* constantly sought after order and equity among the dark-headed people whom *[the god Marduk]* made him conquer.
The Cyrus Cylinder, 529 B.C.

40. That our title to the whole of the Territory of Oregon is clear and unquestionable; that no portion of the same ought to be ceded to England or any other power, and that the reoccupation of Oregon and the reannexation of Texas at the earliest and practicable period are great American measures, which this convention recommends to the cordial support of the Democracy of the Union.
Democratic Party Platform. Adoped in Baltimore, MD, May 29, 1844.

41. We hold that the Constitution follows the flag, and denounce the doctrine that an Executive or Congress deriving their existence and their powers from the Constitution can exercise lawful authority beyond it, or in violation of it. We assert that no nation can long endure half Republic and half empire, and we warn the American people that imperialism abroad will lead quickly and inevitably to despotism at home.
Democratic Party Platform. Adopted in Kansas City, MO, July 5, 1900.

42. Mexico seems a doomed victim to Anglo-Saxon cupidity and love of dominion.
Frederick Douglass (c.1817-1895), Recorder of Deeds, District of Columbia, and U.S. Minister to Haiti. Comment on the Mexican War. *Rochester North Star*, Jan. 21, 1848.

43. All empire is no more than power in trust.
John Dryden (1631-1700), English poet and dramatist. *Absalom and Achitophel*, I, 1681.

44. Whatever America hopes to bring to pass in this world must first come to pass in the heart of America.
Dwight D. Eisenhower (1890-1969), 34th President of the United States (R-KS). First inaugural address, Jan. 20, 1953.

45. We Americans know and we observe the differences between world leadership and imperialism.
Dwight D. Eisenhower. *Ibid.*

46. Civilized men arrived in the Pacific, armed with alcohol, syphilis, trousers, and the Bible.
Havelock Ellis (1859-1939), British writer. *The Dance of Life*, 1923.

47. Alaska ... is an inhospitable, wretched, God-forsaken region, worth nothing, but a positive injury and incumberance as a colony of the United States.... Of what possible commercial importance can this territory be to us?
Orange Ferriss (1814-1894), U.S. Congressman and Auditor of the U.S. Treasury (R-NY). Congressional debate on the acquisition of Alaska, 1868.

48. I don't believe that the Poles consider themselves dominated by the Soviet Union.
Gerald R. Ford, 38th President of the United States (R-MI). Televised debate with presidential candidate Jimmy Carter, Oct. 6, 1976.

49. The Castro regime is a thorn in the flesh, but it is not a dagger in the heart.... I have no evidence that the Cuban people are able and willing at this time to assist any invasion from the outside.
J. William Fulbright, U.S. Senator (D-AR). Statement at State Department meeting with President Kennedy and top advisors to discuss the Central Intelligence Agency's proposal to invade Cuba at the Bay of Pigs; the Senator was the sole dissenter. Apr. 4, 1962.

50. If America is to become an empire, there is very little chance that it can avoid becoming a virtual dictatorship as well.
J. William Fulbright. *Congressional Record*, June 19, 1969.

51. Knavery seems to be so much the striking feature of its *[America's]* inhabitants that it may not in the end be an evil that they become aliens to this Kingdom.
George III (1738-1820), King of Great Britain. 1782.

52. We must march from ocean to ocean. We must march from Texas straight to the Pacific Ocean, and be bounded only by its roaring wave.. It is the destiny of the white race, it is the destiny of the Anglo-Saxon race.
William F. Giles (1807-1879), U.S. Congressman (D-MD). House debate on Mexico, Feb. 11, 1847.

53. We don't have much to say about your Arab-Arab border differences such as you have with Kuwait. All we hope is that you solve this quickly.
April Glaspie, U.S. Ambassador to Iraq. Statement to Saddam Hussein just prior to the Iraqi invasion of Kuwait. July 1990.

54. You have introduced Western education, with freedom of speech and freedom of writing.... Side by side with these there have been great evils. One such evil is a steady dwarfing of the race in consequence of its exclusion from power.
Gopan Krishna Gokhale (1866-1915), Member, Indian Legislative Council and Nationalist leader. Speech, New Reform Club, London, England, 1905.

55. ... one of the most unjust wars ever waged by a stronger nation against a weaker nation. It was an instance of a republic following the bad example of European monarchies in not considering justice in their desire to acquire additional territory.
Ulysses S. Grant (1822-1885), 18th President of the United States (R-OH). In reference to the Mexican War. *Personal Memoirs*, 1885.

56. Who believes that a score of victories over Mexico, the annexation of half her provinces, will give us more Liberty, a purer Morality?
Horace Greeley (1811-1872), U.S. Congressman (Whig-NY) and newspaper editor. Editorial, *New York Tribune*, 1846.

57. Proceed northward by interior channels, devastating, laying waste, sacking and burning whatever settlements, plantations, and towns there may be ... and taking possession of the entire country, for ... these parts hold no hostile troops able to resist those under your command.
Juan Francisco Güemes de Horcasitas (1682-1768), Spanish Governor of Cuba. Orders to Don Manuel de Monteano, Governor of Florida, in his expedition against the Carolinas. June 1742.

58. The politician, who measures the interests of his country by her preponderance in the scale of empire, regards all consideration of individual happiness as a weakness.
Elizabeth Hamilton (1761?-1815), Irish writer. *The Cottagers of Glenburnie*.

59. We stole it fair and square.
S. I. Hayakawa (1906-1992), U.S. Senator (R-CA). Comment on why the U.S. should keep control of the Panama Canal. Campaign speech, 1973.

60. The economic cost of empire is higher than the economic gain.
Denis Healey, Minister of Defense and Chancellor of the Exchequer, Great Britain (Labour). *The Time of My Life*, 1990.

61. The expression "World Power" has been made an occasion for ridicule and sneers, but it has a real meaning and a real significance. It means an influence throughout the world, and so long as that influence is wielded for the betterment of mankind, for the uplifting of our unfortunate fellow creatures, for the maintenance of peace, for the promotion of morality and civilization, we may be proud to have taken part in the change of our national policy which made us a world power.
Charles Evans Hughes (1862-1948), Chief Justice, U.S. Supreme Court, and U.S. Secretary of State (R). Speech, Tippecanoe Club, Cleveland, OH, Jan. 29, 1908.

62. We Arabs, especially the educated among us, look with the deepest sympathy on the Zionist movement.... We are working together for a reformed and revived Near East, and our two movements complete one another. The Jewish movement is national and not imperialist, and there is room in Syria for us both. Indeed I think that neither can be a real success without the other.
Feisal ibn Husein (1885-1933), Emir of Iraq. Letter to Felix Frankfurter, Mar. 3, 1919.

63. An Arab country does not have the right to occupy another Arab country. God forbid, if Iraq should deviate from the right path, we would want the Arabs to send their armies to put things right. If Iraq should become intoxicated by its power and move to overwhelm another Arab state, the Arabs would be right to deploy their armies to check it.
Saddam Hussein, President of Iraq. Speech to Arab lawyers, Nov. 28, 1988.

64. Size is not grandeur, and territory does not make a nation.
Thomas H. Huxley (1825-1895), British biologist and President of the Royal Society. *On University Education*, 1876.

65. Let it be signified to me through any channel ... that the possession of Florida is desirable to the United States, and in sixty days it will be accomplished.
Andrew Jackson (1767-1845), 7th President of the United States (D-TN). Secret letter to President Monroe, Jan. 6, 1818.

66. The waves of population and civilization are rolling to the westward, and we now propose to acquire the countries occupied by the red men of the South and West by a fair exchange.
Andrew Jackson. Message to Congress, Dec. 1830.

67. We never make conquests or ask any other nation to let us establish ourselves in their country as the English, the French and the Dutch have done.
Andrew Jackson. Instruction to Edmond Roberts, a New Hampshire sea captain sent to arrange commercial treaties with Burma, Indo-China, Siam, and Japan. 1832.

68. Great Britain's governing principles are conquest, colonialization, commerce, monopoly.
Thomas Jefferson (1743-1826), 3rd President of the United States (Democratic Republican-VA). Letter to William Carmichael, Aug. 2, 1790.

69. If there be one principle more deeply rooted than any other in the mind of every American, it is that we should have nothing to do with conquest.
Thomas Jefferson. Letter to William Short, July 28, 1791.

70. U.S. foreign policy at bottom is to bring Canada into as many situations affecting themselves as possible with a view to leading ultimately to the annexation of our two countries.
Mackenzie King (1874-1950), Prime Minister of Canada (Liberal). *Diary*, June 30, 1950.

71. All colonies are oppressed peoples.
V. I. Lenin (1870-1924), Premier of the U.S.S.R. Speech to the Soviet of Workers' and Soldiers' Deputies, May 19, 1917.

72. Imperialism is the monopoly stage of capitalism.
V. I. Lenin. *Imperialism, the Highest Stage of Capitalism*.

73. Oh, honest Americans, as Christians hear me for my downtrodden people! Their form of government is as dear to them as yours is precious to you.
Lydia Kamekeha Liliuokalani (1838-1917), Queen of Hawaii. Proclamation, 1898.

74. From the Rio Grande to the Arctic Ocean there should be but one flag and one country.
Henry Cabot Lodge (1850-1924), U.S. Congress-

man and U.S. Senator (R-MA). Quoted in Foster Rhea Dulles, *The United States Since 1865*, 1959.

75. Colonialism, imperialism, tribalism and religious separatism – all of which seriously hinder the flowering of a harmonious and fraternal African society.
Patrice Lumumba (1925-1961), 1st Prime Minister of the Congo (later Zaire). Speech, Accra Conference, Dec. 11, 1958.

76. We're not your monkeys now.
Patrice Lumumba. Remark to King Baudouin of Belgium, 1970.

77. Whether we are massacred by our own people or are massacred by foreigners does not amount to exactly the same thing.... If a man slaps his own face, he will not feel insulted, whereas if someone else slaps him, he will feel angry.
Lu Xun (1881-1936), Chinese writer. June 16, 1925.

78. The departure of the fleet was momentous. It drove me to prayer. I could see in it America's assertion of her right to control the Pacific in the interest of civilization and humanity.
Robert MacArthur, minister, Calvary Baptist Church, New York. Statement when Pres. Theodore Roosevelt dispatched sixteen battleships (the Great White Fleet) around the world to impress the Japanese and others with American naval strength. Dec. 16, 1907.

79. National pride may be a valuable possession, but when it becomes consciousness of racial superiority it ceases to be an Imperial virtue.
James Ramsay MacDonald (1866-1937), Prime Minister of Great Britain (Labour). *Labour and the Empire*, 1907.

80. The *[U.S.]* government possesses the power of acquiring territory, either by conquest or by treaty.
John Marshall (1755-1835), Chief Justice, U.S. Supreme Court. *American Insurance Co.* v. *Canter*, 1928.

81. There was nothing left for us to do *[after the Spanish-American War]* but to take them all, and to educate the Filipinos, and uplift and civilize and christianize them, and by God's grace do the very best we could by them.
William McKinley (1843-1901), 25th President of the United States (R-OH). Statement to visiting clergymen, 1896.

82. You may be sure there will be no jingo nonsense under my administration.
[Soon thereafter the Spanish-American War began, and when McKinley favored taking the Philippines from Spain, the New York Sun *stated, "We are all jingoes now, and the head jingo is the Hon. William McKinley."]*
William McKinley. Remark to Sen. Carl Schurz, 1897.

83. We want no wars of conquest; we must avoid the temptation of territorial aggression.
William McKinley. First inaugural address, Mar. 4, 1897.

84. I speak not of forcible annexation, for that cannot be thought of. That by our code of morality would be criminal aggression.
William McKinley. In reference to Cuba. Message to Congress, Dec. 1897.

85. The mission of the United States *[to the Philippine Islands]* is one of benevolent assimilation, submitting the mild sway of justice and right for arbitrary rule.
William McKinley. Statement on taking over the Philippine Islands from Spain. Letter to General Harrison Otis Gray, Dec. 21, 1898.

86. Annexation *[of Hawaii]* is not a change; it is a consummation.
William McKinley. Quoted in Foster Rhea Dulles, *The United States Since 1865*, 1959.

87. I have not heard that you claim exclusively any part of the moon; but there is not a spot on this inhabitable globe that I could affirm that you do not claim.
James Monroe (1758-1831), 5th President of the United States (Democratic Republican-VA). Statement to Stratford Canning, British Minister to the U.S.

88. We must save America from the missionary idea that you must get the whole world onto the American way of life. This is really a big world danger.
Gunnar Myrdal (1898-1987), Swedish diplomat and writer. 1975.

89. Conquest has made me what I am, and conquest alone can enable me to maintain my position.
Napoléon I (1769-1821), military leader and Emperor of France. *Maxims*.

90. The Empire means peace.
Napoléon III (Louis Napoléon Bonaparte) (1808-1873), Emperor of France. Speech, Bordeaux, 1852.

91. Some races are like children, and require a despot to nurse, and feed, and dress them, to give them pocket money, and to take them out for airings.
John Henry Newman (1801-1890), British Roman

Catholic cardinal and philosopher. *Discussions and Arguments*.

92. *[England is]* the greatest aggressor in modern history.

Gerald P. Nye (1892-1971), U.S. Senator (R-ND). In opposition to pre-World War II aid to Great Britain. Quoted in David Brinkley, *Washington Goes to War*, 1988.

93. Our manifest destiny is to overspread the continent allotted by Providence for the free development of our yearly multiplying millions.

John Louis O'Sullivan (1813-1895), American editor. *United States Magazine and Democratic Review*, July-Aug. 1845.

94. We are governed by the laws under which the universe was created; and therefore, in obedience to those laws, we must of necessity move forward in the paths of destiny shaped for us by the great Ruler of the Universe. Activity and progress is the law of heaven and earth; and in the violation of this law there is danger.

John Louis O'Sullivan. Argument for the acquisition of Cuba as part of the United States. *United States Magazine and Democratic Review*, Apr. 1859.

95. No man has a right to fix the boundary of the march of a nation; no man has a right to say to his country – thus far shall thou go and no further.

Charles Stewart Parnell (1846-1891), Irish politician. Speech, Jan. 21, 1885.

96. What is the use of conquest? Vassalage is impossible in this age. What is a King? Chief Magistrate, Chief Magistrate.

Louis Philippe (1773-1850), King of France. To Benjamin Disraeli, 1840. Quoted in Helen and Marvin Swartz, *Disraeli's Reminiscences*, 1976.

97. There is no need for any nation, however great, leaving the Empire, because the Empire is a Commonwealth of Nations.

Archibald Philip Primrose, 5th Earl of Rosebery (1847-1929), Prime Minister of Great Britain (Liberal). Speech at Adelaide, Australia, Jan. 18, 1884.

98. If this Bill for the admission of Orleans *[the Louisiana]* territory as a State passes, it is my deliberate opinion that it is virtually a dissolution of the Union; that it will free the States from their moral obligation *[to oppose slavery]*; and, as it *[slavery]* will be the right of all, so it will be the duty of some, definitely to prepare for a separation – amicably if they can, violently if they must.

Josiah Quincy (1772-1864), President, Harvard College, Cambridge, MA, and U.S. Congressman (Federalist-MA). Speech, House of Representatives, Jan. 14, 1811.

99. The policy of divide and rule is the sheet-anchor of all imperial governments.

Lala Lajpat Rai (1865-1921), Member of Congress, India, and political exile. *Unhappy India*.

100. We have bought 2 million Malays at two dollars a head unpicked, and nobody knows what it will cost to pick them.

Thomas B. Reed (1839-1902), U.S. Congressman and Speaker of the House (R-ME). Remark to Mark Hanna after the United States acquired the Philippines, 1898.

101. We are the first race in the world, and the more of the world we inherit the better it is for the human race.

Cecil Rhodes (1853-1902), Prime Minister of Cape Colony, South Africa, industrialist, and philanthropist. Press statement, 1899.

102. If there be a God, then what he would like me to do is to paint as much of the map of Africa British red as possible, and to do what I can elsewhere to promote the unity and extend the influence of the English-speaking race.

Cecil Rhodes. Quoted in Emil Ludwig, *Genius and Character*, 1927.

103. The Dominion of Canada is part of the sisterhood of the British Empire. I give to you assurance that the people of the United States will not stand idly by if domination of Canadian soil is threatened by any other empire.

Franklin D. Roosevelt (1882-1945), 32nd President of the United States (D-NY). Statement when accepting an honorary degree at Queens University, Kingston, Ontario, Canada, Aug. 18, 1938.

104. If I had my way we should annex those islands *[Hawaii]* tomorrow.

Theodore Roosevelt (1858-1919), 26th President of the United States (R-NY). To Alfred T. Mahan.

105. You have shown that you were accused of seduction, and you have conclusively proved that you were guilty of rape.

Elihu Root (1845-1937), U.S. Senator (R-NY), U.S. Secretary of War, U.S. Secretary of State, and Nobel Laureate in Peace. Remark to Pres. Theodore Roosevelt after the Panama Canal Zone was established. Cabinet meeting, Nov. 1903.

106. There is no part of the world where if asked to leave, we will not leave.

Henry Rowen, U.S. Assistant Secretary of State. House testimony, Sept. 18, 1990.

107. Give me only this assurance, that there never be an unlawful resistance by an armed force to the President bearing the authority of the United States, and give me fifty, forty, thirty more years of life, and I will engage to give you the possession of the American continent and the control of the world.

William H. Seward (1801-1872), Governor of New York (Whig), U.S. Senator (Whig and R), and U.S. Secretary of State. Speech, Boston, MA, June 24, 1867.

108. Excess of insularity makes a Briton an Imperialist.... Excess of local self-assertion makes a colonist an Imperialist.

George Bernard Shaw (1856-1950), Nobel Laureate in Literature (Great Britain). *Maxims for Revolutionists*, 1903.

109. When we learn to sing that Britons never will be masters we shall make an end of slavery.

George Bernard Shaw. *Ibid.*

110. To found a great empire for the sole purpose of raising up a people of customers may at first sight appear a project fit only for a nation of shopkeepers. It is, however, a project altogether unfit for a nation of shopkeepers; but extremely fit for a nation whose government is influenced by shopkeepers.

Adam Smith (1723-1790), Scottish political economist. Response to Napoléon I's comment that "England is a nation of shopkeepers." *The Wealth of Nations*, 1776.

111. The Hawaiian pear is now fully ripe and this is the golden hour for the United States to pluck it.

John L. Stevens (1820-1895), U.S. Ambassador to Hawaii. Communiqué to the State Department, 1893.

112. The colonies of modern nations owe their origin almost exclusively to the spirit of commerce.

Joseph Story (1779-1845), U.S. Supreme Court Justice. *Miscellaneous Writings*, 1835.

113. Little brown brothers

William H. Taft (1857-1930), 27th President of the United States (R-OH) and Chief Justice, U.S. Supreme Court. His term for Filipinos when he was the first U.S. civilian governor of the Philippine Islands, 1901-1904.

114. California and Oregon are both too far away *[to annex]*.... People out there *[should]* ... form an independent government of their own.

Zachary Taylor (1784-1850), 12th President of the United States (Whig-KY). Remark to outgoing President Polk. Inauguration day, Mar. 5, 1849.

115. We want those islands. We want them because they are the stepping way across the sea.... *[They are]* necessary to our safety, they are necessary to our commerce.

Henry Moore Teller (1830-1914), U.S. Senator (R, D, and Silver Republican-CO) and U.S. Secretary of the Interior. Senate speech when the annexation of Hawaii was under consideration, 1898.

116. At a period which may be said to be near ... the Anglo-Americans alone will cover the immense space contained between the polar region and the tropics, extending from the coasts of the Atlantic to those of the Pacific Ocean.

Alexis de Tocqueville (1805-1859), French writer. *Democracy in America*, 1835.

117. Up to our own day American history has been in a large degree the history of the colonization of the Great West.

Frederick Jackson Turner (1861-1932), American historian. *The Significance of the Frontier in American History*, 1893.

118. Defense of the Canadian frontier will in general be best accomplished by mobile troops and an aggressive offensive action.

U.S. Army, Plan G, 1919.

119. Militant Communism remains dedicated to the destruction of our society.

U.S. Joint Chiefs of Staff, position paper presented to the Senate Foreign Relations Committee, Aug. 15, 1963.

120. This agglomeration which was called and which still calls itself the Holy Roman Empire was neither holy, nor Roman, nor an empire.

Voltaire (François-Marie Arouet) (1694-1778), French historian and dramatist. *Essay on the History, Manners, and Spirit of the Nations*, 1759.

121. Every year's advance of our frontier takes in a territory as large of some of the kingdoms of Europe. We are richer by hundreds of millions. The Indian is poorer by a large part of the little he has. This growth is bringing imperial greatness to the nation; to the Indian it brings wretchedness, destitution, beggary.

Francis A. Walker (1840-1897), U.S. Commissioner of Indian Affairs. Report to Congress, 1870.

122. I don't feel we did wrong in taking this country away from them. There were great numbers of people who needed new land, and the Indians were selfishly trying to keep it for themselves.

John Wayne (1907-1979), American actor. Interview, 1975.

123. What do we want with *[Oregon]* ... this region of savages and wild beasts, of deserts and shifting sand and whirlwinds of dust, of cactus and prairie dogs?

Daniel Webster (1782-1852), U.S. Congressman (Federalist-NH and MA), U.S. Senator (Federalist and Whig-MA), and U.S. Secretary of State. Senate speech, 1841.

124. The United States will never again seek one additional foot of territory by conquest.

Woodrow Wilson (1856-1924), 28th President of the United States (D-NJ). Speech, Oct. 27, 1913.

125. To serve mankind.

Woodrow Wilson. Explanation of his order to send American troops to occupy Veracruz after a Mexican military coup. 1914.

126. I am confident that the nations that have learned the discipline of freedom and that have settled with self-possession of its ordered practice are now about to make conquest of the world by the sheer power of example and of friendly helpfulness.

Woodrow Wilson. Oct. 1918.

127. They had commission to put to death the men of Block Island, but to spare the women and children, and to bring them away, and to take possession of the Island.

John Winthrop (1588-1649), Governor of Massachusetts Bay Colony. Statement when a white trader was killed and an expedition was sent from Boston against the Narragansett Indians on Block Island. Quoted in Howard Zinn, *A People's History of the United States*, 1980.

128. That new revelation of right which has been designated as the right of our manifest destiny to spread over the whole continent.

Robert C. Winthrop (1809-1894), U.S. Congressman and U.S. Senator (Whig-MA). Speech in Congress, Jan. 3, 1846.

Chapter 32

Families, Children, and Family Planning

1. WE WANT TIME TO PLAY!
[In 1903, 75,000 textile workers were on strike in Pennsylvania. They included thousands of children ranging in age from ten to fifteen who worked sixty hours a week. A children's march was organized by Mary Harris (Mother Jones) across New Jersey and through New York to Theodore Roosevelt's home in Oyster Bay, Long Island, carrying banners with this slogan.]
Sign at Children's March, 1903.

2. A WOMAN'S PLACE IS IN THE HOUSE ... AND THE SENATE
Bumper sticker, Washington, DC, 1980.

3. For a number of years I've wondered if people like us are the forgotten. We're not the poor, and we're not the rich. We're not the very young or the aged. We're the average American family.
Donna Alexander, Lorena, TX. Letter to Ann Richards, Treasurer of Texas. Quoted by Richards, keynote address, Democratic National Convention, Atlanta, GA, July 18, 1988.

4. You can be fairly tolerant of people's weirdness but you will be less so when it comes to the protection of your family and neighborhood.
Wick Allison, publisher, *National Review*. PBS, *Firing Line*, Jan. 16, 1989.

5. The American people got fucked.
Frank Annunzio, U.S. Congressman (D-IL). Statement to reporter Al Hunt who asked for his reaction after a beef price control amendment he had introduced was defeated. When the reporter said he couldn't print that in a family newspaper, the Congressman suggested he change it to "The American family got fucked." 1973.

6. If you're going to send the mothers out into the work force, what are you going to do about the children they leave at home?
Bruce Babbitt, Governor of Arizona (D). PBS, *America's Children: Who Should Care?*, Sept. 4, 1990.

7. Education, day care, health care – there's not a parent in the country that doesn't have a stake in one of these issues.
Bruce Babbitt. *Ibid.*

8. Our children are our future. And our future is in jeopardy.
Marion Barry, Mayor of Washington, DC (D). State of the District address, 1988.

9. The family is the original Department of Health, Education and Welfare.
William J. Bennett, Director, Office of National Drug Control Policy, and U.S. Secretary of Education (R). Interview, PBS, *MacNeil-Lehrer News Hour*, Aug. 9, 1989.

10. The States are not free, under the guise of protecting maternal health or potential life, to intimidate women into continuing pregnancy.... A woman's right to make that choice is fundamental.
Harry A. Blackmun, U.S. Supreme Court Justice. *Thornburgh* v. *American College of Obstetricians and Gynecologists*, 1986.

11. You've got to be poor, or unwed, or incompetent to get something from the government. Otherwise you get nothing.
T. Berry Brazelton, pediatrician and member, National Commission on Children. PBS, *Bill Moyers' World of Ideas*, October 24, 1988.

12. Some children need help from the day they are born.
T. Berry Brazelton. *The New York Times Magazine*, Sept. 9, 1990.

13. Can I be a good president not having a wife? I tell you, I grew up in a family, my father had a wife, that's how I came to be here.

Edmund G. (Jerry) Brown, Jr., Governor of California (D). Interview, CBS, *Phil Donahue Show*, Apr. 3, 1992.

14. I am a woman, a Democrat, and a Brown.
Kathleen Brown, Treasurer of California (D), daughter of Gov. Edmund G. (Pat) Brown, and sister of Gov. Edmund G. (Jerry) Brown, Jr. Campaign statement, Sept. 1990.

15. There wasn't a kid in my neighborhood who knew his dad. My mother did it for us, and she still thinks I'm an underachiever.
Willie Brown, Speaker of the Assembly, CA (D). Quoted in *The New York Times*, Oct. 31, 1988.

16. Ours is an individualistic society, indeed, and the state must do for the individual what the family does for the older civilizations.
Pearl S. Buck (1892-1973), Nobel Laureate in Literature (United States). *The Child Who Never Grew*, 1950.

17. If our American way of life fails the child, it fails us all.
Pearl S. Buck. *Children for Adoption*, 1964.

18. When families are broken, neighbors and caring friends must step in.
George Bush, 41st President of the United States (R-TX). Speech, Sept. 5, 1989.

19. The state can destroy families, but it can rarely save families.
Alan Carlson, President, Rockford Institute. PBS, *America's Children: Who Should Care?*, Sept. 4, 1990.

20. I told him that Mrs. Carter and I would be deeply hurt and shocked and disappointed – because our daughter is only seven years old.
Jimmy Carter, 39th President of the United States (D-GA). Reply when asked by a reporter how he and Mrs. Carter would feel if their daughter, Amy, had a premarital affair. Naples, FL, 1975.

21. I am sorry that as leader of the community, San Antonio and my name go together. But I guess human beings just aren't made of plastic and wiring and metal. They are made of flesh and blood and feelings.
Henry G. Cisneros, Mayor of San Antonio, TX (D). Confirmation of rumors that he was having an extramarital affair. Quoted in *The New York Times*, Oct. 16, 1988.

22. I am convinced that every boy, in his heart, would rather steal second base than an automobile.
Thomas C. Clark (1899-1977), U.S. Supreme Court Justice. Favorite statement.

23. I don't believe the American people want a gelding in the White House.
Grover Cleveland (1837-1908), 22nd and 24th President of the United States (D-NY). Response to charges that he had fathered an illegitimate child. Quoted in *Smithsonian*, Oct. 1988.

24. Miserable and almost friendless objects are ushered upon the stage of life, inheriting those vices, which idleness and the bad example of their parents naturally produce.
De Witt Clinton (1769-1828), U.S. Senator (Anti-Federalist Republican-NY), Mayor of New York City, Governor of New York, and "Father of Free Public Schools." Calling for universal free public education. Speech, New York City, Feb. 25, 1805.

25. Politicians are elected for two years or four years at a time, and prevention programs of all kinds are simply not a priority for people whose careers are so short-lived.
Anne H. Cohn, Executive Director, National Committee to Prevent Child Abuse. Quoted in *The New York Times*, Nov. 27, 1990.

26. The human body is not lent out, is not rented out, is not sold.
Cour de cassation (Supreme Court of France). Comment when outlawing contracts for surrogate motherhood. May 31, 1991.

27. God created Adam and Eve, not Adam and Steve.
Robert Dannemeyer, U.S. Congressman (R-CA). In opposition to homosexual marriages. Quoted in *USA Today*, May 1, 1990.

28. Some say quality of life is best defined by spotless parks and litter-free roadways. But for me it is best exemplified by a happy, healthy baby or by a teenager with a diploma in hand and a sparkle in the eye.
David Dinkins, Mayor of New York City (D). Press conference, May 25, 1990.

29. I have always thought that every woman should marry and no man.
Benjamin Disraeli, 1st Earl of Beaconsfield (1804-1881), Prime Minister of Great Britain (Conservative). Quoted in Nancy McPhee, *The Book of Insults*, 1978.

30. Never in the history of American politics has there been a constituency so popular but with so little political clout as the American family.
Christopher J. Dodd, U.S. Senator (D-CT). Quoted in *The Washington Post*, Oct. 8, 1988.

31. We must break the cycle of cynicism that has hold of many of our youth.

Elizabeth H. Dole, U.S. Secretary of Labor and U.S. Secretary of Transportation (R). Quoted in *The Los Angeles Times*, June 30, 1989.

32. Child care is a family issue – not a government issue.

Robert J. Dole, U.S. Senator (R-KS). Senate debate, June 23, 1989.

33. I want guys out there to think when they are in the magic moment of lovemaking that if this woman gets pregnant, I'm going to be on a financial hook for the rest of my life.

Thomas J. Downey, U.S. Congressman (D-NY). Quoted in *The Washington Post*, Apr. 5, 1991.

34. Why should Ontario pay for Quebec's fucking? *[The birth rate for Protestant Ontario was much lower than that of Catholic Quebec.]*

George Drew (1894-1984), Premier, Ontario, Canada. Question of Harry Nixon during Parliamentary debate on family allowances, 1975.

35. So long as little children are allowed to suffer, there is no true love in this world.

Isadora Duncan (1878-1927), American dancer and educator. *Memoirs*, 1924.

36. Just because a child's parents are poor or uneducated is no reason to deprive the child of basic human rights to health care, education, proper nutrition.

Marian Wright Edelman, founder, Children's Defense Fund. Quoted in *Psychology Today*, June 1975.

37. I have no objection to doing anything that is within the law to help children.

Marion Wright Edelman. Interview, CBS, *60 Minutes*, Oct. 22, 1989.

38. If adultery were made a federal crime punishable by fine, the national debt would be wiped out in a year or two.

Eunice Zoghlin Edgar, Director, American Civil Liberties Union, WI. Quoted in *Des Moines Register*, May 6, 1990.

39. The thing that impresses me most about America is the way parents obey their children.

Edward VIII, Duke of Windsor (1894-1972), King of Great Britain. Quoted in Nancy McPhee, *The Book of Insults*, 1978.

40. I'm not so much concerned with the natural bastards as I am with the self-made ones.

Robert Ekhardt, U.S. Congressman (D-TX). Statement during a House debate when conservative Republicans tried to cut funds for illegitimate children. Quoted by Morris K. Udall, *Too Funny to Be President*, 1988.

41. Legalized licentiousness.... Every wife, every mother, every daughter in the land is awaiting the action of the House today.

John F. (Honey Fitz) Fitzgerald (1863-1950), Mayor of Boston, MA, and U.S. Congressman (D). House debate to exclude U.S. Congressman Brigham Roberts (D-UT), a Mormon with three wives who refused to break his vows and leave two. Dec. 5, 1899.

42. Children are born into a society in which they are not a priority.

Keith Geiger, President, National Education Association. "A Time for Hope," *The Washington Post*, Dec. 23, 1990.

43. What has made this nation great? Not its heroes but its households.

Sarah J. Hale (1788-1879), American magazine editor. *Traits of American Life*, 1835.

44. It is better for all the world, if instead of waiting to execute degenerate offspring for crime, or let them starve for their imbecility, society can prevent those who are manifestly unfit from continuing their kind. The principle that sustains compulsory vaccination is broad enough to cover cutting the Fallopian tubes.... Three generations of imbeciles are enough.

Oliver Wendell Holmes, Jr. (1841-1935), U.S. Supreme Court Justice. *Buck* v. *Bell*, 1927.

45. Public employment contributes neither to advantage nor to happiness. It is but honorary exile from one's family and affairs.

Thomas Jefferson (1743-1826), 3rd President of the United States (Democratic Republican-VA). Letter to F. Willis, 1790.

46. Responsible parenting cannot be federally mandated.

Elizabeth Kepley, Director, Legislative Affairs, Concerned Women for America. Testimony, House Education and Labor Committee, Feb. 25, 1987.

47. Our ultimate goal as a nation should be to make available comprehensive, developmental childcare services to all families that wish to use them.... There shouldn't be a single little child in America left alone to fend for himself.

Mary Dublin Keyserling, Director, Women's Bureau, U.S. Department of Labor, and President, National Women's Democratic Club. *Windows on Day Care*, 1972.

48. Many of the people who are most opposed to abortion are also most opposed to contraception which would stop it.

C. Everett Koop, U.S. Surgeon General. Interview, ABC, *20/20*, July 15, 1989.

49. The American home, a steady job, an opportunity for the children to go to school properly nourished is the way to combat communism.

Fiorello H. La Guardia (1882-1947), U.S. Congressman (Republican and Socialist-NY) and Mayor of New York City (Republican and Fusion Party). House Ways and Means Committee hearings, 1932.

50. The history of America is the history of families moving.

Louis L'Amour, American writer. Interview, PBS, *The Struggle for Democracy*, July 18, 1989.

51. Children must be taught to hate their parents if they are not Communists.

V. I. Lenin (1870-1924), Premier of the U.S.S.R. 1923.

52. It is a country's sovereign right to decide its own population policy.

Li Zhaoxing, spokesman, Foreign Ministry of China. Response to U.S. criticism of alleged forced abortions as a part of China's family planning program. News briefing, Beijing, Mar. 16, 1989.

53. When the wages of labour are hardly sufficient to maintain two children, a man marries and has five or six.

Thomas R. Malthus (1766-1834), British political economist. *Essay on the Principle of Population*, 1798.

54. We don't have nearly all the *[day care]* options people want.

Ann McLaughlin, U.S. Secretary of Labor (R). CBS, *Face the Nation*, July 3, 1988.

55. For the first time in human history, there are no elders anymore who know what young people know.

Margaret Mead (1901-1978), American anthropologist. Quoted in *Life*, Fall 1990.

56. When people meet my wife, they think rather better of me. They say: "With a wife like that, he can't be as bad as we thought."

Robert G. Menzies (1894-1978), Prime Minister of Australia (Liberal). Quoted in *The Wit of Sir Robert Menzies*, 1966.

57. Children's television has been grossly overcommercialized. The subtle message is, "Buy me! Buy me!"

Howard M. Metzenbaum, U.S. Senator (D-OH). Quoted on CBS, *West 57th Street*, Jan. 7, 1989.

58. The American dream begins with the American family.

Barbara A. Mikulski, U.S. Congresswoman and U.S. Senator (D-MD). Address, Democratic National Convention, Atlanta, GA, July 20, 1988.

59. Thousands of American children have only a cell, a hospital bed, or a temporary shelter to call home.

George Miller, U.S. Congressman (D-CA). Statement, Dec. 12, 1989.

60. Politicians are waving the diaper as often as they wave the flag.

Bill Moyers, American journalist, Special Assistant to President Lyndon B. Johnson, and White House Press Secretary. In reference to the current political emphasis on family values. PBS, *Bill Moyers' World of Ideas*, Oct. 24, 1988.

61. Every law of this country, state or national, should have for its ultimate purpose getting one man in love with one woman and in a home owned by them, and every law that can be made to secure that home and protect the wife and the mother should be enacted; otherwise this civilization cannot live.

William Henry David Murray (1869-1956), Governor of Oklahoma and U.S. Congressman (D). Speech, Democratic National Convention, Chicago, IL, July 1, 1932.

62. RESOLVED: That the conference go on record reaffirming the legal and moral responsibility of parents for child neglect or contribution to child delinquency, and that parents of delinquents be treated if necessary, but that punishment of parents for their children's misdemeanors is not a desirable form of treatment.

Resolution, National Conference on Juvenile Delinquency, U.S. Department of Health, Education and Welfare, June 28, 1954.

63. I think it's next to impossible to write a constitutional *[teenage]* curfew *[law]*.

Eric Neisser, Director, American Civil Liberties Union, NJ. Quoted in *Governing the States and Localities*, Apr. 1988.

64. Workers have both work responsibilities and family responsibilities, and they need some accommodating of these competing needs.

Helen Norton, Director, Women's Legal Defense Fund. Quoted in *The Wall Street Journal*, May 4, 1990.

65. You talk about wives; which one I throw away? You pick him? You little girl, you go 'way; you got no papa – you pick him? You little fellow, you go 'way; you got no papa – you pick him?

Quanah Parker (1854-1911), Chief, Comanche Indians. Statement to Gen. Hugh Scott, who tried to enforce laws outlawing plural marriages among Indians. Quoted in Hugh Lenox Scott, *Some Memories of a Soldier*, 1928.

66. The only privileged persons in our society are the children.

Eva Perón (1919-1952), First Lady of Argentina. Speech, American Congress of Industrial Medicine, Dec. 5, 1949.

67. If there is one thing we should give every child, it is self-esteem.

David Peterson, Premier of Ontario, Canada (Conservative). PBS, *The Editors*, May 26, 1991.

68. Our national interest is served by programs that direct public resources toward investment and youth, not consumption and age.

Peter G. Peterson, U.S. Secretary of Commerce (R). *The New York Times*, Sept. 16, 1990.

69. The average family exists only on paper and its average budget is a fiction, invented by statisticians for the convenience of statisticians.

Sylvia Porter, American economist and writer. *Sylvia Porter's Money Book*, 1976.

70. Let them laugh at us, but let's keep this *[adultery]* law on the books to strengthen our family values.

Robert Preston, Senate Democratic leader, New Hampshire. Quoted in *The Washington Post*, Apr. 30, 1989.

71. I am poor and naked, but I am chief of the nation. We do not want riches, we do not seek riches, but we want our children properly trained and brought up. Our riches will do us no good; we cannot take away into the other world anything we have.

Red Cloud (1822-1909), Chief, Oglala Sioux Indians. Statement, July 16, 1870.

72. If you don't want to talk about *[parental]* leave and you don't want to talk about child care, what are you pro-family about?

Barbara Roberts, Oregon Democratic gubernatorial candidate. Quoted in *The New York Times*, July 1, 1990.

73. The Republican leaders have not been content with attacks upon me, or on my wife, or on my sons – no, not content with that, they now include my little dog Fala. Unlike the members of my family, he resents this.

Franklin D. Roosevelt (1882-1945), 32nd President of the United States (D-NY). Address, Teamsters Union Convention, Sept. 23, 1944.

74. I don't think that any other family ever enjoyed the White House more than we have.

Theodore Roosevelt (1858-1919), 26th President of the United States (R). Letter to Kermit Roosevelt, June 21, 1904.

75. The republics of Korea, Singapore and Thailand are economic successes in part because, as part of their overall development efforts, strong programs of family planning helped to reduce high rates of population growth.

Nafis Sadik, Director, United Nations Fund for Population Activities. Quoted in *The Washington Post*, May 31, 1989.

76. We have to find the resources to do right by kids and by old people.... I don't want to be asked to choose between my mother and my kids. I don't think the nation should choose between its elderly and its kids.

Lisbeth Schorr, American writer. Interview, *USA Today*, Oct. 20, 1988.

77. From a tax point of view you're better off raising horses or cattle than children.

Patricia R. Schroeder, U.S. Congresswoman (D-CO). PBS, *Firing Line*, Oct. 9, 1988.

78. There may be illegitimate parents but there are no illegitimate children.

Mobuto Sese Seko, President of Zaire. Quoted on PBS, *The Africans*, 1986.

79. Marriage ... is fatal to large states because it puts its ban on the deliberate breeding of man as a political animal.

George Bernard Shaw (1856-1950), Nobel Laureate in Literature (Great Britain). *Maxims for Revolutionists*, 1903.

80. Home is the girl's prison and the woman's workhouse.

George Bernard Shaw. *Ibid.*

81. If it's true that politics is the art of compromise, I've had a good start. My mother was a Republican and a Unitarian, my father was a Democrat and a Presbyterian. I wound up in his party and her church.

Adlai E. Stevenson (1900-1965), Governor of Illinois (D) and U.S. Ambassador to the United Nations.

Quoted in Myers and Martin, *Speeches of Adlai Stevenson*, 1952.

82. My great grandfather *[William H. Taft]* was President and Chief Justice of the United States. My grandfather *[Robert A. Taft]* was a United States Senator. My father *[William H. Taft III]* is the American Ambassador to Ireland. I am a Brownie.

Maria Taft. Description of herself to new classmates in Dublin, Ireland. 1953.

83. Young people ought not to be idle. It is very bad for them.

Margaret Thatcher, Prime Minister of Great Britain (Conservative). 1984.

84. The whole country seems to have melded into one middle class.

Alexis de Tocqueville (1805-1859), French writer. *Democracy in America*, 1835.

85. Children and dogs are as necessary to the welfare of this country as Wall Street and the railroads.

Harry S Truman (1884-1972), 33rd President of the United States (D-MO). Speech, National Conference on Family Life, May 6, 1948.

86. The basic value system of this country is the family.

Maurice T. Turner, Jr., Chief of Police, Washington, DC. Interview, WETA-TV, Mar. 21, 1989.

87. Motherhood and childhood are entitled to special care and assistance.

United Nations, Universal Declaration of Human Rights, 1948.

88. The hand that rocks the cradle is the hand that rules the world.

William Ross Wallace (1819-1891), American lawyer and poet. "The Hand That Rocks the Cradle," *John O'London's Treasure Trove*.

89. You are not to enlist any person who is not an American born, unless such person has a wife and family, and is a settled resident in this country.

George Washington (1732-1799), 1st President of the United States (VA). Footnote to a letter to Peyton Randolph, President of the Second Continental Congress. July 24, 1775.

90. The care and upbringing of children are a natural right of, and a duty primarily incumbent on, the parents.

West German Constitution, 1949.

91. Only one enemy can exist for you – my enemy. With the present Socialist machinations, it may happen that I shall order you to shoot your own relatives, your brothers, or even your parents – which God forbid – and then you are bound in duty implicitly to obey my orders.

Wilhelm II (1859-1941), Emperor of Germany and King of Prussia. Speech to new recruits, 1891.

92. If a woman goes for genetic counseling and the doctor says the child will be born with a defect, do you think the father has a right to know about this condition? If a wife wants to have an abortion, do you think the father has a right to know? We've done a lot to foster women's rights, but not enough for husband's rights.

Jerry Winter, American family law attorney. Quoted in *Trial*, July 1988.

93. The structure of the family has changed quite a bit since the stereotype of "Leave It to Beaver" days.

Michael Woo, City Councilman, Los Angeles, CA (D). Quoted in *The New York Times*, May 28, 1989.

Chapter 33

Flags

1. I despise any flag, not just the American flag. It's a symbol of a piece of land that's considered more important than the human lives on it.

   Joan Baez, American folksinger and pacifist. Interview, *Playboy*, July 1970.

2. And, as the last vessel spread her canvas to the wind, the Americans hoisted a most superb and splendid ensign on their battery.

   Robert J. Barrett, British midshipman. *Diary*, Sept. 14, 1814.

3. *[The American flag]* means the rising up of a valiant young people against an old tyranny, to establish the most momentous doctrine that the world has ever known, or has since known – the right of men to their own selves and to their liberties.

   Henry Ward Beecher (1813-1887), American clergyman and writer. Sermon, Plymouth Church, MA, May 1861.

4. The Republic never retreats. Its flag is the only flag that has never known defeat. Where that flag leads we follow, for we know that the hand that bears it onward is the unseen hand of God.

   Albert J. Beveridge (1862-1927), U.S. Senator (R-IN) and founder, Progressive League. Speech, Philadelphia, PA, Feb. 15, 1899.

5. We do not consecrate the flag by punishing its desecration, for in doing so we dilute the freedom that this cherished emblem represents.

   William J. Brennan, Jr., U.S. Supreme Court Justice. *Texas* v. *Johnson*, 1989.

6. The way to preserve the flag's special role is not to punish those who feel differently about these matters. It is to persuade them that they are wrong.... Our decision is a reaffirmation of the principles of freedom and inclusiveness that the flag best reflects, and of the conviction that our toleration of such criticism *[flag burning]* is a sign and source of our strength.

   William J. Brennan, Jr. *Ibid.*

7. We can imagine no more appropriate response to burning a flag than to waving one's own, no better way to counter a flag-burner's message than by saluting the flag that burns, no surer means of preserving the dignity even of the flag that burned than by, as one witness here did, according its remains a respectful burial.

   William J. Brennan, Jr. *Ibid.*

8. Back under Jimmy Carter and Walter Mondale, times were tough. Flags weren't selling that well. Flag sales have taken off *[during the Reagan-Bush years]*.

   George Bush, 41st President of the United States (R-TX). Press conference, Washington, DC, June 27, 1989.

9. Respect for the flag transcends political party.

   George Bush. *Ibid.*

10. If it *[the American flag]* is not defended, it is defamed. We can't forget the importance of the flag to the ideals of liberty and honor and freedom. To burn the flag, to dishonor it, is simply wrong.

    George Bush. Speech, Iwo Jima Memorial, Arlington, VA. June 30, 1989.

11. Your banner's constellation types
White freedom with its stars,
But what is the meaning of the stripes?
They mean your negroes' scars.

    Thomas Campbell (1777-1844), Scottish poet. *To the United States of North America*, 1838.

12. RESOLVED: That the flag of the United States shall be of thirteen stripes of alternate red and white, with a union of thirteen stars of white in a blue field, representing the new constellation.

    Resolution adopted by the Continental Congress, Philadelphia, PA, June 14, 1777.

13. Who personally has ever witnessed a flag burning?

    Philip M. Crane, U.S. Congressman (R-WI). Quoted in *USA Today*, Sept. 11, 1989.

14. Take away that fool's bauble, the Mace.
[The wood mace, covered with gold leaf and topped by a gold crown symbolizing the King or Queen of Great Britain, rests on the Treasury bench in the House of Commons during each session of Parliament.]
Oliver Cromwell (1599-1658), Lord Protector of England. Remark when dismissing the Rump Parliament, Apr. 20, 1653.

15. Here's to the red of it,
There's not a thread of it,
No, not a shred of it,
In all the spread of it,
From foot to head,
But heroes bled for it,
Faced steel and lead for it,
Precious blood shed for it,
Bathing in red.
John Augustin Daly (1838-1899), American playwright. "A Toast to the Flag."

16. If anyone attempts to haul down the American flag, shoot him on the spot.
John Adams Dix (1798-1879), Governor of New York (R), U.S. Senator (D), U.S. Secretary of the Treasury, and U.S. Minister to France. Message to revenue officials in New Orleans, LA, when southern states seized U.S. government property. Jan. 29, 1861.

17. I think he could defend it at a bar association meeting, but not before real people.
Robert J. Dole, U.S. Senator (R-KS). Comment when asked how a member of Congress could defend voting against a constitutional amendment to protect the flag. Quoted in *The Washington Post*, June 14, 1990.

18. Folks, wear flags on your lapels. Put them on your hats. Get the expensive sticker put on the side of the camper, on the side of your Cadillac Eldorado.
Robert Dornan, U.S. Congressman (R-CA). Reaction to the Supreme Court's flag burning decision, *Texas* v. *Johnson*. Quoted in *The Washington Post*, July 9, 1989.

19. I name thee Old Glory.
William Driver (1803-1886), American sea captain. Remark as the U.S. flag was unfurled on the *Charles Dogget* before a voyage to Asia. Salem, MA, 1831.

20. When you commit the flag, you commit it to win.
Dwight D. Eisenhower (1890-1969), 34th President of the United States (R-KS). Comment before sending American troops to Guatemala in 1956. Quoted in *Newsweek*, Mar. 4, 1963.

21. It's not a very radical thing. I don't think the government should tell people the way to express themselves in public.
Marc Elrich, Takoma Park, MD, City Councilman. Comment on why he introduced a proposal to ban recitation of the Pledge of Allegiance at the Council's meetings, Feb. 6, 1992.

22. We cannot allow the American flag to be shot at anywhere on earth if we are to retain our respect and prestige.
Barry M. Goldwater, U.S. Senator (R-AZ). Press release during the Gulf of Tonkin incident, Aug. 1964.

23. Let cannon and bell at high noon call the people from sport or study or toil, to reflection on that great life so nobly lived. Let the universal display from tenement to State House of the flag of the United States of America remind the people that our country is the United States because of Abraham Lincoln.
Curtis Guild, Jr. (1860-1915), Governor of Massachusetts (R) and U.S. Ambassador to Russia. Lincoln's Birthday proclamation, Feb. 22, 1908.

24. I have seen the glories of art and architecture, and mountain and river; I have seen the sunset on the Jungfrau, and the full moon rise over Mt. Blanc, but the fairest vision on which these eyes ever looked was the flag of my country in a foreign land.
George Frisbie Hoar (1826-1904), U.S. Congressman and U.S. Senator (R-MA). Speech, 1885.

25. It seems like th' less a statesman amounts to th' more he loves th' flag.
Frank McKinney (Kin) Hubbard (1868-1930), American caricaturist and writer. Quoted in Fred C. Kelly, *The Life and Times of Kin Hubbard*, 1952.

26. We all find flag burning repugnant. We find burning crosses repugnant. But they have been burning crosses longer than they have been burning flags, and there has been no rush for a constitutional amendment to stop the burning of crosses.
Jesse L. Jackson, Shadow Senator (D-DC). Response to George Bush's call for a constitutional amendment to make burning of the American flag illegal. Statement, Washington, DC, June 30, 1989.

27. When I look at his gallant services, finding him first in the military school of the United States, educated at the expense of his country – taught to love the principles of the Constitution; afterwards entering its service fighting beneath the Stars and Stripes, I cannot understand how he can be willing to hail another banner, and turn from that of his country.... If I could not unsheathe my sword in vindication of the flag of my country ... I would return the sword to its scabbard; I would never

sheathe it in the bosom of my mother. Never! Never! Never!

Andrew Johnson (1808-1875), 17th President of the United States (War Democrat-TN). Statement when Jefferson Davis accepted the presidency of the Confederate States of America. Feb. 25, 1861.

28. *[The American flag is a symbol]* of oppression, international murder, and plunder ... *[of a]* sick and dying empire.

Gregory Johnson, American flag-burner. Quoted in *The Washington Post*, July 4, 1989.

29. The Supreme Court decision *[Texas* v. *Johnson, 1989]* does not in any way indicate the government is backing off from forcing the flag on people. They just don't want to look too dictatorial in the way they do it.

Gregory Johnson. *Ibid.*

30. It is an unmistakable statement of contempt for a government to burn its flag.

Gregory Johnson. Debate with Congressman Charles Douglas, C-SPAN, Dec. 8, 1989.

31. It is poignant but fundamental that the flag protects those who hold it in contempt.

Anthony M. Kennedy, U.S. Supreme Court Justice. *Texas* v. *Johnson*, 1989.

32. I can assure you that this flag will be returned to this brigade in a free Havana.

John F. Kennedy (1917-1963), 35th President of the United States (D-MA). Comment when holding up a Cuban flag at a reunion of the Bay of Pigs invasion force, Jan. 1963.

33. We should look ... at the two states that do not have anti-flag burning laws. Ask yourself how it is that Alaska and Wyoming have survived without such laws. Is it because they are less patriotic than the citizens of the other forty-eight states? Is it because they simply were not aware of the great danger that exists to them without such laws? Or is it because they simply recognize that no danger exists.

J. Robert Kerrey, Governor of Nebraska and U.S. Senator (D). "The Flag Stands for the Freedom to Be Wrong," *The Washington Post*, July 23, 1989.

34. In the short time I still have to live, I would like to see the day when the Communist flag flies over the whole world.

Nikita S. Khrushchev (1894-1971), Premier of the U.S.S.R. Quoted in *The Washington Post*, July 6, 1960.

35. Offensive or not, those who burn the flag to express their views are exercising a right that our founding generation fought a revolution to secure.

Arthur J. Kropp, Executive Director, People for the American Way. Quoted in *The Washington Post*, June 22, 1989.

36. American labor, whenever it gathers, does so with love for its flag and country and loyalty to its government.

Fiorello H. La Guardia (1882-1947), U.S. Congressman (R and Socialist) and Mayor of New York City (R and Fusion Party). Labor Day Speech, Chicago World's Fair, Chicago, IL, Sept. 3, 1934.

37. I am unable to agree that the benefits that may accrue to society from the compulsory flag-salute are sufficiently definite and tangible to justify the invasion of freedom and privacy that is entailed.

Frank Murphy (1890-1959), Governor of Michigan (D), U.S. Attorney General, and U.S. Supreme Court Justice. *West Virginia State Board of Education* v. *Barnette*, 1943.

38. A "loyalty oath" such as the pledge harks back to the McCarthy era.

Hank Prensky, Takoma Park, MD, City Councilman. Comment on why he introduced a proposal to ban recitation of the Pledge of Allegiance at the Council's meetings, Feb. 6, 1992.

39. For more than two hundred years, the American flag has occupied a unique position as the symbol of our nation, a uniqueness that justifies a governmental prohibition against flag burning.

William H. Rehnquist, Chief Justice, U.S. Supreme Court. *Texas* v. *Johnson*, 1989 (dissent).

40. Flag burning is the equivalent of an inarticulate grunt or roar that ... is most likely to be indulged in not to express any particular idea but to antagonize others.

William H. Rehnquist. *Ibid.*

41. While it is now apparently the law that the demonstrators may roll Old Glory and fire her up like a Marlboro if they want, we don't have to permit it in the smoking section. As you know, the park regulations at 36 C.F.R. 2.13 prohibit the lighting or maintaining of fires except in designated areas or receptacles. The regulation is still in effect. It doesn't matter if they want to burn the American Flag or *The Washington Post*, unauthorized fires are still prohibited in the parks.

Richard Robbins, Solicitor, U.S. Department of the Interior. Memorandum to Carl Holmberg, U.S. Park Police, June 1989.

42. I think of the Iwo Jima Memorial – those Marines that raised the flag while their fellow Marines were dying at their feet so that we could have our freedom. That flag is the living symbol of all our freedoms.
Robert W. Spagnole, National Adjutant, American Legion. In reference to the Supreme Court decision *Texas* v. *Johnson*. Quoted in *The Washington Post*, June 22, 1989.

43. There is the National flag. He must be cold, indeed, who can look upon its folds rippling in the breeze without pride of country.... If in a foreign land, the flag is companionship. White is for purity; red, for valor; blue for justice.
Charles Sumner (1811-1874), U.S. Senator (D, R, and Free Soil-MA). Speech, "Are We a Nation?", Nov. 19, 1867.

44. A man may climb Mount Everest for himself, but at the summit he plants his country's flag.
Margaret Thatcher, Prime Minister of Great Britain (Conservative). Quoted in *The Washington Post*, Nov. 25, 1990.

45. The white stripes *[of the American flag should be]* painted black and the stars replaced by the skull and crossbones.
Mark Twain (Samuel Langhorne Clemens) (1835-1910), American writer. Written in opposition to the Spanish-American War, 1898.

46. Our representative is the flag. He is the Republic. He is the United States of America.
Mark Twain. "Diplomatic Pay and Clothes," *Forum*, Mar. 1899.

47. The symbol evokes loyalties to vaguely conceived notions.... The result is that our natures are stirred to suspend all antagonistic impulses.... Symbols acquire ... power to organize the miscellaneous crowd into a smoothly running community.
Alfred North Whitehead (1861-1947), British philosopher and mathematician. *Symbolism: Its Meaning and Effect*, 1927.

48. The flag is the embodiment, not of sentiment, but of history.
Woodrow Wilson (1856-1924), 28th President of the United States (D-NJ). Flag Day speech, June 14, 1915.

49. We meet to celebrate Flag Day because this flag which we honor and under which we serve is the emblem of our unity, our power, our thought and purpose as a nation. It has no other character than that which we give it from generation to generation. The choice is ours.
Woodrow Wilson. *Ibid.*

50. A star for every State, and a State for every star.
Robert C. Winthrop (1809-1894), U.S. Congressman and U.S. Senator (Whig-MA). Address, Boston Common, 1862.

Chapter 34

Food and Nutrition

1. Food: We have more of it and pay less for it than any other country in the world.
   Advertisement, Archer Daniels Midland Company, Feb. 10, 1991.

2. Why be shocked at the drowning of a few if there is no objection to starving a nation?
   William Jennings Bryan (1860-1925), U.S. Secretary of State (D). Question asked of President Wilson when Great Britain began a food blockade against Germany, whose U-boats attacked British civilian liners. 1915.

3. Hunger makes a thief of any man.
   Pearl S. Buck (1892-1973), Nobel Laureate in Literature (United States). *The Good Earth*, 1931.

4. My mother made me eat broccoli. I hate broccoli. I am President of the United States. I will not eat any more broccoli.
   George Bush, 41st President of the United States (R-TX). Mar. 1990.

5. People want to eat. It is that simple.
   Yuri Chernichenko, founder, Russian Peasants' Party. Quoted in *The New York Times*, June 2, 1991.

6. There is no finer investment for any community than putting milk into babies.
   Winston Churchill (1874-1965), Prime Minister of Great Britain (Conservative). Radio broadcast to the nation, Mar. 21, 1943.

7. An empty stomach is not a good political advisor.
   Albert Einstein (1879-1955), Nobel Laureate in Physics (Switzerland). *Cosmic Religion*, 1931.

8. More die in the United States of too much food than too little.
   John Kenneth Galbraith, American economist and U.S. Ambassador to India (D). *The Affluent Society*, 1958.

9. There exists no politician in India daring enough to attempt to explain to the masses that cows can be eaten.
   Indira Gandhi (1917-1984), Prime Minister of India. Statement, 1980.

10. A starving man thinks first of satisfying his hunger before anything else. He will sell his liberty and all for the sake of getting a morsel of food.
    Mohandas K. Gandhi (1869-1948), Indian political and spiritual leader. *Young India*, Mar. 18, 1926.

11. To a man with an empty stomach food is God.
    Mohandas K. Gandhi. Quoted in Edgar Snow, *Journey to the Beginning*, 1958.

12. The human body needs air, water, and food. Only the good Lord makes air and water. Only farmers and ranchers make food.
    Eligio (Kika) de la Garza II, U.S. Congressman (D-TX). Speech, Commodity Club, Washington, DC, June 1990.

13. It's really very simple, Governor. When people are hungry they die. So spare me your politics and tell me what you need and how you're going to get it to these people.
    Robert Geldof, famine relief organizer. Statement to Sudanese regional governor who was using starvation as a political lever. Quoted in *The New York Times*, Jan. 26, 1985.

14. Hunger is not debatable.
    Harry L. Hopkins (1890-1946), U.S. Secretary of Commerce (D); Director, Work Projects Administration; Director, Federal Emergency Relief Administration; and Special Assistant to the President. Quoted in Robert E. Sherwood, *Roosevelt and Hopkins: An Intimate Biography*, 1948.

15. The working class and the employing class have nothing in common. There can be no peace so long as hunger and want are found among millions of working people, and the few who make up the employing class have all the good things of life.
    Constitution, Industrial Workers of the World, June 27, 1905.

16. The war against hunger is truly mankind's war of liberation.
John F. Kennedy (1917-1963), 35th President of the United States (D-MA). Speech, World Food Congress, June 4, 1963.

17. I asked for help and you send me a bulletin. The people of New York cannot feed their children on department bulletins.
Fiorello H. La Guardia (1882-1947), U.S. Congressman (R and Socialist-NY) and Mayor of New York City (R and Fusion Party). Letter to William M. Jardine, U.S. Secretary of Agriculture, asking for an investigation of skyrocketing meat prices. Oct. 14, 1925.

18. Fill the people's bellies and open their hearts.
Lao-tzu (c.604-531 B.C.), Chinese philosopher and founder of Taoism. *Tao Te Ching*.

19. Food is a weapon.
Maxim Litvinov (1876-1951), revolutionist and Commissar of Foreign Affairs, U.S.S.R. Remark to Walter Folger Brown, Riga, Latvia, 1921.

20. You cannot feed the hungry on statistics.
David Lloyd George, 1st Earl of Dwyfor (1863-1945), Prime Minister of Great Britain (Liberal). Tariff Reform speech, House of Commons, 1904.

21. It has been well said that a hungry man is more interested in four sandwiches than four freedoms.
Henry Cabot Lodge, Jr. (1902-1986), U.S. Senator (R-MA), U.S. Ambassador to Vietnam and Germany, and head of American delegation to Paris conference for Vietnam peace negotiations. Jan. 1954.

22. The power of population is indefinitely greater than the power in the earth to produce subsistence for man.
Thomas R. Malthus (1766-1834), British clergyman and political economist. *Essay on the Principle of Population*, 1798.

23. Famine seems to be the last, the most dreadful resource of nature.
Thomas R. Malthus. *Ibid.*

24. A starving man has a right to his neighbor's bread.
Henry Edward Manning (1808-1982), British Roman Catholic cardinal. Quoted in George Seldes, *The Great Quotations*, 1960.

25. We Americans have food in massive oversupply. That oversupply has crushed farm prices. We must dispose of the surpluses in order to strengthen prices, and we should dispose of them by feeding the starving and hungry overseas and the malnourished at home.
John Melcher, U.S. Senator (D-MT). Quoted in *The Washington Post*, Jan. 1, 1989.

26. The next time you feel like complaining, remember that your garbage disposal probably eats better than do 30 percent of the people in this world.
Robert Orben, presidential speech writer (R). Quoted in *Reader's Digest*, Feb. 1979.

27. It is wrong that people like you should be comfortable and well fed while all around you people are starving.
Estelle Sylvia Pankhurst (1882-1960), British suffragist. Quoted in David J. Mitchell, *The Fighting Pankhursts*, 1967.

28. They *[the Russians]* have the Red army but they don't have white potatoes. Can you eat an army?
Shimon Peres, Prime Minister of Israel (Labour). Quoted on CNN, *Waging Peace*, Sept. 16, 1989.

29. Have you ever eaten garbage? Dined on bones sucked dry by strangers' mouths? Bread soaked in the juices of a garbage can?
Adam Clayton Powell (1908-1972), U.S. Congressman (D-NY). *The New York Post*, 1935.

30. Two of the most important duties of a government are to defend its territory and to make sure its people are fed properly.
Derwent Renshaw, agricultural counselor, European Community Mission. In defense of agricultural subsidies. Quoted in *The New York Times*, Mar. 6, 1989.

31. We cannot exist as a little island of well-being in a world where two-thirds of the people go to bed hungry every night.
Anna Eleanor Roosevelt (1884-1962), First Lady and U.S. Delegate to the United Nations. Speech, Democratic Party dinner, Dec. 8, 1959.

32. While it isn't written in the Constitution, nevertheless it is the inherent duty of the federal government to keep its citizens from starvation.
Franklin D. Roosevelt (1882-1945), 32nd President of the United States (D-NY). Quoted in Charles and Mary Beard, *America at Midpassage*, 1939.

33. A hungry people listens not to reason, nor cares for justice, nor is bent by any prayers.
Lucius Annaeus Seneca (The Younger) (4 B.C.-A.D. 65), Roman statesman, dramatist, and philosopher. *De Brevitate Vitae*.

34. Eat less.
Robert A. Taft (1889-1953), U.S. Senator (R-OH). Advice to housewives on how to save money, 1947.

35. Starvation, and not sin, is the parent of modern crime.

Oscar Wilde (1854-1900), Irish writer. Quoted in Alvin Redman, *The Epigrams of Oscar Wilde*, 1954.

36. No one can worship God or love his neighbor on an empty stomach.

Woodrow Wilson (1856-1924), 28th President of the United States (D-NJ). Speech, New York City, 1912.

37. Bolshevism is steadily advancing westward. It cannot be stopped by force, but it can be stopped by food.

Woodrow Wilson. Cable to Sen. George B. Martin (D-KY), Jan. 1919.

Chapter 35

Foreign Aid

1. Since world demand *[for foreign aid]* exceeds our ability to supply, we are going to have to concentrate our emergency assistance in areas where it will be most effective.
   Dean Acheson (1893-1971), U.S. Secretary of State (D). Speech, Cleveland, MS, May 7, 1947.

2. Whatever the amount may be, it is an obligation we cannot escape. It is a part of the obligation that the rich nations of the world, particularly America, must carry out.
   Bernard M. Baruch (1870-1965), Chairman, War Industries Board, and U.S. Delegate to the U.N. Atomic Energy Commission. Letter to President Wilson regarding foreign aid to European nations after World War I, May 7, 1919.

3. We did receive a large amount of aid. Unfortunately, there's not much to show for it. The infrastructure has been depleted.... We would like to see that this time aid can be used honestly.
   Benazir Bhutto, Prime Minister of Pakistan. Interview shortly after taking office. PBS, *MacNeil-Lehrer Report*, Dec. 16, 1988.

4. Obviously there is not money enough in the world to relieve the suffering of the peoples of the underdeveloped areas, but ... there is, for the first time in history, enough knowledge to do the job.
   Jonathan B. Bingham, U.S. Congressman (D-NY). Quoted in Eric F. Goldman, *The Crucial Decade*, 1960.

5. Let it not be said by future historians that in the second decade after World War II, freedom throughout the world died of a balanced budget.
   Chester Bowles (1901-1986), U.S. Undersecretary of State. Quoted in Eric F. Goldman, *The Crucial Decade*, 1960.

6. The answer to too much debt is not more debt; it is less debt.
   William W. Bradley, U.S. Senator (D-NJ). Comment on the practice of making loans to foreign countries to repay the countries' old loans. Interview, PBS, *American Interests*, Mar. 3, 1990.

7. The developing world is poor. It needs capital.
   William W. Bradley. *Ibid.*

8. Foreign aid just doesn't have the constituency that domestic programs do.
   George Bush, 41st President of the United States (R-TX). Press conference, May 8, 1990.

9. Will I lose any aid if I talk?
   José Napoleon Duarte, President of El Salvador. Response when asked what advice he would give the United States on dealing with Panamanian strongman Manuel Noriega. Quoted in *News-week*, May 23, 1988.

10. Foreign aid is like opium. There are withdrawal pains if you remove it.
   John Foster Dulles (1888-1959), U.S. Senator (R-NY) and U.S. Secretary of State. Congressional testimony, 1953.

11. The more money we have to throw around, the better off we're going to be. I think this country doesn't understand its power around the world economically – its ability to buy friends.
   Max Frankel, editor in chief, *The New York Times*. Remark, Apr. 1985.

12. Economic assistance is one of the most effective weapons at our disposal to influence European political events in the direction we desire.
   W. Averell Harriman (1891-1986), Governor of New York (D), U.S. Ambassador-at-Large, and U.S. Secretary of Commerce. Remark to reporters, 1944.

13. Why send money abroad that we all admit we need here at home? Why sacrifice the interests of this country for the benefit of Wall Street?
   William Randolph Hearst (1863-1951), U.S. Congressman (D-NY); founder, Independence League Party; journalist; and publisher. Comment when the British asked for a billion-dollar war loan to be floated by the Morgan Bank. Editorial, Sept. 1915.

14. With every additional shovel of coal, with every additional load of oil that we in Russia obtain through the help of foreign technique, capital will be digging its own grave.

Lev Borisovich Kamenev (1883-1936), Russian Communist leader. Speech, 10th Communist Party Conference, Moscow, Mar. 15, 1921.

15. I feel the happiest when I can light my American cigarettes with Soviet matches.
Mohammed Doud Khan, President of Afghanistan. Quoted in *Newsweek*, July 30, 1973.

16. You cannot preach self-government and liberty to people in a starving land.
Fiorello H. La Guardia (1882-1947), U.S. Congressman (R and Socialist) and Mayor of New York City (R and Fusion Party). In support of food relief as foreign aid. *The Congressional Record*, 65th Congress, 1917-9.

17. I believe that a good portion will in due time be returned, but I am certain that some of it will have to be placed on the profit and loss column of Uncle Sam's books. Let us understand that clearly now and not be deceived later.
Fiorello H. La Guardia. Comment when President Wilson proposed a $3 billion foreign loan bill to the allies after World War I. House debate, 1918.

18. Third World nations will recognize *[their]* debts only so long as they're able to get them rescheduled and have money lent to them.
Richard D. Lamm, Governor of Colorado (D). *Playboy*, Aug. 1984.

19. If we do not watch our step, we shall find the White House en route to England with the Washington Monument as a steering oar.
Emory Scott Land (1879-1971), Admiral, U.S. Navy, and Chief, U.S. Maritime Commission. Expression of concern over the amount of lend-lease and other aid going to England. Quoted in Robert E. Sherwood, *Roosevelt and Hopkins: An Intimate Biography*, 1948.

20. Third World kids are dying today to pay off the debt.
James Madison Leach, U.S. Congressman (D-IA). Interview, PBS, *MacNeil-Lehrer Report*, Mar. 10, 1989.

21. I request that my vote be added in favor of the acceptance of potatoes and arms from the bandits of Anglo-French imperialism.
V. I. Lenin (1870-1924), Premier of the U.S.S.R. Handwritten note, 1917; *Works*, Vol. XXVII.

22. He who helps early helps twice.
Tadeusz Mazowiecki, Prime Minister of Poland. Quoted in *Reader's Digest*, Aug. 1990.

23. We were willing to support almost any scoundrel almost anywhere around the globe provided he was willing to wave an anti-Communist banner.
George S. McGovern, U.S. Congressman and U.S. Senator (D-SD). PBS, *The American Century*, Nov. 21, 1989.

24. Are we Uncle Sam or Uncle Sucker?
George Miller, U.S. Congressman (R-CA). Quoted by Congresswoman Barbara Boxer (D-CA), House debate, Jan. 11, 1991.

25. I would say as emphatically as I can that private enterprise – local and foreign – must respond if the Alliance *[for Progress]* is to succeed.... It must respond by building the factories, the marketing and the service companies which are the manifestations of mature, developed economies. If the private sector fails, then our own public aid programs will have little effect.
Teodoro Moscoso, U.S. Coordinator, Alliance for Progress. Speech, 4th Annual Institute on Private Investments Abroad and Foreign Trade, May 31, 1962.

26. We're a sentimental people. We like a few kind words better than millions of dollars given in a humiliating way.
Gamal Abdel Nasser (1918-1970), President of Egypt. Quoted in *Réalités*, Jan. 1958.

27. I'm opposed to foreign aid. I don't think you buy friends.
T. Boone Pickens, American financier and industrialist. Quoted on PBS, *American Interests*, Oct. 20, 1989.

28. Our foreign policy is an open book – generally a checkbook.
Will Rogers (1879-1935), American humorist. Quoted on PBS, *Will Rogers U.S.A.*, Oct. 3, 1988.

29. Suppose my neighbor's home catches fire, and I have a length of garden hose.
Franklin D. Roosevelt (1882-1945), 32nd President of the United States (D-NY). Remark beginning his proposal for the lend-lease program to provide armaments to Britain in World War II. Press conference, Dec. 17, 1940.

30. The delivery of needed supplies to Britain is imperative. I say this can be done; it must be done; it will be done.
Franklin D. Roosevelt. Radio address, 1941.

31. If you pick up a starving dog and make him prosperous, he will not bite you. That is the principal difference between a dog and a man.
Mark Twain (Samuel Langhorne Clemens) (1835-1910), American writer. *The Tragedy of Pudd'nhead Wilson*, 1894.

32. The English buy peace more than they make it.
Charles Gravier Vergennes (1717-1787), Minister of Foreign Affairs, France. 1782.

33. The supply of words on the world market is plentiful, but the demand is falling.
Lech Walesa, President of Poland, trade unionist, and founder, Solidarity. Address to Congress, Nov. 1989.

34. It seems to me that other parts of the world ought to be concerned about what we are thinking of them instead of what they are thinking about us. After all, we're feeding most of them. And whenever they start rejecting twenty-five cents of each dollar of foreign aid money that we send them, then I'll be concerned about their attitude toward us. But until they reject that twenty-five cents that Southerners pay for foreign aid to these countries, I will never be concerned about their attitude. In the first place, the average man in Africa of Asia doesn't even know where he is, much less where Alabama is.
George C. Wallace, Governor of Alabama (D). May 1963.

35. With God's help, we will lift Shanghai up and up, ever up, until it is just like Kansas City.
Kenneth S. Wherry (1892-1951), U.S. Senator (R-NB). Speech, 1940.

Chapter 36

Foreign Policy

1. OUR FOREIGN POLICY IS ALL LAOSED UP
Bumper sticker, Boston, MA, 1971.

2. In Central America somebody is almost certainly standing around with a large pile of guns, *[and]* the killers tend to win.
Elliott Abrams, U.S. Assistant Secretary of State. Quoted in *The New York Times,* Aug. 14, 1988.

3. This country will never sacrifice humanity in order to carry out any policy.
Dean Acheson (1893-1971), U.S. Secretary of State (D). 1950.

4. The Secretary of State has always stood as much alone as the historian. Required to look far ahead and around him, he measures forces unknown to party managers, and has found Congress more or less hostile since Congress first sat.
Henry Adams (1838-1918), American historian. 1906.

5. The Secretary of State exists only to recognize the existence of a world which Congress would rather ignore... Since the first day the Senate existed, it has always intrigued against the Secretary of State.
Henry Adams. *The Education of Henry Adams,* 1907.

6. Kennedy cooked the soup *[Vietnam]* that Johnson had to eat.
Konrad Adenauer (1876-1967), Chancellor of West Germany. Quoted in *The New York Times,* Jan. 24, 1973.

7. What we have to do in Latin America is learn to raise our own national and regional banners so that our subcontinent doesn't become the ideological battleground of the two superpowers.
Raúl Alfonsín, President of Argentina. Quoted in *Newsweek,* Mar. 10, 1984.

8. A Stevenson with balls
Joseph Alsop (1910-1989), American political columnist. Description of President Kennedy's foreign policy. Quoted in David Halberstam, *The Best and the Brightest,* 1969.

9. We *[the Russians]* are going to do something terrible to you *[America]* – we are going to deprive you of an enemy.
Georgi Arbatrov, Director, Moscow Institute for the Study of the U.S.A. and Canada. Quoted in *Time,* May 23, 1988.

10. The most damning indictment of the United States in Central America is that we have allowed the sterile voices of Marxism-Leninism to claim falsely the mantle of economic justice and hope for ordinary people when it should be carried by the heirs of Thomas Jefferson.
Bernard Aronson, U.S. Assistant Secretary of State. Quoted in *The Washington Post,* Feb. 26, 1989.

11. Mankind is a single body and each nation is a part of that body. We must never say, "What does it matter to me if some part of the world is ailing?" If there is such an illness, we must concern ourselves with it as though we were having that illness.
Kemal Atatürk (1881-1938), 1st President and founder of the Turkish Republic. Quoted in *Atatürk: Creator of Modern Turkey,* 1981.

12. There is no shame in being compelled by force to accept an unjust and undesirable situation. It is shameful to accept such a fact without attempting to prevent it.
Abdul Rahman Azzam, Secretary General of the Arab League. Statement to Abba Eban, 1947.

13. Although the war is over, we are in the midst of a cold war which is getting warmer.
Bernard M. Baruch (1870-1965), Chairman, War Industries Board, and U.S. Delegate to the U.N. Atomic Energy Commission. Testimony, Senate War Investigating Committee, Oct. 24, 1948.

14. We cannot fly from our world duties.
Albert J. Beveridge (1862-1927), U.S. Senator (R-IN) and founder, Progressive League. Senate speech, 1900.

15. We do not believe that good relations with one country precludes good relations with another.
Benazir Bhutto, Prime Minister of Pakistan. PBS, *MacNeil-Lehrer Report*, Dec. 16, 1988.

16. The weak have one weapon: the errors of those who think they are strong.
Georges Bidault (1899-1983), Prime Minister of France. Quoted in *The Observer*, 1962.

17. At this time there was but one among the great nations of the world which adhered to an active and avowed friendship for us. "We desire above all things the maintenance of the American Union as one indivisible nation," was the kindly and always to be remembered greeting that came to us from the Emperor of Russia.
James G. Blaine (1830-1893), U.S. Congressman and U.S. Senator (R-ME). *Twenty Years of Congress: From Lincoln to Garfield*, 1886.

18. There's no such thing as an expert on Russia – only various degrees of ignorance.
Charles E. Bohlen (1904-1974), U.S. Ambassador to the U.S.S.R. Quoted in *The New York Times*, June 3, 1990.

19. The mission of our country is not to make other people like us but to enable them to be free to be themselves.
Daniel Boorstin, American historian and Librarian of Congress. Interview, ABC, *This Week*, Dec. 31, 1989.

20. Congress cannot – nor should it – run foreign policy on a day-to-day basis. That is a truism.
John Brademas, U.S. Congressman (D-IN). Quoted in James L. Sundquist, *The Decline and Resurgence of Congress*, 1981.

21. We should applaud *peristroika* but not pay for it.
William W. Bradley, U.S. Senator (D-NJ). Interview, PBS, *American Interests*, July 21, 1989.

22. When forces hostile to socialism seek to reverse the development of any socialist country ... this becomes the concern of all socialist countries.
Leonid Brezhnev (1906-1982), Premier of the U.S.S.R. Speech, Warsaw, Poland, Nov. 13, 1968 (the Brezhnev Doctrine).

23. This nation is able to legislate for its own people on every question, without waiting for the aid or consent of any other nation on earth.
William Jennings Bryan (1860-1925), U.S. Secretary of State (D). Speech, July 8, 1896.

24. In a democracy the people are entitled to determine the ends or general aims of foreign policy.
James Bryce (1838-1922), British Ambassador to the United States. *Modern Democracies*, 1921.

25. It is important that we get our people back *[from Iran]*, but your greater responsibility is to protect the honor and dignity of our country and its foreign policy interests.
Zbigniew Brzezinski, U.S. Secretary of State and National Security Advisor (D). Comment to President Carter, Nov. 9, 1979.

26. We have a tendency in America to deal with foreign affairs on a day-by-day basis. We are so saturated with facts that we do not look at a longer, broader picture.
Zbigniew Brzezinski. Interview, PBS, *Firing Line*, July 30, 1989.

27. Americans don't stay where they're not wanted.
McGeorge Bundy, presidential assistant for national security (D). Interview, PBS, *America's Century*, Nov. 1989.

28. A wise and salutary neglect *[should be his Majesty's policy toward the American colonies]*.
Edmund Burke (1729-1797), British statesman. Speech on conciliation with America, Mar. 22, 1775.

29. You do not build a foreign policy based on one man.
George Bush, 41st President of the United States (R-TX). Interview with David Frost, PBS, Sept. 5, 1989.

30. We should not conduct a war of nerves to achieve strategic ends.
James F. Byrnes (1879-1972), U.S. Congressman (D), U.S. Senator, U.S. Supreme Court Justice, and U.S. Secretary of State. Comment on George F. Kennan's "containment" policy memorandum, 1946.

31. There is no reason why we should not have peaceful relations with the world if we cease playing the role of international Meddlesome Mattie.
Arthur Capper (1865-1951), Governor of Kansas and U.S. Senator (R). Statement, 1941.

32. The core of détente *[with the U.S.S.R.]* is the reduction in arms.
Jimmy Carter, 39th President of the United States (D-GA). Apr. 1976.

33. Under Nixon-Ford there evolved a secretive "Lone Ranger" foreign policy – a one-man international adventure. This is not appropriate.
Jimmy Carter. June 1976.

34. Because of the greatness of the Shah, Iran is an island of stability in the Middle East.
Jimmy Carter. Dec. 31, 1977.

35. Our fear of communism led us to embrace any dictator that joined us in that fear.
Jimmy Carter. PBS, *America's Century*, Nov. 1989.

36. The *[foreign]* policy of the United States is modeled on interventionism and aggression. It is logical that we should always be very suspicious.
Fidel Castro, Premier of Cuba. Interview, *Playboy*, Jan. 1967.

37. It is always best and safest to count on nothing from America but words.
Neville Chamberlain (1869-1940), Prime Minister of Great Britain (Conservative). Quoted in David Brinkley, *Washington Goes to War*, 1988.

38. I would guess that he *[Soviet Pres. Mikhail Gorbachev]* would ultimately fail – that is to say, that he will not be able to reform the Soviet economy. And when that happens, he's likely to be replaced by somebody who will be far more hostile *[to the United States]*.
Richard B. Cheney, U.S. Congressman (R-WY), White House Chief of Staff, and U.S. Secretary of Defense. PBS, *Evans & Novak*, Apr. 29, 1989.

39. Do not criticize your government when out of the country. Never cease to do so when at home.
Winston Churchill (1874-1965), Prime Minister of Great Britain (Conservative). Attributed.

40. That old town clerk *[Prime Minister Neville Chamberlain]*, looking at foreign affairs through the wrong end of a municipal drainpipe.
Winston Churchill. After Munich, 1938.

41. I cannot forecast to you the action of Russia. It is a riddle wrapped in a mystery inside an enigma; but perhaps there is a key. That key is Russian national interest.
Winston Churchill. Radio address, BBC, Oct. 1, 1939.

42. All we can do is apply the physical stimuli which we have at our disposal to bring about a change of mind in these recalcitrant persons. Of this you may be sure: we shall continue to operate on the Italian donkey at both ends, with a carrot and a stick.
Winston Churchill. Response when asked how the collapsing Italy should be treated. Press conference, Washington, DC, May 25, 1943.

43. From Stettin in the Baltic to Trieste in the Adriatic, an iron curtain has descended across the continent.
Winston Churchill. Speech, Westminster College, Fulton, MO, Mar. 5, 1946.

44. The reason for having diplomatic relations *[with Communist China]* is not to confer a compliment, but to secure a convenience.... British policy has always been that you recognize when ... government truly has control. It's not a question of whether you like them or not.
Winston Churchill. Speech in Parliament, Nov. 17, 1949.

45. The price of greatness is responsibility.
Winston Churchill. Quoted in *Forbes*, Jan. 23, 1989.

46. To disregard what the world thinks of us is not only arrogant but utterly shameless.
Marcus Tullius Cicero (106-43 B.C.), Roman statesman and writer. *De Officiis*.

47. War is regarded as nothing but the continuation of state policy with other means.
Karl von Clausewitz (1780-1831), Prussian general and military writer. Preface, *On War*, 1833.

48. If you wish to avoid foreign collision, you had better abandon the ocean.
Henry Clay (1777-1852), U.S. Congressman (R and Whig-KY), U.S. Senator, Speaker of the House, and U.S. Secretary of State. Speech, House of Representatives, Jan. 22, 1812.

49. I am firm in my conviction that there is no calamity which a great nation can invite which equals that which follows from a supine submission to wrong and injustice, and the consequent loss of national self-respect and honor, beneath which are shielded and defended a people's safety and greatness.
Grover Cleveland (1837-1908), 22nd and 24th President of the United States (D-NY). Statement on the Venezuela boundary dispute, which widened the scope of the Monroe Doctrine. 1888.

50. The Constitution is an invitation to struggle for the privilege of directing American foreign policy.
Edward S. Corwin (1878-1963), American constitutional scholar. *The President: Office and Powers*, 1940.

51. Boldness, more boldness, and always boldness, and France is saved.
Georges-Jacques Danton (1759-1794), French revolutionary. Speech, National Assembly, Aug. 1792.

52. Congress has a constitutional right to an authoritative voice in declaring and prescribing the foreign policy of the United States ... and it is the constitutional duty of the President to respect that policy.
Henry W. Davis (1817-1865), U.S. Congressman (American Party and Unconditional Unionist-MD). House resolution, passed Dec. 21, 1865.

53. Isolationism has been a calamity.
Jean-Pascal Delamuraz, President of Switzerland. Quoted in Malachi Martin, *The Keys of This Blood*, 1990.

54. Foreign policy is always a sticking point between Congress and the executive.
David Demarest, presidential assistant (R). Symposium, "The Press and a Divided Government," National Press Foundation, Washington, DC, Dec. 6, 1989.

55. The only thing wrong with NATO *[North Atlantic Treaty Organization]* is that we don't belong to it.
Jiri Dienstbier, Foreign Minister of Czechoslovakia. Quoted in *The Washington Post*, June 17, 1990.

56. You never say what you're not going to do.
Christopher J. Dodd, U.S. Congressman and U.S. Senator (D-CT). Remark on foreign policy announcements and statements. Interview, ABC, *This Week*, May 14, 1989.

57. The policy of the United States does not flow from transitory considerations.
John Foster Dulles (1888-1959), U.S. Senator (R-NY) and U.S. Secretary of State. Remark, Feb. 16, 1957.

58. Jesus teaches us that nothing is unforgivable.
John Foster Dulles. On normalization of relations with Japan. Quoted in Leonard Mosley, *Dulles*, 1978.

59. The government of Israel is not an aviary.
Abba Eban, Foreign Secretary of Israel (Labor) and Ambassador to the United Nations. Response to reporters when asked if his government's policy was "hawk" or "dove." New York City, July 8, 1967.

60. In most nations, public opinion is in revolt against foreign policy.
Abba Eban. *An Autobiography*, 1977.

61. We shall never acquiesce in the enslavement of any people in order to purchase fancied gain for ourselves.
Dwight D. Eisenhower (1890-1969), 34th President of the United States (R-KS). Comment on agreements such as those at Yalta. Annual message to Congress, Feb. 1953.

62. Any nation's right to form a government and an economic system of its own choosing is *inalienable*.... Any nation's attempt to dictate to other nations their form of government is *indefensible*.
Dwight D. Eisenhower. Apr. 16, 1953.

63. You have broader considerations that might follow what you would call the "falling domino" principle. You have a row of dominoes set up, you knock over the first one, and what will happen to the last one is the certainty that it will go over very quickly. So you have the beginning of a disintegration that would have the most profound influences.
Dwight D. Eisenhower. Explanation as to why Indochina should not be allowed to fall to the Communists. Press conference, Washington, DC, Apr. 7, 1954.

64. Nothing guides Russian policy so much as a desire for friendship with the United States.
Dwight D. Eisenhower. Statement at the end of World War II. Quoted in Lawrence Wittner, *Rebels Against War*, 1969.

65. America should affirm and establish that in no instance should the guns go in advance of the perfect right.
Ralph Waldo Emerson (1803-1882), American writer. *Journals*, May 1866.

66. Make Latin America a partner, not a peon.
Paul Erdman, American economist. "How to Solve the Problems of the Reagan Legacy," *Manhattan,inc.*, Apr. 1989.

67. If we find what we need *[arms]* among friendly nations and if they give us what we ask, they do so for money. We are not getting anything for free. So, if things become complicated with a certain country, we will find other countries, regardless of whether they are Eastern or Western.
Fahd, King of Saudi Arabia. Quoted in *The New York Times*, July 27, 1988.

68. When you're dealing with the Middle East, two thousand years is the normal wait for something to happen.
Marlin Fitzwater, White House spokesman (R). Quoted in *Newsweek*, Nov. 27, 1989.

69. This country is not looking for prestige. It has all it can use. It is not looking for power. It has, likewise, all that it knows how to use .... *[But]* are we willing to live behind a Maginot Line or a Great Wall of China here on the North American continent, and trade and travel in the rest of the world only as permitted by a stronger power than we are?

Ralph E. Flanders (1880-1970), U.S. Senator (R-VT). Argument against isolationism. Senate speech, 1948.

70. A *[foreign]* government is to be judged by what it does for people. It is to be assisted or combatted with reference to people, and is to be approached through those people.

Ralph E. Flanders. *Senator from Vermont*, 1961.

71. But we cannot expect the Soviet Union to show restraint in the face of United States weakness or irresolution. As long as I am President, we will not permit détente to become a license to fish in troubled waters. Détente must be, and I trust will be, a two-way street.

Gerald R. Ford, 38th President of the United States (R-MI). Message to Congress, Apr. 12, 1975.

72. There is no Soviet domination in Eastern Europe, and there never will be under a Ford administration.

Gerald R. Ford. Televised debate with presidential candidate Jimmy Carter, Oct. 6, 1976.

73. As long as we can outproduce the world, can control the sea and can strike inland with the atomic bomb, we can assume certain risks otherwise unacceptable in an effort to restore world trade, to restore the balance of power – military power – and to eliminate some of the conditions which breed war.

James V. Forrestal (1892-1949), Admiral, U.S. Navy, U.S. Secretary of the Navy, and U.S. Secretary of Defense. Letter to J. Chandler Gurney, Chairman, Senate Armed Services Committee, Dec. 8, 1947.

74. Strong nations cooperate to the harmony and wealth of the world. Weak nations are a perpetual cause of disturbances and perils.

Anatole France (Jacques Anatole François Thibault) (1844-1924), Nobel Laureate in Literature (France). *Penguin Island*, 1908.

75. It is never easy to play "chicken" when you face a driver alone in his car while you have passengers in the front and back seats who tend to grab for the steering wheel whenever a collision appears imminent.

Thomas L. Friedman, American journalist. On the problem for a democratic leader dealing with a dictator in an international crisis. *The New York Times*, Dec. 16, 1990.

76. Our foreign policy is inadequate, outmoded, and misdirected.... If we go on as we are, soon – in the fashion of the cat on a hot tin roof – we shall be skipping from one crisis to another all over the globe, unable to get our footing anywhere.

J. William Fulbright, U.S. Senator (D-AR). 1958.

77. For foreign policy it is necessary to have men who inspire confidence.

John Kenneth Galbraith, American economist and U.S. Ambassador to India (D). *The Triumph*.

78. Any President must depend upon congressional support in order to implement his foreign policy, for Congress has power to regulate foreign commerce, to raise armies and maintain navies, to lay and collect taxes for the common defense, and to declare war.

George B. Galloway (1898-1967), historian, Library of Congress. *History of the United States House of Representatives*, 1962.

79. A great country worthy of the name does not have any friends.

Charles de Gaulle (1890-1970), President of France. Quoted in *Time*, May 28, 1965.

80. There are two groups of people in the world, the Anglo-Saxons and the Soviets, who have been stockpiling nuclear weapons. France will not accept a position of permanent and massive inferiority.

Charles de Gaulle. Quoted on PBS, *War and Peace in the Nuclear Age*, Feb. 13, 1989.

81. No nation can ever be safe in the position it holds among nations, however great and however imposing, unless it recognizes those principles of justice and equality which bind together the nations of the world.

William E. Gladstone (1809-1898), Prime Minister of Great Britain (Liberal). Speech, Dec. 9, 1879.

82. War is but an instrument of international policy.

Barry M. Goldwater, U.S. Senator (R-AZ). Speech, Apr. 28, 1955.

83. I'd drop a low-yield atomic bomb on Chinese supply lines in North Vietnam.

Barry M. Goldwater. Quoted in *Newsweek*, May 20, 1963.

84. I have always favored withdrawing recognition from Russia.

Barry M. Goldwater. Quoted in *U.S. News & World Report*, Sept. 2, 1963.

85. There is one phase of our competition which should be brought under control – competing with each other in fueling the arms race in the Third World.... Most of these countries are desperately poor, and they need economic assistance

far more than they need additional arms.... Even though these are only non-nuclear arms, they are instrumentalities of war, and small wars always have the potential of escalating into nuclear wars.
Mikhail Gorbachev, Premier of the U.S.S.R. *Foreign Affairs*, Fall 1985.

86. England and the United States are natural allies, and should be the best of friends.
Ulysses S. Grant (1822-1885), 18th President of the United States (R). *Personal Memoirs*, 1885.

87. Nations of great genius exhibit great patience.
William H. Grey III, U.S. Congressman (D-PA). House debate, Jan. 12, 1991.

88. Deutschland über Allah.
Philip Guedalla (1889-1944), British writer. In reference to Germany's influence in Turkey prior to World War II. *The Hundred Years*, 1936.

89. *[British Foreign Minister Lord Carrington is a]* duplicitous bastard. European friends, just plain cowardly. British, lying through their teeth.
Alexander M. Haig, General, U.S. Army, U.S. Secretary of State, and White House Chief of Staff (R). Comment to reporters, 1982.

90. Military security and a policy of détente are not contradictory but complementary.
Pierre Harmel, Foreign Minister of Belgium. Report, North Atlantic Treaty Organization, 1968.

91. We must recognize that our objectives and the Kremlin's objectives are irreconcilable. The Kremlin wants to promote Communist dictatorships controlled from Moscow, whereas we want as far as possible to see a world of governments responsive to the will of the people.
W. Averell Harriman (1891-1986), Governor of New York (D), U.S. Secretary of Commerce, and U.S. Ambassador-at-Large. Press conference, 1945.

92. No foreign policy will stick unless the American people are behind it. And unless Congress understands it the American people aren't going to understand it.
W. Averell Harriman. Testimony, Senate Judiciary Committee, 1971.

93. We Americans have no commission from God to police the world.
Benjamin Harrison (1833-1901), 23rd President of the United States (R-IN). 1888.

94. The enthusiasm for colonies is dead.
David Haskins, Treasurer, British Anti-Imperialist League. Statement, 1908.

95. What happens in the Philippines, Japan, and Korea has a greater impact on us than most events in Massachusetts.
S. I. Hayakawa (1906-1992), U.S. Senator (R-CA). Quoted in *Newsweek*, Sept. 19, 1979.

96. We recognized the imperial government of Russia, but when Russia secured a democratic government *[after the Revolution]* we have so far not recognized it.
William Randolph Hearst (1863-1951), U.S. Congressman (D-NY); founder, Independence League Party; journalist; and publisher. Telegram to Congressmen, 1918.

97. There are bad people all over the place, and we really can't have a war each time just to get rid of one of these bad people.
Edward Heath, Prime Minister of Great Britain (Conservative). Testimony on Iraq crisis, U.S. House Armed Services Committee, Dec. 19, 1990.

98. It was not lust for honor, nor a seeking after fame, nor blind obstinacy, nor power-seeking that demanded of the *Führer [Adolf Hitler]* our resignation from the League of Nations, but simply the clear determination to be unconditionally responsible to ourselves in enduring and mastering our own destiny.
Martin Heidegger (1899-1976), German philosopher. Speech to German university professors, Leipzig, Nov. 11, 1933.

99. You can't deal with rattlesnakes. You can't deal with Communist governments.
Jesse Helms, U.S. Senator (R-NC). Statement, June 5, 1989.

100. Many Western officials are comfortable with confrontation, and discount or ignore the rising risks and costs of continued arms modernization. They would be intellectually and programmatically bereft without the focal point of a major "enemy."... Can the West get over its need to have an enemy?
Townsend Hoops, Director, American Committee on U.S.-Soviet Relations. *The New York Times*, Sept. 2, 1988.

101. If the world is to keep the peace, then we must keep the peace with dictatorships as well as popular governments.
Herbert Hoover (1874-1964), 31st President of the United States (R-IA). Statement to reporters, 1938.

102. Our Russian policy must not be dictated by people who have already made up their minds there is no possibility of working with the Russians and

that our interests are bound to conflict and ultimately lead to war. From my point of view, this is an untenable position and can but lead to disaster.

Harry L. Hopkins (1890-1946), U.S. Secretary of Commerce (D); Director, Work Projects Administration; and Special Assistant to the President. Quoted in Robert E. Sherwood, *Roosevelt and Hopkins: An Intimate Biography*, 1948.

103. Never insult an alligator until after you have crossed the river.

Cordell Hull (1871-1955), U.S. Congressman and U.S. Senator (D-TN), U.S. Secretary of State, and Nobel Laureate in Peace. Advice to Pres. Franklin D. Roosevelt on dealing with Benito Mussolini, 1934.

104. Public opinion has controlled foreign policy in all democracies.

Cordell Hull. 1936.

105. Congress cannot and should not run foreign policy.

Hubert H. Humphrey (1911-1978), Vice President of the United States and U.S. Senator (D-MN). Senate debate, 1976.

106. Protectionism is the ally of isolationism, and isolationism is the Dracula of American foreign policy.

William G. Hyland, National Security Advisor. Speech, Washington University, St. Louis, MO. Quoted in *The New York Times*, May 17, 1987.

107. Keep the windows open to the East.

Hypatia (370-415), Greek philosopher. Quoted in Elbert Hubbard, *Little Journeys to the Homes of Great Teachers*, 1908.

108. The best politics is no politics.

Henry M. Jackson (1912-1983), U.S. Congressman and U.S. Senator (D-WA). Comment on foreign policy. Speech, American Bar Association, Chicago, IL, Feb. 3, 1980.

109. The very nature of executive decisions as to foreign policy is political, not judicial.

Robert H. Jackson (1892-1954), U.S. Attorney General (D) and U.S. Supreme Court Justice. *Chicago and S. Airlines* v. *Waterman S. S. Corp.*, 1948.

110. The only way we want to give them *[the Iranians]* arms is dropping them from the bay of a B-1 bomber.

William Janklow, Governor of South Dakota (R). In reference to the Iran-Contra arms scandal. Quoted in *Newsweek*, Mar. 16, 1987.

111. The President being the only channel of communication between this country and foreign nations, it is from him alone that foreign nations or their agents are to learn what is or has been the will of the nation.

Thomas Jefferson (1743-1826), 3rd President of the United States (Democratic Republican-VA). Letter to Edmund Genet, Minister of the French Republic, 1793.

112. Peace, commerce, and honest friendship with all nations – entangling alliances with none.

Thomas Jefferson. First inaugural address, Mar. 4, 1801.

113. We consider the interests of Cuba, Mexico, and ours as the same, and that the object of both must be to exclude all European influence from this hemisphere.

Thomas Jefferson. Letter to William C. Claiborne, Oct. 1808.

114. I hope no American patriot will ever lose sight of the essential policy of interdicting in the seas and territories of both Americas the ferocious and sanguinary contests of Europe.

Thomas Jefferson. Letter to William Short, Aug. 4, 1820.

115. The whole responsibility for an honest, realistic American foreign policy ... rests on the Congress. Congress lays down policy, by law; and the President is supposed to carry it out.

William E. Jenner (1908-1985), U.S. Senator (R-IN). Senate debate, Mar. 19, 1951.

116. *[There are]* some Nervous Nellies ... who will ... break ranks under the strain *[of the Vietnam war]*. And some will turn on their own leaders and their own country, and on our own fighting men.

Lyndon B. Johnson (1908-1973), 36th President of the United States (D-TX). In reference to Sen. J. William Fulbright. May 17, 1966.

117. Shit, man, he's the only boy we've got out there.

Lyndon B. Johnson. Expressing caution about support of a coup against President Diem of South Vietnam. Quoted in Nathan Miller, *Spying for America*, 1989.

118. There could be no greater act of madness than to imagine that we can reform Communists by marrying them.

Walter H. Judd, U.S. Congressman (R-MN). Speech, Taft School, Watertown, CT, 1953.

119. We've had administrations where our State Department was an outpost of the British Foreign Office for altogether too long.

Walter H. Judd. Quoted in Leonard Mosley, *Dulles*, 1978.

120. The U.S. should not recognize a governmental entity which is the agent of a group which hold it as their mission to bring about the overthrow of the existing political, economic, and social order throughout the world.

Frank B. Kellogg (1856-1937), U.S. Senator (R-MN), U.S. Ambassador to Great Britain, and U.S. Secretary of State. Statement justifying U.S. refusal to recognize the Soviet government during the 1920's. Quoted in Foster Rhea Dulles, *The United States Since 1865*, 1959.

121. We have historically avoided taking a position on border disputes or internal organization of OPEC *[Organization of Petroleum Exporting Countries]* deliberations, but we have certainly, as have all administrations, resoundingly called for the peaceful settlement of disputes and differences in the area.

John Kelly, U.S. Assistant Secretary of State for Near Eastern and South Asian Affairs. Testimony, House Foreign Affairs Subcommittee on Europe and the Middle East two days before Iraq invaded Kuwait. July 31, 1990.

122. It's tough to tell the Third World how to do things and then have a Third World economy in the Bronx and in our barrios.

Jack F. Kemp, U.S. Congressman and U.S. Secretary of Housing and Urban Development (R-NY). Interview, PBS, *Firing Line*, July 22, 1989.

123. In a sensitive matter, where its own ignorance could scarcely have been greater, Congress would have been better advised to leave the conduct of foreign policy in the hands of those who have been constitutionally charged with it.

George F. Kennan, U.S. Ambassador to the U.S.S.R. and Yugoslavia. *Memoirs: 1950-1963*.

124. The best thing we can do if we want the Russians to let us be Americans is let the Russians be Russian.

George F. Kennan. Quoted on PBS, *U.S.-Soviet Relations: The First Fifty Years*, 1984.

125. I am frankly of the belief that no amount of American military assistance in Indo-China can conquer an enemy which is everywhere, and at the same time nowhere, an enemy of the people which has the sympathy and covert support of the people.

John F. Kennedy (1917-1963), 35th President of the United States (D-MA). Senate speech, Apr. 6, 1954.

126. Every time a country, regardless of how far away from our borders ... passes behind the Iron Curtain, the security of the United States is thereby endangered.

John F. Kennedy. Campaign speech, 1960.

127. It is the President alone who must make the major decisions of our foreign policy.

John F. Kennedy. Campaign speech, Jan. 14, 1960.

128. Let every nation know, whether it wishes us well or ill, that we shall pay any price, bear any burden, meet any hardship, support any friend, oppose any foe to assure the survival and the success of liberty.

John F. Kennedy. Inaugural address, Jan. 20, 1961.

129. Geography has made us neighbors. History has made us friends. Economics has made us partners, and necessity has made us allies. Those whom God has so joined together, let no man put asunder.

John F. Kennedy. Address to Canadian Parliament, Ottawa, May 17, 1961.

130. Domestic policy can only defeat us; foreign policy can kill us.

John F. Kennedy. Quoted in Arthur M. Schlesinger, Jr., *The Imperial Presidency*, 1973.

131. We, too, are giants. You want to threaten – we will answer threats with threats.

Nikita S. Khrushchev (1894-1971), Premier of the U.S.S.R. Remark to Vice President Richard M. Nixon, Moscow, 1955.

132. You don't know anything about Communism – except fear.

Nikita S. Khrushchev. Remark to Vice President Richard M. Nixon, Moscow, 1959.

133. A government is not legitimate merely because it exists.

Jeane J. Kirkpatrick, U.S. Ambassador to the United Nations (R). In reference to Nicaragua's Sandinista government. Quoted in *Time*, June 17, 1985.

134. Peace may be the extension of war by other means.

Jeane J. Kirkpatrick. *The New York Post*, Aug. 15, 1988.

135. The Communist campaign, finely attuned to prevailing fears, almost imperceptibly shifted the primary concern away from Soviet aggression – the real security problem – to the immorality of

the use of nuclear weapons, which happened to be the most effective way of resisting it.

Henry M. Kissinger, U.S. Secretary of State and National Security Advisor (R). *Nuclear Weapons and Foreign Policy*, 1957.

136. All governments ... sometimes do strange things.

Henry M. Kissinger. Remark to Abba Eban, Oct. 1973.

137. I believed that I should do what I could to maintain the dignity of American values and to give Americans some pride in the conduct of their affairs.

Henry M. Kissinger. Press conference, June 10, 1974.

138. Most Communist governments are failing sooner or later anyway.

Henry M. Kissinger. NBC, *Meet the Press*, July 31, 1988.

139. I will not have died unfulfilled if it does not occur in my lifetime.

Henry M. Kissinger. His opinion on the desirability of German unification. Interview, ABC, *This Week*, Nov. 19, 1989.

140. The art of foreign policy is to help guide the inevitable.

Henry M. Kissinger. PBS, *The Secretaries of State*, Nov. 30, 1989.

141. I don't believe foreign policy is about altruism.

Henry M. Kissinger. *Ibid.*

142. We should not pretend that we can remake the domestic structures of governments all over the world.

Henry M. Kissinger. Interview, ABC, *This Week*, Apr. 22, 1990.

143. Americans must not be given the impression that they have a duty to go to war against every evil leader in the world and against every transgression of the international order.

Henry M. Kissinger. *The Washington Post*, Nov. 11, 1990.

144. The purpose of American forces overseas is not to fight prolonged conventional wars but to share the risks of our allies.

Stanley Kober, American foreign policy analyst and writer. *The Washington Post*, July 11, 1988.

145. War and peace are not a city's business – only the process of living.

Teddy Kollek, Mayor of Jerusalem, Israel. Interview, CBS, *60 Minutes*, Oct. 14, 1990.

146. The expression "positive neutrality" is a contradiction in terms. There can no more be positive neutrality than there can be a vegetarian tiger.

V. K. Krishna Menon (1897-1974), Foreign Minister of India. Quoted in *The New York Times*, Oct. 18, 1960.

147. The great nations have always acted like gangsters, and the small nations like prostitutes.

Stanley Kubrick, American film director. *The Guardian*, June 5, 1963.

148. *Glasnost* has given us all a headache.

Yevgeny Lanfang, deputy editor, *Moscow News*. Quoted in *Newsweek*, May 2, 1988.

149. If you want our aid, you must call us to your Councils.

Wilfred Laurier (1841-1919), Prime Minister of Canada (Liberal). Remark to Prime Minister Joseph Chamberlain of Great Britain during the Boer War, 1902.

150. We must be ready to employ trickery, deceit, lawbreaking, withholding and concealing truth.

V. I. Lenin (1870-1924), Premier of the U.S.S.R. Quoted in Max F. Eastman, *Reflections on the Failure of Socialism*, 1955.

151. Undertaking to explain our foreign policy in terms of our public opinion is to explain one mystery in terms of another.

Walter Lippmann (1889-1974), American political columnist. 1952.

152. Lunacy is always distressing, but sometimes it is dangerous; and when you get it manifested in the head of state, and it has become the policy of a great empire, it is about time that it should be ruthlessly put away.

David Lloyd George, 1st Earl of Dwyfor (1863-1945), Prime Minister of Great Britain (Liberal). Speech, Sept. 19, 1914.

153. Personally, I would have dealt with the Soviets as the de facto government of Russia. So would President Wilson. But we both agreed that we could not carry to that extent our colleagues at the *[Versailles]* Congress, nor the public opinion of our countries which was frightened by Bolshevik violence and feared its spread.

David Lloyd George. *The Truth About Peace Treaties*, 1938.

154. The United States is the world's best hope; but if you fetter her in the interests and quarrels of

other nations, if you tangle her in the intrigues of Europe, you will destroy her power for good and endanger her very existence.

Henry Cabot Lodge (1850-1924), U.S. Congressman and U.S. Senator (R-MA). Statement of opposition to the covenant of a League of Nations Covenant proposed by Pres. Wilson. Senate speech, Aug. 12, 1919.

155. Our foreign policy doesn't follow events in the world. It follows the dictates of Congress.

Richard G. Lugar, U.S. Senator (R-IN). Interview, PBS, *MacNeil-Lehrer News Hour*, Jan. 25, 1990.

156. I don't care if he's got two horns and a tail. As long as he's anti-Communist, we can use him.

Douglas MacArthur (1880-1964), General, U.S. Army, and Supreme Commander, U.N. forces in Korea. In reference to the involvement of Chiang Kai-shek in the Korean War. Quoted in Courtney Whitney, *MacArthur: His Rendezvous with History*, 1955.

157. Europe is a dying system. It is worn out and run down, and will become an economic and industrial hegemony of Soviet Russia.... The lands touching the Pacific with thirty billions of inhabitants will determine the course of history for the next ten thousand years!

Douglas MacArthur. Quoted by Arthur Spanier, *The Truman-MacArthur Controversy*, 1959.

158. Once the bear's hug has got you, it is apt to be for keeps.

Harold Macmillan (1894-1986), Prime Minister of Great Britain (Conservative). Quoted in *New York Herald Tribune*, Oct. 15, 1961.

159. The management of foreign relations appears to be the most susceptible of abuse of all the trusts committed to a government.

James Madison (1751-1836), 4th President of the United States (Democratic Republican-VA). Letter to Thomas Jefferson, May 13, 1798.

160. The bloke who ends up sitting in the White House partially controls what we *[the British]* get up to.

John Mahoney, foreign news editor, BBC. Quoted in *USA Today*, Oct. 11, 1988.

161. People of the world, unite and defeat the U.S. aggressors and all their running dogs! People of the world, be courageous, dare to fight, defy difficulties and advance wave upon wave. Then the whole world will belong to the people. Monsters of all kinds shall be destroyed.

Mao Tse-tung (1893-1976), Chairman, Communist Party of China. "People of the World, Unite and Defeat the U.S. Aggressors and All Their Lackeys," speech supporting the people of the Congo against U.S. aggression, Nov. 28, 1964.

162. Our policy *[the Marshall Plan]* is not directed against any country or doctrine, but is directed against hunger, poverty, desperation and chaos. Its purpose should be the revival of a working economy in the world so as to permit the emergence of political and economic conditions in which free institutions can exist.

George C. Marshall (1880-1959), General, U.S. Army, U.S. Secretary of State (D), and U.S. Secretary of Defense. Commencement speech, Harvard University, Cambridge, MA, June 5, 1947.

163. I like Germany so much that I want there to be two of them.

François Mauriac, French writer. Quoted in *The New York Times*, Nov. 9, 1989.

164. Great prosperity is coming. It will be tremendously increased if we can extend reasonable credit to our customers.... To maintain our prosperity we must finance it.

William Gibbs McAdoo (1863-1941), U.S. Senator (D-CA) and U.S. Secretary of the Treasury. Letter to Pres. Wilson requesting American loans to the allies to purchase American arms, Aug. 21, 1915.

165. We need Hawaii as much and a good deal more than we did California; it is Manifest Destiny.

William McKinley (1843-1901), 25th President of the United States (R-OH). Remark when submitting to Congress a treaty to annex the Hawaiian islands. June 16, 1897.

166. *[Russia is]* the most realistic regime in the world – no ideals.

Golda Meir (1898-1978), Prime Minister of Israel (Labour). Oct. 7, 1969.

167. We self-righteously expect all others to admire us for our democracy and our traditions. We are so smug about our superiority, we fail to see our own glaring faults, such as prejudice and poverty amidst affluence.

Patsy Takemoto Mink, U.S. Congresswoman (D-HI). Speech, National Association for Student Affairs, Atlanta, GA, May 1972.

168. A strong Germany is an indispensable condition for a durable peace in Europe.

Vyacheslav Mikhailovich Molotov (1890-1990), Foreign Minister, U.S.S.R. Speech, Fifth Extraordinary Session of the Supreme Soviet, Moscow, Oct. 31, 1939.

169. Mr. President, we need to be strong and firm, but that doesn't mean you have to commit political suicide.

Walter F. Mondale, Vice President of the United States and U.S. Senator (D-MN). Advice to President Carter, who imposed an American grain export embargo against the U.S.S.R. after the invasion of Afghanistan. Jan. 11, 1980.

170. The American continents ... are henceforth not to be considered as subjects for future colonization by any European powers.... We should consider any attempt *[by European countries]* to extend their system to any portion of this hemisphere as dangerous to our peace and safety. With the existing colonies or dependencies of any European Power we have not interfered, and shall not interfere. But with the governments who have declared their independence, and maintained it ... we could not view any interposition for the purpose of oppressing them, or controlling, in any other manner, their destiny, by any European Power, in any other light than as the manifestations of an unfriendly disposition toward the United States.

James Monroe (1758-1831), 5th President of the United States (Democratic Republican-VA). Message to Congress, Dec. 2, 1823 (the Monroe Doctrine).

171. *Perestroika* and *glasnost* mean more nationalism, more fascism.

Gracie Moreno, organizer, Progressive Labor Party (Communist Party U.S.A.). Quoted in *The Washington Post*, Apr. 3, 1990.

172. We are pursuing neither law nor peace in Southeast Asia. We are not even pursuing freedom.

Wayne L. Morse (1900-1974), U.S. Senator (R and Ind-OR). Senate debate, 1966.

173. A dangerous place.

Daniel P. Moynihan, Chief American Delegate to the United Nations and U.S. Senator (D-NY). In reference to the United Nations. *The New York Times*, Aug. 7, 1988.

174. The Constitution provided an invitation to the President and Congress to struggle for the privilege of directing American foreign policy.

Daniel P. Moynihan. Quoted in *The New York Times*, Nov. 9, 1989.

175. International law seeks to avoid the use of force but does not preclude it.

Daniel P. Moynihan. Speech, National Press Club, Washington, DC, Mar. 1990.

176. The problem of indebtedness is part of a larger and more comprehensive problem, namely the existing imbalances in the international economic order.

Hosni Mubarak. President of Egypt. Speech, United Nations, Sept. 30, 1989.

177. Isn't it better to be talking about the relative merits of our washing machines than the relative strength of our rockets?

Richard M. Nixon, 37th President of the United States (R-CA). Remark to Nikita Krushchev, Moscow, 1955.

178. A weak *[foreign]* policy is a war policy; a strong *[foreign]* policy is a peace policy.

Richard M. Nixon. Statement on the landing of U.S. Marines in Lebanon. July 15, 1958.

179. America will not tolerate being pushed around by anybody, anyplace.

Richard M. Nixon. Presidential nomination acceptance speech, Republican National Convention, Chicago, IL, July 27, 1960.

180. Now I know there are those who say the domino theory is obsolete. They haven't talked to the dominoes. They should talk to the Thais, to the Indonesians, to the Singaporans, to the Japanese, and the rest.

Richard M. Nixon. *Papers of the Presidents: Nixon*, 1970.

181. We seek friendly relations with all nations. Any nation can be our friend without being any other nation's enemy.

Richard M. Nixon. July 15, 1971.

182. Communist leaders believe in Lenin's precept: Probe with bayonets. If you encounter mush, proceed; if you encounter steel, withdraw.

Richard M. Nixon. *Memoirs*, 1978.

183. We must accept the fact that our relations to other countries should be determined primarily by what they do outside, not inside, their borders.

Richard M. Nixon. *In the Arena*, 1990.

184. Panama's sovereignty is not negotiable.

Manuel Noriega, President of Panama. Statement rejecting U.S. efforts encouraging him to resign. Quoted in *Time*, May 23, 1988.

185. Already the propagandists of the international bankers and of others seeking profit bring forth their song of Circe in eagerness to befuddle and beguile the minds of the American people, to soften them for the killing.

James C. Oliver (1895-1986), U.S. Congressman (R and D-ME). Congressional speech, June 28, 1939.

186. The United States is practically sovereign on this continent, and its fiat is law upon the subjects to which it confines its interposition.

Richard Olney (1835-1917), U.S. Attorney General and U.S. Secretary of State (R). Communiqué to the British Foreign Office regarding the Venezuela boundary dispute, Feb. 6, 1895.

187. It is the true interest of America to steer clear of European contentions.

Thomas Paine (1737-1809), American political philosopher. *Common Sense*, Jan. 10, 1776.

188. Foreign policy is merely domestic policy with its hat on.

Lester B. Pearson (1897-1972), Prime Minister of Canada (Liberal) and Nobel Laureate in Peace. Quoted in *The Toronto Star*, Oct. 23, 1975.

189. *[Joseph Stalin is]* a man Americans can trust.

Claude D. Pepper (1901-1989), U.S. Senator and U.S. Congressman (D-FL). 1945.

190. The only way for a nation to be respected – by itself as well as the rest of the world – is to be respectable.

Charles H. Percy, U.S. Senator (R-IL). Interview, *Playboy*, Apr. 1968.

191. Millions for defense, but not one cent for tribute.

Charles C. Pinckney (1746-1825), U.S. Ambassador to France. 1796.

192. England has saved herself by her exertions, and will, as I trust, save Europe by her example.

William Pitt (The Younger) (1759-1806), Prime Minister of Great Britain. Speech, Guildhall, London, 1805.

193. Violence is a way of life in the Middle East.

Colin L. Powell, General, U.S. Army; National Security Advisor; and Chairman, Joint Chiefs of Staff. NBC, *Meet the Press*, Dec. 18, 1988.

194. You'd better be ready to respond if someone challenges your interest.

Colin L. Powell. Speech, National Press Club, Washington, DC, June 24, 1990.

195. Americans' scandalous incompetence in foreign languages also explains our dangerously inadequate understanding of world affairs.

Report, Presidential Commission on Foreign Languages. 1979.

196. Why are the nations in an uproar?

Old Testament, *Psalms* 2:1.

197. I have no reason to do anything but hate the Japanese. But we must remember that God put us both in the same ocean and we've got to get along with each other in the future.

Elpidio Quirino (1890-1956), President of the Philippines. Statement to John Foster Dulles, 1951.

198. Are we, sir, to go on a crusade in another hemisphere, for the propagation of two objects as dear and delightful to my heart as to that of any gentleman in this or any other assembly – Liberty and Religion – and in the name of those holy words – by this powerful spell, is this nation to be conjured and beguiled out of the high way of heaven – out of its present comparatively happy state, into all the disastrous conflicts arising from the policy of the European powers, with all the consequences which flow from them?

John Randolph (1773-1833), U.S. Congressman (D-VA), U.S. Senator, and U.S. Minister to Russia. Senate speech, Jan. 24, 1824.

199. Hurting white people is not the same as helping black people.

William Raspberry, American journalist. Comment on proposed economic sanctions against South Africa. Quoted in *Conservative Digest*, Nov. 1987.

200. My fellow Americans: I'm pleased to tell you today that I've signed legislation that will outlaw Russia forever. We begin bombing in five minutes.

Ronald Reagan, 40th President of the United States (R-CA). Jesting comment while testing a microphone before a broadcast. Aug. 11, 1984.

201. When the Senate of the United States tries to direct the nation's foreign policy, it almost always gets into trouble.

James Reston, American journalist. Quoted in Alexander DeConde, *The American Secretary of State*, 1963.

202. Foreign relations are like human relations. They are endless. The solution of one problem usually leads to another.

James Reston. *Sketches in the Sand*, 1967.

203. This is the devilish thing about foreign affairs: They are foreign and will not always conform to our whim.

James Reston. *The New York Times*, Dec. 30, 1969.

204. Free trade has proven to be very expensive, and continual reliance on it is pure folly.

Thomas J. Ridge, U.S. Congressman (R-PA). Testimony, House Education and Labor Committee, Feb. 25, 1987.

205. France gave its word. It will be kept.
Michel Rocard, Premier of France. In reference to Middle East negotiations. Quoted in *Time*, May 30, 1988.

206. We will send Marines to any nation that can get ten people to say they want it.
Will Rogers (1879-1935), American humorist. Quoted on PBS, *Will Rogers U.S.A.*, Oct. 3, 1988.

207. What would we say if the Chinese sent a gunboat with their marines up the Mississippi River claiming they were protecting their laundries in Memphis?
Will Rogers. *Ibid.*

208. Today the world is entering an age of reconciliation and cooperation transcending ideologies and political systems.
Roh Tae Woo, President of South Korea. In reference to his new policy of allowing more contact between North and South Korea. Quoted in *The New York Times*, July 7, 1988.

209. With good will and realistic attitudes, states having different social systems can reach agreement on major international issues.
Rudolf Rohlicek, Deputy Prime Minister of Czechoslovakia. Quoted in *The Washington Post*, June 26, 1988.

210. We must be willing to learn the lesson that cooperation may imply compromise.
Anna Eleanor Roosevelt (1884-1962), First Lady and U.S. Delegate to the United Nations. Speech, Pilgrim Society, Jan. 21, 1946.

211. I would dedicate this nation to the policy of the good neighbor.
Franklin D. Roosevelt (1882-1945), 32nd President of the United States (D-NY). First inaugural address, Mar. 4, 1933.

212. The American people want their government to act, and not merely to talk, whenever and wherever there is a threat to world peace.
Franklin D. Roosevelt. Speech, Foreign Policy Association, Oct. 21, 1944.

213. We have learned that we cannot live alone, at peace; that our own well-being is dependent upon the well-being of other nations far away.
Franklin D. Roosevelt, Fourth inaugural address, Jan. 20, 1945.

214. We in the Americas will decide for ourselves whether, and when, and where, our American interests are attacked or our security threatened.
Franklin D. Roosevelt. Quoted in Foster Rhea Dulles, *The United States Since 1865*, 1959.

215. I have constantly preached what our opponents are pleased to call "jingo doctrines" for a good many years.
Theodore Roosevelt (1858-1919), 26th President of the United States (R-NY). Remark, Mar. 1898.

216. There is a homely adage which runs, "Speak softly and carry a big stick." If the American nation will speak softly and yet build and keep at a pitch of the highest training a thoroughly efficient navy, the Monroe Doctrine will go far.
Theodore Roosevelt. Labor Day address, Minnesota State Fair, Sept. 2, 1901.

217. I wish that all Americans would realize that American politics is world politics.
Theodore Roosevelt. Remark to André Tardieu, 1905.

218. I am interested in the Panama Canal because I started it. If I had followed traditional, conservative methods I would have presented a dignified state paper to Congress and the debates on it would have been going on yet; but I took the Canal Zone and let Congress debate; and while the debate goes on the Canal does also.
Theodore Roosevelt. Speech, Berkeley, CA, 1911.

219. We have no choice, we the people of the United States, as to whether or not we shall play a great part in the world. That has been decided for us by fate, by the march of events. All that we can decide is whether we shall play it well or ill.
Theodore Roosevelt. Quoted in Archibald Carey Coolidge, *The United States as a World Power*, 1912.

220. Let American cities be bombarded and razed rather than pay a dollar to any foe for their safety.
Theodore Roosevelt. Remark to a *New York Sun* reporter, 1916.

221. While we are sleeping, two-thirds of the world is plotting to do us in.
Dean Rusk, U.S. Secretary of State (D). Attributed.

222. I wouldn't make the slightest concession for moral leadership. It's much overrated.
Dean Rusk. Advice to President Kennedy, 1962.

223. It is not healthy for a regime or group of regimes to incur, by their lawlessness and aggressive conduct, the implacable opposition of the American people.
Dean Rusk. Quoted in David Halberstam, *The Best and the Brightest*, 1969.

224. We and the Russians should not play games of "chicken" with each other.

Dean Rusk. Quoted on PBS, *War and Peace in the Nuclear Age*, Feb. 1989.

225. Why do you in the United States tell me not to cut down our rain forest when you cut down your rain forest?

José Sarney, President of Brazil. Quoted on PBS, *Great Decisions, 1990*, Mar. 3, 1990.

226. To hell with Europe and the rest of those nations!

Thomas D. Schall (1878-1935), U.S. Congressman and U.S. Senator (R-MN). Senate debate on Pres. Franklin Roosevelt's proposal that the United States join the World Court, 1935.

227. To move out of its isolationism, American society historically has required a crusade, and crusaders need to focus on infidels and rascals.

James R. Schlesinger, U.S. Secretary of Defense (R), U.S. Secretary of Energy, and Director, Central Intelligence Agency. Quoted in *Time*, Sept. 3, 1990.

228. We won't have the new world order. We'll have the old world disorder.

James R. Schlesinger. Quoted on PBS, *Agony of Decision*, Feb. 23, 1991.

229. If the world gangs up *[diplomatically]* on them *[the Russians]*, then they're going to start shaping up.

Patricia R. Schroeder, U.S. Congresswoman (D-CO). PBS, *Firing Line*, Sept. 7, 1988.

230. Throughout history it has been the inaction of those who could have acted, the indifference of those who should have known better, the silence of the voice of justice when it mattered most, that has made it possible for evil to triumph.

Haile Selassie (1891-1975), Emperor of Ethiopia. Speech, U.N. General Assembly, Oct. 4, 1963.

231. The elections will determine our foreign policy.

Yitzhak Shamir, Prime Minister of Israel (Likud). Quoted in *The New York Times*, Oct. 2, 1988.

232. No nation has the right to play global policeman.

Eduard Shevardnadze, Foreign Minister, U.S.S.R. Commencement speech, Brown University, Providence, RI, June 1991.

233. Say there's a fire. You have to get the fire out. Now at the same time there are various ways you can do it. If you don't have any strategy you just get the fire out. Now if you have a strategy you say to yourself, "Well, all right, I'm going to get this out, but I'm going to do it in such a way that I do it in a manner that is compatible, or at least not incompatible, with my general thrust." So what you try to build is the implementation of your strategy by these incremental little things.

George P. Shultz, U.S. Secretary of State (R). Quoted in *The Washington Post*, Mar. 19, 1989.

234. The main business of Canada in foreign relations is to remain friendly with the United States while preserving its own self-respect.

Clifford Sifton (1861-1929), Member of Parliament, Canada (Liberal). 1921.

235. We yearn to turn away from foreign entanglements and to begin making our own house a better place to live in.

Margaret Chase Smith, U.S. Congresswoman and U.S. Senator (R-ME). *Reader's Digest*, Mar. 1972.

236. No country has ever been brought to its knees by sanctions alone.

Stephen J. Solarz, U.S. Congressman (D-NY). Interview, CNN, *Larry King Live*, Sept. 3, 1990.

237. They *[the Russians]* are trying to engage us in collective procedures, international organizations and multilateral arrangements that will constrain our ability to act on our own.

Richard Solomon, Director, Policy and Planning, U.S. Department of State. Quoted in *Time*, May 23, 1988.

238. The Republicans would like to be the copilots in the foreign policy take-offs as well as in the crash landings.

Harold E. Stassen, Governor of Minnesota (R). 1946.

239. We cannot expect that all nations will adopt like systems, for conformity is the jailer of freedom and the enemy of growth.

Adlai E. Stevenson (1900-1965), Governor of Illinois (D) and U.S. Ambassador to the United Nations. Speech, U.N. General Assembly, Sept. 25, 1961.

240. I am prepared to wait for my answer *[as to whether Russia had placed offensive missiles in Cuba]* until hell freezes over.

Adlai E. Stevenson. Statement to the Soviet delegate to the United Nations during Cuban missile crisis debate, Oct. 1962.

241. We must steel ourselves to forego the unholy profit that comes from dealing in blood traffic. We must treat war as a contagious disease. We must isolate those who have it and refrain from all intercourse with them.

Donald W. Stewart, Commander, American Legion, Department of Kansas. *America*, Apr. 1938.

242. We were fighting Germany to tear down the Nazi system – one-party government supported by the Gestapo.... China, our ally, was being run by a one-party government *[the Koumintang]*, supported by a Gestapo *[Tai Li's organization]*.... To reform such a system it must be torn to pieces.

Joseph W. Stilwell (1883-1946), General, U.S. Army. Quoted in David Horowitz, *The Free World Colossus*, 1965.

243. If at any time the United States had been willing to concede to Japan a free hand in China, there would have been no war in the Pacific.

Henry L. Stimson (1867-1950), U.S. Secretary of State (R), U.S. Secretary of War, and Governor General of the Philippines. Quoted in Foster Rhea Dulles, *The United States Since 1865*, 1959.

244. Our American friends are sometimes in too much of a hurry to get results yesterday.

Bandar Bin Sultan, Ambassador of Saudi Arabia to the United States. Interview, CBS, *Meet the Press*, Aug. 12, 1990.

245. Drive a wedge between a sovereign and his ministers; on other occasions separate his allies from him. Make them mutually suspicious so that they drift apart.

Sun-tzu (c.400 B.C.), Chinese writer of the Age of Warring States. *The Art of War*.

246. The diplomacy of the present administration has sought to respond to modern ideas of commercial intercourse. This policy has been characterized as substituting dollars for bullets *[dollar diplomacy]*. It is one that appeals alike to idealistic humanitarian sentiments, to the dictates of sound policy and strategy, and to legitimate commercial aims.

William H. Taft (1857-1930), 27th President of the United States (R-OH) and Chief Justice, U.S. Supreme Court. Annual message to Congress, Dec. 3, 1912.

247. Americans are poker players, which means they tend to think that as long as you've got money you can stay in the game. It's a very quick game and a hand doesn't last long. Also, a poker player is a reactionary in that you are dealt the hand, you pick it up, and you react to the cards as given. There is no need for long-term planning. Our country plays foreign policy like a poker hand.

Lewis Tambs, U.S. Ambassador to Colombia and Costa Rica. Interview, *Conservative Digest*, Oct. 1987.

248. If we want to control China in the future, we must first crush the United States.

Gi-ichi Tanaka (1893-1929), Premier of Japan. July 25, 1927.

249. Every possible effort of our delegates to the United Nations Organization be directed toward the ultimate goal of establishing a world republic based on democratic principles and universal suffrage regardless of race, color, or creed.

Glen Hearst Taylor (1904-1984), U.S. Senator (D-ID). Resolution introduced into the Senate, Oct. 24, 1945.

250. England has no permanent friends; she has only permanent interests.

Henry John Temple, 3rd Viscount Palmerston (1784-1865), Prime Minister of Great Britain (Whig). Quoted in *The New York Times Magazine*, May 20, 1956.

251. I don't much like abroad.

Margaret Thatcher, Prime Minister of Great Britain (Conservative). Campaign remark, 1980.

252. Fear is no basis for foreign policy.

Margaret Thatcher. Remark in Parliament, 1983.

253. It was essential to the safety of France that Spain should be under her control; if Spain continued constitutional, that is to say, if the feelings of the people were to influence her policy, the antipathy of the Spaniards toward the French would make her a rival or an enemy instead of an ally. Thus it was the duty therefore of every French government to put down every Spanish constitution.

Louis Adolphe Thiers (1797-1877), 1st President of the Third Republic of France. 1823.

254. It was for the sake of France; it was to plant the French flag on the Castle of St. Angelo; it was to maintain our right to have one half of Italy if Austria seized the other. Rather than see the Austrian eagle on the flagstaff that rises above the Tiber, I would destroy a hundred constitutions and a hundred religions. I repeat, therefore, that we, the planners of the Roman expedition, acted as statesmen.

Louis Adolphe Thiers. To justify France's invasion of Rome. 1870.

255. The United States is not a nation of people which in the long run allows itself to be pushed around.

Dorothy Thompson (1894-1961), American journalist. *Let the Record Speak*, 1939.

256. Foreign policy is determined by internal domestic influences.

George Thompson, officer, U.S. Foreign Service, and journalist. *USA Today*, Nov. 3, 1988.

257. America is a large friendly dog in a small room. Every time it wags its tail, it knocks over a chair.

Arnold J. Toynbee (1899-1975), British historian. BBC, July 14, 1954.

258. The socialist revolution begins on national grounds, but it cannot be completed on these grounds. Its maintenance within a national framework can only be a provisional state of affairs.

Leon Trotsky (1879-1940), Russian revolutionary theorist. Introduction, *The Permanent Revolution*, 1932.

259. Coexistence is not a choice – it is a fatal disease.

Arthur G. Trudeau (1903-1991), Lieutenant General, U.S. Army, Chief of Army Intelligence, and Director, U.S. Army Office of Research and Development. Testimony, Senate Armed Services Subcommittee, 1962.

260. Living next to you *[the United States]* is in some ways like sleeping with an elephant. No matter how friendly and even-tempered is the beast, one is affected by every twitch and grunt.

Pierre Elliott Trudeau, Prime Minister of Canada (Liberal). Quoted in *The New York Times*, Mar. 26, 1969.

261. We live in this country ... in which we can get along with our neighbors. Now, we must do that nationally. It will be just as easy for nations to get along in the republic of the world as it is for you to get along in the republic of the United States.

Harry S Truman (1884-1972), 33rd President of the United States (D-MO). Speech, Kansas City, MO, 1945.

262. The responsibility of great states is to serve and not to dominate the world.

Harry S Truman. Message to Congress. Apr. 16, 1945.

263. The State Department doesn't have a policy unless I support it.

Harry S Truman. Remark to a reporter, Jan. 31, 1946.

264. I believe that it must be the policy of the United States to support free peoples who are resisting attempted subjugation by armed minorities or by outside pressures.

Harry S Truman. Speech to Congress, Mar. 12, 1947 (the Truman Doctrine).

265. Isolationism is the road to war. Worse than that, isolationism is the road to defeat in war.

Harry S Truman. Speech, St. Louis, MO, June 10, 1950.

266. If former President Eisenhower had understood the Monroe Doctrine, we would not have any trouble in Cuba today.

Harry S Truman. Statement during the Cuban missile crisis. Oct. 14, 1962.

267. I make American foreign policy.

Harry S Truman, Quoted in Melvin I. Urofsky, *A March of Liberty*, 1988.

268. America shall be self-contained and self-sustained: no foreign entanglements, be they political, economic, financial or military.

Union Party Platform, 1936.

269. We like to have a moral imperative in our foreign policy.

Garrick Utley, American TV journalist. NBC, *Meet the Press*, Apr. 7, 1990.

270. I do not believe that any nation hereafter can immunize itself *[from war]* by its own exclusive action.

Arthur H. Vandenberg (1884-1951), U.S. Senator (R-MI). Senate speech, 1945.

271. If Truman wants it *[involvement in Greece]* he will have to go and scare hell out of the country.

Arthur H. Vandenberg. Mar. 1947.

272. We can only cooperate with one Secretary of State at a time.

Arthur H. Vandenberg. Remark to reporters after Vice President Henry Wallace gave a speech criticizing the foreign policy of the U.S. Secretary of State. 1948.

273. No nation can be healthy in an unhealthy world.

Earl Warren (1891-1974), Chief Justice, U.S. Supreme Court, and Governor of California (R). Quoted in Earl Katcher, *Earl Warren: A Political Biography*, 1967.

274. The great rule of conduct for us in regard to foreign nations is, in extending our commercial relations, to have with them as little political connection as possible.

George Washington (1732-1799), 1st President of the United States (VA). Farewell address, Sept. 17, 1796.

275. I have no confidence in the system of *isolement [isolation]*. It does not answer in social life for individuals, nor in politics for nations. Man is a social animal.

Arthur Wellesley, 1st Duke of Wellington (1769-1852), Chief General at Waterloo, Ambassador to France and Prime Minister of Great Britain (Tory). Letter to Thomas Raikes, Mar. 1, 1841.

276. There's nothing wrong with appeasement if it appeases.

George F. Will, American political columnist. ABC, *This Week*, Apr. 22, 1990.

277. Do everything possible to kill Russians as painfully as possible.
Charles Wilson (1895-1961), U.S. Congressman (D-TX). Quoted in *Roll Call*, May 28, 1990.

278. It is a very perilous thing to determine the foreign policy of a nation in the terms of material interest.
Woodrow Wilson (1856-1924), 28th President of the United States (D-NJ). 1913.

279. We shall not, I believe, be obliged to alter our policy of watchful waiting.
Woodrow Wilson. In reference to Mexico. Annual message to Congress, Dec. 2, 1913.

280. No nation is fit to sit in judgment upon any other nation.
(Said at the beginning of World War I. Wilson reversed himself at the Paris Peace Conference in 1919.)
Woodrow Wilson. Speech, New York City, Apr. 20, 1915.

281. The world must be made safe for democracy. Its peace must be planted upon the tested foundations of political liberty. We have no selfish ends to serve. We desire no conquest, no dominion. We seek no indemnities for ourselves, no material compensation for the sacrifices we shall freely make. We are but one of the champions of the rights of mankind. We shall be satisfied when those rights have been made as secure as the faith and the freedom of nature can make them.
Woodrow Wilson. Message to Congress asking for a declaration of war against Germany, Apr. 2, 1917.

282. This blatant group of misguided, misinformed, misdirected, and moronic individuals are infringing the personal liberties of the first citizen of this nation. For more than a month the White House has been picketed by a group of mentally unbalanced, publicity-seeking morons.
Stephen Young (1889-1984), U.S. Congressman and U.S. Senator (D-OH). In reference to isolationists picketing the White House to oppose aid to Great Britain. 1940.

Chapter 37

Foreign Trade

1. We're part of a global economy whether we like it or not.
   Gerald Baliles, Governor of Virginia (D). Interview, C-SPAN, July 29, 1989.

2. The political boundaries of nation-states are too narrow and constricted to define the scope and activities of modern business.
   George Ball, U.S. Undersecretary of State (D). Speech, International Chamber of Commerce, 1967.

3. The United States is rapidly becoming a colony of Japan.
   Helen D. Bentley, U.S. Congresswoman (R-MD). Quoted in *Time*, June 25, 1990.

4. When trade legislation seeks to protect one industry at the expense of another, then the economic well-being of everyone in this country is adversely affected.
   Douglas K. Bereuter, U.S. Congressman (R-NB). Testimony, House Education and Labor Committee, Feb. 25, 1987.

5. Whence comes this demand for tariff tinkering. Aren't all our fellows happy?
   Joseph G. Cannon (1836-1926), U.S. Congressman and Speaker of the House (R-IL). Advice to party leaders. Quoted in *The Washington Post*, Nov. 17, 1905.

6. No matter how great an improvement the new tariff may be, it almost always results in the party in power losing the election.
   Joseph G. Cannon. Advice against altering duty rates for imports. Quoted in L. W. Busbey, *Uncle Joe Cannon*, 1927.

7. International borders are as uninteresting to large business as the equator.
   William Sloane Coffin, Jr., American clergyman and President, SANE/Freeze. Quoted on CNN, *Waging Peace*, Sept. 16, 1989.

8. The Japanese sit up all night thinking of ways to screw the Americans and the Europeans.
   Edith Cresson, Prime Minister of France. Remark, 1991.

9. Unfair foreign trade practices are not isolated acts.
   John Dingell, U.S. Congressman (D-MI). House debate, Apr. 29, 1987.

10. Free trade is not a principle, it is an expedient.
    Benjamin Disraeli, 1st Earl of Beaconsfield (1804-1881), Prime Minister of Great Britain (Conservative). Speech, House of Commons, Apr. 25, 1843.

11. The way to conquer the foreign artisan is not to kill him, but to beat his work.
    Ralph Waldo Emerson (1803-1882), American writer. *The Conduct of Life*, "Worship," 1860.

12. It's the nation that's at risk, not just Oklahoma or Pennsylvania. It's the whole country that's competing with Korea, Germany, and Japan.
    Chester E. Finn, Jr., U.S. Assistant Secretary of Education. *The Washington Post*, July 16, 1989.

13. No nation was ever ruined by trade.
    Benjamin Franklin (1706-1790), Member, Continental Congress and Constitutional Convention, Governor of Pennsylvania, and U.S. Minister to France. *Thoughts on Commercial Subjects*.

14. Free trade ideas often look great in prospect but less in retrospect.
    John Kenneth Galbraith, American economist and U.S. Ambassador to India (D). PBS, *Firing Line*, Dec. 9, 1989.

15. Demanding freedom of access to other markets isn't protectionism, it's free trade.
    Richard A. Gephardt, U.S. Congressman (D-MO). House debate, May 21, 1986.

16. I am ferociously protectionist. I am not the man you need.
    Horace Greeley (1811-1872), U.S. Congressman (Whig-NY), journalist, and editor. Response to sugges-

tion that he run for President. Quoted in Don C. Seitz, *Horace Greeley*, 1926.

17. The spirit of commerce has a tendency to soften the manners of men and to extinguish those inflammable humors which have so often kindled into wars.

Alexander Hamilton (1755-1804), Member, Continental Congress and Constitutional Convention, and U.S. Secretary of the Treasury (Federalist-NY). *The Federalist*, No. 6, Nov. 14, 1787.

18. Free markets work better when information is available.

Lee Hamilton, U.S. Congressman (D-IN). Argument for less secrecy about the workings of the Federal Reserve Bank. Remark, Dec. 18, 1989.

19. I would rather have indissoluble ties of righteous trade promote international friendship than all the compacts ever written in the world.

Warren G. Harding (1865-1923), 29th President of the United States (R-OH). Speech, Jacksonville Chamber of Commerce, Jacksonville, FL, 1921.

20. We know full well we cannot sell where we do not buy and we cannot sell successfully where we do not carry.

Warren G. Harding. Inaugural address, Mar. 4, 1921.

21. The United States should adopt a protective tariff of such a character as will help the struggling industries of Europe to get on their feet.

Warren G. Harding. Quoted in William Allen White, *Autobiography*, 1946.

22. Tough trade policies make good political fodder back home.

Joel Hefley, U.S. Congressman (R-CO). Testimony, House Education and Labor Committee, Feb. 25, 1987.

23. Merchants throughout the world have the same religion.

Heinrich Heine (1797-1856), German writer. *Letters from Berlin*, Mar. 16, 1822.

24. Our nation has moved from the cold war to the trade war.

Ernest F. Hollings, Governor of South Carolina and U.S. Senator (D). *The New York Times*, Oct. 5, 1990.

25. The public is too damned dumb to understand.

Harry L. Hopkins (1890-1946), U.S. Secretary of Commerce (D); Director, Work Projects Administration; and Special Assistant to the President. Response when asked to explain why the United States had supplied eleven billion dollars to the Soviet Union in lend-lease aid during World War II. Attributed.

26. We're the only dinosaurs left who maintain that the myth of "free trade" really exists.

Lee Iacocca, Chairman, Chrysler Corp., and member, National Economic Commission. *Talking Straight*, 1988.

27. Demanding reciprocity from our trade partners, and retaliating if we don't get it, doesn't undermine free trade, it defends free trade.

Lee Iacocca. "OK, OK, Call Me a Protectionist," *The New York Times*, Feb. 10, 1991.

28. For more than a century, Americans enjoyed unchallenged superiority in virtually everything we turned our hands to. We could afford the luxury of ignoring the seers and experts who urged us to learn the tongues and ways of other lands. But those days have gone the way of leaded gas and the nickel phone call.

Thomas H. Kean, Governor of New Jersey (R). Speech, National Governors Association, Feb. 25, 1989.

29. It is not a fair trade bill, it is a less trade bill.

Jack F. Kemp, U.S. Congressman and Secretary of Housing and Urban Development (R-NY). House debate on proposed trade legislation, May 20, 1986.

30. The country is as strong abroad *[economically]* only as it's strong at home.

John F. Kennedy (1917-1963), 35th President of the United States (D-MA). Speech, St. Paul, MN, Oct. 6, 1962.

31. How can 9 million people enter into such arrangements as are proposed with 90 million strangers on an open frontier of four thousand miles and at the same time preserve their national integrity?... It is her own soul Canada risks today. Once that soul is pawned for any consideration Canada must inevitably conform to the commercial, legal, financial, social, and ethical standards which will be imposed upon her by the sheer admitted weight of the United States.

Rudyard Kipling (1865-1936), Nobel Laureate in Literature (Great Britain). Statement on a proposed treaty of reciprocity whereby most trade barriers between Canada and the United States would be virtually eliminated. 1911.

32. When fifty nations attempt to export simultaneously, some will win and some will lose. This may exacerbate international tension.

Henry M. Kissinger, U.S. Secretary of State and U.S. National Security Advisor (R). Quoted on CNN, *Waging Peace*, Sept. 16, 1989.

33. One of the most reprehensible things that we do is export disease, disability, and death to countries that will not be able to afford to pay for them.

C. Everett Koop, U.S. Surgeon General. On the export of tobacco products by American manufacturers. Quoted on PBS, *Nova*, Oct. 10, 1989.

34. To control the American market is to own America.

Robert M. La Follette (1855-1925), Governor of Wisconsin and U.S. Senator (R). *La Follette's Magazine*, Apr. 1918.

35. Practical and obvious interests of all the capitalistic powers have demanded the development, consolidation, and expansion of trade with Russia.

V. I. Lenin (1870-1924), Premier of the U.S.S.R. Speech to metal workers, Mar. 6, 1922.

36. We have failed to restore Russia to sanity by force. I believe we can save her by trade. Commerce has a sobering influence.... Trade, in my opinion, will bring an end to the ferocity, the rapine, and the crudity of Bolshevism surer than any other method.

David Lloyd George, 1st Earl of Dwyfor (1863-1945), Prime Minister of Great Britain (Liberal). Parliamentary debate, 1922.

37. Seek as we may to compromise the issue there is but one way the neutrality of America may be guaranteed, and that is to break off trade and commercial relations entirely with foreign countries at war.

Louis L. Ludlow (1873-1950), U.S. Congressman (D-IN). Speech in favor of the Neutrality Act, Jan. 8, 1936.

38. It's inappropriate for a Japanese company to come over here and run an American concession *[food, drink, and lodging at Yosemite National Park]* when an American company can't run one in a Japanese shrine.

Manuel Lujan, Jr., U.S. Congressman and U.S. Secretary of the Interior (R-NM). Quoted in *The New York Times*, Jan. 2, 1991.

39. No people in the world can be self-sufficient.

Patrice Lumumba (1925-1961), 1st Prime Minister of the Congo (later Zaire). Speech, University of Ibadan, Nigeria, Mar. 22, 1959.

40. Free trade, one of the greatest blessings which a government can confer on a people, is in almost every country unpopular.

Thomas Babington Macaulay, 1st Baron Macaulay (1800-1859), historian and Secretary of War, Great Britain (Liberal). *On Mitford's History of Greece*, Nov. 1824.

41. It might be, gentlemen, that the lion and the lamb would lie down together, but then the lamb would be inside the lion.

John A. MacDonald (1815-1891), 1st Prime Minister of Canada (Conservative). Speech on possible economic union with the United States. Quoted in *The Montreal Gazette*, Nov. 26, 1875.

42. Protection has done so much for me I must do something for protection.

John A. MacDonald. Statement on the eve of his election, 1878.

43. Many farmers drive pickup trucks ... from Japan.... You refuse to accept their rice in payment for your trucks.

Edward Madigan, U.S. Secretary of Agriculture (R). Letter to the Japanese Minister of Agriculture when Japan banned American rice imports and threatened its marketeers with jail. Mar. 1991.

44. It can never be admitted that the trade of a neutral nation in articles not contraband can be legally obstructed to any place not actually blockaded.

James Madison (1751-1836), 4th President of the United States (Democratic Republican-VA). Statement to the British *Chargé d'Affaires*, 1803.

45. There is no purpose in giving countries aid and then denying them trade access. Such policies would leave them on the drip feed of dependence forever.

John Major, Prime Minister of Great Britain (Conservative). Quoted in *The New York Times*, Sept. 15, 1991.

46. Tariff policy is no longer a question of raising revenue or protecting domestic manufacturing. It is the executive's instrument of foreign policy.

John F. Manley, American political scientist. *The Politics of Finance*, 1970.

47. I am a tariff man standing on a tariff platform.

William McKinley (1843-1901), 25th President of the United States (R-OH). Quoted in Wallechinsky and Wallace, *The People's Almanac*, 1975.

48. Can you have a free trade agreement with a country that isn't free?

Daniel P. Moynihan, Chief American Delegate to the United Nations and U.S. Senator (D-NY). Interview, CNN, *Evans & Novak*, May 12, 1991.

49. If we get sufficiently interlaced economically, we will probably not bomb each other off the face of the planet.
John Naisbitt, American futurist and writer. *Megatrends*, 1982.

50. Their whole lives must disclose the fact that they have always advocated an exorbitantly high tariff.
George W. Norris (1861-1944), U.S. Congressman and U.S. Senator (R and Independent Republican-NE). Comment on the necessary qualifications for appointees to the Tariff Commission. Quoted in John Donald Hicks, *Republican Ascendancy*, 1960.

51. You have to give our trade representatives something to negotiate with. If that means barriers, so be it.
T. Boone Pickens, American financier and industrialist. Quoted on PBS, *American Interests*, Oct. 20, 1989.

52. Show me a subsidy that's not trade distorting.
Derwent Renshaw, agricultural counselor, European Community Mission. Quoted in *The New York Times*, Mar. 6, 1989.

53. We are uncompromisingly in favor of the American system of protection.
Republican Party platform, 1888.

54. Our international trade relations, though vastly important, are in point of time and necessity secondary to the establishment of a sound national economy.
Franklin D. Roosevelt (1882-1945), 32nd President of the United States (D-NY). First inaugural address, Mar. 4, 1933.

55. The president must be both an ardent nationalist and an eager internationalist. He must respond to popular anxieties over imports and other foreign influences on U.S. society. Otherwise he risks losing support at home. But he must also embrace global cooperation to defend the world trade and financial systems on which most countries depend.
Robert J. Samuelson, American economist. *The Washington Post*, Nov. 7, 1988.

56. We *[Japan]* cannot have it both ways, growing rich from international trade while remaining aloof from the world.
Mitsuko Shimomura, Japanese editor and writer. *World Press Review*, Oct. 1990.

57. There may be good policy in *[trade]* retaliation when there is a probability that they will procure the repeal of the high duty or prohibition complained of.
Adam Smith (1723-1790), Scottish political economist. *The Wealth of Nations*, 1776.

58. If we *[Mexico]* can't buy, your unemployment goes up and your farms go under. The *[Mexican foreign]* debt cuts both ways.
León García Solér, Mexican political and economic columnist. PBS, *Campaign: A View From Abroad*, Oct. 17, 1988.

59. Governments have been behind the curve in adjusting to the realities of interdependence.
Anthony Solomon, President, Federal Reserve Bank of New York. *U.S. News & World Report*, June 20, 1988.

60. We are not used to *[government-]* managed trade.
Paula Stern, Chairwoman, U.S. International Trade Commission (D). Interview, PBS, *American Interests*, Aug. 5, 1989.

61. A barrier is a barrier whether you call it a cultural difference or anything else.
Margaret Thatcher, Prime Minister of Great Britain (Conservative). In reference to Japanese trade barriers. Quoted on National Public Radio, Sept. 20, 1989.

62. They've learned to play us like a violin.
Lester C. Thurow, Dean, Sloan School of Management, Massachusetts Institute of Technology. Remark on the ability of the Japanese to deal politically with the United States on trade issues. *Business Week*, July 11, 1988.

63. We are the flea market of the world, and we don't even charge them for the stands.
James A. Traficant, Jr., U.S. Congressman (D-OH). Interview, C-SPAN, May 6, 1990.

64. Canada is a country whose main exports *[to the United States]* are hockey players and cold fronts. Our main imports are baseball players and acid rain.
Pierre Elliott Trudeau, Prime Minister of Canada (Liberal). Quoted in Lee Green, *Sportswit*, 1984.

65. You sold us out!
John N. Turner, Prime Minister of Canada (Liberal). Remark to Conservative Prime Minister Brian Mulroney, who negotiated a free-trade treaty with the United States. Televised debate, 1987.

66. We have built a country, east and west and north, on an infrastructure that resisted the continental pressure of the United States. For 120 years we've done it, and with one stroke of the pen you've reversed that, thrown us into the north-south pull

of the United States. And that will reduce us, I'm sure, to an economic colony of the United States, because when the economic levers go, the political independence is sure to follow.

John N. Turner. Debate with Conservative Prime Minister Brian Mulroney on the proposed free trade pact with the United States, Oct. 1988.

67. A protective tariff is a typical conspiracy in restraint of trade.

Thorstein Veblen (1857-1929), American political economist. *The Engineers and the Price System*, 1921.

68. Most Congressmen are torn between an ideological commitment to free enterprise and a compelling need to respond to the special interests in their districts.

Raymond Vernon, professor emeritus of International Affairs, Harvard University. *The New York Times*, Sept. 2, 1988.

69. Columbuses from America, it is time to discover Poland!

Lech Walesa, President of Poland, trade unionist, and founder, Solidarity. Remark on Poland's new interest in foreign investments. Quoted in *The Washington Post*, Nov. 13, 1989.

70. It is you, the West, who have made good business on the Polish revolution.... The West was supposed to to help us in arranging the economy on new principles, but in fact it largely confined its effort to draining our domestic markets.

Lech Walesa. Statement on flooding Poland with consumer goods but refusing to make major investments. Speech, Council of Europe, Strasbourg, France, Feb. 4, 1992.

71. We must abolish everything that bears even the semblance of privilege or of any kind of artificial advantage, and put our businessmen and producers under the stimulation of a constant necessity to be efficient, economical and enterprising, masters of competitive supremacy, better merchants than any in the world.

Woodrow Wilson (1856-1924), 28th President of the United States (D-NJ). Message to Congress, Apr. 8, 1913.

Chapter 38

Freedom and Liberty

1. It is my living sentiment, and by the blessing of God it shall be my dying sentiment – Independence now and Independence forever!

   John Adams (1735-1826), 2nd President of the United States (Federalist-MA). On his deathbed, July 1, 1826.

2. For what is liberty but the unhampered translation of will into act?

   Dante Alighieri (1265-1321), Italian writer. *Letters*, 6.

3. A free and open society is an ongoing conflict, interrupted periodically by compromises.

   Saul D. Alinsky (1909-1972), American community organizer. *Rules for Radicals*, 1971.

4. You'll never know how sweet freedom can be unless you've lost it for eight and a half years.

   Everett Alvarez, Jr., Vietnam POW. Print advertisement, Philip Morris Companies, Inc., 1990.

5. Are there any limitations? Are they going to allow fornication in Times Square at high noon?

   Douglas E. Applegate, U.S. Congressman (D-OH). To protest the Supreme Court *Texas* v. *Johnson* decision protecting the right to burn the American flag as "symbolic speech." Quoted in *Newsweek*, July 3, 1989.

6. Freedom and its blessings are a reality for a minority and an illusion for the many.

   Benigno Aquino, Jr. (1932-1983), Philippine political leader. *Foreign Affairs*, July 1968.

7. There are no dangerous thoughts; thinking itself is dangerous.

   Hannah Arendt (1906-1975), American political philosopher. Quoted in *The New Yorker*, Dec. 5, 1977.

8. Men may die, but the fabric of free institutions remains unshaken.

   Chester A. Arthur (1830-1886), 21st President of the United States (R-OH). Remark following the assassination of President Garfield. Inaugural address, Sept. 22, 1881.

9. Liberty without socialism is privilege and injustice; socialism without liberty is slavery and brutality.

   Mikhail Bakunin (1814-1876), Russian anarchist. *Federalism, Socialism, Anti-Theologism*.

10. It is the indispensable duty of those who maintain for themselves the rights of human nature, and who profess the obligations of Christianity, to extend their power and influence to the relief of every part of the human race, from whatever burden of oppression they may labor under.

    Benjamin Banneker (1731-1806), American publisher and scientist. Letter to Thomas Jefferson. Aug. 19, 1791.

11. No Arab in the Arab world enjoys the civil freedoms that the Arabs in Israel enjoy.

    I. Y. Bar-Itzhack, professor, Israel Institute of Technology (Technion). Letter to *The Washington Post*, Nov. 20, 1988.

12. We do not want to be anybody's pawns. We are an ancient people. We want our autonomy. We want *sarbasti* – freedom. I do not know who will take my place one day. But they cannot crush us.

    Massoud Barzani (c. 1900-1979), Kurdish leader. Interview, *The New York Times*, Mar. 1979.

13. The abetters of slavery are weaving the thread in the loom, but God is adjusting the pattern. They are asses harnessed to the chariot of Liberty, and, whether they will or no, must draw it on.

    Henry Ward Beecher (1813-1887), American clergyman and writer. *Life Thoughts*, 1858.

14. Liberty is the soul's right to breathe.

    Henry Ward Beecher. *Ibid.*

15. Disorder is the child of authority and compulsion. Liberty is the mother of order.

    Alexander Berkman (1870-1936), American anarchist. *What Is Communist Anarchism?*, 1920.

16. Real freedom means opportunity and well-being. If it does not mean that, it means nothing.
Alexander Berkman. *Ibid.*

17. Freedom is not an end. Freedom is a beginning.
Benazir Bhutto, Prime Minister of Pakistan. Address to U.S. Congress, June 5, 1989.

18. The Founding Fathers gave the free press the protection it must have to bare the secrets of government and inform the people.
Hugo L. Black (1886-1971), U.S. Senator (D-AL) and U.S. Supreme Court Justice. Quoted in *The New York Times*, June 30, 1971.

19. No law means no law!
Hugo L. Black. Referring to the First Amendment: "Congress shall make no law abridging the freedom of speech or of the press." Quoted by Nat Hentoff, *The Washington Post*, June 30, 1990.

20. The free man is he who does not fear to go to the end of his thought.
Léon Blum (1872-1950), Premier of France. Attributed.

21. Because I was born a slave, I love liberty more than you.
Ludwig Boerne (1786-1837), German journalist. *Letters from Paris*, Feb. 7, 1832.

22. The difference between liberty and liberties is as great as between God and gods.
Ludwig Boerne. *Fragments and Aphorisms*, No. 54, 1840.

23. It is not slogans or bullets but only institutions that can make (and keep) people free.
Daniel Boorstin, American historian and Librarian of Congress. *U.S. News & World Report*, Feb. 5, 1990.

24. Without an unfettered press, without liberty of speech, all the outward forms and structures of free institutions are a sham, a pretense – the sheerest mockery.
William E. Borah (1865-1940), U.S. Senator (R-ID). Senate speech, Apr. 19, 1917.

25. Those who won our independence by revolution were not cowards. They did not fear political change. They did not exalt order at the cost of liberty.
Louis D. Brandeis (1856-1941), U.S. Supreme Court Justice. *Whitney* v. *California*, 1927.

26. Experience should teach us to be most on our guard to protect liberty when the government's purposes are beneficent.
Louis D. Brandeis. *Olmstead* v. *United States*, 1927 (dissent).

27. Debate on public issues should be uninhibited, robust and wide-open, and ... it may well include vehement, caustic, and sometimes unpleasantly sharp attacks on government and public officials.
William J. Brennan, Jr., U.S. Supreme Court Justice. *New York Times Co.* v. *Sullivan*, 1964.

28. If there is a bedrock principle underlying the First Amendment, it is that the government may not prohibit the expression of an idea simply because society finds the idea itself offensive or disagreeable.
William J. Brennan, Jr. *Texas* v. *Johnson*, 1989.

29. Freedom Danced Before My Eyes
Tom Brokaw, American TV journalist. Title of article describing the breaching of the Berlin Wall. *The New York Times*, Nov. 19, 1989.

30. The right to discuss freely and openly, by speech, by the press, by the pen, all political questions, and to examine and animadvert upon all political institutions ... *[is]* a right as clear and certain, so interwoven with our other liberties, so necessary, in fact, to their existence that without it we must fall at once into despotism and anarchy.
William Cullen Bryant (1794-1878), American poet and editor. *New York Evening Post*, Nov. 18, 1837.

31. None who have always been free can understand the terrible fascinating power of the hope of freedom on those who are not free.
Pearl S. Buck (1892-1973), Nobel Laureate in Literature (United States). *What America Means to Me*, 1943.

32. Equal rights under the law and reproductive freedom are synonymous.
Alan Burke, U.S. Congressman (D-CA). Speech, abortion rights march, Washington, DC, Apr. 9, 1989.

33. Liberty, too, must be limited in order to be possessed.
Edmund Burke (1729-1797), British statesman. *Letter to the Sheriffs of Bristol*, 1777.

34. The people never give up their liberties but under some delusion.
Edmund Burke. Speech, Bucks County, England, 1784.

35. It is ordained in the eternal constitution of things that men of intemperate minds cannot be free. Their passions forge their fetters.
Edmund Burke. *Letter to a Member of the French National Assembly*, 1791.

36. The habit of declaring sympathy for the enemy will not be allowed. Persons committing such offenses will be arrested with a view toward being tried, or sent beyond our lines to the lines of our friends.

Ambrose E. Burnside (1824-1881), General of the Union Army. General Order No. 38.

37. Liberty dearer than Union

John C. Calhoun (1782-1850), U.S. Congressman (D-SC), U.S. Senator, U.S. Secretary of War, U.S. Secretary of State, and Vice President of the United States. Motto. (Compare Abraham Lincoln's "Liberty and Union.")

38. I am a Canadian, a free Canadian, free to speak without fear, free to worship God in my own way, free to stand for what I think right, free to oppose what I believe wrong, or free to choose those who shall govern my country. This heritage of freedom I pledge to uphold for myself and all mankind.

Canadian Bill of Rights, Adopted July 1, 1960.

39. The Republic may not give wealth or happiness; she has not promised these. It is the freedom to pursue these, not their realization, which the Declaration of Independence claims.

Andrew Carnegie (1835-1919), American industrialist and philanthropist. *Triumphant Democracy*, 1886.

40. In a free country there is much clamor with little suffering; in a despotic state there is little complaint, but much suffering.

Lazare Carnot (1753-1823), French statesman and general. Quoted in S. Austin Allibone, *Prose Quotations*, 1876.

41. The very freedom we seek cannot be attained until we chain some of our exaggerated individuality.

Gerald Emmett Carter, Canadian Roman Catholic cardinal. Speech, Toronto, Dec. 6, 1979.

42. History teaches, perhaps, very few clear lessons. But surely one such lesson learned by the world at great cost is that aggression, unopposed, becomes a contagious disease.

Jimmy Carter, 39th President of the United States (D-GA). Speech to the nation about the Russian invasion of Afghanistan. Jan. 4, 1980.

43. When George Washington and the others created U.S. independence, they did not free the slaves; not long ago, a U.S. black athlete could not play baseball in the major leagues. And yet you called yours the freest country in the world.

Fidel Castro, Premier of Cuba. Interview, *Playboy*, Aug. 1985.

44. The majority are not morally free to become a tyranny and destroy the rights of minorities.

Catholic Association for International Peace. *Timeless Rights*, 1948.

45. The cry has been that when war is declared, all opposition should therefore be hushed. A sentiment more unworthy of a free country should hardly be propagated. If the doctrine be admitted, rulers have only to declare war and they are screened at once from scrutiny.

William Ellery Channing (1780-1842), American Unitarian minister and reformer. Quoted in George Seldes, *The Great Quotations*, 1960.

46. We have assembled, as a union of freedom for the sake of freedom, forgetting all past differences in a common resolve to maintain the rights of free labor against the aggressions of Slave Power, and to secure a free soil for a free people.... Our calm but final answer is, no more slave states, and no more slave territory. Let the soil of our extensive domain be kept free.

Salmon P. Chase (1808-1873), Governor of Ohio (Free Soil), U.S. Senator (Free Soil and R), U.S. Secretary of the Treasury, and Chief Justice, U.S. Supreme Court. Free Soil Party platform, 1848.

47. Free I was born, have lived, and will die.

Christina (1626-1689), Queen of Sweden. Motto on a medal struck during her reign.

48. Political freedom is rare enough in the world, but the kind of social and cultural freedom which is the hallmark of Canada is even less common.

Joe Clark, Prime Minister of Canada (Liberal). Speech, House of Commons, Feb. 18, 1977.

49. There is no rest for free peoples; rest is a monarchical idea.

Georges Clemenceau (1841-1929), Premier of France and journalist. Speech, Chamber of Deputies, 1883.

50. Make no laws whatsoever concerning speech, and speech will be free; so soon as you make a declaration on paper that speech will be free, you will have a hundred lawyers proving that "freedom does not mean abuse, nor liberty license"; and they will define and define freedom out of existence.

Voltarine de Cleyre (1866-1912), French poet and essayist. Quoted in Upton Sinclair, *The Cry for Justice*, 1920.

51. The American people ... have a stake in nonconformity, for they know that the American genius is nonconformist.

Henry Steele Commager, American historian. *Harper's Magazine*, Sept. 1947.

52. Books are feeders of brothels.

Anthony Comstock (1844-1915), Founder, New York Society for the Suppression of Vice, and official censor, U.S. Post Office. Quoted in Wallechinsky and Wallace, *The People's Almanac*, 1975.

53. You may rob the army of its commander in chief, but you cannot deprive the humblest peasant of his opinion.

Confucius (551-458 B.C.), Chinese philosopher. *Analects*.

54. Why is my liberty judged by another man's conscience?

New Testament, *1 Corinthians* 10:29.

55. Where the spirit of the Lord is, there is liberty.

New Testament, *2 Corinthians* 3:17.

56. We do not believe in having happiness imposed upon us.

José Correa, Nicaraguan Ambassador to the United Nations. Statement to the U.N. Ambassador from the U.S.S.R.. Quoted in *The New York Times*, Oct. 20, 1960.

57. The condition upon which God hath given liberty to man is eternal vigilance.

John Philpot Curran (1750-1817), Irish barrister and orator. Speech on the right of election of the Lord Mayor of Dublin, July 10, 1790.

58. Liberty and good government do not exclude each other.

John Dahlberg, 1st Baron Acton (1834-1902), historian and Member of Parliament, Great Britain (Whig). *The History of Freedom in Antiquity*, 1877.

59. The Constitution is a delusion and a snare if the weakest and humblest man in the land cannot be defended in his right to speak and his right to think as much as the strongest in the land.

Clarence S. Darrow (1857-1938), American attorney and author. Defense of Communist Labor Party, 1920.

60. If they come for me in the morning, they will come for you at night.

Angela Davis, Communist Party candidate for President of the United States. Speech, Berkeley, CA, 1971.

61. These are strange times when American citizens are to be assailed under cover of a message to Congress for exercising their inalienable right of the discussion of the policies and acts of the administration. If this liberty is taken from us, what is left of the democracy of which we boast? What better are we than Russia?

James R. Day (1845-1923), Chancellor of Syracuse University, NY. Statement in response to Pres. Theodore Roosevelt's castigating him for writing articles in defense of the Standard Oil Company and other monied interests that Roosevelt had attacked in his Jan. 29, 1908, message to Congress. Feb. 1, 1908.

62. While there is a lower class I am in it. While there is a criminal element I am of it. While there is a soul in prison I am not free.

Eugene V. Debs (1855-1926), American Socialist. Address to the court on being sentenced for violation of the U.S. Espionage Act by speaking against World War I, Sept. 14, 1918.

63. Freedom isn't a gift, it's a task.

Jean Paul Desbiens (Brother Anonymous), Canadian priest and author. *For Pity's Sake*, 1965.

64. Freedom is the right to be wrong, not the right to do wrong.

John G. Diefenbaker (1895-1975), Prime Minister of Canada (Conservative). Quoted in *Reader's Digest*, Sept. 1979.

65. Never participate in anything without consulting the American Legion or your local Chamber of Commerce.

Martin Dies (1901-1972), U.S. Congressman (D-TX). Hearings, House Un-American Activities Committee, 1939.

66. We all think our own speech rights are the ones that count, and our neighbors' rights a little less so.

Norman Dorson, President, American Civil Liberties Union. Quoted in *The New York Times Magazine*, Sep 10, 1989.

67. In this nation every writer, actor, or producer ... should be free from the censor.

William O. Douglas (1898-1980), U.S. Supreme Court Justice. *Superior Films* v. *U.S. Department of Education*, 1952-53.

68. Censorship has had a long history in the Western world. Book banning is as old as books.

William O. Douglas. *We the Judges*, 1956.

69. Advocacy and belief go hand in hand. For there can be no true freedom of mind if thoughts are

secure only when they are pent up.
William O. Douglas. *Speiser* v. *Randall*, 1957.

70. My motto is EXTERMINATION.... The slaveholders not only forfeit their right to liberty, but to life itself.
Frederick Douglass (c.1817-1895), Recorder of Deeds, District of Columbia, and U.S. Minister to Haiti. Speech, Free Soil Party convention, Pittsburgh, PA, Aug. 11, 1852.

71. Every one of us should be ashamed to be free while his brother is a slave.
Frederick Douglass. Quoted in Lerone Bennett, Jr., *Pioneers in Protest*, 1968.

72. There can be no liberty where the military is not subordinate to the civil power.
James Duane (1733-1797), member, Continental Congress, and 1st Mayor of New York City; **John Jay** (1745-1829), U.S. Foreign Secretary and 1st Chief Justice, U.S. Supreme Court; **John Alsop** (1724-1794), member, Continental Congress, and President of the New York Chamber of Commerce; **Lewis Morris** (1726-1798), member, Continental Congress. Letter to the New York Provincial Convention, March 1, 1776.

73. You are not alone. You will never be alone as long as you continue to play worthily your part in the great design of human freedom.
John Foster Dulles (1888-1959), U.S. Secretary of State and U.S. Senator (R-NY). Speech to the Korean Parliament, June 19, 1950.

74. I have made the great discovery that liberty is a product of order.
Will Durant (1885-1981), American historian. Remark on winning the Pulitzer Prize (with Ariel Durant). Quoted in *The New York Times*, May 7, 1968.

75. Don't put no constrictions on da people. Leave 'em the hell alone.
Jimmy Durante (1893-1980), American entertainer. Quoted in George Seldes, *The Great Quotations*, 1983.

76. Gentlemen, radical abolitionism must be put down. This great and glorious country will be shattered into fragments if it is not, or else we shall find ourselves at last brought under the iron rule of military despotism.
Ira A. Eastman, New Hampshire Copperhead gubernatorial candidate. Nomination acceptance speech, 1864.

77. The real guarantee of freedom is an equilibrium of social forces in conflict, not the triumph of any one force.
Max F. Eastman (1883-1969), American writer and editor. *Reflections on the Failure of Socialism*, 1955.

78. Man should be master of his environment, not its slave. That is what freedom means.
Anthony Eden (1897-1977), Prime Minister of Great Britain (Conservative). Speech, Conservative Conference, Oct. 1946.

79. True liberty consists only in the power of doing what we ought to well, and in not being constrained to do what we ought not to do.
Jonathan Edwards (1703-1758), American clergyman. Quoted in *The Congressional Record*, June 29, 1950.

80. Everything that is really great and inspiring is created by the individual who can labor in freedom.
Albert Einstein (1879-1955), Nobel Laureate in Physics (Switzerland). *Out of My Later Years*, 1950.

81. Don't join the book burners. Don't think you are going to conceal faults by concealing evidence that they ever existed. Don't be afraid to go into your library and read every book so long as any document does not offend your own ideas of decency. That should be the only censorship.
Dwight D. Eisenhower (1890-1969), 34th President of the United States (R-KS). Commencement address, Dartmouth College, Hanover, NH, June 14, 1953.

82. The word *liberty* in the mouth of Mr. *[Daniel]* Webster sounds like the word *love* in the mouth of a courtesan.
[Webster, a Senator from South Carolina, was a supporter of the Fugitive Slave Law.]
Ralph Waldo Emerson (1803-1882), American writer. *Journals*, May 1851.

83. Intellect annuls fate. So far as a man thinks, he is free.
Ralph Waldo Emerson. *The Conduct of Life*, 1860.

84. When it becomes possible to speak of freedom, the state, as such, will cease to exist.
Friedrich Engels (1820-1895), German Socialist and revolutionary theorist. Letter to A. Bebel, Mar. 18, 1875.

85. Freedom is a noble thing.
Who loseth his freedom, he loseth all.
Who hath freedom hath all sufficient.
Freedom and liberty should not be sold for all the gold and silver in the world.
English proverbs, c. 1375-1484.

86. The liberty of the press would be an empty sound, and no man would venture to write on any subject, however pure his purpose, without an attorney at one elbow and a counsel at the other. From minds thus subdued by the fear of punishment, there could issue no works of genius to expand the empire of human reason, nor any masterly compositions on the general nature of government.

Thomas Erskine (1750-1823), Lord Chancellor of Great Britain. Trial of John Stockdale, Dec. 9, 1789.

87. Let my people go!

Old Testament, *Exodus* 5:1.

88. We must be free not because we claim freedom, but because we practice it.

William Faulkner (1897-1962), American writer. *Harper's Magazine*, June 1956.

89. Freedom is not worth fighting for if it means no more than license for everyone to get as much as he can for himself. And freedom is worth fighting for. Because it does mean more than unrestricted grabbing.

Dorothy Canfield Fisher (1879-1958), American writer. *Seasoned Timber*, 1939.

90. What freedom? To be wage-slaves, hired and fired at the will of a soulless corporation?

Elizabeth Gurley Flynn (1890-1964), labor leader, International Workers of the World. *The Rebel Girl*, 1955.

91. Nothing confers freedom like a buck in the bank.

Malcolm S. Forbes (1919-1990), publisher, *Forbes* magazine. Quoted on CBS, *Evening News*, Feb. 25, 1990.

92. We are for liberty, but liberty with order, the kind of liberty which will not threaten the basic principles of our nation, nor threaten its faith and unity.

Francisco Franco (1892-1975), President of Spain. Speech, Vitoria, Spain, 1939.

93. The safeguards of liberty have frequently been forged in cases involving not very nice people.

Felix Frankfurter (1882-1965), U.S. Supreme Court Justice. Quoted in Edward Bennett Williams, *One Man's Freedom*, 1962.

94. In those wretched countries where a man cannot call his tongue his own, he can scarce call anything his own.... Whoever would overthrow the liberty of a nation must begin by subduing the freeness of speech.

Benjamin Franklin (1706-1790), member, Continental Congress and Constitutional Convention, Governor of Pennsylvania, and U.S. Minister to France. *Dogwood Papers*, 1722.

95. Where liberty dwells, there is my country.

Benjamin Franklin. Letter, 1785.

96. Those who would give up essential liberty to purchase a little temporary safety deserve neither liberty nor safety.

Benjamin Franklin. Quoted in *Hoyt's New Cyclopedia of Practical Quotations*, 1922.

97. History suggests that capitalism is a necessary condition for political freedom. Clearly it is not a sufficient condition.

Milton Friedman, Nobel Laureate in Economics (United States). *Capitalism and Freedom*, 1962.

98. As the principle of liberty is better understood, and more nobly interpreted, a broader protest is made in behalf of women.

Sarah Margaret Fuller (1810-1850), American writer. *Woman in the Nineteenth Century*, 1845.

99. Under the privilege of the First Amendment many, many ridiculous things are said.

John Kenneth Galbraith, American economist and U.S. Ambassador to India (D). PBS, *Firing Line*, Dec. 9, 1989.

100. Freedom and slavery are mental states.

Mohandas K. Gandhi (1869-1948), Indian political and spiritual leader. *Non-Violence in Peace and War*, 1948.

101. Freedom is not worth having if it does not connote freedom to err.

Mohandas K. Gandhi. Quoted in *Saturday Review*, Mar. 1, 1959.

102. Rather die freemen than live to be the slaves.

Henry Highland Garnet (1815-1881), American clergyman. "An Address to the Slaves of the United States," National Negro Convention, Buffalo, NY, Aug. 31, 1843. (Held in conjunction with the Liberty [Abolitionist] Party Convention.)

103. The apologist for oppression becomes himself the oppressor. To palliate crime is to be guilty of its perpetuation.

William Lloyd Garrison (1805-1879), American editor and abolitionist. *The Liberator*, Jan. 1, 1831.

104. God never made a tyrant, or a slave.

William Lloyd Garrison. Speech, Fort Sumter, SC, Apr. 15, 1865.

105. He who opposes the public liberty overthrows his own.

William Lloyd Garrison. Quoted in Garrison and Garrison, *William Lloyd Garrison: The Story of His Life Told by His Children*, IV, 1889.

106. For liberty means justice, and justice is the natural law – the law of health and symmetry and strength, of fraternity and cooperation.

Henry George (1839-1897), American political economist. *Progress and Poverty*, 1879.

107. Our country has liberty without license and authority without despotism.

James Gibbons (1834-1921), American Roman Catholic cardinal. Speech, Rome, Italy, Mar. 28, 1887.

108. Unless men are taught to rely upon themselves they can never be truly worthy of the name of freemen.

William E. Gladstone (1809-1898), Prime Minister of Great Britain (Liberal). Speech in the House of Commons, Apr. 26, 1870.

109. And only law can give us freedom.

Johann Wolfgang von Goethe (1749-1832), German poet and dramatist. *Nature and Art*.

110. Extremism in the defense of liberty is no vice.... Moderation in the pursuit of freedom is no virtue.

Barry M. Goldwater, U.S. Senator (R-AZ). Presidential nomination acceptance speech, Republican National Convention, Houston, TX, 1964.

111. Show me a country in which there are no strikes and I'll show you that country in which there is no liberty.

Samuel Gompers (1850-1924), President, American Federation of Labor. *Seventy Years of Life and Labor*, 1925.

112. I hold a jail more roomy ... than would be the whole world if I were to submit to repression.

Samuel Gompers. *Ibid.*

113. Freedom of choice is a universal principle that ... applies both to the capitalist and the socialist system.

Mikhail Gorbachev, President of the U.S.S.R. Speech, United Nations, 1988.

114. Anything less than liberty is inadequate.

Henry Grattan (1746-1820), Member of Parliaments, Ireland and Great Britain. Speech, Irish Parliament, Apr. 19, 1780.

115. Freedom of speech cannot be rationed; it is a single entity that belongs to all.

Vartan Gregorian, President, Brown University. *Brown Alumni Monthly*, May 1991.

116. ... the worst plague of all, namely, unrestrained liberty of opinion and freedom of speech.

Pope Gregory XVI (1765-1846). Encyclical, *Mirari Vos*, 1832.

117. The lamps are going out all over Europe; we shall not see them lit again in our lifetime.

Edward Grey, Viscount Fallodon (1862-1933), Foreign Secretary, Great Britain (Liberal). Aug. 4, 1914.

118. We're not against people demonstrating. We want people to exercise their First Amendment rights. They can do that by simply demonstrating across the street, in a way that doesn't block the door or harass women.

Mary Grundrum, Director, Center for Constitutional Rights. In reference to the tactics of antiabortion activists blocking the entrances of abortion clinics. Quoted in *Ms.*, Apr. 1989.

119. Men will sooner surrender their rights than their customs.

Mortiz Guedemann (1835-1918), German rabbi. *Geschichte des Erziehungswesens*, 1888.

120. Shout *freedom!* and the talismanic word will open all the treasures of the soul.

Sarah J. Hale (1788-1879), American magazine editor. *Traits of American Life*, 1835.

121. New Englanders continue to persecute each other for opinion's sake. Here *[New York City]* you enjoy extensive freedom – freedom in newspaper abuse; freedom to gamble in Wall Street; freedom in marriage; freedom in divorce; free lager; free fights; free voting; free love!

Abraham Oakey Hall (1826-1898), Mayor of New York City (D). Welcoming speech to the New England Society. Quoted in J. Werner, *Tammany Hall*, 1928.

122. What is the liberty of the press? Who can give it any definition that would not leave the utmost latitude for evasion?

Alexander Hamilton (1755-1804), Member, Continental Congress and Constitutional Convention, and U.S. Secretary of the Treasury (Federalist-NY). Argument against explicit guarantees of press freedom in the Constitution. *The Federalist*, No. 84, May 28, 1788.

123. The loss of liberty to a generous mind is worse than death.

Andrew Hamilton (1676-1741), American lawyer and newspaper publisher. Defense argument at the trial of John Peter Zenger, New York City, Aug. 4, 1735.

124. The spirit of liberty is the spirit which is not too sure that it is right.
Learned Hand (1872-1961), Federal Judge. Speech, I Am an American Day, New York City, May 21, 1944.

125. A society is which men recognize no check upon their freedom soon becomes a society where freedom is a possession of a savage few.
Learned Hand. *Life*, July 1, 1944.

126. Liberty dies in the hearts of men and women: when it dies there, no constitution, no law, no court can save it.
Learned Hand. Quoted in *Brown Alumni Monthly*, May 1991.

127. Liberty regulated by law is the underlying principle of our institutions.
John Marshall Harlan (1833-1911), U.S. Supreme Court Justice. *Sparf* v. *United States*, 1894.

128. Socialism was embraced by the greater part of the intelligentsia as the apparent heir of the liberal tradition: therefore it is not surprising that to them the idea of socialism's leading to the opposite of liberty should appear inconceivable.
Friedrich A. Hayek (1899-1992), Nobel Laureate in Economics (United States). *The Road to Serfdom*, 1944.

129. If we had American-style personal freedom, then China would fall into terrible chaos.
He Xin, Chinese social commentator. Quoted in *The New York Times*, Mar. 20, 1990.

130. The greatest right in the world is the right to be wrong.... No person or set of persons can properly establish a standard of expression for others.
William Randolph Hearst (1863-1951), U.S. Congressman (D-NY); founder, Independence League Party; journalist; and publisher. Independence League platform, 1924.

131. The history of the world is none other than the progress of the consciousness of freedom.
Georg Wilhelm Friedrich Hegel (1770-1831), German philosopher. *The Philosophy of History*, 1832.

132. Whenever books are burned, men also in the end are burned.
Heinrich Heine (1797-1856), German writer. *Almansor*, 1823.

133. Since the Exodus, Freedom has always spoken with a Hebrew accent.
Heinrich Heine. *Germany to Luther*, 1834.

134. Freedom and equality! They are not to be found on the earth below or in heaven above. The stars on high are not alike, and all obey an ironlike law.
Heinrich Heine. *English Fragments*, No. 1.

135. I really do not know whether I deserve that a laurel wreath be laid on my coffin. But you may lay a sword on my coffin, for I was a brave soldier in the war of freedom for mankind.
Heinrich Heine. *Journey from Munich to Genoa*, No. 31.

136. Is life so dear, or peace so sweet, as to be purchased at the price of chains and slavery? Forbid it, Almighty God! I know not what course others may take, but as for me, give me liberty or give me death.
Patrick Henry (1736-1799), Member, Virginia House of Burgesses and Continental Congress, Governor of Virginia, and member, Virginia Constitutional Ratification Convention. Speech, St. John's Church, Richmond, VA, Mar. 23, 1775.

137. Guard with jealous attention to the public liberty. Suspect everyone who approaches that jewel. Unfortunately, nothing will preserve it but downright force.
Patrick Henry. Remark to militiamen, 1778.

138. I never knew I had so many rights.
Shawn Hinton, student. Remark after attending bicentennial conference on the New York ratification of the Constitution. Quoted in *The New York Times*, July 27, 1988.

139. The National Socialist Party will prevent in the future, by force if necessary, all meetings and lectures which are likely to exercise a depressing influence on the German state.
Adolf Hitler (1889-1945), Führer of the Third German Reich. Speech, Munich, Jan. 4, 1921.

140. The tendency of all strong governments has always been to suppress liberty, partly in order to ease the processes of rule, partly from sheer disbelief in innovation.
John A. Hobson (1858-1940), British economist. *Free Thought in the Social Sciences*, 1926.

141. Where men cannot freely convey their thoughts to one another, no other liberty is secure.
William E. Hocking (1873-1966), professor of philosophy, Harvard University. *Freedom of the Press*, 1947.

142. Where freedom is real, equality is the passion of the masses. Where equality is real, freedom is the passion of a small minority.

Eric Hoffer (1902-1983), American writer and critic. *The True Believer*, 1951.

143. The defendants had as much right to publish *[Bolshevik literature]* as the government has to publish the Constitution.
Oliver Wendell Holmes, Jr. (1841-1935), U.S. Supreme Court Justice. *Abrams* v. *United States*, 1919.

144. The most stringent protection of free speech would not protect a man in falsely shouting "Fire!' in a theater and causing a panic.
Oliver Wendell Holmes, Jr.. *Schenck* v. *United States*, 1919.

145. To silence criticism is to silence freedom.
Sidney Hook (1902-1989), American philosopher. *The New York Times Magazine*, Sept. 30, 1951.

146. Economic freedom cannot be sacrificed if political freedom is to be preserved.
Herbert Hoover (1874-1964), 31st President of the United States (R-IA). Campaign speech, New York City, Oct. 31, 1932.

147. Freedom cannot long service where defiance and contempt are tolerated or condoned. That is why our country can ill-afford the binge of so-called civil disobedience which has erupted on the streets ... and across the campuses of many colleges and universities.
J. Edgar Hoover (1895-1972), Director, Federal Bureau of Investigation. Speech, Michigan Bar Association, Lansing, MI, June 8, 1967.

148. Rights are useless unless the possessor knows about them.
Charles Horsky, President, Council for Court Excellence. Quoted on C-SPAN, Mar. 25, 1990.

149. What we cannot do in a courtroom via criminal prosecutions to curtail the activities of some of these groups *[anti-administration, dissident political groups]*, IRS could do by administrative action. Moreover, valuable intelligence-type information could be turned up by IRS as a result of their field audits.
Tom Charles Houston, presidential assistant (R). Memorandum to White House Chief of Staff H. R. Haldeman, Sept. 21, 1970.

150. We talk about "rugged individualism" and "personal liberty." My dear friends, both of those disappeared from the earth the day the first colony of cave men held a conference around a community fire.
Louis McHenry Howe (1871-1935), presidential assistant (D). Speech, Progressive Education Association, Nov. 1933.

151. If the President takes away from the strong man the right to hit the little man over the head with a club, is that too great curtailment of liberty? We must assure the little man's right not to be clubbed.
Louis McHenry Howe. Interview, Associated Press, 1935.

152. The right to be heard does not include the right to be taken seriously.
Hubert H. Humphrey (1911-1978), Vice President of the United States and U.S. Senator (D-MN). Attributed.

153. The one reason we know that every totalitarian government must fail is that no totalitarian government is prepared to face the consequence of free universities.
Robert M. Hutchins (1899-1977), President, University of Chicago, and President, Center for the Study of Democratic Institutions. Quoted in William O. Douglas, *An Almanac of Liberty*, 1954.

154. The policy of repression of ideas cannot work and has never worked.
Robert M. Hutchins. Testimony, Illinois Subversive Activities Committee, Apr. 1949.

155. A thirst for liberty seems to be the ruling passion not only of America but of the present age.... It must work anarchy and confusion.
Thomas Hutchinson (1711-1780), Colonial Governor of Massachusetts. Letter to John H. Hutchinson, Jan. 18, 1769.

156. Free speech is meaningless unless it tolerates the speech that we hate.
Henry J. Hyde, U.S. Congressman (R-IL). Speech, May 3, 1991.

157. One should never put on one's best trousers to go out to fight for freedom.
Henrik Ibsen (1828-1906), Norwegian writer. *An Enemy of the People*, 1882.

158. While they shriek for "freedom of the press" when there is no slightest threat to that freedom, they deny to citizens that freedom *from* the press to which the decencies of life entitle them. They misrepresent, they distort, they color, they blackguard, they lie.
Harold L. Ickes (1874-1952), U.S. Secretary of the Interior (R). *America's House of Lords*.

159. You have no right to erect your toll gate upon the highways of thought.
Robert Green Ingersoll (1833-1899), Attorney General of Illinois (R). *The Gods*, 1872.

160. By intellectual liberty I mean the right to think and the right to think wrong.
Robert Green Ingersoll. Attributed.

161. There is no slavery but ignorance. Liberty is the child of intelligence.
Robert Green Ingersoll. Motto.

162. The price of freedom of religion or of speech or of the press is that we must put up with and even pay for a good deal of rubbish.
Robert H. Jackson (1892-1954), U.S. Attorney General (D) and U.S. Supreme Court Justice. *United States* v. *Ballard*, 1943.

163. Our forefathers found the evils of free thinking more to be endured than the evils of inquest or suppression. This is because thoughtful, bold, independent minds are essential to wise and considered self-government.
Robert H. Jackson. Quoted in *Atlantic Monthly*, Jan. 1955.

164. We prefer death to slavery.
Eleazar ben Jair (d. 73), Jewish zealot who led 960 men, women, and children in a mass suicide at Masada. Quoted by Josephus, *War*, VII, viii, 6.

165. The God who gave us life, gave us liberty at the same time.
Thomas Jefferson (1743-1826), 3rd President of the United States (Democratic Republican-VA). *Summary View of the Rights of British America*, 1774.

166. The sheep are happier of themselves than under the care of the wolves.
Thomas Jefferson. *Notes on the State of Virginia*, 1784.

167. The tree of liberty must be refreshed from time to time with the blood of patriots and tyrants. It is its natural manure.
Thomas Jefferson. Letter to William Stevens Smith, Nov. 13, 1787.

168. The natural progress of things is for liberty to yield and government to gain ground.
Thomas Jefferson. Letter to Edward Carrington, May 27, 1788.

169. To give liberty to, or rather, to abandon persons whose habits have been formed in slavery is like abandoning children.
Thomas Jefferson. Letter to E. Bancroft, 1789.

170. Error of opinion may be tolerated where reason is left free to combat it.
Thomas Jefferson. First inaugural address, Mar. 4, 1801.

171. We are bound, you and I, and everyone, to make common cause, even with error itself, to maintain the common right of freedom of conscience.
Thomas Jefferson. Letter to Dr. Benjamin Rush, 1813.

172. People are hung sometimes for speaking the truth.
Joan of Arc (1412-1431), French military hero. Statement at her trial, Feb. 23, 1431.

173. The truth shall make you free.
New Testament, *John* 8:32.

174. Communism is the wave of the past, and freedom is the wave of the future.
Lyndon B. Johnson (1908-1973), 36th President of the United States (D-TX). Campaign speech, Springfield, IL, Oct. 7, 1964.

175. Free speech, free press, free religion, the right of free assembly, yes, the right of petition – well, they are still radical ideas.
Lyndon B. Johnson. Speech, International Platform Association, Aug. 3, 1965.

176. Every man has a right to utter what he thinks truth, and every other man has a right to knock him down for it.
Samuel Johnson (1709-1784), British writer and lexicographer. Quoted in James Boswell, *The Life of Samuel Johnson*, 1780.

177. The danger of unbounded liberty *[of printing]*, and the danger of bounding it, have produced a problem in the science of government, which human understanding seems hitherto unable to solve.
Samuel Johnson. *Lives of the English Poets*, 1781.

178. The Supreme Court has always been the last bastion of the protection of our freedoms.
Barbara Jordan, U.S. Congresswoman (D-TX). PBS, *MacNeil-Lehrer Report*, June 23, 1989.

179. Freedom for all; but the power and welfare of the fatherland above all.
Wilhelm Jordan (1819-1904), Prussian writer and Liberal politician. Speech, July 1848.

180. Freedom is that faculty which enlarges all other faculties.

Immanuel Kant (1724-1804), German philosopher. Lecture at Königsberg, 1775.

181. We must be willing to sacrifice a small measure of our liberties to preserve the great bulk of them.

Clarence M. Kelley, Director, Federal Bureau of Investigation. Aug. 9, 1975.

182. There are no limits to our future if we don't put limits on our people.

Jack F. Kemp, U.S. Congressman and U.S. Secretary of Housing and Urban Development (R-NY). Quoted in *The 1989 Conservative Calendar*.

183. We are not against any man – or any nation – or any system – except as it is hostile to freedom.

John F. Kennedy (1917-1963), 35th President of the United States (D-MA). Address to Congress, May 25, 1961.

184. All free men, wherever they may live, are citizens of Berlin. And therefore, as a free man, I take pride in the words, *Ich bin ein Berliner ["I am a Berliner"].*

John F. Kennedy. Speech, Berlin, West Germany, June 26, 1963.

185. Freedom is the ability to defend yourself.

Alan L. Keys, Maryland Republican candidate for U.S. Senate. Symposium, Federalist Society, Mar. 1990.

186. Human rights means that unsuitable individuals should be liquidated so that others can live free.

Sadeq Khalkhali, Iranian judge. Quoted in Robin Wright, *The Khomeini Decade*, 1989.

187. Freedom is never voluntarily given by the oppressor; it must be demanded by the oppressed.

Martin Luther King, Jr. (1929-1968), American clergyman and civil rights leader. *Why We Can't Wait*, 1964.

188. Our freedom was not won a century ago, it is not won today; but some small part of it is in our hands, and we are marching no longer by ones and twos but in legions of thousands, convinced now it cannot be denied by any human force.

Martin Luther King, Jr. Speech to the United Nations, Apr. 15, 1967.

189. The principle of free speech is no new doctrine born of the Constitution of the United States. It is a heritage of English-speaking peoples, which has been won by incalculable sacrifice, and which they must preserve so long as they hope to live as free men.

Robert M. La Follette (1855-1925), Governor of Wisconsin and U.S. Senator (R-WI). Senate speech, Oct. 6, 1917.

190. Only a well-fed, well-housed, well-schooled people can enjoy the blessings of liberty.

Fiorello H. La Guardia (1882-1947), U.S. Congressman (R and Socialist) and Mayor of New York City (R and Fusion Party). Campaign speech, 1922.

191. In every state, good or bad, there will be a number of restless, subtle, crafty, turbulent and ungovernable spirits; who by writings and intrigues will be exciting discontent and stirring up mischief: and will molest and embarrass the best as well as the worst administration.

Samuel Langdon (1723-1797), President, Harvard College. Election sermon, Massachusetts Bay Colony Congress, Watertown, MA, May 31, 1775.

192. Every State is known by the rights it maintains.

Harold J. Laski (1893-1950), British political scientist. *A Grammar of Politics*, 1925.

193. When men hold their peace, the stones will cry out.

Ferdinand Lassalle (1825-1864), founder, German Social Democratic Party. Speech, Assize Court, Aug. 11, 1848.

194. The spirit of liberty is not the result of culture. It may be found in the lowest man.

Wilfrid Laurier (1841-1919), Prime Minister of Canada (Liberal). Speech, Toronto, Dec. 10, 1886.

195. Freedom of speech only exists in proportion to indifference to the thing spoken of.

Stephen Leacock (1869-1944), Canadian writer and economist. *The Revision of Democracy*, 1934.

196. Is it not strange that the descendants of those Pilgrim Fathers who crossed the Atlantic to preserve their own freedom of opinion have always proved themselves intolerable of the spiritual liberty of others?

Robert E. Lee (1807-1870), General-in-Chief of the Confederate Army. Letter to Mrs. Lee, 1856.

197. Why should freedom of speech and freedom of the press be allowed? Why should a government which is doing what it believes is right allow itself to be criticized? It would not allow opposition by lethal weapons. Ideas are much more fatal things than guns.

V. I. Lenin (1870-1924), Premier of the U.S.S.R.. Quoted in *Nieman Reports*, 1956.

198. Liberty belongs only to those who have the gift of reason.
Pope Leo XIII (1810-1903). Encyclical, *Libertas Praestantissimum*, June 20, 1888.

199. Our people need affirmative faith and material security more than they need rights and true science.
Konstantin Nikolaevich Leontiev (1831-1891), Russian Socialist philosopher. Letter, 1890.

200. PROCLAIM LIBERTY THROUGHOUT THE LAND UNTO ALL THE INHABITANTS THEREOF.
Old Testament, *Leviticus* 25:10. Inscribed on the Liberty Bell.

201. Liberty and Union
Abraham Lincoln (1809-1865), 16th President of the United States (R-IL). Motto during his presidency. (Compare John C. Calhoun's "Liberty dearer than Union.")

202. No man is good enough to govern another without the other man's consent. I say this is the leading principle, the sheet anchor of American republicanism.
Abraham Lincoln. Speech, Peoria, IL, Oct. 16, 1854.

203. When we were the political slaves of King George and wanted to be free, we called the maxim that "all men are created equal" a self-evident truth, but now that we have grown fat, and have lost all dread of being slaves ourselves, we have become so greedy to be masters that we call the same maxim "a self-evident lie."
Abraham Lincoln. Letter to George Robertson, Aug. 15, 1855.

204. If we lose Kansas to freedom, an example will be set which will prove fatal to freedom in the end. We, therefore, in the language of the Bible, must "lay the ax to the root of the tree" *[see Matthew 3:10, Luke 3:9]*. Temporizing will not do longer; now is the time for decision – for firm, persistent, resolute action.
Abraham Lincoln. Speech, Bloomington, IN, May 29, 1856.

205. There is this vital difference between all those states *[of the North originally permitting slavery]* and the judge's *[Douglas's]* Kansas experiment; that they sought to disestablish slavery which had already been established, while the judge seeks, so far as he can, to disestablish freedom, which had been established there by the Missouri Compromise.
Abraham Lincoln. *Ibid.*

206. The principles of Jefferson are the definitions and maxims of free society.
Abraham Lincoln. Speech, Chicago, IL, Mar. 1, 1859.

207. Those who deny freedom to others deserve it not for themselves; and, under the rule of a just God, cannot long retain it..
Abraham Lincoln. Letter to H. L. Pierce and others, Apr. 6, 1859.

208. I intend no modification of my oft-expressed wish that all men everywhere could be free.
Abraham Lincoln. Letter to Horace Greeley, Aug. 22, 1862.

209. It was not only the Negro that I freed, but the white man no less.
Abraham Lincoln. Remark to John A. Bingham and Simon Wolf after signing the Emancipation Proclamation, Sept. 1862.

210. Private property was the original source of freedom. It still is its main bulwark.
Walter Lippmann (1889-1974), American political columnist. *The Good Society*, 1937.

211. We must protect the right of our opponents to speak, because we must hear what they have to say.
Walter Lippmann. Quoted in *Reader's Digest*, Dec. 1987.

212. Beware how you trifle with your marvelous inheritance, this great land of ordered liberty, for if we stumble and fall, freedom and civilization everywhere will go down in ruin.
Henry Cabot Lodge (1850-1924), U.S. Congressman and U.S. Senator (R-MA). Announcement of his opposition to the covenant of a League of Nations. Senate speech, Aug. 12, 1919.

213. Ernest to make others free!
James Russell Lowell (1819-1891), U.S. Ambassador to Spain and England. *Stanzas on Freedom*, 1843.

214. Money cannot buy freedom, but freedom can be sold for money.
Lu Xun (1881-1936), Chinese writer. Quoted in *The New York Times*, Aug. 19, 1990.

215. Freedom for supporters of the government only, for the members of one party only – no matter how big its membership may be – is no freedom at all. Freedom is always freedom for the man who thinks differently.
Rosa Luxemburg (1880-1919), German revolutionist. Quoted in Paul Froelich, *Rosa Luxemburg*, 1940.

216. To argue against any breach of liberty from the ill use that may be made of it, is to argue against liberty itself, since all is capable of being abused.

George Lyttelton, 1st Baron Lyttleton of Frankley (1709-1773), Member of Parliament and Chancellor of the Exchequer, Great Britain. Speech, House of Commons, 1752.

217. There are more instances of the abridgement of the freedom of the people by gradual and silent encroachments of those in power than by violent and sudden usurpations.

James Madison (1751-1836), 4th President of the United States (Democratic Republican-VA). Speech, Virginia Ratification Convention, June 6, 1788.

218. Perhaps it is a universal truth that the loss of liberty at home is to be charged to provisions against danger real or pretended from abroad.

James Madison. Letter to Thomas Jefferson, May 1798.

219. Wherever the real power in a government lies, there is the danger of oppression. In our government the real power lies in the majority of the community.

James Madison. Quoted in Richard Hofstadter, *The American Political Tradition*, 1948.

220. Dr. King, Malcolm X,
Freedom of speech is as good as sex.

Madonna, American singer and entertainer. Public service ad, MTV. Quoted (without first line) in *Newsweek*, Nov. 26, 1990.

221. All creatures fight for freedom.

Mao Tse-tung (1893-1976), Chairman, Communist Party of China. "Changsha," 1925.

222. What should our policy be towards non-Marxist ideas? As far as unmistakable counter-revolutionaries and saboteurs of the socialist cause are concerned, the matter is easy: We simply deprive them of their freedom of speech.

Mao Tse-tung. Speech, "On the Correct Handling of Contradictions Among the People," Feb. 27, 1957.

223. There is no true liberty for the individual except as he finds it in the liberty of all. There is no true security for the individual except as he finds it in the security of all.

Edwin Markham (1852-1940), American poet. 1902.

224. Our whole constitutional heritage rebels at the thought of giving government the power to control men's minds.

Thurgood Marshall, U.S. Supreme Court Justice. Apr. 7, 1969.

225. We're not free. We're not nearly free.

Thurgood Marshall. In reference to African-Americans. Interview with Carl Rowan, 1990.

226. Sometimes the truth is inflammatory.

B. Herbert Martin, Chairman, Chicago Housing Authority. Quoted in *The American Spectator*, Oct. 1988.

227. Persecution for opinion ... is still as common *[in America]* as women who have opinions.

Harriet Martineau (1802-1876), British reformer. *Society in America*, 1837.

228. The principles of the Declaration of Independence bear no relation to half of the human race *[females]*.

Harriet Martineau. *Ibid.*

229. Blasphemy against God, denying our Savior Jesus Christ to be the son of God, or denying the Holy Trinity, or the Godhead of any of the Three Persons *[are]* to be punished with Death, and Confiscation of Lands and Goods.

Law passed by Maryland Colonial Assembly, Apr. 21, 1649.

230. Getting involved in politics was a quest for freedom.

Rafael Mazarrasa, Governor of Cuenca, Spain. Interview, *Hispanic*, June 1990.

231. Without doubt, it *[the Fourteenth Amendment]* denotes not merely freedom from bodily restraint, but also the right of the individual to contract, to engage in any of the common occupations of life, to acquire useful knowledge, to marry, establish a home and bring up children, to worship God according to the dictates of his conscience, and generally to enjoy those privileges long recognized at common law as essential to the orderly pursuit of happiness by free men.

James C. McReynolds (1862-1946), U.S. Supreme Court Justice. *Meyer* v. *Nebraska*, 1923.

232. Communism of every type and stripe brings with it an ideological straitjacket. Thought control, brain-washing, censorship, imprisonment, exile, mental and physical torture are the indispensable weapons of Communist rule.

George Meany (1894-1980), President, AFL-CIO. Speech, New York City, Mar. 13, 1957.

233. We Americans are the peculiar, chosen people – the Israel of our time – we bear the ark of liberties of the world.

Herman Melville (1819-1891), American author. *White Jacket*, 1850.

234. England is the freest land on earth because it is the best disciplined.

Klemens von Metternich (1773-1859), Austrian statesman and diplomat. Letter from London, Sept. 7, 1848.

235. Only Americans can say, My homeland is freedom.

Mihajlo Mihajlov, Yugoslav dissident. 1980.

236. Liberty consists in doing what one desires.

John Stuart Mill (1806-1873), Member of Parliament, Great Britain, and political economist. *On Liberty*, 1859.

237. The liberty of the individual must be thus far limited: He must not make himself a nuisance to other people.

John Stuart Mill. *Ibid.*

238. There is a limit to the legitimate interference of collective opinion with individual independence; and to find that limit, and maintain it against encroachment, is as indispensable to a good condition of human affairs as protection against political despotism.

John Stuart Mill. *Ibid.*

239. The only freedom which deserves the name is that of pursuing our own good in our own way, so long as we do not attempt to deprive others of theirs or impede their efforts to obtain it.

John Stuart Mill. *Ibid.*

240. No man who knows aught can be so stupid to deny that all men naturally were born free.

John Milton (1608-1674), English writer. *Tenure of Kings and Magistrates*, 1649.

241. I will not speak of tolerance. The freedom of conscience is a right so sacred that even the name of "tolerance" involves a species of tyranny.

Honoré de Mirabeau (1749-1791), French revolutionary and President of the National Assembly. Speech, National Convention, 1791.

242. No society can give people free choice in economic affairs and deny it to them in political affairs.

George J. Mitchell, U.S. Senator (D-ME). Interview, ABC, *This Week*, Sept. 24, 1989.

243. We lack many things, but we possess the most precious of all – liberty!

James Monroe (1758-1831), 5th President of the United States (Democratic Republican-VA). Response when his daughter observed that the French roads were much better than those in America. Remark to Elisa Monroe, Paris, 1795.

244. God and Liberty – these are the two great motive-powers of my existence. To reconcile these two perfections shall be the aim of my life.

Charles Montalembert (1810-1870), French statesman and writer. *Commonplace Book*, Apr. 23, 1827.

245. Freedom: ah! I can say it without phrases ... and it is my belief that I have never loved her more, never served her better on this day when I am doing my best to unmask her enemies, who deck themselves out in her colors, who usurp her flag to soil it, to dishonor it.

Charles Montalembert. Address on Switzerland, Chamber of Peers, Jan. 11, 1848.

246. America's dissidents are not committed to mental hospitals and sent into exile; they thrive and prosper and buy a house in Nantucket and take flyers in the commodities market.

Ted Morgan, American writer. *On Becoming American*, 1978.

247. Up, you mighty race. You can accomplish what you will! build your future on these foundations: Freedom, Justice, and Equality.

Elijah Muhammad (1896-1975), Messenger, Nation of Islam. Motto, Nation of Islam.

248. Of what use is political liberty to those who have no bread? It is of value only to ambitious theorists and politicians.

Jean-Paul Murat (1743-1793), French revolutionist. Letter, June 24, 1790.

249. Freedom of speech, freedom of the press, and freedom of religion all have a double aspect – freedom of thought and freedom of action.

Frank Murphy (1890-1959), Governor of Michigan (D), U.S. Attorney General, and U.S. Supreme Court Justice. *Jones* v. *Opelika*, 1941.

250. The strength of this nation is weakened more by those who suppress the freedom of others than by those who are allowed freely to think and act as their consciences dictate.

Frank Murphy. *Bridges* v. *Wixon*, 1944-45.

251. The air of England has long been too pure for a slave, and every man is free who breathes it. Every man who comes to England is entitled to the protection of English law, whatever oppression he may heretofore have suffered, and whatever may be the colour of his skin.

William Murray, 1st Earl of Mansfield (1705-1793), Lord Chief Justice of Great Britain. *Case of James Somersett, a Negro*, 1772.

252. We cannot defend freedom abroad by deserting it at home.
Edward R. Murrow (1908-1965), American broadcast journalist and Director, United States Information Agency. CBS, *See It Now*, 1954.

253. It is necessary to be very intelligent in the work of oppression.
Benito Mussolini (1883-1945), dictator of Italy (Fascist). Speech, May 26, 1926.

254. We have buried the putrid corpse of liberty.
Benito Mussolini. 1934.

255. From church to Congress, America has become a nation of self-indulgent, what's-in-it-for-me individual freedom seekers.
Susan Myrick, Mayor of Charlotte, NC (D). Quoted in *USA Today*, Oct. 19, 1990.

256. LIVE FREE OR DIE
New Hampshire license plate motto.

257. We prefer self-government with danger to servility with tranquility.
Kwame Nkrumah (1909-1972), Prime Minister of Ghana. Quoted in *The New York Times Magazine*, July 2, 1958.

258. Liberty in this world is scarcer than oil.
Michael Novak, Fellow, The American Enterprise Institute. C-SPAN, *Immigration Issues*, Dec. 6, 1989.

259. Unless I can meet at least some of these aspirations [for freedom], my support will wane and my head will roll just as sure as the tickbird follows the rhino.
Julius Nyerere, Prime Minister of Tanzania. Quoted in *Time*, Dec. 15, 1961.

260. As long as men are free to ask what they must, free to say what they think, free to think what they will, freedom can never be lost, and science can never regress.
J. Robert Oppenheimer (1904-1967), American physicist and Scientific Director, Manhattan Project. Quoted in *Life*, Oct. 10, 1949.

261. I sometimes think that the price of liberty is not so much eternal vigilance as eternal dirt.
George Orwell (Eric Blair) (1903-1950), British writer. *The Road to Wigan Pier*, 1937.

262. If liberty means anything at all, it means the right to tell people what they do not want to hear.
George Orwell. Introduction, *Animal Farm*, 1944. (The Introduction was suppressed, and was published in *The New York Times* in 1972.)

263. If large numbers of people believe in freedom, there will be freedom of speech, even if the law forbids it.
George Orwell. Quoted in *Brown Alumni Monthly*, May 1991.

264. It is a clear truth that those who barter away other men's liberty will soon care little for their own.
James Otis (1725-1783), Member, Colonial Massachusetts legislature. *The Rights of the British Colonies Asserted and Proved*, 1764.

265. Those who expect to reap the blessing of freedom must, like men, undergo the fatigue of supporting it.
Thomas Paine (1737-1809), American political philosopher. *The American Crisis*, Dec. 19, 1776.

266. Freedom is not for the timid.
Vijaya Lakshmi Pandit (1900-1990), Member of Parliament, India, and President of U.N. General Assembly. Quoted in Vera Mary Brittain, *Envoy Extraordinary*, 1965.

267. Let the voice of the people be heard.
Albert Parsons (1848-1887), American anarchist and Haymarket Trial defendant. Last words before his execution, 1887.

268. Man was not born to go down on his belly before the state.
Alan Paton (1903-1988), South African novelist. Speech, South African Liberal Party meeting, 1968.

269. Happiness is freedom, and freedom is courage.
Pericles (c.500-429 B.C.), Athenian statesman. Quoted by Thucydides, *History of the Peloponnesian War*, II.

270. Slowly but surely, the greater part of formerly closed literature is being transferred from special storehouses into rooms that are open to all readers. Journalists are *[now]* permitted to write about the ills of our society that were formerly kept secret – prostitution, drug addiction, corruption. But it is with patent reluctance that the bureaucratic clans give up the right to a monopoly of information, continuing to conceal it "with a view to the protection of state interests."
S. Pestov, Russian political writer. *Argumenty I Fakty* (Russian Communist Party weekly), Aug. 13-19, 1988.

271. Freedom to preach was first gained, dragging in its train freedom to print.
Wendell Phillips (1811-1884), American orator and reformer. Speech, Boston, MA, Dec. 8, 1837.

272. Eternal vigilance is the price of liberty.
Wendell Phillips. Speech to the Massachusetts Anti-Slavery Society, Jan. 28, 1852.

273. Those who do not want the sexual aspect of life included in the portrayal of real-life situations had better burn their Bibles as well as abstain from the movies.
James A. Pike (1913-1969), American Anglican bishop. Quoted in *The New York Times*, Dec. 1956.

274. I am at last in a free country.
Pinckney Benton Stewart Pinchback (1837-1921), Governor of Louisiana (R), U.S. Congressman (not seated) and U.S. Senator (not seated). Remark on visiting Baltimore, MD, 1891.

275. I love the Americans because they love liberty.
William Pitt, 1st Earl of Chatham (1708-1778), Secretary of State, Great Britain, Lord Privy Seal, and leader of the House of Commons. Speech, House of Lords, Mar. 2, 1770.

276. If I were an American, as I am an Englishman, while a foreign troop was landed in my country, I never would lay down my arms – never – never – never!
William Pitt. Speech, House of Lords, Nov. 18, 1777.

277. Necessity is the plea for every infringement of human freedom. It is the argument of tyrants; it is the creed of slaves.
William Pitt (The Younger) (1759-1806), Prime Minister of Great Britain. Speech on the India Bill, House of Commons, Nov. 18, 1783.

278. The vitality of our race still persists. We have not lived for naught. We are the original discoverers of this continent ... and on it first taught the arts of war and peace, and first planted the institutions of virtue, truth, and liberty.
Pleasant Porter, Chief, Creek Indians. Speech, Creek Council, 1900.

279. We've fought long and hard against censorship. But when it comes to the safety of our employees, one sometimes has to compromise.
Bonnie Predd, Executive Vice President, Walden Books, Inc.. Explanation for her company's pulling copies of Salman Rushdie's *Satanic Verses* from the shelves after death threats from Iranian religious leaders. Quoted in *Newsweek*, Feb. 27, 1989.

280. Freedom of speech only works with a skeptical public.
James (The Amazing) Randi, American magician. Speech, National Institutes of Health, Washington, DC, July 8, 1989.

281. Liberty is always unfinished business.
Joseph L. Rauh, Jr. (1911-1992), American attorney and civil rights activist. Nov. 1988.

282. Freedom is the recognition that no single person, no single authority or government has a monopoly on truth, but that every individual life is infinitely precious, that every one of us put on this world has been put there for a reason and has something to offer.
Ronald Reagan, 40th President of the United States (R-CA). Quoted in *The 1989 Conservative Calendar*.

283. Whether I am or am not a Communist or Communist sympathizer is irrelevant. The question is whether American citizens, regardless of their political beliefs or sympathies, may enjoy their constitutional rights.
Paul Robeson (1898-1976), American musician, pacifist, and civil rights leader. Speech, Council on African Affairs, New York City, 1947.

284. The defenders of liberty will be but outlaws so long as a horde of knaves shall rule.
Maximilien-François-Marie de Robespierre (1758-1794), French revolutionist. Last words before his execution, July 28, 1794.

285. O Liberty! How many crimes are committed in thy name!
Manon Jeanne Roland (1754-1793), French Republican and Girondist. Comment as she walked to the guillotine, Nov. 10, 1793.

286. Certain rights can never be granted to the government, but must be kept in the hands of the people.
Anna Eleanor Roosevelt (1884-1962), First Lady and U.S. Delegate to the United Nations. Quoted in *The New York Times*, May 3, 1948.

287. Where after all do human rights begin? In small places close to home – so close and so small that they cannot be seen on any map of the world. Yet they are the world of the individual persons; the neighborhood he lives in; the school or college he attends; the factory, farm, or office where he works. Such are the places where every man, woman, and child seeks equal justice, equal opportunity, equal dignity without discrimination. Unless these rights have meaning there, they have

little meaning anywhere.
Anna Eleanor Roosevelt. 1958.

288. I am not for a return to that definition of liberty under which for many years a free people were being gradually regimented into the service of the privileged few.
Franklin D. Roosevelt (1882-1945), 32nd President of the United States (D-NY). Fireside Chat, Sept. 30, 1934.

289. Freedom means the supremacy of human rights everywhere.... In the future days, which we seek to make secure, we look forward to a world founded upon four essential freedoms.

The first is freedom of speech and expression – everywhere in the world.

The second is freedom of every person to worship God in his own way – everywhere in the world.

The third is freedom from want – which, translated into world terms, means economic understandings which will secure to every nation peaceful life for its inhabitants – everywhere in the world.

The fourth is freedom from fear – which, translated into world terms, means a worldwide reduction of armaments to such a point and in such a thorough fashion that no nation will be in a position to commit any act of aggression against any neighbor – anywhere in the world.
Franklin D. Roosevelt. Annual message to Congress, Jan. 6, 1941.

290. Necessitous men are not free men.
Franklin D. Roosevelt. Quoted in Foster Rhea Dulles, *The United States Since 1865*, 1959.

291. The only sure bulwark of continuing liberty is a government strong enough to protect the interests of the people, and a people strong enough and well informed enough to maintain its sovereign control over its government.
Franklin D. Roosevelt. *Ibid.*

292. Man is born free, and everywhere he is in fetters. (*L'homme est né libre, et partout il est dans les fers.*)
Jean Jacques Rousseau (1712-1778), French philosopher. *The Social Contract*, 1762.

293. To renounce liberty is to renounce being a man, to surrender the rights of humanity and even its duties.
Jean Jacques Rousseau. *Ibid.*

294. Free people, remember this: You may acquire liberty, but once lost it is never regained.
Jean Jacques Rousseau. *Ibid.*

295. Freedom in general may be defined as the absence of obstacles to the realization of desires.
Bertrand Russell, 3rd Earl Russell of Kingston (1872-1970), British philosopher and reformer. Quoted in Ruth Nanda Anderson, *Freedom*, 1940.

296. Those who talk of liberty in Britain on any other principles than those of the British constitution talk impertinently at best, and much charity is requisite to believe no worse of them.
Henry St. John, 1st Viscount Bolingbroke (1678-1751), Secretary for War and Foreign Secretary, England (Tory). Quoted in S. Austin Allibone, *Prose Quotations*, 1876.

297. Men of ideas vanish first when freedom vanishes.
Carl Sandburg (1878-1967), American poet and political biographer. Quoted on CBS, *Sunday Morning*, Oct. 30, 1988.

298. That a State in the exercise of its police power may punish who abuse this freedom *[of speech]* by utterances inimical to the public welfare, tending to corrupt public morals, incite to crime, or disturb the public peace, is not open to question. *[Edward Gitlow had been convicted of anarchy for publishing and distributing* The Left Wing Manifesto, *which advocated forceful overthrow of the U.S. government.]*
Edward T. Sanford (1865-1930), U.S. Supreme Court Justice. *Gitlow* v. *New York*, 1925.

299. No woman can call herself free who does not own and control her own body.
Margaret Sanger (1883-1966), American family planning advocate. *Woman and the New Race*, 1920.

300. Man is condemned to be free. Condemned, because he did not create himself, yet nevertheless at liberty, and from the moment he is thrown into the world, he is responsible for everything he does.
Jean-Paul Sartre (1905-1980), French philosopher. *Existentialism*, 1947.

301. I love the land and the buffalo and will not part with it. I want the children raised as I was. You want to settle us on a reservation. I don't want to settle. I love to roam over the prairies. There I feel free and happy, but when I settle down I feel pale and die.
Satana (1830-1878), Chief, Kiowa Indians. Statement to the Medicine Lodge Grand Council, Oct. 1867.

302. Liberty can neither be got, nor kept, but by so much Care, that Mankind generally are unwilling to give the Price for it. And therefore, in the Contest between Ease and Liberty, the first hath generally prevailed.
George Savile, 1st Marquess of Halifax (1633-1695), Lord Privy Seal of England. *Political Thoughts and Reflections*, 1750.

303. If none were to have liberty but those who understand what it is, there would not be many free men in the world.
George Savile. *Ibid.*

304. Man is created free, and is free, even though born in chains.
Johann Friedrich von Schiller (1759-1805), German historian and poet. *Die Worte des Glaubens*, 1797.

305. If you want to be free, there is but one way; it is to guarantee an equally full measure of liberty to all your neighbors.
Carl Schurz (1829-1906), U.S. Senator (R-MO). Quoted in George Seldes, *The Great Quotations*, 1983.

306. Liberty: Civilization's highest concept.
Norman Schwartzkopf, General, U.S. Army, and Commander of Forces, Desert Storm. Commencement address, U.S. Naval Academy, Annapolis, MD, June 1, 1991.

307. The fundamental rights of man are, first, the right of habitat; secondly, the right to move freely; thirdly, the right to the soil and the subsoil, and to the use of it; fourthly, the right to freedom of labor and exchange; fifthly, the right to justice; sixthly, the right to live within a natural, national organization; and seventhly, the right to education.
Albert Schweitzer (1875-1965), German musician, philosopher, and physician. Quoted in *The New York Times Magazine*, Jan. 9, 1955.

308. Who ever walked behind anyone to freedom?
Hazel Scott (1920-1981), American musician. Quoted in *Ms.*, Nov. 1974.

309. Liberty is the right of doing whatever the law permits.
Charles-Louis de Secondat, Baron de La Brède et de Montesquieu (1689-1755), French writer. *The Spirit of the Laws*, 1748.

310. When the legislative and executive powers are united in the same person, or in the same body of magistrates, there can be no liberty.
Charles-Louis de Secondat, Baron de La Brède et de Montesquieu. *Ibid.*

311. The fundamental American tradition is that we came away from the fixed world of Europe to create a dynamic country, with freedom to move, to change, to work; with opportunity to learn; with a chance to rise in the world; with a duty to keep the free spirit of the country free.
Gilbert V. Seldes (1893-1970), American writer and anthologist. *The Great Audience*, 1950.

312. Freedom can not be bought for nothing; if you hold her precious, you must hold all else of little value.
Lucius Annaeus Seneca (The Younger) (4 B.C.-A.D. 65), Roman statesman, dramatist, and philosopher. *Epistolae Morales*.

313. Liberty means responsibility. That is why most men dread it.
George Bernard Shaw (1856-1950), Nobel Laureate in Literature (Great Britain). *Maxims for Revolutionists*, 1903.

314. He who confuses political liberty with freedom, and political equality with similarity has never thought for five minutes about either.
George Bernard Shaw. *Ibid.*

315. All Liberty consists only in being subject to no man's will, and nothing denotes a slave but a dependence on the will of another.
Algernon Sidney (1622-1683), Member of Parliament, England. *Discourses Concerning Government*, 1698.

316. When we expand a liberty for one of us, we expand a liberty for all of us.
Paul Simon, U.S. Congressman and U.S. Senator (D-IL). Senate Judiciary Committee, confirmation hearings, Sept. 17, 1990.

317. There is no "slippery slope" toward loss of liberties, only a long staircase where each step downward must first be tolerated by the American people and their leaders.
Alan K. Simpson, U.S. Senator (R-WY). Quoted in *The New York Times*, Sept. 26, 1982.

318. Individual freedom, individual independence of mind, individual participation in the difficult work of government seems to be essential to all true progress.
Jan Christian Smuts (1870-1950), Prime Minister of South Africa. Address, St. Andrews University, Fifeshire, Scotland, Oct. 17, 1934.

319. Censorship is more depraving and corrupting than anything pornography can produce.
Tony Smythe, Chairman, British National Council for Civil Liberties. Quoted in *The Observer*, Sept. 18, 1972.

320. The freedom of America is the freedom to live your own life and take your own chances.
Thomas Sowell, Fellow, The Hoover Institution. Scripps-Howard News Service, July 1, 1986.

321. A man's liberties are none the less aggressed upon because those who coerce him do so in the belief that he will be benefitted.
Herbert Spencer (1820-1903), British social philosopher. *Social Statics*, 1850.

322. The ultimate aim of government is ... to free every man from fear, that he may live in all possible security.... In fact, the true aim of government is liberty.
Benedict Spinoza (1632-1677), Dutch philosopher. *Theological-Political Treatise*, 1670.

323. The most tyrannical governments are those which make crimes of opinions, for everyone has an inalienable right to his thoughts.
Benedict Spinoza. *Ibid.*

324. What can be the personal freedom of an unemployed person who goes hungry and finds no use for his toil?
Joseph Stalin (1879-1953), Premier of the U.S.S.R. Interview with Roy Howard, 1936.

325. My definition of a free society is a society where it is safe to be unpopular.
Adlai E. Stevenson (1900-1965), Governor of Illinois (D) and U.S. Ambassador to the United Nations. Campaign speech, Detroit, MI, Oct. 7, 1952.

326. Only a government which fights for civil liberties and equal rights for its own people can stand for freedom in the rest of the world.
Adlai E. Stevenson. Speech, Feb. 14, 1953.

327. The dichotomy between personal liberties and property rights is a false one. Property does not have rights. People have rights.
Potter Stewart (1915-1985), U.S. Supreme Court Justice. *Lynch* v. *Household Finance Corporation*, 1972.

328. Freedom cannot be granted; it must be taken.
Max Stirner (Johann Kaspar Schmidt) (1806-1856), German anarchist. *The Ego and His Own*, 1845.

329. The government is mild. The press is free. Knowledge reaches, or may reach, every home. What fairer prospect of success could be presented?
Joseph Story (1779-1845), U.S. Supreme Court Justice. *Miscellaneous Writings*, 1835.

330. By definition, individual rights are not going to be popular.
Nadine Strossen, President, American Civil Liberties Union. Interview, C-SPAN, Mar. 23, 1991.

331. To give liberty to the Jews will be very detrimental.... Giving them liberty, we cannot refuse the Lutherans and Papists.
Peter Stuyvesant (1592-1672), Governor of New Amsterdam (later Manhattan). Letter to Directors of the Dutch East India Company, 1626.

332. The liberty of the individual to do as he pleases, even in innocent matters, is not absolute. It must frequently yield to the common good.
George Sutherland (1862-1942), U.S. Supreme Court Justice. *Adkins* v. *Children's Hospital*, 1925.

333. All government without the consent of the governed is the very definition of slavery.
Jonathan Swift (1667-1745), Irish clergyman and satirist. *Drapier's Letters*, IV.

334. We must never forget in the present day that those people who have got their political freedom are not necessarily free, they are merely powerful.
Rabindranath Tagore (1861-1941), Nobel Laureate in Literature (India). *Nationalism*, 1917.

335. The role of government is to strengthen our freedom – not deny it.
Margaret Thatcher, Prime Minister of Great Britain (Conservative). Quoted on National Public Radio, Jan. 27, 1989.

336. When liberty is taken away by force it can be restored by force. When it is relinquished voluntarily by default it can never be recovered.
Dorothy Thompson (1894-1961), American journalist. 1958.

337. America is said to be the arena on which the battle of freedom is to be fought; but surely it cannot be freedom in a merely political sense that is meant. Even if we grant that the American has freed himself from a political tyrant *[England]*, he is still the slave of an economical and moral tyrant *[slavery]*.
Henry David Thoreau (1817-1862), American naturalist and philosopher. "Life Without Principle," published posthumously in *The Atlantic Monthly*, 1863.

338. I know of no country in which there is so little independence of mind and real freedom of discussion as in America.
Alexis de Tocqueville (1805-1859), French writer. *Democracy in America*, 1835.

339. Rights must be given to every citizen, or none at all to anyone ... save one, who is the master of all.
Alexis de Tocqueville. *Ibid.*

340. Happy for America that she has been successful in her struggle for liberty, but unhappy that she has not fully completed her design.
Daniel D. Tompkins (1774-1825), Governor of New York (Democratic Republican), U.S. Congressman, and Vice President of the United States. "On Slavery," written while a student at Columbia College, New York City, June 22, 1793.

341. Those prepared to die for freedom's cause, come across to me.
William Barret Travis (1809-1836), Commandant of the Alamo, San Antonio, TX. Remark made while drawing a line in the sand with his sword. Statement to troops at the Alamo, 1836.

342. If there was one thing I had a right to, it was liberty or death. If I could not have one, I would have the other.
Harriet Tubman (c.1820-1913), American abolitionist. Quoted on PBS, *The American Experience*, Dec. 20, 1988.

343. The struggle to be free is paramount. You cannot suppress it without it taking over your heart.
Samuel Wilbert Tucker (1913-1990), American civil rights leader. 1986.

344. We are not interested in your elections. We are interested in freedom.
Desmond M. Tutu, Anglican archbishop of South Africa and Nobel Laureate in Peace. Quoted on CBS, *News*, Sept. 1, 1989.

345. Of all God's creatures there is only one that cannot be made the slave of the lash. That one is the cat. If man could be crossed with the cat it would improve man, but it would deteriorate the cat.
Mark Twain (Samuel Langhorne Clemens) (1835-1910), American writer. Albert Bigelow Paine, ed., *Mark Twain's Notebook*, 1935.

346. If any person shall knowingly publish and circulate ... any writing or pamphlet, printed or unprinted, among the free black or slave population of this district, tending to excite a discontented or insurrectionary spirit, such a person, for every such act ... *[that person will be committed]* without bail or mainprize ... to undergo a trial for the same at the next superior court of law ...; and upon conviction thereof, shall be punished by confinement in the penitentiary for not less than two, not more than seven years.
U.S. Senate. *A System of Civil and Criminal Law for the District of Columbia and the Organization of the Courts Therein*. Document 85, 22C, 2S (275-276), Feb. 28, 1833.

347. The dead, the dead, the numerous dead ... let us make peace. Let the armies fraternize and go home.... I have the most supreme contempt for King *[Abraham]* Lincoln. Come up united and hurl the tyrant from his throne. The men in power are attempting to establish a despotism.
Clement L. Vallandigham (1820-1871), U.S. Congressman (Peace Democrat-OH) and Copperhead leader. Remark, 1863.

348. Law, the noblest invention of reason, could not contrive to secure the tranquility of people without curtailing their freedom.
Marquis de Vauvenargues (1715-1747), French soldier and moralist. *Réflexions et Maximes*, .

349. The basis of the First Amendment is the hypothesis that speech can rebut speech, propaganda will answer propaganda, free debate of ideas will result in the wisest governmental policies.
Frederick M. Vinson (1890-1953), Chief Justice, U.S. Supreme Court. *Dennis* v. *United States*, 1951.

350. It is dangerous to be right when the government is wrong.
Voltaire (François-Marie Arouet) (1694-1778), French historian and dramatist. Attributed.

351. Monsieur l'abbé, I detest what you write, but I would give my life for you to continue to write.
Voltaire. Letter to M. de Riche, Feb. 6, 1770.

352. All the citizens of a state cannot be equally powerful, but they may be equally free.
Voltaire. *Philosophical Dictionary*, art. "Government."

353. Respect for human rights is a fundamental tenet of our own society and the yardstick against which we measure the actions of friends and foes alike.
William G. Walker, U.S. Ambassador to El Salvador. Letter to *The New York Times*, Jan. 19, 1990.

354. If you accept the idea that Communists have no right to express their opinions, then you don't believe in democracy.
Henry A. Wallace (1888-1965), U.S. Secretary of Agriculture (D-IA), Vice President of the United States,

and U.S. Secretary of Commerce. Campaign remark, 1948.

355. Liberty is the most contagious force in the world. It will eventually abide everywhere. No people of any race will remain slaves.

Earl Warren (1891-1974), Chief Justice, U.S. Supreme Court, and Governor of California (R). Columbia University bicentennial address, New York City, 1954.

356. Liberty, when it begins to take root, is a plant of rapid growth.

George Washington (1732-1799), 1st President of the United States (VA). Letter to James Madison, Mar. 2, 1788.

357. Liberty consists in the ability to choose.

Simone Weil (1910-1943), French revolutionist and political philosopher. *The Need for Roots*, 1952.

358. Freedom does not come from the heavens. It must be fought for every day.

Simon Weisenthal, Nazi war criminal hunter. Interview, PBS, *MacNeil-Lehrer News Hour*, Apr. 24, 1990.

359. Independence is never given to a people, it has to be earned; and having been earned, it has to be defended, again and again.

Chaim Weizmann (1874-1952), 1st President of Israel. To Leon Crestohl, 1951.

360. Think and let think.

John Wesley (1703-1791), British clergyman and founder of Methodism. Constant admonition to his followers.

361. In every human breast, God has implanted a principle, which we call love of freedom; it is impatient of oppression and pants for deliverance.

Phillis Wheatley (1754-1785), American poet. Quoted in *Boston Post-Boy*, Mar. 21, 1774.

362. Enact peacetime conscription and no longer will this be a free land – no longer will a citizen be able to say that he disagrees with a government edict. Hushed whispers will replace free speech – secret meetings in dark places will supplant free assemblage – labor and industry, men and women will be shackled by the chains they have themselves forged.

Burton K. Wheeler (1882-1975), U.S. Senator (D-MT). Quoted in *The New York Times*, Aug. 13, 1940.

363. Liberty is the only thing you cannot have unless you are willing to give it to others.

William Allen White (1868-1944), American writer and editor. Quoted in *Dwight D. Eisenhower's Favorite Poetry, Prose and Prayers*, 1957.

364. And when all life and all the souls of men and women are discharged from any part of the earth, then only shall liberty or the idea of liberty be discharged from that part of the earth.

Walt Whitman (1819-1902), American writer. *To a Foil'd European Revolutionaire.*

365. There can be no safety for these States without innovators – without free tongues, and ears willing to hear the tongues.

Walt Whitman. *Ibid.*

366. There is no week nor day nor hour when tyranny may not enter upon this country, if the people lose their supreme confidence in themselves.

Walt Whitman. Quoted in C. J. Furness, *Walt Whitman's Workshop*, 1928.

367. Let us be dogmatic about tolerance. It was blasphemy that made us free.

Leon Wieseltier, editor, *The New Republic*. Quoted in *The New York Times*, Feb. 23, 1989.

368. It is to be regretted that a portion of our community should be practically in slavery, but to propose to solve the problem by enslaving the entire community is childish.

Oscar Wilde (1854-1900), Irish writer. *The Soul of Man Under Socialism*, 1881.

369. American liberty is a religion. It is a thing of the spirit.

Wendell L. Willkie (1892-1944), Republican candidate for President (IN). Radio address, July 4, 1941.

370. Freedom is an indivisible word.

Wendell L. Willkie. *One World*, 1943.

371. When we talk of freedom and opportunity for all nations, the mocking paradoxes in our own society become so clear they can no longer be ignored.

Wendell L. Willkie. *Ibid.*

372. All creatures embrace liberty and fly servitude.

Catharine Bertie Willoughby (c.1519-1580), Duchess of Suffolk. Letter to Queen Elizabeth I, 1558.

373. Liberty has never come from the government. Liberty has always come from the subjects of government. The history of liberty is a history of the limitation of government power, not the increase of it.

Woodrow Wilson (1856-1924), 28th President of the United States (D-NJ). Campaign speech, New York Press Club, 1912.

374. Freedom exists only where the people take care of the government.
Woodrow Wilson. Campaign speech, Sept. 4, 1912.

375. If America is not to have free enterprise, then she can have freedom of no sort whatever.
Woodrow Wilson. Quoted in Arthur Stanley Link, *Wilson*. Vol. 1: *The Road to the White House*, 1947.

376. A liberty to that only which is good, just, and honest.
John Winthrop (1588-1649), Governor of Massachusetts Bay Colony. *Life and Letters*, II.

377. Liberty is the mother of virtue.
Mary Wollstonecraft (1759-1797), British writer and feminist. *A Vindication of the Rights of Women*, 1792.

378. If liberty has any meaning it means freedom to improve.
Philip G. Wylie (1902-1971), American writer. *A Generation of Vipers*, 1942.

379. Nobody can give anybody the right to free association – or deny it. By merely existing, each man has the right.
Stefan Wyszynski (1901-1981), Polish Roman Catholic cardinal. Quoted in Malachi Martin, *The Keys of This Blood*, 1990.

380. You'll get freedom by letting your enemy know that you'll do anything to get your freedom.... It's the only way you'll get it.
Malcolm X (Malcolm Little) (1925-1965), American black power advocate. Speech to visiting Mississippi students, Harlem, NY, 1964.

381. The Liberty of the Press is a Subject of the greatest Importance, and in which every Individual is as much concern'd as he is in any other Part of Liberty.
John Peter Zenger (1697-1746), American printer and publisher. *New-York Weekly Journal*, Nov. 12, 1733.

382. Beneath the yoke of barbarism one must not keep silence; one must fight. Whoever is silent at such a time is a traitor to humanity.
Stefan Zweig (1881-1942), Austrian writer. Statement after his books were burned by Nazi students and professors at the University of Freiburg, May 1933.

Chapter 39

Fund Raising and Campaign Financing

1. It is campaign money that calls the tune, a fact recognized by every politician within a few minutes after getting into politics.
   James G. Abourezk, U.S. Congressman and U.S. Senator (D-SD). *Advise and Dissent*, 1989.

2. If Frank *[Franklin D. Roosevelt]* is nominated, I won't give one cent to the Democratic Party. He's so wishy-washy.
   Bernard M. Baruch (1870-1965), Chairman, War Industries Board, and U.S. Delegate to U.N. Atomic Energy Commission. Remark to Henry Morganthau, Sr., 1931.

3. We have become part-time Senators and full time fund-raisers. Even the schedule of the Senate itself is now arranged around the need to raise money for the next political campaign, rather than around the need to solve the nation's problems and do the people's business.
   David L. Boren, Governor of Oklahoma and U.S. Senator (D). Senate debate, May 13, 1990.

4. You've outlined the problem very well. Solutions are much more difficult to come by.
   Rudolph E. Boschwitz, U.S. Senator (R-MN). Comment on the problems of campaign financing. Interview, ABC, *This Week*, Oct. 9, 1988.

5. Don't come in *[to the Senate]* without assets and remain that way.... Go out and accumulate some capital and then try and run for the Senate.
   William S. Cohen, U.S. Senator (R-ME). Advice to Peter Dawkins. Quoted in *The New York Times*, Sept. 15, 1988.

6. Money has made it more difficult for Democrats to define an economic agenda that is different than the Republican agenda; we are taking from the same contributors.
   Dan Glickman, U.S. Congressman (D-KS). Quoted in *The Washington Post*, Oct. 30, 1989.

7. Power by the Hour
   (Registered Democrats were asked to give one hour's wage to the governor's campaign.)
   Samuel P. Goddard, Jr., Governor of Arizona (D). Fund-raising slogan. John L. Myers, *The Arizona Governors 1912-1990*, 1989.

8. I don't care if you keep this a secret or not. I've always supported you, and I think it's time this old Republican quit hiding behind the bush *[George Bush]*.
   Barry M. Goldwater, U.S. Senator (R-AZ). Note with a $500 check for Arizona Democrat Morris K. Udall's reelection campaign. Aug. 1990.

9. When somebody contributes to a campaign, that is democracy at work.
   Phil Gramm, U.S. Congressman and U.S. Senator (R-TX). *The Congressional Digest*, Feb. 1987.

10. There are two things that are important in politics. The first is money, and I can't remember what the second one is.
    Mark A. Hanna (1837-1904), U.S. Senator (R-OH). Remark, 1895.

11. I am still writing my own checks for more or less substantial amounts every week in order to squeeze by the weekend.
    Cordell Hull (1871-1955), U.S. Congressman and U.S. Senator (D-TN), U.S. Secretary of State, and Nobel Laureate in Peace. Written while Chairman of the Democratic National Committee. Letter to Bernard M. Baruch, Nov. 12, 1923.

12. State party central committees were not providing very much help or raising much money, so the legislative leadership people started stepping in.
    Malcolm E. Jewell, professor of political science, University of Kentucky. Quoted in *Governing the States and Localities*, May 1988.

13. It's our own money, and we're free to spend it any way we choose. It's part of this campaign business. If you have money, you spend it to win. And the more you can afford, the more you'll spend.

Rose Kennedy, mother of John, Robert, and Edward Kennedy. Quoted by Ralph G. Martin, *A Hero for Our Time*, 1983.

14. Our democratic system is slowly being corroded and eroded by the influence of PAC money.

John F. Kerry, U.S. Senator (D-MA). In reference to Political Action Committees. *The Congressional Digest*, Feb. 1987.

15. A politician taking campaign money from gamblers in Nevada is like one taking campaign money from the auto people in Michigan.

Paul D. Laxalt, Governor of Nevada (R) and U.S. Senator. Response when criticized for taking campaign contributions from gambling interests. Quoted in *The New York Times*, Oct. 21, 1984.

16. I've never been able to look someone in the eye and say, "Can you give me $500?"

James Madison Leach, U.S. Congressman (R-IA). Interview, CNN, *An American Profile*, Sept. 3, 1990.

17. I don't have any real opposition against me in my state because the Republicans can't raise enough money to run a decent race.

Warren Magnuson, U.S. Congressman and U.S. Senator (D-WA). Quoted in James G. Abourezk, *Advise and Dissent*, 1989.

18. Spending limits have proven a monumental failure at limiting campaign spending in presidential elections, merely diverting the money underground.

Mitch McConnell, U.S. Senator (R-KY). *The Washington Post*, June 25, 1988.

19. In 1984, one out of four campaign dollars was budgeted for accountants and lawyers to circumvent – or comply with – the law.

Mitch McConnell. *Ibid.*

20. It's a Catch-22. If you don't have money, you can't get the media to focus on what you're saying. And without the focus of the media, you can't raise the money.

Robert R. McMillan, Republican candidate for U.S. Senator (NY). Quoted in *The New York Times*, Oct. 30, 1988.

21. In order to survive politically, you've got to have a big-buck fund-raiser at least once a year.

Harris N. Miller, Democratic Party Chairman, Fairfax County, VA. Quoted in *The Washington Post*, Dec. 2, 1988.

22. My fortune, my magazines, my newspapers are with you.

Frank Andrew Munsey (1854-1925), American newspaper publisher. To urge Theodore Roosevelt to form a new party after failing to win the Republican presidential nomination in 1912. Quoted in Richard Hofstadter, *The American Political Tradition*, 1948.

23. Royal Feast of Belshazzar Blaine and the Money Kings

New York World cartoon title depicting Sen. James G. Blaine at a dinner with wealthy New Yorkers. Oct. 30, 1884.

24. A paltry consideration infinitely outweighed by the service he was rendering to his country.

Samuel A. Otis (1740-1814), Member, Continental Congress and U.S. Senator (Federalist-MA). Comment when Congressman (later Senator) John Milledge (GA) requested extra funds for clerks while he was electioneering for John Adams for the presidency. Quoted in *The National Intelligencer*, Aug. 14, 1801.

25. We must have some ceilings on how much money can be spent *[on campaigns]*. We cannot have the Senate of the United States a body that is composed of all millionaires. We are coming to that. Why? Because it is easier for a wealthy person to run. He can spend all the money he wants. It is much more difficult for someone who is a schoolteacher or a small businessman to go out and raise the millions of dollars that it takes to be competitive.

Harry Reid, U.S. Congressman and U.S. Senator (D-NV). Remarks in the Senate, May 4, 1989.

26. The need for collecting large campaign funds would vanish if Congress provided an appropriation for the proper and legitimate expense of the great national parties.

Theodore Roosevelt (1858-1919), 26th President of the United States (R-NY). Message to Congress, Dec. 3, 1907.

27. When you need the money, it's too late to raise it.

Daniel D. Rostenkowski, U.S. Congressman (D-IL). Explanation of the need for substantial campaign war chests. Quoted in *Newsweek*, June 6, 1988.

28. Shakespeare once said, "Neither a borrower nor a lender be." That's why Shakespeare could never run for Congress.

Mark Russell, American political humorist. PBS, *Mark Russell's Washington*, Feb. 22, 1989.

29. Tom Bradley *[Mayor of Los Angeles]* simply doesn't make policy to please the people that send him checks. He's the Mayor of a big city. A lot of companies want to see him reelected.
Irene Tritschler, mayoral fund raiser, Los Angeles, CA. *Business Week*, July 11, 1988.

30. Money is the mother's milk of politics.
Jesse Unruh (1922-1987), California State Legislator (D). Favorite saying.

31. If you want to challenge an incumbent *[Congressman]* in an urban area, you have to be prepared to drop a lot of cash.
Jim Weber, congressional campaign manager (R). Quoted in *The Washington Post*, Aug. 28, 1988.

32. An arms race mentality *[of campaign financing]* always benefits the incumbents. They can always outraise the challengers.
Fred Wertheimer, President, Common Cause. Interview, ABC, *This Week*, Oct. 9, 1988.

33. The price of running for the Senate today is spending more time than you'd like to spend asking people for more money than they'd like to give.
Harriett Woods, Lieutenant Governor of Missouri and Democratic senatorial candidate. Quoted in *The New York Times*, Dec. 9, 1986.

Chapter 40

Growth, Change, and Development

1. In differentiation, not uniformity, lies the path of progress.
   Louis D. Brandeis (1856-1941), U.S. Supreme Court Justice. *Business – A Profession*, 1914.

2. Liberty is the great developer.
   Louis D. Brandeis. Quoted in Osmond K. Fraenkel, *The Curse of Bigness*, 1934.

3. Limits *[to growth]* are indeed imposed by the impact of present technologies and social organization on the biosphere, but we must have the ingenuity to change. And change we must.
   Gro Harlem Brundtland, Prime Minister of Norway. *Scientific American*, Sept. 1989.

4. We are rapidly – I was about to say, fearfully – growing.
   John C. Calhoun (1782-1850), U.S. Congressman and U.S. Senator (D-SC), U.S. Secretary of War, U.S. Secretary of State, and Vice President of the United States. Quoted on PBS, *The Congress*, 1989.

5. Our infrastructure is just barely adequate to support our current level of economic activity, and our current rate of infrastructure improvement and investment falls vastly short of tomorrow's needs.
   Bill Clinton, 42nd President of the United States (D-AR). *The New York Times*, June 24, 1988.

6. Free enterprise is the only way for substantial growth.
   Fernando Collor de Mello, President of Brazil. Speech, Brasilia, Mar, 16, 1990.

7. The city ... is involved in the fight for its life. One of the critical battlegrounds is the struggle to preserve middle-class residential neighborhoods.
   Mario Cuomo, Governor of New York (D). *New York Daily News*, Feb. 26, 1980.

8. "More goods and fewer people" is the slogan I should like to see carried at the head of humanity's march into the future.
   Max F. Eastman (1883-1969), American editor and writer. *Reflections on the Failure of Socialism*, 1955.

9. All that is valuable in human society depends upon the opportunity for development accorded to the individual.
   Albert Einstein (1879-1955), Nobel Laureate in Physics (Switzerland). Sept. 15, 1933.

10. Mental power is the motor of progress ... the mental power which is devoted to the extension of knowledge, the improvement of methods, and the betterment of social conditions.
    Henry George (1839-1897), American political economist. *Progress and Poverty*, 1879.

11. The association of poverty with progress is the enigma of our times.
    Henry George. *Ibid.*

12. The government must get out of the "protective" business and the "subsidy" business and the "improvement" and the "development" business. It must let trade, and commerce, and manufactures, and steamboats, and railroads, and telegraphs alone. It cannot touch them without breeding corruption.
    Edwin Lawrence Godkin (1831-1902), editor, *New York Evening Post*. 1891.

13. I don't think we should allow our growth to overwhelm the qualities that are bringing it here, and some of those qualities will be overwhelmed if we just allow it to happen haphazardly.
    Judd Gregg, New Hampshire State legislator (R). Quoted in *The New York Times*, Oct. 23, 1988.

14. It is with nations as with nature which knows no pause in progress and development, and attaches her curse on all inaction.

Wilhelm von Humboldt (1767-1835), Prussian statesman. 1812.

15. We must consider each generation as a distinct nation, with a right, by the will of its majority, to bind themselves, but none to bind the succeeding generation, more than the inhabitants of another country.

Thomas Jefferson (1743-1826), 3rd President of the United States (Democratic Republican, VA). Letter to John W. Eppes, June 24, 1813.

16. You can't inflate your way to economic growth.

Jack F. Kemp, U.S. Congressman and Secretary of Housing and Urban Development (R-NY). Interview with Hobart Rowan, *The Washington Post*, May 28, 1991.

17. The United States has to move very fast to even stand still.

John F. Kennedy (1917-1963), 35th President of the United States (D-MA). Quoted in *The Observer*, July 21, 1963.

18. Human progress is neither automatic nor inevitable. Even a superficial look at history reveals that no social advance rolls in on the wheels of inevitability.

Martin Luther King, Jr. (1929-1968), American clergyman and civil rights leader. Speech, Washington, DC, Aug. 5, 1965.

19. In most people's minds "planning" and "free enterprise" have often been at odds. Planners have traditionally been accused of creating a bureaucratic overlay to stymie healthy growth.

Madeleine M. Kunin, Governor of Vermont (D). *The Christian Science Monitor*, Sept. 22, 1988.

20. The American electorate has come to expect a growing pie, with politicians arguing about how to distribute the growth dividend every year.

Richard D. Lamm, Governor of Colorado (D). *Playboy*, Aug. 1984.

21. What is Communism? The Soviet Republic plus electrification.

V. I. Lenin (1870-1924), Premier of the U.S.S.R. Quoted in Emil Ludwig, *Genius and Character*, 1927.

22. The dogmas of the quiet past are inadequate to the stormy present. The occasion is piled high with difficulty, and we must rise with the occasion. As our case is new, so we must think anew and act anew.

Abraham Lincoln (1809-1865), 16th President of the United States (R-IL). Second annual Message to Congress. In reference to the pending final Emancipation Proclamation. Dec. 1, 1862.

23. We will not develop the country by begging for capital, but by working ourselves with our own hands.... It is not money that creates progress. It is man who creates progress.

Patrice Lumumba (1925-1961), 1st Prime Minister of the Congo (later Zaire). Press conference, Léopoldville (later Kinshasa), Aug. 9, 1960.

24. Population, when unchecked, increases in a geometrical ratio. Subsistence increases only in an arithmetical rate. A slight acquaintence with numbers will show the intensity of the first power in comparison to the second.

Thomas R. Malthus (1766-1834), British clergyman and political economist. *Essay on the Principle of Population*, 1798.

25. In transforming a backward agricultural China into an advanced industrialized country, we are confronted with arduous tasks and our experience is far from adequate. So we must be good at learning.

Mao Tse-tung (1893-1976), Chairman, Communist Party of China. Opening address, 8th National Congress of the Communist Party of China. Sept. 15, 1956.

26. Any man who is a bear on the future of this country will go broke. There may be times when things are dark and cloudy in America ... but remember that the growth of this vast country will take care of all.

J. Pierpont Morgan (1837-1913), American industrialist and financier. Remarks during a depression, Chicago Club, Dec. 11, 1908.

27. *All that Latin America needs is a friendly climate for private enterprise.* This view disregards the need for building roads, ports, power plants, and communications systems which must be built in great part with public funds and which in many areas are a prerequisite for the effective and profitable investment of private capital.

Teodoro Moscoso, U.S. Coordinator, Alliance for Progress. Speech, Detroit Economic Club, Apr. 1, 1963.

28. Each federal dollar has been repaid over and over in taxes collected, in jobs created, and in helping to attract other investment, redevelopment, jobs, and tax-base growth to blighted urban areas.

National League of Cities. Statement in reference to federal grants, July 13, 1988.

29. The nuclear weapons industry is a very unstable, capital-intensive one. Towns are washed out when there's a shift of *[federal]* government priorities.... We feel it's better to build our economy around something that's more labor intensive and has some stability.

David Orr, Alderman of Chicago, IL (D). Quoted in *Governing*, Sept. 1988.

30. Every step of progress the world has made has been from scaffold to scaffold, and from stake to stake.

Wendell Phillips (1811-1884), American orator and reformer. Speech on women's rights, 1851.

31. Development is not paying its way in taxes. We must set up a system in which development pays for the costs it adds to the county.

Neil Potter, County Executive, Montgomery Co., MD (D). Quoted in *Regardie's*, Dec. 1990.

32. Zero defects in products plus zero pollution plus zero risk on the job is equivalent to maximum growth of government plus zero economic growth plus runaway inflation.

Dixy Lee Ray, Governor of Washington and Chairman, U.S. Atomic Energy Commission (D). Speech, Scientists and Engineers for Secure Energy, 1980.

33. Our obligation to the world is primarily our obligation to our own future. Obviously, we cannot develop beyond a certain point unless other nations develop, too.

Anna Eleanor Roosevelt (1884-1962), First Lady and U.S. Delegate to the United Nations. Remark on her 75th birthday, Oct. 11, 1959.

34. If we accept the phrase "the best government is the least government," we must understand that it applies to the simplification of governmental machinery, and to the prevention of improper interference with the legitimate private acts of citizens, but a nation or State which is unwilling to tackle new problems, caused by the immense increase of population and by the astounding strides of modern science, is headed for decline and ultimate death from inaction.

Franklin D. Roosevelt (1882-1945), 32nd President of the United States (D-NY). Press release, Sept. 27, 1926.

35. The test of our progress is not whether we add more to the abundance of those who have much; it is whether we provide enough for those who have too little.

Franklin D. Roosevelt. Second inaugural address, Jan. 20, 1937.

36. What does the country ultimately gain if we encourage businessmen to enlarge the capacity of American industry to produce unless we see to it that the income of our working population actually expands sufficiently to create markets to absorb the increased production?

Franklin D. Roosevelt. Message to Congress, Nov. 1937.

37. Whenever the Corps of Engineers has some dam to dedicate in Georgia, I make it a point to be out of state because those people don't seem to like the economic improvement as much as they dislike being moved off their land.

Richard B. Russell, Jr. (1897-1971), U.S. Senator (D-GA). Remark to Lyndon B. Johnson, 1960.

38. Women are the key not only to patterns of future population growth but also the goal of attainable development.

Nafis Sadik, Director, U.N. Fund for Population Activities. Quoted in *The Washington Post*, May 31, 1989.

39. In order for an economic program to advance, there has to be a social consensus.

Carlos Salinas de Gortarì, President of Mexico. Quoted in *The New York Times*, June 3, 1990.

40. Predatory development is destroying our flora and fauna. We must contain the predatory actions of man.

José Sarney, President of Brazil. Quoted in *The New York Times*, Oct. 13, 1988.

41. The core problems for political and economic security are job creation and education.

L. Ronald Scheman, Asst. Director, Organization of American States. *The Washington Post*, Mar. 27, 1990.

42. All progress has resulted from people who took unpopular positions.

Adlai E. Stevenson (1900-1965), Governor of Illinois (D) and U.S. Ambassador to the United Nations. Speech, Mar. 22, 1954.

43. Environmentally sustainable development will open up more opportunities than it will negate.

Maurice Strong, Member of Parliament, Canada (Liberal), and Secretary General, U.N. Conference on Environment and Development. Interview, *The Financial Post*, Nov. 29, 1990.

44. The old imperialism – exploitation for foreign profit – has no place in our plans. What we envisage is a program of development based on the democratic concepts of fair-dealing.

Harry S Truman (1884-1972), 33rd President of the United States (D-MO). Inaugural address, Jan. 20, 1949.

45. Yankees are a wonderful people. If they emigrated to hell itself they would somehow manage to change the climate.

Mariano G. Vallejo (1808-1890), California politician. 1855.

46. Discontent is the first step in the progress of a man or a nation.

Oscar Wilde (1854-1900), Irish writer. *A Woman of No Importance*, 1894.

47. The American security presence allows them *[Asian countries]* not to concentrate on their security needs but allows them to concentrate on *[economic]* development.

Paul D. Wolfowitz, U.S. Undersecretary of Defense and Assistant Secretary of State. Interview, PBS, *American Interest*, Feb. 24, 1990.

Chapter 41

Guns and Gun Control

1. GUN RIGHTS ARE CIVIL RIGHTS
CHINA HAS GUN CONTROL
ONLY FREE PEOPLE OWN GUNS
GOD AND THE CONSTITUTION: YOUR GUN PERMIT
Signs carried by demonstrators against a proposed partial ban on assault weapons in Maryland. Annapolis, MD, Mar. 10, 1992.

2. GUN CONTROL IS BEING ABLE TO HIT WHAT YOU AIM AT
Bumper sticker, Austin, TX, 1990.

3. This Constitution shall never be construed ... to prevent the people of the United States who are peaceable citizens from keeping their own arms.
Samuel Adams (1722-1803), Member, Continental Congress, and Governor of Massachusetts. Proposed but rejected constitutional amendment.

4. In 1789, when used without any qualifying adjective, "the militia" referred to all Citizens capable of bearing arms.... The "militia" is identical to "the people."
Akhil Amar, professor, Yale University School of Law. "The Bill of Rights as a Constitution," *Yale Law Journal*, Mar. 1991.

5. The Union agrees with the Supreme Court's longstanding interpretation of the Second Amendment that the individual's right to keep and bear arms applies only to the preservation or efficiency of a "well-regulated militia." Except for lawful police and military purposes, the possession of weapons by individuals is not constitutionally protected.
American Civil Liberties Union. Policy #43.

6. The National Rifle Association are the gun nuts of the world.
Cecil D. Andrus, Governor of Idaho and U.S. Secretary of the Interior (D). Quoted in *The New York Times*, Apr. 2, 1990.

7. I have told myself that gun control isn't crime control. But more and more my argument in my own ears sounded threadbare.
Les AuCoin, U.S. Congressman (D-OR). Comment on altering his position on gun control legislation. Quoted in *The New York Times*, Mar. 27, 1991.

8. If we are not going to punish criminals, I will never vote to take away a person's right to bear arms.
Walter M. Baker, Maryland State Senator and Chairman, Judicial Proceedings Committee (D). Senate debate, Annapolis, MD, Mar. 12, 1992.

9. Our neighbors in Virginia are just as responsible for these killings as the criminals are because they won't pass strong gun control legislation.
Marion Barry, Mayor of Washington, DC (D). Comment on a rash of gun murders in Washington, DC, when most of illegal guns confiscated in Washington had been procured legally in neighboring Virginia. Interview, ABC, *This Week*, Mar. 19, 1989.

10. We don't need more assault rifles on our streets right now.
William J. Bennett, Director, Office of National Drug Control Policy, and U.S. Secretary of Education (R). Comment defending the administration's ban on imported assault rifles. Quoted on NBC, *Meet the Press*, Mar. 19, 1989.

11. You've got to protect your legitimate sportsman and hunter, but by God, you've got to protect your police officers too.
William J. Bennett. Comment in support of gun control. *Ibid.*

12. The Second Amendment protects the right of the people to bear arms. That doesn't mean that they should be able to bear any arms, at any time, under any circumstances.
William J. Bennett. Quoted on CBS, *Sunday Morning*, Apr. 23, 1989.

13. How miserable that man is that Governes a People where six parts of seaven at least are Poore Endebted Discontented and Armed.
William Berkeley (1606-1677), Colonial Governor of Virginia. Letter, 1676.

14. We are literally out of our minds to allow 2.5 million new weapons to be manufactured every year for the sole purpose of killing people.
Jonathan B. Bingham, U.S. Congressman (D-NY). Statement to the House Judiciary Committee, Feb. 20, 1975.

15. It *[gun control]* is not a loss of freedom. It's a measure to protect it.
James Brady, White House Press Secretary (R). Congressional testimony, Mar. 21, 1991.

16. The gun lobby finds waiting periods inconvenient. You have only to ask my husband how inconvenient he finds his wheelchair from time to time.
Sarah Brady, wife of White House Press Secretary James Brady and handgun control activist. Quoted on National Public Radio, June 6, 1990.

17. Free men and women have the right to own a gun to protect their home.
George Bush, 41st President of the United States (R-TX). Quoted in *Time*, Feb. 6, 1989.

18. We all know the NRA's *[National Rifle Association's]* position: guns don't kill people – grapes do.
George Bush. Speech, The Gridiron Club, Apr. 1, 1989.

19. Arms and laws do not flourish together.
Julius Caesar (102-44 B.C.), Emperor of Rome. Quoted in Plutarch, *The Parallel Lives: Julius Caesar*.

20. If we're going to let irrational people vote, then we ought to let them own guns too.
Ernie Chambers, Nebraska State Representative. In opposition to an interpretation of the state constitution that would restrict gun ownership for those with histories of mental problems. Quoted in *The New York Times*, Apr. 2, 1989.

21. Nothing is so exhilarating as to be shot at without result.
Winston Churchill (1874-1965), Prime Minister of Great Britain (Conservative). *Recollection of the Boer War*, 1922.

22. Gun manufacturers are not selling guns to kill people, but they don't care if they kill people.
Dave Clark, Chairman, Washington, DC, City Council (D). Interview, WETV, Washington, DC, Dec. 14, 1990.

23. All persons ... shall have in continuall readiness, a good muskitt or other gunn, fitt for service.
Connecticut Code, 1650.

24. What if they had to wait seven days to get their rifles to come to the Alamo and fight?
Robert Corbin, Attorney General of Arizona. Speech, National Rifle Association, Apr. 12, 1991.

25. Show me a man who doesn't want his gun registered and I'll show you a man who ought not to have a gun.
Homer S. Cummings (1870-1956), Mayor of Stamford, CT, and U.S. Attorney General (D). Quoted on CNN, *Capital Gang*, May 11, 1991.

26. You have a right to possess in your home and in your business a rifle, a pistol, and King George can't take it away from you, or Uncle Sam either.
Edward M. Davis, Chief of Police, Los Angeles, CA. Quoted in *The Dallas Times Herald*, July 13, 1975.

27. ... anyone else who can afford them shall keep bows and arrows.
Edward I (1239-1307), King of England. Statute of Winchester, 1253.

28. I'm completely opposed to selling automatic rifles. I don't see any reason why they ever made semiautomatics. I've been a member of the NRA *[National Rifle Association]*; I collect, make, and shoot guns. I've never used an automatic or semiautomatic for hunting. There's no need to. They have no place in anybody's arsenal. If any SOB can't hit a deer with one shot, then he ought to quit shooting.
Barry M. Goldwater, U.S. Senator (R-AZ). Quoted in *The Washington Post*, Jan. 1, 1990.

29. I am not hurt.
Ulysses S. Grant (1822-1885), 18th President of the United States (R-OH). Said to family and officers who rushed to his hotel room after he accidentally discharged a new breech-loading rifle into his own hand. This was Grant's only injury during a long military career. Feb. 25, 1866.

30. A lot of children know absolutely nothing about guns other than what they see on TV, and those are the wrong things.
Marion Hammer, spokeswoman, National Rifle Association (FL). Quoted in *The New York Times*, Oct. 10, 1988.

31. The great object is that every man be armed.
Patrick Henry (1736-1799), Member, Continental Congress, and Governor of Virginia. Debate, Virginia convention on ratification of the U.S. Constitution, 1788.

32. I do not consider firearms as weapons. When I think weapon, I mean bazooka.

James Huber, gun control opponent, Yonkers, NY. Quoted in *Newsweek*, Apr. 28, 1986.

33. It makes no sense for the police of this country to be outgunned by criminals or for our citizens to live in fear of criminals armed with assault rifles.

William J. Hughes, U.S. Congressman (D-NJ). House Judiciary Committee hearings, June 12, 1990.

34. What we're aiming at is the simple, stupid carelessness that leads an adult to leave a loaded gun where a 3-year-old child can pick it up and shoot somebody.

David Iannucci, chief lobbyist for Gov. William Donald Schaefer (D-MD). Statement on proposed legislation that would penalize adults who leave loaded guns within the reach of children under 16. Quoted in *The Washington Post*, Mar. 6, 1992.

35. To make inexpensive guns impossible to get is to say you're putting a money test on getting a gun. It's racism in its worst form.

Roy Innis, President, Congress of Racial Equality. Quoted in *The Washington Post*, Sept. 5, 1988.

36. To preserve liberty, it is essential that the whole body of the people always possess arms, and be taught alike, especially when young, how to use them.

Richard Henry Lee (1732-1794), Member, Continental Congress; signer of the Declaration of Independence; and U.S. Senator (VA). Quoted in Walter Hartwell Bennett, ed., *Letters from the Federal Farmer to the Republican*, 1975.

37. The advantage of being armed ... the Americans possess over the people of all other nations.... Notwithstanding the military establishments in the several Kingdoms of Europe, which are carried as far as the public resources will bear, the governments are afraid to trust the people with arms.

James Madison (1751-1836), 4th President of the United States (Democratic Republican-VA). *The Federalist*, No. 26.

38. To disarm the people – that was the best and most effective way to enslave them.

George Mason (1725-1792), Member, Virginia and Federal constitutional conventions. Debate, Virginia convention for the ratification of the U.S. Constitution, 1788.

39. *[Each man must]* have ... a sufficient musket or other serviceable peece for war ... for himself and each man servant he keeps able to bear arms.

Massachusetts Code, 1632.

40. Registering a gun is like registering to exercise the right of free speech.

Michael McCabe, general counsel, National Rifle Association. Quoted in *The New York Times*, Apr. 2, 1989.

41. I don't like the idea that the police department seems bent on keeping a pool of unarmed victims available for the predations of the criminal class.

David Mohler, orthopedic surgeon. Comment on being denied a permit to carry a handgun by New York City police. Quoted in *Manhattan,inc.*, Apr. 1989.

42. Politicians can be quite disarming.

National Rifle Association. Advertisement, *The Washington Post*, Apr. 5, 1990.

43. It's harder in Florida to rent a car than to buy an AK-47 *[military assault rifle]*.

William Nelson, U.S. Congressman (D-FL). Florida gubernatorial TV campaign ad, 1990.

44. The people have a right to bear arms for the defense of themselves and the State.

Pennsylvania Constitution, 1790.

45. They'll have to shoot me first to take my gun.

Roy Rogers, American cowboy, singer, and actor. 1982.

46. We desire the peace which comes as of right to the just man armed – not the peace granted on terms of ignominy to the craven weakling.

Theodore Roosevelt (1858-1919), 26th President of the United States (R-NY). Dec. 3, 1901.

47. Let ... others call me a hypocrite because I fired a gun in a moment of personal peril. I shall still be for strict gun control. But as long as authorities leave this society awash in drugs and guns, I will protect my family.

Carl T. Rowan, Jr., U.S. Ambassador to Finland and political columnist. Quoted in *Conservative Digest*, Aug. 1988.

48. Our police officers are the victims of those guns. Our citizens are the victims of those guns.

Warren B. Rudman, U.S. Senator (R-NH). Comment advocating the banning of automatic assault rifles. Interview, ABC, *This Week*, Mar. 19, 1989.

49. Next to having stout and friendly comrades, a man is chiefly emboldened by finding himself well armed in case of need.

Walter Scott (1771-1832), Scottish writer. *The Fortunes of Nigel*, 1822.

50. To give arms to all men who offer an honest price for them, without respect of persons or principles: to Royalist and Republican, to Communist and Capitalist, to Protestant and Catholic, to burglar and policeman, to black man, white man and yellow man.

George Bernard Shaw (1856-1950), Nobel Laureate in Literature (Great Britain). *Major Barbara*, 1905.

51. Feminism is about the empowerment of women in all areas of culture and society.... Feminism should be with the gun lobby, not against it.

Mary Zeiss Stange, American attorney and writer. "Feminism and the Second Amendment," *Guns & Ammo Annual*, 1992.

52. The police are definitely outgunned in this country.

Dewey Stokes, President, Fraternal Order of Police. Remark advocating gun control. Quoted in *Time*, Feb. 6, 1989.

53. *[The Second Amendment is]* the palladium of the liberties of the republic.

Joseph Story (1779-1845), U.S. Supreme Court Justice. *Commentaries on the Constitution*, 1833.

54. Handguns are a public-health problem.

Josh Sugarman, spokesman, Coalition to Ban Handguns. Debate, *The Morton Downey, Jr. Show*, 1988.

55. The pattern in these 464 deaths is depressingly clear: Guns most often kill the people who own them or people the owners know well.

Editorial, *Time*, July 17, 1989.

56. I could shoot every member of this assembly with this weapon in the twenty seconds it takes to show you this.

John Van de Kamp, Attorney General of California. Remark while brandishing an automatic weapon in an effort to promote gun control. Address, California Assembly, Feb. 13, 1989.

57. *[It is required that]* every man able to beare armes have in his house a fixt gunn.

Virginia law, 1658.

58. The right to buy weapons is the right to be free.

A. E. van Vogt, American science fiction writer. "The Weapon Shops," *Astounding Science-Fiction*, Dec. 1942.

59. Before a standing army can rule, the people must be disarmed; as they are in almost every kingdom of Europe. The supreme power in America cannot enforce unjust laws by the sword, because the whole body of the people are armed and constitute a force superior to any bands of regular troops.

Noah Webster (1758-1843), American writer and lexicographer. *An Examination into the Leading Principles of the Federal Constitution*, 1787.

60. I'll be damned if I'm going to let them collect guns in the city of Detroit while we're surrounded by hostile suburbs.

Coleman Young, Mayor of Detroit, MI (D). In reaction to a gun control proposal for Detroit. Quoted in *Newsweek*, Oct. 20, 1986.

Chapter 42

Health and Health Care

1. Health is the first of all liberties.
   Henri Amiel (1821-1881), Swiss poet and philosopher. *Diary*, Apr. 3, 1865.

2. Cost containment too often becomes *[health]* care containment. And it affects the least powerful population sector with the quietest voice.
   Ron Anderson, physician and President, Parkland Hospital, Dallas, TX. Quoted in *The New York Times*, Oct. 23, 1988.

3. There is no wealth like health.
   Apocrypha, *Wisdom of Ben Sira* 30:16.

4. When a company owns a drug, it has a responsibility to make sure that the drug is available to all who need it.
   Samuel Broder, Director, National Cancer Institute. Quoted in *The New York Times*, Sept. 23, 1989.

5. It bothers me when people smoke three packs of cigarettes a day for thirty years and then stick me with their health bill.
   Edmund G. (Jerry) Brown, Jr., Governor of California (D). Quoted in *Trends & Forecasts*, Jan. 27, 1981.

6. Medicine, the only profession that labours incessantly to destroy the reason for its own existence.
   James Bryce (1838-1922), British Ambassador to the United States. Speech, Mar. 23, 1914.

7. With 80,000 dead of AIDS, 3,000 more buried each month, our promiscuous homosexuals appear literally hell-bent on Satanism and suicide.
   Patrick Buchanan, White House speech writer (R) and syndicated columnist. *From the Right* (newsletter), Oct. 22, 1990.

8. What is the use of discussing a man's abstract right to food or medicine? The question is upon the method of procuring and administering them.
   Edmund Burke (1729-1797), British statesman. *Reflections on the Revolution in France*, 1790.

9. At least 25 percent of the money Americans spend on health care is wasted.
   Joseph A. Califano, Jr., U.S. Secretary of Health, Education and Welfare (D). "Billions Blown on Health," *The New York Times*, Apr. 12, 1989.

10. The old ethic for medicine *[regarding new drugs]* used to be: Is it safe and what are the risks? That is no longer adequate. Now people ask, "What goal are we reaching for?"
    Arthur Caplan, Director, Center for Biomedical Ethics, University of Minnesota. Quoted in *The Washington Post*, Oct. 30, 1988.

11. When catastrophic illness wipes out a middle-class family's income, they come to the government for help and they come in a hurry.
    Gregory Coler, Director, Illinois Department of Public Aid (R). PBS, *America's Children: Who Should Care?*, Sept. 4, 1990.

12. America's health care system is neither healthy, caring, nor a system.
    Walter Cronkite, American TV journalist. PBS, *Borderline Medicine*, Dec. 17, 1990.

13. The health of the people is really the foundation upon which all their happiness and all their powers as a State depend.
    Benjamin Disraeli, 1st Earl of Beaconsfield (1804-1881), Prime Minister of Great Britain (Conservative). Speech, July 24, 1877.

14. I proceed, gentlemen, briefly to call your attention to the present state of insane persons within the Commonwealth, in cages, closets, cellars, stalls, pens – chained naked, beaten with rods, and lashed into obedience.
    Dorothea L. Dix (1802-1887), mental health reformer and superintendent of women nurses for the Union Army. Memorandum to the Massachusetts legislature, 1841.

15. It is unrealistic to attempt to establish a utopia free from any hazards. Absolute *[industrial]* safety is an impossibility.
    Pete V. Domenici, U.S. Senator (R-CO). Senate debate, 1972.

16. Whether we, as individuals, are motivated by simple humanity or by simple economics, we can no longer permit profits to be dependent upon an unsafe or unhealthy work site.

Thomas F. Eagleton, U.S. Senator (D-MO). Senate debate, 1985.

17. The Department of Energy's nuclear weapons production programs have direct and potentially devastating medical implications.... A public health emergency exists.

H. Jack Geiger, President, Physicians for Social Responsibility. Comment on nuclear plant safety violations. Letter to President Reagan, Oct. 27, 1988.

18. The same people who tell us that smoking doesn't cause cancer are now telling us that advertising cigarettes doesn't cause smoking.

Ellen Goodman, American syndicated columnist. *The Boston Globe*, July 16, 1986.

19. In the future we may have to ration health care, but we're not there now.

Albert A. Gore, Jr., U.S. Senator (D-TN) and Vice President of the United States. Quoted on ABC, *The Health Show*, Feb. 4, 1990.

20. It is a lot easier to find gaps in the health care system than to find ways to fill them.

Willis D. Gradison, U.S. Congressman (R-OH). Interview, PBS, *Frontline*, Apr. 30, 1991.

21. When you have 25 percent of the city not being able to afford care, health becomes everyone's responsibility.... What is the moral responsibility of a hospital? Do you assure basic services for the many, or do you retain complex sophisticated services that tend to affect the relatively few?

Robert D. Grumbs, Director, New York City Health Systems Agency. Quoted in *The New York Times*, Mar. 12, 1989.

22. The state must concern itself with all institutions for those with damaged minds.

Karl August von Hardenberg (1750-1822), Foreign Minister and Chancellor of Prussia. Statement establishing German mental hospital system, 1805.

23. Infectious diseases ... have probably been the most dangerous of enemies of mankind, much more so than war and mass murder. When one studies the constant epidemics of the past and the deficiency diseases on land and at sea, one realizes that the whole of civilization could have succumbed, and one is constantly surprised that mankind has survived.

Folke Henschen, Swedish pathologist. *The History and Geography of Disease*, 1966.

24. AIDS killed him, but our health care system tortured him.

Howard W. Hiatt, American physician and dean, Harvard School of Public Health. *The New York Times*, Aug. 4, 1988.

25. Incurably sick persons should be granted mercy death.

Adolf Hitler (1889-1945), Führer of the Third German Reich. Edict, Sept. 1, 1939.

26. Socialized medicine by the back door.

Oveta Culp Hobby, Director, U.S. Women's (Auxiliary) Army Corps, and U.S. Secretary of Health, Education and Welfare (R). Comment on a bill introduced in Congress to provide free Salk vaccine to all children. Quoted in Eric F. Goldman, *The Crucial Decade*, 1960.

27. It is the duty of the doctor to prolong life. It is not his duty to prolong dying.

Thomas Horder (1871-1955), Member of Parliament, Great Britain (Conservative). Speech, House of Lords, Dec. 1936.

28. Let us be brave and change our life-style. Let us stick to our single partners and stop overindulging. If we cannot do it, let us use condoms.

Tsungiraya Hungwe, Deputy Minister for Political Affairs, Zimbabwe. Speech to Parliament, 1990.

29. If the AMA *[American Medical Association]* is against you, you must be doing something right.

Andrew Jacobs, Jr., U.S. Congressman (D-IN). Quoted on PBS, *The Power Game*, Jan. 2, 1989.

30. Health is the first requisite after morality.

Thomas Jefferson (1743-1826), 3rd President of the United States (Democratic Republican-VA). Letter to Peter Carr, Aug. 1787.

31. I am proposing that every person over sixty-five years of age be spared the darkness of sickness without hope.

Lyndon B. Johnson (1908-1973), 36th President of the United States (D-TX). Message to Congress, 1965.

32. The two most dangerous words in the English language are not "nuclear war." They are "socialized medicine."

Lyndon B. Johnson. Quoted on PBS, *LBJ*, Aug. 2, 1989.

33. A sound mind in a sound body. (*Mens sana in corpore sano.*)

Decimus Junius Juvenal (c.60-c.140), Roman poet. *Satires*.

34. No other industrial nation in the world leaves its citizens in fear of financial ruin because of illness.

Edward M. Kennedy, U.S. Senator (D-MA). Senate speech, Sept. 24, 1970.

35. We've been educating people for forty years on the dangers of cigarette smoking, and millions are still smoking even though they know they are going to die.

Edward I. Koch, U.S. Congressman and Mayor of New York City (D). Interview, PBS, *Tony Brown's Journal*, Oct. 1, 1988.

36. I am the surgeon general of the heterosexuals and the homosexuals, of the young and the old, of the moral and the immoral, the married and the unmarried. I don't have the luxury of deciding which side I want to be on. So I can tell you how to keep yourself alive no matter what you are. That's my job.

C. Everett Koop, U.S. Surgeon General. Quoted in *The Washington Post*, Mar. 25, 1987.

37. Some of you find it unpleasant to recommend condoms to young people. So do I. Acquired Immune Deficiency Syndrome is an unpleasant disease, and recommending condoms to those who need protection is preferable to treating AIDS.

C. Everett Koop. Editorial, *Journal of the American Medical Association*, Oct. 1987.

38. We are fighting a deadly disease. We are not fighting the people who have that disease. Homosexuality does not produce AIDS.

C. Everett Koop. Speech to students, Cardoza High School, Washington, DC, Feb. 1988.

39. There no longer can be any doubt about the link between diet and disease. Your choice of diet can influence your long-term health prospects more than any other action you might take.

C. Everett Koop. July 1988.

40. Cigarettes are the single most important preventable cause of death, responsible for one out of every six deaths in the United States.

C. Everett Koop. Quoted in *Time*, Jan. 23, 1989.

41. It's broken.

C. Everett Koop. Characterization of the American health delivery system. Interview, PBS, *MacNeil-Lehrer Report*, July 21, 1989.

42. I think a laissez-faire economy works best for all of our citizens, but the health care marketplace, although laissez-faire, is not freely competitive and has virtually no moderating controls working on behalf of the patient.

C. Everett Koop. *Newsweek*, Aug. 28, 1989.

43. Until everyone knows someone who has died of AIDS this prejudice and discrimination will continue.

C. Everett Koop. Interview, ABC, *Nightline*, Apr. 11, 1990.

44. It is inevitable that we are going to have to ration health care in the United States.

Richard D. Lamm, Governor of Colorado (D). *Playboy*, Aug. 1984.

45. Whatever the costs are, we can't measure health and lives in economic terms.

Thomas A. Luken, U.S. Congressman (D-OH). House hearings, Aug. 27, 1990.

46. I thought, wait and see – maybe it *[AIDS]* is not as hot as some are making it appear. I definitely admit to a gross underestimate. We're running scared.

Halfdan Mahler, Director, World Health Organization. Quoted in *Newsweek*, Dec. 1, 1986.

47. What we're saying is that if you are poor, you can die.

Tom Mason, Oregon State Senator (D). Criticism of restrictive policies regarding organ transplantation. Quoted on ABC, *The Health Show*, Feb. 4, 1990.

48. I owe my tolerable health to having selected my parents well.

Robert G. Menzies (1894-1978), Prime Minister of Australia (Liberal). Quoted in *The Wit of Sir Robert Menzies*, 1966.

49. We are being medically mugged by these laboratories.

Barbara A. Mikulski, U.S. Congresswoman and U.S. Senator (D-MD). On support of legislation for standards and quality control in medical laboratories. Quoted on NBC, *Newscenter 4*, Washington, DC, Nov. 1, 1988.

50. Each person is the proper guardian of his own health, whether bodily, or mental, or spiritual.

John Stuart Mill (1806-1873), Member of Parliament, Great Britain, and political economist. *On Liberty*, 1859.

51. The United States has the best health system in the world. Unfortunately this is true only for those who can afford it.

George J. Mitchell, U.S. Senator (D-ME). Speech, American Group Practice Association, Apr. 12, 1991.

52. Our hospitals, clinics and social services are already strained to the limit, and many HIV-infected persons are not receiving adequate care. How is the system going to manage in the future?
New York City AIDS Task Force. Quoted in *The New York Times*, Oct. 16, 1988.

53. The United States is now engaged in an insane, but terribly effective, effort to destroy the American people and Western civilization by subsidizing, both at home and abroad, the breeding of the intellectually, physically, and morally unfit.
Revilo P. Oliver, cofounder, John Birch Society. Quoted in Epstein and Forster, *The Radical Right*, 1967.

54. The success we have achieved *[in treating AIDS]* is dramatic and encouraging. But we should not make a naive declaration of triumph at the very outset of a long and difficult campaign.
June Osborne, American physician and dean, University of Michigan School of Public Health. Quoted in *The Montgomery Journal*, June 12, 1989.

55. The cost benefit analysis approach to whether we live or die is generally unappealing.
John O'Sullivan, editor, *National Review*. PBS, *Firing Line*, Jan. 16, 1989.

56. The first thing we should do is pass a long-term care bill for the chronically ill men, women, and children, and I insist, Mr. Chairman, that we include children on that list.
Claude D. Pepper (1901-1989), U.S. Senator and U.S. Congressman (D-FL). Congressional hearings on long-term care insurance, Aug. 2, 1988.

57. We need to make violence a public health issue, just like drunk driving, just like heart disease, just like AIDS.
Deborah Prothrow-Stith, physician and Commissioner of Public Health, Massachusetts. Quoted in *The Washington Post*, Dec. 18, 1990.

58. If the U.S. population were five times its current size, it would be fairly easy for members of Congress to agree on China's family planning policy.
Qian Qichen, Foreign Minister, China. In reference to China's "one couple, one child" policy. Press conference, Beijing, Mar. 27, 1989.

59. The only way to guarantee that more infants do not fall victim to inadequate health care services is to establish a system of universal access to comprehensive prenatal and infant care services.
Lynda Johnson Robb, member, National Commission to Prevent Infant Mortality. *The Washington Post*, July 23, 1989.

60. We go from budget to budget, crisis to crisis, and election to election without deciding as a nation what is right for health care and what we're willing to sacrifice.
Carolyn Roberts, President, Copley Hospital, Vermont. Quoted in *The New York Times*, Oct. 23, 1988.

61. We rebuke this virus and we command your immune system to function in the name of Jesus.
Pat Robertson, American televangelist and candidate for Republican presidential nomination. Said while attempting to heal a person with AIDS. Quoted in *Newsweek*, Jan. 12, 1987.

62. Health insurance has become a cataclysm that threatens to bankrupt the family budget, the corporate budget, and the national budget.
John D. Rockefeller IV, U.S. Senator and Governor of West Virginia (D). Remark, Mar. 3, 1990.

63. If you had spent two years in bed trying to wiggle your big toe, after that anything else would seem easy!
(Roosevelt was paralyzed from the waist down by polio.)
Franklin D. Roosevelt (1882-1945), 32nd President of the United States (D-NY). Quoted in Paul F. Boller, Jr., *Presidential Anecdotes*, 1981.

64. Until recently we believed that more is better - one surgery is good for you, but two is better.
William L. Roper, Director, U.S. Health Care Financing Administration. Quoted in *The New York Times*, Oct. 23, 1988.

65. The Constitution of the Republic should make provision for medical freedom as well as religious freedom. To restrict the art of healing to one class of men and deny equal privilege to others will constitute the Bastille of medical science.
Benjamin Rush (1745-1813), physician and Member, Continental Congress. 1788.

66. It makes you wonder what they're smoking at the Tobacco Institute.
Charles E. Schumer, U.S. Congressman (D-NY). Comment on an accusation that the Surgeon General's recommendation to ban indoor smoking was personal and political rather than scientific. Quoted in *Newsweek*, Feb. 2, 1987.

67. Give us a healthy world – in the full sense – and Communism will finally disappear in every sense.
R. Sargent Shriver, Director, Office of Economic Opportunity (D). Quoted in *The New York Times*, Nov. 16, 1964.

68. Typhoid, cholera, yellow fever, summer diarrhea, dysentery, tuberculosis, anthrax, intestinal worms, and many other diseases are still with us and could again return as plagues of old. During the garbage strike in New York in 1968, public health officials geared up to give massive immunizations against typhoid fever, so great was the potential hazard from garbage in the streets.

William E. Small, editor, *Biomedical News. Third Pollution*, 1974.

69. The fact is that New Yorkers are being asked to play every day a game of Russian roulette, in effect a lotto system where they just don't know, if they, God forbid, need an ambulance, how long they are going to have to wait.

Andrew J. Stein, President of the City Council, New York City (D). Reaction to the news that 45 percent of the city's public ambulance fleet was out of service on that day. Quoted in *The New York Times*, July 26, 1988.

70. People who do not see a future for themselves, who live day to day, do not put a premium on longevity.

Reed V. Tucker, physician and Commissioner of Public Health, Washington, DC. Quoted in *The Washington Post*, Aug. 28, 1988.

71. If it hits me this hard, and I make a governor's salary, how can a man who earns so much less pay his bills?

Earl Warren (1891-1974), Chief Justice, U.S. Supreme Court, and Governor of California (R). Comment on receiving his hospital bill for treatment of a kidney infection. Remark to Robert Kenny, 1945.

72. We do not want to put the medical profession on the public payroll, nor do we want to deprive the individual of the right to select his own physician.... Our major purpose is to spread the cost of medical care among all the people of the state.

Earl Warren. Insurance message to the California legislature, 1946.

73. We have studied this *[health insurance]*... for thirty years.... When you go beyond a certain point, study ceases to be a virtue and becomes a device to destroy progress rather than make progress. I think we have arrived at that point.

Earl Warren. Statement to reporters, 1946.

74. If the President is going to take the chief recommendations of his *[AIDS]* commission and just ignore them, why did he bother having a commission?

Henry A. Waxman, U.S. Congressman (D-CA). Quoted in *The Washington Post*, Aug. 3, 1988.

75. It is good public policy to err on the side of public health.

Henry A. Waxman. Quoted in *The Washington Post*, Feb. 7, 1990.

76. What we had to do was ... to make medical treatment not a favour granted to those in desperate need but to compel all sick persons to submit to it ... to treat illness, in fact, as a public nuisance to be suppressed in the interests of the community.

Beatrice Potter Webb (1858-1943), British Socialist and cofounder, Fabian Society. Quoted by Anne Fremantle in Frederick Giffin, ed., *Woman as Revolutionary*, 1973.

77. Behaviorally based illness *[AIDS, lung cancer, cirrhosis of the liver]* is not the result of bad luck but of bad choices.

George F. Will, American political columnist. *The Washington Post*, July 16, 1989.

78. Prolongation of life should not be the aim of medicine. Health is the aim of medicine.

George F. Will. ABC, *This Week*, June 10, 1990.

79. If criminals have the right to a lawyer, I think working Americans should have the right to a doctor.

Harris Wofford, U.S. Senator (D-PA). *The Washington Post*, Nov. 19, 1991.

80. Swords and lances, arrows, machine guns, and even high explosives have had far less power over the fates of nations than the typhus louse, the plague flea, and the yellow fever mosquito.... War and conquest ... have merely set the stage for these more powerful agents of human tragedy.

Hans Zinsser (1878-1940), American bacteriologist and health researcher. *Rats, Lice and History*, 1935.

Chapter 43

History and Historians

1. Young man, I have lived in this house many years and have seen the occupants of the White House across the square come and go, and nothing you minor officials or the occupant of that house can do will affect the history of the world for long.

Henry Adams (1838-1918), American historian. Remark to Franklin D. Roosevelt, then U.S. Assistant Secretary of the Navy, 1913. Quoted by Eleanor Roosevelt, *This Is My Story*, 1937.

2. The history of our Revolution will be one continued lie from one end to the other.

John Adams (1735-1826), 2nd President of the United States (Federalist-MA). Letter to Dr. Benjamin Rush, Apr. 4, 1790.

3. History is the sum total of things that could have been avoided.

Konrad Adenauer (1876-1967), Chancellor of West Germany. Favorite saying.

4. It is the champions of "left-wing liberal socialism" who shape the tendency toward falsifying the history of socialism. They try to make us believe that the country's past was nothing but mistakes and crimes, keeping silent about the greatest achievements of the past and the present.

Nina Andreyeva, Lecturer, Leningrad College, U.S.S.R. In reference to Soviet advocates of *glasnost*. *Sovetskaya Rossiya*, Mar. 13, 1988.

5. History does not repeat itself. Historians repeat each other.

Arthur J. Balfour, 1st Earl of Balfour (1848-1930), Prime Minister of Great Britain (Conservative). Attributed.

6. We have a national memory in this country of about seven minutes.

Carl Bernstein, American journalist. Interview, CNN, *Larry King Live*, Feb. 7, 1991.

7. The past is buried and I mourn it with greater pain than many among you, because no human power can awaken it when the Crown itself has scattered ashes upon the coffin.

Otto von Bismarck-Schoenhausen (1815-1898), Chancellor of Germany. Remark after the French Revolution of 1848, when the Napoleonic dynasty was ended. 1849.

8. History is simply a piece of paper covered with print; the main thing is still to make history, not to write it.

Otto von Bismarck-Schoenhausen. Quoted in Curtis and Greenslet, *The Practical Cogitator*, 1953.

9. Those who mill around at the crossroads of history do so at their own peril.

David L. Boren, Governor of Oklahoma and U.S. Senator (D). Quoted in *The Chicago Tribune*, Jan. 5, 1990.

10. No one is free from the history he has inherited.

Willy Brandt (1913-1992), Chancellor of West Germany and Nobel Laureate in Peace. 1964.

11. One faces the future with one's past.

Pearl S. Buck (1892-1973), Nobel Laureate in Literature (United States). Nobel address, Oct. 13, 1942.

12. A time of historic change is no time for recklessness.

George Bush, 41st President of the United States (R-TX). Address on national television, Nov. 22, 1989.

13. Posterity will give a man a fair hearing; his own times will not do so if he is attacking vested interests.

Samuel Butler (1835-1902), British writer. *The Note-Books of Samuel Butler*, 1912.

14. History will absolve me.

Fidel Castro, Premier of Cuba. Statement at his trial for attempting to overthrow the Batista dictatorship, 1953.

15. What is past cannot be rewritten, but it is within our power to rewrite the future.

Catherine II (The Great) (1729-1796), Empress of Russia. Quoted on TNT, *The Young Catherine*, Feb. 18, 1991.

16. Study the past, if you would divine the future.
Confucius (551-479 B.C.), Chinese philosopher. *Analects.*

17. Assassination has never changed the history of the world.
Benjamin Disraeli, 1st Earl of Beaconsfield (1804-1881), Prime Minister of Great Britain (Conservative). Speech, House of Commons, May 1, 1865.

18. History teaches us that men and nations behave wisely once they have exhausted all other alternatives.
Abba Eban, Foreign Secretary of Israel (Labour) and Ambassador to the United Nations. Quoted in *The Observer,* Dec. 20, 1970.

19. Neither a wise man nor a brave man lies down on the tracks of history to wait for the train of the future to run over him.
Dwight D. Eisenhower (1890-1969), 34th President of the United States (R-KS). Campaign speech, Oct. 6, 1952.

20. There is no history; only biography.
Ralph Waldo Emerson (1803-1882), American writer. *Journals,* May 28, 1839.

21. History is all party pamphlets.
Ralph Waldo Emerson. *Journals,* Feb. 18, 1855.

22. All history has been a history of class struggles, of struggles between dominated and dominating classes at various stages of social development.
Friedrich Engels (1820-1895), German Socialist and revolutionary theorist. Preface, *The Communist Manifesto,* 1883.

23. History does not disclose to us its alternatives.
Thomas S. Foley, U.S. Congressman and Speaker of the House (D-WA). TV interview, Feb. 1991.

24. History is past politics and politics present history.
Edward Augustus Freeman (1823-1892), British historian. Quoted in John Robert Seeley, *The Growth of British Policy,* 1903.

25. There are moments in history when brooding tragedy and its dark shadows can be lightened by recalling great moments of the past.
Indira Gandhi (1917-1984), Prime Minister of India. Letter to Richard M. Nixon, Dec. 16, 1971.

26. Events rather than politicians have put important issues on the table.
Geoffrey Garin, American political pollster (D). Quoted in *The New York Times,* Nov. 4, 1990.

27. My argument is that war makes rattling good history; but peace is poor reading.
Thomas Hardy (1840-1928), British writer. *The Dynasts,* I, 1904.

28. Falsifiers of history do not safeguard history but imperil it.
Vaclav Havel, President of Czechoslovakia. Quoted in *The New York Times,* July 29, 1990.

29. Governments have never learned anything from history, or acted on principles deduced from it.
Georg Wilhelm Friedrich Hegel (1770-1831), German philosopher. *Philosophy of History,* 1832.

30. It is not the neutrals or the lukewarms who make history.
Adolf Hitler (1889-1945), Führer of the Third German Reich. Speech to the Reichstag celebrating the "legal revolution" that brought him and his Nazi party to power, Berlin, Apr. 23, 1933.

31. The history of most countries has been that of majorities – mounted majorities, clad in iron, armed with death, treading down the tenfold more numerous minorities.
Oliver Wendell Holmes (1809-1894), American physician and writer. May 30, 1860.

32. He who influences the thought of his times, influences all the times that follow. He has made his impress on eternity.
Hypatia (370-415), Greek philosopher. Quoted in Elbert Hubbard, *Little Journeys to the Homes of Great Teachers,* 1908.

33. The infidels of one age have been the aureoled saints of the next.
Robert Green Ingersoll (1833-1899), Attorney General of Illinois (R). *The Great Infidels.*

34. History, in general, only informs us of what bad government is.
Thomas Jefferson (1743-1826), 3rd President of the United States (Democratic Republican-VA). C.1800. *Writings,* XI.

35. Assassins have never changed history.
Robert F. Kennedy (1925-1968), U.S. Senator and U.S. Attorney General (D-NY). Remark after the death of President Kennedy, 1963.

36. It is from numberless diverse acts of courage and belief that human history is shaped.
Robert F. Kennedy. Speech, University of Capetown, South Africa, June 6, 1966.

37. Few will have the greatness to bend history itself. But each of us can work to change a small portion of events, and in the total of all those acts will be written the history of this generation.
Robert F. Kennedy. Quoted in *Conservative Digest*, Nov. 1987.

38. History is on our side. We will bury you.
Nikita S. Khrushchev (1894-1971), Premier of the U.S.S.R. Quoted in *U.S. News & World Report*, Dec. 27, 1957.

39. History is the memory of states.
Henry M. Kissinger, U.S. Secretary of State and National Security Advisor (R). *A World Restored: Castlereagh, Metternich and the Restoration of Peace, 1812-1822*, 1957.

40. Let us avoid the temptation to assume that a solution to the German question can be arranged in advance with a script and a calendar. History doesn't follow a schedule.
Helmut Kohl, Chancellor of West Germany. Quoted in *The Chicago Tribune*, Nov. 16, 1989.

41. People who want to get into history books don't get into them.
Helmut Kohl. Quoted in *Time*, June 25, 1990.

42. I cannot deny our history.
Helmut Kohl. July 24, 1990.

43. It is a great piece of folly to attempt to make anything out of me or my early life. It can all be condensed into a single sentence, and that sentence you will find in Gray's *Elegy [in a Country Churchyard]*: "The short and simple annals of the poor." That's my life, and that's all you or anyone can make out of it.
Abraham Lincoln (1809-1865), 16th President of the United States (R-IL). Letter to J. L. Scripps, 1860.

44. The history of England is emphatically the history of progress.
Thomas Babington Macaulay, 1st Baron Macaulay (1800-1859), historian and Secretary of War, Great Britain (Liberal). "Sir James Mackintosh's History of the Revolution," *Edinburgh Review*, July 1835.

45. Historical experience is written in blood and iron.
Mao Tse-tung (1893-1976), Chairman, Communist Party of China. *Yu Chi Chan*, 1937.

46. The people, and the people alone, are the motive force in the making of world history.
Mao Tse-tung. Speech, "On Coalition Government," Apr. 24, 1945.

47. The history of all hitherto existing society is the history of class struggles.
Karl Marx (1818-1883), German economist and Socialist. *The Communist Manifesto*, 1848.

48. History didn't begin yesterday.
Robert Maynard, American editor and journalist. ABC, *This Week*, Jan. 14, 1990.

49. The press are the chroniclers of history as it is made.
Maryanne Means, American journalist. Symposium, "The Press and a Divided Government," National Press Foundation, Dec. 6, 1989.

50. In a hundred years the historian will understand me better.
Klemens von Metternich (1773-1859), Austrian statesman and diplomat. *Lettres de Prince de Metternich à la Comtesse de Lieven, 1818-1819*.

51. Blood alone moves the wheels of history.
Benito Mussolini (1883-1945), dictator of Italy (Fascist). Speech, Parma, Dec. 13, 1914.

52. We must not pass through this world without leaving traces which may commend our memory to posterity.
Napoléon I (1769-1821), military leader and Emperor of France. *Maxims*.

53. You don't change the course of history by turning the faces of portraits to the wall.
Jawaharlal Nehru (1889-1964), Prime Minister of India. Statement to Premier Nikita Khrushchev of the U.S.S.R. Quoted in *The New York Post*, Apr. 1, 1959.

54. Will history treat me more kindly than my contemporaries?
Richard M. Nixon, 37th President of the United States (R-CA). Question he asked of Henry Kissinger. Quoted in Woodward and Bernstein, *The Final Days*, 1976.

55. Once you get into this great stream of history, you can't get out.
Richard M. Nixon. Quoted in Barbara Rowes, *The Book of Quotes*, 1979.

56. There is no reason to repeat bad history.
Eleanor Holmes Norton, Delegate to U.S. Congress (D-DC) and Chair, Equal Employment Opportunity Commission. "For Sadie and Maude," in *Sisterhood Is Powerful*, 1970.

57. Who controls the past controls the future. Who controls the present controls the past.

George Orwell (Eric Blair) (1903-1950), British writer. *1984*, 1949.

58. Had Cleopatra's nose been shorter, the whole history of the world would have been different.
Blaise Pascal (1623-1662), French mathematician and philosopher. *Pensées*, No. 2.

59. Peace is better than a place in history.
Justo Pastor Benitez (1895-1962), Paraguayan diplomat and journalist. Speech, Asunción, 1935.

60. Those who tell the stories also rule society.
Plato (427-347 B.C.), Greek philosopher.

61. There is a mysterious cycle in human events. To some generations much is given. Of other generations much is expected. This generation has a rendezvous with destiny.
Franklin D. Roosevelt (1882-1945), 32nd President of the United States (D-NY). Presidential nomination acceptance speech, Philadelphia, PA, June 26, 1936.

62. They *[young people]* think Huey Long is a Chinese restaurant.
Mark Russell, American political humorist. Quoted on *NBC Sunday*, July 16, 1988.

63. Progress, far from consisting in change, depends on retentiveness.... Those who cannot remember the past are condemned to fulfil it.
George Santayana (1863-1952), American philosopher. *The Life of Reason*, 1906.

64. World history is the world's judgment.
Johann Friedrich von Schiller (1759-1805), German historian and poet. Inaugural lecture as professor of history, University of Jena, May 26, 1789.

65. Tribe follows tribe, and nation follows nation, like the waves of the sea. It is the order of nature, and regret is useless. Your time of decay may be distant – but it will surely come, for even the White Man whose God walked and talked with him as with a friend, cannot be exempt from the common destiny. We may be brothers after all. We will see.
Seattle (c.1786-1866), Chief, Duwamish Indians. Message to Isaac Stevens, Governor of Washington Territory, 1855.

66. Nothing is certain except the past.
Lucius Annaeus Seneca (The Younger) (4 B.C.-A.D. 65), Roman statesman, dramatist, and philosopher. *De Consolatione ad Marciam*.

67. The evil that men do lives after them;
The good is oft interred with their bones.
William Shakespeare (1564-1616), English writer. *Julius Caesar*, III, ii.

68. History will speak well of me because I will write it.
Joseph R. Smallwood, Premier of Newfoundland, Canada, and historian. Quoted in *The Globe and Mail*, Dec. 24, 1985.

69. It is not heroes that make history, but history that makes heroes.
Joseph Stalin (1879-1953), Premier of the U.S.S.R. Attributed.

70. Now he belongs to the ages.
Edwin M. Stanton (1814-1869), U.S. Attorney General (D), U.S. Secretary of War, and U.S. Supreme Court Justice. Remark on the death of Abraham Lincoln, Apr. 15, 1865.

71. Every nation, race, and creed, which contributed toward the building up of this great continent and country, should, from motives of patriotism, gather up its records and chronicles, so that our historians may be able to examine and describe the forces that our national and political existence have amalgamated.
Oscar S. Straus (1845-1926), U.S. Secretary of Commerce (Progressive-NY), U.S. Secretary of Labor, and U.S. Ambassador to Turkey. Presidential address, American Jewish Historical Society, New York City, 1892.

72. And what I want to say to historians is that any Monday morning quarterback can win a ball game next Monday, but he can't do it on Saturday.
Harry S Truman (1884-1972), 33rd President of the United States (D-MO). Press conference, Washington, DC, Apr. 27, 1952.

73. If a man is acquainted with what other people have experienced at this desk it will be easier for him to go through a similar experience. It is ignorance that causes most mistakes. The man who sits here ought to know his American history, at least.
Harry S Truman. Quoted in Laurin L. Henry, *Presidential Transitions*, 1960.

74. Do your duty, and history will do you justice.
Harry S Truman. Quoted by Congressman Edward T. Roybal, in a memorial tribute to Truman, U.S. House of Representatives, Jan. 3, 1973.

75. The history of the great events of this world are scarcely more than the history of crimes.

Voltaire (François-Marie Arouet) (1694-1778), French historian and dramatist. *On the Morals and the Spirit of Nations*, 1756.

76. He who puts out his hand to stop the wheel of history will have his fingers crushed.

Lech Walesa, President of Poland, trade unionist, and founder, Solidarity. Interview, *CBS News*, July 10, 1989.

77. The destruction of the past is perhaps the greatest of all crime.

Simone Weil (1910-1943), French revolutionist and political philosopher. *The Need for Roots*, 1952.

78. Whoever refuses to remember the inhumanity *[of the Holocaust]* is prone to new risks of infection.

Richard von Weizsächer, President of West Germany. Quoted in *The New York Times*, May 12, 1985.

79. Anybody can make history. Only a great man can write it.

Oscar Wilde (1854-1900), Irish writer. *The Critic as Artist*, 1890.

80. The one duty we owe to history is to rewrite it.

Oscar Wilde. *Ibid*.

81. The main essentials of a successful Prime Minister are sleep and a sense of a history.

Harold Wilson, Prime Minister of Great Britain (Labour). *The Governance of Britain*, 1977.

82. I am more interested in the opinion the country will have of me ten years from now than the opinion it may be willing to express today.

Woodrow Wilson (1856-1924), 28th President of the United States (D-NJ). Remark to Joseph P. Tumulty, 1916.

Chapter 44

Housing and the Homeless

1. A ghetto can be improved in only one way: out of existence.
   James Baldwin (1924-1987), American writer. *Nobody Knows My Name*, 1961.

2. Every bird dwells with its own kind.
   Apocrypha, *Wisdom of Ben Sira*, 27:9.

3. There are thousands on thousands in New York who have no assignable home.
   Charles L. Brace (1855-1905), founder, Children's Aid Society. Statement, 1872.

4. There isn't profit to be made off low-rent housing, and it's time we acknowledge that, instead of perverting a system around maintaining private ownership.
   Bonnie Brower, Executive Director, Association of Neighborhood and Housing Development. *The New York Times*, Oct. 2, 1988.

5. If we provide four hundred new beds, we get four hundred new tramps.
   Ed Burkhart, Seattle, WA, police officer. Comment on the city's problem with the homeless. Quoted in *Newsweek*, Dec. 15, 1986.

6. Inflation is not all bad. After all, it has allowed every American to live in a more expensive neighborhood without moving.
   Alan Cranston, U.S. Senator (D-CA). Remark, 1979.

7. I know we haven't cleaned up all the slums, but I didn't create the slums, did I?
   Richard J. Daley (1902-1976), Mayor of Chicago, IL (D). Quoted in *Look*, Sept. 3, 1968.

8. Housing and the allotment of drinkable water to the greatest number of people will be the immediate objectives of my administration.
   Gustavo Díaz Ordaz (1911-1979), President of Mexico. Campaign speech, 1963.

9. Property has its duties as well as its rights.
   Thomas Drummond (1797-1840), British colonial administrator. Letter to the Earl of Donoughmore. May 22, 1838.

10. He *[Congressman Mike Synar]* has never owned a home in the 2nd Congressional District *[of Oklahoma]*, but he owns a home here. It goes to his ties to the district.... We just wanted a graphic to illustrate our point.
    Drew Enmondson, Democratic Congressional candidate. Explanation of why he camped in front of Synar's Washington, DC, home with a photographer. Feb. 23, 1992.

11. My constituents tell me they want a fight, and that's what I'm here to do.
    Edward Fagan, City Councilman, Yonkers, NY (D). Comment on voting against a construction plan ordered by a federal court to remedy housing discrimination. Quoted in *The Washington Post*, Aug. 3, 1988.

12. There is plenty of affordable housing – it is simply occupied by the wrong people.... The problem in New York is not high rents, but low incomes.
    John J. Gilbert III, President, Rent Stabilization Association of New York (a landlord group). Letter to *The New York Times*, July 12, 1988.

13. As you move away from mass transit you become more dependent on the automobile, so you have to spread the housing out more to accommodate the cars.
    Sandy Hornick, Director of City Planning, New York City. Quoted in *The New York Times*, May 21, 1989.

14. Look what we have built ... low-income projects that became worse centers of delinquency, vandalism, and general social hopelessness than the slums they were supposed to replace.
    Jane Jacobs, American architectural writer. *The Death and Life of Great American Cities*, 1961.

15. It's all part of character building.
    Edward I. Koch, U.S. Congressman and Mayor of New York City (D). Explanation of why homeless people living in city shelters should be charged rent. Dec. 6, 1988.

16. Let your brother live beside you.
Old Testament, *Leviticus* 25:31.

17. Let those who compile riches from the misery of slums hear this message as their eviction notice: There will be no compromise with the profiteers of poverty.
John V. Lindsay, U.S. Congressman (R) and Mayor of New York City (R and Liberal). Mayoral inaugural address, Jan. 1966.

18. So I'll be used to living in it.
Huey P. Long (1893-1935), Governor of Louisiana and U.S. Senator (D). Explanation of why he rebuilt the governor's mansion in Baton Rouge as a replica of the White House. 1930.

19. People who are homeless are not social inadequates. They are people without homes.
Sheila McKechnie, Director, Shelter National Campaign for the Homeless, Great Britain. Quoted in *The Christian Science Monitor,* May 7, 1985.

20. *[Home]* ownership gives a sense of pride and dignity to people; it helps them integrate into the community.
Charles H. Percy, U.S. Senator (R-IL). Interview, *Playboy,* Apr. 1968.

21. We have to desegregate housing before we desegregate schools.
Anna Eleanor Roosevelt (1884-1962), First Lady and U.S. Delegate to the United Nations. Letter to Adlai E. Stevenson, June 13, 1956.

22. The building of houses for us is all nonsense.
Satana (1830-1878), Chief, Kiowa Indians. Statement to the Medicine Lodge Grand Council, Oct. 1867.

Chapter 45

Human Nature

1. The elemental human desire for self-government knows no geographical or racial boundaries.
   Joseph F. Ada, Governor of Guam. *Los Angeles Times*, July 5, 1989.

2. It's always the good men who do the most harm in the world.
   Henry Adams (1838-1918), American historian. Comment on Robert E. Lee, 1899.

3. Knowledge of human nature is the beginning and end of political education.
   Henry Adams. *The Education of Henry Adams*, 1907.

4. Men and nations cannot bear to feel inferior.
   Alfred Adler (1870-1937), Austrian psychiatrist. Quoted in George Seldes, *You Can't Print That*, 1929.

5. Pride, envy, avarice – these sparks
   Have set on fire the hearts of all men.
   Dante Alighieri (1265-1321), Italian writer. *The Inferno*, Canto VI.

6. Men regard it as their right to return evil for evil – and if they cannot, feel they have lost their liberty.
   Aristotle (384-322 B.C.), Greek philosopher and teacher. *Nicomachean Ethics*.

7. The Devil invented gambling.
   St. Augustine (345-430), Church Father and philosopher. *The City of God*, IV.

8. The desire for fame tempts even noble minds.
   St. Augustine. *Ibid.*, V.

9. "Tradition" is very often an excuse word for people who don't want to change.
   Red Barber (1908-1992), American baseball announcer. Interview, PBS Radio, Aug. 4, 1988.

10. All true ambition and aspiration are without comparisons.
    Henry Ward Beecher (1813-1887), American clergyman and writer. *Life Thoughts*, 1858.

11. Government and business are simple. It's only people that make them complicated.
    W. A. C. Bennett (1900-1979), Premier of British Columbia, Canada (Social Credit). Quoted in Roger Keene, *Conversations with W. A. C. Bennett*, 1980.

12. A man's heart tells him his opportunities better than seven watchmen on a tower.
    Apocrypha, *Wisdom of Ben Sira* 37:14.

13. Ambition is the mother of hypocrisy and prefers to skulk in corners and dark places. It cannot endure the light of day. It is an unclean vice wallowing in the depths, always hidden, but with ever an eye to advancement.
    St. Bernard of Clairvaux (c.1090-1153), French ecclesiastic. *Letters*.

14. Consistency frequently launches its devotees into obstinacy.
    Otto von Bismarck-Schoenhausen (1815-1898), Chancellor of Germany. Remark to M. Jules Favre, 1871.

15. When I want a thing, I want it dreadfully.
    James G. Blaine (1830-1893), U.S. Congressman and U.S. Senator (R-ME). Remark to his wife.

16. There is nothing that dies so hard and rallies so often as intolerance.
    William E. Borah (1865-1940), U.S. Senator (R-ID). Senate speech, Apr. 24, 1929.

17. The marvel of all history is the patience with which men and women submit to burdens unnecessarily laid upon them by their governments.
    William E. Borah. Quoted in Otto L. Bettmann, *A Word from the Wise*, 1977.

18. Life is lived on a slippery slope. You are constantly making judgments.
    Robert H. Bork, U.S. Solicitor General and Judge, U.S. Court of Appeals, Washington, DC. Interview, PBS, *The Open Mind*, Dec. 23, 1988.

19. Washington is a pool of money surrounded by people who want some.
    David Brinkley, American TV journalist. ABC, *This Week*, July 31, 1988.

20. Government can try to make the world a little better, but can we alter the human condition? No. We can't make saints out of sinners. St. Augustine had something to say about that.
Edmund G. (Jerry) Brown, Jr., Governor of California (D). *Thoughts*, 1976.

21. Ambition has no rest!
Edward Bulwer-Lytton, 1st Baron Lytton of Knebworth (1803-1873), Colonial Secretary, Great Britain (Conservative), and writer. *Richelieu*, III, 1839.

22. Hearts are strongest when they beat in response to noble ideals.
Ralph J. Bunche (1904-1971), U. N. Undersecretary General and Nobel Laureate in Peace (United States). Quoted in *Forbes*, Jan. 23, 1989.

23. Those who have much to hope and nothing to lose will always be dangerous.
Edmund Burke (1729-1797), British statesman. *Letters on a Regicide Peace*, 1797.

24. Hate breeds violence.
George Bush, 41st President of the United States (R-TX). Quoted in *Response: The Weisenthal Center's World Report*, Aug. 1990.

In extreme danger, fear feels no pity.
Julius Caesar (102-44 B.C.), Emperor of Rome. *Gallic War*.

26. I am one of the great army of mediocrity which constitutes the majority.
Joseph G. Cannon (1836-1926), U.S. Congressman and Speaker of the House (R-IL). Remark, 1919.

27. The spirit of the age, as it is revealed to each of us, is too often only the spirit of the group in which the accidents of birth or education or occupation or fellowship have given us a place.
Benjamin N. Cardozo (1870-1938), U.S. Supreme Court Justice. *The Nature of the Judicial Process*, 1921.

28. The man who cannot laugh is fit for treasons, stratagems, and spoils, but his whole life is already a treason and a stratagem.
Thomas Carlyle (1795-1881), Scottish essayist and historian. *Sartor Resartus*, I, 1836.

29. We are all striving to acquire riches of honor or power, or some other object, whose possession is to realize the daydreams of our imaginations; and the aggregate of these efforts constitutes the advance of our society.
Lewis Cass (1782-1866), U.S. Senator (D-MI), U.S. Secretary of State, and U.S. Secretary of War. Quoted in Howard Zinn, *A People's History of the United States*, 1980.

30. Necessity, which even makes cowards brave.
Catiline (108-62 B.C.), Roman politician. Speec
Pistoria, 62 B.C.

31. If the past is any guide our *[current]* beliefs will b
wrong as our past beliefs have been wrong.
Noam Chomsky, professor of linguistics, Ma
sachusetts Institute of Technology, and political activis
Interview, PBS, *Bill Moyers' World of Ideas*, Nov. 4, 1988.

32. A fanatic is one who can't change his mind an
won't change the subject.
Winston Churchill (1874-1965), Prime Minister o
Great Britain (Conservative). Quoted in *The New Yo
Times*, July 5, 1954.

33. Some people have more sense than other peopl
think they have.
Perl D. Decker (1875-1934), U.S. Congressman (D
MO). House hearings on price regulation, Jan. 9, 1915.

34. Science has brought forth this danger *[the atomi
bomb]*, but the real problem is in the minds an
hearts of men.
Albert Einstein (1879-1955), Nobel Laureate i
Physics (Switzerland). Quoted in *The New York Tim
Magazine*, June 23, 1946.

35. Brass shines as fair to the ignorant as gold to th
goldsmith.
Elizabeth I (1533-1603), Queen of England. Lette
c.1581.

36. In America the geography is sublime, but the me
are not.
Ralph Waldo Emerson (1803-1882), America
writer. *The Conduct of Life*, 1860.

37. The hazards of politics come not from campaign
and elections, as might be supposed, but rathe
from the nature of the creature that engages i
politics. Ambition, love, jealousy, hate and th
many emotions and reactions man is heir to fre
quently affect the course of nation and world mor
than principles or circumstances or events.
James A. Farley (1888-1976), Chairman, Democrati
National Committee, and U.S. Postmaster General. *Th
Sign*, Aug. 1948.

38. Governments never learn. Only people learn.
Milton Friedman, Nobel Laureate in Economic
(United States). Favorite saying.

39. Ambition is bondage.
Solomon Ibn Gabirol (Avicebron) (1021-1069)
Spanish poet and philosopher. *The Choice of Pearls*.

40. Idealism increases in direct proportion to one's
distance from the problem.

John Galsworthy (1867-1933), British writer. Quoted in *Forbes*, June 26, 1989.

41. The better I get to know men, the more I find myself loving dogs.
Charles de Gaulle (1890-1970), President of France. Quoted in *Time*, Dec. 8, 1967.

42. It is a maxim of wise government to deal with men not as they ought to be but as they are.
Johann Wolfgang von Goethe (1749-1832), German poet and dramatist. Quoted in Johann Peter Eckermann, *Conversations with Goethe*, 1833.

43. I sincerely wish ingratitude was not so natural to the human heart as it is.
Alexander Hamilton (1755-1804), Member, Continental Congress and Constitutional Convention, and U.S. Secretary of the Treasury (Federalist-NY). Letter to George Washington, Mar. 25, 1783.

44. We must take man as we find him, and if we expect him to serve the public, we must interest his passions in doing so.
Alexander Hamilton. Debate, Constitutional Convention, Philadelphia, PA, 1787.

45. Nothing is more fallacious than to expect to produce any valuable or permanent results in political projects by relying merely on the reason of men. Men are ... for the most part governed by the impulses of passion.
Alexander Hamilton. Letter to Sen. James A. Bayard, Apr. 1802.

46. The depraved nature of man is well known. He has a natural bias toward his own interest, which will prevail ... unless checked.
Patrick Henry (1736-1799), Member, Continental Congress and Virginia House of Burgesses, and Governor of Virginia. Debate, Virginia convention on the ratification of the U.S. Constitution, 1788.

47. In the nature of man we find three principal causes of quarrel. First, competition; second, diffidence; thirdly, glory.
Thomas Hobbes (1588-1679), English philos-opher. *Leviathan*, 1651.

48. To have done more hurt to a man than he can, or is willing to expiate, inclineth the doer to hate the sufferer. For he must expect revenge or forgiveness; both of which are hateful.
Thomas Hobbes. *Ibid.*

49. The fanatic ... sacrifices his life to prove his worth.
Eric Hoffer (1902-1983), American longshoreman and philosopher. *The True Believer*, 1951.

50. Certitude is not the test of certainty. We have been cock sure of many things that were not so.
Oliver Wendell Holmes, Jr. (1841-1935), U.S. Supreme Court Justice. *The Common Law*, 1881.

51. The best test of truth is the power of the thought to get itself accepted in the competition of the market.
Oliver Wendell Holmes, Jr.. *Abrams* v. *United States*, 1919 (dissent).

52. One has to have hope. Without hope you can't get anywhere.
Hussein ibn Talal, King of the Hashemite Kingdom of Jordan. Statement to the press, Aug. 16, 1990.

53. Little minds are tamed and subdued by misfortune; but great minds rise above it.
Washington Irving (1783-1859), American writer and U.S. Diplomatic Attaché to Spain. *The Sketch Book*, "Philip of Pokanoket," 1820.

54. Distrust naturally creates distrust.
John Jay (1745-1829), Governor of New York (Federalist); President, Continental Congress; U.S. Foreign Secretary; and 1st Chief Justice, U.S. Supreme Court. *The Federalist*, No. 5, Nov. 10, 1787.

55. I have not observed men's honesty to increase with their riches.
Thomas Jefferson (1743-1826), 3rd President of the United States (Democratic Republican-VA). Letter to Jeremiah Moor, Aug. 14, 1800.

56. When there is no hope, there can be no endeavor.
Samuel Johnson (1709-1784), British writer and lexicographer. *The Rambler*, No. 110.

57. By golly, there's something unusual going on here. Generally, fish don't attack people.
Weldon E. Jones, Director, Department of Fish and Game, CA. Comment on hearing reports of people bitten by fish in Lake Mendocino. Quoted in *The New York Times*, July 28, 1988.

58. We forget how quickly the American people forget.
Hamilton Jordan, White House Chief of Staff (D). Quoted in *Newsweek*, Dec. 22, 1986.

59. Men have always looked before and after, and rebelled against existing order. But for their divine discontent men would not have been men, and there would have been no progress in human affairs.
Humayun Kabir (1488-1512), Hindu religious leader. Quoted in *The American Scholar*, 1957.

60. Victory has a hundred fathers and defeat is an orphan.

John F. Kennedy (1917-1963), 35th President of the United States (D-MA). Remark after the Bay of Pigs debacle, Apr. 1961.

61. The American is by nature optimistic.
John F. Kennedy. Quoted on NBC, *Real Life*, Apr. 13, 1991.

62. People don't want to hear bad news. They don't want their institutions criticized.
Paul Kennedy, professor of American history, Yale University, New Haven, CT. Interview, *American Heritage*, Sept.-Oct. 1988.

63. If you live among wolves you have to act like a wolf.
Nikita S. Khrushchev (1894-1971), Premier of the U.S.S.R. 1964.

64. Even a paranoid can have enemies.
Henry M. Kissinger, U.S. Secretary of State and National Security Advisor (R). Quoted in *Time*, Jan. 24, 1977.

65. People's expectations of what government should provide ... are very high.
Madeleine M. Kunin, Governor of Vermont (D). Interview, CBS, *Sunday Morning*, Feb. 6, 1990.

Man is a gaming animal.
Charles Lamb (1775-1834), British writer. *Mrs. Battle's Opinions on Whist*, 1820.

67. How can you compare the masses of Western Europe with our people – so patient, so accustomed to privation?
V. I. Lenin (1870-1924), Premier of the U.S.S.R. Quoted in Angelica Balabanoff, *My Life as a Rebel*, 1938.

68. To believe with certainty, we must begin with doubting.
Stanislaus Leszczynski (1677-1766), King of Poland. *Maxims and Moral Sentences*.

69. Nothing is so sure of itself as fanaticism.
Ludwig Lewisohn (1883-1955), American writer and critic. *The Creative Life*, 1924.

70. You can fool some of the people all of the time, and all of the people some of the time, but you cannot fool all the people all the time.
Abraham Lincoln (1809-1865), 16th President of the United States (R-IL). Speech, Clinton, IL, Sept. 8, 1858.

71. Human action can be modified to some extent, but human nature cannot be changed.
Abraham Lincoln. Speech, Cooper Institute, New York City, Feb. 27, 1860.

72. Men are not flattered by being shown that there has been a difference of purpose between the Almighty and them.
Abraham Lincoln. Reply to Thurlow Weed, 1861.

73. He who believes that new benefits make great men forget old injuries deceives himself.
Niccolò Machiavelli (1469-1527), Florentine statesman and political philosopher. *The Prince*, VII, 1513.

74. But what is government itself but the greatest of all reflections on human nature? If men were angels, no government would be necessary. If angels were to govern men, neither external controls nor internal controls on government would be necessary.
James Madison (1751-1836), 4th President of the United States (Democratic Republican-VA). *The Federalist*, No. 51, Feb. 8, 1788.

75. The road to Hell is paved with good intentions.
Karl Marx (1818-1883), German economist and Socialist. *Das Kapital*, 1867.

76. We always live under the weight of the old and odious customs ... of our barbarous ancestors.
Guy de Maupassant (1850-1893), French writer. *Sur l'Eau*.

77. It needs courage to throw oneself forward, but it needs no less to hold oneself back.
Desiré Joseph Mercier (1851-1926), Belgian Roman Catholic cardinal. Sermon, German-occupied Brussels, July 21, 1916.

78. But what will not ambition and revenge descend to?
John Milton (1608-1674), English writer. *Paradise Lost*, IX, 1665.

79. In order to endure death and horror one tends to kill one's own humanity, which is a much greater danger than not being able to bear it.
Helmuth James von Moltke (1907-1944), German anti-Nazi. Letter to his wife, 1943.

80. On the most exalted throne in the world, we are still seated on nothing but our arse.
Michel Eyquem de Montaigne (1533-1592), Mayor of Bordeaux, France, philosopher, and writer. *Essays*, 1558.

81. Heavens, Mary, of course we'll laugh again. It's just that we'll never be young again.
Daniel P. Moynihan, Chief American Delegate to the United Nations and U.S. Senator (D-NY). Reply to Mary McGrory, who said that after John Kennedy's assasination "We'll never laugh again." Nov. 1963.

82. It is better to have an open enemy than a doubtful ally.
Napoléon I (1769-1821), military leader and Emperor of France. *Maxims*.

83. Men err not so much in prompt action but in hasty judgment.
Napoléon I. *Ibid.*

84. I have never had much sympathy for the point of view "it isn't whether you win or lose that counts, but how you play the game." How you play the game does count. But one must put top consideration on the will, the desire, and the determination to win.
Richard M. Nixon, 37th President of the United States (R-CA). Remark to reporters, 1960.

85. When you let your feelings, your heart, get in the way of your head, that's when you make mistakes.
Richard M. Nixon. TV interview with David Frost, 1977.

86. It is a myth that powerful men's aides do not want to be the bearers of bad tidings ... it is their favorite indoor sport. Most seem to take a visceral pleasure from seeing their boss's face fall at the news of some political or policy disaster.
Richard M. Nixon. *In the Arena*, 1990.

87. The Mediterraneans, who do not think clearly, see clearly.
José Ortega y Gasset (1883-1955), Spanish philosopher and statesman. *Meditations on Quixote*, 1911.

88. Our senses can grasp nothing that is extreme. Too much noise deafens us; too much light blinds us; too far or too near prevents us seeing; too long or too short is beyond understanding; too much truth stuns us.
Blaise Pascal (1623-1662), French mathematician and philosopher. *Pensées*, I.

89. As a man thinketh in his heart, so he is.
Old Testament, *Proverbs* 23:7.

90. Who is able to stand against envy?
Old Testament, *Proverbs* 27:14.

91. 'Tis a political maxim that all government tends to despotism, and like the human frame brings at its birth the latent seed which finally shall destroy the constitution. This is a melancholy truth – but such is the lot of humanity.
Josiah Quincy (1772-1864), President, Harvard College, and U.S. Congressman (Federalist-MA). 1862.

92. Fear makes men believe the worst.
Curtius Rufus Quintus (2nd century A.D.), Roman historian. *De Rebus Gestis Alexandri Magni.*

93. There's no trick to being a humorist when you've got the whole government working for you.
Will Rogers (1879-1935), American humorist. 1926.

94. Everybody wants something.
Anna Eleanor Roosevelt (1884-1962), First Lady and U.S. Delegate to the United Nations. Interview with Maureen Corr, 1960.

95. Never underestimate a man who overestimates himself.
Franklin D. Roosevelt (1882-1945), 32nd President of the United States (D-NY). In reference to General Douglas MacArthur. 1944.

96. The most savage controversies are those about matters as to which there is no good evidence.
Bertrand Russell, 3rd Earl Russell of Kingston (1872-1970), British philosopher and reformer. *Unpopular Essays*, 1950.

97. Hope is generally a wrong Guide, though it is very good Company by the way. It brusheth through Hedge and Ditch till it cometh to a great Leap, and there it is apt to fall and break its Bones.
George Savile, 1st Marquess of Halifax (1633-1695), Lord Privy Seal of England. *Moral Thoughts and Reflections*, 1750.

98. Ambition hath no Mean, it is either upon *all four [begging]* or *Tiptoes [grasping]*.
George Savile. *Ibid.*

99. Malice, like Lust, when it is at the Height, doth not knoe Shame.
George Savile. *Ibid.*

100. Men generally do so love the Taste of Flattery, their Stomach can never be overcharged with it.
George Savile. *Ibid.*

101. It is a self-flattering Contradiction, that wise Men despise the Opinion of Fools, and yet are proud of having their Esteem.
George Savile. *Miscellaneous Thoughts and Reflections*, 1750.

102. Human nature is rarely uniform.
Walter Scott (1771-1832), Scottish writer. *Quentin Durward*, 1823.

103. Vulgarity in a king flatters the majority of the nation.
George Bernard Shaw (1856-1950), Nobel Laureate in Literature (Great Britain). *Maxims for Revolutionists*, 1903.

104. Liars ought to have good memories.
Algernon Sidney (1622-1683), Republican and Member of Parliament, England. *Discourses Concerning Government*, 1698.

105. The Republican form of government is the highest form of government; but because of this it requires

the highest type of human nature – a type nowhere at present existing.
Herbert Spencer (1820-1903), British social philosopher. *Essays*, "The Americans," 1891.

106. You can tell the size of a man by the size of the thing that makes him mad.
Adlai E. Stevenson (1900-1965), Governor of Illinois (D) and U.S. Ambassador to the United Nations. Speech, Liberal Party State Committee, New York City, Aug. 28, 1952.

107. The only way you can make a man truswortny is to trust him.
Henry L. Stimson (1867-1950), U.S. Secretary of State (R), U.S. Secretary of War, and Governor General of the Philippine Islands. Maxim.

108. When a man dies, he wants to die for something important.
Richard L. Strout (1898-1990), American journalist. Quoted in *The Washington Post*, Aug. 28, 1990.

109. Communism really exists nowhere, least of all in the Soviet Union. Communism is an ideal that can be achieved only when people cease to be selfish and greedy.
Josip Broz Tito (1892-1980), President of Yugoslavia. Quoted in Eleanor Roosevelt, *On My Own*, 1958.

110. Ideas that enter the mind under fire remain there securely and forever.
Leon Trotsky (1879-1940), Russian revolutionary theorist. *My Life*, 1930.

111. Man is the only animal that blushes. Or needs to.
Mark Twain (Samuel Langhorne Clemens) (1835-1910), American writer. *Following the Equator*, 1897.

112. It may be called the Master Passion, the hunger for self-approval.
Mark Twain. *What Is Man?*, 1906.

113. Once the people begin to reason, all is lost.
Voltaire (François-Marie Arouet) (1694-1778), French historian and dramatist. Letter to Damilaville, Apr. 1, 1766.

114. How I hate this crooked business! This intercourse with the world, which obliges one to see the worst side of human nature!
Mary Shelley Wollstonecraft (1759-1797), Brit-ish writer and feminist. Letter to Captain Gilbert Imlay, Dec. 29, 1794.

115. You can change a government but you cannot change people.
Yevgeny Yevtushenko, Member, Russian Congress of People's Deputies. Quoted in James Reinbold, "The Weapon of Freedom," *Brown Alumni Monthly*, May 1991.

Chapter 46

Immigration and Naturalization

1. WE WANT ORDER ON OUR BORDER

Bumper sticker on a car near the San Diego-Tijuana border, protesting illegal immigration to the United States. 1990.

2. Freedom of thought and the right to private judgment, in matters of conscience, driven from every corner of the earth, direct their course to this happy country as their last asylum. Let us cherish the noble guests, and shelter them under the wings of universal toleration.

Samuel Adams (1722-1803), Governor of Massachusetts and member, Continental Congress. Speech, Philadelphia, PA, Aug. 1, 1776.

3. We need the immigrants.

Daniel K. Akaka, U.S. Congressman (D-HI). *Ask Congress*, July 31, 1988.

4. This is not the 1890's. We can't have open borders anymore.

Howard L. Berman, U.S. Congressman (D-CA). Interview, PBS, *American Interest*, Mar. 15, 1989.

5. Denaturalization consequences may be more grave than consequences that flow from conviction of crime *[in the United States]*.

Hugo L. Black (1886-1971), U.S. Senator (D-AL) and U.S. Supreme Court Justice. *Klapprott* v. *United States*, 1947-1948.

6. The deportation of a race may be within the inherent powers of a despotism.

David J. Brewer (1837-1910), U.S. Supreme Court Justice. *Fong Yue Ting* v. *New York City*, 1892.

7. I think God made all people good, but if we had to take a million immigrants in, say Zulus, next year, or Englishmen, and put them in Virginia, what group would be easier to assimilate and would cause less problems for the people of Virginia?

Patrick Buchanan, White House speech writer (R) and syndicated columnist. ABC, *This Week with David Brinkley*, Dec. 8, 1991.

8. No immigration scheme, no matter how generous, will satisfy the number of applicants for admission.

Walter D. Cadman, District Director, U.S. Immigration and Naturalization Service. "Driving and Discrimination," *The Washington Post*, Nov. 11, 1990.

9. I am not here as having one vote in the national legislature to shut the door in the face of any of the Caucasian race that are willing to come, whether they be educated or uneducated, and under the hand of honest, earned bread, the common *[that is, public]* schools will take care of the children.

Joseph G. Cannon (1836-1926), U.S. Congressman and Speaker of the House (R-IL). Address, General Convention of the International Order of B'nai B'rith, Washington, DC, Apr. 6, 1910.

10. We are, of course, a nation of immigrants, but some of us too often forget that fact. Sometimes we forget that the question isn't when we came here, but why we came here.

Jimmy Carter, 39th President of the United States (D-GA). Speech, Alfred E. Smith Memorial Dinner, New York City, Oct. 1976.

11. We find ourselves ordered by the government to cast out those we have tried for so long to help. The effort of a parent to feed his or her children is criminalized.

Steven G. Cary, Chairman, American Friends Service Committee (Quaker). Statement when filing a lawsuit against the federal government's enforcement of a law preventing undocumented aliens from being hired for jobs. Los Angeles, CA, Nov. 23, 1988.

12. It is said that the quality of recent immigration is undesirable. The time is quite within recent memory when the same thing was said of immi-

grants who, with their descendants, are now numbered among our best citizens.

Grover Cleveland (1837-1908), 22nd and 24th President of the United States (D-NY). 1897.

13. What did they come here for? Why do not they go back *[to Italy]* and stay there?

William E. Cox (1861-1942), U.S. Congressman (D-IN). In reference to Italian immigrants. House debate, 1917.

14. They *[the Americans]* are a mixture of British, Scotch, Irish, French, Dutch, Germans, and Swedes. From this promiscuous breed, that race called Americans have now arisen.

Michel-Guillaume-Jean de Crèvecoeur (J. Hector St. John) (1735-1813), French Consul in New York City, writer, and agriculturalist. *Letters from an American Farmer*, 1782.

15. Immigrants are alone, ignorant strangers, a prey to all manner of anarchical and wild notions. Except to their employer they have no value until they get a vote.

Richard Croker (1841-1922), Tammany Hall leader, New York City. Quoted by William Thomas Stead, *The Review of Reviews*, Oct. 1897.

16. If you want me to release ten million Chinese to come to the United States, I'll be glad to do so.

Deng Xiaoping, Premier of China. Quoted by Jimmy Carter, *Keeping Faith*, 1982.

17. The silly ancestors of the Americans called it "national development" when they imported millions of foreigners to take up the public lands and left nothing for their own children.

Ignatius Donnelly (1831-1901), U.S. Congressman (Populist-MN). *Caesar's Way*, 1891.

18. Citizenship obtained through naturalization is not a second-class citizenship.

William O. Douglas (1898-1980), U.S. Supreme Court Justice. *Knauer* v. *United States*, 1945.

19. Don't forget, we have a disposal problem.

Allen W. Dulles (1893-1969), Director, Central Intelligence Agency. Remark to President Kennedy in 1961 about the fifteen thousand Cubans recruited for the Bay of Pigs invasion who were still in the United States. Quoted in *The New York Times*, Aug. 20, 1989.

20. *America. Emigration.* In the distinctions of the genius of the American race it is to be considered that it is not indiscriminate masses of Europe that are shipped hitherward, but the Atlantic is a sieve through which only or chiefly the liberal, adventurous, sensitive, *America-loving* part of each city, clan, family are brought. It is the light complexion, the blue eyes of Europe that come: the black eyes, the black drop, the Europe of Europe, is left *[in Europe]*.

Ralph Waldo Emerson (1803-1882), American writer. *Journals*, June 1851.

21. I see with joy the Irish emigrants landing at Boston, at New York, and say to myself, There they go – to school.

Ralph Waldo Emerson. *Journals*, July 1866.

22. The typical immigrant of the present does not really live in America at all, but, from the point of view of nationality, in Italy, Poland, Czecho-Slovakia, or some other foreign country.

Henry Pratt Fairchild (1880-1956), professor, New York University. *Immigration*, 1913.

23. A closed country is a dying country.

Edna Ferber (1887-1968), American novelist. Radio broadcast, 1947.

24. Asia is the continent of origination; Europe the continent of differentiation; and America the continent of reunions.

François Guizot (1787-1874), Premier of France. 1871.

25. My whole family has been having trouble with immigrants ever since we came to this country.

Edgar Y. Harburg (1896-1981), American playwright and songwriter. *Finian's Rainbow*.

26. The banishment *[of Russian Jews]*, whether by direct decree or by not less certain indirect methods, of so large a number of men and women is not a local question. A decree to leave one's country is in the nature of things an order to enter another – some other.

Benjamin Harrison (1833-1901), 23rd President of the United States (R-IN). Message to Congress, Dec. 9, 1891.

27. Make it *[the United States]* the home of the skillful, the industrious, the fortunate, the happy, as well as the asylum of the distressed.... Let but this, our celebrated goddess, Liberty, stretch forth her fair hand toward the people of the old world – tell them to come, and bid them welcome.

Patrick Henry (1736-1799), Member, Continental Congress and Virginia House of Burgesses, Governor of Virginia, and Member of the Virginia Constitutional Ratification Convention. Speech, Virginia House of Delegates, 1783.

28. The melting pot failed to function in one crucial area. Religions and nationalities, however differ-

ent, generally learned to live together, even to grow together, in America. But color was something else. Reds were murdered like wild animals. Yellows were characterized as a peril and incarcerated en masse during World War II for no really good reason by our most liberal President. Browns have been abused as the new slave labor on farms. The blacks, who did not come here willingly, are now, more than a century after emancipation by Lincoln, still suffering a host of slavelike inequalities.

Theodore M. Hesburgh, President, University of Notre Dame. *The New York Times Magazine*, Oct. 29, 1972.

29. We are the Romans of the modern world – the great assimilating people.

Oliver Wendell Holmes (1809-1894), American writer and physician. *The Autocrat of the Breakfast Table*, 1858.

30. Deportation is not a punishment; it is simply a refusal by the government to harbor persons whom it does not want.

Oliver Wendell Holmes, Jr. (1841-1935), U.S. Supreme Court Justice. *Bugajewitz* v. *Adams*, 1912.

31. The boast that our country is the asylum for the oppressed in other parts of the world is very philanthropic and sentimental, but I fear that we shall before long derive little comfort from being made the almshouse and place of refuge for the poor of other countries.

Philip Hone (1780-1851), Mayor of New York City (Whig). *Diary*, Sept. 20, 1833.

32. Efforts to concentrate immigrants in social groups and to retard their Americanization should be steadily frowned down.

John Ireland (1838-1918), American Roman Catholic bishop. Speech, Chicago, IL, Feb. 22, 1895.

33. Surely a race of people, desiring to preserve the integrity of that race ... may be permitted to protect themselves, if in no other way by emigration.... The white man came to this country to avoid conditions which to him were not as bad as the present conditions are to us... All we ask is that we may be permitted to exercise the same privilege.

Jacob B. Jackson, leader, Choctaw Indians. Letter to U.S. Senate, 1906.

34. Our ancestors who migrated hither were laborers, not lawyers.

Thomas Jefferson (1743-1826), 3rd President of the United States (Democratic Republican-VA). *Summary View of the Rights of British America*, 1774.

35. The fundamental, longtime American attitude has been to ask not where a person comes from but what are his personal qualities. On this basis men and women migrated from every quarter of the globe. By their hard work and their enormously varied talents they hewed a great nation out of a wilderness. By their dedication to liberty and equality they created a society reflecting man's most cherished ideas.

Lyndon B. Johnson (1908-1973), 36th President of the United States (D-TX). Message to Congress, Jan. 13, 1965.

36. *A Nation of Immigrants*

John F. Kennedy (1917-1963), 35th President of the United States (D-MA). Title of book, 1964.

37. I was born here. My children were born here. What the hell do I have to do to be called an American?

Joseph P. Kennedy (1888-1969), U.S. Ambassador to Great Britain (D). Response when a Boston newspaper referred to him as an "Irishman." Quoted in O'Neil and Brink, *The World According to Breslin*.

38. Every Jew has the right to immigrate to Israel.

Knesset (Parliament) of Israel. *Law of the Return*, adopted July 5, 1950.

39. A fixed obsession on Anglo-Saxon superiority.

Fiorello H. La Guardia (1882-1947), U.S. Congressman (R and Socialist-NY) and Mayor of New York City (R and Fusion Party). Description of the ethnic immigration quotas that Congress was considering. House debate, 1924.

40. Give me your tired, your poor,
Your huddled masses yearning to breathe free,
The wretched refuse of your teeming shore,
Send these, the homeless, tempest-tossed to me:
I lift my lamp beside the golden door.

Emma Lazarus (1849-1887), American poet. "The New Colossus," poem inscribed on a plaque affixed to the base of the Statue of Liberty, New York Harbor.

41. We are a nation of immigrants. It is immigrants who brought to this land the skills of their hands and brains to make it a beacon of opportunity and of hope for all men.

Herbert H. Lehman (1878-1963), Governor of New York (D); Director, U.N. Foreign Relief and Rehabilitation Administration; and U.S. Senator. Testimony, House Subcommittee on Immigration and Naturalization, July 2, 1947.

42. It is our turn to guard our heritage from Mongol, and Persian and Moor, before we become engulfed in a limitless foreign sea.

Charles A. Lindbergh, Jr. (1902-1974), American aviator. Quoted in *Reader's Digest*, Nov. 1939.

43. We *[native-born]* could not choose, but they *[immigrants]* could and did choose to be Americans.
Henry B. F. Macfarland (1861-1921), American jurist and historian. Flag Day speech, Washington, DC, June 14, 1901.

44. The United States's moral responsibility to accept immigrants is not unlimited.
Romano Mazzoli, U.S. Congressman (D-KY). Quoted in *Time*, Feb. 27, 1989.

45. We were very scared. Going to America was almost like going to the moon.
Golda Meir (1898-1978), Prime Minister of Israel (Labor). Description of her family's immigration to America from Russia. Quoted in *Life*, Fall 1990.

46. America is not a melting pot. It is a sizzling cauldron.
Barbara A. Mikulski, U.S. Congresswoman and U.S. Senator (D-MD). Speech, First National Conference, National Center for Urban and Ethnic Affairs, Apr. 1990.

47. We need employer sanctions to avoid illegal immigration so that legal immigration may dominate.
Bruce Morrison, U.S. Congressman (D-CT). Quoted on ABC, *It's Your Business*, Apr. 8, 1990.

48. Immigration is the sincerest form of flattery.
A. F. K. Organski, political scientist, University of Michigan. Lecture, Brooklyn College, April 1964.

49. Immigration is a privilege which we have a perfect right to grant or deny as we see fit ... like someone applying for membership in a club.
J. W. Pickersgill, Minister of Immigration, Canada. Statement, 1955.

50. In the Soviet Union people are trying to get out. In the United States people are trying to get in. Freedom is the beacon that draws them.
J. Danforth Quayle, Vice President of the United States and U.S. Senator (R-IN). Nomination acceptance speech, Republican National Convention, New Orleans, LA, August 18, 1988.

51. For the protection of the quality of our American citizenship and of the wages of our workingmen against the fatal competition of low-priced *[immigrant]* labor we demand that the immigration laws be thoroughly enforced, and so extended as to exclude from entrance to the United States those who can neither read nor write.
Republican Party platform, 1896.

52. The Italian and the poor Jew rise only by compulsion.
Jacob August Riis (1840-1914), American writer and photographer. *How the Other Half Lives*, 1890.

53. It is not fair to ask of others what you are not willing to do yourself.
Anna Eleanor Roosevelt (1884-1962), First Lady and U.S. Delegate to the United Nations. Comment when the United States asked the British to accept European refugees in Palestine when American immigration laws limited them. "My Day," June 15, 1946.

54. Remember always that all of us, and you and I especially, are descended from immigrants and revolutionists.
Franklin D. Roosevelt (1882-1945), 32nd President of the United States (D-NY). Speech, Daughters of the American Revolution. Quoted in *The New York Times*, Apr. 21, 1938.

55. Observe immigrants ... low browed, big-faced persons of obviously low mentality.... They clearly belong in skins ... at the close of the great Ice Age.
Edward Alsworth Ross (1866-1951), professor of sociology, Stanford University, Palo Alto, CA. *Changing America*, 1912.

56. The U.S. economy demands Mexican workers.
Carlos Salinas de Gortarì, President of Mexico. Quoted in *Business Week*, July 4, 1988.

57. For a big immigration, we need a big and strong state.... We will need a lot of room to absorb everyone.
Yitzhak Shamir, Prime Minister of Israel (Likud). Jan. 14, 1990.

58. If you don't think that racism is deep down in there, you're crazier than hell.
Alan K. Simpson, U.S. Senator (R-WY). Comment on opposition to immigration. C-SPAN, *Immigration Issues*, American Enterprise Institute, Dec. 6, 1989.

59. We have a national interest in knowing how many people our country can accommodate.
Alan K. Simpson. Quoted on ABC, *It's Your Business*, Apr. 8, 1990.

60. An unprejudiced study of immigration justifies me in saying that the evils are temporary and local, while the benefits are permanent and national.
Oscar S. Straus (1845-1926), U.S. Secretary of

Commerce (Progressive-NY), U.S. Secretary of Labor, and U.S. Ambassador to Turkey. Speech, May 22, 1907.

61. Seldom has a bill exhibited the distrust evidenced here for citizens and aliens alike.

Harry S Truman (1884-1972), 33rd President of the United States (D-MO). Statement on vetoing the McCarren-Walter Act which would have restricted immigration, 1952.

62. If any people of other Nations professing the true Christian Religion shall flee to us from the Tiranny or oppression of their persecutors, or from famyne, warres, or the like necessary and cumpulsarie cause, They shall be entertayned and succoured amongst us.

Nathaniel Ward (c.1578-1652), Puritan leader and codifier. *The Massachusetts Body of Liberties*, 1641.

63. Against the insidious wiles of foreign influence, I conjure you to believe me, fellow-citizens, the jealousy of a free people ought to be *constantly* awake, since history and experience prove that foreign influence is one of the most baneful foes of republican Government.

George Washington (1732-1799), 1st President of the United States (VA). Farewell address, Sept. 17, 1796.

64. We have become the world's melting pot. The scum of creation has been dumped on us. Some of our principal cities are more foreign than American. The most dangerous and corrupting hordes of the Old World have invaded us.... The manufacturers are mainly to blame. They wanted cheap labor; and they didn't care a curse how much harm to our future might be the consequence of their heartless policy.

Thomas E. Watson (1856-1922), U.S. Congressman and U.S. Senator (D-GA). *The Life and Times of Thomas Jefferson*, 1912.

65. The world is divided into two groups of nations – those that want to expel the Jews and those that do not want to receive them.

Chaim Weizmann (1874-1952), 1st President of Israel. Comment to Leon Crestohl, 1940.

66. If Jesus tried to get into this country, they'd exclude him on a 212(a)(15).

Sam Williamson, American immigration attorney. In reference to the clause of the Immigration and Nationality Act that permits the exclusion of an alien who is likely to be a public charge. Quoted in *The New Yorker*, May 28, 1984.

67. Some Americans need hyphens in their names because only half of them has come over.

Woodrow Wilson (1856-1924), 28th President of the United States (D-NJ). Speech, Washington, DC, May 16, 1914.

68. ... we may lawfully refuse to receive those whose dispositions suite not ours and whose society will be hurtful to us.

John Winthrop (1588-1649), Governor of Massachusetts Bay Colony. *A Declaration in Defense of an Order of Court*, May 1637.

69. America is the crucible of God. It is the melting pot where all the races are fusing and re-forming.... Into the crucible with you all. God is making the American.

Israel Zangwill (1864-1926), British writer. *The Melting Pot*, 1908.

Chapter 47

Insults and Compliments

1. *[U.S. Secretary of State Dean Acheson]* is the Red Dean of Fashion.

   Joseph R. McCarthy (1908-1957), U.S. Senator (R-WI). Quoted in *The New York Times*, June 2, 1951.

2. *[Pres. John Adams]* is vain, irritable, and a bad calculator of the force and probable effect of the motives which govern men.

   Thomas Jefferson (1743-1826), 3rd President of the United States (Democratic Republican-VA). Letter to James Madison, Jan. 30, 1787.

3. *[Pres. John Quincy Adams]* has a continual grasp for power *[and an]* unbounded thirst for ridiculous pomp, foolish adulation and selfish avarice. *(For writing this, Lyon was convicted under the Sedition Act. He was fined $1,000 and served four months in jail.)*

   Matthew Lyon (1749-1822), U.S. Congressman (R-VT and KY)). Quoted in Melvin I. Urofsky, *A March of Liberty*, 1988.

4. *[Americans]* are all liars. You cannot believe anything they say.

   Sitting Bull (1831?-1890), Chief, Sioux Indians. Remark to James McLeod, Commissioner, Canadian Northwest Mounted Police, Sept. 1877.

5. *[Prime Minister Clement Attlee]* brings to the fierce struggle of politics the tepid enthusiasm of a lazy summer afternoon at a cricket match.

   Aneurin Bevan (1897-1960), Minister of Health, Great Britain (Socialist). *Tribune*, 1945.

6. *[Prime Minister Clement Attlee]* combines a limited outlook with strong qualities of resistance.

   Winston Churchill (1874-1965), Prime Minister of Great Britain (Conservative). Speech, House of Commons, Apr. 27, 1951.

7. *[Lee Atwater]* saw politics as a cutthroat game and didn't mind holding the blade.

   David Gergen, American journalist and White House assistant (R). Comment after Republican National Committee Chairman Atwater's death. PBS, *MacNeil-Lehrer News Hour*, Mar. 29, 1991.

8. *[Prime Minister Stanley Baldwin]* simply takes one jump in the dark, looks round, and then takes another.

   Frederick Edwin Smith, 1st Earl of Birkenhead (1872-1930), Member of Parliament, Great Britain (Conservative) and Lord Chancellor of Britain. In reference to domestic economy. Letter to Austen Chamberlain, 1923.

9. *[Prime Minister Stanley Baldwin]* decided only to be undecided, resolved to be irresolute, adamant for drift, solid for fluidity.

   Winston Churchill (1874-1965), Prime Minister of Great Britain (Conservative). Speech, House of Commons, 1936.

10. *[U.S. Secretary of State William Jennings Bryan]* is a charlatan, a mountebank, a zany without sense or dignity.

    H. L. Mencken (1880-1956), American journalist. Quoted in Foster Rhea Dulles, *The United States Since 1865*, 1959.

11. *[Vice President Aaron Burr]* has no principles, public or private. As a politician, his sole spring of action is an inordinate ambition.

    Alexander Hamilton (1755-1804), Member, Continental Congress and Constitutional Convention, and U.S. Secretary of the Treasury (Federalist-NY). Quoted in Nancy McPhee, *The Book of Insults*, 1978.

12. *[Pres. George Bush]* was born with a silver foot in his mouth.

    Ann Richards, Governor of Texas (D). Keynote address, Democratic National Convention, Atlanta, GA, July 18, 1988.

13. *[Pres. George Bush]* was born on third base and somehow got the idea that he hit a triple.

Jim Hightower, Texas State Agriculture Commissioner (D). Quoted on PBS, *Convention Week in Review*, July 20, 1988.

14. *[Pres. George Bush]* is the resumé that walks like a man.

Pete Hamill, American political columnist. *The New York Post*, Aug. 15, 1988.

15. *[Pres. George Bush]* will antagonize you. To that extent he is steady.

William F. Buckley, Jr., American political columnist and publisher. PBS, *Firing Line*, Jan. 16, 1989.

16. *[U.S. Senator John C. Calhoun]* looks as if he had never been born and could not be extinguished.

Harriet Martineau (1802-1876), British reformer. *Society in America*, 1837.

17. *[U.S. Senator John C. Calhoun]* is a rigid, fanatic, ambitious, selfishly partisan and sectional turncoat with too much genius and too little common sense, who will either die a traitor or a madman.

Henry Clay (1777-1852), U.S. Senator (R and Whig-KY), Speaker of the House, and U.S. Secretary of State. Remark.

18. *[Prime Minister Winston Churchill]* is a man suffering from petrified adolescence.

Aneurin Bevan (1897-1960), Minister of Health, Great Britain (Socialist). Remark.

19. *[Sen. Henry Clay]* is a bad man, an imposter, a creator of wicked schemes.

John C. Calhoun (1782-1850), U.S. Congressman (D-SC), U.S. Senator, U.S. Secretary of War, U.S. Secretary of State, and Vice President of the United States. Quoted in Nancy McPhee, *The Book of Insults*, 1978.

20. *[Pres. Calvin Coolidge]* looks as if he had been weaned on a pickle.

Alice Roosevelt Longworth (1884-1980), American socialite and Washington, DC, hostess; daughter of Pres. Theodore Roosevelt; cousin of Pres. Franklin D. Roosevelt. 1924.

21. *[Pres. Calvin Coolidge]* is at bottom simply a cheap and trashy fellow, deficient in sense and almost devoid of any notion of honor – in brief, a dreadful little cad.

H. L. Mencken (1880-1956), American journalist. *The Baltimore Evening Sun*, Nov. 3, 1924.

22. *[Pres. Calvin Coolidge]* is the greatest man who ever came out of Plymouth, Vermont.

Clarence S. Darrow (1857-1937), American attorney and writer. 1925.

23. *[Americans]* will commit all the stupidities they can think of, plus some that are beyond imagination.

Charles de Gaulle (1890-1970), President of France. Quoted in *Time*, Dec. 8, 1967.

24. *[Confederate President Jefferson Davis]* is as cold as a lizard with the ambition of Lucifer, and what he touches will not prosper.
[Houston was deposed on Mar. 18, 1861, because he refused to take an oath of allegiance to the Confederate States]

Sam Houston (1793-1863), Governor of Tennessee (D), 1st President of the Republic of Texas, U.S. Congressman, and U.S. Senator. Remark, 1861.

25. *[Gov. Thomas E. Dewey]* is a political streetwalker accosting men with "come home with me dear."

Harold L. Ickes (1874-1952), U.S. Secretary of the Interior (R). 1947.

26. *[Gov. Thomas Dewey]* looks exactly like the little man on the wedding cake.

Alice Roosevelt Longworth (1884-1980), American socialite and Washington, DC, hostess; daughter of Pres. Theodore Roosevelt; cousin of Pres. Franklin D. Roosevelt. Quoted on PBS, *The Great Upset of '48*, Nov. 2, 1988.

27. *[U.S. Congresswoman Helen Gehagen Douglas]* is pink right down to her underwear.

Richard M. Nixon, 37th President of the United States (R-CA). Quoted on PBS, *The Unauthorized Biography of Richard M. Nixon*, Mar. 9, 1989.

28. *[Gov. Michael J. Dukakis]* is the smartest clerk in the world.

Peter Jennings, American TV journalist. Quoted in *The Washington Post*, Oct. 11, 1988.

29. *[U.S. Secretary of State John Foster Dulles]* is the world's longest range misguided missile.

Walter P. Reuther (1907-1970), President, United Auto Workers of America. Remark, July 1956.

30. *[U.S. Secretary of State John Foster Dulles]* is the only case I know of a bull who carries his china shop with him.

Winston Churchill (1874-1965), Prime Minister of Great Britain (Conservative), Quoted in Leonard Mosley, *Dulles*, 1978.

31. *[U.S. Secretary of State John Foster Dulles]* is a slab-faced bastard.

Winston Churchill. Quoted in Martin Gilbert, *Winston Churchill*, 1988.

32. *[King Edward VIII]* was at his best only when the going was good.
Alistair Cooke, British TV host. *Six Men*, 1977.

33. *[Pres. Dwight D. Eisenhower]* was far more complex and devious than most people realized.
Richard M. Nixon, 37th President of the United States (R-CA). Remark, 1960.

34. *[Pres. Dwight D. Eisenhower]* wasn't used to being criticized, and he never did get it through his head that's what politics is all about.
Harry S Truman (1884-1972), 33rd President of the United States (D-MO). Quoted in Merle Miller, *Plain Speaking*, 1974.

35. *[Chinese Premier Chou En-lai]* has a pleasant smile, a brain of steel, and blood on his hands.
Dag Hammerskjöld (1905-1961), Secretary-General of the United Nations (Sweden). Quoted on Arts & Entertainment television, *Biography*, Oct. 21, 1990.

36. *[Pres. Gerald R. Ford]* is the only man I ever knew who can't walk and chew gum at the same time.
Lyndon B. Johnson (1908-1973), 36th President of the United States (D-TX). Remark, 1965.

37. *[Pres. Gerald R. Ford]* played too much football with his helmet off.
Lyndon B. Johnson. Remark, 1968.

38. *[Pres. Gerald R. Ford]* is cordial and gracious. But he's consistently wrong and consistency is a virtue of small minds. He's never proposed a constructive solution to anything.
Robert F. Drinan, U.S. Congressman (D-MA). Remark, 1975.

39. *[Benjamin Franklin]* is one continued insult to good manners and decency.
John Adams (1735-1826), 2nd President of the United States (Federalist-MA). Quoted in Phyllis Lee Levin, *Abigail Adams*, 1988.

40. *[Charles de Gaulle]* is one of the biggest sons of bitches who ever straddled a pot.
Charles E. Bohlen (1904-1974), U.S. Ambassador to the U.S.S.R. *Witness to History, 1929-1969*, 1973.

41. *[Prime Minister William E. Gladstone]* made his conscience not his guide but his accomplice.
Benjamin Disraeli, 1st Earl of Beaconsfield (1804-1881), Prime Minister of Great Britain (Conservative). Remark.

42. *[Sen. John Glenn]* is not the brightest guy in Washington.
John G. Tower (1925-1991), U.S. Senator (R-TX). *Consequences: A Political Memoir*, 1991.

43. *[Samuel Gompers]* is a grand national joke ... the greatest political Mr. Facingbothways this country has ever had.
Eugene V. Debs (1855-1926), American Socialist. *Locomotive Fireman's Magazine*, Apr. 1889.

44. *[Pres. Ulysses S. Grant]* is a drunken Democrat who the Republicans dragged out of the Galena gutter, besmeared with the blood of his countrymen slain in domestic broil ... and rules over the prostrate ruins of Washington's Republic.
Harper's Weekly, 1870.

45. *[Pres. Warren G. Harding]* was not a bad man. He was just a slob.
Alice Roosevelt Longworth (1884-1980), American socialite and Washington, DC, hostess; daughter of Pres. Theodore Roosevelt; cousin of Pres. Franklin D. Roosevelt. 1923.

46. *[Sen. Gary Hart]* is just Jerry Brown without the fruit flies.
Robert S. Strauss, Chairman, Democratic National Committee, and U.S. Ambassador to the U.S.S.R. Quoted in *Conservative Digest*, May 1987.

47. *[Pres. Rutherford B. Hayes]* is a third rate nonentity whose only recommendation is that he is obnoxious to no one.
Henry Adams (1838-1918), American historian. Quoted in George B. Tindall, *America: A Narrative History*, 1984.

48. *[William Randolph Hearst]* is a moral pervert, a political degenerate.
Joseph W. Bailey (1862-1929), U.S. Congressman and U.S. Senator (D-TX). Senate speech, 1913.

49. *[William Randolph Hearst]* is a mean man, a particularly low type of man.
Alfred E. Smith (1873-1944), Governor of New York (D). Quoted in *The New York Times*, Oct. 19, 1919.

50. *[Adolf Hitler]* is a queer fellow who will never become Chancellor. The best he can hope for is to head the Postal Department.
Paul von Hindenburg (1847-1934), General, German Army, and President of Germany. 1931.

51. *[Adolf Hitler]* is the repository and embodiment of many forms of soul-destroying hatred, this monstrous product of former wrongs and shame.
Winston Churchill (1874-1965), Prime Minister of Great Britain (Conservative). Radio broadcast, BBC, Sept. 11, 1940.

52. *[Pres. Herbert Hoover]* made a speech Saturday at Valley Forge. He found somebody that was worse off than we are but he had to go back 150 years in history to do it.

Will Rogers (1879-1935), American humorist. May 31, 1931.

53. *[J. Edgar Hoover]* is a moralistic bastard.

William J. Donovan (1883-1959), Director, Office of Strategic Services (precursor to Central Intelligence Agency), and U.S. Assistant Attorney General. Quoted in L. Mosley, *Dulles*, 1978.

54. *[J. Edgar Hoover]* seemed to me like an old boxer who had taken too many punches. He had stayed in the fight past his time, feebly counterpunching. But he had lost his judgement and vigor. He had become an embarrassment.

John Ehrlichman, presidential assistant (R). *Witness to Power*, 1982.

55. *[Harry L. Hopkins]* is the Rasputin of the White House.

Dewey Short (1898-1979), U.S. Congressman (R-MO). *The Chicago Tribune*, Aug. 29, 1943.

56. *[Rev. Jesse L. Jackson]* can't run nothing but his mouth.

Marion Barry, Mayor of Washington, DC (D). Aug. 1990.

57. *[President Andrew Johnson]* is that dead dog in the White House.

William G. Brownlow (1805-1877), Governor of Tennessee and U.S. Senator (Whig). Quoted in Claude F. Bowers, *The Tragic Era*, 1929.

58. *[Pres. Lyndon B. Johnson]* was one of the few politicians with whom I found it uncomfortable to be in the same room.

Denis Healey, Minister of Defense, Great Britain (Labour). Chancellor of the Exchequer. *The Time of My Life*, 1990.

59. *[Sen. Edward Kennedy]* is an overstuffed empty suit, unable to function without a text prepared by his talented staff because he cannot articulate his thoughts or because his own thoughts lack profundity.

William Safire, American political columnist and presidential speech writer (R). Sept. 1987.

60. *[Pres. John F. Kennedy]* is sort of an Indian snake charmer.

Dean Acheson (1893-1971), U.S. Secretary of State (D). Quoted in McLellan and Acheson, *Among Friends*, 1980.

61. *[Pres. John F. Kennedy]* went to his grave and he could never get anything through the Congress.

James Reston, American political columnist. Interview, PBS, *Newsleaders*, Nov. 23, 1989.

62. *[Pres. John F. Kennedy]* must be a strange character – obstinate, sensitive, ruthless, and highly sexed.

Harold Macmillan (1894-1986), Prime Minister of Great Britain (Conservative). Comment to U.S. Ambassador Jock Whitney. Quoted on PBS, *Firing Line*, Dec. 9, 1989.

63. *[Martin Luther King, Jr.]* is a tom cat with obsessive, degenerate, sexual urges.

J. Edgar Hoover (1895-1972), Director, Federal Bureau of Investigation. Handwritten comment on FBI memorandum from W. C. Sullivan to A. H. Belmont. June 27, 1964.

64. *[Martin Luther King, Jr.]* is Martin Loser King.

Adam Clayton Powell (1908-1972), U.S. Congressman (D-NY). Quoted on PBS, *The American Experience*, Nov. 28, 1989.

65. *[Pres. Abraham Lincoln]* is a filthy story-teller, despot, liar, thief, braggart, buffoon, usurper, monster, ignoramus, old scoundrel, perjurer, robber, swindler, tyrant, field-butcher, land-pirate.

Harper's Weekly, 1860.

66. *[Pres. Abraham Lincoln]* is nothing more than a well-meaning baboon.... I went to the White house where I found "the original Gorilla" about as intelligent as ever. What a specimen to be at the head of our affairs now!

George B. McClellan (1826-1885), General, U.S. Army, and Governor of New Jersey (D). 1864.

67. *[Pres. Abraham Lincoln]* is a first-rate second-rate man ... a mere convenience waiting like any other broomstick to be used.

Wendell Phillips (1811-1884), American orator and reformer. Quoted in Richard Hofstadter, *The American Political Tradition*, Vintage, 1948.

68. *[Prime Minister David Lloyd George]* couldn't see a belt without hitting below it.

Margot Asquith (1864-1945), British writer and socialite. *Autobiography*, 1922.

69. *[Sen. Huey P. Long]* is suffering from halitosis of the intellect. That's presuming Emperor Long has an intellect.

Harold L. Ickes (1874-1952), U.S. Secretary of the Interior (R). Remark at a press conference, Apr. 18, 1935.

70. *[Gen. Douglas MacArthur]* is the type of man who thinks that when he gets to heaven, God will step down from the great white throne and bow him into His vacated seat.
Harold L. Ickes. *Diary*, 1943.

71. *[Sen. Joseph R. McCarthy]* dons his warpaint. He goes into his war dance. He emits his war-whoops. He goes forth to battle and proudly returns with the scalp of a pink Army dentist. We may assume that this represents the depth and seriousness of the Communist penetration in this country at this time.
Ralph E. Flanders (1880-1970), U.S. Senator (R-VT). Senate speech, Mar. 9, 1954.

72. *[Sen. Joseph R. McCarthy]* is the most unlovely political character in our history since Aaron Burr.
Dean Acheson (1893-1971), U.S. Secretary of State (D). Quoted in Celebrity Research Group, *The Bedside Book of Celebrity Gossip*, 1984.

73. *[Sen. George McGovern]* couldn't carry Texas even if they caught Dick Nixon fucking a Fort Worth sow.
Lyndon B. Johnson (1908-1973), 36th President of the United States (D-TX). Remark to Bobby Baker, 1972; quoted in *Playboy*, June 1978.

74. *[Sen. George McGovern]* was nominated by the cast of *Hair*.
Thomas P. (Tip) O'Neill, Jr., U.S. Congressman and Speaker of the House (D-MA). Quoted on PBS, *America's Political Parties – the Democrats*, Oct. 17, 1988.

75. *[Pres. William McKinley]* has no more backbone than a chocolate eclair.
Theodore Roosevelt (1858-1918), 26th President of the United States (R-NY). Remark to H. H. Kohlsaat.

76. *[Pres. William McKinley]* walked among men a bronze statue, for thirty years determinedly looking for his pedestal.
William Allen White (1868-1944), American writer and editor. Quoted in Ralph G. Martin, *Ballots & Bandwagons*, 1964.

77. *[Pres. William McKinley]* kept his ear so close to the ground that it was full of grasshoppers.
Joseph G. Cannon (1836-1926), U.S. Congressman and Speaker of the House (R-IL). Quoted in Paul F. Boller, Jr., *Presidential Anecdotes*, 1981.

78. *[Gov. Evan Mecham]* proves that Darwin was wrong.
Bruce Babbitt, Governor of Arizona (D). Quoted in *Newsweek*, Nov. 16, 1987.

79. *[U.S. Attorney General Edwin Meese III]* has never been more than two steps ahead of the law.
Arthur J. Kropp, President, People for the American Way. Quoted in *The New York Times*, July 10, 1988.

80. *[Vice Pres. Richard M. Nixon]* is a shifty-eyed goddamn liar, and people know it. He's one of the few in the history of this country to run for high office talking out of both sides of his mouth and lying out of both sides.
Harry S Truman (1884-1972), 33rd President of the United States (D-MO). 1961.

81. *[Pres. Richard M. Nixon]* bleeds people. He draws every drop of blood and then drops them from a cliff. He'll blame any person he can put his foot on.
Martha Mitchell (1918-1976), wife of U.S. Attorney General John Mitchell during the Nixon administration. Telephone conversation with UPI reporter Helen Thomas, 1973.

82. *[Pres. Richard M. Nixon]* impeached himself. He gave us Gerald Ford as his revenge.
Bella Abzug, U.S. Congresswoman (D-NY). 1974.

83. *[Pres. Richard M. Nixon]* has no style. No style at all.
Benjamin C. Bradlee, editor, *The Washington Post*. Quoted in Theodore H. White, *Breach of Faith*, 1975.

84. *[Pres. Richard M. Nixon]* is an unpleasant man.... What I never understood is why he became a politician.
Henry M. Kissinger, U.S. Secretary of State and National Security Advisor (R). Oct. 1975.

85. *[Pres. Richard M. Nixon]* was more lacking in self-confidence than any leading politician I have known.
Denis Healey, Minister of Defense, Great Britain, and Chancellor of the Exchequer (Labour). *The Time of My Life*, 1990.

86. *[Speaker of the House Thomas P. (Tip) O'Neill, Jr.]* with his massive corpulence and scarlet, varicose nose, was a Hogarthian embodiment of the super-state he had labored for so long to maintain.
David A. Stockman, Director, U.S. Office of Management and Budget and U.S. Congressman (R-MI). *The Triumph of Politics: Why the Reagan Revolution Failed*, 1986.

87. *[Wendell Phillips]* cannot conceive of a tempest outside a teapot.
Horace Greeley (1811-1872), American newspaper editor and abolitionist. Quoted in Richard Hofstadter, *The American Political Tradition*, 1948.

88. *[Pres. James K. Polk]* is a victim of the use of water as a beverage.
Sam Houston (1793-1863), Governor of Tennessee (D), 1st President of the Republic of Texas, U.S. Congressman, and U.S. Senator. In reference to the fact that Polk was a teetotaler. Quoted in Llerena Beauf Friend, *Sam Houston, the Great Designer*, 1954.

89. *[Vice Pres. J. Danforth Quayle]* is not a crisis manager. He's a crisis that needs to be managed.
Michael J. Dukakis, Governor of Massachusetts (D). Presidential campaign speech, Nov. 6, 1988.

90. *[Vice Pres. J. Danforth Quayle]* thinks that *Roe* v. *Wade* are two ways to cross the Potomac.
Patricia R. Schroeder, U.S. Congresswoman (D-CO). Speech, abortion rights march, Washington, DC, Apr. 9, 1989.

91. *[Pres. Ronald Reagan]* won because he ran against Jimmy Carter. If he had run unopposed he would have lost.
Mort Sahl, American comedian. 1981.

92. *[Pres. Ronald Reagan]* is a triumph of the embalmer's art.
Gore Vidal, American writer. Quoted in *The Observer*, Apr. 26, 1981.

93. *[Pres. Ronald Reagan's]* body of knowledge is primarily impressionistic: he registers anecdotes rather than concepts.
David A. Stockman, Director, U.S. Office of Management and Budget and U.S. Congressman (R-MI). *The Triumph of Politics: Why the Reagan Revolution Failed*, 1986.

94. *[Pres. Ronald Reagan]* is a foolish and petulant old man.
James C. Wright, Jr., U.S. Congressman and Speaker of the House (D-TX). Quoted in John M. Barry, *The Ambition and the Power*, 1989.

95. *[Pres. Ronald Reagan]* doesn't retain very much of what comes his way on a given day.
Robert C. McFarlane, National Security Advisor (R). Quoted on CBS, *Sunday Morning*, Nov. 24, 1990.

96. *[Pres. Franklin D. Roosevelt]* is a chameleon on plaid.
Herbert Hoover (1874-1964), 31st President of the United States (R-IA). Quoted in James MacGregor Burns, *Roosevelt: The Lion and the Fox*, 1956.

97. *[Pres. Franklin D. Roosevelt]* is a second-class intellect – but a first-class temperament.
Oliver Wendell Holmes, Jr. (1841-1935), U.S. Supreme Court Justice. Quoted in Arthur M. Schlesinger, Jr., *The Coming of the New Deal*, 1959.

98. *[Pres. Theodore Roosevelt]* is pure act.
Henry Adams (1838-1918), American historian. *The Education of Henry Adams*, 1907.

99. *[Pres. Theodore Roosevelt]* is half St. Paul, half St. Vitus.
John Morley, Viscount Morley of Blackburn (1838-1923), Member of Parliament, Great Britain, Chief Secretary for Ireland, and Secretary of State for India (Liberal). Quoted in Ralph G. Martin, *Ballots & Bandwagons*, 1964.

100. *[U.S. Congresswoman Patricia R. Shroeder]* is a real pain in the ass.
Felix E. Hébert (1901-1979), U.S. Congressman (D-LA). Remark to the press, 1973.

101. *[Gov. Adlai E. Stevenson]* has about as much backbone as *[U.S. Secretary of State Dean]* Acheson and that is as little as a man can have, in my opinion.
Richard M. Nixon, 37th President of the United States (R-CA). Campaign speech, Philadelphia, PA, Oct. 9, 1952.

102. *[U.S. Director of the Budget David Stockman]* is a pathological finagler.
Ernest F. Hollings, U.S. Senator (D-SC). Quoted in Celebrity Research Group, *The Bedside Book of Celebrity Gossip*, 1984.

103. People say I'm arrogant, but I know better.
John Sununu, Governor of New Hampshire and White House Chief of Staff (R). Quoted on PBS, *MacNeil-Lehrer News Hour*, Apr. 26, 1991.

104. *[White House Chief of Staff John H. Sununu's]* idea of open space was a K Mart parking lot.
Patrick Jackson, Chairman, Southeast New Hampshire Regional Planning Commission. Quoted in *The New York Times*, May 14, 1990.

105. *[Pres. William H. Taft]* is a fathead with the brains of a guinea pig.
Theodore Roosevelt (1858-1919), 26th President of the United States (R-NY). Remark.

106. *[Pres. William H. Taft]* meant well, but he meant well feebly.
Theodore Roosevelt. Quoted in Wallechinsky and Wallace, *The People's Almanac*, 1975.

107. *[Prime Minister Margaret Thatcher]* is democratic enough to talk down to anyone.
Austin Mitchell, British writer. *Westminster Man*, 1982.

108. *[Prime Minister Margaret Thatcher]* is a brilliant tyrant surrounded by mediocrities.
Harold Macmillan (1894-1986), Prime Minister of Great Britain (Conservative). Quoted in *Newsweek,* Jan. 12, 1987.

109. If I were married to her *[Prime Minister Margaret Thatcher],* I'd be sure to have dinner ready for her when she came home.
George P. Shultz, U.S. Secretary of State (R). Attributed.

110. *[Pres. Harry S Truman]* is that shirt salesman from Kansas City.
John Foster Dulles (1888-1959), U.S. Secretary of State and U.S. Senator (R-NY). Quoted in Leonard Mosley, *Dulles,* 1978.

111. *[Congressman Morris K. Udall]* wanted to run for President *[in 1976]* in the worst way, and he did.
David S. Broder, American political columnist. 1976.

112. *[Pres. Martin Van Buren]* is an artful, cunning, intriguing, selfish, speculating lawyer, who, by holding lucrative offices for more than half his life, has contrived to amass a princely fortune, and is now seeking the presidency, principally for sordid gain, and to gratify the most selfish ambition.
David Crockett (1786-1836), U.S. Congressman (Anti-Jacksonian-TN). *The Life of Davy Crockett,* 1889.

113. *[New York City Mayor James J. Walker]* is a Paris gigolo ... an English fop.
Fiorello H. La Guardia (1882-1947), U.S. Congressman (R and Socialist), and Mayor of New York City (R and Fusion Party). Campaign speech, 1929.

114. *[Gov. Earl Warren]* has little genuine depth, or coherent political philosophy; a man who has probably never bothered with an abstract thought twice in his life.
John Gunther (1901-1970), American writer. *Inside U.S.A.,* 1947.

115. *[Sen. Daniel Webster]* struck me much like a steam-engine in trousers.
Sydney Smith (1771-1845), British clergyman and writer. Quoted in Lady Holland, *Memoir,* 1855.

Chapter 48

Intergovernmental Relations

1. You understand that, by making these records available to you I do not acknowledge that you or any grand jury have any right to records of the Vice President. Nor do I acknowledge the propriety of any grand jury investigations of possible wrongdoing on the part of the Vice President as long as he occupies that office. These are difficult constitutional questions which need not at this moment be confronted.

   Spiro T. Agnew, Governor of Maryland and Vice President of the United States (R). Letter to U.S. Attorney George Ball, Aug. 14, 1972.

2. The legal grounds are not near as important as the moral and political grounds, and I can use the courts till you can step on my beard.

   Cecil D. Andrus, Governor of Idaho and U.S. Secretary of the Interior (D). Comment when refusing to let a railroad car filled with radioactive waste enter a federal storage site in his state. Quoted in *The New York Times*, Oct. 23, 1988.

3. The current situation *[in Washington, DC]* will shortly and irresistibly tempt the Congress to reassert federal control over the nation's capital city. If the mayor *[Marion Barry]* can't restore order, the federal government must.

   Douglas Bereuter, U.S. Congressman (R-NB). In response to the city's crime and inefficiency. Speech in Congress, Feb. 22, 1989.

4. Almost everyone has heard of ... the practice indulged in by Congress of coercing the President to approve a bill he does not want by coupling it with one that is necessary or highly desirable.

   Emanuel Celler (1888-1981), U.S. Congressman (D-NY). *Congressional Record*, Feb. 25, 1952.

5. How can I run an agency at the same time?

   Douglas Costle, Administrator, Environmental Protection Agency. Comment on the time he had to spend testifying before Congress. Quoted in Tolchin and Tolchin, *Dismantling America: The Rush to Deregulate*, 1983.

6. The federal courts do not sit as an ombudsman, refereeing the disputes between the other two branches.

   William O. Douglas (1898-1980), U.S. Supreme Court Justice. *United States* v. *Gravel*, 1972 (dissent).

7. The President can't deliver us. I'm not a package to be picked up at a department store.

   Mickey Edwards, U.S. Congressman (R-OK). Quoted in *The New York Times*, Oct. 7, 1990.

8. Our best protection against bigger government in Washington is better government in the states.

   Dwight D. Eisenhower (1890-1969), 34th President of the United States (R-KS). Speech, National Governors' Conference, Cleveland, OH, June 8, 1964.

9. We are now an occupied territory. Evidence of the naked force of the federal government is here apparent in these unsheathed bayonets in the backs of schoolgirls.

   Orval E. Faubus, Governor of Arkansas (D). Reaction to federal troops sent to Little Rock, AR, to enforce desegregation orders. Statement, Sept. 27, 1957.

10. Americans are naturally suspicious of too much government and they see divided government as a safeguard.

    Sarah Fritz, American journalist. Symposium, "The Press and a Divided Government," National Press Foundation, Dec. 6, 1989.

11. It may safely be received as an axiom in our political system that the state governments will in all possible contingencies afford complete security against invasions of the public liberty by the national authority.

    Alexander Hamilton (1755-1804), Member, Continental Congress and Constitutional Convention, and

U.S. Secretary of the Treasury (Federalist-NY). *The Federalist*, No. 28, Dec. 26, 1787.

12. *[Chief Justice]* John Marshall has made his decision: *now let him enforce it!*

Andrew Jackson (1767-1845), 7th President of the United States (D-TN). Remark when the Supreme Court held that the state of Georgia could not remove Creek and Cherokee Indians from lands that had been guaranteed to them by federal treaty. March 4, 1832.

13. An elective despotism *[that is, of the Congress]* was not the government we fought for; but one which should not only be founded on free principles, but in which the powers of government should be so divided and balanced among several bodies of magistracy as that no one could transcend their legal limits without being effectually checked and restrained by the others.

Thomas Jefferson (1743-1826), 3rd President of the United States (Democratic Republican-VA). *Notes on the State of Virginia*, Query XIII, 1784.

14. This is buck passing without the bucks.

Richard D. Lamm, Governor of Colorado (D). Criticism of federal curtailment of funds to states while leaving states with the obligations. Quoted in *Newsweek*, Jan. 20, 1986.

15. I have always thought the act of secession is legally nothing, and needs no repealing.

Abraham Lincoln (1809-1865), 16th President of the United States (R-IL). Letter to B. F. Flanders, Nov. 9, 1863.

16. Experience has instructed us that no skill in the science of government has yet been able to discriminate and define, with sufficient certainty, its three great provinces – the legislative, executive, and judiciary; or even the privileges and powers of the different legislative branches. Questions daily occur in the course of practice which prove the obscurity which reigns in these subjects, and which puzzle the greatest adepts in political science.

James Madison (1751-1836), 4th President of the United States (Democratic Republican-VA). *The Federalist*, No. 37, Jan. 11, 1788.

17. The people have not chosen to be governed by one branch of government alone.

Mike Mansfield, U.S. Ambassador to Japan and U.S. Senator (D-MT). Speech, Senate Democratic Conference, quoted in *Congressional Record*, Jan. 4, 1973.

18. The great principle of separation of powers has become separation of responsibility.

Mark Phillips, American TV journalist. CBS, *Evening News*, Oct. 5, 1990.

19. I'm not going to be a rubber stamp to anybody including the President.

Carl D. Pursell, U.S. Congressman (R-MI). Interview, PBS, *MacNeil-Lehrer News Hour*, Oct. 3, 1990.

20. States' rights was only important because of civil rights. They wanted the state's right to discriminate against blacks.

Joseph L. Rauh, Jr. (1911-1992), American attorney and civil rights activist. Comment on Strom Thurmond and his States' Rights Party of 1948. Quoted on PBS, *The Great Upset of '48*, Nov. 2, 1988.

21. It will be my intention to curb the size and influence of the federal government and to demand recognition of the distinction between the powers granted to the federal government and those reserved to the states or the people.

Ronald Reagan, 40th President of the United States (R-CA). First inaugural address, Jan. 20, 1981.

22. I am sure the nation would be better served if each of us in the government does his job to his utmost and refrains from gratuitous advice to others on how they should conduct themselves.

Donald T. Regan, U.S. Secretary of the Treasury and White House Chief of Staff (R). Letter to Edwin J. Gray, Chairman, Federal Home Loan Bank Board, Sept. 11, 1984.

23. Quit mandating what Louisiana has to do. If you're not going to provide the money, let us decide what to do.

Charles E. Roemer III, U.S. Congressman and Governor of Louisiana (D). Interview, C-SPAN, Sept. 4, 1989.

24. The government of the United States is one of delegated and limited powers; it derives its existence and authority altogether from the Constitution; and neither of its branches, executive, legislative, or judicial, can exercise any of the powers of government beyond those specified and granted.

Roger B. Taney (1777-1864), U.S. Secretary of the Treasury (D) and Chief Justice, U.S. Supreme Court. *Ex parte Milligan*, June 1, 1861.

25. The politics of federalism are the politics of accommodation on the part of the governments and, it needs to be said, of people.

Pierre Elliott Trudeau, Prime Minister of Canada (Liberal). Speech to the First Ministers' Conference, Ottawa, Canada, Dec. 14, 1976.

26. I see in the greatest number *[of the American state constitutions]* an unreasonable imitation of the usages of England. Instead of bringing all the authorities into one, that of the nation, they have established different bodies – a House of Representatives, a council, a governor – because England has the House of Commons, lords, and a king. They undertake to balance these different authorities, as if the same equilibrium of powers which has been thought necessary to balance the enormous preponderance of royalty could be of any use in republics, formed upon the equality of all citizens; and as if every article which constitutes different bodies was not a source of divisions. By striving to escape imaginary dangers, they had created real ones.
   Anne Robert Jacques Turgot (1727-1781), French Finance Minister, statesman, and economist. Letter to Robert Price, Mar. 22, 1778.

27. The Executive is as independent of either House of Congress as either House of Congress is independent of him, and they cannot call for the records of his actions, or the action of his officers against his consent, any more than he can call for any of the journals or records of the House or Senate.
   U.S. House of Representatives Judiciary Committee, House Report 141, 45th Congress, 3rd Session, Mar. 3, 1879.

28. One branch of the Government cannot encroach on the domain of another without danger. The safety of our institutions depends in no small degree on a strict observance of this salutary rule.
   Morrison R. Waite (1816-1888), Chief Justice, U.S. Supreme Court. *Sinking Fund Cases*, 1878.

29. The federal government should give leadership and not allow important issues to be decided at the state level.
   Maxine Waters, U.S. Congresswoman (D-CA). Quoted in *Governing*, Mar. 1988. (Said when she was a member of the California Assembly.)

30. It was probably constitutionally unnecessary, but what actually passed by the Congress put the executive branch and the congressional branch in the same bed.
   Earle G. Wheeler, General, U.S. Army, and Chairman, Joint Chiefs of Staff. In reference to the Gulf of Tonkin Resolution. Quoted in Merle Miller, *Lyndon: An Oral Biography*, 1980.

31. We have states' rights. We have the right to go broke without any assistance from the Federal government.
   John Wilson, Chairman, City Council, Washington, DC (D). Interview, CNN, *Newsmaker Sunday*, May 12, 1991.

Chapter 49

Jails and Correction

1. Mandatory prison terms is easy to say, but where are we going to put people?
   William J. Bennett, Director, Office of National Drug Control Policy, and U.S. Secretary of Education (R). Quoted on NBC, *Meet the Press*, Mar. 19, 1989.

2. All punishment is mischief; all punishment in itself is evil.
   Jeremy Bentham (1748-1832), British jurist and philosopher. *Principles of Morals and Legislation*, 1789.

3. It is economic slavery, the savage struggle for a crumb, that has converted mankind into wolves and sheep.... My prison-house is but an intensified replica of the world beyond, the larger prison locked with the levers of Greed, guarded by the spawn of Hunger.
   Alexander Berkman (1870-1936), American anarchist. *Prison Memoirs of an Anarchist*, 1912.

4. Prisons are built with stones of law, brothels with bricks of religion.
   William Blake (1757-1827), British poet and engraver. *The Marriage of Heaven and Hell*, 1790.

5. I don't know, it may be that poor people are the only ones who commit crimes, but I do know that they are the only ones who serve prison sentences.
   Jimmy Carter, 39th President of the United States (D-GA). Speech, May 4 1974.

6. We spend ninety-five cents of every dollar for prisons on pure custody; iron bars and stone walls; and they dehumanize. We spend five cents on hope – health, mental health, education, vocational training, employment services, family guidance, community services. Most of these inmates have never been to a dentist. Psychoses and neuroses – a major cause of crime – are immense.
   Ramsey Clark, U.S. Attorney General (D). Speech, Atlantic City, NJ, 1970.

7. Jails and prisons are designed to break human beings, to convert the population into specimens in a zoo – obedient to our keepers, but dangerous to each other.
   Angela Davis, Communist Party candidate for President of the United States. "Reflections on the Black Woman's Role in the Community of Slaves," *The Black Scholar*, Dec. 1971.

8. There are no furloughs for victims. There is no return from the grave.
   Ralph Fine, Judge, Wisconsin Court of Appeals. Interview, ABC, *Nightline*, Nov. 25, 1988.

9. Punishment is not for revenge, but to lessen crime and reform the criminal.
   Elizabeth Fry (1780-1845), British prison reformer. *Journal*, 1839.

10. No penal or political system which multiplies the population of the prisons at the rate of 10 percent every year will solve a problem which is growing to be more and more of a danger to the social and moral life of the nation.
    William Randolph Hearst (1863-1951), U.S. Congressman (D-NY); founder, Independence League Party; journalist; and publisher. Speech, Dec. 1929.

11. The prison system of the United States is an unendurable disgrace to a civilized country.
    William Randolph Hearst. Editorial, June 29, 1930.

12. If a man is in a minority of one we lock him up.
    Oliver Wendell Holmes, Jr. (1841-1935), U.S. Supreme Court Justice. Speech, Feb. 15, 1913.

13. Ninety percent of prison riots start from stupid wardens.
    Louis McHenry Howe (1871-1935), presidential assistant (D). Radio address, Oct. 1934.

14. There are only two classes of persons in New South Wales. Those who have been convicted and those ought to have been.
    Laclan Macquaire, Governor of New South Wales, Austrialia (Tory). New South Wales was originally a penal colony. Letter to Lord Bathurst, 1822.

15. All my major works have been written in prison.... I would recommend prison not only to aspiring writer but to aspiring politicians, too.

Jawaharlal Nehru (1889-1964), 1st Prime Minister of India. Quoted in *Look*, Apr. 5, 1955.

16. Whereas the Necessity, Number and Continual Increase of the Poor within this City is very Great and ... frequently Commit divers misdemeanors ... who living Idly and unimployed, become debauched and Instructed in the Practice of Thievery ... For Remedy Whereof ... Resolved that there be forthwith built ... A good, Strong and Convenient House and Tenement.

New York City Council. Resolution to build "The Poor House, Work House, and House of Correction," c. 1730.

17. The best political writing in this century has been done from jail.

Richard M. Nixon, 37th President of the United States (R-CA). In reference to Lenin and Gandhi. Remark, Aug. 8, 1974.

18. The most anxious man in a prison is the governor.

George Bernard Shaw (1856-1950), Nobel Laureate in Literature (Great Britain). *Maxims for Revolutionists*, 1903.

19. If Robert Kennedy were alive today, he would not countenance singling me out for this kind of treatment.

Sirhan Sirhan, convicted assassin of Robert F. Kennedy. Statement after his request for parole was rejected by the California Parole Board, May 11, 1982.

20. Would citizens rather have violent offenders at large in their own back yard or incarcerated in their own back yard?

Richard Thornburgh, U.S. Attorney General and Governor of Pennsylvania (R). Speech, May 15, 1990.

Chapter 50

Justice

1. JUSTICE IN THE LIFE AND CONDUCT OF THE STATE IS POSSIBLE ONLY AS FIRST RESIDES IN THE HEARTS AND SOULS OF THE CITIZENS
   Inscription over the 10th Street entrance of the U.S. Department of Justice Building, Washington, DC.

2. EQUAL JUSTICE UNDER THE LAW
   Inscription at the entrance to the Supreme Court, Washington, DC.

3. THE UNITED STATES WINS ITS CASE WHENEVER JUSTICE IS DONE ONE OF ITS CITIZENS IN THE COURTS
   Inscription in the Attorney General's Rotunda, U.S. Department of Justice Building, Washington, DC.

4. Justice is not a prize tendered to the good-natured, nor is it to be withheld from the ill-bred.
   Charles L. Aarons (1872-1952), Wisconsin State Supreme Court Justice. *Hach* v. *Lewinsky*, 1945.

5. I'm a perpetually mad person. I hate injustice. As far as I'm concerned, I'm living to fight injustice. I'm living to fight the goddamned thing. I'm too mad to sleep.
   Sammie Abbott (1908-1990), Mayor of Takoma Park, MD (D). Quoted in *The Washington Post*, Jan. 6, 1991.

6. Justice discards party, friendship, kindred, and is therefore always represented as blind.
   Joseph Addison (1672-1719), Secretary of State, Great Britain (Whig). *The Guardian*, No. 99.

7. Much law, but no justice.
   American proverb.

8. Let justice roll down like waters and righteousness in an everlasting stream.
   Old Testament, *Amos* 5:24.

9. Effective action is always unjust.
   Jean Anouilh (1910-1987), French writer. *Catch as Catch Can.*

10. Revenge is a kind of wild justice; which the more man's nature runs to, the more ought law to weed it out.
    Francis Bacon, 1st Baron Verulam and Viscount St. Albans (1561-1626), Lord Chancellor of England. *Essays*, "Of Revenge," 1597.

11. We administer justice according to law. Justice in a larger sense, justice according to morality, is for Congress and the President to administer, if they see fit, through the creation of new law.
    Robert H. Bork, U.S. Solicitor General and Judge, U.S. Court of Appeals, Washington, DC. *Hohri* v. *United States*, 1986.

12. America's insistent demand in the twentieth century is for social justice.
    Louis D. Brandeis (1856-1941), U.S. Supreme Court Justice. Letter to Frederick Wehle, Oct. 28, 1924.

13. I am skeptical of the ability of black revolutionaries to achieve a fair trial anywhere in the United States.
    Kingman Brewster, Jr., U.S. Ambassador to England and President, Yale University. Comment during the murder trial of Black Panther leader Bobby Seale. 1970.

14. Punishments do not reach up to the Lords.
    Chinese saying.

15. Justice is not synonymous with speed.
    Alfredo Cristiani, President of El Salvador. Quoted in *The Washington Post*, Nov. 19, 1990.

16. It is such an important thing to shake the public's faith in justice so that we take greater concern with justice. Without skepticism, we tend to believe that justice is always done and that you can trust the legal system.
    Alan Dershowitz, professor, Harvard Law School. Speech, University of Pennsylvania, Philadelphia, PA, Apr. 3, 1991.

17. You shall not be partial in judgment: hear out low and high alike.
    Old Testament, *Deuteronomy* 1:17.

18. Justice, justice shall you pursue.
    Old Testament, *Deuteronomy* 16:20.

19. Justice is truth in action.
Benjamin Disraeli, 1st Earl of Beaconsfield (1804-1881), Prime Minister of Great Britain (Conservative). Speech, Feb. 11, 1851.

20. What then to the American black Slave is your Fourth of July? I answer, a day that reveals to him ... constant injustice.
Frederick Douglass (c.1817-1895), Recorder of Deeds, District of Columbia, and U.S. Minister to Haiti. Speech, Rochester, NY, July 5, 1852.

21. We're going to have a Justice Department that understands what the word justice means.
Michael Dukakis, Governor of Massachusetts (D). Presidential nomination acceptance speech, Democratic National Convention, Atlanta, GA, July 21, 1988.

22. It is mad and preposterous to bring to the standard of justice and humanity the exercise of a dominion founded upon violence and terror.
Thomas Erskine (1750-1823), Lord Chancellor of Great Britain . Trial of John Stockdale, Dec. 9, 1789.

23. The business of government is justice.
Millicent Fenwick (1910-1992), U.S. Congresswoman (R-NJ). PBS, *Mrs. Fenwick Goes to Washington,* June 26, 1991.

24. Let justice be done though the world perish.
Ferdinand I (1503-1564), Holy Roman Emperor. Attributed.

25. The power of the people ... to make and alter their laws at pleasure is the greatest security for liberty and justice.
Felix Frankfurter (1882-1965), U.S. Supreme Court Justice. *Bridges* v. *California,* 1941.

26. That which is not just is not law.
William Lloyd Garrison (1805-1879), American editor and abolitionist. Quoted on PBS, *The Civil War,* Sept. 23, 1990.

27. For every social wrong there must be a remedy.
Henry George (1839-1897), American political economist. *Social Problems,* 1883.

28. National injustice is the surest road to national downfall.
William E. Gladstone (1809-1898), Prime Minister of Great Britain (Liberal). Speech, 1878.

29. A government can fall because of one injustice.
Israel Hacohen (Chaim Chofetz) (1838-1933), Jewish theologian. *The Chofetz Chaim.*

30. Justice should not only be done, but should manifestly and undoubtedly be seem to be done.
Gordon Hewart, 1st Viscount Hewart (1870-1943), Member of Parliament and Lord Chief Justice of Great Britain (Liberal). Dictum.

31. The just man and firm of purpose – not the heat of fellow citizens clamoring for what is wrong, not presence of threatening tyrant can shake – in his rocklike soul.
Horace (65-8 B.C.), Roman poet. *Odes.*

32. The injustice to an individual is sometimes of service to the public. Facts are apt to alarm us more than the most dangerous principles.
Junius (Prob. Philip Francis) (1740-1818), British writer (Whig). *Letters,* No. 41, "To the Right Honourable Lord Mansfield," Nov. 14, 1770.

33. Justice delayed is democracy denied.
Robert F. Kennedy (1925-1968), U.S. Senator and U.S. Attorney General (D-NY). *The Pursuit of Justice,* 1964.

34. Injustice anywhere is a threat to justice everywhere.
Martin Luther King, Jr. (1929-1968), American clergyman and civil rights leader. Quoted in *The Atlantic Monthly,* Aug. 1963.

35. He made you king to do justice and righteousness.
Old Testament, *1 Kings* 10:9.

36. A judge's duty is to grant justice, but his practice is to delay it; even those judges who know their duty adhere to the general practice.
Jean de La Bruyère (1644-1696), French writer. *Les "Caractères" de Théophraste,* 1688.

37. The love of justice in most men is simply the fear of suffering injustice.
François de La Rochefoucauld (1613-1680), French nobleman and writer. *Réflexions ou Sentences et Maximes Morales,* 1665.

38. I wish to do justice to all.
Abraham Lincoln (1809-1865), 16th President of the United States (R-IL). Speech, U.S. Congress, July 27, 1848.

39. Why should there not be a patient confidence in the ultimate justice of the people? Is there any better or equal hope in the world?
Abraham Lincoln. First inaugural address, Mar. 4, 1861.

40. To no one will we sell, to no one will we refuse or delay, right or justice.
Magna Carta, 1215.

41. Shall any man be above justice? Above all shall that man be above it who can commit the most extensive injustice?
George Mason (1725-1792), Member, Virginia and Federal Constitutional Conventions. Debate, Constitutional Convention, Philadelphia, PA, 1787.

42. Justice is beyond definition, but the humblest citizen traveling the highways of life has a fairly clear idea of what injustice is in any particular circumstance.
James C. McRuer, Chief Justice, Ontario, Canada. Quoted in *The Globe and Mail*, Jan. 22, 1977.

43. If the parties will at my hands call for justice, then, all ... stood on the one side, and the Devil on the other, his cause being good, the Devil should have the right.
Thomas More (1478-1535), Speaker of the House of Commons and Lord Chancellor of England. Quoted in R. W. Chambers, *Thomas More*, 1935.

44. The constitution *[of England]* does not allow reasons of State to influence our judgment: God forbid it should! We must not regard political consequences, how formidable soever they might be; if rebellion was the certain consequence, we are bound to say, *Fiat justitia, ruat coelum ["Let justice be done, though the heavens fall."]*
William Murray, 1st Earl of Mansfield (1705-1793), Lord Chief Justice of Great Britain . *Rex* v. *Wilkes*, 1770.

45. Civilization is built on a number of ultimate principles: respect for human life, the punishment of crimes against property and persons, the equality of all good citizens before the law – or, in a word, justice.
Max Nordau (1849-1923), German physician, writer, and Zionist. Address, 7th World Zionist Congress, Basel, Switzerland, 1905.

46. An act against natural equity is void.
James Otis (1725-1783), attorney and Member, Colonial Massachusetts legislature. Admiralty Court Trial, Feb. 1761.

47. Justice without power is inefficient; power without justice is tyranny.
Blaise Pascal (1623-1662), French mathematician and philosopher. *Pensées*.

48. Impartiality is the *Life* of Justice, as that is of government.
William Penn (1644-1718), founder of Pennsylvania. *Some Fruits of Solitude, in Reflections and Maxims*, 1693.

49. The fruits of the toil of millions are boldly stolen to build up colossal fortunes for a few; and the possessors of these, in turn, despise the Republic and endanger liberty. From the same prolific womb of governmental injustice we breed the two great classes – tramps and millionaires.
People's (Populist) Party platform, 1892.

50. Those who buy justice wholesale can sell it retail.
Armand Jean du Plessis (Cardinal Richelieu) (1585-1642), French ecclesiastic and statesman. *Political Testament*, I, 4, 1687.

51. Justice cannot reach all wrongs; its hands are tied by the restrictions of the law.
Melville Davisson Post (1869-1930), American writer and attorney. *The Strange Schemes of Randolph Mason*, "The Sheriff of Gullmore," 1896.

52. Terror is nothing else than justice, prompt, secure, and inflexible.
Maximilien-François-Marie de Robespierre (1758-1794), French revolutionist. Speech, Paris, Feb. 5, 1794.

53. Justice cannot be for one side alone, but must be for both.
Anna Eleanor Roosevelt (1884-1962), First Lady and U.S. Delegate to the United Nations. "My Day," Oct. 15, 1947.

54. The passage from the state of nature to the civil state produces a very remarkable change in man, by substituting justice for instinct in his conduct.
Jean-Jacques Rousseau (1712-1778), French philosopher. *The Social Contract*, 1762.

55. Let me have justice, and I will then trust the law.
Elizabeth Hoby Russell (1528-c.1603), English courtier. Statement to King James I, 1603.

56. Where the Generality are Offenders, Justice cometh to be Cruelty.
George Savile, 1st Marquess of Halifax (1633-1695), Lord Privy Seal of England. *Moral Thoughts and Reflections*, 1750.

57. Expedience and justice frequently are not even on speaking terms.
Arthur H. Vandenberg (1884-1951), U.S. Senator (R-MI). Senate speech, Mar. 8, 1948.

58. Severity is commoner than justice.
Marquis de Vauvenargues (1715-1747), French soldier and moralist. *Réflexions et Maximes.*

59. The term "social justice" is not an evil one. It comes to us from the Holy Bible.
Earl Warren (1891-1974), Chief Justice, U.S. Supreme Court, and Governor of California (R). Address, Middlesex Republican Club, Boston, MA, 1952.

60. Justice, sir, is the great interest of man on earth.
Daniel Webster (1782-1852), U.S. Congressman (Federalist-NH and MA), U.S. Senator (Federalist and Whig-MA), and U.S. Secretary of State. Speech, "On Mr. Justice Story," 1845.

61. There may be times when we are powerless to prevent injustice, but there must never be a time when we fail to protest.
Elie Wiesel, Nobel Laureate in Literature (United States). Quoted in *Reader's Digest*, Feb. 1988.

62. There is only one thing worse than injustice, and that is justice without her sword in her hand. When right is not might it is evil.
Oscar Wilde (1854-1900), Irish writer. In conversation.

Chapter 51

Labor and the Labor Force

1. ARBEIT MACHT FREI (Work will make you free)
Inscription over entrance to Auschwitz concentration camp, Oswiecim, Poland, 1940's.

2. The unemployed have rights that are above charity. They have the right to work.
Bernard M. Baruch (1870-1965), Chairman, War Industries Board, and U.S. Delegate to U.N. Atomic Energy Commission. Speech, Nov. 1931.

3. They who are deft with their hands and skilled in their work are indispensable in a city; wherever they dwell, they hunger not.
Apocrypha, *Wisdom of Ben Sira* 38:31.

4. Employment, which Galen calls "nature's physician," is so essential to human happiness that Indolence is justly considered as the mother of Misery.
Robert Burton (1577-1640), vicar of St. Thomas's, Oxford, England. *The Anatomy of Melancholy*, 1621.

5. The golf links lie so near the mill
That almost every day
The laboring children can look out
And see the men at play.
Sarah N. Cleghorn (1876-1959), American writer. "The Golf Links," 1915.

6. Honor lies in honest toil.
Grover Cleveland (1837-1908), 22nd and 24th President of the United States (D-NY). Letter accepting presidential nomination, Aug. 18, 1884.

7. What you earn is largely determined by what you learn.
Bill Clinton, 42nd President of the United States (D-AR). Quoted on C-SPAN, May 5, 1991.

8. When more and more people are thrown out of work, unemployment results.
Calvin Coolidge (1872-1933), 30th President of the United States (R-MA). Remark, 1930.

9. We often wonder how things are made so cheap among the Yankees. Come here and you will see women doing men's work, and happy and cheerful as the day is long, and why not?
David Crockett (1786-1836), U.S. Congressman (D-TN). *The Life of Davy Crockett*, 1889.

10. What this country needs is more unemployed politicians.
Angela Davis, Communist Party candidate for President of the United States. Speech, Oakland, CA, 1967.

11. Oppress not a hired servant ... whether he be of thy brethren or of thy strangers in the land.
Old Testament, *Deuteronomy* 24:14.

12. The young Americans of today are the work force of tomorrow.
Elizabeth H. Dole, U.S. Secretary of Labor and U.S. Secretary of Transportation (R). ABC, Public Service Announcement, Aug. 9, 1990.

13. It is essential that the worker in industry should have the status of an individual and not be a mere cog in a soulless machine.
Anthony Eden (1897-1977), Prime Minister of Great Britain (Conservative). Speech, Conservative Conference, Oct. 1946.

14. Man exists for his own sake, and not to add a laborer to the State.
Ralph Waldo Emerson (1803-1882), American writer. *Journals*, 1839.

15. The capability of the nation's work-force is a national security matter.
Arthur A. Fletcher, Chairman, U.S. Commission on Civil Rights. "For Civil Rights, It's Back to the Future," *The New York Times*, Aug. 19, 1990.

16. The workingmen have been exploited all the way up and down the line by employers, landlords, everybody.
Henry Ford (1863-1947), American industrialist and philanthropist. Quoted in George Seldes, *The Great Quotations*, 1983.

17. When men are employed, they are best contented.
Benjamin Franklin (1706-1790), Member, Conti-

nental Congress and Constitutional Convention, Governor of Pennsylvania, and U.S. Minister to France. *Autobiography*, 1791.

18. We can no longer ignore that voice within women that says: "I want something more than my husband and my children and my home...." And work can now be seen as the key to the problem that has no name.
Betty Friedan, American writer and feminist. *The Feminine Mystique*, 1963.

19. The sad fact is that in communities such as mine, the minimum wage is the maximum wage.
Robert Garcia, U.S. Congressman (D-NY). House debate, June 14, 1989.

20. By the sweat of your brow shall you get bread to eat.
Old Testament, *Genesis* 3:19.

21. Human labor is becoming the cheapest of commodities.
Henry George (1839-1897), American political economist. Speech, Young Men's Hebrew Association, San Francisco, CA, June 1878.

22. The fact is that most people who have no skill have no education for the same reason--low intelligence or ambition.
Barry M. Goldwater, U.S. Senator (R-AZ). Speech, Economics Club, New York City, Jan. 15, 1964.

23. The periods of unemployment accompanying depression in the business cycle ... present a challenge to all our claims to progress, humanity, and civilization.
Samuel Gompers (1850-1924), President, American Federation of Labor. *Seventy Years of Life and Labor*, 1925.

24. The labor of a human being is not a commodity or article of commerce.
[This phrase was incorporated into the Clayton Anti-Trust Act, 1914.]
Samuel Gompers. *Ibid.*

25. Labor disgraces no man; unfortunately you occasionally find men disgrace labor.
Ulysses S. Grant (1822-1885), 18th President of the United States (R-OH). Speech, Birmingham, England, 1877.

26. If the American working people were as I would like them to be, they would all be Socialists and I would be President.
Michael Harrington (1928-1989), American writer and Socialist Party leader. Debate, Minnesota, 1978. Quoted on PBS, *Firing Line*, Sept. 23, 1989.

27. Industrial homework is a dead end, perpetuating the misery and poverty of those it traps. It creates a subclass of workers who receive none of the benefits for which America's working people have fought, sometimes at the cost of their lives.
Neil F. Hartigan, Attorney General of Illinois. Press statement, Chicago, IL, Mar. 11, 1989.

28. To the working class there is no foreigner but the capitalist.
William Dudley Haywood (1868-1928), American labor leader. *International Socialist Review*, 1910.

29. The first duty of this government is to give the workers work.
William Randolph Hearst (1863-1951), U.S. Congressman (D-NY); founder, Independence League Party; journalist; and publisher. Letter to the *New York American*, 1929.

30. The wealth of a country is in its working people.
Theodor Herzl (1860-1904), Austrian journalist and political Zionist. *Altneuland*, 1902.

31. No! I stand by the man who works. To hell with kings!
Daniel Webster Hoan (1881-1961), Mayor of Milwaukee, WI (Socialist). Remark when it was suggested that King Albert of Belgium be invited to the city, 1919.

32. If there is any matter upon which civilized countries have agreed ... it is the evil of premature and excessive child labor.
Oliver Wendell Holmes, Jr. (1841-1935), U.S. Supreme Court Justice. *Hammer* v. *Dagenhart*, 1917.

33. The working class and the employing class have nothing in common.
Industrial Workers of the World, Constitution, June 27, 1905.

34. Any job that can be done by an illiterate can be done by a machine.
John E. Jacob, President, Urban League. Quoted in *Youth: 2000*, 1986.

35. All people shall have the right and the obligation to work.
Japanese Constitution, 1947.

36. In Europe the object is to make the most of the land, labor being abundant; here it is to make the most of our labor, land being abundant.

Thomas Jefferson (1743-1826), 3rd President of the United States (Democratic Republican-VA). *Notes on Virginia*, Query VIII, 1782.

37. Man is born to labor.
Old Testament, *Job* 5:7.

38. All of government is just a device to protect man so that he may earn his bread in the sweat of his labor.
Hugh Samuel Johnson (1882-1942), Director, National Recovery Administration. *The American*, July 1935.

39. The greatest untapped natural resource in the United States today is woman power.
Lyndon B. Johnson (1908-1973), 36th President of the United States (D-TX). Frequent statement to his daughter Luci.

40. When you have 7 percent unemployed, you have 93 percent working.
John F. Kennedy (1917-1963), 35th President of the United States (D-MA). Quoted in Barbara Rowes, *The Book of Quotes*, 1979.

41. Call it what you will, incentives are what get people to work harder.
Nikita S. Khrushchev (1894-1971), Premier of the U.S.S.R. Remark to Sen. Hubert H. Humphrey. Quoted in *The New Republic*, Jan. 5, 1959.

42. The question of the protection of childhood *[child labor legislation]* is not a political one. It is not even an American question. It is just simply a humane problem in which all decent ... loving men and women should be deeply interested.
Fiorello H. La Guardia (1882-1947), U.S. Congressman (R and Socialist-NY) and Mayor of New York City (R and Fusion Party). Letter to Eleanor Roosevelt, Jan. 13, 1928.

43. This is 1930, not 1898. We have not only arrived at a forty-four-hour week but in this machine age we are arriving at the time when all workers will soon be given a forty-hour week.
Fiorello H. La Guardia. Speech to Congress, July 1, 1930.

44. Wages ought not to be insufficient to support a frugal and well-behaved wage earner.
Pope Leo XIII (1810-1903), Encyclical, *Rerum Novarum*, May 15, 1891.

45. We must draw ahead of Europe on the question of labor, and we must set the example.
Konstantin Nikolaevich Leontiev (1831-1891), Russian Socialist and philosopher. Letter, 1890.

46. Labor and capital may be partners in theory, but they are enemies in fact.
John L. Lewis (1882-1947), President, United Mine Workers of America. Speech to rubber workers, Akron, OH, 1935.

47. If the Almighty had ever made a set of men that should do all the eating and none of the work, He would have made them with mouths only and no hands.
Abraham Lincoln (1809-1865), 16th President of the United States (R-IL). 1854.

48. The working people are the basis of all government, for the plain reason that they are the most numerous.
Abraham Lincoln. Speech, Cincinnati, OH, Feb. 12, 1861.

49. Labor is prior to, and independent of, capital. Capital is only the fruit of labor, and could never have existed if labor had not first existed.
Abraham Lincoln. Message to Congress, Dec. 3, 1861.

50. The strongest bond of human sympathy outside the family relation should be one uniting all working peoples of all nations and tongues and kindreds.
Abraham Lincoln. Reply to a committee of the Workingman's Association of New York City, Mar. 21, 1864.

51. Labor was truly said by the ancients to be the price which the gods set upon everything worth having.
John Lubbock, 1st Baron Avebury (1834-1913), Member of Parliament, Great Britain (Liberal), banker, and scientist. *Pleasures of Life*, 1887-1889.

52. The laborer is worthy of his hire.
New Testament, *Luke* 10:7.

53. A laborer who marries without being able to support a family may in some respects be considered as an enemy of all his fellow-laborers.
Thomas R. Malthus (1766-1834), British clergyman and political economist. *Essay on the Principle of Population*, 1798.

54. Enable every woman who can work to take her place on the labor front, under the principle of equal pay for equal work. This should be done as quickly as possible.
Mao Tse-tung (1893-1976), Chairman, Communist Party of China. Introduction, *On Widening the Scope of Women's Work in the Agricultural Co-operative Movement*, 1955.

55. Is it not a cruel civilization that allows little hearts and little shoulders to strain under these grown-up responsibilities.
Edwin Markham (1852-1940), American poet. Argument against child labor. *Cosmopolitan*, Jan. 1907.

56. Disregard for workers' health protection is not what American industry is supposed to be about.
Lynn M. Martin, U.S. Congresswoman and U.S. Secretary of Labor (R-IL). Quoted in *The Washington Post*, Apr. 5, 1991.

57. The workingmen of Europe felt instinctively that the Star Spangled Banner carried the destiny of their class.
Karl Marx (1818-1883), German economist and Socialist. Letter to Abraham Lincoln, 1865.

58. I know of only three ways of living in society: one must be a beggar, a thief, or a wage earner.
Honoré de Mirabeau (1749-1791), French revolutionist and President of the National Assembly. Speech, 1788.

59. State government has followed Washington's misguided lead in another direction – the tendency to serve as an employment program. Few of us have noticed that the increases in much ballyhooed government jobs have occurred in the states, not in Washington.
John Naisbitt, American futurist and writer. *Megatrends*, 1982.

60. Security of the workingman as against unemployment, old age, sickness, accident and death, must be frankly accepted as a special responsibility of industry jointly with society.
Bishops' Administrative Board, National Catholic Welfare Council, *The Church and Social Order*, 1940.

61. Government enterprise is the most inefficient and costly way of producing jobs.
Richard M. Nixon, 37th President of the United States (R-CA). *The Memoirs of Richard M. Nixon*, 1978.

62. The wage paid to the working man must be sufficient for the support of himself and his family.
Pope Pius XI (1857-1939), Encyclical, *Quadragesimo Anno*, May 15, 1931.

63. He who renders service to society and develops its wealth should himself have his proportionate share of the increased public riches.
Pope Pius XI. *Ibid.*

64. Under the influence of either poverty or wealth, workmen and their work are equally liable to degenerate.
Plato (427-347 B.C.), Greek philosopher. *The Republic.*

65. They *[American industries]* can't get a labor force out of our jails, they can't get a labor force out of our rehabilitation centers.
Charles B. Rangel, U.S. Congressman (D-NY). Quoted in *Newsday*, Jan. 29, 1990.

66. The social system in which a man, willing to work, is compelled to starve, is a blasphemy, an anarchy, and no system.
Thomas Devlin Reilly (1824-1854), Irish revolutionist. *The Irish Felon*, 1848.

67. Like all other contracts, wages should be left to the fair and free competition of the market and should never be controlled by the interference of the legislature.
David Ricardo (1772-1823), British political economist. *Principles of Political Economy and Taxation*, 1817.

68. A society in which everyone works is not necessarily a free society and indeed may be a slave society.
Anna Eleanor Roosevelt (1884-1962), First Lady and U.S. Delegate to the United Nations. U.N. speech, Paris, Sept. 27, 1948.

69. These unhappy times call for the building of plans that rest upon the forgotten, the unorganized but indispensable unities of economic power, for plans like those of 1917 that build from the bottom up, and not from the top down, that put their faith once more in the forgotten man ... the forgotten man at the bottom of the economic pyramid.
Franklin Delano Roosevelt (1882-1945), 32nd President of the United States (D-NY). Radio address, Albany, NY, Apr. 7, 1932.

70. No man can be a good citizen unless he has a wage more than enough to cover the bare cost of living, and hours of labor short enough so that after his day's work is done he will have time and energy to bear his share in the management of the community.
Theodore Roosevelt (1858-1919), 26th President of the United States (R-NY). Speech, "The New Nationalism," Osawatomie, KS, Aug. 31, 1910.

71. Never forget that men who labor cast the votes, set up and pull down governments.
Elihu Root (1845-1937), U.S. Senator (R-NY), U.S. Secretary of War, U.S. Secretary of State, and Nobel Laureate in Peace. Quoted in George Seldes, *The Great Quotations*, 1983.

72. Most of our kids are looking for jobs--not looking for trouble.

Kurt Schmoke, Mayor of Baltimore, MD (D). Quoted on ABC, *This Week*, Apr. 30, 1989.

73. It *[the conflict over slavery]* is an irrepressible conflict between opposing and enduring forces, and it means that the United States must and will, sooner or later, become either entirely a slave-holding nation or entirely a free-labor nation.

William H. Seward (1801-1872), Governor of New York (Whig), U.S. Senator (R and Whig-NY), and U.S. Secretary of State. Speech, Rochester, NY, Oct. 25, 1858.

74. Human labor is not a commodity.

Alfred E. Smith (1873-1944), Governor of New York (D). Campaign speech, 1922.

75. Surely no capitalist would ever agree to the complete abolition of unemployment, to the abolition of the reserve army of unemployed, the purpose of which is to bring pressure on the labor market, to ensure a supply of cheap labor.

Joseph Stalin (1879-1953), Premier of the U.S.S.R. Interview with H. G. Wells, July 23, 1934.

76. The State rests upon the *slavery of labor*. If labor becomes *free*, the State is lost.

Max Stirner (Johann Kaspar Schmidt) (1806-1856), German anarchist. *The Ego and His Own*, 1845.

77. The cheapest labor is that which is most productive.

Oscar S. Straus (1845-1926), U.S. Secretary of Commerce (Progressive-NY), U.S. Secretary of of Labor, and U.S. Ambassador to Turkey. Speech, May 22, 1907.

78. Legislation has been the only force which has improved the working conditions of any large number of women wage-earners.

Helen L. Sumner (1876-1933), economist, U.S. Department of Labor. Senate report, *History of Women in Industry in the United States*, 1911.

79. Wealth only comes from production, and all that the wrangling grabbers, loafers, and jobbers get to deal with comes from somebody's toil and sacrifice. Who, then, is he who provides it all? The Forgotten Man.

William Graham Sumner (1840-1910), professor of political and moral sciences, Yale University. *What Social Classes Owe to Each Other*, 1883.

80. Government doesn't employ the bulk of people in the city. You have to have a reliable and vital private sector to do that for you.

Alair A. Townsend, Deputy Mayor of New York City (D). Quoted in *Governing the States and Localities*, May 1988.

81. Work in the U.S.S.R. is an obligation and a matter of honor of each citizen who is fit for work, according to the principle: "He who does not work does not eat."

U.S.S.R. Constitution, Dec. 5, 1936.

82. Speaking of the masses, who in the end govern elections and most other things, we are a nation of Workers. Nothing is therefore better calculated to win their respect and favor, political as well as personal ... than to be a man of business, one who as they do, gets his bread and acquires his substance by his own exertions.... Politics is not regarded by the masses as making an honest livelihood.

Martin Van Buren (1782-1862), 8th President of the United States (D). Letter of political advice to his son, John, Mar. 16, 1858.

83. There is as much dignity in tilling a field as in writing history.

Booker T. Washington (1856-1915), American educator and President, Tuskegee Institute, AL. *Up from Slavery*, 1901.

84. If the people can attain a fair compensation for their labor, they will have good homes, good clothing, and good food.

Daniel Webster (1782-1852), U.S. Congressman (Federalist-NH and MA), U.S. Senator (Federalist and Whig-MA), and U.S. Secretary of State. Quoted in *C.I.O. News*, May 5, 1941.

85. Women must remain in industry despite all narrow-minded caterwauling; in fact the circle of their industrial activity must become broader.

Clara Zetkin (1857-1933), cofounder, German Communist Party. *The Question of Women Workers and Women at the Present Time*, 1889.

Chapter 52

Labor Unions

1. Union gives strength.
   Aesop (620-560 B.C.), Greek fabulist. *The Bundle of Sticks.*

2. The rights and interests of the laboring man will be protected and cared for – not by the labor agitators, but by the Christian men to whom God in His infinite wisdom has given the control of the property interests of the country.
   George F. Baer (1842-1914), President, Philadelphia and Reading Railroad. Statement when refusing to bargain or negotiate with labor. Letter to W. F. Clark, July 17, 1902.

3. The trade union, which originated under the European system, destroys liberty.
   Henry Ward Beecher (1813-1887), American clergyman and writer. Quoted in *Harper's Weekly*, May 8, 1886.

4. Labor cannot on any terms surrender the right to strike.
   Louis D. Brandeis (1856-1941), U.S. Supreme Court Justice. 1913.

5. Neither the common law nor the Fourteenth Amendment confers the absolute right to strike.
   Louis D. Brandeis. *Dorchy* v. *Kansas*, 1926.

6. Don't assume that the interests of employer and employee are necessarily hostile – that what is good for one is necessarily bad for the other. The opposite is more apt to be the case. While they have different interests, they are likely to prosper or suffer together.
   Louis D. Brandeis. Quoted in Alpheus T. Mason, *Brandeis: A Free Man's Life*, 1946.

7. *[The capitalist wants a standing army]* to supplement the local government in protecting his property when he enters into a contest with his employees.
   William Jennings Bryan (1860-1925), U.S. Secretary of State (D). Quoted in Richard Hofstadter, *The American Political Tradition*, 1948.

8. I am always on the side of labor when there is any compromise to be made.
   Plutarco Elías Calles (1877-1945), President of Mexico. Statement to the press, 1927.

9. "Solidarity Forever"
   Ralph Chaplin (1887-1961), American labor organizer. Title of Communist anthem, 1915.

10. If you ever saw a cat and a dog eating out of the same plate, you can bet your ass it was the cat's food.
   William F. Clay, U.S. Congressman (D-MO). Reaction to a suggestion that unions representing public employees form a coalition with presidential candidate Jimmy Carter. 1980.

11. There can be no distress, there can be no hard times, when labor is well paid. The man who raises his hand against the progress of the workingman raises his hand against prosperity.
   William B. Cockran (1854-1923), U.S. Congressman (D-NY). Speech, Aug. 18, 1896.

12. There is no right to strike against the public safety by anybody, anywhere, any time.
   Calvin Coolidge (1872-1933), 30th President of the United States (R-MA). In response to strike by Boston police. Telegram to Samuel Gompers, Sept. 14, 1919.

13. I don't propose to let either the NAM *[National Association of Manufacturers]* or labor unions hand me a bill and say: "Take it or leave it."
   Norris H. Cotton (1901-1989), U.S. Congressman and U.S. Senator (R-NH). In reference to the Taft-Hartley Act. Quoted in his obituary, *The Washington Post*, Feb. 25, 1989.

14. Labor unions are often brutal, they are often cruel, they are often unjust.... I don't care how many brutalities they are guilty of. I know that their cause is just.
   Clarence S. Darrow (1857-1937), American attorney. 1907.

15. No strike has ever been lost.
Eugene V. Debs (1855-1926), American Socialist. Favorite remark.

16. The American motto is "fair play." Boycotting is not *fair play* – it is *not* in consonance with American ideas of justice. It does not recognize *personal* liberty and *personal* rights.
Eugene V. Debs. *Locomotive Fireman's Magazine* June 1886.

17. Organize! Educate! Agitate!
Eugene V. Debs. Apr. 1919.

18. With respect to government service, we hold distinctly that the rights of the people are paramount to the right to strike.
Democratic Party platform, 1920.

19. If the workers of the world want to win, all they have to do is recognize their own solidarity. They have nothing to do but fold their arms and the world will stop.
Joseph Ettor (1885-1945), Industrial Workers of the World labor organizer. Quoted in Howard Zinn, *A People's History of the United States*, 1980.

20. Industrial relations are like sexual relations. It's better between two consenting parties.
Victor Feather (1908-1976), leader, British Labour Party. Quoted in *Guardian Weekly*, Aug. 8, 1976.

21. Labor unions are the worst thing that ever struck the earth because they take away a man's independence.
Henry Ford (1863-1947), American industrialist and philanthropist. 1940.

22. Strikes are a crime ... the law of jungles and primitive societies.
Francisco Franco (1892-1975), President of Spain. Quoted in *Time*, May 21, 1951.

23. I will never recognize the union, never, never!
Henry Clay Frick (1849-1919), American industrialist. Quoted in G. B. M. Harvey, *Henry Clay Frick: The Man*, 1928.

24. The methods by which a trade union can alone act are necessarily destructive; its organization is necessarily tyrannical.
Henry George (1839-1897), American political economist. *Progress and Poverty*, 1879.

25. If it becomes a question of destruction of this union *[the United Mine Workers of America]* or the preservation of the country, the country is going to be preserved.
Thomas Alan Goldsborough (1877-1951), Federal judge. Remark on sentencing United Mine Workers president John L. Lewis, Dec. 5, 1946.

26. The toilers have awakened to the new found power of organized effort.
Samuel Gompers (1850-1924), President, American Federation of Labor. Labor Day address, New York City, 1910.

27. Many of those who helped to lay the foundations of the trade union movement were men who had been through the experience of Socialism and found their way to sounder policies.
Samuel Gompers. *Seventy Years of Life and Labor*, 1925.

28. Labor organizations had been the victims of so much political trickery that we felt that the only way to keep this new organization *[the American Federation of Labor]* free from taint was to exclude all political partisan action.
Samuel Gompers. *Ibid.*

29. What does labor want? We want more schoolhouses and less jails; more books and less arsenals; more learning and less vice; more leisure and less greed; more justice and less revenge; in fact, more of the opportunities to cultivate our better natures, to make manhood more noble, womanhood more beautiful, and childhood more happy and bright.
Samuel Gompers. Quoted in *Labor*, Aug. 4, 1956.

30. I can hire one-half of the working class to kill the other half.
Jay Gould (1836-1892), American industrialist. Comment on the Knights of Labor strike. Remark, 1886.

31. Pray for the dead, but fight like hell for the living.
Mary Harris (Mother Jones) (1830-1930), American labor organizer. Favorite remark.

32. The strike is the weapon of the industrial jungle.
Sidney Hillman (1887-1946), President, Amalgamated Clothing Workers of America, and chief, Labor Division, U.S. War Production Board. Attributed.

33. What labor is demanding all over the world today is not a few material things like more dollars and fewer hours of work, but the right to a voice in the conduct of industry.
Sidney Hillman. Labor Day speech, Baltimore, MD, 1918.

34. Don't mourn for me – organize!
Joseph Hillstrom (Joe Hill) (1879-1915), American

labor organizer, poet, and songwriter. Last words before his execution, Utah, Nov. 1915.

35. The Committee on Un-American Activities calls upon the American labor movement ... to amend its constitutions where necessary in order to deny membership to a member of the Communist party or any other group which dedicates itself to the destruction of America's way of life.
House Un-American Activities Committee, H.R. Reports No. 57, 84th Congress, 1st Session, 1954.

36. ONLY DANGER SAN FRANCISCO STRIKE IS THAT MAYOR IS BADLY FRIGHTENED AND HIS FEAR INFECTED ENTIRE CITY
Louis McHenry Howe (1871-1935), presidential assistant (D). In reference to a general strike in San Francisco, CA. Radiogram to Pres. Franklin D. Roosevelt, July 1934.

37. I don't think the labor movement ever acts in unison. That has been proven in election after election where leaders endorse one candidate and the rank and file vote otherwise.
Theodore Kheel, American labor mediator. Quoted in *The New York Times*, Dec. 23, 1990.

38. We affirm, as a fundamental principle, that labor, the creator of wealth, is entitled to all it creates.
Resolution passed by the Labor-Reform Convention, Worcester, MA, Sept. 1870.

39. It has happened, in all ages of the world, that some have labored and others have, without labor, enjoyed a large proportion of the fruits. This is wrong and should not continue. To secure to each laborer the whole product of his labor, or as nearly as possible, is a worthy object of any good government. That's my platform, but when the average Republican leader in the East *[the progressive Republicans were then mostly in the West]* hears it, he thinks I am quoting from Karl Marx. I did quote it, but not from Karl Marx. I quoted it from Abraham Lincoln.
Fiorello H. La Guardia (1882-1947), U.S. Congressman (R and Socialist) and Mayor of New York City (R and Fusion Party). Campaign speech, 1922.

40. We must have modern conditions to meet modern machinery. As labor-saving devices are installed and used for production we must necessarily shorten the number of hours per day, and we are now at the stage where we will necessarily have to come to a five-day week because, gentlemen, you cannot have prosperity unless you have employment.
Fiorello H. La Guardia. Speech to Congress, May 3, 1930.

41. Trade unionism means the enslavement of the workers by the bourgeoisie.
V. I. Lenin (1870-1924), Premier of the U.S.S.R. *What Is to Be Done?*, 1902.

42. The history of all countries shows that, by its own efforts, the working class can develop only a trade-union consciousness – that is, the realization of the need of getting together in unions in order to fight employers and to demand from the government the passing of laws necessary for the workers.
V. I. Lenin. *Ibid.*

43. Every worker receives from society as much as he has given it.
V. I. Lenin. *The State and Revolution*, 1917.

44. The future of labor is the future of America.
John L. Lewis (1882-1947), President, United Mine Workers of America. Speech, 1937.

45. No tin hat brigade of goose-stepping vigilantes or Bible-babbling mob of blackguarding and corporation paid scoundrels will prevent the onward march of labor.
John L. Lewis. Quoted in *Time*, Sept. 9, 1937.

46. If we must grind up human flesh and bones in the industrial machine, then, before God, I assert that those who consume coal, and you and I who benefit from that service, owe protection to those men *[the miners]* first, and we owe security to their families after, if they die. I say it! I proclaim it! And I care not who in heaven or hell oppose it!
John L. Lewis. Testimony, House Labor Committee, Apr. 1947.

47. You can't dig coal with bayonets.
John L. Lewis. In response to calls for the military to work the mines during labor unrest. Quoted in *The New York Post*, Mar. 1, 1956.

48. And inasmuch as most good things are produced by labor, it follows that all such things of right belong to those whose labor has produced them.
Abraham Lincoln (1809-1865), 16th President of the United States (R-IL). Notes for a tariff discussion in Congress, Dec. 1, 1847.

49. Thank God we have a system of labor where there can be a strike.
Abraham Lincoln. Speech to striking shoe-factory workers, New Haven, CT, Mar. 6, 1860.

50. If this government has not the power to outlaw strikes of this character *[the coal miners]*, then this government has no power of self-preservation.

Scott Wike Lucas (1892-1968), U.S. Congressman and U.S. Senator (D-IL). Speech in Congress, Apr. 1946.

51. We back Solidarity *[the Polish trade union]*, and bust our unions.
Eric Mann, American writer and member, United Automobile Workers. Quoted in *The New York Times*, May 7, 1988.

52. The Sabbath was made for man, and not man for the Sabbath.
New Testament, *Mark* 2:27.

53. You can't mine coal without machine guns.
Richard B. Mellon (1858-1933), American industrialist. Congressional testimony on labor relations in the coal-mining industry. Quoted in *Time*, June 14, 1937.

54. I believe not only in the right of the laboring man to organize in unions but also in the duty of the government which that laboring man supports, to protect these organizations against the vested interests of wealth and intellect.
National Union for Social Justice (precursor to the Union Party). Pledge, 1934.

55. Capital has a right to a just share of the profits, but only a just share.
William Henry O'Connell (1859-1944), American Roman Catholic cardinal. Pastoral letter, Nov. 23, 1912.

56. I don't know any union in the world that does not want more money in wages. That is what unions are for.
Daniel Ortega, President of Nicaragua. Interview, CBS, *Face the Nation*, Mar. 4, 1990.

57. My opponent called me a cream puff. Well, I rushed out and got the baker's union to endorse me.
Claiborne Pell, U.S. Senator (D-RI). Remembrance of his first political campaign in 1960. Quoted in *The New York Times*, Feb. 3, 1987.

58. Compulsion should be a moral compulsion brought about by public opinion rather than by statute.
Frances Perkins (1882-1965), U.S. Secretary of Labor (D). Communication to Governor Alfred E. Smith (NY) on compulsory labor arbitration, 1920.

59. Only organize, and stand together. Claim something together, and at once; let the nation hear a unified demand from the laboring voice, and then, when you have got that, go on after another; but get something.
Wendell Phillips (1811-1884), American orator and reformer. Speech, Labor-Reform Convention, Worcester, MA, Sept. 4, 1870.

60. The labor movement means just this: It is the last noble protest of the American people against the power of incorporated wealth.
Wendell Phillips. *The Foundation of the Labor Movement*, 1871.

61. In all labor there is profit; but the talk of the lips tends only to poverty.
Old Testament, *Proverbs* 14:23.

62. We cannot, as citizens, pick and choose the laws we will or will not obey.
Ronald Reagan, 40th President of the United States (R-CA). Comment when dismissing U.S. air-traffic controllers who had gone on strike contrary to federal law. Chicago, IL, Sept. 3, 1981.

63. No labor leader can deliver the vote. If any labor leader says he can deliver the vote, he is kidding you or himself.
Walter P. Reuther (1907-1970), President, United Auto Workers of America. Quoted in *The Nation*, Dec. 3, 1952.

64. I will not be the Prime Minister of a mistaken generosity who would ruin our chances of economic recovery.
Michel Rocard, Prime Minister of France. Response to critics of his policy of holding the line on wages of government workers. Quoted in *The New York Times*, Oct. 23, 1988.

65. A strike of public employees manifests nothing less than an attempt to prevent or obstruct the operations of government until their demands are satisfied. Such action, looking toward the paralysis of government by those who have sworn to support it, is unthinkable and intolerable.
Franklin D. Roosevelt (1882-1945), 32nd President of the United States (D-NY). 1937.

66. Only in free lands have free labor unions survived.
Franklin D. Roosevelt. Speech, International Brotherhood of Teamsters, 1939.

67. I believe now, as I have all my life, in the right of workers to join unions and to protect their unions.
Franklin D. Roosevelt. Speech, May 2, 1943.

68. Labor organizations are like organizations of capitalists; sometimes they act very well and sometimes they act badly. We should consistently favor them when they act well, and as fearlessly oppose them when they act badly.

Theodore Roosevelt (1858-1919), 26th President of the United States (R-NY). 1911.

69. Where the union movement gets weak is where you have all those goddamn paid union staff organizers, who are no longer workers. They build a union bureaucracy which is just as decadent and as inflexible as management bureaucracy.
Benjamin S. Rosenthal (1923-1983), U.S. Congressman (D-NY). Quoted in Daniel Rapoport, *Inside the House*, 1975.

70. Unions bring democracy to the workplace.
Vikki Saporta, Director of Organizing, International Brotherhood of Teamsters. Interview, PBS, *The Business File*, Nov. 23, 1989.

71. There is more Strength in *Union* than in *Number*; witness the People that in all Ages have been scurvily used, because they could so seldom agree to do themselves Right.
George Savile, 1st Marquess of Halifax (1633-1695), Lord Privy Seal of England. *Political Thoughts and Reflections*, 1750.

72. Union workers know the meaning of getting something now and something later, as opposed to trying to get everything now and getting nothing.
Rick Scott, Political Director, American Federation of State, County and Municipal Employees, Minnesota. Quoted in *Governing the States and Localities*, Feb. 1988.

73. For seventy-five years big business has been sitting down on the American people, and now I am delighted to see the process reversed.
Upton Sinclair (1878-1968), American novelist and politician. Remark during a nationwide union strike, 1937.

74. The strike is a phenomenon of war.
Georges Sorel (1847-1922), French journalist and political philosopher. *Reflections on Violence*, 1908.

75. A red is any son of a bitch who wants thirty cents when we're paying twenty-five.
John Steinbeck (1864-1946), Nobel Laureate in Literature (United States). *The Grapes of Wrath*, 1939.

76. *[A worker has]* an inalienable right to bestow his labor where he will.
William H. Taft (1857-1930), 27th President of the United States (R-OH) and Chief Justice, U.S. Supreme Court. Quoted in William E. Nelson, *The Roots of American Bureaucracy, 1830-1900*, 1982.

77. The crisis of Pearl Harbor was the result of action by a foreign enemy. The crisis tonight *[a national railroad strike]* is caused by ... men within our own country who place their private interests above the welfare of the nation.
Harry S Truman (1884-1972), 33rd President of the United States (D-MO). Radio address, May 1946.

78. We in labor have to start giving some of our friends a message. And the message is that FDR and John Kennedy and Hubert Humphrey never negotiated any kind of permanent lease on our support. And the message is that if you want us to work on your phone banks and put up your yard signs and pay for your campaigns, then you better focus to fight big business, to stand up for strong labor laws, to win health care.
Richard L. Trumka, President, United Mine Workers of America. Quoted in *Rolling Stone*, Oct. 17, 1991.

79. Long Live the Strike! (*Viva la Huelga!*)
Slogan, United Farm Workers of America, 1970's.

80. "Solidarity" means taking care of the person standing next to you.
Lech Walesa, President of Poland, trade unionist, and founder, Solidarity. Speech to striking shipyard workers, Gdansk, Poland, May 1988.

81. Labor is the great producer of wealth.
Daniel Webster (1782-1852), U.S. Congressman (Federalist-NH and MA), U.S. Senator (Federalist and Whig-MA), and U.S. Secretary of State. Speech, House of Representatives, Apr. 2, 1824.

82. I always say we're like any other rats – when we're cornered, we fight back. Down and dirty if we have to. That's what we're like now – cornered rats.
William Wimpsinger, President, International Brotherhood of Machinists. Quoted in *Rolling Stone*, Oct. 17, 1991.

Chapter 53

Law and the Courts

1. NO FREE GOVERNMENT CAN SURVIVE THAT IS NOT BASED ON THE SUPREMACY OF LAW
Inscription on the Justice Department Building, Washington, DC.

2. I desire you would remember the ladies, and be more generous and favorable to them than your ancestors.... If particular care and attention is not paid to the ladies, we are determined to foment a rebellion and will not hold ourselves bound by any laws in which we have no voice or representation.
Abigail Adams (1744-1818), First Lady. In reference to new laws that would be necessary after a proposed Declaration of Independence. Letter to her husband, John Adams, 1774.

3. Good government is an empire of laws.
John Adams (1735-1826), 2nd President of the United States (Federalist-MA). *Thoughts on Government*, 1776.

4. Law is a bottomless pit, it is a cormorant, a Harpy that devoures everything.
John Arbuthnot (1667-1735), Scottish physician and humorist. *The History of John Bull*, 1712.

5. That judges of important causes should hold office for life is not a good thing, for the mind grows old as well as the body.
Aristotle (384-322 B.C.), Greek philosopher and teacher. *Politics*.

6. Where the laws are not supreme, there demagogues spring up.... The law ought to be supreme over all.
Aristotle. *Ibid*.

7. The law is reason unaffected by desire.
Aristotle. *Ibid*.

8. Law is order, and good law is good order.
Aristotle. *Ibid*.

9. Judges ought to remember that their office is *Ius dicere* and not *Ius dare;* to interpret law, and not to make law, or give law.
Francis Bacon, 1st Baron Verulam and Viscount St. Albans (1561-1626), Lord Chancellor of England. *Essays*, "Of Judicature," 1597.

10. The laws of an absolute monarchy are not its legislative acts; they are the will and pleasure of the monarch.
Henry Baldwin (1780-1844), U.S. Supreme Court Justice. *United States* v. *Arredondo*, 1832.

11. The soul of liberty is love of law.
Honoré de Balzac (1799-1850), French writer. *Epigrams*.

12. When laws, customs, or institutions cease to be beneficial to man, they cease to be obligatory.
Henry Ward Beecher (1813-1887), American clergyman and writer. *Life Thoughts*, 1858.

13. A law is valuable, not because it is law, but because there is right in it.
Henry Ward Beecher. *Ibid*.

14. ... organized, institutional liberty – liberty through law, and laws for liberty.
Henry Ward Beecher. Sermon, Plymouth Church, Plymouth, MA, May 1861.

15. Take all the robes of all the good judges that have ever lived on the face of the earth, and they would not be large enough to cover the iniquity of one corrupt judge.
Henry Ward Beecher. *Proverbs from Plymouth Pulpit*, 1887.

16. If we *[federal judges]* had to run for election in the South in the 1960's we would have had a new set of judges every year.
Griffin Bell, U.S. Attorney General (D). Quoted on ABC, *Nightline*, Aug. 3, 1988.

17. A judge is just a lawyer who somebody's blessed.
William J. Bennett, Director, Office of National Drug Control, and U.S. Secretary of Education (R). Interview, CNN, *Evans & Novak*, Dec. 16, 1989.

18. Every law is an evil, for every law is an infraction of liberty.

Jeremy Bentham (1748-1832), British jurist and philosopher. *An Introduction to the Principles of Morals and Legislation,* 1789.

19. The Law! It is the arch-crime of the centuries. The path of Man is soaked with the blood it has shed. Can this great criminal determine Right? Is a revolutionist to respect such a travesty? It would mean the perpetuation of human slavery.

Alexander Berkman (1870-1936), American anarchist. *Prison Memoirs of an Anarchist,* 1912.

20. Laws are like sausages. It is better not to see them being made.

Otto von Bismarck-Schoenhausen (1815-1898), Chancellor of Germany. Attributed.

21. Retribution is no longer the dominant objective of the criminal law. Reformation and rehabilitation of offenders have become important goals of criminal jurisprudence.

Hugo L. Black (1886-1971), U.S. Senator (D-AL) and U.S. Supreme Court Justice. *Williams* v. *New York,* 1948.

22. In this distinct and separate existence of the judicial power in a peculiar body of men, nominated indeed, but not removable at pleasure, by the crown, consists one main preservative of the public liberty; which cannot subsist long in any state unless the administration of justice be in some degree separated from the legislative and also from the executive power.

William Blackstone (1723-1780), British jurist. *Commentaries on the Laws of England,* I, 1765.

23. It is infinitely easier to suffer in obedience to a human command than to accept suffering as free, responsible men.

Dietrich Bonhoeffer (1906-1945), German theologian executed by the Nazis. *Letters and Papers from Prison,* 1953.

24. No more fatuous chimera ever infected the brain of man than that you can control opinions by law or direct belief by statute.

William E. Borah (1865-1940), U.S. Senator (R-ID). Senate speech, Apr. 19, 1917.

25. In a constitutional democracy the moral content of law must be given by the morality of the framer or legislator, never by the morality of the judge.

Robert H. Bork, U.S. Solicitor General and Judge, Federal Court of Appeals, Washington, DC. Quoted in *The 1989 Conservative Calendar.*

26. But the king should not be under any man, only under God and the law, for the law makes the king. Let the king therefore attribute to the law what the law attributes to him, namely lordship and power, for there is no king where will rules and not the law.

Henry de Bracton (d.1268), English ecclesiastic and jurist. *On the Laws and Customs of England,* I.

27. Our government is the potent, the omnipresent teacher. For good or for ill, it teaches the whole people by example. If the government becomes a lawbreaker, it breeds contempt for law; it invites every man to become a law unto himself; it invites anarchy.

Louis D. Brandeis (1856-1941), U.S. Supreme Court Justice. *Olmstead* v. *United States,* 1927 (dissent).

28. Law cannot stand apart from the social changes around it.

William J. Brennan, Jr., U.S. Supreme Court Justice. Lecture, Georgetown University, Washington, DC, Nov. 25, 1957.

29. The American system of criminal prosecution is accusatorial, not inquisitional, and the Fifth Amendment is its essential mainstay.

William J. Brennan, Jr.. *Malloy* v. *Hogan,* 1964.

30. Our federal judicial rulings have come to reek with the snap judgments of New Dealers.... The Supreme Court of the United States has assumed quasi-legislative authority.

John W. Bricker (1893-1986), Governor of Ohio and U.S. Senator (R). Speech, San Francisco, CA, 1942.

31. The Supreme Court is the living voice of the Constitution – that is, of the will of the people expressed in the fundamental law they have enacted. It is ... the conscience of the people.... It is the guarantee of the minority who, when threatened by the impatient vehemence of the majority, can appeal to this permanent law, finding the interpreter and enforcer thereof in a Court set high above the assaults of faction.

James Bryce (1838-1922), British Ambassador to the United States. *The American Commonwealth,* 1888.

32. Instead of allowing the political processes to run their course ... the Court seeks to do Congress's job for it, compensating for congressional inaction. It is not unreasonable to think that this encourages the political branches to pass their problems to the judiciary.

Warren E. Burger, Chief Justice, U.S. Supreme Court. *Plyler* v. *Doe,* 1982 (dissent).

33. Law is whatever is boldly asserted and plausibly maintained.
Aaron Burr (1756-1836), U.S. Senator (D-NY) and Vice President of the United States. Attributed.

34. The *[Supreme]* Court did not interpret the Constitution – the court amended it.
James F. Byrnes (1879-1972), U.S. Congressman and U.S. Senator (D-SC), U.S. Supreme Court Justice, U.S. Secretary of State, and Governor of South Carolina. In reference to *Brown* v. *Board of Education*. Remark, 1954.

35. "Whate'er is best administered is best," may truly be said of a juridical system, and the due distribution of justice depends more upon the rules by which suits are to be conducted than on the perfection of the code by which rights are defined.
John Campbell (1779-1861), British jurist and statesman. *Lives of the Lord Chancellors: Somers*, 1847.

36. The great tides and currents which engulf the rest of men do not turn aside in their course and pass the judges by.
Benjamin N. Cardozo (1870-1938), U.S. Supreme Court Justice. *The Nature of the Judicial Process*, 1921.

37. The supreme rule of the road is the rule of mutual forbearance.
Benjamin N. Cardozo. *Ward* v. *Clark*, 1921.

38. Expediency may tip the scales when arguments are nicely balanced.
Benjamin N. Cardozo. *Woolford Realty Co.* v. *Rose*, 1931.

39. We are in bondage to the law so that we may be free.
Marcus Tullius Cicero (106-43 B.C.), Roman statesman and writer. *De legibus*.

40. The law is silent during war. (*Silent leges inter arma.*)
Marcus Tullius Cicero. *Oratio Pro Annio Milone*, IV.

41. Court rules do not cause crime.
Ramsey Clark, U.S. Attorney General (D). Quoted in Melvin I. Urofsky, *A March of Liberty*, 1988.

42. Trial by television is ... foreign to our system.
Thomas C. Clark (1899-1977), U.S. Supreme Court Justice. June 7, 1965.

43. No man has ever been hanged for breaking the spirit of the law.
Grover Cleveland (1837-1908), 22nd and 24th President of the United States (D-NY). Quoted in Paxton Hibben, *Peerless Leader*, 1929.

44. I don't care what the law is, tell me who the judge is.
Roy M. Cohn (1927-1986), special counsel, House Un-American Activities Committee. Quoted in *Time*, Apr. 4, 1988.

45. Magna Carta is such a fellow that he will have no sovereign.
Edward Coke (1552-1634), Solicitor General, Attorney General, and Speaker of the House of Commons, England. Speech to Parliament on the amendment to the Petition of Right, May 17, 1628.

46. The victim to too severe a law is considered as a martyr rather than a criminal.
Charles Caleb Colton (c.1780-1832), British clergyman and writer. *Lacon*, I, 1825.

47. Necessity hath no law.
Oliver Cromwell (1599-1658), Lord Protector of England. Speech to Parliament, Sept. 12, 1654.

48. The case *[of the Railroad Retirement Act]* was always a difficult one, but the form the opinions took would seem to indicate such a marked cleavage in the Supreme Court that it may be, and probably is, a forecast of what we may expect with reference to almost any form of social legislation that Congress may enact. Apparently there are at least four justices who are against any attempt to use the power of the federal government for bettering general conditions, except within the narrowest limitations. This is a terrific handicap and brings up again, rather acutely, matters we have previously discussed, including a proposed constitutional amendment *[to expand the Supreme Court to fifteen justices]*.
Homer S. Cummings (1870-1956), U.S. Attorney General (D). Memorandum to Pres. Franklin D. Roosevelt, May 1935.

49. Delay in the administration of justice is the outstanding defect of our federal judicial system. It has been a cause of concern to practically every one of my predecessors in office. It has exasperated the bench, the bar, the business community and the public.... To speed justice, to bring it within the reach of every citizen, to free it of unnecessary entanglements and delays, are primary obligations of our government.
Homer S. Cummings. Letter to Pres. Franklin D. Roosevelt, Nov. 1936.

50. If the Constitution, as interpreted by the Court, prevents the proper solution of our social and

economic problems, should we do something to the Constitution to meet the difficulty, or should we do something to the Supreme Court?

Robert Eugene Cushman (1889-1969), American jurist. In reference to the Supreme Court "packing" legislation proposed by Pres. Franklin D. Roosevelt. *The Supreme Court and the Constitution*, 1936.

51. The key to the *[Supreme]* Court's critical constitutional role lies in the mystery of its future actions.

Lloyd N. Cutler, counsel to the President (D). "In Justice, Mystery Is Essential," *The Washington Post*, Aug. 2, 1990.

52. The tort system has correctly been called the lottery system.

John C. Danforth, U.S. Senator (R-MO). Senate debate, Sept. 17, 1986.

53. Custom, that unwritten law,
By which the people keep even kings in awe.

William D'Avenant (1606-1668), English writer. *Circe*.

54. The law ought to prohibit only actions hurtful to society. What is not prohibited by the law should not be hindered, nor should anyone be compelled to that which the law does not require.

Declaration of the Rights of Man, French National Assembly, 1789.

55. Every dictator is an enemy of freedom, an opponent of law.

Demosthenes (385?-322 B.C.), Athenian orator and statesman. *Philippic*.

56. We do not sit as a superlegislature to weigh the wisdom of legislation.

William O. Douglas (1898-1980), U.S. Supreme Court Justice. Remark, Mar. 3, 1952.

57. The fact that there is a five-to-four decision usually means that there is at hand a five-to-four problem. Judges are not perverse; they look for unanimity, not disagreement.

William O. Douglas. *We the Judges*, 1956.

58. I am not willing to trust the *[Supreme]* Court because very much of the trouble in which we are now involved *[the Civil War]* may be attributed to the fact that we had a pro-slavery judiciary.

W. McKee Dunn (1814-1887), U.S. Congressman (R-IN). Quoted in Melvin I. Urofsky, *A March of Liberty*, 1988.

59. It's a good process. It takes a while, and it should. Life tenure is one of our most important safeguards.... I want to make it *[impeachment]* as our founders had in mind – very difficult.

Don Edwards, U.S. Congressman (D-CA). In reference to impeachment of federal judges. Quoted in *The Washington Post*, Apr. 7, 1989.

60. All of us know that if an individual, a community, or a state is going continuously and successfully to defy the rulings of the courts, then anarchy results.

Dwight D. Eisenhower (1890-1969), 34th President of the United States (R-KS). Statement, Newport, RI, Sept. 1958.

61. Let a man keep the law, – any law, – and his way will be strewn with satisfactions.

Ralph Waldo Emerson (1803-1882), American writer. *Essays*, First Series, "Prudence," 1865.

62. I am just a country lawyer from way down in North Carolina, and I probably make inquiries with a little bit more vigor than some of these high-falutin' city lawyers do.

Samuel J. Ervin, Jr. (1896-1985), U.S. Congressman and U.S. Senator (D-NC). Response when asked about the thoroughness of his committee's investigations into the Watergate break-in, July 17, 1983.

63. One law for the native and the stranger among you.

Old Testament, *Exodus* 12:49.

64. When it is left entirely to a judge to decide whether he should give place to another, he becomes a judge in his case.

Charles Fairman, professor, Harvard Law School. *Harvard Law Review*, 51, 1938.

65. To go against a torrent of public passion is not easy even for independent judges.

Yuri Feofanov, Russian legal scholar. *Isvestia*, Sept. 1, 1988.

66. The law, in its majestic equality, forbids the rich as well as the poor to sleep under bridges, to beg in the streets, and to steal bread.

Anatole France (Jacques-Anatole-François Thibault) (1844-1924), Nobel Laureate in Literature (France). *Le Lys rouge*, 1894.

67. Those who wrote our Constitution well knew the danger inherent in special legislative acts which take away the life, liberty or property of particular named persons because the legislature thinks them guilty of conduct which deserves punishment. They *[the authors of the Constitution]* intended to safeguard the people of this country from punishment without trial by duly constituted courts.

Felix Frankfurter (1882-1965), U.S. Supreme Court Justice. *United States* v. *Lovett*, 1945.

68. Due process is not a mechanical instrument. It is not a yardstick. It is a process.

Felix Frankfurter. *Joint Anti-Fascist Refugee Committee* v. *McGrath*, 1951.

69. The *[Supreme]* Court's authority – possessed neither of the purse nor the sword – ultimately rests on sustained public confidence in its moral sanction. Such feeling must be nourished by the Court's complete detachment, in fact and appearance, from political entanglements and by abstention from injecting itself into the clash of political forces and political settlements.

Felix Frankfurter. Quoted in Earl Katcher, *Earl Warren: A Political Biography*, 1967.

70. We ought to have a bill ... to close the law schools. Think of the public service we could do. We could take away their *[lawyers']* licenses to steal.

Jake Garn, U.S. Senator (R-UT). Senate debate, June 6, 1990.

71. The Supreme Court, when it decides a new legal question, does not make illegal what was previously legal; it gives a final authoritative determination of whether an action was legal when it took place.

Arthur J. Goldberg (1908-1990), U.S. Supreme Court Justice, U.S. Secretary of Labor (D), and U.S. Ambassador to the United Nations. *The Washington Post*, June 1, 1973.

72. No great idea in its beginning can ever be within the law.

Emma Goldman (1869-1940), American anarchist. "Address to the Jury," *Mother Earth*, July 1917.

73. Laws grind the poor and rich men rule the law.

Oliver Goldsmith (1728-1774), British writer. *The Traveller*, 1764.

74. I say that the responsibility of the judiciary is to uphold the Constitution, not rewrite it.

Barry M. Goldwater, U.S. Senator (R-AZ). Quoted in *The Baltimore Sun*, Apr. 17, 1964.

75. My measures will not be sickled over with legalistic doubts.... Here I do not have to exercise justice; here I have only to annihilate.

Hermann Goering (1893-1946), German Field Marshal, founder of the Gestapo, President of the Reichstag (Nazi Parliament), and convicted war criminal. Speech to German police, 1934.

76. The Navy and the foreign office had to find the argument to support the action; it was anxious work.

Edward Grey, Viscount Grey of Fallodon (1862-1933), Foreign Secretary of Great Britain (Liberal). Comment when the British extended the traditional legal concept of a blockade early in World War I. *Twenty-Five Years, 1892-1916*, 1925.

77. If the law commands me to sin, I will break it.

Angelina Grimké (1805-1879), American abolitionist and suffragist. *Appeal to the Christian Women of the South*, 1836.

78. It was a glorious day of triumph for the working people of this country when the odious decision of the Supreme Court forbidding the enactment of state minimum-wage laws for women was swept aside; and let me say that the man responsible for that great humane victory, singly and alone, is President Franklin D. Roosevelt.

Joseph F. Guffey (1870-1959), U.S. Senator (D-PA). Senate speech supporting President Roosevelt's Supreme Court-packing proposal, Aug. 20, 1937.

79. I want no one to plead my cause, because I do not wish to defend myself. All that I have done I did with an unflinching will to help destroy the autocratic regime.

Leivick Halpern (1886-1962), Yiddish writer and Bund activist. Explanation for his refusal to have a defending counsel in court during his trial as a Socialist workers' agitator. Minsk, Russia, 1908.

80. The inflexible and uniform adherence to the rights of the Constitution and of individuals, which we perceive to be indispensable in the courts of justice, can certainly not be expected from judges who hold their offices by a temporary commission.

Alexander Hamilton (1755-1804), Member, Continental Congress and Constitutional Convention, and U.S. Secretary of the Treasury (Federalist-NY). *The Federalist*, No. 78, May 28, 1788.

81. I established law and justice in the land.

Hammurabi (c.1955-1913 B.C.), King of Babylon. Prologue, *Code of Hammurabi*.

82. The tradition of English-speaking freedom has depended in no small part upon the merely procedural requirement that the state point with exactness to just that conduct which violates the law. It is difficult and often impossible to meet the charge that one's general ethos is treasonable.

Learned Hand (1872-1961), Federal Judge. *Masses Publishing Co.* v. *Patten*, 1917.

83. The law, the will of the majority expressed in orderly, constitutional methods, is the only king to which we bow.

Benjamin Harrison (1833-1901), 23rd President of the United States (R-IN). Speech, Topeka, KS, Oct. 10, 1890.

84. No one can demand that you be neutral toward the crime of genocide. If there is a judge in the whole world who can be neutral toward this crime, that judge is not fit to sit in judgment.

Gideon Hausner, Chief Justice, Supreme Court of Israel. In defense of Israel's legal right to try Adolf Eichmann. Quoted in *The New York Times*, June 27, 1961.

85. Doctrines and "ideas" shall no longer govern your existence. The *Führer* himself, and only he, is the current and future reality of Germany, and his word is your law.

Martin Heidegger (1899-1976), German philosopher. Open letter to students of the University of Freiburg, Nov. 3, 1933.

86. The people should fight for their law as for their city wall.

Heraclitus of Ephesus (c.500 B.C.), Greek philosopher. *Fragments.*

87. The life of the law has not been logic; it has been experience.

Oliver Wendell Holmes, Jr. (1841-1935), U.S. Supreme Court Justice. *The Common Law*, 1881.

88. Great cases like hard cases make bad law.

Oliver Wendell Holmes, Jr. *Northern Securities Company* v. *United States*, 1904.

89. I have spent seventy years finding out that I am not God.

Oliver Wendell Holmes, Jr. Response when asked by what great principle his judicial decisions were guided. Quoted by Adlai E. Stevenson, *The New York Times Magazine*, Nov. 4, 1962.

90. To live by one man's will became the cause of all men's misery.

Richard Hooker (1553-1600), English theologian. *The Laws of Ecclesiastical Polity*, 1594.

91. Law enforcement does not ask an advantage in its struggle with the lawless. It asks only that the scales of justice be balanced. The cause of justice is not served when hardened criminals are allowed to go free through legal technicalities.

J. Edgar Hoover (1895-1972), Director, Federal Bureau of Investigation. Quoted in Earl Katcher, *Earl Warren: A Political Biography*, 1967.

92. There are a lot of mediocre judges and people and lawyers, and they are entitled to a little representation *[on the Supreme Court]*, aren't they? We can't have all Brandeises, Frankfurters, and Cardozos and stuff like that.

Roman L. Hruska, U.S. Congressman and U.S. Senator (R-NB). In defense of the nomination of G. Harold Carswell to the U.S. Supreme Court by President Nixon. Quoted in *The New York Times*, Mar. 17, 1970.

93. I desire to know wherefore *[why]* I am banished. *[John Winthrop, Governor of Massachusetts Bay Colony, who presided at Hutchinson's trial, answered: "Say no more. The Court knows wherefore, and is satisfied."]*

Anne Hutchinson (1591-1643), American religious leader. Mar. 22, 1638.

94. The highest test of a people's fitness for free institutions is their willingness to obey law.

John Ireland (1838-1918), American Roman Catholic bishop. Speech, Chicago, Feb. 22, 1895.

95. The authority of the Supreme Court must not ... be permitted to control the Congress, or the Executive, when acting in their legislative capacities.

Andrew Jackson (1767-1845), 7th President of the United States (D-TN). Speech, 1832.

96. There is only one excuse for packing the *[Supreme]* Court and that is to change it.

Robert H. Jackson (1892-1954), U.S. Attorney General (D) and U.S. Supreme Court Justice. Advice to Pres. Franklin D. Roosevelt against the appointment of a popular Senator who might be too conservative. 1937.

97. This Court may fall into error as may other branches of the Government.... The Court differs, however ... in its ability to extricate itself from error. It can reconsider.

Robert H. Jackson. *Helvering* v. *Gerhardt*, 1938.

98. The ultimate function of the Supreme Court is nothing less than the arbitration between fundamental and ever-present rival forces or trends in our organized society.

Robert H. Jackson. *The Struggle for Judicial Supremacy*, 1941.

99. Conflicts which have divided the justices *[of the U.S. Supreme Court]* always mirror a conflict which pervades society.

Robert H. Jackson. *Ibid.*

100. No longer may the head of a state consider himself outside the law, and impose inhuman acts on the peoples of the world.

Robert H. Jackson. Statement explaining the Nuremberg trials. 1946.

101. That means that I shall be under the law, which it is treason to affirm.

James I (1566-1625), King of England. Remark to Sir Edward Coke, who opined that since His Majesty was not learned in the law, he should leave legal matters to judges and lawyers. Nov. 13, 1608.

102. Swear not, neither by heaven, neither by the earth, neither by any other oath. But let your yea be yea, and your nay, nay.

New Testament, *James* 5:12. Often invoked by religious persons in courts as a justification for not swearing on a Bible and in opposition to loyalty or other oath requirements.

103. Laws provide against injury from others. God himself will not save men against their wills.

Thomas Jefferson (1743-1826), 3rd President of the United States (Democratic Republican-VA). *Notes on Religion*, Oct. 1776.

104. Juries are not qualified to *judge* questions of *law*, but they are very capable of judging questions of *fact*.

Thomas Jefferson. Letter to M. L'Abbé Arnoud, July 19, 1789.

105. This business of removing judges by impeachment is a bungling way.

Thomas Jefferson. Remark after the impeachment of John Pickering of New Hampshire, 1804.

106. A strict observance of the written laws is doubtless *one* of the high duties of a good citizen, but it is not *the highest*. The laws of necessity, of self preservation, of saving the country when in danger, are of higher obligation.

Thomas Jefferson. Letter to John B. Colvin, Sept. 20, 1810.

107. Our judges are as honest as other men and not more so. They have, with others, the same passions for party, for power, and the privilege of their corps.

Thomas Jefferson. Letter to William Charles Jarvis, Sept. 28, 1820.

108. The great object of my fear is the Federal Judiciary. That body, like gravity, ever acting, with noiseless foot, and alarming advance ... is engulfing insidiously the special governments *[the states]* into the jaws of that which feeds them.

Thomas Jefferson. Letter to Spencer Roane, Mar. 9, 1821.

109. There is an international law just as there has always been a law against theft, but because the thief gets away with his booty at times is no reason why we should say that the law against theft has been abrogated.

Hiram W. Johnson (1866-1945), Governor of California (R), U.S. Senator (R and Progressive-CA), and founder, Progressive Party. Statement, Senate Foreign Relations Committee meeting, 1936.

110. Law is the greatest human invention. All the rest give man mastery over his world, but law gives him mastery over himself.

Lyndon B. Johnson (1908-1973), 36th President of the United States (D-TX). Speech, Conference on World Peace Through Law, Washington, DC, Sept. 16, 1965.

111. One precedent creates another. They soon accumulate and constitute law. What yesterday was fact, today is doctrine.

Junius (Prob. Philip Francis) (1740-1818), British writer (Whig). Dedication, *Letters*, "To the English Nation," Jan. 1769.

112. Law is the strongest link between man and freedom.

John F. Kennedy (1917-1963), 35th President of the United States (D-MA). Law Day proclamation, May 1, 1961.

113. Americans are free ... to disagree with the law, but not to disobey it.

John F. Kennedy. Speech, Sept. 30, 1962.

114. There comes a time when a moral man can't obey a law which his conscience tells him is unjust. And the important thing is that when he does that, he willingly accepts the penalty.

Martin Luther King, Jr. (1929-1968), American clergyman and civil rights leader. In reference to segregated buses. Speech, Montgomery, AL, Dec. 21, 1956.

115. The legal system is a lousy way to handle a great political quarrel.

Morton Kondrake, American political journalist. NBC, *The McLaughlin Group*, May 6, 1989.

116. It is the judge's role to resolve grievances and the role of the legislature to supply the answers for the social and economic problems facing the community.

Shirley Wohl Kram, Federal Judge. Senate confirmation hearing, Feb. 23, 1983.

117. The law has no claim to human respect; its only purpose is to protect exploitation.

Peter A. Kropotkin (1842-1921), Russian prince and anarchist. *Memoirs of a Revolutionist*, 1899.

118. Where is the society that does not struggle along under the dead weight of tradition and law inherited from its grandfathers?
Suzanne La Follette (1893-1983), American politician and writer. *Concerning Women*, 1926.

119. It is ingrained into our national life that the rule of law makes us free.
Patrick J. Leahy, U.S. Senator (D-VT). Senate address, Mar. 4, 1988.

120. Extreme law is extreme injury. (*Summum jus, summa injuria.*)
Legal maxim.

121. Custom is the best interpreter of the law. (*Consuetudo est optima legum interpres.*)
Legal maxim.

122. Ancient custom has the force of law. (*Vetustas pro lege semper habetur.*)
Legal maxim.

123. Where there is a right, there is a remedy. (*Ubu jus, ibi remedium.*)
Legal maxim.

124. The king ought not to be under any man, but under God and under the law, for the law makes the king. (*Rex non debet esse sub homine sed sub Deo et lege, quia lex facit regem.*)
Legal maxim.

125. The Supreme Court has acted as the final barricade against the assaults of democratic majorities.
Max Lerner, American journalist and historian. *Ideas Are Weapons*, 1939.

126. More rogues than honest men find shelter under habeas corpus.
Abraham Lincoln (1809-1865), 16th President of the United States (R-IL). Quoted on PBS, *The Civil War*, Sept. 23, 1990.

127. Wherever law ends, tyranny begins.
John Locke (1632-1704), English philosopher. *Second Treatise on Government*, 1690.

128. I have been told that there is no precedent for admitting a woman to practice in the Supreme Court of the United States. The glory of each generation is to make its own precedents.
Belva Ann Lockwood (1830-1917), American attorney and cofounder, Equal Rights Party. Quoted in Mary Virginia Fox, *Lady for the Defense*, 1975.

129. The Germans *[in America]* could create a civil order which would liberate America from the chains and confusion of the near-dying English law which is a mockery of the young Republic, and striking testimony to American inefficiency.
Franz Loeher (1818-1892), German political journalist. *History and Situation of the Germans in America*, 1847.

130. It is legal because I wish it.
Louis XIV (1638-1715), King of France. Statement.

131. When a prince is wrong, are his people bound to follow him then also? I answer, No, for it is not one's duty to do wrong.
Martin Luther (1483-1546), German Protestant theologian. *Secular Authority: To What Extent It Should Be Obeyed.*

132. The Habeas Corpus Act is the most stringent curb that ever legislation imposed on tyranny.
Thomas Babington Macaulay, 1st Baron Macaulay (1800-1859), historian and Secretary of War, Great Britain (Liberal). *History of England*, I, 1848.

133. The judges must be many, for, if few, they will always follow the behests of the few.
Niccolò Machiavelli (1469-1527), Florentine statesman and political philosopher. *Discourses on the First Ten Books of Livy*, 1531.

134. All new laws, though penned with the greatest technical skill, and passed on the fullest and most mature deliberation, are considered as more or less obscure and equivocal, until their meaning be liquidated and ascertained by a series of particular discussions and adjudications.
James Madison (1751-1836), 4th President of the United States (Democratic Republican-VA). *The Federalist*, No. 37, Jan. 11, 1788.

135. The rules of legal interpretation are rules of common sense, adopted by the courts in the construction of the laws.
James Madison. *The Federalist*, No. 83, 1788.

136. To none will we sell, to none deny or delay, right or justice.
Magna Carta, 1215.

137. No freeman shall be taken, or imprisoned, or disseized, or outlawed, or exiled, or in any way harmed, nor will we go upon or send upon him, save by the lawful judgment of his peers or by the law of the land.
Magna Carta, 1215.

138. Natural law is not a written law.... Natural law is the ensemble of things to do and not to do ... *from the simple fact that man is man*, nothing else being taken into account.
Jacques Maritain (1882-1973), philosopher and Ambassador of France to the Holy See. *The Rights of Man*, 1944.

139. It is emphatically the province and duty of the judicial department to say what the law is.
John Marshall (1755-1835), Chief Justice, U.S. Supreme Court. *Marbury* v. *Madison*, 1803.

140. The very essence of civil liberty is the right of every individual to claim the protection of the laws whenever he receives an injury.
John Marshall. *Ibid.*

141. You have to be angry to write a dissent.
Thurgood Marshall, U.S. Supreme Court Justice. Interview, ABC, *Nightline*, June 27, 1991.

142. Every person within this jurisdiction, whether inhabitant or foreigner, shall enjoy the same justice and law that is general for the plantation, which we constitute and execute one toward another without partiality or delay.
Massachusetts Body of Liberties, No. 2, 1641.

143. All constitutional laws are binding on all the people, in the new States and in the old ones, whether they consent to be bound by them or not.
John McKinley (1780-1852), U.S. Supreme Court Justice. *Pollard* v. *Hagan*, 1845.

144. Strength in Law *[or: Force within Law]* (*Kraft im Recht.*)
Klemens von Metternich (1773-1859), Austrian statesman and diplomat. Motto for his personal coat of arms.

145. In Germany, under the law everything is prohibited except that which is permitted. In France, under the law everything is permitted except that which is prohibited. In the Soviet Union, everything is prohibited including that which is permitted. And in Italy, under the law everything is permitted, especially that which is prohibited.
Newton N. Minow, Chairman, Federal Communications Commission. Quoted in *Time*, Mar. 18, 1985.

146. When is conduct a crime, and when is a crime not a crime? When somebody up there – a monarch, a dictator, a Pope, a legislator – so decrees.
Jessica Mitford, British writer and critic. *Kind and Unusual Punishment*, 1971.

147. All laws are promulgated for this end: that every man may know his duty; and therefore the plainest and most obvious sense of the words is that which must be put upon them.
Thomas More (1478-1535), Speaker of the House of Commons and Lord Chancellor of England. *Utopia*, 1516.

148. *[The Utopians]* have no lawyers among them, for they consider them as a sort of people whose profession it is to disguise matters.
Thomas More. *Ibid.*

149. Jury service is a duty as well as a privilege of citizenship; it is a duty that cannot be shirked on a plea of inconvenience or decreased earning power.
Frank Murphy (1890-1959), Governor of Michigan (D), U.S. Attorney General, and U.S. Supreme Court Justice. *Thiel* v. *Southern Pacific Co.*, 1945.

150. The *[English]* constitution does not allow reasons of state to influence our *[the judges']* judgment. God forbid that it should. We must not regard political consequences, however formidable they may be.
William Murray, 1st Earl of Mansfield (1705-1793), Lord Chief Justice of Great Britain. *Rex* v. *Wilkes*, 1770.

151. Give your decisions, never your reasons; your decisions may be right, your reasons are sure to be wrong.
William Murray. Advice to Middle Temple barristers, 1790.

152. We can only escape the arbitrariness of the judge by placing ourselves under the despotism of the law.
Napoléon I (1769-1821), military leader and Emperor of France. *Maxims*.

153. My code *[the Code Napoléon]* alone, from its simplicity, has been more beneficial to France than the whole mass of laws which preceded it.
Napoléon I. 1815.

154. Our chief justices have probably had more profound and lasting influences on their times and on the direction of the nation than most presidents.
Richard M. Nixon, 37th President of the United States (R-CA). Speech, May 21, 1969.

155. The only way that justice can truly be done in any society is for each member of that society to subject himself to the rule of law – neither to set himself above the law in the name of justice nor to set

himself outside the law in the name of justice.

Richard M. Nixon. Speech, National Conference of the Judiciary, Mar. 11, 1972.

156. When the president does it, that means it is not illegal.

Richard M. Nixon. Quoted on PBS, *The Secret Government*, Sept. 14, 1988.

157. Monopoly, special privilege, the interests of predatory selfishness have lost their old commanding influence at the White House and Capitol. They are making their last stand in the federal courts. There too often they still have their way.

George W. Norris (1861-1944), U.S. Congressman and U.S. Senator (R and Independent Republican-NE). Quoted in *The New York Times Magazine*, May 30, 1937.

158. Yet that we may not appear defective in earthly honors, let a day be solemnly set apart for proclaiming the charter; let it be brought forth, placed on the divine law, the work of God; let a crown be placed thereon, by which the world may know that so far as we approve of monarchy, in America the law is king.

Thomas Paine (1737-1809), American political philosopher. *Common Sense*, Jan. 10, 1776.

159. A judge is not supposed to know anything about the facts of life until they have been presented in evidence and explained to him at least three times.

Hubert Lister Parker (1900-1972), Lord Chief Justice of Great Britain. Quoted in *The Observer*, Mar. 12, 1961.

160. Justice is justly represented Blind, because she sees no Difference in the Parties concerned. She has but one Scale and Weight, for Rich and Poor, Great and Small. Her sentence is not guided by the Person, but by the Cause.

William Penn (1644-1718), founder of Pennsylvania. *Some Fruits of Solitude, in Reflections and Maxims*, 1693.

161. Our Law says well, to delay Justice is Injustice.

William Penn. *Ibid*.

162. The essential principle contained in the actual notion of an illegal act ... is that reparation must, as far as possible, wipe out all the consequences of the illegal act and reestablish the situation which would, in all probability, have existed if that act had not been committed.

Permanent Court of International Justice. *Case Concerning the Factory at Chorzow*, 1928.

163. There is a written and an unwritten law. The one by which we regulate our constitutions in our cities is the written law; that which arises from custom is the unwritten law.

Plato (427-347 B.C.), Greek philosopher. Quoted by Diogenes Laertius, *Plato*, 51.

164. The Law is a light.

Old Testament, *Proverbs* 6:23.

165. A judge is not measured by his capacity to come up with instant answers to impromptu questions. Judges should not and do not behave like legislators, or anyone else who is free to commit himself to a reason apart from the merits.

William H. Rehnquist, Chief Justice, U.S. Supreme Court. In reference to the Senate confirmation process for federal judges. *Roll Call*, Sept. 11, 1988.

166. You can't hardly find a law school in this country that don't, through some inherent weakness in the school, turn out a Senator or Congressman from time to time – or if their rating is real low, even a President.

Will Rogers (1879-1935), American humorist. Quoted on PBS, *Will Rogers U.S.A.*, Oct. 3, 1988.

167. Where there is no law there is no transgression.

New Testament, *Romans* 4:15.

168. We want a Supreme Court which will do justice under the Constitution – not over it. In our courts we want a government of laws and not of men.

Franklin D. Roosevelt (1882-1945), 32nd President of the United States (D-NY). Address, Mar. 9, 1937.

169. We cannot yield our constitutional destiny to the personal judgment of a few men who, fearful of the future, would deny us the necessary means of dealing with the present.

Franklin D. Roosevelt. In reference to the Supreme Court. Fireside Chat, 1937.

170. When a judge decides a Constitutional question, when he decides what the people as a whole can or cannot do, the people should have the right to recall that decision if they think it wrong.

Theodore Roosevelt (1858-1919), 26th President of the United States (R-NY). Speech, "A Charter of Democracy," Ohio Constitutional Convention, Columbus, OH, 1912.

171. Law is a very good thing for men with property and a very bad thing for men without property.

Jean-Jacques Rousseau (1712-1778), French philosopher. *The Social Contract*, 1762.

172. I would say that about one-third of all the new members we get join because of the *[impeachment]* campaign against Earl Warren.
John H. Rousselot, U.S. Congressman (R-CA) and Publicity Director, John Birch Society. Quoted in Earl Katcher, *Earl Warren: A Political Biography*, 1967.

173. The President is not above the law. Nor does he contend that he is. What he *[Richard M. Nixon]* does contend is that as President the law can be applied to him in only one way, and that is by impeachment.
James D. St. Clair, special counsel to President Nixon. Oral argument before the Supreme Court, July 8, 1974.

174. The reason of any Law is, that no Man's Will should be a Law.
George Savile, 1st Marquess of Halifax (1633-1695), Lord Privy Seal of England. *Political Thoughts and Reflections*, 1750.

175. If the Laws could speak for themselves, they would complain of the Lawyers in the first place.
George Savile. *Ibid*.

176. A Prince that exalts his own *Authority* above his *Laws*, is like letting in his *Enemy* to surprise his *Guards*: The *Laws* are the only Guards he can be sure will never run away from him.
George Savile. *Maxims of State*, No. 2.

177. Reverence for life is the highest court of appeal.
Albert Schweitzer (1875-1965), French philosopher, musician, and physician. *The Philosophy of Civilization*, 1923.

178. There is no liberty if the judiciary power be not separated from the legislative and executive. Were it joined with the legislative, the life and liberty of the subject would be exposed to arbitrary control; for the judge would then be the legislator. Were it joined to the executive power, the judge might behave with violence and oppression.
Charles-Louis de Secondat, Baron de La Brède et de Montesquieu (1689-1755), French writer. *The Spirit of the Laws*, XXV, 2, 1748.

179. Generally to pretend Conscience against Law is dangerous; in some Cases haply we may.
John Selden (1584-1654), English jurist and Member of Long Parliament. *Table-Talk: Conscience*.

180. The King's Oath is not security enough for our Property, for he swears to Govern according to Law; now the judges they interpret the Law; and what Judges can be made to do we know.
John Selden. *Table-Talk: The King*.

181. A man may plead not guilty, and yet tell no Lie; for by the Law, no Man is bound to accuse himself; so that when I say Not Guilty, the meaning is, as if I should say by way of paraphrase, I am not so guilty as to tell you; if you will bring me to a Trial, and have me punished for this you lay to my Charge, prove it against me.
John Selden. *Table-Talk: Law*.

182. Some laws, though unwritten, are more firmly established than all the written laws.
Lucius Annaeus Seneca (The Elder) (54 B.C.-A.D.39), Roman orator and rhetorician. *Controversiae*.

183. We must not make a scarecrow of the law,
Setting it up to fear the birds of prey,
And let it keep one shape, till custom make it
Their perch and not their terror.
William Shakespeare (1564-1616), English writer. *Measure for Measure*, ii, 1.

184. The jury, passing on the prisoner's life,
May in the sworn twelve have a thief or two
Guiltier than him they try.
William Shakespeare. English writer. *Measure for Measure*, ii, 1.

185. The majesty and power of law and justice.
William Shakespeare. *II King Henry IV*, v, ii.

186. The first thing we do, let's kill all the lawyers.
William Shakespeare. *King Henry VI*, Pt. 2, iv, 1.

187. Law, in a democracy, means the protection of the rights and liberties of the minority.
Alfred E. Smith (1873-1944), Governor of New York (D). 1920.

188. The right to enjoy property without unlawful deprivation, no less than the right to speak out or the right to travel, is, in truth, a "personal" right.
Potter Stewart (1915-1985), U.S. Supreme Court Justice. *Lynch* v. *Household Finance Corporation*, 1972.

189. Property exists by force of the law. It is not a fact, but a legal fiction.
Max Stirner (Johann Kaspar Schmidt) (1806-1856), German anarchist. *The Ego and His Own*, 1845.

190. Corruption abounding in the commonwealth, the commonwealth abounded in laws.
Cornelius Tacitus (c.55-c.117), Roman historian. *Annals of the Julian Emperors*, III.

191. Presidents come and go, but the Supreme Court goes on forever.
William H. Taft (1857-1930), 27th President of the

United States (R-OH) and Chief Justice, U.S. Supreme Court. Attributed.

192. Take, for instance, the four places likely to be filled by Wilson's successor on the Supreme Court. Think of the danger of another Brandeis and Clark. The power and usefulness of that Court would be broken down under such appointments if the majority of the Court were to be made up of them.

William H. Taft. Written to Republican Senators in support of Warren G. Harding as President. Sept. 8, 1920.

193. We will kill you with legality.

Louis-Adolphe Thiers (1797-1877), 1st President of the Third French Republic. Remark to Comte Arman de Polignac, Jan. 1830.

194. It is not desirable to cultivate a respect for the law, so much as for the right. The only obligation which I have a right to assume is to do at any time what I think is right.

Henry David Thoreau (1817-1862), American philosopher and naturalist. *On the Duty of Civil Disobedience*, 1849.

195. The man for whom law exists – the man of forms, the conservative – is a tame man.

Henry David Thoreau. *Journal*, Mar. 30, 1851.

196. The law will never make men free; it is men who have got to make the law free.

Henry David Thoreau. *Slavery in Massachusetts*, 1854.

197. Problems of definition are what laws are about.

Richard Thornburgh, U.S. Attorney General and Governor of Pennsylvania (R). Interview, CNN, *Evans & Novak*, July 8, 1989.

198. The law is good if a man use it lawfully.

New Testament, *Timothy* 1:8.

199. *[Lawyers are]* ... the democratic aristocracy *[of America]*.

Alexis de Tocqueville (1805-1859), French writer. *Democracy in America*, 1835.

200. Scarcely any question arises in the United States which does not, sooner or later, become the subject of judicial debate.

Alexis de Tocqueville. *Ibid.*

201. Whenever you put a man on the Supreme Court he ceases to be your friend.

Harry S Truman (1884-1972), 33rd President of the United States (D-MO). Quoted in *The New York Times*, May 8, 1959.

202. In the United States we have a society pervaded from top to bottom by contempt for the law.

Barbara Tuchman (1912-1989), American historian. *Newsweek*, July 12, 1976.

203. One puts on black robes to scare white people, while the other puts on white robes to scare the hell out of blacks.

Morris K. Udall, U.S. Congressman (D-AZ). Comparison between judges and the Ku Klux Klan. Speech, Gridiron Club, Washington, DC, Mar. 27, 1982.

204. Limit as you will the sovereign power in a State, no law is capable of hindering a tyrant from abusing the powers conferred on him by his place.

Marquis de Vauvenargues (1715-1747), French soldier and moralist. *Réflexions et Maximes*.

205. No man shall be twise sentenced by Civill Justice for one and the same Crime, offence, or Trespasse.

Nathaniel Ward (c.1578-1652), Puritan codifier. *The Massachusetts Body of Liberties*, 1641.

206. Our system of justice will not be adequate unless every state in the Union requires a man to be given counsel if he does not have it.

Earl Warren (1891-1974), Chief Justice, U.S. Supreme Court, and Governor of California (R). Remark, San Francisco Bar Association, 1954.

207. Interminable and unjustifiable delays in our courts are today compromising the legal rights of thousands of Americans and imperceptibly corroding the foundations of constitutional government in the United States.

Earl Warren. Speech, Conference of Chief State Justices, 1958.

208. Too often we find people who believe fervently in that portion of the rule of law that protects them ... but who are intolerant of that portion which protects other people.

Earl Warren. 1963.

209. The Supreme Court must be recognized as the keystone of our political fabric.

George Washington (1732-1799), 1st President of the United States (VA). Letter to John Jay inviting him to be U.S. Supreme Court Chief Justice, Oct. 5, 1789.

210. The very idea of the power and the right of the People to establish Government presupposes the duty of every individual to obey the established Government.

George Washington. Farewell address, Sept. 17, 1796.

211. Whatever government is not a government of laws, is a despotism, let it be called what it may.

Daniel Webster (1782-1852), U.S. Congressman (Federalist-NH and MA), U.S. Senator (Federalist and Whig-MA), and U.S. Secretary of State. Speech at a public dinner honoring George Washington's centennial birthday, Bangor, ME, Feb. 22, 1832.

212. This court will not deny the equal protection of the law to the unwashed, unshod, unkempt, and uninhibited.

Herman Weinkrantz, New York City Judge. Quoted in *The New York Times*, July 1, 1968.

213. We're the only branch of government that explains itself in writing every time it makes a decision.

Byron R. White, U.S. Supreme Court Justice. Quoted in *Time*, Oct. 8, 1984.

214. An incompetent attorney can delay a trial for years or months. A competent attorney can delay one even longer.

Evelle J. Younger, Attorney General, California. Quoted in *The Los Angeles Times*, Mar. 3, 1971.

Chapter 54

Law Enforcement and Crime

1. You can go much further with a kind word and a gun than with a kind word alone.

   Law enforcement maxim, pre-statehood Arizona.

2. AMNESTY – AN ACT THROUGH WHICH SOVEREIGNS FORGIVE THE INJUSTICES THEY HAVE COMMITTED

   Poster displayed at the Paris School of Fine Arts during the student uprising, May 1968.

3. He *[Richard M. Nixon]* told us he was going to take crime out of the streets. He did. He took it into the damn White House.

   Ralph Abernathy, American clergyman and Director, Southern Christian Leadership Conference. Remark, 1973.

4. Drug people are the very vermin of humanity.... Occasionally we must adopt their dress and tactics.

   Miles J. Ambrose, Special Attorney General, U.S. Office of Drug Abuse. Defense of illegal and questionable law enforcement tactics, 1973.

5. The essence and almost the quintessence of good government is to protect property and its rights.... The major business of government becomes, therefore, the problem of keeping in due subjection to law and order the dangerous mass of poor and vicious.

   Fisher Ames (1758-1808), U.S. Congressman (Federalist-MA). *Works*, 1809.

6. Written laws are like spiders' webs and will, like them, only entangle and hold the poor and weak, while the rich and powerful easily break through them.

   Anarcharsis (c.600 B.C.), Scythian philosopher. Quoted by Plutarch, *The Parallel Lives: Solon*.

7. Law has the power to compel: indeed, the ability to enforce is a condition of the ability to command.

   Thomas Aquinas (c.1225-1274), Italian scholastic philosopher. *Summa Theologica*, I, 2.

8. Good laws, if they are not obeyed, do not constitute good government.

   Aristotle (384-322 B.C.), Greek philosopher and teacher. *Politics*.

9. Trying to solve the crime problem by building more prison cells is like trying to solve the problem of AIDS by building more hospitals.

   James Austin, Director of Research, National Council on Crime and Delinquency. Quoted in *The Washington Post*, Apr. 14, 1988.

10. Lay no burden on the public which the majority cannot bear.

    Babylonian Talmud, *Baba Bathra* 60b.

11. Gentlemen, you are trampling on the sovereignty of this great state.... You are destroying the Constitution of this great nation.... May God have mercy on your souls.

    Ross Barnett, Governor of Mississippi (D). Comment addressing federal officials enforcing a court order integrating the University of Mississippi. Speech, Sept. 1962.

12. It is better to prevent crimes than to punish them.

    Caesare Bonesana di Beccaria (1738-1794), Italian political and economic writer. *Dei Dilitti e Delle Pene*, 1764.

13. Why does everyone think that he can be decent enough without the policeman, but that the club is needed for "the others"?

    Alexander Berkman (1870-1936), American anarchist. *What Is Communist Anarchism?*, 1920.

14. Without the burden on the police to adhere to the requirements of the Fourth Amendment, you loose the dogs.

Joseph R. Biden, Jr., U.S. Senator (D-DE). Remark to Nat Hentoff, 1986. Quoted in *The Washington Post*, Oct. 8, 1988.

15. My chief constructive work was devoted to securing a system by which I could compel the body of men under me – against its old custom and obvious self-interest – really to enforce the law.
Theodore A. Bingham (1858-1934), Police Commissioner, New York City. *McClure's Magazine*, Nov. 1909.

16. It goes without saying that a law to be valid must be clear enough to make its commands understandable.
Hugo L. Black (1886-1971), U.S. Senator (D-AL) and U.S. Supreme Court Justice. *Barenblatt* v. *United States*, 1958 (dissent).

17. It is better that ten guilty persons escape than one innocent suffer.
William Blackstone (1723-1780), British jurist. *Commentaries on the Laws of England*, I, 1765.

18. The statutes are never enforced, but legislators, who would be aghast at any enforcement effort, nevertheless often refuse to repeal them.
Robert H. Bork, U.S. Solicitor General and Judge, U.S. Court of Appeals, Washington, DC. Comment on many statutes covering personal sexual activity. *The Tempting of America*, 1991.

19. The government may set decoys to entrap criminals. But it may nor provoke or create a crime, and then punish the criminal, its creature.
Louis D. Brandeis (1856-1941), U.S. Supreme Court Justice. *Casey* v. *United States*, 1927.

20. Society, by setting forth clear penalties for certain kinds of conduct sets its public ratification on moral judgments that this is wrong behavior and that it is deserving of punishment irrespective of whether the punishment will deter, rehabilitate or anything else. It is a way of society defining what is wrong and what is seriously wrong.
Edmund G. (Jerry) Brown, Jr., Governor of California (D). *Thoughts*, 1976.

21. Obedience to the law is itself a moral duty.
Benjamin N. Cardozo (1870-1938), U.S. Supreme Court Justice. *People* v. *Schmidt* (NY), 1909.

22. The punishment of the wrongdoer is not designed as atonement for a crime; it is a solace to the individual who has suffered a private wrong.
Benjamin N. Cardozo. *Loucks* v. *Standard Oil Co.* (NY), 1911.

23. Crime is contagious.
Benjamin N. Cardozo. *Olmstead* v. *United States*, 1927.

24. The difference between rape and seduction is salesmanship.
Bill Carpenter, Mayor of Independence, MO. Quoted in *Newsweek*, July 16, 1990.

25. I see no reason why big-shot crooks should go free while the poor ones go to jail.
Jimmy Carter, 39th President of the United States (D-GA). Reaction to Gerald Ford's pardon of Richard Nixon. Presidential nomination acceptance speech, Democratic National Convention, 1976.

26. A State is not morally free to allow anarchy and license ... even if the majority should so desire.
Catholic Association for International Peace, *Timeless Rights*, 1948.

27. Obedience to laws can only be justly enforced on the certainty that those who are called on to obey them have had, either personally or by their representatives, the power to enact, amend, or repeal them.
Chartist petition, Great Britain, 1837.

28. I would fill the penitentiaries and jails of the United States so full of Trust magnates that their arms and legs would stick out the windows.
James B. (Champ) Clark (1850-1921), U.S. Congressman and Speaker of the House (D-MO). Quoted in Foster Rhea Dulles, *The United States Since 1865*, 1959.

29. Who will protect the public when the police violate the law?
Ramsey Clark, U.S. Attorney General (D). Remark after the Democratic National Convention, Chicago, IL, Aug. 1968.

30. The people become more observant of justice, and do not refuse to submit to the laws when they see them obeyed by their enactor.
Claudian (c.365-c.408), Roman poet. *De Quarto Consulatu Honorii Augusti Panegyris*.

31. Oppressive government is more terrible than tigers.
Confucius (551-479 B.C.), Chinese philosopher. *Analects*.

32. The terrorist and the policeman both come from the same basket.
Joseph Conrad (1857-1924), British writer. *The Secret Agent*, 1907.

33. It is the duty of a citizen not only to observe the law but to let it be known that he is opposed to its violation.
Calvin Coolidge (1872-1933), 30th President of the United States (R-MA). Message to Congress, Dec. 6, 1923.

34. Instead of a government of law we have a government of lawlessness. Against the continuation of such a condition I enter my solemn protest.
Calvin Coolidge. Comment on the abuses of investigatory probes of big business by Congress. Quoted in Edward Bennett Williams, *One Man's Freedom*, 1962.

35. We have a great many chiefs and headmen but, be they ever so great, they must all abide by the laws.... These laws are not made for any person in particular but for all.
Creek Indian Nation, Declaration of Policy and Law, Tuckabatchee, AL, 1824.

36. I would rather risk myself in an Indian fight than venture among these creatures after night. God deliver me from such constituents or from a party supported by such.
David Crockett (1786-1836), U.S. Congressman (D-TN). Comment on Martin Van Buren's political stronghold, the sixth ward, in New York City. Remark to S. D. Jackson, 1834.

37. The criminal justice system is not working, and people want something that works.
Mario Cuomo, Governor of New York (D). Quoted in *The Washington Post*, June 27, 1989.

38. The policeman isn't there to create disorder, the policeman is there to preserve disorder.
Richard J. Daley (1902-1976), Mayor of Chicago, IL (D). Statement on riots during the Democratic National Convention, Aug. 1968.

39. *[Police]* officers fought so hard for career advancement that they had little time for fighting crime.
Robert Daley, Deputy Police Commissioner, New York City. "That's Me Behind the Machine Gun," *The New York Times*, Aug. 19, 1990.

40. The man who was excellent, I rewarded him well; who was evil, I punished him well.
Darius I (The Great) (549-485 B.C.), King of Persia. *The Beihistun Inscription*.

41. There are too many people with a Father Flanagan philosophy that there is no such thing as a bad boy. There are plenty of bad boys.
Edward M. Davis, Chief of Police, Los Angeles, CA. Quoted in *The Los Angeles Herald-Examiner*, Feb. 27, 1975.

42. The lifeblood of organized crime is gambling, and although I have no scruples about a couple of fellows making a wager, the fact of the matter is that organized crime thrives on illicit income from gambling.
Edward M. Davis. Quoted in *The National Observer*, July 19, 1975.

43. Ye shall not do ... every man what is right in his own eyes.
Old Testament, *Deuteronomy* 12:8.

44. I don't hang anyone – the law does.
Marshal Matt Dillon, *Gunsmoke*, 1950's.

45. The Bible says you should keep the Sabbath day holy. Well, in the Bible the penalty for not doing so is death. We don't go that far. We just give you a summons.
Joseph S. DiMaria, borough attorney, Paramus, NJ. Comment on local "blue laws." Quoted in *Governing*, Oct. 1988.

46. What is crime among the multitude is only vice among the few.
Benjamin Disraeli, 1st Earl of Beaconsfield (1804-1881), Prime Minister of Great Britain (Conservative). *Tancred*, 1847.

47. It is better, so the Fourth Amendment teaches us, that the guilty sometimes go free than the citizens be subject to easy arrest.
William O. Douglas (1898-1980), U.S. Supreme Court Justice. *Henry* v. *United States*, 1959.

48. An arrest is not justified by what the subsequent search discloses.
William O. Douglas. *Ibid*.

49. Every time there is a perceived crisis, law-enforcement agencies and legislators overreact, and usually due process and civil liberties suffer.
Don Edwards, U.S. Congressman (D-CA). Quoted in *The New York Times*, June 3, 1990.

50. I cannot imagine any set of circumstances that would ever induce me to send federal troops ... to enforce the orders of a federal court, because I believe the common sense of Americans will never require it.
[Later that year he sent federal troops to Little Rock, AR, to enforce a desegregation order.]
Dwight D. Eisenhower (1890-1969), 34th President of the United States (R-KS). Statement, July 1957.

51. Good men must not obey the laws too well.
Ralph Waldo Emerson (1803-1882), American writer. *Essays*, Second Series: "Politics," 1876.

52. The real answer to the problem of crime committed by persons on bail, and indeed the solution to the general problem of crime, lies not in preventive detention of individuals presumed innocent, but in the speedy trial of the accused and the swift and sure punishment of the guilty.
Samuel J. Ervin, Jr. (1896-1985), U.S. Congressman and U.S. Senator (D-NC). Oct. 16, 1969.

53. In other words, in order to capture criminals, the law enforcement agencies must act criminally – a little lawbreaking does wonders for law and order.
Samuel J. Ervin, Jr.. Comment on the Omnibus Crime Bill, May 10, 1973.

54. Law is not self-executing. Unfortunately, at times its execution rests in the hands of those who are faithless to it. And even when its enforcement is committed to those who revere it, law merely deters some human beings from offending, and punishes other human beings for offending. This does not make men good. This task can be performed only by ethics or religion or morality.
Samuel J. Ervin, Jr.. Statement on submitting the final report of the Senate Select Committee on Watergate, July 12, 1974.

55. In many parts of Italy the only revolutionary factor would be the full application of the rule of law.
Giovanni Falcone, prosecutor, Palermo, Italy, and Mafia fighter. Press conference, 1989.

56. What we had to do was to make it more dangerous for the federal government *not* to enforce federal law.
James Farmer, National Director, Congress of Racial Equality. Explanation of his civil rights strategy in the 1947 "Journey of Reconciliation." Quoted in Juan Williams, *Eye on the Prize*, 1986.

57. If I do nothing else, I'm going to make this a safe state.
Dianne Feinstein, Mayor of San Francisco, CA (D). Gubernatorial campaign speech. Quoted in *The New York Times Magazine*, Sept. 30, 1990.

58. A convict is not to be scourged until the flesh fall from his body and he die under the lash, though he may have committed a hundred offenses, for each of which, separately, a whipping of twenty stripes might be inflicted.
Stephen J. Field (1816-1899), U.S. Supreme Court Justice. *O'Neil* v. *Vermont*, 1891.

59. If you're riding down somewhere, and a cop stops you and starts to put you under arrest, even though you haven't committed any crime, go to jail. Mississippi is not the place to start conducting constitutional law classes for the policemen, many of whom don't have a fifth-grade education.
James Forman, Executive Director, Student Non-Violent Coordinating Committee. Advice to Mississippi civil rights workers, 1964.

60. He must be a bold man indeed who is confident that he knows what causes crime.
Felix Frankfurter (1882-1965), U.S. Supreme Court Justice. *Winters* v. *New York*, 1947.

61. Human nature is weak enough and sufficiently beset by temptations without government adding to them and generating crime.
Felix Frankfurter. *Sherman* v. *United States*, 1957.

62. My twenty-six years experience as a police officer and official, including command of two police districts, tells me that unfortunately the only short-term response that can counter the on-street violence and offer neighborhoods relief from crime and drugs is aggressive law enforcement.... Cities and states have made police the institution of first response rather than of last resort in addressing this crisis.
Isaac Fulwood, Jr., Chief of Police, Washington, DC. *The Washington Post*, Dec. 31, 1990.

63. Nonviolence implies voluntary submission to the penalty for noncooperation with evil.
Mohandas K. Gandhi (1869-1948), Indian political and spiritual leader. Speech, Mar. 23, 1922.

64. The choice is de Gaulle or anarchy.
Charles de Gaulle (1890-1970), President of France. Campaign speech, 1968.

65. He who murders a black man shall be hanged.... He who robs the black man of his liberty or his property shall be punished like other criminals.
Joshua Reed Giddings (1795-1864), U.S. Congressman (Anti-Slavery Whig-OH) and Consul General to the British North American Provinces (Canada). Senate debate, 1859.

66. All lawyers are the natural enemies of the police.
Michael Gilbert, British crime novelist. *Blood and Judgment*, 1959.

67. If you hang them all, you will get the guilty. But that's not the American way of doing things.
Ira Glasser, Executive Director, American Civil Liberties Union. Quoted in *Governing the States and Localities*, Feb. 1988.

68. Today there's law and order in everything. You can't beat anybody for nothing. If you do beat anyone, it's got to be for the sake of order.
Maxim Gorky (1868-1936), Russian writer. *The Lower Depths*, 1903.

69. The FBI would rather be a little heavy handed than empty handed.
Kenneth de Graffenreid, Intelligence Director, National Security Agency. Interview, ABC, *This Week*, July 30, 1989.

70. I know of no method to secure the repeal of bad or obnoxious laws so effective as their stringent execution.
Ulysses S. Grant (1822-1885), 18th President of the United States (R-OH). First inaugural address, Mar. 4, 1869.

71. Let no guilty man escape, if it can be avoided. No personal considerations should stand in the way of performing a public duty.
Ulysses S. Grant. Instructions to federal officers investigating the Whiskey Ring, July 29, 1875.

72. We all must follow the rule of law, not the rule of aldermen.
Harvey Grossman, attorney, American Civil Liberties Union. Comment when three Chicago aldermen demanded that a painting they found offensive be removed from an art school. Quoted in *The New York Times*, June 25, 1988.

73. Police abuse is a constant problem.
Phil Gutis, national spokesman, American Civil Liberties Union. Quoted in *The Washington Post*, Mar. 8, 1991.

74. Well, summary executions would be very effective. But we have impediments – they're called the Constitution and due process. And we have a responsibility to uphold the Constitution.
Francis C. Hall, Commander, Narcotics Division, New York City Police Department. Response to suggestions that drug traffickers be summarily executed. Interview, *The New York Times*, Mar. 12, 1989.

75. Public safety is too important to be left to psychiatry.
Russell E. Hamill, Vice Chairman, Maryland Criminal Justice Coordinating Committee. Address on the role of psychiatrists in parole and prison furlough decisions. Quoted in *The Washington Post*, Nov. 27, 1988.

76. If a man destroy the eye of another man, they shall destroy his eye.
Hammurabi (c.1955-1913 B.C.), King of Babylon. *Code of Hammurabi*.

77. If it makes people mad, they'll forget it by 1990 *[the year he came up for reelection]*.
Jack Hampton, Texas Judge. Remark on giving a short sentence to a murderer on the grounds that the murder victim was gay. Quoted in *Newsweek*, Jan. 2, 1989.

78. For the middle class, the police protect property, give directions, and help old ladies. For the urban poor, the police are those who arrest you.
Michael Harrington (1928-1989), American writer and Socialist Party leader. *The Other America*, 1962.

79. The time for the State to protect himself against the criminal is before the criminal is made. Most criminals are not born, they are made.... What a State really punishes in a criminal is its own neglect, its own failure to do its duty to the citizens.
William Randolph Hearst (1863-1951), U.S. Congressman (D-NY); founder, Independence League Party; journalist; and publisher. Editorial, Apr. 1926.

80. I'm not against the police; I'm just afraid of them.
Alfred Hitchcock (1899-1980), British film director. Remark.

81. The aim of the law is not to punish sins but to prevent certain external results.
Oliver Wendell Holmes, Jr. (1841-1935), U.S. Supreme Court Justice. *Commonwealth* v. *Kennedy* (MA), 1897.

82. If public officers will infringe men's rights, they ought to pay greater damages than other men, to deter and hinder other officers from the like offences.
John Holt (1642-1710), Member of Parliament and Lord Chief Justice of the King's Bench, England. Judgment, *Ashby* v. *Aylesbury*, 1702.

83. Respect for law is fading from the sensibilities of our people. Twenty times as many people in proportion to the population are lawlessly killed in the United States as in Great Britain. There are fifty times as many robberies. Life and property are relatively more unsafe than in any civilized country in the world.
Herbert Hoover (1874-1964), 31st President of the United States (R-IA). Speech, Associated Press Luncheon, New York City, 1929.

84. Rigid and expeditious justice is the first safeguard of freedom, the basis of all ordered liberty, the vital force of progress.... Justice must not fail because the agencies of enforcement are either delinquent or inefficiently organized.

Herbert Hoover. Inaugural address, Mar. 4, 1929.

85. Law enforcement, however, in defeating the criminal, must maintain inviolate the historic liberties of the individual.

J. Edgar Hoover (1895-1972), Director, Federal Bureau of Investigation. *Iowa Law Review*, Winter 1952.

86. We *[the FBI]* are a fact-gathering organization only. We don't clear anybody. We don't condemn anybody..... The minute the FBI begins making recommendations on what should be done with its information, it becomes a Gestapo.

J. Edgar Hoover. Quoted in *Look*, June 14, 1956.

87. No amount of law enforcement can solve a problem that goes back to the family.

J. Edgar Hoover. Quoted on PBS, *America Goes to War*, Nov. 10, 1990.

88. The Director of the FBI is paid to take risks where the security of the country is at stake.... What Hoover is doing here is putting himself above the President.

Tom Charles Houston, presidential assistant (R). Memorandum to H. R. Haldeman on J. Edgar Hoover's refusal to cooperate with the Nixon "Houston Plan" of illegal surveillance of certain Americans, Aug. 5, 1970.

89. Laws that do not embody public opinion can never be enforced.

Frank McKinney (Kin) Hubbard (1868-1930), American caricaturist and writer. *Epigrams*.

90. There are not enough jails, not enough policemen, not enough courts to enforce a law not supported by the people.

Hubert H. Humphrey (1911-1978), Vice President of the United States and U.S. Senator (D-MN). Speech, Williamsburg, VA, May 1, 1965.

91. Woe unto them ... who acquit the guilty for a bribe, and deprive the innocent of his right!

Old Testament, *Isaiah* 5:22-23.

92. The laws of the United States must be executed. I have no discretionary power on this subject; my duty is emphatically pronounced in the Constitution.

Andrew Jackson (1767-1845), 7th President of the United States (D-TN). *Proclamation to the People of South Carolina*, Dec. 10, 1832.

93. The duty to disclose knowledge of crime rests upon all citizens.

Robert H. Jackson (1892-1954), U.S. Attorney General (D) and U.S. Supreme Court Justice. *Stein* v. *New York*, 1952-53.

94. I cannot say that our country could have no secret police without becoming totalitarian, but I can say with great conviction that it cannot become totalitarian without a centralized national police.

Robert H. Jackson. *The Supreme Court in the American System of Government*, 1955.

95. The prosecutor has more control over life, liberty, and reputation than any other person in America.

Robert H. Jackson. Quoted in *The Washington Post*, Aug. 26, 1990.

96. When any one state in the American union refuses obedience to the Confederation, by which they have bound themselves, the rest have a natural right to compel them to obedience.

Thomas Jefferson (1743-1826), 3rd President of the United States (Democratic Republican-VA). Written when the thirteen states were united only by the loose bonds of the Confederation, 1786.

97. The execution of the laws is more important than the making them.

Thomas Jefferson. Letter to Abbé Arnoud, July 19, 1789.

98. For them, an iota of forgiveness should not be given.

Jiang Zemin, Communist Party leader, China. In reference to leaders of the democratic protests in Tiananmen Square. June 28, 1989.

99. There is no American right to loot stores, or to burn buildings, or to fire rifles from the rooftops. That is crime – and crime must be dealt with forcefully and swiftly, and certainly – under law.

Lyndon B. Johnson (1908-1973), 36th President of the United States (D-TX). Television address to the nation on rioting in New York City, July 27, 1967.

100. Every society gets the kind of criminal it deserves. What is equally true is that every community gets the kind of law enforcement it insists on.

Robert F. Kennedy (1925-1968), U.S. Senator and U.S. Attorney General (D-NY). *The Pursuit of Justice*, 1964.

101. The agents are white southerners who have been influenced by the mores of the community. To maintain their status, they have to be friendly with the local police and people who have been promoting segregation.

Martin Luther King, Jr. (1929-1968), American clergyman and civil rights leader. Criticism of southern FBI agents for not enforcing civil rights laws and protecting blacks, Nov. 18, 1962.

102. When a criminal is in jail for two more years, the people are safe for two more years.
Edward I. Koch, U.S. Congressman and Mayor of New York City (D). Press conference, 1982.

103. We'll never have enough cops.
Edward I. Koch. Remark, 1983.

104. If God should punish men according to what they deserve, he would not leave on the back of the earth so much as a beast.
Koran, Sura 35.

105. The executive *[President]* could have saved the people from the appalling conditions which confront us today, if all the power of this government had been put forth to enforce the *[Sherman]* Anti-Trust law.
Robert M. La Follette (1855-1925), Governor of Wisconsin and U.S. Senator (R-WI). *Autobiography*, 1913.

106. The clemency of princes is often but an act of policy to win the affection of their subjects.
François de La Rochefoucauld (1613-1680), French nobleman and writer. *Réflexions ou Sentences et Maximes Morales*, 1665.

107. Do not favor the poor or show deference to the rich; judge your neighbor fairly.
Old Testament, *Leviticus* 19:15.

108. You shall not stand idly by the blood of your neighbor.
Old Testament, *Leviticus* 19:16.

109. You shall have one law for the stranger and citizen alike.
Old Testament, *Leviticus* 24:22.

110. Obviously crime pays, or there would be no crime.
G. Gordon Liddy, convicted Watergate conspirator. Quoted in *Newsweek*, Nov. 10, 1986.

111. Let every man remember that to violate the law is to trample on the blood of his father, and to tear the charter of his own and his children's liberty.
Abraham Lincoln (1809-1865), 16th President of the United States (R-IL). Speech, Springfield, IL, Jan. 27, 1837.

112. We must make good in essence as well as in form Madison's avowal that "the word *slave* ought not to appear in the Constitution"; and we must even go further and decree that only local law, and not that time-honored instrument *[the Constitution]*, shall shelter a slave-holder.
Abraham Lincoln. Speech, Bloomington, IN, May 29, 1856.

113. No law is stronger than is the public sentiment where it is to be enforced.
Abraham Lincoln. Letter to John J. Crittenden, Dec. 22, 1859.

114. It is as much the duty of government to render prompt justice against itself, in favor of citizens, as it is to administer the same between private individuals.
Abraham Lincoln. First annual message to Congress, Dec. 3, 1861.

115. If a king did not, without tiring, inflict punishment on those deserving to be punished, the stronger would roast the weaker like fish on a spit.
Code of Manu (India), c. 200 B.C.

116. You cannot control a free society by force.
Robert Mark, Commissioner, Scotland Yard, London. Quoted in *The Observer*, July 25, 1976.

117. It is better that Ten Suspected Witches should escape than that one Innocent Person should be condemned.
Increase Mather (1639-1723), Massachusetts clergyman. *Case of Conscience Concerning Evil Spirits*, 1693.

118. What constitutes a cruel and unusual punishment has not been exactly decided. It has been said that ordinarily the terms imply something inhuman and barbarous.
Joseph McKenna (1843-1926), U.S. Supreme Court Justice. *Weems* v. *United States*, 1909.

119. The purpose of punishment is fulfilled, crime is repressed by penalties of just, not tormenting, severity, its repetition is prevented, and hope is given for the reformation of the criminal.
Joseph McKenna. *Ibid.*

120. Courts, not mobs, must execute the penalties of the law.
William McKinley (1843-1901), 25th President of the United States (R-OH). Annual message to Congress, Dec. 5, 1899.

121. To punish the same act by the two governments *[state and federal]* would violate, not only the common principles of humanity, but would be repugnant to the nature of both governments.

John McLean (1785-1861), U.S. Supreme Court Justice. *Fox* v. *Ohio*, 1847.

122. But it's the men who are attacking the women. If there's to be a curfew, let the men stay home, not the women.

Golda Meir (1898-1978), Prime Minister of Israel (Labor). Comment when an outbreak of assaults on women at night prompted a Cabinet minister to suggest a curfew for women. Quoted in Medea and Thompson, *Against Rape*, 1974.

123. Government's first responsibility is the safety of its citizens.

James P. Moran, Jr., U.S. Congressman (D-VA). Interview, *Metro Week in Review*, May 13, 1989.

124. I am anxious that the Justice Department should be a force for the protection of the people's liberties.

Frank Murphy (1890-1949), Governor of Michigan (D), U.S. Attorney General, and U.S. Supreme Court Justice. Remark to Roger Baldwin, 1939.

125. There was more violent crime among poor Irish immigrants in New York City one hundred years ago than there is among blacks and Puerto Ricans today.

Patrick Murphy, Police Commissioner, New York City. Press conference, 1974.

126. I have to do my fighting within the four corners of the Constitution.

Nick Navarro, sheriff, Broward County, FL. Quoted in *USA Today*, Nov. 15, 1989.

127. The Most potent cause of increase in crime *[in New York City]* has been, without doubt, due to the inefficiency and corruption of the police force, which is demonstrated by the flourishing existence of pickpockets, forgers, counterfeiters, and burglars.

New York State Assembly, Report of the Select Committee on Crime, February 11, 1876.

128. Appoint cities of refuge *[asylum]* ... that the manslayer ... through error may flee there.

Old Testament, *Numbers* 35:11.

129. Order is not pressure which is imposed on society from without, but an equilibrium which is set up from within.

José Ortega y Gasset (1883-1955), Spanish philosopher and statesman. *Mirabeau and Politics*, 1927.

130. When crime is taught from early years, it becomes a part of nature.

Publius Ovid (43 B.C.-A.D.17), Roman poet. *Heroides*.

131. The proper end of ... punishment is not the satisfaction of justice, but the prevention of crimes.

William Paley (1743-1805), British clergyman and philosopher. *The Principles of Moral and Political Philosophy*, 1785.

132. The strength of a man's virtue should not be measured by his special exertions, but by his habitual acts.

Blaise Pascal (1623-1662), French mathematician and philosopher. *Pensées*.

133. To hell with habeas corpus until the danger is over.

Westbrook Pegler (1894-1969), American political columnist. Defense of the forced removal of Japanese Americans to concentration camps during World War II. Quoted in Melvin I. Urofsky, *A March of Liberty*, 1988.

134. Happy that King who is great by *Justice*, and that People who are free by *Obedience*.

William Penn (1644-1718), founder of Pennsylvania. *Some Fruits of Solitude, in Reflections and Maxims*, 1693.

135. He who ... tries to disturb order in opposition to the established authorities or contrary to the law of the Constitution may be slain by any Argentine.

Juan Domingo Perón (1895-1974), President of Argentina. Speech, Sept. 1955.

136. Order is heaven's first law.

Alexander Pope (1688-1744), British poet and Tory activist. *An Essay on Man*, IV, 1733.

137. A man's respect for law and order exists in precise relationship to the size of his paycheck.

Adam Clayton Powell (1908-1972), U.S. Congressman (D-NY). *Keep the Faith, Baby!*, 1967.

138. The criminal justice system in the United States is more protective of the rights of criminal defendants than any country in the world.

Lewis F. Powell, Jr., U.S. Supreme Court Justice. Interview, PBS, *MacNeil-Lehrer News Hour*, Jan. 2, 1989.

139. The streets are safe in Philadelphia; it's only the people who make them unsafe.

Frank Rizzo (1920-1991), Chief of Police (D) and Mayor of Philadelphia, PA (R). Remark to reporters, 1975.

140. The leaders of this country can call out the Army and Navy to stop the railroad workers and stop

the maritime workers; why can't they stop the lynchers?

Paul Robeson (1898-1976), American opera singer, pacifist, and civil rights leader. Speech, Madison Square Garden, New York City, Sept. 12, 1946.

141. No man is above the law and no man is below it; nor do we ask any man's permission when we require him to obey it.

Theodore Roosevelt (1858-1919), 26th President of the United States (R-NY). Speech, Jan. 1905.

142. It should be as much the aim of those who seek social betterment to rid the business world of crimes of cunning as to rid the entire body politic of crimes of violence.

Theodore Roosevelt. Annual message to Congress, Dec. 5, 1905.

143. The successful prosecution of one device to evade the law immediately develops another device to accomplish the same purpose.

Theodore Roosevelt. In reference to antitrust law enforcement. "The Standard Oil Decision and After," *Outlook*, 1911.

144. I have a rule of thumb *[regarding new legislation]*. After about twelve months, if I haven't heard anything, that means either there are no problems surfacing or no one knows about the law because it's not being enforced.

Ralph Rosenberg, Iowa State Representative (D). Quoted in *Governing the States and Localities*, Feb. 1988.

145. You can't have people killed and blood running through the streets like it *[Washington, DC]* was the capital of some Third World country run by a despot.

Warren B. Rudman, U.S. Senator (R-NH). Interview, ABC, *This Week*, Mar. 19, 1989.

146. Those who enforce the law are always right.

Russian proverb.

147. As mankind is made, the keeping it in order is an ill-natured office.

George Savile, 1st Marquess of Halifax (1633-1695), Lord Privy Seal of England. *Political Thoughts and Reflections*, 1750.

148. Practices that can only be considered abhorrent in a free society.

William B. Saxbe, U.S. Attorney General (R). Comment characterizing the FBI COINTELPRO program of infiltration and disruption of "suspect" American organizations, 1974.

149. The dirt rubs both ways.

Russell Schmidt, Senior Sergeant, Police Department, Austin, TX. Comment on the potential of police to use excessive violence in apprehending suspects. Quoted in *The Washington Post*, Apr. 12, 1991.

150. Even after all our talk of danger, Mickey Schwerner was incapable of believing that a police officer in the United States would arrest him on a highway for the purpose of murdering him, then and there, in the dark.

Rita Schwerner, American civil rights worker. Comment after Michael Schwerner and two other civil rights workers were arrested and murdered in Mississippi, June 1964 . Quoted in Cagin and Dray, *We Are Not Afraid*, 1988.

151. Ignorance of the law excuses no man; not that all men know the law, but because 'tis an excuse every man will plead, and no man can tell how to refute him.

John Selden (1584-1654), English jurist and Member of Long Parliament. *Table Talk: Law.*

152. While crime is punished it yet increases.

Lucius Annaeus Seneca (The Younger) (4 B.C.-A.D.65), Roman statesman, dramatist, and philosopher. *Thyestes*.

153. He who does not prevent a crime when he can, encourages it.

Lucius Annaeus Seneca. *Troades*.

154. Condemn the fault, and not the actor of it.

William Shakespeare (1564-1616), English writer. *Measure for Measure*, II, ii.

155. The thieves had their revenge when *[Karl]* Marx convicted the bourgeoisie of theft.

George Bernard Shaw (1856-1950), Nobel Laureate in Literature (Great Britain). *Maxims for Revolutionists*, 1903.

156. Wrongdoing can only be avoided if those who are not wronged feel the same indignation at it as those who are.

Solon (c. 638-559 B.C.), Athenian lawgiver. Quoted in Frederick Paley, *Greek Wit*.

157. Written laws are like spiders' webs and will, like them, only entangle and hold the poor and weak, while the rich and powerful easily break through them.

Solon. Quoted by Plutarch, *The Parallel Lives: Solon*.

158. Laws can never be enforced unless fear supports them.

Sophocles (c.496-406 B.C.), Greek tragedian. *Ajax*.

159. Policemen are soldiers who act alone; soldiers are policemen who act in unison.
Herbert Spencer (1820-1903), British social philosopher. *Social Statics*, 1850.

160. In the enforcement of law, politics is public enemy number one.
Lloyd Stark (1886-1972), Governor of Missouri (D). Quoted in *Kansas City Star*, Mar. 23, 1939.

161. The state always calls its own violence law, but that of the individual, crime.
Max Stirner (Johann Kaspar Schmidt) (1806-1856), German anarchist. *The Ego and His Own*, 1845.

162. There is always the possibility that a secret police may become a menace to free government and free institutions, because it carries with it the possibility of abuses of power which are not always quickly apprehended or understood.
Harlan Fiske Stone (1872-1946), U.S. Attorney General (R), and Chief Justice, U.S. Supreme Court. Statement, 1924.

163. We do not obtain authorization for "black bag" jobs from outside the Bureau *[FBI]*. Such a technique involves trespass and is clearly illegal; therefore, it would be impossible to obtain any legal sanction for it. Despite this, "black bag" jobs have been used because they represent an invaluable technique in combating subversive activities of a clandestine nature aimed directly at undermining and destroying our nation.
William Sullivan, Director, Domestic Intelligence Division, and Assistant Director, Federal Bureau of Investigation. Memorandum to Cartha DeLoach, July 19, 1966.

164. Terror is useful when it is supported by sufficient force.
Louis-Adolphe Thiers (1797-1877), 1st President of the Third French Republic. Remark to Louis Napoléon III, 1848.

165. If you think it's easy to fire a police chief, think again.
Richard Thoesen, Mayor of Herndon, VA. Quoted in *The Washington Post*, Nov. 24, 1988.

166. Under a government which imprisons any unjustly, the true place for a just man is also a prison.
Henry David Thoreau (1817-1862), American philosopher and naturalist. *On the Duty of Civil Disobedience*, 1849.

167. Crime does not pay
Little crimes lead to big crimes
Dick Tracy (1931-present), American comic strip detective. Anticrime slogans.

168. Every policeman knows that though governments change, the police remain.
Leon Trotsky (1879-1940), Russian revolutionary theorist. *What Next?*, 1932.

169. In a free country we punish men for the crimes they commit but never for the opinions they have.
Harry S Truman (1884-1972), 33rd President of the United States (D-MO). Message to Congress, vetoing the McCarran Act, Sept. 22, 1950.

170. The rich rob the poor and the poor rob one another.
Sojourner Truth (c.1797-1883), American abolitionist. Remark.

171. The Mobile Guard will deal with those hotheads. A republic is the only system of government that has the right to show no mercy to such wild beasts, since it is the government chosen by the majority of the flock.
Jules Verne (1828-1905), French writer and politician. In reference to the Socialist partisans of the *Commune*. Letter to Pierre Jules Hetzel, 1871.

172. You take all those pseudo-intellectuals, those sociologists, and they'll tell you, "That man is a criminal – a rapist, a robber – because his daddy didn't give him a pony when he was a little boy." Well, I was poor, too. My daddy didn't give me no pony – and I never rioted.
George C. Wallace, Governor of Alabama (D). Quoted in David Caute, *The Year of the Barricades*, 1988.

173. No man shall be forced by Torture to confesse any Crime against himselfe nor any other.
Nathaniel Ward (c.1578-1652), Puritan codifier. *The Massachusetts Body of Liberties*, 1641.

174. No man's life shall be taken away, no man's honour or good name shall be stayned, no man's person shall be arrested, restrayned, banished, dismembred, nor any wayes punished ... under colour of law or Countenance of Authoritie, unless it be by vertue or equitie of some express law of the country waranting the same, established by a general Court and sufficiently published.
Nathaniel Ward. *Ibid.*

175. Organized crime does not exist anywhere unless someone is being paid off.
Earl Warren (1891-1974), Chief Justice, U.S. Supreme Court, and Governor of California (R). Speech, American Bar Association, 1950.

176. The function of law enforcement is the prevention of crime and the apprehension of criminals. Manifestly, that function does not include the manufacturing of crime.
Earl Warren. *Sherman* v. *United States*, 1957.

177. The police must obey the law while enforcing the law.
Earl Warren. Quoted in *The Milwaukee Journal*, Sept. 20, 1964.

178. A free government without adequate provision for personal security is an absurdity.
Daniel Webster (1782-1852), U.S. Congressman (Federalist-NH and MA), U.S. Senator (Federalist and Whig-MA), and U.S. Secretary of State. Speech, 1811.

179. A law is something which must have a moral basis, so that there is an inner compelling force for every citizen to obey.
Chaim Weizmann (1874-1952), 1st President of Israel. *Trial and Error*, 1949.

180. Are the police governable? Yes. Do I control the police right now? No.
Kevin White, Mayor of Boston, MA (D). Quoted in *Report of the National Commission on the Causes and Prevention of Violence*, 1969.

181. Starvation, and not sin, is the parent of modern crime.
Oscar Wilde (1854-1900), Irish writer. *The Soul of Man Under Socialism*, 1881.

182. Excessive bail ought not to be required nor excessive fines imposed; nor unusual punishment inflicted.
William III (1650-1702), Stadholder of Holland, and King of England, Scotland, and Ireland. *English Bill of Rights*, Feb. 13, 1689.

Chapter 55

Leadership

1. The king is dead, long live the king! (*Le roi est mort, vive le roi.*)
   Official announcement by the Herald-at-Arms from the balcony of the palace, of the death of one King and the accession of his successor during the *ancien régime* in France.

2. You are afraid of the one, I, of the few.... You are apprehensive of monarchy, I, of aristocracy.
   John Adams (1735-1826), 2nd President of the United States (Federalist-MA). Letter to Thomas Jefferson, Dec. 6, 1787.

3. Pardon me if I add that I think him *[President Madison]* a little too much of a book politician, and too timid in his politics, for prudence and caution are opposites of timidity.
   Fisher Ames (1758-1808), U.S. Congressman (R-MA). Quoted in Irving Brant, *The Fourth President*, 1950.

4. God save the king!
   Apocrypha, *Letter of Aristeas*, No. 178.

5. What is the essence of kingship? *[It is]* to rule oneself well, and not be led astray by wealth or fame.
   Ibid., No. 211.

6. Men are marked out from the moment of birth to rule or to be ruled.
   Aristotle (384-322 B.C.), Greek philosopher and teacher. *Politics*, I.

7. The caliber of talent attracted to the public service will depend in substantial measure upon the excitement that can be conveyed by presidential leadership.
   Stephen K. Bailey, dean, Maxwell School of Business, Syracuse University, and President, American Society of Public Administration. *Agenda for the Nation*, 1968.

8. A political leader must keep looking over his shoulder all the time to see if the boys are still there. If they aren't still there, he's no longer a political leader.
   Bernard M. Baruch (1870-1965), Chairman, War Industries Board, and U.S. Delegate to the U.N. Atomic Energy Commission. Quoted in obituary, *The New York Times*, June 21, 1965.

9. There is always somebody to believe in anyone who is uppermost.
   Henry Ward Beecher (1813-1887), American clergyman and writer. *Life Thoughts*, 1858.

10. The extreme scarcity of political leaders of any caliber is owing to the fact that they are called upon to decide at any moment, and in detail, problems which the increased size of societies may well have rendered insoluble.
    Henri Bergson (1859-1941), Nobel Laureate in Literature (France). *The Two Sources of Morality and Religion*, 1935.

11. One cannot move so fast as to invite a backlash.
    Benazir Bhutto, Prime Minister of Pakistan. Interview, ABC, *20/20*, Sept. 29, 1989.

12. Earthly majesty is always akin to the fallen angel, who is proud and unhappy, beautiful but troubled, and whose plans and efforts, though vast, are denied access.
    Otto von Bismarck-Schoenhausen (1815-1898), Chancellor of Germany. Quoted in Emil Ludwig, *Genius and Character*, 1927.

13. The path to glory is rough, and many gloomy hours obscure it.
    Black Hawk (1767-1838), Chief, Sac and Fox Indians. Remark to General Atkinson, 1833.

14. That the king can do no wrong is a necessary and fundamental principle of the English constitution.
    William Blackstone (1723-1780), British jurist. *Commentaries on the Laws of England*, III, 1767.

15. To rule is an art, not a science.
    Ludwig Boerne (1786-1837), German journalist. *Fragments and Aphorisms*, No. 7.

16. The children won't leave without me; I won't leave without the King *[George VI]*; and the King will never leave.

Elizabeth Angela Marguerite Bowes-Lyon, Queen of England (George VI). Statement to reporters when asked about the possibility of the royal family evacuating London during the blitz, 1943.

17. I am convinced that the best service a retired general can perform is to turn in his tongue along with his suit, and to mothball his opinions.
Omar N. Bradley (1893-1981), General, U.S. Army, and Permanent Chairman, Joint Chiefs of Staff. Armed Forces Day address, May 16, 1959.

18. Solutions aren't going to come out of Washington, but leadership can.
William Brock, U.S. Congressman (R-TN), U.S. Senator, and U.S. Secretary of Labor. Quoted in *Youth: 2000*, 1986.

19. In a democracy, a man who does not listen cannot lead.
David S. Broder, American columnist. *The Washington Post*, Nov. 7, 1988.

20. Many have ruled well who could not perhaps define a commonwealth.
Thomas Browne (1605-1682), English physician and writer. *Christian Morals*, 1716.

21. There are no honorable rulers.
Pearl S. Buck (1892-1973), Nobel Laureate in Literature (United States). *Sons*, 1932.

22. Magnanimity in politics is not seldom the truest wisdom; and a great empire and little minds go ill together.
Edmund Burke (1729-1797), British statesman. Speech on conciliation with America, Mar. 22, 1775.

23. There are no deliverers. They're all dead.
Nannie Helen Burroughs (1883-1961), American journalist. *The Louisiana Weekly*, Dec. 23, 1933.

24. One should be constantly looking for the broader vision.
Kim Campbell, Minister of Justice, Canada (Conservative). Speech, Johns Hopkins University, Baltimore, MD, Mar. 19, 1991.

25. Every noble crown is, and on Earth will forever be, a crown of thorns.
Thomas Carlyle (1795-1881), Scottish essayist and historian. *Past and Present*, 1843.

26. It is time for our government leaders to respect the law no less than our humblest citizen, so that we can end the double standard of justice in America.
Jimmy Carter, 39th President of the United States (D-GA). Presidential nomination acceptance speech, Democratic National Convention, 1976.

27. If you fear making anyone mad, then you ultimately probe for the lowest common denominator of human achievement.
Jimmy Carter. Speech, Future Farmers of America, Kansas City, KS, Nov. 9, 1978.

28. The true grandeur and excellence of a prince ... does not consist in honors, in gold, in purple, and other luxuries of fortune, but in prudence, wisdom, and knowledge.
Catherine de Médicis (1519-1589), Queen of France. Letter to Mary, Queen of Scots, c.1554.

29. He who goes ahead is always the one that wins.
Catherine II (The Great) (1729-1796), Empress of Russia. Letter, Aug. 11, 1778.

30. You must preserve supreme calm in the midst of all agitation, never appearing disturbed or anxious about anything that may occur.
Catherine II. *Mémoire sur la Révolution*.

31. Leadership means making people feel good.
Jean Chrétien, Minister of Finance, Canada (Liberal). Speech, June 3, 1984.

32. Dictators ride to and fro upon tigers which they dare not dismount. And the tigers are getting hungry.
Winston Churchill (1874-1965), Prime Minister of Great Britain (Conservative). *While England Slept*, 1938.

33. I have nothing to offer but blood, toil, tears, and sweat.
Winston Churchill. Speech during the Battle of Britain, House of Commons, May 13, 1940.

34. The last time you and I sat across a conference table in Potsdam *[July-Aug. 1945]*, I must confess, Sir, I held you in very low regard. I loathed your taking the place of Franklin Roosevelt. I misjudged you badly. Since that time, you more than any other man have saved Western Civilization.
Winston Churchill. Remark to Harry S Truman. Quoted by Congressman Lawrence H. Fountain in a memorial tribute to Truman, House of Representatives, Jan. 3, 1973.

35. Victory finds a hundred fathers, but defeat is an orphan.
Galeazzo Ciano (1903-1944), Foreign Minister of Italy. *Diary*, Sept. 9, 1942. Paraphrased by President Kennedy after the Bay of Pigs fiasco.

36. It takes skill to benefit from luck.
William Colby, Director, Central Intelligence Agency. Quoted on ABC, *This Week*, Mar. 22, 1990.

37. To the same enthusiastic sensibilities which made a fool of him with regard to his Emma, his country owed the victories of the Nile, Copenhagen, and Trafalgar.
Samuel T. Coleridge (1772-1834), British writer. Of Admiral Horatio Nelson. Quoted in John Livingston Lowes, *The Road to Xanadu*, 1927.

38. The superior man is easy to serve and difficult to please.
Confucius (551-479 B.C.), Chinese philosopher. *Analects*.

39. Tell the people not to depend on me anymore.
Crazy Horse (d. 1877), Chief, Oglala Sioux Indians. His dying words. Quoted in Bill Moeller, *Crazy Horse: His Life and Times*, 1988.

40. The danger is not that a particular class is unfit to govern. Every class is unfit to govern.
John Dahlberg, 1st Baron Acton (1834-1902), British historian. Letter to Mary Gladstone, Mar. 24, 1881.

41. When I become mayor it will not be of LaSalle Street nor of State Street, but of all the people.
Richard J. Daley (1902-1976), Mayor of Chicago, IL (D). Campaign speech, Feb. 1955.

42. Good political leadership is good government. What we need is more good political leadership.
Richard J. Daley. Quoted in *Chicago Sun-Times*, Mar. 24, 1989.

43. We have leadership – there's just no followership.
George Danielson, U.S. Congressman (D-CA). Quoted in *The Wall Street Journal*, Dec. 14, 1979.

44. Demagogues are the mob's lackeys.
Diogenes (412-323 B.C.), Greek philosopher. Quoted by Diogenes Laertius, *Diogenes*.

45. A smile for a friend and a sneer for the world, is the way to govern mankind.
Benjamin Disraeli, 1st Earl of Beaconsfield (1804-1881), Prime Minister of Great Britain (Conservative). *Vivian Gray*, 1827.

46. We live in an age of prudence. The leaders of the people now generally follow.
Benjamin Disraeli. *Coningsby*, 1844.

47. I know the Haitian people because I am the Haitian people.
François (Papa Doc) Duvalier (1907-1971), President-for-Life of Haiti. Remark, 1968.

48. The President is here, strong and firm as a monkey's tail.
[One week later, he resigned and fled his country.]
Jean-Claude (Baby Doc) Duvalier, President-for-Life of Haiti. Quoted in *The New York Times*, Feb. 1, 1986.

49. Few strong leaders are enthusiastic about their successors.
Abba Eban, Foreign Secretary of Israel (Labor) and Israeli Ambassador to the United Nations. *An Autobiography*, 1977.

50. Effective leadership may now well require the strength to accept rejection and hostility from a substantial segment of the electorate, while making sure that the disaffected remain a functional minority, especially on election day.
Thomas B. Edsall, American political journalist. *The Washington Post Book World*, Nov. 11, 1990.

51. We, the people, elect leaders not to rule but to serve.
Dwight D. Eisenhower (1890-1969), 34th President of the United States (R-KS). First inaugural address, Jan. 20, 1953.

52. Leadership involves persuasion, and conciliation, and education and patience. It's long, slow, tough work. That is the only kind of leadership I know or will believe in, or will practice.
Dwight D. Eisenhower. Quoted in Peter Lyon, *Eisenhower: Portrait of the Hero*, 1974.

53. There are men whose presence infuses trust and reverence.
George Eliot (Mary Ann Evans) (1819-1880), British writer. *Romola*, 1863.

54. They are most deceived that trusteth most in themselves.
Elizabeth I (1533-1603), Queen of England. Letter to Lord Protector Edward Seymour, Feb. 21, 1549.

55. I know I have the body of a weak and feeble woman, but I have the heart and stomach of a King, and of a King of England too.
Elizabeth I. Speech to English troops at Tilbury on the approach of the Spanish Armada, 1588.

56. I cannot lead you into battle. I do not give you laws or administer justice but I can do something else – I can give my heart and my devotion to these old islands and to all the peoples of our brotherhood of nations.

Elizabeth II, Queen of England. Television address, Dec. 25, 1957.

57. When the team is running away, I prefer to be on the seat with my hands on the lines rather than in front of the runaway.

Stephen Benton Elkins (1841-1911), Delegate, Territory of New Mexico, U.S. Secretary of War, and U.S. Senator (R-WV). Explanation of why he reversed his position on a crucial bill, 1906.

58. There is always room for a man of force, and he makes room for many.

Ralph Waldo Emerson (1803-1882), American writer. *Power, Wealth, Illusions*, "Power," 1876.

59. Toughness doesn't have to come in a pinstripe suit.

Dianne Feinstein, Mayor of San Francisco, CA (D). Quoted in *Time*, June 4, 1984.

60. Ninety percent of leadership is the ability to communicate something that people want.

Dianne Feinstein. Quoted in *Time*, June 18, 1990.

61. Legislatures react. Executives initiate.

James J. Florio, U.S. Congressman and Governor of New Jersey (D). Quoted in *Time*, May 2, 1990.

62. Rule, and change nothing.

Francis I (1768-1835), Emperor of Austria. Directions to his son and successor, Ferdinand I.

63. Men are of no importance. What counts is who commands.

Charles de Gaulle (1890-1970), President of France. Quoted in *The New York Times Magazine*, May 12, 1968.

64. Faced with crisis, the man of character falls back upon himself.

Charles de Gaulle. Quoted in *Forbes*, Jan. 23, 1989.

65. Thank God for a good people!

George VI (1895-1952), King of England and Ireland, and Emperor of India. Response during a rally for wartime unity when someone in the crowd called out, "Thank God for a good King!" London, 1943.

66. Faith in the Führer is enveloped, it could almost be said, in a mysterious, unfathomable mysticism.

Joseph Goebbels (1897-1945), Minister for Propaganda and National Enlightenment, Third German Reich. *The Struggle Over Berlin*.

67. You must either conquer and rule or lose and serve, suffer or triumph, and be the anvil or the hammer.

Johann Wolfgang von Goethe (1749-1832), German poet and dramatist. *Der Gross-Cophta*, II.

68. Nobody obeys my instructions.

Mikhail Gorbachev, President of the U.S.S.R. Quoted in *The Chicago Tribune*, Dec. 3, 1990.

69. Leaders often find themselves temporarily alone.

Ernest Gruening (1887-1974), Governor of Alaska and U.S. Senator (D). Quoted by Morris K. Udall, *Too Funny to Be President*, 1988.

70. I am not better or cleverer than any one of you. But I remain undaunted, and that is why the leadership belongs to me. In darker moments than the present I did not lose courage – indeed I made still greater sacrifices.

Theodor Herzl (1860-1904), Austrian journalist and political Zionist. *The Diaries of Theodore Herzl*, Dec. 20, 1898.

71. The efficiency of the truly national leader consists primarily in preventing the division of the attention of a people, and always in concentrating it on a single enemy.

Adolf Hitler (1889-1945), Führer of the Third German Reich. *Mein Kampf*, 1933.

72. The world's great men have not commonly been great scholars, nor its great scholars great men.

Oliver Wendell Holmes (1809-1894), American physician and author. *The Autocrat of the Breakfast Table*, 1858.

73. A democracy delegates leadership. It cannot surrender to it.... The genuinely democratic community rightfully views the hero with suspicion and is notoriously ungrateful.

Sidney Hook (1902-1989), American philosopher. Speech, "Where Have All the Heroes Gone?" Washington, DC, Feb. 27, 1977.

74. Above all, we know that although Americans can be led to make great sacrifices, they do not like to be driven.

Herbert Hoover (1874-1964), 31st President of the United States (R-IA). *Memoirs*, 1952.

75. I've always preferred to make my decisions without the involvement of others. My decisions are hard, harsh, just like the desert. I've always related my behavior to the desert. Usually it looks so quiet and kind, but suddenly it erupts with rage, mightily fighting the gusts of storms and gales. And this outburst of the desert's rage gave me the feeling that I was on the brink of the end of time.

Saddam Hussein, President of Iraq. *Autobiography.*

76. The leaders of the people cause them to err.
Old Testament, *Isaiah* 11:16.

77. One man with courage makes a majority.
Andrew Jackson (1767-1845), 7th President of the United States (D-TN). Attributed.

78. I know what I am fit for. I can command a body of men in a rough way: but I am not fit to be President.
Andrew Jackson. Quoted in Richard Hofstadter, *The American Political Tradition*, 1948.

79. We submit ourselves to rulers only if under rules.
Robert H. Jackson (1892-1954), U.S. Attorney General (D) and U.S. Supreme Court Justice. *Youngstown Sheet & Tube Co.* v. *Sawyer*, 1951.

80. The state of Monarchy is the supremest thing upon earth: for Kings are not only God's lieutenants, and sit upon God's throne, but even by God himself they are called Gods.
James I (1566-1625), King of England. Speech in Parliament, Mar. 21, 1609.

81. Concern for individual well-being is for private citizens.... Princes, who enjoy public possessions, should be concerned with public good.
Marie de Jars (1565-1645), French writer. *Proumenoir*, 1594.

82. As a soldier I know that the commander is responsible for every man and every thing. The words "I apologize" may sound banal, but I cannot find any other words.
Wojciech Jaruzelski, General and President of Poland. In reference to Poland's economic distress. Retirement speech, Dec. 21, 1990.

83. On great occasions every good officer must be ready to risk himself in going beyond the strict line of the law, when the public preservation requires it; his motives will be a justification.
Thomas Jefferson (1743-1826), 3rd President of the United States (Democratic Republican-VA). 1807.

84. All the world looks to this nation for its future, for the leadership that is required at this moment. And we cannot give that leadership, and we cannot offer it if we are split up in guerilla groups chewing on each other.
Lyndon B. Johnson (1908-1973), 36th President of the United States (D-TX). Aug. 10, 1964.

85. Fear created gods; boldness created kings.
Prosper Jolyot (Sieur de Crébillon) (1674-1762), French poet and dramatic censor. *Xerxès*, 1714.

86. We are given to the cult of personality. When things go badly we look to some messiah to save us.... If by chance we think we have found one, it will not be long before we destroy him.
Constantine Karamanlis, Premier of Greece. Quoted in *The New York Times*, Nov. 17, 1974.

87. One person, serving a group of people, can make a difference.
Nancy Landon Kassebaum, U.S. Senator (R-KS). Interview, C-SPAN, Oct. 9, 1989.

88. Let the word go forth from this time and place, to friend and foe alike, that the torch has been passed to a new generation of Americans – born in this century, tempered by war, disciplined by a hard and bitter peace, proud of our ancient heritage.
John F. Kennedy (1917-1963), 35th President of the United States (D-MA). Inaugural address, Jan. 20, 1961.

89. It is time for a new generation of leadership to cope with new problems and new opportunities. For there is a world to be won.
John F. Kennedy. Quoted in *Time*, Nov. 6, 1989.

90. We never knew, when called to his *[Joseph Stalin's]* office, if we'd ever see our families again. You know, people don't do their best in that atmosphere.
Nikita S. Khrushchev (1894-1971), Premier of the U.S.S.R. Quoted in Celebrity Research Group, *The Bedside Book of Celebrity Gossip*, 1984.

91. There is a spirit and a need and a man at the beginning of every great human advance. Each of these must be right for that particular moment in history, or nothing happens.
Coretta Scott King, widow of Martin Luther King, Jr. *My Life with Martin Luther King, Jr.*, 1969.

92. Grant, then, to Your servant an understanding mind to judge Your people, to distinguish between good and bad; for who can judge this vast people of yours?
[This passage was read to the young Queen Victoria by Prime Minister William Lamb soon after her succession to the throne in 1837.]
Old Testament, *1 Kings* 3:5-9.

93. There has to be a feeling of confidence that the senior officials of the government are not playing with the lives of the public.

Henry M. Kissinger, U.S. Secretary of State and National Security Advisor (R). Press conference, 1972.

94. The Pentagon doesn't need six hundred ships. It needs a damn rudder.

Noel C. Koch, U.S. Deputy Assistant Secretary of Defense. Quoted in *Newsweek*, Mar. 13, 1987.

95. I have been underestimated for decades. I've done very well that way.

Helmut Kohl, Chancellor of West Germany. Quoted in *The New York Times*, Jan. 25, 1987.

96. You must not be a drunkard. You must not be a prison convict. You must be sober, wise, fearless, and bold. You must enforce customary laws of the village, but you must also understand the rules of the government.

Amakuade Wyete Ajeman Labie II, Paramount Chief, Awutu tribe of Ghana. Description of the qualities that make a successful tribal leader. Quoted in *The Washington Post*, July 21, 1990.

97. In governing the people, the leader empties their minds but fills their stomachs, weakens their wills but strengthens their bones. He always keeps them innocent of knowledge and free from desire; he sees that the clever never dare to act *[against him]*.

Lao-tzu (c.604-53 B.C.), Chinese philosopher and founder of Taoism. *Tao Te Ching*.

98. One who takes on the humiliation of the State is called a Ruler; worthy of offering sacrifices to the gods of earth millet. One who takes on himself the calamity of the State is called a King; worthy of dominion over the entire Empire.

Lao-tzu. *Ibid*.

99. The best of all Rulers is only a shadowy presence to his subjects. Next comes the Ruler they love and praise. Then comes one they fear. And then one with whom they take liberties.

Lao-tzu. *Ibid*.

100. I must follow them. I am their leader.

Andrew Bonar Law (1858-1923), Prime Minister of Great Britain (Conservative). Attributed.

101. The king never dies. (*Rex nunquam moritur.*) *[As soon as the king dies, his successor is immediately vested in the king's rights, duties, and prerogatives.]*

Legal maxim.

102. Any cook should be able to run the country.

V. I. Lenin (1870-1924), Premier of the U.S.S.R. Quoted in Alexander Solzhenitsyn, *The First Circle*, 1968.

103. Only a strong monarchical authority, limited solely by its conscience and sanctified by faith, can solve the contemporary problem which seems to us insoluble – the conciliation of capital and labor.

Konstantin Nikolaevich Leontiev (1831-1891), Russian Socialist philosopher. Letter, 1890.

104. Even the best laws can only be respected and feared, not loved. Good rulers are respected, feared, and loved. What mighty sources of happiness for a nation good rulers are!

Georg Christoph Lichtenberg (1741-1799), German physicist and writer. *Aphorisms*, 1793-96.

105. That people *[the Founding Fathers]* were few in number and without resources, save only their wise heads and stout hearts.

Abraham Lincoln (1809-1865), 16th President of the United States (R-IL). Speech, Springfield, IL, July 16, 1852.

106. I am, as you know, only the servant of the people.

Abraham Lincoln. Letter to James Gilmore, Mar. 13, 1861.

107. I do the best I know how, the very best I can,
And I mean to keep doing so until the end.
If the end brings me out all right,
What is said against me won't count;
If it brings me out wrong,
All the angels swearing that I was right
Would have made no difference.

Abraham Lincoln. Quoted by President William Tubman of Liberia, Nov. 5, 1950.

108. The genius of a good leader is to leave behind him a situation which common sense, without the grace of genius, can deal with successfully.

Walter Lippmann (1889-1974), American political columnist. "Roosevelt Has Gone," Mar. 14, 1945.

109. Enthusiasm is good material for the orator, but the statesman needs something more durable to work in.

James Russell Lowell (1819-1891), U.S. Ambassador to Spain and England. Quoted in *Forbes*, May 4, 1987.

110. *[Franklin]* Roosevelt lied us into war because he did not have the political courage to lead us into it.

Clare Boothe Luce (1903-1987), U.S. Congresswoman and Ambassador to Italy and Brazil (R-CT). Campaign speech, Sept. 1944.

111. It is essential for a prince to be on a friendly footing with his people, since, otherwise, he will have no resource in adversity.

Niccolò Machiavelli (1469-1527), Florentine statesman and political philosopher. *The Prince*, 1513.

112. A ruler must learn to be other than good.
Niccolò Machiavelli. *Ibid.*

113. It is in vain to say that enlightened statesmen will always be able to adjust their interests. Enlightened men will not always be at the helm.
James Madison (1751-1836), 4th President of the United States (Democratic Republican-VA). Quoted in *Smithsonian*, Sept. 1987.

114. His own self must be conquered by the king for all time; then only are his enemies to be conquered.
The Mahabharata (c.1000 B.C.), India.

115. Learn from the masses and then teach them.
Mao Tse-tung (1893-1976), Chairman, Communist Party of China. Speech, 1938.

116. Democracy needs leaders, not masters.
Tomas G. Masaryk (1850-1937), 1st President of Czechoslovakia. Quoted in Karyl Capek, *Masaryk on Thought and Life*, 1938.

117. My greatest task is to convince people that things can be better.
Tadeusz Mazowiecki, Prime Minister of Poland. Quoted on CBS, *Face the Nation*, Aug. 20, 1989.

118. A leader who does not hesitate before he sends his nation into battle is not fit to be a leader.
Golda Meir (1898-1978), Prime Minister of Israel (Labor). Remark to reporters, 1973.

119. I never did anything alone. Whatever was accomplished in this country was accomplished collectively.
Golda Meir. Remark to Egyptian Pres. Anwar Sadat, 1977.

120. Leadership involves finding a parade and getting in front of it.
John Naisbitt, American futurist and writer. *Megatrends*, 1982.

121. What is the throne? Four pieces of wood covered over with velvet.
Napoléon I (1769-1821), military leader and Emperor of France. *Maxims*.

122. I have had enough of playing the part of a soldier; the time has come to play that of a king.
Napoléon I. Remark following the Battle of Wagram, 1809.

123. France has more need of me than I of France.
Napoléon I. Address to the French Senate, 1814.

124. It's fundamental in politics and it's a matter of intuition – trust. If the people trust a man, it doesn't matter much what he does or says.
Richard M. Nixon, 37th President of the United States (R-CA). Quoted in *Life*, May 28, 1956.

125. If an individual wants to be a leader and isn't controversial, that means he never stood for anything.
Richard M. Nixon. Quoted in *Dallas Times Herald*, Dec. 10, 1978.

126. Some public men are destined to be loved. Other public men are destined to be disliked.... What is important ... is that you be respected.
Richard M. Nixon. Quoted on PBS, *The Unauthorized Biography of Richard Nixon*, Mar. 9, 1989.

127. To rule is not so much a question of the heavy hand as the firm seat.
José Ortega y Gasset (1883-1955), Spanish philosopher and statesman. *The Revolt of the Masses*, 1930.

128. My advisors built a wall between myself and my people.... When I woke up, I had lost my people.
Mohammed Reza Pahlavi (1919-1980), Shah of Iran. Remark to Egyptian Pres. Anwar Sadat. Quoted in *Time*, Dec. 10, 1979.

129. In a democracy things happen by leadership or by crisis.
Leon E. Panetta, U.S. Congressman (D-CA). 13th Annual Policy Conference, American Enterprise Institute, Nov. 1989.

130. I am not one of those who think that commanders ought at no time to receive advice; on the contrary, I should deem that man more proud than wise who regulated every proceeding by the standard of his own single judgment.
Lucius Aemilius Paulus (c.229-160 B.C.), General and Consul of Rome. Quoted in Plutarch, *The Parallel Lives: Aemilius Paulus*.

131. Leading the Jewish people is not easy – we are a divided, obstinate, highly individualistic people who have cultivated faith, sharp-wittedness, and polemics to a very high level.
Shimon Peres, Prime Minister of Israel (Labour). *The New York Times*, Oct. 5, 1986.

132. It is not that we were so good, but those who followed us were so bad that they made us seem better than we were.

Juan Domingo Perón (1895-1974), President of Argentina. Remark on his return to power, July 1973.

133. It is easy to be independent when all behind you agree with you, but the difficulty comes when nine hundred and ninety-nine of your friends think you wrong.
Wendell Phillips (1811-1884), American orator and reformer. *Orations, Speeches, Lectures and Letters,* 1863.

134. *[The tyrant]* is always stirring up some war or another, in order that the people may require a leader.
Plato (427-347 B.C.), Greek philosopher. *The Republic.*

135. Not the least of the qualities that go to make up a great ruler is the capacity for letting others serve him.
Armand-Jean du Plessis (Cardinal Richelieu) (1585-1642), French ecclesiastic and statesman. *Political Testament,* I, 6, 1687.

136. In an oration to the people he *[Cato the Younger, 95-46 B.C.]* so highly extolled Cicero's consulate that the greatest honors were decreed him, and he was publicly declared the Father of his Country, which title he seems to be the first man to have obtained.
Plutarch (c.46-c.120) Greek biographer. *The Parallel Lives: Cicero.*

137. Where there is no vision, the people perish.
Old Testament, *Proverbs* 29:18.

138. We cannot legislate leadership.
Charles B. Rangel, U.S. Congressman (D-NY). PBS, *MacNeil-Lehrer News Hour,* Nov. 8, 1990.

139. You take people as far as they will go, not as far as you would like them to go.
Jeanette Rankin (1880-1973), U.S. Congresswoman (R-MT). Quoted in Hannah Josephson, *Jeannette Rankin: First Lady in Congress,* 1974.

140. If we are not to shoulder the burdens of leadership in the free world, then who will?
Ronald Reagan, 40th President of the United States (R-CA). Speech, Conservative Political Action Conference, Mar. 17, 1978.

141. Timorous minds are much more inclined to deliberate than to resolve.
Cardinal de Retz (1614-1679), French cleric and politician. *Political Maxims.*

142. Slow and hesitating, he was governed more than he himself governed.
Johann Reuchlin (1455-1522), German scholar and translator. Description of Maximilian I (1459-1519). Letter to Questenberg, Feb. 12, 1519.

143. Responsibility is unique.... You may share it with others but your portion is not diminished. You may delegate it, but it is still with you. You may disclaim it, but you cannot divest yourself of it.
Hyman G. Rickover (1900-1986), Admiral, U.S. Navy. Quoted in G. Michael Durst, *Napkin Notes on the Art of Living,* 1988.

144. What passes for national leadership now consists mostly of viewing with alarm and exhorting governors, mayors, and private institutions to "do something."
Alice Rivlin, Director, Congressional Budget Office. *The Washington Post,* Nov. 5, 1989.

145. I feel like a dentist pulling a tooth every morning.
Charles E. Roemer III, U.S. Congressman and Governor of Louisiana (D). Interview, C-SPAN, Sept. 4, 1989.

146. A leader may chart the way, may point out the road to lasting peace, but many leaders and many peoples must do the building.
Anna Eleanor Roosevelt (1884-1962), First Lady and U.S. Delegate to the United Nations. "My Day," Mar. 16, 1945.

147. We need our heroes.
Anna Eleanor Roosevelt. Letter to Joseph Lash, Jan. 21, 1952.

148. I believe it is a great mistake not to stand up for people, even when you differ with them, if you feel that they are trying to do things that will help our country.
Anna Eleanor Roosevelt. *The Nation,* June 7, 1952.

149. You cannot be a great leader unless the people are great.
Anna Eleanor Roosevelt. Remark, 1956.

150. Without leadership alert and sensitive to change, we are bogged up or lose our way.
Franklin D. Roosevelt (1882-1945), 32nd President of the United States (D-NY). Interview, *The New York Times,* Nov. 13, 1932.

151. There's only one issue in this campaign – it's myself – and people must be either for me or against me.
Franklin D. Roosevelt. July 19, 1936.

152. In the event the Congress should fail to act, and act adequately, I shall accept the responsibility, and I will act.

Franklin D. Roosevelt. Request for a wartime wage and price control act. Message to Congress. Sept. 7, 1942.

153. It is a terrible thing to look over your shoulder when you are trying to lead – and to find no one there.

Franklin D. Roosevelt. Quoted in James MacGregor Burns, *Roosevelt: The Lion and the Fox*, 1956.

154. The leader works in the open, and the boss in covert. The leader leads, and the boss drives.

Theodore Roosevelt (1858-1919), 26th President of the United States (R-NY). Speech, Binghamton, NY, Oct. 24, 1910.

155. Disaster is ahead of us if we trust to the leadership of men whose souls are seared and whose eyes are blinded, men of cold heart and narrow mind, who believe we can find safety in dull timidity and dull inaction.

Theodore Roosevelt. Campaign speech, June 17, 1912.

156. There is something to be said for government by a great aristocracy which has furnished leaders to the nation in peace and war for generations; even a democrat like myself must admit this.

Theodore Roosevelt. Letter to Edward Grey, Nov. 15, 1913.

157. A *People* may let a *King* fall, yet still remain a *People*; but if a *King* let his *People* slip from him, he is no longer *King*.

George Savile, 1st Marquess of Halifax (1633-1695), Lord Privy Seal of England. *Maxims of State*, No. 33.

158. Americans, as opposed to Europeans, care what their *[prospective]* leaders are really like, as opposed to what they'll govern like.

Daniel Schorr, American journalist. National Public Radio, *Weekend Edition*, Oct. 15, 1988.

159. There are times when you as a leader will have to design the procedures and write the manual.

Norman Schwartzkopf, General, U.S. Army, and Commander of Forces in "Desert Storm." Commencement address, U.S. Naval Academy, Annapolis, MD, June 1, 1991.

160. It was a maxim of Queen Caroline to bear herself towards her political friends with such caution, as if there was a possibility of their one day being her enemies, and towards political opponents with the same degree of circumspection, as if they might again become friendly to her measures.

Walter Scott (1771-1832), Scottish writer. In reference to Caroline of Anspach, Wilhelmina Carolina, Queen of England (1638-1737). *The Heart of Midlothian*, 1818.

161. In the infancy of societies, the chiefs of the state shape its institutions; later, the institutions shape the chiefs of state.

Charles-Louis de Secondat, Baron de La Brède et de Montesquieu (1689-1755), French writer. *Considérations sur les Causes de la Grandeur et des Romains et de Leur Décadence*, 1734.

162. A King is a thing men have made for their own sakes, for quietness' sake. Just as in a family one man is appointed to buy the meat.

John Selden (1584-1654), English Jurist and Member of Long Parliament. *Table Talk: King*.

163. They that govern most, make least noise.

John Selden. *Table-Talk: State Power*.

164. If you judge, investigate; if you reign, command.

Lucius Annaeus Seneca (The Younger) (4 B.C.-A.D. 65), Roman statesman, dramatist, and philosopher. *Medea*.

165. Give every man your ear, but few your voice; take each man's censures, but reserve your judgment.

William Shakespeare (1564-1616), English writer. *Hamlet*, I, iii.

166. I give this heavy weight from off my head,
And this unwieldy scepter from my hand,
The pride of kingly sway from out my heart;
With mine own tears I wash away my balm,
With mine own hands I give away my crown,
With mine own tongue deny my sacred state,
With mine own breath release all duteous oaths.

William Shakespeare. *King Richard II*, IV, i.

167. Let them obey that know not how to rule.

William Shakespeare. *King Henry VI*, Pt. 2, V, i.

168. A limited monarchy is a device for combining the inertia of a wooden idol with the credibility of a flesh and blood one.

George Bernard Shaw (1856-1950), Nobel Laureate in Literature (Great Britain). *Maxims for Revolutionists*, 1903.

169. When a man is able to take abuse with a smile, he is worthy to become a leader.

Nachman ben Simcha (1770-1811), Polish rabbi. Quoted in Leo Rosten, *Treasury of Jewish Quotations*, 1972.

170. In today's society Bill Cosby has a lot more influence than Ronald Reagan.
Steve Sippel, student, Withrow High School, Cincinnati, OH. Quoted in *The Washington Post*, June 12, 1988.

171. I am no cooing dove, and what is more I never will be. The people want clear-headed, strong-minded fighting men at the head of the government, and not doves. Let the doves roost in the eaves of the Capitol, and not in the Executive Chamber.
[His opponent, Congressman Ogden L. Mills, had criticized Smith for being too bellicose with the state legislature and claimed he would get along with the legislature like a "cooing dove."]
Alfred E. Smith (1873-1944), Governor of New York (D). Campaign speech, 1926.

172. I think chaos is inevitable. I want to get as many people as I can now, so that when chaos comes, I'll be the leader.
Gerald L. K. Smith (1898-1976), American clergyman and cofounder, Union Party. Interview, 1936.

173. Leadership is not manifested by coercion, even against the resented.
Margaret Chase Smith, U.S. Congresswoman and U.S. Senator (R-ME). Speech, National Republican Women's Conference, Mar. 16, 1961.

174. An able man shews his spirit by gentle words and resolute actions; he is neither hot nor timid.
Philip Dormer Stanhope, 4th Earl of Chesterfield (1694-1773), Member of Parliament, Great Britain (Whig), and Lord-Lieutenant of Ireland. *Maxims*.

175. Isn't a strong man *[politician]*, however bad, socially better than a weak man, however good?
Joseph Lincoln Steffens (1866-1936), American journalist and reformer. *Autobiography*, 1931.

176. Every age needs men who will redeem the time by living with a vision of things that are to be.
Adlai E. Stevenson (1900-1965), Governor of Illinois (D) and U.S. Ambassador to the United Nations. Speech, 1964.

177. If the general is unable to control his patience and orders his troops to swarm up the wall like ants, one-third of them will be killed without taking the city.
Sun-tzu (c.400 B.C.), Chinese writer of the Age of Warring States. *The Art of War*.

178. The disdain that political leaders show the ordinary citizen is reciprocated.
Barry Sussman, American political analyst and writer. *What Americans Really Think and Why Our Politicians Pay No Attention*, 1988.

179. I am not, and never claimed to be a leader.... I am sort of an advisor; I try to harmonize the interests of the party ... as I understand them.... I am simply a passenger on a ship, with the privilege of going ashore if I do not like its management or its course.
Peter B. Sweeny (1824-1911), leader, Tammany Hall, NY (D). Quoted in M. R. Werner, *Tammany Hall*, 1928.

180. Forethought and prudence are the proper qualities of a leader.
Cornelius Tacitus (c.55-c.117), Roman historian. *Annals of the Julian Emperors*, XIII.

181. You wish to rise: Make enemies.
Charles-Maurice de Talleyrand-Périgord (Prince de Bénévent) (1754-1838), French diplomat and statesman. Advice to Louis-Adolphe Thiers, 1827.

182. The command in war is given to the strongest or to the bravest; and in peace, taken up and exercised by the boldest.
William Temple (1628-1699), English statesman and writer. Quoted in S. Austin Allibone, *Prose Quotations*, 1876.

183. I don't care how much my ministers talk – as long as they do what I say.
Margaret Thatcher, Prime Minister of Great Britain (Conservative). Remark to reporters, 1987.

184. When a woman is strong, she is strident. If a man is strong, gosh, he's a good guy.
Margaret Thatcher. Quoted in *Time*, Dec. 3, 1990.

185. The king reigns but does not govern. (*La roi règne et ne gouverne pas.*)
Louis-Adolphe Thiers (1797-1877), 1st President of the Third French Republic. Maxim of State.

186. The King *[Napoléon III]* was personally a hero, but politically a coward.
Louis-Adolphe Thiers. 1840.

187. The king is the country made man.
Louis-Adolphe Thiers. Quoted in Hayward, *Eminent Statesmen and Writers*, I, 1880.

188. I have fought a good fight, I have finished my course, I have kept the faith.
New Testament, *2 Timothy* 4:7.

189. A man who is influenced by the polls or is afraid to make decisions which may make him unpop-

ular is not a man to represent the welfare of the country. If he is right, it makes no difference whether the press and the special interests like what he does, or what they have to say about him.

Harry S Truman (1884-1972), 33rd President of the United States (D-MO). *Memoirs: The Years of Decision*, 1955.

190. Men make history and not the other way 'round. In periods where there is no leadership, society stands still. Progress occurs when courageous, skillful leaders seize the opportunity to change things for the better.

Harry S Truman. Quoted by Congressman Wright Patman in a memorial tribute to Truman, House of Representatives, Jan. 3, 1973.

191. It is amazing what you can accomplish if you do not care who gets the credit.

Harry S Truman. Quoted in *Time*, Nov. 7, 1988.

192. The Right says let the Left run the government, and we and the country will draw its conclusions; and the Left says, let the Right take hold, and we and the country will draw its conclusions.... Each side hopes that the other will make a failure, and the country will turn to it for leadership.

I. G. Tsereteli (1881-1959), provisional government minister, Russia. Speech, Congress of Soviets, June 1917.

193. Think like men of action and act like men of thought.

William V. S. Tubman (1895-1971), 18th President of Liberia. Message to the graduating class, College of West Africa, Monrovia, Nov. 1950.

194. All kings is mostly rapscallions.

Mark Twain (Samuel Langhorne Clemens) (1835-1910), American writer. *The Adventures of Huckleberry Finn*, 1885.

195. To be a king all you need to know is how to sign your name, read a manuscript *[deliver a speech]*, and mount a horse.

Umberto I (1844-1900), King of Italy. Advice to his son, Victor Emmanuel.

196. Great men undertake great things because they are great; and fools because they think them easy.

Marquis de Vauvenargues (1715-1747), French soldier and moralist. *Réflexions et Maximes*.

197. For bad kings to flourish is death to their peoples.

Marquis de Vauvenargues. *Ibid.*

198. It is now demonstrably harder for us to propose something and expect the rest of the world to follow.

Paul A. Volcker, Chairman, Federal Reserve Board. Interview, *Time*, Jan. 23, 1989.

199. I did not lead the Alliance. I followed the Alliance.

Thomas E. Watson (1856-1922), U.S. Congressman and U.S. Senator (D-GA). In reference to the Farmers' Alliance. Quoted in Norman Pollack, ed., *The Populist Mind*, 1967.

200. An aristocracy that shirks its leadership is done for. Its only excuse for existence is that it takes the lead.

Alfred North Whitehead (1861-1947), English philosopher and mathematician. Quoted in Lucien Price, *Dialogues of Alfred North Whitehead*, 1954.

201. The people are always ahead of their leaders.

L. Douglas Wilder, Governor of Virginia (D). Interview, ABC, *This Week*, Jan. 14, 1990.

202. I rule by the favor of God, and of no one else.

Wilhelm I (1797-1888), King of Prussia and Emperor of Germany. Statement on becoming King, 1861.

203. There is one certain means by which I can be sure never to see my country's ruin: I will die in the last ditch.

William III (1650-1702), King of England. Remark to the Duke of Buckingham.

204. The only real leadership in governmental affairs must be legislative leadership.... The leaders, if there be any, must be those who suggest the opinions and rule the actions of the representative body.

Woodrow Wilson (1856-1924), 28th President of the United States (D-NJ). *Congressional Government, A Study in American Politics*, 1885.

205. The whole art and practice of government consists, not in moving individuals, but in moving masses.

Woodrow Wilson. Speech, Woman Suffrage Convention, Atlantic City, NJ, Sept. 8, 1916.

Chapter 56

Legislating and Legislation

1. We have chosen you our next representative at the next General Assembly, and when we did so we expected and still do expect that you will speak our sense in every case when we shall expressly declare it, or when you can by any other means discover it.

   Instructions from voters to their Assembly delegates, Orange County, NC. 1773.

2. This is a pity, for I had many other things of great interest to say. But, as my time has expired, and not wishing to further interrupt the proceedings, I would at least like to have permission to print some remarks in the *[Congressional] Record* and insert "laughter and applause" in appropriate places. Now I will retire to the cloak-room to receive congratulations.

   John Mills Allen (1846-1917), U.S. Congressman (D-MS). Comment when informed that his speaking time had expired. Speech, House Committee on Rivers and Harbors, Apr. 1885.

3. Even when laws have been written down, they ought not always to remain unaltered.

   Aristotle (384-322 B.C.), Greek philosopher and teacher. *Politics.*

4. Readiness to change from old law to new law enfeebles the power of the law.

   Aristotle. *Ibid.*

5. Don't call the question unless you've got the votes.

   Richard K. Armey, U.S. Congressman (R-TX). ABC, *It's Your Business*, Feb. 5, 1989.

6. We have all the mistakes of one-sex legislation.

   Nancy Astor (1879-1964), American-born Mayor of Plymouth, England, and first woman to sit in the House of Commons. *My Two Countries*, 1923.

7. One cannot legislate problems out of existence. It has been tried.

   Norman R. Augustine, President and CEO, Martin Marietta Corp.. *Augustine's Laws*, 1987.

8. His laws, whoso marks them well, are deep, and not vulgar; not made upon the spur of a particular occasion for the present, but out of providence of the future, to make the estate of his people still more and more happy; after the manner of the legislators in ancient and heroical times.

   Francis Bacon, 1st Baron Verulam and Viscount St. Albans (1561-1626), Lord Chancellor of England. *History of King Henry VII*, 1622.

9. A Parliament is nothing less than a big meeting of more or less idle people.

   Walter Bagehot (1826-1877), British economist and historian. *The English Constitution*, 1867.

10. We live in a world of specialists in every phase of our lives. While the congressional system with its high degree of specialization *[the committee system]* may appear fragmented and disorderly to those who admire the symmetry of the parliamentary system, I would submit that the congressional system is peculiarly adapted to the world in which we live today.

    Joseph W. Barr, U.S. Congressman (D-IN); Chairman, Federal Deposit Insurance Corporation; and U.S. Undersecretary of the Treasury. Speech, American Society for Public Administration, Sept. 22, 1965.

11. The political party having the majority ... *[will]* necessarily control all the committees ... because they ... must, as a party, protect themselves against the chance of the control of the business of the body going into the hands of their opponents.

    James A. Bayard, Jr. (1799-1880), U.S. Senator (D-DE). Quoted in *The Congressional Globe*, 1857.

12. As I look back on it I am very ashamed of my vote *[supporting]* the McCarran Act. I do have some excuses and alibis, though in retrospect they are not very good ones.

William Benton (1900-1973), U.S. Senator (D-CT) and U.S. Ambassador to UNESCO. Letter to Sen. Ralph Flanders, Feb. 17, 1954.

13. The Board of Education met on Tuesday evening and shamefully disappointed the hopes of the public. Not a man was called a liar, not a spitoon was cast, there was never an inkstand flung. We would like to know what these men are for, if not to furnish their quota of city amusement and contribute to the sensational literature of the town?

Ambrose Bierce (1842-1914?), American journalist. *News Letter*, Apr. 10, 1869.

14. If we think it necessary to wage war, we shall do so with or without your consent.

Otto von Bismarck-Schoenhausen (1815-1898), Chancellor of Germany. To deputies of the Prussian Parliament, 1864.

15. My responsibility is not to the public. It is to the chairman alone.

John Blandford, chief counsel, House Armed Services Committee. Quoted in *The Nation*, Jan. 19, 1970.

16. We can't get any new thinking because we can't get any new thinkers.

David Boas, Vice President, CATO Institute. In reference to the 98 percent reelection rate of congressional incumbents. Quoted on National Public Radio, *The Fred Fisk Show*, Jan. 14, 1989.

17. An investigation in which the processes of law-making and law-evaluating are submerged entirely in exposure of individual behavior – in adjudication, of a sort, through the exposure process – is outside the constitutional pale of congressional inquiry.

William J. Brennan, Jr., U.S. Supreme Court Justice. Comment on a celebrated case involving the right of the House Un-American Activities Committee to "expose" someone as a Communist. *Barenblatt* v. *United States*, 1958 (dissent).

18. It is the duty of Parliament to look at the men as well as the measures.

Henry Peter Brougham, Baron Brougham and Vaux (1778-1868), Scottish jurist and Member of Parliament, Great Britain (Whig). Speech, House of Commons, Nov. 1830.

19. The House *[of Representatives]* has become not so much a legislative assembly as a huge panel from which committees are selected.

James Bryce (1838-1922), British Ambassador to the United States. *The American Commonwealth*, 1888.

20. In all forms of government the people is the true legislator.

Edmund Burke (1729-1797), British statesman. *Tracts on the Popery Laws*, III, i.

21. Laws, like houses, lean on one another.

Edmund Burke. *On the Sublime and Beautiful*, 1756.

22. In effect, to follow, not to force, the public inclination – to give a direction, a form, a technical dress, and a specific sanction, to the general sense of the community, is the true end of legislation.

Edmund Burke. Letter to the Sheriffs of Bristol, Apr. 3, 1777.

23. The chairman of a committee should be in harmony with the majority who constitute it.

Benjamin Franklin Butler (1818-1893), U.S. Congressman (R-MA) and Governor of Massachusetts (D and Greenback). Explanation of refusal to serve as chairman of a committee to investigate the Ku Klux Klan. House debate, 1871.

24. Man is the only animal that laughs and has a state legislature.

Samuel Butler (1835-1902), British writer. Quoted in Herbert V. Prochnow, *A Dictionary of Wit, Wisdom and Satire*, 1962.

25. If you know an amendment *[you are opposed to]* will pass you don't want a roll call *[vote]* because that makes it *[the amendment]* harder to drop in conference.

Harry F. Byrd, Jr., U.S. Senator (D and Ind.-VA). 1965.

26. The rules of the Senate are made for the convenience of those who wish to delay.

Robert C. Byrd, U.S. Congressman and U.S. Senator (R-WV). *Congressional Record*, 94th Congress, Aug. 31, 1976.

27. One has to be available, very much available, and ready to protect the interests of his colleagues.

Robert C. Byrd. Explanation of his success as Majority Leader. Quoted in *Regardie's*, Jan. 1987.

28. You can go to Hell! It makes no difference what a majority of you decide; I am the Committee.

Philip P. Campbell (1862-1941), U.S. Congressman (R-KS). Statement blocking an investigation of military procurement even though every other member of the committee wanted to pursue the investigation. House Rules Committee meeting, 1922.

29. A majority can do anything.

Joseph G. Cannon (1836-1926), U.S. Congressman and Speaker of the House (R-IL). Quoted in *Congressional Record*, Mar. 4, 1923.

30. When it comes to listening to my constituents or to the governor's staff, who are more interested in their pet projects and their government cars, I'll vote for my constituents every time.

Gerald Cardinale, New Jersey State Senator (R). Quoted in *The New York Times*, Oct. 27, 1988.

31. So you *[Romans]* when you have got together in a body, let yourselves be guided by those whom singly you would never think of being advised by.

Marcus Porcius Cato (The Elder) (234-149 B.C.), Roman censor. Quoted in Plutarch, *The Parallel Lives: Cato the Censor*.

32. You had better have one king than five hundred.

Charles II (1630-1685), King of England. Statement dissolving Parliament, Mar. 28, 1681.

33. The fundamental principle of all just legislation is that the legislature shall not take the property of A and give it to B.

Salmon P. Chase (1808-1873), Governor of Ohio (Free Soil), U.S. Senator (Free Soil and R-OH), U.S. Secretary of the Treasury, and Chief Justice, U.S. Supreme Court. *Legal Tender Cases*, 1871 (dissent).

34. I cannot subscribe to the omnipotence of a State Legislature.

Samuel Chase (1741-1811), American revolutionary leader and U.S. Supreme Court Justice. *Calder* v. *Bull*, 1798 (dissent).

35. All legislation is founded upon the principle of mutual concession.

Henry Clay (1777-1852), U.S. Senator (National Republican and Whig-KY), Speaker of the House, and U.S. Secretary of State. Quoted on PBS, *The Congress*, 1989.

36. The science of legislation is like that of medicine in one respect: that it is far more easy to point out what will do harm than what will do good.

Charles Caleb Colton (c.1780-1832), British clergyman and writer. *Lacon*, I, 1825.

37. Exhaustion and exasperation are frequently the handmaidens of legislative decision.

Barber D. Conable, U.S. Congressman (R-NY) and Chairman, World Bank. Quoted in *Time*, Oct. 22, 1984.

38. Men do not make laws. They do but discover them. Laws must be justified by something more than the will of the majority. They must rest on the eternal foundation of righteousness. That state is the most fortunate which has the aptest instruments for the discovery of laws.

Calvin Coolidge (1872-1933), 29th President of the United States (R-MA). Presidential address to the Massachusetts State Senate, Jan. 20, 1914.

39. If I have to invade the sacred precincts of the White House to find out what is behind this paralysis of the Senate, I will.

Norris H. Cotton (1901-1989), U.S. Congressman and U.S. Senator (R-NH). In response to administration tactics to delay a vote on the Church-Cooper proposal to limit American involvement in Cambodia after June 30, 1970. Quoted in his obituary, *The Washington Post*, Feb. 25, 1989.

40. Woe betide a bill that is opposed! It is laid aside for further time, and that never comes.

David Crockett (1786-1836), U.S. Congressman (D-TN). *The Life of Davy Crockett*, 1889.

41. Do you know what it takes to get a good piece of legislation passed ... one that everyone agrees on? The egos. The turf battles.... It's incredible.

Alfonse D'Amato, U.S. Senator (R-NY). Quoted on PBS, *The Power Game*, Jan. 2, 1989.

42. We have a lame-duck Congress, we have a lame-duck administration, we have a lame-duck Secretary of Defense, all of whom support this legislation. If we do not pass this bill and allow these *[military]* base closures to be named this year, it will be another ten years before such an opportunity comes again.

William L. Dickenson, U.S. Congressman (R-AL). Speech, House Armed Services Committee, July 12, 1988.

43. You start from the broad premise that all of us have a common duty to the country to perform. Legislation is always the art of the possible. You could, of course, follow a course of solid opposition, of stalemate, but that is not in the interest of the country.

Everett M. Dirksen (1896-1969), U.S. Congressman and U.S. Senator (R-IL). Quoted in his obituary, *Times-Dispatch*, Richmond, VA, Sept. 8, 1969.

44. A precedent embalms a principle. The principle may be right or may be wrong – that is a question for discussion; but at the first glance it is right to conclude that it is a principle that has been acted upon and recognized by those who preceded us.

Benjamin Disraeli, 1st Earl of Beaconsfield (1804-1881), Prime Minister of Great Britain (Conservative). Speech in Parliament, Feb. 22, 1848.

45. If we're going to be treated like a bunch of bums on this side of the aisle, then say so.
Robert J. Dole, U.S. Senator (R-KS). Quoted on NBC, *The McLaughlin Group*, July 22, 1990.

46. *[There is]* no right of Congress ... to force a good thing upon a people who are unwilling to receive it. The great principle is the right of every community to judge and decide for itself whether a thing is right or wrong, whether it would be good or evil to adopt it.... Whenever you put a limitation upon the right of any people to decide what laws they want, you have destroyed the fundamental principle of self-government.
Stephen A. Douglas (1813-1861), U.S. Congressman and U.S. Senator (D-IL). Speech, Chicago, IL, July 9, 1858.

47. *[America]* is so awash in rights that we are virtually unable to pass legislation reflecting traditional religious and moral views. Moral relativism will then be the rule, at law; and what is true at law will shape what is practiced.
Terry Eastland, special assistant to U.S. Attorney General Edwin Meese III. In Charles Horn, ed., *Whose Values?*, 1985.

48. No one's going to admit they're in favor of adulterers, although it may not be a group unfamiliar to the Senate. There have been some remarkably lecherous people in the Senate over the years.
Claire Ebel, representative, American Civil Liberties Union in Concord, NH. Comment when New Hampshire's Senate defeated a bill that would have decriminalized adultery. Quoted in *The Washington Post*, Apr. 30, 1989.

49. I do not object to butchering quite so much if everybody gets a fair share of the hog. But when a favored few get all the ham and pork chops, and the rest of the people get just plain old sow belly, at least the people are entitled to know what they are swallowing.
Herman P. Eberharter (1892-1958), U.S. Congressman (D-PA). In reference to the fate of his bill in a House-Senate conference committee. *Congressional Record*, Oct. 16, 1951.

50. I asked for more information because I am unable to unscrew the inscrutable.
Samuel J. Ervin, Jr. (1896-1985), U.S. Congressman and U.S. Senator (D-NC). To Everett M. Dirksen. Senate debate, Mar. 15, 1960.

51. It really is not that important to most evangelicals who's governor *[of Virginia]*. Nothing of significance to us is decided at the Statehouse. Issues that concern us are decided at the White House and the Supreme Court.
Jerry Falwell, American clergyman and founder, Moral Majority. Quoted in *The Washington Post*, Mar. 19, 1989.

52. You change laws by changing lawmakers.
Frances (Sissy) Farenthold, Texas State Legislator (D). Interview, *The Bakersfield Californian*, Apr. 22, 1978.

53. A Senator who wants to stir up trouble ... can do so by introducing on the floor amendments which he was duty bound to present in committee. But presentation in committee makes no headlines.
Ralph E. Flanders (1880-1970), U.S. Senator (R-VT). *Senator from Vermont*, 1961.

54. Sometime between elections we should concentrate on doing something.
Thomas S. Foley, U.S. Congressman and Speaker of the House (D-WA). Interview, ABC, *This Week*, Mar. 9, 1991.

55. A voting record is your work product. It tells people where you stand on issues, and for better or worse it implies you're there doing what you're elected to do. It's the only litmus test available.
Peter Franchot, Delegate, Maryland House of Representatives (D). Quoted in *The Montgomery Journal*, July 12, 1990.

56. Tact, respect, and generosity toward variant views will always commend themselves to those charged with the duties of legislation so as to achieve a maximum of good will and to require a minimum of unwilling submission to a general law.
Felix Frankfurter (1882-1965), U.S. Supreme Court Justice. *West Virginia Board of Education* v. *Barnette*, 1942.

57. Those who govern, having much business on their hands, do not generally like to take the trouble of considering and carrying into execution new projects. The best public measures are therefore seldom adopted from previous wisdom, but forced by the occasion.
Benjamin Franklin (1706-1790), Member, Continental Congress and Constitutional Convention, Governor of Pennsylvania, and U.S. Minister to France. *Autobiography*, 1867.

58. The greatest single virtue of a strong legislature is not what it can do, but what it can prevent.
J. William Fulbright, U.S. Senator (D-AR). Speech, Georgetown University School of Law, Washington, DC, 1971.

59. The trouble today is that we have too many laws.
John Nance Garner (1868-1967), U.S. Congressman (D-TX), Speaker of the House, and Vice President of the United States. Campaign speech, 1932.

60. Mr. Speaker, I have introduced a resolution declaring July Ice Cream Month. Ice cream is good for you. If the legislative process frustrates you, eat ice cream.
Eligio (Kika) de la Garza II, U.S. Congressman (D-TX). House debate, June 7, 1984.

61. To say that sovereignty vests with the people, and that they have not a right to instruct and control their representative is absurd to the last degree.
Elbridge Gerry (1744-1814), U.S. Congressman (Anti-Federalist-MA) and Vice President of the United States (D). House debate, 1st Congress, 1790.

62. The rankest form of hypocrisy. Laws that are good enough for everybody else ought to be good enough for us.
John H. Glenn, U.S. Senator (D-OH). Comment alluding to Congress's common practice of exempting itself and its members from many laws imposed on everyone else. Quoted in *Time*, May 23, 1988.

63. At a time of tight budgets, unless something is really broken and not working, they *[Congress]* just don't get excited about it.
John H. Glenn. Quoted in *The New York Times*, Oct. 16, 1988.

64. It used to be people came here, did their work for three months or so, then went home. Now we have these huge staffs we created and an atmosphere of being a full-time legislature.... Now things just drift without any direction or urgency.
Emmanuel R. Gold, Deputy Democratic leader, New York State Senate. Quoted in *The New York Times*, July 17, 1988.

65. The conference committee, that wonderful wrestling ring of compromise where House and Senate versions of bills are wrenched into law.
Ellen Goodman, American columnist. *The Boston Globe*, July 16, 1988.

66. I needed the good will of the legislatures of four states. I formed the legislative bodies with my own money. I found it was cheaper that way.
Jay Gould (1836-1892), American industrialist. Congressional testimony, 1891.

67. You cannot dictate to those whose sense you are entrusted to represent.
Henry Grattan (1746-1820), Irish politician. Speech to Irish Parliament, Apr. 19, 1780.

68. Our fathers waged a bloody conflict with England, because *they* were taxed without being represented.... *They* were not willing to be governed by laws which *they* had no voice in making; but this is the way in which women are governed in this Republic.
Angelina Grimké (1805-1879), American abolitionist and suffragist. *Letters to Catherine Beecher*, No. 11, 1836.

69. I am president of Congress, not the director of an insane asylum.
Ulysses Guimaraes, President (Majority Leader), Brazilian National Congress. Response when asked to have the assembly remove items in the proposed constitution at the last minute. Quoted in *The New York Times*, July 28, 1988.

70. It is disturbing to see that people have to take the legislative process into their own hands.
Mark Haarer, Director, California Common Cause. In reference to California voter initiatives. Quoted in *The Washington Post*, July 17, 1988.

71. Men will pursue their interest. It is as easy to change human nature as to oppose the strong current of selfish passions. A wise legislature will gently divert the channel, and direct it, if possible, to the public good.
Alexander Hamilton (1755-1804), Member, Continental Congress and Constitutional Convention, and U.S. Secretary of the Treasury (Federalist-NY). Speech, New York Ratifying Convention, June 21, 1788.

72. When I cease to harmonize with the majority ... I feel that I ought no longer to hold that respectable position *[of Senate Commerce Committee chairman]*.
Hannibal Hamlin (1809-1891), U.S. Congressman (D-ME), U.S. Senator, and Vice President of the United States. On breaking with his party on the issue of slavery in the territories. Senate debate, 1856.

73. A consolidation of unchecked and despotic power in the House of Representatives.
Rutherford B. Hayes (1822-1893), 19th President of the United States (R-OH). Description of the rules of the House of Representatives. Quoted in William E. Nelson, *The Roots of American Bureaucracy*, 1982.

74. You use whatever lever you have.
Jesse Helms, U.S. Senator (R-NC). Explanation for his threat to block Senate approval of an appointment he favored in order to achieve another political objective. Quoted in *Time*, May 30, 1988.

75. We ought as Legislatures to meet with national feelings, and our Legislation ought to be for the general good; and as far as practicable equity and

justice to all sections of our country.

Andrew Jackson (1767-1845), 7th President of the United States (D-TN). Letter to Rachel Donelson Jackson, Apr. 12, 1823.

76. This is all that we want ... to nullify the nullifyers *[in Congress]*.

Andrew Jackson. Letter to Martin Van Buren, Nov. 18, 1832.

77. Shame! Shame on this House! A civilized society does not stifle opposition. It meets it.

Andrew Jacobs, Jr., U.S. Congressman (D-IN). Comment when limited to forty-five seconds to argue against the largest military appropriations bill in U.S. history. House debate, Oct. 1969.

78. They who make laws may without doubt amend or repeal them.

John Jay (1745-1829), President of the Continental Congress, Governor of New York (Federalist), U.S. Foreign Secretary, and 1st Chief Justice, U.S. Supreme Court. *The Federalist*, No. 64, Mar. 5, 1788.

79. The legitimate acts of government extend to such acts only as are injurious to others.

Thomas Jefferson (1743-1826), 3rd President of the United States (Democratic Republican-VA). *Notes on the State of Virginia*, 1784.

80. The tendency of the legislation of this country is to build up monopolies ... to concentrate power in the hands of the few.

Andrew Johnson (1808-1875), 17th President of the United States (War Democrat-TN). Quoted in Frederick Moore, *Andrew Johnson: Life and Speeches*, 1875.

81. In all political regulations, good cannot be complete, it can only be predominant.

Samuel Johnson (1709-1784), British writer and lexicographer. *Journey to the Western Islands*, 1775.

82. When you see a *[legislative]* situation you cannot understand, look for the financial interest.

Tom L. Johnson (1854-1911), U.S. Congressman and Mayor of Cleveland, OH (D). Interview, 1894.

83. If you're going to play the game properly you'd better know every rule.

Barbara Jordan. U.S. Congresswoman (D-TX). Quoted in *Ebony*, Feb. 1975.

84. The cry of losers.

Jack F. Kemp, U.S. Congressman and U.S. Secretary of Housing and Urban Development (R-NY). In reference to proposals to limit the terms of legislators. Quoted on PBS, *Washington Week in Review*, Dec. 14, 1990.

85. Man, you could make a lot of friends real fast on those supercommittees.

Joseph Kennedy III, U.S. Congressman (D-MA). In reference to the major congressional committees of the House of Representatives. Quoted in *Spy*, Feb. 1989.

86. Legislatures now pass statutes because of, not despite, their lack of clarity. By using vague language, legislators can avoid making the difficult political choices that they have to confront when drafting a statute precisely.

Alex Kozinski, U.S. Federal Appeals Judge. Quoted in *The Washington Post*, Apr. 28, 1991.

87. Parliamentarianism is nauseating to anyone who has ever seen it at close range.

Peter A. Kropotkin (1842-1921), Russian prince and anarchist. *Memoirs of a Revolutionist*, 1899.

88. Every member present must behave like a gentleman, and those who are not must try to.

Fiorello H. La Guardia (1882-1947), U.S. Congressman (R and Socialist-NY) and Mayor of New York City (R and Fusion Party). Remark to Ald. Bruce M. Falconer, 1920.

89. This is beginning to sound more like a canonization hearing than a confirmation hearing.

Patrick Leahy, U.S. Senator (D-VT). Comment on the Senate confirmation hearings for William Sessions, who had overwhelming support to be confirmed as director of the Federal Bureau of Investigation. Quoted in *Newsweek*, Sept. 21, 1987.

90. It is natural for men, who wish to hasten the adoption of a measure to tell us now is the crisis – now is the crucial moment which must be seized, or all will be lost.

Richard Henry Lee (1732-1794), Member, Continental Congress; signer of the Declaration of Independence; and U.S. Senator (VA). Letter, Oct. 8, 1787.

91. Senator, if you vote for us, maybe we could get a battleship into Arizona.

John F. Lehman, U.S. Secretary of the Navy. Remark to Sen. Barry Goldwater, quoted on PBS, *The Power Game*, Jan. 2, 1989.

92. If elected, I shall consider the whole people of Sangamon my constituents, as well those that oppose as those that support me. While acting as their representative I shall be governed by their will on all subjects upon which I have the means of knowing what their will is.

Abraham Lincoln (1809-1865), 16th President of the United States (R-IL). Campaign speech, Sangamon, IL, 1836.

93. When you sit in council for the welfare of the people, you council for the seventh generation yet unborn.

Oren Lyons, Chief, Onondaga Indians. Interview with Bill Moyers, PBS, July, 1990.

94. To legislate in advance of public opinion is merely to produce anarchy.

Alexander MacKenzie (1822-1892), Prime Minister of Canada (Conservative). Debate, House of Commons, 1877.

95. The *[House of]* Commons, faithful to their system, remained in a wise and masterly inactivity *[during the French Revolution]*.

James Mackintosh (1765-1832), Scottish physician, judge, and historian. *Vindiciae Gallicae*, 1791.

96. Respect for character is always diminished in proportion to the number among whom the blame or praise is to be divided.

James Madison (1751-1836), 4th President of the United States (Democratic Republican-VA). Argument against a popular and large lower House. Debate, Constitutional Convention, Philadelphia, PA, 1787.

97. In all legislative assemblies, the greater the number composing them may be, the fewer will be the men who will in fact direct their proceedings.

James Madison. *The Federalist*, No. 58, Feb. 22, 1788.

98. Their ideas *[those of the voters of a particular district]* may contradict the sense of the whole people; hence the consequence that instructions are binding on the representative is of a doubtful, if not a dangerous nature.

James Madison. Debate, 1st Congress, 1790.

99. Laws and customs may be creative of vice; and should be therefore perpetually under process of observation and correction.

Harriet Martineau (1802-1876), British reformer. *Society in America*, 1837.

100. Being military governor was a pretty heady job. You could turn to your secretary and say, "Take a law."

John J. McCloy (1895-1989), U.S. Assistant Secretary of War (D); President, World Bank; and Military Governor of Germany. Quoted in *The New York Times*, July 29, 1990.

101. You don't compromise principles, but you harmonize tactics to preserve unity.

John W. McCormack (1891-1980), U.S. Congressman and Speaker of the House (D-MA). Quoted in Charles Henning, *The Wit and Wisdom of Politics*, 1989.

102. I don't think we can let such an outlandish result stand. I think to do so is to leave every civil official in the land open for somebody to say, "Well I don't like him."

Evan Mecham, Governor of Arizona (R). In reference to his recent impeachment as Governor. Quoted in *The Washington Post*, June 26, 1988.

103. I entered Parliament with what I thought to be the lowest possible opinion of the average member. I came out with one still lower.

John Stuart Mill (1806-1873), Member of Parliament, Great Britain, and political economist. *Autobiography*, 1873.

104. Sports is a metaphor for life recognized by us in the masculine world. People play basketball like they legislate.

George Miller, U.S. Congressman (D-CA). Quoted in *The Washington Post*, June 26, 1991.

105. I'm a typical Maryland legislator. I've voted both ways on the issue.

V. Mike Miller, Jr., President of the Maryland Senate (D). Quoted in *The Washington Post*, Aug. 3, 1988.

106. Our whole system was to settle disputes within the *[congressional]* committees. It's a waste of time to bring out a bill if you can't pass it. I just don't like to have a record vote for the sake of having a vote.

Wilbur D. Mills (1909-1992), U.S. Congressman (D-AR). Quoted in *The New York Times Magazine*, Feb. 25, 1968.

107. Bipartisanship means you work together to work it out.

George J. Mitchell, U.S. Senator (D-ME). PBS, *MacNeil-Lehrer News Hour*, Jan. 23, 1989.

108. Do you want to make a statement or do you want to make a law?

George J. Mitchell. Comment to Senate leaders, when there were not enough votes to override a presidential veto of a budget bill with a tax provision opposed by the President. Senate debate, Oct. 18, 1990.

109. This legislation is in the President's interest, if only the President could be brought to see it.

Daniel P. Moynihan, Chief American Delegate to the United Nations and U.S. Senator (D-NY). In reference to a transportation bill with a tax provision opposed by the President. Quoted in *The New York Times*, Nov. 9, 1989.

110. You have come here by the sovereign will of the people to cooperate with me in carrying out the mandate recently pronounced at the polls.

William Henry David Murray (1869-1956), Governor of Oklahoma and U.S. Congressman (D). Message to the Oklahoma legislature, 1931.

111. Citizen initiatives frequently tackle the tough sensitive issues that legislators avoid to protect their popularity.... After all, the electorate need not concern itself with staying in office; it must only live with the results of its own decisions.
John Naisbitt, American futurist and writer. *Megatrends*, 1982.

112. Large legislative bodies resolve themselves into coteries, and coteries into jealousies.
Napoléon I (1769-1821), military leader and Emperor of France. *Maxims*.

113. What holds the place of the Deity on earth? The legislature.
Napoléon I. *Ibid*.

114. A politician knows that more important than the bill that is proposed is the law that is passed.
Richard M. Nixon, 37th President of the United States (R-CA). Eulogy for Everett M. Dirksen, Sept. 8, 1969.

115. A lot of yesterday's solutions are today's problems.
Samuel A. Nunn, U.S. Senator (D-GA). Quoted in *The Washington Post*, June 22, 1988.

116. The only way you ever get anything done in this town is to have the moderates of both parties get together. The extremes of the parties get all the attention but they can't pass legislation.
Samuel A. Nunn. Interview, NBC, *Meet the Press*, July 23, 1989.

117. Anyone who assumes that a member of Congress is only working when he is on the House floor is either a charter member of the flat-earth society or he is just about as uninformed about the legislative process as I would be about business if I suggested that the only time a hardware dealer is working is when he is standing behind the cash register.
David R. Obey, U.S. Congressman (D-WI). Letter to constituent, May 19, 1975.

118. Do not be willing to strike up the band unless you are willing to listen to the music.
David R. Obey. House debate, Jan. 12, 1991.

119. I strongly condemn the shooting which should never have happened under Parliament's roof.
Turgut Ozal, Prime Minister of Turkey. Comment when a member of the Prime Minister's party shot and killed an opposition member on the floor of Parliament. Press conference, Ankara, Mar. 30, 1989.

120. To doubt the authority of the people to instruct their representatives will give them just cause to be alarmed for their fate.
John Page (1744-1808), U.S. Congressmen and Governor of Virginia (R). House debate, 1st Congress, 1790.

121. If Congress must do a painful thing, the thing must be done in an odd-numbered year *[because congressional elections are in even-numbered years]*.
James J. (Jake) Pickle, U.S. Congressman (D-TX). 1974.

122. There are those in Wisconsin who say we'd be better off if I missed all those votes.
William Proxmire, U.S. Senator (D-WI). Comment on his Senate record of 10,500 consecutive roll calls. Quoted in *USA Today*, Oct. 13, 1988.

123. Everyone *[in Congress]* is paddling his own canoe while the nation suffers.
James Quillen, U.S. Congressman (R-TN). Quoted in *USA Today*, Oct. 19, 1990.

124. It's awfully easy to get a law passed. It's very difficult to get it unpassed.
Dixy Lee Ray, Governor of Washington and Chairman, U.S. Atomic Energy Commission (D). Interview, C-SPAN, *Booknotes*, June 16, 1991.

125. Let the other fellow get the headlines. I'll take the laws.
Samuel T. Rayburn (1882-1961), U.S. Congressman and Speaker of the House (D-TX). Quoted in H. B. Dulaney, *Speak, Mr. Speaker*, 1978.

126. I never bother with details. First, I don't know them – I'm not smart enough. Second, if the chairman of a committee has a problem, he'll come in and spell it out for me.
Samuel T. Rayburn. Quoted in Charles Henning, *The Wit and Wisdom of Politics*, 1989.

127. I will veto again and again until spending is brought under control.
Ronald Reagan, 40th President of the United States (R-CA). Quoted in *Time*, Mar. 18, 1985.

128. Gentlemen, we *[Republicans]* have decided to perpetrate the following outrage.
Thomas B. Reed (1839-1902), U.S. Congressman and Speaker of the House (R-ME). Showing Democratic colleagues in the Rules Committee a new bill. Attributed.

129. One of the greatest delusions in the world is the hope that the evils of the world can be cured by legislation. I am happy in the belief that the solution of the great difficulties of the world are in better hands even than those of Congress.

Thomas B. Reed. Speech, House of Representatives, 1891.

130. The rules of this House are not for the purpose of protecting the rights of the minority, but to promote the orderly conduct of the business of the House.

Thomas B. Reed. House debate, 1894.

131. The right of the minority is to draw its salaries, and its function is to make a quorum.

Thomas B. Reed. Quoted in *Conservative Digest*, Nov. 1987.

132. If you can't fill the till, then don't pass the bill.

Ann Richards, Governor of Texas (D). Gubernatorial election debate, C-SPAN, Nov. 4, 1990.

133. The desire is there, but the wallet is weak.

Cokie Roberts, American broadcast journalist. Description of the status of some proposed legislation before Congress. National Public Radio, Sept. 7, 1988.

134. Time after time, in meeting legislative opposition in my own state, I have taken an issue directly to the voters by radio, and invariably I have met a most heartening response.

Franklin D. Roosevelt (1882-1945), 32nd President of the United States (D-NY). Quoted in Arthur M. Schlesinger, Jr., *The Coming of the New Deal*, 1959.

135. This action *[of Congress]* is a benefit only to the criminal classes.

Theodore Roosevelt (1858-1919), 26th President of the United States (R-NY). Comment on signing an appropriations bill to keep the federal government in business. 1909.

136. People who don't want to do anything can find a million reasons why not.

Daniel D. Rostenkowski, U.S. Congressman (D-IL). Interview, PBS, *Adam Smith's Money World*, June 30, 1990.

137. The ability to foresee that some things cannot be foreseen is a very necessary quality *[of legislators]*.

Jean-Jacques Rousseau (1712-1778), French philosopher. Quoted in Arthur M. Schlesinger, Jr., *The Imperial Presidency*, 1973.

138. Government neither subsists nor arises because it is good or useful, but solely because it is inevitable.

George Santayana (1863-1952), American philosopher. *The Life of Reason*, 1906.

139. I'm not one of those who subscribe to the theory that making a lot of noise is the best way to get things done.

Paul S. Sarbanes, U.S. Congressman and U.S. Senator (D-MD). Campaign debate, 1988.

140. Don't wait until the *[legislative]* crisis occurs. Jump in there.

Claudine Schneider, U.S. Congresswoman (R-RI). Harvard Fellows Seminar, C-SPAN, May 27, 1991.

141. All might go well in the Commonwealth, if everyone in the Parliament would lay down his own interest, and aim at the general good.

John Selden (1584-1654), English jurist and Member of Long Parliament. *Table-Talk: Public Interest.*

142. Dissensions in Parliament may at length come to a good end, though first there be a deal to do, and a great deal of noise, which mad wild folks make.

John Selden. *Table-Talk: Parliament.*

143. The brain may devise laws for the blood, but a hot temper leaps o'er a cold decree.

William Shakespeare (1564-1616), English writer. *The Merchant of Venice*, I,ii.

144. The approach of waiting until something is an immense crisis is just not a responsible one, but that appears to be the way things work.

Larry Shapiro, Executive Director, New York Environmental Planning Lobby. In reference to the New York State Legislature. Quoted in *The New York Times*, July 17, 1988.

145. If they *[elected representatives]* were to be guided by instructions, there would be no use in deliberation; all that a man would have to do would be for him to produce his instruction, and lay them on the table, and let them speak for him.

Roger Sherman (1721-1793), Delegate, Constitutional Convention; U.S. Congressman; and U.S. Senator (Federalist-CT). Debate, 1st Congress, 1790.

146. When the people have chosen a representative, it is his duty to meet with others from different parts of the Union, and consult, and agree with them as to such acts as are for the general benefit of the whole community.

Roger Sherman. *Ibid.*

147. I've done things in legislating that have alienated almost every single interest group in the United States.

Alan K. Simpson, U.S. Senator (R-WY). Explanation for his not being a good selection for Vice President. ABC, *Nightline*, Aug. 12, 1988.

148. Compromise is the cement that holds our family together. It holds our society together, and it holds our democracy together.

James C. Slattery, U.S. Congressman (D-KS). House debate, Oct. 7, 1990.

149. I think if I can get a vast majority of the membership of the Ways and Means Committee to agree upon something, that I've got a vast majority of the House agreed upon the same thing. Because our committee is a cross-section of the people of the United States.

Dennis A. Smith, U.S. Congressman (R-OR). Interview with Stephen Horn, Oct. 11, 1967.

150. I do a lot of fussing about it, but when the chips are down I think the only feasible and practical way we can operate is under a closed rule *[with no individual amendments]*.

Howard W. Smith (1883-1976), U.S. Congressman (D-VA). Congressional debate, Mar. 28, 1962.

151. Every law which originated in ignorance and malice, and gratifies the passions from which it sprang, we call the wisdom of our ancestors.

Sydney Smith (1771-1845), British clergyman and essayist. *Letters of Peter Plymley*, 1807.

152. Legislation is a business in which you do something, then wait to see who hollers, and then relieve the hollering as best you can to see who else hollers.

Thomas V. Smith (1890-1964), U.S. Congressman (D-IL). *The Legislative Way of Life*, 1940.

153. Precedents are not only to be followed; they are to be created.

Stephen J. Solarz, U.S. Congressman (D-NY). Television interview, 1991.

154. Because I live among mortals and not among angels.

Thaddeus Stevens (1792-1868), U.S. Congressman (Whig and R-PA). Explanation for his willingness to accept Reconstruction legislation that was inconsistent with his basic principles. Quoted in *Congressional Globe*, June 13, 1866.

155. If you had allowed me to have my rights, I would not have been compelled to make a corrupt bargain in order to get them.

Thaddeus Stevens. Comment when reproached by a legislative foe for a base parliamentary trick. Quoted in George Sewall Boutwell, *Reminiscences of Sixty Years of Public Affairs*, 1902.

156. The essence of a republican government is not command. It is consent.

Adlai E. Stevenson (1900-1965), Governor of Illinois (D) and U.S. Ambassador to the United Nations. Presidential campaign speech, Springfield, IL, Aug. 14, 1952.

157. We all know what Parliament is, and we are all ashamed of it.

Robert Louis Stevenson (1850-1894), Scottish writer. *Ethical Studies*.

158. Truth is confirmed by inspection and delay; falsehood by haste and uncertainty.

Cornelius Tacitus (c.55-c.117), Roman historian. *Annals of the Julian Emperors*, XIII.

159. We have got to break with the corrupting idea that we can legislate prosperity, legislate equality, legislate opportunity.

Robert A. Taft (1889-1953), U.S. Senator (R-OH). Quoted in Eric F. Goldman, *The Crucial Decade*, 1960.

160. Men, too often in their revenge, set the example of doing away with those general laws to which all alike can look for salvation in adversity.

Thucydides (c.460-c.400 B.C.), Greek historian. *History of the Peloponnesian War*, II.

161. Let us have quiet. If we cannot have quiet, we will have to put you out. This is no place to show any feelings on the matter.

James Strom Thurmond, U.S. Senator (D and R-SC). In response to enthusiastic applause for the statements of an opposition Senator. Senate Judiciary Committee hearing, Apr. 6, 1983.

162. No one ever told me ... that I had to vote. Sometimes you simply don't want to go on record for either side, or you don't really care.

Judith C. Toth, Delegate, Maryland House of Representatives (D). Explanation for missing so many votes during the legislative session. Quoted in *The Montgomery Journal*, July 12, 1990.

163. The fact that we have had a Republican Congress *[the 80th]* for two years has at least given you a chance to see what they are like and what they will do. I call it the worst Congress, except one, this country has ever had. Because I was in the White House, however, they didn't get to walk backwards quite as fast as they wanted to.

Harry S Truman (1884-1972), 33rd President of the United States (D-MO). Campaign remark, Grand Rapids, MI, Sept. 6, 1948.

164. Everywhere the strong have made the laws and oppressed the weak.

Anne Robert Jacques Turgot (1727-1781), Finance Minister of France, statesman, and economist. Quoted in George Seldes, *The Great Quotations*, 1960.

165. I was elected to the State Senate; I found it was impossible to do anything there without paying for it, and money had to be raised for the passage of bills up there; that was the way the *[Tweed]* Ring first became organized – to pay for bills to protect ourselves in the city.
William Marcy Tweed (1823-1878), U.S. Congressman and leader, Tammany Hall, NY (D). Testimony, corruption investigation, 1878.

166. The difference between a cactus and a caucus: On a cactus, the pricks are on the outside.
Morris K. Udall, U.S. Congressman (D-AZ). *Too Funny to Be President*, 1988.

167. If you don't know one of these new fellows, just call him "Mr. Chairman" and you're safe.
Morris K. Udall. Comment on the proliferation of congressional committees and subcommittees. Quoted on PBS, *The Power Game*, Jan. 2, 1989.

168. The nature and principles of right and wrong ... must stand as boundaries to the sphere of every legislative operation.
Vermont Supreme Court, *Langdon* v. *Strong*, 1829.

169. If God Almighty has stricken one member so that he cannot be here to uphold the dictation of a despot, I thank Him for his interference and I will take advantage of it if I can.
Benjamin Franklin Wade (1800-1878), U.S. Senator (Whig and R-OH). Comment when one of Pres. Andrew Johnson's supporters took ill during impeachment hearings and requested a postponement, Apr. 1866.

170. The way to a man's Aye is through his stomach.
Samuel Ward (1814-1932), Washington lobbyist. Quoted in *The Saturday Evening Post*, Dec. 23, 1950.

171. In our political capacity we, that is, the House of Representatives, have done little or nothing.... Before anything is attempted to be done here, it must be arranged elsewhere.
Daniel Webster (1782-1852), U.S. Congressman (Federalist-NH and MA), U.S. Senator (Federalist and Whig-MA), and U.S. Secretary of State. On caucuses in the Congress. Letter, June 4, 1813.

172. Inconsistencies of opinion, arising from changes of circumstance, are often justifiable.
Daniel Webster. Senate speech, July 25, 1846.

173. I am one of the men who create and maintain the prosperity of the nation and who enable it to survive even the affliction of wrong-headed and cranky legislators.
Joseph Wharton (1826-1909), American industrialist and philanthropist. Quoted in Richard Hofstadter, *The American Political Tradition*, 1948.

174. If you can expel whom you please, and reject those disagreeable to you, the House will be self-created and self-existing.
John Wilkes (1727-1797), Member of Parliament, Great Britian, and Lord Mayor of London. Comment when denied a seat for sympathizing with the American colonists. Speech, House of Commons, Feb. 22, 1775.

175. For redress of all grievances, and for the amending, strengthening, and preserving of the laws, Parliaments ought to be held frequently.
William III (1650-1702), King of England. *English Bill of Rights*, Feb. 13, 1689.

176. Never amend a bad bill. Just kill it.
Pete Wilson, U.S. Senator and Governor of California (R). Senate debate, July 18, 1990.

177. Quite as important as legislation is vigilant oversight of administration.
Woodrow Wilson (1856-1924), 28th President of the United States (D-NJ). *Congressional Government*, 1885.

178. The veto power is the people's tribunative prerogative speaking again through their executive.
Levi Woodbury (1789-1851), U.S. Senator (D), U.S. Secretary of the Navy, U.S. Secretary of the Treasury, and U.S. Supreme Court Justice. Speech, Faneuil Hall, Boston, MA, Oct. 19, 1841.

179. I may have been a little high-handed.... I have employed the rules *[of the House of Representatives]* in order to have the legislative program go through rather than let it be obstructed.
James C. Wright, Jr., U.S. Congressman and Speaker of the House (D-TX). ABC, *This Week with David Brinkley*, June 12, 1988.

180. Are we to be eternally bound by the follies of a law which ought never to have been passed?
Robert Wright (1782-1826), U.S. Senator (R), U.S. Congressman, and Governor of Maryland. Senate debate, 1805.

181. In America, we only work on crises. If you want to fund earthquake engineering research, you have to have an earthquake.
Tom Zimmie, professor of engineering, Rensselaer Polytechnic Institute, NY. Quoted in *Governing the States and Localities*, May 1988.

Chapter 57

Liberals and Conservatives

1. Constituency drives out consistency.
[Liberal senators defend military spending in their states; conservatives support social spending – in their own states.]
Anonymous political dictum, Washington, DC.

2. A Liberal is a Conservative who has been mugged by reality.
Anonymous, 1970s.

3. Liberals seem to be able to deal with every kind of person except those who don't understand them.
Anonymous.

4. I have never really liked Lowell Weicker personally, but I think that those of us who are Conservative have wasted entirely too much effort fighting him over the years.
James F. Altham, Jr., Chairman, Republican Party, Hamden County, CT. Comment on Weicker's nomination for a fourth term as U.S. Senator. Speech, State Republican Convention, Hartford, CT, July 16, 1988.

5. I said to my Liberal friend that we are fundamentally the same. I spend money like it's my money and you spend money like it's my money.
Richard K. Armey, U.S. Congressman (R-TX). PBS, *Firing Line*, Sept. 14, 1990.

6. When a nation's young men are conservative, its funeral bell has already rung.
Henry Ward Beecher (1813-1887), American clergyman and writer. *Proverbs from Plymouth Pulpit*, 1887.

7. It's like being criticized by Liberals. You wake up the next morning and you get over it.
William J. Bennett, Director, Office of National Drug Control Policy, and U.S. Secretary of Education (R). Comment on being criticized by fellow Conservatives. Interview, CNN, *Larry King Show*, June 15, 1989.

8. A Liberal is a man or woman or child who looks forward to a better day, a more tranquil night, and a bright, infinite future.
Leonard Bernstein (1918-1990), American musician. *The New York Times*, Oct. 30, 1988.

9. A Democrat is a progressive individual who believes in regenerating the National Government by inaugurating a system of wholesale plunder in place of the policy which now obtains. A Republican is a conservative person who favors leaving matters as they are. Of the two policies, that of the Democrat is safer and the more economical, but that of the Republican is the more practical at present.
Ambrose Bierce (1842-1914?), American journalist. *News Letter*, May 29, 1869.

10. Conservative: A statesman who is enamored of existing evils, as distinguished from the Liberal, who wishes to replace them with others.
Ambrose Bierce. *The Devil's Dictionary*, 1911.

11. Left-wing confusion spawns right-wing reaction.
A. Alan Borovoy, general counsel, Canadian Civil Liberties Union. Quoted in *Weekend Magazine*, Sept. 4, 1976.

12. Because there can be no real individual freedom in the presence of economic insecurity, liberalism carries a heavy responsibility in fighting continuously to expand our economy.
Chester Bowles (1901-1986), U.S. Undersecretary of State. Quoted in *The New Republic*, July 22, 1946.

13. A Liberal is a man who leaves the room when a fight begins.
Heywood C. Broun (1888-1939), American journalist. Quoted in Fred Metcalf, *The Penguin Dictionary of Modern Humorous Quotations*, 1986.

14. The American people will always be progressive as well as conservative.
Orestes Augustus Brownson (1803-1876), American clergyman, writer, and founder, Working-men's Party. *The American Republic*, 1865.

15. The future belongs to Conservatives. They are younger, they are more energetic, they dominate the party caucuses, they dominate the nominating process. They are committed to ideas, not simply personal aggrandizement or title.

Patrick Buchanan, White House speech writer (R) and syndicated columnist. Quoted in *The 1989 Conservative Calendar*.

16. Conservatism is the politics of reality.
William F. Buckley, Jr., American writer and publisher. Interview, *Playboy*, May 1970.

17. All Socialists are either dumb or romantic.
William F. Buckley, Jr. PBS, *Firing Line*, July 7, 1990.

18. I'm a Liberal when it comes to human rights, the poor; so's George Bush.... But Liberal and Conservative don't mean much to me anymore. Does that mean we care about people and are interested and want to help? And if that makes you a Liberal, so be it.
Barbara Bush, First Lady. Interview with Jim Miklaszewski, NBC, Nov. 15, 1989.

19. I'm conservative but I'm not a nut about it.
George Bush, 41st President of the United States. Remark, Republican National Convention, Dallas, TX, Aug. 21, 1984.

20. What the Liberal really wants is to bring about change which will not in any way endanger his position.
Stokley Carmichael (Kwame Toure), Chairman, Student Non-Violent Coordinating Committee. Quoted in Fred Metcalf, *The Penguin Dictionary of Modern Humorous Quotations*, 1986.

21. If you're not a liberal at twenty, you have no heart, and if you're not a conservative at forty, you have no head.
Winston Churchill (1874-1965), Prime Minister of Great Britain (Conservative). Attributed.

22. If the Democratic Party is to win in November, it will have to fly with both its wings – the liberal and the conservative.
John Conyers, Jr., U.S. Congressman (D-MI). Quoted in *The New York Times*, July 16, 1988.

23. I know that liberalism isn't dead in this country. It simply has, temporarily we hope, lost its voice.
Walter Cronkite, American TV journalist. Quoted in *Newsweek*, Dec. 5, 1988.

24. I consider it a great homage to public opinion to find every scoundrel nowadays professing himself a Liberal.
Benjamin Disraeli, 1st Earl of Beaconsfield (1804-1881), Prime Minister of Great Britain (Conservative). *The Infernal Marriage*, 1834.

25. A Conservative government is an organized hypocrisy.
Benjamin Disraeli. Speech, Mar. 17, 1845.

26. The philosophical conservative is someone willing to pay the price of other people's suffering for his principles.
E. L. Doctorow, American writer. Commencement address, Brandeis University, Waltham, MA, May 21, 1989.

27. You do not have to be a wastrel to be a Liberal.
Paul H. Douglas (1892-1976), U.S. Senator (D-IL). Motto.

28. I'm a Liberal in the tradition of Franklin Roosevelt and Harry Truman and John Kennedy.
Michael Dukakis, Governor of Massachusetts (D). Presidential campaign speech, Oct. 30, 1988.

29. I suppose I am a Conservative where business is concerned and a Liberal with regard to people.
Dwight D. Eisenhower (1890-1969), 34th President of the United States (R-KS). Quoted in Ralph E. Flanders, *Senator from Vermont*, 1961.

30. Whatever tends to preserve the wealth of the wealthy is conservatism, and whatever favors anything else, no matter what, they call Socialism.
Richard T. Ely (1854-1943), American economist. Quoted in Beard and Beard, *The Beards' Basic History of the United States*, 1944.

31. All conservatives are such from personal defects. They have been effeminated by position of nature, born halt and blind, through luxury of their parents, and can only, like invalids, act on the defensive.
Ralph Waldo Emerson (1803-1882), American writer. *The Conduct of Life*, 1860.

32. Men are conservatives when they are least vigorous, or when they are most luxurious. They are conservatives after dinner.
Ralph Waldo Emerson. *Essays*, Second Series, "New England Reformers," 1876.

33. The Democrat is a young conservative; the conservative is an old Democrat. The aristocrat is the Democrat ripe and gone to seed.
Ralph Waldo Emerson. *Representative Men*, "Napoleon," 1876.

34. The castle which conservatism is set to defend is the actual state of things, good and bad.
Ralph Waldo Emerson. Quoted in *The New York Times Magazine*, Mar. 4, 1956.

35. Conservatives must move from stop to go, from making points to making change.
Edwin Feulner, President, The Heritage Foundation. "Conservatism: The Agony of Victory," *The New York Times*, Oct. 27, 1989.

36. American political life has reached the stage where a vocal and powerful group uses "Liberal" as a term of contempt.... Never before in our history has this been true. Liberals and Conservatives have disagreed and, on occasion, have stoutly fought each other; but not in the lifelong recollection of the speaker has any similar attempt been made to convert an honorable word for a socially useful attitude into a sling of mud to be thrown at a political opponent.
Ralph E. Flanders (1880-1970), U.S. Senator (R-VT). Speech, St. Louis, MO, 1954.

37. Vote Labour and you can build castles in the air. Vote Conservative and you can live in them.
David Frost, British TV journalist. BBC, *That Was the Year That Was*, Dec. 1962.

38. A Conservative is someone who demands a square deal for the rich.
David Frost. BBC, *TVam*, 1983.

39. I never dared be radical when young for fear it would make me conservative when old.
Robert Frost (1874-1963), U.S. Poet Laureate. "Precaution."

40. A Liberal is a man who's too broadminded to take his own side in a quarrel.
Robert Frost. Quoted on CBS, *News Election Night*, Nov. 8, 1988.

41. The modern conservative is engaged in one of man's oldest exercises in moral philosophy, that is the search for a superior moral justification for selfishness.
John Kenneth Galbraith, American economist and U.S. Ambassador to India (D). Quoted in Fred Metcalf, *The Penguin Dictionary of Modern Humorous Quotations*, 1986.

42. Liberalism is, I think, resurgent. One reason is that more and more people are becoming so painfully aware of the alternative.
John Kenneth Galbraith. Quoted in *The New York Times Book Review*, Oct. 8, 1989.

43. Conservatives look to deeds. They're not bought off by rhetoric.
David Gergen, American journalist and White House assistant (R). PBS, *MacNeil-Lehrer News Hour*, Dec. 8, 1989.

44. Liberalism is trust of the people tempered by prudence; conservatism is distrust of the people tempered by fear.
William E. Gladstone (1809-1898), Prime Minister of Great Britain (Liberal). Speech, May 31, 1866.

45. A Liberal is a man who is willing to spend somebody else's money.
Carter Glass (1858-1946), U.S. Congressman (D-VA), U.S. Senator, and U.S. Secretary of the Treasury. Sept. 24, 1938.

46. Many Americans don't like the simple things. That's what they have against Conservatives.
Barry M. Goldwater, U.S. Senator (R-AZ). Remark to reporters, Oct. 20, 1964.

47. I think that your being the leader of the Tory *[Conservative]* party is the greatest triumph that liberalism has achieved.
François Guizot (1787-1874), Premier of France. Comment to Benjamin Disraeli. Quoted in Swartz and Swartz, *Disraeli's Reminiscences*, 1976.

48. The Liberals of both the Democratic and Republican Parties are the instruments of Satan to destroy the former great principles of these two political parties.
Billy James Hargis, American clergyman and founder, Christian Crusade. Quoted in Epstein and Forster, *The Radical Right*, 1967.

49. Any man who has the brains to think and the nerve to act for the benefit of the people of the country is considered a radical by those who are content with stagnation and willing to endure disaster.
William Randolph Hearst (1863-1951), U.S. Congressman (D-NY); founder, Independence League Party; journalist; and publisher. Interview, Cleveland *Plain Dealer*, Oct. 24, 1932.

50. Some people say we Democrats have to nominate a moderate in 1988, someone who doesn't say much, who says it with a slightly southern accent, who espouses strong conservatism with just a lit-

tle dash of compassion thrown in. They've described a liberal Republican basically, sort of a George Bush with chest hair.

Jim Hightower, Commissioner of Agriculture, Texas (D). Quoted in Morris K. Udall, *Too Funny to Be President*, 1988.

51. Powerful imaginations are conservative.

Hugo von Hofmannsthal (1874-1929), Austrian writer. *The Book of Friends*, 1922.

52. *[British]* Conservatives do not believe that political struggle is the most important thing in life.... The simplest among them prefer fox hunting, the wisest religion.

Douglas McGarel Hogg, 2nd Viscount Hailsham of Marylebone, British politician. Quoted in *The Wall Street Journal*, Nov. 27, 1990.

53. Man is by nature a conservative animal, and government is his instrument for preventing rapid change.

J. Herbert Holloman (1919-1985), U.S. Assistant Secretary of Commerce. Eastern Mohawk Valley Development Study Committee, *The Valley Tomorrow*, 1961.

54. We will have a government where Liberals will stay in power until they get radical and Conservatives will have the power until they get reactionary.

Louis McHenry Howe (1871-1935), presidential assistant (D). Speech, Columbia University, New York City, Jan. 17, 1933.

55. Some fellows get credit for being conservative when they are only stupid.

Frank McKinney (Kin) Hubbard (1868-1930), American caricaturist and writer. Quoted in Fred Metcalf, *The Penguin Dictionary of Modern Humorous Quotations*, 1986.

56. As the refugees stream north, history is going to assign you folks *[Liberals]* the role of pallbearers at the funeral of freedom in Central America.

Henry J. Hyde, U.S. Congressman (R-IL). Quoted in *The 1989 Conservative Calendar*.

57. Liberal leadership exhausts its power to persuade the discontented and the have-nots to accept ballot-box disappointments or compromises *[as in the case of New Deal legislation struck down by the Supreme Court]* if their victories are to be nullified and if elections are effective in shaping policy only when Conservatives win.

Robert H. Jackson (1892-1954), U.S. Attorney General (D) and U.S. Supreme Court Justice. *The Struggle for Judicial Supremacy*, 1941.

58. A Conservative on the House Education and Labor Committee is one who spends conservatively. A Liberal on the House Education and Labor Committee is one who spends liberally. A Conservative on the House Armed Services Committee is one who spends liberally. A Liberal on the House Armed Services Committee is one who spends conservatively.

Andrew Jacobs, Jr., U.S. Congressman (D-IN). House debate, Jan. 28, 1987.

59. In truth, the parties of Whig *[Liberal]* and Tory *[Conservative]* are those of nature. They exist in all countries, whether called by these names, or by those of Aristocrats and Democrats, Coté Droite and Coté Gauche, Ultras and Radicals, Serviles, and Liberals.

Thomas Jefferson (1743-1826), 3rd President of the United States (Democratic Republican-VA). Letter to the Marquis de Lafayette, Nov. 4, 1823.

60. I have always said, the first Whig *[Liberal]* was the Devil.

Samuel Johnson (1709-1784), British writer and lexicographer. Quoted in James Boswell, *The Life of Samuel Johnson*, Apr. 28, 1778.

61. *[Barry]* Goldwater made conservatism so unattractive I wouldn't have voted for it myself.

Walter H. Judd, U.S. Congressman (R-MN). Quoted in *The New York Herald Tribune*, Nov. 15, 1964.

62. I do not know which makes a man more conservative – to know nothing but the present, or nothing but the past.

John Maynard Keynes (1883-1946), British economist and diplomat. *The End of Laissez-Faire*, 1926.

63. Conservatives are always looking for converts, whereas Liberals are always looking for heretics.

Michael Kinsley, American journalist. 1990.

64. I think of myself as a Liberal with sanity. I believe in liberalism without dogmatism. I try to understand the problems of others, and find a way to accommodate them without compromising my basic point of view.

Edward I. Koch, U.S. Congressman and Mayor of New York City (D). Quoted in *The New York Times*, Apr. 18, 1975.

65. The liberals are the people you can least count on for personal support when the chips are down. To them it's "What have you done for me lately?" Conservatives take a longer view.

Edward I. Koch. *How'm I Doing?*, 1981.

66. I don't believe in half their *[Liberals']* crap. That government has to become bigger. That government is better if it does more. It's the New Deal out of the thirties – that government solves all problems. I once believed that. I have contempt for government. I should know. I'm in it.
Edward I. Koch. 1984.

67. The worst enemy of the new radicals are the old liberals.
V. I. Lenin (1870-1924), Premier of the U.S.S.R. Quoted in Michael Jackman, *Crown's Book of Political Quotations*, 1982.

68. The worst effect of student violence has been to excite Liberals who assume that behind every act of violence there is a condition of injustice, and who take it as their guilty responsibility to eradicate the cause.
William Letwin, American political economist. *The Public Interest*, Fall 1969.

69. The ancient Liberal faith is that our course be governed not by the dead hand of yesterday's facts and prejudices but by the living realities of today and our aspiration for tomorrow. It is this genius for making change serve the eternal unchanging values we cherish that is the very essence of American liberalism.
David E. Lilienthal (1899-1981), Chairman, Tennessee Valley Authority, and Chairman, U.S. Atomic Energy Commission. *Big Business*, 1952.

70. What is conservatism? Is it not adherence to the old and tried against the new and untried?
Abraham Lincoln (1809-1865), 16th President of the United States (R-IL). Speech, Cooper Institute, New York City, Feb. 27, 1860.

71. Communism is the opiate of the intellectuals.
Clare Boothe Luce (1903-1987), U.S. Congresswoman and Ambassador to Italy and Brazil (R-CT). Quoted in *Newsweek*, Jan. 24, 1955.

72. It was the Conservatives who invented the game of "Swallow the Leader."
Charles Lynch, Canadian columnist and writer. *Race for the Rose: Election 1984*.

73. All reactionaries are paper tigers.
Mao Tse-tung (1893-1976), Chairman, Communist Party of China. "Talk with the American Correspondent Anna Louise Strong," Aug. 1946.

74. A young man under twenty-five who is not a Socialist has no heart; one above twenty-five who remains a Socialist has no head.
André Maurois (1885-1967), French writer. Favorite saying.

75. Conservatives should be in power when the country has no problems.
George S. McGovern, U.S. Congressman and U.S. Senator (D-SD). PBS, *Firing Line*, Oct. 9, 1988.

76. The conservative principles are applicable to the most diverse situations.
Klemens von Metternich (1773-1859), Austrian statesman and diplomat. Letter to François Guizot, June 15, 1847.

77. Let no one say that radicalism is the exaggeration of liberalism; no, it is its antipodes, its extreme opposite. Radicalism is nothing more than an exaggeration of despotism; and never has despotism taken a more odious form.
Charles Montalembert (1810-1870), French statesman and writer. Address on Switzerland in the Chamber of Peers, Jan. 11, 1848.

78. The Liberal, emphasizing the civil and property rights of the individual, insists that the individual must remain so supreme as to make the state his servant.
Wayne L. Morse (1900-1974), U.S. Senator (R and Ind-OR). Quoted in *The New Republic*, July 22, 1946.

79. Somehow Liberals have been unable to acquire from birth what Conservatives seem to be endowed with at birth: namely, a healthy skepticism of the powers of government to do good.
Daniel P. Moynihan, Chief American Delegate to the United Nations and U.S. Senator (D-NY). Quoted in *The New York Post*, May 14, 1969.

80. People on the left know the answers before they know the problems.
V. S. Naipul, British writer. Interview, PBS, *American Interests*, Mar. 21, 1989.

81. Conservatism is primarily based on a proper recognition of human limitations.
Lewis B. Namier (1888-1960), British historian. *Vanished Supremacies*, 1958.

82. A Socialist is a Communist who just got back from Russia; a Liberal is a Socialist who just got back from Britain; a Conservative is a Liberal who just got back from New York; a Fascist is a Conservative who just got back from Detroit.
Richard J. Needham, Canadian columnist. *The Globe and Mail*, Aug. 19, 1976.

83. The only clause in the Constitution the Conservatives seem to see is the one that provides for the

common defense. The forget about the one that provides for equal justice.

Robert Ness, Executive Director, Leadership Conference for Civil Rights. Speech, Women's Democratic Club, Feb. 16, 1991.

84. If being a Liberal means federalizing everything, then I'm no Liberal. If being a Conservative means turning back the clock, denying problems that exist, then I'm no Conservative.

Richard M. Nixon, 37th President of the United States (R-CA). *Memoirs*, 1978.

85. The giving away of other men's goods is called liberality.

John Northbrook (1568-1579), English clergyman and writer. Remark, 1577.

86. All organizations that are not actually right-wing will over time become left-wing.

John O'Sullivan, editor, *National Review. National Review*, Oct. 27, 1989.

87. Your Tory *[Conservative]* is always a Fascist at heart.

Vernon L. Parrington (1871-1929), American historian. *Main Currents in American Thought*, 1927-30.

88. It isn't that Liberals are ignorant. It's just that they know so much that isn't so.

Ronald Reagan, 40th President of the United States (R-CA). Speech, Nov. 1964.

89. You'll never hear that "L" word – Liberal – from them *[the Democrats]*. They've put on political trench coats and dark glasses and slipped their platform into a plain brown wrapper.

Ronald Reagan. Comment on the Democratic National Convention of 1988.

90. ... the political liberalism of the upper middle class, the university- and professional-school educated ... the liberalism of a verbal elite ... out of touch with the mass of Americans today.

William Bradford Reynolds, Assistant U.S. Attorney General for Civil Rights (R). *Harvard Journal of Law and Public Policy*, 8, 1985.

91. For liberalism, the individual is the end, and society the means. For Fascism, society is the end, individuals the means, and its whole life consists in using individuals as instruments for its social ends.

Alfredo Rocco (1875-1935), Minister of Justice, Italy (Fascist). *The Political Doctrine of Fascism*, 1930.

92. I can remember way back, when a Liberal was generous with his own money.

Will Rogers (1879-1935), American humorist. 1935.

93. Wise and prudent men – intelligent conservatives – have long known that in a changing world worthy institutions can be conserved only by adjusting them to the changing time.

Franklin D. Roosevelt (1882-1945), 32nd President of the United States (D-NY). Campaign speech, Syracuse, NY, Sept. 29, 1936.

94. A radical is a man with both feet firmly planted – in the air. A conservative is a man with two perfectly good legs who, however, has never learned to walk forward. A reactionary is a somnambulist walking backward. But a liberal is a man who uses his legs and his hands at the behest – at the command – of his head.

Franklin D. Roosevelt. Radio address, Oct. 26, 1939.

95. The true conservative seeks to protect the system of private property and free enterprise by correcting such injustices and inequalities as arise from it.

Franklin D. Roosevelt. Quoted in Foster Rhea Dulles, *The United States Since 1865*, 1959.

96. The essence of the liberal outlook lies not in what opinions are held, but in how they are held; instead of being held dogmatically, they are held tentatively, and with a consciousness that new evidence may at any moment lead to their abandonment.

Bertrand Russell, 3rd Earl Russell of Kingston (1872-1970), British philosopher and reformer. *Unpopular Essays*, 1950.

97. Liberals don't believe they deserve anything they have. Conservatives believe they deserve everything they've stolen.

Mort Sahl, American comedian. 1984.

98. White Liberals are closer to white Conservatives than either of them are to blacks.

Gus Savage, U.S. Congressman (D-IL). Interview, CNN, *Crossfire*, Aug. 24, 1989.

99. Every Liberal is in revolt against the last revolt.

Fulton J. Sheen (1895-1979), American Roman Catholic archbishop and television personality. *Life Is Worth Living*, 1954.

100. A liberal is one who has both feet firmly planted in mid air.

Adlai E. Stevenson (1900-1965), Governor of Illinois (D) and U.S. Ambassador to the United Nations. Attributed.

101. An independent is a guy that wants to take the politics out of politics.
Adlai E. Stevenson. 1955.

102. I am a lawyer. I have some difficulty understanding what those terms *[Liberal and Conservative]* mean even in the field of political life or in the legislative or executive branches. And I find it impossible to know what they mean when they are carried over to judicial life.
Potter Stewart (1915-1985), U.S. Supreme Court Justice. Response when asked at the time of his appointment if he was a Liberal or a Conservative, May 18, 1959.

103. A conservative is a man who will not change things until he studies things. The radical wants to change regardless.
Robert A. Taft (1889-1953), U.S. Senator (R-OH). Quoted in *Fortune*, Aug. 1953.

104. The radical of one century is the conservative of the next.
Mark Twain (Samuel Langhorne Clemens) (1835-1910), American writer. Albert Bigelow Paine, ed., *Mark Twain's Notebook*, XXXI, 1935.

105. *[Tammany Hall is]* the cradle of modern liberalism.
Robert F. Wagner (1877-1953), U.S. Senator (D-NY). In reference to the fact that Tammany Hall politicians supported expanded public works programs. Speech, New York City, July 5, 1937.

106. Pointy headed intellectuals
George C. Wallace, Governor of Alabama (D). Frequent disparaging remark for Liberals.

107. No one can be a conservative unless he has something to lose.
James P. Warburg (1896-1932), American banker and financier. Favorite saying.

108. I never use the words Democrats and Republicans. It's Liberals and Americans.
James G. Watt, U.S. Secretary of the Interior (R). Quoted in *The Washington Post*, May 4, 1989.

109. Conservatives have failed to turn the clock back by even a single minute.
Evelyn Waugh (1903-1966), British writer. Quoted on PBS, *Firing Line*, Sept. 23, 1989.

110. Socialism is an expression of the inferiority feeling of the perpetually disinherited.
H. G. Wells (1866-1945), British writer. Quoted in George Seldes, *You Can't Print That*, 1929.

111. A Liberal is a person who believes that water can be made to run uphill. A Conservative believes everybody should pay for his water. I'm somewhere in between. I believe that water should be free, but that water flows downhill.
Theodore H. White (1915-1986), American political writer. Attributed.

112. Advance or decadence are the only choices offered to mankind. The pure conservative is fighting against the essence of the universe.
Alfred North Whitehead (1861-1947), British philosopher and mathematician. Quoted in George Seldes, *The Great Quotations*, 1983.

113. He thinks like a Tory and talks like a Radical, and that's so important nowadays.
Oscar Wilde (1854-1900), Irish writer. *Lady Windermere's Fan*, 1892.

114. They *[Conservatives]* define themselves in terms of what they oppose.
George F. Will, American political columnist. *Newsweek*, Sept. 30, 1974.

115. Most bad government has grown out of too much government.
John Sharp Williams (1854-1932), U.S. Congressman and U.S. Senator (D-MS). Lecture, Columbia University, New York City, 1912; published as *Thomas Jefferson: His Permanent Influence on American Institutions*, 1913.

116. In politics nothing radically novel may safely be attempted. No result of value can ever be reached ... except through slow and gradual development.
Woodrow Wilson (1856-1924), 28th President of the United States (D-NJ). *The State*, 1889.

117. By a Progressive I do not mean a man who is ready to move but a man who knows where he is going *when* he moves.
Woodrow Wilson. Speech, St. Paul, MN, Sept. 9, 1919.

Chapter 58

Lobbying and Special Interests

1. The principal reasons that special interests can extract their price from government is money.... Those who do not accept money from PACs *[Political Action Committees]* are those who have other sources.
   James G. Abourezk, U.S. Congressman and U.S. Senator (D-SD). *Advise and Dissent*, 1989.

2. No politician can sit on a hot issue if you make it hot enough.
   Saul D. Alinsky, American community organizer. *Rules for Radicals*, 1971.

3. This, Mr. Chairman, is a proposition to establish there *[in Tupelo, MS]* a *[federal]* fish hatchery. We have the ideal place for a fish hatchery. Why, sir, fish will travel over land for miles to get into the water we have at Tupelo. Thousands and millions of unborn fish are clamoring to this Congress this day for an opportunity to be hatched at the Tupelo hatchery.
   John Mills Allen (1846-1917), U.S. Congressman (D-MS). Said in favor of a bill he introduced, Feb. 20, 1901.

4. State legislatures tend to be dominated by suburban and rural interests.
   William J. Althaus, Mayor of York, PA (R). In opposition of federal funds going through the states rather than directly to cities. Quoted in *The New York Times*, Feb. 10, 1991.

5. Farmers who are legislators are the easiest to buy and seduce.
   Henry Ward Beecher (1813-1887), American clergyman and writer. Quoted in Earl Katcher, *Earl Warren: A Political Biography*, 1967.

6. *[Lobbying]* has reached such a position of power that it threatens the government itself. Its size, its power, its capacity for evil; its greed, trickery, deception, and fraud condemn it to the death it deserves.
   Hugo L. Black (1886-1971), U.S. Senator (D-AL) and U.S. Supreme Court Justice. Radio address, 1935.

7. Who do you have coming to see you about the subsidies? Business people, no one else.
   Thomas Hale Boggs, Sr. (1914-1973), U.S. Congressman (D-LA). House hearings on the President's tax proposals, 1963.

8. Congress has become a Stop and Shop for every greedy interest in America.
   Edmund G. (Jerry) Brown, Jr., Governor of California (D). Speech, Las Vegas, NV, Sept. 1991.

9. Toshiba was able to purchase access to those who were writing the legislation. They won, but what they did was very offensive.
   [In 1987, after Toshiba Corporation of Japan illegally sold sophisticated technical equipment to the Soviets, Congress considered legislation to punish Toshiba, but the proposed sanctions were softened.]
   John Bryant, U.S. Congressman (D-TX). Quoted in *Business Week*, July 11, 1988.

10. All legislative bodies which control pecuniary interests are as sure to have a lobby as an army to have camp followers. Where the body is, there will the vultures be gathered together.
    James Bryce (1838-1922), British Ambassador to the United States. *The American Commonwealth*, 1888.

11. The power of the crown, almost dead and rotten as prerogative, has grown up anew, with much more strength and far less odium, under the name of influence.
    Edmund Burke (1729-1797), British statesman. *Thoughts on the Present Discontents*, 1770.

12. Not all special interest groups are bad.
    Robert C. Byrd, U.S. Congressman and U.S. Senator (D-WV). Quoted in *The Congressional Digest*, Feb. 1987.

13. Women are not a special interest group in the usual sense of the term. We are half the population.

Virginia Anne Carabillo, Vice President, National Organization of Women. Speech, National Association of Broadcasters, 1974.

14. As government grows bigger and more directly involved in the economy, the question of who gets what, through the medium of the lobbyist as broker, is of paramount importance.

Marquis Childs (1903-1990), American political columnist. Introduction to James Deakin, *The Lobbyists*, 1966.

15. They *[General Motors's lobbyists]* bullshit all the time.

Joan Claybrook, Administrator, U.S. National Highway Safety Administration. Quoted in Tolchin and Tolchin, *Dismantling America: The Rush to Deregulate*, 1983.

16. When I bought a new car, the folks back home were sure the lobbyists had gotten to me already.

Silvio O. Conte (1922-1991), U.S. Congressman (R-MA). Quoted in *Roll Call*, Feb. 18, 1959.

17. We're frightened by the interest groups;
We act like silly nincompoops.
We can't make cuts that cause some sting;
We cannot even do a thing.

Silvio O. Conte. Poem written for the House budget debate, Oct. 1990.

18. In their hours of timidity the Congress becomes so subservient to the importunities of organized minorities that the President comes more and more to stand as the champion of the rights of the whole country.

Calvin Coolidge (1872-1933), 30th President of the United States (R-MA). "The President Lives Under a Multitude of Eyes," *American Magazine*, Aug. 1929.

19. A majority of Senators placed on the Committee on Interstate Commerce were men whose sympathies were with the railroads.

Shelby M. Cullom (1829-1914), Governor of Illinois (R), U.S. Congressman, and U.S. Senator. *Fifty Years of Public Service*, 1911.

20. It seemed to be the custom of the attachés, when in doubt *[regarding favors]*, to refer the stranger to Mr. Judah P. Benjamin, the "Poo Bah" of the Confederate government.

Varina Howell Davis (1826-1906), Confederate First Lady. Letter to Francis Lawley, June 8, 1898.

21. Two thousand years of painful experiences have forced us into round-the-clock political activity.

Thomas A. Dine, Executive Director, American Israel Political Action Committee. Quoted in *The Washington Lobby*, 1987.

22. They who possess the prince possess the laws.

John Dryden (1631-1700), English poet and dramatist. *Absalom and Achitophel*, I.

23. There's the stench of money around this building *[the Capitol]*.

Thomas F. Eagleton, U.S. Senator (D-MO). Comment on his retirement from the Senate. Quoted in *Newsweek*, Dec. 1, 1986.

24. Political action committees *[PACs]* first and foremost want winners. They're not sentimentalists. They're not theorists. They're not philosophers.... They want to buy a piece of a winner.

Thomas F. Eagleton. Quoted on PBS, *The Power Game*, Jan. 2, 1989.

25. A people that values its privileges above its principles soon loses both.

Dwight D. Eisenhower (1890-1969), 34th President of the United States (R-KS). First inaugural address, Jan. 20, 1953.

26. I can't think of a better way to spend a morning with somebody than riding around a golf course, letting 'em win.

Steven Eure, Washington lobbyist. Quoted in *The Washington Post Magazine*, Nov. 13, 1988.

27. I'll get thirty thousand post cards on an issue before I can even find out that a bill has been introduced.

Wyche Fowler, Jr., U.S. Congressman (D-GA). Quoted in *The Washington Post*, July 11, 1988.

28. I hope I use them more than they use me.

Barney Frank, U.S. Congressman (D-MA). On Political Action Committees. PBS, *Ethics in America*, Feb. 14, 1989.

29. It is now possible to say that the judgment of the people has often been wiser than the judgment of Congressmen or even of the experts. For one thing, the public has no axes to grind. Pressure groups aren't at work on the general public, as they are on legislators.

George Gallup (1901-1984), American statistician and pollster. Quoted in Robert M. Hutchins, *The Power of Reason*, 1964.

30. The Constitution would not actually be a live enterprise without lobbies because that's the way one petitions for the redress of grievances.

Leonard Garment, counselor to the President (R). Quoted in *The Washington Post*, May 12, 1986.

31. I don't know why you're not involved in their *[politicians']* business; they're involved in our *[expletive]* business every day.

Thomas M. Gaubert, Texas businessman and political fund-raiser. Quoted in *The Washington Post*, May 8, 1988.

32. Lobbying is declared to be a crime.

Constitution, State of Georgia, 1877.

33. We do not engage in lobbying as such. However, I do make contact with members of Congress when requested to do so.

Royce L. Givins, Executive Director, International Association of Chiefs of Police. Quoted in William W. Turner, *Power on the Right*, 1971.

34. As one voice must labor speak – to reward its friends and punish its enemies.

Samuel Gompers (1850-1924), President, American Federation of Labor. Quoted in *Labor*, Aug. 4, 1956.

35. The oil and gas lobby, with the vast amount of money at its disposal, is, I believe, the most diabolical influence at work in the nation's capital. It has for years succeeded in blocking the assignment of public-spirited members to the tax-writing committees of the House and Senate, and also intervened in the election of leaders and assistant leaders in both Houses.

Albert A. Gore, Jr., U.S. Senator (D-TN) and Vice President of the United States. *The New York Times Magazine*, Apr. 11, 1965.

36. Parties in Washington are a natural extension of the working day.... Everybody uses everybody.

Katharine Graham, Chairman of the Board, Washington Post Company. PBS, *The Politics of Privacy*, Sept. 26, 1988.

37. There are two Americas. One which influences government and economic policy and the other which must live with the results.

William Greider, American TV journalist. PBS, *Frontline*: "Campaign, The Politics of Prosperity," Oct. 10, 1988.

38. Access is an earned, essential raw material for the lobbying process but vastly overrated as a finished product all by itself. No dam was ever built ... solely on the basis of access.

Robert K. Grey, Washington lobbyist. "In Defense of Lobbyists," *The New York Times*, Apr. 25, 1986.

39. I know that you do not make the laws, but I also know that *you are the wives and mothers, the sisters and daughters of those who do.*

Angelina Grimké (1805-1879), American abolitionist and suffragist. "Appeal to the Christian Women of the South," *The Anti-Slavery Examiner*, Sept. 1836.

40. Corporate power ... is not only economic – the ability to set prices without regard to market pressures or to manipulate consumer demand. It is also political – the ability to use the public government to obtain private economic goals. Corporate power means the ability of big corporations to have more than their fair share of influence over the decisions of government.

Fred R. Harris, U.S. Senator (D-OK). *Corporate Power in America*, 1973.

41. What is being bought *[by Political Action Committees]* is access.... Can my Uncle Fred walk into a Senator's office? Of course not!

Gary Hart, U.S. Senator (D-CO). Quoted on PBS, *The Power Game*, Jan. 2, 1989.

42. The people are weary of detecting the voice of a corporation manager in every political utterance, in the legislature, the Governor's messages, in the expressed opinions of mayors of cities and the Senators sent by the state to Washington, and even in the decisions of judges on the bench.

William Randolph Hearst (1863-1951), U.S. Congressman (D-NY); founder, Independence League Party; journalist; and publisher. Speech, Independence League Conference, Albany, NY, Feb. 28, 1906.

43. Resolved that all persons or corporations employing counsel or agents to represent their interests in regard to any measure pending at any time before this House or any committee thereof shall cause the name and authority of such counsel to be filed with the clerk of the House.

George F. Hoar (1826-1904), U.S. Congressman and U.S. Senator (R-MA). House Resolution, 1875.

44. I believe with $200,000 I can pass our bill. I do not think we can get any legislation this session for land grants or changing line of road unless we pay more for it than it is worth.

Collis Potter Huntington (1821-1900), President, Southern Pacific Railroad. Letter to railroad magnates, 1877.

45. All know the influence of interest on the mind of man, and how unconsciously his judgment is warped by that influence.

Thomas Jefferson (1743-1826), 3rd President of the United States (Democratic Republican-VA). *Notes for an Autobiography*, Jan. 6, 1821.

46. I have never seen such lobbying before as we have had in the last few weeks and such crookedness and complicity among members *[of Congress]*.

George Washington Julian (1817-1899), U.S. Congressman (Free Soil and R-IN). *Diary*, Aug. 1852.

47. The consumer is the only man in our economy without a high-powered lobbyist in Washington.

John F. Kennedy (1917-1963), 35th President of the United States (D-MA). Campaign speech, Wittenberg College, Springfield, OH, 1960.

48. I am sure the power of vested interests is vastly exaggerated compared with the gradual encroachment of ideas.

John Maynard Keynes (1883-1946), British economist and diplomat. *The General Theory of Employment, Interest and Money*, 1936.

49. A faction may beat a faction, at a pretty fair and even conflict; but in a fair and full contest, it can never beat the people. The great art of factions is to keep the decision from the body of the people.

Samuel Langdon (1723-1797), President, Harvard College. Election sermon, Massachusetts Bay Colony Congress, Watertown, MA, May 31, 1775.

50. The munitions manufacturers and the war lords are in the saddle.

William Lemke (1878-1943), U.S. Congressman (R and Nonpartisan-ND), and candidate for President, Union Party. Speech in Congress on the hostilities in Europe, June 29, 1939.

51. I represent whomever I work for.

Ronald C. Marlenee, U.S. Congressman (R-MT). 1984.

52. The national interest is not simply the sum of our special interests and attachments.

Charles McC. Mathias, Jr., U.S. Senator (R-MD). "Ethnic Groups and Foreign Policy," *Foreign Affairs*, Summer 1981.

53. Whenever I tell people I am a lobbyist, there is an embarrassed pause.

Arnold Mayer, Washington lobbyist. Quoted in James Deakin, *The Lobbyists*, 1966.

54. I wasn't there for one constituent; I was there for a major economic interest of my state.

John McCain III, U.S. Senator (R-AZ). Statement on intervening in the regulatory process on behalf of Lincoln Savings and Loan, Nov. 17, 1989.

55. On Capitol Hill money doesn't talk. It bellows.

Ed McMahon, Executive Director, Coalition for Scenic Beauty. Interview, National Public Radio, Sept. 8, 1988.

56. Don't beg, don't threaten, and don't assume you're always right.

George Meany (1894-1980), President, AFL-CIO. Advice to AFL-CIO lobbyist Andrew J. Biemiller.

57. Gucci Gulch

Daniel P. Moynihan, Chief American Delegate to the United Nations and U.S. Senator (D-NY). Reference to the Dirksen Senate Office Building, frequented by so many well-dressed lobbyists. Senate hearings, Mar. 4, 1991.

58. Ten persons who speak make more noise than ten thousand who are silent.

Napoléon I (1769-1821), military leader and Emperor of France. *Maxims*.

59. The politics of courts are so mean that private people would be ashamed to act in the same way; all is trick and finesse, to which the common cause is sacrificed.

Horatio Nelson (1758-1805), British Admiral. Comment on becoming Rear Admiral, 1797.

60. The President must have the courage to stand against the pressures of the few for the good of the many.

Richard M. Nixon, 37th President of the United States (R-CA). Presidential nomination acceptance speech, Republican National Convention, Chicago, IL, July 27, 1960.

61. With Morgan and Company's attorney on the Supreme bench, with the Sugar Trust running the Attorney General's office, with the railroads themselves operating the Interstate Commerce Commission, with the greatest reactionary of the country sitting on the Federal Trade Commission, tell me, O God – tell me! – where the toiling millions of the honest, common people of this country are going to be protected in their rights as against big business?

George W. Norris (1861-1944), U.S. Congressman and U.S. Senator (R and Ind-NE). Statement objecting to the nomination of Attorney General Harlan Fiske Stone as U.S. Supreme Court Associate Justice. *Congressional Record*, 68th Congress, 2nd Sess., 1925.

62. We have a PAC *[Political Action Committee]* because there's a lot of money on the other side.

Alan Parker, spokesperson, Association of Trial Lawyers of America. Quoted in *The Washington Post,* Nov. 7, 1989.

63. The people who work in good faith at the local level don't understand what well-financed lobbyists can do *[to reverse their gains]* at the state level.
Lana Pollack, Michigan State Senator. Quoted in *Governing the States and Localities*, Apr. 1988.

64. Laws go where money pleases.
Portuguese proverb.

65. The railroads own many of our courts and public bodies. Not because they have of necessity bought them by the expenditure of money; they have a different way of doing things. They see to it that the right men, the men of friendly inclinations, are elected.
Charles A. Prouty (1853-1921), American attorney and member, Interstate Commerce Commission. Interview, *Chicago Record-Herald*, Dec. 31, 1904.

66. A lobbyist is anyone who opposes legislation I want. A patriot is anyone who supports me.
James A. Reed (1861-1944), U.S. Senator (D-MO). Quoted in Charles Henning, *The Wit and Wisdom of Politics*, 1989.

67. I think it is a rule followed by most politicians that you never antagonize any group, no matter how small, if you can avoid it. If you have to choose between two groups, you always choose to antagonize the one that is less vindictive and organized than the others.
James Reston, American political columnist. Letter to John Howe, Sept. 29, 1954.

68. Lobbying is the art of the possible.
Tony Rice, chief lobbyist, U.S. Chamber of Commerce. Quoted in James Deakin, *The Lobbyists*, 1966.

69. Lobbying is good information early; it is a presence when minds are being made up.
Charles E. Roemer III, Governor of Louisiana and U.S. Congressman (D-LA). Quoted in *The Washington Lobby*, 1987.

70. Government by organized money is just as dangerous as government by organized mob.
Franklin D. Roosevelt (1882-1945), 32nd President of the United States (D-NY). Campaign speech, Madison Square Garden, New York City, 1936.

71. Okay, you've convinced me. Now go on out and bring some pressure on me.
Franklin D. Roosevelt. Remark to a delegation of citizens. Quoted in Saul D. Alinsky, *Rules for Radicals*, 1971.

72. The most powerful, dangerous lobby that has ever been created.
Franklin D. Roosevelt. In reference to the nation's private utility companies. Quoted in *The Washington Lobby*, 1987.

73. I am genuinely independent of the big monied men in all matters where I think the interests of the public are concerned, and probably I am the first President of recent times of whom this could be truthfully said.... But where I do not grant any favors to these big monied men which I do not think the country requires that they should have, it is out of the question for me to expect them to grant favors to me in return... The sum of this is that I can make no private or special appeals to them, and I am at my wits' end how to proceed.
Theodore Roosevelt (1858-1919), 26th President of the United States (R-NY). Letter to Sen. Henry Cabot Lodge, 1906.

74. We must drive special interests out of politics.
Theodore Roosevelt. Speech, "The New Nationalism," Osawatomie, KS, Aug. 31, 1910.

75. The White House is a bully pulpit.
Theodore Roosevelt. Recalled on his death by George Haven Putnam in his Eulogy, The Century Club, New York City, 1919.

76. Nothing is more dangerous than the influence of private interests in public affairs.
Jean-Jacques Rousseau (1712-1778), French philosopher. *The Social Contract*, 1762.

77. I'm the governor of the legislature. The hell with the Governor of the state *[Earl Warren]*.
Arthur H. Samish (1897-1974), California lobbyist. Quoted in Earl Katcher, *Earl Warren: A Political Biography*, 1967.

78. Toddlers don't have political action committees.
Patricia R. Schroeder, U.S. Congresswoman (D-CO). Quoted in *The New York Times Magazine*, July 1, 1990.

79. The halls of kings are full of men but void of friends.
Lucius Annaeus Seneca (The Younger) (4 B.C.-A.D.65), Roman statesman, dramatist, and philosopher. *Epistolae Morales*.

80. I am not saying to you, sir, that you broke the law. I am saying to you that this is a smelly system and you participated in it.

Christopher Shays, U.S. Congressman (R-CT). Statement to former U.S. Secretary of the Interior James Watt. Congressional hearings, June 1989.

81. It was the political clubs that people who were powerless looked to for gaining an opportunity to have access to government.
Percy Sutton, Borough President, Manhattan, NY (D). Quoted in *The New York Times*, Oct. 10, 1989.

82. Of all forms of government and society, those of free men and women are in many respects the most brittle. They give the fullest freedom for activities of private persons and groups who often identify their own interests, essentially selfish, with the general welfare.
Dorothy Thompson (1894-1961), American journalist. *On the Record*, May 1958.

83. Fifteen million people in the United States are represented by lobbyists. The other 150 million have only one man who is elected at large to represent them – that is, the President of the United States.
Harry S Truman (1884-1972), 33rd President of the United States (D-MO). Quoted in James Deakin, *The Lobbyists*, 1966.

84. I am the lobbyist for the people.
Harry S Truman. Favorite saying.

85. If you can't drink their booze, take their money, fool with their women, and then vote against 'em, you don't belong in politics.
Jesse Unruh (1922-1987), California legislative leader (D). Quoted in Charles Henning, *The Wit and Wisdom of Politics*, 1989.

86. The best lobbying tool in the world is merit and a good cause.
Jack Valenti, special assistant to the President (D). Interview, C-SPAN, *An American Profile*, Feb. 19, 1990.

87. The profession of lobbying is not commendable. But I have endeavored to make it respectable by avoiding all measures without merit.
Samuel Ward (1814-1884), Washington lobbyist. Quoted in *The Saturday Evening Post*, Dec. 23, 1950.

88. The thing that distresses me most is that the lobbyists are so callous to the needs of our people.
Earl Warren (1891-1974), Chief Justice, U.S. Supreme Court, and Governor of California (R). Remark, 1949.

89. Influence is not government.
George Washington (1732-1799), 1st President of the United States (VA). *Political Maxims*.

90. In our society it's the citizens who should have the most *[political]* influence – not the special interests and the PAC's *[Political Action Committees]*.
Fred Wertheimer, President, Common Cause. Interview, ABC, *This Week*, Oct. 9, 1988.

91. The business of government is to organize the common interest against the special interest.
Woodrow Wilson (1856-1924), 28th President of the United States (D-NJ). Presidential campaign speech, 1912.

92. The government of the United States is a foster child of the special interests. It is not allowed to have a will of its own.
Woodrow Wilson. Presidential campaign speech. 1916.

Chapter 59

Loyalty

1. I had a visit from Mr. James Buchanan, Secretary of State. He told me that he had formerly visited my father *[John Adams, 2nd President of the U.S.]* at Quincy, *[MA,]* and said that in speaking to him of some of the Tories during our Revolutionary War, he said they were men of great respectability, fine talents, and excellent private character, but that they were all deplorably loyal – an epithet which Mr. Buchanan said had greatly diverted him.

   John Quincy Adams (1767-1848), 6th President of the United States (Ind-MA). *Diary*, Dec. 25, 1845.

2. The man who is always watching for his own gain is a traitor at heart.

   Apocrypha, *Letter of Aristeas* 270.

3. Everyone thinks chiefly of his own, hardly ever of the public interest.

   Aristotle (384-322 B.C.), Greek philosopher and teacher. *Politics*.

4. A fox in its hour – bow to it.

   Babylonian Talmud, *Megillah* 16b.

5. How useless oaths are has been shown by experience.

   Caesare Bonesana di Beccaria (1738-1794), Italian political and economic writer. *Dei Dilitti e Delle Pene*, 1764.

6. Be on guard against your friends.

   Apocrypha, *Wisdom of Ben Sira* 6:13.

7. Harry Hopkins is nice and likable, but would commit murder for the President *[Franklin D. Roosevelt]*.

   Adolph A. Berle, Jr. (1895-1971), U.S. Assistant Secretary of State (D). *Diary*, Oct. 25, 1940.

8. There are in the United States many persons of Japanese extraction whose loyalty to the country, even in the present emergency *[the attack on Pearl Harbor]*, is unquestioned. It would therefore be a serious mistake to take any action against these people.

   Francis B. Biddle (1886-1968), U.S. Attorney General (D). Statement, Dec. 8, 1941.

9. What matter if they hang me, provided the rope by which I am hung bind this new Germany firmly to your throne.

   Otto von Bismarck-Schoenhausen (1815-1898), Chancellor of Germany. Remark to Frederick II, June 1866.

10. I have been taught by experience, and never hesitate to sacrifice personal feeling to the requirements of the hour.

    Otto von Bismarck-Schoenhausen. Remark to M. Jules Favre, 1871.

11. My friends are not worth the powder and shot it would take to kill them. If there were two Henry Clays, one of them would make the other President of the United States.

    Henry Clay (1777-1852), U.S. Senator (National Republican and Whig-KY), Speaker of the House, and U.S. Secretary of State. Remark after losing the Whig presidential nomination to William H. Harrison, Dec. 8, 1839.

12. Party faithlessness is party dishonor.

    Grover Cleveland (1837-1908), 22nd and 24th President of the United States (D). Speech, Business Man's Democratic Association, New York City, Jan. 8, 1892.

13. Who would be cleared by their committees? Not Washington, who was a rebel. Not Jefferson, who wrote that "rebellion to tyrants is obedience to God." Not Garrison, who publicly burned the Constitution; or Wendell Phillips, a philosophical anarchist; nor *[William]* Seward of the Higher Law.... Not Lincoln or Wilson or Justice Holmes.

    Henry Steele Commager, American historian. Comment on congressional investigations such as those carried out by the House Un-American Activities Committee. *Harper's Magazine*, Sept. 1947.

14. A few honest men are better than numbers.

    Oliver Cromwell (1599-1658), Lord Protector of England. Letter, Sept. 1643.

15. The most striking thing is the absence of personal loyalty to the President. He has no admirers, no

enthusiastic supporters, none to bet on his head.
Richard Henry Dana (1815-1882), American writer and cofounder, Free Soil Party. Comment on the status of the Lincoln administration in 1864. Quoted in David H. Donald, *Lincoln Reconsidered*, 1961.

16. In politics, loyalty is everything.
James O. Eastland, U.S. Senator (D-MS). Quoted in Larry Speakes, *Speaking Out*, 1988.

17. It does no harm to throw the occasional man overboard, but it does not do much good if you are steering full speed ahead for the rocks.
Ian Gilmour, Member of Parliament, Great Britain (Conservative). Remark on being fired as Deputy Foreign Secretary, Sept. 1981.

18. We cannot legislate morality. No, and we cannot legislate loyalty, for loyalty is a kind of morality. We cannot produce these things by decrees or commissions or public inquisitions.
Alfred Whitney Griswold (1909-1963), President, Yale University, New Haven, CT. *Essays on Education*.

19. Community is already in process of disillusion where each man begins to eye his neighbor as a possible enemy.
Learned Hand (1872-1961), Federal Judge. Speech, New York Board of Regents, Oct. 24, 1952.

20. In politics you can't be true to all of your friends all the time.
Perry S. Heath (1857-1927), Secretary, Republican National Committee. Recalled on his death.

21. Compelled speech isn't worth much.
Nat Hentoff, American political and legal columnist. *The Washington Post*, Jan. 5, 1991.

22. He serves me most who serves his country best.
Homer (c.1000 B.C.), Greek poet. *The Iliad*.

23. I was Chairman Mao's dog. Whomever he told me to bite, I bit.
Jiang Qing (1914-1991), widow of Mao Tse-tung and member, "Gang of Four." Comment at her trial for complicity in 34,000 deaths and 700,000 persecutions, Nov. 1980.

24. Greater love has no man than this, that a man lay down his life for his friends.
New Testament, *John* 15:13. "No Greater Love" is the name of a group of relatives and friends of American MIA's and POW's who served in Vietnam.

25. I expect a kiss-my-ass-at-high-noon-in-Macy's-window loyalty.
Lyndon B. Johnson (1908-1973), 36th President of the United States (D). Remark to White House staff, 1964.

26. All friendship is preferring the interest of a friend to the neglect or, perhaps, against the interest of others; so that an old Greek said, "He that has *friends* has no *friend*."
Samuel Johnson (1709-1784), British writer and lexicographer. Quoted in James Boswell, *The Life of Samuel Johnson*, Apr. 15, 1778.

27. Those who like Italy better than America should return to Italy.
Fiorello H. La Guardia (1882-1947), U.S. Congressman (R and Socialist) and Mayor of New York City (R and Fusion Party). Remark addressed to his Italian constituents. Quoted in *The New York Evening World*, 1917.

28. Any service rendered to the temporal King to the prejudice of the eternal King is, without doubt, an act of treachery.
Stephen Langton (c.1150-1228), Archbishop of Canterbury, England. Letter to English Barons, 1207.

29. A healthy loyalty is not passive and complacent, but active and critical.
Harold J. Laski (1893-1950), English political scientist. *The Dangers of Obedience*, 1930.

30. A union that can only be maintained by swords and bayonets has no charm for me.
Robert E. Lee (1807-1870), General-in-Chief, Confederate Army. Remark to his son.

31. The Union we intend to keep, and loyal states will not let disloyal ones break it.
Abraham Lincoln (1809-1865), 16th President of the United States (R-IL). Letter to John J. Crittenden, Dec. 22, 1859.

32. In my devotion to the Union I hope I am behind no man in the nation.
Abraham Lincoln. Speech, New York City, Feb. 20, 1861.

33. I will pardon Jeff Davis, if he asks for it.
Abraham Lincoln. Letter to W. C. Bibb, Apr. 12, 1865.

34. I have never had but one allegiance; I cannot divide it now. I have never loved but one flag, and I cannot share that devotion and give affection to the mongrel banner invented for a league.
Henry Cabot Lodge (1850-1924), U.S. Congressman and U.S. Senator (R-MA). Comment announcing

his opposition to the covenant of a League of Nations. Speech to Senate, Aug. 12, 1919.

35. He that is not with me is against me.
New Testament, *Luke* 11:23.

36. The greatest virtue in a prince is to know his friends.
Martial (Marcus Valerius Martialis) (c.40-104), Roman poet and epigrammatist. *Epigrams*, VII, 15.

37. No man can serve two masters.
New Testament, *Matthew* 6:24.

38. A man's enemies are the men of his own house.
Old Testament, *Micah* 7:6.

39. I am a man of a thousand faces, all of them blacklisted.
Zero Mostel (1915-1977), American actor. After refusing to cooperate with the House Un-American Activities Committee investigations into alleged Communist activity in Hollywood, 1947.

40. The FBI is full of Fordham graduates keeping tabs on Harvard men in the State Department.
Daniel P. Moynihan, Chief American Delegate to the United Nations and U.S. Senator (D-NY). Remark to reporters, 1971.

41. I have been a conspirator for so long that I mistrust all around me.
Gamal Abdel Nasser (1918-1970), President of Egypt. Quoted in *Time*, July 28, 1958.

42. Traitors in the high councils of our own government have made sure that the deck is stacked on the Soviet side of the diplomatic tables.
Richard M. Nixon, 37th President of the United States (R-CA). Speech, 1950.

43. Nobody is a friend of ours. Let's face it.
Richard M. Nixon. Remark to John Dean, Sept. 15, 1972.

44. Most men will proclaim to everyone their own goodness; but a faithful man who can find?
Old Testament, *Proverbs* 20:6.

45. Confidence in an unfaithful man in time of trouble is like a broken tooth, and a foot out of joint.
Old Testament, *Proverbs* 25:19.

46. Put not your trust in princes, nor in the sons of men, for in them there is no salvation.
Old Testament, *Psalms* 146:3.

47. I believe in loyalty down and loyalty up. I live by that credo.
Donald T. Regan, U.S. Secretary of the Treasury and White House Chief of Staff (R). Quoted in *Regardie's*, Jan. 1987.

48. If the government is sincerely concerned about saving America from subversive forces, let our officials stop worrying about the Communists they suspect of subversive activities and start doing something about the fascists who are openly parading their disdain of civil rights and democratic procedures here in America today.
Paul Robeson (1898-1976), American opera singer, pacifist, and civil rights leader. Speech, Council on African Affairs, New York City, 1947.

49. President Taft has not only been disloyal to our past friendship, but he has been disloyal to every canon of decency and fair play.... President Taft served under me for over seven years without finding fault with me. He only discovered I was dangerous when I discovered he was useless to the American people.
Theodore Roosevelt (1858-1919), 26th President of the United States (R-NY). Speech, Worcester, MA, Apr. 26, 1912.

50. Loyalty *[of staff]* is easy to feign. A chief executive who has a fetish for demonstrations and protestations of fealty should buy a collie.
Ed Rovner, Chief of Staff for Governor William Donald Schaffer of Maryland (D). *Governing the States and Localities*, Apr. 1988.

51. All of us have a loyalty greater than our own interest.
Dean Rusk, U.S. Secretary of State (D). Remark to Adlai Stevenson, 1962.

52. Whose side are you on?
Dean Rusk. Question of reporter John Scali, who asked a particularly difficult and embarrassing question at the height of the Vietnam War. 1966.

53. Suspicion is rather a Virtue than a Fault, as long as it doth like a Dog that *watcheth*, and doth *not* bite.
George Savile, 1st Marquess of Halifax (1633-1695), Lord Privy Seal of England. *Miscellaneous Thoughts and Reflections*, 1750.

54. A Prince who will not undergo the Difficulty of Understanding, must undergo the danger of Trusting.
George Savile. *Political Thoughts and Reflections*, 1750.

55. It is safer for a *Prince* to Judge of *Men* by what they do to one another, than what they do to him.
George Savile. *Maxims of State*, No. 13.

56. No enemy can be so dangerous as an offended friend and confidant.
Walter Scott (1771-1832), Scottish writer. *Quentin Durward*, 1823.

57. Fidelity bought with money is overcome by money.
Lucius Annaeus Seneca (The Younger) (4 B.C.-A.D.65), Roman statesman, dramatist, and philosopher. *Agamemnon*.

58. Every subject's duty is the King's, but every subject's soul is his own.
William Shakespeare (1564-1616), English writer. *Henry V*, IV, i.

59. Trust not him that hath once broken faith.
William Shakespeare. *King Henry VI*, Pt. 3, IV, iv.

60. *[Ulysses S.]* Grant stood by me when I was crazy, and I stood by him when he was drunk, and now we stand by each other.
William Tecumseh Sherman (1820-1891), General of the Army. 1872.

61. Many a friend will tell us our faults without reserve, who will not so much as hint at our follies.
Philip Dormer Stanhope, 4th Earl of Chesterfield (1694-1773), Member of Parliament, Great Britain (Whig), and Lord-Lieutenant of Ireland. *Letters to His Son*, July 1, 1748.

62. Ministers *[of state]* love a personal more than a party attachment *[in their closest aides]*.
Philip Dormer Stanhope. *Maxims*.

63. The whole notion of loyalty inquisitions is a natural characteristic of the police state, not of a democracy.
Adlai E. Stevenson (1900-1965), Governor of Illinois (D) and U.S. Ambassador to the United Nations. Veto message of Illinois Senate Bill 102, a wide-ranging "anti-subversive" measure, June 27, 1951.

64. If you want to cut your own throat, don't come to me for a bandage.
Margaret Thatcher, Prime Minister of Great Britain (Conservative). Remark to Prime Minister Robert Mugabe of Zimbabwe. Quoted in *Time*, July 7, 1986.

65. Greater love hath no man than this, that he lay down his friends for his life.
Jeremy Thorpe, Member of Parliament, Great Britain (Conservative). Comment following the dismissal of Selwyn Lloyd as Chancellor of the Exchequer by Prime Minister Harold Macmillan, July 13, 1962.

66. I have learned in these last two months that not everybody loves me.
John G. Tower (1925-1991), U.S. Senator (R-TX). Remark during his Senate confirmation hearings for U.S. Secretary of Defense, Jan. 26, 1989.

67. Only rats desert a sinking ship.
Harry S Truman (1884-1972), 33rd President of the United States (D-MO). Remark on why he attended the funeral of his early political patron and old friend, convicted Missouri Democratic boss Thomas Pendergast. Quoted by Edward J. Derwinski at the memorial tribute to Truman, House of Representatives, Jan. 3, 1973.

68. My kind of loyalty was loyalty to one's country, not to its institutions or its office-holders. The country is the real thing, the substantial thing, the eternal thing; it is the thing to watch over, and care for, and be loyal to.
Mark Twain (Samuel Langhorne Clemens), (1835-1910), American writer. *A Connecticut Yankee in King Arthur's Court*, 1889.

69. You squeeze an orange for its juice, you throw away the skin.
Voltaire (François-Marie Arouet) (1694-1778), French historian and dramatist. In reference to his break with Frederick II, King of Prussia. Letter to Mme. Denis, Sept. 2, 1751.

70. Confidence is a thing not to be produced by compulsion. Men cannot be forced into trust.
Daniel Webster (1782-1852), U.S. Congressman (Federalist-NH and MA), U.S. Senator (Federalist and Whig-MA), and U.S. Secretary of State. Senate speech, 1833.

Chapter 60

Managing Government

1. THE BUCK STOPS HERE
Sign on President Truman's desk.

2. You people *[field commanders]* are telling me what you think I want to know. I want to know what is actually happening.
Creighton W. Abrams, Jr. (1914-1974), General, U.S. Army, and Commander of American forces in Vietnam. Quoted in *Time*, Mar. 8, 1971.

3. While all other sciences have advanced, that of government is at a standstill – little better understood, little better practiced now than three or four thousand years ago.
John Adams (1735-1826), 2nd President of the United States (Federalist-MA). Letter to Thomas Jefferson, 1813.

4. Dictators are the last to know.
Fouad Ajami, American political scientist. CBS, *Evening News*, Jan. 17, 1990.

5. What is the greatest achievement in ruling an empire? That the subjects should live continually in a state of peace, and justice be administered speedily in cases of dispute.
Apocrypha, *Letter of Aristeas*, No. 291.

6. It's a mammoth place that makes an incredible number of mistakes.
Leslie Aspin, U.S. Congressman (D-CO). In reference to the Pentagon. Quoted in *Playboy*, Nov. 1973.

7. I can conceive of nothing worse than a man-governed world – except a woman-governed world.
Nancy Astor (1879-1964), American-born Mayor of Plymouth, England, and first woman to sit in the House of Commons. *My Two Countries*, 1923.

8. The vices of authority are chiefly four: delays, corruption, roughness, and facility *[weakness]*.
Francis Bacon, 1st Baron Verulam and Viscount St. Albans (1561-1626), Lord Chancellor of England. *Essays. Of Great Place*, 1597.

9. Administration is the essence of government, and its quality is a prime condition of civic comfort.
Stanley Baldwin, 1st Earl Baldwin of Bewdley (1867-1947), Prime Minister of Great Britain (Conservative). Empire Day (Queen Victoria's birthday) speech, Hyde Park, May 24, 1929.

10. Government is not guaranteed to work right.
Marion Barry, Mayor of Washington, DC (D). Quoted in *Washingtonian*, Apr. 1989.

11. Action is typical of the American style, thought and planning are not; it is considered heresy to state that some problems are not immediately or easily solvable.
Daniel Bell, sociologist, Harvard University, Cambridge, MA. *Daedalus*, Summer 1967.

12. Government is the art of the momentarily feasible, of the least bad attainable, and not of the rationally most desirable.
Bernard Berenson (1865-1959), American art critic and historian. *Rumor and Reflection*, 1952.

13. The state of affairs in our nation's capital is a national disgrace. It is an international embarrassment and dishonors the name of our first president, George Washington.
Douglas Bereuter, U.S. Congressman (R-NB). Speech in Congress, Feb. 22, 1989.

14. Please don't be deterred in the fanatic application of your sterile logic.
Aneurin Bevan (1897-1960), Minister of Health, Great Britain (Socialist). Criticism of the suggestions of some of his fellow Socialists. Quoted in Nancy McPhee, *The Book of Insults*, 1978.

15. If you are a U.S. Senator, you can give an ideological response to a serious problem and probably never be held accountable for it. Whereas the governors are dealing with the real world – they have to run things, to make them work.
James J. Blanchard, U.S. Congressman and Governor of Michigan (D). Quoted in *The Washington Post*, Nov. 27, 1988.

16. As I watched some of the Watergate hearings I kept asking myself what all these people – *[John]*

Dean and others – were doing there in the first place. Was there really an honest job that needed doing?

Daniel Boorstin, American historian and Librarian of Congress. Testimony, U.S. Senate Select Committee on Watergate, July 7, 1973.

17. Government is not an exact science.

Louis D. Brandeis (1856-1941), U.S. Supreme Court Justice. *Truax* v. *Corrigan*, 1921.

18. I know of no group or class that we do not reach – and we please none.

Prentiss M. Brown (1899-1973), Director, Office of Production Administration, U.S. Congressman, and U.S. Senator (D-MI). In reference to the wartime OPA. Remark, 1943.

19. The actions you plan to take and the actions you actually decide to take *[in a crisis]* are not always the same.

McGeorge Bundy, presidential assistant for national security (D). Quoted on PBS, *War and Peace in the Nuclear Age*, Feb. 1989.

20. "Not men but measures" – a sort of charm by which many people get loose from every honorable engagement.

Edmund Burke (1729-1797), British statesman. *Thoughts on the Cause of the Present Discontents*, 1770.

21. Public life is a situation of power and energy; he trespasses against his duty who sleeps upon his watch as he that goes over to the enemy.

Edmund Burke. *Ibid.*

22. A whistle-blower is a public servant of the highest order.

George Bush, 41st President of the United States (R-TX). Statement, Mar. 1989.

23. People say I'm indecisive, but I don't know about that.

George Bush. Speech, Gridiron Club, Washington, DC, Apr. 1, 1989.

24. Government functions best as a catalyst, not a cure. We need a smarter, more effective government, not a bigger one.

George Bush. Quoted in *The 1989 Conservative Calendar*.

25. The characteristic feature of the experiment in Russia ... is not that it is communist, but that it is being carried on with a plan in the face of a planless opposition.

Nicholas Murray Butler (1862-1947), President, Columbia University and Nobel Laureate in Peace. Commencement address, Columbia University, New York City, June 11, 1931.

26. Life is the art of drawing sufficient conclusions from insufficient premises.

Samuel Butler (1835-1902), British writer. *The Note-Books of Samuel Butler*, 1912.

27. No government at any level has all the answers.

Kim Campbell, Minister of Justice, Canada. Speech, Johns Hopkins University, Baltimore, MD, Apr. 19, 1991.

28. Disclosure is the antidote to partiality and favor.

Benjamin N. Cardozo (1870-1938), U.S. Supreme Court Justice. *People ex rel. Fordham M. R. Church* v. *Walsh*, 1911.

29. If I could find out who leaked the contents of this report, he or she would be a former employee of the Pentagon.

Frank C. Carlucci, U.S. Secretary of Defense and National Security Advisor (D). PBS, *MacNeil-Lehrer News Hour*, Aug. 8, 1988.

30. *[The test of government]* is not how popular it is among the powerful and privileged few, but how honestly and fairly it deals with the many who must depend upon it.

Jimmy Carter, 39th President of the United States (D-GA). Inaugural address as Governor of Georgia, Jan. 1971.

31. I praise loudly; I blame softly.

Catherine II (The Great) (1729-1796), Empress of Russia. Quoted in Evdokimov, *The Complete Works of Catherine II*, 1893.

32. Staff expands to fill the office space available.... The basic obligation of Congress is to the taxpayers, not to its own creature comforts.

John H. Chafee, U.S. Senator and Governor of Rhode Island (R). In opposition to appropriations for the new Hart Senate Office Building. *Reader's Digest*, Feb. 1979.

33. The great secret in life, I think, is to choose the right people around you to do the job.

Charles, Prince of Wales and Duke of Cornwall. Interview, PBS, Oct. 2, 1988.

34. I voted for them *[weapons systems]* when I was in Congress. Now that I'm Secretary *[of Defense]* I have to figure out a way to pay for them.

Richard B. Cheney, U.S. Congressman (R-WY), White House Chief of Staff, and U.S. Secretary of Defense. Interview, 1989.

35. Perhaps it is better to be irresponsible and right than to be responsible and wrong.
Winston Churchill (1874-1965), Prime Minister of Great Britain (Conservative). Radio broadcast, Aug. 26, 1950.

36. It never occurred to any of us to consult in this emergency farmers, doctors, lawyers, shoemakers, or even statesmen. We could not escape the belief that the prospect of obtaining what we needed might be somewhat improved by making application to those whose business and surroundings qualified them to intelligently respond.
Grover Cleveland (1837-1908), 22nd and 24th President of the United States (D-NY). Statement made after his administration borrowed money from J. P. Morgan and other bankers at extremely unfavorable rates, 1904.

37. You cannot bring inexperienced men into the government and expect the government to run well.
Clark P. Clifford, U.S. Secretary of Defense and Special Counsel to the President (D). Interview with Bill Moyers, PBS, 1981.

38. As we seek to improve the management of the federal government, we should keep in mind that the government is not a private corporation. What may make sense for a large corporation may not always make sense for the federal government. In our quest for efficiency, we must not lose sight of the reasons why we enacted certain federal programs in the first place.
William S. Cohen, U.S. Senator (R-ME). Testimony, Senate Committee on Governmental Affairs, May 13-14, 1986.

39. The ruler over a country of a thousand chariots must give diligent attention to business; he must be sincere; he must be economical; he must love his people; and he must provide employment for them at the proper season.
Confucius (551-479 B.C.), Chinese philosopher. *Analects.*

40. There is one rule of action more important than all others. It consists in never doing anything that someone else can do for you.
Calvin Coolidge (1872-1933), 30th President of the United States (R-MA). *Autobiography*, 1929.

41. Perhaps one of the most important accomplishments of my administration has been minding my own business.
Calvin Coolidge. Remark to reporters just before leaving office, Mar. 1929.

42. Mr. President, we can't advise you properly on what we should seek with the Soviets until we know what we're planning for on our side.
William Crowe, Admiral, U.S. Navy, and Chairman, Joint Chiefs of Staff. Remark to President Reagan. Quoted in *Time*, May 30, 1988.

43. To his own people he did evil; in yokes without relief he ruined them all.
Cyrus (The Great) (c.600-529 B.C.), King of Persia. Said of Nabodonius, last king of Babylonia. *The Cyrus Cylinder*, 529 B.C.

44. Look at our Lord's disciples. One denied Him, one doubted Him, one betrayed Him. If our Lord couldn't have perfection, how are you going to have it in city government?
Richard J. Daley (1902-1976), Mayor of Chicago, IL (D). Mar. 1967.

45. Government simply has no bottom line.
Donald Devine, Director, U.S. Office of Personnel Management (R). *National Review*, Oct. 27, 1989.

46. I live by my principles, and one of my principles is flexibility.
Everett M. Dirksen (1896-1969), U.S. Congressman and U.S. Senator (R-IL). Quoted in the *Miami Herald*, Sept. 9, 1969.

47. The greatest of all evils is a weak government.
Benjamin Disraeli, 1st Earl of Beaconsfield (1804-1881), Prime Minister of Great Britain (Conservative). *Coningsby*, 1844.

48. The Communist leaders handle national property as their own, but at the same time they waste it as if it were somebody else's. Such is the nature of ownership and government of the system.
Milovan Djilas, writer and Vice President of Yugoslavia under Marshall Tito. Quoted by Vaclav Havel, *Disturbing the Peace: A Conversation with Karel Hvizdala*, 1990.

49. We must have a Secretary of Defense who will manage, and not be managed, by the Pentagon.
Michael Dukakis, Governor of Massachusetts (D). Presidential nomination acceptance speech, Democratic National Convention, Atlanta, GA, July 21, 1988.

50. This election is not about ideology. It's about competence.
Michael Dukakis. *Ibid.*

51. No Secretary of State can give constant personal care to more than a few problems among the global abundance.
Abba Eban, Foreign Secretary, Israel (Labor) and

Israeli Ambassador to the United Nations. *An Autobiography*, 1977.

52. Unlike presidential administrations, problems rarely have terminal dates.
Dwight D. Eisenhower (1890-1969), 34th President of the United States (R-KS). Annual message to Congress, Jan. 12, 1961.

53. Government has come to be a trade, and is managed solely on commercial principles. A man plunges into politics to make his fortune, and only cares that the world shall last his days.
Ralph Waldo Emerson (1803-1882), American writer. Letter to Thomas Carlyle, Oct. 7, 1835.

54. The more reason, the less government.
Ralph Waldo Emerson. *Essays*, Second Series. "Character," 1876.

55. Our government wasn't created to be efficient. It was created to preserve the individual.
Samuel J. Ervin, Jr. (1896-1985), U.S. Congressman and U.S. Senator (D-NC). Quoted in Marshall Frady, *Southerners*, 1980.

56. It isn't easy, you know, to govern Egypt.
Farouk I (1920-1965), King of Egypt. Statement when he was deposed and sent into exile, 1952.

57. There was a time that you could say the least government was the best – but not in the nation's most populous state.
Dianne Feinstein, Mayor of San Francisco, CA (D). Campaign speech, Mar. 15, 1990.

58. The issue isn't more or less government. It's dumb vs. smart government.
James J. Florio, U.S. Congressman and Governor of New Jersey (D). Comment to justify government initiatives and increasing taxes. Quoted in *Time*, May 2, 1990.

59. Thanks to my football experience, I know the value of team play. It is, I believe, one of the most important lessons to be learned and practiced.
Gerald R. Ford, 38th President of the United States (R-MI). Remark, 1969.

60. Truth is the glue that holds government together. Compromise is the oil that makes governments go.
Gerald R. Ford. 1973.

61. Government ... is neither business nor technology nor applied science. It is the art of making men live together in peace and with reasonable happiness.
Felix Frankfurter (1882-1965), U.S. Supreme Court Justice. *The New Republic*, Oct. 31, 1928.

62. With respect to the true monarchical government, it is the best or the worst of all others, accordingly as it is administered.
Frederick II (The Great) (1712-1786), King of Prussia. *Essay on Forms of Government*.

63. While Washington's establishment ... is whipped into motion by the mere whiff of an emotional issue or scandal, there is no reward in today's Capitol for fixing the broken mechanics of government or solving the huge problems that haunt us.
Tom Freedman, Legislative Director for Congressman Charles E. Schumer (D-NY). "While Journalists Chase Sexy Issues," *The New York Times*, Sept. 16, 1990.

64. Most of the energy devoted to political work is devoted to correcting the effects of mismanagement of government.
Milton Friedman, Nobel Laureate in Economics (America). Quoted on PBS, *Firing Line*, Oct. 9, 1988.

65. Meetings are indispensable when you don't want to do anything.
John Kenneth Galbraith, American economist and U.S. Ambassador to India (D). *Ambassador's Journal*, 1969.

66. To govern is always to choose among disadvantages.
Charles de Gaulle (1890-1970), President of France. Quoted in *The New York Times*, Nov. 14, 1965.

67. Whenever people get frustrated with substance, they tend to want to move boxes around *[that is, reorganize]*.
Dan Glickman, U.S. Congressman (D-KS). Interview, CNN, *Newsmaker*, July 3, 1988.

68. Without *glasnost* there is not, and there cannot be, democratism, the political creativity of the masses and their participation in management.
Mikhail Gorbachev, President of the U.S.S.R. Speech, Communist Party Congress, Moscow, Feb. 1986.

69. There are many people who want simple solutions, but there are none ... nor will there be.
Mikhail Gorbachev. Speech, Communist Party Central Committee, Moscow, Feb. 7, 1990.

70. Actually, I'm going around in circles.
Mikhail Gorbachev. Response when asked if he was moving to the right. Quoted in *The Washington Post*, Dec. 19, 1990.

71. We need citizens willing to make Congress accountable for the travesty which passes for government today.
J. Peter Grace, Chairman, W. R. Grace and Co., and Chairman, President's Commission on Government Productivity. Quoted in *Conservative Digest*, Apr. 1988.

72. We shall either find a way or make one.
Hannibal (c.247-183 B.C.), Carthaginian general. Attributed.

73. I expect you to be a leader, to supervise by example, to lead, not simply order others to do hard jobs. I will hold you personally responsible for the operations under you. If one of your men makes an error, you as well as he will be accountable.
J. Edgar Hoover (1895-1972), Director, Federal Bureau of Investigation. Quoted by Wannall, "J. Edgar Hoover Was My Boss," *Conservative Digest*, June 1987.

74. I pretend to be a gentleman, and when the other fellow finds out, it is too late.
Harry L. Hopkins (1890-1946), U.S. Secretary of Commerce (D), Director, Work Projects Administration, and special assistant to the President. Remark to Charles E. Merriam on how he managed to contend with the infighting of political types in the government.

75. I'm not going to last six months here, so I'll do as I please.
Harry L. Hopkins. Remark on assuming his duties as Federal Emergency Relief Administrator. Quoted in Robert E. Sherwood, *Roosevelt and Hopkins: An Intimate Biography*, 1950.

76. We have moved toward a kind of scorpions-in-a-bottle government where you have two branches *[Executive and Legislative]* that don't understand many of the legitimate needs of the other branch.
Michael J. Horowitz, general counsel, U.S. Office of Management and Budget. Quoted in *The New York Times*, Oct. 23, 1988.

77. The government is mainly an expensive organization to regulate evildoers, and tax those who behave; government does little for fairly respectable people except annoy them.
Edgar Watson Howe (1853-1937), American writer and editor. *Notes for My Biographer*, 1926.

78. I'm a person who believes in close monitoring and knowing what everyone on the staff is doing.
Henry E. Hudson, U.S. Attorney, Arlington, VA. Quoted in *The Washington Post*, June 26, 1988.

79. In government, consensus is more important than command; persuasion not only works better than arrogance, it's vital to the democratic process.
Ellen Hume and **Jane Mayer**, White House correspondents for *The Wall Street Journal*. *Regardie's*, Jan. 1987.

80. There are no necessary evils in government. Its evils exist only in its abuses.
Andrew Jackson (1767-1845), 7th President of the United States (D-TN). Remark when vetoing the Bank Renewal Bill, July 10, 1832.

81. Be swift to hear, slow to speak, slow to wrath.
New Testament, *James* 1:19.

82. That government is best which governs least.
[This quotation has not been found in Jefferson's writings, but it is entirely consistent with his philosophy and practice.]
Thomas Jefferson (1743-1826), 3rd President of the United States (Democratic Republican-VA). Quoted by Henry David Thoreau, *Of Civil Disobedience*, 1849.

83. I will do my best. That's all I can do. I ask for your help and God's.
Lyndon B. Johnson (1908-1973), 36th President of the United States (D-TX). Comment on arriving in Washington, DC, on the evening of President Kennedy's assassination, Nov. 22, 1963.

84. Sure we make mistakes. But point them out and we will correct them. Let's not throw the baby out, though, with the dishes.
Lyndon B. Johnson. June 22, 1967.

85. There are no favorites in my office. I treat them all with the same general inconsideration.
Lyndon B. Johnson. Quoted in Paul F. Boller, Jr., *Presidential Anecdotes*, 1981.

86. The new city manager will take over one of the most backward, rottenest governments in the country.
Kansas City Star, Editorial, 1940.

87. Our Washington reflex is to discover a problem and then throw money at it, hoping it will go away.
Kenneth B. Keating (1900-1975), U.S. Congressman (R-NY), U.S. Senator, and U.S. Ambassador to Israel. Quoted in *The New York Times*, Dec. 24, 1961.

88. You run them or they'll run you.
Edward J. Kelly (1876-1950), Mayor of Chicago, IL (D). Remark on the relationship between the Mayor and the City Council. Quoted in O'Conner, *Clout: Mayor Daley and His City*, 1975.

89. All my life I've known better than to depend on the experts. How could I have been so stupid, to let them go ahead?
John F. Kennedy (1917-1963), 35th President of the United States (D-MA). Reflection on the Bay of Pigs debacle, Apr. 21, 1961.

90. When we got into office, the thing that surprised me most was to find that things were just as bad as we'd been saying they were.
John F. Kennedy. Speech at a dinner honoring his 44th birthday, May 27, 1961.

91. The cabinet can't decide anything. The Secretary of Defense knows nothing about farm legislation. The Secretary of Agriculture knows nothing about the situation in Saigon. The head of HEW *[Dept. of Health, Education and Welfare]* can't advise the Attorney General about civil rights in Alabama. And the Attorney General can't advise the Postmaster General about the employees you should have in the Post Office. So, therefore, what subjects are there in common?
Robert F. Kennedy (1925-1968), U.S. Senator and U.S. Attorney General (D-NY). Interview, Feb. 29, 1964.

92. There is not only a right thing to do. There is a right time to do it.
Mackenzie King (1874-1950), Prime Minister of Canada (Liberal). Remark to Louis St. Laurent.

93. I have to take decisions – not back hunches.
Tom King, Secretary of State for Defense, Great Britain (Conservative). Parliamentary hearings, Mar. 1990.

94. Our government is a little more chaotic than most other governments in the world.
Jeane J. Kirkpatrick, U.S. Ambassador to the United Nations (R). PBS, *Report on the United Nations*, June 21, 1989.

95. A lot can be accomplished with current resources if we don't stand around wringing our hands because of lack of funding or complex requirements.
Dennis Kissinger, City Manager, Salina, KS. Quoted in *Governing the States and Localities*, Apr. 1988.

96. There cannot be a crisis next week. My schedule is already full.
Henry M. Kissinger, U.S. Secretary of State and National Security Advisor (R). Quoted in *The New York Times Magazine*, 1969.

97. To focus on everything is to focus on nothing.
Mark A. R. Kleiman, Director, Policy and Management Analysis, U.S. Department of Justice. Quoted in *The New York Times*, Oct. 16, 1988.

98. I believe in the rule of common sense. That means doing what makes the most sense when it comes time for you to do it.
Edward I. Koch, U.S. Congressman and Mayor of New York City (D). 1981.

99. I'm not the type to get ulcers. I give them.
Edward I. Koch. Quoted in *The New York Times*, Jan. 20, 1984.

100. I say that the most inefficient, wasteful self-government is worth more than the most efficient dictatorship.
Fiorello H. La Guardia (1882-1947), U.S. Congressman (R and Socialist) and Mayor of New York City (R and Fusion Party). Speech in Congress against Hitler and Mussolini, Apr. 15, 1932.

101. It is axiomatic in politics that the earlier one addresses a problem, the more the alternatives and the easier the solutions.
Richard D. Lamm, Governor of Colorado (D). *Playboy*, Aug. 1984.

102. In government it is order that matters.
Lao-tzu (c.604-531 B.C.), Chinese philosopher and founder of Taoism. *Tao Te Ching*.

103. The people are difficult to govern: It is because those in authority are too fond of action *[change]*.
Lao-tzu. *Ibid.*

104. Govern the state by being straightforward; wage war by being crafty; win the empire by not meddling.
Lao-tzu. *Ibid.*

105. The instruments of state prove too big to do the small things and too small to do the big things.
Lewis Lapham, American journalist. PBS, *America's Century*, Nov. 1989.

106. Men too involved in details usually become unable to deal with great matters.
François de La Rochefoucauld (1613-1680), French nobleman and writer. *Réflexions ou Sentences et Maximes Morales*, 1665.

107. One technical expert is worth twenty Communists.
V. I. Lenin (1870-1924), Premier of the U.S.S.R. Quoted in Emil Ludwig, *Genius and Character*, 1927.

108. We need government to do for the people what they cannot do for themselves.
Abraham Lincoln (1809-1865), 16th President of the United States (R-IL). Fragment, July 1, 1854; quoted

by Mario Cuomo in a speech to New York Financial Writers Association, May 15, 1991.

109. Have you already in your mind a plan wholly or partially formed? If you have, prosecute it without interference from me. If you have not, please inform me, so that I, incompetent as I may be, can try and assist you in the formation of some plan for the army.
Abraham Lincoln. Letter to Gen. Joseph Hooker, May 7, 1863.

110. I claim not to have controlled events, but confess plainly that events have controlled me.
Abraham Lincoln. Letter to A. G. Hodges, Apr. 4, 1864.

111. We have not fully pleased anybody and that's a good sign.
Solomon Liss, Chairman, Maryland Critical Areas Commission. Quoted in *The Washington Post*, June 25, 1988.

112. Mr. *[William Jennings]* Bryan thinks that to say something is to do something, which is an imperfect view of administration.
Henry Cabot Lodge (1850-1924), U.S. Congressman and U.S. Senator (R-MA). Letter to Sturgis Bigelow, May 28, 1913.

113. That is the best government which desires to make the people happy, and knows how to make them happy.
Thomas Babington Macaulay, 1st Baron Macaulay (1800-1859), historian and Secretary of War, Great Britain (Liberal). "On Mitford's History of Greece," *Knight's Quarterly*, Nov. 1824.

114. The Navajo Nation spends most of its time jumping through hoops.
Peter MacDonald, Chairman, Navajo Tribal Council. Remark on the administrative procedures required by the U.S. Bureau of Indian Affairs. Quoted in *Governing the States and Localities*, Apr. 1988.

115. It is the duty of Her Majesty's government neither to flap nor to falter.
Harold Macmillan (1894-1986), Prime Minister of Great Britain (Conservative). Quoted in *The London Observer*, Nov. 19, 1961.

116. But the great security against a gradual concentration of the several powers in the same department consists in giving to those who administer each department the necessary constitutional means and personal motives to resist encroachments of the others.
James Madison (1751-1836), 4th President of the United States (Democratic Republican-VA). *The Federalist*, No. 51, Feb. 8, 1788.

117. They say, and do not.
New Testament, *Matthew* 23:3.

118. Our system of checks and balances.... The people keep the politicians from stealing too much, and the politicians keep the people from getting too crazy.
H. L. Mencken (1880-1956), American journalist. *Generally Political*, 1944.

119. The worst government is the most moral. One composed of cynics is often very tolerant and human. But when fanatics are on top there is no limit to oppression.
H. L. Mencken. *Notebooks*, 1956.

120. My constant efforts are directed against ultras of all kinds.
Klemens von Metternich (1773-1859), Austrian statesman and diplomat. Letter to Heinrich Gentz, Mar. 30, 1825.

121. You can't run a city by people who do not live there.
Harvey Milk (1930-1978), City Supervisor, San Francisco, CA. Quoted in Edward Shilts, *The Mayor of Castro Street*, 1982.

122. But political checks will no more act of themselves than a bridle will direct a horse without a rider.
John Stuart Mill (1806-1873), Member of Parliament, Great Britain, and political economist. *Representative Government*, 1861.

123. Don't be so foolish as to ask for more time: Calamities will not wait.
Honoré de Mirabeau (1749-1791), revolutionary and President of the National Assembly, France. Speech, Sept. 28, 1789.

124. A public fund is collected by no fewer than two *[persons]*, and disbursed by no fewer than three.
Mishna, *Peah* 8:7.

125. Your report! 'Tis my report. It is no report at all until I have accepted it.
James Monroe (1758-1831), 5th President of the United States (Democratic Republican-VA). Remark to John Quincy Adams and quoted in Adams's *Diary*, Apr. 30, 1822.

126. The essence of government is making necessary choices between competing uses of public resources.

Jonathan Moore, U.S. Coordinator for Refugee Affairs. Quoted in *The New York Times*, Aug. 21, 1988.

127. When the mayor's concerned about something, eveybody's concerned about it.
Mary Moran, Mayor of Bridgeport, CT (R). CBS, *60 Minutes*, June 16, 1991.

128. Waste of public money is like a sin against the Holy Ghost.
John Morley, Viscount Morley of Blackburn (1838-1923), Member of Parliament, Great Britain (Liberal), Chief Secretary for Ireland, and Secretary of State for India. *Recollections*, 1917.

129. If you can't get along with the head of the government with which you are working, you won't get anything done – nothing!
Robert Moses (1888-1981), Chairman, Port Authority, New York City. Quoted on PBS, *The World That Moses Built*, Jan. 16, 1989.

130. I believe in limited objectives and in getting things done.
Robert Moses. *Ibid.*

131. It has proved politically wiser to set goals than to start programs.
Daniel P. Moynihan, Chief American Delegate to the United Nations and U.S. Senator (D-NY). *The New York Times*, July 16, 1990.

132. You can ask me for anything you like, except time.
Napoléon I (1769-1821), military leader and Emperor of France. Remark to aide, 1803.

133. States are governed by reason and policy, and not by acrimony and weakness.
Napoléon I. *Maxims.*

134. The art of governing consists in not letting men grow old in their jobs.
Napoléon I. *Ibid.*

135. Ambassadors cost a good deal of money, and do very little good. It is better for a sovereign to manage his affairs himself.
Napoléon I. 1814.

136. Debating societies are out. We are going to have action.
Donald Marr Nelson (1888-1959), Director, U.S. War Production Board. Remark when he came from Sears-Roebuck to direct war production for the nation, 1942.

137. I don't give a shit what happens. I want you all to stonewall it, let them plead the Fifth Amendment, cover up, or anything else, if it'll save it – save the plan. We're going to protect our people if we can.
Richard M. Nixon, 37th President of the United States (R-CA). White House meeting, Mar. 22, 1973.

138. The end of the government being the good of mankind, points out its great duties: It is above all things to provide for the security, the quiet, the happy enjoyment of life, liberty, and property.
James Otis (1725-1783), Member, Colonial Massachusetts legislature. *The Rights of the British Colonies Asserted and Proved*, 1764.

139. Behold, my son, with how little wisdom the world is governed.
Axel Gustafsson Oxenstierna (1583-1654), guardian of Queen Christina and Chancellor of Sweden. Letter to his son, reflecting on the Thirty Years' War, 1648.

140. Never tell people how to do things. Tell them what you want them to achieve, and they will surprise you with their ingenuity.
George S. Patton (1885-1945), General, U.S. Army. Quoted in *The Washington Post Magazine*, Dec. 9, 1990.

141. We'll cross that bridge when we fall off it.
Lester B. Pearson (1897-1972), Prime Minister of Canada (Liberal) and Nobel Laureate in Peace. 1964.

142. The End of every thing should direct the Means: Now that of Government being the *Good of the whole*, nothing less should be the *Aim* of the Prince.
William Penn (1644-1718), founder of Pennsylvania. *Some Fruits of Solitude, in Reflections and Maxims*, 1693.

143. You start by saying no to requests. Then if you have to go to yes, okay. But if you start with yes, you can't go to no.
Mildred Perlman, Commissioner, Civil Service, New York State. Quoted in *The New York Times*, Dec. 1, 1975.

144. It's the oldest political cop-out there is. If you don't want to do anything, you appoint a commission.
Gordon Peterson, American TV journalist. CBS, *Inside Washington*, Dec. 31, 1988.

145. Nothing is more dangerous to the state than persons who try to govern kingdoms according to maxims drawn from books.
Armand-Jean du Plessis (Cardinal Richelieu)

(1585-1642), French ecclesiastic and statesman. *Political Testament*, I, 8, 1687.

146. I prefer to supervise the whole operations of the government myself rather than entrust the public business to subordinates, and this makes my duties very great.

James K. Polk (1795-1849), 11th President of the United States (D-TN). Quoted in Wallechinsky and Wallace, *The People's Almanac*, 1975.

147. For forms of government let fools contest;
Whatever's best administered is best.

Alexander Pope (1688-1744), British poet. *An Essay on Man*, III, 1734.

148. The best way to cure a problem is to know what the truth is – what the facts are.

Dixy Lee Ray, Governor of Washington and Chairman, U.S. Atomic Energy Commission (D). Interview, C-SPAN, *Booknotes*, June 16, 1991.

149. Government should do only those things the people cannot do for themselves.

Ronald Reagan, 40th President of the United States (R-CA). June 23, 1971.

150. When you go to bed with the federal government you get more than a good night's sleep.

Ronald Reagan. 1983.

151. I didn't know what was going on there.

Ronald Reagan. Remark to a caller who asked why he never informed the public about the 1989 savings and loan scandal. Interview, CNN, *The Larry King Show*, Jan. 10, 1990.

152. I read all these stories that I don't know anything about politics. But I must know something. I've had some good victories in Congress, and I've survived this town for four years.

Donald T. Regan, U.S. Secretary of the Treasury and White House Chief of Staff (R). Quoted in *The New York Times*, Jan. 25, 1985.

153. In the corporate world, you can arrive at conclusions a lot faster. You can stick to plans a lot better than you can in government.

Donald T. Regan. Quoted in *Regardie's*, Jan. 1987.

154. Flexibility is the most requisite qualification for the management of great affairs.

Cardinal de Retz (1614-1679), French ecclesiastic and politician. *Political Maxims*.

155. No one who is near the king *[Maximilian I (1459-1519]* knows what is going on. I do not believe he himself knows what he is doing.

Johann Reuchlin (1455-1522), German scholar and translator. Letter to Füssen, Mar. 28, 1492.

156. No shoulders can carry responsible burdens if they are already loaded with partisan chips.

Abraham A. Ribicoff, U.S. Congressman (D), U.S. Senator, Governor of Connecticut, and U.S. Secretary of Health, Education and Welfare. Quoted in *Look*, Sept. 20, 1955.

157. Tinkering with the organization has always been a preoccupation with Department of Defense reformers.... Generally the only result is a new, impressive chart. But neat charts don't produce better organizations.

Hyman G. Rickover (1900-1986), Admiral, U.S. Navy. Quoted in *Playboy*, Nov. 1974.

158. As everyone knows, there are overruns on everything. Overruns are no mortal sin.

L. Mendel Rivers (1905-1970), U.S. Congressman (D-SC). Debate, House Armed Services Committee, Oct. 1969.

159. The job of a cabinet minister is to tell the civil service what the public won't stand for.

Duff Roblin, Premier of Manitoba, Canada. Attributed.

160. Thank heavens we don't get all the government we pay for.

Will Rogers (1879-1935), American humorist. Quoted on PBS, *Will Rogers U.S.A.*, Oct. 3, 1988.

161. Say as little as possible while appearing to be awake.

William P. Rogers, U.S. Secretary of State (D). Advice on how to behave in committee meetings.

162. I get my fingers into about everything and there's no law against it.

Franklin D. Roosevelt (1882-1945), 32nd President of the United States (D-NY). Description of his job as U.S. Assistant Secretary of the Navy, 1913. Quoted in Josephus Daniels, *The Wilson Era*, 1946.

163. Do what you can, with what you have, where you are.

Theodore Roosevelt (1858-1919), 26th President of the United States (R-NY). Favorite saying.

164. *[Government]* management is hard to discuss, hard to comprehend, hard to legislate.

William V. Roth, Jr., U.S. Congressman and U.S. Senator (D-DE). May 14, 1986.

165. When you solve a problem, you ought to thank God and go on to the next one.

Dean Rusk, U.S. Secretary of State (D). Quoted in *Look*, Sept. 6, 1966.

166. Where was there time for long-range planning, for quiet reflection, for reconsidering the directions of foreign policy as well as operational detail?

Dean Rusk. *As I Saw It*, 1990.

167. An administration, like a machine, does not create. It carries on.

Antoine de Saint-Exupéry (1900-1944), French writer and aviator. *Flight to Arras*, 1942.

168. To govern, after all, means to do what has to be done.

Carlos Salinas de Gortarì, President of Mexico. Quoted in *The New York Times Magazine*, Nov. 20, 1988.

169. Government watchdogs have become political lapdogs.

James R. Sasser, U.S. Senator (D-TN). Quoted in *The New York Times*, Sept. 9, 1990.

170. Malice may help a Fool to aggravate, but there must be *Skill* to know how to extenuate.

George Savile, 1st Marquess of Halifax (1633-1695), Lord Privy Seal of England. *Moral Thoughts and Reflections*, 1750.

171. The Government of the World is a great thing; but it is a very coarse one too, compared with the Fineness of Speculative Knowledge *[philosophy, mathematics, and science]*.

George Savile. *Ibid.*

172. I am working on one crisis at a time.

William Donald Schaefer, Mayor of Baltimore, MD, and Governor of Maryland (D). Statement to reporters, Dec. 21, 1990.

173. You measure a government by how few people need help.

Patricia R. Schroeder, U.S. Congresswoman (D-CO). PBS, *Firing Line*, Sept. 13, 1989.

174. Here in America you can see how slightly a people needs to be governed.... Here are governments, but no rulers – governors, but they are clerks.

Carl Schurz (1829-1906), U.S. Senator (R-MO). "The Political Life of America," *The Patriotic Anthology*, 1941.

175. "*Yet* and *but*," said the Templar, "are words for fools; wise men neither hesitate nor retract: They resolve and they execute."

Walter Scott (1771-1832), Scottish writer. *The Talisman*, 1825.

176. The system, if it is operating properly, is designed to save the President from himself.

Brent Scowcroft, Admiral, U.S. Navy, and National Security Advisor (R). Quoted on PBS, *The Power Game*, Jan. 4, 1989.

177. The chief cause of problems is solutions.

Eric A. Severeid (1913-1992), American TV journalist. Quoted in Charles E. Silberman, *Criminal Violence, Criminal Justice*, 1986.

178. A planned society is a slave society.

Fulton J. Sheen (1895-1979), American Roman Catholic archbishop and television personality. *On Being Human*, 1982.

179. The people should have as little to do as may be with the government.

Roger Sherman (1721-1793), delegate to Constitutional Convention, U.S. Congressman (Federalist-CT), and U.S. Senator. Debate, Constitutional Convention, Philadelphia, PA, 1787.

180. Putting trust in people will produce trustworthy people. That is the foremost of the many reasons against the widespread and routine use of lie detector tests. Management through fear and intimidation is not the way to promote honesty and protect security.

George P. Shultz, U.S. Secretary of State (R). Speech, Washington, DC, Jan. 9, 1989.

181. He was an extraordinarily successful businessman and very interested in the State Department. He worked hard at it, but finally he just left. He said, "Around here, when you decide something, that's just the beginning. Anybody who doesn't like it goes to Congress, goes to the press or something. It's a different process."

George P. Shultz. Remark on appointing a friend who was a successful businessman to the State Department. Quoted in *The Washington Post*, Mar. 19, 1989.

182. About two-fifths of the upper-level management of this state could be eliminated, and they would not be missing in action because there is no action from which they could be missing.

John Silber, President, Boston University, MA. Comment during the Massachusetts gubernatorial race. ABC, *This Week*, Nov. 4, 1990.

183. At court, many more people can hurt than can help you; please the former, but engage the latter.

Philip Dormer Stanhope, 4th Earl of Chesterfield (1694-1773), Member of Parliament, Great Britain (Whig), and Lord-Lieutenant of Ireland. *Maxims.*

184. There are only three rules of sound administration: Pick good men, tell them not to cut any corners, and back them to the limit.
Adlai E. Stevenson (1900-1965), Governor of Illinois (D) and U.S. Ambassador to the United Nations. Quoted by Joseph Alsop, *The Saturday Evening Post*, June 28, 1952.

185. The only way to make a man trustworthy is to trust him.
Henry L. Stimson (1867-1950), U.S. Secretary of State (R), U.S. Secretary of War, and Governor General of the Philippine Islands. Advice to President Truman.

186. You can't give someone your checkbook without oversight.
Roger R. Stolz, Deputy Director, U.S. General Accounting Office. Quoted in *The New York Times*, July 31, 1989.

187. ... a government like ours, founded by the people, managed by the people.
Joseph Story (1779-1845), U.S. Supreme Court Justice. *Commentaries on the Constitution*, 1833.

188. He who excels at resolving difficulties does so before they arise. He who excels in conquering his enemies triumphs before threats materialize.
Sun-tzu (c.400 B.C.), Chinese writer of the Age of Warring States. *The Art of War.*

189. Any woman who understands the problems of running a home will be nearer to understanding the problems of running a country.
Margaret Thatcher, Prime Minister of Great Britain (Conservative). *The Observer*, May 8, 1979.

190. It must be a "conviction" government. I couldn't waste time having any internal arguments.
Margaret Thatcher. Quoted in *The New York Times*, Oct. 2, 1988.

191. One doesn't always have the luxury of proceeding on purely ideological grounds in the Justice Department.
Richard Thornburgh, U.S. Attorney General and Governor of Pennsylvania (R). Quoted on CBS, *Face the Nation*, Aug. 14, 1988.

192. The more conflict in government, the more openness in government.... Conflict makes government understandable.
Martin Tolchin, American journalist. Symposium, "The Press and a Divided Government," National Press Foundation, Washington, DC, Dec. 6, 1989.

193. I hope for cooperation from farmers, from labor, and from business. Every segment of our population has a right to expect from our government a fair deal.
Harry S Truman (1884-1972), 33rd President of the United States (D-MO). Annual message to Congress, Jan. 5, 1949.

194. If you want an efficient government, why then go someplace where they have a dictatorship and you'll get it.
Harry S Truman. Lecture, Columbia University, New York City, Apr. 28, 1959.

195. I never sit on a fence. I am on either one side or another.
Harry S Truman. Favorite saying.

196. There isn't anything in the world that can't be made better.
Jack Valenti, special assistant to the President (D). Quoted in *Time*, Aug. 20, 1990.

197. My only purpose is to make myself useful and to bring certain urban reforms to a satisfactory conclusion. Why must politics and Christianity always intrude into administrative matters?
Jules Verne (1828-1905), French writer and politician. Comment when elected to the Town Council of Amiens. Quoted by Mme. Allotte de La Fuÿe, *Jules Verne, sa vie, son ouevre*, 1928.

198. Government needs to have both shepherds and butchers.
Voltaire (François-Marie Arouet) (1694-1778), French historian and dramatist. *Notebooks.*

199. FDR could keep all the balls in the air without losing his own.
Henry A. Wallace (1888-1965), U.S. Secretary of Agriculture, U.S. Secretary of Commerce, and Vice President of the United States (D-IA). Quoted in Arthur M. Schlesinger, Jr., *The Imperial Presidency*, 1973.

200. A governor who can't work with the *[state]* legislature can't get results.
Earl Warren (1891-1974), Chief Justice, U.S. Supreme Court, and Governor of California (R). Campaign speech, 1942.

201. To err is nature; to rectify error is glory.
George Washington (1732-1799), 1st President of the United States (VA). Remark to William Payne, 1754.

202. When you're running a department with three million people in it, you're at the mercy of one or two dishonest people.
Caspar Weinberger, U.S. Secretary of Defense,

and U.S. Secretary of Health, Education and Welfare (R). Comment on Defense Department procurement scandals that occurred during his administration. Interview, ABC, *This Week*, Sept. 26, 1988.

203. Miracles do happen, but one has to work very hard for them.

Chaim Weizmann (1874-1952), 1st President of Israel. To Isaiah Berlin.

204. Fewer rules and more results--that's my definition of entrepreneurial government.

William F. Weld, Governor of Massachusetts (R). Inaugural address, Boston, MA, Jan. 3, 1991.

205. Trust nothing to the enthusiasm of the people. Give them a strong and a just and, if possible, a good government; but above all, a strong one.

Arthur Wellesley, 1st Duke of Wellington (1769-1852), British Chief General at Waterloo, Ambassador to France, and Prime Minister of Great Britain (Tory). Letter to Lt.-Gen. Lord William Bentnick, Dec. 24, 1811.

206. They're creating a new political class that knows how to administer but doesn't know the people in the neighborhoods.

Kevin White, Mayor of Boston, MA (D). In reference to the Kennedy School of Government of Harvard University, Cambridge, MA. Quoted in *The New York Times Magazine*, Mar. 12, 1989.

207. People say the city should be run like a business. If it were a business, it would have moved out. It would have gone South.

Thomas J. White, City Alderman, Bridgeport, CT. Comment after the city filed for bankruptcy. Quoted in *The New York Times*, June 10, 1991.

208. To govern is to aggravate.

George F. Will, American political columnist. *The Washington Post*, Feb. 26, 1989.

209. The only really self-governing people is that people which discusses and interrogates its administration.

Woodrow Wilson (1856-1924), 28th President of the United States (D-NJ). *Congressional Government, A Study in American Politics*, 1885.

210. Responsible government means government by those whom the people trust, and trust at the time of decision and action.

Woodrow Wilson. Letter to Robert Lansing, Nov. 1916.

211. Why has not Jesus Christ so far not succeeded in inducing the world to follow His teachings ...? It is because He taught the ideal without devising any practical scheme to carry out His aims.

Woodrow Wilson. Remark at the Versailles Peace Conference, Jan. 1919.

212. My computer in Washington doesn't talk to my computer in Colorado.

Timothy E. Wirth, U.S. Congressman and U.S. Senator (D-CO). Quoted in *The Washington Post*, July 11, 1988.

Chapter 61

The Media and the Press

1. There is not one of them *[newspaper editors]* whose friendship is worth buying, nor one whose enmity is not formidable. They are a sort of assassins who sit with loaded blunderbusses at the corner of streets and fire them off for hire or for sport at any passenger whom they select. They are principally foreigners.

   John Quincy Adams (1767-1848), 6th President of the United States (Ind.-MA). *Diary*, Sept. 7, 1820.

2. They *[the press]* consume a considerable quantity of our paper manufacture, employ our artisans in printing, and find business for great numbers of indigent persons.

   Joseph Addison (1672-1719), Secretary of State, Great Britain (Whig). *The Spectator*, No. 367, May 1, 1712.

3. I think you should be able to have a press conference without having reporters key in on certain divisive issues.

   Spiro T. Agnew, Governor of Maryland and Vice President of the United States (R). Press conference, Omaha, NE, June, 1972.

4. You hope the American people are fair. We recognize journalists have to kill somebody each week.

   Roger Ailes, campaign media consultant (R). Quoted in *Newsweek*, Aug. 29, 1988.

5. The *[TV evening]* news usually defines the candidate for the public.

   Roger Ailes. Quoted on Bill Moyers, PBS, *Television in Politics*, Oct. 1988.

6. The image of one country and its people amongst peoples of another country is largely created and sustained by the media.

   Fouad A. Al-Farsy, Deputy Minister of Information, Saudi Arabia. *Arab American Affairs*, Winter 1989-1990.

7. To a newspaperman, a human being is an item with the skin wrapped around it.

   Fred Allen (John F. Sullivan) (1894-1956), American comedian. Favorite saying.

8. Unless I am gravely mistaken, I am the only reporter in this city, teeming with reporters, who goes to bed every night praying that he is dead wrong. I see danger – fearful danger – hanging over this country that I love. I keep hoping it is a mirage, in which case I shall indeed be dead wrong.

   Joseph Alsop (1910-1989), American political columnist. 1971.

9. The press is new and certainly a powerful agent in human affairs. It will change societies; but it is difficult to conceive how, by rendering men indocile and presumptuous, it can change them for the better.... It has inspired ignorance with presumption, so that those who cannot be governed by reason are no longer awed by authority.

   Fisher Ames (1758-1808), U.S. Congressman (Federalist-MA). *Works*, 1809.

10. I don't like to hurt people, I really don't like it at all. But in order to get a red light at the intersection, you sometimes have to have an accident.

    Jack Anderson, American political columnist. Quoted in *Newsweek*, Mar. 3, 1972.

11. You, the foreign media, have been the companion of my people in its long and painful journey to freedom.

    Corazon C. Aquino, President of the Philippines. Quoted in *Time*, Sept. 29, 1986.

12. The newspaper *[in the United States]* now is a lame thing, and quite uniform from New York to Maine, Arkansas and Mississippi.

    The Atlantic Monthly Review, Editorial, Jan. 1838.

13. I send you the newspapers; but they do not always speak true.

    Sarah Bache (1744-1808), daughter of Benjamin Franklin. Letter to her father, Feb. 23, 1777.

14. We "muckraked" not because we hated our world but because we loved it.

    Ray S. Baker (1870-1946), American journalist. *American Chronicle*, 1945.

15. What the proprietorship of these papers is aiming at is power, and power without responsibility – the prerogative of the harlot throughout the ages.
Stanley Baldwin, 1st Earl Baldwin of Bewdley (1867-1947), Prime Minister of Great Britain (Conservative). Campaign speech, Mar. 18, 1931.

16. Journalism is a giant catapult set in motion by pygmy hatreds.
Honoré de Balzac (1799-1850), French writer. *Droll Stories*, 1837.

17. *[Press]* Photographers are the only dictators in America.
Celâl Bayar, President of Turkey. Statement on U.S. visit, Feb. 1, 1954.

18. During the *[Communist]* party conference *[television]* should broadcast live from the conference hall. We want to see and hear each "Yea" and "Nay."
A. Belov, Member, Communist Party, U.S.S.R. *Pravda*, June 7, 1988.

19. It is tempting to deny, but if you deny you confirm what you won't deny.
Anthony Wedgewood Benn (formerly Lord Stansgate), Member of Parliament, Great Britain (Labour). Remark, 1966.

20. The freedom to persuade and suggest is the essence of the democratic process.
Edward L. Bernays, American publicist and advertising executive. Quoted in *Freedom & Union*, Oct. 1947.

21. The commercial press is not a free press, and it is not a public service organization. It is business, big business, and as such is motivated by one principle – profit.
Jules E. Bernfeld, American civil rights activist. *Hairdresser's Odyssey*, 1976.

22. I read the newspapers avidly; it is my one form of continuous fiction.
Aneurin Bevan (1897-1960), Minister of Health, Great Britain (Socialist). Attributed.

23. When I see an idiot in high station I will add such terrors to his elevation as I can. I will put as many thorns in his crown as the leisure that I can snatch from the pressure of other pleasures will permit me to weave in; and neither the deprecation of his friends nor his own retaliatory lies shall stop the good work.
Ambrose Bierce (1842-1914?), American journalist. *Wasp*, Jan. 13, 1883.

24. Criticism of government finds sanctuary in several portions of the First Amendment. It is part of the right of free speech. It embraces freedom of the press.
Hugo L. Black (1886-1971), U.S. Senator (D-AL) and U.S. Supreme Court Justice. *Wilkinson* v. *United States*, 1960.

25. The liberty of the press is indeed essential to the nature of a free state, but this consists in laying no previous restraints upon publications, and not in freedom from censure for criminal matter when published.
William Blackstone (1723-1780), British jurist. *Commentaries on the Laws of England*, IV, 1765.

26. When a dog bites a man that is not news, but when a man bites a dog, that is news.
John B. Bogart (1845-1920), American journalist. Attributed.

27. Injecting new ideas into public debate is the supreme function of the newspaper columnist. Politicians and civil servants absolutely will not take the risk.
Peter Brimelow, Canadian editor and writer. "Mon Dieu! Montreal!" *National Review*, June 25, 1990.

28. The news media more and more considered the politicians to be props in their entertainment shows.
Herbert Brownell, U.S. Attorney General (R). Quoted on Bill Moyers, PBS, *Television in Politics*, Oct. 1988.

29. We have a two-party, three-network system.
Art Buchwald, American political humorist. Interview, *Playboy*, Apr. 1965.

30. Everybody in Washington works for me.
Art Buchwald. Interview, PBS, *MacNeil-Lehrer News Hour*, Nov. 28, 1989.

31. Beneath the rule of men entirely great,
The pen is mightier than the sword.
Edward Bulwer-Lytton, 1st Baron Lytton of Knebworth (1803-1873), Colonial Secretary, Great Britain (Conservative), and writer. *Richelieu*, 1838.

32. The press conference is as much a White House fixture as the cabinet meeting.
James MacGregor Burns, American political historian. *Presidential Government*, 1966.

33. A bullpen seething with mischief.
George Bush, 41st President of the United States (R-TX). In reference to the reporters covering his 1984

vice-presidential campaign. Quoted in *The New York Times*, Oct. 7, 1984.

34. Never answer a hypothetical question. It gets you beyond where you want to be.
George Bush. PBS, interview with David Frost, Sept. 5, 1989.

35. Twenty-five years in Washington has taught me never to tell a lie to a reporter.
Joseph A. Califano, Jr., U.S. Secretary of Health, Education and Welfare (D). PBS, *Ethics in America*, Feb. 14, 1989.

36. The newspapers of your country seem to be more powerful than the government.
Antonio Canovas del Castillo (1826-1897), Prime Minister of Spain. Remark to an American reporter just before the Spanish-American War.

37. *[Edmund]* Burke said there were three estates in Parliament; but in the reporter's gallery yonder, there sat a fourth estate more important far than they all.
[The other three "estates" were the Lords Spiritual (Clergy), Lords Temporal (Aristocracy), and the Commons.]
Thomas Carlyle (1795-1881), Scottish essayist and historian. *Of Heroes and Hero Worship, and the Heroic in History*, 1841.

38. I look forward to these confrontations with the press to kind of balance up the nice and pleasant things that come to me as President.
Jimmy Carter, 39th President of the United States (D-GA). First presidential press conference, Feb. 7, 1977.

39. Freedom of the Press and Constitutional Liberty must live or perish together.
Salmon P. Chase (1808-1873), U.S. Senator (Free Soil and R-OH), Governor of Ohio (Free Soil), U.S. Secretary of the Treasury, and Chief Justice, U.S. Supreme Court. Quoted in the *Cincinnati Daily Gazette*, Aug. 4, 1836.

40. We do not need a censorship of the press. We have a censorship by the press.
G. K. Chesterton (1874-1936), British writer. *Orthodoxy*, 1908.

41. Most "off the record" never continues to be "off the record."
George Christian, White House Press Secretary (D). PBS, *Presidency, Press, and People*, Apr. 2, 1990.

42. I am no enthusiast for the TV age, in which I fear mass thought and action will be taken too much in charge of by machinery.
Winston Churchill (1874-1965), Prime Minister of Great Britain (Conservative). Quoted in Martin Gilbert, *Winston Churchill*, 1988.

43. Those bastards *[the press]* can rip a single page out of the Bible, and if they play it right, they can make Jesus Christ sound like the devil.
Ken Clawson, White House Director of Communications (R). Quoted in Theodore White, *Breach of Faith*, 1975.

44. The press, like fire, is an excellent servant, but a terrible master.
James Fenimore Cooper (1789-1851), American writer. *The American Democrat*, 1838.

45. By evil report and by good report.
New Testament, *2 Corinthians* 6:8.

46. 1952 was the last year that television covered a political event as if television weren't there.
Walter Cronkite, American TV journalist. Quoted on Bill Moyers, PBS, *Television in Politics*, Oct. 1988.

47. Not yet. But I've been regularly depressed every time I have a press conference.
Mario Cuomo, Governor of New York (D). Response to a reporter's question of whether he ever underwent psychiatric treatment. CBS, *Morning*, Aug. 3, 1988.

48. We cannot admit that a newspaper's purpose is to share the labors of statesmanship or that it is bound by the same limitations, the same duties, the same liabilities as that of Ministers. The purpose and duties of the two powers are constantly separate, generally independent, sometimes diametrically opposite. The dignity and freedom of the press are trammeled from the moment it accepts an ancillary position.
John T. Delane (1817-1879), publisher and editor, *The London Times*. Comment on printing details of secret negotiations between Britain and Louis Napoleon III, to the anger of the Prime Minister, 1852.

49. Most of the media's stories are accurate. My problem is that they are not complete.
David Demarest, presidential assistant (R). Symposium, "The Press and a Divided Government," National Press Foundation, Dec. 6, 1989.

50. It is not a good idea to make an enemy of anyone who buys ink by the barrel.
Robert Denniston, Director of Communication Programs, Office for Substance Abuse Prevention, U.S. Public Health Service. Advice to staff on press relations, March 17, 1992.

51. NEWS is that which comes from North, East, West, and South, and if it comes from only one point of the compass, then it is a class publication and not news.

Benjamin Disraeli, 1st Earl of Beaconsfield (1804-1881), Prime Minister of Great Britain (Conservative). Speech, House of Commons, Mar. 26, 1855.

52. Communism has been so thoroughly exposed in this country that it has been crippled as a political force. Free speech has destroyed it as an effective political party.

William O. Douglas (1898-1980), U.S. Supreme Court Justice. *Dennis* v. *United States*, 1950.

53. I was taught that newspapers were supposed to find out if rumors were true, and if not, not print them.

Dayton Duncan, press secretary to Gov. Michael Dukakis during the 1988 presidential campaign. Quoted in *The Washington Post*, June 8, 1989.

54. What is a reporter except a kind of house detective, scavenging through the bureau drawers of men's lives, searching for the minor vice, the half-forgotten lapse that is stored away like a dirty pair of drawers.

John Gregory Dunne, American writer. *Vegas*, 1974.

55. I had to try and talk in thirty-second clips. The modern young candidates ... can talk in ten seconds or twenty. You just tell them what you want. The old politicians like me take three weeks to answer a question.

Thomas F. Eagleton, U.S. Senator (D-MO). Quoted on PBS, *The Power Game*, Jan. 2, 1989.

56. I'm not going to censor you fellows. I'm just leaving it up to each man's sense of responsibility.

Dwight D. Eisenhower (1890-1969), 34th President of the United States (R-KS). Comment when reporters found out where the next Allied attack was planned. Quoted in Jules Archer, *Battlefield President: Dwight D. Eisenhower*, 1967.

57. Truth is the greatest of all national possessions. A state, a people, a system which suppresses the truth or fears to publish it deserves to collapse.

Kurt Eisner (1867-1919), President of the Bavarian Republic, Germany. Quoted in George Seldes, *The Great Quotations*, 1983.

58. The press must be free; it has always been so and much evil has been corrected by it. If government finds itself annoyed by it, let it examine its own conduct and it will find the cause.

Thomas Erskine, 1st Baron Erskine of Restormel (1750-1823), Lord Chancellor of Great Britain. Dec. 20, 1792.

59. I am one of the few men in public life who doesn't complain much about his treatment at the hands of the press. The press takes me to task every once in a while, but they have always been very kind, not attributing my hypocrisy to bad motives. They have always attributed it to a lack of mental capacity.

Samuel J. Ervin, Jr. (1896-1985), U.S. Congressman and U.S. Senator (D-NC). Herb Altman, *Quotations from Chairman Sam*, 1973.

60. If you don't think a television news show represents the truth, you can turn off your TV. If you don't think a magazine represents the truth, you can cancel your subscription. You have the right to expose yourself to whatever information you want. But to have the government prescribing what the truth is or limiting the information available for the citizen is contrary to the First Amendment.

Samuel J. Ervin, Jr. Speech, Feb. 16, 1973.

61. Once one news organization goes with it, it's tough to keep the lid on *[a rumor]*.

Susan Estrich, professor, Harvard Law School, and director of Gov. Michael Dukakis's 1988 Presidential campaign (D). Quoted in *The Washington Post*, June 8, 1989.

62. *[Ronald Reagan]* turned the White House into a soft focus TV studio.

Harold Evans, British TV journalist. Quoted on Bill Moyers, PBS, *Television in Politics*, Oct. 1988.

63. With the stroke of a pen the political cartoonist can affect public policy.

Gerald R. Ford, 38th President of the United States (R-MI). Interview, CBS, *Sunday Morning*, June 2, 1991.

64. I'd rather be on the sports page than on the front page.

Gerald R. Ford. Attributed.

65. *[Drew]* Pearson and *[Walter]* Winchell are a high price to pay for freedom of the press, but I guess you've got to do it.

James V. Forrestal (1892-1949), U.S. Secretary of Defense. Remark, Bethesda Naval Hospital, Jan. 1949.

66. Freedom of the press is not an end in itself, but a means to the end of a free society.

Felix Frankfurter (1882-1965), U.S. Supreme Court Justice. *The New York Times*, Nov. 28, 1954.

67. When men differ in opinion, both sides ought equally to have the advantage of being heard by the public.

Benjamin Franklin (1706-1790), Member, Continental Congress and Constitutional Convention, Governor of Pennsylvania, and U.S. Minister to France. *Apology for Printers*, 1731.

68. Public men are all amenable to the tribunal of the press in a free state. The greater, indeed, their trust, the more respectable are they.

Benjamin Franklin. 1794.

69. When it comes to the media, the Congress is no match for the President.

Sarah Fritz, American journalist. Symposium, "The Press and a Divided Government," National Press Foundation, Dec. 6, 1989.

70. I have to always worry about my credibility in the black community, realizing that as a black columnist working for a white-owned newspaper, I can easily be dismissed as "the white man's tool."

Dorothy Gilliam, columnist, *The Washington Post*. Quoted in *Washingtonian*, Apr. 1989.

71. Practice whatever the big truth is so that you can say it in forty seconds on camera.

Newton L. Gingrich, U.S. Congressman (R-GA). Advice to Republican Congressmen, 1989.

72. This is a print administration, not a television administration.

Newton L. Gingrich. In reference to George Bush's administration. Quoted in *The Washington Post*, Apr. 30, 1989.

73. Not every item of news should be published; rather those who control news policies endeavor to make every item of news serve a certain purpose.

Joseph Goebbels (1897-1945), Minister of Propaganda and National Enlightenment, Third German Reich. *Diary*, Mar. 14, 1943.

74. With the instrument of radio you can make public opinion. Perhaps even conquer a country.

Joseph Goebbels. Quoted on TNT, *The Nightmare Years*, Sept. 19, 1989.

75. Where there is official censorship it is a sign that speech is serious.

Paul Goodman (1911-1972), American philosopher. *Growing Up Absurd*, 1960.

76. If any paper should print in gigantic type, "The cholera has come," I believe half its readers would be in collapse before tea time.

Abraham Oakey Hall (1826-1898), Mayor of New York City (Whig). Welcoming speech to the New England Society. Quoted in M. R. Werner, *Tammany Hall*, 1928.

77. The hand that rules the press, the radio, the screen, and the far-spread magazine rules the country.

Learned Hand (1872-1961), Federal Judge. Memorial address for Justice Louis D. Brandeis, Dec. 21, 1942.

78. Please remain. You furnish the pictures and I'll furnish the war.

[Hearst's newspapers had called for war and Congress shortly thereafter declared such.]

William Randolph Hearst (1863-1951), U.S. Congressman (D-NY); founder, Independence League Party; journalist; and publisher. Reply to artist Frederic Remington whom Hearst dispatched to Cuba following the sinking of the battleship *Maine* to paint war scenes but, not finding any, had cabled Hearst. Apr. 1898.

79. The newspaper is a moral force second only to the church. It is a political power superior to parties. It is an instrument of justice coequal with the court.

William Randolph Hearst. Quoted in Older, *William Randolph Hearst: American*, 1936.

80. There's good news tonight.

Gabriel Heatter (1890-1972), American radio journalist. Standard lead-in for his news program during the 1940's.

81. There is no lie too improbable, no distortion too great, no smear campaign too dirty for the State Department and the media to embrace.

Jesse Helms, U.S. Senator (R-NC). Quoted in *Newsweek*, Aug. 18, 1986.

82. The state must not ... let itself be confused by the drivel about so-called freedom of the press ... it must make sure of this instrument of popular education, and place it in the service of the state.

Adolf Hitler (1889-1945), Führer of the Third German Reich. *Mein Kampf*, 1933.

83. So you're from the press? Well, your newspapers can all go to hell. You lied yesterday and you're getting ready to lie again today. Go climb down my back.

Daniel Webster Hoan (1881-1961), Mayor of Milwaukee, WI (Socialist). Remark to a reporter who asked if he was going to bolt the Socialist Party, 1932.

84. A modern revolutionary group heads for the television station.

Abbie Hoffman (1936-1989), American revolutionary and founder, Yippie International Party. Quoted in *Current Biography*, 1981.

85. The United States may give up the Post Office when it sees fit, but while it carries it on, the use of the mails is almost as much a part of free speech as the right to use our tongues.
Oliver Wendell Holmes, Jr. (1841-1935), U.S. Supreme Court Justice. *Milwaukee Social Democratic Publishing Co.* v. *Burleson*, 1921.

86. The President of the United States will not stand and be questioned like a chicken thief by men whose names he does not even know.
Herbert Hoover (1874-1964), 31st President of the United States (R-IA). Response when asked if he would take questions from the floor during a press conference. Quoted in David Brinkley, *Washington Goes to War*, 1988.

87. In the coming three years ... *The People's Daily* should publish ten thousand examples for emulation and expose three thousand for criticism.
Hu Yaobang, General Secretary, Communist Party of China. Directive to the newspapers, 1983.

88. Visual images *[in TV political advertising]* have the capacity of disassociating themselves from their source.
Kathleen Hall Jamieson, dean, Annenberg School of Communications, University of Pennsylvania, Philadelphia, PA. Interview, NBC, *Meet the Press*, Oct. 23, 1988.

89. Television has shortened our political discourse.
Kathleen Hall Jamieson. Quoted on Bill Moyers, PBS, *Television in Politics*, Oct. 1988.

90. The basis of our government's being the opinion of the people, the very first object should be to keep that right; and were it left to me to decide whether we should have a government without newspapers or newspapers without a government, I should not hesitate for a moment to prefer the latter.
Thomas Jefferson (1743-1826), 3rd President of the United States (Democratic Republican-VA). Letter to Col. Edward Carrington, Jan. 16, 1787.

91. To the press alone, chequered as it is with abuses, the world is indebted for all the triumphs which have been gained by reason and humanity over error and oppression.
Thomas Jefferson. *Virginia and Kentucky Resolutions*, 1799.

92. From forty years' experience of the wretched guess-work of the newspapers of what is not done in the open daylight, and of their falsehood even as to that, I rarely think them worth reading, and almost never worth notice.
Thomas Jefferson. Letter to James Monroe, Feb. 4, 1816.

93. This man here *[Walter Lippmann]* is the greatest journalist in the world, and he's a friend of mine.
Lyndon B. Johnson (1908-1973), 36th President of the United States (D-TX). 1964.

94. I enjoy seeing the press. I learn much from reporters. In the White House press corps alone there are at least half a dozen experts already on animal husbandry.
Lyndon B. Johnson. May 11, 1964.

95. Somebody ought to do an article on you, on your damn profession, your First Amendment.
Lyndon B. Johnson. To Walter Lippmann, July 14, 1965.

96. The fact that a man is a newspaper reporter is evidence of some flaw in character.
Lyndon B. Johnson. Quoted in *People*, Feb. 2, 1987.

97. I can't deal with all her questions and also be President.
Lyndon B. Johnson. In reference to reporter Sarah McClendon. Quoted in *Modern Maturity*, July 30, 1988.

98. The liberty of the press is the *Palladium* of all the civil, political, and religious rights of an Englishman.
Junius (Prob. Philip Francis) (1740-1818), British writer (Whig). "Dedication to the English Nation," *The Letters of Junius*, George Woodfall, ed., 1812.

99. Maybe if you had printed more about the *[Bay of Pigs]* operation, you would have saved us from a colossal mistake.
John F. Kennedy (1917-1963), 35th President of the United States. Conversation with *New York Times* managing editor Turner Catledge, Apr. 1961.

100. Even though we never like it, and even though we wish they didn't write it, and even though we disapprove, there isn't any doubt that we could not do the job at all in a free society without a very, very active press.
John F. Kennedy. Dec. 17, 1962.

101. Just as an army cannot fight without arms, so the *[Communist]* Party cannot do ideological work successfully without such a sharp and militant weapon as the press. We cannot put the press in unreliable hands. It must be in the hands of the

most faithful, most trustworthy, most politically steadfast people devoted to our cause.

Nikita S. Khrushchev (1894-1971), Premier of the U.S.S.R. Quoted in *The New York Times Magazine*, Sept. 29, 1957.

102. Only one problem to a customer.

Edward I. Koch, U.S. Congressman and Mayor of New York City (D). Admonition to reporters shouting questions at him during a press conference, 1981.

103. Why on earth does anybody watch that stuff *[television violence]*?

C. Everett Koop, U.S. Surgeon General. Speech, National Coalition on Television Violence, Oct. 1983.

104. Warning: This ad has not been cleared for truth and fairness as ads for commercial products are.

Alex Kroll, Chairman, Young and Rubicam Advertising Agency. Suggested "warning label" for negative or misleading political ads. Quoted in *Advertising Age*, Apr. 29, 1991.

105. The highest reach of a newswriter is an empty reasoning on policy, and vain conjectures on the public management.

Jean de La Bruyère (1644-1696), French writer. *Les "Caractères" de Théophraste*, 1688.

106. There is nothing unnatural about kissing. If more husbands would learn from the stage and pictures just how to kiss, and then go home and practice on their wives, there would be happier homes and fewer divorces.

Fiorello H. La Guardia (1882-1947), U.S. Congressman (R and Socialist-NY) and Mayor of New York City (R and Fusion Party). U.S. House hearings on the Upshaw-Swope bill providing for federal censorship of movies which showed too much kissing. Quoted in *The New York Times*, May 5, 1926.

107. The media have entered government as a revolutionary force.

Michael Ledeen, American author and intelligence official. Speech, "Intelligence and Free Society," National Forum Foundation, Washington, DC, May 30, 1989.

108. We are going to have to endure an imperial media with a government by public opinion poll.

Michael Ledeen. *Ibid.*

109. The freedom of the press throughout the world where the capitalists rule is the freedom to buy up papers, the freedom to buy writers, to buy and manufacture public opinion in the interest of the capitalists.

V. I. Lenin (1870-1924), Premier of the U.S.S.R. 1921.

110. Freedom of the press is guaranteed only to those who own one.

A. J. Liebling (1904-1963), American journalist and writer. Quoted in *The Washington Post*, June 19, 1989.

111. Those villainous reporters *[Stephen]* Douglas has with him.

Abraham Lincoln (1809-1865), 16th President of the United States (R-IL). Letter to M. P. Sweet, Sept. 16, 1858.

112. When distant and unfamiliar and complex things are communicated to great masses of people, the truth suffers a considerable and often a radical distortion.

Walter Lippmann (1889-1974), American political columnist. *The Public Philosophy*, 1955.

113. As a rule I don't care a damn what any crooked newspaperman says about me, because they're mostly goddamn liars.

Huey P. Long (1893-1935), Governor of Louisiana and U.S. Senator (D). Statement in the Senate, 1932.

114. In a world of daily – nay, almost hourly – journalism every clever man, every man who thinks himself clever, is called upon to deliver his judgment point-blank and at the word of command on every conceivable subject of human thought.

James Russell Lowell (1819-1891), U.S. Ambassador to Spain and England. "Democracy," 1884.

115. The gallery in which the reporters sit has become a fourth estate of the realm.

Thomas Babington Macaulay, 1st Baron Macaulay (1800-1859), historian and Secretary of War, Great Britain (Liberal). "Hallam's Constitutional History," *Edinburgh Review*, Sept. 1828.

116. I have read a great number of press reports and find comfort in the fact that they are nearly always conflicting.

Harold Macmillan (1894-1986), Prime Minister of Great Britain (Conservative). Quoted in *The London Observer*, Dec. 20, 1959.

117. To the press alone, chequered as it is with abuses, the world is indebted for all the triumphs which have been gained by reason and humanity, over error and oppression.

James Madison (1751-1836), 4th President of the United States (Democratic Republican-VA). *Report of the Resolutions of the Virginia House of Delegates in 1799* (Virginia Report of 1799).

118. A popular government, without popular information or the means of acquiring it, is but a Prologue to a Farce or a Tragedy; or, perhaps both.

James Madison. Letter to W. T. Barry, Aug. 4, 1832.

119. In America a reporter thinks first of the story. But in Japan, if someone is covering political issues for a long time, he thinks first of the national interest, second about his company, and third about his job as a reporter.

Takeshi Maezawa, Japanese editor. Quoted in *Columbia Journalism Review*, Sept.-Oct. 1990.

120. The real problem ... is to get to this unfair *[press]* coverage.... Use the antitrust division *[of the Justice Department]* to investigate various media relating to antitrust violations. Even the threat of antitrust action I think would be effective in changing their views.

Jeb Stuart Magruder, presidential assistant (R). Memorandum to White House Chief of Staff H. R. Haldeman, Oct. 17, 1969.

121. Every journalist who is not too stupid or too full of himself to notice what is going on knows that what he does is morally indefensible. He is a kind of confidence man, preying on people's vanity, ignorance, or loneliness, gaining their trust and betraying them without remorse.

Janet Malcolm, American writer. *The New Yorker*, Mar. 1989.

122. There are comrades without elementary knowledge of politics, and this brings them to entertain absurd ideas, such as the idea that we live in a time where critical journalism remains a necessity.

Mao Tse-tung (1893-1976), Chairman, Communist Party of China. Quoted in Butterfield, *China: Alive in the Bitter Sea*.

123. Of all newspaper presses, I never heard anyone deny that the American is the worst.... Nothing is easier than to make the people know only one side of a question; few things are easier than to keep them altogether from the knowledge of any particular affair; and, worse than all, on them *[the American people]* may easily be practiced the discovery that lies may work their intended effect, before the truth can overtake them. It is hard to tell which is worse, the wide diffusion of things that are not true or the suppression of things that are.

Harriet Martineau (1802-1876), British reformer. *Society in America*, 1837.

124. To say that the newspaper press represents public opinion is to administer insult to intelligent men. It is the property of speculators, political leaders, large contractors, and railway directors.

Karl Marx (1818-1883), German economist and Socialist. Quoted in George Seldes, *The Great Quotations*, 1983.

125. That the freedom of the press is one of the great bulwarks of liberty and can never be restrained but by despotic governments.

George Mason (1725-1792), Member, Virginia and Federal Constitutional Conventions. *Virginia Bill of Rights*, XII, June 12, 1776.

126. Reporters are like blackbirds sitting on a telephone wire. One flies off and they all fly off. One flies back and they all fly back.

Eugene J. McCarthy, U.S. Congressman and U.S. Senator (D-WI). Remark, 1968.

127. He *[President Kennedy]* was very well informed. I think that's why he wasn't afraid of the press.

Sarah McClendon, American journalist. *Modern Maturity*, July 30, 1988.

128. Every time I talk to the press, I put my foot in my mouth.

Robert S. McNamara, U.S. Secretary of Defense (D). *The Washington Post Magazine*, June 12, 1988.

129. Stop crapping all over my husband.

Maureen McTeer, wife of Prime Minister Joe Clark, of Canada. Statement to reporters. Quoted in *Atlantic*, Dec. 1977.

130. Don't you ever ask me for a true statement again!

Evan Mecham, Governor of Arizona (R). Remark to reporters, 1986.

131. All successful newspapers are ceaselessly querulous and bellicose.

H. L. Mencken (1880-1956), American journalist. *Prejudices*, First Series, 1919.

132. Years ago, a South Australian Premier, Sir Thomas Playford, told me: "You never get into trouble for what you don't say." There's a great deal of truth in that, though in my experience what you don't say is frequently reported.

Robert G. Menzies (1894-1978), Prime Minister of Australia (Liberal). Quoted in *The Wit of Sir Robert Menzies*, 1966.

133. Sit down in front of your television set when your station goes on the air and stay there without a book, magazine, newspaper, profit-and-loss

sheet, or rating book to distract you – and keep your eyes glued to that set until the station signs off. I can assure you that you will observe a vast wasteland.

Newton N. Minow, Chairman, Federal Communications Commission. Speech, National Association of Broadcasters, May 9, 1961.

134. All that crap you're putting in the paper *[about Watergate]*.... Katie Graham *[Chairman of the Board of The Washington Post]* is gonna get her tit caught in a big fat wringer if that's published.

John N. Mitchell (1913-1988), U.S. Attorney General (R). Quoted in *Columbia Journalism Review*, July-Aug. 1973.

135. I'd have to set my hair on fire to get on the news.

Walter F. Mondale, Vice President of the United States and U.S. Senator (D-MN). Campaign remark, 1980.

136. Persecuted truth has triumphed everywhere over protected and powerful error.

Charles Montalembert (1810-1870), French statesman and writer. Argument for freedom of the press for his liberal Catholic journal. *L'Avenir*, 1832.

137. Then there is the newspaper press, that huge engine for making the political test final.

John Morley, Viscount Morley of Blackburn (1838-1923), Member of Parliament, Great Britain (Liberal), Chief Secretary for Ireland, and Secretary of State for India. *On Compromise*, 1874.

138. What draws the press is conflict, corruption and scandal.

Bill Moyers, journalist, Special Assistant to Pres. Lyndon B. Johnson, and White House Press Secretary. PBS, *The Public Mind*, Nov. 22, 1989.

139. We see more and more of our Presidents and know less and less about what they do.

Bill Moyers. Comment on television coverage of the President. PBS, *The Presidency, the Press, and the People*, Apr. 2, 1990.

140. Our job *[White House Press Secretary]* is to serve the interest of the President while recognizing the interests of the press.

Bill Moyers. *Ibid.*

141. Television has become the primary precinct of politics.

Bill Moyers. Quoted on ABC, *It's Your Business*, Apr. 8, 1990.

142. *The Washington Post* is the first and prime source of information for the national government.... It can come very close to setting the nation's agenda.

Roger Mudd, American TV journalist. Quoted in *The Washington Post*, June 4, 1989.

143. Most of us probably feel we couldn't be free without newspapers, and that is the real reason we want the newspapers to be free.

Edward R. Murrow (1908-1965), American broadcast journalist and Director, United States Information Agency. *New York Herald Tribune*, Mar. 12, 1958.

144. A journalist is a grumbler, a censurer, a giver of advice, a regent of sovereigns, a tutor of nations.

Napoléon I (1769-1821), military leader and Emperor of France. *Maxims*.

145. Four hostile newspapers are more to be feared than ten thousand bayonets.

Napoléon I. *Ibid.*

146. It must be forbidden to publish papers that are not conducive to the general welfare.

National Socialist [Nazi] Party. Original program, Feb. 25, 1920.

147. In Czechoslovakia there is no such thing as freedom of the press. In the United States there is no such thing as freedom from the press.

Martina Navratalova, American professional tennis player. Quoted in Lee Green, *Sportswit*, 1984.

148. Nobody believes the official spokesman but everybody trusts an unidentified source.

Ron Nessen, White House Press Secretary (R). 1977.

149. As you observe a *[political]* phenomenon with television you modify it somewhat.

Benjamin Netanyahu, Deputy Foreign Minister, Israel. Interview, CNN, *The Larry King Show*, Jan. 18, 1991.

150. We are what we read.

The New York Times Book Review. Headline, Sept. 18, 1988.

151. You won't have Dick Nixon to kick around anymore.

Richard M. Nixon, 37th President of the United States (R-CA). Remark after losing the California gubernatorial race. Press conference, Nov. 7, 1962.

152. Journalists have a fetish about fairness, and once they are caught being unfair they ... try to compensate.

Richard M. Nixon. Quoted in *Newsweek*, Feb. 25, 1991.

153. You're always looking for the hole in the doughnut.

Fritz Nolting, U.S. Ambassador to Vietnam. Remark to a reporter who was pressing him for information, 1962.

154. The sewer system of American journalism.

George W. Norris (1861-1944), U.S. Congressman and U.S. Senator (R and Ind.-NE). Open letter to William Randolph Hearst on his newspapers' tactics. *The New York Times*, Dec. 20, 1927.

155. To give the news impartially, without fear or favor, regardless of any party, sect, or interest involved.

Adolph S. Ochs (1858-1935), American newspaper publisher. Credo, *The New York Times*, Aug. 18, 1896.

156. I don't meet very many politicians. I'm afraid I might like them.

Pat Oliphant, American political cartoonist. Quoted in *The New York Times Magazine*, Aug. 5, 1990.

157. In recent years, both print and broadcast journalism have been the subject of a growing if irrational suspicion – sometimes expressed in high places – that the press is somehow to blame for unhappy events and trends merely because it performs its duty of reporting them.

William S. Paley (1901-1990), founder and Chairman, Columbia Broadcasting System. Dec. 7, 1976.

158. There's a tendency on the part of government to want to get the best of the break.

William S. Paley. Quoted on CBS, *William S. Paley*, Oct. 31, 1990.

159. When my public activities are reported it is very annoying to read how I looked, if I smiled, if a particular reporter liked my hair style.

Vijaya Lakshmi Pandit (1900-1990), Member of Parliament, India, and President of the U.N. General Assembly. Quoted in *The Scotsman*, Aug. 29, 1955.

160. Never lose your temper with the press or the public is a major rule of political life.

Christabel Pankhurst (1880-1958), British suffragist. *Unshackled*.

161. We live under a government of men and morning newspapers.

Wendell Phillips (1811-1884), American orator and reformer. Speech, Jan. 28, 1852.

162. The penny papers of New York do more to govern this country than the White House at Washington.

Wendell Phillips. Quoted in *Hoyt's New Cyclopedia of Practical Quotations*, 1922.

163. I don't pay them so that they can beat up on me. *[Mexico has heavily subsidized newsprint and supplies to newspapers.]*

José López Portillo, President of Mexico. Quoted in *The New York Times*, Dec. 4, 1989.

164. Our Republic and its press will rise or fall together!

Joseph Pulitzer (1847-1911), U.S. Congressman (D-NY) and newspaper publisher. Salutatory, the *New York World*, May 10, 1883; also quoted on 3-cent U.S. commemorative stamp, 1947.

165. Always fight for progress and reform, never tolerate injustice or corruption, always fight demagogues of all parties, never belong to any party, always oppose privileged classes and public plunderers, never lack sympathy for the poor, always remain devoted to the public welfare, ... never be afraid to attack wrong, whether by predatory plutocracy or predatory poverty.

Joseph Pulitzer. Message to employees on retiring as editor of the *St. Louis Post Dispatch*, Oct. 16, 1890.

166. ... for the encouragement of public service, public morals, American literature, and the advancement of education.

Joseph Pulitzer. Terms of his bequest to Columbia University, New York City, establishing the Pulitzer Prize; first awarded in May 1917.

167. Congressmen make inviting targets in the press because they are often sanctimonious about what other's conduct ought to be and are hypocritical about their own.

Daniel Rapoport, American political journalist. *Inside the House*, 1975.

168. Never trust a reporter who has a nice smile.

William Rauch, press secretary, New York City. Quoted in *The New York Times*, Jan. 18, 1984.

169. Radio talk-show hosts undermine their potentially valuable role by playing partisan politics.

Dianne Rehm, American radio talk-show host. *The Washington Post*, Feb. 26, 1989.

170. We do not expect journalists to be political eunuchs.

Dorothy Ridings, President, League of Women Voters. Quoted in *Time*, Oct. 22, 1984.

171. I hope we never live to see the day when a thing is as bad as some of our newspapers make it.

Will Rogers (1879-1935), American humorist. Remark, 1934.

172. There is no news on that today.
Franklin D. Roosevelt (1882-1945), 32nd President of the United States (D-NY). Frequent remark at press conferences when he did not wish to respond.

173. In this country there is a free and sensational press.
Franklin D. Roosevelt. Letter to Ray Stannard Baker, Mar. 20, 1935.

174. The men with the muckrakes are often indispensable to the well-being of society; but only if they know when to stop raking the muck.
Theodore Roosevelt (1858-1919), 26th President of the United States (R-NY). Speech, Washington DC, Apr. 14, 1906.

175. A singularly able, trustworthy and public-spirited body of men, and the most useful of all agents in the fight for efficient and decent government.
Theodore Roosevelt. Description of Washington journalists. *Autobiography*, 1919.

176. What happens today is no longer news – it is what is going to happen tomorrow that is the object of interest and concern.
Dean Rusk, U.S. Secretary of State (D). Quoted in *Time*, May 17, 1963.

177. The most successful *[newspaper]* column is one that causes the reader to throw down the paper in a fit of pique.
William Safire, Presidential speech writer and political columnist (R). Quoted in *Vanity Fair*, Sept. 1984.

178. We are moving from a parliamentary democracy to a television democracy.
Helmut Schmidt, Chancellor of West Germany. Interview, C-SPAN, *Booknotes*, Apr. 15, 1990.

179. In America the press rules the country; it rules its politics, its religion, its social practice.
Edward W. Scripps (1854-1926), American newspaper publisher. Quoted in *Damn Old Crank*, 1951.

180. Give light and the people will find their own way.
Motto of the Scripps-Howard newspapers.

181. They *[the press]* can get a story either from you or your worst enemy. You're not helping yourself if you stonewall them.
John P. Sears, deputy counsel to the President (R). Quoted in David Wise, *The American Police State*, 1976.

182. I know and every officer knows that no army or detachment moves ... that is not attended by correspondents of hundreds of newspapers.... They encumber our transports ... eat our provisions ... publish without stint ... information of movements past and prospective.... No matter how rapidly we move, our enemy has notice in advance.... Never had an enemy a better corps of spies than our army carries along, paid, transported, and fed by the United States.
William Tecumseh Sherman (1820-1891), General, Union Army. Letter to Sen. Thomas Ewing (Whig-OH), Feb. 6, 1863.

183. I know as I candidate I should kiss your ass, but I haven't learned to do that with equanimity yet.
John Silber, President, Boston University, Boston, MA. Addressing reporters during his Democratic gubernatorial nomination for Governor of Massachusetts. Quoted in *Time*, June 18, 1990.

184. There is but one way for a newspaper man to look at a politician, and that is down.
Frank Herbert Simonds (1878-1936), American journalist and editor. Advice to reporters, *New York Tribune*, 1917.

185. What is it about the word "No" that you do not understand?
Alan K. Simpson, U.S. Senator (R-WY). To reporters. ABC, *Nightline*, Aug. 12, 1988.

186. They didn't let them within one hundred yards of the building. That's what the founding fathers in Philadelphia thought of the press.
Alan K. Simpson. Seminar, National Press Club, Washington, DC, Mar. 28, 1990.

187. Good news is not news as a rule. Bad news is interesting.... Bad information seems to flow quicker through the press than it does through official channels.
Robert B. Sims, U.S. Assistant Secretary of Defense. Quoted on PBS, *The Power Game*, Jan. 4, 1989.

188. YOU DON'T TELL US HOW TO STAGE THE NEWS, AND WE DON'T TELL YOU HOW TO COVER IT
Larry Speakes, White House Press Secretary (R). Sign on his desk during the Reagan administration.

189. I'm not the AP *[Associated Press.]* You can tell me.
Larry Speakes. Remark to Pres. Ronald Reagan, 1985.

190. I was not the original muckraker; the prophets of the Old Testament were ahead of me.
Joseph Lincoln Steffens (1866-1936), American journalist and reformer. *Autobiography*, 1931.

191. I'm convinced that most of the press in this country follow Joseph Pulitzer's admonition that accuracy is to a newspaper what virtue is to a lady. Except, as someone pointed out, a newspaper can always print a retraction.
Adlai E. Stevenson (1900-1965), Governor of Illinois (D) and U.S. Ambassador to the United Nations. Awards dinner speech, Joseph P. Kennedy, Jr. Foundation, Washington, DC, Dec. 7, 1962.

192. Feed him. He's a hungry dog. If you don't feed him lots of red meat, he'll eat you.
Monica Stewart, Illinois State Legislator. Advice on dealing with an investigative reporter. Quoted in *The New York Times Magazine*, Mar. 12, 1989.

193. To write the truth as I see it; to defend the weak against the strong; to fight for justice; and to seek, as best as I can, to bring healing perspective to bear on the terrible hates and fears of mankind, in the hope of some day bringing about one world, in which men will enjoy the differences of the human garden instead of killing each other over them.
I. F. Stone (1908-1989), American investigative journalist and political writer. Credo.

194. It is a newspaper's duty to print the news, and raise hell.
Wilbur F. Storey (1818-1884), American newspaper editor. Statement of editorial purpose, *The Chicago Times*, 1861.

195. Our danger is that the virtual monopolization of the media of mass expression by big capital will distort and finally abort the democratic process.
Evelyn John St. Loe Strachey (1901-1963), Member of Parliament, Great Britain (Labour), and Secretary of War. *Contemporary Capitalism*, 1956.

196. If a man is pictured chopping off a woman's breast, it only gets an "R" rating; but if, God forbid, a man is pictured kissing a woman's breast, it gets an "X" rating. Why is violence more acceptable than tenderness?
Sally Struthers, American actress. Quoted in *Life*, 1984.

197. Every time you blink, somehow it makes news.
Louis W. Sullivan, U.S. Secretary of Health and Human Services (R). Quoted in *The Washington Post Magazine*, May 14, 1989.

198. Freedom of the press ... is freedom to print such of the proprietor's prejudices as the advertisers don't object to.
Hannen Swaffer (1879-1962), British journalist. Attributed.

199. The people elected me – not the press.
William H. Taft (1857-1930), 27th President of the United States (R-OH) and Chief Justice, U.S. Supreme Court. Remark to Archie Butt, 1909.

200. The people can handle the truth, and they deserve no less.
Helen Thomas, chief White House correspondent, United Press International. CBS, *60 Minutes*, June 26, 1988.

201. Criticizing a political satirist for being unfair is like criticizing a nose guard for being physical.
Gary Trudeau, American cartoonist. Quoted in *Newsweek*, Oct. 15, 1990.

202. I certainly have many sins, but I generally confess them to a priest and not to the press.
Pierre Elliott Trudeau, Prime Minister of Canada (Liberal). Remark, Nov. 2, 1972.

203. I'm kind of sorry I won't have you to kick around any more.
Pierre Elliott Trudeau. Statement to reporters upon his retirement, Nov. 21, 1979.

204. My grandson was on the front page of newspapers when he was only three days old. It took me fifty years to make it.
Harry S Truman (1884-1972), 33rd President of the United States (D-MO). Remark to reporters, June 23, 1957.

205. I always learned more about what was on the minds of the people from the reporters' questions than they could possibly learn from me.
Harry S Truman. "My View of the Presidency," *Look*, Nov. 11, 1958.

206. To hell with them *[the press]*. When history is written they will be the sons of bitches – not I.
Harry S Truman. Quoted in Margaret Truman, *Bess W. Truman*, 1986.

207. My constituents don't know how to read, but they can't help seeing them damned pictures.
William Marcy Tweed (1823-1878), U.S. Congressman (D-NY) and political leader, Tammany Hall, New York City (D). In reference to Thomas Nast's cartoons in *Harper's Weekly* attacking him. Quoted in *American Heritage*, Dec. 1986.

208. It should be recognized that news is not the sacred property of the press, but something in the public domain. In time of war the armed forces themselves are the creators of news and have therefore a vested interest in the way it is reported and edited.

U.S. Army, *Guide to the Use of Information Materials,* World War II publication.

209. If politicians are to be able to decide what the electorate wants, they have to have the parameters of the debate communicated to them by the scriveners.

Jude Wanniski, editor, *The Media Guide.* Quoted in *The New York Times,* Sept. 23, 1990.

210. The people have a keen and accurate sense that much of editorial anxiety about the freedom of the press rises out of editorial greed.

William Allen White (1868-1944), American writer and editor. Speech, University of Pennsylvania, Philadelphia, PA, May 2, 1938.

211. Station managers and network officials who fail to correct imbalances or consistent bias from the networks – or who acquiesce by silence – can only be considered willing participants, to be fully accountable ... at license-renewal time.

Clayton Whitehead, White House Director of Telecommunications (R). Quoted in *The New York Times,* Dec. 31, 1972.

212. In the old days the men had the rack, now they have the press.

Oscar Wilde (1854-1900), Irish writer. *The Soul of Man Under Socialism,* 1881.

213. We're like radio politicians without having to run.

Jerry Williams, American radio talk-show host. Quoted in *The Washington Post,* Feb. 26, 1989.

214. The Liberty of the Press is a Subject of the greatest Importance, and in which every Individual is as much concern'd as he is in any other Part of Liberty.

John Peter Zenger (1697-1746), American printer and publisher. *The New-York Weekly Journal,* Nov. 12, 1733.

215. Television looks for conflict and tries to amplify it.

Clifford Zukin, Director, Eagleton Institute of Politics, Rutgers University, New Brunswick, NJ. Quoted in *The Washington Post,* July 21, 1988.

Chapter 62

Memorials, Monuments, and Medals

1. THIS TOMB IS ERECTED TO THE MEMORY OF THAYENDANEGEA, OR CAPTAIN JOSEPH BRANT, PRINCIPAL CHIEF AND WARRIOR OF THE SIX NATIONS INDIANS, BY HIS FELLOW SUBJECTS, ADMIRERS OF HIS FIDELITY AND ATTACHMENT TO THE BRITISH CROWN.

   Gravestone of Joseph Brant (1742-1807), Warrior Chief, Mohawk Indians. Branford, Ontario, Canada.

2. JOHN BROWN OF KANSAS: HE DARED BEGIN; HE LOST, BUT LOSING, WON.

   Inscription on statue of abolitionist John Brown (1800-1859), Osawatomie, KS.

3. With monuments as with men, position means everything.

   Honoré de Balzac (1799-1850), French writer. *Droll Stories*, 1837.

4. For years our opponents were hoping to see President Reagan's back against the wall here in the White House. I don't think this is exactly what they had in mind.

   George Bush, 41st President of the United States (R-TX). Statement at the unveiling of Ronald Reagan's official portrait. White House, Nov. 15, 1989.

5. I would much rather be asked why I do not have one than why I do have one.

   Marcus Porcius Cato (The Elder) (234-149 B.C.), Roman censor. Response when asked why there was no statue of him in Rome. Quoted in Plutarch, *The Parallel Lives: Cato the Censor*.

6. Never make people laugh. If you would succeed in life, you must be solemn, solemn as an ass. All great monuments are built over solemn asses.

   Thomas Corwin (1794-1865), Governor of Ohio (Whig), U.S. Congressman, U.S. Senator, U.S. Secretary of the Treasury, and U.S. Minister to Mexico. Advice to freshman Congressman James Garfield, 1864.

7. Mr. Lely, I desire you would use all your skill to paint my picture truly like me, and not flatter me at all; but remark all these roughnesses, pimples, warts, and everything as you see me; otherwise I will never pay a farthing for it.

   Oliver Cromwell (1599-1658), Lord Protector of England. Quoted in Robert Walpole, *Anecdotes of Painting in England*, 1762.

8. We do not have orders or decorations. We have no tradition of formality. One thing, however, is within the power of Israel to confer. It is the gift of immortality. We are now writing the name of President Truman upon the map of our country. In a village near the gateway to Israel, we establish a monument not of dead stone but of living hope *[Truman Village]*.

   Abba Eban, Foreign Secretary, Israel (Labour) and Israeli Ambassador to the United Nations. Speech, Washington, DC, May 1952.

9. A bird of questionable moral character.

   Benjamin Franklin (1706-1790), Member, Continental Congress and Constitutional Convention, Governor of Pennsylvania, and U.S. Minister to France. In opposition to the eagle as the national bird of the United States.

10. The great Napoléon who devised the Legion of Honor knew human weakness, and recognized the irrepressible inclination of the citizens of a republic to covet the titles and insignia their democracy teaches them to disdain.

    William Randolph Hearst (1863-1951), U.S. Congressman (D-NY); founder, Independence League Party; journalist; and publisher. 1930.

11. Gallant heroes lived before Agamemnon, not a few; but on all alike, unwept and unknown, eternal night lies heavy because they lack a sacred poet.

    Horace (Quintus Horatius Flaccus) (65-8 B.C.), Roman poet. *Satires*, II.

12. Civic courage is the kind of valor to which the monuments of nations should most of all be reared.
    William James (1842-1910), American psychologist and philosopher. Quoted in *The New York Times*, Jan. 15, 1989.

13. HERE WAS BURIED THOMAS JEFFERSON, AUTHOR OF THE DECLARATION OF INDEPENDENCE, OF THE STATUTE OF VIRGINIA FOR RELIGIOUS FREEDOM AND FATHER OF THE UNIVERSITY OF VIRGINIA
    Thomas Jefferson (1743-1826), 3rd President of the United States (Democratic Republican-VA). Epitaph written by himself.

14. One of the first bits of protocol I learned was that when awarding a woman a medal, you hand it to her.
    C. Everett Koop, U.S. Surgeon General. Quoted on PBS, *Nova*, Oct. 10, 1989.

15. To the memory of the man, first in war, first in peace, first in the hearts of his countrymen.
    Henry Lee (1756-1818), Member, Continental Congress, Governor of Virginia, and U.S. Congressman (Federalist-VA). Congressional resolution on the death of George Washington, Dec. 14, 1799.

16. This is surprising. If anyone had named a raspberry after me I could have understood it.
    Robert G. Menzies (1894-1978), Prime Minister of Australia (Liberal). Remark on having a pelargonium named after him by the Los Angeles Garden Club. Quoted in *The Wit of Sir Robert Menzies*, 1966.

17. We must not pass through this world without leaving traces which may commend our memory to posterity.
    Napoléon I (1769-1821), military leader and Emperor of France. *Maxims*.

18. For to famous men the whole earth is a sepulcher.
    Pericles (c.500-429 B.C.), Athenian statesman. Quoted by Thucydides, *History of the Peloponnesian War*, II.

19. I declare this thing open – whatever it is.
    Philip, Duke of Edinburgh, Prince Consort of Elizabeth II. Dedication ceremony, City Hall Annex, Vancouver, Canada.

20. Since it is not granted to us to live long, let us transmit to posterity some memorial that we have at least lived.
    Pliny (The Younger) (62-113), Roman orator and writer. *Letters*, III.

21. They're sure different than a lot of those cartoons we had to put up with.
    Ronald Reagan, 40th President of the United States (R-CA). Remark to Nancy Reagan at the unveiling of their official portraits. The White House, Nov. 15, 1989.

22. Men's evil manners live in brass; their virtues we write in water.
    William Shakespeare (1564-1616), English writer. *Henry VIII*, IV, ii.

23. There's hope a great man's memory may outlive his life by half a year.
    William Shakespeare. *Hamlet*, III, ii.

24. You have set up in New York Harbor a monstrous idol which you call Liberty. The only thing that remains to complete that monument is to put on its pedestal the inscription written by Dante on the gate of Hell: "All hope abandon, ye who enter here."
    George Bernard Shaw (1856-1950), Nobel Laureate in Literature (Great Britain). Speech, New York City, Apr. 11, 1933.

25. I am weary seeing our laboring classes so wretchedly housed, fed, and clothed, while thousands of dollars are wasted ever year over unsightly statues. If these great men must have outdoor memorials let them be in the form of handsome blocks of buildings for the poor.
    Elizabeth Cady Stanton (1815-1902), 1st President, National Woman Suffrage Association. 1886.

26. It is contrary to the usages of civilized nations to perpetuate the memory of civil war.
    Charles Sumner (1811-1874), U.S. Senator (R, D and Free Soil-MA). In opposition to statues for Civil War generals. Quoted in Claude F. Bowers, *The Tragic Era*, 1929.

27. You spoke so flatteringly about me that for a moment I thought I was dead.
    Harry S Truman (1884-1972), 33rd President of the United States (D-MO). Thank-you letter to Abba Eban, May 1952 (see above).

28. The cross of the *[French]* Legion of Honor has been conferred upon me. However, few escape that distinction.
    Mark Twain (Samuel Langhorne Clemens), (1835-1910), American writer. *A Tramp Abroad*, 1880.

29. There is hardly a single person in the House of Commons worth painting; though many of them would be better for a little whitewashing.
    Oscar Wilde (1854-1900), Irish writer. *The Picture of Dorian Gray*, 1890.

Chapter 63

The Military

1. TO CARE FOR HIM WHO SHALL HAVE BORNE THE BATTLE AND FOR HIS WIDOW, AND HIS ORPHAN.
   Inscription at the entrance of the U.S. Veterans Administration, Washington, DC (See *Psalms* 82:3).

2. IS THIS A POPULAR WAR? WHY CONSCRIPTION?
   Antiwar parade banner, Boston, MA, July 1, 1917.

3. Over-paid
   Over-fed
   And over here.
   British parody of the popular World War I song, "Over There." In reference to U.S. soldiers, 1918.

4. Join the Army, see the world, meet interesting people – and kill them.
   Pacifist slogan, 1978.

5. COST WHAT IT MAY. THE NATION MUST BE SAVED
   DON'T WAIT TO BE DRAFTED
   Recruiting posters for the Union Army, 1862.

6. Taxpayers are burdened with so-called defense spending that is used not for defense but to create or hold jobs in someone's congressional district, or to continue to pile up profits for an arms manufacturer.
   James G. Abourezk, U.S. Congressman and U.S. Senator (D-SD). *Advise and Dissent*, 1989.

7. I will not steal a victory.
   Alexander III (The Great) (356-323 B.C.), King of Macedonia. Quoted in Plutarch, *The Parallel Lives: Alexander*.

8. It almost seems an institutional phenomenon that *[military weapons]* projects start with gross underestimates by both government and the contractor.
   James Ambrose, U.S. Undersecretary of the Army. Quoted in *Time*, Feb. 22, 1982.

9. This is not a fix; it's a prayer.
   Leslie Aspin, U.S. Congressman (D-WI). Letter questioning Air Force corrections of the problem-ridden B-1 bomber program, 1987.

10. Full service-connected disability and medical care *[for veterans]* ought to be absolutely inviolate and is.
    Steve Bartlett, U.S. Congressman (R-TX). Interview, C-SPAN, Jan. 30, 1991.

11. There were the giants, great of stature and expert in war.... They perished because they had no wisdom; they perished through their own foolishness.
    Apocrypha, *Wisdom of Ben Sira* 3:26-7.

12. The great questions of the day are not to be decided by speeches and majorities, but by iron and blood.
    Otto von Bismarck-Schoenhausen (1815-1898), Chancellor of Germany. Speech to Prussian Parliament, Sept. 29, 1862.

13. Nothing ... ought to be more guarded against in a free state than making the military power ... a body too distinct from the people.
    William Blackstone (1723-1780), British jurist. *Commentaries on the Laws of England*, I, 1765.

14. Generals who can write always make me nervous.
    Benjamin C. Bradlee, editor, *The Washington Post*. Quoted in *American Heritage*, July-Aug. 1987.

15. Universal suffrage, furloughs, and whiskey have ruined us.
    Braxton Bragg (1817-1876), General, Confederate Army. Remark after the Battle of Shiloh, 1862.

16. An army is not a deliberative body. It is the executive arm. Its law is that of obedience.
    David J. Brewer (1837-1910), U.S. Supreme Court Justice. *In re Grimley*, 1890.

17. The government has the right to the military service of all its able-bodied citizens.
    David J. Brewer. *Ibid.*

18. I have alreddy given Two cousins to the war, and I stand reddy to sacrifiss my wife's brother ruther'n not to see the rebellion krusht. And if

wuss comes to wuss, I'll shed ev'ry drop of blud my able-bodid relashuns has got.

Charles Ferrar Browne (1834-1867), American journalist. *Artemus Ward: To the Prince of Wales*, 1863.

19. A nuclear exchange confined to military targets seems more possible, not less, when both sides have a sure second strike capability. Then you might have a more stable balance of terror.

McGeorge Bundy, presidential assistant for National Security (D). Interview, *The Saturday Evening Post*, Dec. 1, 1962.

20. I have a premonition which sounds like utter folly, and yet it will not leave me: The military state will become one vast factory.

Jakob Burkhardt (1818-1897), Swiss historian. In Freund, ed., *Kultur und Macht*, 1934.

21. The first time I raised the issue *[of rigged weapons tests]*, my job was eliminated.

James Burton, Colonel, U.S. Army. Quoted on PBS, *The Power Game*, Jan. 2, 1989.

22. Competitive strategies *[in managing and developing American military strength]* is a concept or philosophy that's as American as apple pie.

George Bush, 41st President of the United States (R-TX). Campaign speech, Aug., 1988.

23. God is ordinarily for the big battalions against the little ones.

Roger de Bussy-Rabutin (1618-1693), French soldier and writer. Letter to the Comte de Limoges, Oct. 18, 1677.

24. The Old Guard dies and never surrenders. (*La Vieille Garde meurt et ne se rend pas*.)

Pierre Cambronne (1770-1842), Commander of Napoléon I's Old Guard at Waterloo. Reply to Colonel Halkett's demand for surrender, 1815.

25. With Freedom's lion-banner
Britannia rules the waves.

Thomas Campbell (1777-1844), Scottish poet, editor, and anthologist. *Ode to the Germans*.

26. Why turn this country into an armed camp?

Arthur Capper (1865-1951), Governor of Kansas and U.S. Senator (R-KS). Arguing against the draft before World War II, 1940.

27. The only way to make budget cuts is to bring down force structure.

Frank C. Carlucci, U.S. Secretary of Defense and National Security Advisor (D). PBS, *Third Annual Report of the Secretaries of Defense*, Jan. 19, 1990.

28. The purchase of unnecessary military hardware is undoubtedly the most wasteful element in American government.

Jimmy Carter, 39th President of the United States (D-GA). *Keeping Faith*, 1982.

29. The stationing of U.S. troops abroad on a permanent basis in foreign military installations is the kind of thing that should not be done without the approval of the Senate.

Clifford P. Case (1904-1982), U.S. Congressman and U.S. Senator (R-NJ). Senate debate, June 14, 1973.

30. The cost overrun *[for the C-5A]* here is so much smaller as a percentage of what we expected it to be when we let the contract, that it is a great improvement.

Robert Charles, U.S. Assistant Secretary of the Air Force. Testimony, House Armed Services Committee hearing, 1969.

31. Never in the field of human conflict was so much owed by so many to so few.

Winston Churchill (1874-1965), Prime Minister of Great Britain (Conservative). A tribute to RAF pilots for saving the nation in the Battle of Britain. Speech, House of Commons, Aug. 20, 1940.

32. The poop of the French nation.

Winston Churchill. Description of the French army. *The Gathering Storm*, 1948.

33. First, I want to thank you, not just for saving me from the draft, but for being so kind and decent to me last year.... Please say hello to Col. Jones for me.

Bill Clinton, 42nd President of the United States (D-AR). Letter to Col. Eugene Holmes, Arkansas ROTC, 1969.

34. We have neglected to develop an offensive capability in chemical war and have no defense worthy of the name.... In biological warfare we have neither an offensive nor a defensive capability.

Cecil Coggins, Admiral and Chief, Atomic, Bacteriology, and Chemical Warfare, U.S. Navy. Pearl Harbor Day speech, Commonwealth Club, San Francisco, CA, Dec. 7, 1962.

35. Leading an uninstructed people to war is to throw them away.

Confucius (551-479 B.C.), Chinese philosopher. *Analects*.

36. The military market is based on human folly, not normal market precepts. Human folly goes up and down, but it always exists. Its depths have never been plumbed.

Sam Cummings, President, Interarms, Inc. (the world's largest international arms dealer). Quoted in *Fortune*, Feb. 16, 1987.

37. How much of this junk shall we buy?
Josephus Daniels (1862-1948), U.S. Secretary of the Navy and U.S. Minister to Mexico (D). Response to being asked to approve an ever-expanding set of weapons and supplies. *Diary*, 1917.

38. Damn it all, the business of an army is to win the way, not quibble around with a lot of cheap buying. Hell and Marih! We weren't trying to keep a set of books, we were trying to win a war.
Charles G. Dawes (1865-1951), Brigadier General, Allied Expeditionary Forces, Vice President of the United States (R-IL), U.S. Ambassador to Great Britain, and Nobel Laureate in Peace. Response when called to testify about improper military spending and sloppy accounting during World War I. Congressional testimony, Feb. 4, 1921.

39. No worker has any business to enlist in the capitalist class war *[World War I]* or fight a capitalist class battle. It is our duty to enlist in our own war and fight our own battle.
Eugene V. Debs (1855-1926), American Socialist. Speech, 1914.

40. They bum-rapped me for being a patriot. I'm happy to be a patriot.
Lawrence DiPrima (1910-1991), Illinois State Representative (D) and Chairman, Illinois Democrats for the Reagan-Bush Committee. Response to criticism that he was a one-issue legislator (veterans). Quoted in obituary, *Chicago Tribune*, May 25, 1991.

41. Morale is the greatest single factor in successful wars.
Dwight D. Eisenhower (1890-1969), 34th President of the United States (R-KS). Quoted in *The New York Post*, June 23, 1945.

42. Americans, indeed all free men, remember that in the final choice a soldier's pack is not so heavy a burden as a prisoner's chains.
Dwight D. Eisenhower. First inaugural address, Jan. 20, 1953.

43. In the councils of government we must guard against the acquisition of unwarranted influence, whether sought or unsought, by the military-industrial complex. The potential for the disastrous rise of misplaced power exists and will persist. We must never let the weight of this combination endanger our liberties or democratic processes.
Dwight D. Eisenhower. Farewell address, Jan. 17, 1961.

44. When our young officers come back from the army, on a forty days' furlough, they find apathy and opposition in the cities.
Ralph Waldo Emerson (1803-1882), American writer. *Journals*, Oct. 1863.

45. The Founding Fathers were not foolish enough to place the command of American troops engaged in combat operations in a Congress of the United States which is now composed of 100 Senators and 435 Representatives.
Samuel J. Ervin, Jr. (1896-1985), U.S. Congressman and U.S. Senator (D-NC). Senate debate, Cambodia resolution, 1970.

46. If this country ever had a military of the poor, it no longer does.
Richard L. Fernandez, senior analyst, Congressional Budget Office. *The Washington Post*, Dec. 18, 1990.

47. The army is the only power to preserve the *[Soviet]* Union.
Valentin Filatov, Soviet General. Remark on the hostilities between the Baltic states and the Soviet government. Quoted in *The Washington Post*, Dec. 23, 1990.

48. The military mind always imagines that the next war will be on the same lines as the last.
Ferdinand Foch (1851-1929), French General. Quoted in George Seldes, *The Great Quotations*, 1960.

49. Possession by an American citizen of the rights and privileges that constitute citizenship imposes correlative obligations, of which the most indispensable may well be "to take his place in the ranks of the army of his country and risk the chance of being shot down in its defense."
Felix Frankfurter (1882-1965), U.S. Supreme Court Justice. *Trop* v. *Dulles*, 1957.

50. The sky does not rest more firmly on the shoulders of Atlas than the Prussian state does on the Prussian army.
Frederick II (The Great) (1712-1786), King of Prussia. 1760.

51. If my soldiers were to begin to think, not one of them would remain in the army.
Frederick II. Quoted by Leo Tolstoy, *Bethink Yourselves!*.

52. Wars ruin armies.
Frederick William I (1688-1740), King of Prussia. Attributed.

53. There has been a strong tradition in this country that it is not the function of the military to educate the public on political issues.

J. William Fulbright, U.S. Senator (D-AR). Remark, 1961.

54. Deployed on the sands of Saudi Arabia and facing possible extinction are young men and women drawn, in the main, from the poorer families of our republic.

John Kenneth Galbraith, American economist and U.S. Ambassador to India (D). *The New York Times*, Nov. 7, 1990.

55. *[A state militia is necessary]* to prevent the establishment of a standing army, the bane of liberty.... Whenever governments mean to invade the rights and liberties of the people, they always attempt to destroy the militia in order to raise an army upon their ruins.

Elbridge Gerry (1744-1814), U.S. Congressman (Anti-Federalist-MA) and Vice President of the United States (D). Debate in 1st Congress on James Madison's proposed Bill of Rights, 1789. Quoted by U.S. Chief Justice Warren E. Burger, *Parade*, Jan. 14, 1990.

56. We can live without butter, but not without arms. One cannot shoot with butter, but with guns.

Joseph Goebbels (1897-1945), Minister of Propaganda and National Enlightenment, Third German Reich. Speech, Berlin, Jan. 17, 1936.

57. Guns will make us powerful; butter will only make us fat.

Hermann Goering (1893-1946), Field Marshal, German Army; founder, Gestapo; President of the Reichstag (Nazi parliament); and convicted war criminal. Radio address, 1936.

58. Before they got through with this thing *[Grenada]*, everybody got in the act.... They ordered over seven thousand medals to be awarded for an action that probably would have required twelve hundred or fifteen hundred people.

Barry M. Goldwater, U.S. Senator (R-AZ). In reference to the U.S. invasion of Grenada. Quoted on PBS, *The Power Game*, Jan. 2, 1989.

59. The trouble with military rule is that every colonel or general is soon full of ambition. The navy takes over today and the army tomorrow.

Yakubu Gowon, Prime Minister of Nigeria. Quoted in *The Chicago Daily News*, Aug. 29, 1970.

60. The person to protect is the American taxpayer. We deserve to be protected, not Lockheed.

Martha Griffiths, U.S. Congresswoman and Lieutenant Governor of Michigan (D). Quoted in Rice, *The C-5A Scandal*, 1971.

61. There is always a perception on the part of the military that organizations voicing dissent are communist fronts.

Venencio Guarduce, Member, Philippine House of Representatives. Quoted in *The Washington Post*, Nov. 27, 1988.

62. Strategy must dominate tactics, not the other way around.

Yehoshafat Harkabi, Chief of Intelligence, Israel Defense Forces, and military writer. *Arab Strategies and Israel's Response*, 1977.

63. The only way we'll ever get a volunteer army is to draft 'em.

Felix E. Hébert (1901-1979), U.S. Congressman (D-LA). Quoted in Morris K. Udall, *Too Funny to Be President*, 1988.

64. A Cadmean victory

Herodotus (c.480-425 B.C.), Greek "Father of History." Description of a victory in which the victor suffers as much as the loser. *History of the Persian Wars*, I.

65. Woe to them ... that trust in chariots!

Old Testament, *Isaiah* 31:1.

66. Our soldiers in combat should have the same insurance policies that the Congress has.

Jesse L. Jackson, Shadow Senator (D-DC). In reference to the Persian Gulf War. Radio interview, WAMU-FM, *The Diane Rehm Show*, Washington, DC, Feb. 5, 1991.

67. A country may be conquered from the back of a horse but may not be ruled therefrom.

Japanese proverb.

68. The spirit of this country is totally averse to a large military force.

Thomas Jefferson (1743-1826), 3rd President of the United States (Democratic Republican-VA). Letter to Chandler Price, 1807.

69. The guns and the bombs, the rockets and the warships, are all symbols of human failure. They are necessary symbols. They protect what we cherish. But they are witnesses to human folly.

Lyndon B. Johnson (1908-1973), 36th President of the United States (D-TX). Speech, The Johns Hopkins University, Baltimore, MD, Apr. 7, 1965.

70. God was on the Roman side.

Flavius Josephus (37-105), Roman-Jewish general

and historian. Written after the destruction of Jerusalem, A.D. 70 *Wars*, V.

71. Be strong, and of good courage.
Old Testament, *Joshua* 1:9.

72. Who is to guard the guards themselves? (*Quis custodiet ipsos custodes?*)
Decimus Junius Juvenal (c. 60-c. 140), Roman poet. *Satires*, No. 347.

73. Militarism ... is one of the chief bulwarks of capitalism, and the day that militarism is undermined, capitalism will fall.
Helen Keller (1880-1968), American writer. *The Story of My Life*, 1902.

74. We couldn't go to war without them, and we couldn't win without them.
Lawrence J. Korb, U.S. Assistant Secretary of Defense (D). In reference to women in the armed forces. Interview, CBS, *60 Minutes*, Jan. 1, 1989.

75. We might better reexamine the reasons for entering the war than abolish volunteers and substitute for them men dragged into the ranks by draft.
Robert M. La Follette (1855-1925), Governor of Wisconsin and U.S. Senator (R). Argument against a draft in World War I. Senate speech, Apr. 27, 1917.

76. Incompetency, criminal negligence, and almost treasonable administration of national defense.
Fiorello H. La Guardia (1882-1947), U.S. Congressman (R and Socialist-NY) and Mayor of New York City (R and Fusion Party). Testimony on Air Force leaders at the court martial of Gen. Billy Mitchell, Nov. 1925.

77. You must bear constantly in mind not to hazard unnecessarily your command ... but be content to accomplish all the good you can, without feeling it necessary to obtain all that might be desired.
Robert E. Lee (1807-1870), General-in-Chief, Confederate Army. Advice to Jeb Stuart, June 1862.

78. There is so much crap going on over there *[the Pentagon]*, I could run the Navy Department on the cost-of-living increases alone.
John Lehman, U.S. Secretary of the Navy (R). Remark to Stuart Spencer. Quoted in Mayer and McManus, *Landslide: The Unmasking of the President, 1984-1988*.

79. We confused the warriors with the war.
Thomas Lewis, Director of Veterans Affairs, New York. Comment on the hostility that greeted some returning Vietnam veterans. Interview, PBS, *Inside Albany*, Aug. 20, 1989.

80. If I had fifty thousand additional troops here now, I believe I could substantially close the war in two weeks.
Abraham Lincoln (1809-1865), 16th President of the United States (R-IL). Letter to Union governors, July 3, 1862.

81. The desertion of the army is now the most serious evil we have to encounter.
Abraham Lincoln. Letter to Mary A. Livermore, Sept. 1862.

82. I can't spare this man – he fights.
Abraham Lincoln. Letter to A. K. McClure, when informed that General Ulysses S. Grant was an alcoholic, 1862.

83. The strength of the rebellion *[the Confederacy]* is in its military, its army. That army dominates all the country and all the people within its range.
Abraham Lincoln. Letter to Sen. Roscoe Conkling, Aug. 26, 1863.

84. I shall at all times be ready to recognize the paramount claims of the soldiers of the nation in the disposition of public trusts *[patronage]*.
Abraham Lincoln. Message to General Winfield Scott, Mar. 1, 1865.

85. What is our task? To make Britain a fit country for heroes to live in.
David Lloyd George, 1st Earl of Dwyfor (1863-1945), Prime Minister of Great Britain (Liberal). Speech, Wolverhampton, Nov. 24, 1918.

86. They talk about conscription as being a democratic institution. Yes; so is a cemetery.
Meyer London (1871-1926), U.S. Congressman (Socialist-NY). Speech to U.S. Congress, Apr. 25, 1917.

87. A standing army is one of the greatest mischiefs that can possibly happen.
James Madison (1751-1836), 4th President of the United States (Democratic Republican-VA). Speech in the Virginia Convention. 1787.

88. No person religiously scrupulous of bearing arms shall be compelled to render military service.
James Madison. Draft of constitutional amendment dropped by 1st Congress when creating the Bill of Rights, 1789-91.

89. A standing military force, with an overgrown Executive will not long be safe companions to liberty.
James Madison. Speech, Virginia Convention to ratify the Constitution. June 14, 1788.

90. The only possible way to provide for standing armies is to make them unnecessary. The way to do this is to organize and discipline our militia, so as to render them capable of defending the country against external invasions, and internal insurrections.

James Madison. *Ibid.*

91. Always remember that an armed and trained militia is the firmest bulkwark of republics – that without standing armies their liberty can never be in danger, nor with large ones safe.

James Madison. First inaugural address, Mar. 4, 1809.

92. The enemy advances, we retreat.
The enemy camps, we harass.
Th enemy tires, we attack.
The enemy retreats, we pursue.

Mao Tse-tung (1893-1976), Chairman, Communist Party of China. Written during his revolutionary battles in Kaingsi. Quoted in Engle and Engle, *Poems of Mao Tse-tung*, 1972.

93. I warn you not to accept military advice too easily.

George C. Marshall (1880-1959), General, U.S. Army, U.S. Secretary of State, and U.S. Secretary of Defense. Advice to Moshe Sharette, May 12, 1947.

94. That a well-regulated militia, composed of the body of the people trained to arms, is the proper, natural, and safe defense of a free State; that standing armies in time of peace should be avoided as dangerous to liberty; and that in all cases the military should be under strict subordination to, and governed by, the civil power.

George Mason (1725-1792), Member, Virginia and Federal Constitutional Conventions. *The Virginia Bill of Rights*, XIII, June 12, 1776.

95. Military men are the scourges of the earth.

Guy de Maupassant (1850-1893), French writer. *Sur l'Eau*.

96. I must have money to get ready for war. I am doing everything possible to prevent war but it must come, and we are not prepared.

William McKinley (1843-1901), 25th President of the United States (R-OH). Remark to House Appropriations Committee Chairman Joseph G. Cannon (D-IL) shortly after the *Maine* blew up in Havana Harbor, Mar. 6, 1898.

97. The military thinks about weapons the way women think about perfume.

Robert S. McNamara, U.S. Secretary of Defense (D). Quoted in Rice, *The C-5A Scandal*, 1971.

98. There is a great danger that you will try to solve political problems through military action.

Robert S. McNamara. Quoted on PBS, *War and Peace in the Nuclear Age*. Feb. 1989.

99. You can kill ten of my men for every one I kill of yours, but even then, you will lose and I will win.

Ho Chi Minh (1890-1969), Premier of North Vietnam. Statement to the French, 1952.

100. I can stand by no longer and see these disgusting performances by the Navy and War Departments at the expense of the lives of our people, and the delusion of the American public.

William (Billy) Mitchell (1879-1936), General, U.S. Army. Statement, Oct. 1925.

101. The threat is there, and we get paid to tell Americans it is there.

Thomas Moorer, Admiral, U.S. Navy, and Chairman, Joint Chiefs of Staff. Quoted in Fox, *Arming America: How the U.S. Buys Weapons*, 1974.

102. Some members of Congress have dealt so long with the military and with the defense contractors that they begin to think they are without faults.

William S. Moorhead (1923-1987), U.S. Congressman (D-PA). Speech, House of Representatives, 1969.

103. To make a people great it is necessary to send them to battle even if you have to kick them in the ass.

Benito Mussolini (1883-1945), dictator of Italy (Fascist). 1940.

104. The great mass of eighteen-year olds ... are given no choice.... The older generation immolates the younger, on the altar of Moloch [see *Leviticus 20:2*; *Jeremiah 32:35*; II *Kings 23:10*]. What God, centuries ago, forbade Abraham to do even to his own son, – "Lay not thy hand upon the lad, neither do thou anything unto him" [*Genesis 22:12*] – this we do by decree to the entire youth of a nation.

A. J. Muste (1885-1967), American clergyman and pacifist. *Of Holy Disobedience*, 1952.

105. In war morale counts for three quarters, the balance of manpower counts for only one quarter.

Napoléon I (1769-1821), military leader and Emperor of France. *Maxims*.

106. Never has so much military, economic, and diplomatic power been used as ineffectively as in Vietnam.

Richard M. Nixon, 37th President of the United States (R-CA). Campaign speech, 1968.

107. If they go to such lengths for fruitcakes, can you imagine what the standards and specifications would be for even the most basic weapons system?

Samuel A. Nunn, U.S. Senator (D-GA). Comment on a Pentagon eighteen-page recipe and specification sheet for fruitcakes to be supplied to the armed forces. Quoted in *Newsweek*, Jan. 6, 1986.

108. We must not only have the right *[military]* forces, we must manage those forces effectively and efficiently.

Samuel A. Nunn. *The New York Times*, July 10, 1988.

109. Every time we get in the selling stage, the costs go down. When we get into the building stage, the costs go up.

Samuel A. Nunn. In reference to weapons systems. Quoted in *Newsweek*, Oct. 17, 1988.

110. Am I wrong in listening to women who live in Nicaragua and follow the Sermon on the Mount? Or am I supposed to just sit here and believe generals?

Thomas P. (Tip) O'Neill, Jr., U.S. Congressman and Speaker of the House (D-MA). Comment when several Maryknoll nuns doing missionary work in Nicaragua testified against aid to the Contras in opposition to the position of U.S. military leadership. Quoted in *The New York Daily News*, June 29, 1986.

111. One could do just as good a job ... in awarding the major contracts by putting the names of qualified bidders on a wall and throwing darts.

David Packard, U.S. Deputy Secretary of Defense. Quoted in *The Washington Post*, July 31, 1988.

112. Stand your ground. Don't fire unless fired upon, but if they mean to have a war, let it begin here.

John Parker (1729-1775), American revolutionary militia captain. Orders to Minute Men, in anticipation of the arrival of English troops, Lexington, MA, Apr. 19, 1775.

113. If anyone wishes to give me free *[military]* advice, let him come with me into Macedonia. He shall be furnished with a ship, a horse, a tent, even his traveling charges shall be defrayed. But if he thinks this is too much trouble, and prefers the repose of city life to the toils of war, let him not, on land, assume the duties of pilot.

Lucius Aemilius Paulus (c. 229-160 B.C.), Roman General and Consul. Quoted in Plutarch, *The Parallel Lives: Aemilius Paulus*.

114. My military experience has given me the confidence which anybody needs to know that the military ain't perfect. I have seen the military waste so much with my own eyes. I have seen them screw up so badly with my own eyes.

Otis Pike, U.S. Congressman (D-NY). Quoted in Daniel Rapoport, *Inside the House*, 1975.

115. I certainly agree that we should not go around saying we are the world's policemen. But guess who gets called when suddenly someone needs a cop?

Colin L. Powell, General, U.S. Army, U.S. National Security Advisor, and Chairman, Joint Chiefs of Staff. Quoted in *The New York Times*, Aug. 17, 1990.

116. Our formula to prevent this *[nuclear war]* has been a successful one to date, and it is a really simple formula. We have had overwhelming military superiority to the point where it is ridiculous for Mr. Khrushchev to even seriously contemplate attacking this country. Now I maintain that it is possible to hold this kind of lead, and that is what I recommend.

Thomas S. Power, Commander, U.S. Strategic Air Command. Testimony, U.S. Senate Armed Forces Committee, Sept. 6, 1963.

117. A king is not saved by the multitudes of a host *[army]*.

Old Testament, *Psalms* 33:16.

118. I did not know in 1969 that I would be standing in this room today, I guess.

J. Danforth Quayle, U.S. Senator and Vice President of the United States (R-IN). Response when asked why he joined the National Guard in 1969 instead of fighting in Vietnam. Press conference, Washington, DC, Aug. 1988.

119. If you have a weapons overrun by 50 percent, which is the average, you are not getting 50 percent more defense, you are getting 50 percent more waste.

Dina Rasor, Director, Project on Military Procurement. *The New York Times*, Feb. 5, 1989.

120. We're in greater danger today than we were the day after Pearl Harbor. Our military is absolutely incapable of defending this country.

Ronald Reagan, 40th President of the United States (R-CA). Quoted in *The New York Times*, Apr. 12, 1980.

121. The only way we could get rid of the problems in the Pentagon is in a nuclear exchange. But that presumes that the Russians would be stupid enough to destroy it. Because their only hope would be to leave it standing.

Jeffrey Record, defense analyst, Hudson Institute.

Quoted in D. Morrison, *Government Executive,* Nov. 1988.

122. The claim that the draft is democratic is the very antithesis of the truth. The draft is not democratic, it is autocratic; it is not republican, it is despotic; it is not American, it is Prussian. Its essential feature is that of involuntary servitude.
James A. Reed (1861-1944), U.S. Senator (D-MO). Senate speech, 1917.

123. The quarrels which other nations have we did not have. Our drumbeat did not encircle the world with our martial airs. Our guns were not called upon to throw projectiles which cost each of them the price of a happy home.
Thomas B. Reed (1839-1902), U.S. Congressman and Speaker of the House (R-ME). In opposition to war with Spain, 1899.

124. To be neutral you must be ready to be highly militarized.
Edwin O. Reischauer (1911-1990), U.S. Ambassador to Japan. Quoted in *The New York Times,* Sept. 2, 1990.

125. We did what we had to do when we had to do it.
Will C. Rogers III, Captain, U.S. Navy. Remark after returning from duty patrolling the Persian Gulf where his ship accidentally shot down an Iranian airliner. San Diego, CA, Oct. 24, 1988.

126. We can afford all we need; but we cannot afford all we want.
Franklin D. Roosevelt (1882-1945), 32nd President of the United States (D-NY). Remark when vetoing the Soldier's Bonus Bill. May 22, 1935.

127. We would rather die on our feet than live on our knees.
Franklin D. Roosevelt. Third inaugural address, Jan. 20, 1941.

128. To change something in the Navy is like punching a feather bed. You punch it with your right and you punch it with your left until you are finally exhausted, and then you find the damn bed just as it was before you started punching.
Franklin D. Roosevelt. Quoted in *American Heritage,* Feb. 1988.

129. The man who has not raised himself to be a soldier, and the woman who has not raised her boy to be a soldier for the right, neither one of them is entitled to citizenship in the Republic.
Theodore Roosevelt (1858-1919), 26th President of the United States (R-NY). Speech to U.S. Army troops, Camp Upton, Yaphank, NY, Nov. 18, 1917.

130. In my own judgment the most important service that I rendered to peace was the voyage of the battle fleet around the world.
Theodore Roosevelt. *Autobiography,* 1919.

131. If defense contractors can't hack it, they ought to be terminated for default. If they lose money and go bankrupt, let them do it. Maybe a couple of bankruptcies and defaults in the industry will do them good.
Gordon Rule, chief civilian procurement official, U.S. Navy. Quoted in *The New Republic,* Mar. 28, 1970.

132. There is something about preparing for destruction that causes men to be more careless in spending money than they would be if they were building for constructive purposes.
Richard B. Russell, Jr. (1897-1971), U.S. Senator (D-GA). Quoted in *Baltimore News American,* May 9, 1969.

133. We have to realize that military spending is not a public works project.
James Sasser, U.S. Senator (D-TN). Quoted on ABC, *Nightline,* Jan. 29, 1990.

134. We called it the Lone Star Air Show. If it was made in Texas you bought it; if it wasn't you went after it.
Patricia R. Schroeder, U.S. Congresswoman (D-CO). In reference to Sen. John Tower's cutting the defense budget when he was chairman of the Armed Services Committee. Quoted on PBS, *MacNeil-Lehrer News Hour,* Dec. 16, 1988.

135. The welfare queens of the 80's are the military-industrial complex.
Patricia R. Schroeder. *Ibid.*

136. An empire founded by arms must likewise have arms for its support.
Charles-Louis de Secondat, Baron de La Brède et de Montesquieu (1689-1755), French writer. *Considérations sur les causes de la grandeur et des Romains et de leur décadence,* XVIII, 1734.

137. Trumpets and bagpipes, those clamorous harbingers of blood and death.
Walter Scott (1771-1832), Scottish writer. *A Legend of Montrose,* 1819.

138. When the military man approaches, the world locks up its spoons and packs off its womankind.
George Bernard Shaw (1856-1950), Nobel Laureate in Literature (Great Britain). *Man and Superman,* 1903.

139. In all armies there must be wide differences of opinion and partial causes of disaffection.
William Tecumseh Sherman (1820-1891), General, U.S. Army. Letter from Vicksburg, MS, Feb. 17, 1863.

140. The job of the Marines is not to be anti-Communist. It is to wait until the President says, "Saddle up and go," and then to saddle up and go.
David Shoup, Commandant, U.S. Marine Corps. Quoted in David Halberstam, *The Best and the Brightest*, 1969.

141. They *[the defense department]* are cheating on the *[weapons]* tests.
Dennis A. Smith, U.S. Congressman (R-OR). Quoted on PBS, *The Power Game*, Jan. 2, 1989.

142. We are sick to death of war, defense spending, and all things military.
Margaret Chase Smith (1897-1954), U.S. Congresswoman and U.S. Senator (R-ME). Quoted in *Reader's Digest*, Mar. 1972.

143. Whatever fosters militarism makes for barbarism.
Herbert Spencer (1820-1903), British social philosopher. *Social Statics*, 1851.

144. In a showdown between the interests of the military industrial complex and the nation's school children, I wouldn't bet on the school children.
Richard L. Strout (1898-1990), American journalist. Quoted on CBS, *Sunday Morning*, Aug. 26, 1990.

145. Thus while we have heard of blundering swiftness in war, we have not yet seen a clever operation that was prolonged.
Sun-tzu (c. 400 B.C.), Chinese writer of the Age of Warring States. *The Art of War*.

146. For to win one hundred victories is not the acme of skill. To subdue the enemy without fighting is the acme of skill.
Sun-tzu. *Ibid*.

147. It is said that a compulsory draft is a democratic system. I deny that it has anything to do with democracy. It is neither democratic nor undemocratic. It is far more typical of totalitarian nations than of democratic nations. The theory behind it leads directly to totalitarianism. It is absolutely opposed to the principles of individual liberty which have always been considered a part of American democracy.
Robert A. Taft (1889-1953), U.S. Senator (R-OH). Senate debate, 1948.

148. War is much too serious a thing to be left to military men.
Charles-Maurice de Talleyrand-Périgord (Prince de Bénévent) (1754-1838), French diplomat and statesman. Attributed.

149. If the authority which the Constitution has confided to the judiciary department ... may ... be usurped by the military power, at its discretion, the people of the United States are no longer living under a government of laws, but every citizen holds life, liberty, and property at the will and pleasure of the army officer in whose military district he may happen to be found.
Roger B. Taney (1777-1864), Chief Justice, U.S. Supreme Court, and U.S. Secretary of the Treasury. *Ex parte Milligan*, June 1, 1861.

150. The first and most imperative necessity in war is money, for money means everything else – men, guns, ammunition.
Ida M. Tarbell (1857-1944), American writer. *The Tariff in Our Times*, 1906.

151. The army is a nation within the nation; it is a disease of our time.
Alfred de Vigny (1797-1863), French writer and soldier. *Servitude et grandeur militaires*, 1835.

152. We must let our young men know that they owe some responsibility to this country.
James W. Wadsworth (1846-1926), U.S. Congressman (R-NY). Remark urging compulsory military training for all young males, 1916.

153. To place any dependence upon Militia is, assuredly, resting upon a broken staff. Men just dragged from the tender Scenes of domestick life; unaccustomed to the din of Arms; totally unacquainted with every kind of military skill, which being followed by a want of confidence in themselves, when opposed by Troops regularly train'd, disciplined, and appointed, superior in knowledge and superior in Arms, makes them timid, and ready to fly from their own shadows.
George Washington (1732-1799), 1st President of the United States (VA). Letter to Congress, Sept. 24, 1776.

154. A free government with an uncontrolled power of military conscription, is a solecism.
Daniel Webster (1782-1852), U.S. Congressman (Federalist-NH and MA), U.S. Senator (Federalist and Whig-MA), and U.S. Secretary of State. Speech, 1811.

155. Military conscription is incompatible with any notion of personal liberty.

Daniel Webster. Anti-draft speech, House of Representatives, Dec. 9, 1814.

156. The struggle of the defense budget is a serious problem, because that budget speaks volumes to the world about what kind of a people we are, what kind of a nation we will be, how strongly we will stand as protectors of freedom, and whether we will be able to negotiate successfully with the Soviet Union.

Caspar Weinberger, U.S. Secretary of Defense and U.S. Secretary of Health, Education and Welfare (R). Quoted in *The 1989 Conservative Calendar*.

157. The professional military mind is by necessity an inferior and unimaginative mind; no man of high intellectual quality would willingly imprison his gifts in such a calling.

H. G. Wells (1866-1945), British writer. *The Outline of History*, 1920.

158. Militarism does not consist in the existence of an army.... Militarism is a spirit. It is a point of view. It is a system. It is a purpose. The purpose of militarism is to use armies for aggression.

Woodrow Wilson (1856-1924), 28th President of the United States (D-NJ). Speech, West Point, NY, June 13, 1916.

159. Standing armies can never consist of resolute robust men; they may be well-disciplined machines, but they will seldom contain men under the influence of strong passions.

Mary Wollstonecraft (1759-1797), British writer and feminist. *A Vindication of the Rights of Women*, 1792.

160. It *[the military procurement system]* produces almost none of the stability enjoyed by most regulated utilities and very little of the positive incentives to lower costs and increase creativity that are the hallmarks of competition.

R. James Woolsey, U.S. Undersecretary of the Navy. Testimony, Senate Armed Services Committee, July 28, 1988.

Chapter 64

Minorities and Women

1. THEY MADE US MANY PROMISES, MORE THAN I CAN REMEMBER, BUT THEY NEVER KEPT BUT ONE; THEY PROMISED TO TAKE OUR LAND, AND THEY TOOK IT.
Sign painted on a wall of the U.S. Bureau of Indian Affairs, Washington, DC, 1970.

2. I must not write a word to you about politics, because you are a woman.
John Adams (1735-1826), 2nd President of the United States (Federalist-MA). Letter to Abigail Adams, Feb. 13, 1779.

3. You will be well advised to infect the Indians with sheets upon which smallpox patients have been lying, or by any other means which may serve to exterminate this accursed race.
Jeffery Amhurst (1717-1797), British Commander in Chief of North America. Quoted in John Robert Colombo, *New Canadian Quotations*, 1987.

4. The only question left to be settled now is: Are women persons?
Susan B. Anthony (1820-1906), American suffragist. Frequent question in speeches.

5. Men, their rights and nothing more; women, their rights and nothing less.
Susan B. Anthony. Motto, *Revolution*, 1868.

6. Everything we see in the world is the creative work of women.
Kemal Atatürk (1881-1938), 1st President of the Turkish Republic. Quoted in *Atatürk: Creator of Modern Turkey*, 1981.

7. When we have congressmen and top state politicians all working together with powerful interests, what have we got to fight against them? Not much, except to ask for justice.
George Aubid, Jr. (Egiwaateshkang) (1930-1990), Chief of the Chippewa Indians. Statement to reporters, 1985.

8. If they want fifteen left-handed, Lithuanian lesbians, they can have them.
Haley Barbour, American political consultant (R). Reaction to a reporter's observation that the Republican delegates to the 1988 convention did not include many blacks, poor, or women. CBS, *Face the Nation*, Aug. 14, 1988.

9. Anti-Semitism is the Socialism of fools.
August F. Bebel (1840-1913), German Social Democratic leader. Speech quoting Ferdinand Kronawetter, Berlin, Oct. 27, 1893.

10. If our people are to fight their way up out of bondage, we must arm them with the sword and the shield and the buckler of pride.
Mary McLeod Bethune (1875-1955), American educator. *Journal of Negro History*, Jan. 1938.

11. Dear Nigger-lover.
Theodore G. Bilbo (1877-1947), Governor of Mississippi and U.S. Senator (D). Frequent beginning of official letters he sent to those who took exception to his position on civil rights.

12. An Indian who is as bad as the white men could not live in our nation.... The white men do not scalp the head; but they do worse. They poison the heart.
Black Hawk (1767-1838), Chief of Sac and Fox Indians. 1832.

13. My reason teaches me that land cannot be sold. The great Spirit gave it to his children to live upon. So long as they occupy and cultivate it they have a right to the soil. Nothing can be sold but such things as can be carried away.
Black Hawk. *Autobiography*, 1833.

14. There can be no doubt that our nation has had a long and unfortunate history of sex discrimination. Traditionally, such discrimination was rationalized by an attitutde of "romantic paternalism" which, in practical effect, put women not on a pedestal, but in a cage.
William J. Brennan, Jr., U.S. Supreme Court Justice. *Frontiero* v. *Richardson*, 1973.

15. The enslavement of Africans *[in America]* built the world's strongest economy.

Tony Brown, American TV journalist. PBS, *Tony Brown's Journal*, July 8, 1989.

16. *[Rape]* is nothing more or less than a conscious process of intimidation by which *all men* keep *all women* in a state of fear.
Susan Brownmiller, American feminist writer. *Against Our Will*, 1975.

17. When the curtain dropped on the *[Marcus]* Garvey theatricals, the black man of America was exactly where Garvey had found him, though a little bit sadder, perhaps a bit poorer – if not wiser.
Ralph J. Bunche (1904-1971), Undersecretary General of the United Nations and Nobel Laureate in Peace. Quoted in Gunnar Myrdal, *The American Dilemma*, 1944.

18. A woman is but an animal, and an animal not of the highest order.
Edmund Burke (1729-1797), British statesman. *Reflections on the Revolution in France*, 1790.

19. The very look and temperament of women will be altered.
Horace Bushnell (1802-1876), American clergyman. Prediction of the outcome if women voted. *Women's Suffrage: the Reform against Nature*, 1869.

20. I don't think the approach is to simply give them *[the Indian tribes]* money, because too much money has disappeared in Indian country, too much has been mismanaged. The history of Indian country is the disappearance of money.
Ben Nighthorse Campbell, U.S. Congressman (D-CO). Quoted in *Governing the States and Localities*, Apr. 1988.

21. Be it said to the honor of the Hebrew race, we very rarely find one in the poorhouse, they are willing to work, and they add so much to the progress of the country.
Joseph G. Cannon (1836-1926), U.S. Congressman and Speaker of the House (R-IL). Address, General Convention of the International Order of B'nai B'rith, Washington, DC, Apr. 6, 1910.

22. The United States will never ask for your land there. This I promise you in the name of your great father, the President. That country he assigns to his red people, to be held by them and their children's children forever.
Lewis Cass (1782-1866), U.S. Senator (D-MI), U.S. Secretary of State, and U.S. Secretary of War. Statement during negotiations with the Shawnee and Cherokee Indians to persuade them to move to land west of the Mississippi. Treaty negotiation, 1825.

23. We must frequently promote their *[Indians]* interest against their inclination.
Lewis Cass. Quoted in Howard Zinn, *A People's History of the United States*, 1980.

24. Our young men will marry your daughters and we shall be one people.
Samuel de Champlain (1567?-1635), French colonist of Canada. Statement to the Iroquois Indians, Tadoussac, 1633.

25. Coercion alone will remove them *[the Indians]* to the western country allotted for the Indians.
Editorial, *Cherokee Phoenix*, July 15, 1828.

26. Except in Haiti, nowhere in the world have we resisted you. We have suffered, we have grown dull, and like cattle under a whip, obeyed. Why? Because, m'sieu, we have no pride! And we have no pride because we have nothing to remember.... While I live I shall try to build that pride we need, and build it in terms white men as well as black can understand. I am thinking of the future, m'sieu, not of now. I will teach pride if my teaching breaks every back in my kingdom.
Henri Christophe (1767-1820), President and King of Haiti. Quoted in John W. Vandercook, *Black Majesty*, 1928.

27. My number one priority is to save the black man.
Barbara-Rose Collins, U.S. Congresswoman (D-MI). Quoted in *Ebony*, Jan. 1991.

28. Do not receive overtures of peace or submission.... Kill every male Indian over twelve years of age.
Patrick E. Connor (1820-1891), General, U.S. Army. Instructions, Platte River campaign, 1865.

29. A black public official must be held to the same standard *[as anyone else]* ... a lower standard would be patronizing, a higher standard would be racist.
John Conyers, Jr., U.S. Congressman (D-MI). Statement, House Judiciary Committee hearings, July 26, 1988.

30. They tell us they want to civilize us. They lie. They want to kill us.
Crazy Horse (1849?-1877), Chief, Sioux Indians. 1876.

31. We do not want your civilization. We would live as our fathers did, and their fathers before them.
Crazy Horse. Statement on surrendering, 1877.

32. This is the land of our fathers; we love it ... and on no account whatever will we consent to sell one foot ... neither by exchange or otherwise.

Creek Indian Nation, Declaration of Policy and Law, Tuckabatchee, AL, 1824.

33. There must be in their *[the Indian's]* social bond, something singularly captivating, and far superior to anything to be boasted among us; for thousands of Europeans are *[now]* Indians, and we have no examples of even one of those Aborigines having from choice become Europeans.
Michel-Guillaume-Jean de Crèvecoeur (J. Hector St. John) (1735-1813), French Consul in New York City, writer, and agriculturalist. *Letters from an American Farmer*, 1782.

34. Some day an Italian and a Jew will be mayors of New York, and the Italian will come first.
Richard Croker (1841-1922), Tammany Hall leader, New York City (D). 1919.

35. I want no peace till the Indians suffer more.
Samuel R. Curtis (1805-1866), General, U.S. Army. Speech to his troops, Council Bluffs, IA, 1866.

36. The Army is the Indian's best friend.
George Armstrong Custer (1839-1876), Major General, U.S. Army. 1870.

37. I would be glad if the whites would pick out a place for themselves and not come into our grounds.
Cut Nose, Chief, Arapaho Indians. Statement, Horse Creek Council, Wyoming, 1851.

38. The most certain test by which we judge whether a country is really free is the amount of security enjoyed by minorities.
John Dahlberg, 1st Baron Acton (1834-1902), British historian. *The History of Freedom in Antiquity*, 1877.

39. The law has made the Negro equal, but man has not.
Clarence S. Darrow (1857-1937), American attorney. 1926.

40. They have got as far as they can go, because they own their land in common.... There is no enterprise to make your home any better than that of your neighbors. There is no selfishness, which is at the bottom of civilization. Till this people will consent to give up their lands, and divide them among their citizens ... they will not make much more progress.
Henry L. Dawes (1816-1903), U.S. Congressman and U.S. Senator (R-MA). Description of the Cherokee Indians. Speech, Lake Mohonk, NY, 1883.

41. The history of mankind is a history of repeated injuries and usurpations on the part of man toward woman, having in direct object the establishment of an absolute tyranny over her.
Declaration of Sentiments, Women's Rights Convention, Seneca Falls, NY, 1848.

42. The time has come to allow tribal governments to stand free – independent, responsible, and accountable.
Dennis DeConcini, U.S. Senator (D-AZ). Press conference, Nov. 17, 1989.

43. We call it taco politics. They *[U.S. government officials]* come to us, speaking Spanish, offering Hispanic rhetoric. But they're not really getting down to specifics of the problems we have.
Jose Garcia De Laua, President, League of United Latin Citizens (LULAC). Quoted in *USA Today*, Nov. 3, 1988.

44. A Jap is a Jap. It makes no difference whether the Japanese is theoretically a citizen. He is still a Japanese. Giving him a scrap of paper won't change it.
John L. De Witt, General, U.S. Army, West Defense Command. Remark in favor of removal of Japanese American citizens to detention camps, 1942.

45. Racism in America has not been completely eradicated. It is a sturdy pestilence. Racism and intolerance raise their heads repeatedly, not only in America but in every land.
William O. Douglas (1898-1980), U.S. Supreme Court Justice. *We the Judges*, 1956.

46. What does it amount to if the black man, after having been made free by the letter of your law ... is to be subject to the *[former]* slaveholder's shotgun?
Frederick Douglass (c.1817-1895), Recorder of Deeds, District of Columbia, and U.S. Minister to Haiti. In reference to the Ku Klux Klan. Speech, Republican National Convention, Cincinnati, OH, June 14, 1876.

47. The destiny of colored Americans is the destiny of America. We shall never leave you.
Frederick Douglass. Quoted in Lerone Bennett, Jr., *Pioneers in Protest*, 1968.

48. One ever feels his twoness – an American, a Negro; two souls, two thoughts, two unreconciled stirrings.
W. E. B. Du Bois (1868-1963), American educator and writer. *The Souls of Black Folk*, 1903.

49. The problem of the twentieth century is the color line.
W. E. B. Du Bois. *Ibid.*

50. We are Americans, not only by birth and by citizenship, but by our political ideals, our language, our religion. Farther than that, our Americanism does not go. At that point, we are Negroes, members of a vast historic race that from the very dawn of creation has slept, but half awakening in the dark forests of its African fatherland.
W. E. B. Du Bois. *Occasional Papers*, No. 2, American Negro Academy.

51. The black world squirms beneath the feet of the white in impotent fury or sullen hate.
W. E. B. Du Bois. Quoted in *The Nation*, Jan. 25, 1958.

52. There is now a recognition that there are three sovereigns in this country, and they are the federal government, the state governments, and the tribal governments.
John E. Echohawk, Executive Director, Native American Rights Fund. Quoted in *The New York Times*, June 24, 1988.

53. You, sir, will bring down that renowned chair in which you sit into infamy if your seal is set to this instrument of perfidy; and the name of this nation, hitherto the sweet omen of religion and liberty, will stink to the world.
Ralph Waldo Emerson (1803-1882), American writer. Letter to Pres. Van Buren protesting the westward removal of the Cherokee Indians, Apr. 1838.

54. Today is holden at Worcester, *[MA]*, the "Woman's Convention." I think that as long as they have not equal rights of property and right of voting they are not on the right footing.
Ralph Waldo Emerson. *Journals*, Oct. 14, 1861.

55. The pious ones of Plymouth, reaching the Rock, first fell upon their knees and then upon the aborigines.
William Maxwell Evarts (1818-1901), U.S. Senator (R-NY), U.S. Attorney General, and U.S. Secretary of State. Attributed.

56. The abortion thing is not going to change until ... the pro-life people look on the unborn as a disenfranchised minority, make it a civil rights issue, *[and]* go to the same level of commitment the civil rights people did – civil disobedience.
Jerry Falwell, American clergyman and founder, The Moral Majority. Interview, *Newsweek*, Aug. 29, 1988.

57. If I were not a woman, I would not have been the vice presidential candidate.
Geraldine A. Ferraro, U.S. Congresswoman (D-NY). PBS, *America's Political Parties – the Democrats*, Oct. 17, 1988.

58. We wish to plead our own cause. Too long have others spoken for us.
[The first issue of the first black newspaper in America.]
Editorial, *Freedom's Journal*, Mar. 16, 1827.

59. We have crowded the tribes upon a few miserable acres on our southern frontier; it is all that is left to them of their once boundless forest: and still, like the horse-leech, our insatiated cupidity cries, Give! Give!... Do the obligations of justice change with the color of the skin?
Theodore Frelinghuysen (1787-1862), U.S. Senator (Whig-NJ). Senate debate, 1829.

60. If the Negro be a soul, if the woman be a soul, apparelled in flesh, to one master only are they accountable.
Sarah Margaret Fuller (1810-1850), American feminist, writer, and critic. *The Dial*, July 1843.

61. In order that she may be able to give her hand with dignity, she must be able to stand alone.
Sarah Margaret Fuller. *Women in the Nineteenth Century*, 1845.

62. When a respectable minority objects to any rule of conduct, it would be dignified for the majority ... to yield.... Numerical strength savors of violence when it acts in total disregard of any strongly felt opinion of the minority.
Mohandas K. Gandhi (1869-1948), Indian political and spiritual leader. *Young India*, June 9, 1927.

63. I have been derisively called a "Woman's Rights Man." I know no such distinction. I claim to be a Human Rights Man; and wherever there is a human being, I see God-given rights inherent in that being, whatever may be the sex or complexion.
William Lloyd Garrison (1805-1879), American editor and abolitionist. Quoted in Garrison and Garrison, *William Lloyd Garrison: The Story of His Life Told by His Children*, III, 1889.

64. The reliance of our race upon the progress and achievements of others for a consideration in sympathy, justice, and rights is like a dependence upon a broken stick, resting upon which will eventually consign you to the ground.
Marcus Garvey (1887-1940), American black nationalist. Quoted in Essien-udom, *Black Nationalism*, 1962.

65. When the white man came we had the land and they had the Bibles; now they have the land and we have the Bibles.

Dan George (1899-1982), Canadian Indian Chief.

66. We are vanishing from the earth, yet I cannot think we are useless or Usen *[God]* would not have created us.

Geronimo (1829-1909), War Shaman, Apache Indians. Quoted in Angie Debo, *A History of the Indians of the United States*, 1970.

67. By arming the Negro we have added a powerful ally. They will make good soldiers.

Ulysses S. Grant (1822-1885), 18th President of the United States (R-OH). Quoted on PBS, *The Civil War*, Sept. 23, 1990.

68. Slavery always has, and always will, produce insurrections wherever it exists, because it is a violation of the natural order of things, and no human power can much longer perpetuate it.

Angelina Grimké (1805-1879), American abolitionist and suffragist. "Appeal to the Christian Women of the South," *The Anti-Slavery Examiner*, Sept. 1836.

69. If we surrender the right to speak in public this year, we must surrender the right to petition next year, and the right to write the year after that.... What then can women do for the slave, when she herself is under the feet of man and shamed into silence?

Angelina Grimké. Quoted in Howard Zinn, *A People's History of the United States*, 1980.

70. The American economy, the American society, the American unconscious are all racist.

Michael Harrington (1928-1989), American writer and Socialist leader. *The Other America*, 1962.

71. I am one of them. I am a black woman, the daughter of a dining car waiter. You do not seem to understand who I am.

Patricia R. Harris, U.S. Secretary of Health, Education and Welfare (D). Statement to Sen. William Proxmire, Senate confirmation hearings, July 1979.

72. The Indians were the original occupants of the lands we now possess. They have been driven from place to place.... In many instances, when they had settled down upon lands assigned to them by compact and begun to support themselves by their own labor, they were rudely jostled off and thrust into the wilderness again. Many, if not most, of our Indian wars have had their origin in broken promises and acts of injustice on our part.

Rutherford B. Hayes (1822-1893), 19th President of the United States (R). Message to Congress, 1877.

73. Women were really the backbone of the civil rights movement, although the leadership was predominantly male. At the rallies, the audience was women and children. The platform was predominantly men.

Dorothy Height, President, National Council of Negro Women. Quoted in *USA Today*, Oct. 13, 1988.

74. All Latins are volatile people.

Jesse Helms, U.S. Senator (R-NC). Quoted in *Newsweek*, June 23, 1986.

75. Brother, when we came here to relate our grievances about our lands, we expected to have something done for us.... You are not to expect to hear of me any more, and brother, we desire to hear no more of you.

Hendrick (Tiyanoga) (1680?-1755), Chief, Mohawk Indians, and member, New York State Colonial Congress. Statement to Governor George Clinton and the Provincial Council of New York, 1753.

76. There are no such things as women's issues. All issues are women's issues.

Aileen Clarke Hernandez, President, National Organization of Women. Speech, NOW Conference, Los Angeles, CA, Sept. 1971.

77. You will see how little time we shall need in order to upset the ideas and the criteria of the whole world, simply and purely by attacking Judaism.... Anti-Semitism is a useful revolutionary expedient.

Adolf Hitler (1889-1945), Führer of the Third German Reich. 1929.

78. It would need more than the Nineteenth Amendment to convince me that there are no differences between men and women, or that legislation cannot take those differences into account.

Oliver Wendell Holmes, Jr. (1841-1935), U.S. Supreme Court Justice. *Adkins* v. *Children's Hospital*, 1923 (dissent).

79. The hostility to all Indian ways and culture that characterized so much of government policy now appears to have been a mistake.

Report, Hoover Commission to Study and to Advise the Congress of the United States on Matters of Organization of the Executive Branch of Government, 1948.

80. Mistreatment of Jews in Germany may be considered virtually eliminated.

Cordell Hull (1871-1955), U.S. Congressman (D-

TN), U.S. Senator, U.S. Secretary of State, and Nobel Laureate in Peace. Quoted in *Time*, Apr. 3, 1933.

81. You don't run a feminist agenda and achieve political power.

Loila Hunking, City Commissioner, Sioux Falls, SD. Quoted in *Governing the States and Localities*, Feb. 1988.

82. *Be it enacted....* That all non-citizen Indians born within the territorial limits of the United States be, and they are hereby, declared to be citizens of the United States: *Provided*, That the granting of such citizenship shall not in any manner impair or otherwise affect the right of any Indian to tribal or other property.

Indian Citizenship Act, *Congressional Record*, 68th Congress, 1st Session, June 2, 1924.

83. There will never be a generation of great men until there has been a generation of free women.

Robert Green Ingersoll (1833-1899), Attorney General of Illinois (R). *Workers Should Be Free.*

84. Solutions to Indian problems in Indian country made in Washington very rarely work.

Daniel K. Inouye, U.S. Senator (D-HI). Speech, National Indian Council, June 1991.

85. All preceding experiments for the improvement of the Indians have failed. It seems now to be an established fact that they cannot live in contact with a civilized community and prosper.

Andrew Jackson (1767-1845), 7th President of the United States (D-TN). Comment justifying the settling of all Indians west of the Mississippi River. Message to Congress, 1835.

86. *A Century of Dishonor*

Helen Hunt Jackson (1830-1885), American writer and special commissioner to investigate conditions among the mission Indians of California. Title of her report documenting the wrongful treatment of the Indians by the U.S. government, 1881.

87. The purer a people, the better; the more mixed, the worse.

Friedrich Ludwig Jahn (1778-1852), Prussian gymnast and nationalist. *Folkdom.*

88. My children, persevere in your friendship to the United States. We will never injure you nor permit you to be injured by any white people, and we trust that you will take care that none of our people are injured by yours. Encourage among you the cultivation of the earth, raising of cattle, spinning and weaving, and we will assist you in it. With plenty of food and clothing you will raise many children, multiply, be strong and happy. May the Great Spirit protect and prosper you in all your just pursuits. Farewell.

Thomas Jefferson (1743-1826), 3rd President of the United States (Democratic Republican-VA). Letter to the brothers of the Choctaw Nation. Mar. 13, 1805.

89. The appointment of a woman to office is an innovation for which the public is not prepared, nor am I.

Thomas Jefferson. Letter to U.S. Secretary of the Treasury Albert Gallatin, Jan. 1807.

90. The rights of the first Americans to remain Indians while exercising their rights as Americans.

Lyndon B. Johnson (1908-1973), 36th President of the United States (D-TX). Special message to Congress, Mar. 6, 1968.

91. Your father never sold his country – never forget my dying words.... This country holds your father's body. Never sell the bones of your father and mother.

Joseph (1790-1871), Chief, Nez Percé Indians. To his son, Joseph, 1871.

92. If we ever owned the land we own it still, for we never sold it.

Joseph. Quoted in A. M. Josephy, *Nez Percé Indians and the Opening of the Northwest*, 1965.

93. Indians have heard fine words and promises long enough. They are right in asking for deeds.

John F. Kennedy (1917-1963), 35th President of the United States (D-MA). Letter to Oliver La Farge of the Association on American Indian Affairs, 1960.

94. There are no "white" or "colored" signs on the foxholes or graveyards of battle.

John F. Kennedy. Message to Congress on civil rights, June 19, 1963.

95. Obviously, Miss Craig, not enough.

John F. Kennedy. Response when reporter May Craig asked him what he had done lately for women. Quoted in Morris K. Udall, *Too Funny to Be President*, 1988.

96. All too many white Americans are horrified not with conditions of Negro life but with the product of these conditions, the Negro himself.

Martin Luther King, Jr. (1929-1968), American clergyman and civil rights leader. *American Psychologist*, 1968.

97. A repressed minority is an angry one, which may ultimately threaten the government's stability.

Jeri Laber, Executive Director, Helsinki Watch. Letter to *The New York Times*, Aug. 15, 1989.

98. In this enlightened age there are few, I believe, but what will acknowledge that slavery as an institution is a moral and political evil in any country.... I think it, however, a greater evil to the white than to the black race, and while my feelings are strongly enlisted in behalf of the latter, my sympathies are more strong for the former.
Robert E. Lee (1807-1870), General in Chief, Confederate Army. Letter to his wife, Dec. 6, 1856.

99. You shall not curse the deaf.
Old Testament, *Leviticus* 19:14.

100. A *[minority or ethnic]* group is best defined as a dynamic whole based on interdependence rather than on similarity.
Kurt Lewin (1890-1947), American social psychologist. *Menorah Journal*, 1940.

101. Raising the self-esteem of minority groups is one of the most strategic means for the improvement of intergroup relations.
Kurt Lewin. *Journal of Social Issues*, 1946.

102. Our progress in degeneracy appears to me to be pretty rapid. As a nation we began by declaring that "all men are created equal." Now we practically read it, "all men are created equal except Negroes." When the Know Nothings get control, it will read "all men are created equal except Negroes and foreigners and Catholics." When it comes to this I should prefer emigrating to some country where they make no pretense of loving liberty – to Russia for instance where despotism can be taken pure and without the base alloy of hypocrisy.
Abraham Lincoln (1809-1865), 16th President of the United States (R-IL). Letter to James Speed, Aug. 24, 1855.

103. There is an unwillingness on the part of our people for you free colored people to remain with us. Whether it is right or wrong I do not propose to discuss, but to propose it as a fact with which we have to deal. It is better for us both, therefore, to be separated.
Abraham Lincoln. Meeting with a delegation of black leaders to discuss a program for Negroes freed by the Civil War to emigrate to Africa, Aug. 1862.

104. I know not how much is within the legal power of the government in this case; but it is certainly true in equity, that the laboring women in our employment should be paid at the least as much as they were at the beginning of the war. Will the Secretary of War please have the cases fully examined, and so much relief given as can be consistently with the law and the public service.
Abraham Lincoln. Letter to U.S. Secretary of War Edwin M. Stanton, July 27, 1864.

105. Let every man honor and love the land of his birth and the race from which he springs and keep their memory green.... If a man is going to be an American at all, let him be so without any qualifying adjectives; and if he is going to be something else, let him drop the word American from his personal description.
Henry Cabot Lodge (1850-1924), U.S. Congressman and U.S. Senator (R-MA). Speech, Brooklyn, NY, Dec. 21, 1888.

106. It's the other end of me that you'd better start paying attention to.
Clare Boothe Luce (1903-1987), U.S. Congresswoman and Ambassador to Italy and Brazil (R). Response when, at the end of her maiden speech in the House of Representatives, a Congressmen observed that she had nice legs. 1943.

107. Look at the Pentagon. Women are almost 41 percent of the Defense Department. Yet, out of the 855 career and appointive employees in the top three grade levels, only 5 are women. Over 80 percent of the employes in the three lowest grades are women. Our Defense Department seems more scared of giving a break to women than of giving it to the Russians.
Clare Both Luce. Quoted in *U.S. News & World Report*, June 24, 1974.

108. If the United States is indeed the great melting pot, the Negro either didn't get in the pot or he didn't get melted down.
Thurgood Marshall, U.S. Supreme Court Justice. *Newsweek*, Sept. 21, 1987.

109. I spent most of my life getting the word "Negro" to be spelled with a capital "N." By the time I finally got that done people were using the word "black" with a small "b."
Thurgood Marshall. Quoted on CBS, *Evening News*, Oct. 17, 1989.

110. Mr. Speaker, there is no real persecution of Jews in Germany.
Louis Thomas McFadden (1876-1936), U.S. Congressman (R-PA). House debate, 1933.

111. Freedom is the red man's heritage, the precious boon of his nomadic life; and retaining that, he will assume a friendly attitude toward other men if assured of their good will and love of peace.

John McLean (1799-1890), British North American missionary. *The Methodist Magazine*, Feb. 1891.

112. They *[the American Indians]* have claims on the magnanimity and, I may add, on the justice of this nation which we must all fill. We should become their real benefactors; we should perform the office of their Great Father, the endearing title which they emphatically give to the Chief Magistrate of our Union.

James Monroe (1758-1831), 5th President of the United States (Democratic Republican-VA). Second inaugural address, Mar. 5, 1821.

113. The issue of race could benefit from a period of benign neglect.

Daniel P. Moynihan, Chief American Delegate to the United Nations and U.S. Senator (D-NY). Memorandum to President Nixon, 1971.

114. The main and basic responsibility for effecting a solution of the black man's problems rests upon American Negroes themselves. They should supply the money and pay the price, make the sacrifice and endure suffering to realize full manhood as Black Men.

Elijah Muhammad (1896-1975), messenger, Nation of Islam. Quoted in Essien-udom, *Black Nationalism*, 1962.

115. She who has borne the greatest number of children.

Napoléon I (1769-1821), military leader and Emperor of France. Reply to Mme. de Staël's question, "Who was the greatest woman?"

116. This book is dangerous for the Negro to read, for it will only excite discontent and fill his imagination with things that do not exist, or things that should not bear upon his mind.

Editorial, *Nashville Banner*, 1903. In reference to *The Souls of Black Folk* by W. E. B. DuBois.

117. Noe Negro or Slave be suffered to work ... as a Porter about any goods either imported or Exported from or into this Citty.

New York City Council. Law, 1686.

118. All Indyans here are free and not Slaves, nor can bee forc'd to be servants.

New York Colonial Council. Order, Dec. 5, 1679.

119. Mixed races are the sources of great civilizations.

Friedrich Wilhelm Nietzsche (1844-1900), German philosopher. Quoted in George Seldes, *The Great Quotations*, 1960.

120. I want to emphasize here my deep and abiding respect for the values of Indian culture and for the undeniable right of Indian people to preserve their traditional heritage. Our overriding aim ... should not be to separate the Indians from the richness of their past.

Richard M. Nixon, 37th President of the United States (R-CA). Campaign speech, Association on American Indian Affairs, 1960.

121. If *[Jesse Jackson]* is nominated *[for President by the Democratic Party]*, it goes without saying he cannot win. But everyone is overplaying the fact that he would be a liability because he is black. That is simply not true. Jackson would be a liability because his views are radical.

Richard M. Nixon. Interview, *The Washington Times*, Apr. 4, 1988.

122. Many of our ancestors have died because they've trusted the white government.

Joe Norton, Grand Chief, Kahnawake Mohawk Indians, Canada. To explain why Canadian Mohawks took up arms in a land dispute with the Quebec government at Oka. Quoted in *The Montgomery Journal*, July 23, 1990.

123. How can we plan our future when the Indian Bureau threatens to wipe us out as a race?

Earl Old Person, Tribal Chairman, Blackfoot Indians. Remark to the Director of the U.S. Bureau of Indian Affairs, 1966.

124. A society without an aristocracy, without an elite minority, is not a society.

José Ortega y Gasset (1883-1955), Spanish philosopher and statesman. *Invertebrate Spain*, 1922.

125. Minorities are individuals or groups of individuals especially qualified. The masses are the collection of people not specially qualified.

José Ortega y Gasset. Prologue, *The Revolt of the Masses*, 1930.

126. We fight that our pride, our self-respect, our dignity may not be sacrificed in the future as they have been in the past.

Christabel Pankhurst (1880-1958), British suffragist. Speech, Mar. 23, 1911.

127. We who campaigned for *[Al]* Smith in 1928, and also the candidate himself, were not prepared for the degree of *[anti-Catholic]* prejudice we encountered ... and were shocked and surprised by the way our opponents appealed to the basest passions and the lowest motives of the people.

Frances Perkins (1882-1965), U.S. Secretary of Labor (D). Quoted in Josephson, *Al Smith: Hero of the Cities*, 1969.

128. Governments exist to protect the rights of minorities. The loved and the rich need no protection. They have many friends and few enemies.
Wendell Phillips (1811-1884), American orator and reformer. Speech, Boston, MA, Dec. 21, 1860.

129. We *[women]* are half the people; we should be half the Congress.
Jeanette Rankin (1880-1973), U.S. Congresswoman (R-MT). Quoted in *Newsweek*, Feb. 14, 1966.

130. Those who demand *[racial]* sensitivity have a duty to practice it.
William Raspberry, American columnist. *The Washington Post*, Oct. 30, 1989.

131. You could call them Fritz and Tits because then there'd be three boobs in the White House.... Geraldine Ferraro – big deal! Let's put a woman in the White House! May I tell you something? Can we talk here for a second? It's no big deal to have a woman in the White House. John F. Kennedy had a thousand of them.
Joan Rivers, American comedian and TV talk show host. Speech, GOP women's luncheon, Dallas, TX, Aug. 22, 1984.

132. They have found the forgotten man. There's nine of him and one woman.
Will Rogers (1879-1935), American humorist. Comment after Franklin D. Roosevelt appointed his Cabinet, which included nine men and one woman, Frances Perkins, Secretary of Labor. 1933.

133. Too often the great decisions are originated and given form in bodies made up wholly of men, or so completely dominated by them that whatever of special value women have to offer is shunted aside without expression.
Anna Eleanor Roosevelt (1884-1962), First Lady and U.S. Delegate to the United Nations. Speech, United Nations, Dec. 1952.

134. The moment a mere numerical superiority by either states or voters in this country proceeds to ignore the needs and desires of the minority ... that moment will mark the failure of our constitutional system.
Franklin D. Roosevelt (1882-1945), 32nd President of the United States (D-NY). 1930.

135. No democracy can long survive which does not accept as fundamental to its very existence the recognition of the rights of minorities.
Franklin D. Roosevelt. Letter to the National Association for the Advancement of Colored People, June 25, 1938.

136. I don't go so far as to think that the only good Indians are dead Indians, but I believe nine out of ten are, and I shouldn't like to inquire too closely into the case of the tenth.
Theodore Roosevelt (1858-1919), 26th President of the United States (R-NY). 1886.

137. To divide along the lines of section or caste or creed is un-American.
Theodore Roosevelt. 1917.

138. A woman's place is in the House and the Senate.
Gloria Schaffer, Secretary of State, Connecticut (D). 1976.

139. Every people, every creed, every class of society has contributed its share to that wonderful mixture out of which is to grow the great nation of the new world.
Carl Schurz (1829-1906), U.S. Senator (R-MO). Speech, Faneuil Hall, Boston, MA, Apr. 1859.

140. Indian Territory south of Kansas must be vacated by the Indian.
William H. Seward (1801-1872), Governor of New York (Whig), U.S. Senator (Whig and R-NY), and U.S. Secretary of State. Campaign speech, 1860.

141. Douglas, no man who spells Negro with two g's will ever be elected President of the United States.
William H. Seward. Remark to Sen. Stephen A. Douglas who used the word "nigger" in his speeches. Quoted in *American Heritage*, Nov. 1988.

142. We must act with vindictive earnestness against the Sioux, even to their extermination, men, women, and children.
William Tecumseh Sherman (1820-1891), General, U.S. Army. Quoted in Angie Debo, *A History of the Indians of the United States*, 1970.

143. One wonders why it is that if we maintain civilized dialogue with representatives from other countries, we sometimes are unable to do that with various members of our own society.
Eduard Shevardnadze, Foreign Minister, U.S.S.R. Comment on Russia's problems with its ethnic minorities. Interview, *Time*, May 15, 1989.

144. No people goes down until their women are weak and dishonored.
Traditional Sioux Indian female puberty ceremony.

145. Well, the time hasn't come when a man can say his beads in the White House.

Alfred E. Smith (1873-1944), Governor of New York (D). Remark after losing the presidential election to Herbert Hoover, Nov. 6, 1928.

146. The rule of the many by the few we call tyranny; the rule of the few by the many is tyranny also, only of a less intense kind.

Herbert Spencer (1820-1903), British social philosopher. *Social Statics*, 1850.

147. Anti-Semitism is the most dangerous survival of cannibalism.

Joseph Stalin (1879-1953), Premier of the U.S.S.R. Remark on the German Nazi Party. Jan. 12, 1931.

148. God wrote it. I merely wrote His dictation.

Harriet Beecher Stowe (1811-1896), American writer. Comment on her book, *Uncle Tom's Cabin*, 1852.

149. The Jew is neither a newcomer nor an alien in this country or on this continent.... He came in the caravels of Columbus, and he knocked at the gates of New Amsterdam only thirty-five years after the Pilgrim Fathers stepped ashore on Plymouth Rock.

Oscar S. Straus (1845-1926), U.S. Secretary of Commerce and Labor and U.S. Ambassador to Turkey (Progressive-NY). Speech, Jan. 18, 1911.

150. Anti-Semitism is a noxious weed that should be cut out. It has no place in free America.

William H. Taft (1857-1930), 27th President of the United States (R-OH) and Chief Justice, U.S. Supreme Court. 1920.

151. Congress has no power to abolish or prevent slavery in any of its territories.

Roger B. Taney (1777-1864), Chief Justice, U.S. Supreme Court and U.S. Secretary of the Treasury. *Dred Scott* v. *Sanford*, 1857.

152. It is my determination nor will I give rest to my feet until I have united all the red men.

Tecumseh (1768-1813), Leader, Shawnee Indians. Statement to William Henry Harrison, Governor of the Indiana Territory. Aug. 1809.

153. You try and prevent the Indians from doing what we, their leaders, wish them to do – unite and consider their land the common property.

Tecumseh. *Ibid.*

154. The white people have no right to take the land from the Indians, because they had it first.... It belongs to the first who sits down upon his blanket or skins which he has thrown upon the ground; and till he leaves it no other has a right.

Tecumseh. Statement to Harrison, 1810.

155. I owe nothing to women's lib.

Margaret Thatcher, Prime Minister of Great Britain (Conservative). Quoted in *The Observer*, Dec. 1, 1974.

156. In politics, if you want anything said, ask a man. If you want anything done, ask a woman.

Margaret Thatcher. Quoted in *People*, Sept. 15, 1975.

157. The earth is part of my body and I never gave up the earth.

Toohoolhoolzote (1810-1877), Chief, Nez Percé Indians. Quoted in Angie Debo, *A History of the Indians of the United States*, 1970.

158. I've said for a long time that women have everything else, they might as well have the presidency.

Harry S Truman (1884-1972), 33rd President of the United States (D-MO). Quoted by Cong. Edward J. Derwinski, memorial tribute to Truman in the House of Representatives, Jan. 3, 1973.

159. Domestic dependent nations

U.S. Congress. Description of Indian tribes. Public Law No. 280, 1953.

160. It is the policy of Congress ... to make the Indians ... subject to the same laws and entitled to the same privileges and responsibilities as ... other citizens ... and to end their status as wards of the United States, and to grant them all the rights and privileges pertaining to American citizenship.

U.S. House of Representatives, House Resolution No. 108, Aug. 1, 1953.

161. The paramount destiny and mission of woman are to fulfill the noble and benign office of wife and mother. This is the law of the Creator.

[Myra Bradwell, publisher of the Chicago Legal News, *had been denied admission to the Illinois bar because she was a married woman and therefore not an independent agent. She was finally admitted in 1890.]*

U.S. Supreme Court, *Bradwell* v. *Illinois*, 1873.

162. The Queen is most anxious to enlist everyone who can speak or write to join in checking this mad, wicked folly of "Women's Rights," with all its attendant horrors, on which her poor feeble sex is bent, forgetting every sense of womanly feeling and propriety. It is a subject which makes the Queen so furious that she cannot contain herself. God created men and women different – then let them remain each in their own position.

Victoria (1819-1901), Queen of Great Britain and Ireland and Empress of India. Memorandum on Women's Suffrage, 1870.

163. The white man, who possesses this whole vast country from sea to sea, who roams over it at pleasure and lives where he likes, cannot know the cramp we feel in this little spot *[the reservation]*, with the undying remembrance of the fact ... that every foot of what you proudly call America not very long ago belonged to the Red man.

Washakie (1804?-1900), Chief, Shoshoni Indians. Speech, Wyoming Governor's Conference, 1878.

164. To those of my race who depend on bettering their condition in a foreign land or who underestimate the importance of cultivating friendly relations with the southern white man, who is their next-door neighbor, I would say, "Cast down your bucket where you are."

Booker T. Washington (1856-1915), American educator and President, Tuskegee Institute. Speech, Cotton States International Exposition, Atlanta, GA, 1895.

165. One of its *[anti-Semitism's]* fundamental causes is that the Jews exist.

Chaim Weizmann (1874-1952), 1st President of Israel. Testimony, Anglo-American Committee, Mar. 8, 1946.

166. Different races and nationalities cherish different ideals of society that stink in each other's nostrils.

Rebecca West (Cicily Isabel Fairfield) (1892-1983), British writer and critic. *Black Lamb, Grey Falcon*, 1941.

167. Whatever women do they must do twice as well as men to be thought half as good. Luckily, this is not difficult.

Charlotte Whitton, Mayor of Ottawa, Canada. Quoted in Nancy McPhee, *The Book of Insults*, 1978.

168. It's like the weather. If it's inevitable, just relax and enjoy it.

Clayton Williams, Republican candidate for Governor of Texas. Response when reporters asked his views on rape, Apr. 1990.

169. We cannot make a homogeneous population of a people who do not blend with the Caucasian race.

Woodrow Wilson (1856-1924), 28th President of the United States (D-NJ). Campaign speech, 1912.

170. Tonight there are some Americans sharing the same grave who in the United States could not have shared the same hotel.

Walter Winchell (1897-1972), American columnist and radio commentator. World War II radio broadcast.

171. It's a minority anyone can join.

Pat Wright, Director, Disability Rights and Education Fund. In reference to the disabled. Quoted in *The New York Times*, Sept. 17, 1989.

172. After four hundred years of slave labor, we have some back pay coming.

Malcolm X (Malcolm Little) (1925-1965), American black power advocate. 1964.

173. We don't judge you because you're white; we don't judge you because you're black. We judge you because of what you do.... We're not against people because they're white. We're against people who practice racism.

Malcolm X. Quoted in *The Washington Post*, Jan. 5, 1991.

Chapter 65

Minting, Money, and Coins

1. In God We Trust
   Motto on United States currency. First appeared on two-cent coin, 1864.

2. I believe gold and silver coin to be the money of the Constitution. No power was conferred on Congress to declare that either metal should not be money. Congress has therefore no power to demontize silver any more than to demonitize gold.
   James G. Blaine (1830-1893), U.S. Congressman and U.S. Senator (R-ME). Feb. 7, 1878.

3. Cannot the poor man's cattle, and horses, and corn be thus taken by the government when the public exigency requires it, and cannot the rich man's bonds and notes be in like manner taken to reach the same end? If the government enacts that the certificates of indebtedness which it gives the farmer for his cattle and provender shall be receivable by the farmer's creditors in payment of his bonds and notes, is it anything more than transferring the government loan from the hands of one man to the hands of another – perhaps far more able to advance it? Is it anything more than putting the securities of the capitalist on the same platform as the farmer's stock?
   [During the Civil War the government issued paper money and made it legal tender for the payment of all government debts. It was argued that the government was, in effect, taking citizens' valuable property and only giving them worthless paper in exchange.]
   Joseph P. Bradley (1813-1892), U.S. Supreme Court Justice. *Legal Tender Cases*, 1871.

4. However plenty silver dollars may become, they will not be distributed as gifts among the people.
   Grover Cleveland (1837-1908), 22nd and 24th President of the United States (D-NY). Annual message to Congress, Dec. 8, 1885.

5. Money can never circulate freely and actively unless there be absolute confidence in its value.
   William B. Cockran (1854-1923), U.S. Congressman (D-NY). Speech, Madison Square Garden, New York City, Aug. 18, 1896.

6. We believe in honest money, the gold and silver coinage of the Constitution, and a circulating medium convertible into such money without loss.
   Democratic Party platform, 1884.

7. Susan B. Anthony need not hold us hostage forever.
   Pete V. Dominici, U.S. Senator (R-NM). Remark when introducing a bill to create a gold-colored dollar coin, stamped in copper, despite the failure of the Susan B. Anthony dollar piece in the late 1970s. June 1990.

8. It makes me look so old.
   Elizabeth II, Queen of Great Britain. Comment on a new bank note with her portrait. Quoted in *The New York Times*, June 7, 1990.

9. The law may do what it will with the owner of property, its just power will still attach to the cent.
   Ralph Waldo Emerson (1803-1882), American writer. *Essays*, Second Series. "Politics," 1876.

10. The crown has the sole right to issue money.
    English Privy Council, 1603.

11. Whoever controls the volume of money in any country is absolute master of all industry and commerce.
    James A. Garfield (1831-1881), 20th President of the United States (R-OH). Attributed.

12. The suggestion that we may devaluate the gold dollar 50 percent means national repudiation. To me, it means dishonor. In my conception of it, it is immoral.
    Carter Glass (1858-1946), U.S. Congressman and U.S. Senator (D-VA). Quoted in Smith and Beasley, *Carter Glass*, 1939.

13. We have lost control over the financial system ... by printing much more money than in previous years.
Mikhail Gorbachev, President of the U.S.S.R. Quoted in *The Washington Post*, Dec. 23, 1990.

14. The Almighty Dollar, that great object of universal devotion throughout our land, seems to have no genuine devotees in these peculiar villages.
Washington Irving (1783-1859), American writer and U.S. Diplomatic Attaché to Spain. *Wolfert's Roost and Miscellanies: The Creole Roost*, 1835.

15. A great deal of small change is useful in a state, and tends to reduce the price of small articles.
Thomas Jefferson (1743-1826), 3rd President of the United States (Democratic Republican-VA). *Notes on the Establishment of a Money Unit, and of a Coinage for the United States*, 1784.

16. The best way to destroy the capitalist system is to debauch the currency. By a continuing process of inflation governments can confiscate, secretly and unobserved, an important part of the wealth of their citizens.
John Maynard Keynes (1883-1946), British economist and diplomat. *Essays in Persuasion*, 1931.

17. You take care of the Treasury and I will take care of the Constitution.
Abraham Lincoln (1809-1865), 16th President of the United States (R-IL). Remark to Secretary of the Treasury Salmon P. Chase, who insisted that printing paper money to pay the troops because of silver and gold shortages was unconstitutional, 1863.

18. Let the influx of money be ever so great, if there be no confidence, property will sink in value.... The circulation of confidence is is better than the circulation of money.
James Madison (1751-1836), 4th President of the United States (Democratic Republican-VA). Speech, Virginia Convention, June 20, 1788.

19. The American dollar must never again be a hostage in the hands of international speculators.
Richard M. Nixon, 37th President of the United States (R-CA). Remark on removing U.S. currency from the gold standard. PBS, *The American Century*, Nov. 21, 1989.

20. Inflation fears constantly assail him *[Sen. Arthur H. Vandenberg]*; he carries German marks printed with 1 million signs to give colleagues visual warning of its danger.
The Philadelphia Record, June 23, 1937.

21. If we must use gold and silver all the time, a lady can scarcely carry enough money with her *[because of the weight]*.
Sarah Childress Polk (1803-1891), First Lady. Remark to her husband, Pres. Polk, a staunch opponent of the use of paper money as opposed to gold and silver coins. Quoted in Nelson and Nelson, *Memorials of Sarah Childress Polk*, 1892.

22. ... the Susan B. Anthony experience, a lesson that every other nation has learned in introducing a high-denomination coin: People prefer paper currency to coins when offered the choice.
Donna Pope, Director, U.S. Mint. *The Washington Post*, July 21, 1990.

23. We women have to put first things first. Why should we mind if men have their faces on the money, as long as we get our hands on it?
Ivy Baker Priest (1905-1975), Treasurer of the United States. *Green Grows Ivy*, 1958.

24. We have always recommended the best money known to the civilized world; and we urge that efforts should be made to unite all commercial nations in the establishment of an international standard, which shall fix for all the relative value of gold and silver coinage.
Republican Party platform, 1884.

25. Think what kind of internal market you'd have in the United States if there were ten different currencies between Seattle and Boston.
Helmut Schmidt, Chancellor of West Germany. In reference to the European Common Market. Quoted in *Forbes*, June 12, 1989.

26. All money is a matter of belief.
Adam Smith, American economist and financial advisor. *Paper Money*, 1981.

27. I am for gold dollars as against baloney dollars.
Alfred E. Smith (1873-1944), Governor of New York (D). Interview, Nov. 24, 1933.

28. Of all the contrivances for cheating the laboring classes of mankind, none has been more effectual than that which deludes them with paper money.
Daniel Webster (1782-1852), U.S. Congressman (Federalist-NH and MA), U.S. Senator (Federalist and Whig-MA), and U.S. Secretary of State. Quoted in *The Congressional Record*, Mar. 4, 1946.

29. Too great a quantity of cash in circulation is a much greater evil than too small a quantity.
Noah Webster (1758-1843), American writer and lexicographer. Letter to *The Maryland Journal*, Aug. 9, 1785.

Chapter 66

Nationalism, Patriotism, and Treason

1. Think of your forefathers! Think of your posterity!
   John Quincy Adams (1767-1848), 6th President of the United States (Ind-MA). Speech, Plymouth, MA, Dec. 22, 1802.

2. Unless our conception of patriotism is progressive, it cannot hope to embody the real affection and real interest of the nation.
   Jane Addams (1860-1935), American settlement worker and Nobel Laureate in Peace. *Newer Ideals of Peace*, 1907.

3. For God and Country, we associate ourselves together for the following purposes: To uphold and defend the Constitution of the United States of America; to maintain law and order; to foster and perpetuate a one hundred percent Americanism.
   Preamble to Constitution, American Legion, 1919.

4. Let me die in my old uniform. God forgive me for ever putting on any other.
   Benedict Arnold (1741-1801), Major General, Continental Army, and traitor. Last words, London, England. Attributed.

5. A traitor is a good fruit to hang from the boughs of the tree of liberty.
   Henry Ward Beecher (1813-1887), American clergyman and writer. *Life Thoughts*, 1858.

6. There's an element of truth in every idea that lasts long enough to be corny.
   Irving Berlin (1888-1988), American song writer and composer of "God Bless America." Remark to Eleanor Roosevelt, 1938.

7. *Sic temper tyranis!* The South is avenged!
   John Wilkes Booth (1838-1865), American actor. Words shouted after he shot President Lincoln. Ford's Theater, Washington, DC, Apr. 14, 1865.

8. Patriotism is a little like strength. If you've got it, you don't have to wear it on your sleeve.
   William W. Bradley, U.S. Senator (D-NJ). Commencement address, Middlebury College, Middlebury, VT, May 1989.

9. I know of no more patriotic group than television journalists.
   Tom Brokaw, NBC news anchorman. Newspaper ad, Mar. 1985.

10. To make us love our country, our country ought to be lovely.
    Edmund Burke (1729-1797), British statesman. *Reflections on the Revolution in France*, 1790.

11. That which distinguishes this day from all others is that both orators and artillerymen shoot blank cartridges.
    John Burroughs (1837-1921), American naturalist and writer. *Journal*, July 4, 1859.

12. You make men love their country by giving them the kind of government and the kind of country that inspire respect and love.
    Zechariah Chafee, Jr. (1885-1957), professor of law, Harvard University. *Free Speech in the United States*, 1942.

13. "My country, right or wrong," is a thing that no patriot would think of saying, except in a desperate case. It is like saying, "My mother, drunk or sober."
    G. K. Chesterton (1874-1936), British writer. *The Defendant*.

14. Our country is wherever we are well off.
    Marcus Tullius Cicero (106-43 B.C.), Roman statesman and writer. *Tusculan Disputations*.

15. It is every man's duty to leave his country as good as he found it.

William Cobbett (1763-1835), British journalist. *Cobbett's Political Register*, Dec. 22, 1832.

16. Patriotism is easy to understand in America. It means looking out for yourself while looking out for your country.
Calvin Coolidge (1872-1933), 30th President of the United States (R-MA). Attributed.

17. I hope to find my country in the right; however, I will stand by her, right or wrong.
John J. Crittendon (1787-1863), U.S. Congressman (Whig and Unionist-KY), U.S. Senator, and U.S. Attorney General. *On the Mexican War.*

18. The man who prefers his country before any other duty shows the same spirit as the man who surrenders every right to the state. They both deny that right is superior over authority.
John Dahlberg, 1st Baron Acton (1834-1902), British historian. *The Home and Foreign Review*, July 1862.

19. Patriotism is in political life what faith is in religion.
John Dahlberg. *Ibid.*

20. It is bad to be oppressed by a minority, but it is worse to be oppressed by a majority.... From the absolute will of an entire people there is no appeal, no redemption, no refuge but treason.
John Dahlberg. *The History of Freedom in Antiquity*, 1877.

21. I'm not afraid to make a patriotic speech. There should be more of them.
Richard J. Daley (1902-1976), Mayor of Chicago, IL (D). Campaign dinner, Mercy Hospital, Sept. 24, 1968.

22. Our country! In her intercourse with foreign nations may she always be in the right; but our country, right or wrong.
Stephen Decatur (1779-1820), Commodore, U.S. Navy. Toast given at Norfolk, VA, Apr. 1816.

23. The heart of America is right.
Everett M. Dirksen (1896-1969), U.S. Congressman and U.S. Senator (R-IL). Speech, Jacksonville, FL, 1967.

24. There can be no neutrals in this war *[the Civil War]* – only patriots or traitors.
Stephen A. Douglas (1813-1861), U.S. Congressman and U.S. Senator (D-IL). 1861.

25. Nationalism is an infantile disease. It is the measles of mankind.
Albert Einstein (1879-1955), Nobel Laureate in Physics (Switzerland). Letter to George Sylvester Viereck, 1921.

26. Patriotism means equipped forces and a prepared citizenry.
Dwight D. Eisenhower (1890-1969), 34th President of the United States (R-KS). First inaugural address, Jan. 20, 1953.

27. I offer neither pay, nor quarters, nor provisions; I offer hunger, thirst, forced marches, battles, and death. Let him who loves his country in his heart and not with his lips only, follow me.
Giuseppe Garibaldi (1807-1882), Italian patriot, general, and politician. To members of the *Cacciatori della Alpi*, 1859.

28. Our country is the world – our countrymen are all mankind.
William Lloyd Garrison (1805-1879), American editor and abolitionist. Motto of *The Liberator*, 1837-1839.

29. Where is the black man's government? Where is his king and his kingdom? Where is his President, his country, and his ambassador, his army, his navy, his men of big affairs? I could not find them, and then I declared, "I will help to make them."
Marcus Garvey (1887-1940), American black nationalist leader. Quoted in Cronon, *Black Moses*, 1957.

30. Patriotism is when love of your own people comes first; nationalism is when hate for people other than your own comes first.
Charles de Gaulle (1890-1970), President of France. Quoted in *Life*, May 9, 1969.

31. I desire what is good. Therefore, everyone who does not agree with me is a traitor.
George III (1738-1820), King of Great Britain, and King of Hanover. Quoted in Gerald Tomlinson, *Speaker's Treasury of Political Stories, Anecdotes, and Humor*, 1990.

32. I love my country and I am fighting for my country, but if this war *[the Civil War]* ever ends, I'll be dad-burned if I'll ever love another country.
John Brown Gordon (1832-1904), General, Confederate Army, U.S. Senator (D-GA), and Governor of Georgia. Quoted by Woodrow Wilson to Joseph Tumulty upon German acceptance of the World War I armistice, 1918.

33. Some men and all cattle lack patriotism.
George Monro Grant (1835-1902), Canadian clergyman and historian. *Principal Grant*.

34. I only regret that I have but one life to lose for my country.

Nathan Hale (1755-1776), Captain, Continental Army. Last words before being hanged as a spy by the English, Sept. 22, 1776.

35. I had rather take my chances that some traitors will escape detection than spread abroad a spirit of general suspicion and distrust, which accepts rumor and gossip in place of undismayed and unintimidated inquiry.

Learned Hand (1872-1961), Federal Judge. Address, New York University Law School, New York City, Oct. 24, 1952.

36. Treason doth never prosper: What's the reason?
Why, if it prosper, none dare call it treason.

James Harrington (1611-1677), English writer and political theorist. *Epigrams.*

37. Let us exalt patriotism and moderate our party contentions. Let those who would die for the flag on the field of battle give a better proof of their patriotism and a higher glory to their country by promoting fraternity and justice.

Benjamin Harrison (1833-1901), 23rd President of the United States (R-IN). Inaugural address, Mar. 4, 1889.

38. Have you not learned that not stocks or bonds or stately houses, or products of the mill or field are our country? It is a spiritual thought that is in our minds.

Benjamin Harrison. Speech, July 4, 1893.

39. I think there is one higher office than President, and I would call that patriot.

Gary Hart, U.S. Senator (D-CO). Interview, ABC, *Nightline*, Sept. 8, 1987.

40. A politician will do anything to keep his job – even become a patriot.

William Randolph Hearst (1863-1951), U.S. Congressman (D-NY); founder, Independence League Party; journalist; and publisher. Signed editorial, Aug. 28, 1933.

41. There exists only one single German way of life. It is that which is rooted in the enduring core of the people and in a way of work freely offered to the will of the State, a way whose enrichment is being shaped in the National Socialist Revolution.

Martin Heidegger (1899-1976), German philosopher. Speech to students, University of Freiburg, Jan. 22, 1934.

42. Truth made you a traitor as it often does in a time of scoundrels.

Lillian Hellman (1905-1984), American writer. In reference to the United States during the McCarthy period. *Scoundrel Time*, 1976.

43. *Deutschland über alles* (Germany over all)

August Hoffman (1789-1874), German writer. Popular song that became the official anthem of the Third German Reich.

44. Prevent the rise of a "messiah" who could unify, and electrify the militant black nationalist movement.

J. Edgar Hoover (1895-1972), Director, Federal Bureau of Investigation. In reference to Martin Luther King, Jr. Memorandum to FBI offices, Mar. 3, 1968.

45. It is a sweet and glorious thing to die for one's country. (*Dulce et decorum est pro patria mori.*)

Horace (Quintus Horatius Flaccus) (65-8 B.C.), Roman poet. *Satires*, II.

46. *Saving souls* was once the most popular work; but now *saving the country* takes the lead.

Edgar Watson Howe (1853-1937), American editor and writer. *Ventures in Common Sense*, 1919.

47. As a matter of fact, it is the Fascist-minded men of America who are the real enemies of our institutions.... It is these men who, pretending that they would save us from Communism, would superimpose upon America an equally dreaded Fascism.

Harold L. Ickes (1874-1952), U.S. Secretary of the Interior (R). Speech, American Civil Liberties Union, Dec. 8, 1937.

48. Political rights have been preserved by traitors.

Robert Green Ingersoll (1833-1899), Attorney General of Illinois (R). *Liberty of Man, Woman and Child.*

49. Disunion by armed force is treason.

Andrew Jackson (1767-1845), 7th President of the United States (D-TN). Warning to John Calhoun and other South Carolinians about the implications of their nullification of the Tariff Act. *Proclamation to the People of South Carolina.* Dec. 10, 1832.

50. I think it fortunate for the United States to have become the asylum for so many virtuous patriots of different denominations.

Thomas Jefferson (1743-1826), 3rd President of the United States (Democratic Republican-VA). Letter to M. de Meusnier, Apr. 29, 1795.

51. A nation united can never be conquered.
Thomas Jefferson. Letter to John Adams, Jan. 11, 1816.

52. Robbery is a crime; rape is a crime; murder is a crime; treason is a crime and crime must be punished. The law provides for it, and the courts are open. Treason must be made infamous and traitors must be impoverished.
Andrew Johnson (1808-1875), 17th President of the United States (War Democrat-TN). Quoted in George W. Julian, *Recollections*, 1884.

53. Patriotism is the last refuge of the scoundrel.
Samuel Johnson (1709-1784), British writer and lexicographer. Quoted in James Boswell, *The Life of Samuel Johnson*, Apr. 7, 1775.

54. I criticize America because I love her. I want to see her stand as a moral example to the world.
Martin Luther King, Jr. (1929-1968), American clergyman and civil rights leader. Quoted on National Public Radio, Apr. 21, 1989.

55. Pacifism is patriotism.
Fiorello H. La Guardia (1882-1947), U.S. Congressman (R and Socialist) and Mayor of New York City (R and Fusion Party). Quoted in *The Harlemite*, Apr. 23, 1923.

56. Treason is more often the result of weakness than of a deliberate plan to betray.
François de La Rochefoucauld (1613-1680), French nobleman and writer. *Reflexions ou Sentences et Maximes Morales*, 1665.

57. True patriotism sometimes requires of men to act exactly contrary, at one period, to that which it does at another.
Robert E. Lee (1807-1870), General in Chief, Confederate Army. Quoted in *The New York Times*, Jan. 19, 1957.

58. Gold is good in its place, but living, brave, patriotic men are better than gold.
Abraham Lincoln (1809-1865), 16th President of the United States (R-IL). Quoted by Carl Schurz in Simon Wolf's 70th Year Book, 1903.

59. Hope is the mainspring of patriotism.
David Lloyd George, 1st Earl of Dwyfor (1863-1945), Prime Minister of Great Britain (Liberal). Speech, House of Commons, Oct. 30, 1919.

60. Let us abandon this narrow conception of patriotism, which consists of the doctrine, "My country right or wrong." There is a nobler doctrine ... "My country must always be right."
Meyer London (1871-1926), U.S. Congressman (Socialist-NY). Speech to Congress, Jan. 18, 1916.

61. If Fascism ever came to America it would be on a program of Americanism.
Huey P. Long (1893-1935), Governor of Louisiana and U.S. Senator (D-LA). Quoted in *U.S. Army Orientation Fact Sheet No. 64*, Mar. 24, 1945.

62. Newfangled and artificial treasons have been the great engines by which violent factions, the natural offspring of free government, have usually wreaked their alternate malignity on each other.
James Madison (1751-1836), 4th President of the United States (Democratic Republican-VA). *The Federalist*, No. 10, Nov. 23, 1787.

63. Patriotism is a kind of religion; it is the egg from which wars are hatched.
Guy de Maupassant (1850-1893), French writer. *My Uncle Sosthenes*.

64. The issue between the Republicans and the Democrats is clearly drawn. It has been deliberately drawn by those who have been in charge of twenty years of treason.
Joseph R. McCarthy (1908-1957), U.S. Senator (R-WI). Speech, Charleston, WV, Feb. 4, 1954.

65. Every Frenchman has two mistresses: his own, and France.
Napoléon I (1769-1821), military leader and Emperor of France. *Maxims*.

66. While it is dangerous to see nothing wrong in America, it is wrong to see nothing right in America.
Richard M. Nixon, 37th President of the United States (R-CA). Presidential nomination acceptance address, Republican National Convention, Chicago, IL, July 27, 1960.

67. There are things a man must not do to save a nation.
John O'Leary (1830-1907), Irish patriot and separatist. Quoted by W. B. Yeats, *Autobiographies*, 1927.

68. The Communism of the English intellectual is something explicable enough. It is the patriotism of the deracinated.
George Orwell (Eric Blair) (1903-1950), English writer. *A Collection of Essays*, 1954.

69. Patriotism is usually stronger than class-hatred, and always stronger than internationalism.
George Orwell. *A Collection of Essays*, 1954.

70. I believe in the United States of America as a government of the people, by the people, for the people; whose just powers are derived from the consent of the governed; a democracy in a republic; a sovereign nation of many sovereign states; a perfect union, one and inseparable; established upon those principles of freedom, equality, justice, and humanity for which American patriots sacrificed their lives and fortunes. I therefore believe it is my duty to my country to love it, to support its constitution, to obey its laws, to respect its flag, and to defend it against all enemies.
   William Tyler Page (1868-1942), clerk, U.S. House of Representatives. *The American's Creed.* Adopted by the House, Apr. 3, 1918.

71. These are the times that try men's souls. The summer soldier and the sunshine patriot will, in this crisis, shrink from the service of their country; but he that stands it *now* deserves the love and thanks of man and woman.
   Thomas Paine (1737-1809), American political philosopher. *The Pennsylvania Journal*, Dec. 19, 1776.

72. Unawed by Opinion,
Unseduced by Flattery:
Undismayed by disaster,
He confronted Life with antique Courage:
And Death with Christian Hope:
In the Great Civil War
He withstood his People for his Country.
   James Louis Petigru (1789-1863), Member, South Carolina House of Representatives (Union and Anti-Nullification). Written by himself and inscribed on his tombstone, Charleston, SC.

73. We rode together in a streetcar marked "Socialism," but I got off at the stop "Independent Poland."
   Josif Pilsudski (1867-1935), General, Polish Army, and President of Poland. Quoted in *Time*, Aug. 14, 1933.

74. America is too great for small dreams.
   Ronald Reagan, 40th President of the United States (R-CA). 1983.

75. Americanism is a question of principle, of purpose, of idealism, of character. It is not a matter of birthplace or creed or line of descent.
   Theodore Roosevelt (1858-1919), 26th President of the United States (R-NY). Speech, Washington, DC, 1909.

76. There are men walking about the streets of this city tonight who ought to be taken out at sunrise tomorrow and shot for treason.
   Elihu Root (1845-1937), U.S. Senator (R-NY), U.S. Secretary of War, U.S. Secretary of State, and Nobel Laureate in Peace. Quoted in *The New York Times*, 1917.

77. Patriots always talk of dying for their country and never of killing for their country.
   Bertrand Russell, 3rd Earl Russell of Kingston (1872-1970), British philosopher and reformer. *Autobiography*, 1967.

78. Patriotism is the passion of fools and the most foolish of passions.
   Arthur Schopenhauer (1788-1860), German philosopher. *The American Freeman.*

79. Our country, right or wrong! When right to be kept right; when wrong, to be put right!
   Carl Schurz (1829-1906), U.S. Senator (R-MO). Speech, Oct. 17, 1899.

80. When our actions do not, our fears do make us traitors.
   William Shakespeare (1564-1616), English writer. *Macbeth*, IV, ii.

81. You'll never have a quiet world until you knock the patriotism out of the human race.
   George Bernard Shaw (1856-1950), Nobel Laureate in Literature (Great Britain). *O'Flaherty, V. C.*

82. Patriotism is a pernicious, psychopathic form of idiocy.
   George Bernard Shaw. *L'Esprit Français.*

83. I like to be in America
OK by me in America
Everything free in America
For a small fee in America!
   Stephen Sondheim, American composer. Song, "America," *West Side Story*, 1957.

84. Patriotism, like charity, begins at home.
   John L. Spaulding (1840-1916), American Roman Catholic archbishop. *Opportunity and Other Essays*, 1899.

85. The virtue of patriotism is subordinant in most souls to individual and family aggrandizement.
   Elizabeth Cady Stanton (1815-1902), 1st President, National Woman Suffrage Association. *History of Woman Suffrage*, 1881.

86. Patriotism is not a short and frenzied outburst of emotion but the tranquil and steady dedication of a lifetime.
   Adlai E. Stevenson (1900-1965), Governor of Illinois (D) and U.S. Ambassador to the United Nations. Speech, American Legion, New York City, Aug. 27, 1952.

87. You should have as much faith in America as I have.

Margaret Thatcher, Prime Minister of Great Britain (Conservative). CBS, *Face the Nation*, July 19, 1987.

88. I am not liberal, but I am national.

Louis-Adolphe Thiers (1797-1877), 1st President of the Third French Republic. July 1836.

89. We must stand for America, America, forever.

James Strom Thurmond, U.S. Senator (D and R-SC). Supporting a Senate resolution of "profound disappointment" over the Supreme Court's *Texas* v. *Johnson* flag-burning decision, July 1989.

90. It is good to die for our country!

Joseph Trumpeldor (1882-1920), Russian military hero and founder, Jewish Legion. Dying words, Tel Hai, Palestine, Mar. 1, 1920.

91. Our country is that spot to which our heart is bound.

Voltaire (François-Marie Arouet) (1694-1778), French historian and dramatist. *Le Fanatisme*, I.

92. Put none but Americans on guard tonight.

George Washington (1732-1799), 1st President of the United States (VA). Instructions, Apr. 30, 1777.

93. Thank God, I – I also – am an American!

Daniel Webster (1782-1852), U.S. Congressman (Federalist-NH and MA), U.S. Senator (Federalist and Whig-MA), and U.S. Secretary of State. Speech at the completion of the Bunker Hill Monument, Breed's Hill, Boston, MA, June 17, 1843 (2nd Bunker Hill oration).

94. Patriotism has become a mere self-assertion, a sentimentality of flag-cheering with no constructive duties.

H. G. Wells (1866-1946), British writer. *The Future in America*.

95. Patriotism is the virtue of the vicious.

Oscar Wilde (1854-1900), Irish writer. In conversation.

96. Some people are arguing that the Negro has nothing to celebrate in this *[U.S.]* Bicentennial. He has everything to celebrate. He has overcome all kinds of obstacles; if he cannot celebrate, no American can.

Roy Wilkins, Executive Director, National Association for the Advancement of Colored People. Quoted in *San Francisco Examiner & Chronicle*, Nov. 30, 1975.

97. The nation's honor is dearer than the nation's comfort; yes, than the nation's life itself.

Woodrow Wilson (1856-1924), 28th President of the United States (D-NJ). Speech, Jan. 29, 1916.

98. You're not supposed to be so blind with patriotism that you can't face reality. Wrong is wrong no matter who does it or says it.

Malcolm X (Malcolm Little) (1925-1965), American black power advocate. *Malcolm X Speaks Out*.

99. *J'accuse!* (I accuse!)

Émile Zola (1840-1902), French writer. Beginning of an open letter to Félix Faure, President of France, accusing government and military officials of conspiracy, complicity, and "high treason against humanity" in the Dreyfus case. *L'Aurore*, Jan. 13, 1898.

Chapter 67

Negotiation and Compromise

1. As long as there is a great disparity of power which makes negotiations seem to be unnecessary to one side, that causes them to believe that they can accomplish their purposes without it.
   Dean Acheson (1893-1971), U.S. Secretary of State (D). Quoted by David Horowitz, *The Free World Colossus*, 1965.

2. The one sure way to conciliate a tiger is to allow oneself to be devoured.
   Konrad Adenauer (1876-1967), Chancellor of West Germany. Quoted in Fred Metcalf, *The Penguin Dictionary of Modern Humorous Quotations*, 1986.

3. Please all and you please none.
   Aesop (620-560 B.C.), Greek fabulist. *The Miller, His Son, and Their Ass.*

4. The telephone number is 1-202-456-1414 *[The White House]*. When you're serious about peace, call us.
   James A. Baker III, U.S. Secretary of the Treasury (R), U.S. Secretary of State, White House Chief of Staff, and presidential campaign manager. Statement to Israeli officials, June 1990.

5. You are not supposed to begin negotiations with concessions. You start with differences of opinion and you narrow them down. Sadat and I know what our differences are and we are prepared to negotiate an accord.
   Menachem Begin (1913-1992), Prime Minister of Israel (Likud), and Nobel Laureate in Peace. Remark after Egyptian President Anwar Sadat's visit to Jerusalem, Sept. 1975.

6. Lord, if only I could have talked with Hitler, all this might have been avoided.
   William E. Borah (1865-1940), U.S. Senator (R-ID). Remark on hearing of Germany's invasion of Poland, Sept. 1, 1939.

7. All government – indeed, every human benefit and enjoyment, every virtue and every prudent act, – is founded on compromise and barter.
   Edmund Burke (1729-1797), British statesman. Speech on Conciliation with America, Mar. 22, 1775.

8. The people await action. They did not send us here to bicker. Let us negotiate soon – and hard. But in the end, let us produce.
   George Bush, 41st President of the United States (R-TX). Inaugural address, Jan. 20, 1989.

9. You're constantly trading assets back and forth to get your program.
   Clark P. Clifford, U.S. Secretary of Defense and Special Counsel to the President (D). Interview with Bill Moyers, PBS, 1981.

10. A workable solution should have no losers.
    Chester A. Crocker, U.S. Assistant Secretary of State. In reference to conflict between Cuba, Angola, and South Africa. Quoted in *The New York Times*, Dec. 18, 1988.

11. When you accept our views, we shall be in full agreement with you.
    Moshe Dayan (1915-1981), Chief of Staff, Israel Defense Forces, and Minister of Defense (Labour). Comment to U.S. Secretary of State Cyrus Vance. Quoted in *The New York Times*, Aug. 11, 1977.

12. As long as we are still talking, that's progress.
    Kamu De Almida, Ambassador of Angola to Egypt. Quoted in *The Washington Post*, June 26, 1988.

13. Finality is not the language of politics.
    Benjamin Disraeli, 1st Earl of Beaconsfield (1804-1881), Prime Minister of Great Britain (Conservative). Speech, House of Commons, Feb. 28, 1859.

14. Public men have, however, to pick their steps as best they may, for the straight path would lead too often to the cliff-edge.

Arthur Conan Doyle (1859-1930), British writer and Conservative candidate for Parliament. *Micah Clarke*, 1888.

15. If you are scared to go the brink, you are lost.
John Foster Dulles (1888-1959), U.S. Secretary of State and U.S. Senator (R-NY). Quoted in *Life*, 1956.

16. Since negotiation would have to take place after the war, why not have negotiations before and instead of the war?
Abba Eban, Foreign Secretary of Israel, and Israeli Ambassador to the United Nations (Labor). Statement to Abdul Rahman Azzam, Secretary General of the Arab League, 1947.

17. Time and again governments have rejected proposals today – and longed for them tomorrow.
Abba Eban. Quoted in *The New York Times*, Oct. 9, 1968.

18. You may gain temporary appeasement by a policy of concession to violence, but you do not gain lasting peace that way.
Anthony Eden (1897-1977), Prime Minister of Great Britain (Conservative). 1939.

19. A kingdom knows no kindred.
Elizabeth I (1533-1603), Queen of England. Letter to Henry Sidney, 1565.

20. We lost the American colonies because we lacked the statesmanship to know the right time and the manner of yielding what is impossible to keep.
Elizabeth II, Queen of Great Britain. Speech, Philadelphia, PA, July 1976.

21. Nothing astonishes men so much as common sense and plain dealing.
Ralph Waldo Emerson (1803-1882), American writer. *Essays*, First Series, "Art," 1865.

22. Issuing an ultimatum is not negotiation.
Thomas M. Foglietta, U.S. Congressman (Ind and D-PA). House debate, Jan. 10, 1991.

23. You're bombing that little piss-ant country up there *[Vietnam]*, and you think you can blow them up. You've been doing this all the time. It's a bunch of crap about wanting to negotiate.
J. William Fulbright, U.S. Senator (D-AR). Comment on meeting with Johnson administration strategists, 1967. Quoted in Merle Miller, *Lyndon: An Oral Biography*, 1980.

24. You have a solid state behind you, a united nation, a great army. For my part, I am too poor to afford bending.
Charles de Gaulle (1890-1970), President of France. Remark to Winston Churchill, who advocated flexibility in dealing with Pres. Franklin Roosevelt. Quoted in Jean Lacouture, *De Gaulle: The Rebel*, 1990.

25. Hot heads and cold hearts never solved anything.
Billy Graham, American evangelist. 1980.

26. No terms except an unconditional and immediate surrender can be accepted. I propose to move immediately on your works.
Ulysses S. Grant (1822-1885), 18th President of the United States (R-OH). Message to Confederate general Simon Bolivar Buckner, who had suggested a negotiated surrender of Fort Donaldson, TN, Feb. 16, 1862.

27. The decision *[to partition Palestine into Jewish and Arab lands]* is not directed against either of the two national groups that inhabit Palestine. On the contrary, it corresponds to the fundamental interests of both peoples.
Andrei A. Gromyko (1909-1989), Soviet Foreign Minister, Ambassador to the United States and to the United Nations. Speech, U.N. General Assembly, 1947.

28. Wars are ... often the product of the conflicting intentions of decent men who have lost the patience to negotiate.
Vance Hartke, U.S. Senator (D-IN). *Playboy*, May 1970.

29. When a man tells me he's going to put all his cards on the table, I always look up his sleeve.
Leslie Hore-Belisha (1893-1957), Minister of Transport and Secretary of War, Great Britain. Remark to Winston Churchill regarding Mussolini, 1938.

30. Come now, and let us reason together.
Old Testament, *Isaiah* 1:18. Favorite quotation of Pres. Lyndon Johnson during congressional negotiations of civil rights legislation, 1964-1965.

31. I'm a compromiser and a maneuverer. I try to get *something*. That's the way our system works.
Lyndon B. Johnson (1908-1973), 36th President of the United States (D-TX). Quoted in *The New York Times*, Dec. 8, 1963.

32. Don't spit in the soup. We've all got to eat.
Lyndon B. Johnson. Political advice, 1965.

33. A dialogue is more than two monologues.
Max M. Kampelman, U.S. arms negotiator. Quoted in *Time*, Mar. 11, 1985.

34. The Soviets approach arms control much the same way Andy Warhol approached art: anything you can get away with.

Jack F. Kemp, U.S. Congressman and U.S. Secretary of Housing and Urban Development (R-NY). Quoted in *Newsweek*, May 16, 1987.

35. Let us never negotiate out of fear, but let us never fear to negotiate.
John F. Kennedy (1917-1963), 35th President of the United States (D-MA). Inaugural address, Jan. 20, 1961.

36. We cannot negotiate with those who say, "What's mine is mine, and what's yours is negotiable."
John F. Kennedy. Speech, July 25, 1961.

37. The Soviet Union prepared to test *[nuclear weapons]* while we were at the table negotiating with them. If they fooled us once, it is their fault; if they fool us twice, it is our fault.
John F. Kennedy. Press conference, Nov. 8, 1961.

38. I'm against any deal I'm not in on.
Robert S. Kerr (1896-1963), U.S. Senator and Governor of Oklahoma (D). Attributed.

39. However acute the ideological differences between the two systems – the Socialist and the Capitalist – we must solve questions in dispute among states not by war, but by peaceful negotiation.
Nikita S. Khrushchev (1894-1971), Premier of the U.S.S.R. Speech, Moscow, Dec. 21, 1957.

40. If you cannot catch a bird of paradise, better take a wet hen.
Nikita S. Khrushchev. Quoted in *Time*, Jan. 6, 1958.

41. I did not know anybody cared any longer about these sorts of things. Now I have a hold on the fools.
William Lamb, 2nd Viscount Melbourne (1779-1848), Prime Minister of Great Britain (Tory). Comment when a list of would-be baronets was shown to him, 1839.

42. The French monarchist and I shook hands, knowing that each of us would gladly have hung the other. But at the moment, our interests coincided.
V. I. Lenin (1870-1924), Premier of the U.S.S.R. Description of negotiations with a French officer in 1917. *Works*, Vol. XXVIII.

43. Before going into a room, make sure you can get out again.
Yegor Ligachev, Communist Party member, U.S.S.R. Speech, Communist Party Congress, Moscow, June 1988.

44. The genius of America is in its ability to make adjustments.
David E. Lilienthal (1899-1981), Chairman, Tennessee Valley Authority, and Chairman, U.S. Atomic Energy Commission. Quoted in *The New Dictionary of American Thoughts*, 1957.

45. Compromise makes a good umbrella but a poor roof; it is a temporary expedient often wise in party politics, almost sure to be unwise in statesmanship.
James Russell Lowell (1819-1891), U.S. Ambassador to Spain and Great Britain. Speech, Birmingham, England, Oct. 6, 1884.

46. We will be criticized tomorrow if we do not manage to understand each other today.
Patrice Lumumba (1925-1961), 1st Prime Minister, the Congo (Zaire). Cable to political opponent Moise Tshombe, June 15, 1960.

47. Jaw-jaw is better than war-war.
Harold Macmillan (1894-1986), Prime Minister of Great Britain (Conservative). Speech, 1958.

48. Only free men can negotiate; prisoners cannot enter into contracts. Your freedom and mine cannot be separated.
Nelson Mandela, founder, African National Congress, South Africa. Comment about an offer to set him free if he would agree to desist from anti-government activities. Quoted in *Time*, Feb. 25, 1985.

49. We should support whatever the enemy opposes and oppose whatever the enemy supports.
Mao Tse-tung (1893-1976), Chairman, Communist Party of China. *Selected Works*, II, 1954.

50. I could sit down and talk with the devil if necessary.
Donald McHenry, U.S. Ambassador to the United Nations. Response to a question about how he, as a black man, could talk with the President of South Africa, Aug. 1985.

51. War should never be entered upon until every agency of peace has failed; peace is preferable to war in almost every contingency. Arbitration is the true method of settlement of international as well as local or individual differences.
William McKinley (1843-1901), 25th President of the United States (R-OH). First inaugural address, Mar. 4, 1897.

52. Give your opponent an out. Look at the crises from his point of view.... Try to pick an option that achieves your purpose at minimal cost to him – military, political, or otherwise.

Robert S. McNamara, U.S. Secretary of Defense (D). Quoted on PBS, *War and Peace in the Nuclear Age,* Feb. 1989.

53. We should not check American ideals at the door when we engage in discussions with other nations.

George J. Mitchell, U.S. Senator (D-ME). Interview, PBS, *MacNeil-Lehrer News Hour,* June 1, 1990.

54. I propose that we insert a "not" before every verb in the text.

Vyacheslav Mikhailovich Molotov (1890-1990), Foreign Minister of the U.S.S.R. Procedural motion during negotiations with the U.S. delegation. Quoted in Leonard Mosley, *Dulles,* 1978.

55. One interest must be opposed to another interest. Vices, as they exist, must be turned against each other.

Gouverneur Morris (1752-1816), U.S. Senator (Federalist-NY), U.S. Commissioner to England, and U.S. Minister to France. Debate, Constitutional Convention, Philadelphia, PA, 1787.

56. The term negotiation implies compromise; painful concessions on the part of both parties.

Edward R. Murrow (1908-1965), American broadcast journalist and Director, United States Information Agency. Feb. 6, 1953.

57. To negotiate with effect, force should be at hand, and in a situation to act.

Horatio Nelson, Viscount Nelson (1758-1805), British admiral. Quoted in Robert Southey, *Life of Nelson,* 1813.

58. A politician knows that the best way to be a winner is to make the other side feel it does not have to be a loser.

Richard M. Nixon, 37th President of the United States (R-CA). Eulogy for Everett M. Dirksen, Sept. 8, 1969.

59. You can't make a deal with him, and you can't make one without him.

Richard M. Nixon. Comment on the possibility of peace negotiations with Yasser Arafat, Chairman of the Palestine Liberation Organization. Interview, *The Washington Times,* Apr. 4, 1988.

60. To militate against the compromising mentality and the plans it spawns, which are either contrary to our people's cause of national liberation or aim to liquidate this cause through "proposed Palestinian entities" or through a Palestinian state on part of the Palestinian national soil. Also to oppose these plans through armed struggle and political struggle of the masses connected to it.

Palestine Liberation Organization. Political program adopted at the Palestinian Popular Congress and Eleventh Extraordinary Council, Jan. 1973.

61. The tyranny of tactics (*Taughian at-taktit*)

Palestinian slogan, 1970's. Derogatory reference to tactics (negotiation) versus strategy (armed struggle) in the conflict with Israel.

62. A fool uttereth all his mind; but a wise man keeps it until afterwards.

Old Testament, *Proverbs* 29:11.

63. You are a rare good fellow and you have got the American spirit.... You are dead honest, and I like that too; but in the great office to which you are being so certainly called, you have got to remember that nobody is ever surely right and nobody ever absolutely wrong. You have got to remember that compromise and adjustment are unfailingly necessary to all human progress.

Lemuel E. Quigg (1863-1919), U.S. Congressman (R-NY). Letter to Pres. Theodore Roosevelt, 1904.

64. You always talk "no compromise" at a convention until you get the best you can. Then you quit.

Joseph L. Rauh, Jr. (1911-1992), American attorney and civil rights activist. Remark to reporters during the Democratic National Convention, 1964.

65. Insist more on the heart of the matter rather than the procedures.

Michel Rocard, Prime Minister of France. Quoted on ABC, *This Week,* Mar. 9, 1991.

66. We never won a conference.

Will Rogers (1879-1935), American humorist. *Ziegfield Follies,* 1922.

67. When you know when to laugh and when to look upon things as too absurd to be taken seriously, the other person is ashamed to carry through even though he was serious about it.

Anna Eleanor Roosevelt (1884-1962), First Lady and U.S. Delegate to the United Nations. Letter to President Truman, May 14, 1945.

68. When you write an international document, you try not to let the words interfere with getting as much agreement as possible and as much acceptance as possible to obtain the ends you want.

Anna Eleanor Roosevelt. Speech, "The Declaration of Human Rights," 1949.

69. The Soviets look on this *[compromise]* as evidence of weakness rather than as a gesture of good will.

Anna Eleanor Roosevelt. Statement, 1949.

70. To accomplish almost anything worthwhile it is necessary to compromise between the ideal and the practical.

Franklin D. Roosevelt (1882-1945), 32nd President of the United States (D-NY). Quoted in Pearson and Allen, "How the President Works," *Harper's Magazine*, June 1936.

71. No man can tame a tiger into a kitten by stroking it. There can be no appeasement with ruthlessness. There can be no reasoning with an incendiary bomb.

Franklin D. Roosevelt. In reference to Hitler's Germany. Fireside Chat, Dec. 29, 1940.

72. Jesse Jackson wants to be a crisis negotiator. If there isn't a crisis, Jesse will negotiate one.

Louis Rukeyser, American economist and journalist. PBS, *Wall Street Week*, July 22, 1988.

73. We were eyeball-to-eyeball and the other fellow just blinked.

Dean Rusk, U.S. Secretary of State (D). Remark during Cuban missile crisis, Oct. 1962.

74. One of the best ways to persuade others is with your ears – by listening to them.

Dean Rusk. Quoted in Dee Danner Barwick, *Great Words of Our Time*, 1970.

75. I do not want to place my cards before the microphones.

Anwar Sadat (1918-1981), President of Egypt and Nobel Laureate in Peace. In reference to negotiations with Israel. Quoted on Cairo Radio, Sept. 8, 1975.

76. There are some things that it is important to do quietly – not in the eye of the television cameras.

Brent Scowcroft, Admiral, U.S. Navy, and National Security Advisor (R). Interview, CNN, Apr. 7, 1991.

77. A skillful negotiator will most carefully distinguish between the little and the great objects of his business, and will be as frank and open in the former, as he will be secret and pertinacious in the latter.

Philip Dormer Stanhope, 4th Earl of Chesterfield (1694-1773), Member of Parliament, Great Britain (Whig), and Lord-Lieutenant of Ireland. *Maxims*.

78. A temporary compromise is a diplomatic act, but a permanent compromise is an abandonment of a goal.

Leo Stein (1872-1947), American writer. *Journey into the Self*, 1950.

79. Arbitration should become a substitute for war in reality as well as in name.

Charles Sumner (1811-1874), U.S. Senator (D, R, and Free Soil-MA). Resolution introduced in the Senate, May 31, 1872.

80. The King of Tung Hai said: Now you have massed troops and enriched the enemy who is determined to fight to the death. This is no strategy! Let them know that an escape route is open and they will flee and disperse. Show him there is a road to safety, and create in his mind the idea that there is an alternative to death.

Sun-tzu (c.400 B.C.), Chinese writer of the Age of Warring States. *The Art of War*.

81. Turmoil can be very disturbing.

Margaret Thatcher, Prime Minister of Great Britain (Conservative). Remark on negotiating. Press conference, NATO meeting, Brussels, Dec. 4, 1989.

82. I want my money back.

Margaret Thatcher. Expression of dissatisfaction with the way the European Common Market was progressing. Quoted in *The Washington Post*, Nov. 25, 1990.

83. The lion and the lamb can lie down together ... but the lamb won't get much sleep.

Morris K. Udall, U.S. Congressman (D-AZ). *Too Funny to Be President*, 1988.

84. It is not important with whom I sit down at the table. I'll hold talks with the cleaning lady if she's properly authorized.

Lech Walesa, President of Poland, trade unionist, and founder, Solidarity. Remark, Lenin Shipyard, Gdansk, Poland, Aug. 29, 1988.

85. Conversations and negotiations with Arabs are not unlike chasing a mirage in the desert: full of promise and good to look at, but likely to lead you to death by thirst.

Chaim Weizmann (1874-1952), 1st President of Israel. *Trial and Error*, 1949.

86. I believe in taking half a loaf until the full loaf comes along.

L. Douglas Wilder, Governor of Virginia (D). Interview, ABC, *This Week*, Jan. 14, 1990.

87. Better to go down fighting than to dip your colors in dishonorable compromise.

Woodrow Wilson (1856-1924), 28th President of the United States (D-NJ). Remark to his wife on the Senate discussions of the League of Nations treaty he offered, 1919.

Chapter 68

Nicknames

1. Warhawks
   Pro-war Members of Congress, 1812.

2. Hunkers
   Democrats with no political principles, but with a "hunkering" for public office. 1847.

3. Know Nothings
   American Party, 1850's.

4. Copperheads
   Northern "Peace Democrats" who opposed battle with the South in the Civil War, 1861-1865.

5. Goo-goos
   Civil Service reformers, Early 1900's.

6. The Great Assassin
   Abdul the Damned
   Abdul Hamid II (1842-1918), Sultan of Turkey.

7. Battling Bella
   Bellicose Bella
   Hurricane Bella
   Mother Courage
   The Mouth that Roared
   Bella Abzug, U.S. Congresswoman (D-NY).

8. Mrs. President
   Abigail Adams (1744-1818), First Lady.

9. Mr. President by Three Votes
   His Rotundity
   Old Sink or Swim
   The Colossus of Independence
   John Adams (1735-1826), 2nd President of the United States (Federalist-MA).

10. Every city and town at which he *[John Quincy Adams]* arrives sends out its multitudes to welcome "the old man eloquent."
    [The phrase originated in John Milton's Sonnet to the Lady Margaret Ley.*]*
    John Quincy Adams (1767-1848), 6th President of the United States (Ind-MA). Philip Hone, *Diary*, Nov. 10, 1843.

11. *Der Alte* (The Old Man)
    Konrad Adenauer (1876-1967), Chancellor of West Germany.

12. The Emancipator
    Alexander II (1818-1881), Czar of Russia.

13. The Young Steer
    The Old Steer
    Alexander III (1845-1894), Czar of Russia.

14. Private John
    John M. Allen (1846-1917), U.S. Congressman (D-MS).

15. The Ohio Gong
    Fog Horn
    William Allen (1803-1879), U.S. Congressman (D), U.S. Senator, and Governor of Ohio.

16. Big Daddy
    Idi Amin, President of Uganda.

17. Randy Andy
    Andrew, Prince of Great Britain.

18. The Traitorous Hero
    The Traitor
    Benedict Arnold (1741-1801), Major General, Continental Army.

19. Dear Alben
    The Veep
    Alben W. Barkley (1877-1956), U.S. Congressman (D-KY), U.S. Senator, and Vice President of the United States.

20. The Veepess
    Elizabeth J. Barkley (1912-1964), Second Lady.

21. Mayor Barely
    Marion Barry, Mayor of Washington, DC (D). 1990.

22. The Brains of the Confederacy

Judah P. Benjamin (1811-1884), U.S. Senator (Whig and Democrat-LA); Confederate Attorney General, Secretary of War, and Secretary of State.

23. Old Bullion
The Gold Humbug
Thomas Hart Benton (1782-1858), U.S. Senator and U.S. Congressman (D-MO).

24. Loophole Lloyd
Tax Man
Lloyd M. Bentsen, Jr. U.S. Congressman and U.S. Senator (D-TX).

25. Emperor Nick
Emperor Nick of the Bribery Bank
Nicholas Biddle (1786-1844), President, Second Bank of the United States.

26. The Man
The Edged Knife
Theodore G. Bilbo (1877-1947), U.S. Senator and Governor of Mississippi (D).

27. The Iron Chancellor
The Man of Blood and Iron
Otto von Bismarck-Schoenhausen (1815-1898), Chancellor of Germany.

28. The Plumed Knight
The Uncrowned King
The Tattooed Man
Phryne of the Senate
James G. Blaine (1830-1893), U.S. Congressman, U.S. Senator, and Speaker of the House (R-ME).

29. Silver Dick
Richard P. Bland (1835-1899), U.S. Congressman (D-MO). Leader of the House "free silver" bloc, 1890's.

30. Old Dutch Cleanser
Richard Blankenburg (1843-1918), Mayor of Philadelphia, PA.

31. Boleslav the Mighty
The Charlemagne of Poland
Boleslav I (c.966-1025), King of Poland.

32. The Liberator
The Washington of Colombia
Simón Bolívar (1783-1830), Supreme Chief of Colombia, President of Peru, and founder of Bolivia.

33. The Lone Lion of Idaho
The Great Opposer
William E. Borah (1865-1940), U.S. Senator (R-ID).

34. The People's Attorney
Louis D. Brandeis (1856-1941), U.S. Supreme Court Justice.

35. Governor Moonbeam
Edmund G. (Jerry) Brown, Jr., Governor of California (D).

36. Boy Orator of the Platte
The Black Eagle of Nebraska
The Silver Knight of the West
The Great Commoner
William Jennings Bryan (1860-1925), U.S. Secretary of State (D).

37. The Bachelor President
Ten Percent Jimmy
The Sage of Wheatland
James Buchanan (1791-1868), 15th President of the United States (D-PA).

38. I am an old public functionary *[O. P. F.]*.
James Buchanan. Presidential campaign speech, Lancaster, PA, 1856.

39. The Dinner Bell
Edmund Burke (1729-1797), British statesman.

40. The Napoleon of the West
The Great American Rascal
The Mephistopheles of American Politics
Aaron Burr (1756-1836), U.S. Senator and Vice President of the United States (D-NY).

41. The Warhawk
The Napoleon of Slavery
The Great Nullifier
John C. Calhoun (1782-1850), U.S. Congressman (D-SC), U.S. Senator, U.S. Secretary of War, U.S. Secretary of State, and Vice President of the United States.

42. Foul-mouthed Joe
Uncle Joe
Czar Cannon
Joseph G. Cannon (1836-1926), U.S. Congressman and Speaker of the House (R-IL).

43. The Peanut President
Hot Shot
Jimmy Who?
Jimmy Carter, 39th President of the United States (D-GA).

44. The Iron Magnolia
Rosalynn Carter, First Lady.

45. The Great Father at Detroit

Lewis Cass (1782-1866), Governor of Michigan (D), U.S. Senator, U.S. Secretary of State, and U.S. Secretary of War.

46. The Yankee Castro
Raul H. Castro, Governor of Arizona, and U.S. Ambassador to El Salvador, Bolivia, and Argentina (D).

47. Ten Percent Tony
Anton J. Cermak (1873-1933), Mayor of Chicago, IL (D).

48. Happy
Albert B. Chandler (1898-1991), Governor of Kentucky (D), U.S. Senator, and U.S. Baseball Commissioner.

49. The Man of Blood
The Royal Martyr
Charles I (1600-1649), King of England.

50. The Merry Monarch
Old Rowley
Charles II (1630-1685), King of England.

51. Millboy of the Slashes
The Cock of Kentucky
The War Hawk
The Great Kentuckian
Harry of the West
Prince Hal
The Great Compromiser
The Farmer of Ashland
The Old Prince
The Great Commoner
The Great Pacificator
Henry Clay (1777-1852), U.S. Senator (National Republican and Whig-KY), Speaker of the House, and U.S. Secretary of State.

52. The Tiger
Georges Clemenceau (1841-1929), Premier of France and journalist.

53. The Beast of Buffalo
The Buffalo Hangman
The Veto President
The Pretender
Backbone
Uncle Jumbo
The Stuffed Prophet
The Dumb Prophet
The People's President
The Man of Destiny
Grover Cleveland (1837-1908), 22nd and 24th President of the United States (D-NY).

54. Peter Porcupine
William Cobbett (1763-1835), Member of Parliament, Great Britain (Tory) and political journalist.

55. Silent Cal
Calvin Coolidge (1872-1933), 30th President of the United States (R-MA).

56. Tommy the Cork
The Cork
Thomas G. Corcoran (1900-1981), special assistant to the U.S. Attorney General, and special counsel, Reconstruction Finance Corporation (D).

57. King of the Wild Frontier
The Munchhausen of the West
David Crockett (1786-1836), U.S. Congressman (Anti-Jacksonian-TN).

58. The Pothole Senator
Alfonse D'Amato, U.S. Senator (R-NY).

59. The President-Maker
Foxy Harry
Harry M. Daugherty (1860-1941), U.S. Attorney General (R).

60. Old Pint-a-Day
Jeff Davis (1862-1913), U.S. Senator and Governor of Arkansas (D).

61. King Jeff the First
Jefferson Davis (1808-1889), U.S. Congressman (D-MS), U.S. Senator, (D-MS), U.S. Secretary of War, and President, Confederate States of America. 1862.

62. The Bishop of Tammany
The Pope of Tammany
The Last of the New York Bosses
Mr. Tammany
Carmine De Sapio, Tammany Hall leader, New York City (D).

63. The Lover of Mankind
No. 9653
Eugene V. Debs (1855-1926), American Socialist.

64. Gangbuster
Buster
The Little Man on the Wedding Cake
The Boy Scout
Thomas E. Dewey (1902-1971), Governor of New York (R).

65. Loaded Dies
Martin Dies (1901-1972), U.S. Congressman (D-TX).

66. The Wizard of Ooze
Everett M. Dirksen (1896-1969), U.S. Congressman and U.S. Senator (R-IL).

67. The Pocket Dictator
Englebert Dollfuss (1892-1943), anti-Nazi Chancellor of Austria.

68. The Pink Lady
Helen Gahagan Douglas (1900-1980), U.S. Congresswoman (D-CA).

69. The Little Giant
Stephen A. Douglas (1813-1861), U.S. Congressman and U.S. Senator (D-IL).

70. Papa Doc
The Voodoo President
François Duvalier (1907-1971), President-for-Life, Haiti.

71. Baby Doc
Jean-Claude Duvalier, President-for-Life, Haiti.

72. Ike
Dwight D. Eisenhower (1890-1969), 34th President of the United States (R-KS).

73. The American Carlyle
The Sage of Concord
Ralph Waldo Emerson (1803-1882), American writer.

74. Hanoi Jane
The Rottenest American
Jane Fonda, American actress and political activist.

75. First Mama
Betty Ford, First Lady.

76. Calico Charlie
Charles Foster (1828-1904), U.S. Congressman (R-OH), Governor of Ohio, and U.S. Secretary of the Treasury.

77. Honey Fitz
John F. Fitzgerald (1863-1950), U.S. Congressman and Mayor of Boston, MA (D).

78. The Chief
The Old Fascist
The Enduring Fascist
Francisco Franco (1892-1975), President of Spain.

79. Poor Richard
Father of the Mail Order Catalog
The American Socrates
The Jolly Imbiber
Benjamin Franklin (1706-1790), Member, Continental Congress and Constitutional Convention, Governor of Pennsylvania, and U.S. Minister to France.

80. The Pathfinder
John Charles Frémont (1813-1890), American explorer, army officer, and U.S. Senator (R-CA).

81. Senator Halfbright
J. William Fulbright, U.S. Senator (D-AR).

82. Foghorn Funston
Edward H. Funston (1836-1911), U.S. Congressman (R-KS).

83. The Teacher President
The Preacher President
The Available Man
The Martyr President
James A. Garfield (1831-1881), 20th President of the United States (R-OH).

84. The Grand Old Man
William E. Gladstone (1809-1898), Prime Minister of Great Britain (Liberal).

85. The Fat One
Sawdust Caesar
Hermann Goering (1893-1946), German Field Marshal, founder of the Gestapo, President of the Reichstag (Nazi Parliament), and convicted war criminal.

86. The Hammerer
The Butcher
The Wooden-Indian President
The Hero of Fort Donalson
The Hero of Appomattox
Uncle Sam
Useless Grant
The American Caesar
Ulysses S. Grant (1822-1885), 18th President of the United States (R-OH).

87. The Hoosier Shakespeare
Finley H. Gray (1863-1947), U.S. Congressman (D-IN).

88. Old Figgers
Charles Henry Grosvenor (1833-1917), U.S. Congressman (R-OH).

89. The Father of the Tariff
The Little Lion
The Adulterer
Alexander Hamilton (1755-1804), Member, Continental Congress and Constitutional Convention, and U.S. Secretary of the Treasury (Federalist-NY).

90. King Hancock
King of the Smugglers
Old Mother Hancock
The Yankee Doodle Dandy
John Hancock (1737-1793), President of the Continental Congress, and Governor of Massachusetts.

91. Dollar Mark
Mark A. Hanna (1837-1904), U.S. Senator (R-OH) and Chairman, Republican National Committee.

92. The Terror of the House
Benjamin Hardin (1784-1852), U.S. Congressman (R-KY).

93. Little Ben
His Grandfather's Son
Kid-Gloves Harrison
Chinese Harrison
Timid Harrison
Benjamin Harrison (1833-1901), 23rd President of the United States (R-IN).

94. General Mum
The Farmer President
Log Cabin Harrison
The Hero of Tippecanoe
Old Tippecanoe
The Washington of the West
Hard Cider Harrison
William Henry Harrison (1773-1841), 9th President of the United States (Whig-OH).

95. Samurai Sam
Sleeping Sam
S. I. Hayakawa (1907-1992), U.S. Senator (R-CA).

96. Lemonade Lucy
Lucy Ware Webb Hayes (1831-1889), First Lady.

97. His Fraudulency
Old 8-to-7
Rutherfraud B. Hayes
Boss Thief
Granny Hayes
Rutherford B. Hayes (1822-1893), 19th President of the United States (R-OH).

98. The Little Corporal
The Paperhanger
Schickelgruber
The Buffoon
Adolf Hitler (1889-1945), Führer of the Third German Reich.

99. The Great Dissenter
Oliver Wendell Holmes, Jr. (1841-1935), U.S. Supreme Court Justice.

100. Ice Lady
Liz the Lion Killer
Virgin Liz
Elizabeth Holtzman, U.S. Congresswoman (D-NY), and District Attorney, Brooklyn, NY.

101. The Chief
The Great Engineer
The Man of Great Heart
Herbert Hoover (1874-1964), 31st President of the United States (R-IA).

102. The Master of Deceit
J. Edgar Hoover (1895-1972), Director, Federal Bureau of Investigation.

103. The Father of Texas
The Big Drunk
Samuel Houston (1793-1863), U.S. Congressman (D-TN), U.S. Senator (D-TX), 1st President of the Republic of Texas, and Governor of Texas.

104. The Great Survivor
Little Hussi
Abdul ibn Hussein, King of the Hashemite Kingdom of Jordan.

105. The Great Resigner
Harold L. Ickes (1874-1952), U.S. Secretary of the Interior (D).

106. The Modern Cincinnatus
Old Hickory
The Duel Fighter
King Andrew the First
Andrew Jackson (1767-1845), 7th President of the United States (D-TN).

107. Scoop
The Last of the Cold War Liberals
Henry M. Jackson (1912-1983), U.S. Congressman and U.S. Senator (D-WA).

108. The Confederate Cromwell
Stonewall
Tom Fool Jackson
Old Blue Light
The Sword of the Confederacy
Thomas J. Jackson (1824-1863), General, Confederate Army.

109. The Apostle of Liberty
The Friend of the People
The Pen of the Revolution
The Philosopher of Democracy
Infidel Jefferson
Oliver Jefferson Cromwell
The Sage of Monticello

Thomas Jefferson (1743-1826), 3rd President of the United States (Democratic Republican-VA).

110. Father of the Homestead Act
His Accidency
Sir Veto
The Unfortunate
Andrew Johnson (1808-1875), 17th President of the United States (War Democrat-TN).

111. LBJ
Landslide Lyndon
Lucky Lyndon
Lyndon B. Johnson (1908-1973), 36th President of the United States (D-TX).

112. The Nevada Commoner
John P. Jones (1829-1912), U.S. Senator (R-NV).

113. The Orator of Free Dirt
The Apostle of Disunion
Wolly-head
George Washington Julian (1817-1899), U.S. Congressman (Free Soil-IN).

114. King of the District *[of Columbia]*
William H. King (1863-1949), U.S. Congressman and U.S. Senator (D-UT).

115. Sleepy Phil
Philander Chase Knox (1853-1921), U.S. Senator (R-PA), U.S. Attorney General, and U.S. Secretary of State.

116. I won't be intimidated. They call me the *Mayatolla.*
Edward I. Koch, U.S. Congressman and Mayor of New York City (D). 1981.

117. The soldier's friend
Marquis de Lafayette (1757-1834), French statesman and Major General, Continental Army.

118. The Little Flower
Butch
Fiorello H. La Guardia (1882-1947), U.S. Congressman (R and Socialist) and Mayor of New York City (R and Fusion Party).

119. Wild Bill
William Langer (1886-1959), Governor of North Dakota and U.S. Senator (Independent Republican).

120. The Unknown Prime Minister
Andrew Bonar Law (1858-1923), Prime Minister of Great Britain (Conservative).

121. Uncle Robert
Marse Robert
The Gentle General
The Gentleman General
Old Ace of Spades
Robert E. Lee (1807-1870), General in Chief, Confederate Army.

122. Moratorium Bill
William Lemke (1878-1943), U.S. Congressman (R and Nonpartisan-ND).

123. The Labor Baron
John L. Lewis (1880-1969), President, United Mine Workers of America.

124. Honest Abe
The Rail-Splitter
The Great Emancipator
The Buffoon
The Baboon
The Jester
Massa Linkum
Monster
Ignoramus
The Monkey in the White House
The Hat
The Ugliest Man in Washington
The Fool in the White House
Abraham Lincoln (1809-1865), 16th President of the United States (R-IL).

125. The She-Wolf
Mary Todd Lincoln (1818-1882), First Lady.

126. The Happy Warrior of Squandermania
David Lloyd George, 1st Earl of Dwyfor, 1863-1945, Prime Minister of Great Britain (Liberal).

127. The Kingfish
Hooey Long
Huey P. Long (1893-1935), U.S. Senator and Governor of Louisiana (D).

128. Inferior Secretary
Manuel Lujan, Jr., U.S. Secretary of the Interior (R).

129. The Boneless Wonder
Ramsay MacDonald (1866-1937), Prime Minister of Great Britain (Labour).

130. Father of the Constitution
Master builder of the Constitution
The Sage of Montpelier
Jemmy
James Madison (1751-1836), 4th President of the United States (Democratic Republican-VA).

131. Madame Deficit
Marie Antoinette (1755-1793), Queen of France and wife of Louis XVI.

132. Emperor Max
Maximilian I (1459-1519), King of Germany and Holy Roman Emperor.

133. Little Mac
Mac the Unready
The Little Corporal of Unsought Fields
The Young Napoleon
George B. McClellan (1826-1885), General, U.S. Army, and Governor of New Jersey (D).

134. The Gangster's Enemy
The Gangster's Nightmare
The Man Behind the Frown
John L. McClellan (1896-1977), U.S. Congressman and U.S. Senator (D-AR).

135. The Stocking-foot Orator
The Napoleon of Protection
Prosperity's Advance Agent
William McKinley (1843-1901), 25th President of the United States (R-OH).

136. Evan the Terrible
Evan Mecham, Governor of Arizona (R).

137. King of the New Dealers
Sherman Minton (1890-1965), U.S. Senator (D-IN) and U.S. Supreme Court Justice.

138. The Last Cocked Hat
James Monroe (1758-1831), 5th President of the United States (Democratic Republican-VA).

139. The Lone Wolf of the Senate
The Wrecker
Wayne L. Morse (1900-1974), U.S. Senator (R-OR).

140. The Leaning Tower of Putty
Karl E. Mundt (1900-1974), U.S. Congressman and U.S. Senator (R-SD).

141. Silent Charlie
The Colossus of Graft
The Black Hand of Tammany
Charles F. Murphy (1858-1924), Tammany Hall leader, New York City (D).

142. Alfalfa Bill
William Murray (1869-1956), U.S. Congressman and Governor of Oklahoma (D).

143. The Lady with the Hatchet
Carry A. Nation (1846-1911), American temperance agitator.

144. Tricky Dick
Iron Butt
Gloomy Gus
Richard M. Nixon, 37th President of the United States (R-CA).

145. I've been called everything.
Richard M. Nixon. Quoted in *The Chicago Tribune*, Feb. 11, 1968.

146. Grocer George
George W. Norris (1861-1944), U.S. Senator (R and Independent Republican-NE).

147. Pass the Biscuits, Pappy
Pappy
Wilbert Lee O'Daniel (1890-1969), Governor of Texas and U.S. Senator (D).

148. Tip
Thomas P. O'Neill, Jr., U.S. Congressman and Speaker of the House (D-MA).

149. The uncrowned king of Ireland
Charles Stewart Parnell (1846-1891), nationalist leader and Member of Parliament, Ireland (Liberal).

150. The Red Pepper
Old Salt and Pepper
Claude D. Pepper (1901-1989), U.S. Senator and U.S. Congressman (D-FL).

151. Evita
Eva Perón (1919-1952), First Lady of Argentina.

152. Governor Goofy
Rudy Perpich, Governor of Minnesota (D).

153. *Roi Citoyen* (The Citizen King)
Louis Philippe (1773-1850), King of France.

154. Honest John
John C. Phillips (1870-1943), Governor of Arizona (R).

155. Handsome Frank
The Hero of Many a Well-Fought Bottle
Franklin Pierce (1804-1869), 14th President of the United States (D-NH).

156. Silent Sam
Samuel Pierce, U.S. Secretary of Housing and Urban Development (R).

157. The Great Commoner
The Napoleon of Oratory
William Pitt, 1st Earl of Chatham (1708-1778), Secretary of State, Lord Privy Seal, and leader of the House of Commons, Great Britain.

158. The Endless Pitt
The Bottomless Pit
William Pitt (The Younger) (1759-1806), Prime Minister of Great Britain.

159. The Easy Boss
Thomas Collier Platt (1833-1910), U.S. Congressman and U.S. Senator (R-NY).

160. The Napoleon of the Stump
Young Hickory
The Dark Horse
James K. Polk (1795-1849), 11th President of the United States (D-TN).

161. Quisling
Vidkun Quisling (1887-1945), Minister of Defense, Norway. He actively supported the invasion of his country by the Nazis in 1940.

162. First Mannequin
Queen Nancy
Nancy Reagan, First Lady.

163. The Teflon President
The Great Communicator
Rambling Ron
Ronald Ray Gun
Sleepy
Dopey
Ronald Reagan, 40th President of the United States (R-CA).

164. Czar Reed
The Terrible Turk
Thomas B. Reed (1839-1902), U.S. Congressman and Speaker of the House (R-ME).

165. Richard the Lionheart (*Coeur de Lion*)
Richard I (1157-1199), King of England.

166. Mr. Secretary of Everything
Mr. Clean
Elliot L. Richardson, U.S. Secretary of Defense (R), U.S. Secretary of Health, Education and Welfare, U.S. Attorney General, and U.S. Undersecretary of State.

167. Rocky
Nelson A. Rockefeller (1908-1979), Governor of New York and Vice President of the United States (R).

168. First Lady of the 20th Century
First Lady of the Free World
Mrs. Assistant President
Public Enemy Number One
Hatchet Face
Anna Eleanor Roosevelt (1884-1962), First Lady and U.S. Delegate to the United Nations.

169. That Man in the White House
Franklin D. Roosevelt (1882-1945), 32nd President of the United States (D-NY).

170. The Trustbuster
The Rough Rider
The Happy Warrior
Teddy
Teddy the Meddler
That Damned Cowboy
The Patron Saint of Dry Sundays
King Roosevelt I
Theodore Roosevelt (1858-1919), 26th President of the United States (R-NY).

171. I feel as fit as a bull moose.
Theodore Roosevelt. Remark at a press conference, Aug. 6, 1912.

172. Short-weight Jim
James S. Sherman (1855-1912), U.S. Congressman and Vice President of the United States (R-NY).

173. Sockless Jerry
Jeremiah Simpson (1842-1905), U.S. Congressman (Populist-KS).

174. The Happy Warrior
Alfred E. Smith (1873-1944), Governor of New York (D).

175. Watchdog of the Treasury
Francis Elias Spinner (1802-1890), U.S. Secretary of the Treasury.

176. Uncle Joe
The Man of Steel
Joseph Stalin (1879-1953), Premier of the U.S.S.R.

177. The Prince of Wits
Tea-Table Scoundrel
Philip Dormer Stanhope, 4th Earl of Chesterfield (1694-1773), Member of Parliament, Great Britain (Whig) and Lord-Lieutenant of Ireland.

178. The King of the Muckrakers
Joseph Lincoln Steffens (1866-1936), American journalist and reformer.

179. The prairie Franklin Roosevelt
Woordrow Wilson with warmth
Egghead
Adlai E. Stevenson (1900-1965), Governor of Illinois (D) and U.S. Ambassador to the United Nations.

180. The Slasher
The Grim Reaper
David A. Stockman, Director, Office of Management and Budget, and U.S. Congressman (R-MI).

181. The Great Persuader
Robert S. Strauss, Chairman, Democratic National Committee, and U.S. Ambassador to the U.S.S.R.

182. Big Tim
The Big Feller
The Last of the Big Time Grafters
The Boxing King of New York
Timothy D. Sullivan (1862-1913), Tammany Hall leader, New York City (D), New York boxing czar, and U.S. Congressman.

183. Mr. Republican
Mr. America
Mr. Integrity
Robert A. Taft (1889-1953), U.S. Senator (R-OH).

184. The Big Chief
His Acreage
William H. Taft (1857-1930), 27th President of the United States (R-OH), and Chief Justice, U.S. Supreme Court.

185. Old Rough and Ready
Old Buena Vista
Zachary Taylor (1784-1850), 12th President of the United States (Whig-KY).

186. The Iron Lady
Tina *[There Is No Alternative]*
The Cold War Witch
Margaret Thatcher, Prime Minister of Great Britain (Conservative).

187. The Sage of Greystone
The Sage of Gramercy Park
Old Usufruct
Slippery Sam
Samuel J. Tilden (1814-1886), Governor of New York (D).

188. Pitchfork Ben
Benjamin Ryan Tillman (1847-1918), Governor of South Carolina and U.S. Senator (D).

189. The New Missouri Compromise
Give 'Em Hell, Harry
The Man from Missouri
The Man of Independence
High Tax Harry
Harry the Haberdasher
Harry S Truman (1884-1972), 33rd President of the United States (D-MO).

190. Old Daddy
William V. S. Tubman (1895-1971), 18th President of Liberia.

191. His Accidency
The Executive Ass
Old Veto
John Tyler (1790-1862), 10th President of the United States (Whig-VA).

192. The American Talleyrand
The Little Magician
Old Kinderhook *[O.K.]*
The Kinderhook Fox
King Martin the First
Martin Van Ruin
The Panic of 1837
Whiskey Van
Martin Van Buren (1782-1862), 8th President of the United States (D-NY).

193. The Ice Man
Robert A. Van Wyck (1849-1918), Mayor of New York City (D).

194. The Great White Chief
James K. Vardaman (1861-1930), Governor of Mississippi and U.S. Senator (D).

195. Backstage Boss of the Pentagon
Carl Vinson (1883-1981), U.S. Congressman and Speaker of the House (D-GA).

196. Beau James
The Playboy Mayor
Midnight Mayor
The Wiseacre
James J. Walker (1881-1946), Mayor of New York City (D).

197. Some folks call me the "night mayor" of New York.
James J. Walker. Quoted in Charles Hurd, *A Treasury of Great American Quotations*, 1964.

198. King of the Lobby
Samuel Ward (1814-1884), Washington lobbyist.

199. Superchief
Earl Warren (1891-1974), Chief Justice, U.S. Supreme Court, and Governor of California (R).

200. The Lucifer of the lobby
The Wizard of the lobby
Lord Thurlow
Thurlow Weed (1797-1882), American journalist and politician.

201. Fighting Joe
Joseph Wheeler (1836-1906), U.S. Congressman (D-AL); Lieutenant General, Confederate Army; and Chief, U.S. Volunteer Calvary, Cuba and the Philippines.

202. Whispering John
John J. Williams (1904-1988), U.S. Senator (R-DE).

203. Goodtime Charlie
Charles Wilson, U.S. Congressman (D-TX).

204. Presidentress of the United States
Edith Bolling Wilson (1872-1961), First Lady.

205. The Prince of the Fire-Eaters
William L. Yancey (1814-1863), U.S. Congressman (D-AL), and Confederate Senator.

Chapter 69

Nuclear Weapons and Energy

1. What regrets I have about being a party to killing and maiming thousands of Japanese civilians this morning are tempered with the hope that the terrible weapon we have created may bring the countries of the world together and prevent further wars.

   Luis Alvarez (1911-1988), American atomic scientist assigned to the Manhattan Project. Letter to his son, 1945.

2. We are here to make a choice between the quick and the dead.... We must elect World Peace or World Destruction.

   Bernard M. Baruch (1870-1965), Chairman, War Industries Board, and U.S. Delegate to the U.N. Atomic Energy Commission. Speech, U.N. Atomic Energy Commission. June 14, 1946.

3. I would not recommend the use of any atomic weapon, no matter how small, when both sides have the power to destroy the world.

   Charles R. Brown, Admiral, U.S. Navy. Quoted in *The New Yorker*, Oct. 17, 1983.

4. In the real world of real political leaders a decision that would bring even one hydrogen bomb on one city of one's own country would be recognized as a catastrophic blunder.

   McGeorge Bundy, Presidential Assistant for National Security (D). *Foreign Affairs*, 1969.

5. We were in the presence of a new factor in human affairs. We possessed powers which were irresistible ... our outlook on the future was transformed.

   Winston Churchill (1874-1965), Prime Minister of Great Britain (Conservative). Statement after the first atomic bomb test, the day before the Potsdam Conference began. Quoted in *The New York Times*, Aug. 17, 1945.

6. There will one day spring from the brain of science a machine or force so fearful in its potentialities, so absolutely terrifying, that even man, the fighter who will dare torture and death in order to inflict torture and death, will be appalled, and so abandon war forever.

   Thomas A. Edison (1847-1931), American inventor. 1921.

7. We are still at the stumbling stage in atomic weapons.

   Charles de Gaulle (1890-1970), President of France. Quoted in *Life*, Nov. 15, 1963.

8. The agency *[Nuclear Regulatory Commission]* still emphasizes reactor designs, instead of the more important safety problems, which focus on the soft spots: ongoing maintenance of the reactors and operator training.

   Victor Gilinsky, Commissioner, Nuclear Regulatory Commission. Quoted in Tolchin and Tolchin, *Dismantling America: The Rush to Deregulate*, 1983.

9. I have one more problem for your computer. How long will take five hundred thousand angry Americans to climb that White House wall out there and lynch their President if he does something like that?

   Lyndon B. Johnson (1908-1973), 36th President of the United States (D-TX). Remark to military leaders who suggested using atomic weapons in Vietnam, 1965.

10. We know enough about broken negotiations, secret preparations, and the *[Soviet]* advantage gained from a long test series never to offer again an uninspected moratorium.

    John F. Kennedy (1917-1963), 35th President of the United States (D-MA). Press conference, Mar. 2, 1962.

11. The Communist campaign, finely attuned to prevailing fears, almost imperceptibly shifted the primary concern away from Soviet aggression – the real security problem – to the immorality of the use of nuclear weapons, which happened to

be the most effective way of resisting it.

Henry M. Kissinger, U.S. Secretary of State and National Security Advisor (R). *Nuclear Weapons and Foreign Policy*, 1957.

12. The atom bomb is a paper tiger which the U.S. reactionaries use to scare people. It looks terrible, but in fact it isn't. Of course, the atom bomb is a weapon of mass slaughter, but the outcome of a war is decided by the people, not by one or two new types of weapons.

Mao Tse-tung (1893-1976), Chairman, Communist Party of China. *Talk with the American Correspondent Anna Louise Strong*, Aug. 1946.

13. If an SDI *[Strategic Defense Initiative]* system were to keep out ninety percent of incoming nuclear missiles, it would be a ninety percent success and most Americans would be dead.

George S. McGovern, U.S. Congressman and U.S. Senator (D-SD). PBS, *Firing Line*, Sept. 7, 1988.

14. Going underground is no answer. What kind of world would they come up to? What would they use for air? What would they use for food? What would they use for people?

Robert B. Meyner, Governor of New Jersey (D). Response to suggestions for building underground fallout shelters. Speech, Mar. 1960.

15. Nuclear power is a political question, not just a question of whether the plumbing works.

Editorial, *The New York Times*, Sept. 11, 1982.

16. I am become death, the destroyer of worlds.

J. Robert Oppenheimer (1904-1967), American physicist and Scientific Director of the Manhattan Project. Statement at the first atomic bomb test; quoting from the *Baghavad-Gita*. Alamogordo, NM, July 16, 1945.

17. In some crude sense, which no vulgarity, no humor, no overstatement can quite extinguish, the physicists have known sin and this is a knowledge which they cannot lose.

J. Robert Oppenheimer. In reference to the atomic bomb. Nov. 25, 1947.

18. The American people are backing you and the President to the limit, determined that now is the time to exterminate the Yellow Peril for all time.... Let the rats squeal.

Charles A. Plumley (1875-1964), U.S. Congressman (R-VT). Telegram to U.S. Secretary of State James Byrnes encouraging the administration to drop the atomic bomb on Japan in World War II, Aug. 1945.

19. It *[nuclear power]* is an inherently dangerous technology, with risks only comparable to a nuclear war.

Robert Pollard, nuclear engineer, Nuclear Regulatory Commission. Quoted in Tolchin and Tolchin, *Dismantling America: The Rush to Deregulate*, 1983.

20. A nuclear power plant is infinitely safer than eating, because three hundred people choke to death on food every year.

Dixy Lee Ray, Governor of Washington and Chairman, U.S. Atomic Energy Commission (D). Statement, 1977.

21. Unfortunately, the federal government has created a regulatory environment that is forcing many utilities to rule out nuclear power as a source of new generating capacity.

Ronald Reagan, 40th President of the United States (R-CA). Campaign speech, 1980.

22. What is this massive *[nuclear]* retaliation? It's extinction without representation.

James Reston, American political columnist. Remark, Nov. 3, 1989.

23. It is difficult to determine in the organization scheme ... where the *[Atomic Energy]* Commission ends and the industry begins.

Abraham A. Ribicoff, Governor of Connecticut (D), U.S. Congressman, U.S. Senator, and U.S. Secretary of Health, Education and Welfare. Quoted in *The New Yorker*, Apr. 13, 1981.

24. I think that if the atomic bomb did nothing more, it scared the people to the point where they realized that either they must do something about preventing war or there is a chance that there might be a morning when we would not wake up.

Anna Eleanor Roosevelt (1884-1962), First Lady and U.S. Delegate to the United Nations. Press conference, Jan. 3, 1946.

25. Matters relative to foreign policy are given to the national government, but that doesn't mean municipalities have to be political eunuchs. After all, a nuclear war will have a dramatic local effect.

David Rosenberg, City Councilman, Davis, CA. Defense of local government ordinances for nuclear-free zones. Quoted in *Governing*, Sept. 1988.

26. It's all very complicated, isn't it? You never know whether those things will really work when it comes right down to it, do you?

Dean Rusk, U.S. Secretary of State (D). Comment after a briefing by Glenn Seaborg of the Atomic Energy Commission on nuclear weapons. Quoted in David Halberstam, *The Best and the Brightest*, 1969.

27. If we have to start over again with another Adam and Eve, I want them to be Americans, not Russians.

Richard B. Russell, Jr. (1897-1971), U.S. Senator (D-GA). On the prospects of nuclear war, 1968.

28. The atomic bomb is a marvelous gift that was given to our country by a wise God.

Phyllis Schlafly, American political activist and President, Eagle Forum. Quoted in Erwin Knoll, *No Comment*, 1984.

29. The word "nuclear" is a fear word.

Tony Schwartz, American political TV ad producer. Quoted on CBS, *West 57th Street*, Nov. 5, 1988.

30. Cogito ergo boom.

Susan Sontag, American writer and critic. In reference to atomic weapons. *Styles of Radical Will*, 1969.

31. There is no evil in the atom, only in men's souls.

Adlai E. Stevenson (1900-1965), Governor of Illinois (D) and U.S. Ambassador to the United Nations. Speech, Hartford, CT, Sept. 18, 1952.

32. The atomic bomb ... has profoundly affected political considerations in all sections of the globe. In many quarters it has been interpreted as a substantial offset to the growth of Russian influence on the *[European]* continent.... The temptation will be strong for the Soviet political and military leaders to acquire this weapon in the shortest possible time.

Henry L. Stimson (1867-1950), U.S. Secretary of State, U.S. Secretary of War, and Governor General of the Philippine Islands (R). Memorandum to President Truman, Sept. 11, 1945.

33. Atmospheric nuclear tests do not seriously endanger either present or future generations.

Edward Teller, American nuclear physicist. *Life*, Feb. 10, 1958.

34. A world without nuclear weapons would be less stable and more dangerous for all of us.

Margaret Thatcher, Prime Minister of Great Britain (Conservative). Remark to Mikhail Gorbachev. Quoted in *Time*, Apr. 27, 1987.

35. Sixteen hours ago an American plane dropped one bomb on Hiroshima, an important Japanese army base. That bomb had more power than twenty thousand tons of TNT.

Harry S Truman (1884-1972), 33rd President of the United States (D-MO). Announcement of the dropping of the first atomic bomb, Aug. 6, 1945.

36. This is the greatest thing in history.

Harry S Truman. Remark upon hearing of the world's first atomic bomb being dropped on Hiroshima. Addressed to the crew of the U.S.S. *Augusta*, Aug. 6, 1945.

37. Never in history has society been confronted with a power so full of promise for the future of man and for the peace of the world.

Harry S Truman. Message to Congress, Oct. 3, 1945.

38. There is only one thing worse than one nation having the atomic bomb – that's two nations having it.

Harold C. Urey (1893-1980), Nobel Laureate in Physics (United States). Remark to reporters, 1949.

39. Fallout is nothing more than particles of matter in the air. Radioactivity is nothing new.... The whole world is radioactive.

U.S. Civil Defense Administration, *Facts About Fallout*, 1955.

40. Mushroom clouds make lousy umbrellas.

Paul Warnke, Director, U.S. Arms Control and Disarmament Agency; Chief Negotiator, SALT II. In reference to the continued testing of "nuclear umbrella" defensive weapons. *The Washington Post*, Dec. 22, 1990.

Chapter 70

Obscenity, Prostitution, and Pornography

1. If this be true, General Pinckney has kept them all for himself and cheated me out of my two.

   John Adams (1735-1826), 2nd President of the United States (Federalist-MA). Response when asked about a rumor that he had dispatched Charles Pinckney to England to obtain four young women of "easy virtue" – two for each of them. Quoted in *Conservative Digest*, Nov., 1987.

2. I finally gave up. If you can't define it *[pornography]*, you can't prosecute people for it.

   William J. Brennan, Jr., U.S. Supreme Court Justice. Remark to Nat Hentoff. Quoted in *Time*, July 30, 1990.

3. The First Amendment is about how we govern ourselves – not about how we titillate ourselves sexually.

   Robert H. Bork, U.S. Solicitor General and Judge, U.S. Court of Appeals, Washington, DC. Argument for greater restrictions on pornography. Interview, ABC, *This Week*, June 25, 1989.

4. Pornography is the undiluted essence of anti-female propaganda.

   Susan Brownmiller, American feminist and writer. *Against Our Will*, 1975.

5. It seems strange to put prostitutes in prison for selling something that is perfectly legal to give away for free.

   George Carlin, American comedian. Lecture, George Washington University, Washington, DC, 1990.

6. The trouble with this wide-open pornography ... is not that it corrupts but that it desensitizes; not that it unleashes the passions but that it cripples the emotions; not that it encourages a mature attitude but that it is a reversion to infantile obsessions; not that it removes the blinders but that it distorts the view. Progress is proclaimed but love is denied. What we have is not liberation but dehumanization.

   Norman Cousins, American writer and editor. *Saturday Review*, Sept. 20, 1975.

7. Women are as varied as any citizens of a democracy; there is no agreement or feminist code as to what images are distasteful or even sexist.

   Betty Friedan, American feminist and writer. Quoted in *The Washington Post*, Apr. 4, 1992.

8. The economic and social inferiority of women is responsible for prostitution.

   Emma Goldman (1869-1940), American anarchist. *The Tragedy of Women's Emancipation*, 1911.

9. We're going to call it the John Hour.

   Edward I. Koch, U.S. Congressman and Mayor of New York City (D). Comment when it was suggested that the names of prostitutes' patrons be broadcast on radio. *How'm I Doing?*, 1981.

10. The issue we take with pornography has nothing to do with the First Amendment. It seems to me that our country has never permitted or condoned speech that endangers the lives of others.

    C. Everett Koop, U.S. Surgeon General. Speech to a group of Roman Catholic physicians, Chicago, IL, Sept. 1986.

11. Sexual imagery causes arousal, not violence. Eliminating arousal is no goal of feminism or of law enforcement.

    Marcia Pally, American writer and editor. In opposition to the U.S. Senate Pornography Victims' Compensation Act. *The Washington Post*, Feb. 11, 1992.

12. Hostile forces at home and abroad have never abandoned their hope of subverting ... they plot to win without firing a shot, and one of their methods is to distribute pornography.

    Front page editorial, *People's Daily*, Chinese Communist Party newspaper, Oct. 27, 1990.

13. Politics I supposed to be the second oldest profession. I have come to realize that it bears a very close resemblance to the first.

Ronald Reagan, 40th President of the United States (R-CA). Quoted in *The Los Angeles Herald-Examiner*, Mar. 3, 1978.

14. Obscenity is what happens to shock some elderly and ignorant magistrate.

Bertrand Russell, 3rd Earl Russell of Kingston (1872-1970), British philosopher and reformer. Quoted in *Look*, 1954.

15. Unto the lewd all things are lewd.

Theodore Albert Schroeder (1864-1953), American Libertarian activist. *A Challenge to the Sex Censors*, 1938.

16. Pornography is a malady to be diagnosed and an occasion for judgment. It's something one is for or against. And taking sides about pornography is hardly like being against aleatoric music or Pop Art, but quite a bit like being for or against legalized abortion or federal aid to parochial schools.

Susan Sontag, American writer and critic. In Day and Bloom, eds., *Perspectives on Pornography*, 1988.

17. The long history of antiobscenity laws makes it very clear that such laws are most often invoked against political and life-style dissidents.

Gloria Steinem, American editor and feminist. *Ms.*, Oct. 1973.

18. I shall not today attempt further to define the kinds of material ... embraced within that shorthand description; and perhaps I could never succeed in intelligibly doing so. But I know it when I see it, and the motion picture involved in this case is not that.

Potter Stewart (1915-1985), U.S. Supreme Court Justice. In reference to obscenity. *Jacobellis* v. *Ohio*, 1964.

19. Every obscene, lewd, or lascivious, and every filthy book, pamphlet, picture, paper, letter, writing, print or other publication of an indecent character ... is hereby declared to be nonmailable matter.

U.S. Criminal Code, Mar. 4, 1909.

20. The worst that can be said about pornography is that it leads not to "antisocial" acts but to the reading of more pornography.

Gore Vidal, American writer. *Reflections upon a Sinking Ship*, 1969.

21. It is another case of burning the house to roast the pig.

Byron R. White, U.S. Supreme Court Justice. Explanation for the Supreme Court's unanimously striking down part of a 1988 law that banned "indecent" speech on the telephone out of concern that children would hear the sexually explicit messages of some "dial-a-porn" lines. *Sable Communications of California* v. *Federal Communications Commission*, 1989.

Chapter 71

Oratory and Debate

1. I never said I had no idea about most of the things you said I said I had no idea about.

Elliott Abrams, U.S. Assistant Secretary of State (R). Statement to Congressman Jack Brooks at the Iran-Contra hearings, 1987.

2. This shuffling trick of misstating the question, and setting up a man of straw to make a pompous demonstration of knocking him down, is the measure of the capacity of *[Congressman]* Edward Black *[of Georgia]* and of the majority of the House *[of Representatives]*.

John Quincy Adams (1767-1848), 6th President of the United States (Ind.-MA). *Diary*, Feb. 12, 1841.

3. At the *[U. S.]* House *[of Representatives]*, Stephen A. Douglas of Illinois, the author of the majority report from the Committee of Elections, had taken the floor last evening, and now raved out his hour in abusive invective upon the members who had pointed out its slanders, and upon the Whig Party. His face was convulsed, his gesticulations frantic, and he lashed himself into such a heat that if his body had been made of combustible matter it would have burnt out. In the midst of his roaring, to save himself from choking, he stripped off and cast away his cravat, unbuttoned his waistcoat, and had the air and aspect of a half-naked pugilist. And this man comes from a judicial bench, and passes for an eloquent orator!

John Quincy Adams. *Diary*, Feb. 14, 1844.

4. His tongue drips poison.

John Quincy Adams. In reference to John Randolph of Virginia. Quoted in Nancy McPhee, *The Book of Insults*, 1978.

5. Ridicule is man's most potent weapon.

Saul D. Alinsky, American community organizer. *Rules for Radicals*, 1971.

6. Mr. Chairman, I desire to say to those present that their perfect attention will not embarrass me in the least.

John Mills Allen (1846-1917), U.S. Congressman (D-MS). Maiden speech in Congress, Apr. 1885.

7. By words the mind is winged.

Aristophanes (c.450-385 B.C.), Greek dramatist. *The Birds*.

8. The demagogue ... is a good showman, whether at Nuremberg at a youth conference, or in Georgia at a political barbecue. He knows the tricks of the ham actor, the gestures, the tones of voice that can arouse passions. Always he dresses himself up as the little man come to life, grown to Brobdingnagian stature and becomes the "Duce" or the "Leader" or, maybe, "Ploughboy Pete."

Ellis G. Arnall (1907-1992), Governor of Georgia (D). *The Shores Dimly Seen*, 1946.

9. I used to recite my speeches walking up a hill. It gives you wind power. I could throw fifty-six-pound words across the Grand Canyon.

Henry Fountain Ashurst (1874-1962), U.S. Senator (D-AZ). Quoted in Morris K. Udall, *Too Funny to Be President*, 1988.

10. Do not prove things too much.

Henry Ward Beecher (1813-1887), American clergyman and writer. Quoted in Kenneth Cmiel, *The Fight Over Popular Speech in Nineteenth-Century America*, 1990.

11. The whole art of a political speech is to put *nothing* into it. It is much more difficult than it sounds.

Hilaire Belloc (1870-1953), British writer and political biographer. *A Conversation with an Angel*.

12. Why do Republicans fear debate? For the same reason baloney fears the slicer.

Lloyd M. Bentsen, Jr., U.S. Congressman and U.S. Senator (D-TX). Quoted on NBC, *The McLaughlin Group*, Oct. 15, 1988.

13. The mediocrity of his *[Winston Churchill's]* thinking is concealed by the majesty of his language.... He mistakes verbal facilities for mental inspiration.

Aneurin Bevan (1897-1960), Minister of Health, Great Britain (Socialist). Quoted in Fred Metcalf, *The Penguin Dictionary of Modern Humorous Quotations*, 1986.

14. Better pointed bullets than pointed words.
Otto von Bismarck-Schoenhausen (1815-1898), Chancellor of Germany. Speech, Erfurt Parliament, 1850.

15. When you make speeches you elicit expectations against which you will be held accountable.
William W. Bradley, U.S. Senator (D-NJ). Interview, PBS, *American Interests*, Mar. 3, 1990.

16. He managed to hit all the keys on the great American political piano.
David Brinkley, American TV journalist. In reference to the 1988 presidential nomination acceptance speech of Gov. Michael Dukakis. ABC news coverage, Democratic National Convention, Atlanta, GA, July 20, 1988.

17. An orator is a man who says what he thinks and feels what he says.
William Jennings Bryan (1860-1925), U.S. Secretary of State (D). Quoted in Paxton Hibben, *Peerless Leader*, 1929.

18. If you want to get across an idea, wrap it up as a person.
Ralph J. Bunche (1904-1971), Undersecretary General of the United Nations and Nobel Laureate in Peace. Favorite saying.

19. He that wrestles with us strengthens our nerves and sharpens our skill. Our antagonist is our helper.
Edmund Burke (1729-1797), British statesman. *Reflections on the Revolution in France*, 1790.

20. I am the voice of my people.
Captain Jack (1837-1873), Chief, Modoc Indians. 1873.

21. Speech that leads not to action, still more that hinders it, is a nuisance on the earth.
Thomas Carlyle (1795-1881), Scottish essayist and historian. Letter to Jane Welsh, Nov. 4, 1825.

22. Discuss anything, argue anything, but without bitterness or hot temper.
Catherine II (The Great) (1729-1796), Empress of Russia. Sign in her Pavilion Hall, written in her own hand.

23. I will begin to speak when I have that to say which had not better be unsaid.
Marcus Porcius Uticensis Cato (Cato the Younger) (95-46 B.C.), Roman soldier and philosopher. Quoted in Plutarch, *The Parallel Lives: Cato the Younger*.

24. He generally speaks about facts, issues, and if he's got a fault in speaking, it's probably that he knows so much about what he's talking about, sometimes he talks over people's heads.
George Christian, White House press secretary (D). In reference to Sen. Lloyd Bentsen, Jr. (D-TX). Quoted in *The New York Times*, July 22, 1988.

25. He *[Lord Charles William Beresford]* is one of those orators of whom it was well said, "Before they get up to speak they do not know what they are going to say; when they are speaking, they do not know what they are saying; and when they sit down, they do not know what they have said."
Winston Churchill (1874-1965), Prime Minister of Great Britain (Conservative). Speech, House of Commons, Dec. 20, 1912.

26. The practice of public speaking flourishes in every peaceful and free state.
Marcus Tullius Cicero (106-43 B.C.), Roman statesman and orator. *Of Oratory*, II.

27. The ideologue does not perform miracles. Very fittingly he confines himself to the deceptive charm of the realized abstraction.
Georges Clemenceau (1841-1929), Premier of France and journalist. *In the Evening of My Thought*, 1929.

28. It wasn't my finest hour. It wasn't even my finest hour and a half.
Bill Clinton, 42nd President of the United States (D-AR). Reflection on his too-long speech at the Democratic National Convention in Atlanta, GA, nominating Gov. Michael Dukakis for President. Quoted in *The Washington Post*, Dec. 27, 1988.

29. It appears to me that since I have been sitting here I have heard a great deal of unprofitable discussion.
William Cobbett (1763-1835), Member of Parliament, Great Britain (Tory) and political journalist. Maiden speech in the House of Commons, Feb. 2, 1833.

30. Some of mankind's most terrible misdeeds have been committed under the spell of certain magic words or phrases.
James B. Conant (1893-1978), U.S. High Commissioner for Germany and President, Harvard University, Cambridge, MA. Speech, 1934.

31. Unless one understands the power of words, he will never understand men.
Confucius (551-479 B.C.), Chinese philosopher. *Analects*.

32. Draco wrote his laws in blood; the Senate writes its laws in wind.

Thomas T. Connally (1877-1963), U.S. Congressman and U.S. Senator (D-TX). Remark on his 80th birthday, 1957.

33. I have noticed that nothing that I never said ever did me any harm.

Calvin Coolidge (1872-1933), 30th President of the United States (R-MA). Attributed.

34. One of the reasons for retiring from public life was to avoid further speechmaking.

Calvin Coolidge. Remark, 1924.

35. Many times I only say yes or no and even that winds them up for twenty minutes more.

Calvin Coolidge. Remark to Bernard Baruch, 1924.

36. If you don't say anything, you can't be called upon to repeat it.

Calvin Coolidge. Quoted in Louis Untermeyer, *A Treasury of Laughter*, 1946.

37. The New Englanders by their canting, whining, insulting tricks have persuaded the rest of the *[American]* colonies that the government *[of George III]* is going to make absolute slaves of them.

Nicholas Cresswell (1729-1786), Member of Parliament, Great Britain (Tory). Speech, House of Commons, 1774.

38. Some of my constituents let me know that they would not listen to me on such a dry subject as the welfare of the nation, until they had something to drink, and that I must treat them.

David Crockett (1786-1836), U.S. Congressman (Anti-Jacksonian-TN). *The Life of Davy Crockett*, 1889.

39. Debates measure abilities you don't need to govern, like glibness. To govern you should be thoughtful, not glib. A debater has a sense of humor, but what's it got to do with governing? The ability to think on your feet? You make a budget sitting on your tush.

Mario Cuomo, Governor of New York (D). Quoted in *The New York Times*, July 31, 1989.

40. When I get into an argument I generally could get something out of Shakespeare which I could put on an opponent to his disadvantage. He has helped me out of many a tight place.

James M. Curley (1874-1958), U.S. Congressman and Mayor of Boston, MA (D). Quoted in Reinhard H. Luthin, *American Demagogues*, 1959.

41. We will reach greater and greater platitudes of achievement.

Richard J. Daley (1902-1976), Mayor of Chicago, IL (D). Quoted in *The New York Times*, Feb. 21, 1989.

42. Then there was a maiden speech, so inaudible that it was doubted whether, after all, the young orator really did lose his virginity.

Benjamin Disraeli, 1st Earl of Beaconsfield (1804-1881), Prime Minister of Great Britain (Conservative). *The Young Duke*, 1831.

43. It is said that a bird never makes so much noise as when she lays her first egg. I will sit down now, but the time will come when you will hear me.

Benjamin Disraeli. Maiden speech, House of Commons, 1837.

44. A majority is always the best repartee.

Benjamin Disraeli. *Tancred*, 1847.

45. We like to make tough speeches, but we don't like to make tough choices.

Robert J. Dole, U.S. Senator (R-KS). *The New York Times*, Oct. 7, 1990.

46. Sit down, Lincoln, your time is up.

Stephen A. Douglas (1813-1861), U.S. Congressman and U.S. Senator (D-IL). Remark to Abraham Lincoln, during the Great Debate of 1858.

47. They depended far more on their physical power of oratory than upon any semblance of argument ... with small regard for modesty, truth or time.

Walter E. Edge (1874-1956), U.S. Senator and Governor of New Jersey (R). Description of political orators of his day. Quoted in Reinhard H. Luthin, *American Demagogues*, 1959.

48. Only two people are permitted to refer to themselves as "We" – a king, and a man with a tapeworm inside of him.

Edward VII (1841-1901), King of Great Britain and Ireland. Attributed.

49. We live in a sea of semantic disorder in which old labels no longer faithfully describe. Police states are called "people's democracies." Armed conquest of free people is called "liberation."

Dwight D. Eisenhower (1890-1969), 34th President of the United States (R-KS). Annual message to Congress, Jan. 7, 1960.

50. One of our statesmen said, "The curse of this country is eloquent men."

Ralph Waldo Emerson (1803-1882), American writer. *Letters and Social Aims*. "Eloquence," 1875.

51. I would hope that ... this Senate does return to the decorum that calls for courtesy when one is speaking and others should be listening, the decorum of people in their seats rather than straggling in the aisles when debate is going on.
Daniel J. Evans, U.S. Senator (R-WA). Farewell speech, Oct. 19, 1988.

52. I *[Moses]* am not a man of words.
Old Testament, *Exodus* 4:10.

53. Some of the finest speeches in the Senate *[Congressional]* Record have been delivered to a scattering half-dozen of listeners. Nine-tenths of the verbal proceedings are "for the record" rather than with any expectation of changing votes. Yet the most important of the speeches "for the record" have their effect on public opinion, when reported in the press ... or when distributed as reprints.
Ralph E. Flanders (1880-1970), U.S. Senator (R-VT). *Senator from Vermont*, 1961.

54. When a man is asked to make a speech, the first thing he has to decide is what to say.
Gerald R. Ford, 38th President of the United States (R-MI). Quoted in Wallechinsky and Wallace, *The People's Almanac*, 1975.

55. During five whole sessions I spoke every night but one; and I regret only that I did not speak on that night too.
Charles James Fox (1749-1806), British statesman and orator. Explanation of the secret of his oratorical success in the House of Commons. Quoted by Macaulay, "William Pitt," *Encyclopedia Britannica*, 8th ed., 1859.

56. Would you persuade, speak of interest, not of reason.
Benjamin Franklin (1706-1790), Member, Continental Congress and Constitutional Convention, Governor of Pennsylvania, and U.S. Minister to France. *Poor Richard's Almanack*, 1746.

57. Tell candidates who desire total control *[of televised debates]* that in a democracy elections belong to the voters.
Barbara Friedman, debates manager, League of Women Voters. To advocate less candidate control of presidential debates. Letter to *Ms.* magazine, Apr., 1989.

58. I think we Americans tend to put too high a value on unanimity, as if there were something dangerous and illegitimate about honest differences of opinion honestly expressed by honest men.
J. William Fulbright, U.S. Senator (D-AR). Senate speech on American policy in Vietnam, Oct. 22, 1965.

59. There is one rule for politicians all over the world: Don't say in Power what you say in Opposition; if you do, you only have to carry out what the other fellows have found impossible.
John Galsworthy (1867-1933), British writer. *Maid in Waiting*, 1931.

60. On this subject *[slavery]* I do not wish to think, or speak, or write, with moderation. No! No! Tell a man whose house is on fire to give a moderate alarm; tell him to moderately rescue his wife from the hands of the ravisher; tell the mother to gradually extricate her babe from the fire into which it has fallen; but urge me not to use moderation in a cause like the present.
William Lloyd Garrison (1805-1879), American editor and abolitionist. *The Liberator*, Jan. 1, 1831.

61. Since a politician never believes what he says, he is surprised when others believe him.
Charles de Gaulle (1890-1970), President of France. Attributed.

62. In every election in American history both parties have their clichés. The party that has the clichés that ring true wins. And if the clichés continue to ring true when the party governs, then that party and those clichés can change history.
Newton L. Gingrich, U.S. Congressman (R-GA). Quoted in *The New York Times*, July 31, 1988.

63. Self-vindication never does a man any good unless he has been assailed.
William E. Gladstone (1809-1898), Prime Minister of Great Britain (Liberal). Remark, House of Commons, Mar. 12, 1877.

64. When ideas fail, words come in very handy.
Johann Wolfgang von Goethe (1749-1832), German poet and dramatist. *Faust*, 1808.

65. Here comes another spell-binder.
William Cassius Goodloe (1841-1899), Kentucky State Representative (R). Remark during the Harrison-Cleveland campaign, 1888.

66. I've learned to mumble with great incoherence.
Alan Greenspan, Chairman, Federal Reserve Board. 1987.

67. I do not share all the ideas of the honorable speaker; I do not accept the reproaches he has addressed to the government. But he has given expression to too many great, good, and useful truths, and he has spoken with a sentiment too

sincere and profound to make it possible to raise any debate with him at the moment. I cannot introduce a purely political and still less a personal question, after what he has just said. I have no reply to M. de Montalembert.

François Guizot (1787-1874), Premier of France. Reply to Charles Montalembert's speech on Switzerland, Chamber of Peers, Jan. 11, 1848.

68. I never saw this before. I didn't write this speech and I don't believe what I just read.

Warren G. Harding (1865-1923), 29th President of the United States (R-OH). Remark after stumbling over a passage in a campaign speech written for him, Sept. 1920.

69. Progression is not proclamation nor palaver. It is not pretense nor play on prejudice. It is not of personal pronouns, nor perennial pronouncement. It is not the perturbation of a people passion-wrought, nor a promise proposed.

Warren G. Harding. Quoted in Russell, *The Shadow of Blooming Grove*, 1968.

70. I am not a professional speaker nor a studied orator, but I am an old soldier and a farmer, and as my sole objective is to speak what I think, you will excuse me if I do it in my own way.

William Henry Harrison (1773-1841), 9th President of the United States (Whig-OH). Campaign speech, 1840.

71. Next to fried foods, the South has suffered most from oratory.

Lawrence B. Hays (1898-1981), U.S. Congressman (D-AK). Quoted by Morris K. Udall, *Too Funny to Be President*, 1988.

72. Mr. Speaker, having received unanimous consent to extend my remarks in the *Record*, I would like to indicate that I am not really speaking these words. Try as I might, I could not get the floor to deliver my plea on behalf of the coal miners.... I do not want to kid anybody into thinking that I am now on my feet delivering a stirring oration. As a matter of fact, I am back in my office typing this out on my own hot little typewriter . Such is the pretense of the House that it would have been just as easy to quietly include these remarks in the Record, issue a brave press release, and convince thousands of cheering constituents that I was in there every step of the way, influencing the course of history in the heat of debate.

Kenneth Hechler, U.S. Congressman (D-WV). *Congressional Record*, Oct. 18, 1971.

73. Be calm in arguing; for fierceness makes error a fault, and truth discourtesy.

William Herbert, 3rd Earl of Pembroke (1580-1630), English Ambassador to Paris and Chancellor of Oxford University. *Temple*.

74. When the fox preacheth then beware your geese.

John Heywood (1497-1580), English writer. *Proverbs*, ii, 7.

75. Only constant repetition will finally succeed in imprinting an idea on the memory of the crowd.

Adolf Hitler (1889-1945), Führer of the Third German Reich. *Mein Kampf*, 1933.

76. All epoch-making revolutionary events have been produced not by the written word but by the spoken word.

Adolf Hitler. *Ibid*.

77. Words are wise men's counters – they do but reckon by them; but they are the money of fools.

Thomas Hobbes (1588-1679), English political philosopher. *Leviathan*, 1651.

78. Eloquence may set fire to reason.

Oliver Wendell Holmes, Jr. (1841-1935), U.S. Supreme Court Justice. *Gitlow* v. *New York*, 1924.

79. He that goeth about to persuade a multitude, that they are not so well governed as they ought to be, never wants attentive and favourable hearers.

Richard Hooker (1553-1600), English theologian. *The Laws of Ecclesiastical Polity*, 1594-1595.

80. I struggle to be brief, and become obscure. (*Brevis esse laboro, obscurus fio.*)

Horace (Quintus Horatius Flaccus) (65-8 B.C.), Roman poet. *Ars Poetica*, XXV.

81. There's not a problem we have that we can't talk out. We can't shout it out.

Hubert H. Humphrey (1911-1978), Vice President of the United States and U.S. Senator (D-MN). Remark to protesters and demonstrators. Presidential campaign, 1968.

82. Hubert, a speech does not need to be eternal to be immortal.

Muriel Humphrey. Reminder to her husband, Hubert H. Humphrey. Quoted in Max Kampelman, *Entering New Worlds*, 1991.

83. A tart temper never mellows with age, and a sharp tongue is the only edge tool that grows keener with constant use.

Washington Irving (1783-1859), American writer and U.S. Diplomatic Attaché to Spain. *The Sketch Book: Rip Van Winkle*, 1819-1820.

84. Don't I deserve just as much credit for picking out the man who could write it?
[His first annual message to Congress was articulate and well received, but one of his close associates told him that nobody believed he had written it.]
Andrew Jackson (1767-1845), 7th President of the United States (D-TN). Statement to General Robert Armstrong, Dec. 7, 1829.

85. Deliberation and debate is the way you stir the soul of our democracy.
Jesse L. Jackson, Shadow Senator (D-DC). Interview, CBS, July 16, 1988.

86. If you use words to rebut a visual image, we know the visual image is dominant.
Kathleen Hall Jamieson, dean, Annenberg School of Communications, University of Pennsylvania, Philadelphia, PA. Quoted on PBS, Bill Moyers, *Television in Politics*, Oct. 1988.

87. I observe that the House of Representatives are sensible of the ill effects of the long speeches in their house on their proceedings. But they have a worse effect in the disgust they excite among the people, and the disposition they are producing to transfer their confidence from the legislature to the executive branch, which would soon sap our Constitution. These speeches, therefore, are less and less read, and if continued, will cease to be read at all.
Thomas Jefferson (1743-1826), 3rd President of the United States (Democratic Republican-VA). Letter to John W. Eppes, Jan. 17, 1810.

88. I don't believe the President of the United States should debate with anybody.
Lyndon B. Johnson (1908-1973), 36th President of the United States (D-TX). Dec. 15,1963.

89. YOU AIN'T LEARNING NOTHING WHEN YOU'RE TALKING.
Lyndon B. Johnson. Sign in his Senate office.

90. Come on down to the speakin' tonight!
Lyndon B. Johnson. Repeatedly shouted to crowds during his 1964 presidential campaign.

91. Give me some jokes for my statement on behalf of retarded children.
Lyndon B. Johnson. Request to his press Secretary. Quoted in George E. Reedy, *Lyndon B. Johnson: A Memoir*, 1982.

92. Pretty damn good speech. Now if all you had to do to run for and be president was talk, Adlai'd be the best. But it ain't.
Lyndon B. Johnson. Remark to Sam Houston Johnson about Adlai Stevenson, 1955. Quoted in Merle Miller, *Lyndon: An Oral Biography*, 1980.

93. Attack is the reaction; I never think I have hit hard unless it rebounds.
Samuel Johnson (1709-1784), British writer and lexicographer. Remark on his debating style. Quoted in James Boswell, *Life of Samuel Johnson*, Apr. 2, 1775.

94. *[Judah P. Benjamin spoke]* like Daniel Webster after taking a pint of brandy.
J. B. Jones (1810-1866), clerk, Confederate War Department. *Diary*, I, 1866.

95. There happened in my time one noble speaker *[Francis Bacon]* who was full of gravity in his speaking. His language (where he could spare or pass by a jest) was nobly censorious. No man ever spake more neatly, more weightily, or suffered less emptiness, less idleness, in what he uttered. His hearers could not cough, or look aside from him, without loss. The fear of every man that heard him was, lest he should make an end.
Ben Jonson (c.1573-1637), English writer. *Sylva*.

96. The persons who control the President's rhetoric exert an enormous influence over his actions and policies.
Hamilton Jordan, White House Chief of Staff (D). *Crisis: The Last Year of the Carter Presidency*, 1982.

97. There is a holy mistaken zeal in politics as religion. By persuading others, we convince ourselves.
Junius (Prob. Philip Francis) (1740-1818), British writer (Whig). *Letters*, No. 35, Dec. 19, 1769.

98. Senator, we're speaking English, but we're not talking the same language.
Robert F. Kennedy (1925-1968), U.S. Senator (D-NY) and U.S. Attorney General. Remark to Sen. Sam Ervin. Quoted on PBS, *Senator Sam*, Oct. 25, 1988.

99. Tone can be as important as text.
Edward I. Koch, U.S. Congressman and Mayor of New York City (D). *The Washington Post*, May 14, 1988.

100. God loveth not the speaking ill of any one in public.
The Koran, *Sura* 4.

101. I always hate a speech after I make it.
Robert M. La Follette (1855-1925), Governor of Wisconsin and U.S. Senator (R). Letter to his family, Mar. 1919.

102. I will say that I never had a more respectful hearing or fewer interruptions.

Robert M. La Follette. Remark on delivering his first radio address. Quoted in *The Madison Capital Times*, Sept. 29, 1924.

103. I'd rather split an infinitive than split an idea.
Fiorello H. La Guardia (1882-1947), U.S. Congressman (R and Socialist) and Mayor of New York City (R and Fusion Party). Remark to aides who criticized his grammar.

104. *[Everett M. Dirksen's]* voice was the sound gravel makes in a jar of honey.
Odin Elsford Langen (1913-1976), U.S. Congressman (R-MN). Tribute to Everett M. Dirksen, Sept. 8, 1969.

105. What Thucydides said of the Greeks at the time of the Peloponnesian War applies to us at present *[1860]*. The Greeks did not understand each other any longer, though they spoke the same language; words received a different meaning in different parts.
Francis Lieber (1800-1872), American political philosopher, publicist, and educator. Theodore Perry, ed., *Life and Letters*, 1882.

106. The point – the power to hurt – of all figures *[of speech]* consist in the truthfulness of their application.
Abraham Lincoln (1809-1865), 16th President of the United States (R-IL). Speech in Congress, July 27, 1848.

107. Henry Clay's eloquence did not consist, as many fine specimens of eloquence do, of types and figures, of antitheses and elegant arrangements of words and sentences, but rather of that deeply earnest and impassioned tone and manner which can proceed only through conviction in the speaker of the justice and importance of his cause. This it is that truly touches the chords of sympathy; and those who heard Mr. Clay never failed to be moved by it, or ever after forgot the impression. All his *[oratorical]* efforts were made for practical effect. He never spoke merely to be heard.
Abraham Lincoln. Speech, Springfield, IL, July 16, 1852.

108. I am very little inclined on any occasion to say anything unless I hope to produce some good by it.
Abraham Lincoln. Speech, Washington, DC, Aug. 6, 1862.

109. *[Woodrow Wilson]* could state a principle better than the expert from whom he had borrowed it.
Walter Lippmann (1889-1974), American political columnist. *A Preface to Politics*, 1913.

110. We have a Sunday code and a weekday code. We preach good and practice evil. We clothe the wolf of our actions in the sheep's clothing of our beautiful phrases.
Meyer London (1871-1926), U.S. Congressman (Socialist-NY). Speech in Congress, 1915.

111. Most people would rather laugh than weep. When I'm making a political speech, I'd like to cut around the opposition with a joke.
Huey P. Long (1893-1935), Governor of Louisiana and U.S. Senator (D). Quoted in Reinhard H. Luthin, *American Demagogues*, 1959.

112. The politicians were talking themselves red, white, and blue in the face.
Clare Boothe Luce (1903-1987), U.S. Congresswoman and Ambassador to Italy and Brazil (R-CT). Remark at the Republican National Convention, Chicago, IL, July 26, 1960.

113. Out of thine own mouth will I judge thee.
New Testament, *Luke* 19:22.

114. It's kinda like the House except the Senators use a little better English.
E. B. Lyon, Port Orange, FL. Commenting on the first Senate session the public could view on TV. Quoted in *Newsweek*, June 16, 1986.

115. The object of oratory alone is not truth, but persuasion.
Thomas Babington Macaulay, 1st Baron Macaulay (1800-1859), historian and Secretary of War, Great Britain (Liberal). *Essay on the Athenian Orators*, 1824.

116. It is a foolish thing to make a long prologue and be short in the story itself.
Apocrypha, 2 *Maccabees*, 2:32.

117. Nothing he *[a Foreign Secretary]* can say can do very much good, and almost anything he may say may do a great deal of harm. Anything he says that is not obvious is dangerous; whatever is not trite is risky. He is forever poised between the cliché and the indiscretion.
Harold Macmillan (1894-1986), Prime Minister of Great Britain (Conservative). Speech, House of Commons, July 27, 1955.

118. The Fascists kill because they cannot argue.
Victor Margueritte (1866-1942), French writer. Speech to the French Academy, 1940.

119. I once said that democracy is a discussion. But real discussion is only possible where men trust one another, and honestly seek the truth. Democracy is a conversation among equals, the thinking of free people open to complete publicity – the word "parliament" has a fine meaning, if only we could give it body!

Tomas G. Masaryk (1850-1937), 1st President of Czechoslovakia. Quoted in Karyl Capek, *Masaryk on Thought and Life*, 1938.

120. Out of the abundance of the heart the mouth speaks.

New Testament, *Matthew* 12:34.

121. Charitably, you could say it was a little long. In fact, it was a lot long.

Jim Mattox, Attorney General of Texas (D). Evaluation of a nominating speech at the Democratic National Convention. Quoted in *The Washington Post*, July 21, 1988.

122. Mr. Speaker, I rise today to make one statement, two observations, and one conclusion.

Maury Maverick (1895-1954), U.S. Congressman (D-TX). Opening remarks on the Judicial Reform Bill, Feb. 22, 1937.

123. He *[Pres. Warren G. Harding]* spoke in a big bow-wow style of oratory. His speeches leave the impression of an army of pompous phrases moving over the landscape in search of an idea. Sometimes these meandering words would actually capture a straggling thought and bear it triumphantly, a prisoner in their midst, until it died of servitude and overwork.

William Gibbs McAdoo (1863-1941), U.S. Secretary of the Treasury and U.S. Senator (D-CA). 1921.

124. One has to watch the new words that are introduced into politics – you never know what you are admitting to.

Eugene J. McCarthy, U.S. Congressman and U.S. Senator (D-WI). Campaign speech, Hartford, CT, Apr. 3, 1968.

125. The bully pulpit is not an open microphone. You have to target it very carefully.

Michael McCurry, American political consultant (D). Quoted in *The New York Times*, Oct. 21, 1990.

126. When I am in office I always keep members of Parliament talking. If they stopped they might start thinking.

Robert G. Menzies (1894-1978), Prime Minister of Australia (Liberal). Quoted in *The Wit of Sir Robert Menzies*, 1966.

127. It is only by the collision of adverse opinions that the remainder of the truth has any chance of being supplied.

John Stuart Mill (1806-1873), Member of Parliament, Great Britain, and political economist. *On Liberty*, 1859.

128. Sometimes hyperbole and lying are not easily distinguishable *[in politics]*.

Merle Miller, American journalist and author. *Lyndon: An Oral Biography*, 1980.

129. Though all the winds of doctrine were let loose to play upon the earth, so Truth be in the field, we do injuriously, by licensing and prohibiting, to misdoubt her strength. Let her and Falsehood grapple; who ever knew Truth put to the worse, in a free and open encounter.

John Milton (1608-1674), English writer. *Areopagitica*, 1644.

130. Success depends on three things: who says it, what he says, how he says it; and of these three things, what he says is the least important.

John Morley, Viscount Morley of Blackburn (1838-1923), Member of Parliament, Great Britain (Liberal), Chief Secretary for Ireland, and Secretary of State for India. *Recollections*, 1917.

131. Statistics is the plural of anecdote.

Daniel P. Moynihan, Chief American Delegate to the United Nations and U.S. Senator (D-NY). Quoted in *Public Opinion*, Sept./Oct. 1988.

132. The politician is ... trained in the art of inexactitude. His words tend to be blunt or rounded, because if they have a cutting edge, they may later return to wound him.

Edward R. Murrow (1908-1965), American broadcast journalist and Director, United States Information Agency. Speech, London, Oct. 19, 1959.

133. I still believe with Adlai Stevenson that you can win elections by talking sense to the American people.

Edmund S. Muskie, U.S. Secretary of State and U.S. Senator (D-ME). Quoted in *The Washington Post*, Nov. 4, 1990.

134. I pay attention only to what people say. I have little interest in what they think.

Napoléon I (1769-1821), military leader and Emperor of France. Remark to Gaspard Gourgaud, Jan. 20, 1818.

135. The great orators who rule the assemblies by the brilliance of their eloquence are, in general, men of the most mediocre political talents: I always

defeated them with this simple argument – two and two makes four.
Napoléon I. *Maxims*.

136. The power to persuade is the power to bargain.
Richard E. Neustadt, American political scientist. Quoted in *The Washington Post*, Nov. 19, 1990.

137. A good off-the-cuff informal speech takes more preparation than a speech.
Richard M. Nixon, 37th President of the United States (R-CA). Speech, Radio and Television Executives Society, New York City, 1955.

138. A politician knows that his words are his weapons, but that his word is his bond.
Richard M. Nixon. Eulogy for Everett M. Dirksen, Sept. 8, 1969.

139. Let us again learn to debate our differences with civility and decency, and let each of us reach for that precious quality government cannot provide – a new level of respect for the rights of one another.
Richard M. Nixon. 2nd inaugural address, Jan. 20, 1973.

140. A great speech is literature.
Peggy Noonan, presidential speech writer (R). Quoted in *Ms.*, Dec. 1988.

141. *[A political speech is]* a moment of prepared self-revelation.
Peggy Noonan. *Ibid.*

142. Words are weapons, and it is dangerous in speculation, as in politics, to borrow them from our enemies.
José Ortega y Gasset (1883-1955), Spanish philosopher and statesman. *Obiter Scripta*, 1936.

143. In our time, political speech and writing are largely the defense of the indefensible.
George Orwell (Eric Blair) (1903-1950), British writer. *Animal Farm*, 1945.

144. Who can refute a sneer?
William Paley (1743-1805), British clergyman and philosopher. *The Principles of Moral and Political Philosophy*, 1785.

145. There are those who speak well, and do not write well. It is because the place, the audience, warms them, and elicits from their mind more than they find in it without this warmth.
Blaise Pascal (1623-1662), French mathematician and philosopher. *Pensées*, IX.

146. In every generation there has to be some fool who will speak the truth as he sees it.
Boris Pasternak (1890-1960), Nobel Laureate in Literature (U.S.S.R.). Quoted in *The New York Times*, Feb. 2, 1959.

147. If after my talk you are still confused, as you may well be, I dare to hope that it is at least confusion on a higher plane.
Lester B. Pearson (1897-1972), Prime Minister of Canada (Liberal) and Nobel Laureate in Peace. Speech, Ottawa, July 13, 1961.

148. I have this unfortunate faculty, perhaps, of making the most exciting subject gray.
Claiborne Pell, U.S. Senator (D-RI). Quoted in *Newsweek*, Feb. 16, 1987.

149. There is a Truth and Beauty in Rhetorick; but it oftener serves ill Turns than good ones.
William Penn (1644-1718), founder of Pennsylvania. *Some Fruits of Solitude, in Reflections and Maxims*, 1693.

150. The demagogue, mounting the platform, like a slave in the market, is a slave *[himself]* ... and because of the honors he seems to receive, is the captive of ten thousand masters.
Philo Judaeus (c.20 B.C.-c.A.D. 40), Alexandrian philosopher and diplomat. *Joseph*, VII.

151. The proudest of politicians have the strongest desire to write speeches and bequeath compositions.... When an orator or a king succeeds in acquiring the power of a Lycurgus, a Solon, or a Darius *[the First]*, and so winning immortality among his people as a speech writer, doesn't he deem himself a peer of the gods while still living, and do not people in later ages hold the same opinion of him when they contemplate his writings?
Plato (427-347 B.C.), Greek philosopher and teacher. *Phaedrus*.

152. Rhetoric is the art of ruling the minds of men.
Plato. Quoted in Plutarch, *The Parallel Lives: Pericles*.

153. Kings must be spoken to with silken words.
Armand-Jean du Plessis (Cardinal Richelieu) (1585-1642), French ecclesiastic and statesman. *Political Testament*, I, 8, 1687.

154. In their declamations and speeches they made use of words to veil and muffle their design.
Plutarch (c.46-c.120), Greek biographer. In reference to the Sophists. *On Hearing*.

155. A political speech should be like a woman's skirt – long enough to be respectable and short enough to be interesting.
Adam Clayton Powell (1908-1972), U.S. Congressman (D-NY). Quoted on PBS, *The American Experience*, Nov. 28, 1989.

156. Few speeches which have produced an electrical effect on an audience can bear the colorless photography of a printed record.
Archibald Philip Primrose, 5th Earl of Rosebery (1847-1929), Prime Minister of Great Britain (Liberal). *Life of Pitt*, 1891.

157. A fool's lips enter into contention, and his mouth calls for strokes.
Old Testament, *Proverbs* 18:6.

158. Answer not a fool according to his folly, lest you become like him.
Old Testament, *Proverbs* 26:4.

159. Day after day pours forth speech.
Old Testament, *Psalms* 19:3.

160. The words of his mouth were smoother than butter, but war was in his heart; his words were softer than oil, yet they were drawn swords.
Old Testament, *Psalms* 55:21.

161. It's not so much what you say but how you say it, and what kind of overall impression you convey.
Jerry Rafshoon, presidential media advisor (D). Quoted in Hamilton Jordan, *Crisis: The Last Year of the Carter Presidency*, 1982.

162. *[Lyndon]* Johnson had ... little respect for the integrity of words. I think he thought words were just something you used as weapons.
George E. Reedy, White House press secretary (D). Quoted in Merle Miller, *Lyndon: An Oral Biography*, 1980.

163. The talent of insinuation is much more useful than that of persuasion; as everybody is open to insinuation, but scarce any to persuasion.
Cardinal de Retz (1614-1679), French cleric and politician. *Political Maxims*.

164. The situation does not call for a stand-up comic.
Ann Richards, Governor of Texas (D). In reference to her plans for the 1988 keynote speech to the Democratic National Convention. Quoted in *The Washington Post*, July 18, 1988.

165. The keynoter is someone who opens the door and says "come on in."
Ann Richards. Interview, NBC, July 18, 1988.

166. *[Sen. Joseph]* Biden's a great speaker – for the first hour.
Phil Roeder, Communications Director, Iowa Democratic Party. Quoted in *Newsweek*, June 22, 1987.

167. We pay for wisdom and get wind.
Will Rogers (1879-1935), American humorist. In reference to Senate oratory. Quoted on PBS, *Will Rogers U.S.A.*, Oct. 3, 1988.

168. I used to tell my husband that, if he could make me understand something, it would be clear to all the other people in the country.
Anna Eleanor Roosevelt (1884-1962), First Lady and U.S. Delegate to the United Nations. "My Day," Feb. 12, 1947.

169. If you can speak to the mass of the people as though you were talking to any one individual in your living room, you will reach their hearts and that is all that you have to bother about.
Anna Eleanor Roosevelt. Advice to Adlai Stevenson, Oct. 10, 1956.

170. Things depend so much on the way they are put.
Franklin D. Roosevelt (1882-1945), 32nd President of the United States (D-NY). Letter to Sen. Harry Byrd, Aug. 20, 1928.

171. I fully expect to give personal talks from time to time on all kinds of subjects of national interest.
Franklin D. Roosevelt. Letter to the National Broadcasting Company, 1933.

172. And he wrote all those speeches himself!
Franklin D. Roosevelt. Remark to Raymond Massey after a special White House screening of *Abe Lincoln of Illinois*, 1940.

173. Be sincere; be brief; be seated.
Franklin D. Roosevelt. Advice to his son, James, on political speechmaking.

174. One of our defects as a nation is a tendency to use what have been called "weasel words." When a weasel sucks an egg, the meat is sucked out of the egg; and if you use a "weasel word" after another there is nothing left of the other.
Theodore Roosevelt (1858-1919), 26th President of the United States (R-NY). Speech, St. Louis, MO, May 31, 1916.

175. Make your point as clear as possible and thrust the steel well home.
Theodore Roosevelt. Quoted in Kenneth Cmiel, *The Fight Over Popular Speech in Nineteenth-Century America*, 1990.

176. Jargon is not insight.
Leo Rosten, American political scientist and Deputy Director, Office of War Information. *A Trumpet for Reason*, 1970.

177. It is Ill-manners to silence a Fool, and Cruelty to let him go on.
George Savile, 1st Marquess of Halifax (1633-1695), Lord Privy Seal of England. *Moral Thoughts and Reflections*, 1750.

178. Anger is never without an Argument, but seldom with a good one.
George Savile. *Ibid.*

179. Men's Words are Bullets that their Enemies take up and make use of against them.
George Savile. *Miscellaneous Thoughts and Reflections*, 1750.

180. A patient Hearer is a good Speaker.
George Savile. *Ibid.*

181. No one over forty should be a speech writer.
Arthur M. Schlesinger, Jr., American historian and presidential advisor (D). Quoted by Republican speech writer Peggy Noonan, interview, CNN, *Evans & Novak*, Mar. 4, 1990.

182. No man possessed a gayer and more playful wit in society; no one, since *[William]* Pitt's time, had more commanding sarcasm in debate; in the House of Commons he was the terror of that species of orators called the Yelpers. His lash fetched away both skin and flesh, and would have penetrated the hide of a rhinoceros. In his conduct as a statesman he had a great fault: he lent himself too willingly to intrigue.
Walter Scott (1771-1832), Scottish writer. In reference to British Prime Minister George Canning. Quoted in John Gibson Lockhart, *Life of Scott*, 1837.

183. Wise men say nothing in dangerous times.
John Selden (1584-1654), English jurist and Member of Long Parliament. *Table-Talk: Wisdom.*

184. It is in the nature of politics that candidates make statements which they afterward regret.
Stephen Shaddeg, presidential campaign manager for Sen. Barry M. Goldwater. *How to Win an Election: The Art of Political Victory*, 1964.

185. No man dares say so much of what he thinks as to appear to himself an extremist.
George Bernard Shaw (1856-1950), Nobel Laureate in Literature (Great Britain). *Maxims for Revolutionists*, 1903.

186. It is said that every people has the government it deserves. It is more to the point that every government has the electorate it deserves; for the orators of the front bench can edify or debauch an ignorant electorate at will.
George Bernard Shaw. Preface, *Heartbreak House*, 1917.

187. I am the King of Rome, and above grammar. (*Ego sum rex Romanus, et supra grammaticam.*)
Sigismund (1368-1437), King of Hungary and Bohemia, and Holy Roman Emperor of the House of Luxembourg. Exclamation at the Council of Constance, 1414.

188. The reduction of political discourse to sound bites is one of the worst things that's happened in American political life.
John Silber, President of Boston University, Boston, MA, and Democratic gubernatorial candidate. Quoted in *USA Today*, Oct. 1, 1990.

189. The thirty-second sound bite is a fact of life, but we don't have to be prisoners of it.
Adam Smith, American economic journalist. PBS, *Adam Smith's Money World*, June 30, 1990.

190. If I keep on making these funny speeches, people will think I can't do anything else. There is nothing more dangerous to the reputation of a public man than that of being consistently humorous.
Alfred E. Smith (1873-1944), Governor of New York (D). 1916.

191. No. I'm going to campaign as I am. I wouldn't change now even to get into the White House.
Alfred E. Smith. Response when urged to change his New York diction when campaigning for the presidency in the Midwest. Remark to Charles Michelson, 1928.

192. The governor has a tendency to put his foot in his mouth.
Ken Smith, press secretary to Evan Mecham, Governor of Arizona (R). Quoted in John L. Myers, *The Arizona Governors 1912-1990*, 1989.

193. Truth is always the strongest argument.
Sophocles (c.496-406 B.C.), Greek tragedian. *Phaedra.*

194. It is much easier to modify an opinion if one has not already persuasively declared it.
David H. Souter, U.S. Supreme Court Justice. Confirmation hearings, Senate Judiciary Committee, Sept. 14, 1990.

195. Speech was given to the ordinary sort of men whereby to communicate their mind, but to wise men whereby to conceal it.

Robert South (1634-1716), English clergyman. Sermon, Westminster Abbey, Apr. 30, 1676.

196. The business of oratory is to persuade people; and you easily feel that to please people is a great step toward persuading them. You must, then, consequently, be sensible how advantageous it is for a man who speaks in public, whether it be in Parliament, in the pulpit, or at the bar, to please his hearers so much as to gain their attention: which he can never do without the help of oratory. It is not enough to speak the language he speaks in utmost purity, and according to the rules of grammar; but he must speak it elegantly; that is, he must choose the most expressive words, and put them in the best order. He should likewise adorn what he says by proper metaphors, similes, and other figures of rhetoric; and he should enliven it, if he can, by quick and sprightly turns of wit.

Philip Dormer Stanhope, 4th Earl of Chesterfield (1694-1773), Member of Parliament, Great Britain (Whig) and Lord-Lieutenant of Ireland. *Letters to His Son*, Nov. 1, 1739.

197. Man does not live by words alone, despite the fact that sometimes he has to eat them.

Adlai E. Stevenson (1900-1965), Governor of Illinois (D) and U.S. Ambassador to the United Nations. Speech, Denver, CO, Sept. 5, 1952.

198. When political ammunition runs low, inevitably the rusty artillery of abuse is always wheeled into action.

Adlai E. Stevenson. Campaign speech, New York City, Sept. 22, 1952.

199. I want you to bear with me while I try to make a speech. I never made one in my life, but with the way things are going in this campaign, with vilification for everyone and the degrading of good men for the sake of a few offices, I want to make a speech.

Timothy D. (Big Tim) Sullivan (1862-1913), Tammany Hall leader, New York City, New York boxing czar, and U.S. Congressman (D). Speech, Miner's Bowery Theater, New York City, Oct. 31, 1909.

200. Proper words in proper places make the true definition of a style.

Jonathan Swift (1667-1745), Irish clergyman and satirist. *Letter to a Young Clergyman*, Jan. 9, 1720.

201. Be silent as a politician, for talking may beget suspicion.

Jonathan Swift. Quoted in Otto L. Bettmann, *A Word from the Wise*, 1977.

202. Was it honest, was it fair in Theodore Roosevelt to seize one sentence from a speech, to garble it, and then give it a meaning which he knew from context it could not bear?

William H. Taft (1857-1930), 27th President of the United States (R-OH) and Chief Justice, U.S. Supreme Court. Presidential campaign speech, 1912.

203. Speech was given to man to disguise his thoughts.

Charles-Maurice de Talleyrand-Périgord (Prince de Bénévent) (1754-1838), French diplomat and statesman. Attributed.

204. Platitudes are there because they are true.

Margaret Thatcher, Prime Minister of Great Britain (Conservative). Response when criticized for using platitudes. Quoted in *The London Times*, June 1, 1984.

205. If they attack one personally, it means they have not a single political argument left.

Margaret Thatcher. Quoted in *The London Daily Telegraph*, Mar. 21, 1986.

206. Beaten today, beaten tomorrow; it is the fate of the soldier and the orator.

Louis-Adolphe Thiers (1797-1877), 1st President of the Third French Republic. Dec. 10, 1830.

207. I always get more applause than votes.

Norman Thomas (1884-1968), Director, League for Industrial Democracy, and Socialist Party candidate for President. Interview, *Playboy*, Nov. 1966.

208. In 1957 I spoke for twenty-four hours and eighteen minutes *[the longest speech in Senate history]*. I could have spoken another twelve hours but I thought twenty-four hours had dramatized the situation sufficiently.

James Strom Thurmond, U.S. Senator (D and R-SC). Quoted on PBS, *Congress: We the People*, 1989.

209. I can think of nothing more boring, for the American public, than to have to sit in their living rooms for a whole half an hour looking at my face on their television screens.

Harry S Truman (1884-1972), 33rd President of the United States (D-MO). Quoted in Wallechinsky and Wallace, *The People's Almanac*, 1975.

210. O Lord, help me to utter words that are tender and gentle, for at some future time I may have to eat them.

Morris K. Udall, U.S. Congressman (D-AZ). Quoted on PBS, *MacNeil-Lehrer News Hour*, July 20, 1988.

211. I'm from a state that raises corn and cotton and cockleburs and Democrats, and frothy eloquence neither convinces nor satisfies me. I'm from Missouri, you've got to show me.

William Duncan Vandiver (1852-1932), U.S. Congressman (D-MO). Speech, Five O'Clock Club, Philadelphia, PA, 1902.

212. As quick as I'd talk politics, he'd talk horses. In these times a man may be all right on horses and all wrong on politics.

Benjamin Franklin Wade (1800-1878), U.S. Senator (Whig and R-OH). Comment on debating Ulysses S. Grant. Quoted in *The New York Tribune*, Nov. 9, 1867.

213. Be not tedious in discourse; make not many digressions, nor repeat often the same manner of discourse.

George Washington (1732-1799), 1st President of the United States (VA). *Moral Maxims*.

214. We are not unmindful of his genius for disruption.

Arthur V. Watkins (1886-1973), U.S. Senator (R-UT) and Chairman, Select Committee on the Censure of Joseph McCarthy. In reference to Sen. Joseph R. McCarthy. Remark, Sept. 12, 1954.

215. It *[eloquence]* comes, if it comes at all, like the outbreaking of a fountain from the earth.

Daniel Webster (1782-1852), U.S. Congressman (Federalist-NH and MA), U.S. Senator (Federalist and Whig-MA), and U.S. Secretary of State. Quoted in S. Austin Allibone, *Prose Quotations*, 1876.

216. I like to do all the talking myself. It saves time and prevents arguments.

Oscar Wilde (1854-1900), Irish writer. *The Remarkable Rocket*.

217. All Americans lecture.... I suppose it is something in their climate.

Oscar Wilde. *A Woman of No Importance*, 1893.

218. In order to represent all the people you've got to talk to all of the people.

L. Douglas Wilder, Governor of Virginia (D). Interview, ABC, *This Week*, Jan. 14, 1990.

219. Politicians employ speech writers as ventriloquists.

George F. Will, American political columnist. *Newsweek*, Dec. 31, 1990.

220. A good catchword can obscure analysis for fifty years.

Wendell L. Willkie (1892-1944), Republican candidate for President (IN). Debate, 1938.

221. If I am to speak ten minutes, I need a week of preparation; if fifteen minutes, three days; if half an hour, two days; and if an hour, I am ready now.

Woodrow Wilson (1856-1924), 28th President of the United States (D-NJ). Quoted in Josephus Daniels, *The Wilson Era, 1856-1924*, 1924.

Chapter 72

Parties and Machines

1. The difference between Eastern Europe and the United States is that the United States still has a Communist party.
Popular joke in Czechoslovakia, 1990.

2. The system of building up, by corruption, political machines dominated by a boss whom the corporations believe essential to them for corrupt purposes of their own, is too deeply entrenched even yet in our national life.
James Truslow Adams (1878-1949), American historian. *The March of Democracy*, II, 1933.

3. My friends Sir Roger de Coverly and Sir Andrew Freeport are of different principles, the first of them inclined to the *landed* and the other to the *monied* interest.
Joseph Addison (1672-1719), Secretary of State, Great Britain (Whig). *The Spectator*, No. 126, July 25, 1711.

4. There are but two divisions of party in the United States; and he is a very weak or very presumptuously vain man who can think of organizing a third party that shall rule them both.
Fisher Ames (1758-1808), U.S. Congressman (Federalist-MA). 1801.

5. I'm for making the Republican Party conservative or making it die.
Tom Anderson, member, National Council, John Birch Society. Quoted in Epstein and Forster, *The Radical Right*, 1967.

6. All political parties die at last of swallowing their own lies.
John Arbuthnot (1667-1735), Scottish physician and humorist. Quoted in *Hoyt's New Cyclopedia of Practical Quotations*, 1922.

7. Those who think that all virtue is to be found in their own party principles push matters to extremes: They do not consider that disproportion destroys a state.
Aristotle (384-322 B.C.), Greek philosopher and teacher. *Politics*.

8. Never you mind about the country, or about the state, or the city, or about the ward. You take care of your precinct.
Jacob L. Arvey (1895-1977), Chicago, IL, political leader (D). Advice to precinct workers, 1940's.

9. David Duke is not a Republican. He is a pretender, a charlatan, and a political opportunist who is looking for any organization he can find to try to legitimize his views of racial and religious bigotry and intolerance.
[Duke, a former Imperial Wizard of the Ku Klux Klan, won election to the Louisiana legislature on the Republican ticket.]
Lee Atwater (1950-1991), Chairman, Republican National Committee. Quoted in *The Washington Post*, Feb. 19, 1989.

10. When great questions end, little parties begin.
Walter Bagehot (1826-1877), British economist and writer. *The English Constitution*, 1867.

11. Adversity in politics does not encourage cohesiveness, it seems. Deprived of the fruits of power, a national political party seems to break down into regional or other factions. Unity can only be regained by victory – yet victory is forestalled by disunity.
Bernard M. Baruch (1870-1965), Chairman, War Industries Board, and U.S. Delegate to the U.N. Atomic Energy Commission. *The Public Years*, 1960.

12. You can't build a lasting political movement based on hostility to government.
Gary Bauer, U.S. Assistant Secretary of Education (R). Quoted in *U.S. News & World Report*, Feb. 5, 1990.

13. Not parties, but principles.
Henry Ward Beecher (1813-1887), American clergyman and writer. *Life Thoughts*, 1858.

14. There are but two parties. There never have been but two parties ... founded in the radical question, whether people or property shall govern?
Thomas Hart Benton (1782-1858), U.S. Senator and U.S. Congressman (D-MO). Senate speech, 1835.

15. This party *[the Progressive]* comes from the grass roots. It has grown from the soil of the people's hard necessities.

Albert J. Beveridge (1862-1927), U.S. Senator (R-IN) and founder, Progressive League. Keynote address, Progressive Party (Bull Moose Party) Convention, Chicago, IL, Aug. 5, 1912.

16. The passion which all Democrats seem to have for writing in Republican papers, and vice versa, is something astonishing, and it is only exceeded by their unconquerable desire to censure men of their own party.

Ambrose Bierce (1842-1914?), American journalist. *News Letter*, June 12, 1869.

17. Here lies the body of the Republican party –
Corrupt, and generally speaking, hearty.

Ambrose Bierce. *Wasp*, Oct. 7, 1882.

18. What is a platform?
An elaborate, exhaustive, minute and accurate statement of a candidate's political beliefs.
Does he write it?
Oh no; it is published before it is known who he will be.

Ambrose Bierce. *Wasp*, Aug. 27, 1884.

19. What is a Democrat? One who believes that the Republicans have ruined the country. What is a Republican? One who believes that the Democrats would ruin the country.

Ambrose Bierce. *Ibid.*

20. Important issues do not always split along party lines.

Christopher Bond, Governor of Missouri and U.S. Senator (R). Interview, C-SPAN, June 15, 1991.

21. The disagreement among American political parties, with only a few exceptions, has been over the practical question of how to secure the agreed objective, while conciliating different interests, rather than over ultimate values or over what interest is paramount.

Daniel Boorstin, American historian and Librarian of Congress. *The Genius of American Politics*, 1953.

22. Any man who can carry a Republican primary is a man.

William E. Borah (1865-1940), U.S. Senator (R-ID). Attributed, 1923.

23. The Republicans throw money at crime and military defense the way the Democrats do at poverty and welfare.

Tony Bouza, Chief of Police, Minneapolis, MN. Quoted in *The New York Times*, May 28, 1989.

24. Your paper is now a power in the land. Advocate calling together in every church and schoolhouse in the free states all the opponents of the Kansas-Nebraska Bill, no matter what their previous party affiliations and to band together under the name I suggested to you ... in 1852. I mean the name "Republican."

Alvan E. Bovay (1818-1903), Secretary, National Reform Association, and founder, Republican Party. Letter to Horace Greeley, Feb. 26, 1854.

25. We went in Whigs, Free Soilers, and Democrats. We came out of it Republicans.

Alvan E. Bovay. Remark on the birth of the Republican Party, Rippon, WI, Mar. 20, 1854.

26. When we say vote with the party or else, we don't have much on the all else side of the equation.

John Brademas, U.S. Congressman (D-IN). Speech, National Democratic Club, Washington, DC, Mar. 6, 1979.

27. Republicans lobby; Democrats march.

Donna Brazile, political consultant (D). Quoted in *Campaigns & Elections*, Oct. 1989.

28. We don't win or lose elections because of *[party]* rules.

Ron Brown, Chairman, Democratic National Committee. Quoted on PBS, *MacNeil-Lehrer Report*, Feb. 13, 1989.

29. I hope the two wings of the Democratic Party may flap together.

William Jennings Bryan (1860-1925), U.S. Secretary of State (D). 1891.

30. A national convention is not the best place in the world to decide questions of abstract justice. The temptation to gain an unfair advantage is so great that it is not always resisted.

William Jennings Bryan. Quoted in Ralph G. Martin, *Ballots & Bandwagons*, 1964.

31. We are Republicans, and don't propose to have our party identify itself with the party whose antecedents are rum, Romanism, and rebellion.

Samuel D. Burchard (1812-1891), American clergyman. Speech, Fifth Avenue Hotel, New York City, Oct. 9, 1884.

32. Party divisions, whether on the whole operating for good or evil, are things inseparable from free government.

Edmund Burke (1729-1797), British statesman. *Observations on a Publication, "The Present State of a Nation,"* 1769.

33. *[A party is]* a body of men united, for promoting by their joint endeavors the national interest, upon some particular principle on which they are all agreed.
Edmund Burke. *Thoughts on the Cause of the Present Discontents*, 1770.

34. When bad men combine, the good must associate; else they will fall, one by one, an unpitied sacrifice in a contemptible struggle.
Edmund Burke. *Ibid.*

35. We *[the Republican Party] are* the change.
George Bush, 41st President of the United States (R). Remark during his 1988 presidential campaign.

36. Potholes know no party.
Robert C. Byrd, U.S. Congressman and U.S. Senator (D-WV). 1987.

37. Being of no party, I shall offend all parties: – never mind!
My words at least, are more sincere and hearty
Than if I sought to sail before the wind.
George Gordon Byron, 6th Baron Byron (1788-1824), poet and Member of Parliament, Great Britain. *Don Juan*, 1818-20.

38. Party organization, party discipline, party proscription, and their offspring, the spoils system, have been unknown to the state *[of South Carolina]*. Nothing of the kind is necessary to produce concentration.
John C. Calhoun (1782-1850), U.S. Congressman (D), U.S. Senator, U.S. Secretary of War, U.S. Secretary of State, and Vice President of the United States. 1849.

39. With money we will get partisans, with partisans votes, and with votes money, is the maxim of our political pilferers.
John C. Calhoun. Quoted in Lord, *Beacon Lights of History*.

40. We only need one *[political party]*, in the same way that Lenin only needed one.
Fidel Castro, Premier of Cuba. Quoted in *The New York Times*, July 31, 1988.

41. We join ourselves to no party that does not carry the flag and keep step to the music of the Union.
Rufus Choate (1779-1859), U.S. Congressman and U.S. Senator (Whig-MA). Letter to the Whig Convention, Worcester, MA, Oct. 1, 1855.

42. The duty of an Opposition is to oppose.
Randolph Churchill (1849-1895), Chancellor of the Exchequer, Great Britain (Conservative). Favorite saying.

43. Anyone who can bring the Conservative Party together can bring the country together.
Joe Clark, Prime Minister of Canada (Conservative). Remark to reporters, 1978.

44. Party honesty is party expediency.
Grover Cleveland (1837-1908), 22nd and 24th President of the United States (D-NY). Interview, *New York Commercial Advisor*, Sept. 19, 1889.

45. We must raise our hands against the nominee of our party *[William Jennings Bryan]*, and we must do it to preserve the future of the party itself.
William B. Cockran (1854-1923), U.S. Congressman (D-NY). Speech, Democratic National Convention, New York City, Aug. 18, 1896.

46. We are told the Republican party is a machine. Yes. A government is a machine ... the school system of the State of New York is a machine; a political party is a machine.
Roscoe Conkling (1829-1888), U.S. Congressman and U.S. Senator (R-NY). Quoted in Richard Hofstadter, *The American Political Tradition*, 1948.

47. Parties are not built by deportment.
Roscoe Conkling. *Ibid.*

48. There's no place for a third party in the United States.
Thomas T. Connally (1877-1963), U.S. Congressman and U.S. Senator (D-TX). Quoted in *The New York Times*, July 14, 1936.

49. It is the business of the President as party leader to do the best he can to see that the declared party platform purposes are translated into legislative and administrative action.
Calvin Coolidge (1872-1933), 30th President of the United States (R-MA). *Autobiography*, 1929.

50. You run the party or the party runs you.
Richard J. Daley (1902-1976), Mayor of Chicago, IL (D). 1955.

51. This must be a contingent of Republicans.
Richard J. Daley. Response when he was booed by the crowd at a national convention of the National Association for the Advancement of Colored People, Chicago, IL, July 4, 1963.

52. Organization, not machine. Get that? Organization, not machine.
Richard J. Daley. Remark to reporters, 1968.

53. You try it!
Richard J. Daley. To a reporter who suggested that His Honor feared dismantling of the Chicago

Democratic organization. Quoted in *The Chicago Tribune*, Nov. 14, 1968.

54. I figured it out real early: How can you control the city unless you're the leader of your party?
Richard J. Daley. Quoted in Len O'Connor, *Clout: Mayor Daley and His City*, 1975.

55. The captains of the *[political]* system become the captives of the system.
Alfonse D'Amato, U.S. Senator (R-NY). Quoted in *The New York Times*, Mar. 17, 1989.

56. No member shall be bound upon questions involving a construction of the Constitution of the United States or upon which he made contrary pledges to his constituents prior to his election or received contrary instructions by resolutions or platform from his nominating authority.
Democratic Party, *Caucus Rules*, 1909.

57. There are at least eighty liars in the convention.
Chauncey M. Depew (1834-1928), U.S. Senator (R-NY). Remark to reporters when told that both the Taft and Roosevelt camps claimed a majority of forty delegates, Republican National Convention, Chicago, IL, June 18, 1912.

58. Political action alone will not suffice. A new political party cannot win by conventional means. A new political party can win if it serves its proper function as the political arm of a complete patriotic resistance movement.
Robert DePugh, founder, Patriotic Party (Minutemen). *Blueprint for Victory*, 1966.

59. Governments propose, and oppositions dispose.
John G. Diefenbaker (1895-1975), Prime Minister of Canada (Conservative). Speech, House of Commons, Nov. 2, 1962.

60. Damn your principles! Stick to your party.
Benjamin Disraeli, 1st Earl of Beaconsfield (1804-1881), Prime Minister of Great Britain (Conservative). Attributed.

61. Party is organized opinion.
Benjamin Disraeli. Speech, Oxford, Nov. 25, 1864.

62. Without party, parliamentary government is impossible.
Benjamin Disraeli. Speech, Manchester, England, Apr. 4, 1872.

63. The friends of the court and the advocates of lineal succession are, by the Republican Party, branded with the title of *Tories*, which was the name of certain Irish robbers: while the court party in return would find no other revenge than by appropriating to covenanters and the Republicans of that class, the name of the Scotch beverage of sour milk, whose virtue they considered so expressive of their disposition and which is called *Whigg*.
Isaac D'Israeli (1766-1848), British writer. *Curiosities of Literature*, III, 1834.

64. Democrats give away their old clothes; Republicans wear theirs. Republicans employ exterminators; Democrats step on the bugs. Democrats eat the fish they catch; Republicans stuff 'em and hang 'em on the wall.
Sean Donlon, Ambassador of Ireland to the United States. Quoted in *The Washington Post*, Oct. 23, 1981.

65. To die for faction *[party]* is a common evil.
John Dryden (1631-1700), English poet and dramatist. *Absalom and Achitophel*, II.

66. A sect or party is an elegant incognito devised to save a man from the vexation of thinking.
Ralph Waldo Emerson (1803-1882), American writer. *Journals*, 1831.

67. If we don't like what the Republicans do, we need to get in there and change it.... By the turn of the century it'll be a 95 percent white Republican Party and a 99 percent black Democratic Party. That's not what we need.
Medgar Evers, Mayor of Fayette, MS. Explanation for his joining the Republican Party, May 12, 1989.

68. Party organization matters. When the door of a smoke-filled room is closed, there's hardly ever a woman inside.
Millicent Fenwick (1910-1992), U.S. Congresswoman (R-NJ). Interview, CBS, *60 Minutes*, Feb. 1, 1981.

69. Sworn to no party,
Of no sect am I;
I won't keep quiet
And I will not lie.
William Fisher (1780-1852), Rear-Admiral, British Navy. Motto.

70. Never again must America allow an arrogant, elite guard of political adolescents to bypass the regular party organization and dictate the terms of a national election.
Gerald R. Ford, 38th President of the United States (R-MI). Comment on Watergate. Quoted in *The New York Times*, Mar. 31, 1974.

71. We are against political parties and we have none.
Francisco Franco (1892-1975), President of Spain. Speech, Pamplona, Spain, 1953.

72. All free governments are party governments.
James A. Garfield (1831-1881), 20th President of the United States (R-OH). Speech, House of Representatives, Jan. 18, 1878.

73. I am an organization Democrat. I never in my life cast a vote against my own judgment, except I had to go along with the Democratic organization. I have done that. I will do it again. You must have organization.
John Nance Garner (1868-1967), U.S. Congressman (D-TX), Speaker of the House, and Vice President of the United States. Telegram accepting vice-presidential nomination, 1932.

74. The party or sect that will suffer by the triumph of injustice cannot exist with safety to mankind.
William Lloyd Garrison (1805-1879), American editor and abolitionist. *The Liberator*, Jan. 1, 1831.

75. How can one conceive of a one-party system in a country that has over two hundred varieties of cheeses?
Charles de Gaulle (1890-1970), President of France. Attributed.

76. Party leaders must have not only the confidence of the party, but the confidence of the people.
Gennadi I. Gerasimov, spokesman, Foreign Ministry, U.S.S.R. Comment when Russia held contested elections for the first time since the 1917 revolution and numerous incumbents lost. Statement, Moscow, Mar. 28, 1989.

77. I always voted at my party's call,
And never thought of thinking for myself at all.
William S. Gilbert (1836-1911), British dramatist. *H. M. S. Pinafore*, 1878.

78. I don't necessarily vote a straight ticket in my own state because there are sometimes Democrats out there who are better than Republicans. It's hard to believe but it's true.
Barry M. Goldwater, U.S. Senator (R-AZ). Quoted in *The Sacramento Bee*, Jan. 8, 1964.

79. No party has a monopoly over what is right.
Mikhail Gorbachev, President of the U.S.S.R. Speech, Congress of the Soviet Communist Party, Moscow, Feb. 1986.

80. There are but two parties now – traitors and patriots.
Ulysses S. Grant (1822-1885), 18th President of the United States (R-OH). Statement at the outbreak of the Civil War, 1861.

81. I have long held that this is a one-party government, the incumbent party.
Mark Green, unsuccessful candidate for the U.S. Senate. Quoted in *The New York Times*, Aug. 9, 1988.

82. All Democrats recognize we do have differences because we are a big family.
William H. Grey III, U.S. Congressman (D-PA). Quoted in *The New York Times*, June 25, 1988.

83. Party spirit was ... and always will be, wherever indulged, the bane of society and good neighborhood.
Sarah J. Hale (1788-1879), American magazine editor. *Sketches of American Character*, 1829.

84. Political controversies are never entered into with any wish to gain knowledge, but only a triumph for the party.
Sarah J. Hale. *Ibid.*

85. *[The Bank of the United States would be]* a political machine of the greatest importance of the state.
Alexander Hamilton (1755-1804), Member, Continental Congress and Constitutional Convention, and U.S. Secretary of the Treasury (Federalist-NY). *Proposal to Establish a Bank of the United States*, Jan. 1791.

86. Believing as I do in political parties, I had rather that the party ... should, in its conferences, make a declaration than to assume a leadership or take an individual position on the question.
Warren G. Harding (1865-1923), 29th President of the United States (R-OH). Quoted in Ralph G. Martin, *Ballots & Bandwagons*, 1964.

87. If parties in a republic are necessary to secure a degree of vigilance sufficient to keep the public functionaries within the bounds of law and duty, at that point their usefulness ends.
William Henry Harrison (1773-1841), 9th President of the United States (Whig-OH). Inaugural address, Mar. 4, 1841.

88. I cannot answer your question because I am neither a Democrat or a Republican. I am a constitutional monarchy.
Hassan II, King of Morocco. Statement to Sen. Clifford Case, 1978.

89. He serves his party best who serves the country best.
Rutherford B. Hayes (1822-1893), 19th President of the United States (R). Inaugural address, Mar. 5, 1877; also his personal motto.

90. The Grey Poupon crowd, the Gucci-shoe wearing, Mercedes-driving, polo-playing, Jacuzzi-soaking, Perrier-drinking, Aspen-skiing, ritzy rich.

Howell T. Heflin, U.S. Senator (D-AL). Quoted in *The Washington Post*, Oct. 28, 1990.

91. None is so crazy but that he may find a crazier comrade who will understand him.

Heinrich Heine (1797-1856), German writer. *Harz Journey*, 1824.

92. Republicans hate government ... so they let us *[Democrats]* run it for them.

David Helbach, Wisconsin State Senator (D). Quoted in Alan Ehrenhalt, *The United States of Ambition*, 1991.

93. Weak natures have to be told that it simply means "to be *[with the Nazi Party]* or not to be *[at all]*."

Adolf Hitler (1889-1945), Führer of the Third German Reich. *Mein Kampf*, 1933.

94. When a third party's demands become popular enough, they are appropriated by one or both of the major parties and the third party disappears. Third parties are like bees: Once they have stung, they die.

Richard Hofstadter, American historian. *The Age of Reform*, 1955.

95. The election was held today. Besides the two great party tickets, there is a new party which has polled most unexpectedly five or six thousand votes. They call themselves the American Party, and are opposed to the extension of suffrage to foreigners; ... with this powerful demonstration of popular opinion in their favor, I should not be surprised if ere long they should swallow up the Whig Party. This new movement has occasioned a great defection from both parties.

Philip Hone (1780-1851), Mayor of New York City (Whig). *Diary*, Nov. 7, 1843.

96. Honor is not the exclusive property of any political party.

Herbert Hoover (1874-1964), 31st President of the United States (R-IA). Quoted on his death.

97. The basic tactics of the Communist Party are deceit and trickery.

J. Edgar Hoover (1895-1972), Director, Federal Bureau of Investigation. Testimony, House Un-American Activities Committee, 1955.

98. The mission of parties is to keep the people divided into factions, that they may be unable to do anything for themselves.

Edgar Watson Howe (1853-1937), American editor and writer. *Ventures in Common Sense*, 1919.

99. Every man that lowered our flag was a Democrat.... Every preacher that said slavery was a divine institution was a Democrat. Recollect it! Every man that shot a Union soldier was a Democrat. Every wound borne by you Union soldiers is a souvenir of a Democrat.

Robert Green Ingersoll (1833-1899), Attorney General of Illinois (R). Campaign speech, 1890.

100. People who won those states wanted to see their states in the victory column last night. They won elections in the streets and lost them in the suites.

Jesse L. Jackson, Shadow Senator (D-DC). Comment when unpledged delegates tipped the balance against him in several states where he had won the majority of delegates in the 1988 Democratic presidential primary elections. Quoted in *The New York Times*, July 22, 1988.

101. This election isn't about race; it's about the direction of the *[Democratic]* party. They say, "You're not supporting the party nominee." I endorsed Daley twice over Republican opponents. He didn't endorse me once. This is about reciprocal voting and mutual support.

Jesse L. Jackson. Comment on supporting a black third-party candidate for Mayor of Chicago while ignoring the regular Democratic nominee, Richard J. Daley, Jr.. Speech, Faith Tabernacle Church, Chicago, IL, Mar. 29, 1989.

102. It doesn't matter whether you're riding an elephant or a donkey if you're going in the wrong direction.

Jesse L. Jackson. Speech, C-SPAN, July 22, 1990.

103. Our American elections have been fought between parties which, roughly, have represented the forces advocating change and those preferring stability.

Robert H. Jackson (1892-1954), U.S. Attorney General (D) and U.S. Supreme Court Justice. *The Struggle for Judicial Supremacy*, 1941.

104. Democrats make up plans and then do something else. Republicans follow the plans their grandfathers made.... Republican boys date Democratic girls. They plan to marry Republican girls, but feel they're entitled to a little fun first.

Andrew Jacobs, Jr., U.S. Congressman (D-IN). House debate, July 19, 1983.

105. If I could not go to heaven but with a party, I would not go there at all.

Thomas Jefferson (1743-1826), 3rd President of

the United States (Democratic Republican-VA). Letter to Francis Hopkinson, Mar. 13, 1789.

106. We are all Republicans; we are all Federalists.
Thomas Jefferson. First inaugural address, Mar. 4, 1801.

107. Men by their constitutions are naturally divided into two parties: 1). Those who fear and distrust the people and wish to draw all powers from them into the hands of the higher classes. 2). Those who identify themselves with the people, have confidence in them.... In every country these two parties exist.... Call them, therefore, Liberals and Serviles, Jacobins and Ultras, Whigs and Tories, Republicans and Federalists, Aristocrats and Democrats, or by whatever name you please, they are the same party still and pursue the same object.
Thomas Jefferson. Letter to Henry Lee, Aug. 10, 1824.

108. They have the Republican Party of President Eisenhower. They have the Republican Party of Senator Taft. They have the Republican Party of Senator Morse. And somewhere – way out behind the *Chicago Tribune* tower is – the Republican Party of Senator McCarthy with one foot heavy in Greece and the other foot in Secretary Dulles's security files. It makes bipartisanship right difficult. We Democrats need to know which one of the Republican parties to be bipartisan *with;* and which one of the Republican parties to be bipartisan *against.*
Lyndon B. Johnson (1908-1973), 36th President of the United States (D-TX). Speech, Gridiron Club, Washington, DC, Apr. 11, 1953.

109. I'm a fellow that likes small parties, and the Republican Party is about the size I like.
Lyndon B. Johnson. Apr. 21, 1964.

110. Lincoln was right about not fooling all the people all of the time. But the Republicans haven't given up trying.
Lyndon B. Johnson. Oct. 7, 1966.

111. The people will turn to us *[the Republicans]* and the country will be saved.
Walter H. Judd, U.S. Congressman (R-MN). Keynote address, Republican National Convention, Chicago, IL, July 24, 1960.

112. When you try to make an issue of religion or conscience a matter of party policy, you run into trouble.
Thomas H. Kean, Governor of New Jersey (R). In reference to abortion. Speech, Republican Governors' Conference, Hilton Head, SC, Nov. 13, 1989.

113. We need Democrats. They are on this earth to distribute wealth. But we first need a party that can create the wealth to distribute.
Jack F. Kemp, U.S. Congressman and Secretary of Housing and Urban Development (R-NY). PBS, *Firing Line*, Oct. 9, 1988.

114. Our duty as a party is not to our party alone, but to the nation and, indeed, to all mankind. Our duty is not merely the preservation of political power but the preservation of peace and freedom.
John F. Kennedy (1917-1963), 35th President of the United States (D-MA). Undelivered speech, Nov. 1963.

115. Parties are instruments of government.... The business of parties is not just to win elections. It is to govern. And a party cannot govern if it is disunited.
Robert F. Kennedy (1925-1968), U.S. Senator and U.S. Attorney General (D-NY). Speech, Kings County Democratic Party dinner, Brooklyn, NY, May 20, 1965.

116. A Communist has no right to be a mere onlooker.
Nikita S. Khrushchev (1894-1971), Premier of the U.S.S.R. 1956.

117. It's been challenging, but I can't say it's been fun.
Paul G. Kirk, Jr., National Chairman, Democratic Party. In regard to his job as party chairman. Quoted in *The Washington Post*, July 17, 1988.

118. When Marxist dictators shoot their way into power in Central America, the San Francisco Democrats don't blame the guerillas and their Soviet allies, they blame United States policies of one hundred years ago, but then they always blame America first.
Jeane J. Kirkpatrick, U.S. Ambassador to the United Nations (R). Quoted in *The 1989 Conservative Calendar*.

119. Party loyalty lowers the greatest of men to the petty level of the masses.
Jean de La Bruyère (1644-1696), French writer. *Les "Caractères" de Théophraste*, 1688.

120. I long for the time when the public service will get onto a higher plane than that of serving political parties, and come to serve the public interest instead.
Robert M. La Follette (1855-1925), Governor of Wisconsin and U.S. Senator (R). Senate speech, June 28, 1917.

121. Permanent political parties have been born in this country after, and not before, national campaigns, and they have come from the people, not from the proclamations of individual leaders.

Robert M. La Follette. Platform statement presented to the Progressive Conference, Cleveland, OH, July 4, 1924.

122. Women in politics are the hope of American politics. They are either going to break the control of the bosses or put the political parties out of business.

Fiorello H. La Guardia (1882-1947), U.S. Congressman (R and Socialist) and Mayor of New York City (R and Fusion Party). Speech, 1921.

123. I am a Republican. But I am not running on the Republican platform. I'm running on my own platform. I stand for the Republicanism of Abraham Lincoln.

Fiorello H. La Guardia. Campaign speech, 1922.

124. There comes a time in the life of every public official when he must decide between right and regularity.

Fiorello H. La Guardia. Speech, Erasmus Hall High School, Brooklyn, NY, 1923.

125. I loathe the professional politician. I have never been a regular. I have fought political machines and party politics at every opportunity.

Fiorello H. La Guardia. 1931.

126. I'm a loyal Republican. I support the President *[Ronald Reagan]* when he's right – and I just keep quiet the other 95 percent of the time.

John LeBoutiller, U.S. Congressman (R-NY). Quoted in Larry Wilde, *The Official Politicians Joke Book*, 1984.

127. When we are reproached for exercising the dictatorship of party, we say, yes.... We stand by it and cannot do without it.

V. I. Lenin (1870-1924), Premier of the U.S.S.R. Quoted in *The New York Times*, Feb. 11, 1990.

128. We hold the true republican position. In leaving the people's business in their hands, we cannot be wrong.

Abraham Lincoln (1809-1865), 16th President of the United States (R-IL). Speech in Congress, July 27, 1848.

129. As to politics, I am doing what I can for the cause.

Abraham Lincoln. Letter to Albert Parker, Aug. 10, 1858.

130. I am not, nor ever have been, connected with the party called the Know Nothing party, or the party calling themselves the American Party.

Abraham Lincoln. Letter to Edward Lusk, Oct. 30, 1858.

131. As to the matter of fusion *[with the other three parties]* I am for it if it can be had on Republican grounds; and I am not for it on any other terms. A fusion on any other terms would be as foolish as unprincipled. It would lose the whole North, while the common enemy would carry the whole South.... I am against letting down the Republican standard a hair's breadth.

Abraham Lincoln. Letter to Dr. Theodore Canisius, May 17, 1859.

132. No party can command respect which sustains this year what it opposed last.

Abraham Lincoln. Letter to Samuel Galloway, July 28, 1859.

133. There was once in this country a man by the name of Thomas Jefferson, supposed to be a Democrat – a man whose principles and policies are not very prevalent among Democrats today.

Abraham Lincoln. Speech, Columbus, OH, Sept. 16, 1859.

134. We *[the Republicans]* hold no doctrine, and make no declaration, which was not held to and made by "our fathers who framed the government under which we live."

Abraham Lincoln. Address, Cooper Institute, New York City, Feb. 27, 1860.

135. The opposition is indispensable. A good statesman, like any other sensible human being, always learns more from his opponents than from his fervent supporters.

Walter Lippmann (1889-1974), American political columnist. *The Atlantic Monthly*, Aug. 1939.

136. The Founding Fathers did not foresee the party system as it has developed, and what they knew about its early beginnings they disliked intensely.

Walter Lippmann. Quoted in Gladwin Hill, *Dancing Bear*, 1968.

137. I relate to both parties. I eat like an elephant and act like a jackass.

Rich Little, American comedian and impersonator. CBS, *Sunday Morning*, Aug. 16, 1988.

138. The only difference I ever found between the Democratic leadership and the Republican leadership is that one of them is skinning you from the ankle up and the other, from the neck down.

Huey P. Long (1893-1935), Governor of Louisiana and U.S. Senator (D). Quoted on CBS, *Sunday Morning*, Aug. 14, 1988.

139. One party takes us *[blacks]* for granted. The other just takes us.

Joseph Lowery, President, Southern Christian Leadership Council. SCLC National Convention, Aug. 9, 1990.

140. Whenever a Republican leaves one side of the aisle and goes to the other, it raises the intelligence quotient of both parties.

Clare Boothe Luce (1903-1987), U.S. Congresswoman and U.S. Ambassador to Italy and Brazil (R-CT). Remark when Senator Wayne Morse of Oregon switched from the Republican to the Democratic Party, 1956.

141. The wish to have unified parties or movements in our young countries must not be interpreted as a tendency toward political monopoly or a certain brand of dictatorship.

Patrice Lumumba (1925-1961), Prime Minister of The Congo (Zaire). Speech, University of Ibadan, Nigeria, Mar. 22, 1959.

142. No sophism is too gross to delude minds distempered by party spirit.

Thomas Babington Macaulay, 1st Baron Macaulay (1800-1859), historian and Secretary of War, Great Britain (Liberal). *History of England*, V, 1861.

143. But the most common and durable source of faction *[political parties]* has been the various and unequal distribution of property. Those who hold and those who are without property have ever formed distinct interests in society.

James Madison (1751-1836), 4th President of the United States (Democratic Republican-VA). *The Federalist*, No. 10, Nov. 23, 1787.

144. I did not clash with the National Party. I clashed with my conscience. And in the end, conscience wins.

Wynand Malan, Member of Parliament, South Africa (National Party). Comment on resigning from the party. Quoted in *Time*, May 4, 1987.

145. Every political organization has a right to exist and to advocate its own point of view.

Nelson Mandela, founder, African National Congress, South Africa. Testimony at his treason trial, Pretoria, South Africa, 1962.

146. Our principle is that the Party commands the gun, and the gun must never be allowed to command the Party.

Mao Tse-tung (1893-1976), Chairman, Communist Party of China. *Problems of War and Strategy*, Nov. 6, 1938.

147. If there is to be a revolution, there must be a revolutionary party.

Mao Tse-tung. *Revolutionary Forces of the World Unite, Fight Against Imperialist Aggression!*, Nov. 1948.

148. In the hour of danger there is no partisanship.

Joseph W. Martin, Jr. (1884-1968), U.S. Congressman and Speaker of the House (R-MA). Statement, Dec. 7, 1941.

149. The brighter the presidential prospect of victory *[for a particular party]*, the greater the crop of available candidates.

Ralph G. Martin, American political historian. *Ballots & Bandwagons*, 1964.

150. Mr. Chairman, I am from the South, and I never knew a Republican was white until I was twenty-one years old.

Maury Maverick (1895-1954), U.S. Congressman (D-TX). Speech, House Committee of the Whole, for the Gavagan antilynching bill, Apr. 15, 1937.

151. On those rare occasions when successful *[political]* reform organizations have been welded together they have developed techniques of political astuteness, leadership, and discipline not unlike political machines.

Robert S. Maxwell, American historian. *Indiana Magazine of History*, Mar. 1952.

152. Have you ever tried to split sawdust?

Eugene J. McCarthy, U.S. Congressman and U.S. Senator (D-WI). Remark when accused of splitting the Democratic Party, Oct. 23, 1969.

153. We opened the door of the Democratic Party, and 30 million Democrats walked out.

George S. McGovern, U.S. Congressman and U.S. Senator (D-SD). Speech, Gridiron Club, Washington, DC, 1973.

154. For me party discipline is a sacred matter, not just lust for power.

Golda Meir (1898-1978), Prime Minister of Israel (Labour). Apr. 11, 1974.

155. A party of order and stability, and a party of progress or reform, are both necessary elements of a healthy state of political life.

John Stuart Mill (1806-1873), Member of Parliament, Great Britain, and political economist. *On Liberty*, 1859.

156. It is not healthy to have a country governed by just one political party. There should be other political families taking part in government.
François Mitterand, President of France (Socialist). Quoted in *Time*, June 20, 1988.

157. You have done more than elect a President *[Franklin D. Roosevelt]*. You have created a new party that ought to hold power for twenty-five years.
Raymond Moley (1886-1975), U.S. Assistant Secretary of State and presidential assistant (D). Remark to Louis McHenry Howe, Nov. 12, 1932.

158. Any party which takes credit for the rain must not be surprised if its opponents blame it for the drought.
Dwight Whitney Morrow (1873-1931), U.S. Ambassador to Mexico and U.S. Senator (R-NJ). Campaign speech, Oct. 1930.

159. As a partisan Republican, I am concerned by the fact that the John Birch Society has picked my party ... as a vehicle to promulgate its monolithic philosophy. There are three organizations in this country which give me grave doubts as a citizen: the Communist Party, the Ku Klux Klan, and the John Birch Society.
Thurston B. Morton (1907-1982), U.S. Congressman and U.S. Senator (R-KY). Statement, Washington, DC, 1965.

160. The Democrats have prevailed because at heart we have embodied a great idea, which is that an elected government can be the instrument of the common purpose of a free people; that government can embrace great causes and do great things.
Daniel P. Moynihan, Chief American Delegate to the United Nations and U.S. Senator (D-NY). Speech, Gridiron Club, Washington, DC, 1981.

161. Today the national political parties are in name only; on Capitol Hill there are 535 political parties.
John Naisbitt, American futurist and writer. *Megatrends*, 1982.

162. Democrats are to the manna born.
Ogden Nash (1902-1971), American poet and humorist. *Vive le Postmaster General.*

163. The Republican Party is not strong enough to elect a President. We have to have a Presidential candidate strong enough to get the Republican Party elected.
Richard M. Nixon, 37th President of the United States (R-CA). Quoted in *The New York Times*, Mar. 15, 1955.

164. In the Democratic Party, about half of their representatives get elected by being for civil rights and the other half by being against civil rights.
Richard M. Nixon. Speech, New York City, Jan. 20, 1958.

165. The direct primary *[election]* will lower party responsibility. In its stead it establishes individual responsibility.
George W. Norris (1861-1944), U.S. Congressman and U.S. Senator (R and Independent Republican-NE). *Annals of the American Academy of Political and Social Science*, Mar. 1923.

166. Party-mindedness is a form of feeble-mindedness.
George W. Norris. Quoted in *Harper's Magazine*, Oct. 1936.

167. When it comes to deciding between losing an election and losing control of the party – lose the election.
Benjamin B. Odell, Jr. (1854-1926), U.S. Congressman and Governor of New York (R). Quoted in Ralph G. Martin, *Ballots & Bandwagons*, 1964.

168. As with the Christian religion, the worst advertisement for Socialism is its adherents..
George Orwell (Eric Blair) (1903-1950), British writer. *The Road to Wigan Pier*, 1937.

169. *[Pres. Theodore]* Roosevelt is trying to make his *[Republican]* Party radical, which is impossible; don't let us *[Democrats]* be forced into the mistake of trying to make our party conservative, which is equally impossible.
Thomas Mott Osborne (1859-1926), penologist and warden of Sing Sing Prison; Mayor of Auburn, NY; and founder, Democratic League. Letter to John A. Dix, Oct. 8, 1910.

170. It is better ... to have a small, united group than an immense debating society.
Alice Paul (1885-1977), founder, National Women's Party. Letter to Eunice R. Oberly, Mar. 6, 1914.

171. Here we sit, a group of supposedly practical men, trying to deceive ourselves that the people want us..... They're tired of the whole damned lot of us. We're going to lose this election; for God's sake, don't let us lose control of ourselves. There's only one way to go and that's straight ahead.... I know damn well it leads straight over a precipice. You know it, too. But that's what we've got to do. All right, let's drive the old machine into the chasm. After the crash, we can pick ourselves out of the

wreck – those of us who survive. With what's left of the machine, we can begin building another.... In the reconstructed machine we'll ride back home.
Boies Penrose (1860-1921), U.S. Senator (R-PA). Remarks at a meeting of Republican party leaders, 1912.

172. We're not going to make the mistake this time that we made four years ago *[with Charles Evans Hughes]*. Our fellows are going to put in *[nominate]* a man *[Warren G. Harding]* who will listen .
Boies Penrose. 1920. Quoted in Ralph G. Martin, *Ballots & Bandwagons*, 1964.

173. Negroes are slowly but surely taking over the apparatus of the Democratic Party in a growing number of deep southern black belt counties, and this cannot but push whites into the alternative party structure – that of the GOP.
Kevin Phillips, political consultant (R). *The Emerging Republican Majority*, 1969.

174. First, this great and glorious country was built up by political parties; second, parties can't hold together if their workers don't get offices when they win; third, if the parties go to pieces, the government they build up must go to pieces too; fourth, then there'll be hell to pay.
George Washington Plunkitt (1842-1924), Tammany Hall leader, New York City (D). Quoted by U.S. Supreme Court Justice Antonin Scalia, *Rutan* v. *Republican Party of Illinois*, 1990 (dissent).

175. Party spirit ... at best is the madness of many for the gain of a few.
Alexander Pope (1688-1744), British poet and Tory activist. Letter to Martha Blount, Aug. 27, 1714.

176. There never was any party, faction, sect or cabal whatsoever in which the most ignorant were not the most violent.... However, such instruments are necessary to politicians; and perhaps it may be with states as with clocks, which must have some dead weight hanging at them to help and regulate the motion of the finer and more useful parts.
Alexander Pope. *Thoughts on Various Subjects*, 1741.

177. We have witnessed for more than a quarter of a century the struggles of the two great political parties for power and plunder, while grievous wrongs have been inflicted upon the suffering people. We charge that the controlling influences dominating both these parties have permitted the existing dreadful conditions to develop without serious effort to prevent or restrain them.... They propose ... to destroy the multitude in order to secure corruption funds from the millionaires.
Populist Party platform, 1892.

178. In Congress today everyone runs for office as a political entity of his own.
Joel M. Pritchard, U.S. Congressman (R-WA). Quoted in *The Washington Post*, Jan. 6, 1991.

179. A party of doom and gloom.
J. Danforth Quayle, U.S. Senator and Vice President of the United States (R-IN). In reference to the Democratic Party. Interview, ABC, *This Week*, Aug. 14, 1988.

180. The Democratic Party *[in Connecticut]*, both by inertia and design, had shifted so far to the right it made the Republican Party unnecessary.
Miles S. Rapoport, Connecticut Assemblyman (D). Quoted in *Governing*, Sept. 1988.

181. From negation arises party, not movement.
Walther Rathenau (1867-1922), Foreign Minister, Germany. 1917.

182. My answer to why did I choose the Democratic Party is that I spent three years in Washington under a Republican administration.
Dixy Lee Ray, Governor of Washington and Chairman, U.S. Atomic Energy Commission (D). Quoted in *The Wall Street Journal*, Mar. 15, 1976.

183. Republicans believe every day is the Fourth of July, but Democrats believe every day is Apr. 15.
Ronald Reagan, 40th President of the United States (R-CA). Quoted in *The Los Angeles Herald-Examiner*, Mar. 3, 1978.

184. The best system is to have one party govern and the other party watch, and on general principles I think it would be best for us to govern and the Democrats watch.
Thomas B. Reed (1839-1902), U.S. Congressman and Speaker of the House (R-ME). House debate, Apr. 22, 1880.

185. A hopeless assortment of discordant differences as incapable of positive action as it is capable of infinite clamor.
Thomas B. Reed. In reference to the Democratic party. 1892.

186. The Democratic Party is like a man riding backward in a railroad car – it never sees anything until he has got past it.
Thomas B. Reed. 1896.

187. A good party is better than the best man that ever lived.

Thomas B. Reed. Quoted in W. A. Robinson, *Life of Thomas B. Reed*, 1930.

188. The Republicans must be put down at the point of the bayonet.
William A. Richardson (1811-1875), U.S. Congressman (D-IL), U.S. Senator, and U.S. Secretary of War. Speech, Concord, NH, Mar. 6, 1863.

189. This is a party *[Democratic]* that is hungry to win the White House – and winning looks so close now we can almost taste it. There's nobody here who's going to fight and die for some platform plank if it looks like it could hurt ... in the election.
William B. Richardson, U.S. Congressman (D-NM). Quoted in *The Washington Post*, June 26, 1988.

190. The Republicans have their splits right after the election and the Democrats have theirs just before an election.
Will Rogers (1879-1935), American humorist. Column, Dec. 29, 1930.

191. While the Republicans are smart enough to make money, the Democrats are smart enough to get in office every two or three times a century and take it away from them.
Will Rogers. Radio broadcast, 1934.

192. The more you read about politics, you got to admit that each party is worse than the other. The one that's out always looks the best.
Will Rogers. *Illiterate Digest*. "Breaking into the Writing Game," 1924.

193. I don't belong to any organized political party. I'm a Democrat.
Will Rogers. Quoted on PBS, *Will Rogers U.S.A.*, Oct. 3, 1988.

194. There is no way in this world you're going to make a political party respectable unless you keep it out of office.
Will Rogers. *Ibid.*

195. I want unity but above everything else, I want a party that will fight for the things that we know to be right at home and abroad.
Anna Eleanor Roosevelt (1884-1962), First Lady and U.S. Delegate to the United Nations. Speech, Democratic National Advisory Committee, New York City, 1959.

196. Until we get rid of these political manchus who now control the *[Democratic]* Party, we might as well not go to the polls.
Franklin D. Roosevelt (1882-1945), 32nd President of the United States (D-NY). Quoted in *The Poughkeepsie Daily Eagle*, Mar. 14, 1912.

197. They call the system *[of party bosses]* ... invisible government.... The ruler of the state *[New York]* during the greater part of the forty years of my acquaintance with the state government has not been any man authorized by the Constitution or by the law.
Elihu Root (1845-1937), U.S. Senator (R-NY), U.S. Secretary of War, U.S. Secretary of State, and Nobel Laureate in Peace. Speech, New York State Constitutional Convention, 1915.

198. No matter how fondly or how often we may long for a President who is above the heat of political strife, we must acknowledge resolutely his right and duty to be the leader of his party.
Clinton Rossiter (1917-1970), American political historian. *The American Presidency*, 1956.

199. Beware the man who sees himself as bigger than the political party.
John G. Rowland, Connecticut State Legislator (R). Quoted in *The New York Times*, July 22, 1990.

200. This is the week the Democrats had a love feast *[the 1988 National Convention]*, and the stock market had indigestion. The two may, or may not, be connected.
Louis Rukeyser, American economic journalist. PBS, *Wall Street Week*, July 22, 1988.

201. An Englishman has to have a Party, just as he has to have trousers.
Bertrand Russell, 3rd Earl Russell of Kingston (1872-1970), British philosopher and reformer. Letter to Maurice Amos, June 16, 1936.

202. It's nice to be here in the great state of Georgia, where Republicans are real Republicans and so are Democrats.
Mark Russell, American political humorist. Quoted on NBC, *Sunday*, July 16, 1988.

203. A conservative Republican is one who doesn't believe anything new should be tried for the first time. A liberal Republican is one who does believe something should be tried for the first time – but not now.
Mort Sahl, American comedian. 1980.

204. The best Party is but a kind of a Conspiracy against the rest of the Nation. They put everybody else out of their Protection..
George Savile, 1st Marquess of Halifax (1633-1695), Lord Privy Seal of England. *Political Thoughts and Reflections*, 1750.

205. But to be turned off by the unfairness of the system is not equivalent to understanding why the system works that way or, better yet, what can be done about it. What we are witnessing is the emergence of a radicalism or populism that is apolitical and cynical.
Robert Scheer, American political scientist. *America After Nixon*, 1974.

206. Television has replaced the political party.
Arthur M. Schlesinger, Jr., American historian and presidential advisor (D). Quoted in *Time*, Oct. 24, 1988.

207. The only things the *[congressional]* party leadership controls are the keys to the washrooms.
Patricia R. Schroeder, U.S. Congresswoman (D-CO). Interview, CBS, *Nightwatch*, Oct. 24, 1988.

208. A leader should be true to his principles, his convictions of right, and the commands of his conscience even against the behests of his party.
Carl Schurz (1829-1906), U.S. Senator (R-MO). Memorial address for Congressman Carlton B. Curtis (R-PA), Mar. 1883.

209. The three parties are ABC, NBC, and CBS.
Tony Schwartz, American political TV ad producer. Interview, PBS, *A Walk Through the 20th Century: The 30 Second President*, July 23, 1990.

210. It is not a question of who we should prefer but whom can we elect.
William H. Seward (1801-1872), Governor of New York (Whig), U.S. Senator (Whig and R), and U.S. Secretary of State. Comment on Henry Clay, who was the most popular Whig but who had already lost two presidential elections. Letter to Whig leaders, 1852.

211. A *[political]* party is in one sense a joint stock company in which those who contribute the most, direct the action and management of the concern.
William H. Seward. Quoted in Richard Hofstadter, *The American Political Tradition*, 1948.

212. That's something we have to get used to, that it's a normal thing to have a group playing the role of the opposition.
Georgy K. Shakhnazarov, Soviet political advisor. Quoted in *The New York Times*, June 4, 1989.

213. The narrower the view of a political party gets, the smaller it gets.
Christopher Shays, U.S. Congressman (R-CT). Quoted on PBS, *Firing Line*, Dec. 4, 1988.

214. True patriotism is of no party.
Tobias Smollett (1721-1771), British novelist. *Adventures of Sir Launcelot Greaves*, 1762.

215. He shall be disenfranchised who, in time of faction, takes neither side.
Solon (c. 638-559 B.C.), Athenian lawgiver. *Tables of the Law*.

216. As soon as classes have been abolished, and the dictatorship of the proletariat has been done away with, the *[Communist]* Party will have fulfilled its mission and can be allowed to disappear.
Joseph Stalin (1879-1953), Premier of the U.S.S.R. Speech to students at Sverdloff University, Apr. 1924.

217. The duty of an opposition is very simple – it is to oppose everything and propose nothing.
Edward Stanley, 15th Earl of Derby (1799-1869), Member of Parliament, Great Britain (Conservative, Liberal, and Liberal Union), Foreign Secretary, and Colonial Secretary. Debate, Parliament, June 4, 1841.

218. Republicans sleep in twin beds – some even in separate rooms. That is why there are more Democrats.
Will Stanton, American writer. "How to Tell a Democrat from a Republican," *Ladies' Home Journal*, 1962.

219. Republicans study the financial pages of the newspaper. Democrats put them in the bottom of the bird cage.
Will Stanton. *Ibid*.

220. Conscience indeed! Throw conscience to the devil and stand by your party.
Thaddeus Stevens (1792-1868), U.S. Congressman (Whig and Republican-PA). Remark to a party colleague who was troubled at a particular course of action. Quoted in *Lancaster Intelligencer*, Jan. 17, 1866.

221. The principles of the Constitution, under which we live; the principles, upon which republics generally are founded, by which they are sustained, and through which they must be saved; the principles of public policy, by which national prosperity is secured, and national ruin averted; these, certainly, are not party creeds or party dogmas.
Joseph Story (1779-1845), U.S. Supreme Court Justice. *Miscellaneous Writings*, 1835.

222. The platform defines the norms of the party but is not a litmus test on each and every issue.
John Sununu, Governor of New Hampshire and White House Chief of Staff (R). Interview, ABC, *This Week*, Feb. 4, 1990.

223. A Whig, but not an ultra-Whig.

Zachary Taylor (1784-1850), 12th President of the United States (Whig-KY). Description of his party position. Quoted in Bernard Dyer, *Zachary Taylor*, 1946.

224. Those only are regarded *[in the House of Commons]* who are true to their party; and all the talent required is to be hot, to be heady, to be violent on one side or the other.

William Temple (1628-1699), English statesman and writer. Quoted in S. Austin Allibone, *Prose Quotations*, 1876.

225. Two rival messiahs *[Father Charles Coughlin and Rev. Gerald L. K. Smith]* plus one ambitious politician *[William Lemke]* plus some neopopulists plus a platform which reminds me of the early efforts of Hitler.

Norman Thomas (1884-1968), Director, League for Industrial Democracy. Description of the Union Party. *After the New Deal, What?*, 1936.

226. Justices of the Supreme Court do not act as Republicans or Democrats.

Richard Thornburgh, U.S. Attorney General and Governor of Pennsylvania (R). Interview, PBS, *John McLaughlin's One on One*, June 25, 1989.

227. In politics, shared hatreds are almost always the basis of friendships.

Alexis de Tocqueville (1805-1859), French writer. *Democracy in America*, 1835.

228. Fellow Americans, let us not put our trust in either of the old political parties. Both of them are owned and controlled by the same set of men. Self-interest is their God and their guide in every political move that they make.... Let us never again be such fools as to permit them to deceive us.

Francis E. Townsend (1867-1960), American physician; founder, Old Age Revolving Pensions; and cofounder, Union Party. 1936.

229. I'm a Democrat. I do not have enough money to be a Republican.

James A. Traficant, Jr., U.S. Congressman (D-OH). Interview, C-SPAN, May 6, 1990.

230. I didn't run on the bipartisan ticket.

James A. Traficant, Jr. House debate, Oct. 8, 1990.

231. The dictatorship of the Communist Party is maintained by recourse to every form of violence.

Leon Trotsky (1879-1940), Russian revolutionary theorist. *Terrorism and Communism*, 1924.

232. The party organization first substitutes itself for the party as a whole. Then the central committee substitutes itself for the party organization, and finally a single dictator substitutes himself for the central committee.

Leon Trotsky. 1926.

233. The *[Communist]* Party is always right.

Leon Trotsky. Favorite saying.

234. GOP stands for "Gluttons of Privilege."

Harry S Truman (1884-1972), 33rd President of the United States (D-MO). Campaign speech, 1948.

235. In this era of industrial and social unrest both parties are in disrepute with the average man.

Joseph Tumulty (1879-1954), presidential assistant (D). Advice to Woodrow Wilson, 1919.

236. Not long ago we had two men running for the President. There was Mr. McKinley on the one hand and Mr. Bryan on the other. If we'd have had an "Anti-Doughnut Party" neither would have been elected.

Mark Twain (Samuel Langhorne Clemens) (1835-1910), American writer. Quoted in Paul Foner, *Mark Twain, Social Critic*, 1958.

237. The power of the ballot ... may be rendered ineffective by the tyranny of party.

Martin Van Buren (1782-1862), 8th President of the United States (D). Quoted in William E. Nelson, *The Roots of American Bureaucracy, 1830-1900*, 1982.

238. It is easier to construct a new party than to rise gradually to the head of an old one.

Marquis de Vauvenargues (1715-1747), French soldier and moralist. *Réflexions et Maximes*.

239. We are the party of the people's anger.

Lech Walesa, President of Poland, trade unionist, and founder, Solidarity. Quoted in *The Washington Post*, Nov. 13, 1989.

240. No man should be permitted to be both Governor and political boss.

Earl Warren (1891-1974), Chief Justice, U.S. Supreme Court, and Governor of California (R). Statement, 1946.

241. Good Americans are to be found in both parties.... Party affiliation does not change human instincts, or affect loyalty to country or transcend the fond hope of Americans for their children. No party has a patent on progress, a copyright on governmental principles, or a proprietary interest in the advances made in former days.... Both parties have at times served their country well.

Earl Warren. Speech, Salt Lake City, UT, Sept. 1948.

242. ... the demon of party spirit.
George Washington (1732-1799), 1st President of the United States (VA). Quoted in John C. Fitzpatrick, *The Writings of George Washington*, 1940.

243. I'm against the Democratic platform because it doesn't say anything. I'm against the Republican platform because it says too much.
Lowell P. Weicker, Jr., U.S. Congressman and U.S. Senator (R-CT), and Governor of Connecticut (Ind.). Quoted in *The New York Times*, Aug. 16, 1988.

244. Let the Afro-American depend on no party, but on himself for his salvation... When he has money, and plenty of it, parties and races will become his servants.
Ida B. Wells (1862-1931), American educator and cofounder, National Association for the Advancement of Colored People. *The New York Age*, Nov. 11, 1892.

245. We heard and read what *[Governor Earl]* Warren was saying at the time, and it proved to us that he never was a Republican. I felt that he had deceived the party. Each year he came up with something new that was contrary to Republican philosophy.... By 1950, we were ready to fight him *[in the primary election]*. Our problem was that we couldn't come up with a candidate.
Thomas H. Werdel (1905-1966), U.S. Congressmen (R-CA). Quoted in Earl Katcher, *Earl Warren: A Political Biography*, 1967.

246. We have an incumbent party today.
Fred Wertheimer, President, Common Cause. Interview, CBS, *Sunday Morning*, Nov. 4, 1990.

247. I don't know a lot about politics, but I know a good party man when I see one.
Mae West (1893-1979), American actress. *Every Day's a Holiday*, 1938.

248. You're the fireplug in a dog kennel.
John C. White, Jr., National Chairman, Democratic Party. Remark on the party chairmanship. Quoted in *The Washington Post*, July 17, 1988.

249. You should be very careful about mixing the will of the people and the will of the party.
Hans-Jochim Willerding, Member, Politburo, East Germany. Interview, ABC, *This Week*, Nov. 19, 1989.

250. A vital element in the balanced opposition of a democracy is a strong, alert, and watchful opposition. That is our task for the next four years. We must constitute ourselves a vigorous, loyal and public-spirited opposition party.
Wendell L. Willkie (1892-1944), Republican candidate for President (IN). Radio address following his defeat by Franklin D. Roosevelt, Nov. 11, 1940.

251. Our parties marshal their adherents with the strictest possible discipline for the purpose of carrying elections, but their discipline is very slack and indefinite when dealing with legislation.
Woodrow Wilson (1856-1924), 28th President of the United States (D-NJ). *Congressional Government, A Study in American Politics*, 1885.

252. The only bond for cohesion is the caucus, which occasionally whips a party together for cooperative action against the time for casting its vote upon some critical question
Woodrow Wilson. *Ibid.*

253. The success of a party means little except when the nation is using that party for a large and definite purpose.
Woodrow Wilson. First inaugural address, Mar. 4, 1913.

254. Before we proceed I wish it clearly understood that I owe you nothing.... God ordained that I should be the next President of the United States. Neither you nor any other mortal could have prevented that.
Woodrow Wilson. Statement to William F. McCoombs, Chairman of the Democratic National Committee. Quoted in McCoombs, *Making Woodrow Wilson President*, 1921.

255. There must not be a party monopoly on power.
Boris Yeltsin, President of the Russian Republic and President of the U.S.S.R. Speech, Feb. 5, 1990.

256. If the Senate holds a trial *[impeachment of President Nixon]*, then the Republican Party goes down with it.
Milton R. Young (1897-1983), U.S. Senator (R-ND). Quoted in Woodward and Bernstein, *The Final Days*, 1976.

Chapter 73

Patronage and Pork Barrel

1. No man who ever held the office of President would congratulate a friend on obtaining it. He will make one man ungrateful, and a hundred men his enemies, for every office he can bestow.

   John Adams (1735-1826), 2nd President of the United States (Federalist-MA). Comment upon learning that his son, John Quincy Adams, had been chosen President of the United States. Quoted by Josiah Quincy, *Figures from the Past*, 1883.

2. I will devote none of my time to developing laws to increase my own patronage and multiply canvassers *[electors]* in my favor.

   John Quincy Adams (1767-1848), 6th President of the United States (Ind.-MA). *Diary*, Feb. 25, 1821.

3. *[President]* Van Buren says he considers it as a misfortune when any office to be filled by him becomes vacant, and thinks patronage rather a burden than a benefit.

   John Quincy Adams. *Diary*, Dec. 9, 1837.

4. Political appointees *[to civil service positions]* are talented, able people. They are not lepers; they are not diseased.

   Lon Anderson, spokesman, U.S. Department of Education. Quoted in *The Washington Post*, Oct. 9, 1988.

5. Sooner or later you have to reach down into that old pork barrel.

   Richard K. Armey, U.S. Congressman (R-TX). PBS, *Firing Line*, Sept. 14, 1990.

6. Where the public money runs deepest the hogs fight each other to get their snouts in the trough, and the big trough nowadays runs through the Pentagon.

   Russell Baker, American columnist. *The New York Times*, June 25, 1988.

7. To the victor belong only those spoils that may be constitutionally obtained.

   William J. Brennan, Jr., U.S. Supreme Court Justice. Comment when declaring unconstitutional the requiring of particular political party affiliation for government jobs. *Rutan* v. *Republican Party of Illinois*, 1990.

8. Can you let me know what positions you have at your disposal with which to reward deserving Democrats?

   William Jennings Bryan (1860-1925), U.S. Secretary of State (D). Letter to Walker W. Vick, Receiver-General of the Dominican Republic, Aug. 20, 1913.

9. I am glad to have the public know that I appreciated services of those who work in politics and feel an interest in seeing them rewarded.

   William Jennings Bryan. Interview, *The New York Times*, Jan. 15, 1915.

10. The host of contractors, speculators, stockjobbers, and lobby members which haunt the halls of Congress, all desirous ... to get their arm into the public treasury, are sufficient to alarm every friend of this country. Their progress must be arrested.

    James Buchanan (1791-1868), 15th President of the United States (D-PA). Letter to Franklin Pierce, 1852.

11. The trouble with *[President]* Taft is that if he were Pope he would think it necessary to appoint a few Protestant cardinals.

    Joseph G. Cannon (1836-1926), U.S. Congressman and Speaker of the House (R-IL). Quoted in Mark Sullivan, *Our Times: The United States, 1900-1925*, 1927.

12. Jimmy *[Carter]*'s still mad because I wouldn't take secretary of state. I want to be director of alcohol and firearms.

    Billy Carter (1937-1988), President Jimmy Carter's brother. Rifkin and Howard, *Redneck Power: The Wit and Wisdom of Billy Carter*, 1977.

13. The Senate has no army, no navy, no patronage, no lucrative offices, nor glittering honors to be-

stow. Around us there is no swarm of greedy expectants rendering us homage, anticipating our wishes, and ready to execute our commands. How is it with the President *[Andrew Jackson]*? Is he powerless? He is felt from one extremity to the other of this republic. By means of principles which he has introduced *[the spoils system]*, and innovations which he has made in our institutions, alas! but too much countenanced by Congress and a confiding people, he exercises uncontrolled the power of the state. In one hand he holds the purse and in the other brandishes the sword of the country! Myriads of dependents and partisans scattered over the land are ever ready to sing hosannahs to him and to laud to the skies whatever he does. He has swept over the government like a tropical tornado.

Henry Clay (1777-1852), U.S. Senator (National Republican and Whig-KY), Speaker of the House, and U.S. Secretary of State. Senate speech on expunging the censure of President Jackson, Jan., 1837.

14. Congressmen have their noses right in the trough, and they're slurping it up for their districts at the expense of all the taxpayers.

Silvio O. Conte (1922-1991), U.S. Congresman (R-MA). Comment made while wearing a pig's snout and ears. House debate, 1983.

15. Politics are impossible without spoils.... You have to deal with men as they are.... You must bribe the masses with spoils.

Richard Croker (1841-1922), Tammany Hall leader, New York City (D). 1900.

16. Every time you do a favor for a constituent, you make nine enemies and one ingrate.

James Michael Curley (1874-1958), Mayor of Boston, MA, Governor of Massachusetts, and U.S. Congressman (D). Quoted in *Conservative Digest*, Feb. 1987.

17. I favor putting the responsibility for the dispensing of patronage squarely on the organizations *[parties]*. Let the organizations be held strictly accountable for the endorsements. After the appointment is made the appointee ought to fit the job, so that the appointing power can rest assured that the work entrusted to him will be done right.

Harry M. Daugherty (1860-1941), U.S. Attorney General (R). 1920.

18. Local groups demand that their Representatives and Senators bring home the "bacon" or else.... They want economy practiced on the other fellow but not on themselves.

Paul H. Douglas (1892-1976), U.S. Senator (D-IL). Senate debate, 1964.

19. Good patronage.

Maurice L. Duplessis (1890-1959), Premier of Quebec, Canada (Union Nationale). Favorite phrase.

20. The Republicans in my state are expressing impatience and disappointment that so little progress has been made during the last eight months in calling to the support of the administration men loyal to it and in full sympathy with it.

Davis Elkins (1876-1959), U.S. Senator (R-WV). Statement to President Harding. Quoted in *The New York Times*, Oct. 15, 1921.

21. Take from the United States the appointment of postmasters and let the towns elect them, and you deprive the federal government of half a million defenders.

Ralph Waldo Emerson (1803-1882), American writer. *Journals*, 1860.

22. He is great who confers most benefits.

Ralph Waldo Emerson, *Essays*, First Series, "Compensation," 1865.

23. *[The legislature]* has no right to give monopolies of legal privilege – to bestow unequal portions of our common inheritance on favorites.

William Findley (1741-1821), U.S. Congressman (R-PA). Argument against rechartering the Bank of North America. *Debates and Proceedings of the General Assembly of Pennsylvania*, 1786.

24. One person's pork barrel project is another person's wise investment in the local infrastructure.

Thomas S. Foley, U.S. Congressman and Speaker of the House (D-WA). Quoted in Charles Henning, *The Wit and Wisdom of Politics*, 1989.

25. In the military budget, regionalism overcomes partiotism.

William Frenzel, U.S. Congressman (R-MN). Speech, Economics Club, C-SPAN, Sept. 18, 1990.

26. There is something in the heart of every politician that loves a dam, or a harbor, or a bridge or a military installation.

William P. Gramm, U.S. Congressman and U.S. Senator (R-TX). Quoted in *The New York Times*, Oct. 13, 1988.

27. All *patronage* is perilous to men of real ability and merit. It aids only those who lack other claims to support.

Rutherford B. Hayes (1822-1893), 19th President of the United States (R-OH). Letter to Gov. William McKinley of Ohio. Dec. 27, 1892.

28. I am firmly against the kind of logrolling which would subject our defense program to narrowly sectional or selfish pulling or hauling. But I am growing pretty hot under the collar about the way my state of West Virginia is being shortchanged by the Army, Navy, and Air Force.

Kenneth Hechler, U.S. Congressman (D-WV). Speech, House of Representatives, 1959.

29. I have heard in highest places the shameless doctrine avowed by men grown old in public office that the true way by which power should be gained in the Republic is to bribe the people with the offices created for their service.

George Frisbie Hoar (1826-1904), U.S. Congressman and U.S. Senator (R-MA). Statement at the impeachment trial of U.S. Secretary of War W. W. Belknap, 1876.

30. Major parties have lived more for patronage than principles; their goal has been to bind together a sufficiently large coalition of diverse interests to get into power; and once in power, to arrange sufficiently satisfactory compromises of interest to remain there.

Richard Hofstadter, American historian. *The Age of Reform*, 1955.

31. It is a handicap to any man to succeed a member of his own party as President. He has little patronage with which to reward his personal supporters.

Herbert Hoover (1874-1964), 31st President of the United States (R-IA). *Memoirs*, 1952.

32. I take it for granted that all who do not support the present administration, you will not consider your friends, and of course will lose your confidence.... All personal considerations and private friendships must yield to political justice.

Jesse Hoyt, tax collector, Port of New York. Remark to Martin Van Buren, Mar. 21, 1829.

33. Politics makes strange postmasters.

Frank McKinney (Kin) Hubbard (1868-1930), American caricaturist and writer. Cartoon, 1925.

34. If I had a teat for every one of these pigs to suck at, they would still be my friends.

Andrew Jackson (1767-1845), 7th President of the United States (D-TN). Comment when abandoned by some of his political supporters. Quoted in Carl B. Swisher, *Roger B. Taney*, 1935.

35. Okay, Frank, next time you need a dam in Idaho, ask Walter Lippmann for one.

Lyndon B. Johnson (1908-1973), 36th President of the United States (D-TX). Response To Sen. Frank Church (D-ID) when he explained his opposition to the President's Vietnam policy by showing him an article by columnist Walter Lippmann, who was also critical of the war. Quoted in *Esquire*, Aug. 1967.

36. Were it believed that vacant places could be had at the North Pole, the road there would be lined with dead Virginians.

Abraham Lincoln (1809-1865), 16th President of the United States (R-IL). Letter to Donn Piatt, Feb. 11, 1861.

37. Not knowing whether he *[Charles Wiegand]* is fit for any place, I could not with propriety recommend him for any.

Abraham Lincoln. Memorandum, Mar. 24, 1863.

38. Too many pigs; two few teats.

Abraham Lincoln. Remark when despondent over the number of job seekers who assailed the White House. Quoted on PBS, *The Civil War*, Sept. 23, 1990.

39. When I first came to Washington ... my charge was to cut the cost of government, to get government off our backs.... Thirty years later, the local newspaper says, "We want you to be a pork provider and we don't mean the farm kind."

Robert H. Michel, U.S. Congressman (R-IL). Quoted in *The Washington Post*, Nov. 1, 1988.

40. The root of most all problems we have today is the uncontrollable appetite of politicians in Washington to dish it out.

Wilbur D. Mills (1909-1992), U.S. Congressman (D-AR). Speech, Commonwealth Club, San Francisco, CA, June 2, 1972.

41. What we called the civil service was, in the main, merely a mass of Republican political appointees frozen into office by act of Congress.

Raymond Moley (1886-1975), U.S. Assistant Secretary of State and presidential assistant (D). *After Seven Years*, 1939.

42. *[It is]* indispensable that public affairs be conducted on business principles, and that the dangerous custom of giving public posts to political paupers and partisan servants, regardless of their fitness, should be discontinued, as such custom absorbs a large share of the public revenue.

National Manufacturers Association, Resolution, first annual meeting, 1868.

43. When you have a Republican administration in office, you have Republicans making money off it. When a Democratic administration, Democrats make money off it. Everyone knows that's the way it works.

Lynn Nofziger, White House Political Director (R). Statement to reporters, July 2, 1989.

44. To be popular, you must have a lot of programs, a lot of money for everyone.
Samuel Pierce, U.S. Secretary of Housing and Urban Development (R). Interview, *Time,* Sept. 18, 1989.

45. A government builds for the people.
Robert A. Roe, U.S. Congressman (R-NJ). House debate, June 6, 1991.

46. Our magnificent river system, with its superb possibilities for public usefulness, was dealt with by the national government not as a unit, but as a disconnected series of problems, whose only real interest was in their effect upon the reelection of a congressman here and there.
Theodore Roosevelt (1858-1919), 26th President of the United States (R-NY). *Autobiography,* 1919.

47. The spoils system, that practice which turns public offices, high and low, from public trusts into objects of prey and booty for the victorious party, may without extravagance of language be called one of the greatest criminals in our history, if not the greatest. In the whole catalogue of our ills there is none more dangerous to the vitality of our free institutions.
Carl Schurz (1829-1906), U.S. Senator (R-MO). Speech, Chicago, IL, Dec. 12, 1894.

48. You roll my log, and I will roll yours.
Lucius Annaeus Seneca (The Younger) (4 B.C.-A.D.65), Roman statesman, dramatist, and philosopher. *Apocolocynyosis.*

49. O, that estates, degrees, and offices
Were not deriv'd corruptly, and that clear honor
Were purchased by the merit of the wearer!
William Shakespeare (1564-1616), English writer. *The Merchant of Venice,* II, ix.

50. I do not condemn nepotism, provided the relatives really work.
Margaret Chase Smith, U.S. Congresswoman and U.S. Senator (R-ME). Speech, Republican National Women's Conference, Apr. 16, 1962.

51. It *[the defense budget]* bought jobs, votes in elections, and votes in Congress. Complicated weapons designs and success-oriented weapons testing combined with astute political engineering to convert the defense budget into a giant, self-perpetuating public works budget.
Franklin C. Spinney, staff member, Office of the U.S. Secretary of Defense. *The Washington Post,* Oct. 30, 1988.

52. They are either rogues or fools who think benefits are merely gifts.
Publilius Syrus (c.43 B.C.), Syrian writer. *Maxims.*

53. Either take your pork out or put our pork in.
William Thompson, U.S. Congressman (R-CA). His formula for appropriations legislation. Quoted in *USA Today,* Oct. 19, 1990.

54. Public servant: Persons chosen by the people to distribute the graft.
Mark Twain (Samuel Langhorne Clemens) (1835-1910), American writer. Quoted in Merle DeVore Johnson, ed., *More Maxims of Mark,* 1927.

55. He delivers to each group what each group needs.
Robert F. Wagner, Jr., Deputy Mayor, New York City (D), and President, New York City Board of Education. In reference to Howard Golden, Brooklyn Borough President (D). Quoted in *The New York Times,* July 16, 1988.

Chapter 74

Policy and Policy Making

1. Policy bubbles up from the bottom. Decisions are made at the top.

   Dean Acheson (1893-1971), U.S. Secretary of State (D). Quoted in Theodore White, *Breach of Faith*, 1975.

2. We must take great risks to avoid greater ones.

   Dean Acheson. Letter to Anthony Eden.

3. We have generals working on worst-case scenarios; we need statesmen on best cases.

   Gary Ackerman, U.S. Congressman (D-NY). Quoted in *The Washington Post*, Nov. 14, 1989.

4. Just because you change administrations doesn't mean you have to change *[foreign]* policy.

   James A. Baker III, U.S. Secretary of the Treasury (R), U.S. Secretary of State, White House Chief of Staff, and presidential campaign manager. Interview, CBS, *Face the Nation*, Feb. 26, 1989.

5. We should not, however, proceed with the adventure simply because we are wound up and cannot stop.

   Chester Bowles (1901-1986), U.S. Undersecretary of State (D). Memorandum to Dean Rusk, urging cancellation of the Bay of Pigs invasion, 1962.

6. It is time we steered by the stars, not by the light of each passing ship.

   Omar N. Bradley (1893-1981), General, U.S. Army, and Permanent Chairman, Joint Chiefs of Staff. Remark.

7. You can't build a foreign policy on the presence of an individual.

   George Bush, 41st President of the United States (R-TX). In reference to Mikhail Gorbachev. Press conference, May 8, 1990.

8. In the policy of nations there are two extremes: one extreme, in which justice and moderation may sink in feebleness; another, in which the lofty spirit which ought to animate all nations, particularly free ones, may mount up to military violence. These extremes ought to be equally avoided; but of the two, I consider the first far more dangerous.

   John C. Calhoun (1782-1850), U.S. Congressman (D-SC), U.S. Senator, U.S. Secretary of War, U.S. Secretary of State, and Vice President of the United States. Speech, House of Representatives. Jan. 31, 1816.

9. National policy must depend on correct predictions concerning the international future.

   Marlborough Churchill (1878-1942), General, U.S. Army, and Director, U.S. Military Intelligence. Quoted in Nathan Miller, *Spying for America*, 1989.

10. No one starts a war – or rather, no one in his senses ought to do so – without first being clear in his mind what he intends to achieve by that war, and how he intends to conduct it.

    Karl von Clausewitz (1780-1831), Prussian general and military writer. *On War*, 1833.

11. How can we decide matters of public policy when we cannot understand them?

    Richard Cohen, American columnist. In reference to scientific and technological public policy issues such as the Space Defense Initiative. *The Washington Post Magazine*, June 26, 1988.

12. The dead govern the living.

    Auguste Comte (1798-1857), French mathematician and philosopher. *Catéchisme positiviste*, 1852.

13. Not what they want but what is good for them.

    Oliver Cromwell (1599-1658), Lord Protector of England. Attributed.

14. What we anticipate seldom occurs; what we least expected generally happens.

    Benjamin Disraeli, 1st Earl of Beaconsfield (1804-1881), Prime Minister of Great Britain (Conservative). *Henrietta Temple*, 1837.

15. Never take anything for granted.
Benjamin Disraeli. Debate, House of Commons, Oct. 5, 1864.

16. Too many policy decisions over the years have been made by men in closed rooms not thinking about the dead bodies. When bullets fly, people die. Pictures ram that message home.
Sam Donaldson, American journalist. Interview, *Playboy*, Mar. 1983.

17. Only by decisions of national policy based upon accurate information can we have the chance that peace will endure.
William J. Donovan (1883-1959), Director, Office of Strategic Services (precursor to CIA), and U.S. Assistant Attorney General. Farewell address, Sept. 28, 1945.

18. Men and nations behave wisely once they have exhausted all other alternatives.
Abba Eban, Foreign Secretary of Israel and Israeli Ambassador to the United Nations (Labour). Quoted in *The Observer*, Dec. 20, 1970.

19. Changing social policy is just dogged hard work.
Marion Wright Edelman, Director, Children's Defense Fund. Interview, CBS, *60 Minutes*, Oct. 22, 1989.

20. People at the political extremes have an advantage over the rest of us. Only they seem to know exactly who and what is wrong with America and precisely what policies and programs should be adopted to fix it.
Lewis D. Eigen, Associate Director, U.S. Job Corps. Speech, Washington, DC, 1964.

21. I have one yardstick by which I test every major problem – and that yardstick is: Is it good for America?
Dwight D. Eisenhower (1890-1969), 34th President of the United States (R-KS). Veto message on farm bill, Apr. 16, 1956.

22. A foolish consistency is the hobgoblin of little minds.
Ralph Waldo Emerson (1803-1882), American writer. *Essays*, First Series, "Self-Reliance," 1865.

23. There is no practical question on which anything more than an approximate solution can be had.
Ralph Waldo Emerson. *Representative Men*, "Montaigne," 1876.

24. This strategy represents our policy for all time. Until it's changed.
Marlin Fitzwater, White House spokesman (R). Quoted in *Newsweek*, Apr. 2, 1990.

25. Let's sleep on it.
Francis I (1768-1835), Emperor of Austria. Frequent remark when faced with policy decisions.

26. United States policy *[concerning Vietnam]* was marred by a lack of candor and by misinformation.
J. William Fulbright, U.S. Senator (D-AR). Statement, Senate Foreign Relations Committee, 1965.

27. Let us study our misfortunes and go back to the causes.
Leon Michel Gambetta (1838-1882), Member, French Chamber of Deputies. Speech, June 26, 1871.

28. Sentiment inspires me no less than reason.
Charles de Gaulle (1890-1970), President of France. Quoted in Abba Eban, *An Autobiography*, 1977.

29. You don't determine what is good policy by polling.
Jack Germond, American political columnist. NBC, *The McLaughlin Group*, Jan. 13, 1990.

30. Public policy should be conducted on those principles which constitute virtue in private life.
William E. Gladstone (1809-1898), Prime Minister of Great Britain (Liberal). Speech, Dec. 9, 1879.

31. Momentary passions and immediate interests have a more active and imperious control over human conduct than general or remote considerations of policy, utility, or justice.
Alexander Hamilton (1755-1804), Member, Continental Congress and Constitutional Convention, and U.S. Secretary of the Treasury (Federalist-NY). *The Federalist*, No. 6.

32. A policy ought to start with some principle.
Tom Hayden, founder, Students for a Democratic Society, and California State Senator (D). ABC, *After Vietnam*, Apr. 27, 1990.

33. Abhorrence of apartheid is a moral attitude. It is not a policy.
Edward Heath, Prime Minister of Great Britain (Conservative). Speech, Nov. 16, 1970.

34. Most politicians will not stick their necks out unless they sense grass-roots support.... Neither you nor I should expect someone else to take our responsibility.
Katherine Hepburn, American actress. Planned Parenthood fund-raising letter, Nov. 1981.

35. Make a habit of two things – to help, or at least to do no harm.

Hippocrates (c.460-c.377 B.C.), Greek physician. *Epidemics*.

36. Until nations are generous they will never be wise; true policy is generous policy. All bitterness, selfishness, etc., may gain small ends, but lose great ones.
Washington Irving (1783-1859), American writer and U.S. Diplomatic Attaché to Spain. Mar. 1823.

37. When I want your advice, I'll give it to you.
Lyndon B. Johnson (1908-1973), 36th President of the United States (D-TX). Remark to Vice President Hubert Humphrey during the 1964 campaign.

38. We cannot divide ourselves between right and expedience. Policy must bow the knee before morality.
Immanuel Kant (1724-1804), German philosopher. Lecture at Königsberg, 1775.

39. Having elected a government, we will be best advised to let it govern and to let it speak for us as it will in the councils of the nations.
George F. Kennan, U.S. Ambassador to Russia and Yugoslavia. *Realities of American Foreign Policy*, 1954.

40. It is much easier to make the speeches than to finally make the judgments.
John F. Kennedy (1917-1963), 35th President of the United States (D-MA). Interview, 1962.

41. Our policy is not to use chemical weapons, but each rule has an exception.
Adnan Khairallah, Minister of Defense, Iraq. Comment on accusations that Iraq had utilized chemical weapons outlawed by international law, Baghdad, Sept. 15, 1988. Quoted in *The Washington Post*, Sept. 25, 1988.

42. The most useful things I've done are the things I refused to do.
Mackenzie King (1874-1950), Prime Minister of Canada (Liberal). Quoted in Bruce Hutchison, *The Unfinished Country: To Canada with Love*, 1985.

43. If we have as a clear certainty with which to plan total uncertainty, then that would be helpful.
Tom King, Secretary of State for Defense, Great Britain (Conservative). Parliamentary hearings, Mar. 1990.

44. If time is not pressing on you, there are more options than otherwise.
Henry M. Kissinger, U.S. Secretary of State and National Security Advisor (R). Remark to Abba Eban, Oct. 1973.

45. Moderation is a virtue only in those who are thought to have an alternative.
Henry M. Kissinger. Quoted in *The Observer*, Jan. 24, 1982.

46. Political unity should be given great weight, but it also should be related to some sensible program.
Henry M. Kissinger. Quoted on PBS, *MacNeil-Lehrer News Hour*, May 30, 1989.

47. Most important ideas aren't exciting. Most exciting ideas aren't important. Not every problem has a good solution. Policies have unwanted side effects.
Mark A. R. Kleiman, Director, Policy and Management Analysis, U.S. Department of Justice. Reasons most often given for making no changes in policy. Quoted in *The New York Times*, Oct. 16, 1988.

48. Whether it's in the military or in the export arena, you'd better have a long-term strategy in your pocket. You need to develop a plan, to figure out where your strengths are and to stop thinking about the quarterly report.
Dennis Kloske, Pentagon analyst and Undersecretary for Export Administration, U.S. Department of Commerce. Quoted in *Regardie's*, May 1989.

49. One cannot guarantee that if we have good intelligence, good policy will necessarily follow. But we can guarantee that if we have poor intelligence, poor policy will necessarily follow.
Michael Ledeen, American author and intelligence official. Speech, "Intelligence and Free Society Conference," National Forum Foundation, Washington, DC, May 30, 1989.

50. Policy making is not as easy as slurping down cabbage soup.
Yegor Ligachev, member, Communist Party, U.S.S.R.. Speech, Communist Party Congress, Moscow, June 1988.

51. No policy that does not rest upon philosophical public opinion can be permanently maintained.
Abraham Lincoln (1809-1865), 16th President of the United States (R-IL). Speech, New Haven, CT, Mar. 6, 1860.

52. My policy is to have no policy.
Abraham Lincoln. Remark to his secretary, 1861.

53. The American people cannot be driven to do anything that they do not want to do. The way to promote happiness is by moral suasion and not by force.
Abraham Lincoln. Quoted by William Randolph Hearst, NBC, *Colliers Radio Hour*.

54. Your ideas will not have any impact this year and maybe not even next. The way government works is you have to sow seeds.

David W. Lloyd, Director, National Center on Child Abuse and Neglect. Speech, National Child Maltreatment Prevention Symposium, June 7, 1991.

55. No quarrel ought ever be converted into a policy.

David Lloyd George, 1st Earl of Dwyfor (1863-1945), Prime Minister of Great Britain (Liberal). Attributed.

56. Self-interest is not only a legitimate but a fundamental cause for national policy – one which needs no cloak of hypocrisy.

Alfred Thayer Mahan (1840-1914), Admiral, U.S. Navy, and writer on naval affairs. 1902.

57. When you're trying to make decisions in the executive branch, sometimes these news reports get inside your decision-making cycle.

Jack Marsh, U.S. Secretary of the Army (R). Interview, CNN, *The Larry King Show*, Jan. 24, 1991.

58. Avoid trivia.

George C. Marshall (1880-1959), General, U.S. Army, U.S. Secretary of State, and U.S. Secretary of Defense. Instructions to George F. Kennan on developing policy options with respect to the U.S.S.R., 1947.

59. Now, decisions with a major impact on health care are made in conjunction with budgetary decisions. Before we debated health policy. Now we debate fiscal policy.

Carol McCarthy, President, American Hospital Association. Quoted in *The New York Times*, Oct. 23, 1988.

60. Our differences are policies, our agreements principles.

William McKinley (1843-1901), 25th President of the United States (R-OH). Speech, Des Moines, IA, 1901.

61. Never forget posterity when devising a policy. Never think of posterity when making a speech.

Robert G. Menzies (1894-1978), Prime Minister of Australia (Liberal). 1970.

62. The great axioms of political science are deduced from the knowledge of the true political interests of all States: In these general interests lies the security for their existence, while the individual interests, – to which the daily or transitory political movements occasionally lend a great importance, and the promotion of which constitutes political wisdom in the eyes of a restless and short-sighted policy – possess only a relative and secondary worth.

Klemens von Metternich (1773-1859), Austrian statesman and diplomat. Quoted by Anthony Trollope, *Vienna and the Austrians*, 1838.

63. I don't think we ought to base our policy on what the conventional wisdom is.... The conventional wisdom usually is wrong.

George J. Mitchell, U.S. Senator (D-ME). Interview, ABC, *This Week*, Sept. 24, 1989.

64. When a President decides he's going to do something, a vast array of forces contrary to his purpose begin to organize to thwart him.

Bill Moyers, American journalist, Special Assistant to President Lyndon B. Johnson, and White House Press Secretary (D). Quoted on ABC, *It's Your Business*, Apr. 8, 1990.

65. The struggle between Communism and capitalism has been perverting people's analysis of social issues.

Yoweri Museveni, President of Uganda. Interview, *Time*, Nov. 6, 1989.

66. We cannot change our policy now. After all, we are not political whores.

Benito Mussolini (1883-1945), dictator of Italy (Fascist). Quoted in Alan Bullock, *Hitler, A Study in Tyranny*, 1964.

67. Events ought not to govern policy, but policy events.

Napoléon I (1769-1821), military leader and Emperor of France. *Maxims*.

68. My policy is to govern men as the greatest number wish to be governed.

Napoléon I. *Ibid*.

69. I don't think we are very much driven by the question of equity, other than in the broad sense. We would not back off from an interest rate because we thought there were major inequities involved.

J. Charles Partee, member, Federal Reserve Board of Governors. Quoted in *The New Yorker*, Nov. 23, 1987.

70. The U.S. government is like a car with two drivers.

Wright Patman (1893-1976), U.S. Congressman (D-TX). In reference to the independent status of the Federal Reserve Board. Quoted in *The New Yorker*, Nov. 23, 1987.

71. National policy should be determined by the need for a healthy economy rather than a need for accounting neatness.

Thomas E. Petri, U.S. Congressman (R-WI). Letter to *The Washington Post*, Oct. 22, 1988.

72. Congress's separate power is an obstacle to modern policymaking.
Kevin Phillips, Republican political strategist. *Newsweek*, Apr. 23, 1973.

73. Policy must come from us; from within ourselves; from our own minds. All natures grow from within. Communities have the same growth from within, not from without.
Pleasant Porter (1840-1907), Chief, Creek Indians. Speech, Indian Council, Fort Gibson, OK, June 19, 1888.

74. We always tend to focus on the dramatic.
Colin L. Powell, General, U.S. Army, National Security Advisor, and Chairman, Joint Chiefs of Staff. Speech, National Press Club, C-SPAN, June 24, 1990.

75. You'd have to be a cretin not to have doubts about any major decision that was made.
Jody Powell, White House Press Secretary (D). PBS, *The Presidency, the Press and the People*, Apr. 2, 1990.

76. I was chosen by the Almighty to play a more important and demanding role – to save our nation. I had to remove the government and rewrite the repugnant Constitution.
Sitivena Rabuka, military strongman of Fiji. Quoted in *The New York Times*, July 22, 1988.

77. An indefinable something is to be done, in a way that nobody knows how, at a time nobody knows when, that will accomplish nobody knows what.
Thomas B. Reed (1839-1902), U.S. Congressman and Speaker of the House (R-ME). Comment on Pres. Theodore Roosevelt's trust-busting policy, 1901.

78. If a policy is wrong, there's no way to handle it.
George E. Reedy, White House Press Secretary (D). PBS, *The Presidency, the Press and the People*, Apr. 2, 1990.

79. What is necessary is never a risk.
Cardinal de Retz (1614-1679), French cleric and politician. *Mémoires*.

80. It is not desirable for the outcome of public policy to be determined by money.
Alice Rivlin, Director, Congressional Budget Office. Speech, Women's Democratic Club, Feb. 16, 1991.

81. It is common sense to take a method and try it. If it fails, admit it frankly and try another. But above all, try something.
Franklin D. Roosevelt (1882-1945), 32nd President of the United States (D-NY). Campaign speech, 1932.

82. The consequences of both escalation and withdrawal are so bad that we simply must make our present policy work.
Dean Rusk, U.S. Secretary of State (D). Quoted by McGeorge Bundy in a memorandum to Pres. Lyndon B. Johnson, Jan. 27, 1965.

83. It is better to turn back than to lose your way.
Russian proverb.

84. A Prince who followeth his own Opinion too soon, is in danger of repenting it too late.
George Savile, 1st Marquess of Halifax (1633-1695), Lord Privy Seal of England. *Maxims of State*, No. 18.

85. We implicitly recognize that reducing risks to zero is impossible, and trying to do it would impose unbearably large losses in our living standards.... Zero risk is simply an unrealistic goal.
Charles L. Schultze, Chairman, Council of Economic Advisors, and Director, U.S. Bureau of the Budget (D). Speech, Commonwealth Club, San Francisco, CA, Apr. 13, 1979.

86. Policy sits above conscience.
William Shakespeare (1564-1616), English writer. *Timon of Athens*, III, ii.

87. Let's not base policy on a self-fulfilling prophecy.
George P. Shultz, U.S. Secretary of State (R). Quoted in *Time*, May 30, 1988.

88. You've got to dream a little bit if you're going to get somewhere.
George P. Shultz. Interview, PBS, *MacNeil-Lehrer News Hour*, Feb. 1991.

89. He never even feigned an interest in policy. But then he was busy stage-managing the upcoming inaugural – hiring elephants and Frank Sinatra.
David A. Stockman, Director, U.S. Office of Management and Budget, and U.S. Congressman (R-MI). Description of presidential assistant Michael Deaver. *The Triumph of Politics: Why the Reagan Revolution Failed*, 1986.

90. Policy and the budget are inextricable.
David A. Stockman. *Ibid.*

91. Any administration worth its salt does not make policy decisions based on the ups and downs of a poll.

John Sununu, Governor of New Hampshire and White House Chief of Staff (R). Interview, *CNN Newsmaker Saturday*, Oct. 27, 1990.

92. U-turn if you want to. The lady's not for turning.
Margaret Thatcher, Prime Minister of Great Britain (Conservative). Remark on policy shifts dictated by public opinion. Speech, Conservative Conference, 1980.

93. They condemn us for straddling when we try to be thoughtful.
James R. Thompson, Governor of Illinois (R). Quoted in *The New York Times*, July 31, 1989.

94. All these things are vital policy matters which can only be decided by the President of the United States, but I would prefer not to make firm decisions on these matters without your concurrence, though the decisions will have to be made.
Harry S Truman (1884-1972), 33rd President of the United States (D-MO). Letter to President-elect Dwight D. Eisenhower, Nov. 6, 1952.

95. The spirit of this Administration shall be: *No Reprisals; No Pay-Backs; No Get-Even-With; but let the dead past bury its dead.*
William V. S. Tubman (1895-1971), 18th President of Liberia. First inaugural address, Jan. 3, 1944.

96. We must not let our Russian policy be guided or influenced by those inside or outside the United States who want war with Russia. This does not mean appeasement.
Henry A. Wallace (1888-1965), U.S. Secretary of Agriculture (D-IA), Vice President of the United States, and U.S. Secretary of Commerce. Speech, 1946.

97. The President can formulate no policy and try to implement it without Congress appropriating the dollars in order to make that possible.
Malcolm Wallop, U.S. Senator (R-WY). Senate speech, Mar. 15, 1988.

98. Whenever I'm caught between two evils, I take the one I've never tried.
Mae West (1892-1980), American actress. Attributed.

99. Seek simplicity and distrust it.
Alfred North Whitehead (1861-1947), British philosopher and mathematician. *The Concept of Nature*, 1920.

100. Words do not constitute policy.
George F. Will, American political columnist. *The Washington Post*, Oct. 12, 1988.

101. While the deck chairs can be rearranged rapidly, the ship of state itself can only gradually change direction.
Richard S. Williamson, U.S. Assistant Secretary of State (R). *Governing the States and Localities*, Feb. 1988.

102. Governmental decisions must be taken in the light of their anticipated consequences abroad as well as at home.
Adam Yarmolinsky, Deputy Director, U.S. Office of Economic Opportunity (D). *Organizing for Interdependence: The Role of Government*, 1976.

Chapter 75

Political Philosophies

1. Communism is a system that takes from the Stone Age its technical level, from slavery its social relations, from feudalism its hierarchy, from capitalism its exploitation, and from socialism its name.
   Popular joke in Poland, 1965.

2. WE OWE ALL TO SOCIALISM
   Government wall poster placed next to a line of citizens waiting for meat rations. Albania, 1990.

3. Democracy + Private Ownership = Capitalism
   Democracy + Public Ownership = Socialism
   Dictatorship + Private Ownership = Fascism
   Dictatorship + Public Ownership = Communism
   Anonymous.

4. Dictatorship: A system of government where everything that isn't forbidden is obligatory.
   Anonymous.

5. What is the difference between Capitalism and Communism? Capitalism is the exploitation of man by man. Communism is the opposite.
   Widely circulated joke in Russia, Poland, Hungary, Yugoslavia, and Romania, 1960's.

6. A communist is a man who has nothing and wishes to share it with the world.
   Anonymous.

7. I am not a centrist.
   Bella Abzug, U.S. Congresswoman (D-NY). Quoted in *Newsweek,* Nov. 3, 1986.

8. ... a government of laws, not of men.
   John Adams (1735-1826), 2nd President of the United States (Federalist-MA). Part I, Article 30 (*Declaration of Rights*), Massachusetts Constitution, 1780.

9. The essence of a free government consists in an effectual control of rivalries.
   John Adams. *Discourses on Davila,* 1790.

10. It is easier to fight for one's principles than to live up to them.
    Alfred Adler (1870-1937), Austrian psychiatrist. Quoted in Phyllis Bottome, *Alfred Adler,* 1939.

11. A spirit of national masochism prevails, encouraged by an effete corps of impudent snobs who characterize themselves as intellectuals.
    Spiro T. Agnew, Vice President of the United States and Governor of Maryland (R-MD). Quoted in *The New York Times,* Oct. 20, 1969.

12. We *[Americans]* like to believe we can do anything, and we usually can.
    Lamar Alexander, Governor of Tennessee and U.S. Secretary of Education (R). CNN, *Crossfire,* June 7, 1991.

13. It is a favorite maxim of despotick power, that mankind are not made to govern themselves.
    Fisher Ames (1758-1808), U.S. Congressman (Federalist-MA). Quoted in *Boston Independent Chronicle,* Mar. 1, 1787.

14. Russian communism is the illegitimate child of Karl Marx and Catherine the Great.
    Clement R. Attlee, Viscount Prestwood (1883-1967), Prime Minister of Great Britain (Labour). Speech, Apr. 11, 1956.

15. Non-violence is a flop. The only bigger flop is violence.
    Joan Baez, American folksinger and pacifist. 1974.

16. I would rather be an opportunist and float than go to the bottom with my principles around my neck.
    Stanley Baldwin, 1st Earl Baldwin of Bewdley (1867-1947), Prime Minister of Great Britain (Conservative). Attributed.

17. The worst thing in this world, next to anarchy, is government.
    Henry Ward Beecher (1813-1887), American clergyman and writer. *Proverbs from Plymouth Pulpit,* 1867.

18. The greatest happiness of the greatest number is the foundation of morals and legislation.

Jeremy Bentham (1748-1832), British jurist and philosopher. *An Introduction to the Principles of Morals and Legislation*, 1789.

19. We know what happens to people who stay in the middle of the road. They get run over.
Aneurin Bevan (1897-1960), Minister of Health, Great Britain (Socialist). Speech, House of Commons, Apr. 2, 1946.

20. If some imaginative practical joker had been appointed by the malevolent gods to devise, for our sins, a system of municipal government, he would have invented something like what we have, though better.
Ambrose Bierce (1842-1914?), American journalist. *Wasp*, Sept. 9, 1881.

21. We will protect ourselves from the force and violence of the racist police and the racist military, by whatever means necessary.
Black Panther Party platform, 1966.

22. Governments are sails, the people is the wind, the state is the boat, and time is the sea.
Ludwig Boerne (1786-1837), German journalist. *Fragments and Aphorisms*, No. 194, 1840.

23. America should have a big ambition.
William W. Bradley, U.S. Senator (D-NJ). Commencement address, Middlebury College, Middlebury, VT, May 1989.

24. Government isn't a religion. It shouldn't be treated as such. It's not God; it's humans, fallible people, feathering their nests most of the time.
Edmund G. (Jerry) Brown, Jr., Governor of California (D). *Thoughts*, 1976.

25. By the next century Communism's irreversible historical decline will have made its practice and its dogma largely irrelevant to the human condition.
Zbigniew Brzezinski, U.S. Secretary of State and National Security Advisor (D). *The Grand Failure*, 1989.

26. There is no society, however free and democratic, where wealth will not create an aristocracy.
Edward Robert Bulwer-Lytton, 1st Earl of Lytton (1831-1891), Viceroy of India and British Ambassador to France. Quoted in Susan Teltser-Schwartz, *Money Talks*, 1988.

27. Believe in something larger than yourself.
Barbara Bush, First Lady. Commencement address, Wellesley College, Wellesley, MA, 1990.

28. We are not the sum of our possessions.
George Bush, 41st President of the United States (R-TX). Inaugural address, Jan. 20, 1989.

29. All the calamities we have experienced, and those which are yet to come, are the result of the consolidating tendency of this government; and unless this tendency be arrested, all that has been foretold will certainly befall us, – even to the pouring out of the last vial of wrath, military despotism.
John C. Calhoun (1782-1850), U.S. Congressman (D-SC), U.S. Senator, U.S. Secretary of War, U.S. Secretary of State, and Vice President of the United States. Quoted in Lord, *Beacon Lights of History*.

30. Principles that have served their day expire, and new principles are born.
Benjamin N. Cardozo (1870-1938), U.S. Supreme Court Justice. *The Nature of the Judicial Process*, 1921.

31. France was a long despotism tempered by epigrams.
Thomas Carlyle (1795-1881), Scottish essayist and historian. *History of the French Revolution*, I, 1837.

32. Government cannot solve our problems. It can't set our goals. It cannot define our vision. Government cannot eliminate poverty or provide a bountiful economy or reduce inflation or save our cities.
Jimmy Carter, 39th President of the United States (D-GA). Annual message to Congress, 1978.

33. Discovering Marxism ... was like finding a map in the forest.
Fidel Castro, Premier of Cuba. Speech, Chile, Nov. 18, 1971.

34. The office of government is not to confer happiness, but to give men opportunity to work out happiness for themselves.
William Ellery Channing (1780-1842), American Unitarian minister and reformer. *The Life and Character of Napoleon Bonaparte*.

35. All men are democrats when they are happy.
G. K. Chesterton (1874-1936), British writer. *What's Wrong with the World?*, 1936.

36. The final end of government is not to exert restraint but to do good.
Rufus Choate (1779-1859), U.S. Congressman and U.S. Senator (Whig-MA). Senate speech, July 2, 1841.

37. Democratic societies can't force people. Therefore they have to control what they think.

Noam Chomsky, American linguist and political activist. Interview, PBS, *Bill Moyers' World of Ideas*, Nov. 4, 1988.

38. The inherent vice of capitalism is the unequal sharing of blessings; the inherent virtue of socialism is the equal sharing of miseries.

Winston Churchill (1874-1965), Prime Minister of Great Britain (Conservative). Quoted in *Conservative Digest*, Aug. 1988.

39. One is always somebody's reactionary.

Georges Clemenceau (1841-1929), Premier of France and journalist. Quoted in Emil Ludwig, *Genius and Character*, 1927.

40. Ideology knows no boundaries.

Georges Clemenceau. *In the Evening of My Thought*, 1929.

41. Communism is a hateful thing and a menace to peace and organized government; but the communism of combined wealth and capital, the outgrowth of over weening cupidity and selfishness, which insidiously undermines the justice and integrity of free institutions, is not less dangerous than the communism of oppressed poverty and toil, which, exasperated by injustice and discontent, attacks with wild disorder the citadel of rule.

Grover Cleveland (1837-1908), 22nd and 24th President of the United States (D-NY). Annual message to Congress, Dec. 3, 1888.

42. The political philosophy of one generation becomes the political anathema of another.

Frank I. Cobb (1869-1923), American editor and writer. *La Follette's Magazine*, Jan. 1920.

43. It has long been a fashion amongst you ... to call every friend of reform, every friend of freedom, a *Jacobin*, and to accuse him of *French principles*.... What are these principles? That governments were made for the people, and not the people for governments. That sovereigns reign legally only by virtue of the people's choice. That birth without merit ought not to command merit without birth. That all men ought to be equal in the eye of the law. That no man ought to be taxed or punished by any law to which he has not given his assent by himself or by his representative. That taxation and representation ought to go hand in hand. That every man ought to be judged by his peers, or equals. That the press ought to be free. Now, I should be glad to know, how these came to be *French* principles.... The principles are the *growth of England*.

William Cobbett (1763-1835), Member of Parliament, Great Britain (Tory) and political journalist. *Cobbett's Weekly Political Register*, Apr. 16, 1815.

44. I'm not 100 percent anybody's ideological prism.

J. Marshall Coleman, Attorney General of Virginia (R). Remark, 1981.

45. We justify the greater and greater accumulation of capital because we believe that therefrom flows the support of all science, art, learning, and the charities which minister to the humanities of life, all carrying their beneficent effects to the people as a whole. Unless this is measurably true our system of civilization ought to stand condemned.

Calvin Coolidge (1872-1933), 30th President of the United States (R-MA). *The Price of Freedom*.

46. The principal business of government is to further and promote human strivings.

Wilbur L. Cross (1862-1948), professor of English, Yale University, and Governor of Connecticut (D). Quoted in *The New York Times*, Mar. 29, 1931.

47. Government can have both a heart and a head.

Mario Cuomo, Governor of New York (D). Quoted in *The New Yorker*, Mar. 23, 1987.

48. The issue is Socialism versus Capitalism. I am for Socialism because I am for humanity.

Eugene V. Debs (1855-1926), American Socialist. Speech, Jan. 1, 1897.

49. Throughout history there have been no ideal ends which were attained with nonideal, inhumane means, just as there has been no free society which was built by slaves. Nothing so well reveals the reality and greatness of ends as the methods used to obtain them.

Milovan Djilas, writer and Vice President of Yugoslavia under Marshall Tito. *The New Class*, 1957.

50. The Socialist who is a Christian is more to be dreaded than a Socialist who is an atheist.

Fyodor Dostoyevsky (1821-1881), Russian writer. *The Brothers Karamazov*, 1880.

51. The American political creed rests on the sovereignty of good-will.

William O. Douglas (1898-1980), U.S. Supreme Court Justice. *We the Judges*, 1956.

52. White people ... have got to unite ... and we're not going to stop until we win.

David Duke, Louisiana State legislator (Ind.). Statement at a meeting of the Ku Klux Klans, 1986.

53. People of Haiti. I am the heir to the political philosophy, the doctrine and the revolution which my late father *[François Duvalier]* incarnated as President-for-Life. I have decided to continue his work with the same fierce energy and the same intransigence.
Jean-Claude (Baby Doc) Duvalier, President-for-Life of Haiti. Radio address, Apr. 21, 1971.

54. A world authority and an eventual world state are not just desirable in the name of brotherhood, they are necessary for survival.
Albert Einstein (1879-1955), Nobel Laureate in Physics (Switzerland). 1946.

55. We face a hostile ideology *[Communism]* – global in scope, atheistic in character, ruthless in purpose, and insidious in method.
Dwight D. Eisenhower (1890-1969), Farewell address to the nation. Jan. 17, 1961.

56. The middle of the road is all of the usable surface. The extremes, right and left, are in the gutters.
Dwight D. Eisenhower. Quoted in *The New York Times*, Nov. 10, 1963.

57. What is a communist? One who has yearnings for equal division of unequal earnings.
Ebenezer Elliott (1781-1849), British poet. *Corn Law Rhymes*, 1828.

58. The less government we have, the better – the fewer laws, and the less confided power.
Ralph Waldo Emerson (1803-1882), American writer. *Essays*, Second Series, "Politics," 1876.

59. A government big enough to give you everything you want is a government big enough to take from you everything you have.
Gerald R. Ford, 38th President of the United States (R-MI). Address to Congress, Aug. 12, 1974.

60. Keep yourselves to what is old, for that is good; our ancestors have proved it to be good; why should not we do as they did? New ideas *[democracy, parliamentary reform]* are now coming forward of which I do not nor ever shall approve. Mistrust these ideas and keep to the positive.
Francis I (1768-1835), Emperor of Austria. Address to professors, 1821.

61. If I wished to punish a province, I would have it governed by philosophers.
Frederick II (The Great) (1712-1786), King of Prussia. Attributed.

62. I am prepared to die, but there is no cause for which I am prepared to kill.
Mohandas K. Gandhi (1869-1948), Indian political and spiritual leader. Attributed.

63. I see a society learning new ways as a baby learns to walk. He stands up, falls, stands again, falls and bumps his nose, cries, and tries again – and eventually walks. Some of the critics now sounding off about the Great Society would stop the baby after his first fall and say, "That'll teach you. Stick to crawling."
John W. Gardner, U.S. Secretary of Health, Education and Welfare, and Chairman, Common Cause. Letter to Harry Middleton.

64. It is not government that makes society; it is society that makes government.
Henry George (1839-1897), American political economist. *Protection or Free Trade*, 1885.

65. All the world over, I will back the masses against the classes.
William E. Gladstone (1809-1898), Prime Minister of Great Britain (Liberal). Speech, Liverpool, June 28, 1866.

66. Since government, even in its best state is an evil, the object principally to be aimed at is that we should have as little of it as the general peace of human society will permit.
William Godwin (1756-1836), British philosopher. *An Inquiry Concerning Political Justice*, 1793.

67. What government is best? That which teaches us to govern ourselves.
Johann Wolfgang von Goethe (1749-1832), German writer. *Sprüche in Prosa*.

68. Anarchy stands for the liberation of the human mind from the dominion of religion; the liberation of the human body from the dominion of property; liberation from the shackles and restraints of government.
Emma Goldman (1869-1940), American anarchist. *Anarchism*, 1917.

69. I don't want to see this country run by big business and big labor.
Barry M. Goldwater, U.S. Senator (R-AZ). CBS, *Face the Nation*, Apr. 19, 1959.

70. Socialism holds nothing but unhappiness for the human race. It destroys personal initiative, wipes out national pride ... and plays into the hands of the autocrats.... Socialism is the end of fanatics, the sophistry of so-called intelligentsia, and it has no place in the hearts of those who would secure and fight for freedom and preserve democracy.

Samuel Gompers (1850-1924), President, American Federation of Labor. *Seventy Years of Life and Labor*, 1925.

71. The organization of American society is an interlocking system of semi-monopolies, notoriously venal, an electorate notoriously unenlightened, misled by mass media notoriously phony.

Paul Goodman (1911-1972), American philosopher. *The Community of Scholars*, 1962.

72. Whatever is good for the People is bad for their Governors; and what is good for the Governors is pernicious for the People.

Thomas Gordon (d.1750), British essayist. *Cato's Letters*, 1748.

73. I am ... one of a different sort: one of those who risks his skin to prove his platitudes.

Ernesto G. (Che) Guevara (1928-1967), Cuban revolutionary leader. Letter to his parents, 1965.

74. All communities divide ... into the few and the many. The 1st are the rich and well-born; the other are the mass of the people *[who are]* ... turbulent and changing, they seldom judge or determine right. Give, therefore, to the 1st class a distinct, permanent share in the government.

Alexander Hamilton (1755-1804), Member, Continental Congress and Constitutional Convention, and U.S. Secretary of the Treasury (Federalist-NY). 1789.

75. The People cannot see, but they can feel. The People, having felt the difference between a Government of Laws and a Government of Arms, will always desire the Government of Laws, and abhor that of arms.

James Harrington (1611-1677), English writer. *Aphorisms*.

76. Socialists are firmly committed to the principles of democracy.

Michael Harrington (1928-1989), American Socialist and writer. Quoted on PBS, *Firing Line*, Sept. 23, 1989.

77. We are the people of this generation, bred in at least modest comfort, looking uncomfortably to the world we inherit.

Tom Hayden, California State Representative (D) and founder, Students for a Democratic Society. Port Huron Statement, 1962.

78. These Russians *[Communists]* attach a hell of a lot to ideological theory ... most of them would sooner talk than work, or even eat.

William Dudley Haywood (1868-1928), American labor leader. Statement to Walter Duranty, 1920s.

79. Zionism aims to create for the Jewish people a publicly recognized and legally secured home in Palestine.

Theodor Herzl (1860-1904), Austrian journalist and political Zionist. *The Basle Program*, 1897.

80. There is nothing in the middle of the road but yellow stripes and dead armadillos.

Jim Hightower, Agriculture Commissioner, Texas. Quoted in *The New York Times*, May 28, 1989.

81. If you wish the sympathy of broad masses then you must tell them the crudest and most stupid things.

Adolf Hitler (1889-1945), Führer of the Third German Reich. *Mein Kampf*, 1933.

82. My job was to nurture the frail plants of democracy in Europe against anarchy or Communism. And Communism was the pit into which all governments were in danger of falling when frantic peoples were driven by the Horsemen of Famine and Pestilence.

Herbert Hoover (1874-1964), 31st President of the United States (R-IA). Comment on the American relief effort to feed the starving of Europe after World War I. Quoted in Richard Hofstadter, *The American Political Tradition*, 1948.

83. The doctrines of Karl Marx are a destroyer of all mortals.

Hubert H. Humphrey (1911-1978), Vice President of the United States and U.S. Senator (D-MN). Address, 1960 Democratic National Convention, Los Angeles, CA, July 12, 1960.

84. Our friends on the left never met an anti-Communist they liked.

Henry J. Hyde, U.S. Congressman (R-IL). Quoted in *The 1989 Conservative Calendar*.

85. Heresy is what the minority believe; it is the name given by the powerful to the doctrines of the weak.

Robert Green Ingersoll (1833-1899), Attorney General of Illinois (R). *Heretics and Heresies*.

86. The care of human life and happiness and not their destruction, is the first and only legitimate object of good government.

Thomas Jefferson (1743-1826), 3rd President of the United States (Democratic Republican-VA). Message to the people of Washington County, MD, Mar. 31, 1809.

87. I am sensible that there are defects in our federal government, yet they are so much lighter than those of monarchies, that I view them with much

indulgence. I rely, too, on the good sense of the people for remedy, whereas the evils of monarchical government are beyond remedy. If any of our countrymen wish for a King, give them Aesop's fable of the frogs who asked a King; if this does not cure them, send them to Europe. They will go back good republicans.

Thomas Jefferson. Letter to David Ramsay, Aug. 4, 1787.

88. We will have differences. Even in our own country we do not see everything alike. If we did, we would all want the same wife – and that would be a problem, wouldn't it!

Lyndon B. Johnson (1908-1973), 36th President of the United States (D-TX). Feb. 11, 1964.

89. I'm not a hawk. I'm a dove – a heavily armed dove.

Jack F. Kemp, U.S. Congressman and U.S. Secretary of Housing and Urban Development (R-NY). Debate, Rivier College, Nashua, NH, 1987.

90. Wealth is the means and people are the ends.

John F. Kennedy (1917-1963), 35th President of the United States (D-MA). Attributed.

91. The people of this country come first – not the institutions.

Joseph Kennedy III, U.S. Congressman (D-MA). Interview, May 7, 1989.

92. One-fifth of the people are against everything all the time.

Robert F. Kennedy (1925-1968), U.S. Senator and U.S. Attorney General (D-NY). 1964.

93. The ideas of economists and political philosophers, both when they are right and when they are wrong, are more powerful than is commonly understood.... Practical men, who believe themselves to be quite exempt from any intellectual influences, are usually the slaves of some defunct economist. Madmen in authority, who hear voices in the air, are distilling their frenzy from some academic scribbler of a few years back.

John Maynard Keynes (1883-1946), British economist and diplomat. *The General Theory of Employment, Interest and Money*, 1936.

94. Any people searching for independence must remember that it can't be achieved without suffering.

Ali Abdul Khadar Khalil, Palestinian activist. Quoted in *Time*, May 23, 1988.

95. If there is to be peace on earth and good will towards men, we must finally believe in the ultimate morality of the universe, and believe that all reality hinges on moral foundations.

Martin Luther King, Jr. (1929-1968), American clergyman and civil rights leader. Speech, Howard University, Washington, DC, Mar. 2, 1965.

96. Government is just people acting on behalf of others rather than acting on behalf of themselves.

Jeane J. Kirkpatrick, U.S. Ambassador to the United Nations (R). PBS, *Firing Line*, Sept. 13, 1989.

97. True stability is best established not by military, but by economic and social forces.... The problem of good government is inextricably interwoven with economic prosperity and sound finance; financial stability contributes perhaps more than any one other factor to political stability.

Philander Chase Knox (1853-1921), U.S. Senator (R-PA), U.S. Secretary of State, and U.S. Attorney General. Speech, University of Pennsylvania, Philadelphia, PA, June 15, 1910.

98. The supreme issue, involving all others, is the encroachment of the powerful few on the rights of the many. It is against the system built up by privilege that we must make unceasing warfare.

Robert M. La Follette (1855-1925), Governor of Wisconsin and U.S. Senator (R-WI). Quoted in Mark Sullivan, *Our Times*, 1927.

99. The middle class serves as a bridge between the haves and the have-nots. If it goes, so goes political stability.

Richard D. Lamm, Governor of Colorado (D). *Playboy*, Aug. 1984.

100. The theory of Socialism grew out of the philosophic, historical, and economic theories that were elaborated by the educated representatives of the propertied classes, the intellectuals. The founders of modern scientific Socialism, Marx and Engels, belonged to the *bourgeois* intelligentsia.

V. I. Lenin (1870-1924), Premier of the U.S.S.R. *What Is To Be Done?*, 1902.

101. *[Capitalism is]* a special machine for the suppression of one class by another.

V. I. Lenin. *The State and Revolution*, 1917.

102. Fascism is Capitalism in decay.

V. I. Lenin. 1923.

103. The main tenet of Socialism, namely the community of goods, must be rejected without qualification, for it would injure those it pretends to benefit, it would be contrary to the rights of man, and it would introduce confusion and disorder into the commonwealth.

Pope Leo XIII (1810-1903). Encyclical, *Rerum Novarum*, May 15, 1891.

104. If all men were just, there still would be some, though not so much, need of government.
Abraham Lincoln (1809-1865), 16th President of the United States (R-IL). Fragment, July 1, 1854.

105. A house divided against itself cannot stand. I believe this government cannot endure half slave and half free.
Abraham Lincoln. Senatorial nomination acceptance speech, Illinois Republican Convention, Springfield, IL, June 16, 1858 (see *Mark* 3:25; also *Matthew* 12:25).

106. Important principles may and must be flexible.
Abraham Lincoln. His last speech, Apr. 11, 1865.

107. A radical is one who speaks the truth.
Charles A. Lindbergh (1859-1924), U.S. Congressman (R-MN). Quoted in *Labor*, June 15, 1957.

108. The reason why men enter into *[political]* society is the preservation of their property.
John Locke (1632-1704), English political philosopher. *Second Treatise on Government*, 1690.

109. Ultimately we will win the world struggle on a spiritual basis or victory will elude us.... We have the most glorious purposes of any nation in history.
Henry Cabot Lodge, Jr. (1902-1986), U.S. Senator (R-MA), U.S. Ambassador to Vietnam and Germany, and head of American delegation to Paris Peace Conference for Vietnam peace negotiations. Address, Republican National Convention, Chicago, IL, July 28, 1960.

110. I am the State. (*L'État, c'est moi.*)
Louis XIV (1638-1715), King of France. Reminder to his ministers.

111. Truly there is a tide in the affairs of men, but there is no gulfstream setting forever in one direction.
James Russell Lowell (1819-1891), U.S. Ambassador to Spain and Great Britain. *Among My Books*. "New England Two Centuries Ago," 1876.

112. There are too many political moderates in America.
Barry Lynn, radio talk show host. Apr. 14, 1990.

113. Communism might be likened to a race in which all competitors come in first with no prizes.
James Lyle Mackay, 1st Earl of Inchcape (1852-1932), Chairman, British India Committee. Remark to reporters, 1924.

114. Criticism in a free man's country is made on certain assumptions, one of which is the assumption that the government belongs to the people and is at all times subject to the people's correction and criticism.
Archibald MacLeish (1892-1982), American poet, writer, and Librarian of Congress. *A Time to Speak*, 1941.

115. The safety and happiness of society are the objects at which all political institutions aim and to which all such institutions must be sacrificed.
James Madison (1751-1836), 4th President of the United States (Democratic Republican-VA). *The Federalist*, No. 45.

116. Every nation has the government it deserves. (*Toute nation a le gouvernement qu'elle mérite.*)
Joseph Marie de Maistre (1753-1821), French philosopher and statesman. Letter from St. Petersburg, Aug. 15, 1811.

117. Communism is not love. Communism is a hammer which we use to crush the enemy.
Mao Tse-tung (1893-1976), Chairman, Communist Party of China. Quoted in *Time*, Dec. 18, 1950.

118. Let a hundred flowers blossom and let one hundred schools of thought contend is the policy for promoting the progress of the arts and sciences and a flourishing socialist culture in our land.
Mao Tse-tung. *On the Correct Handling of Contradictions Among the People*, Feb. 27, 1957.

119. Philosophers have only interpreted the world in various ways; the point is to change it.
Karl Marx (1818-1883), German economist and Socialist. *Theses on Feuerbach*.

120. The theory of Communism may be summed up in one sentence: Abolish all private property.
Karl Marx. *The Communist Manifesto*, 1848.

121. Absolutism did not consist in the existence of a monarch but in his assertion of infallibility
Tomas G. Masaryk (1850-1937), 1st President of Czechoslovakia. *The Making of a State, 1914-1918*, 1927.

122. The happy ending is our national belief.
Mary McCarthy (1912-1989), American writer. *On the Contrary*, 1961.

123. I remember thinking that there was no problem that we *[government]* couldn't resolve.
George S. McGovern, U.S. Congressman and U.S. Senator (D-SD). PBS, *America's Political Parties – the Democrats*, Oct. 17, 1988.

124. In a sense, the police power is but another name for the power of government.
Joseph McKenna (1843-1926), U.S. Supreme Court Justice. *Mutual Loan Co.* v. *Martell*, 1911.

125. The urge to save humanity is almost always a false-face for the urge to rule it.
H. L. Mencken (1880-1956), American journalist. *Minority Report*, 1956.

126. What men value in this world is not rights but privileges.
H. L. Mencken. *Ibid.*

127. Whoever has a principle must go with it to the extreme, not hold by a middle.
Klemens von Metternich (1773-1859), Austrian statesman and diplomat. Remark to Varnhagen von Ense, Baden, 1835.

128. In human affairs the solution to every problem contains within it the seeds of a new problem.
George J. Mitchell, U.S. Senator (D-ME). Interview, ABC, *Sunday Morning*, Jan. 1, 1989.

129. Those who would treat politics and morality apart will never understand the one or the other.
John Morley, Viscount Morley of Blackburn (1838-1923), Member of Parliament, Great Britain (Liberal), Chief Secretary for Ireland, and Secretary of State for India. *Rousseau*, 1783.

130. We believe in American government, and we fully expect that those who now denigrate it, and even despise it, will soon or late find themselves turning to it in necessity, even desperation.
Daniel P. Moynihan, Chief American Delegate to the United Nations and U.S. Senator (D-NY). Speech, Gridiron Club, Washington, DC, 1981.

131. The struggle between Fascism and Democracy can permit no compromises.... Either we or they.
Benito Mussolini (1883-1945), dictator of Italy (Fascist). Speech, Oct. 27, 1930.

132. Events are not a matter of chance.
Gamal Abdel Nasser (1918-1970), President of Egypt. *The Philosophy of the Revolution*, 1954.

133. Its *[Communism's]* contempt for what might be called the moral and spiritual side of life not only ignores something that is basic in man but also deprives human behavior of standards and values. Its unfortunate association with violence encourages a certain evil tendency in human beings.
Jawaharlal Nehru (1889-1964), Prime Minister of India. *The New York Times Magazine*, Sept. 7, 1958.

134. The United States must never settle for second best in anything.
Richard M. Nixon, 37th President of the United States (R-CA). Presidential nomination acceptance speech. Republican National Convention, Los Angeles, CA, July 27, 1960.

135. Don't demand socialism tomorrow. Demand, instead, that capitalism ... begin creating for itself a more human heart ... demand that the old elites at once start behaving better.
Carl Oglesby, President, Students for a Democratic Society. Quoted in David Caute, *The Year of the Barricades*, 1988.

136. Man is a social rather than a political animal; he can exist without a government.
José Ortega y Gasset (1883-1955), Spanish philosopher and statesman. *Obiter Scripta*, 1936.

137. Government, even in its best state, is but a necessary evil; in its worst state, an intolerable one.
Thomas Paine (1737-1809), American political philosopher. *Common Sense*, Jan. 10, 1776.

138. Marxism is too uncertain of its grounds to be a science. I do not know a movement more self-centered and further removed from the facts than Marxism.
Boris Pasternak (1890-1960), Nobel Laureate in Literature (Russia). *Doctor Zhivago*, 1958.

139. You can't have government like this without an income tax, but we don't want a government like this.
Ronald E. Paul, U.S. Congressman (R-TX) and Libertarian candidate for President. Interview, ABC, *Frontline*, Oct. 24, 1988.

140. A people does not marry its government for an eternity, as in a church wedding. They are tied together in a modern way that allows a change of relationship when things do not work.
Octavio Paz, Mexican writer. Quoted in *The New York Times*, Apr. 2, 1989.

141. No class is safe unless government is so arranged that each class has in its own hands the means of protecting itself. That is the idea of republics.
Wendell Phillips (1811-1884), American orator and reformer. Quoted in Richard Hofstadter, *The American Political Tradition*, 1948.

142. Our object in the construction of the state is the greatest happiness of the whole, and not that of any one class.
Plato (427-347 B.C.), Greek philosopher. *The Republic.*

143. You cannot do political philosophy on television. Its form works against its content.

Neil Postman, professor of communications, New York University, New York City. *Amusing Ourselves to Death: Public Discourse in the Age of Show Business*, 1985.

144. The existing concentration of vast wealth under a corporate system ... has placed in the hands of a few men enormous, secret, irresponsible power over the daily life of the citizen – a power insufferable in a free government.

Progressive Party platform, 1912.

145. The state governments must be swept away.

George Read (1733-1798), Delegate, Constitutional Convention, and U.S. Senator (DE). Debate, Constitutional Convention, Philadelphia, PA, 1787.

146. Government is not the solution to our problem; government *is* the problem.

Ronald Reagan, 40th President of the United States (R-CA). First inaugural address, Jan. 1981.

147. A society is great not because of promises made by its government but by progress made by its people.

Ronald Reagan. Address, Republican National Convention, New Orleans, LA, Aug. 14, 1988.

148. Communism is like Prohibition, it's a good idea but it won't work.

Will Rogers (1879-1935), American humorist. *Autobiography*, 1927.

149. In the future the State ... will assume a much larger role in the lives of its citizens.

Franklin D. Roosevelt (1882-1945), 32nd President of the United States (D-NY). Quoted in *The New York Times*, Dec. 30, 1928.

150. Our government is not the master but the creature of the people. The duty of the state toward the citizens is the duty of the servant to its master. The people have created it; the people, by common consent, permit its continual existence.

Franklin D. Roosevelt. Message to the New York State Legislature, Aug. 1931.

151. We want to get for the American people two great human values – work and security. To achieve this end I invite you all. It is no mere party slogan. It is a philosophy of life.

Franklin D. Roosevelt. Speech, New York City, Nov. 3, 1932.

152. I have never sought and I do not welcome the support of any person or group committed to Communism, or Fascism, or any other foreign ideology which would undermine the American system of government, or the American system of free competitive enterprise and private property.

Franklin D. Roosevelt. Radio campaign broadcast, Oct. 5, 1944.

153. Philosophy? I am a Christian and a Democrat – that's all.

Franklin D. Roosevelt. Quoted in Frances Perkins, *The Roosevelt I Knew*, 1946.

154. I am advocating a corrective to Socialism and an antidote to anarchy.

Theodore Roosevelt (1858-1919), 26th President of the United States (R-NY). Presidential nomination acceptance speech, Progressive (Bull Moose) Party National Convention, Chicago, IL, June 7, 1916.

155. I am in every fiber of my body a radical.

Theodore Roosevelt. Attributed.

156. U for Unity must precede V for Victory. Those who play this game forget that U and V are both preceded by P for principle.

Phyllis Schlafly, President, Eagle Forum, and conservative activist. *Safe, Not Sorry*, 1967.

157. Germans have an enormous capacity for idealism and the perversion of it.

Helmut Schmidt, Chancellor of West Germany. Quoted in *The New Yorker*, Oct. 17, 1983.

158. Humanitarianism consists in never sacrificing a human being to a purpose.

Albert Schweitzer (1875-1965), French musician, philosopher, and physician. *The Philosophy of Civilization*, 1923.

159. The people are responsible for what their government does.

William Seidman, Chairman, Federal Deposit Insurance Corporation. Comment on the taxpayer bailout in the 1989 savings and loan scandal. Quoted on ABC, *Nightline*, Aug. 9, 1989.

160. The golden rule is that there are no golden rules.

George Bernard Shaw (1856-1950), Nobel Laureate in Literature (Great Britain). *Maxims for Revolutionists*, 1903.

161. Any State which concentrates property in its hands is the enemy of the people.

Fulton J. Sheen (1895-1979), American Roman Catholic archbishop and television personality. *Seven Pillars of Peace*, 1944.

162. I am not a neo-anything. I'm a Democrat.
Paul Simon, U.S. Senator (D-IL). Speech announcing his presidential candidacy, 1987.

163. Labor laws are enacted for the preservation of the health of the men of the State, because after all what is the State? Green fields, and rivers and lakes and mountains and cities? Why not at all. It is the people, all the people of the State, and anything that tends to make the members of the State strong and vigorous helps to make the State so.
Alfred E. Smith (1873-1944), Governor of New York (D). Speech to the New York State legislature. Quoted in M. and H. Josephson, *Al Smith: Hero of the Cities*, 1969.

164. All Socialism involves slavery.
Herbert Spencer (1820-1903), British social philosopher. *The Man Versus the State*, 1884.

165. Government by the consent of the governed is the most difficult system of all because it depends for its success and viability on the good judgments of so many of us.
Adlai E. Stevenson (1900-1965), Governor of Illinois (D) and U.S. Ambassador to the United Nations. *Major Campaign Speeches of Adlai E. Stevenson*, 1953.

166. If I were asked to choose a single principle which underlies more than any other the difference between the Communist and the free philosophy, it would be this issue of criticism which we in the West not only tolerate, but esteem.
Adlai E. Stevenson. *What I Think*, 1955.

167. Communism has yet to be the popular choice of one single nation anywhere on the face of the globe. In the few places where it has extended its control – in Czechoslovakia, North Vietnam, or Cuba – it has been in the same classic role: as the scavenger of war and of ruined revolutions.
Adlai E. Stevenson. *The New York Times Magazine*, Nov. 4, 1962.

168. Upon subjects of government it has always appeared to me, that metaphysical refinements are out of place.
Joseph Story (1779-1845), U.S. Supreme Court Justice. *Commentaries on the Constitution of the United States*, 1833.

169. It is dissatisfaction with the attainable, which leads to fanaticism and at last to social fury.... When great masses are ready to believe the impossible, that is an ominous political fact.
Raymond Gram Swing (1887-1968), American journalist and radio commentator. *Forerunners of American Fascism*, 1935.

170. Government by unanimous vote of the electorate is impossible, and therefore the majority of the electorate must rule. We find, therefore, that government by a majority of one-fourth of those whose rights and happiness are to be affected by the course and conduct of the Government. This is the nearest to government by the whole people we have ever had.
William H. Taft (1857-1930), 27th President of the United States (R-OH), and Chief Justice, U.S. Supreme Court. Speech, Mar. 8, 1912.

171. Political principles resemble military tactics; they are usually designed for a war which is over.
Richard H. Tawney (1880-1962), British economic historian. *Equality*, 1931.

172. These lands are ours. No one has a right to remove us, because we were the first owners. The Great Spirit above has appointed this place for us, on which to light our fires, and we will remain ... the Great Spirit knows no boundaries, nor will His red children acknowledge any.
Tecumseh (1768-1813), Chief, Shawnee Indians. Reply to President Madison's messenger, 1810.

173. It is a great error, in my opinion, to believe that a government is more firm or assured when it is supported by force, than when founded on affection.
Terence (c.190-159 B.C.), Roman poet. *Adelphi*.

174. The war we have to wage today has only one goal and that is to make the world safe for diversity.
U Thant (1909-1974), Burmese diplomat and Secretary General of the United Nations. Quoted in *The New York Times*, Jan. 8, 1964.

175. I think in no country in the civilized world is less attention paid to philosophy than in the United States.... Their life is so practical, so confused, so excited, so active, that little time remains for them for thought.
Alexis de Tocqueville (1805-1859), French writer. *Democracy in America*, 1835.

176. Government is an association of men who do violence to the rest of us.
Leo Tolstoy (1828-1910), Russian writer and philosopher. *The Kingdom of God Is Within You*, 1893.

177. The greatest happiness of the greatest number – on the rock of this principle let this society rest, and by this let it judge and determine every political question.
Wolfe Tone (1763-1798), Irish revolutionary. *Manifesto to the Friends of Freedom in Ireland*, 1791.

178. Communism is based on the belief that man is so weak and inadequate that he is unable to govern himself, and therefore requires the rule of strong masters.

Harry S Truman (1884-1972), 33rd President of the United States (D-MO). Inaugural address, Jan. 20, 1949.

179. I don't pretend to be a philosopher. I'm just a politician from Missouri and proud of it.

Harry S Truman. Oct. 23, 1955.

180. Human rights of the masses take precedence over the financial rights of the classes.

Union Party platform, 1936.

181. What's socialistic in limiting hours of labor to give workers more leisure and to raise their standard of living?

Robert F. Wagner (1877-1953), U.S. Senator (D-NY). Comment on his support of New Deal legislation, 1937.

182. The radical does not want to see progress because he hopes that our democratic institutions will fail and that he will be able to take over with some form of alien tyranny.

Earl Warren (1891-1974), Chief Justice, U.S. Supreme Court, and Governor of California (R). *The New York Times Magazine*, Apr., 1948.

183. I shall allow no man to belittle my soul by making me hate him.

Booker T. Washington (1856-1915), American educator and President, Tuskegee Institute. 1891.

184. The aggregate happiness of society, which is best promoted by the practice of a virtuous policy is, or ought to be, the end of all government.

George Washington (1732-1799), 1st President of the United States (VA). *Political Maxims*.

185. Liberty and Union, now and forever, one and inseparable!

Daniel Webster (1782-1852), U.S. Congressman (Federalist-NH and MA), U.S. Senator (Federalist and Whig-MA), and U.S. Secretary of State. Debate with Robert Y. Hayne, Jan. 1830.

186. The people's government, made for the people, made by the people, and answerable to the people.

Daniel Webster. Second speech on Foote's Resolution in support of state's rights, Jan. 26, 1830.

187. Government is not an alien force, it is us – with all our strengths and weaknesses.

Fred Wertheimer, President, Common Cause. Quoted in *The New York Times*, July 10, 1988.

188. If Socialism is Authoritarianism; if there are governments armed with economic power as they are now with political power; if, in a word, we are to have Industrial Tyrannies, then the last state of man will be worst than the first.

Oscar Wilde (1854-1900), Irish writer. *The Soul of Man Under Socialism*, 1881.

189. The value of an idea has nothing whatsoever to do with the sincerity of the man who expresses it.

Oscar Wilde. *The Picture of Dorian Gray*, 1891.

190. *One World*

Wendell L. Willkie (1892-1944), Republican candidate for President (IN). Title of his book, 1943.

191. I'm an optimist, but I'm an optimist who carries a raincoat.

Harold Wilson, Prime Minister of Great Britain (Labour). Attributed.

192. No government could long subsist without the confidence of the people.

James Wilson (1742-1798), U.S. Supreme Court Justice. Debate, Constitutional Convention, Philadelphia, PA, 1787.

193. The cure for bad politics is the same as the cure for tuberculosis. It is living in the open air.

Woodrow Wilson (1856-1924), 28th President of the United States (D). Speech, Minneapolis, MN, Sept. 18, 1912.

194. Only free peoples can hold their purpose and their honor steady to a common end, and prefer the interests of mankind to any narrow interest of their own.

Woodrow Wilson. Statement when asking Congress for a declaration of war against Germany, Apr. 2, 1917.

195. Life is essentially illogical.... We should pray God that the good passions should outvote the bad passions. But the movement of impulse, of motive, is the stuff of passion, and therefore clear thinking about life is not logical, symmetrical thinking, but it is interpretive thinking, thinking that sees the secret motive of things, thinking that penetrates deepest places where there are pulses of life.

Woodrow Wilson. Quoted in William G. Hoffman, *The Public Speaker's Scrapbook*, 1935.

Chapter 76

Politics and Politicians

1. Your politicians will always be there when they need you.
   Seen on a T-shirt in Phoenix, AZ, 1990.

2. Political promises go in one year and out the other.
   Anonymous.

3. You're not going to have a society that understands its humanity if you don't have more women in government.
   Bella Abzug, U.S. Congresswoman (D-NY). Quoted in *Redbook*, Apr. 1974.

4. Politics are a very unsatisfactory game.
   Henry Adams (1838-1918), American historian. Letter to Charles Milnes Gaskell, Mar. 26, 1874.

5. When the day comes when it will be considered as disgraceful to be seen in a caucus as to be seen in a gambling house or brothel, then my interest will wake up again and legitimate politics will get a new birth.
   Henry Adams. Letter to Sen. Henry Cabot Lodge, June 24, 1876.

6. The political field is amusing though somewhat saddening to the believer in human perfectibility.
   Henry Adams. Letter to Sen. Henry Cabot Lodge, Aug. 31, 1876.

7. Practical politics consists in ignoring facts.
   Henry Adams. *The Education of Henry Adams*, 1907.

8. Politics, as a practice, whatever its professions, has always been the systematic organization of hatreds.
   Henry Adams. *Ibid.*

9. A great soldier might be a baby politician.
   Henry Adams. *Ibid.*

10. In this country, politicians of desperate private fortunes always find the means of keeping themselves above water as public men.
    John Quincy Adams (1767-1848), 6th President of the United States (Ind-MA). *Diary*, Apr. 6, 1820.

11. And so I am launched again upon the faithless wave of politics.
    John Quincy Adams. Comment when nominated for the House of Representatives as a Whig after serving as President as an Independent. *Diary*, Oct. 13, 1830.

12. He *[Stalin]* is gone, but his shadow still stands over us today. It still dictates to us and we, very often, obey.
    Svetlana Allilueva, daughter of Joseph Stalin. *Twenty Letters to a Friend*, 1967.

13. Man is ... a political animal.
    Aristotle (384-322 B.C.), Greek philosopher and teacher. *Politics*, I.

14. Politics will sooner or later make fools of everybody.
    Richard K. Armey, U.S. Congressman (R-TX). PBS, *Firing Line*, Sept. 14, 1990.

15. Politics is the art of putting people under obligation to you.
    Jacob L. Arvey (1895-1977), Chicago, IL, political leader (D). Quoted in *The New York Times*, July 1, 1990.

16. Politics is like roller skating. You go partly where you want to go, and partly where the damned things take you.
    Henry Fountain Ashurst (1874-1962), U.S. Senator (D-AZ). 1921.

17. The clammy hand of consistency has never rested for long upon my shoulder.
    Henry Fountain Ashurst. Quoted in Morris K. Udall, *Too Funny to Be President*, 1988.

18. Any time a political movement shrinks dramatically, very quickly, it is almost impossible to unify.
    Lee Atwater (1950-1991), Chairman, Republican National Committee. *Campaign for the President: The Manager's Look at '88*, 1989.

19. Politics is people.

Lee Atwater. Quoted in *The New York Times*, Mar. 17, 1990.

20. Bull permeates everything.... American people think politics and politicians are full of baloney.

Lee Atwater. Quoted in *The New York Times*, Mar. 18, 1990.

21. A group of politicians deciding to dump a president because his morals are bad is like the Mafia getting together to bump off the Godfather for not going to church on Sunday.

Russell Baker, American columnist. In reference to Watergate. *The New York Times*, 1974.

22. The politician is an acrobat. He keeps his balance by saying the opposite of what he does.

August Maurice Barrès (1862-1923), French writer and Nationalist politician. *Mes Cahiers*, XII.

23. There's no crime in being a poor role model.

Marion Barry, Mayor of Washington, DC (D). Quoted on PBS, *Washington, DC*, June 2, 1990.

24. An elder statesman is somebody old enough to know his own mind and keep quiet about it.

Bernard M. Baruch (1870-1965), Chairman, War Industries Board, and U.S. Delegate to the U. N. Atomic Energy Commission. 1959.

25. The field of politics always presents the same struggle. There are the Right and the Left, and in the middle is the Swamp. The Swamp is made up of know-nothings, of them who are without ideas, of them who are always with the majority.

August Bebel (1840-1913), German Social Democratic leader. Speech, Dresden, 1903.

26. Issues are a problem for politicians most of the time; the reason is that somebody won't like what you say when you start talking issues.

Gerald Benjamin, New York State legislator (R). Quoted in *The New York Times*, July 31, 1989.

27. You're either moving the ball on them or they're moving the ball on you. It's important to move the ball on them.

William J. Bennett, Director, Office of National Drug Control Policy, and U.S. Secretary of Education (R). Remark on politics in Washington. Heritage Foundation dinner, Washington, DC, Dec. 1, 1988.

28. *[Political]* prophets of doom, like physicians who smoke, often do not believe in their own prophecies.

Meron Benvenisti, Israeli historian and Deputy Mayor of Jerusalem. *The New York Times Magazine*, Oct. 16, 1988.

29. Politics is a blood sport.

Anuerin Bevan (1897-1960), Minister of Health, Great Britain (Socialist). Quoted by Jennie Lee, *My Life With Nye*.

30. Politics is the business of managing perceptions.

Donald S. Beyer, Jr., Lieutenant Governor of Virginia (D). Remark to reporters, Oct. 19, 1989.

31. Politics: A strife of interests masquerading as a contest of principles. The conduct of public affairs for private gain.

Ambrose Bierce (1842-1914?), American journalist. *The Devil's Dictionary*, 1911.

32. Politician: An eel in the fundamental mud upon which the superstructure of organized society is reared.

Ambrose Bierce. *Ibid.*

33. Politics are not an exact science.

Otto von Bismarck-Schoenhausen (1815-1898), Chancellor of Germany. Speech, Prussian Parliament, Dec. 1863.

34. Politics is the art of the possible, the attainable, the art of the next best.

Otto von Bismarck-Schoenhausen. Remark to Count Meyer von Waldeck, Aug. 11, 1867.

35. Politics ruins the character.

Otto von Bismarck-Schoenhausen. Attributed.

36. Of course, in my country most political leaders are really, well, I suppose I think of them as being, well, not gangsters but more or less the same kind of thing, no? I mean – people who go in for getting elected. What can you expect of a man like that?

Jorge Luis Borges (1899-1986), Argentine writer. Quoted in *The New York Times*, Apr. 6, 1971.

37. Only in politics do resurrections occur.

[Turned out of office in 1976, he was reelected in 1985.]

Robert Bourassa, Premier of Quebec, Canada (Liberal). Aug. 12, 1982.

38. My life has told me that I do owe another human being. I owe him part of my life. That's why I'm in politics.

William W. Bradley, U.S. Senator (D-NJ). Commencement address, Middlebury College, Middlebury, VT, May 1989.

39. They love him for the enemies he has made.
Edward S. Bragg (1827-1912), U.S. Congressman (D-WI). Presidential nomination speech for Grover Cleveland, Democratic National Convention, Chicago, IL, July 9, 1884.

40. Politics. Where fat, bald, disagreeable men, unable to be a candidate themselves, teach a president how to act on a public stage.
Jimmy Breslin, American columnist. *Table Money*, 1986.

41. It's theater now, not politics.
William Brock, U.S. Congressman (R-TN), U.S. Senator, and U.S. Secretary of Labor. Interview, *Newsweek*, Aug. 29, 1988.

42. Very few *[Americans]* ... take an active part in politics, however interested they may be in public affairs.
James Bryce (1838-1922), British Ambassador to the United States. *The American Commonwealth*, 1888.

43. *[Communism]* is the 20th century's most extraordinary political aberration.
Zbigniew Brzezinski, U.S. Secretary of State and National Security Advisor. Interview, PBS, *Firing Line*, July 30, 1989.

44. A race-transcendent politics is most likely to succeed when the white community takes responsibility for overcoming its racism, not when the black community decides to forget it.
Haywood Burns, dean, City University of New York Law School at Queens College, Flushing, NY. Quoted in *The Washington Post*, Dec. 18, 1990.

45. Politics is the art of the possible.
Richard A. Butler (1902-1984), British politician. Epigraph, *The Art of the Possible*.

46. I hold them *[politics]* to be subject to laws as fixed as matter itself, and to be as fit a subject for the application of the highest intellectual power.
John C. Calhoun (1782-1850), U.S. Congressman (D-SC), U.S. Senator, U.S. Secretary of War, U.S. Secretary of State, and Vice President of the United States. Senate speech, 1833.

47. True consistency, that of the prudent and wise, is to act in conformity with circumstances, and not to act always the same way under a change of circumstances.
John C. Calhoun. Senate speech, Mar. 16, 1848.

48. A week is a long time in politics. A month is an eternity.
Kim Campbell, Minister of Justice, Canada. Speech, Johns Hopkins University, Baltimore, MD, Apr. 19, 1991.

49. Sometimes in politics one must duel with skunks, but no one should be fool enough to let the skunks choose the weapons.
Joseph G. Cannon (1836-1926), U.S. Congressman and Speaker of the House (R-IL). Attributed.

50. Politicians don't make things – they occasionally have ideas and mostly see them frustrated. But at Cadbury-Schweppes, you can actually go into a factory and see something come out the other end, like a bottle of tonic water or a bar of chocolate. It is a completely different feeling.
Lord Carrington, Foreign Minister, Great Britain, and Secretary General of the North Atlantic Treaty Organization. Remark, Apr. 1984.

51. Politicians are half ego and half humility.
Jimmy Carter, 39th President of the United States (D-GA). Apr. 11, 1975.

52. For myself and for our nation I want to thank my predecessor for all he has done to heal our land.
Jimmy Carter. In reference to Pres. Ford. Inaugural address, Jan. 20, 1977.

53. I'm glad it was me instead of you, Frank. The country needs you.
Anton J. Cermak (1873-1933), Mayor of Chicago, IL (D). Deathbed remark to Franklin D. Roosevelt, Miami, FL, Feb. 15, 1933.

54. Those people who have done me wrong – well, I try to outlive them.
Albert B. (Happy) Chandler (1898-1991), Governor of Kentucky (R), U.S. Senator, and U.S. Baseball Commissioner. Remark, 1982.

55. Politicians have no politics.
G. K. Chesterton (1874-1936), British writer. *Autobiography*, 1936.

56. If when I die I am still a dictator I will certainly go down into the oblivion of all dictators. If, on the other hand, I succeed in establishing a stable base for a democratic government, I will be remembered forever in every home in China.
Chiang Kai-shek (1887-1975), Chinese general and statesman. Attributed.

57. He *[Lord Rosebery]* would not stoop *[to common politics]*; he did not conquer.
Winston Churchill (1874-1965), Prime Minister of Great Britain (Conservative). *Great Contemporaries*, 1937.

58. I have nothing to offer but blood, toil, tears, and sweat.
Winston Churchill. Speech on becoming Prime Minister, May 13, 1940.

59. Persistence in one opinion has never been considerd a merit in political leaders.
Marcus Tullius Cicero (106-43 B.C.), Roman statesman and writer. *Ad Familares*, I.

60. I'm not the greatest. I'm the best available.
Joe Clark, Prime Minister of Canada (Conservative). Interview, *Maclean's*, Feb. 21, 1977.

61. Once Canadians get to know me better, they'll learn to like me.
Joe Clark. Quoted in *Toronto Star*, May 23, 1979.

62. The difference between a politician and a statesman is: A politician thinks of the next election and a statesman thinks of the next generation.
James F. Clarke (1810-1888), American clergyman and writer. *Self-Culture*, 1882.

63. What is the use of being elected or reelected unless you stand for something?
Grover Cleveland (1837-1908), 22nd and 24th President of the United States (D-NY). Remark to advisors cautioning him against aggressiveness on the tariff question, 1887.

64. Politics is a very important part of our government. It must not be denigrated. It's the way our country runs. It's the lubricant that keeps things running smoothly.
Clark P. Clifford, U.S. Secretary of Defense and Special Counsel to the President (D). Interview with Bill Moyers, PBS, 1981.

65. In politics, what begins in fear usually ends in folly.
Samuel Taylor Coleridge (1772-1834), British writer. *Table Talk*, 1830.

66. A chess tournament disguised as a circus.
Alistair Cooke, British TV host. Remark on politics in America. PBS, *America*, 1980.

67. It is impossible to take politics out of politics.
Thomas G. Corcoran (1900-1981), special assistant to the U.S. Attorney General, and special counsel, Reconstruction Finance Corporation (D). Testimony, U.S. Senate Judiciary Committee, 1972.

68. If you want to go into politics, first get your name known.
David Crockett (1786-1836), U.S. Congressman (Anti-Jacksonian, TN). Quoted on PBS, *American Adventure*, Dec. 26, 1988.

69. An ingrate in politics is no good.
Richard Croker (1841-1922), Tammany Hall leader, New York City (D). Quoted in Richard Hofstadter, *The American Political Tradition*, 1948.

70. Politics begins when you have two people in a room or when you have one person looking in a mirror.
Linda Cropp, President, School Board, Washington, DC (D). Quoted in *The Washington Post*, June 14, 1988.

71. One of the failures of our politics is that it has been simplistic.
Mario Cuomo, Governor of New York (D). Quoted in *The New York Times Magazine*, Feb. 10, 1991.

72. I always win.
Richard J. Daley (1902-1976), Mayor of Chicago, IL (D). Remark, Dec. 1974.

73. Politicians worry about downside political risks. Generally speaking, they are risk minimizers.
Richard G. Darman, Director, U.S. Office of Management and Budget (R). Quoted in *The Washington Post*, May 14, 1989.

74. I thought his genius was military, but that as a party manager, he would not succeed. He did not know the arts of the politician and would not practice them if understood, and he did know those of war.
Varina Howell Davis (1826-1906), Confederate First Lady. Said of her husband, Jefferson Davis. *Jefferson Davis ... A Memoir*, II, 1890.

75. Some say politics means destruction to labor organizations, but the reverse is the fact.
Eugene V. Debs (1855-1926), American Socialist. Speech to workers, 1894.

76. Oppositions clean and purify those in office, and we in the opposition are in fact the detergents of democracy.
John G. Diefenbaker (1895-1975), Prime Minister of Canada (Conservative). Nov. 14, 1964.

77. In politics there is no honor.
Benjamin Disraeli, 1st Earl of Beaconsfield (1804-1881), Prime Minister of Great Britain (Conservative), *Vivian Grey*, 1824.

78. We cannot learn men from books.
Benjamin Disraeli. *Ibid*.

79. Next to knowing when to seize an opportunity, the most important thing in life is to know when to forego an advantage.
Benjamin Disraeli. *Infernal Marriage*, 1828.

80. Principle is ever my motto, not expediency.
Benjamin Disraeli. *Sybil*, 1845.

81. This career *[politics]* of plundering and blundering.
Benjamin Disraeli. Letter to Lord Grey de Wilton, Oct. 1873.

82. You will find that in politics that you are much exposed to the attribution of false motives. Never complain and never explain.
Benjamin Disraeli. Quoted by Stanley Baldwin to Harold Nicolson, 1943.

83. Political life must be taken as you find it.
Benjamin Disraeli. Quoted in Saul D. Alinsky, *Rules for Radicals*, 1971.

84. Politics. The art of governing mankind by deceiving them.
Isaac D'Israeli (1766-1848), British writer. *Curiosities of Literature*, III, 1834.

85. Politics is not a spectator sport. You can't just sit on the sidelines.
Robert J. Dole, U.S. Senator (R-KS). Speech, CNN, *Presidential Classroom*, June 15, 1991.

86. Our rulers do wrong from choice and right from necessity.
Frederick Douglass (c.1817-1895), Recorder of Deeds, District of Columbia, and U.S. Minister to Haiti. Speech, Washington, DC, 1885.

87. For politicians neither love nor hate.
John Dryden (1631-1700), English poet and dramatist. *Absalom and Achitophel*, I.

88. All politics is local.
Finley Peter Dunne (1867-1936), American humorist and newspaper editor. Favorite saying of Speaker of the House Thomas P. (Tip) O'Neill, Jr.

89. American politics is money and thirty second spots.
Thomas F. Eagleton, U.S. Senator (D-MO). Quoted on PBS, *The Power Game*, Jan. 2, 1989.

90. I don't want to be politically correct. I want to be humanly correct.
Ramona Edelin, President, National Urban Coalition. Speech, American Indian Council, June 10, 1991.

91. Politics, you will observe, is the science of guessing right.
Robert C. Edwards (1864-1922), Canadian newspaper publisher and editor. *The Eye Opener*, Nov. 16, 1912.

92. Politics are for the moment. An equation is for eternity.
Albert Einstein (1879-1955), Nobel Laureate in Physics (Switzerland). Quoted in *Life*, Fall 1990.

93. I'm a soldier and I'm positive no one thinks of me as a politician.
Dwight D. Eisenhower (1890-1969), 34th President of the United States (R-KS). Remark to reporters, 1945.

94. The blessed work of helping the world forward, happily, does not wait to be done by perfect men.
George Eliot (Mary Ann Evans) (1819-1880), British writer. *Janet's Repentance*, 1857.

95. A mugwump is a fellow with his mug on one side of the fence and his wump on the other.
Albert J. Engel (1888-1959), U.S. Congressman (R-MI). Speech, House of Representatives, Apr. 23, 1936.

96. American politics is not, as is that of Europe, "a prelude to civil war"; it cannot become either entirely irresponsible or entirely dogmatic; and it must not try to be logical. It is a rocking sea of checks and balances in which uncompromising absolutes must drown.
Erik H. Erikson, professor of psychology, Harvard University, Cambridge, MA. *Childhood and Society*, 1950.

97. The day may come when we will replace politicians with computers. Judging from some of the reasoning of politicians I've seen over the years, I know I would sooner take the logic of a computer. The machine may suffer the same lack of intelligence as some politicians, but at least there is consistency in its idiocy.
Samuel J. Ervin, Jr. (1896-1985), U.S. Congressman and U.S. Senator (D-NC). Quoted in *The Washington Post*, Aug. 14, 1973.

98. A politician cannot separate his own personal advantage from his own political advantage.
James Farmer, President, Congress of Racial Equality. Interview, PBS, *The American Experience*, Nov. 28, 1989.

99. I got into politics on account of Hitler.... To see the injustice of a system like that drove me crazy. I haven't trusted government since.

Millicent Fenwick (1910-1992), U.S. Congresswoman (R-NJ). Interview, CBS, *60 Minutes*, Feb. 1, 1981.

100. If American politics are too dirty for women to take part in, then there's something wrong with American politics.
Edna Ferber (1887-1968), American writer. *Cimarron*, 1929.

101. I learned a long time ago in politics, never say never.
Gerald R. Ford, 38th President of the United States (R-MI). 1974.

102. Politicians are like horses, they cannot go properly without blinkers.
Anatole France (Jacques-Anatole-François Thibault) (1844-1924), Nobel Laureate in Literature (France). *The Crime of Sylvestre Bonnard*, 1881.

103. There are times in politics when you must be on the right side and lose.
John Kenneth Galbraith, American economist and U.S. Ambassador to India (D). Quoted in *The Observer*, Feb. 11, 1968.

104. Politics is the art of the possible. It consists of choosing between the disastrous and the unpalatable.
John Kenneth Galbraith. *Ambassador's Journal*, 1969.

105. Nothing is so admirable in politics as a short memory.
John Kenneth Galbraith. Quoted in *A Guide to the 99th Congress*, 1985.

106. My father *[Pandit Nehru]* was a statesman. I'm a political woman. My father was a saint. I'm not.
Indira Gandhi (1917-1984), Prime Minister of India. Quoted in *The New York Review of Books*, Sept. 18, 1975.

107. I believe cunning is not only morally wrong but also politically inexpedient, and have therefore always discontinued its use, even from a practical standpoint.
Mohandas K. Gandhi (1869-1948), Indian political and spiritual leader. *The Story of My Experiments with Truth*, 1957.

108. Many who think they are workers in politics are really merely tools.
Robert Gascoyne-Cecil, 3rd Marquess Salisbury (1830-1903), Prime Minister of Great Britain (Liberal). Comment to his successor and nephew, Arthur J. Balfour, after the Boer War, 1902.

109. In order to become the master, the politician poses as the servant.
Charles de Gaulle (1890-1970), President of France. Attributed.

110. I am a man who belongs to no one and who belongs to the whole world.
Charles de Gaulle. Quoted in *New Statesmen*, May 24, 1958.

111. We cannot safely leave politics to politicians, or political economy to college professors.
Henry George (1839-1897), American political economist. *Social Problems*, 1884.

112. All politics is reactive.
Jack Germond, American political columnist. Panel, John F. Kennedy School of Government, Harvard University, C-SPAN, Mar. 3, 1991.

113. Politicians trim and tack in their quest for power, but they do so in order to get the wind of votes in their sails.
Ian Gilmour, Member of Parliament, Great Britain (Conservative), and Deputy Foreign Secretary. *The Body Politic*, 1969.

114. Practical politics is the politics of the coming election.
William E. Gladstone (1809-1898), Prime Minister of Great Britain (Liberal). Speech, Dalkeith, Scotland, 1879.

115. No, I am a military man, not a statesman. I would just like to be mayor of Galena long enough to build a sidewalk from my house to the station.
Ulysses S. Grant (1822-1885), 18th President of the United States (R-OH). Response to a suggestion that he run for President, 1868.

116. Anarchists are a race of highly intelligent and imaginative children.
Alexander Gray (1882-1968), Scottish political economist. *The Socialist Tradition: Moses to Lenin*, 1959.

117. Letting someone else take the blame ... every politician does that if they can, every politician.
Martha Griffiths, U.S. Congresswoman and Lieutenant Governor of Michigan (D). Interview with Connie Chung, CBS, Sept. 7, 1990.

118. Politics makes strange bedfellows rich.
Wayne G. Haisley. *New Teeth in Old Saws*, 1928.

119. I've never concerned myself with the issues. I'm a political mechanic.
Robert H. Haldeman, White House Chief of Staff (R). Quoted in Theodore H. White, *Breach of Faith*, 1975.

120. Few individuals enter into public life who would not be wealthier and happier as private citizens – but then they would not be known, would not see their names in the newspaper, except for raising a curious calf or a mammoth cabbage.

Sarah J. Hale (1788-1879), American magazine editor. *Traits of American Life*, 1835.

121. When shall the softer, saner politics,
Whereof we dream, have play in each proud land?

Thomas Hardy (1840-1928), British writer. *Departures*.

122. There's nothing in politics that's worse than being caught unaware.

Mark O. Hatfield, Governor of Oregon and U.S. Senator (R). PBS, *Congress: We the People*, 1989.

123. I favor antipolitics politics.

Vaclav Havel, President of Czechoslovakia. 1984.

124. Politics is like a race horse. A good jockey must know how to fall with the least possible damage.

Edouard Herriot (1872-1957), Premier of France and President of the National Assembly. Remark to reporters, 1949.

125. He who is involved in *realpolitik* must think only of the last twenty-four hours.

Theodor Herzl (1860-1904), Austrian journalist and political Zionist. Remark to Max Nordau, 1897.

126. There are always choices in politics.

Michael Heseltine, Defense Secretary, Great Britain (Conservative). Nov. 1990.

127. Politics is the science of who gets what, when, and why.

Sidney Hillman (1887-1946), President, Amalgamated Clothing Workers of America, and Chief, Labor Division, War Production Board. *Political Primer for All Americans*, 1944.

128. A great politician has to bother himself less with means than with goals.

Adolf Hitler (1889-1945), Führer of the Third German Reich. *Mein Kampf*, 1933.

129. Scholars know that the processes of politics normally involve exaggeration, myth making, and fierce animosities.

Richard Hofstadter, American historian. *The American Political Tradition*, 1948.

130. During *[President Van Buren's]* stay in New York he has visited most of the public places in the constant custody of a set of men who are not (unless he has greatly changed) the sort of folks he would have chosen for his associates; but party politics, like poverty, bring men "acquainted with strange bedfellows."

Philip Hone (1780-1851), Mayor of New York City (Whig). *Diary*, July 9, 1939.

131. I thought at first I could be completely nonpolitical. Then they told me I had to be part nonpolitical and part political. I found that it was impossible, at least for me. I finally realized there was nothing for it but to be all political.

Harry L. Hopkins (1890-1946), U.S. Secretary of Commerce, Director, Work Projects Administration, and Special Assistant to the President (D). Quoted in Robert E. Sherwood, *Roosevelt and Hopkins: An Intimate Biography*, 1950.

132. There is always a type of man who says he loves his fellow men, and expects to make a living at it.

Edgar Watson Howe (1853-1937), American editor and writer. *Ventures in Common Sense*, 1919.

133. Politics is a profession as certainly as baseball.... The only difference is that baseball is on the square; no baseball hero claims he is working in the interest of the crowd in the bleachers.

Edgar Watson Howe. *Ibid.*

134. Americans ... are ruled by the Boss and the Trust.

William Ralph Inge (1860-1954), Anglican prelate and dean of St. Paul's, London. *Outspoken Essays*, First Series, 1919.

135. I have only two regrets: that I have not shot Henry Clay or hanged John C. Calhoun.

Andrew Jackson (1767-1845), 7th President of the United States (D-TN). Remark when leaving the presidency, 1837.

136. My constituency is the desperate, the damned, the disinherited, the disrespected, and the despised.

Jesse L. Jackson, Shadow Senator (D-DC). Speech, Democratic National Convention, San Francisco, CA, July 17, 1984.

137. A politician ought to be born a foundling and remain a bachelor.

Claudia (Lady Bird) Johnson, First Lady. Quoted in *Time*, Dec. 1, 1975.

138. But I guess as long as I'm here, we might as well talk a little politics.

Lyndon B. Johnson (1908-1973), 36th President of the United States (D-TX). Said to party leaders, Evansville, IN, Oct. 27, 1964.

139. My link to the bomb throwers.
Lyndon B. Johnson. Comment on Vice President Hubert H. Humphrey. Quoted in David Halberstam, *The Best and the Brightest*, 1969.

140. I seldom think of politics more than eighteen hours a day.
Lyndon B. Johnson. Attributed.

141. A crony is a presidential advisor you don't like.
Sam Houston Johnson, brother of Lyndon B. Johnson. Quoted in Merle Miller, *Lyndon: An Oral Biography*, 1980.

142. Politics are now nothing more than the means of rising in the world.
Samuel Johnson (1709-1784), British writer and lexicographer. Quoted in James Boswell, *The Life of Samuel Johnson*, 1775.

143. Politicians respect a lot of things, but nothing so much as success.
Hamilton Jordan, White House Chief of Staff (D). *Crisis: The Last Year of the Carter Presidency*, 1982.

144. Whether it's football or politics, the American people like a winner.
Hamilton Jordan. *Ibid*.

145. That vision thing is so elusive to American politicians.
Bernard Kalb, American journalist and spokesperson, U.S. State Department. Seminar, National Press Club, Washington, DC, Mar. 29, 1990.

146. Forgive your enemies, but never forget their names.
John F. Kennedy (1917-1963), 35th President of the United States (D-MA). Attributed.

147. Mothers may still want their sons to grow up to become President, but they don't want them to become politicians in the process.
John F. Kennedy. Attributed.

148. Don't get mad, get even.
Joseph P. Kennedy (1888-1969), U.S. Ambassador to Great Britain (D). Quoted in Benjamin C. Bradlee, *Conversations with Kennedy*, 1975.

149. People say I am ruthless. I am *not* ruthless. And if I find the man who is calling me ruthless, I shall destroy him.
Robert F. Kennedy (1925-1968), U.S. Senator and U.S. Attorney General (D-NY). Remark during his Senate campaign, New York City, 1964.

150. Now I can go back to being ruthless again.
Robert F. Kennedy. Remark after winning his Senate campaign, Nov. 1964.

151. My babies were rocked to political lullabies.
Rose Kennedy, mother of John, Robert, and Edward Kennedy. Quoted in *The Washington Post Magazine*, Apr. 29, 1990.

152. Politics is now become a complete trade, and what is worse every fellow follows it, fool or knave, and aspires to the best jobs.
John Leeds Kerr (1780-1844), U.S. Congressman and U.S. Senator (Whig-MD). 1837.

153. Politicians. Little Tin Gods on Wheels.
Rudyard Kipling (1865-1936), Nobel Laureate in Literature (Great Britain). *Public Waste*.

154. I don't even agree with myself at times.
Jeane J. Kirkpatrick, U.S. Ambassador to the United Nations (R). When asked why she switched political parties from Democrat to Republican just prior to becoming U.N. Ambassador in Ronald Reagan's administration. Remark to reporters, Apr. 3, 1985.

155. Ninety percent of the politicians give the other 10 percent a bad name.
Henry M. Kissinger, U.S. Secretary of State and National Security Advisor (R). Remark to reporters, 1978.

156. Politics is more than dealing with issues. It also requires a "compass" of principles.
Helmut Kohl, Chancellor of West Germany. Quoted in *The New York Times*, July 1, 1990.

157. I refuse to politicize a health issue.
C. Everett Koop, U.S. Surgeon General. Interview, CBS, *Christian Lifestyle Magazine*, Oct. 28, 1989.

158. America is just the country that shows how all the written guarantees in the world for freedom are no protection against tyranny and oppression of the worst kind. There the politician has come to be looked upon as the very scum of society.
Peter A. Kropotkin (1842-1921), Russian prince and anarchist. Speech, 1891.

159. I would like to be remembered as one who in the world's darkest hours kept a clean conscience and stood at the end for the ideals of American democracy.
Robert M. La Follette (1855-1925), Governor of Wisconsin and U.S. Senator (R). Last writing before his death, 1925.

160. Politics is the management of expectations.
Richard D. Lamm, Governor of Colorado (D). *Playboy*, Aug. 1984.

161. In public affairs skill consists less in creating situations than in profiting from those that arise.
François de La Rochefoucauld (1613-1680), French nobleman and writer. *Réflexions ou sentences et maximes morales*, 1665.

162. *Politics: who gets what, when, how.*
Harold D. Lasswell (1902-1978), American political economist. Title of book, 1936.

163. There are a lot of smart people in politics and government, but character matters ... it is terribly important that the two be melded.
James Madison Leach, U.S. Congressman (R-IA). Interview, CNN, *An American Profile*, Sept. 3, 1990.

164. Politicians have the same occupational hazard as generals – focusing on the last battle and overreacting to that.
Ann F. Lewis, National Director, Americans for Democratic Action. Quoted in *The New York Times*, Sept. 24, 1986.

165. I am a slow walker, but I never walk backward.
Abraham Lincoln (1809-1865), 16th President of the United States (R-IL). Attributed; frequently quoted by Earl Warren.

166. A politician is a person with whose politics you don't agree; if you agree with him he is a statesman.
David Lloyd George, 1st Earl of Dwyfor (1863-1945), Prime Minister of Great Britain (Liberal). Attributed.

167. The kind of thing I'm good at is knowing every politician in the state and remembering where he itches. And I know where to scratch him.
Earl Kemp Long (1895-1960), Governor of Louisiana (D). Quoted in *The New Yorker*, June 4, 1960.

168. I would describe a demagogue as a politician who don't keep his promises. On that basis, I'm the first man to have power in Louisiana who ain't a demagogue because I kept every promise I ever made.
Huey P. Long (1893-1935), Governor of Louisiana and U.S. Senator (D). Quoted in David H. Bennett, *Demagogues in the Depression*, 1969.

169. In politics you must help your friends or you won't have any.
Russell B. Long, U.S. Senator (D-LA). Quoted in Charles Henning, *The Wit and Wisdom of Politics*, 1989.

170. The rich and powerful are robbing us blind, and the politicians in Washington are doing nothing to help us.
Harry Lonsdale, Oregon Democratic senatorial candidate. Campaign TV ad, 1990.

171. Sooner or later all politicians die of swallowing their own lies.
Clare Boothe Luce (1903-1987), U.S. Congresswoman and U.S. Ambassador to Italy and Brazil (R-CT). *Europe in the Spring*, 1940.

172. No woman has ever so comforted the distressed or so distressed the comfortable.
Clare Boothe Luce. Speaking of Eleanor Roosevelt, Nov. 1962.

173. In politics women ... type the letters, lick the stamps, distribute the pamphlets and get out the vote. Men get elected.
Clare Boothe Luce. Quoted in *Saturday Review*, Sept. 15, 1974.

174. I have always been able to take care of the enemy in my front, but I have never been able to protect myself from the enemy in my rear *[domestic politics and politicians]*.
Douglas MacArthur (1880-1964), General, U.S. Army, and Supreme Commander of U.N. forces in Korea. Quoted by Arthur Spanier, *The Truman-MacArthur Controversy*, 1959.

175. A politician must often talk and act before he has thought and read. He may be very ill-informed respecting a question; all his notions about it may be vague and inaccurate, but speak he must; and if he is a man of talents, of tact, and of intrepidity, he soon finds that, even under such circumstances, it is possible to speak successfully.
Thomas Babington Macaulay, 1st Baron Macaulay (1800-1859), historian and Secretary of War, Great Britain (Liberal). "Gladstone on Church and State," *Edinburgh Review*, Apr. 1839.

176. Politics is civil war carried on by other means.
Alisdair MacIntyre, British political philosopher. *After Virtue*, 1984.

177. At home, you always have to be a politician; when you're abroad, you almost feel yourself a statesman.
Harold Macmillan (1894-1986), Prime Minister of Great Britain (Conservative). Quoted in *Look*, Apr. 15, 1958.

178. If people want a sense of purpose, they should get it from their archbishop. They should certainly not get it from their politicians.

Harold Macmillan. Quoted in Henry Fairlie, *The Life of Politics*, 1969.

179. I never found in a long experience of politics that criticism is ever inhibited by ignorance.
Harold Macmillan. Attributed.

180. Politics is not the Business of a Woman.
Mary (de la Rivière) Manley (1663-1724), English writer and political journalist. *The Adventures of Rivella*, 1714.

181. "You are dictatorial." My dear sirs, you are right, that is just what we are.
Mao Tse-tung (1893-1976), Chairman, Communist Party of China. *On the People's Democratic Dictatorship*, June 30, 1949.

182. When you're functioning out of conviction, you can't think of politics.
Bob Martinez, Director, Office of National Drug Control Policy, and Governor of Florida (R). Explanation of his anti-abortion stance. Quoted in *Time*, Oct. 23, 1989.

183. Politics is the art of looking for trouble, finding it everywhere, diagnosing it incorrectly, and applying the wrong remedies.
Groucho Marx (1895-1977), American comedian. 1954.

184. The old guys schmooze; the new guys broadcast.
Christopher Matthews, political columnist, campaign manager, and presidential speech writer (D). Quoted on PBS, *The Power Game*, Jan. 2, 1989.

185. It is very unfair to expect a politician to live in private up to the statements he makes in public.
W. Somerset Maugham (1874-1965), English writer. *The Circle*, 1921.

186. A man must have guts enough to fall out even with his friends.... The only way to play politics is not to play politics.
Maury Maverick (1895-1954), U.S. Congressman (D-TX). Recalled on his death.

187. One of the lines in the Benedictine monastery is to keep death daily before your eyes, which never hurts in politics.
Eugene J. McCarthy, U.S. Congressman and U.S. Senator (D-WI). 1968.

188. Being in politics is like coaching football. You have to be smart enough to understand the game and dumb enough to think it's important.
Eugene J. McCarthy. 1968.

189. One thing about a pig. He thinks he's warm if his nose is warm. I saw a bunch of pigs one time that had frozen together in a rosette, each one's nose tucked under the rump of the one in front. We have a lot of pigs in politics.
Eugene J. McCarthy. Quoted in *Life*, May 1968.

190. Most political accidents happen in the middle of the road.
Eugene J. McCarthy. Quoted in *U.S. News & World Report*, Nov. 26, 1990.

191. He who dallies is a dastard; he who doubts is damned.
George McDuffie (1790-1851), U.S. Congressman and U.S. Senator (D-SC). Quoted by Cong. William Jasper Blackburn (R-KY), House debate of the Hayes-Tilden electoral controversy, Feb. 1877; (compare *Romans* 14:23, "But he who has doubts is condemned ...").

192. Washington likes people who are articulate and look at the big picture and have all the answers.
M. Peter McPherson, U.S. Deputy Secretary of the Treasury (R). Quoted in *The New York Times*, Nov. 19, 1989.

193. The whole aim of practical politics is to keep the populace alarmed (and hence clamorous to be led to safety) by an endless series of hobgoblins.
H. L. Mencken (1880-1956), American journalist. *In Defense of Women*, 1923.

194. For if experience teaches us anything at all it teaches us this: that a good politician, under democracy, is quite as unthinkable as an honest burglar.
H. L. Mencken. *Prejudices*, Fourth Series, "The Politician," 1924.

195. Politics is the science of the vital interests of States in the highest sphere.
Klemens von Metternich (1773-1859), Austrian statesman and diplomat. Quoted by Anthony Trollope, *Vienna and the Austrians*, 1838.

196. For the politician the goal is always to be in the government.... Everything is about the struggle for office. The purpose of power, the problem to solve, is forgotten.
Jean Monnet (1888-1979), French politician and statesman. Quoted in *The New York Times*, Nov. 13, 1988.

197. They can say that you are a liar, a cheat, a crackpot, and a licentious old man, and most politicians don't care. But if they say you can't win, you're through.

Mike Monroney (1902-1980), U.S. Congressman and U.S. Senator (D-OK). Quoted in Ralph G. Martin, *Ballots & Bandwagons*, 1964.

198. The proper memory for a politician is one that knows what to remember and what to forget.

John Morley, Viscount Morley of Blackburn (1838-1923), Member of Parliament, Great Britain (Liberal), Chief Secretary for Ireland, and Secretary of State for India. *Recollections*, 1917.

199. Politics is the science of the second best.

John Morley. Quoted in Ralph G. Martin, *Ballots & Bandwagons*, 1964.

200. The politician in my country seeks votes, affection and respect, in that order.

Edward R. Murrow (1908-1965), American broadcast journalist and Director, United States Information Agency. Speech, London, Oct. 19, 1959.

201. There are only two kinds of politics. They are not radical or reactionary, or conservative and liberal, or even Democratic and Republican. There are only the politics of fear and the politics of trust.

Edmund S. Muskie, U.S. Secretary of State and U.S. Senator (D-ME). Televised speech, Nov. 2, 1970.

202. My program is simple. I want to govern.

Benito Mussolini (1883-1945), dictator of Italy (Fascist). *My Autobiography*, 1939.

203. In politics there is no heart, only head.

Napoléon I (1769-1821), military leader and Emperor of France. Explanation of his divorce from Josephine.

204. Just because people are involved in politics doesn't mean that they don't have intelligence.

Burton Natarus, Alderman of Chicago, IL. Quoted in *The New York Times*, Feb. 21, 1989.

205. A politician knows that his friends are not always his allies and that his adversaries are not his enemies.

Richard M. Nixon, 37th President of the United States (R-CA). Eulogy for Everett M. Dirksen, Sept. 8, 1969.

206. I'm an introvert in an extrovert's profession.

Richard M. Nixon. Quoted in Barbara Rowes, *The Book of Quotes*, 1979.

207. There is one solid and fundamental thing in politics: the law of change. What's up today is down tomorrow.

Richard M. Nixon. Remark, 1979.

208. SEEK YE FIRST THE POLITICAL KINGDOM AND ALL THINGS SHALL BE ADDED UNTO YOU.

Kwame Nkrumah (1909-1972), Prime Minister of Ghana. Inscription on his statue, Accra, Ghana.

209. Politics has always been largely an all male business.

Peggy Noonan, presidential speech writer (R). Interview, C-SPAN, *Bookbeat*, Feb. 18, 1990.

210. It is hard to write about politicians, see them at such close range, and still think of any of them as heroes.

Robert Novak, American political columnist. Interview, *Conservative Digest*, May-June 1988.

211. Is American politics so brain-dead that we are reduced to having political shysters manipulate symbols?

David R. Obey, U.S. Congressman (D-WI). Quoted in *The New York Times*, Mar. 18, 1990.

212. A politician should have a big heart and a bigger stomach to take the punches.

Turgut Ozal, Prime Minister of Turkey. Quoted in *The New York Times*, Mar. 9, 1991.

213. You can do more damage to your cause by lack of manners than by lack of substance.

Robert W. Packwood, U.S. Senator (R-OR). Quoted in Tolchin and Tolchin, *Dismantling America: The Rush to Deregulate*, 1983.

214. Race is the single major issue in life and politics in Chicago.

Lu Palmer, American political organizer (D). Quoted in *The New York Times*, Oct. 16, 1988.

215. Politics is the science of exigencies.

Theodore Parker (1810-1860), American clergyman and abolitionist. *Of Truth*, 1858.

216. Politicians don't see the light until they feel the heat.

Stanford E. Parris, U.S. Congressman (R-VA). House hearing, Aug. 9, 1990.

217. Politics is the skilled use of blunt objects.

Lester B. Pearson (1897-1972), Prime Minister of Canada (Liberal) and Nobel Laureate in Peace. Quoted on CBS, *The Tenth Decade*, 1972.

218. The secret is to always let the other man have your way.

Claiborne Pell, U.S. Senator (D-RI). Quoted in *The New York Times*, Feb. 3, 1987.

219. The mistake a lot of politicians make is in forgetting they've been appointed and thinking they've been anointed.

Claude D. Pepper (1901-1989), U.S. Senator and U.S. Congressman (D-FL). Remark on his 80th birthday.

220. Advice to politicians: Always be sincere, whether you mean it or not.

Charles H. Percy, U.S. Senator (R-IL). Quoted in Skubik and Short, *Republican Humor*, 1976.

221. You've got to be crazy or an optimist to be in politics, and I prefer to think of myself as an optimist.

David Peterson, Premier of Ontario, Canada. Interview, PBS, *MacNeil-Lehrer News Hour*, May 23, 1990.

222. There is no Canaan *[promised land]* in politics.

Wendell Phillips (1811-1884), American orator and reformer. Speech, Jan. 28, 1852.

223. You can always get the truth from an American statesman after he has turned seventy, or given up all hope of the Presidency.

Wendell Phillips. Speech, Nov. 7, 1860.

224. Two kinds of men generally succeed best in political life – men of no principle, but of great talent, and men of no talent, but one principle: of obedience to their superior.

Wendell Phillips. Attributed.

225. I am a good friend to Communists abroad, but I do not like them at home.

Souvanna Phouma. Premier of Laos. Quoted in *Life*, Nov. 3, 1961.

226. I wasn't looking for this job. Destiny gave it to me.

Augusto Pinochet, Captain General and President of Chile. Comment after leading a military coup, bombing the presidential palace, directing the murder of the elected President, and taking over the government. Quoted in *National Geographic*, July 1988.

227. I'll tell you what I really think about politicians. The other night I watched some politicians on television talking about Vietnam. I wanted very much to burst through the screen with a flame thrower and burn their eyes out and their balls off and then inquire from them how they would assess this action from a political point of view.

Harold Pinter, British playwright. Quoted in George Plimpton, *Writers at Work*, 3rd series, 1967.

228. Presumptuousness is one of the greatest vices in a man of public responsibility, and though a political leader need not necessarily be humble, he must absolutely be modest.

Armand Jean du Plessis (Cardinal Richelieu) (1585-1642), French ecclesiastic and statesman. *Political Testament*, I, 8, 1687.

229. Statesmen are not only liable to give an account of what they say or do in public, but there is a busy inquiry made into their very meals, beds, marriages, and every other sportive or serious action.

Plutarch (c.46-c.120), Greek biographer. *Political Precepts*.

230. They are wrong who think that politics is like an ocean voyage or a military campaign, something to be done with some particular end in view, something which leaves off as soon as the end is reached. It is not a public chore to be got over with. It is a way of life.

Plutarch. *Politics and Philosophy*.

231. A statesman is a politician who places himself at the service of the nation. A politician is a statesman who places the nation at his service.

Georges Pompidou (1911-1974), President of France. Quoted in *The Observer*, Dec. 30, 1973.

232. All political lives, unless they are cut off in midstream at a happy juncture, end in failure.

John Enoch Powell, Member of Parliament, Great Britain. Quoted in *The Sunday Times*, Nov. 6, 1977.

233. A lot of politics is timing. Timing and opportunity. And the two are critical to success but you can't necessarily determine either one of them.

J. Danforth Quayle, U.S. Senator and Vice President of the United States (R-IN). Quoted in *The Washington Post*, Jan. 5, 1992.

234. Politics is the art of postponing decisions until they are no longer relevant.

Henri Queuille (1884-1970), Premier of France. Quoted by Frank L. Carlucci, *The Bureaucrat*, Winter 1985-1986.

235. A man must be strong enough to mold the peculiarity of his imperfections into the perfection of his peculiarities.

Walther Rathenau (1867-1922), Foreign Minister, Germany. Quoted in Emil Ludwig, *Genius and Character*, 1927.

236. A hero always presents two choices: to win or to lose.

Moness Razzaz, Jordanian writer. In reference to Iraqi Pres. Saddam Hussein. Quoted in *Newsweek*, Jan. 7, 1991.

237. I must say acting was good training for the political life which lay ahead for us.

Nancy Reagan, First Lady. *Nancy*, 1980.

238. Politics is just like show business. You have a hell of an opening, coast for a while, and then have a hell of a close.

Ronald Reagan, 40th President of the United States (R-CA). Remark to aide Stuart Spencer, 1966.

239. We should all be glad if we could step aside and say: "Now let us have a day of rest. Politics are over and the millennium is begun." But we live in a world of sin and sorrow.

Thomas B. Reed (1839-1902), U.S. Congressman and Speaker of the House (R-ME). Speech, Philadelphia, PA, Feb. 15, 1884.

240. Politics is mostly pill-taking.

Thomas B. Reed. Letter to Cong. John Dalzell (R-PA), Aug. 1, 1896.

241. A statesman is a successful politician who is dead.

Thomas B. Reed. Quoted on PBS, *The Congress*, 1989.

242. All the wisdom in the world consists in shouting with the majority.

Thomas B. Reed. Quoted in Charles Henning, *The Wit and Wisdom of Politics*, 1989.

243. The professional politician is one of the mysteries of American life, a bundle of paradoxes, shrewd as a fox, naive as a schoolboy. He has great respect for the people yet treats them like boobs, and is constitutionally unable to keep his mouth shut.

James Reston, American political columnist. *The New York Times*, Oct. 2, 1955.

244. All politics are based on the indifference of the majority.

James Reston. *The New York Times*, June 12, 1968.

245. In politics as in love, there's a time when you have to kiss the girl.

James Reston. Remark, Nov. 3, 1989.

246. You have only one political death, but you can choose when to use it.

John Jacob Rhodes III, U.S. Congressman (R-AZ). Quoted in *The Washington Post*, Jan. 6, 1991.

247. I've achieved my objective. I'm a has-been.

John P. Robarts, Premier of Ontario, Canada. Retirement speech, Toronto, Feb. 11, 1971.

248. Politics is not a vocation. It is not even an avocation. It's an incurable disease. If it ever gets in one's blood, it can never be eradicated.

Joseph Taylor Robinson (1872-1937), Governor of Arkansas (D), U.S. Congressman, and U.S. Senator. Recalled on his death.

249. Politics, of course, requires sweat, work, combat, and organization. But these should not be ugly words for any free people.

Nelson A. Rockefeller (1908-1979), Governor of New York and Vice President of the United States (R). *The Future of Federalism*, 1962.

250. I don't like Louisiana politics. I like Louisiana.

Charles E. Roemer III, U.S. Congressman and Governor of Louisiana (D). Campaign speech, 1988.

251. I tell you folks, all politics is apple sauce.

Will Rogers (1879-1935), American humorist. *The Illiterate Digest*, 1924.

252. Politics is the best show in America.

Will Rogers. 1933.

253. There is no more independence in politics than there is in jail.

Will Rogers. Quoted in *The New York Times Magazine*, Sept. 8, 1946.

254. I love animals and I love politicians and I love to watch both of 'em play, either back home in their native state or after they have been captured and sent to the zoo or to Washington.

Will Rogers. Quoted in *The New York Times*, Jan. 28, 1984.

255. I have spent many years of my life in opposition, and I rather like the role.

Anna Eleanor Roosevelt (1884-1962), First Lady and U.S. Delegate to the United Nations. Letter to Bernard Baruch, Nov. 18, 1952.

256. Someday you may well be sitting here where I am now as President of the United States. And when you are, you'll be looking at that door over there and knowing that practically everybody who walks through it wants something out of you. You'll learn what a lonely job this is, and you'll discover the need for somebody like Harry Hopkins who asks for nothing except to serve you.

Franklin D. Roosevelt (1882-1945), 32nd President of the United States (D-NY). Remark to Wendell Wilkie. Quoted in Robert E. Sherwood, *Roosevelt and Hopkins: An Intimate Biography*, 1948.

257. This whole political business now is bitterly distasteful to me.

Theodore Roosevelt (1858-1919), 26th President of the United States (R-NY). Letter to Sen. Henry Cabot Lodge, 1910.

258. Our great democracies still tend to think that a stupid man is more likely to be honest than a clever man, and our politicians take advantage of this prejudice by pretending to be even more stupid than nature has made them.

Bertrand Russell, 3rd Earl Russell of Kingston (1872-1970), British philosopher and reformer. *New Hopes for a Changing World*, 1951.

259. If you call your opponent a politician, it's grounds for libel.

Mark Russell, American political comedian. PBS, *Mark Russell Comedy Hour*, Oct. 1990.

260. Man is a social rather than a political animal; he can exist without a government.

George Santayana (1863-1952), American philosopher. *Obiter Scripta*, 1936.

261. There are too many ideologues in politics these days – people who know what they believe and don't want to be confused by the facts.

Paul S. Sarbanes, U.S. Congressman and U.S. Senator (D-MD). Campaign debate, 1988.

262. It is the Fools and the Knaves that make the Wheels of the World turn. *They* are *the World;* those few who have Sense or Honesty sneak up and down single, but never go in Herds.

George Savile, 1st Marquess of Halifax (1633-1695), Lord Privy Seal of England. *Moral Thoughts and Reflections*, 1750.

263. Men often mistake themselves, but they never *forget* themselves.

George Savile. *Ibid.*

264. An injury may more properly be said to be postponed, than to be forgiven.

George Savile. *Ibid.*

265. Where Men get by pleasing, and lose by serving, the choice is so easy that no body can miss it.

George Savile. *Political Thoughts and Reflections*, 1750.

266. I am not a visionary, and I'm skeptical of all visionaries.

Helmut Schmidt, Chancellor of West Germany. Quoted in *The New Yorker*, Oct. 17, 1983.

267. I really wanted to be the mayor. This is the job in politics that I've been interested in for many years, and I thought it was a job that I could do well.... I knew that most of the time mayors don't go on to higher office.

Kurt Schmoke, Mayor of Baltimore, MD (D). Quoted in *The Washington Post Magazine*, May 27, 1990.

268. Politics can be, in some part at least, a creative process, not simply a deterministic response to the myopic self-interest of majorities or special-interest groups.

Charles L. Schultze, Chairman, Council of Economic Advisors, and Director, U.S. Bureau of the Budget (D). *The Public Use of Private Interest*, 1977.

269. In politics you have a one-day sale.

Tony Schwartz, political TV ad producer. Interview, PBS, *A Walk Through the 20th Century: The 30-Second President*, July 23, 1990.

270. Politics are the blowpipe beneath whose influence the best-cemented friendships diffuse.

Walter Scott (1771-1832), Scottish writer. Quoted in John Gibson Lockhart, *Life of Scott*, 1838.

271. A politician ... one that would circumvent God.

William Shakespeare (1564-1616), English writer. *Hamlet*, V, i.

272. Get thee glass eyes;
And, like a scurvy politician, seem
To see the things thou dost not.

William Shakespeare. *King Lear*, IV, vi.

273. He knows nothing and he thinks he knows everything. That points clearly to a political career.

George Bernard Shaw (1856-1950), Nobel Laureate in Literature (Great Britain). *Major Barbara*, 1905.

274. Politics has become so primary in modern life that the masses are more moved by promises than by fulfillments.

Fulton J. Sheen (1895-1979), American Roman Catholic archbishop and television personality. *The Way to Inner Peace*, 1955.

275. Nothing ever gets settled in this town *[Washington]*.... It's not like running a company or even a university. It's a seething debating society in which the debate never stops, in which people never give up, including me, and that's the atmosphere in which you administer.

George P. Shultz, U.S. Secretary of State (R). Testimony in Congress, 1986.

276. In politics the only thing that succeeds is success.

Hugh Sidey, American political columnist. *Time*, May 23, 1988.

277. I am not a professional politician and ... I see that as a badge of honor and will wear it proudly.

John Silber, President of Boston University, Boston, MA, and Massachusetts Democratic gubernatorial candidate. Quoted on CBS, *Face the Nation*, Nov. 4, 1990.

278. Those who travel the high road of humility are not troubled by heavy traffic in Washington, DC.

Alan K. Simpson, U.S. Senator (R-WY). Roast of Sam Donaldson, Sept. 25, 1990.

279. In politics you must know people and know how to work with them.

Alfred E. Smith (1873-1944), Governor of New York (D). Quoted in Frances Perkins's private papers.

280. Can anything live in this country 139 years *[Tammany Hall]* that is not all right?

Alfred E. Smith. Speech, Tammany Hall Independence Day celebration, July 4, 1928.

281. In politics you've got to understand that some things are doable and some are not.

Christopher H. Smith, U.S. Congressman (R-NJ). Interview, CBS, *20/20*, Nov. 4, 1989.

282. *[Huey]* Long's thinking is a correct representation of the mass mind.

Gerald L. K. Smith (1898-1976), American clergyman and cofounder, Union Party. *The New Republic*, Feb. 13, 1935.

283. Before you can become a statesman you first have to get elected, and to get elected you have to be a politician pledging support for what the voters want.

Margaret Chase Smith, U.S. Congresswoman and U.S. Senator (R-ME). *Declaration of Conscience*, 1972.

284. Nature and political responsibility ... abhor a vacuum.

David H. Souter, U.S. Supreme Court Justice. Senate Judiciary Committee, confirmation hearings, Sept. 14, 1990.

285. America has always loved un-politicians.

Leslie Stahl, American TV journalist. CBS, *Face the Nation*, Nov. 4, 1990.

286. At court, people embrace without acquaintance, serve one another without friendship, and injure one another without hatred. Interest, not sentiment, is the growth of that soil.

Philip Dormer Stanhope, 4th Earl of Chesterfield (1694-1773), Member of Parliament, Great Britain (Whig), and Lord-Lieutenant of Ireland. *Maxims*.

287. Affairs of moment.

Philip Dormer Stanhope. Favorite phrase for politics and diplomacy.

288. It is not my appearance but my disappearance that troubles me.

Thaddeus Stevens (1792-1868), U.S. Congressman (Whig and R-PA). Remark during an illness. Quoted in J. W. Forney, *Anecdotes of Public Men*, 1873.

289. A politician is a statesman who approaches every question with an open mouth.

Adlai E. Stevenson (1900-1965), Governor of Illinois (D) and U.S. Ambassador to the United Nations. 1956.

290. After lots of people who go into politics have been in it a while, they find that to stay in politics they have to make all sorts of compromises to satisfy their supporters and that it becomes awfully important for them to keep their jobs because they have nowhere else to go.

Adlai E. Stevenson. 1958.

291. The best politics is good government.

Adlai E. Stevenson. Quoted in *The New York Times*, Aug. 26, 1990.

292. Politics is perhaps the only profession for which no preparation is thought necessary.

Robert Louis Stevenson (1850-1894), Scottish writer. *Familiar Studies of Men and Books*, V, 1882.

293. In a republic, all are masters, and each tyrannizes over the others.

Max Stirner (Johann Kaspar Schmidt) (1806-1856), German anarchist. *The Ego and His Own*, 1845.

294. He practiced the politics of envy, pure and simple.

David A. Stockman, Director, U.S. Office of Management and Budget, and U.S. Congressman (R-MI). In reference to Speaker of the House Jim Wright. *The Triumph of Politics: Why the Reagan Revolution Failed*, 1986.

295. Every government is run by liars and nothing they say should be believed.

I. F. Stone (1908-1989), American investigative journalist and political writer. Remark, 1973.

296. Both life-style and technology has forced politics, for the most part, to sharpen its focus.

John Sununu, Governor of New Hampshire and White House Chief of Staff (R). Quoted in *The New York Times*, Mar. 18, 1990.

297. I cannot give you the formula for success, but I can give you the formula for failure – which is: Try to please everybody.

Herbert Bayard Swope (1882-1958), American war correspondent and political journalist. Speech, St. Louis, MO, Democratic Organization, Dec. 20, 1950.

298. I am not so constituted that I can run with the hare and hunt with the hounds.

William H. Taft (1857-1930), 27th President of the United States (R-OH), and Chief Justice, U.S. Supreme Court. Quoted in Foster Rhea Dulles, *The United States Since 1865*, 1959.

299. I am determined to paddle my own canoe.

William H. Taft. Quoted in Ralph G. Martin, *Ballots & Bandwagons*, 1964.

300. Politics, when I am in it, makes me sick.

William H. Taft. Quoted in Wallechinsky and Wallace, *The People's Almanac*, 1975.

301. I brought down but one brace of pheasants, owing to the high wind which blew; but Lamb was luckier, and always found the wind lower when he fired, which was a knack he had through life, which stood him in good stead in politics as in sporting.

Henry John Temple, 3rd Viscount Palmerston (1784-1865), Prime Minister of Great Britain (Whig). In referring to William Lamb, Lord Melbourne. Quoted in W. Torrens, *Memoirs of ... Viscount Melbourne*, 1878.

302. In politics one must take nothing tragically and everything seriously.

Louis-Adolphe Thiers (1797-1877), 1st President of the Third French Republic. 1856.

303. Politics is the gizzard of society, full of grit and gravel, and the two political parties are its two opposite halves – sometimes split into quarters – which grind on each other. Not only individuals, but states, have this dyspepsia.

Henry David Thoreau (1817-1862), American naturalist and philosopher. "Life Without Principle," *The Atlantic Monthly*, 1863.

304. The choice in politics isn't usually between black and white. It's between two horrible shades of grey.

Peter Thorneycroft, Member of Parliament, Great Britain (Conservative). Quoted in *London Sunday Telegraph*, Feb. 11, 1979.

305. Those of us who are engaged in politics as a profession, I think, recognize that this is probably the most fascinating business in the world. It is also perhaps the most brutal and ruthless business in the world, and those of us who make a career of it have to have pretty tough hides. I think that any number of us are given to question ourselves from time to time as to whether or not it is ice water or human blood that courses through our veins. But I know that to survive in this business you have to be tough. You have to turn and oppose "the slings and arrows of outrageous fortune." I know that we have to steel ourselves against our critics. I know that we have to exercise a degree of cunning, and sometimes a degree of insensitivity.

John G. Tower (1925-1991), U.S. Senator (R-TX). Memorial address for Everett M. Dirksen, Sept. 8, 1969.

306. All politicians are cowards.

Francis E. Townsend (1867-1960), American physician; founder, Old Age Revolving Pensions; and cofounder, Union Party. Quoted in D. H. Bennett, *Demagogues in the Depression*.

307. In politics you seek to accommodate truth to the facts around you.

Pierre Elliott Trudeau, Prime Minister of Canada (Liberal). 1978.

308. I have an old definition for a statesman, a very old one: A statesman is a dead politician.

Harry S Truman (1884-1972), 33rd President of the United States (D-MO). Remark at a buffet supper for Democratic Members of Congress, Washington, DC, Jan. 11, 1951.

309. Partisan politics should stop at the boundaries of the United States.

Harry S Truman. Letter to Dwight D. Eisenhower, Aug. 16, 1952.

310. My choice early in life was either to be a piano-player in a whorehouse or a politician. And to tell the truth, there's hardly any difference.

Harry S Truman. Remark, 1962.

311. Why, this fellow *[Dwight D. Eisenhower]* don't know any more about politics than a pig knows about Sunday.

Harry S Truman. Quoted in Richard M. Nixon, *Memoirs*, 1978.

312. No one, indeed, will ever be able to understand Franklin *[D. Roosevelt]* without understanding Eleanor *[Roosevelt]* as well.

Rexford Guy Tugwell (1891-1979), presidential assistant (D); U.S. Undersecretary of Agriculture; Administrator, Federal Resettlement Administration; Chairman, N. Y. City Planning Commission; and Governor of Puerto Rico. *The Democratic Roosevelt*, 1957.

313. I don't think you can mix politics and police.

Maurice T. Turner, Jr., Police Chief, Washington, DC. Interview, WETA-TV, Mar. 21, 1989.

314. The ability to change one's views without losing one's seat is the mark of a great politician.

Morris K. Udall, U.S. Congressman (D-AZ). *Too Funny to Be President*, 1988.

315. If I had slain all my enemies yesterday, I wouldn't have any friends today.
Jesse Unruh (1922-1987), California legislative leader (D). 1983.

316. I don't think about politics. That's one of my goddamn precious American rights.
John Updike, American writer. *Rabbit Redux*, 1971.

317. Politics is the greatest training ground for anything you do in life because politics is all about the human condition.
Jack Valenti, Special Assistant to the President (D). Interview, C-SPAN, *An American Profile*, Feb. 19, 1990.

318. The most inefficient public servant I know is one who's out of office.
Jack Valenti. *Ibid.*

319. Politics is the art of preventing people from taking part in affairs which properly concern them.
Paul Valéry (1871-1945), French writer. *Tel quel*, 1943.

320. I would make it a point to speak invariably well of ... other would-be great men in the State, particularly those who think they deserve to be well-spoken of; taking no part, and feeling no preference, in their intrigues and intentions about nominations, etc. Seven out of ten of those you benefit will prove ungrateful, all of your opponents will be vindictive, you will fritter away your strength, and worry yourself to no purpose by caring about, and still more by meddling in, any of these matters.
Martin Van Buren (1782-1862), 8th President of the United States (D). Letter of political advice to his son, John, Mar. 16, 1858.

321. Politicians are here today and gone tomorrow.
Fidel Velazques, Mexican labor leader. Quoted in *The New York Times Magazine*, Nov. 20, 1988.

322. Politics is for abnormal people.
Lech Walesa, President of Poland, trade unionist and founder, Solidarity. Quoted in *The Washington Post*, Nov. 13, 1989.

323. If I thought I might serve the taxpayers better by appearing at City Hall clad in overalls, or even a snood, I should do so. But until we have an ordinance to the contrary, I shall bathe frequently, as is my custom; and change my linen often, as is perhaps my eccentric desire; and patronize the tailor of my own choice.
James J. Walker (1881-1946), Mayor of New York City (D). Response to criticism of his "dandy" appearance. Campaign speech, Oct. 1929.

324. I am not a politician, and my other habits are good.
Artemus Ward (Charles Farrar Browne) (1834-1867), American writer and editor. *Artemus Ward, His Book*, "Fourth of July Oration," 1862.

325. Politics makes strange bedfellows.
Charles Dudley Warner (1829-1900), American writer and editor. *My Summer in a Garden*, 1871.

326. Get elected!
Earl Warren (1891-1974), Chief Justice, U.S. Supreme Court, and Governor of California (R). His "first rule" of politics.

327. This will be the commencement of the decline of my reputation.
George Washington (1732-1799), 1st President of the United States (VA). Remark to Patrick Henry after being elected Commander in Chief by the Continental Congress, June 15, 1775.

328. There is a lot of dishonesty in the way people relate to each other, particularly in the political arena. I know it is talked about as diplomacy, it's talked about as getting things done, but I have discovered that honest anger is respected also.
Maxine Waters, U.S. Congresswoman (D-CA). Quoted in *Governing*, Mar. 1988.

329. American politics is one of the noblest arts of mankind; and I cannot do anything else but write about it.
Theodore H. White (1915-1986), American political analyst and writer. Quoted in *The New York Times*, June 22, 1965.

330. Control is what politics is all about.
Theodore H. White. *Breach of Faith*, 1975.

331. Politics in America is the binding secular religion.
Theodore H. White. Quoted in *Time*, Dec. 29, 1986.

332. It is personalities, not principles, that move the age.
Oscar Wilde (1854-1900), Irish writer. In conversation.

333. The only realistic aspiration in Washington is survival. It's a tough town in which to survive with influence because it's a passing show. You see a lot of people flash across the sky.

Edward Bennett Williams (1920-1988), American attorney. Nov. 1985.

334. People live at the local level.

Pete Wilson, U.S. Senator and Governor of California (R). Campaign speech, Oct. 1990.

335. Politics I conceive to be nothing more than the science of the ordered progress of society along the lines of the greatest usefulness to itself.

Woodrow Wilson (1856-1924), 28th President of the United States (D-NJ). Speech, Pan American Scientific Congress, Jan. 6, 1916.

336. Politics is adjourned. The election will go to those who think least of it; to those who go to the constituencies without explanations or excuses, with a plain record of duty faithfully and disinterestedly performed.

Woodrow Wilson. Speech, joint session of the Congress, May 27, 1918.

337. Tolerance is an admirable intellectual gift, but it is of little worth in politics. Politics is a war of *causes*; a joust of principles. Government is too serious a matter to admit of meaningless courtesies.

Woodrow Wilson. Quoted in Richard Hofstadter, *The American Political Tradition*, 1948.

338. You bet I'm prejudiced against those in high office who guessed so wrong before Pearl Harbor. They're still guessing wrong.

Walter Winchell (1897-1972), American columnist and radio commentator. Radio comment, 1943.

339. Here is an animal with a hide two feet thick, and no apparent interest in politics. What a waste.

James C. Wright, Jr., U.S. Congressman and Speaker of the House (D-TX). Description of the rhinoceros. Quoted in *The New York Times*, Dec, 9, 1986.

340. Politics is only productive if it puts bread on your table and money in your pocket.

Andrew Young, U.S. Ambassador to the United Nations, U.S. Congressman (D), and Mayor of Atlanta, GA. Description of Adam Clayton Powell. Interview, PBS, *Politics: The New Black Power*, Aug. 28, 1990.

341. We need not only a new economic order, but also a new political order.

Zhao Ziyang, General Secretary, Communist Party of China. Speech, Henan, Jan. 1989.

342. Good politics is the art of the possible and the desirable.

James Zogby, Executive. Director, Arab-American Anti-Defamation Institute. C-SPAN, Jan. 28, 1991.

Chapter 77

Poverty

1. Private beneficence is totally inadequate to deal with the vast numbers of the city's disinherited.

   Jane Addams (1860-1935), American settlement worker and Nobel Laureate in Peace. *Twenty Years at Hull House*, 1910.

2. Poverty is slavery.

   African proverb.

3. To some extent, if you've seen one city slum you've seen them all.

   Spiro Agnew, Vice President of the United States and Governor of Maryland (R). Speech, Detroit, MI, Oct. 18, 1968.

4. I could persuade a millionaire on a Friday to subsidize a revolution for Saturday out of which he would make a huge profit on Sunday even though he was certain to be executed on Monday.

   Saul D. Alinsky (1909-1972), American community organizer. *Rules for Radicals*, 1971.

5. God help the poor, for the rich can help themselves.

   American proverb, 1876.

6. Poverty is the parent of revolution.

   Aristotle (384-322 B.C.), Greek philosopher and teacher. *Politics*.

7. The old simplifications about "more" schools and "more" housing, or even "better" schools or "better" housing, have not proved very successful in breaking the cycle of poverty or in dealing with the Negro family structure.

   Daniel Bell, professor of sociology, Harvard University, Cambridge, MA. *The Public Interest*, Fall 1968.

8. In the day of prosperity there is a forgetfulness of affliction.

   Apocrypha, *Wisdom of Ben Sira* 11:25.

9. Has every defense contractor yielded a perfect product, at minimal cost? Has every cancer project brought a cure? Has every space launching succeeded? Has every diplomatic initiative brought peace? Why should a less than perfect record for social programs be less tolerable to society than failed economic, military, or diplomatic policies?

   Hyman Bookbinder, Executive Officer, President's Task Force for the War on Poverty. *The New York Times*, Aug. 20, 1989.

10. Los Angeles cannot permanently exist as two cities – one amazingly prosperous, the other increasingly poorer in substance and in hope.... This city, like the nation, is living with an increasing polarization of incomes. A rising tide no longer lifts all boats.

    Thomas Bradley, Mayor of Los Angeles, CA (D). 5th inaugural address, June 30, 1989.

11. Upon the state falls directly the ... burden of the demoralization of its citizenry and of the social unrest which attend destitution and the denial of opportunity.

    Louis D. Brandeis (1856-1941), U.S. Supreme Court Justice. *New York Central Railroad* v. *Winfield*, 1916.

12. Those of us who have been economically successful cannot forget those who have not.

    Ron Brown, Chairman, Democratic National Committee. Lecture, Harvard University, Cambridge, MA, Nov. 1989.

13. Poverty and immorality are not synonymous.

    James F. Byrnes (1879-1972), Governor of South Carolina (D), U.S. Congressman, U.S. Senator, U.S. Supreme Court Justice, and U.S. Secretary of State. *Edwards* v. *California*, 1941.

14. The greatest and best of our race have necessarily been nurtured in the bracing school of poverty – the only school capable of producing the supremely great.

    Andrew Carnegie (1835-1919), American industrialist and philanthropist. *The Gospel of Wealth*, 1910.

15. The poor don't vote all the time.

    Rosalynn Carter, First Lady. PBS, *America's Children: Who Should Care?*, Sept. 4, 1990.

16. Those who claim they are the prisoners of the laws of economics only testify that they are prisoners of the idol.
Catholic bishops of Appalachia, *Pastoral Letter on Powerlessness in Appalachia*, Lent, 1975.

17. There are only two families in the whole world, my old grandmother used to say, the *Haves* and the *Have-Nots*.
Miguel de Cervantes (1547-1616), Spanish writer. *Don Quixote*, II, xx, 1615.

18. The poor are the Negroes of Europe.
Sébastien Chamfort (1741-1794), French writer and Jacobin. *Maxims and Thoughts*, VII, 1794.

19. In a well-governed nation poverty is something to be ashamed of. In a badly governed country wealth is something to be ashamed of.
Confucius (551-479 B.C.), Chinese philosopher. *Analects*.

20. What a miserable place a city is for poor people.
David Crockett (1786-1836), U.S. Congressman (Anti-Jacksonian-TN). *The Life of Davy Crockett*, 1889.

21. The real threat to the democracy is the half a nation in poverty.
Walter Cronkite, American TV journalist. Quoted in *Newsweek*, Dec. 5, 1988.

22. I have lived in Chicago all my life and I still say we have no ghettos in Chicago.
Richard J. Daley (1902-1976), Mayor of Chicago, IL (D). July 8, 1963.

23. Politicians don't like to target benefits to poor people, because poor people don't contribute to their campaigns.
Alfred DelliBovi, U.S. Undersecretary of Housing and Urban Development (R). Quoted in *The Wall Street Journal*, Dec. 18, 1989.

24. The poor will never cease out of the land.
Old Testament, *Deuteronomy* 15:11.

25. The Privileged and the People form Two Nations.
Benjamin Disraeli, 1st Earl of Beaconsfield (1804-1881), Prime Minister of Great Britain (Conservative). *Sybil*, 1845.

26. To be a poor man is hard, but to be a poor race in a land of dollars is the very bottom of hardships.
W. E. B. Du Bois (1868-1963), American educator and writer. *The Souls of Black Folk*, 1903.

27. It is the destiny of the people of Haiti to suffer.
Jean-Claude (Baby Doc) Duvalier, President-for-Life of Haiti. Attributed.

28. I have found out in later years we were very poor, but the glory of America is that we didn't know it then.
Dwight D. Eisenhower (1890-1969), 34th President of the United States (R-KS). Speech, Abilene, TX, June 16, 1952.

29. No man can be wise on an empty stomach.
George Eliot (Mary Ann Evans) (1819-1880), British writer. *Adam Bede*, 1859.

30. Poverty demoralizes.
Ralph Waldo Emerson (1803-1882), American writer. *The Conduct of Life*, 1860.

31. We should remember the poor.
New Testament, *Galatians* 2:10.

32. So long as all the increased wealth which modern progress brings goes but to build up great fortunes, to increase luxury, and make sharper the contest between the House of Have and the House of Want, progress is not real and cannot be permanent.
Henry George (1839-1897), American political economist. *Progress and Poverty*, 1879.

33. Poverty is an open-mouthed, relentless hell which yawns beneath civilized society. And it is hell enough.
Henry George. *Ibid.*

34. People who are much too sensitive to demand of cripples that they run races ask of the poor that they get up and act just like everyone else in society.
Michael Harrington (1928-1989), American Socialist. *The Other America*, 1962.

35. I want there to be no peasant in my kingdom so poor that he is unable to have a chicken in his pot every Sunday.
Henri IV (1553-1610), King of France. Attributed.

36. However badly off a community may be at any given time, someone profits while the community remains in its present conditions. Someone owes his status to retention of the present conditions. Someone's plans and investment in the future depend on everything remaining the same.
J. Herbert Holloman (1919-1985), U.S. Assistant Secretary of Commerce. *The Valley Tomorrow*, 1961.

37. The poorhouse is vanishing from among us.... We ... today are nearer to the final triumph over poverty than ever before in the history of any land.... We shall soon ... be in sight of the day when poverty will be banished from this nation.

Herbert Hoover (1874-1964), 31st President of the United States (R-IA). Speech accepting presidential nomination, Republican National Convention, Kansas City, MO, June 28, 1928.

38. No one has starved.

Herbert Hoover. Assessment of the seriousness of the "Great Depression," 1931. Quoted in Leinwand, *Poverty and the Poor*, 1968.

39. People don't eat in the long run. They eat every day.

Harry L. Hopkins (1890-1946), U.S. Secretary of Commerce, Director, Work Projects Administration, and Special Assistant to the President (D). Quoted in Robert E. Sherwood, *Roosevelt and Hopkins: An Intimate Biography*, 1950.

40. Attacking poverty is very expensive, and means doing things politically that are either impossible or very difficult to bring off.

Harold Howe II, U.S. Commissioner of Education and Chairman, Commission on Work, Family and Citizenship. Quoted in *The New York Times*, Dec. 6, 1989.

41. There may not be as many rich individuals, but there will be far less poor.

Louis McHenry Howe (1871-1935), presidential assistant (D). Remark on the consequences of the New Deal. *Life More Abundant*, 1934.

42. The story every mayor tells is a tale of two cities – of the haves and have-nots.

William H. Hudnut III, Mayor of Indianapolis, IN (R). Quoted in *The Washington Post*, Sept. 22, 1991.

43. Woe to them that take away the right of the poor.

Old Testament, *Isaiah* 10:1.

44. Indigence in itself is neither a source of rights nor a basis for denying them.

Robert H. Jackson (1892-1954), U.S. Attorney General (D) and U.S. Supreme Court Justice. *Edwards* v. *California*, 1941.

45. I never knew an instance of the English parliament's undertaking to relieve the poor by a distribution of bread in time of scarcity.... I think, that according to the principles of their government, they would only vote a sum of money, and address the King to employ it for the best.

Thomas Jefferson (1743-1826), 3rd President of the United States (Democratic Republican-VA). Letter to the Marquis de Lafayette, June 12, 1789.

46. This administration today, here and now, declares unconditional war on poverty.

Lyndon B. Johnson (1908-1973), 36th President of the United States (D-TX). Annual message to Congress, Jan. 8, 1964.

47. For the first time in America's history, poverty is on the run.

Lyndon B. Johnson. Apr. 17, 1964.

48. The wall between rich and poor is a wall of glass which all can see.

Lyndon B. Johnson. *My Hope for America*, 1964.

49. Poverty has many roots, but the tap root is ignorance.

Lyndon B. Johnson. Jan. 12, 1965.

50. People who didn't know the depression just don't know what being poor means.

Lyndon B. Johnson. Quoted in Merle Miller, *Lyndon: An Oral Biography*, 1980.

51. Poverty is a great enemy to human happiness; it certainly destroys liberty, and makes some virtues impracticable and others extremely difficult.

Samuel Johnson (1709-1784), British writer and lexicographer. Letter to James Boswell, Dec. 7, 1782.

52. Everybody suffers when you have more people who have not than who have.

Sharon Pratt Kelly, Mayor of Washington, DC (D). Interview, CBS, *Face the Nation*, May 12, 1991.

53. The ultimate measure of compassion is how few people need food stamps, welfare, and the safety net.

Jack F. Kemp, U.S. Congressman and U.S. Secretary of Housing and Urban Development (R-NY). PBS, *Firing Line*, Sept. 13, 1989.

54. If a free society cannot help the many who are poor, it cannot save the few who are rich.

John F. Kennedy (1917-1963), 35th President of the United States (D-MA). Inaugural address, Jan. 20, 1961.

55. If an American citizen does not have the dollars he has the right to sleep on the pavement at night.

Nikita S. Khrushchev (1894-1971), Premier of the U.S.S.R. Remark to V.P. Richard Nixon, Moscow, 1955.

56. The curse of poverty has no justification in our age. It is socially as cruel and blind as the practice of cannibalism at the dawn of civilization, when

men ate each other because they had not yet learned to take food from the soil or to consume the abundant animal life around them. The time has come for us to civilize ourselves by the total, direct, and immediate abolition of poverty.

Martin Luther King, Jr. (1929-1968), American clergyman and civil rights leader. *Where Do We Go from Here?*, 1967.

57. Compassion is not a sloppy sentimental feeling for people. It is an absolutely practical belief that regardless of a person's background, ability, or ability to pay, he should be provided with the best that society has to offer.

Neil Kinnock, Member of Parliament, Great Britain (Labour). Speech, House of Commons, 1970.

58. If you feel guilty, see a priest.

Edward I. Koch, U.S. Congressman and Mayor of New York City (D). To urge New Yorkers not to give to beggars. Aug. 10, 1988.

59. Poverty in America wears a diaper much more often than it wears a hearing aid. Money desperately needed by poor kids is going to rich elderly.

Richard D. Lamm, Governor of Colorado (D). Interview, *USA Today*, Oct. 20, 1988.

60. One-fourth of the children in this country are poor – and they don't vote.

Patrick J. Leahy, U.S. Senator (D-VT). Quoted in *The Washington Post*, July 27, 1988.

61. Russia is in the advanced stages of poverty.

Juri Liim, Estonian politician and founder of Geneva 49. Quoted in *Newsweek*, May 28, 1990.

62. No men living are more worthy to be trusted than those who toil up from poverty.

Abraham Lincoln (1809-1865), 16th President of the United States (R-IL). 1st annual message to Congress, Dec. 3, 1861.

63. The cry of the poor for bread has been answered by warheads!

Timothy Manning (1910-1989), Catholic archbishop of Los Angeles, CA. Speech on announced increases in military spending, 1981.

64. Poverty divides not only nations but societies within nations.

Malachi Martin, American author and Catholic theologian. *The Keys of This Blood*, 1990.

65. Pauperism is the hospital of the labor army.

Karl Marx (1818-1883), German economist and Socialist. *Das Kapital*, 1867.

66. For you will have the poor with you always.

New Testament, *Matthew* 26:11.

67. I believe in preferring the sanctity of human rights to the sanctity of property rights. I believe that the chief concern of government shall be for the poor, because, as is witnessed, the rich have ample means of their own to care for themselves.

Pledge, National Union for Social Justice (precursor to Union Party), 1934.

68. The war on poverty has been first in promises, first in politics, first in press releases, and last in performance.

Richard M. Nixon, 37th President of the United States (R-CA). Apr. 3, 1966.

69. Poverty ... is a thing created by that which is called civilized life.

Thomas Paine (1737-1809), American political philosopher. Observation of the lack of poverty among the Indians of North America. *Agrarian Justice*.

70. It is hard to think that disparities in wealth can go on widening forever, without the world order one day being affected.

Jean-Claude Paye, Secretary General, Organization for Economic Cooperation and Development. Quoted in *The Globe and Mail*, Nov. 29, 1990.

71. It is a Reproach to Religion and Government to suffer so much Poverty and Excess.

William Penn (1644-1718), founder of Pennsylvania. *Some Fruits of Solitude, in Reflections and Maxims*, 1693.

72. Any ordinary city is in fact two cities, one the city of the poor, the other of the rich, each at war with each other.

Plato (427-347 B.C.), Greek philosopher. *The Republic*.

73. He who is sated with food disdains the honeycomb, but to the hungry man every bitter thing is sweet.

Old Testament, *Proverbs* 27:7.

74. Defend the poor and fatherless; do justice to the afflicted and needy.

Old Testament, *Psalms* 82:3.

75. The comforts and well-being of the poor cannot be permanently secured without some regard on their part, or some effort on the part of the legislature, to regulate the increase of their numbers, and to render less frequent among them early and improvident marriages.

David Ricardo (1772-1823), British political economist. *Principles of Political Economy and Taxation*, 1817.

76. *How the Other Half Lives.*
Jacob A. Riis (1840-1914), American writer and journalist. Book title, 1890.

77. The slum is the measure of civilization.
Jacob A. Riis. *How the Other Half Lives*, 1890.

78. I see one third of a nation ill-housed, ill-clad, ill-nourished.
Franklin D. Roosevelt (1882-1945), 32nd President of the United States (D-NY). 2nd inaugural address, Jan. 20, 1937.

79. People who are hungry and out of a job are the stuff of which dictatorships are made.
Franklin D. Roosevelt. Message to Congress, Jan. 11, 1944.

80. If war no longer occupies men's thoughts and energies, we would, within a generation, put an end to all serious poverty throughout the world.
Bertrand Russell, 3rd Earl Russell of Kingston (1872-1970), British philosopher and reformer. *Unpopular Essays*, 1950.

81. Compassion is not measured by how many people are on food stamps.
Patricia R. Schroeder, U.S. Congresswoman (D-CO). PBS, *Firing Line*, Oct. 9, 1988.

82. Extreme poverty brings ignorance and vice, and these are the mothers of crime.
Walter Scott (1771-1832), Scottish writer. Quoted in John Gibson Lockhart, *Life of Scott*, 1837.

83. When that the poor have cried, Caesar hath wept;
Ambition should be made of sterner stuff.
William Shakespeare (1564-1616), English writer. *Julius Caesar*, III, ii.

84. Poverty is not just an individual affair. It is also a condition, a relationship to society, and to all the institutions which comprise society.
R. Sargent Shriver, Director, Peace Corps, and Director, Office of Economic Opportunity (D). Testimony, House Education and Labor Committee, Apr. 12, 1965.

85. No society can surely be peaceful and happy, of which the far greater part of the members are poor and miserable.
Adam Smith (1723-1790), Scottish political economist. *The Wealth of Nations*, 1776.

86. The great curse in poverty lies in the utter helplessness that goes with it.
Alfred E. Smith (1873-1944), Governor of New York (D). Speech, N.Y. State Legislature. Quoted in M. and H. Josephson, *Al Smith: Hero of the Cities*, 1969.

87. The men who devote themselves to the revolutionary cause know that they must always remain poor.
Georges Sorel (1847-1922), French journalist and political philosopher. *Reflections on Violence*, 1908.

88. A hungry man is not a free man.
Adlai E. Stevenson (1900-1965), Governor of Illinois (D) and U.S. Ambassador to the United Nations. Campaign speech, Kasson, MI, Sept. 6, 1952.

89. Do you want to live under the same conditions as did your parents ten, twenty, fifty, or a hundred years ago? You have got to try to improve your living conditions, and this cannot be done unless you work.
William V. S. Tubman (1895-1971), 18th President of Liberia. Speech to the chiefs and people of Pleebo District, Webbo Township, June 14, 1954.

90. You can't hold a man down without staying down with him.
Booker T. Washington (1856-1915), American educator and President, Tuskegee Institute. Quoted in *Dwight D. Eisenhower's Favorite Poetry, Prose and Prayers*, 1957.

91. Let's redistribute money from the childless to the childbearing, because that's where we have the maximum amount of poverty in America.
Ben Wattenberg, Senior Fellow, American Enterprise Institute, and White House speech writer (D). Interview, *USA Today*, Oct. 20, 1988.

92. There is only one class in the community that thinks more about money than the rich, and that is the poor. The poor can think of nothing else.
Oscar Wilde (1854-1900), Irish writer. *The Soul of Man Under Socialism*, 1881.

93. To recommend thrift to the poor is both grotesque and insulting. It is like advising a man who is starving to eat less.
Oscar Wilde. *Ibid.*

94. If the rich could hire other people to die for them, the poor could make a wonderful living.
Yiddish proverb.

95. God is the poor man's advocate.
Yiddish proverb.

Chapter 78

Power

1. The perception of power is power in Washington.
Anonymous. Quoted in *The Washington Post*, Oct. 6, 1990.

2. FEMINIZE POWER – ELECT WOMEN
Bumper sticker, 1989.

3. ULTIMA RATIO REGUM (THE LAST ARGUMENT OF KINGS)
Inscription engraved on French cannon by order of Louis XIV, c. 1700.

4. The establishment is made up of little men, very frightened.
Bella Abzug, U.S. Congresswoman (D-NY). May 5, 1971.

5. Power, whether vested in many or a few, is ever grasping, and like the grave, cries, "Give, give!"
Abigail Adams (1744-1818), First Lady. Letter to her husband, John Adams, 1774.

6. Remember, all men would be tyrants if they could.
Abigail Adams. Letter to John Adams, Mar. 1776.

7. The effect of power and publicity on all men is an aggravation of self, a sort of tumor that ends by killing the victim's sympathies.
Henry Adams (1838-1918), American historian. *The Education of Henry Adams*, 1907.

8. A friend in power is a friend lost.
Henry Adams. *Ibid.*

9. Power is poison. Its effects on Presidents had always been tragic; chiefly as an almost insane excitement at first, and a worse reaction afterward; but also because no mind is so well balanced as to bear the strain of seizing unlimited force without habit or knowledge of it; and finding it disputed with him by hungry packs of wolves and hounds whose lives depend on snatching the carrion.
Henry Adams. *Ibid.*

10. Fear is the foundation of most governments.
John Adams (1735-1826), 2nd President of the United States (Federalist-MA). *Thoughts on Government*, 1776.

11. It is weakness rather than wickedness which renders men unfit to be trusted with unlimited power.
John Adams. *A Defense of the Constitutions of Government of the United States of America Against the Attack of Mr. Turgot*, 1788.

12. Life without power is death.
Saul D. Alinsky (1909-1972), American community organizer. *Rules for Radicals*, 1971.

13. No one is king by his own power.
Apocrypha, *Letter of Aristeas*, No. 224.

14. No one loves the man whom he fears.
Aristotle (384-322 B.C.), Greek philosopher and teacher. *Politics*.

15. Force in today's world, just as in the past, is what determines rights.
Hafez Assad, President of Syria. Quoted in *The Wall Street Journal*, Dec. 19, 1989.

16. Power to do good is the true and lawful end of aspiring.
Francis Bacon, 1st Baron Verulam and Viscount St. Albans (1561-1626), Lord Chancellor of England. *Essays*. "Of Great Place," 1597.

17. I found early on that having a position of power really doesn't bring the fulfillment that many people think it does.
James A. Baker III, U.S. Secretary of the Treasury (R), U.S. Secretary of State, White House Chief of Staff, and presidential campaign manager. Speech, Congressional National Prayer Breakfast, Feb. 1, 1990.

18. The state is force incarnate, its essence is command and compulsion.
Mikhail Bakunin (1814-1876), Russian anarchist. *God and the State*, 1882.

19. Let a man rise to power, and he has as many virtues as will furnish an epitaph. Let him fall

from power, and he has more vices than the prodigal son.

Honoré de Balzac (1799-1850), French writer. *Droll Stories*, 1837.

20. *[William Randolph]* Hearst's power for evil is immeasurable.

James M. Beck (1861-1936), U.S. Solicitor General and U.S. Congressman (R-PA). Speech, Carnegie Hall, New York City, Nov. 1917.

21. The most striking defect in our system of government is that it divides political power and thereby conceals political responsibility.

Carl L. Becker (1873-1945), American historian. Quoted in *The New Dictionary of American Thoughts*, 1957.

22. Political power, considered in general, not descending in particular to monarchy, aristocracy, or democracy, comes directly from God alone.

Robert Bellarmine (1542-1621), Italian priest. *De Laicis*, V.

23. I have the most important person in the company behind me, and that's the President.

William J. Bennett, Director, Office of National Drug Control Policy, and U.S. Secretary of Education (R). Quoted on NBC, *Meet the Press*, Mar. 19, 1989.

24. Your strength lies in this, that you are not absolute but resolute.

Pierre Antoine Berryer (1790-1868), French lawyer and politician. Remark to Charles Montalembert, 1851.

25. I realized that there is only one way to be right, and that is to be in power.

Georges Bidault (1899-1983), Prime Minister of France. 1962.

26. As to mere power I have been for years in the daily exercise of more personal authority than any President habitually enjoys.

Nicholas Biddle (1786-1844), President, Second Bank of the United States. Letter to Thomas Cooper, 1837.

27. To strengthen a weak government, we must reduce its power.

Ludwig Boerne (1786-1837), German journalist. *Fragments and Aphorisms*, No. 42, 1840.

28. It is the characteristic excellence of the strong man that he can bring momentous issues to the fore and make a decision about them. The weak are always forced to decide between alternatives they have not chosen themselves.

Dietrich Bonhoffer (1906-1945), German Protestant theologian executed by the Nazis. *Letters and Papers from Prison*, 1953.

29. All governments abuse power. Every one of them. It's the duty of citizens to resist those abuses.

Leonard Boudin (1913-1990), American civil rights attorney. Quoted in *The Washington Post*, Jan. 28, 1990.

30. The Soviet Union is a first-rate military power and a fourth-rate economic power.

William W. Bradley, U.S. Senator (D-NJ). Interview, PBS, *American Interest*, July 12, 1989.

31. Silence coerced by law – the argument of force in its worst form.

Louis D. Brandeis (1856-1941), U.S. Supreme Court Justice. *Other People's Money*, 1914.

32. All of our human experience shows that no one with absolute power can be trusted to give it up even in part.

Louis D. Brandeis. Testimony, U.S. Commission on Industrial Relations, 1915.

33. Any who wield a large amount of power should always feel the check of power. The very principle on which the nation exists is that no person shall rise above power.

Louis D. Brandeis. Quoted in Alpheus T. Mason, *Brandeis: A Free Man's Life*, 1946.

34. All private property is held subject to the demands of a public use. The constitutional guarantee of just compensation is not a limitation of the power to take, but only a condition of its exercise.

David J. Brewer (1837-1910), U.S. Supreme Court Justice. *Long Island Water Supply Co.* v. *Brooklyn*, 1896.

35. That which killed my late master, and so many of his predecessors. The responsibility of arbitrary power.

P. I. Brunnow (1797-1875), Russian Ambassador to Great Britain. Comment to Benjamin Disraeli, when asked about the health of Napoleon III, Emperor of France. c. 1860.

36. Power abdicates only under stress of counterpower.

Martin Buber (1878-1965), Jewish philosopher. *Paths in Utopia*, 1950.

37. What strikes me most singular in you is that you are fonder of Power than of Fame.

Edward Bulwer-Lytton, 1st Baron Lytton of Knebworth (1803-1873), Colonial Secretary, Great

Britain (Conservative), and writer. Comment to Benjamin Disraeli, c. 1860.

38. The greater the power, the more dangerous the abuse.
Edmund Burke (1729-1797), British statesman. Speech, House of Commons, Feb. 7, 1771.

39. Law and arbitrary power are in eternal enmity.
Edmund Burke. Speech on the impeachment of Warren Hastings, Feb. 15, 1788.

40. The power of eminent domain is essential to a sovereign government.
Harold Hitz Burton (1888-1964), Mayor of Cleveland, OH (D), U.S. Senator, and U.S. Supreme Court Justice. *United States* v. *Carmack*, 1946.

41. Use power to help people.
George Bush, 41st President of the United States (R-TX). Inaugural address, Jan. 20, 1989.

42. The sudden acquisition of power by those who have never had it before can be intoxicating, and we run the risk of petty power games.
Virginia Anne Carabillo, Vice President, National Organization of Women. Speech, NOW Convention, San Diego, CA, Oct. 28, 1973.

43. We want black power.
Stokley Carmichael (Kwame Toure), President, Student Non-Violent Coordinating Committee. Speech, Greenwood, MS, June 1966.

44. I shall either perish or reign.
Catherine II (The Great) (1729-1796), Empress of Russia. Letter to Sir Charles Hanbury Williams, Aug. 9, 1756.

45. For those who can raise up great evils can best allay them.
Marcus Porcius Uticensis Cato (Cato the Younger) (95-46 B.C.), Roman soldier and philosopher. Advice to the Roman Senate to place even greater powers in the hands of Pompey. Quoted in Plutarch, *The Parallel Lives: Cato the Younger*.

46. I have only to raise a finger and the whole face of Europe is changed.
Neville Chamberlain (1869-1940), Prime Minister of Great Britain (Conservative). Quoted in Keith Middlemas, *Diplomacy of Illusion*.

47. Men are never very wise in the exercise of a new power.
William Ellery Channing (1780-1842), American clergyman and reformer. Address, "The Present Age," 1841.

48. In a republican land the power behind the throne is *the* power.
Maria Weston Chapman (1806-1885), American abolitionist. Speech, New York City, 1855.

49. The less people know about what is going on, the easier it is to wield power and authority.
Charles, Prince of Wales and Duke of Cornwall, Quoted in *The Observer*, Mar. 2, 1975.

50. How a minority, reaching majority, seizing authority, hates a minority.
Paul L. C. Claudel (1868-1955), French diplomat and poet. Quoted in *The New Dictionary of American Thoughts*, 1957.

51. Force is the law of the universe. It implacably determines the outcome of every conflict.
Georges Clemenceau (1841-1929), Premier of France and political journalist. *In the Evening of My Thought*, 1929.

52. Money is power, and you ought to be reasonably ambitious to have it.
Russell H. Conwell (1843-1945), founder and 1st President, Temple University, Philadelphia, PA. Speech, "Acres of Diamonds," delivered more than six thousand times.

53. Almost all that has been done for the good of the people has been done since the right lost the monopoly of power, since the rights of property were discovered to be not unlimited.
John Dahlberg, 1st Baron Acton (1834-1902), historian and Member of Parliament, Great Britain (Whig). *The History of Freedom in Antiquity*, 1877.

54. Power tends to corrupt, and absolute power corrupts absolutely.
John Dahlberg. Letter to Bishop Mandell Creighton, Apr. 5, 1887.

55. Suspect power more than vice.
John Dahlberg. Inaugural lecture, University of Cambridge, June 11, 1895.

56. The ancients understood the regulation of power better than the regulation of liberty.
John Dahlberg. *The History of Freedom*, 1907.

57. The reactionaries are in possession of force, in not only the army and police, but in the press and schools.
John Dewey (1859-1952), American educator and philosopher. Quoted in *The New York World Telegram*, Dec. 31, 1934.

58. The shortest way to ruin a country is to give power to demagogues.
Dionysius of Halicarnassus (c.25 B.C.), Greek writer. *Antiquities of Rome*, VI.

59. Real politics are the possession and distribution of power.
Benjamin Disraeli, 1st Earl of Beaconsfield (1804-1881), Prime Minister of Great Britain (Conservative). *Endymion*. 1880.

60. The power of eminent domain is merely the means to an end.
William O. Douglas (1898-1980), U.S. Supreme Court Justice. *Berman* v. *Parker*, 1954.

61. Power is more satisfying to some than wealth.... Power is, indeed, a heady thing – whether it be a King, a President, a Legislature, a Court, or an Administration agency that is concerned.
William O. Douglas. *We the Judges*, 1956.

62. Those in power need checks and restraints lest they come to identify the common good with their own tastes and desires, and their continuation in office as essential to the preservation of the nation.
William O. Douglas. *Ibid.*

63. Power concedes nothing without a demand. It never did, and it never will.
Frederick Douglass (c.1817-1895), Recorder of Deeds, District of Columbia, and U.S. Minister to Haiti. Letter to Gerrit Smith, Mar. 30, 1849.

64. Government runs by clout. That's how it runs, by clout.
Thomas F. Eagleton, U.S. Senator (D-MO). Testimony, Senate Committee on Governmental Affairs, May 13-14, 1986.

65. I believe it to be invariable rule that tyrants of genius are succeeded by scoundrels.
Albert Einstein (1879-1955), Nobel Laureate in Physics (Switzerland). *The World As I See It*, 1934.

66. Weakness cannot cooperate with anything. Only strength can cooperate.
Dwight D. Eisenhower (1890-1969), 34th President of the United States (R-KS). Annual message to Congress, Feb. 2, 1953.

67. Ignorant power comes in the end to the same thing as wicked power; it makes misery.
George Eliot (Mary Ann Evans) (1819-1880), British writer. *Felix Holt*, 1866.

68. There is always room for a man of force, and he makes room for many.
Ralph Waldo Emerson (1803-1882), American writer. *The Conduct of Life*. "Power," 1860.

69. A man is the prisoner of his power.
Ralph Waldo Emerson. *The Conduct of Life*. "Culture," 1860.

70. Great men are they who see that spiritual is stronger than any material force, that thoughts rule the world.
Ralph Waldo Emerson. *Letters and Social Aims*, "Progress of Culture," 1875.

71. The weak are always at war with the stronger; that is the source of eternal hatreds.
Euripides (480-405 B.C.), Greek dramatist. *Antigone*. Quoted approvingly by Georges Clemenceau, *In the Evening of My Thought*, 1929.

72. Is not this fact enough to alarm the American people? A bank in the heart of the Republic with its branches scattered over the Union; wielding $200 million of capital; owning an immense amount of real property; holding at its command 100,000 debtors; buying up our newspapers, entering the field of politics; attempting to make Presidents and Vice Presidents for the country.
George H. Evans (1805-1856), Founder, National Reform Association. 1842.

73. With our increased birthrates the black man and woman can actually breed ourselves into power.
Louis Farrakhan, chief minister and leader, Nation of Islam. Speech, New Orleans, LA, Apr. 23, 1989.

74. Frequent elections by the people furnish the only protection under the Constitution against the abuse of acknowledged legislative power.
Stephen J. Field (1816-1899), U.S. Supreme Court Justice. *Ex parte Newman*, 9 Cal. 502.

75. The power of the purse always prevails.
Raymond A. Fontaine, Comptroller, U.S. General Services Administration. Quoted in *The Washington Post*, Oct. 21, 1988.

76. All political power is a trust.
Charles James Fox (1749-1806), Lord of the Treasury and Foreign Minister, Great Britain (Tory). Quoted in *Hoyt's New Cyclopedia of Practical Quotations*, 1927.

77. In a democracy, power implies responsibility.
Felix Frankfurter (1882-1965), U.S. Supreme Court Justice. *United States* v. *United Mine Workers*, 1946.

78. Truth is more praiseworthy than power.
John Hope Franklin, American historian. *Race and History*, 1990.

79. The preservation of the laws was the sole reason which induced men to allow of, and to elect, a superior; that is the true origin of sovereign power.
Frederick II (The Great) (1712-1786), King of Prussia. *Essay on Forms of Government*.

80. The lust for power is not rooted in strength but in weakness.
Erich Fromm (1900-1980), American psychoanalyst. *Escape from Freedom*, 1941.

81. Politics is the art of acquiring, holding, and wielding power.
Indira Gandhi (1917-1984), Prime Minister of India. 1969.

82. Power *[in Washington]* is being able to affect the hegemony of existing systems.
Leonard Garment, counselor to the President (R). Quoted in *Regardie's*, Oct. 1987.

83. Don't be deceived. There is no justice but strength.
Marcus Garvey (1887-1940), American black nationalist leader. Quoted in Lerone J. Bennett, Jr., *Pioneers in Protest*, 1968.

84. It's a very popular sport *[in America]* to talk about power struggles in the Kremlin.
Gennadi I. Gerasimov, spokesman, Soviet Foreign Ministry. Quoted on *Nightline*, Sept. 30, 1988.

85. Where might is master, justice is servant.
German proverb.

86. Law not served by power is an illusion. But power not ruled by law is a menace.
Arthur Goldberg (1908-1990), U.S. Supreme Court Justice, U.S. Secretary of Labor (D), and U.S. Ambassador to the United Nations. Speech, Catholic University, Washington, DC, June 1966.

87. The strongest bulwark of authority is uniformity.
Emma Goldman (1869-1940), American anarchist. Quoted in *Forbes*, Aug. 8, 1988.

88. We should get back to the ... doctrine of brinkmanship, where everybody knows we have the power and will use it.
Barry M. Goldwater, U.S. Senator (R-AZ). Presidential campaign speech, Hartford, CT, Oct. 4, 1963.

89. I will never abuse power if elected.... This country can never again fall under the influence of a dictator.
Mikhail Gorbachev, President of the U.S.S.R. Speech, Moscow, May 25, 1989.

90. The only advantage of power is that you can do more good.
Baltasar Gracián y Morales (1601-1658), Spanish Jesuit and writer. *The Art of Worldly Wisdom*, 1651.

91. The thing women must do to rise to power is redefine their femininity. Once, power was considered a masculine attribute. In fact, power has no sex.
Katharine Graham, Chairman of the Board, Washington Post Company. Quoted in Beilenson and Melnick, *Words on Women*, 1987.

92. In Washington it is an honor to be disgraced.... You have to have *been* somebody to fall.
Meg Greenfield, American political columnist. *Newsweek*, June 2, 1986.

93. Americans have always tended to view government as inherently illegitimate. We give it power only grudgingly and then object to its exercise.
Andrew Hacker, American political scientist. *The New York Times*, Nov. 15, 1981.

94. I am the law.
Frank Hague (1876-1956), Mayor of Jersey City, NJ (D). Response when asked by what right he prohibited picketing and the distribution of labor circulars in Jersey City. Testimony, NJ legislative corruption investigation, 1937.

95. Power over a man's support is a power over his will.
Alexander Hamilton (1755-1804), Member, Continental Congress and Constitutional Convention, and U.S. Secretary of the Treasury (Federalist-NY). *The Federalist*, No. 73, Mar. 21, 1788.

96. If government is in the hands of the few, they will tyrannize the many; if in the hands of the many, they will tyrannize over the few. It ought to be in the hands of both, and they should be separated.... They will need a mutual check. This check is a monarch.
Alexander Hamilton. *Works*, II.

97. Liberty is so much latitude as the powerful choose to accord to the weak.
Learned Hand (1872-1961), Federal Judge. Speech, University of Pennsylvania, Philadelphia, PA, May 21, 1944.

98. I always wanted to be number one, but I wanted power solely to help the poor and disadvantaged.
Patricia R. Harris, U.S. Secretary of Health, Education and Welfare (D). Quoted in *The Chicago Tribune*, July 18, 1979.

99. God has placed upon our head a diadem and has laid at our feet power and wealth beyond definition and calculation.
Benjamin Harrison (1833-1901), 23rd President of the United States (R-IN). 1889.

100. A single seemingly powerless person who dares to cry out the word of truth and to stand behind it with all his person and all his life has, surprisingly, greater power, though formally disenfranchised, than do thousands of anonymous voters.
Vaclav Havel, writer and President of Czechoslovakia. Quoted in *The Los Angeles Times*, Feb. 17, 1990.

101. Conkling, the power behind the throne, superior to the throne.
Rutherford B. Hayes (1822-1893), 19th President of the United States (R-OH). In reference to Sen. Roscoe Conkling.

102. Man is a toad-eating animal. The admiration of power in others is as common to man as the love of it in himself; the one makes him a tyrant, the other a slave.
William Hazlitt (1778-1830), British writer and critic. *Political Essays*, "Toad-Eaters and Tyrants," 1819.

103. Our devotion to individual freedom limits our readiness to give central government the power to override our traditional power structure.
Denis Healey, Minister of Defense, Great Britain (Labour), and Chancellor of the Exchequer. *The Time of My Life*, 1990.

104. The force of the newspaper is the greatest force in civilization.... *[Newspapers]* declare wars ... make and unmake statesmen.
William Randolph Hearst (1863-1951), U.S. Congressman (D-NY); founder, Independence League Party; journalist; and publisher. Quoted in Swanberg, *Citizen Hearst*, 1961.

105. The worst of poisons: to mistrust one's power.
Heinrich Heine (1797-1856), German writer. *Sonnets*, 1, 1821.

106. I do not blame those who wish to rule *[the Athenians]*, but those who are overready to serve.
Hermocrates (d.407 B.C.), Syracusan general and politician. Speech at assembly of Sicilian cities at Gela urging unified resistance to Athenian domination, c. 426 B.C. Quoted by Thucydides, *The Peloponnesian War*, IV.

107. Power is precarious.
Herodotus (c.480-425 B.C.), Greek "Father of History." *History of the Persian Wars*, III.

108. No man ever ruled other men for their own good.
George D. Herron (1862-1925), American clergyman. Quoted in Upton Sinclair, *The Cry for Justice*, 1920.

109. Dictators ride to and fro upon tigers from which they dare not dismount.
Hindustani proverb, quoted by Winston Churchill, *While England Slept*, 1936.

110. What will rank Mussolini among the great of this earth is the same determination not to share Italy with Marxism, but to save the fatherland from it by dooming internationalism to annihilation.
Adolf Hitler (1889-1945), Führer of the Third German Reich. *Mein Kampf*, 1933.

111. Power corrupts the few, while weakness corrupts the many.
Eric Hoffer (1902-1983), American philosopher and longshoreman. *The Passionate State of Mind*, 1954.

112. The only prize much cared for by the powerful is power. The prize of the general is not a bigger tent, but command.
Oliver Wendell Holmes, Jr. (1841-1935), U.S. Supreme Court Justice. Letter to Charles Bunn, 1917.

113. To an imagination of any scope the most far-reaching form of power is not money, it is the command of ideas.
Oliver Wendell Holmes, Jr. *The Path of the Law*, 1896.

114. Emergency does not create power.
Charles Evans Hughes (1862-1948), Chief Justice, U.S. Supreme Court, and U.S. Secretary of State (R). *Home Building & Loan Association* v. *Blaisdell*, 1934.

115. There is one thing stronger than all the armies of the world, and that is an idea whose time has come.
Victor Hugo (1802-1885), French writer and Member, Constituent Assembly and National Assembly at Bordeaux. 1861.

116. Idealism is the noble toga that political gentlemen drape over their will to power.
Aldous Huxley (1894-1963), British writer. Quoted in *The New York Herald Tribune*, Nov. 24, 1963.

117. Government is force.
John James Ingalls (1833-1900), U.S. Senator (R-KS). Quoted in *The New York World*, 1890.

118. If there is any power in this country greater than the power of the people, we will destroy it.
Andrew Jackson (1767-1845), 7th President of the United States (D-TN). Quoted by William Randolph Hearst, 1906.

119. Government of limited power need not be anemic government.
Robert H. Jackson (1892-1954), U.S. Attorney General (D) and U.S. Supreme Court Justice. *West Virginia State Board of Education* v. *Barnette*, 1943.

120. Always, as in this case, the government urges hasty decision to forestall some emergency or serve some purpose and pleads that paralysis will result if its claims to power are denied.
Robert H. Jackson. *Woods* v. *Miller*, 1948.

121. No one will question that this power *[the war power]* is the most dangerous one to free government in the whole catalogue of powers.
Robert H. Jackson. *Ibid.*

122. Nothing is more certain than the indispensable necessity of government; and it is equally undeniable that whenever and however it is instituted, the people must cede to it some of their natural rights, in order to vest it with requisite powers.
John Jay (1745-1829), President, Continental Congress, Governor of New York (Federalist), U.S. Foreign Secretary, and 1st Chief Justice, U.S. Supreme Court. *The Federalist*, No. 2.

123. Every government degenerates when trusted to the rulers of the people alone. The people themselves are its only safe depositories.
Thomas Jefferson (1743-1826), 3rd President of the United States (Democratic Republican-VA). *Notes on the State of Virginia:* Query XIV, 1784. Repeated verbatim in a letter to Abbé Arnoud, July 19, 1789.

124. No, my friend, the way to have good and safe government, is not to trust it all to one, but to divide it among the many.
Thomas Jefferson. To Joseph C. Cabell, 1816.

125. Opinion is power.
Thomas Jefferson. Letter to John Adams, Jan. 11, 1816.

126. Telling a man to go to hell and making him go are two different propositions.
Lyndon B. Johnson (1908-1973), 36th President of the United States (D-TX). Remark to aides, 1964.

127. I've just been elected and right now we'll have a honeymoon with Congress... I'll have a good chance to get my program through.... But after I make my recommendations, I'm going to lose the power and authority I have because that's what happened to President Woodrow Wilson, to President Roosevelt and to Truman and to Kennedy. Every day that I'm in office ... I'll be losing part of my ability to be influential.... So I want you guys to get off your asses and do everything possible to get ... my program passed as soon as possible, before the aura and halo that surround me disappear.
Lyndon B. Johnson. Instructions to congressional liaison officers, Jan. 1965.

128. There are many, many people who can recommend and advise, and a few of them consent, but there is only one who has been chosen by the American people to decide.
Lyndon B. Johnson. Speech, Omaha, NB, June 30, 1966.

129. Power is always gradually stealing away from the many to the few, because the few are more vigilant and consistent.
Samuel Johnson (1709-1784), British writer and lexicographer. *The Adventurer*, No. 45.

130. The power of punishment is to silence, not to confute.
Samuel Johnson. *Sermons*, No. 23.

131. Bureaucrats understand ... their real masters are ... not their department heads. The real powers are the chairmen on Capitol Hill.
Gordon S. Jones, Vice President, Heritage Foundation. Quoted in *The New York Times*, Feb. 26, 1989.

132. The enjoyment of power inevitably corrupts the judgment of reason, and perverts its liberty.
Immanuel Kant (1724-1804), German philosopher. *Perpetual Peace*, 1795.

133. For it is power that brings about peace between any two rulers. No piece of iron that is not made red-hot will combine with another piece of iron.
Kautilya (c.300 B.C.), Prime Minister of Chandragupta, India. *Arthasastra.*

134. You want power because it's an opportunity.
Edward M. Kennedy, U.S. Senator (D-MA). Remark to Stephen Smith, 1980.

135. Wilbur Mills knows that he was chairman of Ways and Means before I got here and that he'll still be chairman after I've gone – and he knows I know it.
John F. Kennedy (1917-1963), 35th President of the United States (D-MA). Quoted in Theodore Sorenson, *Kennedy*, 1965.

136. Society is an association for the protection of property as well as of life, and the individual who contributes only one cent to the common stock ought not to have the same power and influence ... as he who contributes his thousands.

James Kent (1763-1847), Chief Judge, New York State Supreme Court. Debate, New York State Constitutional Convention, 1821.

137. Power is the ultimate aphrodisiac.

Henry M. Kissinger, U.S. Secretary of State and National Security Advisor (R). Quoted in *The Washington Post*, Nov. 27, 1976.

138. Whenever there is a new Soviet leader, our experts speculate about the changes as if one man could change a whole society. In their system, power doesn't come with the office. It takes many years to acquire.

Henry M. Kissinger. Remark, July 1984.

139. An expert is someone who is capable of articulating the interests of people with power.

Henry M. Kissinger. Quoted on PBS, *Bill Moyers' World of Ideas*, Nov. 4, 1988.

140. You've got your maximum amount of power in your honeymoon period. The decisions may be wrong, history may prove them wrong, but at least you do it.

Lawrence J. Korb, U.S. Assistant Secretary of Defense (D). Comment on a new presidential administration. Quoted in *Government Executive*, Nov. 1988.

141. The opinion of the strongest is always the best.

Jean La Fontaine (1621-1695), French fabulist. *The Wolf and the Lamb*.

142. Reward and punishment are the twin instruments of power in the state; they must not be revealed to anyone.

Lao-tzu (c.604-531 B.C.), Chinese philosopher and founder of Taoism. *Tao Te Ching*.

143. No one today in Washington doubts the superior firepower of the media over that of the executive branch.

Michael Ledeen, American author and intelligence official. Speech, "Intelligence and Free Society Conference, " National Forum Foundation, Washington, DC, May 30, 1989.

144. It must never be forgotten ... that the liberties of the people are not so safe under the gracious manner of government as by the limitation of power.

Richard Henry Lee (1732-1794), Member, Continental Congress, and U.S. Senator (VA). Remark to Patrick Henry. Quoted in Charles Warren, *The Supreme Court in United States History*, 1935.

145. It was to guard against the encroachment of power, the insatiate ambition of wealth, that this government was instituted by the people themselves.

William Leggett (1801-1839), American journalist and editor. Editorial, *New York Evening Post*, 1834.

146. The people want to exercise power, but what on earth would they do with it if it were given to them?

V. I. Lenin (1870-1924), Premier of the U.S.S.R. *The State and Revolution*, 1917.

147. *All power* to the Soviet of Workers' and Soldiers' Deputies.

V. I. Lenin. Remark advocating a revolution against the Karenski provisional government. *Collected Works*, Vol. XXI, Book II.

148. Our people love and understand authority better than law. They consider a military chief more accessible than an article of a legal code.

Konstantin Nikolaevich Leontiev (1831-1891), Russian Socialist philosopher. Letter, 1890.

149. If I, in my brief connection with public affairs, shall be wicked or foolish, and if you remain true and honest, you cannot be betrayed. My power is temporary; yours as eternal as the principles of liberty.

Abraham Lincoln (1809-1865), 16th President of the United States (R-IL). Speech, Lawrenceburg, IN, Feb. 11, 1861.

150. The man does not live who is more devoted to peace than I am, but it may be necessary to put the foot down firmly.

Abraham Lincoln. Speech to the New Jersey Assembly, Feb. 21, 1861.

151. Power tends to corrupt if you're there too long.

John V. Lindsay, U.S. Congressman and Mayor of New York City (R). PBS, *The World That Moses Built*, Jan. 16, 1989.

152. A mature and great power will make measured and limited use of its power.

Walter Lippmann (1889-1974), American political columnist. Quoted in *The New York Times*, Mar. 17, 1990.

153. The great question which, in all ages, has disturbed mankind, and brought on them the greatest part of those mischiefs which have ruined cities, depopulated countries, and disordered the peace of the world, has been, not whether there be

power in the world, nor whence it came, but who should have it.

John Locke (1632-1704), English political philosopher. *First Treatise on Government*, 1690.

154. The people who run Mississippi can do so only by force. They cannot allow free elections in Mississippi, because if they did, they wouldn't run Mississippi.

Allard Lowenstein (1929-1980), U.S. Congressman (D-NY). Quoted in Juan Williams, *Eyes on the Prize*, 1987.

155. The world is ruled by a certain few, even as a little boy of twelve rules, governs, and keeps a hundred big and strong oxen in a pasture.

Martin Luther (1483-1546), German Protestant theologian. *Table Talk*, CLVII.

156. The injury done to a man ought to be such that vengeance cannot be feared.

Niccolò Machiavelli (1469-1527), Florentine statesman and political philosopher. *The Prince*, III.

157. Those republics which in time of danger cannot resort to a dictatorship, or some similar authority, will generally be ruined when grave emergencies occur.

Niccolò Machiavelli. *The Prince*, V.

158. All men having power ought to be distrusted to a certain degree.

James Madison (1751-1836), 4th President of the United States (Democratic Republican-VA). Debate, Constitutional Convention, Philadelphia, PA, 1787.

159. In framing a government which is to be administered by men over men, the great difficulty lies in this: you must first enable the government to control the governed; and in the next place, oblige it to control itself.

James Madison. *The Federalist*, No. 51, Feb. 8, 1788.

160. Force is never more operative than when it is known to exist but is not brandished.

Alfred Thayer Mahan (1840-1914), Admiral, U.S. Navy, and writer on naval affairs. Speech, Newport War College, 1893.

161. Every Communist must grasp the truth: "Political power grows out of the barrel of a gun."

Mao Tse-tung (1893-1976), Chairman, Communist Party of China. "Problems of War and Strategy," concluding speech, 6th Plenary of the Central Committee of the Communist Party of China, Nov. 6, 1938.

162. We should rid our ranks of all impotent thinking. All views that overestimate the strength of the enemy and underestimate the strength of the people are wrong.

Mao Tse-tung. *The Present Situation and Our Tasks*, Dec. 25, 1947.

163. Whenever anybody is pursuing power, he's got to be funny.

Don Marlette, American political cartoonist. Interview, ABC, July 18, 1988.

164. The government of the Union, then, ... is, emphatically, and truly, a government of the people. In form and in substance it emanates from them. Its powers are granted by them, and are to be exercised directly on them, and for their benefit.

John Marshall (1755-1835), Chief Justice, U.S. Supreme Court. *McCulloch* v. *Maryland*, 1819.

165. There are men who will hold power by any means rather than not hold it; and who would prefer a dissolution of the union to a continuance of an administration not of their own party. They will risk all ills ... rather than permit that happiness which is dispensed by other hands than their own.

John Marshall. Quoted in Albert J. Beveridge, *Life of John Marshall*, II, 1916-1919.

166. Institutions are more powerful than men.

Karl Marx (1818-1883), German economist and Socialist. *Remarks on the Latest Prussian Censorship Instruction*, 1843.

167. Political power, properly so called, is merely the organized power of one class for suppressing another.

Karl Marx. *The Communist Manifesto*, 1848.

168. That all power is vested in, and consequently derived from, the people; that magistrates are their trustees and servants, and at all amenable to them.

George Mason (1725-1792), Member, Virginia and Federal Constitutional Conventions. *Virginia Bill of Rights*, II, June 12, 1776.

169. No branch of government should ever be able to combine the power of the sword with the power of the purse.

George Mason. Quoted by Sen. Samuel Nunn, C-SPAN, Sept. 14, 1990.

170. By some strange operation of magic I seem to have become *the* power of the land.

[At the age of 34 he became the Union's first victorious general after a minor skirmish in West Virginia, and was named Commanding General of the Army of the Potomac.]

George B. McClellan (1826-1885), General in Chief, Union Army, and Governor of New Jersey (D). Letter to his wife, July 1861.

171. Whether it's a blessing or a curse, it's a fact that we have power. Everyone – friend and enemy – looks to see how we use it, how we treat it, how we keep it.

Robert C. McFarlane, National Security Advisor (R). Apr. 1984.

172. The exercise of the power of eminent domain is against common right. It subverts the usual attributes of the ownership of property.

Joseph McKenna (1843-1926), U.S. Supreme Court Justice. *Western Union Telegraph Co.* v. *Pennsylvania Railroad*, 1904.

173. The people who exercise the power are not always the same people over whom it is exercised.

John Stuart Mill (1806-1873), Member of Parliament, Great Britain, and political economist. *On Liberty*, 1859.

174. Was there ever any domination which did not appear natural to those who possessed it?

John Stuart Mill. *The Subjugation of Women*, 1869.

175. While a Vice President of the United States may lack power, he never lacks; his rank is similar to that of a crown prince, though his succession is considerably less certain.

Merle Miller, American journalist and biographer. *Lyndon: An Oral Biography*, 1980.

176. Better to reign in hell than serve in heaven.

John Milton (1608-1674), English writer. *Paradise Lost*, I, 261, 1667.

177. To carry out my mission, I need a stable majority.

François Mitterrand, President of France (Socialist). June 1988.

178. No reasonable man would think more highly of himself because he has office or power in this world; he is no more than a prisoner whom the chief gaoler has set over his fellow-prisoners, until the executioner's cart comes for him too.

Thomas More (1478-1535), Speaker of the House of Commons, Lord Chancellor of England, and writer. *The Four Last Things*, 1522.

179. You have not converted a man because you have silenced him.

John Morley, Viscount Morley of Blackburn (1838-1923), Member of Parliament, Great Britain (Liberal), Chief Secretary for Ireland, and Secretary of State for India. *On Compromise*, 1874.

180. Power has to be insecure to be responsive.

Ralph Nader, American consumer advocate. Quoted in John J. Rhodes, *The Futile System*, 1976.

181. My hand of iron was not at the extremity of my arm; it was immediately connected with my head.

Napoléon I (1769-1821), military leader and Emperor of France. *Maxims*.

182. My power depends on my glory, and my glory on the victories I have gained.

Napoléon I. *Ibid.*

183. Christ was a victim of the people's power, so *[Ferdinand]* Marcos was a victim of the people's power.

Domingo Nebres, Philippine Roman Catholic monsignor. Eulogy for Philippine President Ferdinand Marcos, Honolulu, HI, Oct. 15, 1989.

184. Material force is the *ultima ratio* of political society everywhere. Arms alone can keep the peace.

John Henry Newman (1801-1890), British Roman Catholic cardinal. *Discussions and Arguments*.

185. Wherever I found a living creature, there I found the will to power.

Friedrich Wilhelm Nietzsche (1844-1900), German philosopher. *Thus Spake Zarathustra*, 1883.

186. Use the power we have – while we can.

Richard M. Nixon, 37th President of the United States (R-CA). Robert Haldeman's notes, July 25, 1971.

187. If this is the exercise of power, I liked it better when I didn't have that power.

Samuel A. Nunn, U.S. Senator (D-GA). In reference to his role as Chairman of the Senate Armed Services Committee in the confirmation hearings for former Sen. John Tower as Secretary of Defense. NBC, *Meet the Press*, Feb. 26, 1989.

188. Power is the perception of power.

Thomas P. (Tip) O'Neill, Jr., U.S. Congressman and Speaker of the House (D-MA). Quoted on PBS, *MacNeil-Lehrer News Hour*, Aug. 23, 1991.

189. Power is inflicting pain and humiliation. Power is tearing human minds to pieces and putting them together again in new shapes of our own choosing.

George Orwell (Eric Blair) (1903-1950), British writer. *1984*, 1949.

190. Money is this day the strongest power of the nation.
Theodore Parker (1810-1860), American clergyman and abolitionist. Sermon, 1858.

191. Force rules the world, and not opinion; but opinion is that which makes use of force.
Blaise Pascal (1623-1662), French mathematician and philosopher. *Pensées*, XXIV.

192. The property of power is to protect.
Blaise Pascal. Quoted in *Forbes*, Dec. 14, 1987.

193. If I fall, look out for the crash. There won't be anyone left standing.
Eva Perón (1919-1952), First Lady of Argentina. Quoted on Arts and Entertainment, *Biography*, Mar. 24, 1990.

194. We are no longer interested in elections except as a means to reach our objective.
Juan Domingo Perón (1895-1974), President of Argentina. Remark on his return to power, July 1973.

195. We exceeded our implicit mandate not to challenge power.
Michael Pertschuk, Chairman, Federal Trade Commission. Explanation of why he gets so much criticism from Congress. Interview, *Philadelphia Inquirer*, Oct. 1, 1978.

196. Our role, as I see it, is to redistribute power to the people.
Michael Pertschuk. *Ibid.*

197. Washington is a power-hungry place.... It has to do with wanting to feel strong. That's when you reach the pinnacle in Washington.
Samuel Pierce, U.S. Secretary of Housing and Urban Affairs (R). Interview, *Time*, Sept. 18, 1989.

198. Unlimited power is apt to corrupt the minds of those who posses it.... Unlimited power corrupts the possessor.
William Pitt, 1st Earl of Chatham (1708-1778), Secretary of State, Great Britain, Lord Privy Seal, and leader of the House of Commons. Speech concerning the case of John Wilkes, House of Lords, Jan. 9, 1770.

199. The President's power is negative merely, and not affirmative.
James K. Polk (1795-1849), 11th President of the United States (D-TN). Fourth annual message to Congress, Dec. 5, 1848.

200. Property is exploitation of the weak by the strong. Communism is exploitation of the strong by the weak.
Pierre-Joseph Proudhon (1809-1865), French journalist, Socialist Member, Constituent Assembly, and anarchist. *What Is Property?*, 1840.

201. Tell power the truth.
Quaker proverb.

202. It is much easier to restrain liberty from running into licentiousness than power from swelling into tyranny and oppression.
Josiah Quincy (1744-1775), President, Harvard College, Cambridge, MA, and U.S. Congressman (Federalist-MA). *Observations on the Boston Port Bill*, 1774.

203. Machination is worth more than force.
François Rabelais (1494-1553), French writer. *Pantagruel*, 1533.

204. I don't think we have an establishment anymore.
Susan Randall, City Commissioner, Sioux Falls, SD. Quoted in *Governing the States and Localities*, Feb. 1988.

205. Power alone can limit power.
John Randolph (1773-1833), U.S. Congressman (State's Rights Democrat-VA), U.S. Senator, and U.S. Minister to Russia. Attributed.

206. The secret of the personality is: Strength from weakness.
Walther Rathenau (1867-1922), Foreign Minister, Germany. Quoted in Emil Ludwig, *Genius and Character*, 1927.

207. I've always wanted responsibility because I want the power responsibility brings.
Samuel T. Rayburn (1882-1961), U.S. Congressman and Speaker of the House (D-TX). Quoted in Robert A. Caro, *Lyndon B. Johnson*, 1982.

208. Isolation from reality is inseparable from the exercise of power.
George E. Reedy, White House Press Secretary (D). Conference, "Problems of Isolation of the Presidency," Center for the Study of Democratic Institutions, 1966.

209. It is dangerous to have a known influence over the people; as thereby we become responsible even for what is done against our will.
Cardinal de Retz (1614-1679), French ecclesiastic and politician. *Political Maxims*.

210. Irresolute men are diffident in resolving upon the means, even when they are determined upon the end.
Cardinal de Retz. *Ibid.*

211. It was well understood at the American Founding that all governmental power derived from the people. Nothing other than popular sovereignty could comport ... with the principles of the Revolution.

William Bradford Reynolds, U.S. Assistant Attorney General for Civil Rights (R). *Harvard Journal of Law and Public Policy*, 8, 1985.

212. A city of cocker spaniels. It's a city of people who are more interested in being petted and admired, loved, than rendering the exercise of power.

Elliot L. Richardson, U.S. Attorney General (R), U.S. Secretary of Health, Education and Welfare, and U.S. Secretary of Defense. Description of Washington, DC. Quoted in *The New York Times*, July 13, 1982.

213. Political and economic power is increasingly being concentrated among a few large corporations and their offices.... They often exercise the power of government, but without the checks and balances inherent in our democratic system.

Hyman G. Rickover (1900-1986), Admiral, U.S. Navy. Senate testimony, Jan. 28, 1982.

214. A power has arisen in this country greater than that of government itself.

Elzey Roberts (1892-1962), Publisher, *St. Louis Star-Times*. In reference to Rev. Charles E. Coughlin, 1935.

215. The powers that be are ordained of God.

New Testament, *Romans* 13:1.

216. The liberty of a democracy is not safe if the people tolerate the growth of private power to a point where it becomes stronger than the democratic state itself.

Franklin D. Roosevelt (1882-1945), 32nd President of the United States (D-NY). Message to Congress, 1938.

217. Power must be linked with responsibility and obliged to defend and justify itself within the framework of the general good.

Franklin D. Roosevelt. Message to Congress, Jan. 1945.

218. Power invariably means both responsibility and danger.

Theodore Roosevelt (1858-1919), 26th President of the United States (R-NY). Inaugural address, Mar. 4, 1905.

219. The strongest is never strong enough always to be master, unless he transforms strength into right, and obedience into duty.

Jean-Jacques Rousseau (1712-1778), French philosopher. *The Social Contract*, 1762.

220. All *[political]* power is derived *from* the people. They possess it only on the days of their elections. After this, it is the property of their rulers, nor can they *[the people]* exercise it or resume it, unless it is abused.

Benjamin Rush (1745-1813), American physician and Member, Continental Congress. Quoted in *Boston Independent Chronicle*, Apr. 5, 1787.

221. Those who have seized power, even for the noblest of motives, soon persuade themselves that there are good reasons for not relinquishing it.

Bertrand Russell, 3rd Earl Russell of Kingston (1872-1970), British philosopher and reformer. *Saturday Review*, 1951.

222. By transferring economic power to an oligarchic State, they *[the leaders of the Russian Revolution]* produced an engine of tyranny more dreadful, more vast, and at the same time more minute than any that had existed in previous history. I do not think this was the intention of those who made the Revolution, but it was the effect of their actions. Their actions had this effect because they failed to realize the need for liberty and the inevitable evils of despotic power.

Bertrand Russell. *Portraits from Memory*, 1969.

223. The *[Italian]* Fascist Party is no longer an organization of mercenaries in the service of capitalism, but has become an independent force.... If the capitalists stopped playing with the policy of the *[Fascist]* Party, the Party could easily steer to the Left.... It is not the first time in history that mercenaries have been the masters' masters.

Gaetano Salvemini (1873-1957), Italian anti-Fascist politician and historian. *The Fascist Dictatorship in Italy*, 1927.

224. Power is so apt to be insolent, and Liberty to be saucy, that they are very seldom upon good terms.

George Savile, 1st Marquess of Halifax (1633-1695), Lord Privy Seal of England. *Political Thoughts and Reflections*, 1750.

225. That whatever a man hath a desire to do or hinder, if he hath uncontested and irresistible power to effect it, that he will certainly do it.

George Savile. *Ibid.*

226. The dependence of a great man upon a greater, is a subjection that lower men cannot easily comprehend.

George Savile. *Moral Thoughts and Reflections*, 1750.

227. When a *Prince's Example* ceaseth to have the force of a *Law*, it is a sure sign that his *Power* is wasting, and that there is but little distance between *Men's* neglecting to *Imitate* and their refusing to *Obey*.
George Savile. *Maxims of State*, No. 32.

228. I guess I worry about whether the federal government is taking my power away, but I'm more worried about the state legislature taking my power away. I got 188 governors *[in the State General Assembly]*. I can't do anything until the legislature's out of session – and then I go wild.
William Donald Schaefer, Mayor of Baltimore, MD, and Governor of Maryland (D). Speech, National Governors' Association, Cincinnati, OH, Aug. 9, 1988.

229. The socialist state justifies itself on the ground that the concentration of power is necessary to do good; but it has never solved the problem of how you ensure that power bestowed to do good will not be employed to do harm, especially when you remove all obstacles to its exercise.
Arthur M. Schlesinger, Jr., American historian and presidential advisor (D). *Partisan Review*, 1947.

230. Being a great power is no longer much fun.
David Schoenbaum, American journalist. *The New York Times*, 1973.

231. Japan redefined world power. They showed you could become a world power without having a military.
Patricia R. Schroeder, U.S. Congresswoman (D-CO). Quoted on PBS, *American Defense Monitor*, Aug. 4, 1989.

232. It is dangerous to be witness to the infirmities of men high in power.
Walter Scott (1771-1832), Scottish writer. *Woodstock*, 1826.

233. The principles of statesmen are regulated by their advance toward, or retreat from, power; and from men who are always acting upon the emergencies of the moment, it is vain to expect consistency.
Walter Scott. Quoted in John Gibson Lockhart, *Life of Scott*, 1837.

234. Experience constantly proves that every man who has power is impelled to abuse it.
Charles-Louis de Secondat, Baron de La Brède et de Montesquieu (1689-1755), French writer. *The Spirit of the Laws*, XI, 4, 1748.

235. Power should be a check to power.
Charles-Louis de Secondat, Baron de La Brède et de Montesquieu. *Ibid.*, XXV, 2, 1748.

236. The President says you can have it. You can have it.
Mobuto Sese Seko, President of Zaire. In reference to himself. Quoted in *The Washington Post*, June 26, 1988.

237. There is no stretching of Power. 'Tis a good rule, Eat within your Stomach, act within your Commission.
John Selden (1584-1654), English jurist and Member of Long Parliament. *Table-Talk: State Power*.

238. To learn to endure odium is the first art to be learned by those who aspire to power.
Lucius Annaues Seneca (The Younger) (4 B.C.-A.D.65), Roman statesman, dramatist, and philosopher. *Hercules Furens*.

239. Might makes right.
Lucius Annaeus Seneca (The Younger). *Ibid.*.

240. Men want power in order to do something. Boys want power in order to be something.
Eric A. Sevareid (1913-1992), American TV journalist. CBS, presidential campaign coverage, July 29, 1988.

241. Power does not corrupt men; fools, however, if they get into a position of power, corrupt power.
George Bernard Shaw (1856-1950), Nobel Laureate in Literature (Great Britain). Quoted in Stephen Winsten, *Days with Bernard Shaw*, 1949.

242. If you ask about a characteristic of Ronald Reagan it is that he had these certain things he believed in and he just didn't change. That was his great strength.
George P. Shultz, U.S. Secretary of State (R). Quoted in *The Washington Post*, Mar. 19, 1989.

243. Tyranny is infectious.
Jan Christiaan Smuts (1870-1950), Prime Minister of South Africa. Rectorial address, St. Andrews University, Fifeshire, Scotland, Oct. 17, 1934.

244. Truth and, by consequence, liberty, will always be the chief power of honest men.
Anne Louise de Staël (1766-1817), French writer. Letter to General Moreau.

245. Authority, not majority.
Friedrich Julius Stahl (1802-1861), German jurist and politician. Speech, Erfurt Parliament, Apr. 15, 1850.

246. American efficiency is that indomitable force which neither knows nor recognizes obstacles.
Joseph Stalin (1879-1953), Premier of the U.S.S.R. *Foundations of Leninism*, 1933.

247. You who have read the history of nations, from Moses down to our last election, where have you ever seen one class looking after the interests of another?
Elizabeth Cady Stanton (1815-1902), 1st President, National Woman Suffrage Association. Speech, New York State Legislature, 1860.

248. Power does not corrupt. Fear corrupts, perhaps the fear of a loss of power.
John Steinbeck (1902-1968), Nobel Laureate in Literature (United States). *The Short Reign of Pippin IV*, 1957.

249. We *[women]* are not more moral *[than men]*, we are only less corrupted by power.
Gloria Steinem, American editor and feminist. *The New York Times*, Aug. 26, 1971.

250. Power corrupts, but lack of power corrupts absolutely.
Adlai E. Stevenson (1900-1965), Governor of Illinois (D) and U.S. Ambassador to the United Nations. 1954.

251. Since the beginning of time, governments have been mainly engaged in kicking people around. The astonishing achievement of modern times is the idea that the citizen should do the kicking.
Adlai E. Stevenson. *What I Think*, 1955.

252. Where is there a more enduring monument of political wisdom than the separation of the judicial from the legislative power?
Joseph Story (1779-1845), U.S. Supreme Court Justice. *Miscellaneous Writings*, 1835.

253. Do not put a premium on killing; to capture an enemy's army is better than to destroy it.
Sun-tzu (c. 400 B.C.), Chinese writer of the Age of Warring States. *The Art of War*.

254. Lord Northcliffe ... aspired to power instead of influence, and as a result forfeited both.
A. J. P. Taylor, British historian. *English History, 1914-1945*, 1965.

255. We're not in politics, but we have to be; it's the only way we can survive. Politics is today's method of power.
Vincent Teresa, American Mafia captain. *My Life in the Mafia*, 1974.

256. Wife, the Athenians rule the Greeks, and I rule the Athenians, and you me, and our son, you. Let him then use sparingly the authority which makes him, foolish as he is, the most powerful person in Greece.
Themistocles (c.525-c.460 B.C.), Athenian naval commander and statesman. Quoted in Plutarch, *The Parallel Lives: Themistocles*.

257. Providence must have abundant confidence in me, for every time when I arrive at power she seems to reserve the most embarrassing affairs for me.
Louis-Adolphe Thiers (1797-1877), 1st President of the Third French Republic. 1834.

258. Without hypocrisy, lying, punishments, prisons, fortresses, and murders, no new power can arise and no existing one hold its own.
Leo Tolstoy (1828-1910), Russian writer and philosopher. *The Kingdom of God Is Within You*, 1893.

259. Not believing in force is the same as not believing in gravitation.
Leon Trotsky (1879-1940), Russian revolutionary theorist. *What Next?*, 1932.

260. New York has all the money, and money decides who goes to Washington.
Donald Trump, American financier. Comparison of the relative political power of Washington, DC, and New York City. Quoted in *Newsweek*, June 29, 1988.

261. We have, I fear, confused power with greatness.
Stewart L. Udall, U.S. Congressman (D-AZ) and U.S. Secretary of the Interior. Commencement address, Dartmouth College, Hanover, NH, June 13, 1965.

262. What do I care about the law. Hain't I got the power?
Cornelius Vanderbilt (1794-1877), American financier and railroad magnate. Quoted in Robert L. Heilbroner, *The Worldly Philosophers*, 1953.

263. The higher you go in the hierarchy of *[political]* posts, the more you are disempowered.
Lech Walesa, President of Poland, trade unionist, and founder, Solidarity. Quoted in *The Washington Post*, Nov. 13, 1989.

264. The balance of power.
Robert Walpole, 1st Earl of Oxford (1676-1745), Prime Minister of Great Britain (Whig). Speech, House of Commons, Feb. 13, 1741.

265. Character is power.

Booker T. Washington (1856-1915), American educator and President, Tuskegee Institute. Quoted on PBS, *Tony Brown's Journal*, Aug. 22, 1987.

266. In the absence of military force, political power naturally and necessarily goes into the hands which hold the property.

Daniel Webster (1782-1852), U.S. Congressman (Federalist-NH and MA), U.S. Senator (Federalist and Whig-MA), and U.S. Secretary of State. Speech, Massachusetts Constitutional Convention, 1820.

267. We are all agents of the same supreme power, the people.

Daniel Webster. Jan. 26, 1830.

268. There is nothing so powerful as truth; and often nothing so strange.

Daniel Webster. Arguments on the murder of Captain White, Apr. 6, 1830.

269. LBJ's *[Lyndon B. Johnson's]* instinct for power is as primordial as a salmon's going upstream to spawn.

Theodore H. White (1915-1986), American political analyst and writer. Quoted in Celebrity Research Group, *The Bedside Book of Celebrity Gossip*, 1984.

270. Whoever is in office, the Whigs are in power.

Harold Wilson, Prime Minister of Great Britain (Labour). Quoted in Arthur M. Schlesinger, Jr., *The Imperial Presidency*, 1973.

271. The size of the modern democracy necessitates the exercise of persuasive power by dominant minds.

Woodrow Wilson (1856-1924), 28th President of the United States (D-NJ). "Character of Democracy in the United States," *Atlantic Monthly*, 1889.

272. If monopoly persists, monopoly will always sit at the helm of government.... If there are men in this country big enough to own the government of the United States, they are going to own it.

Woodrow Wilson. *The New Freedom*, 1913.

273. There must be, not a balance of power, but a community of power.

Woodrow Wilson. Senate address, Jan. 22, 1917.

274. Anyone who opposes me in that *[U.S. entry into the League of Nations]*, I'll crush!"

Woodrow Wilson. Remark to Sen. Thomas Martin (D-VA), 1919.

275. Power only respects power.

Malcolm X (Malcolm Little) (1925-1965), American black power advocate. Speech, Detroit, MI, 1964.

276. The king reigns, but does not govern.

Jan Zamoyski (1541-1605), General, Polish Army. Speech, Polish Parliament, 1605.

277. It is hardly debatable that the power of Napoléon in Europe was broken by disease more effectively than by military opposition or even by Trafalgar.

Hans Zinsser (1878-1940), American bacteriologist and public health researcher. *Rats, Lice and History*, 1935.

Chapter 79

The Presidency and Vice Presidency

1. The most important aspect of the relationship between the President and the Secretary of State is that they both understand who is President.

   Dean Acheson (1893-1971), U.S. Secretary of State (D). Maxim.

2. If there is one certain truth to be collected from the history of all ages, it is this: that the people's rights and liberties, and the democratic mixture in a constitution, can never be preserved without a strong executive, or, in other words, without separating the executive power from the legislature.

   John Adams (1735-1826), 2nd President of the United States (Federalist-MA). *Defense of the Constitutions of Government of the United States of America Against the Attack of Mr. Turgot*, 1787.

3. My country has in its wisdom contrived for me the most insignificant office *[the vice presidency]* that ever the invention of man contrived or his imagination conceived.

   John Adams. Letter to Abigail Adams, Dec. 1789.

4. Methought I heard him say, "Ay! I am fairly out, and you fairly in. See which of us will be the happiest."

   John Adams. Letter to Abigail Adams relating George Washington's great satisfaction at leaving the presidency, Mar. 1797.

5. The presidency of the United States was an office neither to be sought nor declined. To pay money for securing it directly or indirectly was in my opinion incorrect in principle.

   John Quincy Adams (1767-1848), 6th President of the United States (Ind-MA). *Diary*, 1828.

6. The respective powers of the President and Congress of the United States, in the case of war with foreign powers, are yet undetermined. Perhaps they can never be defined.

   John Quincy Adams. Eulogy for James Madison, 1836.

7. Protect the people from the oppression of dictatorships.

   Leo E. Allen (1898-1973), U.S. Congressman (R-IL). Remark advocating presidential term limitation through the Twenty-second Amendment. House debate, 1950.

8. The way you judge presidents is the way you judge plumbing fixtures. It doesn't matter whether plumbing fixtures are orchid or white. What really matters about a plumbing fixture is – does it flush?

   Joseph Alsop (1910-1989), American political columnist. Sept. 1985.

9. Well, there doesn't seem anything else for an ex-President to do but go into the country and raise big pumpkins.

   Chester A. Arthur (1830-1886), 21st President of the United States (R-OH). Quoted in *The New York Herald*, Nov. 19, 1896.

10. The presidency is not an extension of a congressional campaign. The presidency, we must come to understand, is about the larger issues of national destiny, which depend in turn upon our economic power and productivity and America's mission in the world.

    Bruce Babbitt, Governor of Arizona (D). *The New York Times*, Nov. 15, 1988.

11. Because you're a heartbeat away from the big office. That's why.

    James A. Baker III, U.S. Secretary of the Treasury (R), U.S. Secretary of State, White House Chief of Staff, and presidential campaign manager. Explanation for why anyone would want to be Vice President. Interview, ABS, *This Week*, Aug. 14, 1988.

12. When I first came to this town, I didn't think Presidents lied.

Benjamin C. Bradlee, editor, *The Washington Post*. Interview, ABC, *20/20*, Aug. 29, 1991.

13. I don't think that winning the presidency of the United States is a matter of a single issue.
Ron Brown, Chairman, Democratic National Committee. Interview, PBS, *John McLaughlin's One on One*, Nov. 4, 1989.

14. He did not live long enough to prove his incapacity for the office of President.
William Cullen Bryant (1794-1878), American poet and editor. Comment on the death of Pres. William Henry Harrison after only one month in office, Apr. 6, 1841.

15. If you are as happy, my dear sir, on entering this house *[the White House]* as I am in leaving it and returning home, you are the happiest man in this country.
James Buchanan (1791-1868), 15th President of the United States (D-PA). Remark to Abraham Lincoln, Mar. 4, 1861.

16. The office of the President is so staggeringly complicated that nobody can ... be a good President.
William F. Buckley, Jr., American political columnist and publisher. Interview, *Playboy*, May 1970.

17. Someday, someone will follow in my footsteps and preside over the White House as the President's spouse. And I wish him well.
Barbara Bush, First Lady. Commencement address, Wellesley College, Wellesley, MA, 1990.

18. You may think the President is all-powerful, but he is not. He needs a lot of guidance from the Lord.
Barbara Bush. Speech to schoolchildren, Jan. 7, 1991.

19. The first responsibility of any President is to work for peace in the world and prosperity at home.
George Bush, 41st President of the United States (R-TX). Speech, National Association for the Advancement of Colored People, July 12, 1988.

20. When I make a call, we move as a team.
George Bush. Statement to his cabinet nominees just before his inauguration, Jan. 1989.

21. I cannot consult with 535 strong-willed individuals.
George Bush. Response to criticism that he was not consulting sufficiently with the Congress. Press conference, Nov. 30, 1990.

22. As long as there is no chance of my being elected Vice President.
Nicholas Murray Butler (1862-1947), President, Columbia University, and Nobel Laureate in Peace. Response to suggestion that his name be placed on the Progressive (Bull Moose) ticket, Nov. 1, 1912.

23. The problems of the country look very different from the Oval Office than they do from the campaign trail.
Jimmy Carter, 39th President of the United States (D-GA). Remark to Lloyd Cutler, Jan. 19, 1981.

24. There will be a new President in this country someday, and I have as good a chance as anybody.
Albert B. (Happy) Chandler (1898-1991), Governor of Kentucky (D), U.S. Senator, and U.S. Baseball Commissioner. Quoted in the Lexington, KY, *Herald*, July 25, 1937.

25. We are practically an island here *[the White House.]*
Dwight Chapin, presidential appointments secretary (R). Remark to Herbert Porter, 1971.

26. I trust the sentiments and opinions are correct; I had rather be right than President.
Henry Clay (1777-1852), U.S. Senator (National Republican and Whig-KY), Speaker of the House, and U.S. Secretary of State. In reference to impending legislation on Missouri. Quoted by Sen. William Preston (Whig-SC), Philadelphia, PA, 1839; also attributed to Clay during Senate debates on the Compromise of 1850.

27. I'll be back!
Frances Folsom Cleveland, First Lady. Remark to White House staff after her husband Grover Cleveland lost the presidential election, 1888; Cleveland won the Presidency again in 1892, the only President to win a second nonconsecutive term.

28. I am honest and sincere in my desire to do well, but the question is whether I know enough to accomplish what I desire.
Grover Cleveland (1837-1908), 22nd and 24th President of the United States (D-NY). Quoted in Wallechinsky and Wallace, *The People's Almanac*, 1975.

29. In times of crisis, the American citizen tends to back up his President.
Clark P. Clifford, U.S. Secretary of Defense and Special Counsel to the President (D). Campaign memorandum, 1948.

30. A President immunized from political consideration is a President who need not listen to the people.

Clark P. Clifford. Testimony, Senate Judiciary Committee, 1972.

31. *[Jimmy Carter]* had so much going for him. He was elected without any real commitments.... To come in with no commitments gives a President a marvelous, broad, flexible horizon of operation.
Clark P. Clifford. Interview with Bill Moyers, PBS, 1981.

32. The problems of the President of the United States are not susceptible to scientific treatment.
Clark P. Clifford. *Ibid.*

33. I don't care whom you take; Chester Allen Arthur will do as well as any other.
Roscoe Conkling (1829-1888), U.S. Congressman and U.S. Senator (R-NY). Remark refusing to run for Vice President with James A. Garfield, Republican National Convention, Chicago, IL, June 8, 1880; President Garfield was assasinated six months later and Arthur became the 21st President.

34. The public wants a solemn ass as a President. And I think I'll go along with them.
Calvin Coolidge (1872-1933), 30th President of the United States (R-MA). Remark to Ethel Barrymore, 1925.

35. If you keep dead still, they will run down in three or four minutes.
Calvin Coolidge. Advice to his successor Herbert Hoover on how to deal with long-winded White House visitors and dignitaries, 1929.

36. The Presidents who have gone to Washington without first having held some national office have been at great disadvantage. It takes them a long time to become acquainted with the federal officeholders and the federal government.
Calvin Coolidge. *Autobiography*, 1929.

37. Unlike a monarch, the President is not the Sovereign.
Archibald Cox, Watergate special prosecutor. Memorandum, Aug. 13, 1973.

38. The second hardest job in America.
Margaret Truman Daniels, daughter of President Truman. Description of the job of the First Lady. Quoted in Exhibit, "The First Ladies," Hoover Museum, Iowa City, IA, 1990.

39. When I was a boy I was told that anybody could become President; I'm beginning to believe it.
Clarence S. Darrow (1857-1937), American attorney. Attributed.

40. He looked like a President.
Harry M. Daugherty (1860-1941), U.S. Attorney General (R). Statement to reporters when asked why he sponsored Warren G. Harding for the presidency, June 1923.

41. Our nation has no right to expect that it will always have wise and humane rulers, sincerely attached to the principles of the Constitution. Wicked men, ambitious of power, with hatred of liberty and law, may fill the place once occupied by Washington and Lincoln.
David Davis (1815-1886), U.S. Supreme Court Justice. *Ex Parte Milligan*, 1866.

42. This memorandum addresses the matter of how we can maximize the fact of our incumbency in dealing with persons known to be active in their opposition to our administration. Stated a bit more bluntly – how we can use the available federal machinery to screw our political enemies?
John Dean, counselor to the President (R). Memorandum, Aug. 16, 1971.

43. The White House is another world. Expediency is everything.
John Dean. Quoted in *The New York Post*, June 18, 1973.

44. The office of the President is not such a very difficult one to fill, his duties being mainly to execute the laws of Congress. Should I be chosen for this exalted position, I would execute the laws of Congress as faithfully as I have always executed the orders of my superiors.
George Dewey (1837-1917), Admiral, U.S. Navy. Statement on his candidacy, Apr. 1900.

45. History buffs probably noted the reunion at a Washington party a few weeks ago of three ex-Presidents. Carter, Ford and Nixon. See no evil, hear no evil, and evil.
Robert J. Dole, U.S. Senator (R-KS). Speech, Gridiron Club, Washington, DC, Mar. 26, 1983.

46. Inside work with no heavy lifting.
Robert J. Dole. Description of the vice presidency. Quoted on ABC, *This Week*, July 24, 1988.

47. It only takes one vote to win the vice presidential nomination.
Robert J. Dole. Speech, CNN, *Presidential Classroom*, June 15, 1991.

48. President Taft is an amiable man, completely surrounded by men who know exactly what they want.
Jonathan P. Dolliver (1858-1910), U.S. Congress-

man and U.S. Senator (R-IA). Quoted in Mark Sullivan, *Our Times*, 1927.

49. What a President may do as a matter of expediency or extremity may never reach a definitive constitutional decision.
William O. Douglas (1898-1980), U.S. Supreme Court Justice. *Youngstown Sheet & Tube Co.* v. *Sawyer*, 1952.

50. There is one thing about being President – nobody can tell you when to sit down.
Dwight D. Eisenhower (1890-1969), 34th President of the United States (R-KS). Remark to visitors in the Oval Office, 1953.

51. ... this idea that all wisdom is in the President, in me, that's baloney.... I don't believe this government was set up to be operated by anyone acting alone; no one has a monopoly on the truth and on the facts that are affecting this country.
Dwight D. Eisenhower. Quoted in Richardson, *The Presidency of Dwight D. Eisenhower*, 1979.

52. It's really difficult to go out on a date with the Secret Service.... How about the Secret Service on your honeymoon? It's amazing that David and I are still together.
Julie Nixon Eisenhower, daughter of President Nixon. Video interview, Exhibit, "The First Ladies," Hoover Museum, Iowa City, IA, 1990.

53. If a king goes astray the common people pay for the sin.
English proverb, 1393.

54. The President is the government.
John Erlichman, presidential assistant (R). Remark, 1970.

55. You can't have fifteen people coming together to give the President advice in a Cabinet session. They're all arguing with each other for their own interests and he gets confused. What he decides has to come to him in an orderly way.
John Erlichman. Quoted in Theodore H. White, *Breach of Faith*, 1975.

56. Divine right went out with the American Revolution and doesn't belong to the White House aides. What meat do they eat that makes them grow so great?
Samuel J. Ervin, Jr. (1896-1985), U.S. Congressman and U.S. Senator (D-NC). Press conference. Apr. 1973.

57. I do not believe that we *[Congress]* should allow him *[the President]* to nullify acts of Congress by executive fiat. There is not one syllable in the Constitution which authorizes the President to exercise such power.
Samuel J. Ervin, Jr. *Congressional Record*, May 10, 1973.

58. There is nothing in the Constitution that authorizes or makes it the official duty of a President to have anything to do with criminal activities.
Samuel J. Ervin, Jr. Hearings, Senate Select Committee on Watergate, July 24, 1973.

59. I do not believe that the President has any powers at all except such as the Constitution expressly gives him or such as are necessarily inferred.
Samuel J. Ervin, Jr. Hearings, Senate Select Committee on Watergate, July 25, 1973.

60. The President of the U.S. every time he opens his mouth has to mention God – well, my God! I mean, not even the Pope does that.
Oriana Fallaci, Italian journalist. Interview, *Playboy*, Nov. 1981.

61. I wish I'd married a plumber. At least he'd be home by five o'clock.
Betty Ford, First Lady. Remark, 1974.

62. I think a president has to be able to think like the people think.
Betty Ford. Quoted in Wallechinsky and Wallace, *The People's Almanac*, 1975.

63. I am acutely aware that you have not elected me as your President by your ballots. So I ask you to confirm me with your prayers.
Gerald R. Ford, 38th President of the United States (R-MI). Speech to the nation upon assuming the presidency after the resignation of President Nixon, Aug. 9, 1974.

64. The President has a constitutional right to behave like a spoiled child.
Barney Frank, U.S. Congressman (D-MA). House debate, Aug. 3, 1989.

65. The first man put at the helm will be a good one. Nobody knows what sort may come afterward.
Benjamin Franklin (1706-1790), Member, Continental Congress and Constitutional Convention, Governor of Pennsylvania, and U.S. Minister to France. In reference to George Washington. Debate, Constitutional Convention, Philadelphia, PA, 1787.

66. The President has full responsibility, which cannot be shared, for military decisions in a world in which the difference between safety and cataclysm can be a matter of hours or even minutes.

J. William Fulbright, U.S. Senator (D-AR). "American Foreign Policy in the 20th Century Under an 18th Century Constitution," *Cornell Law Quarterly*, Fall 1961.

67. My fellow citizens, the President is dead, but the government lives and God Omnipotent reigns.

James A. Garfield (1831-1881), 20th President of the United States (R-OH). Speech after the death of Abraham Lincoln, Apr. 16, 1865.

68. The President is the last person in the world to know what the people really want and think.

James A. Garfield. Attributed.

69. The vice presidency ain't worth a pitcher of warm spit.

John Nance Garner (1868-1967), Vice President of the United States (D-TX), U.S. Congressman, and Speaker of the House. Quoted in Bascom Timmins, *Garner of Texas: A Personal History*, 1948.

70. Worst damnfool mistake I ever made was letting myself be elected Vice President of the United States. Should have stuck with my old chores as Speaker of the House. I gave up the second most important job in the government for one that didn't amount to a hill of beans. I spent eight long years as Mr. Roosevelt's spare tire. I might still be Speaker if I hadn't let them elect me Vice President.

John Nance Garner. Quoted in *Saturday Evening Post*, Nov. 2, 1963.

71. If the American President had control of the media, his job would be much easier.

April Glaspie, U.S. Ambassador to Iraq. Remark to Iraqi dictator Saddam Hussein, July 25, 1990.

72. A President in his first year has a mandate and some political capital. When he picks an issue, he can practically roll any Congress.

William H. Grey III, U.S. Congressman (D-PA). Quoted in *The Washington Post*, Oct. 4, 1989.

73. Every night, whisper "peace" in your husband's ear.

Andrei A. Gromyko (1909-1989), Foreign Minister, U.S.S.R., Ambassador to the U.S., and Ambassador to the United Nations. Remark to First Lady Nancy Reagan, Sept. 28, 1984.

74. Congress plays to day-to-day headlines. The President can't afford to do that.

Alexander M. Haig, General, U.S. Army, U.S. Secretary of State (R), and White House Chief of Staff. Interview, CNN, *Newsmaker Sunday*, Aug. 27, 1989.

75. By the nature of his office, a President is separated from his natural constituency and from the art of his profession, politics. The office restricts his movements, his access to events and reality.

David Halberstam, American writer. *The Best and the Brightest*, 1969.

76. Every president needs an S.O.B. I'm Nixon's.

H. Robert Haldeman, White House Chief of Staff (R). 1971.

77. Rather than the President telling someone to do something, I'll tell the guy. If he wants to find out something from somebody, I'll do it.

H. Robert Haldeman. Interview, *New York Daily News*, July 29, 1973.

78. Now look, that damned cowboy *[Theodore Roosevelt]* is President of the United States.

Mark A. Hanna (1837-1904), U.S. Senator (R-OH). Remark to H. H. Kohlsaat after Pres. McKinley's funeral, Sept. 15, 1901.

79. When you're in the presidency, and when you've got a major decision to make, you just put everything out of your mind and focus on that decision like a laser beam, and when the decision is finally made you just put everything else out of your mind because there's another one right behind it and then you've got to focus in on that.

Robert Hardesty, presidential assistant and speech writer (D). Quoted in Merle Miller, *Lyndon: An Oral Biography*, 1980.

80. They can't hurt you now.

Florence King Harding (1860-1924), First Lady. Remark to her dead husband in his coffin, Aug. 2, 1923.

81. I am not fit for this office and never should have been here.

Warren G. Harding (1865-1923), 29th President of the United States (R-OH). Quoted in Nicholas Murray Butler, *Across the Busy Years*, 1939.

82. Never with my consent shall an officer of the people, compensated for his services out of their pockets, become the pliant instrument of executive will.

William Henry Harrison (1773-1841), 9th President of the United States (Whig-OH). Inaugural address, Mar. 4, 1841.

83. I consider the veto power to be used only to protect the Constitution from violation; secondly, the people from effects of hasty legislation where their will has been disregarded or not well understood; and thirdly, to prevent the effects of com-

binations violative of the rights of minorities.
William Henry Harrison. *Ibid.*

84. If you do get into the Senate, don't get the presidential mania. It makes mad every man who is at all prominent at Washington either in the House or Senate. Scores of men, usually sound and sensible, fancy they can be President, who has no more right to think so than the autocrat of Russia. I have no knowledge of any tolerably conspicuous politician at Washington whose career is not colored and marred by his ambition to be President. I say this in all seriousness. It makes fools of all sorts from *[Daniel]* Webster and Lewis Campbell.
Rutherford B. Hayes (1822-1893), 19th President of the United States (R-OH). Letter to Guy M. Bryan, July 11, 1858.

85. I see more clearly than ever, and I thought I saw before, that congressional life is not the best introduction to the President's house. Great and fully equipped as the general *[James Garfield]* is, there are embarrassments growing out of his long and brilliant career in Congress, which Jackson and Lincoln, and Grant, and myself, escaped.
Rutherford B. Hayes. *Diary*, Apr. 25, 1881.

86. My old friend Judge Johnson used to say, "The presidency is unlike the Kingdom of Heaven – those who seek shall never find."
Rutherford B. Hayes. Letter to William McKinley, June 27, 1888; alluding to *Matthew* 7:7; *Luke* 11:9, 12:31.

87. Nobody wants to embarrass a President of the United States by discussing the assassination of foreign leaders in his presence. I just think we all had the feeling that we were hired ... to keep those things out of the Oval Office.
Richard Helms, Director, Central Intelligence Agency, and U.S. Ambassador to Iran. Senate hearings, June 13, 1975.

88. In the Middle Ages it was the fashion to wear hair shirts to remind one's self of trouble and sin. Many years ago I concluded that a few hair shirts were part of the mental wardrobe of every man. The President differs only from other men in that he has a more extensive wardrobe. We have had tonight an indication of the great variety of persons and organizations who cheerfully and voluntarily insist on acting as hair-shirts to the President.
Herbert Hoover (1874-1964), 31st President of the United States (R-IA). Speech, Gridiron Club, Washington, DC, Dec. 14, 1929.

89. The Democrats have an answer to the unemployment problem. They're all running for the presidency.
Bob Hope, American actor and comedian. In reference to the crowded field of presidential hopefuls, Dec. 1987.

90. I can say with truth mine is a situation of dignified slavery.
Andrew Jackson (1767-1845), 7th President of the United States (D-TN). Letter to T. R. J. Chester, Nov. 30, 1829.

91. I would rather be a doorkeeper in the house of God than live in that palace at Washington *[the White House.]*
Rachel Donelson Jackson (1767-1828), First Lady. Quoted in William Seale, *The President's House*, 1986.

92. No penance would ever expiate the sin against free government of holding that a President can escape control of executive powers by law through assuming his military role.
Robert H. Jackson (1892-1954), U.S. Attorney General (D) and U.S. Supreme Court Justice. Comment after President Truman seized the steel mills to end a labor dispute that was curtailing critical production. *Youngstown Sheet & Tube* v. *Sawyer*, 1952.

93. Presidents today spend more time speaking than they do reading or thinking.
Kathleen Hall Jamieson, dean, Annenberg School of Communications, University of Pennsylvania, Philadelphia, PA. Quoted on PBS, Bill Moyers, *Television in Politics*, Oct. 1988.

94. No man will ever bring out of the presidency the reputation which carries him into it.
Thomas Jefferson (1743-1826), 3rd President of the United States (Democratic Republican-VA). To Edward Rutledge, 1796.

95. The second office of the government is honorable and easy; the first is but a splendid misery.
Thomas Jefferson. Letter to Elbridge Gerry, 1797.

96. I have here *[at the White House]* company enough, part secretly hostile and a constant succession of strangers.
Thomas Jefferson. Letter to his daughter, Mary Eppes, Oct. 26, 1801.

97. Let them *[Congress]* impeach and be damned!
Andrew Johnson (1808-1875), 17th President of the United States (War Democrat-TN). Remark, 1868.

98. One of the things about the White House is that you know from the moment you walk in there that this has a time limitation. You don't know exactly what it is; it may be the four years you were elected for, or death, but you know it's got a time limitation. And that's one reason why you do as much as you can do, because you know that this will never happen again, and you can drum up the energy from somewhere within you to go more, do more, learn more, for this limited time.

Claudia (Lady Bird) Johnson, First Lady. Quoted in Merle Miller, *Lyndon: An Oral Biography*, 1980.

99. The first lady is, and always will be, an unpaid public servant elected by one person, her husband.

Claudia (Lady Bird) Johnson. Quoted in *U.S. News & World Report*, Mar. 9, 1987.

100. An assassin's bullet has thrust upon me the awesome burden of the Presidency. I am here to say that I need the help of all Americans, in all America.

Lyndon B. Johnson (1908-1973), 36th President of the United States (D-TX). Address to Congress, Nov. 27, 1963.

101. Boys, I've just reminded Hubert that I've got his balls in my pocket.

Lyndon B. Johnson. Remark to reporters after Vice President Humphrey had departed from his presidentially approved speech on education, Nov. 1964.

102. A President's hardest task is not to do what is right, but to know what is right.

Lyndon B. Johnson. Annual message to Congress, Jan. 4, 1965.

103. They're all mine, son.

Lyndon B. Johnson. Remark to an Air Force corporal who, pointing to the presidential helicopter, said, "This one is yours, sir," 1965.

104. What a President says and thinks is not worth five cents unless he has the people and Congress behind him. Without the Congress I'm just a six-feet-four Texan. With the Congress I'm President of the United States in the fullest sense.

Lyndon B. Johnson. Remark to Abba Eban, 1967.

105. If you ever keep *[Vice President]* Hubert *[Humphrey]* waiting again, I'll kick your ass down that hall.

Lyndon B. Johnson. To his secretary. Quoted in *Esquire*, Aug. 1967.

106. The presidency has made every man who occupied it, no matter how small, bigger than he was; and no matter how big, not big enough for its demands.

Lyndon B. Johnson. Quoted in *The New York Times*, Mar. 26, 1972.

107. Being President is like being a jackass in a hailstorm. There's nothing to do but stand there and take it.

Lyndon B. Johnson. Quoted in his obituary, Jan. 22, 1973.

108. The presidency is worse than being in jail.

Lyndon B. Johnson. Remark to Bobby Baker. Quoted in *Playboy*, June 1978.

109. If the ... President has much more than a hangnail, the stock market goes crazy.

Lyndon B. Johnson. Remark to Bobby Baker. *Ibid.*

110. Welcome to your house!

Lyndon B. Johnson. Greeting to White House visitors and tourists.

111. Well, what the hell's the presidency for?

Lyndon B. Johnson. Remark when told that his support of the Voting Rights Act might produce difficulties for the administration. Quoted in Merle Miller, *Lyndon: An Oral Biography*, 1980.

112. A President himself is shaped by an accumulation of policies of previous presidents.

James Jones, U.S. Congressman and White House Chief of Staff (D-OK). Speech, Center for the Study of the Presidency, C-SPAN, Sept. 1991.

113. There was no one at the table *[of a Cabinet meeting]* who could be of help to me except the President, and when I needed to consult him I did not choose a cabinet meeting to do so.

Jesse Holman Jones (1874-1956), Chairman, Reconstruction Finance Corporation, and U.S. Secretary of Commerce (D). In reference to Franklin D. Roosevelt. Quoted in *The New York Times*, May 28, 1989.

114. A growing number of people in this country do not believe that it makes a real difference who is elected President of the United States.

Hamilton Jordan, White House Chief of Staff (D). Memorandum to Jimmy Carter, June 25, 1980.

115. I'm only good at transitions in – not transitions out.

Hamilton Jordan. Response to Jody Powell, when asked to assist the transition team for Ronald Reagan, Dec. 4, 1980.

116. Roosevelt proved a man could be President for life; Truman proved anybody could be President; and Eisenhower proved you don't need to have a President.

Kenneth B. Keating (1900-1975), U.S. Congressman (R-NY), U.S. Senator, and U.S. Ambassador to Israel. Quoted in Morris K. Udall, *Too Funny to be President*, 1988.

117. I don't mind not being President; I just mind that someone else is.

Edward M. Kennedy, U.S. Senator (D-MA). Speech, Gridiron Club, Washington, DC, Mar. 22, 1986.

118. Let the word go forth from this time and place, to friend and foe alike, that the torch has been passed to a new generation of Americans – born in this century, tempered by war, disciplined by a hard and bitter peace, proud of our ancient heritage.

John F. Kennedy (1917-1963), 35th President of the United States (D-MA). Inaugural address, Jan. 20, 1961; compare below, Martin Van Buren.

119. I guess this is the week that I earn my salary.

John F. Kennedy. Remark during the Cuban missile crisis, Apr. 1961.

120. No one in the country is more assailed by divergent advice and clamorous counsel.

John F. Kennedy. Description of the presidency. Introduction to Theodore Sorenson, *Decision Making in the White House*, 1963.

121. Just think of what we'll pass on to the poor fellow who comes after me.

John F. Kennedy. Discussion of problems of the presidency. Quoted in Theodore Sorenson, *Kennedy*, 1965.

122. If anyone is crazy enough to want to kill a President of the United States, he can do it. All he must be prepared to do is give his life for the President's.

John F. Kennedy. Quoted in Pierre Salinger, *With Kennedy*, 1966.

123. So you want this fucking job.

John F. Kennedy. Remark to Sen. Barry M. Goldwater during the Bay of Pigs crisis. Quoted in Woodward and Bernstein, *The Final Days*, 1976.

124. There is no question that in the next thirty or forty years a Negro can achieve the position ... of President of the United States.

Robert F. Kennedy (1925-1968), U.S. Senator and U.S. Attorney General (D-NY). Radio address, Voice of America, May 26, 1961.

125. Mo *[Congressman Udall]* is too funny to be President.

James J. Kilpatrick, American political columnist. Quoted in Morris K. Udall, *Too Funny to Be President*, 1988.

126. We are all the President's men.

Henry M. Kissinger, U.S. Secretary of State and National Security Advisor (R). 1973.

127. This talk of blindly following the President in everything pertaining to war – except as to his conduct of military operation in the field – is blithering idiocy.... The Constitution still abides. It defines the powers and duties of Congress. It gave Congress every war power, except that it left with the President the right to direct all military operation in the field. It gave him no other war power.

Robert M. La Follette (1855-1925), Governor of Wisconsin and U.S. Senator (R). Letter to James C. Kerwin, Jan. 5, 1918.

128. The Founding Fathers wisely concluded that it was not enough for the President to swear to obey the law. He had to "take care that the laws be faithfully executed," which means by his appointees and subordinates.

Arthur L. Liman, chief counsel, Senate Iran-Contra Committee (D). *The New York Times*, Mar. 2, 1990.

129. I must in candor say I do not think myself fit for the presidency.

Abraham Lincoln (1809-1865), 16th President of the United States (R-IL). Letter to T. J. Pickett, Apr. 16, 1859.

130. Nobody has ever expected me to be President. In my poor, lean, lank face nobody has ever seen that any cabbages were sprouting.

Abraham Lincoln. Campaign speech, 1860.

131. The chief magistrate derives all his authority from the people, and they have conferred none upon him to fix terms for the separation of the states *[from the Union]*. The people themselves can do this also if they choose; but the Executive, as such, has nothing to do with it.

Abraham Lincoln. First inaugural address, Mar. 4, 1861.

132. The presidency is not an office to be either solicited or declined.

William Loundes (1782-1822), U.S. Congressman (D-SC). Comment after his state legislature nominated him for the presidency, Dec. 1821.

133. To be seen only in public on stated times, like an eastern Lama would be ... offensive.
William Maclay (1737-1804), U.S. Senator (PA). Advice to President Washington. Quoted in *Smithsonian*, June 1989.

134. You are living in an unreal world when you work there *[the White House]*.
Jeb Stuart Magruder, presidential assistant (R). Quoted in *The Listener*, July 26, 1973.

135. That the President of the United States may be subpoenaed, and examined as a witness, and required to produce any paper in his possession, is not controverted.
John Marshall (1755-1835), Chief Justice, U.S. Supreme Court. Treason trial of Aaron Burr, Aug. 1807.

136. Once there were two brothers. One ran away to sea, the other was elected Vice President, and nothing was ever heard from either of them again.
Thomas Riley Marshall (1854-1925), Governor of Indiana and Vice President of the United States (D). *Recollections*, 1925.

137. I am against giving the power of war to the Executive, because he is not safely to be trusted with it.
George Mason (1725-1792), Member, Virginia and Federal Constitutional Conventions. Debate on Article 1, Section 8 of the proposed Constitution. Constitutional Convention, Philadelphia, PA, 1787.

138. It would be as unnatural to refer the choice of a proper character for chief magistrate to the people as it would be to refer a trial of colors to a blind man.
George Mason. *Ibid.*

139. Presidents ... become hermits only at their peril. Running the executive branch is now a team sport. It is operated best by politicians who thrive on command, possess a fine and sure touch for the levers of power, and enjoy the company of those who serve them.
Christopher Matthews, political columnist, presidential campaign manager, and speech writer for Gov. Michael Dukakis (D). *The New York Times* Nov. 13, 1988.

140. I can no longer be called the President of a party. I am now the President of the whole people.
William McKinley (1843-1901), 25th President of the United States (R-OH). Remark on his reelection, 1900.

141. A Galileo could no more be elected President of the United States than he could be elected Pope of Rome. Both high posts are reserved for men favored by God with an extraordinary genius for swathing the bitter facts of life in bandages of self-illusion.
H. L. Mencken (1880-1956), American journalist. *Minority Report*, 1956.

142. As Chairman of the *[House]* Ways and Means Committee, I can contact the President, whoever he may be, quite readily on the telephone. As a Vice President I don't know whether he'd listen to me or not.
Wilbur D. Mills (1909-1992), U.S. Congressman (D-AR). Explanation for not accepting the vice presidential nomination of his party. CBS, *Face the Nation*, June 4, 1972.

143. Presidents cannot lead if they don't know what's going on in the life of the average American.
Walter F. Mondale, Vice President of the United States and U.S. Senator (D-MN). Presidential campaign speech, 1984.

144. It's very dangerous ... to confuse the identity and fortune of the President with the success and fortune of the nation.
Bill Moyers, American journalist, special assistant to Pres. Lyndon B. Johnson, and White House Press Secretary (D). Interview with Clark Clifford, PBS, 1981.

145. The healthy presidency is one that never lets the press hustle the President's priorities.
Bill Moyers. PBS, *The Presidency, the Press and the People*, Apr. 2, 1990.

146. The more publicized the presidency the less powerful the office.
Bill Moyers. *Ibid.*

147. Only the President has the prestige to step forward and capture the imagination of the nation.
Gaylord Nelson, U.S. Senator and Governor of Wisconsin (D). Speech, National Press Club, C-SPAN, Apr. 16, 1990.

148. With all the power that a President has, the most important thing to bear in mind is this: You must not give power to a man unless, above everything else, he has character. Character is the most important qualification the President of the United States can have.
Richard M. Nixon, 37th President of the United States (R-CA). Campaign TV ad for Barry M. Goldwater, 1964.

149. Surely one of the President's greatest resources is the moral authority of his office.
Richard M. Nixon. Campaign speech, 1968.

150. The presidency has many problems, but boredom is the least of them.
Richard M. Nixon. Interview, Jan. 9, 1973.

151. The constitutional right for the President of the United States to impound funds ... when the spending of money would mean either increasing prices or increasing taxes ... is absolutely clear.
Richard M. Nixon. Press conference, Jan. 31, 1973.

152. I don't give a shit what happens. I want you all to stonewall it.
Richard M. Nixon. Directions to key staff on Watergate, 1973.

153. Unless a President can protect the privacy of the advice he gets, he cannot get the advice he needs.
Richard M. Nixon. Press conference, Jan. 27, 1974.

154. I hereby resign the office of the President of the United States.
Richard M. Nixon. Full text of resignation letter to U.S. Secretary of State Henry M. Kissinger, Aug. 7, 1974.

155. I impeached myself by resigning.
Richard M. Nixon. TV interview with David Frost, May 4, 1977.

156. A Vice President cannot help you *[in a presidential campaign]*, he can only hurt you.
Richard M. Nixon. Remark, 1968. Quoted in *Time*, Aug. 29, 1988.

157. One constantly has the problem of either getting on top of the job *[the presidency]* or letting the job get on top of you.
Richard M. Nixon. PBS, *The American Experience*, Oct. 15, 1990.

158. Being first lady is the hardest unpaid job in the world.
Thelma (Pat) Nixon, First Lady. Statement, Mar. 15, 1972.

159. You see so many of these *[red carpets being rolled out]* you'll get so you'll hate them.
Thelma (Pat) Nixon. Remark to incoming First Lady, Betty Ford, Aug. 1974.

160. Presidents are presidents. They're not kings.
David R. Obey, U.S. Congressman (D-WI). Interview, PBS, *MacNeil-Lehrer News Hour*, Oct. 5, 1990.

161. Are there no carpets made in the United States ... to please the eye of a democratic President? Why does he prefer *Royal* and *Imperial Wiltons* to the fabric of his own countrymen?
Charles Ogle (1798-1841), U.S. Congressman (Whig-PA). Comment after President Van Buren purchased some foreign carpets for the White House. Speech, "On the Regal Splendor of the President's Palace," Apr. 14, 1840.

162. Oh, Bunny, you're President now.
Jacqueline Kennedy Onassis, First Lady. Remark to John F. Kennedy, Nov. 8, 1960.

163. America's banner must never be, "Our President, Right or Wrong."
Claiborne Pell, U.S. Senator (D-RI). *The Washington Post*, September 16, 1990.

164. We are plain folks from Tennessee called here by a national calamity *[the assassination of Abraham Lincoln]*. I hope not too much will be expected from us.
Martha Johnson Petterson (1828-1901), daughter of President Andrew Johnson. Statement upon arriving at the White House, Apr. 1865.

165. There's nothing left but to get drunk.
Franklin Pierce (1804-1869), 14th President of the United States (D-NH). Remark on leaving office, 1857.

166. That is not my house. It's the people's house.
Franklin Pierce. Comment when showing visitors the White House. Quoted in Clay-Copton, *A Belle of the Fifties*, 1904.

167. I am on good terms at the White House, which by the way is no advantage, for the cry of the mad dog is not more fatal to its victim than the cry of executive connections here.
George Poindexter (1779-1855), Governor of Mississippi (D), U.S. Congressman, and U.S. Senator. Letter to William C. Mead, Apr. 10, 1812.

168. No candidate for the presidency ought ever to remain in the cabinet. He is an unsafe adviser.
James K. Polk (1795-1849), 11th President of the United States (D-TN). *Diary*, Feb. 21, 1848.

169. I cannot, whilst President of the United States, descend to enter into a newspaper controversy.
James K. Polk. Comment on newspaper stories linking him to underhanded dealing when Texas was admitted to the Union. *Diary*, July 31, 1848.

170. The President represents in the Executive Department the whole people of the United States, as each member of the Legislative Department represents portions of them.
James K. Polk. Annual message to Congress, Dec. 5, 1848.

171. I am now free from all public cares. I am sure I shall be a happier man in my retirement than I have been during the four years I have filled the highest office in the gift of my countrymen.
James K. Polk. *Diary,* Mar. 5, 1849.

172. If I get to the White House, I expect to live on $25,000 a year, and I will neither keep house nor make butter.
Sarah Childress Polk (1803-1891), First Lady. Response to a reporter, 1844.

173. To dance in these rooms would be undignified, and it would be respectful neither to the house nor to the office.
Sarah Childress Polk. Quoted in William Seale, *The President's House,* 1986.

174. The American people do not spend a lot of time thinking about their Vice President.
J. Danforth Quayle, U.S. Senator and Vice President of the United States (R-IN). Interview, ABC, *Nightline,* Oct. 2, 1990.

175. The fetus of monarchy.
Edmund Jenings Randolph (1753-1813), Member, Continental Congress, Delegate, Constitutional Convention, Governor of Virginia, U.S. Attorney General, and U.S. Secretary of State. Description of the presidency. Quoted in Arthur M. Schlesinger, Jr., *The Imperial Presidency,* 1973.

176. Just because you're married *[to the president]* doesn't mean you've given up your right to have an opinion.
Nancy Reagan, First Lady. Quoted in *The New York Times,* Jan. 15, 1989.

177. For eight years I was sleeping with the President. If that doesn't give you special access, I don't know what does.
Nancy Reagan. Interview, CBS, *60 Minutes,* Oct. 15, 1989.

178. Every woman is entitled to an opinion and the right to express that opinion – especially to the man she's married to.
Nancy Reagan. Interview, CNN, *The Larry King Show,* Dec. 28, 1989.

179. If you need a plumber, you can get a plumber.
Nancy Reagan. Remark on the benefits of living in the White House. Interview, CBS, *The Phil Donahue Show,* 1990.

180. The thought of being President frightens me. I do not think I want the job.
Ronald Reagan, 40th President of the United States (R-CA). Dec. 1973.

181. Shouldn't the people have the right to vote for someone as many times as they want to vote for him?
Ronald Reagan. Arguing against the two-term limit for Presidents. Interview with Barbara Walters, ABC, Mar. 24, 1986.

182. The presidency is an institution over which you have temporary custody.
Ronald Reagan. Interview with Hugh Sidey, *Time,* Apr. 7, 1986.

183. An ordeal I have never ceased to thank the framers of our own Constitution for sparing the President.
Ronald Reagan. Comment on the British practice of House of Commons members grilling the Prime Minister. Preface to Margaret Thatcher, *In Defense of Freedom,* 1987.

184. You go to bed every night knowing that there are things that you are not aware of.
Ronald Reagan. Quoted in *Newsweek,* July 3, 1989.

185. I just thought that in sixteen years I hadn't made any kind of money.
Ronald Reagan. Remark on why he accepted $2 million to make appearances and speeches in Japan. Quoted in *The Chicago Tribune,* Nov. 17, 1989.

186. The result of the *[Twenty-second]* Amendment has been twofold: It has undermined necessary presidential power to conduct the great public business assigned to that office, while simultaneously denying the people their most hallowed democratic right of having whomever they desire hold their offices for as long as the people desire.
Ronald Reagan. *Restoring the Presidency: Reconsidering the 22nd Amendment,* 1990.

187. My average of meeting with people was about eighty a day for eight years.
Ronald Reagan. Testimony, John Poindexter's Iran-Contra trial, Feb. 1990.

188. They could do worse and probably will.

Thomas B. Reed (1839-1902), U.S. Congressman and Speaker of the House (R-ME). Remark when asked if his party would nominate him for President, 1895.

189. A President moves through his days surrounded by literally hundreds of people whose relationship to him is that of doting mother to a spoiled child.

George E. Reedy, White House Press Secretary (D). *The Twilight of the Presidency*, 1970.

190. When the country decides to get rid of a President, they decide not only that he was wrong but also that he was an S.O.B.

George E. Reedy. PBS, *The Presidency, the Press, and the People*, Apr. 2, 1990.

191. The President has to comment on almost anything that happens anywhere in the world.

George E. Reedy. *Ibid.*

192. With respect to the suggestion that the President has a *constitutional* power to decline to spend appropriated funds, we must conclude that such a broad power is supported by neither reason nor precedent.

William H. Rehnquist, Chief Justice, U.S. Supreme Court. Memorandum to the deputy counsel to President Nixon. Written while he was a U.S. Justice Department official, Dec. 19, 1969.

193. I don't believe in social relationships between Presidents and reporters..... If you have sympathy for them ... you can't do your job.

James Reston, American political columnist. Interview, PBS, *Newsleaders*, Nov. 23, 1989.

194. The best part about being Vice President is presiding over the Senate. Where else could I have Barry Goldwater addressing me as "Mr. President"?

Nelson A. Rockefeller (1908-1979), Governor of New York and Vice President of the United States (R). Quoted in Skubik and Short, *Republican Humor*, 1976.

195. The man with the best job in the country is the Vice President. All he has to do is get up every morning and say, "How's the President?"

Will Rogers (1879-1935), American humorist. After-dinner speech, Washington, DC, 1934.

196. But there isn't going to be any First Lady. There is just going to be plain, ordinary Mrs. Roosevelt. And that's that.

Anna Eleanor Roosevelt (1884-1962), First Lady and U.S. Delegate to the United Nations. Remark to reporters, Mar. 1933.

197. Is there anything we can do for *you*? For *you* are the one in trouble now.

Anna Eleanor Roosevelt. Remark to President Truman, Apr. 12, 1945.

198. It isn't really possible under our system, I fear, for the Executive and the Legislative to get along well.

Anna Eleanor Roosevelt. Letter to Joseph P. Lash, Aug. 21, 1952.

199. When we elect a President and a Vice President we must be prepared to face the fact that the Vice President may become President.

Anna Eleanor Roosevelt. Interview, NBC, *Meet the Press*, Sept. 16, 1956.

200. Always be on time. Do as little talking as humanly possible. Remember to lean back in the parade car so everybody can see the President. Be sure not to get too fat, because you'll have to sit three in the back seat.

Anna Eleanor Roosevelt. Campaign advice for candidates' spouses. Quoted in *The New York Times*, Nov. 11, 1962.

201. Can the Vice President Be Useful?

Franklin D. Roosevelt (1882-1945), 32nd President of the United States (D-NY). Title of article, *Saturday Evening Post*, Oct. 16, 1920.

202. The fate of America cannot depend on any one man.

Franklin D. Roosevelt. Speech, New York City, Nov. 5, 1932.

203. The presidency is not merely an administrative office. That is the least of it. It is pre-eminently a place of moral leadership.

Franklin D. Roosevelt. *The New York Times*, Nov. 13, 1932.

204. Never let your left hand know what your right hand is doing.

Franklin D. Roosevelt. Remark to U.S. Secretary of the Treasury Henry Morganthau, Jr., on handling the Cabinet, 1934.

205. Governments can err. Presidents do make mistakes.

Franklin D. Roosevelt. Presidential nomination acceptance speech, Democratic National Convention, Philadelphia, PA, June 27, 1936.

206. Reluctantly, but as a good soldier, I will accept and serve in this office if I am so ordered by the commander-in-chief of us all, the sovereign people of the United States.

Franklin D. Roosevelt. Press conference announcing his run for a fourth term, July 11, 1944.

207. The vice presidency is a most honorable office, but for a young man there is not much to do.
Theodore Roosevelt (1858-1919), 26th President of the United States (R-NY). Letter to Sen. Henry Cabot Lodge, Dec. 11, 1899.

208. I am no longer a political accident.
Theodore Roosevelt. In reference to his first term when President McKinley's assassination elevated him to the presidency. Remark to his wife after he won the election, Nov. 9, 1904.

209. The President should be a very strong man who uses without hesitation every power that the position yields; but because of this fact I believe that he should be sharply watched by the people.
Theodore Roosevelt. Letter to Sen. Henry Cabot Lodge, July 19, 1908.

210. I like my job. The burdens of this great nation I have borne up under for the past seven years will not be laid aside with relief, as all presidents have heretofore said, but will be laid aside with a good deal of regret, for I have enjoyed every moment of this so-called arduous and exacting task.
Theodore Roosevelt. Remark to William Jennings Bryan. 1908.

211. No President has ever enjoyed himself as much as I have enjoyed myself.
Theodore Roosevelt. On leaving the White House, 1909.

212. My belief was that it was not only his *[the President's]* right but his duty to do anything that the needs of the nation demanded unless such action was forbidden by the Constitution or by the laws. Under this interpretation of executive power I did and caused to be done many things not previously done by the President.
Theodore Roosevelt. *Autobiography*, 1919.

213. The favorite indoor sport around Washington – making fun of Vice Presidents.
Dean Rusk, U.S. Secretary of State (D). Quoted in Merle Miller, *Lyndon: An Oral Biography*, 1980.

214. The first ladyship is the only federal office in which the holder can neither be fired nor impeached.
William Safire, presidential speech writer and political columnist (R). *The New York Times*, Mar. 2, 1987.

215. The image of the President abroad is as important as his image in the United States.
Pierre Salinger, White House Press Secretary (D). PBS, *The Presidency, the Press, and the People*, Apr. 2, 1990.

216. The President will always need a small and alert personal staff to serve as his eyes and ears and one lobe of his brain, but he must avoid a vast and possessive staff ambitious to make all the decisions of government.
Arthur M. Schlesinger, Jr., American historian and presidential advisor (D). *The Imperial Presidency*, 1973.

217. No sensible President should give one man control of all the channels of communication.
Arthur M. Schlesinger, Jr. *Ibid.*

218. What the country needs today is a little serious disrespect for the office of the presidency; a refusal to give any more weight to a President's words than the intelligence of the utterance.
Arthur M. Schlesinger, Jr. *Ibid.*

219. The genius of impeachment lay in the fact that it could punish the man without punishing the office.
Arthur M. Schlesinger, Jr. Quoted in Barbara Rowes, *The Book of Quotes*, 1979.

220. Unpopular Presidents such as Hoover, Johnson, Nixon, and Carter have to deliver the goods or they are finished. But the electorate will give popular Presidents, such as Franklin Roosevelt, Eisenhower, Kennedy, and Reagan the benefit of the doubt.
Arthur M. Schlesinger, Jr. *Playboy*, Nov. 1982.

221. You *[Americans]* elect an emperor every four years.
Helmut Schmidt, Chancellor of West Germany. Interview, C-SPAN, *Booknotes*, Apr. 15, 1990.

222. Every presidential election is about values.
William Schneider, political analyst, American Enterprise Institute. ABC, *It's Your Business*, Nov. 19, 1989.

223. The theory of our government is that a specific sum shall be appropriated by a law originating in the House, for a specific purpose, and within a given fiscal year. It is the duty of the executive to use that sum, and no more, especially for that purpose, and no other, and within the time fixed.
John Sherman (1823-1900), U.S. Congressman (R-OH), U.S. Senator, U.S. Secretary of the Treasury, and U.S. Secretary of State. *Recollections of Forty Years in the House, Senate and Cabinet*, 1895.

224. If forced to choose between the penitentiary and the White House for four years, I would say the penitentiary, thank you.
William Tecumseh Sherman (1820-1891), General, U.S. Army. Letter to H. W. Halleck, 1864.

225. *[I would be]* a fool, a madman, an ass, to embark anew, at sixty-five years of age, in a career that may at any moment become tempest-tossed by the perfidy, the defalcation, the dishonesty or neglect of any one of a hundred thousand subordinates.
William Tecumseh Sherman. Statement declining to be considered a candidate for President. Letter to Sen. James G. Blaine, May 25, 1884.

226. A life in Washington cures one of ambition for honors and distinctions, by exhibiting them in all their vanity, instability, and transitoriness, and unveiling at the same time all the pains and some vexations appertaining to them.
Margaret Bayard Smith (Mrs. Samuel Harrison) (1798-1844), Washington hostess and society leader. *The First Forty Years of Washington Society*, 1904.

227. I'd go straight to Mrs. Truman and apologize.
Margaret Chase Smith, U.S. Congresswoman and U.S. Senator (R-ME). Response when asked what she would do if she were to wake up one day in the White House. Quoted in *Lears*, Feb. 1990.

228. It's important for the President to seek a diversity of advice and not simply have cheerleaders.
Theodore Sorensen, presidential assistant and speech writer (D). PBS, *Frontline*, Jan. 15, 1991.

229. You are sleeping on a volcano. The ground is mined all around and under you and ready to explode, and without prompt and energetic action, you will be the last President of the United States.
Edwin M. Stanton (1814-1869), U.S. Attorney General, U.S. Secretary of War, and U.S. Supreme Court Justice. Advice to President Buchanan, 1857.

230. You know how it is in an election year. They pick a President and then for four years they pick on him.
Adlai E. Stevenson (1900-1965), Governor of Illinois (D), and U.S. Ambassador to the United Nations. Aug. 28, 1952.

231. In America, anyone can become President. It's one of the risks we take.
Adlai E. Stevenson. Quoted in Roger Simon, *Road Show*, 1990.

232. How one feels about the "inherent" powers of the presidency has been generally determined throughout our history by how one feels about the use to which they are put and the pressing needs of the time.
I. F. Stone (1908-1989), American investigative journalist and political writer. *The New York Review of Books*, June 28, 1973.

233. I have a constituency of one. I only have to keep the President happy.
John Sununu, Governor of New Hampshire and White House Chief of Staff (R). NBC, *A Day at the White House*, Feb. 28, 1990.

234. Of course there was objection, but I had my way. *[Until her day, it had been the custom for First Ladies to walk behind, not with, their husbands in the inaugural parade.]*
Helen Herron Taft (1861-1943), First Lady. Remark, 1901.

235. The secret service men, like the poor, we had with us always.
Helen Herron Taft. *Recollections*; alluding to *Matthew* 26:11.

236. The White House is a big political asset when used wisely.
William H. Taft (1857-1930), 27th President of the United States (R-OH), and Chief Justice, U.S. Supreme Court. Remark to Archibald Butt on White House entertaining, 1909.

237. The White House is a bigger proposition than one imagines.... One or two breaks and you become a laughing stock.
William H. Taft. Remark to Archibald Butt, 1909.

238. Nobody ever drops in for the evening.
William H. Taft. Remark on the presidency. Quoted in *Harvard Business Review*, May-June 1952.

239. While I'd rather be right than President, at any time I'm ready to be both.
Norman Thomas (1884-1968), American Socialist and Director, League for Industrial Democracy. Attributed.

240. No man is big enough to refuse a nomination for President if it is offered him.
William Hale Thompson (1869-1944), Mayor of Chicago, IL (D). Quoted in Reinhard H. Luthin, *American Demagogues*, 1959.

241. Tell him *[Franklin D. Roosevelt]* to go to hell. I don't want to be Vice President. I bet I can go down the street and stop the first ten men I see and that they can't tell me the names of two of the last ten Vice Presidents of the United States.

Harry S Truman (1884-1972), 33rd President of the United States (D-MO). Remark to Robert E. Hannegan, July 1944.

242. I was getting along fine until I stuck my neck out too far and got too famous – and then they made me V. P. and now I can't do anything.
Harry S Truman. Jan. 1945.

243. Within the first few months I discovered that being a President is like riding a tiger. A man has to keep on riding or be swallowed.
Harry S Truman. Remark to reporters, Dec. 3, 1945.

244. It's almost impossible for a man to be President of the United States without learning something.
Harry S Truman. Aug. 14, 1948.

245. The President spends most of his time kissing people on the cheek in order to get them to do what they ought to do without getting kissed.
Harry S Truman. Quoted in *The Observer*, Feb. 6, 1949.

246. In my opinion eight years as President is enough and sometimes too much for any man to serve in that capacity.
Harry S Truman. Announcement that he would not seek a second full term, Mar. 29, 1952.

247. I have tried my best to give this nation everything I had in me. There are probably a million people who could have done the job better than I did it, but I had the job, and I always quote an epitaph in a cemetery in Tombstone, Arizona: "Here lies Jack Williams. He done his damndest."
Harry S Truman. Statement on leaving office, 1953.

248. Any man who has had the job I've had and didn't have a sense of humor wouldn't still be here.
Harry S Truman. Apr. 1955.

249. What have you done? You have taken a man and put him in the hardest job in the world and sent him out to fight our battles in a life and death struggle – and you have sent him out with one hand tied behind his back, because everyone knows he cannot run for reelection. He is still the President of the whole country, and all of us are dependent upon him to do his job. If he is not a good President, and you do not want to keep him, you do not have to reelect him. There is a way to get rid of him, and it does not require a constitutional amendment to do the job.
Harry S Truman. Testimony about the Twenty-second Amendment, 1959.

250. Some of the Presidents were great and some of them weren't. I can say that because I wasn't one of the great Presidents, but I had a good time trying to be one.
Harry S Truman. Interview, Apr. 27, 1959.

251. He *[the President]* is just as much subject to our *[Congress's]* control as if we appointed him, except that we cannot remove him and place another in his place.
Lyman Trumbull (1813-1896), U.S. Senator (R, D, and Liberal Republican-IL). Quoted in Wilfred E. Binkley, *President and Congress*, 1947.

252. As soon as you breathe the slightest hint of ambition to run for President, you are handed this enormous bullhorn.... If I win, I win, but I also win if my ideas win.
Paul Tsongas, U.S. Senator (D-MA). Quoted in *The Washington Post*, May 15, 1991.

253. The office *[of the President]* has become too complex and its reach too far extended to be trusted to the fallible judgment of any one individual.
Barbara Tuchman (1912-1989), American historian. *The New York Times*, Feb. 13, 1973.

254. Go you now then, Mr. Clay, to your end of the avenue where stands the Capitol, and there perform your duty to the country as you shall think proper. So help me God I shall do mine at this end of it as I shall think proper.
John Tyler (1790-1862), 10th President of the United States (Whig-VA). Statement to Sen. Henry Clay, 1842.

255. With me it is emphatically true that the presidency is no bed of roses.
John Tyler. Quoted in Exhibit, "39 Men."

256. Beware of the presidential candidate who has no friends his own age and confidants who can tell him to go to hell, who has no hobbies and outside interests.... God help us from Presidents who can't be a little bit gentle, and who don't have a sense of humor, and who can't gather friends around and play poker and climb a mountain. You know, these intense workaholics really worry me.
Morris K. Udall, U.S. Congressman (D-AZ). Statement during his bid for the presidential nomination, 1976.

257. I'm against all vice – including the vice-presidency.
Morris K. Udall. *Too Funny to Be President*, 1988.

258. I do solemnly swear *[or affirm]*, that I (name) will faithfully execute the office of President of the United States, and will, to the best of my ability, preserve, protect, and defend the Constitution of the United States.

U.S. Presidential inaugural oath.

259. Richard Nixon has acted in a manner contrary to his trust as President and subversive of constitutional government, to the great prejudice of law and justice and to the manifest injury of the people of the U.S.

U.S. House of Representatives, Judiciary Committee, *Articles of Impeachment*, July 27, 1974.

260. Unlike all who have preceded me, the Revolution that gave us existence as one people was achieved at the period of my birth; and while I contemplated with gratified reverence that memorable event, I feel that I belong to a later age and that I may not expect my countrymen to weigh my actions with the same kind and partial hand.

Martin Van Buren (1782-1862), 8th President of the United States (D-NY). Statement noting that he was the first President to be born after the signing of the Declaration of Independence. Inaugural address, Mar. 4, 1837; compare above, John F. Kennedy.

261. As to the presidency, the two happiest days of my life were those of my entrance upon the office and my surrender of it.

Martin Van Buren. Remark to President Buchanan, 1857.

262. I can see no propriety in precluding ourselves from the service of any man who on some great emergency shall be deemed universally most capable of serving the public.

George Washington (1732-1799), 1st President of the United States (VA). Letter to Lafayette, Apr. 28, 1788.

263. I walk on untrodden ground. There is scarcely any part of my conduct which may not hereafter be drawn into precedent.

George Washington. Quoted in *Smithsonian*, June 1989.

264. A prisoner of state.

Martha Washington (1731-1802), First Lady. Description of her role. Quoted in Exhibit, "The First Ladies," Hoover Museum, Iowa City, IA, 1990.

265. Being related to a President may bring more problems than opportunity. Almost any enterprise is criticized. If successful, it's assumed that it is because of the relationship. If not, the public assumes that the son or daughter is lazy or incompetent.

Douglas Wead, presidential assistant (R). *All the President's Children*, 1990.

266. I foresee a time when the President of the United States will be as powerful and vicious as Caligula.

Theodore H. White (1915-1986), American political analyst and writer. *America At Last*, 1965.

267. Economists are very much like reporters. The best of them can tell you where you are, the exceptional ones can tell you how they got there – but none can predict how you go from where you are to where you want to get. And it is as unwise for a President to let his economists tell him where to go as for a President to let his generals tell him what the aims and purposes of a war should be.

Theodore H. White. *Breach of Faith*, 1975.

268. In America the President reigns for four years, and journalism goes on for ever and ever.

Oscar Wilde (1854-1900), Irish writer. *The Soul of Man Under Socialism*, 1881.

269. I am first of all the wife of Woodrow Wilson and secondly the wife of the President of the United States.

Edith Bolling Wilson (1872-1961), First Lady. Remark to Professor Link about her role as "Mrs. Presidentress," 1919.

270. The President is at liberty, both in law and conscience, to be as big a man as he can. His capacity will set the limit; and if Congress be overborne by him, it will be no fault of the makers of the Constitution – it will be from no lack of constitutional powers on his part, but only because the President has the nation behind him, and Congress has not.

Woodrow Wilson (1856-1924), 28th President of the United States (D-NJ). *Constitutional Government in the United States*, 1908.

271. Men of ordinary physique and discretion cannot be President and live.

Woodrow Wilson. *Ibid.*

272. The idea of the Presidents we have recently had has been that they were Presidents of a National Board of Trustees *[the Cabinet]*. That is not my idea. I have been president of one board of trustees and I do not care to have another on my hands. I want to be President of the people of the United States.

Woodrow Wilson. *The New Freedom*, 1913.

273. The President ... must be Prime Minister, as much concerned with the guidance of legislation as with the just and orderly execution of law.

Woodrow Wilson. Quoted in Wilfred E. Binkley, *President and Congress*, 1947.

274. He *[the President]* is not always, as we know, a real leader before he is chosen to his great office of leadership.

Woodrow Wilson. Quoted in *Review of Reviews*, Apr. 1983.

Chapter 80

Privacy

1. Private faces in public places
Are wiser and nicer
Than public faces in private places.
W. H. Auden (1907-1973), British poet. *Marginalia,* 1943.

2. The only public good is that which assures the private good of the citizens.
Simone de Beauvoir, French author. *The Second Sex,* 1953.

3. I like my privacy as much as the next one, but I am compelled to admit that government has a right to invade it unless prohibited by some specific constitutional provision.
Hugo L. Black (1886-1971), U.S. Senator (D-AL), and U.S. Supreme Court Justice. *Griswald* v. *Connecticut,* 1965 (dissent).

4. This right of privacy, whether it be founded in the Fourteenth Amendment's concept of personal liberty and restrictions upon state action, as we feel it is, or, as the District Court determined, in the Ninth Amendment's reservation of rights to the people, is broad enough to encompass a woman's decision whether or not to terminate her pregnancy.
Harry A. Blackmun, U.S. Supreme Court Justice. *Roe* v. *Wade,* 1973.

5. The states are not free, under the guise of protecting maternal health or potential life, to intimidate women into continuing pregnancy.... A woman's right to make that choice is fundamental.
Harry A. Blackmun. *Thornburgh* v. *American College of Obstetricians and Gynecologists,* 1986.

6. No outward doors of a man's house can in general be broken open to execute any civil process; though in criminal cases the public safety supersedes the private.
William Blackstone (1723-1780), British jurist. *Commentaries on the Laws of England,* IV, 1769.

7. The makers of our Constitution ... conferred, as against the government, the right to be let alone – the most comprehensive of rights and the most valued by civilized men. To protect that right, every unjustifiable intrusion by the government upon the privacy of the individual, whatever the means employed, must be deemed a violation of the Fourth Amendment.
Louis D. Brandeis (1856-1941), U.S. Supreme Court Justice. *Olmstead* v. *United States,* 1927 (dissent).

8. It is clear that in some instances the use of microphone surveillance is the only possible way of uncovering the activities of espionage agents, possible saboteurs, and subversive persons. In such instances I am of the opinion that the national interest requires that microphone surveillance be utilized by the Federal Bureau of Investigation.
Herbert Brownell, U.S. Attorney General (R). Memorandum to J. Edgar Hoover, May 20, 1954.

9. A right of privacy doesn't emerge from any single part of the Constitution. The right of privacy emerges from the Constitution as a whole.
Warren E. Burger, Chief Justice, U.S. Supreme Court. Interview, PBS, *MacNeil-Lehrer News Hour,* Sept. 13, 1990.

10. The "flatfoot mentality" insists that any individual or organization that wants to change anything in our present system is somehow subversive of "the American way," and should be under constant surveillance – a task that seems to absorb most of our resources for fighting genuine crime.
Virginia Anne Carabillo, Vice President, National Organization of Women. "The Flatfoot Mentality," *Hollywood NOW News,* Aug. 1975.

11. Without your knowledge the eyes and ears of many will see and watch you as they have done already.
Marcus Tullius Cicero (106-43 B.C.), Roman statesman and writer. *Orationes in Catilinam.*

12. ... the silly, mean, and cowardly lies that every day are found in the columns of certain newspapers, which violate every instinct of American manliness, and in ghoulish glee desecrate every sacred relation of private life.

Grover Cleveland (1837-1908), 22nd and 24th President of the United States (D-NY). Speech, 250th anniversary, Harvard University, Cambridge, MA, Nov. 8, 1886.

13. For a man's house is his castle ... for where else shall a man be safe, if it be not in his house?
Edward Coke (1552-1634), Solicitor General, Attorney General, and Speaker of the House of Commons, England. *Institutes of the Laws of England*, III, 1644.

14. We are ... so anxious that neither the police nor the security service pry into private lives, that there is no machinery for reporting the moral misbehavior of *[Cabinet]* ministers.... It is perhaps better thus, than we should have a "police state."
Alfred T. Denning, British jurist. Conlusion reached by his official report on the Profumo sex scandal. Quoted in *Life*, Oct. 11, 1963.

15. What a man thinks is of no concern to government.
William O. Douglas (1898-1980), U.S. Supreme Court Justice. *Speiser* v. *Randall*, 1957.

16. Various guarantees *[of the Constitution]* create zones of privacy. The right of association contained in the penumbra of the First Amendment is one, as we have seen. The Third Amendment in its protection against the quartering of soldiers "in any house" in time of peace without the consent of the owner is another facet of that privacy. The Fourth Amendment explicitly affirms the "right of the people to be secure in their persons, houses, papers, and effects against unreasonable searches and seizures." The Fifth Amendment in its Self-Incrimination Clause enables the citizen to create a zone of privacy which the government may not force him to surrender to his detriment.
William O. Douglas. *Griswold* v. *Connecticut*, 1965.

17. There is no communication between the Census Bureau and the IRS *[Internal Revenue Service]* and the INS *[Immigration and Naturalization Service]*. None. Zero. Zilch.
Mervyn Dymally, U.S. Congressman (D-CA). *Ask Congress*, July 31, 1988.

18. We are told here today that what the King of England can't do, the President of the United States can.
Samuel J. Ervin, Jr. (1896-1985), U.S. Congressman and U.S. Senator (D-NC). Response when John Erlichmann claimed that President Nixon could break and enter and burglarize in the interest of national security. Senate Watergate hearings, July 25, 1973.

19. Surely there is not a constitutional right to force unwilling people to listen.
Felix Frankfurter (1882-1965), U.S. Supreme Court Justice. *Saia* v. *New York*, 1947.

20. The right to be let alone is the underlying principle of the Constitution's Bill of Rights.
Erwin N. Griswold, dean, Harvard Law School, and U.S. Solicitor General. Address, Northwestern University School of Law, Evanston, IL, June 11, 1960; see also Louis D. Brandeis, *Olmstead* v. *United States*, 1927.

21. If you want the government off your back, get your hands out of its pockets.
Gary Hart, U.S. Senator (D-CO). PBS, *Firing Line*, Sept. 13, 1989.

22. It behooves every man who values liberty of conscience for himself, to resist invasions of it in the case of others.
Thomas Jefferson (1743-1826), 3rd President of the United States (Democratic Republican-VA). Letter to Dr. Benjamin Rush, 1803.

23. We should outlaw all wiretapping – public and private, wherever and whenever it occurs, except when the security of the nation itself is at stake – and then only with the strictest safeguards.
Lyndon B. Johnson (1908-1973), 36th President of the United States (D-TX). Quoted in Merle Miller, *Lyndon: An Oral Biography*, 1980.

24. Political liberty is good only so far as it produces private liberty.
Samuel Johnson (1709-1784), British writer and lexicographer. Quoted in James Boswell, *The Life of Samuel Johnson*, May 1768.

25. The issue of wiretapping raises the issue of the balance between human liberty and the requirements of national security. I would say that the weight should be on the side of human liberty and that if human liberty is ever to be infringed, the demonstration on the national security side must be overwhelming.
Henry M. Kissinger, U.S. Secretary of State and National Security Advisor (R). Senate Watergate hearings, Sept. 7, 1973.

26. When awesome investigative power is entrusted to so many individuals *[in Congress]*, it is extremely important that they wield it with a proper regard for your constitutional rights, especially your right to privacy.
Edward V. Long (1908-1972), U.S. Senator (D-MS). *Playboy*, Apr. 1967.

27. *[Genetic manipulation may lead to]* the possible emergence of an establishment program to invade the rights and privacy of individuals ... to "perfect" human individuals by "correcting" their genomes in conformity, perhaps, to an "ideal, white, Judeo-Christian, economically successful" genotype.

Salvador A. Luria (1913-1978), Nobel Laureate in Medicine (United States). Letter to the editor, *Science*, Nov. 1990.

28. Please be advised that I cannot authorize the installation of a microphone involving a trespass under existing law.

J. Howard McGrath (1903-1966), U.S. Attorney General (D). Memorandum to J. Edgar Hoover, Feb. 26, 1952.

29. They shall sit every man under his vine and under his fig tree, and none shall make them afraid.

Old Testament, *Micah* 4:4.

30. The right of individual privacy is essential to the well-being of a free society and shall not be infringed without the showing of a compelling state interest.

Montana Constitution, passed June 6, 1972.

31. This principle of confidentiality in presidential communications is what is at stake in the question of the tapes. I shall continue to oppose any efforts to destroy that principle, which is indispensable to the conduct of the presidency.

Richard M. Nixon, 37th President of the United States (R-CA). Television address to the American people, turning over White House tapes to Senate Watergate investigators, Aug. 15, 1973.

32. People are interested in the private lives of public officials as opposed to their public records.

Kirk O'Donnell, Director, Center for National Policy. Quoted in *The Washington Post*, May 28, 1989.

33. Big Brother is watching you.

George Orwell (Eric Blair) (1903-1950), British writer. *1984*, 1949.

34. Now, one of the most essential branches of English liberty is the freedom of one's house. A man's house is his castle; and whilst he is quiet, he is as well guarded as a prince in his castle.

James Otis (1725-1783), Member, Colonial Massachusetts legislature. Argument in Boston Court on writs of assistance, Feb. 24, 1761.

35. A man has a right to pass through this world, if he wills, without having his picture published, his business enterprises discussed, his successful experiments written up for the benefit of others, or his eccentricities commented upon, whether in handbills, circulars, catalogues, newspapers, or periodicals.

Alton Brooks Parker (1852-1926), Chief Justice, New York State Court of Appeals. *Roberson* v. *Rochester Folding Box Co.*, 1902.

36. The poorest man may in his cottage bid defiance to the forces of the Crown. It may be frail; its roof may shake; the wind may blow through it; the storm may enter; the rain may enter; but the King of England cannot enter; all his force dares not cross the threshold of the ruined tenement.

William Pitt, 1st Earl of Chatham (1708-1778), Secretary of State, Lord Privy Seal, and leader of the House of Commons, Great Britain. Speech on the Excise Bill, House of Lords. Quoted in Henry Peter Brougham, *Statesmen in the Time of George III*, First Series, 1839.

37. Civilization is the progress toward a society of privacy. The savage's whole existence is public, ruled by the laws of his tribe. Civilization is the process of setting man free from men.

Ayn Rand (1905-1982), American objectivist philosopher and writer. *The Fountainhead*, 1943.

38. He *[Calvin Coolidge]* is the first President to discover that what the American people want is to be left alone.

Will Rogers (1879-1935), American humorist. Newspaper column, 1924.

39. It is impossible to differentiate between what I say in my individual capacity from what I say as President.

Theodore Roosevelt (1858-1919), 26th President of the United States (R-NY). Letter to Bellamy Storer, 1903.

40. Strangely, so strangely, there was always between us, even in the bed we shared, the shadow of the prying state security.

Suzanne Rosenberg, Soviet trade official and writer. Description of her life as a minor Communist party official in Moscow, 1930's. *A Soviet Odyssey*, 1988.

41. There is but little privacy here *[at the White House]*.... The house belongs to the government and everyone feels at home, and they sometimes stalk into our bedroom and say they are looking at the house.

Joanna Rucker, niece of James K. Polk and frequent White House visitor. Letter, Apr. 7, 1846.

42. A kind of immolation of privacy and human dignity in symbolic opposition to drug use.

Antonin Scalia, U.S. Supreme Court Justice. Description of random drug testing through urinalysis. Quoted in *Newsweek*, June 26, 1989.

43. We fight for simple things, for the little things that are all-important. We fight for the right to lock our house doors and be sure that no bully with official sanction will break the lock.

Brehon Burke Somervell (1892-1955), General, U.S. Army. Quoted in *The New York Post*, Mar. 9, 1944.

44. The state has no business in the bedrooms of the nation.

Pierre Elliott Trudeau, Prime Minister of Canada (Liberal). Quoted in *The New York Times*, June 16, 1968.

45. Each day the public man or woman faces the excavation of his or her past, from which so few can claim a seamless purity.

Jack Valenti, Special Assistant to the President (D). "Who Dares to Enter the Political Woods?" *The New York Times*, June 4, 1989.

46. The uninvited ear of the government hears but is not often seen.

David Wise, American journalist. *The American Police State*, 1976.

Chapter 81

Public Office

1. I will undoubtedly have to seek what is happily known as gainful employment, which I am glad to say does not describe holding public office.
   Dean Acheson (1893-1971), U.S. Secretary of State (D). Comment shortly before the end of his term. Quoted in *Time*, Dec. 22, 1952.

2. My return to public life in a subordinate station is disagreeable to my family, and disapproved by some of my friends.
   [After serving as President, Adams won a seat in the House of Representatives.]
   John Quincy Adams (1767-1848), 6th President of the United States (Ind-MA). *Diary*, Nov. 6, 1830.

3. A thick skin is a gift from God.
   Konrad Adenauer (1876-1967), Chancellor of West Germany. 1964.

4. There is no leisure about politics.
   Thomas Aquinas (c.1225-1274), Italian scholastic philosopher. *Commentary on the Ethics*, X.

5. The son of the ruler is an orphan.
   Arabic proverb.

6. To plunder, to lie, to show your ass, are the three essentials for climbing high.
   Aristophanes (c.450-385 B.C.), Greek dramatist. *The Knights*.

7. No man is fit to be a Senator unless he is willing to surrender his political life for a great principle.
   Henry Fountain Ashurst (1874-1962), U.S. Senator (D-AZ). Quoted in Morris K. Udall, *Too Funny to Be President*, 1988.

8. It is royal to do good and be abused.
   Marcus Aurelius (121-180), Emperor of Rome and Stoic philosopher. *Meditations*.

9. Men in great places are thrice servants: servants of the sovereign or state, servants of fame, and servants of business.
   Francis Bacon, 1st Baron Verulam and Viscount St. Albans (1561-1626), Lord Chancellor of England. *Essays*, "Of Great Place," 1597.

10. It is a miserable state of mind, to have few things to desire and many things to fear; and yet that commonly is the case of Kings.
    Francis Bacon. *Essays*, "Of Empire," 1597.

11. Professionalism is friendly to the qualified performance of precise tasks, but unfriendly to those accommodations and bargains that give coherence and direction to general public objectives.
    Stephen K. Bailey, dean, Maxwell School of Business, Syracuse University, Syracuse, NY, and President, American Society of Public Administration. *Agenda for the Nation*, 1968.

12. The pleasure politicians take in their limelight pleases me with a sort of pleasure I get when I see a child's eyes gleam over a new toy.
    Hilaire Belloc (1870-1953), British writer and political biographer. *A Conversation with a Cat*.

13. Life in Washington is pressure.
    William J. Bennett, Director, Office of National Drug Control Policy, and U.S. Secretary of Education (R). Quoted on NBC, *Meet the Press*, Mar. 19, 1989.

14. It is very rarely that a man of brains, honor, and good manners gets into public life. In most instances the man who holds an office is a rogue, a vulgarian, or an ignoramus; commonly he is all three.
    Ambrose Bierce (1842-1914?), American journalist. *Wasp*, Jan. 13, 1883.

15. I want to get into politics so I can make a decent salary and do something that isn't all that difficult. But if politics don't work out I'm going to be a welder.
    Timothy Birard, high school junior and candidate for Weymouth, MA, school committee. Quoted in *The Boston Globe*, Mar. 1, 1989.

16. In the atmosphere existing in this country today, the charge that someone is Communist is so common that hardly anyone in public life escapes it.
    Hugo L. Black (1886-1971), U.S. Senator (D-AL), and U.S. Supreme Court Justice. *Wilkinson* v. *United States*, 1960.

17. The great happiness in life is not to donate but to serve.
Louis D. Brandeis (1856-1941), U.S. Supreme Court Justice. Speech, Boston, MA, Mar. 20, 1913.

18. I was attracted and repelled by what I saw of politics in my father's house. Attracted by the adventure, the opportunity. Repelled by the grasping, the artificiality, the obvious manipulation and role-playing, the repetition of emotion without feeling, particularly that: the repetition of emotion.
Edmund G. (Jerry) Brown, Jr., Governor of California (D). *Thoughts*, 1976.

19. It is hard to manage a personal life when everything you do is amplified in the public media.
Edmund G. (Jerry) Brown, Jr. Interview, CNN, *Larry King Live*, Aug. 9, 1989.

20. I wouldn't want to be in the government. I wouldn't want people writing about me the way I write about them.
Art Buchwald, American political humorist. Interview, CNN, *Evans & Novak*, Dec. 22, 1990.

21. Government demands the finest training as well as the finest talent, for the successful management of its affairs.
John W. Burgess (1844-1931), American political scientist and civil service reformer. Letter to Frederick A. P. Barnard, Feb. 20, 1880.

22. I could not permit my silence and my inaction to be construed as condonation.... With my tongue tied by the confidentiality demanded of me by law, there was only one way I could make a statement that something was wrong. I chose it. I resigned.
Arnold I. Burns, U.S. Deputy Attorney General (R). Explanation of his resignation from the Justice Department under U.S. Attorney General Edwin Meese III. Testimony, Senate Judiciary Committee, July 26, 1988.

23. The very essence of a free government consists in considering offices as public trusts, bestowed for the good of the country, and not for the benefit of an individual or party.
John C. Calhoun (1782-1850), U.S. Congressman (D-SC), U.S. Senator, U.S. Secretary of War, U.S. Secretary of State, and Vice President of the United States. Speech, July 13, 1835.

24. Men who have greatness within them don't go into politics.
Albert Camus (1913-1960), Nobel Laureate in Literature (France). *Notebooks, 1935-1942*.

25. I think he *[President Carter]* is around too many people that kiss his ass all the time.
Billy Carter (1937-1988), President Carter's brother. Rifkin and Howard, *Redneck Power: The Wit and Wisdom of Billy Carter*, 1977.

26. We want to bring back to Washington people who are more interested in public service than they are in private gain.
Jimmy Carter, 39th President of the United States (D-GA). Address, Democratic National Convention, Atlanta, GA, July 18, 1988.

27. It only hurts for a day.
William J. Casey (1913-1987), Director, Central Intelligence Agency. Remark on public criticism. Quoted in Joseph E. Persico, *Casey: From the OSS to the CIA*, 1990.

28. Can we wonder that all has gone ill with us when our love of office survives in our very ruin?
Marcus Porcius Uticensis Cato (Cato the Younger) (95-46 B.C.), Roman soldier and philosopher. Quoted in Plutarch, *The Parallel Lives: Cato the Younger*.

29. Boy, the things I do for England.
Charles, Prince of Wales and Duke of Cornwall, Remark on sampling snake meat in Australia, 1974.

30. If a man becomes an official, even his chickens and dogs will go to heaven.
Chinese proverb.

31. Fools are more to be feared than the wicked.
Christina (1626-1689), Queen of Sweden. *Maxims*.

32. *[Grover Cleveland]* had a sort of patent way of shaking hands which he probably invented for self-protection. He grabbed the visitor's hand, gave it a slight squeeze, and dropped it like a hot potato. He never under any circumstances whatsoever permitted a visitor to grip his large, fat hand.
James B. (Champ) Clark (1850-1921), U.S. Congressman (D-MO), Speaker of the House, and U.S. Baseball Commissioner. *My Quarter Century of American Politics*, 1920.

33. One of the luxuries of a politician's life is that you see yourself as others see you.
Joe Clark, Prime Minister of Canada (Conservative). Quoted in *Barnes & Noble Book of Quotations*, 1987.

34. Government is a trust, and the officers of the government are trustees; and both the trust and trustees are created for the benefit of the public.

Henry Clay (1777-1852), U.S. Senator (National Republican and Whig-KY), Speaker of the House, and U.S. Secretary of State. Speech, Lexington, KY, May 16, 1829.

35. The conduct of organized humanity requires brains, and, furthermore, educated brains. The right kind of temperament is equally essential. You wish to persuade, to overcome resistance, to impose your will in virtue of a heroic endurance, and you encounter every form of accusation and every degree of hatred with all their consequences. Is it not a task to make any man hesitate?
Georges Clemenceau (1841-1929), Premier of France and journalist. *In the Evening of My Thought*, 1929.

36. Officeholders are the agents of the people, not their masters.
Grover Cleveland (1837-1908), 22nd and 24th President of the United States (D-NY). Speech, July 14, 1886.

37. The damned everlasting clatter for offices makes me feel like resigning.
Grover Cleveland. Remark, 1894.

38. The only problem with running for office is, once you are elected you have to serve.
J. Marshall Coleman, Attorney General of Virginia (R). Remark after his election, 1977.

39. A mayor is a political leader for a city. He doesn't know anything necessarily about city administration, and furthermore he shouldn't have to.
L. P. Cookingham, City Manager, Fort Worth, TX, and Kansas City, MO. Quoted in *Governing the States and Localities*, Feb. 1988.

40. It was the saddest day of my life.
Norris H. Cotton (1901-1989), U.S. Congressman and U.S. Senator (R-NH). When President Nixon called him on the morning of Aug. 4, 1974, to say good-bye. Quoted in his obituary, *The Washington Post*, Feb. 25, 1989.

41. There is no worse heresy than that the office sanctifies the holder of it.
John Dahlberg, 1st Baron Acton (1834-1902), British historian. Letter to Bishop Mandell Creighton, Apr. 3, 1887.

42. No public character has ever stood the revelation of private utterance and correspondence.
John Dahlberg. Letter to Bishop Mandell Creighton, Apr. 5, 1887.

43. They have vilified me, they have crucified me – yes, they have even criticized me!
Richard J. Daley (1902-1976), Mayor of Chicago, IL (D). Quoted in *The New York Times*, Feb. 21, 1989.

44. Success is the child of Audacity.
Benjamin Disraeli, 1st Earl of Beaconsfield (1804-1881), Prime Minister of Great Britain (Conservative). *The Rise of Iskander*, 1834.

45. Yes! I have climbed to the top of that greasy pole.
Benjamin Disraeli. Remark upon becoming Prime Minister, 1868.

46. It would be all right with me. I'd probably get a car and driver out of it.
Robert J. Dole, U.S. Senator (R-KS). Response when asked how he felt about the possibility of his wife, U.S. Secretary of Transportation Elizabeth Dole, becoming Vice President. Quoted in *Newsweek*, Apr. 4, 1988.

47. If you accept the privilege of public service, you had better understand the responsibilities of public service.
Michael Dukakis, Governor of Massachusetts (D). Presidential nomination acceptance speech, Democratic National Convention, Atlanta, GA, July 21, 1988.

48. I think that at the close of next November, I ought to hang up the boxing gloves.
George Dunne, President, Cook County, IL, Board of Aldermen. Quoted in *The Chicago Tribune*, Nov. 29, 1989.

49. If people are going to stay in office because of the money they get there, apart from the attractions of political life, they are going to be more difficult than ever to remove.
Anthony Eden (1897-1977), Prime Minister of Great Britain (Conservative). Memorandum to the Chancellor of the Exchequer, July 13, 1955.

50. I have found it impossible to carry the heavy burden of responsibility and to discharge my duties as King as I would wish to, without the help and support of the woman I love.
Edward VIII, Duke of Windsor (1894-1972), King of Great Britain. Abdication speech, Dec. 11, 1936.

51. To be elected to public office requires no qualifications.
Ed Eilert, Mayor of Overland, KS. Quoted in *Governing the States and Localities*, Feb. 1988.

52. I am deeply moved, though also sad and abashed, that it is impossible for me to accept this offer. Since all my life I have been dealing with the

world of objects, I have neither the natural ability nor the experience necessary to deal with human beings and to carry out official functions.

Albert Einstein (1879-1955), Nobel Laureate in Physics (Switzerland). Response when offered the position of President of Israel. Letter to Abba Eban, Nov. 18, 1952.

53. Politics is a profession; a serious, complicated and, in a true sense, a noble one.

Dwight D. Eisenhower (1890-1969), 34th President of the United States (R-KS). Quoted in *The New Dictionary of American Thoughts*, 1957.

54. You get burned out very quickly. You can sprint one hundred yards, but you can't sprint a mile, and these jobs are all sprints.

Stuart Eizenstat, presidential assistant and chief domestic policy advisor to President Carter (D). Explanation of the short average tenure of high-level government jobs, 1982.

55. Why are people so sensitive about the reputation of General *[George]* McClellan? There is always something rotten about a sensitive reputation. Besides, is not General McClellan an American citizen? And is it not the first attribute and distinction of an American to be abused and slandered as long as he is heard of?

Ralph Waldo Emerson (1803-1882), American writer. *Journals*, July 1862.

56. Take egoism out and you would castrate the benefactors. Luther, Mirabeau, Napoléon, John Adams; and our nearer eminent public servants, – *[Horace]* Greeley, Theodore Parker, *[Henry]* Ward Beecher, Horace Mann, *[William Lloyd]* Garrison would lose their vigor.

Ralph Waldo Emerson. *Journals*, June 1863.

57. To be great is to be misunderstood.

Ralph Waldo Emerson. *Essays*, First Series, "Self-Reliance," 1865.

58. Every hero becomes a bore at last.

Ralph Waldo Emerson. *Representative Men*, "Uses of Great Men," 1876.

59. In politics and in trade, bruisers and pirates are of better promise than talkers and clerks.

Ralph Waldo Emerson. *Essays*, Second Series, "Manners," 1876.

60. It's all in the day's work. (*C'est le métier*.)

Eugénie Marie, Comtesse de Teba (1826-1920), Empress of France. Remark after a bomb destroyed her carriage, killed ten persons and wounded 140, but failed to kill her or her husband, Napoléon III. Paris, Jan. 14, 1858.

61. I am working for the time when unqualified blacks, browns and women join the unqualified men in running our government.

Frances (Sissy) Farenthold, Texas State Legislator (D). Quoted in *The Los Angeles Times*, Sept. 18, 1974.

62. Inside the institution *[Congress]* there's a sense of puzzlement that incumbents have a lock.... The members feel they are targets of a conspiracy, using slick ad techniques and misinformation, to remove them from office, no matter how hard they have worked.

Thomas S. Foley, U.S. Congressman and Speaker of the House (D-WA). Quoted in *The Washington Post*, Dec. 9, 1990.

63. If they think it's such a sacrifice to go into public service, then they should stay the heck out.

Barney Frank, U.S. Congressman (D-MA). ABC, *This Week*, July 31, 1988.

64. If you really wish to be independent and make your own judgments about everything important, it is difficult to be a good team player – because a team has different criteria for making judgments about an issue.

J. William Fulbright, U.S. Senator (D-AR). Comment on being a Cabinet member. *The Price of Empire*, 1989.

65. My God. What is there about this place *[the White House]* that a man should ever want to get into it?

James A. Garfield (1831-1881), 20th President of the United States (R-OH). Quoted in John M. Taylor, *Garfield of Ohio*, 1970.

66. I never did care much for the upholstery of office.

James A. Garfield. Attributed.

67. The highest of distinctions is service to others.

George VI (1895-1952), King of Great Britain and Ireland, and Emperor of India. Coronation greeting, May 12, 1937.

68. It is hardly possible to believe that one is not the greatest scoundrel on earth when one is assured of it on all sides on such excellent authority.

William E. Gladstone (1809-1898), Prime Minister of Great Britian (Liberal). Reaction to his then-current low popularity. Letter to Lord Aberdeen, 1855.

69. We underrate their honesty and overrate their intelligence.

Edwin Lawrence Godkin (1831-1902), editor, *New York Evening Post* and founder, *The Nation*. In reference to new members of the House of Representatives, 1871.

70. There is nothing wrong with a political joke as long as it doesn't get elected.

Miles E. Godwin, Jr., Governor of Virginia (R). Remark to reporters, 1970.

71. Genius develops in quiet places; character out of the full current of human life.

Johann Wolfgang von Goethe (1749-1832), German poet and dramatist. *Torquato Tasso*, I, 1790.

72. If they chased every man or woman out of this town who has shacked up with somebody else or got drunk, there wouldn't be any government left in Washington.

Barry M. Goldwater, U.S. Senator (R-AZ). Comment on the Senate debate over the confirmation of John Tower as U.S. Secretary of Defense. Press statement, Mar. 4, 1989.

73. I was assailed so bitterly that I hardly knew whether I was running for the presidency or the penitentiary.

Ulysses S. Grant (1822-1885), 18th President of the United States (R-OH). Remark after his campaign for a third term, 1880.

74. *[Impeachment is a]* method of national inquest into the conduct of public men.

Alexander Hamilton (1755-1804), Member, Continental Congress and Constitutional Convention, and U.S. Secretary of the Treasury (Federalist-NY). *The Federalist*, No. 65, Mar. 7, 1788.

75. The public official must pick his way nicely, must learn to placate though not to yield too much, to have the art of honeyed words but not to seem neutral, and above all to keep constantly audible, visible, likable, even kissable.

Learned Hand (1872-1961), Federal Judge. Mar. 8, 1932.

76. I believe that the people want an ordinary man as President, being a little tired of supermen.

Warren G. Harding (1865-1923), 29th President of the United States (R-OH). Interview, *New York Herald*, June 12, 1920.

77. For God's sake, man, when you leave State, you'll be overwhelmed with offers. You'll be rich.

W. Averell Harriman (1891-1986), Governor of New York (D), U.S. Ambassador-at-Large, and U.S. Secretary of Commerce. Advice to Dean Rusk, who hesitated about becoming President Kennedy's Secretary of State. Quoted in David Halberstam, *The Best and the Brightest*, 1969.

78. When I first went to Washington, I thought, what is l'il ole me doing with these ninety-nine great people? Now I ask myself, what am I doing with those ninety-nine jerks?

S. I. Hayakawa (1907-1992), U.S. Senator (R-CA). Quoted in Fred Metcalf, *The Penguin Dictionary of Modern Humorous Quotations*, 1986.

79. Not too much hard work, plenty of time to read, good society, etcetera.

Rutherford B. Hayes (1822-1893), 19th President of the United States (R-OH). Remark when he was Governor of Ohio. Quoted in Harry Barnard, *Rutherford B. Hayes and His America*, 1954.

80. I am heartedly tired of this life of bondage, responsibility, and toil.

Rutherford B. Hayes. Remark when he was President. *Diary*, 1879.

81. I regard office as not an end but an opportunity.

William Randolph Hearst (1863-1951), U.S. Congressman (D-NY); founder, Independence League Party; journalist; and publisher. Debate with Elihu Root, Elmira, NY, 1906.

82. Bring back that better era of the republic in which, when men consecrated themselves to the public service, they utterly abnegated all selfish purposes.

Abram S. Hewitt (1882-1903), U.S. Congressman and Mayor of New York City (D). Speech, House of Representatives, May 25, 1876.

83. Politics can bring a lot of happiness, but you can also experience a lot of unhappiness.

Harri Holkeri, Prime Minister of Finland. Quoted in *The New York Times Magazine*, May 8, 1988.

84. When people have recently asked me my profession, I have not dared to reply.

François Hollande, Member of National Assembly, France. Quoted in *The New York Times*, Dec. 23, 1990.

85. They say his arm is so lame at overexercise in shaking hands that he can no longer use it in that way.

Philip Hone (1780-1851), Mayor of New York City (Whig). Remark about President-elect William H. Harrison. *Diary*, Feb. 11, 1841.

86. Men can make a living with far more satisfaction and many less wounds to the souls at some other calling.

Herbert Hoover (1874-1964), 31st President of the United States (R-IA). Quoted in Exhibit, "39 Men".

87. I am busier than a whore working two beds.
C. P. Howe, Minister of Trade and Commerce, Canada. Quoted on PBS, *Canada: True North*, Sept. 12, 1988.

88. May the future bring all the best to you, your family and friends, and may your mother never find out where you work.
William L. Hungate, U.S. Congressman (D-MO). Farewell address, 1976.

89. My best experience was my business training.
George W. P. Hunt (1859-1934), Governor of Arizona (D). Quoted in John L. Myers, *The Arizona Governors, 1912-1990*, 1989.

90. I am wearied with public life. I have been accused of acts I never committed, of crimes I never even thought of.
Andrew Jackson (1767-1845), 7th President of the United States (D-TN). Letter to President Monroe, 1821.

91. There is not a single crowned head in Europe whose talents or merits would entitle him to be elected a vestryman by the people of any parish in America.
Thomas Jefferson (1743-1826), 3rd President of the United States (Democratic Republican-VA). Letter from Paris to George Washington, May 2, 1788.

92. I find the pain of a little censure, even when it is unfounded, is more acute than the pleasure of much praise.
Thomas Jefferson. Remark to Francis Hopkinson, 1789.

93. When a man assumes a public trust, he should consider himself as public property.
Thomas Jefferson. Remark to Baron Alexander von Humboldt, in the President's office, 1807. Quoted in B. L. Rayner, *Life of Jefferson*, 1834.

94. With the rashness of ignorance the uninitiated dare to dabble in affairs of state.
John of Salisbury (c.1115-1180), English ecclesiastic and scholar. *Policraticus*, I.

95. I'm tired. I'm tired of feeling rejected by the American people. I'm tired of waking up in the middle of the night worrying about the *[Vietnam]* war.
Lyndon B. Johnson (1908-1973), 36th President of the United States (D-TX). Remark to a friend. Quoted in *Newsweek*, Apr. 15, 1968.

96. Mr. *[Judah P.]* Benjamin, unquestionably, will have great influence with the President *[Jefferson Davis]*, for he has studied his character most carefully. He will be familiar not only with his "likes" but especially his "dislikes."
J. B. Jones (1810-1866), clerk, Confederate War Department. *Diary*, I, 1866.

97. If people seek the country's most important job, then they should be prepared to submit to a "job interview" – a debate that allows voters to observe candidates in environments not of their own choosing, to hear them respond to questions they did not select, and to see them sweat under a little pressure without the ministrations of media advisors.
Jim Karayn, presidential debate advisor, League of Women Voters. *The Washington Post*, Sept. 25, 1988.

98. I don't think you're going to be a success in anything if you think about losing, whether it's in sports or in politics.
Edward M. Kennedy, U.S. Senator (D-MA). Quoted in Lee Green, *Sportswit*, 1984.

99. They even cut your hair free of charge.
John F. Kennedy (1917-1963), 35th President of the United States (D-MA). Remark to his family when he first entered the Senate, 1953.

100. More Nebraskans approve of her being in the executive mansion than me being there.
J. Robert Kerrey, Governor of Nebraska and U.S. Senator (D). Remark on his dating of actress Deborah Winger, 1987.

101. Scholars are of all men least fitted for politics and its ways. The reason for this is that they are accustomed to intellectual speculation, the search for concepts, and their abstraction and clarification in the mind. These operations aim to attaining the universal aspect of things, not those particular to their material content and peculiarity.... Their judgments and views remain purely speculative.... They do not, in general, seek to make their thoughts conform to external reality, but rather deduce what ought to be outside from what goes on in their minds.... The ordinary sound man, however, whose mind is not given to such speculation ... judges events, and men, and things on their merits and according to the realities of the situation.
Ibn Khaldoun (1332-1406), Arab historian and diplomat. *Kitab al-Ibar* (*The Universal History*).

102. Every politician or public official who is single, male or female, at some time in their lives will be the subject of a slander alleging that they are homosexual or lesbian. I believe that there is nothing wrong with homosexuality. It's whatever God made you. It happens I'm a heterosexual.

Edward I. Koch, U.S. Congressman and Mayor of New York City (D). Quoted in *The New York Times*, Mar. 17, 1989.

103. There is no better job.

Edward I. Koch. Comment after losing his bid for a fourth term as mayor, Sept. 13, 1989.

104. If I am not offered the job of Secretary of Health and Human Services, I will be disappointed for a few days and grateful for the rest of my life.

C. Everett Koop, U.S. Surgeon General. Remark to friends, 1989.

105. If you're in public life, a certain percentage of what you do must be done on television.

Ted Koppel, American TV journalist. 1989.

106. To enjoy a prince's favor does not rule out the possibility of merit, but neither does it argue for its existence.

Jean de La Bruyère (1644-1696), French writer. *Les "Caractères" de Théophraste*, 1688.

107. Politics, like theater, is one of those things where you've got to be wise enough to know when to leave.

Richard D. Lamm, Governor of Colorado (D). Comment when retiring after three terms as governor. Quoted in *U.S. News & World Report*, Jan. 26, 1987.

108. High rank is – like one's body – a source of great trouble.

Lao-tzu (c. 604-531 B.C.), Chinese philosopher and founder of Taoism. *Tao Te Ching*.

109. There are no words which men detest more than "solitary," "desolate," and "hapless." Yet Lords and Princes use them to describe themselves.

Lao-tzu. *Ibid.*

110. No one with a weak heart or delicate digestion should seek the job *[Secretary of the Navy]*.

John F. Lehman, U.S. Secretary of the Navy. *Command of the Seas*, 1989.

111. Being elected to Congress, though I am very grateful to our friends for having done it, has not pleased me as much as I expected.

Abraham Lincoln (1809-1865), 16th President of the United States (R-IL). Letter to Joshua F. Speed, Oct. 22, 1846.

112. I have endured a great deal of ridicule without much malice; and have received a great deal of kindness not quite free from ridicule.

Abraham Lincoln. Letter to James H. Hackett, Nov. 2, 1863.

113. Being Interior Secretary is like being in a sack full of cats clawing at each other.

Manuel Lujan, Jr., U.S. Congressman and U.S. Secretary of the Interior (R-NM). Speech, National Press Club, Washington, DC, June 29, 1990.

114. No man can be a competent legislator who does not add to an upright intention and a sound judgment a certain degree of knowledge on the subjects on which he is to legislate.

James Madison (1751-1836), 4th President of the United States (Democratic Republican-VA). *The Federalist*, No. 53, Feb. 9, 1788.

115. I suppose John ought to be the center of my life, but he's not because he's out of it so much of the time.

Norma Major, wife of John Major, Prime Minister of Great Britain. Quoted in *The Washington Post*, Nov. 28, 1990.

116. The presidential function is difficult and full of responsibility. It calls from the incumbent a plenitude of his physical vigor. I am aware I am no longer strong enough for the task. Wherefore, I resign.

Tomas G. Masaryk (1850-1937), 1st President of Czechoslovakia. Letter of resignation, Dec. 14, 1935.

117. Somebody has to try it.

Tadeusz Mazowiecki, Prime Minister of Poland. Remark alluding to the difficulty of forming a new government. Quoted in *The New York Times*, Aug. 19, 1989.

118. I lived with uncertainty.

Robert S. McNamara, U.S. Secretary of Defense (D). Testimony in *Westmoreland* v. *CBS, Inc.*, 1984.

119. The saddest life is that of a political aspirant under democracy. His failure is ignominious and his success is disgraceful.

H. L. Mencken (1880-1956), American journalist. *The Baltimore Evening Sun*, Dec. 9, 1929.

120. If I didn't have the constitution – and maybe the mentality – of a horse, I couldn't keep going.

Robert G. Menzies (1894-1978), Prime Minister of Australia (Liberal). Quoted in *The Wit of Sir Robert Menzies*, 1966.

121. The man of public life has always at command a sure resource against this danger *[losing political battles]* – that is, retirement.

Klemens von Metternich (1773-1859), Austrian statesman and diplomat. Quoted by Anthony Trollope, *Vienna and the Austrians*, 1838.

122. Since they *[political leaders]* take the risks, they need the laurels.
Jean Monnet (1888-1979), French statesman. Quoted in *The New York Times,* Nov. 13, 1988.

123. You're going to find that, intellectually, they *[governors]* as a whole are a cut or two above what they were ten or twenty years ago.
Arch A. Moore, Jr., Governor of West Virginia (R). Quoted in *Governing the States and Localities,* Feb. 1988.

124. Congressmen will be earning five times what the average American does. That's a hell of a gap between the rulers and the ruled.
Ralph Nader, American consumer advocate. Comment on a proposed pay increase for members of Congress. Quoted on National Public Radio, *The Diane Rheem Show,* Jan. 6, 1989.

125. Great ambition is the passion of a great character.
Napoléon I (1769-1821), military leader and Emperor of France. *Maxims.*

126. The government can't run unless we get the best and the brightest.
Constance Newman, Director, U.S. Office of Personnel Management (R). Interview, PBS, *MacNeil-Lehrer News Hour,* July 4, 1990.

127. ... not brains, loyalty.
Richard M. Nixon, 37th President of the United States (R-CA). Memorandum to George Bush, then U.S. Ambassador to the United Nations. Statement of qualifications he wanted for people on Bush's staff, 1971.

128. Only death or the people of Arizona will remove me from office.
[The governor had ALS disease but continued to work until his death.]
Sidney P. Osborn (1864-1948), Governor of Arizona (D). Quoted in John L. Myers, *The Arizona Governors, 1912-1990,* 1989.

129. No person in the public service is for that reason under any obligations to contribute to any political fund, or to render any political service, and that he will not be removed or otherwise prejudiced for refusing to do so.
George H. Pendleton (1825-1889), U.S. Congressman and U.S. Senator (D-OH). Introduction to the Civil Service Act, Dec. 6, 1881.

130. Public office is the last refuge of the incompetent.
Boies Penrose (1860-1921), U.S. Senator (R-PA). Quoted in *Collier's Weekly,* Feb. 14, 1931.

131. There are some politicians whom the applause of the multitude has deluded into the belief that they are really statesmen.... When a man cannot measure, and a great many others who cannot measure, declare that he is four cubits high, can he help believing them?
Plato (427-347 B.C.), Greek philosopher. *The Republic,* IV.

132. When a man works in politics, he should get something out of it.
George Washington Plunkitt (1842-1924), leader, Tammany Hall, New York City (D). Quoted in William L. Riordon, *Plunkitt of Tammany Hall,* 1905.

133. I stood on my feet shaking hands with the immense crowd from half past eleven o'clock A.M., till three o'clock P.M.... I was very much exhausted by the fatigue of the day.
James K. Polk (1795-1849), 11th President of the United States (D-TN). *Diary,* Jan. 1, 1847.

134. I expect to go back to a nice quiet foxhole where I can serve my country in a more comfortable and perhaps less exposed position.
Colin L. Powell, General, U.S. Army, National Security Advisor, and Chairman, Joint Chiefs of Staff. In reference to his plans when a new administration came into office. Speech, World Affairs Council, Los Angeles, CA, July 19, 1988.

135. We just get out of touch with our constituency if we get $135,000.
William Proxmire, U.S. Senator (D-WI). Reaction to a proposal to raise congressional salaries. Interview, NBC, *Meet the Press,* Dec. 25, 1988.

136. You get killed quicker in government doing your duty than turning your back.
[After arresting renegade Mormons and their polygamous families at Short Creek, he lost the governorship in the next election.]
John Howard Pyle (1878-1987), Governor of Arizona (R). Quoted in John L. Myers, *The Arizona Governors, 1912-1990,* Heritage, 1989.

137. The reins of state may be held by the son of the poorest man, if possessed of abilities equal to that important station.
David Ramsay (1749-1815), Member, Continental Congress (PA). *Orations on the Advantages of American Independence.*

138. I wish that just one of them had run for sheriff in his home county.
Samuel T. Rayburn (1882-1961), U.S. Congressman and Speaker of the House (D-TX). Comment to

Lyndon B. Johnson on President Kennedy's closest advisors, 1961.

139. There are times that I've wondered how you could do the job if you weren't an actor.
Ronald Reagan, 40th President of the United States (R-CA). Interview with David Brinkley, ABC, Dec. 22, 1988.

140. The best minds are not in government. If they were, business would hire them away.
Ronald Reagan. Quoted in *Forbes*, Apr. 16, 1990.

141. It's an ear job, not an eye job.
Donald T. Regan, U.S. Secretary of the Treasury and White House Chief of Staff (R). Description of his job as White House Chief of Staff. Quoted in *The New York Times*, Jan. 25, 1985.

142. My opponents claim that I have a criminal record. This may be true, but no one can accuse me of crimes against the people of Jacques Cartier.
Léo Rémillard, Mayor of Jacques Cartier, Quebec, Canada. Quoted in Pierre Sévigny, *This Game of Politics*, 1965.

143. Like any other human being I goof up occasionally. My family has to read that in the paper.
Charles E. Roemer III, U.S. Congressman and Governor of Louisiana (D). Interview, C-SPAN, Sept. 4, 1989.

144. It is of enormous personal satisfaction to try and do the right thing and occasionally get it done.
Charles E. Roemer III. *Ibid.*

145. We can't all be heroes because somebody has to sit on the curb and clap as they go by.
Will Rogers (1879-1935), American humorist. Quoted in Laurence J. Peter, *Peters's Quotations*, 1977.

146. The cost of being in politics is fine for one's ideals, but it is very high in personal sacrifice, I think.
Anna Eleanor Roosevelt (1884-1962), First Lady and U.S. Delegate to the United Nations. Letter, Oct. 3, 1949.

147. The first twelve years are the hardest.
Franklin D. Roosevelt (1882-1945), 32nd President of the United States (D-NY). Remark on the eve of his fourth inauguration. Press conference, Jan. 19, 1945.

148. If the people should feel that I was the instrument to be used at this time, I should accept *[the presidential nomination]* even though I knew that I should be broken and cast aside in the using.... The right motto for any man is "Spend and be spent"; and if, in order to do a job worth doing from a public standpoint, he must pay with his own life, actual life on the field of battle, or political life in civic affairs, he must not grudge the payment.
Theodore Roosevelt (1858-1919), 26th President of the United States (R-NY). Letter to Frank A. Munsey, Jan. 16, 1912.

149. There isn't a lot of free time here. It's not like a normal life.
Warren B. Rudman, U.S. Senator (R-NH). Interview, C-SPAN, *American Profile*, May 27, 1991.

150. How are the mighty fallen.
Old Testament, 2 *Samuel* 1:27.

151. The World dealeth with Ministers of State as they do with ill Fiddlers, ready to kick them down Stairs for playing ill, though few of the Fault-finders understand their Music enough to be good Judges.
George Savile, 1st Marquess of Halifax (1633-1695), Lord Privy Seal of England. *Political Thoughts and Reflections*, 1750.

152. State-Business is a cruel Trade; Good-nature is a Bungler in it.
George Savile. *Ibid.*

153. Serving Princes will make Men proud at first, and humble at last.
George Savile. *Ibid.*

154. I have a brain and a uterus and I use both.
Patricia R. Schroeder, U.S. Congresswoman (D-CO). Quoted in *The New York Times*, May 6, 1977.

155. No. But then most congresswomen don't have twenty-five-year-old lifeguards throwing themselves at their feet around this place.
Patricia R. Schroeder. Response when asked if she had ever committed adultery. Quoted in *Newsweek*, Aug. 10, 1987.

156. He that would live by traffic *[public or private business]* must hold himself at the disposal of everyone claiming business with him.
Walter Scott (1771-1832), Scottish writer. *Ivanhoe*, 1819.

157. An office holder who loses contact with his constituents soon goes from *Who's Who* to "Who's that?"
William L. Scott, U.S. Congressman and U.S. Senator (R-VA). Quoted in Skubik and Short, *Republican Humor*, 1976.

158. I only ran for mayor because the others were dodos.

John Sewell, Mayor of Toronto, Canada. Quoted in *Toronto Life*, Jan. 1980.

159. Some are born great, some achieve greatness, and some have greatness thrust upon 'em.

William Shakespeare (1564-1616), English writer. *Twelfth Night*, II, v.

160. Titles distinguish the mediocre, embarrass the superior, and are disgraced by the inferior.

George Bernard Shaw (1856-1950), Nobel Laureate in Literature (Great Britain). *Maxims for Revolutionists*, 1903.

161. The written Constitution and the aspirations of democracy are joined together only by the concept of public service – not as the goal, but as the necessary means of fulfilling our common purpose as a community and nation.

George P. Shultz, U.S. Secretary of State (R). Speech, Washington, DC, Jan. 9, 1989.

162. In the closing hours of the campaign Mr. Whitman's sole reply seems to be that I am unfit for the office of Governor because I was born in a tenement on the East Side. It is true. In fact it is one of the few things he said which is true. I not only admit it, but I glory in it. That is one of the things which distinguishes America from all other countries under the sun.

Alfred E. Smith (1873-1944), Governor of New York (D). Campaign speech, New York City, Nov. 1918.

163. Why would Bush want me?

David H. Souter, U.S. Supreme Court Justice. Response when he heard he was being considered by the President for nomination to the U.S. Supreme Court. Quoted in *Newsweek*, Aug. 6, 1990.

164. Your public servants serve you right; indeed, often they serve you better than your apathy and indifference deserve.

Adlai E. Stevenson (1900-1965), Governor of Illinois (D), and U.S. Ambassador to the United Nations. Speech, Los Angeles, CA, Sept. 11, 1952.

165. Flattery is all right so long as you don't inhale.

Adlai E. Stevenson. Remark to reporters, 1961.

166. I regret that I have but one law firm to give to my country.

Adlai E. Stevenson. Comment upon learning that several of his Chicago law firm partners had been invited to join the Kennedy administration, 1962.

167. In a political world one has to accept things that I might perhaps privately wish were otherwise.

Louis W. Sullivan, U.S. Secretary of Health and Human Services. Interview with *Atlanta Constitution* reporter Kevin Sack, 1989.

168. The foundation of the government of a nation must be built upon the rights of the people, but the administration must be trusted to experts.

Sun Yat-sen (1867-1925), Chinese nationalist leader. *The Three Principles of the People*.

169. I've always felt that you should leave when people still think you should stay.

Helen Suzmann, Liberal Party leader, South Africa. Comment on her retirement from politics. Quoted on PBS, *MacNeil-Lehrer News Hour*, Oct. 16, 1989.

170. Censure is the tax a man pays to the public for being eminent.

Jonathan Swift (1667-1745), Irish clergyman and satirist. *Thoughts on Various Subjects*, 1706.

171. Ambition often puts men upon doing the meanest offices, so climbing is performed in the same posture with creeping.

Jonathan Swift. *Miscellanies*, 1711.

172. The horrors of a modern presidential campaign and the political troubles of the successful candidate rob the office of the slightest attraction for me.

William H. Taft (1857-1930), 27th President of the United States (R-OH), and Chief Justice, U.S. Supreme Court. Letter to his brother, 1901.

173. I love being at the center of things.

Margaret Thatcher, Prime Minister of Great Britain (Conservative). Quoted in *Reader's Digest*, 1984.

174. They who are in highest places, and have the most power, have the least liberty, because they are most observed.

John Tillotson (1630-1694), archbishop of Canterbury. *Reflections*.

175. There always is another crisis around the corner.

Harry S Truman (1884-1972), 33rd President of the United States (D-MO). Remark, 1950.

176. "A good public servant" – I hope that will be my epitaph.

Harry S Truman. Quoted by Wright Patman, memorial tribute to Truman, Jan. 3, 1973.

177. I have never yet coveted a seat in Congress – or in any other place where one must be always servant and never master.

Mark Twain (Samuel Langhorne Clemens) (1835-1910), American writer. Letter to Mrs. Fairbanks, Feb. 6, 1880.

178. Some of us first organized a Democratic Club up at Havre de Grace in 1915. I had no idea at all of running for office, but when it was announced that, anyhow, young Millard Tydings couldn't go to the legislature, I just naturally had to go and get myself elected.

Millard E. Tydings (1890-1961), U.S. Congressman and U.S. Senator (D-MD). Quoted in J. Salter, *The American Politician*, 1938.

179. If I may say so without sounding like a demagogue or a prig, the science of government is my study. I spend most of my time reading, for every year I realize how much there is to learn and how little I know.

Millard E. Tydings. *Ibid.*

180. What a heavy burden is a name that has become too famous.

Voltaire (François-Marie Arouet) (1694-1778), French historian and dramatist. *La Henriade*, 1728.

181. Being governor doesn't mean a thing anymore in this country. We're nothing. Just high-paid ornaments is all.

George C. Wallace, Governor of Alabama (D). Quoted in *Life*, July 22, 1986.

182. You have to have a baptism of fire in public service. Then you either fold or are committed for life.

Earl Warren (1891-1974), Chief Justice, U.S. Supreme Court, and Governor of California (R). Remark, 1935.

183. As to pay, sir, I beg leave to assure the Congress that as no pecuniary consideration could have tempted me to accept this arduous employment at the expense of my domestic ease and happiness, I do not wish to make any profit from it.

George Washington (1732-1799), 1st President of the United States (VA). Speech to the Second Continental Congress accepting appointment as Commander-in-Chief of the Continental Army, Philadelphia, PA, June 16, 1775.

184. My movement to the chair of government will be accompanied by feelings not unlike those of a culprit who is going to his place of execution.

George Washington. Remark upon leaving Mt. Vernon to assume the presidency, Feb. 4, 1789.

185. I have learned too much of the vanity of human affairs to expect felicity from the scenes of public life.

Martha Washington (1731-1802), First Lady. Letter to Mrs. Warren, Dec. 26, 1789.

186. There is something utterly nauseating about a system of society which pays a harlot 25 times as much as it pays its Prime Minister – 250 times as much as it pays its Members of Parliament.

Harold Wilson, Prime Minister of Great Britain (Labour). Reaction to the John Profumo sex scandal. Speech, House of Commons, Mar. 1963.

187. Forget about it. We're liberated. We don't have to care what those people say any more. Free at last.

James C. Wright, Jr., U.S. Congressman and Speaker of the House (D-TX). Remark to his wife the day after he announced his resignation, June 1, 1989.

188. If God lived on earth, people would break His windows.

Yiddish proverb.

189. I was elected mayor, not messiah.

Andrew Young, U.S. Congressman (D), U.S. Ambassador to the United Nations, and Mayor of Atlanta, GA. Quoted in *The New York Times*, Jan. 7, 1990.

Chapter 82

Public Opinion and Polling

1. THE VOICE OF THE PEOPLE IS THE SUPREME LAW. (VOCE POPULI LEX SUPREMA.)
Motto on revolutionary flag of East Florida, 1812; East Florida revolted against Spain and in 1819 became part of the United States.

2. Pollsters don't vote. People vote.
Anonymous; quoted by many politicians, usually those behind in the polls.

3. Nor should we listen to those who say "The voice of the people is the voice of God," for the turbulence of the mob is always close to insanity.
Alcuin (Flaccus) of York (c.735-804), English scholar and abbot. Letter to Emperor Charlemagne, 800.

4. In the world of public opinion, the person with the bullhorn is king.
Helen Alvaré, Director of Communications, National Conference of Catholic Bishops. *The Washington Post*, June 2, 1991.

5. The voice of the people hath some divineness in it, else how should so many men agree to be of one mind?
Francis Bacon, 1st Baron Verulam and Viscount St. Albans (1561-1626), Lord Chancellor of England. *De Dignitate et Augmentis Scientiarium*, 1623.

6. Stand not against the stream.
Apocrypha, *Wisdom of Ben Sira* 4:26.

7. Public opinion wavers.
Otto von Bismarck-Schoenhausen (1815-1898) Chancellor of Germany. Speech, Sept. 29, 1862.

8. The problem with polls lies not in turning the heads of voters but in destroying what little spine remains in politicians.... We've created a nation of office seekers and officeholders who operate like wind socks.
Chuck Bowden, editor, *City Magazine*. *USA Today*, Oct. 13, 1988.

9. All law is a dead letter without public opinion behind it.
Louis D. Brandeis (1856-1941), U.S. Supreme Court Justice. Letter to Alice Goldmark, Dec. 28, 1890.

10. Towering over Presidents and State Governors, over Congress and State Legislatures, over conventions and the vast machinery of party, public opinion stands out in the United States, as the great source of Power.
James Bryce (1838-1922), British Ambassador to the United States. *The American Commonwealth*, 1888.

11. Public opinion, which is there *[America]* omnipotent, is generally right in its aims.
James Bryce. *Modern Democracies*, 1921.

12. Our Union rests upon public opinion, and can never be cemented by the blood of its citizens shed in civil war.
James Buchanan (1791-1868), 15th President of the United States (D-PA). Message to Congress, Dec. 3, 1860.

13. The individual is foolish; the multitude, for the moment, is foolish, when they act without deliberation; but the species is wise, and when time is given to it, as a species it always acts right.
Edmund Burke (1729-1797), British statesman. Speech, House of Commons, May 7, 1782.

14. The public buys its opinions as it buys its meat, or takes its milk, on the principle that it is cheaper to do this than to buy a cow. So it is, but the milk is more likely to be watered.
Samuel Butler (1835-1902), British satirist. *The Note-Books of Samuel Butler*, 1912.

15. Reason will conclude that where multitude is, there is the truth.
John Capgrave (1393-1464), English scholar. *Life of St. Katherine of Alexandria*, c. 1450.

16. Vain hope to make people happy by politics!
Thomas Carlyle (1795-1881), Scottish essayist and historian. *Journal*, Oct. 10, 1831.

17. When the people's voice cannot be heard, that's when we make mistakes.
Jimmy Carter, 39th President of the United States (D-GA). Campaign speech, 1980.

18. The only people right now capable of mobilizing the public are talk show hosts.
Tony Coelho, U.S. Congressman (D-CA). Quoted in *The New York Times*, Feb. 15, 1989.

19. Jesus was never moved from the path of duty, however hard, by public opinion.
Anthony Comstock (1844-1915), founder, New York Society for the Suppression of Vice, and official censor, U.S. Postal Service. Quoted in Wallechinsky and Wallace, *The People's Almanac*, 1975.

20. Without the confidence of the people there would be no government.
Confucius (551-479 B.C.), Chinese philosopher. *Analects*.

21. In a democracy, as a matter of course, every effort is made to seize upon and create public opinion, which is, substantially, securing power.
James Fenimore Cooper (1789-1851), American writer. *The American Democrat*, 1838.

22. We talk about the influence of the media on public opinion. But reality has some influence on public opinion too.
David Demarest, presidential assistant (R). Symposium, "The Press and a Divided Government," National Press Foundation, Dec. 6, 1989.

23. Polls are only good for dogs.
John G. Diefenbaker (1895-1975), Prime Minister of Canada (Conservative). Quoted in *The Globe and Mail*, Nov. 28, 1990.

24. The multitude is always in the wrong.
Wentworth Dillon (1633-1684), Irish poet. *Essay on Translated Verse*, 1684.

25. The average American doesn't know the difference between a Contra and a caterpillar or between a Sandinista and a sardine.
John P. East (1931-1986), U.S. Senator (R-NC). Quoted in *The New York Times*, Oct. 12, 1984.

26. Masses are rude, lame, unmade, pernicious in their demands and influence, and need not to be flattered but schooled.
Ralph Waldo Emerson (1803-1882), American writer. *The Conduct of Life*, 1860.

27. I grieve to see that the government is governed by the hurrahs of the soldiers or the citizens. It does not lead opinion, but follows it.
Ralph Waldo Emerson. *Journals*, Aug. 1862.

28. The only sin which we never forgive in each other is difference of opinion.
Ralph Waldo Emerson. *Society and Solitude*, "Clubs," 1870.

29. It is a good part of sagacity to have known the foolish desires of the crowd and their unreasonable notions.
Desiderius Erasmus (c. 1466-1536), Dutch scholar and theologian. *Colloquies*, 1516.

30. The masses are absolutely being manipulated by those in power.
Louis Farrakhan, chief minister, Nation of Islam. Interview, *The Washington Post*, Feb. 28, 1990.

31. Polling is merely an instrument for gauging public opinion. When a President or any other leader pays attention to poll results, he is, in effect, paying attention to the views of the people.
George Gallup (1901-1984), American public opinion pollster. Feb. 1954.

32. The factors that are the long-term influences on opinion in this country are education, social and economic background, and religion. Those are the great constants. People's *basic* attitudes change very little.
George Gallup. Quoted in Robert M. Hutchins, *The Power of Reason*, 1964.

33. Real political issues cannot be manufactured by the leaders of political parties. The real political issues of the day declare themselves, and come out of the depths of that deep which we call public opinion.
James A. Garfield (1831-1881), 20th President of the United States (R-OH). Speech, Boston, MA, Sept. 10, 1878.

34. The public has to have a head, and if the President takes the heads away, the public will have his.
Leonard Garment, counselor to the President (R). Comment when H. R. Haldeman asked for a presidential pardon. Quoted in Woodward and Bernstein, *The Final Days*, 1976.

35. It is the absolute right of the State to supervise the formation of public opinion.

Joseph Goebbels (1897-1945), Minister of Propaganda and National Enlightenment, Third German Reich. Address to party supporters, Berlin, 1923.

36. What the multitude says is so, or soon will be.
Baltasar Gracián y Morales (1601-1658), Spanish Jesuit and writer. *The Art of Worldly Wisdom*, 1647.

37. Nothing is more unjust or capricious than public opinion.... The public have neither shame nor gratitude.
William Hazlitt (1778-1830), British writer. *Characteristics*, 1823.

38. Out of sight, out of mind.
John Heywood (1497-1580), English writer. *Proverbs*, I, iii.

39. That mysterious independent variable of political calculation, Public Opinion.
Thomas H. Huxley (1825-1895), British biologist and President, Royal Society. *Universities, Actual and Ideal*, 1874.

40. Public opinion, a vulgar, impertinent, anonymous tyrant who deliberately makes life unpleasant for anyone who is not content to be the average man.
William Ralph Inge (1860-1965), Anglican prelate and dean of St. Paul's. *Outspoken Essays*, First Series, 1919.

41. The people sometimes may be misled by the lying spirit in the mouths of their prophets, but never perverted; and in the end are always right.
Andrew Johnson (1808-1875), 17th President of the United States (War Democrat-TN). Quoted in *The New York World*, Nov. 14, 1867.

42. After a point it does not matter whether ... perceptions are true or false; it is the perceptions that matter.
Eddie Bernice Johnson, Texas State Senator (D). Quoted in *The New York Times*, Sept. 10, 1989.

43. Opinion and protest are the life breath of democracy – even when it blows heavy.
Lyndon B. Johnson (1908-1973), 36th President of the United States (D-TX). Remark to Presidential Scholars, Washington, DC, June 7, 1966.

44. We don't base our opinions on the Gallup Poll.
Lyndon B. Johnson. July 31, 1967.

45. Not a single person in this country has voted and we already know we've been defeated. Modern technology takes a lot of the honest emotion out of politics.
Hamilton Jordan, White House Chief of Staff (D). Remark to Jimmy Carter, Nov. 4, 1980.

46. Rulers who prefer popular opinion to truth have as much power as robbers in the desert.
Justin Martyr (c.100-c.165), Church father. *First Apology*, XII.

47. The worse I do the more popular I get.
[After the Bay of Pigs debacle, his May 1961 approval rating in the polls was 82 percent, higher than ever.]
John F. Kennedy (1917-1963), 35th President of the United States (D-MA). Quoted in Wallechinsky and Wallace, *The People's Almanac*, 1975.

48. Wouldn't it be wonderful if we didn't have any idea how this election would come out?
Charles Kuralt, American TV journalist. CBS, *Sunday Morning*, Nov. 6, 1988.

49. Free government is government by public opinion. Upon the soundness and integrity of public opinion depends the destiny of democracy.
Robert M. La Follette (1855-1925), Governor of Wisconsin and U.S. Senator (R). *La Follette's Magazine*, Apr. 1918.

50. What you farmers need to do is raise less corn and more hell.
Mary Elisabeth Lease (1853-1933), American agrarian reformer and Populist. Quoted in William E. Connelley, *History of Kansas: State and People*, 1928.

51. We decide what is right. Never mind what the people think.
Lee Kwan Yew, Prime Minister of Singapore. Quoted in *Toronto Globe and Mail*, Nov. 28, 1990.

52. The pollsters are engaged in an ancient and primitive rite – trying to predict the future.
Patricia N. Limerick, historian, University of Colorado, Boulder, CO. "Polls Are A Liability for Our Democracy," *USA Today*, Oct. 20, 1988.

53. Our government rests in public opinion. Whoever can change public opinion can change the government practically just so much.
Abraham Lincoln (1809-1865), 16th President of the United States (R-IL). Speech, Chicago, IL, Dec. 10, 1856.

54. Public opinion in this country is everything.
Abraham Lincoln. Speech, Columbus, OH, Sept. 16, 1859.

55. Mass opinion has acquired mounting power in this century ... a dangerous master of decisions when the stakes are life and death.

Walter Lippmann (1889-1974), American political columnist. *The Public Philosophy*, 1955.

56. Democracy is much too important to be left to public opinion.
Walter Lippmann. Quoted by Abba Eban, speech, Washington, DC, May 1989.

57. All free governments, whatever their name, are in reality governments by public opinion, and it is on the quality of this public opinion that their prosperity depends.
James Russell Lowell (1819-1891), U.S. Ambassador to Spain and Great Britain. Speech, Birmingham, England, Oct. 6, 1884.

58. The larger a country, the less easy for its real opinion to be ascertained, and the less difficult to be counterfeited.
James Madison (1751-1836), 4th President of the United States (Democratic Republican-VA). *National Gazette*, Dec. 19, 1791.

59. In a democracy such as ours military policy is dependent on public opinion.
George C. Marshall (1880-1959), General, U.S. Army, U.S. Secretary of State, and U.S. Secretary of Defense. Quoted in *Yank*, Jan. 28, 1943.

60. I'd rather be underestimated by the polltakers than by the voters.
Eugene J. McCarthy, U.S. Congressman and U.S. Senator (D-WI). Campaign speech, June 12, 1968.

61. It's up to us to mobilize public opinion in such a way that these politicians know their jobs are at stake.
Kate Michelman, Executive Director, National Abortion Rights Action League. Comment after the Supreme Court's *Webster* v. *Reproductive Health Services* decision, which gave the states greater power to control abortion. Quoted in *The Washington Post*, July 26, 1989.

62. The silence of peoples is something kings should study.
Honoré de Mirabeau (1749-1791), French revolutionary and President of the National Assembly. *Discourse on the Constituent Assembly*, July 15, 1789.

63. I've learned a long time ago not to take polls too seriously.
Brian Mulroney, Prime Minister of Canada (Conservative). Quoted in *The New York Times*, Oct. 16, 1988.

64. Imagination rules the world.
Napoléon I (1769-1821), military leader and Emperor of France. *Maxims*.

65. Opinion is everything in France, and most frequently turns on trifles.
Napoléon I. *Ibid.*

66. Public opinion is a mysterious and invisible power which it is impossible to resist: Nothing is more unsteady, more vague, or more powerful; and capricious as it may be, it is, nevertheless, just and reasonable more frequently than is supposed.
Napoléon I. *Ibid.*

67. In war the moral element and public opinion are half the battle.
Napoléon I. *Ibid.*

68. I can calculate the motion of heavenly bodies but not the madness of people.
Isaac Newton (1642-1727), English mathematician and scientist. Attributed.

69. The average American is just like a child.
Richard M. Nixon, 37th President of the United States (R-CA). Interview with Garnett D. Horner, reprinted in *The New York Times*, Nov. 10, 1972.

70. Public opinion responds to threats, not opportunities.
Richard M. Nixon. "We Are Ignoring Our World Role," *Time*, March 16, 1992.

71. I don't have any philosophical disagreements. My opposition has always been rooted in public opposition.
Cornelius O'Leary, Connecticut Senate Majority Leader (D). Explanation of his opposition to state income taxes. Quoted in *USA Today*, Mar. 6, 1991.

72. I took my own informal, politician's poll. I talked to fifty-six people. All fifty-six said that they didn't think that Truman could win, but all fifty-six said they were voting for Truman.
Thomas P. (Tip) O'Neill, Jr., U.S. Congressman and Speaker of the House (D-MA). Reminiscence about the 1948 presidential campaign. Quoted on PBS, *The Great Upset of '48*, Nov. 2, 1988.

73. Public opinion, because of the tremendous urge to conformity in gregarious animals, is less tolerant than any system of law.
George Orwell (Eric Blair) (1903-1950), British writer. *A Collection of Essays*, 1954.

74. Public opinion is a compound of folly, weakness, prejudice, wrong feeling, right feeling, obstinacy, and newspaper paragraphs.
Robert Peel, 2nd Baronet Peel (1788-1850), Prime Minister of Great Britain (Tory). 1835.

75. If polls are so accurate, why are there so many polling companies?
John Peers and Gordon Bennett. *1,001 Logical Laws, Accurate Axioms, Profound Principles, Trusty Truisms, Homey Homilies, Colorful Corollaries, Quotable Quotes, and Rambunctious Ruminations for All Walks of Life*, 1979.

76. In America, public opinion is the leader.
Frances Perkins (1882-1965), U.S. Secretary of Labor (D). *People at Work*, 1934.

77. Governors will never be awed by the voice of the people, so long as it is a mere voice, without overt acts.
Joseph Priestley (1733-1804), British clergyman and chemist. *Essay on the First Principles of Government*, 1768.

78. My esteem in the country has gone up substantially. It is very nice now that when people wave at me, they use all five fingers.
Ronald Reagan, 40th President of the United States (R). Quoted in Larry Wilde, *The Official Politicians Joke Book*, 1984.

79. The dull purblind folly of the very rich men; their greed and arrogance ... the corruption in business and politics, have tended to produce a very unhealthy condition of excitement and irritation in the popular mind, which shows itself in the great increase in the socialistic propaganda.
Theodore Roosevelt (1858-1919), 26th President of the United States (R-NY). Communication to William H. Taft, 1906.

80. Our generals ... had to grapple with a public sentiment which screamed with anguish over the loss of a couple of thousand men ... a sentiment of preposterous and unreasoning mawkishness.
Theodore Roosevelt. Remark to Cecil Spring Rice. Quoted in Richard Hofstadter, *The American Political Tradition*, 1948.

81. The most successful politician is he who says what the people are thinking most often and in the loudest voice.
Theodore Roosevelt. Quoted in *Forbes*, Apr. 2, 1990.

82. Almost everyone in the firm was for Truman. But we saw the future of the firm going down the drain.
Elmo Burns Roper, Jr. (1900-1971), American public opinion pollster. Comment after predicting that Truman would lose to Dewey in 1948. Quoted on PBS, *The Great Upset of '40*, Nov. 2, 1988.

83. The public is just a great baby.
John Ruskin (1819-1900), British art historian. *Sesame and Lilies*, 1865.

84. Men who borrow their Opinions can never repay their Debts.
George Savile, 1st Marquess of Halifax (1633-1695), Lord Privy Seal of England. *Miscellaneous Thoughts and Reflections*, 1750.

85. It is less dangerous for a *Prince* to mind too much what the *People* say, than too little.
George Savile. *Maxims of State*, No. 19.

86. People are polled out.... They don't necessarily tell the truth *[to pollsters]* any more.
Robert Scheifer, American TV journalist. CBS, *Sunday Morning*, Nov. 6, 1988.

87. Opinion is something wherein I go about to give reason why all the world should think as I think.
John Selden (1584-1654), English jurist and Member of Long Parliament. *Table-Talk: Opinion*.

88. A hated government does not last long.
Lucius Anneaus Seneca (The Younger) (4 B.C.-A.D.65), Roman statesman, dramatist, and philosopher. *Phaenissae*.

89. Englishmen never will be slaves; they are free to do whatever the government and public opinion allow them to do.
George Bernard Shaw (1856-1950), Nobel Laureate in Literature (Great Britain). *Man and Superman*, 1903.

90. Whatever people think, is.
Otis Singletary, Director, U.S. Job Corps (D). Quoted in Eigen and Siegel, *The Manager's Book of Quotations*, 1988.

91. I need not say how unfavorable an influence these defeats *[of Confederate forces at Roanoke Island, Fort Henry, and Fort Donaldson]*, following in such quick succession, have produced in public sentiment. If not soon counterbalanced by some decisive success in our arms, we may bid *adieu* to all hopes of seasonable recognition *[from France and England]*.
John Slidell (1793-1871), U.S. Congressman (D-LA), U.S. Senator, and Confederate Ambassador to France. Letter to Confederate Secretary of State Robert Hunter, Mar. 10, 1862.

92. Opinion is ultimately determined by the feelings, and not by the intellect.
Herbert Spencer (1820-1903), British social philosopher. *Social Statics*, 1851.

93. If there is anything for which I have entire indifference, perhaps I might say contempt, it is the public opinion which is founded on popular clamor.

Thaddeus Stevens (1792-1868), U.S. Congressman (Whig and R-PA). Quoted in George Seldes, *The Great Quotations*, 1960.

94. When troops are raised to chastise transgressors, the temple council first considers the adequacy of the rulers' benevolence and the confidence of their peoples; next, the appropriateness of nature's seasons; and finally, the difficulties of the topography.

Sun-tzu (c.400 B.C.), Chinese writer of the Age of Warring States. *The Art of War*.

95. *[Politicians regard public opinion as]* the great gorilla in the political jungle, a beast that must be kept calm.

Barry Sussman, American writer. *What Americans Really Think and Why Our Politicians Pay No Attention*, 1988.

96. There is more wisdom in public opinion than is to be found in Napoleon, Voltaire, or all the ministers of state, present or to come.

Charles-Maurice de Talleyrand-Périgord (Prince de Bénévent) (1754-1838), French diplomat and statesman. Speech, Chamber of Peers, 1821.

97. Polls are information. It's better to know what you're doing than not know what you're doing.

Robert Teeter, political pollster and campaign strategist (R). Interview, NBC, *Meet the Press*, Nov. 6, 1988.

98. It matters not a whit what Mr. Gladstone thinks of me. It is what I think of him that is important.

Victoria (1819-1901), Queen of Great Britain and Empress of India. Response when told that Prime Minister William Gladstone was saying unkind things about her, 1886.

99. Our supreme governors – the mob.

Robert Walpole, 1st Earl of Oxford (1676-1745), Prime Minister of Great Britain (Whig). Letter to Horace Mann, Sept. 7, 1743.

100. Public opinion is stronger than the legislature, and nearly as strong as the ten commandments.

Charles Dudley Warner (1829-1900), American writer and editor. *My Summer in a Garden*, 1871.

101. Eventually, popular support is essential, even in the most dictatorial countries.

John Whitehead, U.S. Deputy Secretary of State. ABC, *This Week*, July 24, 1988.

102. England ... has invented and established Public Opinion, which is an attempt to organize the ignorance of the community, and to elevate it to the dignity of a physical force.

Oscar Wilde (1854-1900), Irish writer. *The Critic as Artist*, 1890.

103. The only poll that counts is the one after the polls have closed.

L. Douglas Wilder, Governor of Virginia (D). Statement to the press, Nov. 6, 1989.

104. The symbol of this *[the Bush]* administration should be a wetted finger held up to the wind.

George F. Will, American political columnist. *The Washington Post*, Oct. 12, 1898.

105. Opinion ultimately governs the world.

Woodrow Wilson (1856-1924), 28th President of the United States (D-NJ). Speech, Associated Press, New York City, Apr. 20, 1915.

106. Not choice
But habit rules the unreflecting herd.

William Wordsworth (1770-1850), British poet. *Grant That by This Unsparing Hurricane*.

Chapter 83

Public Relations, Publicity, and Image

1. An ounce of image is worth a pound of performance.
   Political axiom, *Roll Call*, Sept. 11, 1988.

2. Report uttered by the people is everywhere a great power.
   Aeschylus (525-456 B.C.), Greek poet. *Agamemnon*.

3. Remember this about any slander. Denial only emphasizes and gives added importance to falsehood. Let it alone and it will die for want of nourishment.
   John P. Altgeld (1847-1902), Governor of Illinois (D). Remark to a friend. Quoted in Wallechinsky and Wallace, *The People's Almanac*, 1975.

4. Better known than trusted.
   American proverb.

5. Craft must have clothes, but truth loves to go naked.
   American proverb, 1876.

6. Amongst all the accusations that have ever been made against me, no man ever before imputed to me a lack of candor or charged me with duplicity, and no man ever shall and escape my denunciation. When a man so accuses me, it matters not where I am or who he is, I will write "liar" across his forehead, so that in future years all men may know him and all honest men may shun him.
   Joseph W. Bailey (1862-1929), U.S. Congressman and U.S. Senator (D-TX). Congressional debate, May 17, 1906.

7. A summit is a photo opportunity featuring two or more heads of government who have no business to transact, but believe a set of smiley photos will do them a lot of good politically.
   Russell Baker, American political columnist. Quoted in *Newsweek*, Sept. 22, 1986.

8. If you have to eat crow, eat it while it's hot.
   Alben W. Barkley (1877-1956), U.S. Congressman, U.S. Senator, and Vice President of the United States (D-KY). Advice to politicians.

9. The best audience is intelligent, well educated, and a little drunk.
   Alben W. Barkley. Attributed.

10. Image has become everything.
    Edward L. Bernays, American publicist and advertising executive. Quoted in *Life*, Fall 1990.

11. Public investigating committees formed from the people themselves or from their public representatives ... have always been opposed by groups that seek or have special privileges.... That is because special privilege thrives in secrecy and darkness and is destroyed by rays of pitiless publicity.
    Hugo L. Black (1886-1971), U.S. Senator (D-AL) and U.S. Supreme Court Justice. 1938.

12. Our national politics has become a competition for images or between images, rather than between ideals.
    Daniel Boorstin, American historian and Librarian of Congress. *The Image*, 1961.

13. We all live in a televised goldfish bowl.
    Kingman Brewster, Jr., U.S. Ambassador to Great Britain and President, Yale University, New Haven, CT. Speech, Windsor, England, May 5, 1978.

14. Every politician higher up than assistant water commissioner knows how to avoid tough questions *[from reporters]*: Don't answer them.
    David Brinkley, American TV journalist. ABC, *This Week*, Sept. 25, 1988.

15. I don't believe in the cult of personality, having my portrait hung all over the place like Ronald Reagan or Mao Tse-tung.

Edmund G. (Jerry) Brown, Jr., Governor of California (D). *Thoughts*, 1976.

16. Happily we do not idolize our public men.
John Buchan, 1st Baron Tweedsmuir (1875-1940), Member of Parliament, Great Britain (Liberal), and Governor-General of Canada. Quoted in *The New Dictionary of American Thoughts*, 1957.

17. Let's face it. If I was funnier than Ronald Reagan, I would have won in 1980. And he'd be up here tonight trying to laugh away the Bush deficit.
George Bush, 41st President of the United States (R-TX). Speech, Gridiron Club, Washington, DC, Apr. 1, 1989.

18. I don't care if my popularity rating goes down to zero.
George Bush. Remark to Yitzhak Shamir, Prime Minister of Israel, during the Iraq crisis, Dec. 1990.

19. I have contacted fifteen or twenty of the top *[advertising]* agencies in New York. The reluctance of all of them to take on our account boils down to the fact that they have big business clients who would not approve of them being responsible for the advertising and promotion of the Democratic Party.
Paul M. Butler (1905-1961), Chairman, Democratic National Committee. Memorandum, 1956.

20. I awoke one morning and found myself famous.
George Gordon Byron, 6th Baron Byron (1788-1824), poet and Member of Parliament, Great Britain. Quoted in Thomas Moore, *Life of Byron*, 1830.

21. Because I would have the chastity of my wife clear even of suspicion.
Julius Caesar (102-44 B.C.), Roman statesman. Comment on why he divorced his wife Pompeia. Quoted in Plutarch, *Life of Julius Caesar*.

22. A lie can be halfway round the world before the truth gets its boots on.
James Callaghan, Prime Minister of Great Britain (Labour). Quoting Charles Haddon Spurgeon. Speech, House of Commons, Nov. 1, 1976.

23. If anybody ever finds out where your district is, they'll beat you.
Joseph G. Cannon (1836-1926), U.S. Congressman and Speaker of the House (R-IL). Remark to Congressman John Nance Garner of Texas, c. 1913.

24. This is a town *[Washington, DC]* where sound travels faster than light.
Joseph Canzeri, White House assistant (R). Quoted in *The Washington Post*, Apr. 9, 1991.

25. You make more friends by becoming interested in other people than by trying to interest other people in yourself.
Dale Carnegie (1888-1955), American public speaking teacher. *How to Win Friends and Influence People*, 1936.

26. You need to market whatever it is you're trying to sell.
Tony Coelho, U.S. Congressman (D-CA). Quoted on PBS, *The Power Game*, Jan. 2, 1989.

27. The first twenty stories written about a public figure set the tone for the next two thousand and it is almost impossible to reverse it.
Charles W. Colson, presidential assistant (R). Quoted in *The New York Times*, July 7, 1974.

28. We don't make announcements until we make announcements.
B. J. Cooper, Deputy White House Press Secretary (R). Response when asked by reporters to confirm or deny a rumor regarding the President's selection for a vacant post, Apr. 12, 1989.

29. The people would be just as noisy if they were going to see me hanged.
Oliver Cromwell (1599-1658), Lord Protector of England. Comment when cheered by a large crowd. Quoted in *The Macmillan Dictionary of Quotations*, 1989.

30. A media management policy.
Nicholas Daniloff, American journalist and Moscow correspondent. Description of *glasnost*. *Two Lives, One Russia*, 1988.

31. The public is a bad guesser.
Thomas De Quincy (1785-1859), British writer. *Essays*, "Protestantism."

32. The truth of television is that what people see, they believe.
Michael Deaver, White House Director of Communications (R) and Deputy Chief of Staff for President Reagan. Quoted in *Regardie's*, Oct. 1987.

33. In any battle between what the ear hears and what the eye sees, the eye wins every time.
Michael Deaver. Quoted in *The Washington Post*, Nov. 22, 1989.

34. I am Ronald Reagan.
Michael Deaver. Quoted in Maureen Dowd, "Where's the Rest of Him?" *The New York Times*, Nov. 18, 1990.

35. If you want to be noticed, attack somebody.
Jerry Della Femina, American advertising execu-

tive. Interview, PBS, *Adam Smith's Money World,* July 22, 1989.

36. I am not in a position to say whether we can legislate effectively in reference to this matter *[Communist propaganda]*, but I do know that exposure in a democracy of subversive activities is the most effective weapon that we have in our possession.
Martin Dies (1901-1972), U.S. Congressman (D-TX). Speech, first session of the House Un-American Activities Committee. *Congressional Record,* 1938.

37. Without publicity there can be no public support, and without public support every nation must decay.
Benjamin Disraeli, 1st Earl of Beaconsfield (1804-1881), Prime Minister of Great Britain (Conservative). Speech, House of Commons, Aug. 8, 1871.

38. I was told that people did not like negative ads. So I didn't run any. I lost.
Robert J. Dole, U.S. Senator (R-KS). Description of his race for the Republican presidential nomination against George Bush. Quoted on ABC, *Nightline,* Nov. 10, 1988.

39. This is not politics. This is garbage. And we are disgusted by it. To those who are departed *[at the Republican National Committee, source of the offending letter]*, who sought in some, quote, clever, unquote, way to tarnish the reputation of Tom Foley, I say, good riddance.
Robert J. Dole. Comment after a memo was circulated about House Speaker-elect Tom Foley that implied the Congressman was homosexual. Senate speech, June 7, 1989.

40. Respond to the attacks immediately. Don't let them get away with a thing.
Michael Dukakis, Governor of Massachusetts (D). Interview, Nov. 3, 1988.

41. In upright demeanor there's ever more poise than all disguised shows of good can do.
Elizabeth I (1533-1603), Queen of England. Letter to the King of Scotland, Apr. 6, 1601.

42. As gaslight is found to be the best nocturnal police, so the universe protects itself by pitiless publicity.
Ralph Waldo Emerson (1803-1882), American writer. *The Conduct of Life,* "Worship," 1860.

43. Image is not one way to differentiate yourself, it's the *only* way.
Sean K. Fitzpatrick, American marketing executive. Quoted in *The New York Times,* Oct. 10, 1988.

44. The great leaders have always stage-managed their effects.
Charles de Gaulle (1890-1970), President of France. *The Edge of the Sword,* 1960.

45. My personality doesn't interest me.
Andrei A. Gromyko (1909-1989), Foreign Minister, U.S.S.R., and Russian Ambassador to the United States and the United Nations. Response when asked personal questions by reporters. Quoted in *Newsweek,* Oct. 1, 1984.

46. Once the toothpaste is out of the tube, it's hard to get it back in.
H. Robert Haldeman, White House Chief of Staff (R). In reference to Watergate, Aug. 1973.

47. The rich make you famous; the poor make you a hero.
Theodor Herzl (1860-1904), Austrian journalist and political Zionist. Attributed.

48. No whispered rumors which the many spread can wholly perish.
Hesiod (8th century B.C.), Greek poet. *Works and Days.*

49. The higher a monkey climb, the more he expose.
Jamaican proverb.

50. If you want to know what's going on in America, you have to watch soap operas.
Cyril L. R. James (1901-1989), Trinidad Pan-Africanist. Quoted on WEDH, *Evening Exchange,* Washington, DC, July 10, 1989.

51. While you're trying to save your face, you're losing your ass.
Lyndon B. Johnson (1908-1973), 36th President of the United States (D-TX). 1965.

52. No one person should be bigger than the office he represents.
Sterling Johnson, Jr., New York special prosecuter and Federal Judge. New York City Council Committee meeting, May 21, 1991.

53. Bread and circuses. (*Panem et circenses.*)
Decimus Junius Juvenal (c.60-c.140), Roman poet. The keys to politics. *Satires.*

54. We are what we say.
Justin Kaplan, editor, *Bartlett's Familiar Quotations. The New York Times,* June 2, 1991.

55. It's gotten so out of hand that now reporters are doing stories about the spin control, as opposed to being helped by it.

David Keene, political consultant (R). Quoted in *USA Today*, Oct. 13, 1988.

56. If your enemies see this picture of us together, I'm in big trouble.

Edward M. Kennedy, U.S. Senator (D-MA). Remark to Sen. James G. Abourezk during a photo session.

57. For years I was introduced as the brother of the President of the United States, and then I was introduced as the brother of the Attorney General. And just when I begin to make it on my own, I'm introduced as the father of the recipient.

Edward M. Kennedy. Comment when accepting the Washington Touchdown Club's Gene Brito Award on behalf of his son, Edward, Jr., who had recently lost a leg to cancer. Quoted in Lee Green, *Sportswit*, 1984.

58. I am reading it *[his press coverage]* more and enjoying it less.

John F. Kennedy (1917-1963), 35th President of the United States (D-MA). Quoted in Pierre Salinger, *With Kennedy*, 1966.

59. It's too bad that such crowds can't be turned out in the United States.

Henry M. Kissinger, U.S. Secretary of State and National Security Advisor (R). Remark to Brent Scowcroft and Lawrence Eagleburger on the huge crowds that turned out to welcome President Nixon to Egypt. June 13, 1974. Quoted in Woodward and Bernstein, *The Final Days*, 1976.

60. What you see is what you get.

Edward I. Koch, U.S. Congressman and Mayor of New York City (D). Campaign promise, 1980.

61. No, the Mayor of New York is not a coward, and the Mayor of New York is not a *schmuck*.

Edward I. Koch. Remark when refusing to be photographed with a rare Bengal tiger. *How'm I Doing?*, 1981.

62. We must stop politicians from ruining our reputation with their advertising. It is a disgrace.

Alex Kroll, Chairman, Young and Rubicam Advertising Agency. Quoted in *Advertising Age*, Apr. 29, 1991.

63. Don't worry about people knowing you. Make yourself worth knowing.

Fiorello H. La Guardia (1882-1947), U.S. Congressman (R and Socialist) and Mayor of New York City (R and Fusion Party). Quoted in Arthur Mann, *La Guardia: A Fighter Against His Times*, 1959.

64. Top secret is when you give a press conference and nobody comes.

Michael Ledeen, American writer and intelligence official. Speech, Conference, "Intelligence and Free Society," National Forum Foundation, Washington, DC, May 30, 1989.

65. Truth is generally the best vindication against slander.

Abraham Lincoln (1809-1865), 16th President of the United States (R-IL). Letter to Secretary of War Edwin M. Stanton, July 18, 1864.

66. You may as well know that one American national trait which irritates many Americans and must be convenient for our critics is that we relentlessly advertise our imperfections.

Henry Cabot Lodge, Jr. (1902-1986), U.S. Senator (R-MA), U.S. Ambassador to Vietnam and Germany, and head of the American delegation to the Paris Peace Conference for Vietnam peace negotiations. Remark to Nikita Khrushchev, Sept. 1959.

67. Tell them I lied.

Earl Kemp Long (1895-1960), Governor of Louisiana (D). Response when asked by aides what to tell the public regarding campaign promises that could not be kept. Quoted on ABC, *This Week*, Nov. 14, 1988.

68. Woe unto you when all men shall speak well of you.

New Testament, *Luke* 6:26.

69. The great majority of mankind are satisfied with appearances, as though they were realities, and are often more influenced by the things that seem than by those that are.

Niccolò Machiavelli (1469-1527), Florentine statesman and political philosopher. *The Prince*, 1513.

70. In every dimension, metaphysical, political, psychological, and existential, it was a magnificent victory ... within the context of our defeat.

Clovis Maksoud, Arab League Representative to the United Nations. Statement to the press after defeat of Arab armies by Israel, Oct. 1973.

71. I apologize for what was said even though I didn't say it.

Donald R. Manes (1922-1986), Borough President of Queens, New York City. Comment on reports that he had referred to New York Mayor Edward Koch in derogatory terms. Statement to reporters, Feb. 2, 1986.

72. Dictators always look good until the last ten minutes.

Tomas G. Masaryk (1850-1937), 1st President of Czechoslovakia. 1936.

73. They put out statements to make themselves look good.

Sarah McClendon, American journalist. In reference to White House statements. *Modern Maturity*, July 30, 1988.

74. Watch what we do, instead of what we say.

John N. Mitchell (1913-1988), U.S. Attorney General (R). Remark to reporters at the beginning of President Nixon's administration, Jan. 1969.

75. Our credibility had gotten so bad we couldn't even believe our own leaks.

Bill Moyers, journalist, Special Assistant to President Lyndon B. Johnson, and White House Press Secretary (D). PBS, *The Presidency, the Press and the People*, Apr. 2, 1990.

76. I was tempted to raise this issue in the Senate several weeks ago, but I decided that I would get more attention if I could get it printed in the papers.

Daniel P. Moynihan, Chief American Delegate to the United Nations and U.S. Senator (D-NY). Speech, National Press Club, Washington, DC, Mar. 1990.

77. Political writings are often overexaggerated polemics bearing the imprint of the period and the place in which written.

Frank Murphy (1890-1959), Governor of Michigan (D), U.S. Attorney General, and U.S. Supreme Court Justice. *Schneiderman* v. *United States*, 1942.

78. I am the state.... Even if I had done wrong you should not have reproached me in public – people wash their dirty linen at home.

Napoléon I (1769-1821), military leader and Emperor of France. Address to the French Senate, 1814.

79. The best answer to a smear ... is to tell the truth.

Richard M. Nixon, 37th President of the United States (R-CA). Televised speech, "Checkers," Sept. 23, 1952.

80. You know very well that whether you're on page one or page thirty depends on whether they fear you. It is just as simple as that.

Richard M. Nixon. Remark to Murray Chotiner, 1960.

81. Nobody's going to package me!

Richard M. Nixon. Remark, 1968.

82. I have seen so-called public relations experts ruin many a candidate by trying to make him over into an "image" of something he can never be.

Richard M. Nixon. Quoted in Lurie, *The Running of Richard Nixon*, 1972.

83. Political language – and with variations this is true of all political parties, from Conservatives to Anarchists – is designed to make lies sound truthful and murder respectable and to give an appearance of solidity to pure wind.

George Orwell (Eric Blair) (1903-1950), British writer. *Politics and the English Language*, 1946.

84. Every noble deed dies, if suppressed in silence.

Pindar (522-443 B.C.), Greek poet. *Eulogy on Alexander, Son of Amyntas*.

85. The politician who curries favor with the citizens and indulges them and fawns upon them and has a presentiment of their wishes, and is skillful in gratifying them, he is esteemed as a great statesman.

Plato (427-347 B.C.), Greek philosopher. *The Republic*, IV.

86. Publicity is like power ... it's a rare man who isn't corrupted by it.

Anthony Price, British novelist and newspaper editor. *Colonel Butler's Wolf*, 1972.

87. Let another praise you; and if not, your own mouth.

Old Testament, *Proverbs* 27:2.

88. Publicity, *publicity*, PUBLICITY is the greatest moral factor and force in our public life.

Joseph Pulitzer (1847-1911), U.S. Congressman (D-NY) and newspaper publisher. Letter to editors of the *New York World*, Dec. 29, 1895.

89. Just remember my right side – my far right side.

Ronald Reagan, 40th President of the United States (R-CA). Remark to White House News Photographers Association, May 18, 1983.

90. No gentleman ever weighs more than two hundred pounds.

Thomas B. Reed (1839-1902), U.S. Congressman and Speaker of the House (R-ME). In reference to William H. Taft. 1895.

91. The President is more than just somebody operating the country. The President is the United States for the years he is in office.

George E. Reedy, White House Press Secretary (D). PBS, *The Presidency, the Press, and the People*, Apr. 2, 1990.

92. Businessmen are not accustomed to the glare of publicity.

Donald T. Regan, U.S. Secretary of the Treasury and White House Chief of Staff (R). Quoted in *Regardie's*, Jan. 1987.

93. A government is the only vessel known to leak from the top.
James Reston, American political columnist. Quoted in *Reader's Digest*, Sept. 1988.

94. In this town *[Washington, DC]* everybody wants credit for everything.
James Reston. Remark, Nov. 3, 1989.

95. The best way to compel weak-minded people to adopt our opinion is to terrify them from all others, by magnifying their danger.
Cardinal de Retz (1614-1679), French cleric and politician. *Political Maxims*.

96. The voice of the people, the voice of God.
Walter Reynolds (d.1327), Chancellor of England and Archbishop of Canterbury. Sermon when Edward III ascended the throne, Feb. 1, 1327.

97. Senator *[Joseph R.]* McCarthy would cease to be a headline when the people realize their safety lies in knowledge and not in fear.
Anna Eleanor Roosevelt (1884-1962), First Lady and U.S. Delegate to the United Nations. Statement, Hong Kong, July 25, 1953.

98. You never saw a photograph of me playing tennis. I'm careful about that; photographs on horseback, yes; tennis, no. And golf is fatal.
Theodore Roosevelt (1858-1919), 26th President of the United States (R-NY). Advice to William H. Taft passed through Mark Sullivan, 1912.

99. I wanted to give the people a good show.
Theodore Roosevelt. Request that the Apache war shaman Geronimo, who was a federal prisoner, be transported to Washington, DC, to ride in his inaugural parade. Quoted in Angie Debo, *A History of the Indians of the United States*, 1970.

100. There aren't any embarrassing questions – just embarrassing answers.
Carl T. Rowan, Jr., U.S. Ambassador to Finland and political columnist. Quoted in *The New Yorker*, Dec. 7, 1963.

101. A press secretary is not in charge of handling the image of the President. The President does his own image.
Pierre Salinger, American journalist and White House Press Secretary (D). PBS, *The Presidency, the Press, and the People*, Apr. 2, 1990.

102. What we have is a competition *[among councilmen]* to see who can attract the greatest notoriety and who will be the political martyr.
Leonard B Sand, Federal Judge. In reference to a dispute over housing discrimination with the Yonkers, NY, city council. Quoted in *The Washington Post*, Aug. 3, 1988.

103. *[Popularity]* is stepping very low to get very high.
George Savile, 1st Marquess of Halifax (1633-1695), Lord Privy Seal of England. *Moral Thoughts and Reflections*, 1750.

104. I don't try and please everybody. I can't do that.
Kurt Schmoke, Mayor of Baltimore, MD (D). Interview, PBS, *Politics: The New Black Power*, Aug. 28, 1990.

105. *[Ronald Reagan is]* perfecting the Teflon-coated presidency. Nothing sticks to him. He is responsible for nothing – civil rights, Central America, the Middle East, the economy, the environment. He is just the master of ceremonies at someone else's dinner.
Patricia R. Schroeder, U.S. Congresswoman (D-CO). Aug. 2, 1983.

106. The art of government is organizing idolatry.
George Bernard Shaw (1856-1950), Nobel Laureate in Literature (Great Britain). *Maxims for Revolutionists*, 1903.

107. It is absolutely impossible to slaughter a man in this position without making him a martyr and a hero, even though the day before the rising he may have been only a minor poet.
George Bernard Shaw. In reference to the leaders of the Easter Uprising in Dublin who were sentenced to die. Letter to *The Daily News*, May 10, 1916.

108. Officers find it easier to attain rank, renown, fame, and notoriety by the cheap process of newspapers.
William Tecumseh Sherman (1820-1891), General, U.S. Army. Letter from Vicksburg, MS, to his wife, Feb. 17, 1863.

109. If you tell the same story five times, it's true.
Larry Speakes, White House Press Secretary (R). Dec. 16, 1983.

110. A lie is an abomination unto the Lord and a very present help in trouble.
Adlai E. Stevenson (1900-1965), Governor of Illinois (D) and U.S. Ambassador to the United Nations. Speech, Jan. 1951.

111. What some invent the rest enlarge.
Jonathan Swift (1667-1745), Irish clergyman and satirist. *Journal of a Modern Lady*.

112. The more cynical the news reporters and news consumers have become, the more image-manipulating, demagogic, and risk-adverse the newsmakers have become. And so our cynicism begets their fakery and their fakery our cynicism.
Paul Taylor, American political journalist. *See How They Run: Electing the President in an Age of Mediocrity*, 1990.

113. I will not change just to court popularity.
Margaret Thatcher, Prime Minister of Great Britain (Conservative). Speech, Conservative Party Conference, 1981.

114. In Washington, the truth is never told in daylight hours or across a desk. If you catch people when they're very tired or drunk or weak, you can get some answers. You have to wear the bastards down.
Hunter Thompson, American journalist. Interview, *Playboy*, Nov. 1974.

115. You can fool too many of the people too much of the time.
James Thurber (1894-1961), American writer and humorist. *Fables for Our Time*, 1940.

116. The answer rarely catches up with the charge.
John G. Tower (1925-1991), U.S. Senator (R-TX). Quoted on ABC, *This Week*, Feb. 26, 1989.

117. Mine isn't a bullshit, chrome and polish facade.
James A. Traficant, Jr., U.S. Congressman (D-OH). Interview, CBS, *60 Minutes*, Nov. 11, 1990.

118. A week is a long time in politics.
Harry S Truman (1884-1972), 33rd President of the United States (D). Remark to reporters after the funeral of President Kennedy. Nov. 26, 1963.

119. The public never turned me down. I took my story right to them, told them the facts bluntly, and when we got into a pinch, they stayed with us.
Earl Warren (1891-1974), Chief Justice, U.S. Supreme Court, and Governor of California (R). Quoted in Earl Katcher, *Earl Warren: A Political Biography*, 1967.

120. Some of these councilmen revel in the opportunity. The more press, the more they get caught up in the theatrics of it.... They're at the damn-the-torpedoes stage. No political logic or reasonable negotiation can persuade them at this time.
Nicholas Wasicsko, Mayor of Yonkers, NY. In reference to his city council and its fight with the federal court over housing discrimination. Quoted in *The Washington Post*, Aug. 3, 1988.

121. Let us get off the front pages and back among the obituaries.
Arthur V. Watkins (1886-1973), U.S. Senator (R-UT) and Chairman, Select Committee on the Censure of Joseph McCarthy. In reference to the publicity his Senate committee was getting. Remark, Sept. 12, 1954.

122. The turd in the punchbowl of American politics.
Lowell P. Weicker, Jr., U.S. Congressman (R), U.S. Senator, and Governor of Connecticut (Ind.). Description of his image among his political foes. Quoted on PBS, *Firing Line*, Dec. 4, 1988.

123. The impression of you got by the people is that you do not appreciate their suffering and poverty ... and have your ideas formed by Eastern money power.
William C. Whitney (1841-1904), U.S. Secretary of the Navy and New York City Corporation Counsel (D). Letter to Grover Cleveland, 1892.

124. When we shake hands we shake the world.
Wilhelm II (1859-1941), Emperor of Germany and King of Prussia. Inscription he wrote on photo of him and Theodore Roosevelt shaking hands in Germany.

125. I do wish the various parties would stop submitting their balyhooey to me about their respective candidates. I don't like any of them – and won't devote any part of the column's praise to them. I don't care whether Roosevelt wins or Hoover loses. I know too much about politics to care.
Walter Winchell (1897-1972), American columnist and radio commentator. Column, 1932.

126. I'm still an incumbent because I don't answer this type of question.
Robert E. Wise, Jr., U.S. Congressman (D-WV). Refusal to answer questions about his family and diet. Quoted in *USA Today*, Nov. 3, 1988.

127. The primary role of the press secretary is not to be an image maker, but to be a spokesman.
Ron Ziegler, White House Press Secretary (R). PBS, *The Presidency, the Press, and the People*, Apr. 2, 1990.

Chapter 84

Reform and Reformers

1. No reform Mayor ever served two terms.
Popular wisdom following John Purroy Mitchel's defeat for reelection as Mayor of New York City, 1917.

2. Disobey the rules; ask for more; leave your wretchedness behind; organize with your brothers and sisters; never accept the hand of fate.
Jean-Bertrand Aristede, President of Haiti. Quoted in *The New York Times*, Dec. 18, 1990.

3. An institution or reform movement that is not selfish, must originate in the recognition of some evil that is adding to the sum of human suffering, or diminishing the sum of happiness.
Clara Barton (1821-1912), founder, American Red Cross. *The Red Cross*, 1898.

4. Almost every witness that has been before this committee has opposed that reform which would affect his own industry.
Ross Bass, U.S. Congressman and U.S. Senator (D-TN). House hearings on the President's tax message, 1963.

5. They are not reformers who simply abhor evil. Such men become in the end abhorrent themselves.
Henry Ward Beecher (1813-1887), American clergyman and writer. *Life Thoughts*, 1858.

6. You can't find your way to social reform through the forces that made social reform necessary.
Albert J. Beveridge (1862-1927), U.S. Senator (R-IN) and founder, Progressive League. Quoted in Richard Hofstadter, *The American Political Tradition*, 1948.

7. Man is as the Lord made him. But we can change our institutions.
Louis D. Brandeis (1856-1941), U.S. Supreme Court Justice. Letter to Alfred Lief, Dec. 7, 1940.

8. The humblest citizen of all the land, when clad in the armor of a righteous cause, is stronger than all the hosts of Error.
William Jennings Bryan (1860-1925), U.S. Secretary of State (D). "Cross of Gold" speech, Democratic National Convention, Chicago, IL, July 10, 1896.

9. The dynamic architect of Soviet reform.
George Bush, 41st President of the United States (R-TX). Description of Soviet President Mikhail Gorbachev. Speech, Nov. 21, 1989.

10. What is a rebel? A man who says no.
Albert Camus (1913-1960), Nobel Laureate in Literature (France). *The Rebel*, 1951.

11. I am goddamned tired of listening to all this babble for reform. America is a hell of a success. Why tinker with it? The country don't need any legislation.
Joseph G. Cannon (1836-1926), U.S. Congressman and Speaker of the House (R-IL). 1905.

12. The prophet and the martyr do not see the hooting throng. Their eyes are fixed on the eternities.
Benjamin N. Cardozo (1870-1938), U.S. Supreme Court Justice. *Law and Literature*, 1931.

13. The socialist or anarchist who seeks to overturn present conditions is to be regarded as attacking the foundation upon which civilization itself rests.
Andrew Carnegie (1835-1919), American industrialist and philanthropist. *The Gospel of Wealth*, 1889.

14. It is hard to build a Communist state while reformers are slandering Socialism, destroying its values, discrediting the party and liquidating its leading role, doing away with social discipline, and sowing chaos and anarchy everywhere.
Fidel Castro, Premier of Cuba. Speech, Dec. 8, 1989.

15. Don't be content with things as they are.
Winston Churchill (1874-1965), Prime Minister of Great Britain (Conservative). Quoted in *Time*, Nov. 6, 1989.

16. Reformers and progressives are inevitably iconoclasts.
James B. (Champ) Clark (1850-1921), U.S. Con-

gressman and Speaker of the House (D-MO). Speech on reorganization of the House Speaker system, Mar. 1910.

17. Every new political principle must have its special advocates, just as every new faith has its martyrs.
Richard Cobden (1804-1865), Member of Parliament, Great Britain. Speech, Manchester, Jan. 25, 1846.

18. When Dr. *[Samuel]* Johnson called patriotism the last refuge of a scoundrel, he *[President Hayes]* forgot the possibilities contained in the word *[civil service]* Reform.
Roscoe Conkling (1829-1888), U.S. Congressman and U.S. Senator (R-NY). Remark in the Senate, 1878.

19. *[New York reformers]* tried to stand so straight that they fell over backward.
Richard Croker (1841-1922), leader, Tammany Hall, New York City (D). Quoted in *American Heritage*, Dec. 1986.

20. Reforms are less to be dreaded than revolutions, for they cause less reaction.
Charles John Darling (1849-1936), British Ambassador to the United States and Member of Parliament (Conservative). *Scintillae Juris*, 1889.

21. There is nothing in our government that the ballot cannot remove or amend. It can make and unmake presidents and congresses and courts.... It can sweep over trusts, syndicates, corporations, monopolies and every other development of the money power.
Eugene V. Debs (1855-1926), American Socialist. *The Cooperative Commonwealth*, 1885.

22. Intelligent discontent is the mainspring of civilization.
Eugene V. Debs. Speech, New York City, 1921.

23. The spirit of the age is the very thing a great man changes.
Benjamin Disraeli, 1st Earl of Beaconsfield (1804-1881), Prime Minister of Great Britain (Conservative). *Coningsby*, 1844.

24. In matters relating to business, finance, industrial and labor conditions, health, and the public welfare, great leeway is now granted the legislature, for there is no guarantee in the Constitution that the *status quo* will be preserved against regulation by government.
William O. Douglas (1898-1980), U.S. Supreme Court Justice. *Beauharnais* v. *Illinois*, 1951.

25. We are not rebels. Rebels defy authority and break laws at will.
Frederick T. Dykes, President, Citizens on Sensible Taxation, Montgomery County, MD. *The Washington Post*, July 16, 1989.

26. Self-regulation is a myth.
Thomas F. Eagleton, U.S. Senator (D-MO). "Chicago Markets: Corrupt to the Core," *The New York Times*, Nov. 14, 1989.

27. The martyr cannot be dishonored, every lash inflicted is a tongue of flame, every prison a more illustrious abode.
Ralph Waldo Emerson (1803-1882), American writer. *Essays*, First Series, "Compensation," 1865.

28. Every reform was once a private opinion, and when it shall be a private opinion again, it will solve the problem of the age.
Ralph Waldo Emerson. *Ibid.*, "History."

29. Criticism is the spur of reform; and Burke's admonition that a healthy society must reform in order to conserve has not lost its force.
Felix Frankfurter (1882-1965), U.S. Supreme Court Justice. *Dennis* v. *United States*, 1950.

30. The common people, the toilers, the men of uncommon sense – these have been responsible for nearly all social-reform measures which the world accepts today.
William E. Gladstone (1809-1898), Prime Minister of Great Britain (Liberal). Quoted in Brand, *Gladstone*.

31. We launched *perestroika [openness and restructuring]* with our eyes open. We foresaw the complexity and the special nature of that process, realizing that it would shake up thoroughly our entire society. We were not wrong.... As for the difficulties – and they do exist – we accept them as a natural expression of contradictions inherent in a transition period.
Mikhail Gorbachev, Premier of the U.S.S.R. To reporters, London, Apr. 1989.

32. The apathy of the modern voter is the confusion of the modern reformer.
Learned Hand (1872-1961), Federal Judge. Speech, Washington, DC, Mar. 8, 1932.

33. Reform and renewal come from below, not above. Do not await a reform messiah.
Gary Hart, U.S. Senator (D-CO). *Los Angeles Times*, Feb. 17, 1990.

34. We are returned to office to change the course of history – nothing less.
Edward Heath, Prime Minister of Great Britain

(Conservative). Speech, Conservative Party conference, Oct. 1970.

35. In the eyes of the true believer, people who have no holy cause are without backbone and character.

Eric Hoffer (1902-1983), American philosopher and longshoreman. *The True Believer*, 1951.

36. To have a grievance is to have a purpose in life.

Eric Hoffer. *The Passionate State of Mind*, 1954.

37. I'll say this for reformers – they're mighty patient.

Frank McKinney (Kin) Hubbard (1868-1930), American caricaturist and writer. *Abe Martin: Hoss Sense and Nonesense*, 1926.

38. The results of political changes are hardly ever those which their friends hope or their foes fear.

Thomas H. Huxley (1825-1895), British biologist and President, Royal Society. *Government*, 1890.

39. In the name of "reform" Congress now has its hand in virtually every aspect of military procurement.

David Ignatius, associate editor, *The Washington Post*. *The Washington Post*, June 26, 1988.

40. Change never comes from the White House. It comes from your house and my house.

Jesse L. Jackson, Shadow Senator (D-DC). Speech, Washington DC, Mar. 6, 1990.

41. We can surely boast of having set the world a beautiful example of a government reformed by reason alone, without bloodshed.

Thomas Jefferson (1743-1826), 3rd President of the United States (Democratic Republican-VA). Comment on the Constitution of 1787. Letter to Edward Rutledge, July 18, 1788.

42. Politics, like religion, hold up torches of martyrdom to the reformers of error.

Thomas Jefferson. Letter to James Ogilvie, Aug. 4, 1811.

43. What is objectionable, what is dangerous about extremists is not that they are extreme, but that they are intolerant. The evil is not what they say about their cause, but what they say about their opponents.

Robert F. Kennedy (1925-1968), U.S. Senator and U.S. Attorney General (D-NY). *The Pursuit of Justice*, 1964.

44. The great events of history are often due to secular changes in the growth of population and other fundamental economic causes, which, escaping by their gradual character the notice of contemporary observers, are attributed to the follies of statesmen or the fanaticism of atheists.

John Maynard Keynes (1883-1946), British economist and diplomat. *The Economic Consequences of the Peace*, 1919.

45. Economic reform is impossible without the educated groups.

Henry M. Kissinger, U.S. Secretary of State and National Security Advisor (R). Quoted in *The New York Times*, Aug. 20, 1989.

46. The function of a progressive is to keep on protesting until things get so bad that a reactionary demands reform.

Fiorello H. La Guardia (1882-1947), U.S. Congressman (R and Socialist) and Mayor of New York City (R and Fusion Party). Quoted in Arthur Mann, *La Guardia: A Fighter Against His Times*, 1959.

47. Only force would produce social change.

V. I. Lenin (1870-1924), Premier of the U.S.S.R. Quoted in Malachi Martin, *The Keys of This Blood*, 1990.

48. *[It is]* ... a sound maxim that it is better only sometimes to be right than at all times to be wrong, so as soon as I discover my opinions to be erroneous, I shall be ready to renounce them.

Abraham Lincoln (1809-1865), 16th President of the United States (R-IL). Address, Sangamon County, IL, Mar. 9, 1832.

49. We need reform, but not at the hands of Wall Street.

Charles A. Lindbergh (1859-1924), U.S. Congressman (R-MN). Congressional debate, July 1911.

50. A reforming age is always fertile of imposters.

Thomas Babington Macaulay, 1st Baron Macaulay (1800-1859), historian and Secretary of War, Great Britain (Liberal). *Essay on Moore's Life of Byron*, June 1830.

51. He who desires or attempts to reform the government of a state, and wishes to have it accepted ... must at least retain the semblance of the old forms; so that it may seem to the people that there has been no change in the institutions, even though in fact they are entirely different from the old ones.

Niccolò Machiavelli (1469-1527), Florentine statesman and political philosopher. *The Prince*, 1513.

52. Socialism appeals to Jews because it embraces the interests of the oppressed.

Tomas G. Masaryk (1850-1937), 1st President of Czechoslovakia. *Foundations of Marxism*, No. 126.

53. Beware of false prophets, which come to you in sheep's clothing, but inwardly they are ravening wolves.
New Testament, *Matthew* 7:15.

54. When the object is to raise the permanent condition of a people, small means do not merely produce small effects; they produce no effect at all.
John Stuart Mill (1806-1873), Member of Parliament, Great Britain, and political economist. *Principles of Political Economy*, 1848.

55. The spirit of improvement is not always a spirit of liberty, for it may aim at forcing improvements on an unwilling people.
John Stuart Mill. *On Liberty*, 1859.

56. I am for the restoration of order, not for the restoration of the old order.
Honoré de Mirabeau (1749-1791), French revolutionary and President of the National Assembly. Letter to Comte de la Marck, Oct. 22, 1790.

57. This country is going so far right you are not even going to recognize it.
John N. Mitchell (1913-1988), U.S. Attorney General (R). Quoted in *Women's Wear Daily*, Sept. 8, 1970.

58. Reform means difficulties. History moves often by leaps, then it moves slowly, because the resistance is organizing itself.
François Mitterrand, President of France (Socialist). Quoted in *The New York Times*, May 30, 1989.

59. Great economic and social forces flow with a tidal sweep over communities that are only half conscious of them. Wise statesmen are those who foresee what time is thus bringing, and endeavor to shape institutions and to mold men's thought and purpose in accordance with the change that is silently surrounding them.
John Morley, Viscount Morley of Blackburn (1838-1923), Member of Parliament, Great Britain (Liberal), Chief Secretary for Ireland, and Secretary of State for India. *Life of Richard Cobden*, 1881.

60. The worst we have from the Stalin era is the way we think. We cannot obtain new thinking on credit.
Oazug Nantoy, Moldavian reformer. Quoted in Malachi Martin, *The Keys of This Blood*, 1990.

61. The men who have changed the universe have never accomplished it by changing officials but always by inspiring the people.
Napoléon I (1769-1821), military leader and Emperor of France. *Maxims*.

62. It is the cause, not the death, that makes the martyr.
Napoléon I. *Ibid.*

63. The liberals would have to win every election for twelve years before there would be any liberal tax reform, because that's how long it would take to reform the *[Senate]* Finance Committee.
George W. Norris (1861-1944), U.S. Congressman and U.S. Senator (R and Independent Republican-NE). Quoted in Manley, *The Politics of Finance*, 1970.

64. Liberal reforms in Russia come only in the wake of military defeats and foreign policy setbacks.
William E. Odom, Director, National Security Agency. *The Washington Post*, Mar. 12, 1989.

65. You have to make more noise than anybody else, you have to make yourself more obtrusive than anybody else, you have to fill all the papers more than anybody else; in fact, you have to be there all the time and see that they do not snow you under, if you are really going to get your reforms realized. That is what we women have been doing, and in the course of our desperate struggle we have had to make a great many people uncomfortable.
Emmeline Pankhurst (1858-1928), British suffragist. Speech, Hartford, CT, Nov. 13, 1913.

66. One on God's side is a majority.
Wendell Phillips (1811-1884), American orator and reformer. Speech, Brooklyn, NY, Nov. 1859.

67. The reformer is careless with numbers, disregards popularity, and deals only with ideas, conscience, and common sense.
Wendell Phillips. Quoted in Richard Hofstadter, *The American Political Tradition*, 1948.

68. We knew who was behind Gorbachev. It was *[Boris]* Yeltsin who was committed to a reform agenda. We don't know what the forces are behind Yeltsin.
J. Danforth Quayle, U.S. Senator and Vice President of the United States (R-IN). Quoted in *The Washington Post*, Feb. 11, 1992.

69. There is filth on the floor and it must be scraped up with the muck-rake; and there are times and places where this service is the most needed of all the services that can be performed. But the man who never does anything else, who never thinks or speaks or writes, save of his feats with the muck-rake, speedily becomes, not a help to society, not an incitement to good, but one of the most potent forces for evil.

Theodore Roosevelt (1858-1919), 26th President of the United States (R-NY). Speech at the cornerstone laying of the House Office Building, Apr. 14, 1906.

70. The various admirable movements in which I have been engaged have always developed among their members a large lunatic fringe.
Theodore Roosevelt. Letter to Sen. Henry Cabot Lodge, Feb. 27, 1913.

71. I cannot say that I entered the presidency with any deliberately planned and far-reaching scheme of social betterment.
Theodore Roosevelt. *Autobiography*, 1919.

72. All movements go too far.
Bertrand Russell, 3rd Earl Russell of Kingston (1872-1970), British philosopher and reformer. *Unpopular Essays*, 1950.

73. A thousand reforms have left the world as corrupt as ever, for each succeeding reform has founded a new institution, and this institution as founded bred its new and congenial abuses.
George Santayana (1863-1952), American philosopher. *The Life of Reason*, 1906.

74. There are Men who shine in a Faction, and make a Figure by Opposition, who would stand in a worse light, if they had the Preferments they struggle for.
George Savile, 1st Marquess of Halifax (1633-1695), Lord Privy Seal of England. *Political Thoughts and Reflections*, 1750.

75. You end the pressure, you end the progress.
Harry Schwarz, South African Ambassador to the United States. Quoted in *The Washington Post*, Mar. 1, 1991.

76. The reformer for whom the world is not good enough finds himself shoulder to shoulder with him that is not good enough for the world.
George Bernard Shaw (1856-1950), Nobel Laureate in Literature (Great Britain). *Maxims for Revolutionists*, 1903.

77. The reasonable man adapts himself to the world; the unreasonable one persists in trying to adapt the world to himself. Therefore all progress depends on the unreasonable man.
George Bernard Shaw. *Ibid.*

78. Nothing is ever done in this world until men are prepared to kill each other if it is not done.
George Bernard Shaw. *Major Barbara*, 1905.

79. Reformers can be as bigoted and sectarian and as ready to malign each other as the Church in its darkest periods has been to persecute its dissenters.
Elizabeth Cady Stanton (1815-1902), 1st President, National Woman Suffrage Association. *The Kansas Campaign of 1867*, 1868.

80. Reformers who are always compromising have not yet grasped the idea that truth is the only safe ground to stand upon.
Elizabeth Cady Stanton. *The Woman's Bible*, 1895.

81. There is in such governments *[despotism]* what may be called a desolating calm, a universal indisposition to changes, and a fearfulness of reform on all sides; on the part of the people, lest it should generate some new oppression; and on the part of the ruler, lest it should introduce some jealousy or check of his arbitrary power.
Joseph Story (1779-1845), U.S. Supreme Court Justice. *Miscellaneous Writings*, 1835.

82. There's none so blind as they that won't see.
Jonathan Swift (1667-1745), Irish clergyman and satirist. *Polite Conversation*, II, 1738.

83. If I believed the monarchy possible, I would retire.
Louis-Adolphe Thiers (1797-1877), 1st President of the Third French Republic. Speech, Nov. 29, 1872.

84. There are a thousand hacking at the branches of evil to one who is striking at the root.
Henry David Thoreau (1817-1862), American philosopher and naturalist. *Walden, or Life in the Woods*, 1854.

85. Absolute *[political]* systems are strong as long as they are absolute. When they begin to reform they are lost. Yet they cannot avoid reform, or they will explode.
Alexis de Tocqueville (1805-1859), French writer. Quoted in *The New York Times*, Oct. 16, 1988.

86. Governments hate change.
Brian Urquhart, Undersecretary General, United Nations. Interview, C-SPAN, Dec. 24, 1990.

87. It's almost always the case that the first reformers don't succeed. Only the others who come after succeed.
Lech Walesa, President of Poland, trade unionist, and founder, Solidarity. Interview, *CBS News*, July 10, 1989.

88. A reformer is a guy who rides through a sewer in a glass-bottomed boat.
James J. Walker (1881-1946), Mayor of New York City (D). Attributed.

89. The blare of the bugle drowned the voice of the reformer.
Thomas E. Watson (1856-1922), U.S. Congressman and U.S. Senator (D-GA). In reference to public preoccupation with the Spanish-American War. Quoted in C. Vann Woodward, *Tom Watson*, 1938.

90. The eager and often inconsiderate appeals of reformers and revolutionists are indispensable to counterbalance the inertness and fossilism making so large a part of human institutions.
Walt Whitman (1819-1902), American poet. *Democratic Vistas*, 1870.

91. If you open the door to reform one inch, somebody's going to come all the way through.
Tom Wicker, American political columnist. ABC, *This Week*, Oct. 16, 1988.

92. Nothing is impossible in Russia but reform.
Oscar Wilde (1854-1900), Irish writer. *Vera, or The Nihilists*, 1881.

93. Times never change; people do.
L. Douglas Wilder, Governor of Virginia (D). Interview, PBS, *John McLaughlin's One on One*, May 26, 1991.

94. To Negro Americans "gradual" means either no progress at all, or progress so slow as to be barely perceptible.
Roy Wilkins, Executive Director, National Association for the Advancement of Colored People. Letter to Adlai E. Stevenson, Feb. 9, 1956.

Chapter 85

Regulation and Deregulation

1. Is there anything in the existing condition that makes the duty of Congress to put the liberty of all the people of the United States in jeopardy?... Are we going to take up the question of what a man shall eat and what a man shall drink, and put him under severe penalties if he is eating or drinking something different from what the chemists of the Agricultural Department think desirable?

   Nelson W. Aldrich (1841-1915), U.S. Congressman and U.S. Senator (R-RI). Argument against the Pure Food Act introduced by Pres. Theodore Roosevelt. Senate debate, Dec. 13, 1905.

2. You don't intervene in the regulatory process. It's law enforcement. It's like a parent ... calling the police chief to say, "Don't touch my kid." It's wrong.

   Bruce Babbitt, Governor of Arizona (D). In reference to the savings and loan scandal. Quoted in *The Washington Post*, Nov. 7, 1989.

3. The measures have not yet been devised which can permanently protect men from their folly.

   Bernard M. Baruch (1870-1965), Chairman, War Industries Board, and U.S. Delegate to the U.N. Atomic Energy Commission. *The Public Years*, 1960.

4. Look with favor on the merchants of the land; always care for them; let no one order them about, for through their trading the land becomes prosperous.

   Ahmet Sinan Celebi Behesti (1485-1511), Ottoman (Turkish) writer. *An Ottoman Mirror for Princes*.

5. To save my live I cannot see what right we have to control the air that God Almighty gave the people.

   Coleman L. Blease (1868-1942), Governor of South Carolina and U.S. Senator (D). Argument against regulation of the airwaves used by radio. Senate debate, Mar. 1, 1929.

6. Billboards have a tremendous negative impact on neighborhoods and therefore neighborhoods should have the ability to regulate them.

   John H. Chafee, U.S. Senator and Governor of Rhode Island (R). Press conference, Washington, DC, Apr. 24, 1990.

7. They not only deregulated. They desupervised.

   Tony Coelho, U.S. Congressman (D-CA). Criticism of federal regulators in the savings and loan scandal. ABC, *Money Politics*, Nov. 12, 1989.

8. The city does not have the right to regulate content. That's the First Amendment.

   James A. Eatrides, President, Boisclair Outdoor Advertising Co. Comment on attempts to restrict the number of billboards advertising tobacco and alcohol products in Baltimore, MD, by using special zoning and permit regulations. Quoted in *The Washington Post*, Sept. 12, 1991.

9. Tough enforcement of the antitrust laws can help prevent a recurrence of inflation by attacking abuses of economic power.

   Lewis A. Engman, Chairman, Federal Trade Commission (R). Speech, Commonwealth Club of California, 1973.

10. Well, if the Teamsters and the truckers are against it, it must be a pretty good bill.

    Gerald R. Ford, 38th President of the United States (R-MI). Remark to William Coleman when considering a bill to deregulate the trucking industry, 1974.

11. A king-sized cancer on our economy.

    William Frenzel, U.S. Congressman (R-MN). Description of the Federal Trade Commission. Quoted in *Saturday Review*, Mar. 29, 1980.

12. I don't think you can ask the free market to make sure that airplanes are working or that the cockpit crew is rested.

Dan Glickman, U.S. Congressman (D-KS). Quoted in *Forbes*, Jan. 23, 1989.

13. We do not want to place more power in the hands of government to investigate and regulate the lives, the conduct and the freedom of America's workers.

Samuel Gompers (1850-1924), President, American Federation of Labor. Argument against government imposed minimum wages and unemployment insurance. *American Federationist*, 1915.

14. Work of intellectual daring carries the danger of increased error, in both frequency and consequence.... Intrusive regulation by nonscientists is most frightening for this reason: Innovation and chanciness will die.

Stephen Jay Gould, American geologist. *The New York Times*, July 31, 1989.

15. Regulations are in the eye of the beholder.

Jere Goyan, Commissioner, U.S. Food and Drug Administration. Quoted in *The New York Times*, Dec. 4, 1989.

16. I felt terrified as the chief regulator that I would start a run on my own industry *[by disclosing elements of the 1989 savings and loan scandal]*.

Edwin J. Gray, Chairman, Federal Home Loan Bank Board (R). C-SPAN, *The Media and The Savings and Loan Scandal*, Nov. 3, 1990.

17. It emasculated people to be protected in this way.... They should be used to protecting themselves.

Samuel Gridley Howe (1801-1876), Principal, Perkins School for the Blind, and Chairman of the Massachusetts Board of State Charities. Comment on efforts by the government to regulate working conditions. Quoted in Richards, *Letters and Journals of Samuel Gridley Howe*, 1909.

18. Our government is the most successful contrivance the world has ever known for preventing things from being done.

Charles Evans Hughes (1862-1948), Chief Justice, U.S. Supreme Court, and U.S. Secretary of State (R). Quoted in McCraw, *Regulation in Perspective*, 1981.

19. An instrument of oppression and disturbance and injury instead of help to business.

William E. Humphrey (1862-1934), Chairman, Federal Trade Commission, and U.S. Congressman (R-WA). Description of the Federal Trade Commission, which he had just been nominated to head. 1925.

20. ... a wise and frugal government which shall restrain men from injuring one another, which shall leave them otherwise free to regulate their own pursuits of industry and improvement, and shall not take from the mouth of labor the bread it has earned. This is the sum of good government, and this is necessary to close the circle of our felicities.

Thomas Jefferson (1743-1826), 3rd President of the United States (Democratic Republican-VA). 1st inaugural address, Mar. 4, 1801.

21. I believe in municipal ownership of all public service monopolies for the same reason that I believe in the municipal ownership of waterworks, of parks, of schools. I believe in the municipal ownership of these monopolies because if you do not own them, they will own you. They will rule your politics, corrupt your institutions, and finally destroy your liberties.

Tom L. Johnson (1854-1911), U.S. Congressman (D-OH). Quoted in William O. Douglas, *An Almanac of Liberty*, 1954.

22. It's destructive and it's cruel, but that's the way the market functions.

Alfred E. Kahn, Chairman, Civil Aeronautics Board. Comment on the negative effects of deregulation. Quoted in *The Wall Street Journal*, May 14, 1982.

23. The revolt against regulation that we're experiencing is also a revolt against government compulsion and meddling.... Keep the hand of government as invisible as possible.

Alfred E. Kahn. Quoted in Tolchin and Tolchin, *Dismantling America: The Rush to Deregulate*, 1983.

24. Regulators all too often encourage or approve unreasonably high prices, inadequate service, and anticompetitive behavior. The cost of this regulation is always passed on to the consumer. And that cost is astronomical.

Edward M. Kennedy, U.S. Senator (D-MA). Senate hearings, 1975.

25. If you'd like to buy some of the fruits of deregulation, we have some S&L's we'd like to sell you.

Ted Koppel, American television journalist. Remark to Japanese economist advocating more U.S. deregulation. PBS, *Worlds Without Walls*, University of Pennsylvania, Philadelphia, PA, May 17, 1990.

26. I am conscious each time I ask a question that there is a deep resentment in the heart of the railroad official at being compelled to answer; but that he is compelled to, he recognizes.

Franklin K. Lane (1864-1921), member, Interstate Commerce Commission. Letter, Feb. 1, 1907.

27. The railroad men did not hesitate to dominate government where they could.

Ernest I. Lewis (1873-1947), Chairman, Interstate Commerce Commission. Apr. 30, 1930.

28. There is hardly a section of the community that doesn't in one breath protest undying hostility to Government interference and, in the next breath, pray for it.

Robert G. Menzies (1894-1978), Prime Minister of Australia (Liberal). Quoted in *The Wit of Sir Robert Menzies*, 1966.

29. Regulation rollbacks *[in the automobile industry]* are going to kill a lot of people and ruin the health and environment for others.

Ralph Nader, American consumer advocate. Quoted in Tolchin and Tolchin, *Dismantling America: The Rush to Deregulate*, 1983.

30. When the feds walk away from the problem *[environmental regulation]*, businesses ask, "Why stay in your state? Why not go to a state with very lax standards?"

Norman H. Nosenchuck, Division Director, N. Y. State Department of Environmental Conservation. Quoted in Tolchin and Tolchin, *Dismantling America: The Rush to Deregulate*, 1983.

31. It is not the business of government to prevent capitalistic acts between consenting adults.

Robert W. Packwood, U.S. Senator (R-OR). Interview, 1979.

32. We've got to police virtually the whole economy.

Michael Pertschuk, Chairman, Federal Trade Commission. Statement, FTC hearing, 1977.

33. Regulators should seek to inform women of risks, not deprive them of choices.

Virginia Postrel, editor, *Reason Magazine*. In reference to silicone gel breast implants. *The Washington Post*, Jan. 26, 1992.

34. If the Interstate Commerce Commission were worth buying, the railroads would try to buy it.... The only reason they have not tried to purchase the Commission is that the body is valueless in its ability to correct railroad abuses.

Charles A. Prouty (1853-1921), member, Interstate Commerce Commission. Interview, *Chicago Record-Herald*, Dec. 31, 1904.

35. I think it's important for the government to take some responsibility over the decisions that the corporate sector would rather just make for itself.

Miles S. Rapoport, Connecticut Assemblyman (D). Quoted in *Governing*, Sept. 1988.

36. We *[Congress]* created the regulatory agencies to do what we don't have time to do.

Samuel T. Rayburn (1882-1961), U.S. Congressman and Speaker of the House (D-TX). Quoted in Tolchin and Tolchin, *Dismantling America: The Rush to Deregulate*, 1983.

37. Fewer regulators will necessarily result in fewer regulations and less harassment of the regulated.

Ronald Reagan, 40th President of the United States (R-CA). Speech, Feb. 18, 1981.

38. Government exists to protect us from each other. We can't afford the government it would take to protect us from ourselves.

Ronald Reagan. Quoted in Laurence I. Barrett, *Gambling With History – Reagan in the White House*, 1983.

39. The least responsible ... corporations will seek out and encourage the most permissive regulatory environments.

Elliot L. Richardson, U.S. Attorney General (R), U.S. Secretary of Health, Education and Welfare, and U.S. Secretary of Defense. *The New York Times*, Feb. 7, 1990.

40. The tendency lately has been toward regulation of industry. Something goes wrong somewhere, immediately the public is aroused, the press, the pulpit call for an investigation. That is fine, that is healthy ... but government regulation is not feasible. It is unwieldy, expensive ... it means higher taxes. The public doesn't want it; the industry doesn't want it.

[Roosevelt had just become president of the American Construction Council, an industry association.]

Franklin D. Roosevelt (1882-1945), 32nd President of the United States (D-NY). Speech, American Construction Council, 1922.

41. ... every issue of new securities to be sold in interstate commerce shall be accompanied by full publicity and information, and that no essentially important element attending to the issue shall be concealed to the buying public.

Franklin D. Roosevelt. Message to Congress, Mar. 29, 1933.

42. We must find practical controls over blind economic forces and blindly selfish men.

Franklin D. Roosevelt. 2nd inaugural address, Jan. 20, 1937.

43. Great interests ... which desire to escape regulation rightly see that if they can strike at the heart of modern reform by sterilizing the administrative tribunal which administers them, they will effectively destroy the reform itself.

Franklin D. Roosevelt. Veto message, Walter-Logan Act, Dec. 8, 1940.

44. Corporations engaged in interstate commerce should be regulated, if they are found to harm the public interest.
Theodore Roosevelt (1858-1919), 26th President of the United States (R-NY). Annual message to Congress, Dec. 3, 1902.

45. Somehow or other we shall have to work out methods of controlling the big corporations without paralyzing the energies of the business community.
Theodore Roosevelt. Letter to George Trevelyan, 1905.

46. I recommend that a law be enacted to regulate interstate commerce in misbranded and adulterated foods, drinks, and drugs.... Traffic in foodstuffs which have been debased or adulterated so as to injure health or to deceive purchasers should be forbidden.
Theodore Roosevelt. Annual message to Congress, Dec. 5, 1905.

47. The mechanism of modern business is so delicate that extreme care must be taken not to interfere with it in a spirit of rashness or ignorance.
Theodore Roosevelt. *Ibid.*

48. Nothing ... is gained by breaking up a huge industrial organization which has not offended otherwise than by its size.
Theodore Roosevelt. 1911.

49. Even our *[SEC]* commissioners are feisty and don't always do what I want them to do.
David S. Ruder, Chairman, Securities and Exchange Commission. Interview, PBS, *Wall Street Week*, June 9, 1989.

50. A Man watches himself best when Others watch him too.
George Savile, 1st Marquess of Halifax (1633-1695), Lord Privy Seal of England. *Miscellaneous Thoughts and Reflections*, 1750.

51. *[The U.S. Office of Safety and Health Affairs]* ... regulates the trivial in exquisite detail.
Charles L. Schultze, Chairman, Council of Economic Advisors and Director, U.S. Bureau of the Budget (D). *The Public Use of Private Interest*, 1977.

52. Every contract, combination in the form of a trust or otherwise, or conspiracy in restraint of trade ... is hereby declared to be illegal.
John Sherman (1823-1900), U.S. Senator (R-OH), U.S. Secretary of the Treasury, and U.S. Secretary of State. *Sherman Anti-Trust Act*, July 2, 1890.

53. If there's not competition, then the federal government becomes a surrogate for competition.
Alfred Sikes, Chairman, Federal Communications Commission (R). Quoted in *USA Today*, Mar. 29, 1990.

54. I simply do not favor government regulation when there is a free market option available.
Alfred Sikes. Letter to ABC, *Money Politics*, Apr. 1990.

55. The federal government should have the power to spend money on its people's welfare, but not the power to regulate in those fields.
Robert A. Taft (1889-1953), U.S. Senator (R-OH). Quoted in *Fortune*, Aug. 1953.

56. We can't rely on the free market system anymore. We need rules even if that means that you and I end up being called Communist or Socialist.
Pierre Elliott Trudeau, Prime Minister of Canada (Liberal). Speech, Toronto, Apr. 1975.

57. Freedom is the general rule, and restraint the exception.
Willis Van Devanter (1859-1941), U.S. Supreme Court Justice. *Wolff Packing Co.* v. *Court of Industrial Relations*, 1924.

58. The whole thing *[support of a federal meat inspection bill]* stamps the President *[Theodore Roosevelt]* as unreliable, a faker, and a humbug. For years he has indulged in lofty sentiments, and violates them all for the sake of satisfying his petty spite.... Thank God, he can't fool all the people all the time, and this country is fast awakening to the real character of this bloody hero of Kettle Hill.
James W. Wadsworth (1846-1926), U.S. Congressman (R-NY). 1907.

59. The power to regulate is not a power to destroy.
Morrison R. Waite (1845-1921), Chief Justice, U.S. Supreme Court. *Munn* v. *Illinois*, 1877.

60. The state should take the entire management of commerce, industry, and agriculture into its own hands, with a view of succoring the working classes and preventing their being ground to dust by the rich.
Wang An-shih (c. 11th century), Chinese politician and statesman. Quoted in Upton Sinclair, *The Cry for Justice*, 1920.

61. I have a concern about forcing students into mandatory workshops *[about campus hate-speech policies]*.... It bothers me about our society in gen-

eral that the only way people think they can change behavior is to set up a rule.

Sue Wasiolek, dean for student life, Duke University, Durham, NC. Quoted in *The Chronicle of Higher Education*, Feb. 12, 1992.

62. Liberty exists in proportion to wholesome restraint.

Daniel Webster (1782-1852), U.S. Congressman (Federalist-NH and MA), U.S. Senator (Federalist and Whig-MA), and U.S. Secretary of State. Speech, May 10, 1847.

63. Regulation was born of legislation tailored to promote fair play in a vigorously competitive free market.

Murray Weidenbaum, Chairman, Council of Economic Advisors (R). *Reader's Digest*, Feb. 1979.

64. When you have nothing to do, undo.

Murray Weidenbaum. Addressing Federal regulators. Quoted in Tolchin and Tolchin, *Dismantling America: The Rush to Deregulate*, 1983.

65. Tell the truth on the label and let the consumer judge for himself.

Harvey Washington Wiley (1844-1930), chief chemist, U.S. Dept. of Agriculture. Quoted in Mark Sullivan, *Our Times*, 1927.

66. We do not mean to strike at any essential economic arrangements, but we do mean to drive all beneficiaries of government into the open and demand of them by what principle of national advantage, as contrasted with selfish privilege, they enjoy the extraordinary assistance extended to them.

Woodrow Wilson (1856-1924), 28th President of the United States (D-NJ). Campaign speech, 1911.

67. Without the watchful interference, the resolute interference, of the government there can be no fair play.

Woodrow Wilson. *The New Freedom*, 1913.

68. The promise to get the government off the backs of the industry was a promise to permit drug and medical device companies to more easily be able to injure and kill thousands of people.

Sidney Wolfe, Director, Public Citizen Health Research Group. Quoted in *The New York Times*, Dec. 4, 1989.

69. Regulation is the key to civilized society. The extent to which we take regulations for granted in our daily lives is reflected by the confidence with which we drink our water, eat our food, take our medication, drive our cars, and perform hundreds of other tasks without thought of peril.

Jerry Wurf (1919-1981), President, American Federation of State, County and Municipal Workers. Quoted in Tolchin and Tolchin, *Dismantling America: The Rush to Deregulate*, 1983.

Chapter 86

Religion

1. OUTLAW COMMUNISTS, NOT PRAYERS
PUT GOD BACK IN THE SCHOOLS
Bumper stickers protesting the U.S. Supreme Court's school prayer decisions. 1960's.

2. The Puritans' greatest concern seems to have been to establish a government of the church more consistent with the Scriptures, and a government of the state more agreeable to the dignity of human nature, than any they had seen in Europe, and to transmit such a government down to their posterity, with the means of securing and preserving it forever.
John Adams (1735-1826), 2nd President of the United States (Federalist-MA). *Dissertation on the Canon and Feudal Law*, 1765.

3. I don't think He would want to run a heaven that would keep Henry Fountain Ashurst out.
Henry Fountain Ashurst (1874-1962), U.S. Senator (D-AZ). Quoted in Morris K. Udall, *Too Funny to Be President*, 1988.

4. People call us *[Moslems]* terrorists while ours is a religion of peace.
Dawud Assad, President, U.S. Council of Masajid (Mosques). Quoted in *Time*, May 23, 1988.

5. The greatest vicissitude of things amongst men, is the vicissitude of sects and religions.
Francis Bacon, 1st Baron Verulam and Viscount St. Albans (1561-1626), Lord Chancellor of England. *Essays*, "Of Vicissitudes of Things," 1597.

6. People go to church for the same reasons they go to a tavern: to stupefy themselves, to forget their misery, to imagine themselves, for a few minutes anyway, free and happy.
Mikhail A. Bakunin (1814-1876), Russian prince and anarchist. *A Circular Letter to My Friends in Italy*.

7. Our goal is not ... the provinces, but the restoration of the caliphate and the rule of the Book of God throughout the Islamic nation.
Ali Belhadj, Algerian fundamentalist clergyman. Quoted in *Newsweek*, Jan. 7, 1991.

8. Jesus the Socialist
Francis Bellamy (1855-1931), Vice President, Society of Christian Socialists. Frequent lecture title.

9. An Indiana member of Congress says, "A Sunday in San Francisco will convince anyone that at least two-thirds of the population are composed of heathens and infidels."... But does the Indiana mind suppose that we came all the way to the Pacific to acquire faith and practice virtue? We could have done that sort of stupid business at home.
Ambrose Bierce (1842-1914?), American journalist. *News Letter*, Oct. 16, 1869.

10. The First Amendment has erected a wall between church and state. That wall must be kept high and impregnable. We could not approve the slightest breach.... State power is no more to be used so as to handicap religions than it is to favor them.
Hugo L. Black (1886-1971), U.S. Senator (D-AL) and U.S. Supreme Court Justice. *Everson* v. *Board of Education*, 1947.

11. Christianity is part of the law of England.
William Blackstone (1723-1780), British jurist. *Commentaries on the Laws of England*, IV, 1769.

12. Politics are not the task of a Christian.
Dietrich Bonhoffer (1906-1945), German Protestant theologian executed by the Nazis. *No Rusty Swords*, 1953.

13. The prince must employ his authority to destroy false religions in his state.
Jacques Bossuet (1627-1861), French Roman Catholic bishop. *Oeuvres de Bossuet*.

14. Liberty's chief foe is theology.
Charles Bradlaugh (1833-1891), secularist reformer and Member of Parliament, Great Britain. Remark to Viscount Peel.

15. The door of the Free Exercise Clause *[of the First Amendment]* stands tightly closed against any governmental regulation of religious beliefs as

such. Government may neither compel affirmation of a repugnant belief, nor penalize or discriminate against individuals or groups because they hold religious views abhorrent to the authorities.

William J. Brennan, Jr., U.S. Supreme Court Justice. *Sherbert* v. *Verner*, 1963.

16. The Bible states it. It must be so.

William Jennings Bryan (1860-1925), U.S. Secretary of State (D). Testimony at the trial of John T. Scopes, Dayton, TN, July 20, 1925.

17. No teacher should be allowed on the faculty of any American university unless he is a Christian.

William Jennings Bryan. Oft-quoted on his lecture circuit toward the end of his life.

18. An atheist is a man who has no invisible means of support.

John Buchan, 1st Baron Tweedsmuir (1875-1940), Member of Parliament, Great Britain (Liberal) and Governor-General of Canada. Attributed.

19. Politics and the pulpit are terms that have little agreement.

Edmund Burke (1729-1797), British statesman. *Reflections on the Revolution in France*, 1790.

20. Everything that we are about as African people in terms of our struggle for justice and freedom started in the church. There is no separation of the sacred and secular – of the church and state – in black America. There is no separation.

Calvin Butts, American Baptist minister and political activist. Interview, PBS, *The American Experience*, Nov. 28, 1989.

21. When I signed the Declaration of Independence I had in view not only our independence from England but the toleration of all sects.

Charles Carroll (1737-1832), Member, Continental Congress, and U.S. Senator (Federalist-MD). Letter to G. W. Parke Custis.

22. My earnest regard to preserve inviolate forever, in our new empire, the great principle of religious freedom ... which is independent of any religious doctrine and not restrained by any.

John Carroll (1735-1815), 1st American Roman Catholic bishop. *Gazette of the United States*, June 10, 1789.

23. I do not see my election of 1976 or my defeat in 1980 in the narrow focus of God's will for this specific event. I believe He has a purpose for individual lives as well as for the sweep of human events. He works out those purposes in ways far beyond our understanding. I was His in 1976. I am His in 1980. Now, let's go eat supper.

Jimmy Carter, 39th President of the United States (D-GA). Quoted in *Liberty*, Sept.-Oct. 1981.

24. A free church in a free state.

Camillo Benso di Cavour (1810-1861), Italian nationalist statesman. Speech in Italian Parliament, Mar. 27, 1861; the same phrase was used by Count de Montalembert at a Catholic conference in Malines, Aug. 20, 1863, and is sometimes attributed to him.

25. You shall none of you suffer for your opinions or religion, so long as you live peaceably, and you have the word of a king for it.

Charles II (1630-1685), King of Great Britain and Ireland. Comment to a Puritan delegation, 1662.

26. My ancestors brought the cross to America, and you have made a club of it.

Dennis Chavez (1888-1962), U.S. Congressman and U.S. Senator (D-NM). Comment on use of the cross in Pres. Eisenhower's anti-Communist crusade. Quoted by Eugene J. McCarthy, *Roll Call*, Sept. 18-24, 1989.

27. That it is much in their *[the colonists']* hearts (if they may be permitted) to hold forth a lively experiment that a most flourishing civil state may stand and be best maintained, and that among our British subjects, with full liberty of religious concernments.

John Clarke (1609-1676), English clergyman and physician. Petition to King Charles II of England for a charter for the colony of Rhode Island, 1663. Inscribed on the west front of the capitol in Providence.

28. All religions united with government are more or less inimical to liberty. All separated from government, are compatible with liberty.

Henry Clay (1777-1852), U.S. Senator (National Republican and Whig-KY), Speaker of the House, and U.S. Secretary of State. Congressional debate, Mar. 24, 1818.

29. Whenever the clergy succeeded in conquering political power in any country, the result has been disastrous to the interests of religion and inimical to the progress of humanity.

James Connolly (1870-1916), Irish labor leader. Quoted in George Seldes, *The Great Quotations*, 1960.

30. Too many pulpits have become political rostrums, openly taking sides with party or government as if Jesus Christ Himself, were He living today, would be either a Democrat or a Republican.

Charles E. Coughlin (1891-1979), American Roman Catholic priest and cofounder, Union Party. Address, Chicago, IL, 1930.

31. Christ would advocate what I am advocating; if I am a radical Christ is a radical.
Charles E. Coughlin. Quoted in *The New York Times*, July 26, 1936.

32. The influence which religious motives formerly possessed is now in a great measure exercised by political opinion.
John Dahlberg, 1st Baron Acton (1834-1902), historian and Member of Parliament, Great Britain (Whig). *The History of Freedom*, 1907.

33. *[Jesus]* organized a working class movement ... for no other purpose than to destroy class rule and set up the common people as the sole and rightful inheritors of the earth.
Eugene V. Debs (1855-1926), American Socialist. *Jesus, the Supreme Leader*, 1910.

34. We must not, under the pretext of secularism, chase God out of every public expression in society.
Albert Decourtray, French Roman Catholic cardinal. Quoted in *The New York Times*, Nov. 12, 1989.

35. The moment religion organizes into a specific creed it becomes a political force. From Moses down to Brigham Young, every creed-founder has been a Statebuilder.
Daniel DeLeon (1852-1914), American writer and Socialist. *The Vatican in Politics*, 1891.

36. ... the day intended for rest and cheerfulness *[turned]* into one of universal gloom, bigotry, and persecution ... for ... constables ... invested with arbitrary, vexatious, and the most extensive powers.... You cannot make people religious by act of Parliament, or force them to church by constables; they display their feelings by staying away.
Charles Dickens (1812-1890), British writer. Comment on the Sunday Observance Bill, introduced into the House of Commons by Sir Andrew Agnew. *Sunday Under Three Heads*, 1836.

37. Let us strangle the last king with the guts of the last priest.
Denis Diderot (1713-1784), French philosopher. 1750.

38. Yes, I am a Jew, and when the ancestors of the right honorable gentlemen were brutal savages in an unknown island, mine were priests in the temple of Solomon.
Benjamin Disraeli, 1st Earl of Beaconsfield (1804-1881), Prime Minister of Great Britain (Conservative). Reply to Daniel O'Connell.

39. The question is this: Is man an ape or an angel? I am on the side of the angels. I repudiate with indignation and abhorrence these new-fangled theories.
Benjamin Disraeli. Speech, House of Commons, Nov. 25, 1864.

40. Protestant Christianity ... tutored the first generations of Americans. It provided what we today would call the value system of the society.
Terry Eastland, Special Assistant to Attorney General Edwin Meese III (R). In Charles Horn, ed., *Whose Values?*, 1985.

41. I do not believe that any type of religion should ever be introduced into the public schools of the United States.
Thomas A. Edison (1847-1931), American inventor. *Do We Live Again?*

42. Science without religion is lame, religion without science is blind.
Albert Einstein (1879-1955), Nobel Laureate in Physics (Switzerland). *The World As I See It*, 1934.

43. Our government makes no sense, unless it is founded in a deeply felt religious faith – and I don't care what it is.
Dwight D. Eisenhower (1890-1969), 34th President of the United States (R-KS). 1st inaugural address, Jan. 20, 1953.

44. Who goes to church against his will come home accursed.
English proverb, c. 1450.

45. When religion controls government, political liberty dies; and when government controls religion, religious liberty perishes.
Samuel J. Ervin, Jr. (1896-1985), U.S. Congressman and U.S. Senator (D-NC). Apr. 23, 1971.

46. We *[the clergy]* have a threefold responsibility to people: get them baptized, get them saved, and get them registered to vote.
Jerry Falwell, American televangelist and founder, Moral Majority. PBS, Bill Moyers, *God and Politics*, Aug. 10, 1988.

47. Crime is not the less odious because sanctioned by what any particular sect may designate as religion.
Stephen J. Field (1816-1899), U.S. Supreme Court Justice. *Davis* v. *Beason*, 1889.

48. The great leaders of the American Revolution were determined to remove political support from every religious establishment.

Felix Frankfurter (1882-1965), U.S. Supreme Court Justice. *West Virginia Board of Education* v. *Barnette*, 1943.

49. Separation *[of church and state]* means separation, not something less.
Felix Frankfurter. *McCollum* v. *Board of Education*, 1948.

50. Religious beliefs pervade, and religious institutions have traditionally regulated virtually all human activity. It is a postulate of American life ... that those beliefs ... shall continue ... to exist, to function ... free of the dictates and directions of the state.
Felix Frankfurter. *McGowan* v. *Maryland*, 1961 (concurring).

51. All religions must be tolerated. Every man must get to heaven in his own way.
Benjamin Franklin (1706-1790), Member, Continental Congress and Constitutional Convention, Governor of Pennsylvania, and U.S. Minister to France. *In re the Catholic Schools*, 1740.

52. Religion is the idol of the mob; it adores everything it does not understand.
Frederick II (The Great) (1712-1786), King of Prussia. Letter to Voltaire, July 7, 1737.

53. All religion must be tolerated, for this way everyone may get to heaven in his own way.
Frederick II. Cabinet order, June 22, 1740.

54. It is now widely believed that God is a conservative.
John Kenneth Galbraith, American economist and U.S. Ambassador to India (D). Quoted in *The Toronto Star*, Nov. 15, 1980.

55. We therefore ... are pleased to grant indulgence to these men, allowing Christians the right to exist again and set up their places of worship; provided always that they do not offend against public order. In return ... it will be the duty of Christians to pray to God for our recovery *[and]* ... that the state may be preserved from danger.
Galerius (d. 311), Emperor of Rome. Edict from his deathbed.

56. The most heinous and the most cruel crimes of which history has record have been committed under the cover of religion or equally noble motive.
Mohandas K. Gandhi (1869-1948), Indian political and spiritual leader. *Young India*, July 7, 1927.

57. The Vatican is a dagger in the heart of Italy.
Giuseppe Garibaldi (1807-1882), Italian patriot, general, and politician. 1862.

58. A civilian ruler dabbling in religion is as reprehensible as a clergyman dabbling in politics. Both render themselves odious as well as ridiculous.
James Gibbons (1834-1921), American Roman Catholic cardinal. *The Faith of Our Fathers*, 1876.

59. American Catholics rejoice in our separation of church and state, and I can conceive no combination of circumstances likely to arise which would make a union desirable for either church or state.
James Gibbons. Quoted in *North American Review*, Mar. 1909.

60. We cannot change the profound and resistless tendencies of the age toward religious liberty. It is our business to guide and control their applications.
William E. Gladstone (1809-1898), Prime Minister of Great Britain (Liberal). Speech, Mar. 1851.

61. It is not the Bible that produced religion and morals, but religion and morals that produced the Bible.
William E. Gladstone. *The People's Bible History*, 1881.

62. Somehow I always knew that our first Jewish President would be an Episcopalian.
Harry Golden (1902-1981), American editor and humorist. In reference to Sen. Barry M. Goldwater, whose grandfather was Jewish. Remark during the presidential campaign, 1964.

63. Well, he didn't write it.
Ulysses S. Grant (1822-1885), 18th President of the United States (R-OH). Remark when told that Gen. Edwin Sumner had no faith in the Bible. Quoted by Charles Eliot Norton in a letter to Thomas Carlyle, May 7, 1874.

64. Leave the matter of religion to the family altar, the church, and the private school, supported entirely by private contributions. Keep the church and the state forever separate.
Ulysses S. Grant. Speech, Des Moines, IA, 1875.

65. Our princes take the word of God no more seriously than a cow does the game of chess.
Argula von Grumbach (1492-c.1549), German Lutheran reformer. Letter to Adam von Torring.

66. Never wage war on religion, nor upon seemingly holy institutions, for this thing has too great a force upon the minds of fools.

Francesco Guicciardini (1483-1540), Florentine statesman and historian. *Counsels and Reflections*, 1890.

67. Christianity is part of the Common Law of England.

Matthew Hale (1609-1676), Chief Justice, Court of King's Bench. *History of the Pleas of the Crown*, 1685.

68. I don't think any government can be just if it does not somehow have contact with the Omnipotent God.

Warren G. Harding (1865-1923), 29th President of the United States (R-OH). Primary campaign speech, Ohio, 1920.

69. We admit to no government by divine right.

William Henry Harrison (1773-1841), 9th President of the United States (Whig-OH). Quoted in "39 Men" exhibit.

70. Liberty is a new religion, the religion of our age.

Heinrich Heine (1797-1856), German writer. *English Fragments*, No. 13.

71. I'm not intolerant. I just know what it says in the Scriptures.

Jesse Helms, U.S. Senator (R-NC). Campaign speech, Oct. 1990.

72. Those who follow their conscience directly are of my religion.

Henry IV (1533-1610), King of France. Letter, 1577.

73. The proud monuments of liberty knew that ... intolerance in matters of faith had been from the earliest ages of the world the severest torment by which mankind could be afflicted; and that governments were only concerned about the actions and conduct of man, and not his speculative notions.

Jacob Henry (c. 1776-1823), North Carolina State Legislator. Speech, North Carolina House of Commons, Dec. 6, 1809.

74. Intrude not yourself into ecclesiastical matters.

Hilary (d. 367?), Roman Catholic bishop of Poitiers and Church doctor. Epistle to Emperor Constantine, 355.

75. I believe that I am acting in accordance with the will of the Almighty Creator: *By defending myself against the Jews, I am fighting for the Lord.*

Adolf Hitler (1889-1945), Führer of the Third German Reich. *Mein Kampf*, 1933.

76. They that approve a private opinion, call it opinion; but they that mislike it, heresy, and yet heresy signifies no more than private opinion.

Thomas Hobbes (1588-1679), English political philosopher. *Leviathan*, 1651.

77. Mass movements can rise and spread without belief in a God, but never without belief in a devil.

Eric Hoffer (1902-1983), American philosopher and longshoreman. *The True Believer*, 1951.

78. The Congress should at once submit an amendment to the Constitution which enables the right to religious devotion in all governmental agencies – national, state, or local.

Herbert Hoover (1874-1964), 31st President of the United States (R-IA). Quoted in *The New York Times*, July 1, 1962.

79. The problem for the churches and synagogues of America is ... the tendency to think of religion itself in terms of "usefulness" and "service" to the community, or the contribution faith can make toward guaranteeing personal "peace of mind." Like almost everything else, religion in America is valued for services rendered.

Robert M. Hutchins (1899-1977), President, University of Chicago, and President, Center for the Study of Democratic Institutions. *The Power of Reason*, 1964.

80. To rule by fettering the mind through fear of punishment in another world, is just as base as to use force.

Hypatia (370-415), Greek philosopher. Quoted in Elbert Hubbard, *Little Journeys to the Homes of Great Teachers*, 1908.

81. Freedom to differ is not limited to things that do not matter much.... The test of its substance is the right to differ as to things that touch the heart of the existing order.

Robert H. Jackson (1892-1954), U.S. Attorney General (D) and U.S. Supreme Court Justice. *West Virginia State Board of Education* v. *Barnette*, 1943.

82. The day that this country ceases to be free for irreligion it will cease to be free for religion – except for the sect that can win political power.

Robert H. Jackson. *Zorach* v. *Clauson*, 1951.

83. It does me no injury for my neighbor to say there are twenty Gods, or no God. It neither picks my pocket nor breaks my leg.

Thomas Jefferson (1743-1826), 3rd President of the United States (Democratic Republican-VA). *Notes on the State of Virginia*, Query XVII, 1784.

84. Difference of opinion is advantageous in religion. The several sects perform the office of a *censor morum* over each other.

Thomas Jefferson. *Ibid.*

85. To compel a man to furnish contributions of money for the propagation of opinions which he disbelieves, is sinful and tyrannical.

Thomas Jefferson. *Acts for Establishing Religious Freedom in Virginia,* 1786.

86. *Be it enacted by the General Assembly,* That no man shall be compelled to frequent or support any religious worship, place, or Ministry whatsoever, nor shall be enforced, restrained, molested, or burthened in his body or goods, nor shall otherwise suffer on account of his opinions or belief; but that all men shall be free to profess, and by argument to maintain, their opinions in matters of religion, and that the same shall in no wise diminish, enlarge, or affect their civil capacities.

Thomas Jefferson. *Virginia Statute for Religious Freedom,* Jan. 16, 1786.

87. I never will, by any word or act, bow to the shrine of intolerance, or admit a right in inquiry into the religious opinions of others.

Thomas Jefferson. Letter to Edward Dowse, Apr. 19, 1803.

88. History I believe furnishes no example of a priest-ridden people maintaining a free civil government.

Thomas Jefferson. Letter to Baron Alexander von Humboldt, Dec. 6, 1813.

89. ... the loathsome combination of church and state.

Thomas Jefferson. Letter to the Reverend Charles Clay, Jan. 29, 1815.

90. I never told my own religion nor scrutinized that of another. I never attempted to make a convert, nor wished to change another's creed. I am satisfied that yours must be an excellent religion to have produced a life of such exemplary virtue and correctness. For it is in our lives, and not from our words, that our religion must be judged.

Thomas Jefferson. Letter to Mrs. H. Harrison Smith, 1816.

91. I am of a sect by myself, as far as I know.

Thomas Jefferson. Response when asked his religion. Letter to the Rev. Ezra Styles, 1819.

92. The Catholics had the right secured to them by the Constitution of worshipping the God of their fathers in the manner dictated by their consciences.... This country is not prepared to establish an inquisition to try and punish men for their religious beliefs.

Andrew Johnson (1808-1875), 17th President of the United States (War Democrat-TN). Comment when Catholics were blamed for the defeat of Henry Clay in 1844. Quoted in Claude F. Bowers, *The Tragic Era,* 1929.

93. We allow none ... to be dragged to the altars unwillingly.

Julian (331-363), Emperor of Rome. Edict, 362.

94. I hope that no American ... will waste his franchise and throw away his vote by voting either for me or against me solely on account of my religious affiliation. It is not relevant.

John F. Kennedy (1917-1963), 35th President of the United States (D-MA). Quoted in *Time,* July 25, 1960.

95. I ask you tonight ... to judge me on the basis of fourteen years in the Congress – on my declared stands against an ambassador to the Vatican, against unconstitutional aid to parochial schools, and against any boycott of the public schools (which I attended myself) – instead of judging me on the basis of these pamphlets and publications we have all seen that carefully selected quotations out of context from the statements of Catholic Church leaders, usually in other countries, frequently in other centuries, and rarely relevant to any situation here – and always omitting, of course, that statement of the American bishops in 1948 which strongly endorsed church-state separation.... I do not speak for my church on public matters – and the church does not speak for me.

John F. Kennedy. Speech to the Houston Ministerial Association, Houston, TX, Sept. 12, 1960.

96. I do not accept the right ... of any ecclesiastical official to tell me what I shall do in the sphere of my public responsibility as an elected official.

John F. Kennedy. Response to questioner, Houston, TX, Sept. 12, 1960.

97. I believe in an America where the separation of church and state is absolute – where no Catholic prelate would tell the President, should he be a Catholic, how to act, and no Protestant minister would tell his parishioners how to vote.... I believe in an America that is officially neither Catholic, Protestant, or Jewish ... for while this year it may be a Catholic against whom the finger of suspicion is pointed, in other years it has been, and may someday be again, a Jew – or a Quaker – or a Unitarian – or a Baptist.

John F. Kennedy. Campaign speech, Texas, 1960.

98. We can pray a good deal more at home. We can attend our churches with a good deal more fidelity.

John F. Kennedy. Comment on the Supreme Court's ban on public school prayer, June 1963.

99. My revolution is about Islam. It is not about the price of melons.

Ruhollah Khomeini (1900-1989), Iranian cleric (Ayatollah) and revolutionary leader. Quoted on PBS, *World Without Walls*, May 17, 1990.

100. The church ... is not the master or the servant of the state, but rather the conscience of the state.

Martin Luther King, Jr. (1929-1968), American clergyman and civil rights leader. *Strength to Love*, 1963.

101. You don't have to be Roman Catholic to love the Pope.

Edward I. Koch, U.S. Congressman and Mayor of New York City (D). Remark during the visit of Pope John Paul II to the United States, Oct. 1979.

102. He who owns the land, dictates the religion. (*Cuius regio, eius religio.*)

Latin maxim used to justify wholesale conversion of conquered populations to the religion of the conqueror.

103. Religion is a clumsy sort of whiskey in which the slaves of capital drown their human being and their revenge for an existence little worthy of men.

V. I. Lenin (1870-1924), Premier of the U.S.S.R. *New Life*, Dec. 16, 1905.

104. All oppressing classes of every description need two social functions to safeguard their domination: the function of a hangman and the function of a priest. The hangman is to quell the protest ... the priest reconciles them to class domination, weans them away from revolutionary actions.

V. I. Lenin. 1915.

105. To despise legitimate authority, no matter in whom it is invested, is unlawful; it is rebellion against God's will.

Pope Leo XIII (1810-1903). Encyclical, *Immortale Dei*, Nov. 1, 1885.

106. It is not lawful for the state, any more than for the individual, either to disregard all religious duties, or to hold in equal favor different kinds of religion.

Pope Leo XIII. *Ibid.*

107. That I am not a member of any Christian church is true; but I have never denied the truth of the Scriptures.

Abraham Lincoln (1809-1865), 16th President of the United States (R-IL). Address to voters, July 31, 1846.

108. Certainly there is no contending against the will of God, but still there is some difficulty in ascertaining it, and applying it, to particular cases.

Abraham Lincoln. Quoted in *American Heritage*, Sept.-Oct. 1989.

109. If we allow the Jews to have dwellings amongst us, why should we not allow them to have synagogues?

John Locke (1632-1704), English political philosopher. *Letter Concerning Toleration*, 1689.

110. How could God do this to me after all I have done for Him?

Louis XIV (1638-1715), King of France. Remark after his army was defeated at Blenheim, Bavaria, Aug. 13, 1704.

111. Where church and state are habitually associated it is natural that minds, even of high order, should unconsciously come to regard religion as only a subtler mode of police.

James Russell Lowell (1819-1891), U.S. Ambassador to Spain and Great Britain. *Latest Literary Essays and Addresses*, 1891.

112. For political and intellectual freedom and for all the blessings that political and intellectual freedom have brought in their train, she *[England]* is chiefly indebted to the great rebellion of the laity against the priesthood.

Thomas Babington Macaulay, 1st Baron Macaulay (1800-1859), historian and Secretary of War, Great Britain (Liberal). *History of England*, I, 1848.

113. It is ... the duty of princes and heads of republics to uphold the foundations of the religion of their countries, for then it is easy to keep their people religious and consequently well conducted and united.

Niccolò Machiavelli (1469-1527), Florentine statesman and political philosopher. *The Prince*, 1513.

114. Who does not see that the same authority which can establish Christianity in exclusion of all other religions may establish, with the same ease, any particular sect of Christians in exclusion of all other sects.

James Madison (1751-1836), 4th President of the United States (Democratic Republican-VA). *Memorial and Remonstrance*, 1785.

115. Where there is a variety of *[religious]* sects, there cannot be a majority of any one sect to oppress and persecute the rest.... The United States abound in such a variety of sects, that it is a strong security against religious persecution.

James Madison. Speech, Virginia Convention, June 12, 1788.

116. Religion and government will both exist in greater purity, the less they are mixed together.
James Madison. Letter to Edward Livingston, July 10, 1822.

117. In the papal system, government and religion are in a manner consolidated, and that is found to be the worst of government.
James Madison. 1832.

118. For any human government, then, to attempt to coerce and predetermine the religious opinions of children by law, and contrary to the will of their parents, is unspeakably more criminal than the usurpation of such control over the opinions of men.... The sovereign antidote against these machinations is free schools for all, and the right of every parent to determine the religious education of his children.
Horace Mann (1796-1859), American educator, founder, and 1st President, Antioch College, Yellow Springs, OH. *Report of the Secretary of the Board of Education of Massachusetts*, 1948.

119. Religion is the sign of the oppressed creature, the sentiment of a heartless world, and the soul of soulless conditions. It is the opium of the people.
Karl Marx (1818-1883), German economist and Socialist. *Critique of Hegel's Philosophy of Right*, 1844.

120. That religion, or the duty which we owe to our Creator, and the manner of discharging it, can be directed only by reason and conviction, not by force or violence.
George Mason (1725-1792), Member, Virginia and Federal Constitutional Conventions. *Virginia Bill of Rights*, XVI, June 12, 1776.

121. Any body of men who believe in hell will persecute whenever they have the power.
Joseph M. McCabe (1867-1957), British philosopher. *What Gods Cost Men*.

122. Voluntaryism is the necessary corollary of religious freedom.
Sidney E. Mead, American religious historian. *The Lively Experiment*, 1963.

123. No religious education may be imparted without the consent of the government.
Mexican Constitution, 1917.

124. Although he's regularly asked to do so, God does not take sides in American politics.
George J. Mitchell, U.S. Senator (D-ME). Congressional hearing, July 13, 1987.

125. God doesn't belong in politics.
Walter F. Mondale, Vice President of the United States and U.S. Senator (D-MN). Response to criticisms by Rev. Jerry Falwell about America's moral decline. Campaign remark, 1984; see below, Mark Russell.

126. The powers of the present age both in government and in opposition are, by the grace of Heaven, equally hostile to Catholics.
Charles Montalembert (1810-1870), French statesman and writer. Statement during his trial before the Chamber of Peers, Paris, Sept. 19, 1831.

127. Religion is a species of mental disease.
Benito Mussolini (1883-1945), dictator of Italy (Fascist). Speech, July 1924.

128. A nation must have a religion, and that religion must be under the control of the government.
Napoléon I (1769-1821), military leader and Emperor of France. Remark to Count Thibaudeau, June 6, 1801.

129. Religious fanaticism is a powerful and a successful engine when exercised over an uncivilized people. In France, if we were to resort to such jugglery, we should be laughed at. In Russia, it raises up devoted assassins.
Napoléon I. *Maxims*.

130. I do not believe in forms of religion, but in the existence of a God.
Napoléon I. *Ibid*.

131. An absolutely rigorous separation of church and state means the secularization of the community.
Reinhold Niebuhr (1892-1971), American Protestant theologian. *Christianity and Crisis*, Sept. 17, 1947.

132. Religion is so frequently a source of confusion in political life, and so frequently dangerous to democracy, precisely because it introduces absolutes into the realm of relative values.
Reinhold Niebuhr. Quoted in *Brown Alumni Monthly*, May 1989.

133. Two great European narcotics, alcohol and Christianity.
Friedrich Wilhelm Nietzsche (1844-1900), German philosopher. *The Twilight of the Gods*, 1888.

134. I would have made a good pope.
Richard M. Nixon, 37th President of the United States (R-CA). Quoted in *Loose Talk*, 1980.

135. We live in a pluralistic society with people of widely divergent religious backgrounds or none at all. Government cannot endorse beliefs of one group without sending a clear message to nonadherents that they are outsiders.
Sandra Day O'Connor, U.S. Supreme Court Justice. Speech, Bicentennial Conference on Religion in Public Life, Philadelphia, PA, May 31, 1991.

136. Kingcraft and priestcraft have fell out so often that 'tis a wonder this grand and ancient alliance is not broken off forever. Happy for mankind will it be when such a separation shall take place.
James Otis (1725-1783), Member, Colonial Massachusetts Legislature. *The Rights of the British Colonies Asserted and Proved*, 1764.

137. My country is the world, and my religion is to do good.
Thomas Paine (1737-1809), American political philosopher. *The Rights of Man*, 1792.

138. Persecution is not an original feature in any religion; but it is always the strongly marked feature of all law-religions, or religions established by law.
Thomas Paine. *Ibid.*

139. The adulterous connection of church and state.
Thomas Paine. *The Age of Reason*, 1793.

140. Men never do evil so completely and cheerfully as when they do it from religious conviction.
Blaise Pascal (1623-1662), French mathematician and philosopher. *Pensées*, XIV.

141. Government ... ought indeed to take account of the religious life of the citizenry and show it favor, since the function of government is to make provision for the common welfare.
Pope Paul VI (1897-1978). Declaration, Dec. 7, 1965.

142. There is no law in Pennsylvania against riding on broomsticks.
William Penn (1644-1718), founder of Pennsylvania. Statement dismissing a charge of witchcraft, 1666.

143. *No Cross, No Crown*
William Penn. Title of booklet, 1669.

144. No People can be truly happy, though under the greatest enjoyment of Civil Liberties, if abridged of the Freedom of their Consciences, as to their Religious Profession and Worship.
William Penn. *The Pennsylvania Charter of Privileges*, Oct. 28, 1701.

145. Clericalism, that is the enemy. (*Le cléricalisme, voilà l'ennemi.*)
Alphonse Peyrat (1812-1891), French politician. Speech, National Assembly, 1859.

146. Our lawgiver *[Moses]*... did not make religion a part of virtue, but had the insight to make the virtues part of religion.
Philo Judaeus (c.20 B.C.-c.A.D. 40), Alexandrian philosopher and diplomat. *Against Apion*, II.

147. It belongs to the civil power to define what the rights of the Catholic Church are and the limits within which she may exercise these rights... In the case of conflicting laws enacted by the two powers, the civil law prevails.... The Church ought to be separated from the state, and the state from the Church.
Pope Pius IX (1792-1878). Encyclical, *Venerabilis*, Oct. 17, 1867.

148. It would not be permissible for Catholic Action to become an organization of party politics.
Pope Pius XII (1876-1958). Speech, May 3, 1951.

149. Thank God, under our Constitution there was no connection between church and state.
James K. Polk (1795-1849), 11th President of the United States (D-TN). Remark to a British clergyman, 1845.

150. If you start to say there is error in Scripture, where do you stop?
Paul Pressler, Texas State Judge. PBS, Bill Moyers, *God and Politics*, Aug. 10, 1988.

151. You say there is but one way to worship and serve the Great Spirit. If there is but one way, why do you white people differ so much about it?
Red Jacket (1751-1830), Chief, Seneca Indians. To Christian missionaries, c. 1805.

152. I know of nothing in my lifetime that could give more aid and comfort to Moscow than this bold, malicious, aesthetic, and sacrilegious twist by this unpredictable group of uncontrolled despots.
L. Mendel Rivers (1905-1970), U.S. Congressman (D-SC). Comment on the Supreme Court's decision on school prayer. Quoted in Earl Katcher, *Earl Warren: A Political Biography*, 1967.

153. I think it's wrong to stand up and say you're God's candidate.
Pat Robertson, American evangelist and Republican presidential nomination candidate. Aug. 12, 1986.

154. The Republican convention opened with a prayer. If the Lord can see his way to bless the Republi-

can party the way it's been carrying on, then the rest of us ought to get it without even asking.

Will Rogers (1879-1935), American humorist. June 12, 1928.

155. As Commander-in-Chief, I take pleasure in commending the reading of the Bible to all who serve in the armed forces. Throughout the centuries, men of many faiths and diverse origins have found in the sacred book words of wisdom, words of counsel and inspiration. It is a fountain of strengths, and now as always, an aid in attaining the highest aspirations of the human soul.

Franklin D. Roosevelt (1882-1945), 32nd President of the United States (D-NY). Foreword to the pocket Bible issued by the U.S. armed forces in 1942.

156. As President it is none of my business to interfere for or against the advancement of any man in any church.

Theodore Roosevelt (1858-1919), 26th President of the United States (R-NY). Letter to Amb. Bellamy Storer, 1903.

157. While I am President and you are Ambassador, neither of us in his public relation is to act as Protestant or Catholic, Jew or Gentile.

Theodore Roosevelt. Instruction to Amb. Bellamy Storer, 1903.

158. In my cabinet at the present moment there sit side by side Catholic and Protestant, Christian and Jew.

Theodore Roosevelt. Letter, 1908.

159. Mr. Mondale said that God doesn't belong in politics. And apparently God feels the same way about Walter Mondale.

Mark Russell, American political comedian. Nov. 10, 1984.

160. The Bible is literature, not dogma.

George Santayana (1863-1952), American philosopher. *Introduction to the Ethics of Spinoza*, 1910.

161. The several Sorts of Religion in the World are little more than so many spiritual Monopolies.

George Savile, 1st Marquess of Halifax (1633-1695), Lord Privy Seal of England. *Political Thoughts and Reflections*, 1750.

162. *Scrutamini scripturas [Let us examine the scriptures].* These two words have undone the world.

John Selden (1584-1654), English jurist and Member of Long Parliament. *Table Talk. Scriptures.*

163. If we must admit nothing but what we read in the Bible, what will become of the Parliament? For we do not read of that there.

John Selden. *Table Talk: Human Invention.*

164. There's no such thing as spiritual jurisdiction; all is civil, the church's is the same with the lord mayor's.

John Selden. *Table-Talk: Jurisdiction.*

165. So important has politics become that now men judge religion by its attitude toward politics, rather than politics by its attitude toward religion.

Fulton J. Sheen (1895-1979), American Roman Catholic archbishop and television personality. *Seven Pillars of Peace*, 1944.

166. There is one iron rule in politics. With one exception ministers, rabbis, and priests should stay out of politics. The only exception is when they agree with me.

Mark Shields, American political columnist. PBS, *MacNeil-Lehrer News Hour*, Dec. 8, 1989.

167. When it is said that religious faith is above the Constitution and above law ... that is the basis of a theocratic state.

V. P. Singh, Prime Minister of India. Speech upon leaving office. Quoted in *The Washington Post*, Nov. 7, 1990.

168. There's no chance for a Catholic to be President. Not in my lifetime or yours.
[Smith was the first Catholic to run for President.]

Alfred E. Smith (1873-1944), Governor of New York (D). Remark to Arthur Mullen, 1925.

169. I recognize no power in the institution of my Church to interfere with the operations of the Constitution of the United States or the enforcement of the law of the land.

Alfred E. Smith. Presidential campaign response to an open letter from Charles G. Marshall on the issue of Catholicism, Apr. 17, 1927.

170. Christian theology is the grandmother of Bolshevism.

Oswald Spengler (1880-1936), German philosopher. *The Hour of Decision*, 1934.

171. How many divisions did you say the Pope has?

Joseph Stalin (1879-1953), Premier of the U.S.S.R. Remark to Winston Churchill at the Potsdam Conference, July 1945.

172. I cannot see how an official religion is established by letting those who want to say a prayer say it.

Potter Stewart (1915-1985), U.S. Supreme Court Justice. *Engel* v. *Vitale*, 1962 (dissent).

173. Some say revivals don't last. Neither does a bath, but it's helpful.
Billy Sunday (William Ashley) (1862-1935), American baseball player and evangelist. 1903.

174. If a minister believes and teaches evolution, he is a stinking skunk, a hypocrite, and a liar.
Billy Sunday. 1925.

175. We have just enough religion to make us hate, but not enough to make us love one another.
Jonathan Swift (1667-1745), Irish clergyman and satirist. *Thoughts on Various Subjects*, 1706.

176. I found there a country with thirty-two religions and only one sauce.
Charles-Maurice de Talleyrand-Périgord (Prince de Bénévent) (1754-1838), French diplomat and statesman. Description of England. *Autant en Apportent les Mots*.

177. Nothing is more foreign to us Christians than politics.
Tertullian (c.150-c.225), Christian writer. *Apologetics*.

178. If God did not exist, it would be necessary to invent him. (*Si Dieu n'existait pas, il faudrait l'inventer.*)
Voltaire (François-Marie Arouet) (1694-1778), French historian and dramatist. *Collection of Letters on the Miracles*, XCVI, 1767.

179. The rivers of America will run red with blood filled to their banks before we will submit to them taking the Bible out of our schools.
Davis H. Waite (1825-1901), Governor of Colorado. Quoted by evangelist Billy Sunday. Revival meeting, 1912.

180. Laws are made for the government of actions, and while they cannot interfere with mere religious beliefs and opinions, they may with practices.
Morrison R. Waite (1816-1888), Chief Justice, U.S. Supreme Court. Comment on the Mormon practice of polygamy. *Reynolds* v. *United States*, 1879.

181. The responsibility of the politician is to God.
Dayton Walker, City Councilman, Greenville, SC. Quoted in *Governing*, Sept. 1988.

182. The biblical record is heavily loaded on the side of the Progressive Independents.
Henry A. Wallace (1888-1956), U.S. Secretary of Agriculture (D), U.S. Secretary of Commerce, and Vice President of the United States. *Statesmanship and Religion*, 1948.

183. No church censure shall degrade or dispose any man from any Civill dignitie, office, or Authoritie he shall have in the Commonwealth.
Nathaniel Ward (c.1578-1652), Puritan codifier. *The Massachusetts Body of Liberties*, 1641.

184. Civill Authoritie hath power and libertie to deale with any Church member in a way of Civill Justice, notwithstanding any Church relation, office, or interest.
Nathaniel Ward. *Ibid*.

185. The disconnection of Church and State was a master stroke for freedom and harmony.
Josiah Warren (1798-1874), American reformer and anarchist. *Equitable Commerce*, 1855.

186. Whatever makes good Christians, makes them good citizens.
Daniel Webster (1782-1852), U.S. Congressman (Federalist-NH and MA), U.S. Senator (Federalist and Whig-MA), and U.S. Secretary of State. Speech, Plymouth, MA, Dec. 22, 1820.

187. The Bible is a book of faith, and a book of doctrine, and a book of morals, and a book of religion, of especial revelation from God; but it is also a book which teaches man his own individual responsibility, his own dignity, and his equality with his fellow-man.
Daniel Webster. Speech at completion of Bunker Hill Monument, Breed's Hill, Boston, MA, June 17, 1843.

188. Among politicians, the esteem of religion is profitable, the principles of it are troublesome.
Benjamin Whichcote (1609-1683), English philosopher. Quoted in Ralph L. Woods, *The World Treasury of Religious Quotations*, 1966.

189. God requireth not a uniformity of religion to be enacted and enforced in any civil state.
Roger Williams (c.1603-1683), English clergyman and founder of Rhode Island. *The Bloody Tenet of Persecution for Cause of Conscience*, 1644.

190. ... no person within the said colony *[of Rhode Island]* at any time hereafter shall be in any wise molested, punished, disquieted, or called in question for any difference in opinion in matters of religion ... that all and every person may, from time to time and at all times hereafter, freely and fully have and enjoy his and their own judgments and consciences in matters of religious concernments.
Roger Williams. *Charter of Rhode Island*, 1647.

191. American liberty is a religion. It is a thing of the spirit.

Wendell L. Willkie (1892-1944), American writer and Republican presidential candidate. Radio address, July 4, 1941.

192. I believe in Divine Providence. If I did not, I would go crazy.

Woodrow Wilson (1856-1924), 28th President of the United States (D-NJ). 1919.

193. Woe to the crown that doth the cowl obey!

William Wordsworth (1770-1850), British poet. *Ecclesiastical Sonnets*, 1822.

194. This Bible is for the government of the people, by the people, and of the people.

John Wycliffe (c.1320-1384), English religious reformer and Bible translator. Preface, *Wycliffe English Bible*, 1382.

195. All shades of Sectarians exist here *[in Pennsylvania]* down to open infidelity.

Nikolaus Ludwig von Zinzendorf (1700-1760), bishop, Reformed Moravian Church. Comment after his visit to America, 1742.

Chapter 87

Revolution and Revolutionaries

1. FRIENDS! BRETHREN! COUNTRYMEN! That worst of plagues, the detested TEA, shipped for this port by the East India Company, is now arrived in this Harbor; the Hour of Destruction or manly Opposition to the Maccinations of Tyranny stares you in the face; every Friend to his Country, to Himself, or to his Posterity, is now called upon to meet in Fanueil Hall, at nine o'clock THIS DAY (at which Time the Bells will ring), to make a united and successful Resistance to the last, worst, and most destructive Measure of Administration.
   Anonymous notice, Boston, MA, *Weekly News-Letter*, Dec. 2, 1773.

2. HAVE PATIENCE, RADICALS – ROME WASN'T BURNT IN A DAY.
   Bumper sticker, Berkeley, CA, 1969.

3. The *[American]* Revolution was effected before the war commenced. The Revolution was in the minds and hearts of the people.
   John Adams (1735-1826), 2nd President of the United States (Federalist-MA). Speech, July 4, 1818.

4. In monarchy the crime of treason may admit of being pardoned or lightly punished but the man who dares rebel against the laws of a republic ought to suffer death.
   Samuel Adams (1722-1803), Governor of Massachusetts and Member, Continental Congress. Comment on Shays' Rebellion, 1787.

5. Revolution by the Have-Nots has a way of inducing a moral revelation among the Haves.
   Saul D. Alinsky (1909-1972), American community organizer. *Rules for Radicals*, 1971.

6. There can be no such thing as a successful traitor, for if one succeeds he becomes a founding father.
   Saul D. Alinsky. *Ibid.*

7. We will take up the ball of the Revolution where our fathers stopped it and roll it to the final consummation of freedom and independence for the masses.
   Anti-Renters Resolution, 1839.

8. The most radical revolutionary will become a conservative the day after the revolution.
   Hannah Arendt (1906-1975), American political philosopher. *The New Yorker*, Sept. 12, 1970.

9. Revolution, not elections!
   Jean-Bertrand Aristede, President of Haiti. Prescription for Haiti's political, social, and economic ills, 1990.

10. Poverty is the parent of revolution.
    Aristotle (384-322 B.C.), Greek philosopher and teacher. *Politics*.

11. Revolutions break out when opposite parties, the rich and the poor, are equally balanced, and there is little or nothing between them.
    Aristotle. *Ibid.*

12. Inferiors revolt in order that they may be equal and equals that they may be superior. Such is the state of mind which creates revolutions.
    Aristotle. *Ibid.*

13. Those who are inclined to compromise can never make a revolution.
    Kemal Atatürk (1881-1938), founder and 1st President of the Turkish Republic. Speech in the National Assembly, 1920.

14. You can either have revolution or you can have revival.
    Jim Bakker, American TV evangelist. Praise the Lord (PTL) Club broadcast, 1986.

15. ... wasting the country's time and energy by just talking too much.

Omar Hassan Ahmed Bashir, Brigadier General, leader of coup, and interim Prime Minister of Sudan. Explanation of the ouster of Prime Minister Sadiq Mahdi, June 30, 1989.

16. A government needs one hundred soldiers for every guerilla it faces.

Fulgencio Batista (1901-1973), President of Cuba. Jan. 1, 1959.

17. To die for the revolution is a one-shot deal; to live for the revolution means taking on the more difficult commitment of changing our day-to-day life patterns.

Frances M. Beal, American civil rights leader. "Double Jeopardy: To Be Black and Female," *Sisterhood Is Powerful,* 1970.

18. Rebellion! The very word is a confession; an avowal of tyranny, outrage, and oppression. It is taken from the despot's code, and has no terror for other than slavish souls.

Judah P. Benjamin (1811-1884), U.S. Senator (Whig and D-LA); Confederate Attorney General, Secretary of War, and Secretary of State. Senate speech, "Farewell to the Union," 1861.

19. You know how absurd is the fiction put forward by our enemies in the Northern states that the great Civil War which raged between 1861 and 1865 would never have taken place but for Jefferson Davis and myself. Such mighty convulsions, which amount indeed to revolutions, are never the work of individuals, but of divided nations.

Judah P. Benjamin. Letter to Francis Lawley, 1883.

20. The removal of a tyrant is not merely justifiable; it is the highest duty of every true revolutionist.

Alexander Berkman (1870-1936), American anarchist. *Prison Memoirs of an Anarchist,* 1912.

21. The revolutionist has no personal right to anything. Everything he has or earns belongs to the Cause. Everything, even his affections.

Alexander Berkman. *Ibid.*

22. It can't work – for Lenin and Trotsky are both extremely unpopular.... Lenin ... will never be able to dominate the Russian people.

Herman Bernstein (1876-1935), U.S. Minister to Albania. Statement written while he was Russian correspondent for *The New York Times,* covering the Russian revolution, Nov. 9, 1917.

23. The tree of Liberty only grows when watered by the blood of tyrants. (*L'arbre de la libertè ne croît qu'arrosé par le sang des tyrans.*)

Barère de Vieuzac Bertrand (1755-1841), French lawyer, revolutionary, and supporter of the Terror. Speech, French National Convention, 1792.

24. Liberalism is but childishness, which is easily brought to reason; but revolution is a force, and one must know how to use it.

Otto von Bismarck-Schoenhausen (1815-1898), Chancellor of Germany. 1862.

25. The right of revolution is the inherent right of a people to cast out their rulers, change their policy, or effect radical reforms in their system of government or institutions, by force or a general uprising, when the legal and constitutional methods of making such changes have proved inadequate, or are so obstructed as to be unavailable.

Henry Campbell Black (1860-1927), American legal scholar. *Constitutional Law,* 1910.

26. All the former prisioners are now the government.

Shirley Temple Black, U.S. Chief of Protocol and U.S. Ambassador to Czechoslovakia (R). Interview with Connie Chung, CBS, Jan. 20, 1990.

27. I have no fear of losing the throne through revolution because I could always get a job in the United States as a *[locomotive]* engineer or college professor.

Boris (1895-1943), Czar of Bulgaria. Quoted in David Randall, *Royal Misbehavior.*

28. Americans have always been amongst the most revolutionary people of the world.

Earl Browder (1891-1973), Communist Party candidate for President of the United States. Speech, 1937.

29. If it is deemed necessary that I should forfeit my life for the furtherance of the ends of justice, and mingle my blood further with the blood of my children, and with the blood of millions in this slave country whose rights are disregarded by wicked, cruel, and unjust enactments, I say, let it be done.

John Brown (1800-1859), American abolitionist. Speech at his trial, Nov. 2, 1959.

30. I, John Brown, am now quite certain that the crimes of this guilty land will never be purged away but with blood.

John Brown. Last writing before his execution, Dec. 2, 1859.

31. Civil war has taught them *[Americans]* that "the sacred right of insurrection" is as much out of place in a democratic state as in an aristocratic or a monarchical state; and that the government

should always be clothed with ample authority to arrest and punish whoever plots its destruction.

Orestes Augustus Brownson (1803-1876), American clergyman and writer. *The American Republic*, 1865.

32. Let us look the danger fairly in the face. Secession is neither more nor less than revolution.

James Buchanan (1791-1868), 15th President of the United States (D-PA). Annual message to Congress, Dec. 3, 1860.

33. A reform is a correction of abuses; a revolution is a transfer of power.

Edward Bulwer-Lytton, 1st Baron Lytton of Knebworth (1803-1873), Colonial Secretary, Great Britain (Conservative), and writer. Speech on the Reform Bill, House of Commons, 1866.

34. Revolutions are not made with rose water.

Edward Bulwer-Lytton. *The Parisians*, 1873.

35. Make the revolution a parent of settlement, and not a nursery of future revolutions.

Edmund Burke (1729-1797), British statesman. *Reflections on the Revolution in France*, 1790.

36. Kings will be tyrants from policy when subjects are rebels from principle.

Edmund Burke. *Ibid.*

37. All modern revolutions have ended in a reinforcement of the power of the state.

Albert Camus (1913-1960), Nobel Laureate in Literature (France). *The Rebel*, 1951.

38. Thought once awakened does not again slumber.

Thomas Carlyle (1795-1881), Scottish essayist and historian. *Of Heroes and Hero-Worship*, 1841.

39. No great revolution can happen in a state without revolutions or mutations of private property.

Charles Carroll (1737-1832), U.S. Senator (Federalist-MD). 1781.

40. If there be no right to rebellion against a state of things that no savage tribe would endure without resistance, then I am sure it is better for men to fight and die without right than to live in such a state of right as this.

Roger Casement (1864-1916), Irish revolutionary. Speech at his trial, June 29, 1916.

41. I began the revolution with eighty-two men. If I had to do it again, I would do it with ten or fifteen and absolute faith. It does not matter how small you are if you have faith and a plan of action.

Fidel Castro, Premier of Cuba. Quoted in *The New York Times*, Apr. 22, 1959.

42. There are only two groups I recognize in Cuba: those who wholly support the revolution and those who are joining the reactionaries.

Fidel Castro. Quoted in *Time*, June 22, 1959.

43. A revolution is a struggle to the death between the future and the past.

Fidel Castro. Speech, Havana, Jan. 1961.

44. Every revolutionary movement ... proposes the greatest number of achievements possible.

Fidel Castro. Interview, *Playboy*, Jan. 1967.

45. It is the duty of all revolutionary governments to help all the forces of liberation in whatever part of the world.

Fidel Castro. *Ibid.*

46. We can neither export revolution nor can the United States prevent it.

Fidel Castro. Interview, *Newsweek*, Jan. 9, 1984.

47. One can justifiably say that the decisions unanimously adopted by this great forum of Romanian Communists represents the wisdom and determination of our whole party and all our people.

Nicolae Ceausescu (1918-1989), Chairman, Communist Party of Romania. Speech, 14th Congress of the Romanian Communist Party, Nov. 24, 1989. Spoken one month before a revolution ousted him and he was executed.

48. You can never have a revolution in order to establish a democracy. You must have a democracy in order to have a revolution.

G. K. Chesterton (1874-1936), British writer. *Tremendous Trifles*, 1909.

49. All revolutions must be social revolutions, based upon fundamental changes in society; otherwise it is not a revolution, but merely a change in government.

Chingling Soon (1891-1981), Chinese politician and wife of Sun Yat-sen. *The People's Tribune*, July 14, 1927.

50. The revolt against any oppression usually goes to an opposite extreme for a time; and that is right and necessary.

Tennessee Claflin (1845-1923), American writer and feminist. *Woodhull and Claflin's Weekly*, 1871.

51. An oppressed people are authorized whenever they can to rise and break their fetters.

Henry Clay (1777-1852), U.S. Senator (National Republican and Whig-KY), Speaker of the House, and U.S. Secretary of State. Speech, House of Representatives. Mar. 4, 1818.

52. Loyalty ... is a realization that America was born of revolt, flourished in dissent.
Henry Steele Commager, American political historian. *Freedom, Loyalty, Dissent*, 1959.

53. If the citizens of the United States are to regain their freedom from excessive government, they must do so by means of a counterrevolution.
Robert DePugh, founder, Patriotic Party, and member, John Birch Society. *Blueprint for Victory*, 1966.

54. Then join in hand, brave Americans all. By uniting we stand, by dividing we fall.
John Dickenson (1732-1808), Member, Continental Congress, President of Delaware, and President of Pennsylvania. *The Liberty Song*, 1768.

55. There is only one step from fanaticism to barbarism.
Denis Diderot (1713-1784), French philosopher. Dedication, *Essay on Merit and Virtue*, 1745.

56. In politics experiments mean revolutions.
Benjamin Disraeli, 1st Earl of Beaconsfield (1804-1881), Prime Minister of Great Britain (Conservative). *Popanilla*, 1828.

57. The only books on revolution were published by Communists.
William O. Douglas (1898-1980), U.S. Supreme Court Justice. *The U.S. and Revolution*, occassional paper No. 116, Center for the Study of Democratic Institutions.

58. Outraged men will seek revenge.
Frederick Douglass (c.1817-1895), Recorder of Deeds, District of Columbia, and U.S. Minister to Haiti. Quoted in Lerone Bennett, Jr., *Pioneers in Protest*, 1968.

59. An intelligence service is the ideal vehicle for a conspiracy *[against its own government]*. Its members can travel about at home and abroad under secret orders, and no questions are asked. Every scrap of paper in the files, its membership, its expenditure of funds, its contacts, even enemy contacts, are state secrets.
Allen W. Dulles (1893-1969), Director, Central Intelligence Agency. Writing about the *Abwehr*, the German World War II intelligence service. Quoted in David Wise, *The American Police State*, 1976.

60. The right to rebellion is the right to seek a higher rule, and not to wander in mere lawlessness.
George Eliot (Mary Ann Evans) (1819-1880), British writer. *Felix Holt*, 1866.

61. By the rude bridge that arched the flood,
Their flag to April's breeze unfurl'd,
Here once the embattled farmers stood,
And fired the shot heard round the world.
Ralph Waldo Emerson (1803-1882), American writer. "Concord Hymn," written for the dedication of a monument on Apr. 19, 1836, at Concord bridge in honor of the battles of Lexington and Concord, Apr. 19, 1775.

62. A desperate disease requires a dangerous remedy.
Guy Fawkes (1570-1606), English revolutionary. Statement at his interrogation in the Gunpowder Plot, Nov. 5, 1605.

63. I am not a do-gooder. I am a revolutionary. A revolutionary woman.
Jane Fonda, American actress and political activist. Quoted in *The Los Angeles Weekly*, Nov. 28-Dec. 4, 1980.

64. To die for an idea is to place a pretty high price upon conjecture.
Anatole France (Jacques-Anatole François Thibault) (1844-1924), Nobel Laureate in Literature (France). *The Revolt of the Angels*, 1914.

65. The Americans have escaped from England. (*Les Américains ont échappé à l'Angleterre.*)
Frederick II (The Great) (1712-1786), King of Prussia. Quoted by John Quincy Adams, *Diary*, Nov. 25, 1799.

66. Rebellion must be managed with many swords; treason to his prince's person may be with one knife.
Thomas Fuller (1608-1661), English clergyman and royal chaplain. *Holy and Profane States*, "The Traitor," 1642.

67. Martyrdom does not end something. It is only the beginning.
Indira Gandhi (1917-1984), Prime Minister of India. Speech to Parliament, Aug. 12, 1971.

68. If blood is to be shed, let it be our blood.... For man lives freely only by his readiness to die, if need be, at the hand of his brother, never by killing him.
Mohandas K. Gandhi (1869-1948), Indian political and spiritual leader. *True Patriotism: Some Sayings of Mahatma Gandhi*, 1939.

69. The willing sacrifice of the innocent is the most powerful answer to insolent tyranny that has yet been conceived by God or man.
Mohandas K. Gandhi. *Ibid.*

70. The foundation of our movement rests on complete nonviolence, whereas violence is the final refuge of the government. And as no energy can be created without resistance, our nonresistance to government violence must bring the latter to a standstill.
Mohandas K. Gandhi. *Non-Violence in Peace and War*, 1948.

71. Neither God, nor angels, or just men, command you to suffer for a single moment. Therefore it is your solemn and imperative duty to use every means, both moral, intellectual, and physical, that promise success.... Brethren, arise, arise! Strike for your lives and liberties.... Let your motto be resistance, resistance, resistance!
Henry Highland Garnet (1815-1881), American clergyman and abolitionist. Speech, Liberty Party Convention, Buffalo, NY, Aug. 31, 1843.

72. If the State cannot survive the antislavery agitation, then let the State perish.
William Lloyd Garrison (1805-1879), American editor and abolitionist. *The Liberator*, Jan. 1, 1831.

73. A crank is a little thing that makes revolutions.
Henry George (1839-1897), American political economist. Attributed.

74. The more revolutions occur, the less things change.
Georgie Anne Geyer, American journalist. Introduction, *The New Latins*, 1970.

75. Though a revolution may call itself "national," it always marks the victory of a single party.
André Gide (1869-1951), French writer. *Journals*, Oct. 17, 1941.

76. The American Revolution was a conservative revolution.
William E. Gladstone (1809-1898), Prime Minister of Great Britain (Liberal). *North American Review*, Sept.-Oct. 1878.

77. The past is lying in flames. The future will rise from the flames within our hearts.
Joseph Goebbels (1897-1945), Minister of Propaganda and National Enlightenment, Third German Reich. Speech at a university-organized book-burning, University of Freiburg, May 10, 1933.

78. A great revolution is never the fault of the people, but of the government.
Johann Wolfgang von Goethe (1749-1832), German writer. Quoted in Johann Eckermann, *Conversations with Goethe*, Jan. 4, 1824.

79. Demonstrate before the palaces of the rich; demand work. If they do not give you work, demand bread. If they deny you both, take bread. It is your sacred right.
Emma Goldman (1869-1940), American anarchist. Speech, 1893.

80. The ultimate end of all revolutionary social change is to establish the sanctity of human life, the dignity of man, the right of every human being to liberty and well-being.
Emma Goldman. *My Further Disillusionment*, 1924.

81. A revolution should constant develop, there must be no marking time. Should we again get stuck, we are in for trouble. Therefore only forward!
Mikhail Gorbachev, President of the U.S.S.R. *Perestroika*, 1987.

82. We are opposed to doctrines that seek to justify the export of revolution.
Mikhail Gorbachev. Statement to Fidel Castro. Quoted in *Time*, Apr. 17, 1989.

83. The war is over and the rebels are our countrymen again.
Ulysses S. Grant (1822-1885), 18th President of the United States (R-OH). Quoted on PBS, *The Civil War*, Sept. 23, 1990.

84. I believe in the armed struggle as the only solution for those people who fight to free themselves.
Ernesto G. (Che) Guevara (1928-1967), Cuban revolutionary leader. Letter to his parents, 1965.

85. The men who make revolutions are always despised by those who profit from them.
François Guizot (1787-1874), Premier of France. *Corneille and His Times*, 1855.

86. Revolution is the right of slaves.
Leivick Halpern (1886-1962), Russian writer, Yiddish poet, and Bund activist. *The Golem*, 1921.

87. If the representatives of the people betray their constituents, there is then no recourse left but in the exertion of that original right of self-defense which is paramount to all forms of government.
Alexander Hamilton (1755-1804), Member, Continental Congress and Constitutional Convention, and U.S. Secretary of the Treasury (Federalist-NY). *The Federalist*, No. 28.

88. Shall the majority govern or be governed? Shall the nation rule or be ruled? Shall the general will prevail, or the will of a faction? Shall there be government or no government?

Alexander Hamilton. Comment on Shays' Rebellion, 1794.

89. If you follow this policy *[encouraging liberation movements in Eastern Europe]*, you're going to have the deaths of some brave people on your conscience.

W. Averell Harriman (1891-1986), Governor of New York (D), U.S. Ambassador-at-Large, and U.S. Secretary of Commerce. In reference to Hungary. Letter to U.S. Secretary of State John Foster Dulles, 1956.

90. Tecumseh *[the Shawnee warrior and chief]* is one of those uncommon geniuses which spring up occasionally to produce revolutions.

William Henry Harrison (1773-1841), 9th President of the United States (Whig-OH). Letter to U.S. Secretary of War John Armstrong, 1810.

91. Without a global revolution in the sphere of human consciousness, nothing will change for the better in the sphere of our being.... We still don't know how to put morality ahead of politics, science, and economy.

Vaclav Havel, President of Czechoslovakia and writer. Address to the Congress, Feb. 21, 1990.

92. From the saintly and single-minded idealist to the fanatic is often but a step.

Friedrich A. Hayek (1899-1992), Nobel Laureate in Economics (United States). *The Road to Serfdom*, 1944.

93. Revolutions and *bolts [from the party]* are alike. They are sacred when the facts justify them. When not so justified they are blunders of the sort that is worse than crime.

Rutherford B. Hayes (1822-1893), 19th President of the United States (R-OH). *Diary*, Jan. 28, 1888.

94. If bad institutions and bad men be got rid of only by killing, then the killing must be done.

William Randolph Hearst (1863-1951), U.S. Congressman (D-NY); founder, Independence League Party; journalist; and publisher. Editorial, *New York Evening Journal*, Apr. 10, 1901.

95. We first understand the glory and the greatness of the Hitler revolution when we carry implanted deep within us this reflection: Everything that is great is in the midst of the storm.

Martin Heidegger (1899-1976), German philosopher. Speech on becoming rector of the University of Freiburg, May 28, 1933.

96. The National Socialist revolution is not simply the taking of power in the state by one party from another, but brings a complete revolution of our German existence. Henceforth every matter demands decision, and every act demands responsibility.

Martin Heidegger. Speech to professors of German universities and colleges, Leipzig, Nov. 11, 1933.

97. Tarquin and Caesar each had his Brutus, Charles the First his Cromwell, and George the Third ("Treason!" cried the Speaker) – *may profit by their example*. If *this* be treason, make the most of it.

Patrick Henry (1736-1799), Member, Continental Congress and Virginia Constitutional Ratification Convention, and Governor of Virginia. Debate, Virginia House of Burgesses, May 29, 1765.

98. The first duty of a revolutionist is to get away with it.

Abbie Hoffman (1936-1989), American revolutionary and founder, Yippie International Party. Speech, Brandeis University, Waltham, MA, Oct. 8, 1966.

99. *Revolution for the Hell of It*

Abbie Hoffman. Book title, 1968.

100. I was probably the only revolutionary ever referred to as "cute."

Abbie Hoffman. *Soon to Be a Major Motion Picture*, 1980.

101. They sow the wind, and they shall reap the whirlwind.

Old Testament, *Hosea* 8:7.

102. How the Russian revolutionists loved each other before they had anything to divide!

Edgar Watson Howe (1853-1937), American editor and writer. *Ventures in Common Sense*, 1919.

103. When dictatorship is a fact, revolution becomes a right.

Victor Hugo (1802-1885), French writer, and Member, Constituent Assembly and National Assembly at Bordeaux. Quoted in *Time*, June 3, 1957.

104. It is futile to expect a hungry and squalid population to be anything but violent and gross.

Thomas H. Huxley (1825-1895), British biologist and President, Royal Society. *Joseph Priestley*, 1874.

105. Fire in the lake: The image of revolution.

I Ching: Book of Changes.

106. Better to die on one's feet than live on one's knees. (*Mejor morir a pie que vivir rodillas.*)

Dolores Ibarruri (1895-1989), Spanish revolutionary. Speech, Valencia, Spain, 1936.

107. A little rebellion now and then is a good thing.... Unsuccessful rebellions indeed generally establish the encroachment on the rights of people which have produced them. An observation of this truth should render honest republican governments so mild in their punishment of rebellion so as not to discourage them too much.

Thomas Jefferson (1743-1826), 3rd President of the United States (Democratic Republican-VA). Letter to James Madison, Jan. 30, 1787.

108. Debt and revolution are inseparable as cause and effect.

Thomas Jefferson. Letter to Samuel Smith, 1821.

109. REBELLION TO TYRANTS IS OBEDIENCE TO GOD.

Motto on Thomas Jefferson's seal. Attributed to Benjamin Franklin in Henry S. Randall, *Life of Jefferson*, 1858.

110. Revolution breeds its own excesses.

Roy Jenkens, Home Secretary and Chancellor of the Exchequer, Great Britain (Conservative). PBS, *Worlds Without Walls*, University of Pennsylvania, Philadelphia, PA, May 17, 1990.

111. He who is not against us is with us.

Janos Kadar, 1st Secretary, Communist Party of Hungary. Statement during the Hungarian Revolution, 1956.

112. Every revolution evaporates and only leaves behind the slime of a new bureaucracy.

Franz Kafka (1883-1924), Austrian writer. Quoted on PBS, *American Interest*, Apr. 11, 1990.

113. A new Zimbabwe can only be born out of the barrel of a gun.

Kenneth David Kaunda, President of Zambia. Quoted in *Time*, July 18, 1977.

114. The power which establishes a state is violence; the power which maintains it is violence; the power which eventually overthrows it is violence.

Kenneth David Kaunda. Quoted in Colin M. Morris, ed., *Kaunda on Violence*, 1980.

115. What we have on the streets ... is almost a type of revolution – people who feel no interest, no stake in the world at hand.

Sharon Pratt Kelly, Mayor of Washington, DC (D). Quoted in *The Washington Post*, Sept. 22, 1991.

116. No amount of arms and armies can help stabilize those governments which are unable or unwilling to achieve social and economic reform and development. Military pacts cannot help nations whose social injustice and economic chaos invite insurgency and penetration and subversion.

John F. Kennedy (1917-1963), 35th President of the United States (D-MA). Address to Congress, May 25, 1961.

117. Only those who have felt the pain of deprivation, poverty, and weakness, the poor and the pious are the true creators of and participants in revolutions.

Ruhollah Khomeini (1900-1989), Iranian cleric (Ayatollah) and revolutionary leader. Quoted on Teheran Radio, July 20, 1988.

118. Revolutions are the locomotives of history.

Nikita S. Khrushchev (1894-1971), Premier of the U.S.S.R. Speech to the Supreme Soviet, 1957.

119. No system disappears quickly because habits live on.

Jeane J. Kirkpatrick, U.S. Ambassador to the United Nations (R). Seminar, American Defense Institute, C-SPAN, Feb. 16, 1990.

120. The conventional army loses if it does not win. The guerrilla wins if he does not lose.

Henry M. Kissinger, U.S. Secretary of State and National Security Advisor (R). *Foreign Affairs*, Jan. 1969.

121. Our Revolution is getting on as well as it can with a nation that has attained its liberty at once, and is still liable to mistake licentiousness for freedom.

Marquis de Lafayette (1757-1834), French statesman and Major General, Continental Army. Letter to George Washington from Paris, Mar. 17, 1790.

122. The "have nots" outnumber the "haves." No wonder the ruling class of every country grows more and more alarmed.

Robert M. La Follette (1855-1925), Governor of Wisconsin and U.S. Senator (R). Letter to his family, Dec. 28, 1918.

123. No, Sire, it is a revolution. (*Non, sire, c'est une révolution.*)

François de La Rochefoucauld-Liancourt (1747-1827), French courtier. Response to King Louis XVI's question, "Is it a revolt?" when a mob stormed the Bastille, July 14, 1789.

124. An anarchist is just a bourgeois turned inside out.

V. I. Lenin (1870-1924), Premier of the U.S.S.R. "Party Organization and Party Literature," *Novaya Zhizn*, Nov. 13, 1905.

125. We shall now proceed to construct the socialist order.

V. I. Lenin. Speech after capturing the Winter Palace, Congress of Soviets, Oct. 26, 1917.

126. The revolutionary dictatorship of the proletariat ... *[is a]* state that is democratic for the proletariat and the poor in general.

V. I. Lenin. *The State and Revolution*, 1917.

127. Inciting to revolution is treason, not only against man, but also against God.

Pope Leo XIII (1810-1903), Encyclical, *Immortale Dei*, Nov. 1, 1885.

128. Any people anywhere, being inclined and having the power, have the right to rise up and shake off the existing government, and form a new one that suits them better.

Abraham Lincoln (1809-1865), 16th President of the United States (R-IL). House debate, Jan. 12, 1848.

129. Be not deceived. Revolutions do not go backward.

Abraham Lincoln. May 19, 1856.

130. This country with its institutions belongs to the people who inhabit it. Whenever they shall grow weary of the existing government, they can exercise their constitutional right of amending it, or their revolutionary right to dismember or overthrow it.

Abraham Lincoln. 1st inaugural address, Mar. 4, 1861.

131. Before the revolution *[of 1911]* we were slaves. And now we are the slaves of former slaves.

Lu Xun (1881-1936), Chinese writer. Quoted in *The New York Times*, Aug. 19, 1990.

132. The oppressed never free themselves – they do not have the necessary strengths.

Clare Boothe Luce (1903-1987), U.S. Congresswoman and U.S. Ambassador to Italy and Brazil (R-CT). Quoted in *Saturday Review*, Sept. 15, 1974.

133. Passive fatalism can never be the role of a revolutionary party.

Rosa Luxemburg (1880-1919), German revolutionary. *The Crisis in the German Social Democracy*, 1919.

134. The people are fed up with politics and partisanship.

Omar Hassan Sadek Mahdi, Sudanese military dictator. Explanation for staging a military coup. Quoted in *The Los Angeles Times*, July 1, 1989.

135. Government violence can only do one thing and that is to breed counterviolence.

Nelson Mandela, founder, African National Congress, South Africa. Trial testimony, Pretoria, 1962.

136. The revolutionary war is a war of the masses; it can be waged only by mobilizing the masses and relying on them. Revolution is the proper occupation of the masses.

Mao Tse-tung (1893-1976), Chairman, Communist Party of China. *Be Concerned with the Well-Being of the Masses, Pay Attention to Methods of Work*, Jan. 27, 1934.

137. We Communists are like seeds and the people are like the soil. Wherever we go, we must unite with the people, take root and blossom among them.

Mao Tse-tung. *On the Chungking Negotiations*, Oct. 17, 1945.

138. Grasp Revolution.

Mao Tse-tung. Admonition to students, 1946.

139. Revolution is not a dinner party, not an essay, nor a painting, nor a piece of embroidery; it cannot be advanced softly, gradually, carefully, considerately, respectfully, politely, plainly, and modestly.

Mao Tse-tung. Quoted in *Time*, Dec. 18, 1950.

140. If a house be divided against itself, that house cannot stand.

New Testament, *Mark* 3:25; see *Matthew* 12:25. Quoted by Abraham Lincoln in his speech to the Republican State Convention, Springfield, IL, June 16, 1858.

141. Let the ruling classes tremble at a Communist revolution. The proletarians have nothing to lose but their chains. They have a world to win.

Karl Marx (1818-1883), German economist and Socialist. *The Communist Manifesto*, 1848.

142. Insurrection is an art.

Karl Marx. Quoted by Leon Trotsky, *History of the Russian Revolution*, 1932.

143. That government is, or ought to be instituted for the common benefit, protection, and security of the people, nation, or community; ... and that when any government shall be found inadequate or contrary to these purposes, a majority of the community hath an indubitable, unalienable, and indefeasible right to reform, alter, or abolish it, in such manner as shall be judged most conducive to the public weal.

George Mason (1725-1792), Member, Virginia and Federal Constitutional Conventions. *The Virginia Bill of Rights*, III, June 12, 1776.

144. Every kingdom divided against itself is brought to desolation; and every city or house divided against itself shall not stand.

New Testament, *Matthew* 12:25; compare *Mark* 3:25, above.

145. Since governments take the right of death over people, it is not astonishing that people should sometimes take the right of death over governments.

Guy de Maupassant (1850-1893), French writer. *Sur l'Eau.*

146. The pogroms are oil for the wheels of revolution.

Vladimir Medem (1879-1923), Russian revolutionary. Comment after the Kishinev massacre, Oct. 22, 1905.

147. Never in our history has the country been confronted with so many revolutionary elements determined to destroy by force the government it stands for.

John N. Mitchell (1913-1988), U.S. Attorney General (R). Quoted in *The Washington Post,* May 12, 1973.

148. When you make your peace with authority you become authority.

Jim Morrison (1944-1971), lead singer, The Doors. Quoted in Jonathon Green, *The Book of Rock Quotes,* 1978.

149. We must take things into our own hands. We must return to the Mosaic law of an eye for an eye and a tooth for a tooth. What does it matter if 10 million of us die? There will be 7 million of us left, and they will enjoy justice and freedom.

Elijah Muhammad (1896-1975), Messenger, Nation of Islam. Speech, Washington, DC, May 31, 1959.

150. The reign of terror is not a revolution: it is only a necessary instrument in a determined phase of the revolution.

Benito Mussolini (1883-1945), dictator of Italy (Fascist). Quoted in Gilbert Seldes, *You Can't Print That,* 1929.

151. Revolution is an idea which has found its bayonets.

Napoléon I (1769-1821), military leader and Emperor of France. Maxim frequently quoted by Benito Mussolini.

152. The weapons of revolution are obscenity, blasphemy, and drugs.

Richard Neville, editor, *Oz* (American counterculture newspaper). 1968.

153. Our ambition is to change the American government. I think that will ultimately be done through armed violence, because the American ruling circle will not give up without a bitter struggle.

Huey P. Newton, cofounder, Black Panther Party. *Playboy,* May 1973.

154. All revolutions are the work of a minority.

Max Nordau (1849-1923), German physician, writer, and Zionist. Remark to Theodor Herzl, Basel, Switzerland, 1897.

155. A great revolution ... must ... be productive of hazard, vicissitudes, and perhaps calamity. But the question for you is, whether or not it is not worthwhile to pass through the ordeal of temporary suffering to establish permanent liberty.

Feargus O'Connor (1794-1855), Irish Chartist leader. 1848.

156. A revolution only lasts fifteen years, a period which coincides with the effectiveness of a generation.

José Ortega y Gasset (1883-1955), Spanish philosopher and statesman. *The Revolt of the Masses,* 1930.

157. Most revolutionaries are potential Tories because they imagine that everything can be put to rights by altering the shape of society.

George Orwell (Eric Blair) (1903-1950), British writer. *1984,* 1949.

158. The Independence of America was accompanied by a Revolution in the principles and practices of governments.... Government founded on a moral theory ... on the indefeasible hereditary Rights of Man, is now revolving from West to East.

Thomas Paine (1737-1809), American political philosopher. *The Rights of Man,* 1792.

159. If there be any doubt of the character of the leaders and agitators amongst those avowed revolutionists, a visit to the Department of Justice and an examination of their photographs would dispel it. Out of the sly and crafty eyes of many of them leap cupidity, cruelty, insanity, and crime; from their lopsided faces, sloping brows, and misshapen features may be recognized the unmistakable criminal type.

A. Mitchell Palmer (1872-1936), U.S. Congressman and U.S. Attorney General (D-PA). Congressional testimony, 1918.

160. We are a rebellious nation. Our whole history is treason ... our creeds are infidelity to the mother church; our Constitution, treason to our fatherland.

Theodore Parker (1810-1860), American clergyman and abolitionist. Thanksgiving Day sermon, Boston, MA, 1850.

161. There isn't any science of revolution, and there won't be for a long time. There is only a groping of the life force, partly guided empirically.

Ivan Petrovich Pavlov (1849-1936), Nobel Laureate in Medicine and Physiology (U.S.S.R.). Letter to Max Eastman.

162. *Oppression* makes a *Poor* Country, and a *Desperate* People, who always wait an Opportunity to *change.*

William Penn (1644-1718), founder of Pennsylvania. *Some Fruits of Solitude, in Reflections and Maxims,* 1693.

163. Revolutions are not made. They come.

Wendell Phillips (1811-1884), American orator and reformer. Speech to the Massachusetts Anti-Slavery Society, Boston, MA, Jan. 28, 1852.

164. Politics is but the common pulse-beat, of which revolution is the fever spasm.

Wendell Phillips. Speech to the Massachusetts Anti-Slavery Society, Boston, MA, 1853.

165. Insurrection of thought always precedes insurrection of arms.

Wendell Phillips. Speech on John Brown, Harper's Ferry, WV, Nov. 1, 1859.

166. Perseverance is more prevailing than violence; and many things which cannot be overcome when they are taken together, yield themselves up when taken little by little.

Plutarch (c.46-c.120), Greek biographer. *The Parallel Lives: Sertorius.*

167. I see the ardor for liberty catching and spreading.... Tremble all ye oppressors of the world! You cannot hold the world in darkness.... Restore to mankind their rights; and consent to the correction of abuses, before they and you are destroyed together.

Richard Price (1723-1791), British mathematician, clergyman, and political publisher. Sermon, Revolution Society of Great Britain, Nov. 4, 1789.

168. To resist him that is set in authority is evil.

Ptah-Hotep (c.2675 B.C.), Egyptian writer. *Instruction.*

169. The only justification of rebellion is success.

Thomas B. Reed (1839-1902), U.S. Congressman and Speaker of the House (R-ME). House debate, Apr. 12, 1878.

170. Subversive? Of course we're subversive. But if they really believe that you can start a revolution with a record, they're wrong. I wish we could. We're more subversive at live appearances.

Keith Richard, British rock star. Quoted in Jonathon Green, *The Book of Rock Quotes,* 1978.

171. We were against revolution. And, therefore, we waged war against those conditions which make revolution – against the inequalities and resentments that breed them.

Franklin D. Roosevelt (1882-1945), 32nd President of the United States (D-NY). Speech, New York State Democratic Convention, Sept. 30, 1936.

172. He *[William Randolph Hearst]* spreads the spirit, he follows the methods, and he is guided by the selfish motives of a revolutionist.

Elihu Root (1845-1937), U.S. Senator (R-NY), U.S. Secretary of War, U.S. Secretary of State, and Nobel Laureate in Peace. Debate with William Randolph Hearst, Elmira, NY, 1906.

173. From Berkeley to Wisconsin to Columbia to Harvard, all the evidence reinforces the old maxim of European revolutionists: No demonstration should be considered successful unless it provokes the authorities to use the police against the demonstrators. The more police violence, the easier the charges of brutality – and the better for the cause.

Leo Rosten, American writer and Deputy Director, War Information Office. *A Trumpet for Reason,* 1970.

174. When in doubt, burn. Fire is the revolutionary's god. Fire is instant theater. No words can match fire.

Jerry Rubin, American revolutionary. *Growing Up at 37,* 1976.

175. It was thought by radicals in those days *[the 1920's and 1930's]* that one ought to support the Russian Revolution, whatever it might be doing, since it was opposed by reactionaries, and criticism of it played into their hands. I ... was for some time in doubt as to what I ought to do. But in the end I decided in favor of what seemed to me to be the truth. I stated publicly that I thought the Bolshevik regime abominable, and I have never seen any reason to change this opinion.

Bertrand Russell, 3rd Earl Russell of Kingston (1872-1970), British philosopher and reformer. *Portraits from Memory,* 1969.

176. Revolt and terror pay a price.
Order and law have a cost.

Carl Sandburg (1878-1967), American poet and political biographer. *The People, Yes,* 1936.

177. Freedom of speech and of the press do not protect disturbances to the public peace or the attempt to subvert the government ... or to impede or hinder it in the performance of governmental duties. It does not protect publications prompting the overthrow of the government by force.

Edward T. Sanford (1865-1930), U.S. Supreme Court Justice. *Gitlow* v. *New York*, 1924.

178. Revolutions are ambiguous things. Their success is generally proportionate to their power of adaption and to the reabsorption within them of what they rebelled against.

George Santayana (1863-1952), American philosopher. *The Life of Reason*, 1906.

179. When the people contend for their liberty, they seldom get anything for their victory but new masters.

George Savile, 1st Marquess of Halifax (1633-1695), Lord Privy Seal of England. *Political Thoughts and Reflections*, 1750.

180. The aim of a revolution can be nothing else than to make room for the will of the people.

Carl Schurz (1829-1906), U.S. Senator (R-MO). "The Political Life of America," in *The Patriotic Anthology*, 1941.

181. You can jail a revolutionary but you cannot jail the revolution.

Bobby Seale, Chairman, Black Panther Party. 1969.

182. I know and all the world knows that revolutions never go backwards.

William H. Seward (1801-1872), Governor of New York (Whig), U.S. Senator (Whig and R), and U.S. Secretary of State. Speech, "The Irrepressible Conflict," Rochester, NY, Oct. 25, 1858.

183. Revolutions have never lightened the burden of tyranny; they have only shifted it to another shoulder.

George Bernard Shaw (1856-1950), Nobel Laureate in Literature (Great Britain). *Man and Superman*, 1903.

184. A slave is ... a man who waits for someone else to come and free him.

Anastasia M. Shkilnyk, Canadian writer. *A Poison Stronger Than Love: The Destruction of an Ojibwa Community*, 1985.

185. The only land in these United States which will ever remain in the possession of a British officer will measure but six feet by two.

Mary Slocumb (1760-1836), Revolutionary patriot. Remark to a British colonel. Quoted in *Women of the American Revolution*, 1848.

186. There's going to be a revolution in the country, and I'm going to lead it.

Gerald L. K. Smith (1898-1976), American clergyman and cofounder, Union Party. Remark to T. Semmes Walmsley, Mayor of New Orleans, LA, 1936.

187. Capitalism, not socialism, is the true revolutionary force.

Hernando de Soto, Peruvian economist. Quoted in *Forbes*, Jan. 23, 1989.

188. To bring about a revolution a leading revolutionary minority is required. But the most talented, devoted, and energetic minority would be helpless if it did not rely upon the at least passive support of millions.

Joseph Stalin (1879-1953), Premier of the U.S.S.R. Interview with H. G. Wells, July 23, 1934.

189. The export of revolution is nonsense. Every country makes its own revolution if it wants to, and if it doesn't want to, there will be no revolution.

Joseph Stalin. Interview with Roy Howard, 1936.

190. You cannot make a revolution with silk gloves.

Joseph Stalin. Quoted in John Gunther, *Soviet Russia Today*, 1958.

191. The time to stop a revolution is at the beginning, not the end.

Adlai E. Stevenson (1900-1965), Governor of Illinois (D) and U.S. Ambassador to the United Nations. Campaign speech, Sept. 11, 1952.

192. We are not playing politics with the capitalist system; we are seeking to destroy the system.

John Stonehouse, Member of Parliament, Great Britain (Socialist). Keynote address, Socialist Party conference, Scarborough, England, Oct. 4, 1960.

193. The government of the United States is intrinsically too weak, and the powers of the state governments too strong; that the danger always is much greater of anarchy in the parts, than tyranny in the head.

Joseph Story (1779-1845), U.S. Supreme Court Justice. *Martin* v. *Hunter Lessee*, 1816.

194. If people are willing to endure the horror of war in a quest for freedom, can we abandon them in their fight?

Steven D. Symms, U.S. Congressman and U.S. Senator (R-ID). In reference to congressional support for the "Contra" revolutionaries in Nicaragua. *The Congressional Digest*, Mar. 1988.

195. Whoever did not live in the years neighboring 1789 does not know what the pleasure of living means.

Charles-Maurice de Talleyrand-Périgord (Prince de Bénévent) (1754-1838), French diplomat and statesman. In reference to the "reign of terror" of the French Revolution. Quoted in François Guizot, *Mémoirs,* 1867.

196. For a King, death is better than dethronement and exile.

Theodora (508-548), Empress of Rome. Attributed.

197. The Revolution of the United States was the result of a mature and reflecting preference for freedom, not of a vague or ill-defined craving for independence. It did not contract an alliance with the turbulent passions of anarchy, but its course was marked, on the contrary, by a love of order and law.

Alexis de Tocqueville (1805-1859), French writer. *Democracy in America,* 1835.

198. You can't overthrow a leader if you can't find him.

Omar Torrijos (1926-1981), Panamanian strongman. Explanation for maintaining a dozen residences in different parts of the country. Remark to Hamilton Jordan, Dec. 11, 1979.

199. The revolution is not so obedient, so tame, that it can be led on a leash as we imagined.

Leon Trotsky (1879-1940), Russian revolutionary theorist. Speech, Third Congress of the Communist International, Moscow, 1921.

200. In a country economically backward, the proletariat can take power earlier than in countries where capitalism is advanced.

Leon Trotsky. *The Permanent Revolution,* 1931.

201. The fundamental premise of a revolution is that the existing social structure has become incapable of solving the urgent problems of development of the nation.

Leon Trotsky. *History of the Russian Revolution,* 1932.

202. You are either on the side of the repressed or on the side of the oppressor. You can't be neutral.

Desmond M. Tutu, Anglican archbishop of South Africa and Nobel Laureate in Peace. Quoted in *Newsweek,* Dec. 17, 1984.

203. Progress affects few. Only revolution can affect many.

Alice Walker, American writer and feminist. *Ms.,* Aug. 1979.

204. There is an ultimate violent remedy, above the Constitution and in defiance of the Constitution, which may be resorted to when a revolution is to be justified.

Daniel Webster (1782-1852), U.S. Congressman (Federalist-NH and MA), U.S. Senator (Federalist and Whig-MA), and U.S. Secretary of State. Jan. 26, 1830.

205. The word "revolution" is a word for which you kill, for which you die, for which you send the laboring masses to their death, but which does not possess any content.

Simone Weil (1910-1943), French revolutionist and political philosopher. *Reflections Concerning the Causes of Liberty and Social Oppression,* 1934.

206. Where the populace rise at once against the never-ending audacity of elected persons.

Walt Whitman (1819-1902), American poet. *Leaves of Grass,* "Broad-Axe Poem," 1856.

207. No sympathy with those who seek to seize the power of government to advance their own personal interests or ambition.

Woodrow Wilson (1856-1924), 28th President of the United States (D-NJ). Comment on the Mexican revolutionaries. Press statement, Mar. 11, 1913.

208. The whole heart of the United States is with the people of Russia in their attempt to free themselves forever from autocratic government and become the masters of their own life.

Woodrow Wilson. Comment after the Russian Revolution. Mar. 11, 1918.

209. The Workers Party prides itself on being a Communist Party; that means that it considers its work to build up and lead the forces which will bring about a proletarian revolution in the United States and establish a Soviet form of government and a dictatorship of the Proletariat.

Workers Party of America. Statement, Mar. 31, 1924.

210. Revolution is always based on land.

Malcolm X (Malcolm Little) (1925-1965), American black power advocate. Speech, Militant Labor Forum, New York City, 1964.

211. Who ever heard of angry revolutionists swinging their bare feet together with their oppressors in lily-pad park pools, with gospels and guitars and "I Have a Dream" speeches?

Malcolm X. Quoted in Robert Weisbrot, *Freedom Bound,* 1989.

Chapter 88

Science, Technology, and Space

1. Today's research is tomorrow's future.
University of Arkansas TV advertisement, 1988.

2. We cannot be Neanderthal in a high-tech world.
Douglas E. Applegate, U.S. Congressman (D-OH). House debate, June 6, 1991.

3. That's one small step for a man, one giant leap for mankind.
Neil Armstrong, American astronaut. Comment when first setting foot on the moon, July 21, 1969.

4. We must become a space-faring nation.
Jim Bacchus, U.S. Congressman (R-FL). House debate, June 6, 1991.

5. If this thing *[cold fusion]* is what they say it is, it's better than the gold rush.
Norman H. Bangerter, Governor of Utah (R). Quoted in *The New York Times*, Apr. 23, 1989.

6. Not only am I not persuaded by the testimony, I do not even understand it. For me the charm of quarks is well hidden.
Henry L. Bellmon, Governor of Oklahoma and U.S. Senator (R-OK). In reference to testimony from the Research Director of the U.S. Department of Energy on the importance of funding research on subatomic particles. Senate debate, Mar. 21, 1978.

7. Our technology has already outstripped our ability to control it.
Omar N. Bradley (1893-1981), General, U.S. Army, and Permanent Chairman, Joint Chiefs of Staff. Quoted on *The World Tomorrow*, Apr. 9, 1989.

8. Hell no. The last thing I understood was when the guy said hello.
George Bush, 41st President of the United States (R-TX). Comment after a tour of a scientific research facility at the University of West Virginia, Morgantown, WV. Quoted in *Governing*, Sept. 1988.

9. For the new century, back to the moon, back to the future, and this time back to stay. And then a journey into tomorrow, a journey to another planet, a manned mission to Mars.
George Bush. Statement, July 20, 1989.

10. To pursue science is not to disparage things of the spirit.
Vanevar Bush (1890-1974), presidential science advisor. Speech, Massachusetts Institute of Technology, Cambridge, MA, Oct. 5, 1953.

11. All these remarkable new technologies are starting to make people very uncomfortable with the whole process of science.
Arthur Caplan, Director, Center for Biomedical Ethics, University of Minnesota, Minneapolis, MN. Quoted in *The Washington Post*, Oct. 30, 1988.

12. *[France has to win]* ... the great battle that every country has to fight to ensure its modernization and preserve its independence.
Jean-Pierre Chevenement, Minister of Education, France. Speech announcing the "Computers for Everyone" plan, 1985.

13. The military system is, to a substantial extent, a method whereby the population provides a subsidy to the high technology industry.
Noam Chomsky, American linguist and political activist. Interview, PBS, *Bill Moyers' World of Ideas*, Nov. 4, 1988.

14. The European talks of progress because by the aid of a few scientific discoveries he has established a society which has mistaken comfort for civilization.
Benjamin Disraeli, 1st Earl of Beaconsfield (1804-1881), Prime Minister of Great Britain (Conservative). Quoted by William R. Inge, *Outspoken Essays*, First Series, 1919.

15. We can't defend French culture without a *[computer]* software industry.

Marcel Duhamel, Assistant Director, Ministry of Education, France. Quoted in *The Washington Post*, Mar. 19, 1989.

16. I am proud of the fact that I never invented weapons to kill.

Thomas A. Edison (1847-1931), American inventor. Quoted in *The New York Times*, June 8, 1915.

17. Physicists find themselves in a position not unlike that of Alfred Nobel. Alfred Nobel invented an explosive more powerful than any then known – an exceedingly effective means of destruction. To atone for this "accomplishment" and to relieve his conscience he instituted his awards for the promotion of peace. Today, the physicists who participated in producing the most formidable weapon of all time are harassed by a similar feeling of responsibility, not to say guilt. As scientists, we must never cease to warn against the danger created by these weapons.

Albert Einstein (1879-1955), Nobel Laureate in Physics (Switzerland). Speech, Nobel anniversary dinner, Dec. 10, 1945.

18. It's a kind of Russian roulette.

Richard P. Feynman (1918-1988), Nobel Laureate in Physics (United States) and member, commission investigating the *Challenger* accident. Quoted in *Newsweek*, Apr. 14, 1986.

19. For a successful technology, reality must take precedence over public relations, for Nature cannot be fooled.

Richard P. Feynman. *What Do You Care What Other People Think?*, 1988.

20. More and more Americans feel threatened by runaway technology.

John W. Gardner, U.S. Secretary of Health, Education and Welfare, and Chairman, Common Cause. *No Easy Victories*, 1968.

21. There's no such thing as a free launch.

Richard A. Gephardt, U.S. Congressman (D-MO). In reference to the high cost of the space program. Remark, July 20, 1989.

22. We cannot have as our goal a world that cannot conceivably come to pass unless all scientific knowledge of the atom is erased.

Alexander M. Haig, General, U.S. Army, U.S. Secretary of State, and White House Chief of Staff (R). Testimony, Senate Foreign Relations Committee, Jan. 29, 1988.

23. Marx never saw an electric light bulb.

Hu Yaobang (1915-1989), General Secretary, Communist Party of China. Remark, Nov. 1986.

24. Every great advance in natural knowledge has involved the absolute rejection of authority.

Thomas H. Huxley (1825-1895), British biologist and President, Royal Society. *Lay Sermons, Addresses and Reviews*, 1870.

25. Science commits suicide when it adopts a creed.

Thomas H. Huxley. *Darwiniana*, 1893.

26. I am not afraid of new inventions or improvements, nor bigoted to the practices of our forefathers. It is that bigotry which keeps the Indians in a state of barbarism ... and still keeps Connecticut where their ancestors were when they landed on these shores.... Where a new invention is supported by well-known principles, and promises to be useful, it ought to be tried.

Thomas Jefferson (1743-1826), 3rd President of the United States (Democratic Republican-VA). Letter to Robert Fulton, inventor of the steamboat, Mar. 17, 1810.

27. Science is my passion; politics, my duty.

Thomas Jefferson. Oft-repeated remark.

28. You yourself said to Khrushchev, "You may be ahead of us in rocket thrust, but we're ahead of you in color television." I think that color television is not as important as rocket thrust.

John F. Kennedy (1917-1963), 35th President of the United States (D-MA). Presidential campaign debate with Richard M. Nixon, 1960.

29. What the scientists have in their briefcases is terrifying.

Nikita S. Khrushchev (1894-1971), Premier of the U.S.S.R. Remark, 1960.

30. The *[Lawrence Livermore National]* lab is basically an honest place. But it's filled with human beings who are expected to sell programs.

Ray E. Kidder, scientist, Lawrence Livermore National Laboratory. Quoted in *The New York Times Magazine*, Oct. 9, 1988.

31. Legislators don't want to seem anti-science or anti-progress.

Andrew Kimbrell, counsel, Foundation on Economic Development. Explanation of the difficulty of lobbying for controls on science and technology. Quoted in *The New York Times Magazine*, Oct. 16, 1988.

32. Americans tend to believe that every problem has some technical solution.

Ronald F. Kirby, Director of Transportation Planning, Metropolitan Washington Council of Governments. Quoted in *The Washington Post*, June 12, 1988.

33. Anecdotes do not make good scientific material.
C. Everett Koop, U.S. Surgeon General. Congressional testimony, Mar. 16, 1989.

34. Computer technology is already a powerful ally of the totalitarian.
Raymond Kurzweil, American computer scientist and inventor. *The Age of Intelligent Machines*, 1990.

35. Technologies are political; what technologies finally appear as is not something decided in a laboratory.
Christopher Lasch, American sociologist. Quoted in *The Los Angeles Times*, Jan. 14, 1990.

36. Machines and their development provide the greatest opportunity in the whole history of mankind to improve the lot of the individual human being.
David E. Lilienthal (1899-1981), Chairman, Tennessee Valley Authority, and Chairman, U.S. Atomic Energy Commission. *Big Business*, 1952.

37. Our thanks, and something more substantial than thanks, are due to the man engaged in the effort to produce a successful steam plow.
Abraham Lincoln (1809-1865), 16th President of the United States (R-IL). Speech, Milwaukee, WI, Sept. 30, 1859.

38. All our inventions have endowed material forces with intellectual life, and degraded human life into a material force.
Karl Marx (1818-1883), German economist and Socialist. Speech, London, Apr. 14, 1856.

39. Military technology is like a continuing chess game, with no final move.
David McCurdy, U.S. Congressman (D-OK). Quoted in *Time*, Nov. 6, 1989.

40. It is difficult putting technical developments in a language that policy makers can understand.
Gordon McDonald, chief scientist, Mitre Corporation. Speech, "Intelligence and Free Society Conference," National Forum Foundation, Washington, DC, May 30, 1989.

41. We have a moral obligation to straighten out the world before we mess up space.
Stewart B. McKinney, U.S. Congressman (R-CT). Statement supporting of an extension of the ban on antisatellite weapons. Quoted in *Newsweek*, Aug. 25, 1986.

42. Isn't it strange that as technology advances, the quality of life frequently declines.
Harvey Milk (1930-1978), City Supervisor, San Francisco, CA. Quoted in Edward Shilts, *The Mayor of Castro Street*, 1982.

43. When it comes to action risking war, technology has modified the Constitution.
Richard E. Neustadt, American political scientist. Testimony, Senate Government Operations Committee, 1963.

44. There must be no barriers to freedom of inquiry. There is no place for dogma in science – the scientist is free, and must be free to ask any question, to doubt any assertion, to seek for any evidence, to correct any errors.
J. Robert Oppenheimer (1904-1967), American physicist and Scientific Director, Manhattan Project. Quoted in *Life*, Oct. 10, 1949.

45. Those who control the government can control the flow and content of the information that is communicated electronically.
Robert W. Packwood, U.S. Senator (R-OR). Senate speech, Apr. 21, 1987.

46. The space shuttle has been a fiscal and substantiative disaster.
William Proxmire, U.S. Senator (D-WI). CBS, *Meet the Press*, Oct. 2, 1988.

47. I call upon the scientific community ... those who gave us nuclear weapons, to turn their great talents now to the cause of mankind and world peace – to give us the means of rendering those nuclear weapons impotent and obsolete.
Ronald Reagan, 40th President of the United States (R-CA). Argument for the Strategic Defense Initiative. Speech, Mar. 23, 1983.

48. Here is $100,000 of the people's money wasted on this scientific aerial navigation experiment because some man, perchance a professor wandering in his dreams, was able to convince the *[military]* officers that his aerial scheme had some utility.
James M. Robinson (1861-1942), U.S. Congressman (D-IN). Comment when the government funded Samuel P. Langley, Secretary of the Smithsonian Institution, to try to develop a flying machine. Speech, Jan. 24, 1904.

49. Every advance in civilization has been denounced as unnatural while it was recent.
Bertrand Russell, 3rd Earl Russell of Kingston (1872-1970), British philosopher and reformer. *A History of Western Philosophy*, 1945.

50. Conservative people are undoubtedly right in their distrust and hatred of science, for the scientific spirit is the very spirit of innovation and adventure – the most reckless kind of adventure into the unknown. And such is its aggressive strength that its revolutionary activity can neither be restrained nor restricted within its own field.
Jean-Paul Sartre (1905-1980), French philosopher. *Existentialism*, 1947.

51. Science is inherently neither a potential for good nor for evil. It is a potential to be harnessed by man to do his bidding.
Glenn T. Seaborg, Chairman, U.S. Atomic Energy Commission. Interview, Associated Press, Sept. 29, 1964.

52. When you have a new belief, it's very hard to get economic, scientific, or political support for it.
Bernard Siegel, American physician. PBS, *Search for Common Ground*, Nov. 21, 1989.

53. Science is the great antidote to the poison of enthusiasm and superstition.
Adam Smith (1723-1790), Scottish political economist. *The Wealth of Nations*, 1776.

54. Freedom is absolutely necessary for progress in science and the liberal arts.
Benedict Spinoza (1632-1677), Dutch philosopher. *Theological-Political Treatise*, 1670.

55. Discovery consists of seeing what everybody has seen and thinking what nobody has thought.
Albert Szent-Györgyi, Nobel Laureate in Physiology and Medicine (Hungary). Quoted in Irving John Good, *The Scientist Speculates*, 1963.

56. It is not the scientist's job to determine whether a hydrogen bomb should be constructed, whether it should be used or how it should be used. This responsibility rests with the people and with their ... representatives.
Edward Teller, American nuclear physicist. Quoted in *Newsweek*, Aug. 2, 1954.

57. When civilized man, with his science, his technique, his power, loses his soul, he becomes the most terrible monster the world has ever seen.
Dorothy Thompson (1894-1961), American journalist. *Ladies' Home Journal*, Sept. 1945.

58. Another highly important asset *[for the head of NASA]* is political aptitude – the ability to relate to a wide variety of influential players, from presidents to congressional staff members, from industrial heavy hitters to bench scientists.
John H. Trattner, Chairman, Council for Excellence in Government. *The Prune Book: The 60 Toughest Science and Technology Jobs in Washington*, 1992.

59. We cannot have a first-rate economy with third-rate technology.
Peter Varkonyi, Hungarian Ambassador to the United States. Quoted in *The New York Times*, Mar. 4, 1990.

60. Astronauts! Rotarians in outer space.
Gore Vidal, American writer. *Myra Breckinridge*, 1968.

61. Noncooperation in military matters should be an essential moral principle for all true scientists.
Norbert Wiener (1894-1964), American computer scientist. *Atlantic Monthly*, Jan. 1947.

Chapter 89

Secrecy, Confidentiality, and Classification

1. What is more tempting for a censor than to censor?
   Floyd Abrams, American attorney. PBS, Special on the Persian Gulf War, Jan. 16, 1991.

2. The CIA claims that secrecy is necessary to hide what it's doing from enemies of the United States ... the real reason for secrecy is to hide what the CIA is doing from the American people.
   Phillip Agee, Field officer, Central Intelligence Agency. *Playboy*, Aug. 1975.

3. What did the President know and when did he know it?
   Howard H. Baker, Jr., U.S. Senator and White House Chief of Staff (R-TN). Hearings, Senate Select Committee on Watergate, June 28, 1973.

4. I consulted the President *[Jefferson Davis]* whether it was best for the country that I should submit to unmerited censure or reveal to a congressional committee our poverty and my utter inability to supply the requisitions of General Wise, and thus run the risk that the fact should become known to some of the spies of the enemy, of whose activity we were well assured. It was thought best for the public service that I should suffer the blame in silence and a report of censure on me was accordingly made by the Committee of Congress.
   Judah P. Benjamin (1811-1884), U.S. Senator (Whig and D-LA), Confederate Attorney General, Secretary of War and Secretary of State. Statement after the Confederate defeat at Roanoke Island, Norfolk, VA, Jan. 1862.

5. Secrecy necessarily breeds suspicion.
   Louis D. Brandeis (1856-1941), U.S. Supreme Court Justice. Letter to Cyrus Adler, Aug. 10, 1915.

6. Public disclosure is one of the great disinfectants ever invented.
   Richard Breeden, Chairman, Securities and Exchange Commission. Senate hearings, Sept. 10, 1990.

7. Interdepartmental memoranda, advisory opinions, recommendations of subordinates, informal working papers, material in personnel files, and the like, cannot be subject to disclosure if there is to be any orderly system of government.
   Herbert Brownell, U.S. Attorney General (R). 1954.

8. Though secrecy in diplomacy is occasionally unavoidable, it has its perils.... Publicity may cause some losses, but may avert some misfortunes.
   James Bryce (1838-1922), British Ambassador to the United States. *Modern Democracies*, 1921.

9. If we guard our toothbrushes and diamonds with equal zeal, we will lose fewer toothbrushes and more diamonds.
   McGeorge Bundy, presidential assistant for national security (D). Congressional testimony. Quoted in *The New York Times*, Mar. 6, 1989.

10. The root of the problem *[secrecy in government]* is not so much that our people have lost confidence in government, but that government has demonstrated time and again its lack of confidence in the people.
    Jimmy Carter, 39th President of the United States (D-GA). Dec. 1974.

11. Broad public access, consonant with the right of personal privacy, should be provided to government files. Maximum security declassification must be implemented.
    Jimmy Carter. Statement, May 18, 1976.

12. Alas, what is terrible is not the skeletons, but the fact that I am no longer terrified by them.
    Anton Chekhov (1860-1904), Russian writer. *Notebooks*, 1896.

13. Secrecy is a necessary part of doing business in the modern world.

Richard B. Cheney, U.S. Congressman (R-WY), White House Chief of Staff, and U.S. Secretary of Defense. Quoted on C-SPAN, Jan. 21, 1990.

14. All state affairs which have not yet been decided upon, or which have been decided upon but not yet been made public *[are secret]*.

Chinese law, *Regulations on Guarding State Secrets*, 1951.

15. The secret bombing of Laos was not a secret to the Laotians. Only the American people were kept in the dark.

Warren I. Cohen, Chairman, U.S. State Department Advisory Committee on Historical Diplomatic Documentation. "Stop Falsifying U.S. History," *World Monitor*, Oct. 1990.

16. Leaks usually have more value to the public at large than the harm which they occasionally do.

Lloyd N. Cutler, counsel to the President (D). Speech, Maryland Bar Association, 1990.

17. National security is like that vague term Executive privilege. Both terms have been abused; both concepts have been damaged; they've been used as shields for secrecy.

John Dean, counselor to the President (R). Interview, *Playboy*, Jan. 1975.

18. It is unwise to wish everything explained.

Benjamin Disraeli, 1st Earl of Beaconsfield (1804-1881), Prime Minister of Great Britain (Conservative). *Coningsby*, 1844.

19. One of my own guiding principles in intelligence work was ... not to make a mystery of what is a matter of common knowledge or obvious to friend and foe alike.

Allen W. Dulles (1893-1969), Director, Central Intelligence Agency. Quoted in Leonard Mosley, *Dulles*, 1978.

20. What good does it do to spend millions to protect ourselves against espionage if our secrets just leak away?

Allen W. Dulles. *The Craft of Intelligence*, 1963.

21. If thou hast heard a word, let it die with thee.

Old Testament, *Ecclesiastes* 19:10.

22. Tell never thy counsel to thy foe.

English proverb, c. 1450.

23. I'm not going to let anybody come down at night like Nicodemus and whisper something in my ear that no one else can hear. That's not executive privilege; it is poppycock.

Samuel J. Ervin, Jr. (1896-1985), U.S. Congressman and U.S. Senator (D-NC). Comment when the White House did not want to make information public but offered to communicate it privately to the Senator. Statement, Senate Watergate hearings, 1973.

24. Pontiac *[Chief of the Ottawa Indians]* ... keeps two secretaries, one to write for him, and the other to read the letters he receives, and he manages them so as to keep each of them ignorant of what is transacted by the other.

Thomas Gage (1721-1787), British General and Royal Governor of Massachusetts. Letter to Lord Halifax, 1764.

25. There are more secrets, but there is not more secrecy.

Steven Garfinkel, Director, U.S. Information Security Oversight. Quoted in *The New York Times*, Apr. 15, 1986.

26. We *[press and public affairs officers]* never knew how much we did not know.

Phil Goulding, U.S. Assistant Secretary of Defense. *Confirm or Deny*, 1970.

27. I had never seen a trace of a threat to the national security from the publication.

Erwin N. Griswold, Solicitor General of the United States (R). Statement in 1989 about asking the Supreme Court in 1971 to prohibit *The New York Times* from publishing the Pentagon Papers on grounds of national security. Quoted in *The New York Times*, June 11, 1991.

28. Our government cannot function cloaked in secrecy. It cannot function unless officials tell the truth.

Lee Hamilton, U.S. Congressman (D-IN). Quoted in Nathan Miller, *Spying for America*, 1989.

29. A decent and manly examination of the acts of government should be not only tolerated but encouraged.

William Henry Harrison (1773-1841), 9th President of the United States (Whig-OH). Inaugural address, Mar. 4, 1841.

30. Nothing on paper; paper can be lost or stolen or simply inherited by the wrong people; if you want to keep something secret, don't write it down.

Richard Helms, Director, Central Intelligence Agency, and U.S. Ambassador to Iran. Quoted in *The Economist*, Apr. 12, 1980.

31. Leaks are a cottage industry in this town *[Washington, DC]*.

Henry J. Hyde, U.S. Congressman (R-IL). Quoted on PBS, *American Interest*, Jan. 25, 1989.

32. The leaks can kill you.
Lyndon B. Johnson (1908-1973), 36th President of the United States (D-TX). Advice to Richard M. Nixon, Dec. 1968.

33. General, thank you, but I'm aware that once I look at that information I'll never be able to speak about the program in public again.
Robert W. Kastenmeier, U.S. Congressman (D-WI). Response when an Army Chemical Corps officer at Ft. Detrick, MD, offered to show him classified information on why the military's development of bubonic plague weapons in the early 1960's was so essential. Quoted in *The Washington Post*, Nov. 17, 1990.

34. Secret agreements don't really have the base of popular support they ought to have if you are going to have a commitment.
Nicholas Katzenbach, U.S. Attorney General and U.S. Undersecretary of State (D). Congressional testimony, 1972.

35. Washington officials see secrecy as a secular religion – as an end in itself.... How much secrecy can a democracy stand?
John Keker, special prosecutor at Oliver North's Iran-Contra trial. Speech, Commonwealth Club of California, C-SPAN, Dec. 2, 1989.

36. Executive privilege can be invoked only by the President and will not be used without specific presidential approval.
John F. Kennedy (1917-1963), 35th President of the United States (D-MA). 1962.

37. If there's more than one person – including yourself – in a room, consider anything said to be on the record and a probable headline in the morning paper.
John F. Kennedy. Quoted in *Time*, Feb. 6, 1989.

38. The success of a democracy depends on the enlightenment of its people. The people should know what's going on, and public officials should keep the people informed.
Fiorello H. La Guardia (1882-1947), U.S. Congressman (Socialist and R) and Mayor of New York City (R and Fusion Party). Radio address, 1945.

39. The fight is not over what shall be secret, but over who shall determine what shall be secret.
Michael Ledeen, American author and intelligence official. Speech, "Intelligence and Free Society Conference," National Forum Foundation, Washington, DC, May 30, 1989.

40. If we cannot keep secrets, it is impossible for our leaders to have the adequate information on which to base their policies.
Michael Ledeen. *Ibid.*

41. Truth fears nothing but concealment. (*Veritas nihil veretur nisi abscondi.*)
Legal maxim.

42. Time and chance reveal all secrets.
Mary (de la Rivière) Manley (1663-1724), English writer and political journalist. *Secret Memoirs and Manners of Several Persons of Quality of Both Sexes*, 1709.

43. Once secrecy becomes sacrosanct, it invites abuse.
Mike Mansfield, U.S. Ambassador to Japan and U.S. Senator (D-MT). 1954.

44. There's no such thing as a secret meeting. There's no such thing as a secret document.... That's a fact of life.
John McCain III, U.S. Senator (R-AZ). In reference to appearances of impropriety in the 1989 savings and loan scandal. Interview, PBS, *MacNeil-Lehrer News Hour*, Feb. 22, 1989.

45. They could hang people for what's in there.
Robert S. McNamara, U.S. Secretary of Defense (D). Remark after reading parts of the Pentagon Papers. Quoted in David Halberstam, *The Best and the Brightest*, 1969.

46. National security is the figleaf against freedom of information.
Ralph Nader, American consumer advocate. In protest of Canada's restrictive "right-to-know" legislation. Speech, Winnipeg, Canada, Aug. 30, 1976.

47. Only those who wish to deceive the people and rule them for their own personal advantage would desire to keep them in ignorance; for the more they are enlightened, the more they feel convinced of the utility of laws, and of the necessity of defending them; and the more steady, happy, and prosperous will society become.
Napoléon I (1769-1821), military leader and Emperor of France. 1815.

48. The biggest waste of time in Washington that I know of is trying to track down leaks.
Ron Nesson, White House Press Secretary (R). Quoted on ABC, *It's Your Business*, Apr. 8, 1990.

49. I don't know how accurate they are, but I know they'll scare the hell out of people.
Richard M. Nixon, 37th President of the United States (R-CA). Comment on polygraphing government

employees to intimidate leakers. Quoted in Wise, *The American Police State*, 1976.

50. Some people will believe anything if you whisper it to them.
Louis B. Nizer, American attorney. *Thinking on Your Feet*, 1940.

51. The trouble with secrecy is that it denies to the government itself the wisdom and resources of the whole community, of the whole country.
J. Robert Oppenheimer (1904-1967), American physicist and Scientific Director, Manhattan Project. CBS, *See it Now: A Conversation with J. Robert Oppenheimer*, Jan. 4, 1955.

52. The art of dissembling *[concealing motives]* is the art of kings.
Armand-Jean du Plessis (Cardinal Richelieu) (1585-1642), French ecclesiastic and statesman. *Mirame*.

53. Secrecy is the first essential in affairs of the State.
Armand Jean du Plessis. *Political Testament*, 1687.

54. The experience of every nation on earth has demonstrated that emergencies may arise in which it becomes absolutely necessary for the public safety or the public good to make expenditures, the very object of which would be defeated by publicity.
James K. Polk (1795-1849), 11th President of the United States (D-TN). Comment on U.S. Secretary of State Daniel Webster's secret use of government funds to develop newspaper support for the unpopular Webster-Ashburn treaty of 1842 regarding the Canadian boundary dispute. Statement to congressional investigators, 1846.

55. There appears to be an inverse relationship between the level one attains in the executive branch and one's obligation to comply with the law governing access to, and control of, classified information.
David H. Pryor, U.S. Congressman and U.S. Senator (D-AK). In reference to books written by former secretaries of defense Caspar Weinberger and George Shultz. Quoted in *The Washington Post*, Nov. 14, 1990.

56. I don't want to know. If I don't know a secret I can't let it leak out.
Samuel T. Rayburn (1882-1961), U.S. Congressman and Speaker of the House (D-TX). Response when offered secret information on the atomic bomb, 1943.

57. Whenever the public weal is at stake, it is legitimate for an agency such as ours to suggest the withholding of information.
Fred Reagan, spokesman, Federal Bureau of Investigation. Response when the FBI asked newspapers not to print details of new methods of investigating bank robberies. Quoted in *Columbia Journalism Review*, Sept.-Oct. 1990.

58. The White House is the leakiest place I've ever been in.
Ronald Reagan, 40th President of the United States (R-CA). Apr. 9, 1986.

59. I have to believe that somebody thought he was doing me a favor by not giving me all the information.
Ronald Reagan. In reference to Iran-Contra. Interview, CBS, *Sunday Morning*, June 10, 1989.

60. It *[the Vietnam War]* wasn't a secret from anyone except the American people who were footing the bill.
George E. Reedy, White House Press Secretary (D). PBS, *The Presidency, the Press, and the People*, Apr. 2, 1990.

61. Presidents hate leaks unless they do them.
George E. Reedy. *Ibid.*

62. In the modern world I just don't think there are any more secrets.
George E. Reedy. *Ibid.*

63. One of the greatest difficulties in civil war is that more art is required to know what should be concealed from our friends than what ought to be done against our enemies.
Cardinal de Retz (1614-1679), French cleric and politician. *Political Maxims*.

64. Executive privilege.
William P. Rogers, U.S. Attorney General and U.S. Secretary of State (R). Defense of the Air Force's right not to turn over certain information to the U.S. Controller General for an investigation of procurement practices, 1958.

65. I really don't know of any secrets which have a significant bearing upon the ability of the public to make their judgments about major issues of foreign policy.
Dean Rusk, U.S. Secretary of State (D). Quoted in *Executive Privilege: The Withholding of Information by the Executive*, U.S. Senate Judiciary Committee, 1971.

66. All censorship is designed to protect the policy from the public.
Morley Safer, American journalist. Interview, PBS, *MacNeil-Lehrer News Hour*, Jan. 24, 1991.

67. Information which is a national security problem today may not be a national security problem tomorrow.... Too much information is now still in classified files ... and is being held there long after that information has any impact on national security.

Pierre Salinger, journalist and White House Press Secretary (D). Quoted on ABC, *It's Your Business*, Apr. 8, 1990.

68. A Man in a corrupted Age must make a Secret of his Integrity, or else he will be looked upon as a common Enemy.

George Savile, 1st Marquess of Halifax (1633-1695), Lord Privy Seal of England. *Moral Thoughts and Reflections*, 1750.

69. The People will ever suspect the Remedies for the Diseases of the State, where they are wholly excluded from seeing how they are prepared.

George Savile. *Maxims of State*, No. 26.

70. So I take it that your testimony is, there never was a time when Colonel North said that Paul was sending Aran and the Bookkeeper to the Swimming Pool to get a price so that Orange could send some Dogs through Banana to Apple for some Zebras. Is that correct?

John Saxon, associate counsel, Senate Iran-Contra Committee. Question to Pentagon official Noel Koch using code names for secret or sensitive information during the Iran-Contra hearings, 1987.

71. How quickly Americans establish traditions. What had been for a century and a half sporadic executive practice employed in very unusual circumstances was now in a brief decade hypostatized into sacred constitutional principle.

Arthur M. Schlesinger, Jr., American historian and presidential advisor (D). Comment on the use of executive privilege by the Eisenhower administration. *The Imperial Presidency*, 1973.

72. It is our indispensable duty to keep it a secret even from Congress. We find by fatal experience, the Congress consists of too many members to keep secrets.

Secret Committee of Correspondence of the Continental Congress (Benjamin Franklin and Robert Morris). Committee charged with intelligence information and work during the American Revolution, Oct. 1776.

73. Peacetime censorship exists for one reason only: to hide rotten affairs of state.

George H. Seldes (1890-1970), American writer and correspondent. *You Can't Print That*, 1929.

74. I will continue to share information with appropriate Congressional committees once a process has been established to protect those materials.

Samuel K. Skinner, U.S. Secretary of Transportation (R). Letter to congressional leaders expressing concern about leaks of classified information, Apr. 6, 1989.

75. I fear that the American people are ahead of their leaders in realism and courage – but behind them in knowledge of the facts because the facts have not been given to them.

Margaret Chase Smith, U.S. Congresswoman and U.S. Senator (R-ME). Senate speech, Sept., 21, 1961.

76. Preposterous!

Larry Speakes, White House Press Secretary (R). Response to a reporter when asked if the rumor that the United States would invade Grenada that day was true. Quoted on PBS, *The Presidency, the Press, and the People*, Apr. 2, 1990.

77. Sir, a secret ballot makes a secret government; and a secret government is a government by conspiracy; in which the people at large can have no rights.

Lysander Spooner (1808-1887), American attorney and Libertarian. *A Letter to Thomas F. Bayard*, 1882.

78. A proper secrecy is the only mystery of able men; mystery is the only secrecy of weak and cunning ones.

Philip Dormer Stanhope, 4th Earl of Chesterfield (1694-1773), Member of Parliament, Great Britain (Whig) and Lord-Lieutenant of Ireland. *Maxims*.

79. It is the insidious art of politics and politicians to keep things concealed from the people.

Ezra Stiles (1727-1795), American clergyman and President, Yale College, New Haven, CT. *History of the Three Judges of King Charles I*, 1794.

80. The government produces so much information that they can't hide the truth all the time.

I. F. Stone (1908-1989), American investigative journalist and political writer. Explanation of how he could learn so much about "secret" government affairs. Conversation with Jonathan Siegel, 1981.

81. Walls have tongues, and hedges ears.

Jonathan Swift (1667-1745), Irish clergyman and satirist. *Pastoral Dialogue*.

82. The result of the general practice of secrecy has been to deprive the Senate and Congress of the substance of the powers conferred on them by the Constitution.

Robert A. Taft (1889-1953), U.S. Senator (R-OH). Senate speech, Jan. 5, 1951.

83. Secrecy, once accepted, becomes an addiction.
Edward Teller, American nuclear physicist. *The New York Times*, May 27, 1973.

84. There are truths which are not for all men nor for all times.
Voltaire (François-Marie Arouet) (1694-1778), French historian and dramatist. Letter to Cardinal de Bernis, Apr. 23, 1761.

85. It is to be much wished that our printers be more discreet in their publications.
George Washington (1732-1799), 1st President of the United States (VA). To Alexander Hamilton, 1777.

86. Candor is not a more conspicuous trait in the character of governments than it is in individuals.
George Washington. Letter to U.S. Secretary of State Timothy Pickering. Aug. 29, 1797.

87. Presidents feel that leaks thwart their policies and reduce their options.
Ron Ziegler, White House Press Secretary (R). PBS, *The Presidency, the Press, and the People*, Apr. 2, 1990.

88. The intelligence agencies of the democratic countries suffer from a grave disadvantage that in attempting to damage their adversary they must also deceive their own public.
Victor Zorza, American writer. *The Washington Post*, Nov. 15, 1965.

Chapter 90

Slogans and Mottos

1. Liberty and Property
   Slogan of the Sons of Liberty, pre-American revolution dissident group.

2. Shame to him who evil thinks. (*Honi soit qui mal y pense.*)
   Motto on a one-shilling stamp issued by England and used by American colonists during the administration of Prime Minister George Grenville, 1766.

3. No Quarter for Tories
   Slogan of followers of Revolutionary War general Francis Marion, 1780-1781.

4. He gave up all to serve the republic. (*Omnia relinquit servare rem publican.*)
   Motto of the Society of the Cincinnati, veterans of the Revolutionary War, 1783.

5. Freedom Our Rock
   Motto of the Columbian Order (Tammany Society) of New York, 1789.

6. Liberty and No Excise
   Slogan of Pennsylvania distillers who objected to Federal excise tax on their products, 1791-1794.

7. Jefferson and Liberty
   Presidential campaign slogan for Thomas Jefferson, 1800.

8. Free Trade and Oxen's Rights
   Free Trade and Teamsters' Rights
   Free Trade and Sailors' Rights
   No Impressment
   On to Canada
   The Existing War – The Child of Prostitution
   Slogans during the War of 1812.

9. Victory or Death
   Slogan of American soldiers under Andrew Jackson during the Battle of New Orleans, Jan. 8, 1815.

10. Freemen cheer the Hickory tree,
    In storms its boughs have shelter'd thee.
    Slogan from Maryland campaign poster for Andrew "Old Hickory" Jackson, 1824.

11. John Quincy Adams who can write
    And Andrew Jackson who can fight.
    Presidential campaign ditty, 1828.

12. Remember the Alamo!
    Texas, 1836.

13. Tippecanoe and Tyler Too
    Whig presidential campaign slogan of William Henry Harrison, 1840. Attributed to Orson E. Woodbury.

14. The Log Cabin and Hard Cider Campaign
    Popular description of William Henry Harrison's presidential campaign, 1840.

15. No Union with Slaveholders
    Slogan of the American Anti-Slavery Society, 1841-1865.

16. Fifty-four Forty or Fight
    Popular slogan referring to Oregon Territory, presidential campaign of 1844.

17. Polk's War
    Whig nickname for the Mexican War, 1846-1848.

18. Free Soil, Free Labor, Free Speech
    Slogan of the Free Soil Party and its presidential candidate, Martin Van Buren, 1848.

19. Americans Ruling America
    Know Nothing (American) Party slogan, 1850-1856.

20. The Union Now and Forever
    Campaign slogan of Franklin Pierce, 14th President of the United States (D-NH), 1852.

21. Free Homes for Free Men
    Homesteader's slogan, 1852-1862.

22. Free Soil, Free Men, Fremont, and Victory
    Campaign slogan for Sen. John C. Fremont (D-CA), 1st Republican nominee for President. 1856.

23. Wide Awake
    Union and Liberty

Republican presidential campaign slogans of Abraham Lincoln, 1860.

24. The Union as It Was – The Constitution as It Is
Democratic Party Civil War slogan, 1860's.

25. A Rich Man's War – A Poor Man's Fight
Civil War Southern anti-draft slogan, 1863.

26. Vote as you shoot.
Republican campaign slogan among Union soldiers, 1864.

27. Forty Acres and a Mule
Slogan of carpetbaggers and freed slaves, 1865.

28. Turn the rascals out.
Liberal Republican presidential slogan supporting Horace Greeley against incumbent Ulysses S. Grant, 1872.

29. The Old Guard dies but never surrenders.
(The "Old Guard" were Ulysses S. Grant's supporters for a third term as President.)
Slogan, Republican National Convention, Chicago, IL, June 8, 1880.

30. Anything to Beat Grant
Republican campaign slogan against Ulysses Grant's bid for a third term as President. Republican National Convention, Chicago, IL, June 8, 1880.

31. I carry my sovereignty under my hat.
Slogan of Independent Republicans, 1880.

32. Wealth belongs to him who creates it.
Populist Party slogan, 1892.

33. Long Live Democracy
Slogan, *The Tammany Times*, New York City, 1893-1917.

34. In God we trust – with Bryan we bust.
Republican presidential campaign slogan against Democrat William Jennings Bryan, 1896.

35. Elect *[William]* McKinley, the advance agent of prosperity.
Republican convention slogan, 1896.

36. *[William]* McKinley, Protection, and Prosperity
Republican presidential campaign slogan, 1896.

37. Free Silver and Free Cuba
Democratic Party anti-war slogan, 1898.

38. Four More Years of the Full Dinner Pail
Republican reelection campaign slogan for Pres. William McKinley, 1900.

39. Equal Rights to All – Special Privileges to None
Democratic presidential campaign slogan for William Jennings Bryan, 1900.

40. Protect the country – kill the foreigner.
Slogan of the I Ho Chuan (Boxers), China, 1900.

41. Deeds, Not Words
Motto of the English women's suffrage movement, 1905.

42. The Man of the Hour
Stand Pat
Republican presidential campaign slogans for William H. Taft, 1908.

43. No Truck nor Trade with the Yankees
Campaign slogan, Conservative Party, Canada, 1911.

44. The New Freedom
Democratic Party presidential campaign slogan for Woodrow Wilson, 1912; also the title of a book by Wilson, 1913.

45. A Square Deal All Around
Progressive (Bull Moose) Party presidential campaign slogan for Theodore Roosevelt, 1912.

46. He kept us out of war.
Peace and Preparedness
Democratic Party slogans of Woodrow Wilson's reelection campaign for the presidency, 1916.

47. Politics is adjourned.
Food will win the war – don't waste it.
Work or fight.
Slogans popular after America entered World War I, 1917.

48. Soil and Peace
Slogan of Russian Bolshevik revolutionaries who overthrew the Kerensky government, Nov. 7, 1917.

49. Power to the Soviets
Land to the Peasants
Factories to the Workers
Bread to the Hungry
Bread and Peace
Russian revolutionary slogans, 1917-1918.

50. Give until it hurts.
Liberty Loan slogan, 1917-1919.

51. Steady America
Back to Normalcy
Republican presidential campaign slogans for Warren G. Harding, 1920.

52. The bosses don't want him, but you, Mr. Knickerbocker, do.
New York City Alderman campaign slogan of Fiorello H. La Guardia, 1921.

53. Coolidge or Chaos
Keep Cool with Cal.
Keep Cool and Keep Coolidge.
Let well enough alone.
Republican presidential campaign slogans for Calvin Coolidge, 1924.

54. Kool klammy Kal Koolidge kan't kondemn the Ku Klux Klan.
A vote for Coolidge is a vote for the Klan.
Robert M. La Follette presidential campaign slogans against Calvin Coolidge, 1924.

55. A 100% Investment in a People's Government
The Dawn of a New Day
Slogans on Robert M. La Follette "Emancipation Bonds" sold for his campaign funding, 1924.

56. A vote for Coolidge is a vote for chaos.
Honesty at Home – Honor Abroad
Democratic presidential campaign slogans, 1924.

57. Vote for industrial freedom.
Campaign slogan of the Socialist Labor Party, 1924.

58. You never had it so good.
Four More Years of Proseperity
Republican presidential campaign slogans for Herbert Hoover, 1928.

59. A Chicken in Every Pot *[Often coupled with:]* A Car in Every Garage.
Republican presidential campaign slogan for Herbert Hoover; intended to remind voters of the "Coolidge prosperity," 1928.

60. Elect a full-time Mayor who will sleep at night and work in the daytime.
Campaign slogan of Fiorello H. La Guardia's New York City mayoralty race against Jimmy Walker, 1929.

61. The worst is past.
Republican presidential campaign slogan for Herbert Hoover, 1932.

62. Roosevelt or Ruin
Return the country to the people.
Happy days are here again.
Down with Hoover.
Throw the spenders out.
Remember the forgotten man.
Democratic presidential campaign slogans for Franklin D. Roosevelt, 1932.

63. Prosperity is just around the corner.
Republican presidential campaign slogan for Herbert Hoover, 1932.

64. It's an elephant's job. No time for donkey business.
Republican anti-Democrat presidential campaign slogan, 1932.

65. One good term deserves another.
Senate campaign slogan for Arthur Hendrick Vandenberg, 1934.

66. Don't change the pilot.
International Ladies Garment Workers Union, slogan in support of Franklin D. Roosevelt's second term, 1935.

67. Save the American way of life.
Let's get another deck.
Slogans of Alf Landon's Republican presidential campaign, 1936.

68. *Kirche, Keuche, Kinder* (Church, Kitchen, Children)
Nazi slogan indicating woman's position in the Third German Reich, 1930's.

69. Home Rule – Not Hague Rule
Slogan of opponents of Mayor Frank Hague of Jersey City, NJ, city commissioner election of 1939.

70. Don't be a third termite.
Wendell Willkie for Prosperity
I am a Democrat for Willkie.
We don't want Eleanor either.
Roosevelt for ex-President
Away with the New Deal and its inefficiency.
Win with Willkie.
No man is good three times.
Republican presidential campaign slogans for Wendell L. Willkie, opposing a third term for Franklin D. Roosevelt, 1940.

71. Two good terms deserve another.
Franklin D. Roosevelt campaign slogan for his third term, 1940.

72. America Calls
Slogan of the National Association of Roosevelt-for-1940 Clubs, Inc.

73. Aid the allies by methods short of war.
Britain is fighting our war.
Defend America by aiding the allies
Slogans in favor of Lend-Lease to Britain, 1941.

74. Buy a share of America.
If you can't go over, come across.
Back the attack – buy more than ever before.
Let's go – for the knockout blow.
Let's pave the road to Rome with war bonds.
They give their lives – you lend your money.
You've done your bit, now do your best!
Slogans for the purchase of American World War II bonds, 1941-1945.

75. Speed them back – join the WAAC.
I'd rather be with them than waiting for them.
Back the attack – be a WAAC.
America is calling YOU!
Slogans urging women to enlist in the American armed forces during World War II, 1941-1945.

76. Work, Family, Homeland
Slogan of Vichy France during World War II, sometimes attributed to Marshal Philippe Pétain or to Paul Touvier, head of the Second Service, 1940's.

77. Keep America solvent and sensible.
Republican presidential nomination campaign slogan of Sen. Robert A. Taft, 1947.

78. I'm just mild about Harry.
Anti-Truman slogan at the Democratic National Convention, Philadelphia, PA, July 12-15, 1948.

79. To err is Truman.
Republican Party campaign slogan, 1948.

80. Phooey on Dewey
Democratic presidential campaign slogan against Gov. Thomas E. Dewey, 1948.

81. Bread, Butter, Bacon, Beans
Campaign slogan of William Murray (1869-1956), Governor of Oklahoma and U.S. Congressman (D).

82. I like Ike.
Republican presidential campaign slogan for Dwight D. Eisenhower, 1952.

83. Don't be daft – vote for Taft.
Republican presidential nomination campaign slogan for Sen. Robert A. Taft, 1952.

84. I still like Ike.
Republican presidential campaign slogan for Dwight D. Eisenhower's second term, 1956.

85. Everything's booming but the guns.
Republican presidential campaign slogan, 1956.

86. On the Right Track With Jack
Democratic presidential campaign slogan for John F. Kennedy, 1960.

87. Love That Lyndon
All The Way with LBJ
Let us continue.
Democratic presidential campaign slogans for Lyndon B. Johnson, 1964.

88. Serve the People.
Slogan, Chinese Communist party, 1960's.

89. Sweep away all monsters and demons.
Slogan of the Chinese Cultural Revolution, 1960's. Attributed to Chen Boda, political secretary to Mao Tsetung.

90. We shall overcome.
Slogan of the American civil rights movement, 1960's. Quoted by Pres. Lyndon B. Johnson in his address to Congress proposing the Voting Rights Act, March 15, 1965.

91. Less Government, More Individual Responsibility, and a Better World
Slogan, John Birch Society, 1960's.

92. Impeach Earl Warren!
John Birch Society slogan, 1961.

93. A Choice for a Change
Peace without Surrender
Republican presidential campaign slogans for Sen. Barry M. Goldwater, 1964.

94. In your heart you know he's right.
In your guts you know he's nuts.
Republican presidential campaign slogan for Sen. Barry M. Goldwater and Democratic rejoinder, 1964.

95. The Politics of Joy
Democratic presidential campaign slogan of Hubert H. Humphrey, 1968.

96. Stand up for America.
Presidential campaign slogan of Independent George C. Wallace, 1968.

97. Nixon's the one.
Republican presidential campaign slogan, 1968.

98. Leave fear of red *[i.e., Reds, Communists]* to horned animals.
Slogan during the student riots in France, 1968.

99. Clean for Gene
Youth slogan for Eugene McCarthy's presidential campaign, 1968.

100. WINNING IN POLITICS ISN'T EVERYTHING, IT'S THE ONLY THING
Sign in a restricted room of the Committee to Re-elect the President (CREEP), 1971.

101. Come home, America.
Slogan of George S. McGovern's Democratic presidential campaign, 1972.

102. Self Control – Not State Control
Campaign slogan of Israel Asper, Liberal Party leader, Manitoba, Canada, 1973.

103. IMPEACHMENT WITH HONOR
JAIL TO THE CHIEF
IMPEACH THE COX-SACKER
Bumper stickers displayed in Washington, DC, during the Watergate crisis, 1973-1974.

104. A Government as Good as the People
Slogan of Jimmy Carter's presidential campaign, 1975.

105. Liberation Before Education
Slogan of anti-apartheid blacks in South Africa, urging students to leave their classrooms and take to the streets, 1976-1987.

106. LONG LIVE THE GREAT, GLORIOUS, AND ALWAYS CORRECT CHINESE COMMUNIST PARTY
Sign welcoming delegates, Chinese Communist Party Congress, Canton, Aug. 1977.

107. Vote for Cuomo, not the homo!
Unauthorized New York City mayoral campaign poster for Mario Cuomo against Edward I. Koch, 1977.

108. What Britain needs is an iron lady.
Campaign slogan for Margaret Thatcher, Prime Minister of Great Britain (Conservative), 1979.

109. IT ISN'T WHO YOU KNOW BUT WHO YOU YES.
Desk sign, "The Politician's Motto," 1979.

110. Elect me, I'll fight for you.
Slogan of Alfonse D'Amato's New York senatorial campaign, 1980.

111. Together – A New Beginning
Republican presidential campaign slogan for Ronald Reagan, 1980.

112. For the dead *and* the living we must bear witness.
Motto, U.S. Holocaust Memorial Council, 1980.

113. Labour isn't working.
[The slogan was used with a picture of an unemployment line.]
Slogan of Conservative Party against the Labour Party, Great Britain, 1982.

114. Leadership That's Working
Campaign slogan for Ronald Reagan, 1984, and Mario Cuomo, 1986

115. Where's the beef?
Democratic presidential campaign slogan for Walter Mondale, 1984.

116. Burdick's clout is North Dakota's.
Senate campaign slogan of Quentin Burdick, U.S. Senator (D), 1988.

117. On Your Side
Democratic presidential campaign slogan for Michael Dukakis, 1988.

118. DON'T DUMP THE DONKEY. STOP NOMINATING JACKASSES
Democratic presidential campaign bumper sticker, 1988.

119. Pray for rain but vote for Dukakis.
Billboard in Norwalk, IA, during the 1988 presidential election and drought. Quoted in *Des Moines Register*, July 3, 1988.

120. Let the people speak.
Demonstrators' placard outside the United Nations protesting the Burmese government, Aug. 1988.

121. The Chief is a thief.
Campaign slogan in opposition to Prime Minister Lynden Oscar Pindling of the Bahamas. Quoted in *The Washington Post*, June 25, 1988.

122. Reduce, reuse, recycle.
Slogan of Earth Day, 1990.

123. Evolution, not Revolution
Slogan of Prime Minister Tadeusz Mazowiecki's Polish Communist Party after popular demonstrations brought down his government, July 1990.

124. True Equal Rights for Everyone
Slogan of David Duke's Louisiana gubernatorial campaign, 1990.

125. He's nobody's man but yours.
Connecticut gubernatorial campaign slogan of Lowell P. Weicker, Jr., 1990.

126. Silence = Death
Slogan of ACT UP, AIDS activist group, 1990.

127. Oppressors are not our protectors.
Graffito in Harlem, New York City, 1991.

128. The World Is Too Much Governed
Francis Preston Blair (1791-1876), American editor and publisher. Masthead slogan of his pro-Jacksonian newspaper, *The Washington Globe*, 1830's.

129. Either Caesar or Nothing (*Aut Caesar aut Nihil.*)
Caesar Borgia (1475-1507), Italian ecclesiastic and statesman. Motto.

130. I am for "peace, retrenchment, and reform," the watchword of the great Liberal Party thirty years ago.
John Bright (1811-1829), Member of Parliament, Great Britain (Liberal). Speech, Birmingham, England, Apr. 28, 1859.

131. God bless my country!
James Buchanan (1791-1868), 15th President of the United States (D-PA). Motto.

132. Mexico for the Mexicans
Plutarco Elias Calles (1877-1945), President and dictator of Mexico, 1925. Campaign slogan and personal motto.

133. Move on over or we'll move on over you.
Stokley Carmichael (Kwame Toure), President, Student Non-Violent Coordinating Committee. Frequent slogan, 1960's.

134. Why Not the Best?
Jimmy Carter, 39th President of the United States (D-GA). Personal slogan and title of his book, 1976.

135. The maxim of the British people is "Business as usual."
Winston Churchill (1874-1965), Prime Minister of Great Britain (Conservative). Speech, Guildhall, London, Nov. 9, 1914.

136. The family motto of the House of Marlborough from which I descend is *Faithful but Unfortunate.* But I, by my enterprise, nay daring, have reversed the motto, *[to] Faithless but Fortunate.*
Winston Churchill. Quoted in Kay Halle, *Irrepressible Churchill*, 1966.

137. A Fair Field and No Favor
Grover Cleveland (1837-1908), 22nd and 24th President of the United States (D-NY). Motto.

138. Three Acres and a Cow
Jesse Collings (1831-1920), British politician and land reform leader. Slogan, 1888.

139. If you've got 'em by the balls, their hearts and minds will follow.
Charles W. Colson, presidential assistant (R). Sign over the bar in his den.

140. Slogans are both exciting and comforting, but they are also powerful opiates for the conscience.
James B. Conant (1893-1978), U.S. High Commissioner for Germany and President of Harvard University, Cambridge, MA. Speech, 1934.

141. Do the day's work.
Calvin Coolidge (1872-1933), 30th President of the United States (R-MA). Speech to the Massachusetts State Senate after becoming its presiding officer, and his personal motto.

142. Be sure you are right, then go ahead.
David Crockett (1786-1836), U.S. Congressman (Anti-Jacksonian, TN). Motto.

143. Long live socialism with a human face.
Alexander Dubcek (1921-1992), Premier of Czechoslovakia. Personal slogan during the "Prague Spring" before the Russian invasion, August 1968.

144. Ottawa gives to foreigners, Duplessis gives to his province.
Maurice L. Duplessis (1890-1959), Premier of Quebec, Canada (Union Nationale). Campaign slogan, 1948.

145. Kill the rent hog and the interest hog.
James E. Fergeson (1871-1944), Governor of Texas (D). Campaign slogan, 1922.

146. No Truck nor Trade with the Yankees
George Eulas Foster (1847-1931), Minister of Trade and Commerce, Canada (Conservative), and Vice President of the League of Nations. Election slogan, 1911.

147. Liberty, Equality, Fraternity (*Liberté, Egalité, Fraternité.*)
Benjamin Franklin (1706-1790), Member, Continental Congress and Constitutional Convention, Governor of Pennsylvania, and U.S. Minister to France. Suggested slogan for the French Revolution.

148. More!
Samuel Gompers (1850-1924), President, American Federation of Labor. Motto.

149. Let us have peace.
Ulysses S. Grant (1822-1885), 18th President of the United States (R-OH). Letter to Joseph Hawley, Chairman of the National Republican Convention, May 29, 1868; the phrase became his campaign slogan.

150. When in doubt, fight.
Ulysses S. Grant. Motto.

151. It ain't over yet.
Slogan of the Mississippi Freedom Democratic Party, coined by civil rights activist Fannie Lou Hamer, 1965.

152. There are no footprints backwards.
John Hampden (1594-1643), English statesman. Motto.

153. Neither snow nor rain nor heat nor gloom of night stays these faithful couriers *[the Persian post riders]* from the swift accomplishment of their appointed rounds.
[Slightly adapted, this phrase became the slogan of the U.S. Postal Service.]
Herodotus (c.480-425 B.C.), Greek "Father of History." *History of the Persian Wars*, V.

154. Let the people rule.
Andrew Jackson (1767-1845), 7th President of the United States (D-TN). Slogan.

155. Our Federal Union! It must and shall be preserved.
Andrew Jackson. Toast, in the presence of John C. Calhoun, Apr. 30, 1830.

156. Fair shares for all is Labour's call.
Douglas Jay, Member of Parliament, Great Britain (Labour). Campaign slogan, 1946.

157. Our maxim of that day *[1776]* was "Where annual election ends, tyranny begins."
Thomas Jefferson (1743-1826), 3rd President of the United States (Democratic Republican-VA). To Samuel Adams, 1800.

158. Rebellion to tyrants is obedience to God.
Thomas Jefferson. Motto; attributed to Benjamin Franklin.

159. So what you do is you just reach up there and grab that lever *[in the voting booth]* and say, "All the Way with LBJ."
Lyndon B. Johnson (1908-1973), 36th President of the United States (D-TX). Campaign rally, Wilmington, DE, airport, Oct. 31, 1964.

160. We stand today at the edge of a new frontier – the frontier of the 1960's.
John F. Kennedy (1917-1963), 35th President of the United States (D-MA). Presidential nomination acceptance speech, Democratic National Convention, Los Angeles, CA, July 15, 1960.

161. If you feed the people with revolutionary slogans, they will listen today, they will listen tomorrow, they will listen the day after tomorrow, but on the fourth day they will say "To hell with you."
Nikita S. Khrushchev (1894-1971), Premier of the U.S.S.R. Quoted in *The New York Times*, Oct. 4, 1964.

162. An injury to one is the concern of all.
Motto of the Knights of Labor.

163. After eight years of charisma *[John V. Lindsay]* and four years of the clubhouse *[Abraham S. Beame]*, why not try competence?
Edward I. Koch, U.S. Congressman and Mayor of New York City (D). Slogan when he first ran for Mayor, 1978.

164. A new deal for everyone
David Lloyd George, 1st Earl Lloyd-George of Dwyfor (1863-1945), Prime Minister of Great Britain (Liberal). Campaign slogan, 1919; the phrase was also used by Franklin D. Roosevelt in 1932 and became the appellation for his programs.

165. Every Man a King
Huey P. Long (1893-1935), Governor of Louisiana and U.S. Senator (D). Originated by William Jennings Bryan in a 1900 campaign speech.

166. Divide and govern.
Louis XI (1423-1483), King of France. Motto.

167. No More Wolves, Wilderness, or Welfare
Ronald C. Marlenee, U.S. Congressman (R-MT). Frequent slogan in speeches opposing hunting restrictions to protect endangered species, and federal control of lands and welfare, 1980s.

168. What this country needs is a good five-cent cigar.
Thomas Riley Marshall (1854-1925), Governor of Indiana and Vice President of the United States (D). Slogan.

169. Jesus – Not Caesar
Tomas G. Masaryk (1850-1937), 1st President of Czechoslovakia. Motto.

170. Observe moderation. (*Halt Mass.*)
Maximilian I (1459-1519), King of Germany and Holy Roman Emperor. Motto; also a principle of Aristotle.

171. Strength in Law (*Kraft im Recht*)
Klemens von Metternich (1773-1859), Austrian statesman and diplomat. Motto.

172. Guard well. (*Gardez bien.*)
Richard Montgomery (c. 1738-1775), Revolutionary War general. Motto; also on the coat of arms of Montgomery County, MD.

173. Slogans are apt to petrify man's thinking.
Jawaharlal Nehru (1889-1964), Prime Minister of India. Quoted in George Seldes, *The Great Quotations*, 1983.

174. Submit and obey.
Nicholas I (1796-1855), Czar of Russia. Motto.

175. War is peace.
Freedom is slavery.
Ignorance is strength.
George Orwell (Eric Blair) (1903-1950), British writer. "Slogans for the people," *1984*, 1949.

176. Wealth belongs to him who creates it.
Populist Party slogan, 1892.

177. Property is theft.
Pierre Joseph Proudhon (1809-1865), French journalist, anarchist, Socialist, and Member, Constituent Assembly. Motto.

178. Faith in God and the Peasant's Furrow
Stefan Radic (1871-1928), Croatian politician. Motto.

179. Open to ALL PARTIES, but Influenced by NONE
Clementina Rind (1740-1774), American newspaper editor. Motto of the *Virginia Gazette*, May 16, 1766.

180. People who are least governed are best governed.
Albert C. Ritchie (1876-1936), Governor of Maryland (D). Campaign slogan and personal motto.

181. I pledge you, I pledge myself, to a new deal for the American people.
Franklin D. Roosevelt (1882-1945), 32nd President of the United States (D-NY). Presidential nomination acceptance speech, Democratic National Convention, Chicago, IL, July 2, 1932.

182. Long live the king!
Old Testament, *1 Samuel* 10:24. In reference to Saul, 1st king of Israel.

183. Do it now.
William Donald Schaefer, Mayor of Baltimore, MD, and Governor of Maryland (D). Motto.

184. Give light and the people will find their own way.
Scripps-Howard Newspapers, slogan; attributed to Carl McGee.

185. I found when I arrived in my old home *[Mansfield, OH]* that the papers said I came west seeking the nomination for governor. I came purely on private business – *to repair my fences and look after neglected property*. The reporters seized upon the reference to my fences, and construed it as having a political significance. The phrase *mending fences* became a byword, and every politician engaged in strengthening his position is still said to be *mending his fences*.
John Sherman (1823-1900), U.S. Congressman (R-OH), U.S. Senator, U.S. Secretary of the Treasury, and U.S. Secretary of State. *Recollections of Forty Years in the House, Senate and Cabinet*, 1895.

186. Where liberty is, there is my country.
Algernon Sidney (1622-1683), Republican and Member of Parliament, England. Motto.

187. I am the smith of my fortunes. (*Faber mea fortuna.*)
Frederick Edwin Smith, 1st Earl of Birkenhead (1872-1930), Member of Parliament, Great Britain (Conservative) and Lord Chancellor of England. Motto adopted on becoming a peer, 1922.

188. Keep America solvent and sensible.
Robert A. Taft (1889-1953), U.S. Senator (R-OH). Presidential nomination campaign slogan, 1947.

189. To do the right thing, to do the best we could, never complain, never take advantage, don't give up, don't be afraid.
Harry S Truman (1884-1972), 33rd President of the United States (D-MO). Family motto.

190. Crush the infamous one! (*Écrasez l'infâme!*)
Voltaire (François-Marie Arouet) (1694-1778), French historian and dramatist. Motto; referred to often during the French Revolution.

191. Our whole duty, for the present at any rate, is summed up in the motto: America first.
Woodrow Wilson (1856-1924), 28th President of the United States (D-NJ). Speech, New York City, Apr. 20, 1915.

Chapter 91

States and Nationhood

1. Upon the whole, if we allow two-thirds of the people to have been with us in the revolution, is not the allowance ample? Are not two-thirds of the nation now with the administration? Divided we have ever been, and ever must be. Two-thirds always had and will have more difficulty to struggle with the one-third than with all our foreign enemies.

   John Adams (1735-1826), 2nd President of the United States (Federalist-MA). Letter to Thomas McKean, Aug. 31, 1813.

2. *[U.S. Supreme Court Chief Justice John]* Marshall has cemented the Union which the crafty and quixotic democracy of Jefferson had a perpetual tendency to dissolve.

   John Quincy Adams (1767-1848), 6th President of the United States (Ind-MA). *Diary,* July 10, 1835.

3. *[America should be a]* nation, coextensive with the North American continent, destined by God and nature to be the most populous and powerful people ever combined under one social compact.

   John Quincy Adams. Quoted in *Smithsonian,* 1988.

4. It is inconceivable that we will recognize the right of our enemy *[Israel]* over any piece of territory on Palestinian soil.

   Abu Ayad, deputy to Yassir Arafat, Chairman of the Palestine Liberation Organization. Comment on Israel's right to exist, Oct. 1988. Quoted in *The Washington Post,* Nov. 20, 1988.

5. States are great engines moving slowly.

   Francis Bacon, 1st Baron Verulam and Viscount St. Albans (1561-1626), Lord Chancellor of England. *The Advancement of Learning,*1605.

6. His Majesty's Government view with favor the establishment in Palestine of a national home for the Jewish people, and will use their best endeavor to facilitate the achievement of this object, it being clearly understood that nothing shall be done which may prejudice the civil and religious rights of existing non-Jewish communities in Palestine or the rights and political status enjoyed by the Jews in any other country.

   Arthur J. Balfour, 1st Earl of Balfour (1848-1930), Prime Minister of Great Britain (Conservative). Memorandum to Baron Edmund de Rothschild, Nov. 2, 1917.

7. The country is the people.

   Mann Batson, Chairman, City Council Greenville, SC. Quoted in *Governing,* Sept. 1988.

8. My people have a right to exist ... and this existence is in danger.

   David Ben-Gurion (1886-1973), 1st Prime Minister of Israel. Note to President Kennedy, 1963.

9. *[Czechoslovakia is]* ... the godchild of the great and glorious Republic of the United States.

   Edvard Benes (1884-1948), Foreign Minister, Prime Minister, and President of Czechoslovakia. Speech, Joint Session of Congress, May 13, 1943.

10. The well-being of the nation is in the well-being of the people.

    Benazir Bhutto, Prime Minister of Pakistan. *Daughter of the East,* 1988.

11. The United States is the only country with a known birthday. All the rest began, they know not when, and grew into power, they know not how. If there had been no Independence Day, England and America combined would not be so great as each actually is. There is no "Republican," no "Democrat," on the Fourth of July – all are Americans.

    James G. Blaine (1830-1893), U.S. Congressman and U.S. Senator (R-ME). Quoted in *Dwight D. Eisenhower's Favorite Poetry, Prose and Prayers,* 1957.

12. Thus out of small beginnings greater things have been produced by His hand that made all things of nothing, and gives being to all things that are; and, as one small candle might light a thousand, so the light here *[in Plymouth Colony]* kindled hath shone unto many, yea in some sort to our whole nation.

    William Bradford (1590-1657), Pilgrim father and Governor of Plymouth Colony. *History of Plymouth Plantation,* 1856.

13. What if we as Americans can no longer define ourselves in opposition to a well-defined evil?
William W. Bradley, U.S. Senator (D-NJ). Commencement address, Middlebury College, Middlebury, VT, May 1989.

14. This is a beautiful day after a long voyage, but we are only at a way station. We are not at the end of our way.
Willy Brandt (1913-1992), Chancellor of West Germany and Nobel Laureate in Peace. Comment when the wall between West and East Berlin was opened up. Quoted in *The New York Times*, Nov. 12, 1989.

15. *[America is]* a republic in which every citizen is a sovereign, but in which no one cares or dares to wear a crown.
William Jennings Bryan (1860-1925), U.S. Secretary of State (D). Speech, 1900; compare Huey P. Long, "Every Man a King, but No Man Wears a Crown."

16. To compare us to the Soviet union is like comparing the person who pushes an old lady toward an oncoming bus and the person who pushes the old lady away from the oncoming bus. They both push old ladies around.
William F. Buckley, Jr., American political columnist and publisher. PBS, *Firing Line*, Sept. 7, 1988.

17. A thousand years scarce serve to form a state; an hour may lay it in the dust.
George Gordon Byron, 6th Baron Byron (1788-1824), poet and Member of Parliament, Great Britain. *Childe Harold*, 1812.

18. America is the only nation in history which miraculously has gone from barbarism to degeneracy without the usual interval of civilization.
Georges Clemenceau (1841-1929), Premier of France and journalist. Quoted in *Saturday Review*, Dec. 1, 1945.

19. To give laws unto a people; to institute magistrates and officers over them; to punish and pardon malefactors; to have the sole authority of making war and peace are the true marks of sovereignty.
John Davies (1569-1626), English jurist and poet. Quoted in S. Austin Allibone, *Prose Quotations*, 1876.

20. A nation is a work of art and a work of time.
Benjamin Disraeli, 1st Earl of Beaconsfield (1804-1881), Prime Minister of Great Britain (Conservative). *The Spirit of Whiggism*, 1836.

21. It is a community of purpose that constitutes society.
Benjamin Disraeli. *Sybil*, 1845.

22. Individuals may form communities, but it is institutions alone that can create a nation.
Benjamin Disraeli. Speech, Manchester, England, 1866.

23. The state is no more than a machine for oppression of one class by another. This is as true of democracy as it is of monarchy.
Friedrich Engels (1820-1895), German Socialist and revolutionary theorist. Introduction to Karl Marx, *The Civil War in France*, 1871.

24. I will make them one nation in the land.
Old Testament, *Ezekiel* 37:22.

25. We French are colonized by the cruelest master of all. We are colonized by our past.
Edgar Faure (1908-1988), French politician. Quoted in *The Washington Post*, July 24, 1990.

26. In America, the people govern.
Benjamin Franklin (1706-1790), Member, Continental Congress and Constitutional Convention, Governor of Pennsylvania, and U.S. Minister to France. Quoted on PBS, *The Congress*, 1989.

27. I never met anyone in Ireland who understood the Irish question, except one Englishman who had only been there a week.
Keith Fraser (1876-1935), Member of Parliament, Great Britain. Speech, House of Commons, May 1919.

28. Honest mediocrity is the most suitable condition for states; riches lead to softness and corruption.
Frederick II (The Great) (1712-1786), King of Prussia. Letter to Voltaire, Dec. 28, 1774.

29. The Negro needs a nation and a country of his own, where he can best show evidence of his ability in the art of human progress. Scattered as an unmixed and unrecognized part of alien nations and civilizations is but to demonstrate his imbecility, and point him out as an unworthy derelict, fit neither for the society of Greek, Jew, nor Gentile.
Marcus Garvey (1887-1940), American black nationalist leader. Quoted in E. U. Essien-Udom, *Black Nationalism*, 1962.

30. You must not expect the central government of any country to encourage separatism.
Gennadi I. Gerasimov, spokesman, Foreign Ministry, U.S.S.R. Interview, ABC, *This Week*, Feb. 11, 1990.

31. Sometimes I think this country could be better off if we would just saw off the Eastern seaboard and let it float off to sea.

Barry M. Goldwater, U.S. Senator (R-AZ). Remark, 1963.

32. To exercise self-determination through secession is to blow apart the union, to pit peoples against one another and to sow discord, bloodshed, and death. This is precisely the goal of secessionists in all republics.
Mikhail Gorbachev, President of the U.S.S.R. Speech, Congress of People's Deputies, Moscow, Dec. 23, 1989.

33. Your Majesty, we must do from above what the French have done from below.
Karl August von Hardenberg (1750-1822), Foreign Minister and Chancellor of Prussia. Remark on creating a sense of national unity and destiny, to King Frederick William III after the Battle of Jena, 1806.

34. Nations are what their deeds are.
Georg Wilhelm Friedrich Hegel (1770-1831), German philosopher. *The Philosophy of History*, 1832.

35. A nation is a historical group of men of recognizable cohesion, held together by a common enemy.
Theodor Herzl (1860-1904), Austrian journalist and political Zionist. *The Jewish State*, 1896.

36. Kings are for nations in swaddling clothes.
Victor Hugo (1802-1885), French writer, Member, Constituent Assembly and National Assembly at Bordeaux. 1848.

37. We feel that the Arabs and Jews are cousins in race, having suffered similar oppressions at the hands of powers stronger than themselves, and by a happy coincidence have been able to take the first step toward the attainment of their national ideals together.
Feisal ibn Husein (1885-1933), Emir of Iraq. Letter to U.S. Supreme Court Justice Felix Frankfurter, Mar. 3, 1919.

38. Our nation has a message. That is why it can never be an average nation. Throughout history our nation has either soared to the heights or fallen into the abyss through the envy, conspiracy and enmity of others.
Saddam Hussein, President of Iraq. Quoted in *Newsweek*, Jan. 7, 1991.

39. Size is not grandeur, and territory does not make a nation.
Thomas H. Huxley (1825-1895), British biologist and President, Royal Society. *Aphorisms and Reflections*, CX, 1907.

40. The nations which have put mankind and posterity in their debt have been small states – Israel, Athens, Florence, Elizabethan England.
William Ralph Inge (1860-1965), Anglican prelate and dean of St. Paul's. Quoted in Marchant, *The Wit and Wisdom of Dean Inge*.

41. Is a land born in one day? Is a nation brought forth at once?
Old Testament, *Isaiah* 66:8.

42. Americans are not a perfect people, but we are called to a perfect mission.
Andrew Jackson (1767-1845), 7th President of the United States (D-TN). Quoted by Sen. William W. Bradley (D-NJ), Commencement address, Middlebury College, Middlebury, VT, May 1989.

43. A *Volk [people]* without a state is nothing, a lifelong frivolous phantom like the vagabond Gypsies and Jews.
Friedrich Ludwig Jahn (1778-1852), Prussian gymnast and nationalist. *Folkdom*.

44. The small land-holders are the most precious part of a state.
Thomas Jefferson (1743-1826), 3rd President of the United States (Democratic Republican-VA). Letter to Rev. James Madison, Oct. 28, 1785.

45. ...in the full tide of successful experiment.
Thomas Jefferson. 1st inaugural address, Mar. 4, 1801.

46. Divided as they *[Americans]* are into a thousand forms of policy and religion, there is one point in which they all agree – they equally detest the pageantry of a king and the supercilious hypocrisy of a bishop.
Junius (Prob. Philip Francis) (1740-1818), British writer (Whig). *Letters*, No. 35, Dec. 19, 1769.

47. No sort of new dictatorship is about to come *[in Hungary]*. The old one, the proletarian dictatorship, will persist. People have come to see and know that this is not a bad kind of dictatorship. In it you can live in freedom, bring works about, and can earn esteem, if you are an honest person.
Janos Kadar, 1st Secretary, Communist Party of Hungary. Speech to the Hungarian Communist Party Congress, Budapest, Mar. 21, 1975.

48. I can anticipate no greater calamity for the nation than the dissolution of the Union.
Robert E. Lee (1807-1870), General-in-Chief, Confederate Army. Quoted on PBS, *The Civil War*, Sept. 23, 1990.

49. The kingdom is not divisible. (*Regnum non est divisible.*)
Legal maxim.

50. Under capitalism we have a state in the proper sense of the word, that is, a special machine for the suppression of one class by another.
V. I. Lenin (1870-1924), Premier of the U.S.S.R. *The State and Revolution*, 1917.

51. While the state exists, there is no freedom; when there is freedom, there will be no state.
V. I. Lenin. *Ibid.*

52. Let me say right here that only the unanimous consent of the states can dissolve this Union.
Abraham Lincoln (1809-1865), 16th President of the United States (R-IL). Letter to Alexander H. Stevens, Jan. 19, 1859.

53. The great danger to our general government is the great southern and northern interests of the continent being opposed to each other. *[The states are]* divided into different interests not by their difference in size ... but principally from their having or not having slaves.
James Madison (1751-1836), 4th President of the United States (Democratic Republican-VA). Debate, Constitutional Convention, Philadelphia, PA, 1787.

54. *[Czechoslovakia resembles America because]* ... we have no dynasty of our own and no liking for a foreign dynasty.
Tomas G. Masaryk (1850-1937), 1st President of Czechoslovakia. *The Making of a State, 1914-1918*, 1927.

55. Country is not a mere zone of territory. The true country is the idea to which it gives birth ... the sense of communion which united in one all the sons of that territory.
Giuseppe Mazzini (1805-1872), Italian statesman. *The Duties of Man*, 1858.

56. The cultivation of the ego must recognize bounds in the lives of states as in private life, in order not to be reduced to absurdity.
Klemens von Metternich (1773-1859), Austrian statesman and diplomat. To Friedrich Gentz, 1852.

57. A portion of mankind may be said to constitute a nationality if they are united among themselves by common sympathies which do not exist between them and any others – which make them cooperate more willingly than with other people, desire to be under the same government, and desire that it should be government by themselves or a portion of themselves inclusively.
John Stuart Mill (1806-1873), Member of Parliament, Great Britain, and political economist. *Representative Government*, 1861.

58. National honor is national property of the highest value.
James Monroe (1758-1831), 5th President of the United States (Democratic Republican-VA). 1st inaugural address, Mar. 4, 1817.

59. Canada is our inheritance from our parents and our legacy to our children.
Brian Mulroney, Prime Minister of Canada (Conservative). Speech on the Meech Lake Accord failure, June 1990.

60. There will be no repose in Europe until it is under one head, under an emperor whose officers would be kings.
Napoléon I (1769-1821), military leader and Emperor of France. *Maxims.*

61. Independence, like honor, is a rocky island, without a beach.
Napoléon I. *Ibid.*

62. The system of government must be adapted to the spirit of the nation.
Napoléon I. *Ibid.*

63. The State invariably has its origins in conquest and confiscation.
Albert Jay Nock (1872-1945), American Libertarian. *Our Enemy the State*, 1935.

64. The Palestinian national authority, after its establishment, will struggle for the unity of the confrontation states for the sake of completing the liberation of all Palestinian soil and as a step on the path of comprehensive Arab unity.
Palestine Liberation Organization, Resolution, Article 8, adopted by the Palestine National Council, Cairo, June 1974.

65. Faced with what we consider wrong and profoundly humiliating, it is time for us to have our own country, our own Constitution.
Jacques Parizeau, French-Canadian leader (Parti Québecois). To urge Quebec Premier Robert Bourassa to vote against the Meech Lake Accord giving the Canadian provinces, especially Quebec, more autonomy. Quoted in *Time*, June 25, 1990.

66. Government has many shapes: But 'tis *Sovereignty*, tho' not Freedom, in all of them.
William Penn (1644-1718), founder of Pennsylvania. *Some Fruits of Solitude, in Reflections and Maxims*, 1693.

67. Developing a national identity in our country *[Canada]* is a full time preoccupation.... Americans don't worry about that.
David Peterson, Premier of Ontario, Canada. Interview, PBS, *MacNeil-Lehrer News Hour*, May 23, 1990.

68. States are as its men are: They grow out of human characters.
Plato (427-327 B.C.), Greek philosopher and teacher. *The Republic*, VIII.

69. Well, I learned a lot when I went down there *[Latin America]* to find out from them their views. You'd be surprised. They're all individual countries.
Ronald Reagan, 40th President of the United States (R-CA). Quoted in *The Washington Post*, Dec. 6, 1982.

70. Nationalism is not incompatible with Federalism.
Gil Rémillard, Minister of Justice, Quebec, Canada. Quoted in *The Financial Post*, Nov. 29, 1990.

71. Kings, aristocrats, and tyrants, whoever they may be, are slaves in rebellion against the sovereign of the earth, which is mankind, and against the legislator of the universe, which is nature.
Maximilien-François-Marie de Robespierre (1758-1794), French revolutionist. *Déclaration des Droits de l'homme*, Apr. 24, 1793.

72. Must we go on in many groping, disorganized, separate units to defeat or shall we move as one great team to victory?
Franklin D. Roosevelt (1882-1945), 32nd President of the United States (D-NY). Statement signing the National Recovery Act, June 16, 1933.

73. The government is us; we are the government, you and I.
Theodore Roosevelt (1858-1919), 26th President of the United States (R-NY). Speech, Asheville, NC, Sept. 9, 1902.

74. The European traveler in America ... is struck by two peculiarities: first, the extreme similarity of outlook in all parts of the United States (except the Old South), and secondly, the passionate desire of each locality to prove that it is peculiar and different from every other. The second of these is, of course, caused by the first.
Bertrand Russell, 3rd Earl Russell of Kingston (1872-1970), British philosopher and reformer. "Modern Homogeneity," 1930.

75. If the *[Washington,]* DC, statehood bill passes, I'm going to run for sheriff of Georgetown County.
Mark Russell, American political humorist. Interview, National Public Radio, July 21, 1988.

76. To be or not to be a united government, that is the question.
Nikolai Ryzhkov, Prime Minister of the U.S.S.R. Quoted in *The Washington Post*, Sept. 26, 1990.

77. The melting pot stands open – if you're ready to get bleached first.
Buffy Sainte-Marie, American singer and Indian rights activist. Quoted in *Ms.*, Mar. 1975.

78. Nations, like men, have their infancy.
Henry St. John, 1st Viscount Bolingbroke (1678-1751), Secretary for War and Foreign Secretary, Great Britain (Tory). *Letters on the Study and Use of History*, V, 1752.

79. A Nation is a mass of Dough, it is the Government that kneadeth it into Form.
George Savile, 1st Marquess of Halifax (1633-1695), Lord Privy Seal of England. *Political Thoughts and Reflections*, 1750.

80. There has always been a struggle in the American tradition between those who felt that America was a nation uniquely appointed by the Almighty to redeem unregenerate mankind, and others who felt that America was a nation like other nations with certain advantages and disadvantages but not raised above lesser breeds by some inherent virtue or superior motive.
Arthur M. Schlesinger, Jr., American historian and presidential advisor (D). Speech, Brown University, Providence, RI, May 1989.

81. American nationality ... did not spring from one family, one tribe, one country, but incorporates the vigorous elements of all civilized nations on earth.
Carl Schurz (1829-1906), U.S. Senator (R-MO). Speech, Faneuil Hall, Boston, MA, Apr. 1859.

82. It is only here *[in America]* that you realize how superfluous governments are in many affairs in which, in Europe, they are considered entirely indispensable, and how the possibility of doing something inspires a desire to do it.
Carl Schurz. "The Political Life of America," in *The Patriotic Anthology*, 1941.

83. We cannot expect states to have human feelings. States are cold monsters.
Norodom Sihanouk, Prince of Cambodia and politician. Quoted in *The New York Times*, Oct. 16, 1988.

84. Society exists for the benefit of its members; not the members for the benefit of society.
Herbert Spencer (1820-1903), British social philosopher. *Principles of Ethics*, 1893.

85. The state is an instrument of the ruling class for suppressing the resistance of its class enemies.
Joseph Stalin (1879-1953), Premier of the U.S.S.R.

86. God hath sifted a Nation *[England]* that he might send choice grain into this Wilderness.
William Staughton (1631-1701), Pilgrim father and Governor of Plymouth Bay Colony. 1669.

87. The purpose of the State is always the same: to limit the individual, to tame him, to subordinate him, to subjugate him.
Max Stirner (Johann Kaspar Schmidt) (1806-1856), German anarchist. *The Ego and His Own*, 1845.

88. No state has been built up without force.
Sun Yat-sen (1867-1925), Chinese nationalist leader. Lecture, "The Three Principles of the People," 1924.

89. Anyone who attempts to impose ideas that are contrary to the established traditions of Georgia is a foreigner.
Eugene Talmadge (1884-1946), Governor of Georgia (D). Quoted in Reinhard H. Luthin, *American Demagogues*, 1959.

90. Commonwealths were nothing more in the original but free cities; though sometimes, by force of order and discipline, they have extended themselves into mighty dominions.
William Temple (1628-1699), British statesman and writer. Quoted in S. Austin Allibone, *Prose Quotations*, 1876.

91. The United States is the only great and populous world nation-state and world power whose people are not cemented by ties of blood, race, or original language.
Dorothy Thompson (1894-1961), American journalist. *Ladies' Home Journal*, Oct. 1954.

92. The government of the world I live in was not framed, like that of Britain, in after-dinner conversations over the wine.
Henry David Thoreau (1817-1862), American naturalist and philosopher. *Walden, or Life in the Woods*, 1854.

93. Among democratic nations, each new generation is a new people.
Alexis de Tocqueville (1805-1859), French writer. *Democracy in America*, 1835.

94. The state system of Europe is akin to the system of cages in an impoverished provincial zoo.
Leon Trotsky (1879-1940), Russian revolutionary theorist. *What Next?*, 1932.

95. Americans never can be united into one compact empire, under any species of government whatever. Their fate seems to be – a disunited people till the end of time.
Josiah Tucker (1712-1799), British economist and writer. 1783.

96. Historically, we *[Canadians]* were not born of revolution.... I think that was reflected in the *[American]* Declaration of Independence, which speaks of "life, liberty, and the pursuit of happiness." In the Canadian Constitution, the phrase is "peace, order, and good government."... We are instinctively a consensus people. And we have a less highly centralized government.
John N. Turner, Prime Minister of Canada (Liberal). *The New York Times*, Aug. 7, 1988.

97. We Americans have always been ambivalent about government.
Paul A. Volcker, Chairman, Federal Reserve Board. *Public Opinion*, Sept.-Oct. 1988.

98. But now since these parts have been more extensively explored, and another 4th part has been discovered by Americus Vespucius ... I see no reason why it should not be called Amerigo, after Americus, the discoverer, or indeed America, since both Europe and Asia have a feminine form of name.
Martin Waldseemüller (1470-1521), German cosmographer and cartographer. *Cosmographidae Introductio*, 1507.

99. It is the diversity in human beings that makes a healthy society.
Barbara Walters, American TV journalist. ABC, *News Special*, July 18, 1990.

100. A language is a dialect with an army and a navy.
Max Weinreich (1894-1969), American linguist and Yiddish writer. Attributed.

Chapter 92

Taxes and Taxation

1. No taxation without representation.
Slogan and rallying cry of Colonial opponents of the Stamp Act, 1765.

2. This is a free country but the upkeep is killing us.
Graffito in a New York City subway station, 1986.

3. A power in the individuals who compose legislatures, to fish up wealth from the people, by nets of their own weaving ... will corrupt legislative, executive, and judicial publick servants.
John Adams (1735-1826), 2nd President of the United States (Federalist-MA). 1811.

4. We're not the bosses of taxpayers; they're ours.
T. Coleman Andrews, Director, U.S. Internal Revenue Service. 1955.

5. Governments last as long as the undertaxed can defend them against the overtaxed.
Bernard Berenson (1865-1959), American art critic and historian. *Rumor and Reflection*, 1952.

6. To sell a new tax to the voters you have to be very specific about what it is being used for.
James J. Blanchard, U.S. Congressman and Governor of Michigan (D). Quoted in *The New York Times*, Nov. 27, 1990.

7. Welfare for the wealthy simply can no longer be afforded.
Michael Boskin, Chairman, President's Council of Economic Advisors. *Reagan and the Economy*, 1987.

8. There never has been a new tax that met with public enthusiasm.
John Bowis, Member of Parliament, Great Britain (Conservative). Interview, ABC, *Nightline*, Apr. 2, 1990.

9. Capital gains tax reduction is the ultimate now-nowism.
William W. Bradley, U.S. Senator (D-NJ). Senate debate, Oct. 30, 1989.

10. The tax code was so complicated that it took so long to master it that one lost the will to reform it.
William W. Bradley. Senate committee hearing, Mar. 6, 1991.

11. There is one thing I can promise you about the outer-space program – your tax dollars will go further.
Wernher Von Braun (1912-1977), American rocket scientist. Statement to reporters, 1969.

12. A bad tax is one that is wastefully and poorly spent.
David Brinkley, American TV journalist. ABC, *This Week*, Jan. 14, 1990.

13. I wouldn't minimize the avoidance of tax increases as a contribution to human welfare.
Edmund G. (Jerry) Brown, Jr., Governor of California (D). *Thoughts*, 1976.

14. We should not be a party leading with our chin in the area of taxes.
Ron Brown, Chairman, Democratic National Committee. Interview, PBS, *John McLaughlin's One On One*, Nov. 4, 1989.

15. The progressive feature of the income tax is the most dangerous element of democracy.
William F. Buckley, Jr., American political columnist and publisher. Interview, PBS, *MacNeil-Lehrer News Hour*, 1990.

16. You ought not in a free country to lay a tax on the expression of political opinion.
Edward Bulwer-Lytton, 1st Baron Lytton of Knebworth (1803-1873), Colonial Secretary, Great Britain (Conservative), and writer. Argument for the abolition of taxes on newspapers, 1868.

17. To tax and to please, no more than to love and be wise, is not given to men.
Edmund Burke (1729-1797), British statesman. *Speech on American Taxation*, 1774.

18. Forcing taxpayers to pay their own money out of their own pockets in a building that is paid for by their own taxes for the purpose of answering nature's call is a very restrictive form of taxation.

John L. Burton, U.S. Congressman (D-CA). House debate on a law that would prohibit pay toilets in federal buildings, Nov. 13, 1975.

19. My opponent won't rule out raising taxes, but I will. Congress will push me to raise taxes, and I'll say no, and they'll push, and I'll say no, and they'll push and I'll say, "Read my lips: *no new taxes*."

George Bush, 41st President of the United States (R-TX). Presidential nomination acceptance speech, Republican National Convention, New Orleans, LA, Aug. 18, 1988.

20. Madame, if it is possible, it has already been done; if impossible, it will be done.

Charles-Alexandre de Callone (1734-1802), Minister of Finance under Louis XVI of France. Response when asked by Queen Marie-Antionette to raise taxes again. Quoted in Norbert Guterman, *The Anchor Book of French Quotations*, 1990.

21. I want no money raised by injustice.

Canute (The Great) (994?-1035), King of Denmark and England. 1027.

22. There is one difference between a tax collector and a taxidermist – the taxidermist leaves the hide.

Mortimer Caplin, Commissioner, U.S. Internal Revenue Service. Quoted in *Time*, Feb. 1, 1963.

23. Government is emphatically a machine: to the discontented a "taxing machine," to the contented a "machine for securing property."

Thomas Carlyle (1795-1881), Scottish essayist and historian. *Signs of the Times*.

24. A disgrace to the human race.

Jimmy Carter, 39th President of the United States (D-GA). Description of the American tax system. Presidential nomination acceptance speech, Democratic National Convention, 1976.

25. It's no more logical to tax phone calls than it is to put a tax on letters or any other form of communication.

John E. Chapoton, U.S. Assistant Secretary of the Treasury. Quoted in *The New York Times*, Sept. 4, 1989.

26. Communistic, socialistic ... as populistic as ever have been addressed to any political assembly in the world.

Joseph H. Choate (1832-1917), U.S. Ambassador to Great Britain and President, New York State Constitutional Convention. In reference to principles underlying the income tax. Quoted in Foster Rhea Dulles, *The United States Since 1865*, 1959.

27. All those who gather unto the land of Zion shall be tithed of their surplus properties, and shall observe this law, or they shall not be found worthy to abide among you.

Church of Jesus Christ of Latter-day Saints, *Declarations and Covenants* 119:5.

28. With a cash machine like an income tax, the state legislature will go wild and go on a spending spree.

William J. Cibes, Jr., Connecticut State Legislator (D). Comment on the wisdom of instituting a state income tax. Quoted in *The New York Times*, Mar. 31, 1989.

29. When more of the people's sustenance is exacted through the form of taxation than is necessary to meet the just obligations of government and expenses of its economical administration, such exaction becomes ruthless extortion and a violation of the fundamental principles of a free government.

Grover Cleveland (1837-1908), 22nd and 24th President of the United States (D-NY). 2nd annual message to Congress, Dec. 1886.

30. There's a lot of evidence you can sell people on tax increases if they think it's an investment.

Bill Clinton, 42nd President of the United States (D-AR). Quoted in *Newsweek*, Aug. 1, 1988.

31. Developers play one of us off the other, forcing us to reduce our taxes to attract their development. Everyone is being forced to reduce their tax level to a point where it's not economical.

Rick Cohen, Director, Jersey City, NJ, Department of Housing and Economic Development. Quoted in *Governing the States and Localities*, May 1988.

32. You will see and deal with so much dirt that you will assume everyone is guilty.

Sheldon S. Cohen, Commissioner, U.S. Internal Revenue Service. Speech to new IRS agents, Washington, DC. Quoted in *Government Executive*, May 1990.

33. The art of taxation consists in so plucking the goose as to obtain the largest amount of feathers with the least possible amount of hissing.

Jean-Baptiste Colbert (1619-1683), Chief Minister to Louis XIV of France. Attributed.

34. Collecting more taxes than is absolutely necessary is legalized robbery.

Calvin Coolidge (1872-1933), 30th President of the United States (R-MA). Quoted in *The New York Times*, Mar. 6, 1955.

35. We are blessed by a large middle class in this country, and the middle class will always pay the

lion's share of the taxes.

Carol Cox, spokeswoman, Committee for a Responsible Budget. Interview, CBS, Oct. 2, 1990.

36. Taxes are forever; spending cuts are transitory.

Philip M. Crane, U.S. Congressman (R-WI). House debate, Oct. 4, 1990.

37. Rail against taxes of all kinds.

David Crockett (1786-1836), U.S. Congressman (Anti-Jacksonian-TN). Campaign strategy. *The Life of Davy Crockett*, 1889.

38. I believe you have reached the wrong number.

Richard G. Darman, Director, U.S. Office of Management and Budget (R). Response when House Budget Committee Chairman Leon E. Panetta urged him and the administration to take a more flexible position on taxes. Quoted in *The Washington Post*, May 14, 1989.

39. I'm against sin, but I'm not prepared to discuss sin taxes.

Richard G. Darman. Interview, PBS, *MacNeil-Lehrer News Hour*, May 10, 1990.

40. As certain as death and taxes.

Daniel Defoe (c.1659-1731), British writer. *History of the Devil*, II.

41. Thou shalt truly tithe all the increase of thy seed, that the field bringeth forth year by year.

Old Testament, *Deuteronomy* 14:22.

42. The rich aren't like us – they pay less taxes.

Peter DeVries, American writer. Quoted in *The Washington Post*, July 30, 1989.

43. It was as true ... as taxes is. And nothing's truer than them.

Charles Dickens (1812-1890), British writer. *David Copperfield*, 1850.

44. To tax the community for the advantage of a class is not protection. It is plunder!

Benjamin Disraeli, 1st Earl of Beaconsfield (1804-1881), Prime Minister of Great Britain (Conservative). Debate, House of Commons, May 14, 1850.

45. Why don't we go all the way and simply take the rich off the tax rolls altogether?

Byron Dorgan, U.S. Congressman (D-ND). Comment on proposals to reduce the capital gains tax. Quoted in *The Chicago Tribune*, Sept. 29, 1989.

46. I sometimes suspected that the major qualification for most aspirants for membership on the *[Senate]* Finance Committee was a secret pledge or agreement to defend the *[oil and gas]* depletion allowance against all attacks.... Campaign funds reinforced these pledges.

Paul H. Douglas (1892-1976), U.S. Senator (D-IL). *The American Scholar*, Winter 1967-1968.

47. The power to tax is the power to govern.

Maurice L. Duplessis (1890-1959), Premier of Quebec (Union Nationale). Apr. 26, 1946.

48. When the federal government promises no new taxes, they're promising no new federal taxes.

Robert Ebel, Chairman, President's Advisory Commission on Intergovernmental Relations. Quoted in *Forbes*, Nov. 14, 1988.

49. The American people are willing to invest their money *[taxes]* in things that work.

Marion Wright Edelman, Director, Children's Defense Fund. PBS, *America's Children: Who Should Care?*, Sept. 4, 1990.

50. The hardest thing in the world to understand is the income tax.

Albert Einstein (1879-1955), Nobel Laureate in Physics (Switzerland). Attributed.

51. Reduction in taxes will be justified only as we can show we can succeed in bringing the budget under control.... Until we can determine the extent to which expenditures can be reduced, it would not be wise to reduce our revenues.

Dwight D. Eisenhower (1890-1969), 34th President of the United States (R-KS). Message to Congress, Feb. 1953.

52. Our taxes reflect a continuing struggle among contending interests for the privilege of paying the least.

Louis Eisenstein, American historian and writer. *The Ideologies of Taxation*, 1961.

53. Men's common guise is always to lay the burden on some other back.

English proverb, c. 1515.

54. A good prince will tax as lightly as possible those commodities which are used by the poorest members of society ... staples without which human life could not exist.

Desiderius Erasmus (c. 1466-1536), Dutch scholar and theologian. *The Praise of Folly*, 1509.

55. Every American has the constitutional right not to be taxed or have his tax money expended for the establishment of a religion.

Samuel J. Ervin, Jr. (1896-1985), U.S. Congressman and U.S. Senator (D-NC). Mar. 13, 1968.

56. The present assault upon capital is but the beginning. It will be but a stepping-stone to others, larger and more sweeping, till our political contests will become a war of the poor against the rich.

Stephen J. Field (1816-1899), U.S. Supreme Court Justice. Comment on the newly imposed income tax. Quoted in Foster Rhea Dulles, *The United States Since 1865*, 1959.

57. Why shouldn't the American people take half my money from me? I took all of it from them.

Edward A. Filene (1860-1937), American department store founder. Quoted in *Forbes*, Jan. 22, 1990.

58. If you don't drink, smoke, or drive a car, you're a tax evader.

Thomas S. Foley, U.S. Congressman and Speaker of the House (D-WA). Quoted in *Time*, June 18, 1990.

59. Our Constitution is in actual operation; everything appears to promise that it will last; but nothing in this world is certain but death and taxes.

Benjamin Franklin (1706-1790), Member, Continental Congress and Constitutional Convention, Governor of Pennsylvania, and U.S. Minister to France. Letter to M. Leroy, 1789.

60. No government can exist without taxation.... This money must of necessity be levied on the people; and the grand art consists in levying so as not to oppress.

Frederick II (The Great) (1712-1786), King of Prussia. *Essay on Forms of Government*.

61. Inflation is taxation without legislation.

Milton Friedman, Nobel Laureate in Economics (United States). Comment on President Carter's plan to raise taxes to reduce inflation, 1979.

62. When you smile the world smiles with you, but when you tax you tax alone.

Frank G. Gardiner, Toronto, Canada. Quoted in John Robert Colombo, *New Canadian Quotations*, 1987.

63. We are in favor of raising all public revenues by a single tax upon land values.

Henry George (1839-1897), American political economist. *The Single Tax Theory*.

64. Taxes are a necessary evil of a civilized society.

Richard A. Gephardt, U.S. Congressman (D-MO). Interview, NBC, *Meet the Press*, Nov. 4, 1990.

65. We're not looking for love as tax collectors. We recognize that taxpayers may not be altogether pleased with the bottom line of what we do. But, if they can say to themselves, "I was treated courteously, I was treated promptly, and I was treated professionally," then that is part of a customer service that we think is ... appropriate.

Lawrence B. Gibbs, Commissioner, U.S. Internal Revenue Service. Quoted in *The Washington Post*, May 4, 1987.

66. The income tax created more criminals than any other single act of government.

Barry M. Goldwater, U.S. Senator (R-AZ). Interview, PBS, *Firing Line*, Nov. 18, 1989.

67. I would suggest the taxation of all property equally, whether church or corporation.

Ulysses S. Grant (1822-1885), 18th President of the United States (R-OH). Annual message to Congress, Dec. 7, 1875.

68. Reverse Robin Hood – take from the needy and give to the greedy.

William H. Grey III, U.S. Congressman (D-PA). Description of a proposed capital gains tax cut. Interview, CNN, Sept. 15, 1990.

69. Income tax is a license to spend.

George Gunther, Connecticut State Senator (R). Statement in opposition to a state income tax proposed by Gov. Lowell P. Weicker, Jr. Quoted in *USA Today*, Mar. 6, 1991.

70. Anyone may so arrange his affairs that his taxes shall be as low as possible.

Learned Hand (1872-1961), Federal Judge. Quoted in *The Financial Consultant*, Jan.-Feb. 1989.

71. I can't make a damn thing out of this tax problem. I listen to one side and they seem right – and then I talk to the other side and they seem just as right, and here I am where I started. God, what a job!

Warren G. Harding (1865-1923), 29th President of the United States (R). Quoted in *The New York Times*, Oct. 5, 1952.

72. The delicate duty of devising schemes of revenue should be left where the Constitution has placed it – with the immediate representatives of the people.

William Henry Harrison (1773-1841), 9th President of the United States (Whig-OH). Inaugural address, Mar. 4, 1841.

73. Only the little people pay taxes.

Leona Helmsley, American hotel owner. Attributed to her by an ex-housekeeper who testified at her trial for tax evasion and extortion. Quoted in *The Washington Post*, July 30, 1989.

74. Unnecessary taxation is unjust taxation.
Abram S. Hewitt (1882-1903), U.S. Congressman and Mayor of New York City (D). Democratic Party platform, 1884.

75. If you must call this relief tax, which I have approved to keep the people from starving, "a Hoffman Tax," then I say you should go ahead and do it. I am willing to pay whatever price may be required of me so far as my personal fortunes are concerned.
[In the midst of the Depression he abandoned his party's traditional opposition to taxes.]
Harold G. Hoffman (1896-1954), Governor of New Jersey (R). Speech to businessmen, 1935.

76. The power to tax is not the power to destroy.
Oliver Wendell Holmes, Jr. (1841-1935), U.S. Supreme Court Justice. *Panhandle Oil Co.* v. *Mississippi*, 1930 (dissent).

77. We will spend and spend, and tax and tax, and elect and elect.
Harry L. Hopkins (1890-1946), U.S. Secretary of Commerce, Director, Work Projects Administration, and Special Assistant to the President (D). Remark to Max Gordon at Empire Race Track, Yonkers, NY, Aug. 1938.

78. That system, unequal as it is indefensible, is the mightiest engine of oppression imposed upon an honest yeomanry since the feudal ages. This system places a high premium on wealth and a severe penalty on poverty.
Cordell Hull (1871-1955), U.S. Congressman (D-TN), U.S. Senator, U.S. Secretary of State and Nobel Laureate in Peace. Comment on the proposed nonprogressive personal income tax. Congressional debate, Mar. 16, 1912.

79. I am truly wearied with lounging here; doing nothing but feeding on the public funds – we have really done nothing yet beneficial; and for nine weeks has the House of Representatives been engaged debating the tariff, that could have been as well decided in two.
Andrew Jackson (1767-1845), 7th President of the United States (D-TN). Letter to Rachel Donelson Jackson while he was a U.S. Senator, Apr. 12, 1823.

80. The wisdom of man never yet contrived a system of taxation that would operate with perfect equality.
Andrew Jackson. Comment on nullification of the Tariff Act. *Proclamation to the People of South Carolina*, Dec. 10, 1832.

81. It will be a sad day for the revenues if the good will of the people toward their taxing system is frittered away in efforts to accomplish by taxation moral reforms that cannot be accomplished by direct legislation.
Robert H. Jackson (1892-1954), U.S. Attorney General (D) and U.S. Supreme Court Justice. 1952.

82. Government, as well as religion, has furnished its schisms, its persecutions, and its devices for fattening idleness on the earnings of the people.
Thomas Jefferson (1743-1826), 3rd President of the United States (Democratic Republican-VA). Letter to the Rev. Charles Clay, Jan. 29, 1815.

83. Taxes grow without rain.
Jewish proverb. Quoted in *Leo Rosten's Treasury of Jewish Quotations*, 1972.

84. He would understand it a little better if there were a few oil wells in Cook County *[Chicago]*.
Lyndon B. Johnson (1908-1973), 36th President of the United States (D-TX). Comment on Illinois Sen. Paul Douglas' opposition to the oil and gas depletion allowances. Quoted in David Halberstam, *The Best and the Brightest*, 1969.

85. There is so much emphasis being placed on spending taxpayers' money that little or no consideration has been given on how to effectively collect what is due.
John R. Kasich, U.S. Congressman (R-OH). Testimony, Senate Committee on Governmental Affairs, May 13-14, 1986.

86. Higher income taxes are a razor guillotine poised to descend on the bare neck of prosperity.
Thomas H. Kean, Governor of New Jersey (R). Quoted in *The New York Times*, Jan. 29, 1989.

87. The promises of yesterday are the taxes of today.
Mackenzie King (1874-1950), Prime Minister of Canada (Liberal). Attributed.

88. If there's anyone who's been shafted, it's the middle class.... They pay most of the taxes and get the least *[government]* services.... We *[politicians]* ought to kiss their feet.
Edward I. Koch, U.S. Congressman and Mayor of New York City (D). Quoted on National Public Radio, *All Things Considered*, Nov. 2, 1989.

89. The people who use alcohol and tobacco ought to be the ones who are taxed.
C. Everett Koop, U.S. Surgeon General. Quoted in *The Washington Post*, Oct. 30, 1990.

90. So long as there is an income to be found in the country so large that it yields to its possessor a surplus over and above what he needs for the

comfort or even luxuries of life for himself and his family, I am in favor of taking such portion of the surplus income by taxation as the government needs for war purposes, and if it needs it all I am in favor of taking it all before we take one penny from the slender income of a man who receives only enough to provide himself and family with the bare necessities of life.

Robert M. La Follette (1855-1925), Governor of Wisconsin and U.S. Senator (R). Senate speech, Aug. 21, 1917.

91. Now all of you profiteering "patriots" who have bawled yourself hoarse about "standing back of the President" get into line and support his recommendation for "additional taxes on war profits, incomes, and luxuries."

Robert M. La Follette. *La Follette's Magazine*, June 1918.

92. They *[post-World War I allied leaders]* are all afraid to face high taxation to pay for the war. The rich won't stand it – and the poor can't stand it.

Robert M. La Follette. Jan. 6, 1919.

93. The purpose of the income tax law is to prevent the accumulation of enormous fortunes, and the control of industry and commerce that goes with such large fortunes.

Fiorello H. La Guardia (1882-1947), U.S. Congressman (R and Socialist) and Mayor of New York City (R and Fusion Party). 1924.

94. The people are hungry: It is because those in authority eat up too much in taxes.

Lao-tzu (c.604-531 B.C.), Chinese philosopher and founder of Taoism. *Tao Te Ching*.

95. We are placing the burdens on the broad shoulders. Why should I put more burdens on the people?
[As Chancellor of the Exchequer, he proposed a budget that heavily taxed the wealthy.]

David Lloyd George, 1st Earl of Dwyfor (1863-1945), Prime Minister of Great Britain (Liberal). Speech, July 30, 1909.

96. 'Tis true that governments cannot be supported without great charge, and it is fit everyone who enjoys a share of protection should pay out of his estate his proportion of the maintenance of it.

John Locke (1632-1704), English philosopher. *Of Civil Government*.

97. War should be supported by a conscription of war profits and certain amounts of swollen fortunes, as well as conscription of men.

Huey P. Long (1893-1935), Governor of Louisiana and U.S. Senator (D). 1918.

98. *[A tax loophole is]* something that benefits the other guy. If it benefits you, it is tax reform.

Russell B. Long, U.S. Senator (D-LA). Quoted in *Time*, Nov. 10, 1986.

99. Don't tax you; don't tax me; tax that fellow behind the tree.

Russell B. Long. Quoted in *U.S. News & World Report*, June 6, 1988.

100. The Chancellor of the Exchequer is a man whose duties make him more or less of a taxing machine. He is intrusted with a certain amount of misery which it is his duty to distribute as fairly as he can.

Robert Lowe, 1st Viscount Sherbrooke (1811-1892), Member of Parliament (Liberal), Chancellor of the Exchequer, and Home Secretary, Great Britain. Speech, House of Commons, Apr. 11, 1870.

101. The tax-reduction plan embodied in this bill was conceived in political expediency, nurtured by political demagoguery, and delivered to you today in political desperation.

Walter A. Lynch (1894-1957), U.S. Congressman (D-NY) and Justice, New York Supreme Court. Congressional debate, Mar. 26, 1947.

102. When neither their property nor their honor is touched, the majority of men live content.

Niccolò Machiavelli (1469-1527), Florentine statesman and political philosopher. *The Prince*, 1513.

103. Our ordinary income is barely at a par with our ordinary expenditures and new taxes must be ready.

James Madison (1751-1836), 4th President of the United States (Democratic Republican-VA). Comment when a Congressman, 1796.

104. Render unto Caesar what is Caesar's, and render unto God what is God's.

New Testament, *Mark* 12:17.

105. Considering the utter impracticability of their ever being fully and equally represented in Parliament, and the great expense that must unavoidably attend even a partial representation there *[in England]*, this House thinks that taxation of their constituents, even without their consent, grievous as it is, would be preferable to any representation that could be admitted for them there.

Massachusetts House of Representatives. Circular letter, 1768.

106. We're moving more and more toward user fees, but the people who use social service programs obviously don't have the ability to pay for them.
Scott S. McInnis, majority leader, Colorado House of Representatives (R). Quoted in *The New York Times*, Nov. 27, 1990.

107. "I pay my taxes," says somebody, as if that were an act of virtue instead of one of compulsion.
Robert G. Menzies (1894-1978), Prime Minister of Australia (Liberal). Quoted in *The Wit of Sir Robert Menzies*, 1966.

108. I'm offended by any suggestion that we have to beat groups of people over the head with an economic club to keep them from exercising their freedom of choice in the marketplace.
Walker Merryman, Vice President, Tobacco Institute. Comment on the suggestion that "sin taxes" on alcohol and tobacco be raised. Quoted in *The Washington Post*, Oct. 30, 1990.

109. To ruin those who possess something is not to come to the aid of those who possess nothing; it is only to render misery general.
Klemens von Metternich (1773-1859), Austrian statesman and diplomat. Comment on higher taxes for the wealthier classes. *Mémoires*, VII, 1884.

110. The middle class has no more to give. The poor have nothing. Let's get it from those who've got it.
Barbara A. Mikulski, U.S. Congresswoman and U.S. Senator (D-MD). Senate debate, Oct. 18, 1990.

111. Hideous bankruptcy is here ... yet you deliberate.... Is it so magnanimous ... to give a portion of one's revenue to save all of one's posessions?
Honoré de Mirabeau (1749-1791), French revolutionary and President, National Assembly. Comment when rich nobles rejected the idea of an income tax. Speech, French Assembly, Feb. 3, 1789.

112. Mr. Reagan will raise taxes and so will I. He won't tell you. I just did.
Walter F. Mondale, Vice President of the United States and U.S. Senator (D-MN). Presidential nomination acceptance speech, Democratic National Convention, San Francisco, CA, July 19, 1984.

113. Congress should know how to levy taxes, and if it doesn't know how to collect them, then a man is a fool to pay the taxes.
J. Pierpont Morgan (1837-1913), American financier. Quoted in *The New York Times*, Mar. 6, 1955.

114. Anybody has a right to evade taxes if he can get away with it.
J. Pierpont Morgan. Statement to reporters, Quoted in *Labor*, June 15, 1957.

115. An auction of the treasury.
Daniel P. Moynihan, Chief American Delegate to the United Nations and U.S. Senator (D-NY). Description of the 1981 Reagan tax cuts. Remark, 1981.

116. The tax structure of the United States is fast becoming the most regressive of any Western nation.
Daniel P. Moynihan. Quoted in *Newsday*, Jan. 29, 1990.

117. True civil liberty depends on the safety of property. There is none in a country where the rate of taxation is changed every year. A man who has three thousand francs income does not know how much he will have to live on the next year. His whole substance may be swallowed up by taxes.
Napoléon I (1769-1821), military leader and Emperor of France. *Maxims*.

118. Great accumulations of property should go back to the community and common purpose.
Alfred Bernhard Nobel (1833-1896), Swedish munitions manufacturer and philanthropist. Quoted in *The New Yorker*, Mar. 22, 1958.

119. If Patrick Henry thought that taxation without representation was bad, he should see how bad it is with representation.
The Old Farmer's Almanac, 1881.

120. Taxation without representation is tyranny.
James Otis (1725-1783), Member, Colonial Massachusetts legislature. Attributed to him by John Adams, 1763.

121. Taxes are not to be laid on the people but by their consent in person or by deputation.
James Otis. *The Rights of the British Colonies Asserted and Proved*, 1764.

122. If we don't watch out La Follette's amendments will make this goddamned war unpopular.
[Sen. La Follette kept introducing amendments to Senate bills to require the wealthy and those making profits from military contracts to pay higher taxes to support the cost of the war.]
Boies Penrose (1860-1921), U.S. Senator (R-PA). Remark, 1917. Quoted in La Follette and La Follette, *Robert M. La Follette*, 1953.

123. Everybody hates a tax collector, but we've got to collect over a trillion dollars a year.
James J. (Jake) Pickle, U.S. Congressman (D-TX). Interview, National Public Radio, Mar. 15, 1989.

124. When there is an income tax, the just man will pay more and the unjust less on the same amount of income.

Plato (427-347 B.C.), Greek philosopher. *The Republic.*

125. IRS agents strike fear into the hearts of the little people of America.

David H. Pryor, U.S. Senator (D-AK). Quoted in *The Washington Post*, May 4, 1987.

126. Even Albert Einstein reportedly needed help on his 1040 *[tax]* form.

Ronald Reagan, 40th President of the United States (R-CA). Argument for tax simplification. Speech, May 28, 1985.

127. The current tax code is a daily mugging.

Ronald Reagan. Speech, Independence, MO, Sept. 2, 1985.

128. Taxation under every form presents but a choice of evils.

David Ricardo (1772-1823), British political economist. *Principles of Political Economy and Taxation*, 1817.

129. Almost all taxes on production fall finally on the consumer.

David Ricardo. *On Protection to Agriculture*, 1820.

130. I'm against an income tax because all the rich people hire lawyers and accountants to be sure that they don't pay income tax.

Ann Richards, Governor of Texas (D). Gubernatorial election debate, C-SPAN, Nov. 4, 1990.

131. Nuclear physics is much easier than tax law. It's rational and always works the same way.

Jerold Rochwald, Washington, DC, lobbyist. Quoted in Burdett A. Loomis, *Interest Group Politics*, 1986.

132. I will ask the legislature to lift some business taxes so we can grow some jobs.

Charles E. Roemer III, U.S. Congressman and Governor of Louisiana (D). Quoted in *The New York Times*, Aug. 14, 1988.

133. The income tax has made more liars out of the American people than golf has.

Will Rogers (1879-1935), American humorist. *The Illiterate Digest*, "Helping the Girls with their Income Taxes," 1924.

134. It is the duty of those who have benefited from our industrial and economic system to come to the front in such a grave emergency *[the Depression]* and assist in relieving those who under the same industrial and economic order are the losers and sufferers.

Franklin D. Roosevelt (1882-1945), 32nd President of the United States (D-NY). Governor's message to the New York State Legislature requesting a tax increase, 1931.

135. Taxes ... are the dues that we pay for the privilege of membership in an organized society.

Franklin D. Roosevelt. Speech, Worcester, MA, 1936.

136. I guess we'll have to raise taxes on the rich again.

Franklin D. Roosevelt. Remark to Vincent Astor aboard the Astor yacht. Quoted in Henry Lewis, *Humorous Anecdotes About Famous People*, 1948.

137. Rich people should pay taxes along with poor people.

James C. Rosapepe, Maryland State Legislator (D). In support of a capital gains tax. Quoted in *The Washington Post*, Mar. 10, 1991.

138. You're not going to see any profiles in courage here.

Daniel D. Rostenkowski, U.S. Congressman (D-IL). In reference to behind-the-scenes negotiations over pending tax legislation. PBS, *Frontline*, Apr. 1986.

139. I am not about to tell the wage earners in Chicago that they should pay a higher tax than the stockbrokers.

Daniel D. Rostenkowski. Reaction to a presidential proposal to have a capital gains tax lower than the income tax. Quoted on CBS, *Inside Washington*, Feb. 11, 1989.

140. Pay-as-you-go.

Beardsley Ruml (1894-1960), Treasurer, R. H. Macy & Co., and Chairman, Federal Reserve Bank of New York. Self-coined term for payroll withholding tax, 1941.

141. Taxes are a killer in my district.

Don Saltzman, Illinois State Representative (D). Quoted in *The Washington Post*, July 21, 1988.

142. Thinking about government, most Americans are muddled. Budget gaps reflect a persisting gap between the public's demand for government services and its willingness to be taxed.... No one *[politician]* wants to offend the muddled majority.

Robert J. Samuelson, American economic columnist. *The Washington Post*, July 27, 1988.

143. The question is not taxes or no taxes. The question is who is going to pay the taxes.

Bernard Sanders, U.S. Congressman (Socialist-VT). Interview, ABC, *Nightline*, Nov. 7, 1990.

144. Money hath too great a Preference given to it by States, as well as by particular Men.
George Savile, 1st Marquess of Halifax (1633-1695), Lord Privy Seal of England. *Moral Thoughts and Reflections*, 1750.

145. Heretofore the Parliament was wary what Subsidies they gave to the King ... but now they care not how much they give of their Subjects' money, because they give it with one hand, and receive it with the other *[in taxes]*; and so upon the matter give it themselves.
John Selden (1584-1654), English jurist and Member of Long Parliament. *Table-Talk: Subsidies*.

146. If people in America who've got some bucks can't pay some of their share, then we're in deep trouble.
Alan K. Simpson, U.S. Senator (R-WY). Interview, CNN, *Evans & Novak*, Sept. 17, 1989.

147. Men, who prefer any load of infamy, however great, to any pressure of taxation, however light.
Sydney Smith (1771-1845), British clergyman and writer. *On American Debts*.

148. We do not commonly see in a tax a diminution of freedom, and yet it clearly is one.
Herbert Spencer (1820-1903), British social philosopher. *Social Statics*, 1850.

149. The beer drinkers are buying the rich people champagne.
Peter Stark, U.S. Congressman (D-CA). Description of a proposed reduced capital gains tax. Quoted in *U.S. News & World Report*, Aug. 7, 1989.

150. You can have a lord, you can have a king, but the man to fear is the tax collector.
Sumerian proverb, c. 2000 B.C.

151. I do not see why the schoolmaster should be taxed to support the priest, and not the priest the schoolmaster.
Henry David Thoreau (1817-1862), American naturalist and philosopher. *On the Duty of Civil Disobedience*, 1849.

152. No one wants to go back to the district and say that taxes are going up. That's why I'm in Hong Kong.
Estaban Torres, U.S. Congressman (D-CA]. Quoted in *Newsweek*, Aug. 27, 1990.

153. The Republicans voted themselves a cut in taxes and you a cut in freedom.
Harry S Truman (1884-1972), 33rd President of the United States (D-MO). Campaign speech, 1948.

154. If you don't have any tax revenues, you don't have any education programs.
Paul Tsongas, U.S. Senator (D-MA). Speech, American Business Conference, C-SPAN, Apr. 13, 1991.

155. Congress shall set a limitation upon the net income of any individual in any one year and a limitation on the amount that such an individual may receive as a gift or as an inheritance, which limitation shall be executed through taxation.
Union Party platform, 1936.

156. The choice is not between taxes or no taxes, but between taxes or no services.
Carl Van Horn, Policy Director, Governor's Office, NJ (D). Quoted in *The New York Times*, Oct. 21, 1990.

157. Taxing our addictions can't be all bad.
Paul A. Volcker, Chairman, Federal Reserve Board. Advocating increased alcohol and cigarette taxes. *The Washington Post*, Dec. 17, 1989.

158. In general, the art of government consists in taking as much money as possible from one class of citizens and giving it to the other.
Voltaire (François-Marie Arouet) (1694-1778), French historian and dramatist. *Philosophical Dictionary*, s.v. "Money," 1764.

159. The thing generally raised on city land is taxes.
Charles Dudley Warner (1829-1900), American writer and editor. *My Summer in a Garden*, 1871.

160. An unlimited power to tax involves, necessarily, the power to destroy.
Daniel Webster (1782-1852), U.S. Congressman (Federalist-NH and MA), U.S. Senator (Federalist and Whig-MA), and U.S. Secretary of State. Oral argument before the U.S. Supreme Court. *McCulloch* v. *Maryland*, 1819.

161. We've been selling the wrong things. This is what we were selling in Mississippi: cheap labor, cheap land, and low taxes. And we got exactly what we paid for.
William F. Winter, Governor of Mississippi (D). Quoted in *Governing the States and Localities*, Feb. 1988.

162. We must be willing to abridge ourselves of our superfluities for the supply of others' necessities.
John Winthrop (1606-1676), English colonial governor of Connecticut. Sermon aboard the *Arabella*, 1630.

Chapter 93

Terrorism and Terrorists

1. Torture is a very humiliating experience. The goal is not to obtain information but to punish and break you so that you won't do anything against the authorities. You are made an example to others so that they will be too terrified to do anything either.

   Isabel Allende, Chilean journalist and writer. 1990.

2. It is unconscionable to permit a foreign government to avoid responsibility for acts of terrorism while it benefits from U.S. commerce.

   Howard L. Berman, U.S. Congressman (D-CA). Quoted in *The New York Times*, Oct. 13, 1988.

3. This *[counterterrorism]* is a game of drag bunts and stolen bases, not home runs.

   L. Paul Bremer, U.S. Ambassador-at-Large for Counterterrorism. Quoted in *The Washington Post*, June 26, 1988.

4. If they *[terrorists]* see a Western hostage can be sold for a couple of million dollars, they may conclude that by holding on to an American, they'll get some money out of us.

   L. Paul Bremer. Comment on France's willingness to pay ransom for hostages. Quoted in *The New York Times*, Oct. 10, 1988.

5. If you want to know what a terrorist is doing, you have to put an agent in their camp.

   L. Paul Bremer. Quoted in *The New York Times*, Mar. 6, 1989.

6. The United States position is clear. We do not meet demands.

   George Bush, 41st President of the United States (R-TX). Statement on refusing to negotiate with terrorist kidnappers of Americans. Apr. 19, 1990.

7. We cannot permit hostage taking to shape the foreign policy of this country.

   George Bush. Quoted on CBS, *Inside Washington*, Sept. 1, 1990.

8. Terrorism has become the systematic weapon of a war that knows no borders or seldom has a face.

   Jacques Chirac, Premier of France. Speech, United Nations, Sept. 24, 1986.

9. How can we expect other nations to respect our law if we don't respect theirs?

   Don Edwards, U.S. Congressman (D-CA). Argument against proposals to have the CIA apprehend terrorists in foreign countries against the wishes of the sheltering country. Hearings, House Judiciary Committee, Nov. 8, 1989.

10. If we announced threats *[to airlines and flights]* as we received them, we would be catering to the terrorists' goals.

    Donald Engen, Administrator, U.S. Federal Aviation Administration. Interview, ABC, *This Week*, Dec. 25, 1988.

11. All terrorists, at the invitation of the government, end up with drinks at the Dorchester.

    Hugh Gaitskell (1906-1963), Member of Parliament, Great Britain (Labour). Quoted in *The Guardian*, Aug. 23, 1977.

12. One of the problems of living in a free country is that you have free access to everything.

    Mike Hall, spokesman, Fire Department, Montgomery County, MD. Remark after police uncovered a nation-wide ring of bomb enthusiasts linked by electronic bulletin board. Quoted in *The Montgomery Journal*, Apr. 28, 1989.

13. We won't make concessions *[to terrorists]*, but other governments can make them on our behalf.

    Brian Jenkins, Senior Fellow, Rand Corporation. Quoted in *The New York Daily News*, Aug. 8, 1989.

14. It'll be over in a few hours.

    Hamilton Jordan, White House Chief of Staff (D). Reaction to the taking of sixty-three American hostages by radicals in Teheran, Iran, Nov. 4, 1979.

15. I am saying that the Israelis have two choices: to let all Palestinians return to their land and have this democratic state we propose, or to live in this so-called state of Israel without letting the Palestinians return. If they choose the latter, they will

surely die and we will surely win.
Farouk Kaddoumi, Representative of Palestine Liberation Organization to the U.N. Security Council. Quoted in *Newsweek*, Jan. 5, 1976.

16. The best way to avoid hostages being taken in the future is to devalue the hostages that exist.
Henry M. Kissinger, U.S. Secretary of State and National Security Advisor (R). PBS, *MacNeil-Lehrer News Hour*, Aug. 22, 1990.

17. The violent will not come to a natural end.
Lao-tzu (c.604-531 B.C.), Chinese philosopher and founder of Taoism. *Tao Te Ching*.

18. Terrorism always has the advantage of surprise.
Lewis Lapham, American journalist. PBS, *America's Century*, Nov. 1989.

19. Democracies cannot be intimidated by terrorism.
John Major, Prime Minister of Great Britian (Conservative). Quoted on PBS, *MacNeil-Lehrer News Hour*, Feb. 7, 1991.

20. Because we're so visible, American diplomats are often the biggest target in town.
John McCarthy, U.S. Ambassador to Lebanon. Quoted in *Government Executive*, Feb. 1991.

21. No one can terrorize a whole nation, unless we are all his accomplices.
Edward R. Murrow (1908-1965), American broadcast journalist and Director, United States Information Agency. In reference to Sen. Joseph R. McCarthy (R-WI). CBS, *See It Now*, Mar. 7, 1954.

22. Man can do no harm to one who is willing to die.
Napoléon I (1769-1821), military leader and Emperor of France. *Maxims*.

23. We want to make the death of a collaborator so grotesque that people will never think of it.
Tim Ngubane, Spokesman, African National Congress, South Africa. Response to moral criticism of "necklacing" in South Africa. Speech, California State University, Fullerton, CA, 1985.

24. The PLO will struggle by every means, the foremost of which is armed struggle, to liberate Palestinian land and to establish the people's national, independent and fighting authority on every part of Palestinian land to be liberated.
Palestine Liberation Organization, Resolution, Article 2, adopted by the Palestine National Council, Cairo, June 1974.

25. The altar-lamp of terror must never be extinguished. The people must have fear.
Miroslav Piade, Yugoslavian Communist leader. Quoted in *The New York Times*, Nov. 11, 1946.

26. If Abu Nidal is a terrorist, then so is George Washington.
Muammar Qaddafi, Chief of State of Libya. Quoted in *Newsweek*, Jan. 20, 1986.

27. No one can kill Americans and brag about it. No one.
Ronald Reagan, 40th President of the United States (R-CA). Quoted in *The Observer*, Apr. 27, 1986.

28. America will never make concessions to terrorists, for to do so will only invite more terrorism.
Ronald Reagan. Quoted on ABC, *Nightline*, Aug. 1, 1989.

29. Turn right over and go to sleep. It's just a little bomb.
Anna Eleanor Roosevelt (1884-1962), First Lady and U.S. Delegate to the United Nations. Remark to James Roosevelt when a bomb went off near their home, May 1919. Quoted in Earle Looker, *This Man Roosevelt*, 1932.

30. One difference between French appeasement *[of terrorists]* and American appeasement is that France pays ransom in cash and gets its hostages back while the United States pays ransom in arms and gets additional hostages taken.
William Safire, presidential speech writer and political columnist (R). In reference to Iran-Contra. Quoted in *Newsweek*, Nov. 24, 1986.

31. They weren't human or inhuman. They were nonhuman.
Michel Seurat, French hostage. Description of the Islamic Jihad terrorists who held him hostage in Lebanon. Quoted in *Time*, May 23, 1988.

32. He who slays a king and he who dies for him are alike idolaters.
George Bernard Shaw (1856-1950), Nobel Laureate in Literature (Great Britain). *Maxims for Revolutionists*, 1903.

33. Hundreds of terrorist tragedies did not happen because we had the information to abort or intercept them.
George P. Shultz, U.S. Secretary of State (R). Speech, Anti-Defamation League, New York City, June 1989.

34. The Department of Transportation or the airline industry cannot stop all acts of terrorism.
Samuel K. Skinner, U.S. Secretary of Transportation (R). Statement, June 23, 1989.

35. We must try to find ways to starve the terrorist and the hijacker of the oxygen of publicity on which they depend.

Margaret Thatcher, Prime Minister of Great Britian (Conservative). Speech, American Bar Association, London, July 15, 1985.

36. A President has to expect these things. The only thing you have to worry about is bad luck. I never have bad luck.

Harry S Truman (1884-1972), 33rd President of the United States (D-MO). Remark to reporters after an abortive assassination attempt on him at Blair House, 1950.

37. Freeing hostages is like putting up a stage set, which you do with the captors, agreeing on each piece as you slowly put it together. Then you leave an exit through which both the captor and the captive can walk with sincerity and dignity.

Terry Waite, Middle East emissary of the Archbishop of Canterbury. Interview, ABC, Nov. 3, 1986.

38. The conspiracy theory of assassination – it's historical, particularly with Europeans. Most of their assassinations grew out of palace guard defections and things of that kind. It's the same in South America. Here, on the contrary, practically all of our assassins have just been demented people.

Earl Warren (1891-1974), Chief Justice, U.S. Supreme Court, and Governor of California (R). Quoted in Merle Miller, *Lyndon: An Oral Biography*, 1980.

39. You have to know for certain whom you are retaliating against and you have to limit the number of innocent people you kill.

Caspar Weinberger, U.S. Secretary of Defense and U.S. Secretary of Health, Education and Welfare (R). Comment on retaliation against terrorism. Quoted in *The New York Times*, Aug. 9, 1989.

40. We look on terrorism as a universal evil, even if it is directed toward those with whom we have no political sympathy.

Joe D. Whitley, U.S. Associate Attorney General of the United States. Quoted in *The New York Times*, July 18, 1990.

41. The real test in the government's success in the antisubversion effort is the eradication of fear. People must be infused with enough courage to withstand threats and keep their shops and establishments open.

Ranjan Wijeratne, Foreign Minister, Sri Lanka. Quoted in *The New York Times*, Aug. 20, 1989.

Chapter 94

Transportation and Infrastructure

1. Clinton's Big Ditch

Derisive reference to the Erie Canal, a pet project of De Witt Clinton, Governor of New York (Democratic Republican), c. 1821.

2. In America we don't just drive cars. We inhabit them.

Bernard Beck, professor of sociology, Northwestern University, Evanston, IL. Quoted in *The New York Times*, Oct. 10, 1988.

3. Let us complete the grand design of Columbus by putting Europe and Asia into communication, and that to our advantage, through the heart of our country. Let us give to his ships, converted into cars, a continuous course, unknown to all former times. Let us make the iron road, and make it from sea to sea.

Thomas Hart Benton (1782-1858), U.S. Senator and U.S. Congressman (D-MO). Speech, St. Louis, MO, 1849.

4. Potholes know no party.

Robert C. Byrd, U.S. Congressman and U.S. Senator (D-WV). 1987.

5. Let us then bind the republic together with a perfect system of roads and canals.

John C. Calhoun (1782-1850), U.S. Congressman (D-SC), U.S. Senator, U.S. Secretary of War, U.S. Secretary of State, and Vice President of the United States. Quoted on PBS, *The Congress*, 1989.

6. There's blood on the hands of every member of Congress who decided to do that.

Joan Claybrook, Director, National Highway Traffic Safety Administration. Comment on Congressional repeal of the 55 mph speed limit. Quoted in *Newsweek*, Sept. 8, 1986.

7. In an unpleasant world, a car takes you where you want in an enjoyable way.

David E. Davis, Jr., editor, *Automobile Magazine*. Quoted in *The New York Times*, Oct. 10, 1988.

8. To be immobile is to be in chains.

Abraham ibn Ezra (1097-1167), Spanish Jewish scholar and poet. *Shirat Yisrael*.

9. Competition doesn't work well in the transportation business.

Albert Fink (1827-1897), Vice President, Louisville and Nashville Railroad Co. Congressional testimony, 1883.

10. I don't think you can ask the free market to make sure that airplanes are working or that the cockpit crew is rested.

Dan Glickman, U.S. Congressman (D-KS). Comment on airline deregulation. Quoted in *The New York Times*, Dec. 11, 1988.

11. Any railroad corporation has infinitely more influence in any department of government than all the human beings that live in the territory that the railroad traverses.

William Randolph Hearst (1863-1951), U.S. Congressman (D-NY); founder, Independence League Party; journalist; and publisher. Speech, Independence League Conference, Albany, NY, Feb. 28, 1906.

12. An uncomfortably tight oligopoly.

Alfred E. Kahn, Chairman, Civil Aeronautics Board. Explanation of what deregulation of airlines during the 1980's created. Quoted in *The Washington Post*, Mar. 19, 1989.

13. Better to be inconvenienced and safe than to be convenienced and dead.

Edward I. Koch, U.S. Congressman and Mayor of New York City (D). Explanation of his action closing the Williamsburg Bridge, which carries 250,000 people into Manhattan each day, in order to make repairs. Quoted on CBS, *60 Minutes*, Feb. 19, 1989.

14. We must produce a true American motor, a true American plane.

Fiorello H. La Guardia (1882-1947), U.S. Congressman (R and Socialist) and Mayor of New York City (R and Fusion Party). House debate, 1918.

15. People don't want to cut back on the railroads, and they haven't ridden the damn things in years.

Jean Le Pepin, Minister of Transportation, Canada. Interview, Canadian Broadcasting Corporation, *As It Happens*, June 26, 1989.

16. Every person that you can get on a public transportation vehicle is one less person polluting the air or taking up space on our highways.

Eva Lerner-Lam, member, New Jersey Transit Board. Quoted in *The New York Times*, May 27, 1990.

17. The Father of Waters *[the Mississippi River]* again goes unvexed to the sea.

Abraham Lincoln (1809-1865), 16th President of the United States (R-IL). Remark after the Confederate defeat at Vicksburg, MS. Letter to James C. Conkling, Aug. 26, 1863.

18. Every improvement of the means of locomotion benefits mankind morally and intellectually as well as materially, and not only facilitates the interchange of the various productions of nature and art, but tends to remove national and provincial antipathies, and to bind together all the branches of the great human family.

Thomas Babington Macaulay, 1st Baron Macaulay (1800-1859), historian and Secretary of War, Great Britain (Liberal). *History of England*, I, 1848.

19. We lack many things, but we possess the most precious of all – liberty!

James Monroe (1758-1831), 5th President of the United States (Democratic Republican-VA). Remark when his daughter Elisa observed that the French roads were much finer than those in America, 1795.

20. *Unsafe at Any Speed*

Ralph Nader, American consumer advocate. Title of report on automobile safety, 1965.

21. The vertebrae and spinal cord which would direct, consolidate, and give life to the numerous *[railway]* systems that would eventually connect the vast central highroad *[of Africa]* with the seas.

Cecil Rhodes (1853-1902), Prime Minister of Cape Colony, South Africa, industrialist, and philanthropist. Description of the proposed Cape-to-Cairo railway. Quoted in Emil Ludwig, *Genius and Character*, 1927.

22. A Congressman is never any better than his roads, and sometimes worse.

Will Rogers (1879-1935), American humorist. *Autobiography*, 1927.

23. I do not believe in government ownership of anything which can with propriety be left in private hands, and in particular I should most strenuously object to government ownership of railroads. In my judgment public ownership of railroads is highly undesirable and would probably in this country entail far-reaching disaster.

Theodore Roosevelt (1858-1919), 26th President of the United States (R-NY). Speech, Raleigh, NC, Oct. 19, 1905.

24. Slow pedestrians are killed more than quick ones are.

Victor Ross, spokesman, New York City Department of Transportation. Quoted in *The New York Times*, Aug. 19, 1990.

25. All of the revenue generated by tolls and gasoline taxes does not equal what is being spent on our roads and bridges.

Ross Sandler, Commissioner of Transportation, New York City. Quoted in *The New York Times*, Aug. 20, 1989.

26. Traffic is a sign of success.

Thom Serrani, Mayor of Stamford, CT. Quoted in *The New York Times*, Dec. 31, 1989.

27. The railroads are not run for the benefit of the dear public. That story is all nonsense. They are built for men who invest their money and expect to get a fair percentage on the same.

William H. Vanderbilt (1821-1885), President, New York Central Railroad. Remark, 1882.

28. In their delirium of greed the managers of our *[railway]* transportation system disregard both private right and the public welfare.

James B. Weaver (1833-1912), U.S. Congressman (Greenback, D, and Greenback-Labor-IA). Presidential nomination acceptance speech, People's Party National Convention, Omaha, NE, July 5, 1892.

29. Nothing has spread socialistic feeling in this country more than the use of the automobile ... a picture of the arrogance of wealth, with all its independence and carelessness.

Woodrow Wilson (1856-1924), 28th President of the United States (D-NJ). 1907.

30. *[Washington officials have]* an infinite capacity for taking trains.

Walter Winchell (1897-1972), American columnist and radio commentator. Newspaper column, 1937.

31. When we need to fix a bridge, we inspect it, and when we need to demolish it, we fix it.

Bojidar Yanev, Assistant Commissioner, New York City Department of Transportation. Quoted in *Newsday*, May 22, 1991.

32. I'll fill it myself.

Andrew Young, U.S. Congressman (D-GA), U.S. Ambassador to the United Nations, and Mayor of Atlanta, GA. Challenge to anyone to show him a pothole in Atlanta. Quoted in *The Washington Post*, July 13, 1988.

Chapter 95

Treaties and Agreements

1. A treaty is the promise of a nation.
 Fisher Ames (1758-1808), U.S. Congressman (Federalist-MA). Speech in Congress on conclusion of the treaty with England, Apr. 28, 1796.

2. When a treaty must depend for its execution ... on a law or laws to be passed by Congress ... it is the constitutional duty of the House of Representatives to deliberate on the expediency of carrying such treaty into effect.
 William Blount (1749-1800), Member, Continental Congress, and U.S. Senator (TN). Resolution of the House of Representatives, 1796.

3. We are not put in the Senate to deal only with treaties on copyrights, extradition, stamp collections and minor questions of protocol.
 Clifford P. Case (1904-1982), U.S. Congressman and U.S. Senator (R-NJ). Argument that executive agreements were being used to circumvent the Senate right to ratify treaties. Senate debate, June 19, 1972.

4. I gained the unenviable distinction of being the first United States Army Commander in history to sign an armistice without a victory.
 Mark W. Clark (1896-1984), General, U.S. Army. Remark at the signing of the truce agreement with Korea, July 1953.

5. I am signing my death warrant.
 Michael Collins (1890-1922), Irish revolutionist and soldier. Remark on signing the Irish Treaty, 1921.

6. It is more difficult *[for foreign governments]* to ignore or defy a convention signed by 120 countries than a bilateral treaty with the United States.
 J. Mark Dion, U.S. Assistant Secretary of State (R). Statement advocating a multinational treaty on drug enforcement. Quoted in *The New York Times*, Oct. 2, 1988.

7. A king's word must stand.
 English proverb, 1200.

8. A foolish covenant ought not to be held.
 English proverb, c.1500.

9. Too often ... in statecraft the object is to reach an agreement, which is only sometimes – not always – the way to reach a result.
 Ralph E. Flanders (1880-1970), U.S. Senator (R-VT). *Senator from Vermont*, 1961.

10. Treaties are like roses and young girls. They last while they last.
 Charles de Gaulle (1890-1970), President of France. Quoted in *Time*, July 12, 1963.

11. Treaties were expedients by which ignorant, intractable, and savage people were induced without bloodshed to yield up what civilized peoples had a right to possess.
 George Rockingham Gilmer (1790-1859), U.S. Congressman and Governor of Georgia (D). Quoted in Weinberg, *Manifest Destiny*, 1935.

12. The attitude of the Senate toward public affairs makes all serious negotiations impossible.
 John Milton Hay (1838-1905), U.S. Ambassador to Great Britain and U.S. Secretary of State (R). In reference to the Senate's right to ratify treaties and the effect on negotiations. Quoted in Arthur M. Schlesinger, Jr, *The Imperial Presidency*, 1973.

13. He *[British Prime Minister Neville Chamberlain]* seemed like such a nice old gentleman – I gave him my autograph as a souvenir.
 Adolf Hitler (1889-1945), Führer of the Third German Reich. Comment after signing the Munich Pact by which Czechoslovakia was partitioned and Anglo-German amity was declared. Sept. 1938.

14. Covenants without the sword are but words and of no strength to secure a man at all.
 Thomas Hobbes (1588-1679), English political philosopher. *Leviathan*, 1651.

15. A treaty is only another name for a bargain; and that it would be impossible to find a nation who would make any bargain with us, which would be binding on them *absolutely*, but on us only so long as and so far as we may think proper to be bound by it.... Treaties are made not by one of the contracting parties but by both, and consequently

that as the consent of both was essential to their formation at first, so must it ever afterwards be to alter or cancel them.

John Jay (1745-1829), President, Continental Congress, Governor of New York (Federalist), U.S. Foreign Secretary, and 1st Chief Justice, U.S. Supreme Court. *The Federalist*, No. 64, Mar. 5, 1788.

16. We've got to hit the country while the country's hot. That's the only thing that makes any impression to these goddamned senators.... We don't want to wait just for their convenience.... They'll move as the country moves.

John F. Kennedy (1917-1963), 35th President of the United States (D-MA). Discussion of the ratification strategy for the Limited Test Ban Treaty in the Senate. Telephone conversation with U.S. Secretary of State Dean Rusk, 1963.

17. Pacts ought to be observed. (*Pacta sunt servanda.*)

Legal maxim.

18. Please refresh my memory. Is it Upper or Lower Silesia that we are giving away?

David Lloyd George, 1st Earl of Dwyfor (1863-1945), Prime Minister of Great Britain (Liberal). Question asked of an aide during negotiations for the Treaty of Versailles, 1919.

19. A wise prince cannot, nor ought he to, keep faith *[with a treaty or agreement]* when such observance may be turned against him, and when the reasons that caused him to pledge it exist no longer. If men were entirely good, this precept would not hold, but because they are bad and will not keep faith with you, you are not bound to observe it with them.

Niccolò Machiavelli (1469-1527), Florentine statesman and political philosopher. *The Prince*, 1513.

20. Ever since 1954, when the United States did not sign the Geneva accords but instead started down the road of unilateral military action in South Vietnam, we have become a provocateur of military conflict in Southeast Asia and marched in the opposite direction from fulfilling our obligations under the United Nations Charter.

Wayne L. Morse (1900-1974), U.S. Senator (R and Ind.-OR). Senate debate, Aug. 5, 1964.

21. Illegal agreements are not to be enforced. (*Pacta illegalia non sevanda sunt.*)

Daniel P. Moynihan, Chief American Delegate to the United Nations and U.S. Senator (D-NY). In connection with the transfer of Lithuania from Nazi Germany to Stalinist Russia after World War II, in the context of the breakup of the Soviet empire in 1990. Speech, National Press Club, Mar. 1990; see above, "Legal maxim," for the origin of the word-play.

22. The only true solution *[to war]* would be a convention under which all the governments would bind themselves to defend collectively any country that was attacked.

Alfred Bernhard Nobel (1833-1896), Swedish munitions manufacturer and philanthropist. Quoted in *The New Yorker*, Mar. 22, 1958.

23. Unless you here in the halls of the American Congress, with the support of the American people, concur in the general conclusions reached at a place called Yalta, and give them your active support, the meeting will not have produced lasting results.

Franklin D. Roosevelt (1882-1945), 32nd President of the United States (D-NY). Congressional address after the Yalta Conference, Mar. 1, 1944.

24. The fidelity of the United States to security treaties is not just an empty matter. It is a pillar of peace in the world.

Dean Rusk, U.S. Secretary of State (D). Quoted in *The New York Times*, Apr. 30, 1985.

25. It is my duty to inform the governments of the deadly peril which threatens them *[Fascism and Naziism]*.... It is a question of trust in international treaties and of the value of promises to small states that their integrity shall be respected. In a word, it is international morality that is at stake. Apart from the Kingdom of God, there is not on this earth any nation that is higher than any other.... God and history will remember your judgment.

Haile Selassie (1891-1975), Emperor of Ethiopia. Speech, League of Nations, Geneva, Switzerland, June 30, 1936.

26. We must forsake any hope that the Soviet Union is going to lie still and lick her awful wounds. She's not. Peace treaties that reflect her legitimate demands, friendly governments on her frontiers, and an effective United Nations organization should be sufficient security. But evidently they are not and she intends to advance her aims, many of them objectives of the czars, to the utmost.

Adlai E. Stevenson (1900-1965), Governor of Illinois (D) and U.S. Ambassador to the United Nations. Speech, Louisville, KY, Mar. 1946.

27. The record is clear: treaties, agreements, pledges, and the morals of international relations were never an obstacle to the Soviet Union under Stalin.

Adlai E. Stevenson. Speech, U.N. Security Council, Oct. 23, 1962.

28. Promises and pie crust are made to be broken.
Jonathan Swift (1667-1745), Irish clergyman and satirist. *Polite Conversation*, I, 1738.

29. ... giving the Russians the northern half of the country, with most of the power and a good deal of the industry, and leaving a southern half which could not support itself, except on an agricultural basis.
Robert A. Taft (1889-1953), U.S. Senator (R-OH). Description of the agreement to partition Korea at the 38th parallel. Senate speech, 1950.

30. The Indian treaties will constitute no obstacle.
Robert J. Walker (1801-1869), Territorial Governor of Kansas. Remark on a plan to make the eastern half of the Indian Territory into a state, and to push the Indians into the western part of their land, which was prohibited by federal treaty, 1857.

31. It is our policy to steer clear of permanent alliances with any portion of the foreign world.
George Washington (1732-1799), 1st President of the United States (VA). Farewell address, Sept. 17, 1796.

32. Settlements may be temporary, but the action of the nations in the interest of peace and justice must be permanent. We can set up permanent processes. We may not be able to set up permanent decisions.
Woodrow Wilson (1856-1924), 28th President of the United States (D-NJ). Address to the Paris Peace Conference, Jan. 25, 1919.

33. Dare we reject it and break the heart of the world?
Woodrow Wilson. Statement when presenting the Versailles Treaty to the Senate for ratification, June 10, 1919.

34. I will consent to nothing. The Senate must take its medicine.
Woodrow Wilson. Remark to French Ambassador Jean-Jules Jusserand when the French and British indicated they would be willing to accept the treaty with certain reservations if that would produce Senate ratification. Quoted in Thomas A. Bailey, *Woodrow Wilson and the Great Betrayal*, 1945.

Chapter 96

United Nations

1. Standards violated are better than no standards at all.

   Kenneth Adelman, Director, U.S. Arms Control and Disarmament Agency. C-SPAN, Dec. 5, 1989.

2. It is better for aged diplomats to be bored than for young men to die.

   Warren Austin (1877-1962), U.S. Delegate to the United Nations. Response when asked about long, boring U.N. debates. Quoted in *The Macmillan Dictionary of Quotations*, 1987.

3. No nation can stand against a world united.

   George Bush, 41st President of the United States (R-TX). National address at the start of the war with Iraq, Jan. 16, 1991.

4. The United Nations was not set up to be a reformatory. It was assumed that you would be good before you got in and not that being in would make you good.

   John Foster Dulles (1888-1959), U.S. Secretary of State and U.S. Senator (R-NY). 1954.

5. If the United Nations would not take responsibility in time of peril, by what right should it claim authority when the danger is passed?

   Abba Eban, Foreign Secretary of Israel and Israeli Ambassador to the U.N. (Labour). *My People*, 1968.

6. We must face the fact that the United Nations is not yet the international equivalent of our own legal system and the rule of law.

   Anthony Eden, Earl of Avon (1897-1977), Prime Minister of Great Britain (Conservative). Speech, House of Commons, Nov. 1, 1956.

7. If the United Nations once admits that international disputes can be settled by using force, then we will have destroyed the foundation of the organization and our best hope of establishing a world order.

   Dwight D. Eisenhower (1890-1969), 34th President of the United States (R-KS). Speech, Feb. 20, 1957.

8. We begin by not taking it *[the United Nations]* seriously.

   Barry M. Goldwater, U.S. Senator (R-AZ). Speech, Air War College, Nov. 14, 1960.

9. Without the U. N., world politics is inconceivable.

   Mikhail Gorbachev, President of the U.S.S.R. Speech, U.N. General Assembly, Dec. 7, 1988.

10. The world cockpit of propaganda.

    Fitzhugh Green, American diplomat and political writer. Description of the U.N. Interview, C-SPAN, Jan. 21, 1990.

11. I find it inconceivable that the American Congress would be less willing to confront aggression than the United Nations.

    Alexander M. Haig, General, U.S. Army, U.S. Secretary of State, and White House Chief of Staff (R). Congressional testimony during the Iraq crisis, Jan. 8, 1991.

12. No nation is responsible to itself alone, but that laws of political morality are universal; and that obedience to such laws is incumbent upon all nations.

    Japanese Constitution, 1947.

13. A cesspool.

    Edward I. Koch, U.S. Congressman and Mayor of New York City (D). Quoted in *The New York Times*, Aug. 30, 1991.

14. One thing the United Nations is good at is producing documents.

    Lewis Lapham, American journalist. PBS, *Bookbeat*, Apr. 7, 1990.

15. If in the judicious determination of the members of the United Nations they feel not welcome and treated with the hostly consideration that is their due, the United States strongly encourages member states to seriously consider removing themselves and this organization from the soil of the United States. We will put no impediment in your way and we will be at dockside bidding you a farewell as you set off into the sunset.

    Charles M. Lichenstein, U.S. Delegate to the United Nations, and Issues Coordinator, Nixon 1960 presidential campaign. Comment in the wake of the downing of KAL 107 and the issue of Soviet landing rights at American airfields. Quoted in *The New York Times*, Sept. 20, 1983.

16. My God, this is war against the United Nations.
Trygve Lie (1896-1968), Secretary General of the United Nations (Norway). Remark to U.S. Assistant Secretary of State Jack Hickerson on being informed by telephone of the North Korean attack on South Korea, June 24, 1950.

17. The United Nations is a foolish attempt at world government inspired by Satan.
Paul D. Lindstrom, American clergyman, Church of Christian Liberty. Quoted in *Newsweek*, July 13, 1970.

18. The world state is inherent in the United Nations as an oak tree is in an acorn.
Walter Lippmann (1889-1974), American political columnist. *One World or None*, 1946.

19. This organization *[the United Nations]* is created to prevent you from going to hell. It isn't created to take you to heaven.
Henry Cabot Lodge, Jr. (1902-1986), U.S. Senator (R-MA), U.S. Ambassador to the United Nations, Vietnam, and Germany, and head of the American delegation to the Paris Peace Conference for Vietnam peace negotiations. Jan. 1954.

20. You can accidentally but deliberately bump into someone at a party *[at the United Nations]* whose office you cannot enter.
Roderic Lyne, British Delegate to the United Nations. Quoted in *The New York Times*, Oct. 4, 1985.

21. Only external authority – the United Nations – can bring about the necessary arrangements to prevent both communities from killing one another.
Thomas P. Melady, U.S. Ambassador to Burundi. Discussion of the inter-tribal killings in that country. *The New York Times*, Sept. 1, 1988.

22. It's group therapy for the world.
Antonio Monteiro, Portuguese Delegate to the United Nations. Comment on debates in the U.N. Quoted in *The New York Times*, Sept. 27, 1986.

23. We will not take care. We do not give a damn.
Daniel P. Moynihan, Chief American Delegate to the United Nations and U.S. Senator (D-NY). Remark to the Soviet U.N. delegate who urged him to "take care" lest his strong rhetoric offend other nations, 1976.

24. Few, if any, calamities ... have befallen the world without some advance notice ... from this rostrum.... The end of man in our time may come as a rude shock, but it will no longer come as a complete surprise.
Abdul Rahman Pazwak, Afghan Representative to the United Nations. Speech, Sept. 19, 1967.

25. The United Nations is a little too much of a debating society.
Claiborne Pell, U.S. Senator (D-RI). Interview, C-SPAN, Dec. 24, 1990.

26. It's not enough *[for member governments]* to make expressions of admiration and good will for peacekeeping. We need money as well.
Javier Pérez de Cuéllar, Secretary General of the United Nations (Spain). Speech, Oslo University, Norway, Dec. 10, 1988.

27. If you believe in God, only he knows; if you don't believe, I don't know who knows.
Javier Pérez de Cuéllar. Reply to reporters when asked if he thought there would be a war with Iraq, Jan. 13, 1991.

28. The United Nations isn't a separate thing. It's a collection of nations and governments.
Ronald Reagan, 40th President of the United States (R-CA). Interview, CNN, *The Larry King Show*, Jan. 10, 1990.

29. Can you imagine a policeman being required to secure the assent of parties to a street fight before breaking up the conflict?
Carlos Romulo (1899-1985), Philippines Representative to the United Nations. Comment on the U.N. peacekeeping process, 1984.

30. There is a small articulate minority in this country that advocates changing our national symbol which is the eagle to that of the ostrich and withdrawing from the United Nations.
Anna Eleanor Roosevelt (1884-1962), First Lady and U.S. Delegate to the United Nations. Speech, Democratic National Convention, Chicago, IL, July 23, 1952.

31. Our agenda is now exhausted. The Secretary General is exhausted. All of you are exhausted. I find it comforting that, beginning with our very first day, we find ourselves in such unanimity.
Paul Henri Spaak (1899-1972), Premier of Belgium and President of the U.N. General Assembly. Statement adjourning the first General Assembly meeting, Flushing Meadows, NY, Dec. 15, 1946.

32. After four years at the United Nations I sometimes yearn for the peace and tranquility of a political convention.

Adlai E. Stevenson (1900-1965), Governor of Illinois (D) and U.S. Ambassador to the United Nations. Quoted in *The New York Times*, Aug. 14, 1964.

33. There is no authority to use armed forces in support of the United Nations in the absence of some previous action by Congress dealing with the subject.
Robert A. Taft (1889-1953), U.S. Senator (R-OH). Senate speech, 1950.

34. Since wars begin in the minds of men, it is in the minds of men that the defenses of peace must be constructed.
United Nations Educational, Scientific, and Cultural Organization. Constitution, 1946.

35. Unlike most governments, the United Nations is not allowed to go into debt.
Brian Urquhart, Undersecretary General of the United Nations. Interview, C-SPAN, Dec. 24, 1990.

36. It is so conservative from a nationalist standpoint.... This is anything but a wild-eyed international dream of a world State.
Arthur H. Vandenberg (1884-1951), U.S. Senator (R-MI) and U.S. Delegate to the United Nations. Comment on the U.N. charter. Diary entry, 1946.

37. The greatest nation on earth either justifies or surrenders its leadership. We must choose.
Arthur H. Vandenberg. Comment on America's role in the U.N., Dec. 1947.

38. The United Nations has become a place where many countries seek to achieve a lynching of the United States by resolution.
Vernon A. Walters, General, U.S. Army, and U.S. Ambassador to the United Nations. Quoted in *The New York Times*, May 31, 1985.

Chapter 97

Voters, Voting, and Elections

1. Australian Ballot
[The modern system of secret voting in political elections was introduced in 1855 in Australia. In America, the Australian ballot was called "the kangaroo ballot" or "the kangaroo vote."]

2. A Chinaman running under the star *[the official symbol of the Democratic Party]* was bound to be elected.
Tammany Hall boast, New York City, c. 1910.

3. Voters are people with the God-given right to decide who will waste their money for them.
Anonymous, 1940.

4. One Man. One Vote
Slogan, Student Non-Violent Coordinating Committee. Civil rights protests, Selma, AL, 1965.

5. Festival of Democracy
Indonesian description of elections, 1980's.

6. We don't all sing, we don't all dance and we don't all vote Democratic.
Anonymous black delegate, Republican National Convention, New Orleans, LA. Quoted in *The New York Post*, Aug. 15, 1988.

7. You don't need a home to vote!
Button worn by homeless people, New York City, Nov. 1989.

8. When annual elections end, there slavery begins.
John Adams (1735-1826), 2nd President of the United States (Federalist-MA). *Thoughts on Government*, 1776.

9. How few of the human race have ever enjoyed an opportunity of making an election of government for themselves and their children.
John Adams. Quoted on PBS, *The Congress*, 1989.

10. General *[Thomas]* Metcalfe, member of the House from Kentucky ... is the administration candidate for Governor of the State, and according to the usage of that part of the country, must before the election travel round the State and offer himself to the people and solicit their votes. His competitor has already made his canvassing tour.
John Quincy Adams (1767-1848), 6th President of the United States (Ind-MA). *Diary*, May 20, 1828.

11. Look at this face. Is it black enough? I want you to vote for me.
Oscar Adams, Alabama State Supreme Court Justice. Reelection campaign speech to a black group in Montgomery, AL. Quoted in *USA Today*, Oct. 20, 1988.

12. If voting could change anything, they would have made it illegal.
Anarchist saying.

13. Suffrage is the pivotal right.
Susan B. Anthony (1820-1906), American suffragist. *The Arena*, May 1897.

14. We'll get out the *[black]* vote, but we need the white vote to win.
Richard Arrington, Jr., Mayor of Birmingham, AL (D). In reference to the 1988 presidential election. Quoted in *The Washington Post*, July 21, 1988.

15. When I have to choose between voting for the people or voting for the special interests, I always stick with the special interests. They remember. The people forget.
Henry Fountain Ashurst (1874-1962), U.S. Senator (D-AZ). Quoted in Morris K. Udall, *Too Funny to Be President*, 1988.

16. Voters do not care about those kinds of things. Democrats get totally preoccupied with things that voters don't care about.
Lee Atwater (1950-1991), Chairman, Republican National Committee. In reference to a letter from the

Republican National Committee intimating that Speaker of the House-designate Thomas Foley was homosexual. Quoted in *The Washington Post*, June 18, 1989.

17. Vote for the man who promises least. He'll be the least disappointing.
Bernard M. Baruch (1870-1965), Chairman, War Industries Board, and U.S. Delegate to the U.N. Atomic Energy Commission. Advice.

18. If every man in New York tonight who had broken the seventh commandment voted for Cleveland, he would be elected by a two-hundred-thousand vote majority.
(Grover Cleveland had fathered an illegitimate child and it was an issue in the presidential campaign.)
Henry Ward Beecher (1813-1887), American clergyman and writer. Speech, New York City, 1884.

19. As nearly as practicable one man's vote in a congressional election is to be worth as much as another's.
Hugo L. Black (1886-1971), U.S. Senator (D-AL) and U.S. Supreme Court Justice. *Wesberry* v. *Sanders*, 1964.

20. Your vote will give the government a legitimacy it does not deserve.
Allan Boesak, founder, United Democratic Front of South Africa. Comment urging a boycott of parliamentary election. Quoted on ABC, *Nightline*, Oct. 26, 1988.

21. One goal of empowerment is to gain influence in as many elections as possible.... Beware of plans that pack you into super-minority districts, that ghettoize minorities.
Mark Bohannon, Director, Election Analysis and Planning, Democratic National Committee. Quoted in *The Washington Post*, July 7, 1990.

22. The shop is only open one day a year.
Rudolph E. Boschwitz, U.S. Senator (R-MN). Remark after losing his reelection bid to political novice Paul Wellstone, Nov. 7, 1990.

23. Politicians, even if their motives are not of the purest, come much nearer performing their duties than the so-called "good" citizens who stay at home *[on Election Day]*.
Louis D. Brandeis (1856-1941), U.S. Supreme Court Justice. Quoted in Alpheus T. Mason, *Brandeis: A Free Man's Life*, 1946.

24. The larger percentage of people you have registered, the larger percentage of people you will have voting.
Ron Brown, Chairman, Democratic National Committee. Conference, "The Presidency in the 90's," C-SPAN, Fordham University, Bronx, NY, Sept. 4, 1989.

25. One of the reasons why voters are turned off is the process *[of modern presidential campaigns]*.
Ron Brown. *Ibid.*

26. When voters get a chance to vote, they vote their hopes rather than their fears.
Ron Brown. Interview, ABC, *Nightline*, Nov. 6, 1989.

27. You've got to jump through all kinds of hoops to vote in America.
Ron Brown. Comparison of America's voter registration procedures with those of other industrialized democracies. Lecture, Harvard University, Cambridge, MA, Nov. 9, 1989.

28. I don't know anything about free silver, but the people of Nebraska are for free silver and I am for free silver. I will look up the arguments later.
William Jennings Bryan (1860-1925), U.S. Secretary of State (D). Campaign speech, 1892.

29. I got all the applause, but McKinley got the votes.
William Jennings Bryan. Remark to Simon Wolf, 1913.

30. The ballot box is the surest arbiter of disputes.
James Buchanan (1791-1868), 15th President of the United States (D-PA). 4th annual message to Congress, Dec. 3, 1860.

31. Too many people are voting.
William F. Buckley, Jr., American political columnist and publisher. Interview, *Playboy*, May 1970.

32. I mean to live my life as an obedient man, but obedient to God, subservient to the wisdom of my ancestors; never to the authority of political truths arrived at yesterday at the voting booth.
William F. Buckley, Jr. Quoted in *The 1989 Conservative Calendar*.

33. Why do we want dumb votes?
William F. Buckley, Jr. In support of literacy requirements for voters. Interview, PBS, *MacNeil-Lehrer News Hour*, 1990.

34. Your representative owes you, not his industry only, but his judgment; and he betrays instead of serving you if he sacrifices it to your opinion.
Edmund Burke (1729-1797), British statesman. Speech to the Electors of Bristol, Nov. 3, 1774.

35. It is no exaggeration to say that undecided voters could go either way.

George Bush, 41st President of the United States (R-TX). Remark, presidential campaign, 1988.

36. The danger of democracy has always been the danger of an electorate seized by passivity.
Dalton Camp, Canadian journalist. Introduction, *An Electric Eel*, 1982.

37. This is representative government, and Indians have very little political clout because for the most part, they don't vote. But white ranchers and farmers do vote.
Ben Nighthorse Campbell, U.S. Congressman (D-CO). Quoted in *Governing the States and Localities*, Apr. 1988.

38. As of right now, I have two votes, mine and Jimmy's. I'm sure of Jimmy because he said he is gonna vote for me and Jimmy never tells a lie.
Billy Carter (1937-1988), President Jimmy Carter's brother. Comment when he ran for mayor of Plains, GA. Rifkin and Howard, *Redneck Power: The Wit and Wisdom of Billy Carter*, 1977.

39. If all the things the Republicans are saying about me are true, I wouldn't vote for myself either.
Jimmy Carter, 39th President of the United States (D-GA). Campaign speech, New York City, Oct. 1976.

40. Are you honest people or thieves?
Jimmy Carter. Question of Panamanian election inspectors when some citizens were falsely certifying the election of Gen. Manuel Noriega's hand-picked candidate who had actually lost. Quoted in *The New York Times Magazine*, Dec. 10, 1989.

41. Does any of you believe that we can solve our country's problems in five years? That is why we do not have this nonsense of elections.
Fidel Castro, Premier of Cuba. Comment to Latin American leaders. Quoted by Napoleon Duarte, PBS, *MacNeil-Lehrer News Hour*, Feb. 22, 1990.

42. For you will seem either not to esteem government worth much, or to think few worthy to hold it.
Marcus Porcius Cato (The Elder) (234-149 B.C.), Roman censor. Remark when the Romans chose the same men again and again as their magistrates. Quoted in Plutarch, *The Parallel Lives: Cato the Censor*.

43. Nothing would induce me to vote for giving women the franchise. I am not going to be henpecked into a question of such importance.
Winston Churchill (1874-1965), Prime Minister of Great Britain (Conservative). Quoted in Robert L. Taylor, *The Amazing Mr. Churchill*, 1952.

44. Women will vote by 1917.
James B. (Champ) Clark (1850-1921), U.S. Congressman and Speaker of the House (D-MO). Statement, 1912.

45. Sensible and responsible women do not want to vote. The relative positions to be assumed by man and woman in the working out of our civilization were assigned long ago by a higher intelligence than ours.
Grover Cleveland (1837-1908), 22nd and 24th President of the United States (D-NY). Inaugural address, Mar. 4, 1885.

46. Your every voter, as surely as your chief magistrate, under the same high sanction, though in a different sphere, exercises a public trust.
Grover Cleveland. *Ibid.*

47. I don't care how great your ideas are or how well you can articulate them, people must *like* you before they will vote for you.
William S. Cohen, U.S. Senator (R-ME). Quoted in Morris K. Udall, *Too Funny to Be President*, 1988.

48. Feel the power. Vote America.
Bill Cosby, American entertainer and educator. Public Service TV ad, Oct. 1990.

49. When an upstart dictator in the United States *[Franklin D. Roosevelt?]* succeeds in making this a one-party form of government, when the ballot is useless, I shall have the courage to stand up and advocate the use of bullets.
Charles E. Coughlin (1891-1979), American Roman Catholic priest and cofounder, Union Party. Sept. 25, 1936.

50. You may all go to Hell, and I will go to Texas.
David Crockett (1786-1836), U.S. Congressman (Anti-Jacksonian-TN). Comment after being defeated for reelection to Congress, 1835.

51. When the day of election approaches, visit your constituents far and wide. Treat liberally, and drink freely, in order to rise in their estimation, though you fall in your own. True, you may be called a drunken dog by some of the clean shirt and silk stocking gentry, but the real roughnecks will style you a jovial fellow, their votes are certain, and frequently count double.
David Crockett. *The Life of Davy Crockett*, 1889.

52. Vote early and vote often.
James M. Curley (1874-1958), U.S. Congressman (D), Governor of Massachussetts, and Mayor of Boston, MA. Admonition to constituents, borrowed from John Van Buren.

53. The United States is the only major democracy where divided government has become the norm.... For those who are disappointed in the current performance of our national political system, the fault, dear voters, may not be in our stars but in ourselves, that we are ticket-splitters.

Lloyd N. Cutler, counsel to the President and member, President's Commission on Federal Ethics Law Reform (D). *The Washington Post*, Nov. 1, 1988.

54. He didn't get enough votes.

Richard J. Daley (1902-1976), Mayor of Chicago, IL (D). Reply when reporters asked him why Vice President Hubert H. Humphrey did not carry Illinois in the presidential election, Nov. 13, 1968.

55. The ballot can give our civilization its crowning glory – the Cooperative Commonwealth.

Eugene V. Debs (1855-1926), American Socialist. *The Cooperative Commonwealth*, 1885.

56. *[Freeholders are]* the best guardians of liberty, and the restrictions of the right *[of suffrage]* to them was a necessary defense against the dangerous influence of those multitudes without property and without principle with which our country, like all others, will in time abound.

John Dickenson (1732-1808), Member, Continental Congress (DE and PA), President of Delware, and President of Pennsylvania. Debate, Constitutional Convention, Philadelphia, PA, 1787.

57. All voting systems are capable of being corrupted. Most of them have been or will be ... simply because voting is the way we determine who gets power in this great country.

Craig C. Donsanto, Chief, Election Crimes Branch, U.S. Department of Justice. Quoted in *The Los Angeles Times*, July 4, 1989.

58. When corruption enters, the election is no longer free, and the choice of the people is affected.

William O. Douglas (1898-1980), U.S. Supreme Court Justice. *United States* v. *Classic*, 1940.

59. There is more to the right to vote than the right to mark a piece of paper and drop it in a box or the right to pull a lever in a voting booth.... It also includes the right to have the vote counted at full value without dilution or discount.

William O. Douglas. *South* v. *Peters*, 1949.

60. Whin a man gets to be my age, he ducks political meetin's, an' r-reads th' papers an' weighs th' evidence an' th' argymints – pro-argymints, an' con-argyments – an' makes up his mind ca'mly, an' votes th' Dimmycratic ticket.

Finley Peter Dunne (1867-1936), American humorist and newspaper editor. *Mr. Dooley in Peace and War*, 1898.

61. No matter whether th' Constitution follows th' flag or not, the Supreme Coort follows th' iliction returns.

Finley Peter Dunne. *Mr. Dooley's Opinions*, 1900.

62. My boy, the only place you find unanimity is in the graveyard. And even there, I have heard it said, at election times the dead have been known to vote in various ways.

Maurice L. Duplessis (1890-1959), Premier of Quebec (Union Nationale). Quoted in Charles Lynch, *You Can't Print That!*, 1983.

63. A voter without a ballot is like a soldier without a bullet.

Dwight D. Eisenhower (1890-1969), 34th President of the United States (R). Quoted in *The New York Times*, Oct. 27, 1957.

64. George Minot *[a Concord neighbor]* thinks that it is of no use balloting, for it will not stay, but what you do with the gun will stay so.

Ralph Waldo Emerson (1803-1882), American writer. Referring to the recently-passed Fugitive Slave Law. *Journals*, May 1851.

65. Those who stay away from the election think that one vote will do no good. 'Tis but one step more to think one vote will do no harm.

Ralph Waldo Emerson. *Journals*, May 1854.

66. What they were seeking to steal was not the jewels, money, or other property of American citizens, but something much more valuable – their most precious heritage, the right to vote in a free election.

Samuel J. Ervin, Jr. (1896-1985), U.S. Congressman and U.S. Senator (D-NC). Comment about the men who conceived and carried out the Watergate break-in, May 17, 1973.

67. We *[clergy]* have a threefold responsibility to people: get them baptized, get them saved, and get them registered to vote.

Jerry Falwell, American televangelist and founder, Moral Majority. PBS, *Bill Moyers: God and Politics*, Aug. 10, 1988.

68. War they *[women]* understand least, and from it they instinctively recoil. There is danger in this situation. Women now have the vote, and they outnumber the men.... In spite of themselves we must protect the ladies!

Bradley A. Fiske (1854-1942), Admiral, U.S. Navy. 1925.

69. I am acutely aware that I have received the votes of none of you.

Gerald R. Ford, 38th President of the United States (R-MI). Comment upon assuming office as the only President not elected to the presidency or the vice presidency. National address, Aug. 9, 1974.

70. As to those who have no landed property ... allowing them to vote for legislators is an impropriety.

Benjamin Franklin (1706-1790), Member, Continental Congress and Constitutional Convention, Governor of Pennsylvania, and U.S. Minister to France. Quoted in *The New York Times*, Nov. 8, 1989.

71. Registration is a necessary – but not sufficient – condition for voting.

Curtis Gans, Director, Committee for the Study of the American Electorate. Quoted in *The New York Times*, Oct. 9, 1988.

72. The public will vote if they have something important to vote for or against.

Curtis Gans. Quoted in *USA Today*, Oct. 1, 1990.

73. You cannot fight against the future. Time is on our side.

William E. Gladstone (1809-1898), Prime Minister of Great Britain (Liberal). Speech against those who opposed his efforts to expand the voting franchise, House of Commons, 1866.

74. People vote for their dreams and fears.

Martin Goldfarb, Canadian political pollster. *The Toronto Star*, Apr. 22, 1978.

75. The Democrats want to save more on defense so they can spend more money to buy votes through the welfare state.

Barry M. Goldwater, U.S. Senator (R-AZ). Quoted in *The St. Louis Post-Dispatch*, Feb. 1, 1964.

76. The issue of private ownership of land is too critical a decision to be left to the government.

Mikhail Gorbachev, President of the U.S.S.R. Statement urging a referendum, Sept. 1990.

77. The extension of suffrage will not forbid the supremacy of intelligence.

Ulysses S. Grant (1822-1885), 18th President of the United States (R). 1871.

78. Increased turnout at the polls produces two secondary benefits: more definitive election results and an election that costs less per vote.

Bill Graves, Kansas Secretary of State. *Governing the States and Localities*, May 1988.

79. Politicians in this country have been more concerned with maintaining a positive public opinion of the white electorate than they have with upholding their oath to implement the Constitution.

Dick Gregory, American comedian and writer. *Write Me In*, 1968.

80. In a democracy citizens are entitled to know what is in store for them before they vote.

William Greider, American TV journalist. PBS, *Frontline: Campaign, The Politics of Prosperity*, Oct. 10, 1988.

81. There are a hell of a lot more rednecks out there than people who eat crepes suzette.

Mickey Griffin, presidential campaign aide to Gov. George C. Wallace. Remark, 1972.

82. The voters don't care if you are white, black or green; if you got a $2 raise, you are going to vote for them *[politicians]*.

Luis V. Gutierez, Alderman of Chicago, IL (D). Quoted in *The Washington Post*, July 21, 1988.

83. I know how illusory would be the belief that my vote determined anything; but nevertheless when I go to the polls I have a satisfaction in the sense that we are all engaged in a common venture.

Learned Hand (1872-1961), Federal Judge. *The Bill of Rights*, 1958.

84. When it comes to kids' issues, voters are willing to put their money where their mouth is.

Peter Hart, American political pollster (D). Quoted in *The Washington Post*, July 15, 1988.

85. Anti-Nebraska, Know Nothings, and general disgust with the powers that be have carried this country by between seven and eight thousand majority! How people do hate Catholics, and what happiness it was to thousands to have a chance to show it in what seemed a lawful and patriotic manner.

Rutherford B. Hayes (1822-1893), 19th President of the United States (R-OH). Letter to Sardis Birchard, Oct. 13, 1854.

86. If the Red Shirts can be present at the polls in South Carolina, why cannot the bluecoats *[Federal troops]* be called in also?

Rutherford B. Hayes. Comment when informed that South Carolina "Red Shirts," an armed band organized to restore white supremacy in their state, controlled the elections. *Diary*, Mar. 23, 1879.

87. Voting is a civic sacrament.

Theodore M. Hesburgh, President, University of Notre Dame, IN. *Reader's Digest*, Oct. 1984.

88. I've always voted for Franklin Roosevelt for President. My father before me always voted for Franklin Roosevelt for President.

Bob Hope, American actor and comedian. Comment after Roosevelt was elected to a fourth term as President. White House correspondents' dinner, 1945.

89. The people are always worsted in an election.

Edgar Watson Howe (1853-1937), American editor and writer. *Ventures in Common Sense*, 1919.

90. We receive from America the right to vote as Americans, for America's weal, and if we cannot use our privilege as Americans we should surrender it.

John Ireland (1838-1918), American Roman Catholic bishop. Speech, Chicago, IL, Feb. 22, 1895.

91. Our Constitution sought to leave no excuse for violent attack on the status quo by providing a legal alternative – attack by ballot.

Robert H. Jackson (1892-1954), U.S. Attorney General (D) and U.S. Supreme Court Justice. *Harisiades* v. *Shaughnessy*, 1951.

92. To me, the most compelling reason for lowering the voting age *[to eighteen]* is that American politics needs the infusion that younger voting would give it.

Jacob K. Javits (1904-1986), U.S. Congressman and U.S. Senator (R-NY). *Playboy*, Feb. 1968.

93. A vote for every man, whether he owns property or not.

Thomas Jefferson (1743-1826), 3rd President of the United States (Democratic Republican-VA). Motto.

94. We may lessen the danger of buying and selling votes by making the number of voters too great for any means of purchase.

Thomas Jefferson. Letter to Jeremiah Moor, Aug. 14, 1800.

95. Voting is the first duty of democracy.

Lyndon Baines Johnson (1908-1973), 36th President of the United States (D-TX). Speech, Aug. 11, 1964.

96. The vote is the most powerful instrument ever devised by man for breaking down injustice and destroying the terrible walls which imprison men because they are different from other men.

Lyndon B. Johnson. Speech on signing the Voting Rights Act, Aug. 6, 1965.

97. Public confidence in the elective process is the foundation of public confidence in government.

Lyndon B. Johnson. Message to Congress, May 26, 1966.

98. The age of eighteen, far more than the age of twenty-one, has been and is the age of maturity in America – and never more than now.

Lyndon B. Johnson. Message to Congress, 1968.

99. Though we cannot out-vote them we will out-argue them.

Samuel Johnson (1709-1784), British writer and lexicographer. Quoted in James Boswell, *The Life of Samuel Johnson*, Apr. 3, 1778.

100. The right of election is the very essence of the *[English]* Constitution.

Junius (Prob. Philip Francis) (1740-1818), British writer (Whig). *Letters*, No. 11, Apr. 24, 1769.

101. The point of an election is not to test the fortitude and determination of the voters, but to discern the will of the majority.

Kansas City Consensus (a Missouri citizens organization). Quoted in *Governing the States and Localities*, May 1988.

102. Our democracy is but a name. We vote. What does that mean? It means that we choose between two bodies of real, though not avowed, autocrats. We choose between Tweedledum and Tweedledee.

Helen Keller (1880-1968), American writer. Letter, 1911.

103. If we can lower the voting age to nine, we are going to sweep the state.

John F. Kennedy (1917-1963), 35th President of the United States. Presidential campaign speech, Girard, OH, Oct. 9, 1960.

104. From the vote, from participation in the elections, flow all other rights far, far more easily.

Robert F. Kennedy (1925-1968), U.S. Attorney General and U.S. Senator (D-NY). Interview, Dec. 1964.

105. Universal suffrage once granted, is granted forever and can never be recalled.

James Kent (1763-1847), Chief Judge, New York State Supreme Court. Debate, New York State Constitutional Convention, 1821.

106. This is Selma, Alabama, where there are more Negroes in jail with me than there are on the voting rolls.

Martin Luther King, Jr. (1929-1968), American clergyman and civil rights leader. Letter to *The New York Times*, Feb. 5, 1965.

107. *[President Johnson should]* get a voting bill *[from Congress]* that will end the necessity for any more voting rights bills.

Martin Luther King, Jr. Press conference, Mar. 1965.

108. Because the women's vote is so complicated, it's very hard to organize, but it's also very hard to ignore.

Ethel Klein, political science professor, Columbia University, New York City. *Savvy*, June 1988.

109. I believe that everything that happens on earth is preordained by God, and I believe that, while the people elected me, it was God that selected me.

Edward I. Koch, U.S. Congressman and Mayor of New York City (D). Quoted in *The New Yorker*, Mar. 23, 1987.

110. The people in this country have always been afraid of power. Now, maybe the powerful are becoming a little afraid of the people.

Vitaly Korotich, editor, *Ogonyok*, Kharkov, U.S.S.R. Comment after Russia's first open elections, when liberal delegates replaced many old-line Communists, May 25, 1989.

111. The ballot is the legitimate weapon of the Socialists just as it is of the general public.

Fiorello H. La Guardia (1882-1947), U.S. Congressman (R and Socialist) and Mayor of New York City (R and Fusion Party). Statement when the New York State legislature, at the height of the "Red scare," voted to unseat five legally elected Socialist assemblymen, 1920.

112. The direct primary is the salvation of American politics. It vests responsibility where it belongs – in the people.

Fiorello H. La Guardia. Speech, League of Women Voters, New York City, 1921.

113. That which touches all should be approved by all. (*Quod omnes tangit, debet ab omnibus approbari.*)

Legal maxim.

114. A delegate cannot have a delegate. (*Vicarius non habet vicarium.*)

Legal maxim.

115. I go for sharing the privileges of government with those who assist in the bearing the burdens. Consequently I go for admitting all whites to the rights of suffrage who pay taxes or bear arms, by no means excluding females.

Abraham Lincoln (1809-1865), 16th President of the United States (R-IL). Announcement for the Illinois House of Representatives, July 18, 1836; also in a letter to a newspaper, June 13, 1836.

116. Ballots are the rightful and peaceful successors of bullets.

Abraham Lincoln. July 4, 1861.

117. If we could, somehow, get a vote of the people of Tennessee and have it result properly, it would be worth more to us than a battle gained. How long before we can get such a vote?

Abraham Lincoln. Letter to Governor Johnson, July 11, 1862.

118. If the Constitution does not allow women to vote, then the Constitution should be amended or abolished.

Belva Ann Lockwood (1830-1917), American attorney, feminist, and cofounder, Equal Rights Party. Speech.

119. Take the money and vote for me.

Huey P. Long (1893-1935), Governor of Louisiana and U.S. Senator (D). Advice to voters who had been offered money to vote for his opponent. 1923.

120. We did not fight and die for the Voting Rights Act just to change the color of government but to change the character of government.

Joseph Lowery, President, Southern Christian Leadership Conference. Speech, SCLC National Convention, Aug. 9, 1990.

121. Who are to be the electors? Not the rich more than the poor, not the learned more than the ignorant, not the haughty heirs of distinguished names more than the humble sons of obscure and unpropitious fortune. The electors are to be the great body of the people of the United States.

James Madison (1751-1836), 4th President of the United States (Democratic Republican-VA). *The Federalist*, No. 57, Feb. 19, 1788.

122. If they're not voting, we're not touching their heads and hearts.

Lynn M. Martin, U.S. Congresswoman (R-IL) and U.S. Secretary of Labor. Seminar, The National Press Club, Washington, DC, Mar. 29, 1990.

123. We must demonstrate our power by exercising our right to vote.

Julian Martinez, Special Assistant, Hispanic Affairs, Republican National Committee. Quoted in *Hispanic*, Oct. 1990.

124. You're proving you're a dope who has been duped if you do vote. Hardly a word of truth seems to come from either presidential candidate, and they want me to confirm their opinion of me as an idiot by helping either of them get elected.

Jackie Mason, American comedian. Quoted in *The New York Times*, Aug. 14, 1988.

125. American youth attributes much more importance to arriving at driver's license age than at voting age.

Marshall McLuhan (1911-1980), Canadian educator and media philosopher. *The Mechanical Bride*, 1951.

126. The public always tires of its messiahs, and soon or late invariably turns them out, whether they be good, which is uncommon, or bad, which is the rule.

H. L. Mencken (1880-1956), American journalist. *Generally Political*, 1944.

127. No one ever went broke underestimating the intelligence of the American people.

H. L. Mencken. Attributed.

128. To get an affirmative vote from the Australian people on a referendum proposal is one of the labours of Hercules.

Robert G. Menzies (1894-1978), Prime Minister of Australia (Liberal). Quoted in *The Wit of Sir Robert Menzies*, 1966.

129. Give the votes to people who have no property and they will sell them to the rich, who will be able to buy them.

Gouverneur Morris (1752-1816), U.S. Senator (Federalist-NY), U.S. Commissioner to Great Britain, and U.S. Minister to France. Debate, Constitutional Convention, Philadelphia, PA, Aug. 7, 1787.

130. Governments are like underwear. They start smelling pretty bad if you don't change them once in a while.

Margaret Murray, Canadian publisher. Quoted in *The Toronto Star*, Apr. 26, 1981.

131. These new devices *[voter referenda and initiatives]*, the key instrumentalities of the new participatory democracy, enable the people to leapfrog traditional representative processes and mold the political system with their own hands.

John Naisbitt, American futurist and writer. *Megatrends*, 1982.

132. When people really care about an issue, it doesn't matter how much is spent to influence their vote; they will go with their beliefs. When an issue is inconsequential to the voters, buying their vote is a snap.

John Naisbitt. *Ibid.*

133. People on whom I do not bother to dote
Are people who do not bother to vote.

Ogden Nash (1902-1971), American poet and humorist. "Election Day Is a Holiday," *Happy Days*, 1933.

134. The Soviet Union took a small but symbolically important step today toward increased democracy when a handful of members of the Supreme Soviet ... cast the first "No" votes in more than half a century.

Editorial, *The New York Times*, Oct. 29, 1988.

135. There is only one month left to save America.

Richard M. Nixon, 37th President of the United States (R-CA). Campaign speech, Alexandria, VA, Oct. 1, 1952.

136. It's time for the great silent majority of Americans to stand up and be counted.

Richard M. Nixon. Presidential election speech, Nov. 11, 1968.

137. A politician knows not only how to count votes but how to make his vote count.

Richard M. Nixon. Eulogy for Everett M. Dirksen, Sept. 8, 1969.

138. Why am I opposed to *[Washington, DC]* statehood? I just don't want two senators to come from the one place that supported McGovern and Dukakis without question. If I can prevent that, I will.

Stanford E. Parris, U.S. Congressman (R-VA). Quoted in *Regardie's*, May 1989.

139. A dollar ain't much if you have one.

Claude D. Pepper (1901-1989), U.S. Senator and U.S. Congressman (D-FL). Comment on a $1 poll tax. Quoted by Sen. Daniel P. Moynihan, CNN, *Evans & Novak*, May 12, 1991.

140. Never forgive at the ballot box!

Wendell Phillips (1811-1884), American orator and reformer. Quoted in Richard Hofstadter, *The American Political Tradition*, 1948.

141. If it be said that the representatives in the popular branch of Congress are chosen directly by the people, it is answered, the people elect the President. If both Houses represent the states and the people, so does the President.

James K. Polk (1795-1849), 11th President of the United States (D-TN). Annual message to Congress, Dec. 5, 1848.

142. We are mortgaged. All but our votes.

Populist Party slogan, 1892.

143. Let other Democrats wring their hands about losing racist white votes. If the choice is between racial justice and racist votes, our choice is clear. Let the Republicans have those votes and pay the price. History is on our side. Eventually, the voters will be too.

Robert Rackleff, presidential speech writer (D). *The Washington Post*, Feb. 26, 1989.

144. We did not labor in suffrage just to bring the vote to women but to allow women to express their opinions and become effective in government.

Jeanette Rankin (1880-1973), U.S. Congresswoman (R-MT). Recalled on her death.

145. The United States is a constitutional democracy. Its organic law grants to all citizens a right to participate in the choice of elected officials without restriction by any state because of race.

Stanley F. Reed (1884-1980), U.S. Solicitor General and U.S. Supreme Court Justice. *Smith* v. *Allwright*, 1943.

146. It is not surprising to find that the reasons on which the continuance of the inferiority of women are urged are drawn almost entirely from a tender consideration of their own good. The anxiety felt less they should thereby deteriorate would be an honor to human nature were it not a historical fact that the same sweet solicitude have been put up as a barrier against every progress women have made since civilization began.

Thomas B. Reed (1839-1902), U.S. Congressman and Speaker of the House (R-ME). *Minority Report*, House Judiciary Committee, Apr. 1884.

147. One with God is always a majority, but many a martyr has been burned at the stake while the votes were being counted.

Thomas B. Reed. Remark after losing the Republican presidential nomination to William McKinley, June 18, 1896.

148. An election is a bet on the future, not a popularity test of the past.

James Reston, American political columnist. *The New York Times*, Oct. 10, 1984.

149. Most people wouldn't change their vote if their candidate went on a boat ride to Bimini with a bimbo.

Andy Rooney, TV columnist and humorist. Allusion to Adam Clayton Powell and Gary Hart, CBS, *60 Minutes*, Oct. 9, 1988.

150. A free election is of no use to the man who is too indifferent or too lazy to vote.

Franklin D. Roosevelt (1882-1945), 32nd President of the United States (D-NY). Remark to advisors, 1940.

151. One of the chief principles for which I have stood is the genuine rule of the people. I hope that the people may be given the chance, through direct primaries, to express their preference as to who shall be the nominee.

Theodore Roosevelt (1858-1919), 26th President of the United States (R-NY). Presidential candidacy announcement, 1912.

152. One man one vote does not make Sambo equal to Socrates in the state.

Edward A. Ross (1866-1951), sociology professor, Stanford University, Palo Alto, CA. *Changing America*, 1912.

153. As racial polarization increases, racial voting increases as well.

Larry J. Sabato, political scientist, University of Virginia, Charlottsville, VA. Quoted in *The Washington Post*, Sept. 12, 1989.

154. If we do not fulfill the objectives of free and clean elections, we will not be able to move ahead in the construction of Mexican democracy.

Carlos Salinas de Gortarì, President of Mexico. Comment after narrowly winning an election marked by charges of fraud and corruption against his ruling party. Quoted in *The New York Times Magazine*,Nov. 20, 1988.

155. People tend to vote the present tense – not the subjunctive.

Diane Sawyer, American TV journalist. *CBS News Election Night*, Nov. 8, 1988.

156. Snaring votes means hitting emotions.

Tony Schwartz, American political TV ad producer. Interview, PBS, *A Walk Through the 20th Century: The 30 Second President*, July 23, 1990.

157. The tyranny of a prince in an oligarchy is not so dangerous to the public welfare as the apathy of a citizen in a democracy.

Charles-Louis de Secondat, Baron de La Brède et de Montesquieu (1689-1755), French writer. *The Spirit of the Laws*, XXV, 2, 1748.

158. I stand opposed to the election by the people. The people want *[lack]* information and are constantly liable to be misled.

Roger Sherman (1721-1793), U.S. Congressman and U.S. Senator (Federalist-CT). Debate, Constitutional Convention, Philadelphia, PA, June 26, 1787.

159. Frequent elections are necessary to preserve the good behavior of rulers.
Roger Sherman. *Ibid.*

160. Bad politicians are sent to Washington by good people who don't vote.
William E. Simon, U.S. Secretary of the Treasury (R). LTV Corporation, *A Guide to the 99th Congress*, 1985.

161. Why should we go on voting for a State Treasurer who hasn't a cent, or a State Secretary who is nothing but a clerk?
Alfred E. Smith (1873-1944), Governor of New York (D). Call for the elimination of statewide voting for minor functionaries. Radio address, 1925.

162. No second-rate man should be given the opportunity to steal a ride into the Executive Chamber on the back of the national bandwagon.
Alfred E. Smith. Opposition to a move to make the New York gubernatorial election years coincide with the national presidential elections, 1925.

163. They *[prospective voters]* find that the issues they care most about simply are not being addressed by any of the candidates, so they wonder why take the trouble of going out in the rain or snow in November. The choice no longer has that much meaning to them.
Pricilla Southwell, political science professor, University of Oregon, Eugene, OR. Quoted in *The Washington Post*, Oct. 18, 1988.

164. The secret ballot makes a secret government; and a secret government is a secret band of robbers and murderers. Open despotism is better than this.
Lysander Spooner (1808-1887), American attorney and Libertarian. *No Treason*, No. VI: *The Constitution of No Authority*, 1870.

165. I am for Negro suffrage in every rebel state. If it be just, it should not be denied; if it be necessary, it should be adopted; if it be a punishment to traitors, they deserve it.
Thaddeus Stevens (1792-1868), U.S. Congressman (Whig and R-PA). Speech in Congress, Jan. 3, 1867.

166. When the people rule they must be rendered happy, or they will overturn the state.
Alexis de Tocqueville (1805-1859), French writer. *Democracy in America*, 1835.

167. By their votes ye shall know them.
Harry S Truman (1884-1972), 33rd President of the United States (D-MO). Remark, Sept. 23, 1948.

168. A vote is the best way of getting the kind of country and the kind of world you want.
Harry S Truman. Presidential campaign speech, Grand Rapids, MI, Oct. 10, 1948.

169. I don't want you to vote for me, I want you to get out on election day and vote for yourselves – for your interests.
Harry S Truman. *Ibid.*

170. It's not the hand that signs the laws that holds the destiny of America. It's the hand that casts the ballot.
Harry S Truman. Presidential campaign speech, Raleigh, NC, Oct. 19, 1948.

171. I don't like bipartisans. Whenever a fellow tells me he's bipartisan, I know he's going to vote against me.
Harry S Truman. Speech, Kansas City, MO, Jan. 21, 1962.

172. I am not defying the government. I am obeying God.
Desmond M. Tutu, Anglican archbishop of South Africa and Nobel Laureate in Peace. Comment on his call to boycott elections in South Africa. Quoted in *The New York Times*, Sept. 5, 1988.

173. A patriotic American must do something around election time.
Mark Twain (Samuel Langhorne Clemens), (1835-1910), American writer. Interview, *New York Herald*, Oct. 16, 1900.

174. Vote: The only commodity that is peddleable without a license.
Mark Twain. Quoted in Merle DeVore Johnson, ed., *More Maxims of Mark*, 1927.

175. As long as I count the votes, what are you going to do about it? Say.
William Marcy Tweed (1823-1878), U.S. Congressman and Tammany Hall leader, New York City (D). *The Ballot in 1871.*

176. The ballots made no result; the counters made the result.
William Marcy Tweed. Testimony, New York State corruption investigation, 1878.

177. Some of the policies of the Roosevelt administration are not popular. What can be done about it? We can support the Democratic ticket; we can support the Republican ticket, or we can take a walk. I do not propose to take a walk.
Millard E. Tydings (1890-1961), U.S. Congress-

man and U.S. Senator (D-MD). Statement at a rally, Baltimore, MD, Mar. 5, 1936.

178. The voters have spoken – the bastards.
Morris K. Udall, U.S. Congressman (D-AZ). Remark after losing in New Hampshire's presidential primary election, 1976.

179. To every Southern river shall Negro Suffrage come,
But not to fair New England, for that's too close to home.
Zebulon B. Vance (1830-1894), U.S. Congressman and U.S. Senator (D-NC). Speech, Union Square, New York City, July 11, 1868.

180. In presidential years there are two national elections taking place. The one who sits in the White House. The other, who controls the Congress.
Guy Vander Jagt, U.S. Congressman (R-MI). Symposium, "The Press and a Divided Government," National Press Foundation, Washington, DC, Dec. 6, 1989.

181. The Constitution of the United States does not confer the right of suffrage upon anyone.
Morrison R. Waite (1816-1888), Chief Justice, U.S. Supreme Court. *Minor* v. *Happersett*, 1875.

182. The U.S. Constitution nowhere delegates to men the right to give voting power to women, since they already have it.
Mary Edwards Walker (1832-1919), American physician and suffragist. Testimony, Suffrage Committee, New York State Constitutional Convention, Aug. 12, 1915.

183. The President got too many votes.
Earl Warren (1891-1974), Chief Justice, U.S. Supreme Court, and Governor of California (R). Response when asked why Gov. Thomas Dewey lost to Harry Truman. Press conference, Dec. 1948.

184. The weight of a citizen's vote cannot be made to depend on where he lives.
Earl Warren. *Reynolds* v. *Sims*, 1964.

185. A frequent return to the bar of their constituents is the strongest check against the corruptions to which men are liable.
Mercy Otis Warren (1748-1814), American revolutionary. Criticism of infrequent elections in the Constitution. *Observations on the New Constitution*, 1789.

186. You've got the strongest hand in the world. That's right. Your hand. The hand that marks the ballot. The hand that pulls the voting lever. Use it, will you.
John Wayne (1907-1979), American actor. TV campaign ad, 1964.

187. It is a misfortune in the Southern states that the freemen of a *whole county* assemble at elections. This is one principal cause why the elections are attended with tumults, riots, quarrels, bloody noses, and in a few instances with death. The laws of a republic should guard against all large collections of people for good or bad purposes: They are always dangerous.
Noah Webster (1758-1843), American writer and lexicographer. *A Collection of Essays*, 1790.

188. Act as if the whole election depended on your single vote, and as if the whole Parliament on that single person whom you now choose to be a member of it.
John Wesley (1703-1791), British clergyman and founder of Methodism. *A Word to a Freeholder*, 1748.

189. Today alike are great and small
The nameless and the known;
My palace is the people's hall;
The ballot box my throne.
John Greenleaf Whittier (1807-1892), American poet and reformer. "The Poor Voter on Election Day."

190. Voters don't decide issues, they decide who will decide issues.
George F. Will, American political columnist. *Newsweek*, Mar. 8, 1976.

191. The American political conundrum is that while a lack of defined issues breeds voter indifference, a sharpening of issues breeds political divisiveness and social polarization. Can it be that the American consensus can only be sustained by apathy?
Juan Williams, American journalist. *The Washington Post*, Nov. 7, 1988.

192. The best way to raise voter turnout is to get candidates on the ballot whom people feel represent their interest.
Linda Williams, Director, Joint Center for Political Studies. Quoted in *USA Today*, Nov. 3, 1988.

193. The people will stand for anything. What they can't stand for, they'll fall for.
Ross Winne (1882-1960), American conservationist. Quoted in Bergen Evans, *Dictionary of Quotations*, 1978.

194. If the ballot doesn't work, we'll try something else, but let us try the ballot.
Malcolm X (Malcolm Little) (1925-1965), American black power advocate. Quoted in *Life*, Fall 1990.

Chapter 98

War and Peace

1. Hail, Caesar, we who are about to die salute you. (*Ave Caesar, morituri te salutant.*)

   Gladiators' salute. Quoted by Suetonius, *Lives of the Caesars: Claudius*.

2. THE PRICE OF PRIDE IS HIGH, AND PAID BY THE YOUNG.

   Anonymous inscription, German World War II memorial at El Alamein, Egypt.

3. War is unhealthy for children and other living things.

   Popular slogan, Late 1960's and early 1970's, protesting the Vietnam War.

4. Hey, hey, LBJ, how many kids *[or boys]* did you kill today?

   Anonymous student chant against Pres. Lyndon B. Johnson during the Vietnam War, 1965-1968.

5. Nonviolence or Nonexistence

   Pacifist slogan chanted by pickets of Trident nuclear submarines. Quoted on CBS, *Evening News*, Dec. 17, 1988.

6. PEACE IS NOT A WORD – IT IS A WAY OF LIVING.

   Airport sign, Abidjan, Ivory Coast, 1988.

7. Under our Constitution the Congress alone has the power to declare war.

   Dean Acheson (1893-1971), U.S. Secretary of State (D). Testimony on the North Atlantic Treaty Organization agreement. Senate Foreign Relations Committee, 1949.

8. My voice is still *[silent]* for war.

   Joseph Addison (1672-1719), Secretary of State, Great Britain (Whig). *Cato*, II, 1713.

9. We have won the *[Vietnam]* war in the sense that our armed forces are in control of the field and no potential enemy is in a position to establish authority in South Vietnam.

   George D. Aiken (1892-1984), Governor of Vermont and U.S. Senator (R). Speech, Oct. 19, 1966.

10. Arms once taken up should never be laid down but upon one of three conditions – a safe peace, a complete victory, or an honorable death.

    Jeanne Albret (1528-1572), French Queen of Navarre. Quoted in Sarah Josepha Hale, *Biography of Distinguished Women*, 1876.

11. Why are American boys dying in a war the President refuses to call a war, yet commits our forces to it?

    Bruce R. Alger, U.S. Congressman (R-TX). House debate, 1963.

12. For a war to be just, three conditions are necessary – public authority, just cause, right motive.

    Thomas Aquinas (1225-1274), Italian scholastic philosopher. *Summa Theologica*.

13. If peace should break out, what are we going to do with all these weapons?

    Leslie Aspin, U.S. Congressman (D-WI). Quoted on PBS, *MacNeil-Lehrer News Hour*, July 24, 1989.

14. War is a last and terrible defense of even a righteous cause, and sets at defiance all the ordinary laws and customs of society.

    Lafayette C. Baker (1826-1868), Director, U.S. Secret Service. Defense of torture and other violations of civil and human rights by the Union during the Civil War. *History of the United States Secret Service*, 1868.

15. You have a lot of support right now, but once you get a lot of casualties, this thing is going to change.

    George Ball, U.S. Undersecretary of State (D). Statement to President Lyndon B. Johnson, 1963.

16. A soldier who doesn't like or want war. It's like a whore who believes in chastity.

    Mary Bancroft, American socialite and OSS operative. In reference to Gen. Dwight D. Eisenhower. Quoted in Leonard Mosley, *Dulles*, 1978.

17. It is wise statesmanship which suggests that in time of peace we must prepare for war, and it is no less a wise benevolence that makes preparation in the hour of peace for assuaging the ills that are sure to accompany war.

Clara Barton (1821-1912), founder, American Red Cross. *The Red Cross*, 1898.

18. Take the profits out of war.
Bernard M. Baruch (1870-1965), Chairman, War Industries Board, and U.S. Delegate to the U.N. Atomic Energy Commission. Quoted in George Seldes, *The Great Quotations*, 1983.

19. It takes twenty years or more of peace to make a man. It takes only twenty seconds of war to destroy him.
Baudouin I, King of Belgium. Address, U.S. Congress, May 12, 1959.

20. Whenever there is talk of peace, there is anger in the military-industrial-political complex.
Edward W. Bauman, American televangelist. WJLA-TV, *Bauman Bible Telecast*, Apr. 23, 1989.

21. War is a biological necessity.
Friedrich A. J. von Bernhardi (1849-1930), General, Prussian Army. *Germany and the Next War*, 1911.

22. A short cleansing thunderstorm.
Theobald von Bethmann-Hollweg (1856-1921), Chancellor of Germany. Description of World War I given to Prince Bernhard von Bülow, Aug. 1914.

23. There has never been a war yet which, if the facts had been put calmly before the ordinary folk, could not have been prevented. The common man is the greatest protection against war.
Aneurin Bevan (1897-1960), Minister of Health, Great Britain (Socialist). 1945.

24. Most future wars will be conflicts for commerce.
Albert J. Beveridge (1862-1927), U.S. Senator (R-IN) and founder, Progressive League. Speech, 1900.

25. The Congress decides when to make war and the President decides how to make war.
Joseph R. Biden, Jr., U.S. Senator (D-DE). Senate debate, Jan. 10, 1991.

26. The decision *[to go to war]* can only come from God, the God of battles, when He shall let fall from his hands the iron dice of destiny.
Otto von Bismarck-Schoenhausen (1815-1898), Chancellor of Germany. Speech in the Diet, May 17, 1847.

27. I see in our relation with the *[Austrian]* Bund an error of Prussia's which, sooner or later, we shall have to repair *ferro et igni [sword and fire]*, unless we take advantage betimes of a favorable season to employ a healing remedy *[war]* against it.
Otto von Bismarck-Schoenhausen. Letter to M. de Schleinitz, Mar. 29, 1859.

28. We Germans fear God but nothing else in the world. (*Wir Deutsch fürchten Gott aber sonst nichts in der Welt.*)
Otto von Bismarck-Schoenhausen. Speech, Reichstag, Feb. 6, 1888.

29. We did not expect to conquer the whites. I took up the hatchet to revenge the injuries which my people could no longer endure. Had I borne them without striking, my people would have said, "Black Hawk is a woman; he is too old to be a chief; he is no Sauk."
Black Hawk (1767-1838), Chief, Sac and Fox Indians. Statement to President Jackson, Apr. 1832.

30. *[World War I started]* through the stupidity and ineptitude of old men in the chancelleries of Europe, and there are still a lot of doddering old men over there in positions of power, along with a sorry lot of confirmed megalomaniacs, egomaniacs, and psychopaths, who are literally preparing to dip their hands in blood and drag the whole world into the frightful mess they are creating for themselves.
Homer T. Bone (1883-1970), U.S. Senator (D-WA). Senate speech, Aug. 20, 1935.

31. Peace upon any other basis than national independence, peace purchased at the cost of any part of our national integrity, is fit only for slaves, and even when purchased at such a price it is a delusion, for it cannot last.
William E. Borah (1865-1940), U.S. Senator (R-ID). Statement leading the Senate opposition to the League of Nations Covenant proposed by President Wilson. Senate speech, Nov. 19, 1919.

32. In war there is no second prize for the runner-up.
Omar N. Bradley (1893-1981), General, U.S. Army, and Permanent Chairman, Joint Chiefs of Staff. Statement to troops, 1944.

33. The wrong war, at the wrong place, at the wrong time, and with the wrong enemy.
Omar N. Bradley. Opposition to Gen. Douglas MacArthur's proposal to extend the Korean War into China. Senate testimony, May 1951.

34. We are much in the position of those who love peace so much that they are ready to fight for it.
Louis D. Brandeis (1856-1941), U.S. Supreme Court Justice. Letter to Robert M. La Follette, May 27, 1913.

35. Neutrality is at times a graver sin than belligerence.

Louis D. Brandeis. Quoted in Solomon Goldman, *The Words of Justice Brandeis*, 1954.

36. And even if I were alone ... I should have the consolation ... to the last moment of my existence ... that no word of mine has tended to the squandering of my country's treasure or the spilling of one single drop of my country's blood.

John Bright (1811-1889), Member of Parliament, Great Britain (Liberal). Speech on the Crimean War, House of Commons, Dec. 22, 1854.

37. I started in politics by opposing the war in Vietnam.... I don't think it was right, and I think it has seriously undermined the position of America in the world. It has weakened the social and political fabric of our country. And it is going to take heroic efforts to rebuild America because of it.

Edmund G. (Jerry) Brown, Jr., Governor of California (D). *Thoughts*, 1976.

38. The present administration had no alternative but to accept the war initiated by South Carolina or the Southern Confederacy. The North will sustain the administration almost to a man, and it ought to sustain it at all hazards.

James Buchanan (1791-1868), 15th President of the United States (D-PA). Letter to John A. Dix, Mar. 8, 1861; four days earlier Abraham Lincoln had become President.

39. War is the second worst activity of mankind, the worst being acquiescence in slavery.

William F. Buckley, Jr., American political columnist and publisher. "On the Right," *National Review*, Apr. 1, 1965.

40. I know there is no present evidence and I think there is no present likelihood that the Cubans and the Cuban government and the Soviet government would in combination attempt to install major offensive capability.

McGeorge Bundy, presidential assistant for National Security (D). Speech, Oct. 14, 1962.

41. The greatest enemy to man is man.

Robert Burton (1577-1640), vicar of St. Thomas's, Oxford. *The Anatomy of Melancholy*, 1621.

42. The Commonwealth of Venice in their armoury have this inscription, "Happy is that city which in time of peace thinks of war."

Robert Burton. *Ibid.*

43. War is never cheap or easy.

George Bush, 41st President of the United States (R-TX). Press briefing, Jan. 18, 1991.

44. *[The atomic bomb means]* the end of world war. Fear will prevent it.

Vanevar Bush (1890-1974), presidential science advisor. Quoted in Lawrence Wittner, *Rebels Against War*, 1969.

45. War is a racket.... The only way to stop it is by conscription of capital before conscription of the nation's manhood.... Let the officers and directors of our armament factories, our gun builders and munitions makers and shipbuilders all be conscripted – to get $30 a month, the same wage paid to our lads in the trenches. Give capital thirty days to think it over and you will learn by that time there will be no war. That will stop the racket – that, and nothing else.

Smedley Butler (1881-1940), General and Commandant, U.S. Marine Corps. Quoted in *Forum*, Sept. 1934.

46. None of the Americans I spoke to want to nominate their sons for the Unknown Soldier.

Smedley Butler. Quoted on National Public Radio, May 26, 1990.

47. *[Theodore Roosevelt]* came down here *[to Washington, DC]* looking for war. He did not care whom we fought as long as there was a scrap.

Thomas S. Butler (1855-1928), U.S. Congressman (R-PA). 1900.

48. War, war is still the cry, "War even to the knife."

George Gordon Byron, 6th Baron Byron (1788-1824), poet and Member of Parliament, Great Britain. *Childe Harold*, Canto I, 1812.

49. The only way to save our empires from the encroaching of the people is to engage in war, and thus substitute national passions for social aspirations.

Catherine II (The Great) (1729-1796), Empress of Russia. Quoted in Evdokimov, *The Complete Works of Catherine II*, 1893.

50. We go about peace in a very belligerent way, don't we?

Robert Cecil, Viscount Cecil of Chelwood (1864-1958), drafter of the covenant of the League of Nations and Nobel Laureate in Peace (Great Britain). Remark to Eleanor Roosevelt, Jan. 1946.

51. I believe it is peace for our time.

Neville Chamberlain (1869-1940), Prime Minister of Great Britain (Conservative). In reference to his negotiation of the Munich Pact with Adolf Hitler. Remark, Sept. 1938.

52. There is no such thing as fighting on the winning side; one fights to find out which is the winning side.
G. K. Chesterton (1874-1936), British writer. *What's Wrong with the World?*, 1910.

53. The wars of the peoples will be more terrible than those of kings.
Winston Churchill (1874-1965), Prime Minister of Great Britain (Conservative). 1901.

54. Those who can win a war well can rarely make a good peace and those who make a good peace would never have won the war.
Winston Churchill. *My Early Life: A Roving Commission*, 1930.

55. *[Prime Minister Neville]* Chamberlain has a lust for peace.
Winston Churchill. 1937.

56. France though armed to the teeth is pacifist to the core.
Winston Churchill. 1940.

57. Learn to get used to it *[the German bombings of England]*. Eels get used to skinning.
Winston Churchill. Remark in secret Cabinet session, June 20, 1940.

58. Are we beasts? Are we taking this too far?
Winston Churchill. Remark after viewing films of the effects of Allied bombing on German cities. June 1943.

59. In war: resolution. In defeat: defiance. In victory: magnanimity.
Winston Churchill. Epigraph, *The Second World War: The Gathering Storm*, 1948.

60. In wartime, truth is so precious that she should be attended by a bodyguard of lies.
Winston Churchill. Quoted in *Time*, Dec. 24, 1984.

61. Wars are to be undertaken in order that it may be possible to live in peace without molestation. (*Bella suscipienda sunt ob eam causam, ut sine injuria in pace vivatur.*)
Marcus Tullius Cicero (106-43 B.C.), Roman statesman and writer. *De Officiis*, I.

62. I prefer the most unfair peace to the most righteous war.
Marcus Tullius Cicero. *Epistola ad Atticum*.

63. Endless money forms the sinews of war. (*Nervi belli pecunia infinita.*)
Marcus Tullius Cicero. *Philippics*, V.

64. All great civilizations, in their early stages, are based on success in war.
Kenneth Clark (1903-1983), British art historian and broadcast commentator. *Civilization*, 1969.

65. War is an act of force to compel our enemy to do our will.
Karl von Clausewitz (1780-1831), General, Prussian Army, and military writer. *On War*, 1833.

66. There is only one decisive victory; the last.
Karl von Clausewitz. *Ibid.*

67. Peaceably if we can, forcibly if we must.
Henry Clay (1777-1852), U.S. Senator (National Republican and Whig-KY), Speaker of the House, and U.S. Secretary of State. Speech on the new army bill, 1813; Clay in his speech gave credit for the sentiment to Josiah Quincy of Cambridge, MA.

68. It is not every cause of war that should lead to war.
Henry Clay. House debate, Mar. 24, 1818.

69. My home policy? I wage war. My foreign policy? I wage war. Always, everywhere, I wage war.
Georges Clemenceau (1841-1929), Premier of France and journalist. Speech, Chamber of Deputies, Mar. 8, 1918.

70. We made war to the end – to the very end of the end.
Georges Clemenceau. Message to the American people, referring to the Battle of the Meuse-Argonne. Sept. 30, 1918.

71. War is a series of catastrophes that results in a victory.
Georges Clemenceau. To Woodrow Wilson at the Paris Peace Conference, Jan. 12, 1919.

72. How can I talk to a fellow *[Woodrow Wilson]* who thinks himself the first man in two thousand years to know anything about peace on earth?
Georges Clemenceau. Jan. 14, 1919.

73. War is too serious to be entrusted to generals.
Georges Clemenceau. Quoted in *The New York Times*, July 19, 1944.

74. I am not conscious of falling under any of those ornithological divisions.
Clark P. Clifford, U.S. Secretary of Defense (D) and Special Counsel to the President. Reply when

asked if he was a hawk or a dove. Quoted in *The New York Times*, Jan. 2, 1968.

75. It must be a peace with no losers.
Chester A. Crocker, U.S. Assistant Secretary of State. Comment on mediating the conflict between Cuba, Angola, and South Africa. Quoted in *The New York Times*, Dec. 18, 1988.

76. It's a maxim not to be despised, "Though peace be made, yet it's interest that keeps peace."
Oliver Cromwell (1599-1658), Lord Protector of England. Speech, Parliament, Sept. 4, 1654.

77. War is not neat. It's not tidy. It's a mess.
William Crowe, Admiral, U.S. Navy, and Chairman, Joint Chiefs of Staff. Senate testimony, Nov. 29, 1990.

78. Capitalist wars for capitalist conquest and capitalist plunder must be fought by the capitalists themselves so far as I am concerned.
Eugene V. Debs (1855-1926), American Socialist. Speech, 1914.

79. War seldom enters but where wealth allures.
John Dryden (1631-1700), English poet and dramatist. *The Hind and the Panther*, II, 1687.

80. War is the trade of kings.
John Dryden. *King Arthur*, 1691.

81. No soldier starts a war – they only give their lives to it. Wars are started by you and me, by bankers and politicians, excitable women, newspaper editors, clergymen who are ex-pacifists, and Congressmen with vertebrae of putty.
Francis P. Duffy (1871-1932), American Roman Catholic priest. Sermon, New York City, 1919.

82. Almost every great war has led to a collapse of the coalition that won the victory.
Foster Rhea Dulles, American historian. *The United States Since 1865*, 1959.

83. The world will never have lasting peace so long as men reserve for war the finest human qualities. Peace, no less than war, requires idealism and self-sacrifice and a righteous and dynamic faith.
John Foster Dulles (1888-1959), U.S. Secretary of State and U.S. Senator (R-NY). Mar. 9, 1955.

84. One of the great advances of our time is the recognition that one of the ways to prevent war is to deter it by having the will and the capacity to use force to punish the aggressor.
John Foster Dulles. Speech, Williams College, Williamstown, MA, Oct. 6, 1956.

85. War is one of the constants of history, and it has not diminished with civilization or democracy. In the last 3,421 years of recorded history only 268 have seen no war.
Will Durant (1885-1981) and **Ariel Durant** (1898-1981), American historians. *The Lessons of History*, 1968.

86. We've got a rattlesnake by the tail, and the sooner we pound its damn head in the better.
Charles A. Eaton (1868-1953), U.S. Congressman (R-NJ). In reference to early U.S. action in the Korean War. House speech, 1950.

87. I think this is the first war in history that on the morrow the victors sued for peace and the vanquished called for unconditional surrender.
Abba Eban, Foreign Secretary of Israel and Israeli Ambassador to the U.N. (Labour). Remark after the Six-Day War. Quoted in *The New York Times*, July 9, 1967.

88. We are not at war with Egypt. We are in an armed conflict.
Anthony Eden, Earl of Avon (1897-1977), Prime Minister of Great Britain (Conservative). Speech, House of Commons, Nov. 4, 1956.

89. Peace cannot be kept by force. It can only be achieved by understanding.
Albert Einstein (1879-1955), Nobel Laureate in Physics (Switzerland). *Cosmic Religion*, 1931.

90. As long as there are sovereign nations possessing great power, war is inevitable.
Albert Einstein. Quoted in *The Atlantic Monthly*, Nov. 1945.

91. We have won an armistice on a single battleground, not peace in the world. We may not now relax our guard nor cease our quest.
Dwight D. Eisenhower (1890-1969), 34th President of the United States (R-KS). Remark when signing armistice ending the Korean War, July 27, 1953.

92. There is going to be no involvement of America in war unless it is the result of the constitutional process that is placed upon Congress to declare it.
Dwight D. Eisenhower. Response when asked if the U.S. would become involved in Vietnam after the defeat of the French. Press conference, Mar. 10, 1954.

93. The United States will never take part in an aggressive war.
Dwight D. Eisenhower. Statement at summit meeting, Geneva, Switzerland, 1955.

94. The people who know war, those who have experienced it ... I believe are the most earnest advocates of peace in the world.

Dwight D. Eisenhower. Quoted in Nathan Marsh Pusey, *Eisenhower, the President*, 1956.

95. There are no alternatives to peace.
Dwight D. Eisenhower. Quoted in Lawrence Wittner, *Rebels Against War*, 1969.

96. Monarchs ought to put to death the authors and instigators of war, as their sworn enemies and as dangers to their states.
Elizabeth I (1533-1603), Queen of England. Attributed.

97. But the real and lasting victories are those of peace, and not of war.
Ralph Waldo Emerson (1803-1882), American writer. *The Conduct of Life*, "Worship," 1860.

98. Peace makes plenty.
English proverb, 1425.

99. Ares *[the god of war]* hates those who hesitate.
Euripides (480-405 B.C.), Greek dramatist. *Hericlidae*.

100. Dead men have no victory.
Euripides. *The Phoenician Women*.

101. The essence of war is violence. Moderation in war is imbecility.
William Fisher (1780-1852), Rear-Admiral, British Navy. Remark during the campaign against Villeneuve, 1805.

102. Long, continuous periods of peace and prosperity have always brought about the physical, mental, and moral deterioration of the individual.
Bradley A. Fiske (1854-1942), Admiral, U.S. Navy. Quoted in George Seldes, *The Great Quotations*, 1983.

103. No nation is rich enough to pay for both war and civilization.
Abraham Flexner (1866-1959), American educator and writer. *Universities*, 1930.

104. War is an orgy of money, just as it is an orgy of blood.
Henry Ford (1863-1947), American industrialist and philanthropist. *My Life and Work*, 1924.

105. Get there firstest with the mostest.
Nathan Bedford Forrest (1821-1877), General, Confederate Army. The secret of his military victories. Attributed.

106. It is simply not true that war never settles anything.
Felix Frankfurter (1882-1965), U.S. Supreme Court Justice. 1950.

107. I join with you most cordially in rejoicing at the return of peace. I hope it will be lasting, and that mankind will at length, as they call themselves reasonable creatures, have reason to settle their differences without cutting throats; for, in my opinion, there never was a good war or a bad peace.
Benjamin Franklin (1706-1790), Member, Continental Congress and Constitutional Convention, Governor of Pennsylvania, and U.S. Minister to France. Letter to Josiah Quincy, Sept. 11, 1783.

108. Even peace may be purchased at too high a price.
Benjamin Franklin. Quoted in George Seldes, *The Great Quotations*, 1983.

109. I love war because of the fame that goes with it; but were I not a Prince I should devote myself entirely to philosophy. After all, every one in this world must have his trade.
Frederick II (The Great) (1712-1786), King of Prussia. 1747.

110. Peace we want because there is another war to fight against poverty, disease, and ignorance.
Indira Gandhi (1917-1984), Prime Minister of India. Radio broadcast, Jan. 26, 1966.

111. Unless now the world adopts nonviolence, it will spell certain suicide for mankind.
Mohandas K. Gandhi (1869-1948), Indian political and spiritual leader. Remark after learning of the atomic bombing of Hiroshima, Aug. 1945.

112. In the murder of Mexicans upon their own soil, or in robbing them of their country, I can take no part either now or hereafter. The guilt of these crimes must rest on others. I will not participate in them.
Joshua Reed Giddings (1795-1864), U.S. Congressman (Anti-Slavery Whig-OH), and Consul General to the British North American Provinces (Canada). Comment when refusing to vote any appropriations for the Mexican War, 1847.

113. Pro football is like nuclear warfare. There are no winners, only survivors.
Frank Gifford, American football player and sportscaster. Quoted in *Sports Illustrated*, 1960.

114. War! War! War! I fear it will swallow up everything good and useful.
William E. Gladstone (1809-1898), Prime Minister of Great Britain (Liberal). Letter to his wife, Mar. 1854.

115. Do not listen to those who set up doctrines which are dangerous to the peace of the world.
William E. Gladstone. Speech, Dec. 9, 1879.

116. Naturally the common people don't want war ... but after all, it is the leaders of a country who determine the policy, and it is always a simple matter to drag the people along, whether it is a democracy or a fascist dictatorship, or a parliament or a communist dictatorship. Voice or no voice, the people can always be brought to the bidding of the leaders. That is easy. All you have to do is tell them they are being attacked, and denounce the pacifists for lack of patriotism and exposing the country to danger. It works the same in every country.
Hermann Goering (1893-1946), Field Marshal, German Army, founder of the Gestapo, President of the Reichstag (Nazi Parliament), and convicted war criminal. Speech, 1934.

117. All wars are wars among thieves who are too cowardly to fight and who therefore conscript the young manhood of the whole world to do the fighting for them.
Emma Goldman (1869-1940), American anarchist. "Address to the Jury," *Mother Earth*, July 1917.

118. To insist on strength ... is not war-mongering. It is peace-mongering.
Barry M. Goldwater, U.S. Senator (R-AZ). Quoted in *The New York Times*, Aug. 11, 1964.

119. It gets down to one, little, simple phrase: I am pissed off! This is an act violating international law. It is an act of war.
Barry M. Goldwater. Letter to CIA Director William Casey protesting the mining of Nicaraguan harbors. Apr. 9, 1984.

120. Let us have peace.
Ulysses S. Grant (1822-1885), 18th President of the United States (R). Remark when accepting the nomination for President. National Republican Party Convention, Chicago, IL, May 29, 1868.

121. Peace is bearish.
Joseph E. Granville. American stock market analyst. Quoted in *The Wall Street Journal*, Dec. 18, 1989.

122. War! As soon as possible! Now! We need a voice to lead us without equivocation: Communism must be destroyed.
Robert W. Grow. General, U.S. Army, and U.S. Military Attaché in Moscow. *Diary*, Feb. 5, 1951.

123. We fight to great disadvantage when we fight with those who have nothing to lose.
Francesco Guicciardini (1483-1540), Florentine historian and statesman. *Storia d'Italia*, 1561.

124. Suppose they gave a war and no one came?
Arlo Guthrie, American folk singer and songwriter. 1966.

125. There are things more important than peace.
Alexander M. Haig, General, U.S. Army, U.S. Secretary of State (R), and White House Chief of Staff. Interview, *Le Figaro Magazine*, 1979.

126. The Bible nowhere prohibits war. In the Old Testament we find war and even conquest positively commanded, and although war was raging in the time of Christ and His apostles, still they said not a word of its unlawfulness and immorality.
Henry Wager Halleck (1815-1872), General, U.S. Army. *Elements of Military Art and Science*, 1846.

127. Let us recollect that peace or war will not always be left to our option; that however moderate or unambitious we may be, we cannot count upon the moderation, or hope to extinguish the ambition of others.
Alexander Hamilton (1755-1804), Member, Continental Congress and Constitutional Convention, and U.S. Secretary of the Treasury (Federalist-NY). *The Federalist*, No. 34, Jan. 4, 1788.

128. It is often easier to assemble armies than it is to assemble army revenues.
Benjamin Harrison (1833-1901), 23rd President of the United States (R-IN). Speech, Marquette Club, Chicago, IL, Mar. 20, 1888.

129. War is a dreadful thing, but there are things more dreadful even than war; one of them is dishonor.
William Randolph Hearst (1863-1951), U.S. Congressman (D-NY); founder, Independence League; journalist; and publisher. Editorial, *New York Journal*, Feb. 22, 1897.

130. I believe in war, if the people want war. They have to do the fighting. I believe, first, in a referendum to the people, and failing that, a decision by the people's representatives in Congress.
William Randolph Hearst. Mar. 2, 1917.

131. The abolition of war is like the abolition of slavery, a matter of education and civilization.
William Randolph Hearst. 1918.

132. Frankly, I'd like to see the government get out of war altogether and leave the whole field to private industry.
Joseph Heller, American writer. *Catch-22*, 1961.

133. Peace on earth would mean the end of civilization as we know it.

Joseph Heller. *Good as Gold*, 1988.

134. Once we have a war there is only one thing to do. It must be won. For defeat brings worse things than any that can ever happen in war.

Ernest Hemingway (1898-1961), Nobel Laureate in Literature (United States). *Men at War*, 1942.

135. The step from one degree of violence to the next is imperceptibly taken and cannot be easily taken back.... Wars have a way of getting out of hand.

John Hersey, American writer. Address, White House Festival of the Arts, May 14, 1965.

136. A man who invents a terrible explosive does more for peace than a thousand mild apostles.

Theodor Herzl (1860-1904), Austrian journalist and political Zionist. Letter to Baroness von Suttner, 1895.

137. I cannot bear to see my innocent people suffer any longer. Ending the war is the only way to restore world peace and to relieve the nation from the terrible distress with which it is burdened.

Hirohito (1901-1990), Emperor of Japan. Message to the Japanese Supreme Council, Aug. 9, 1945; Japan surrendered five days later.

138. Older men declare war. But it is youth that must fight and die. And it is youth who must inherit the tribulations, the sorrow, and the triumphs that are the aftermath of war.

Herbert Hoover (1874-1964), 31st President of the United States (R-CA). Speech, Republican National Convention, Chicago, IL, June 27, 1944.

139. Tell our friends the news, that we have beaten the enemy. Tell them to come on and let the people plant corn.

Sam Houston (1793-1863), Governor of Tennessee (D), 1st President of the Republic of Texas, U.S. Congressman, and U.S. Senator. Message to General Gaines after the Battle of San Jacinto, Apr. 26, 1836.

140. Our wars were not fought for the glory of war, but for freedom.

Hubert H. Humphrey (1911-1978), Vice President of the United States and U.S. Senator (D-MN). Address, Democratic National Convention, Los Angeles, CA, July 12, 1960.

141. The nature of American society makes it impossible for the U.S. to bear tens of thousands of casualties in one battle.

Saddam Hussein, President of Iraq. Remark to U.S. Ambassador to Iraq April Glaspie, Baghdad, July 25, 1990.

142. The representative of the Jewish Agency *[for Palestine]* told us yesterday that they were not the attackers, that the Arabs had begun the fighting. We did not deny this. We told the whole world we were going to fight *[against an independent Israel]*.

Jemal Husseini, Chairman, Palestine Higher Committee. Statement to the U.N. Security Council, New York City, Apr. 16, 1948.

143. Men will fight for a superstition as quickly as a living truth – often more so, since a superstition is so intangible you cannot get at it to refute it.

Hypatia (370-415), Greek philosopher. Quoted in Elbert Hubbard, *Little Journeys to the Homes of Great Teachers*, 1908.

144. A man may build himself a throne of bayonets, but he cannot sit on it.

William R. Inge (1860-1965), Anglican prelate and dean of St. Paul's. Quoted in James Marchant, *The Wit and Wisdom of Dean Inge*, 1927.

145. They shall beat their swords into plowshares, and their swords into pruning hooks. And nation shall not take up sword against nation, and they shall not learn war any more.

Old Testament, *Isaiah* 2:4; inscribed on the outside front wall of the United Nations, New York City.

146. Peace, above all things, is to be desired. but blood must sometimes be spilled to obtain it on equable and lasting terms.

Andrew Jackson (1767-1845), 7th President of the United States (D-TN). Quoted in George Seldes, *The Great Quotations*, 1983.

147. Germany needs a war of her own in order to feel her power; she needs a feud with Frenchdom to develop her national way of life in all its fullness. This occasion will not fail to come.

Friedrich Ludwig Jahn (1778-1852), Prussian gymnast and nationalist. C. Euler, ed., *F. L. Jans Werke*, 1884-1887.

148. Capitalism carries in itself war, like clouds carry rain.

Jean Léon Jaurès (1859-1914), French Socialist and Member, Chamber of Deputies. *Studies in Socialism*, 1900.

149. ... not peace at any price. There is a peace more destructive to the manhood of living man than war is destructive of his material body. Chains are worse than bayonets.

Douglas W. Jerrold (1803-1857), English journalist and humorist. *Jerrold's Wit.* "Peace," 1846.

150. War has its evils. In all ages it has been the minister of wholesale death and appalling desolation; but however inscrutable to us, it has been made, by the Allwise Dispenser of events, the instrumentality of accomplishing the great end of human elevation and human happiness.... It is in this view that I subscribe to the doctrine of manifest destiny.

Herschel V. Johnson (1812-1880), U.S. Senator (D-GA), Governor of Georgia, and Senator, Confederate Congress. Quoted in Howard Zinn, *A People's History of the United States*, 1980.

151. The first casualty when war comes is truth.

Hiram W. Johnson (1866-1945), Governor of California (R), U.S. Senator (Progressive and R-CA), and founder, Progressive Party. Speech, 1917.

152. In this age there can be no losers in peace and no victors in war. We must recognize the obligation to match national strength with national restraint.

Lyndon B. Johnson (1908-1973), 36th President of the United States (D-TX). Speech, joint session of Congress, Nov. 27, 1963.

153. Peace is a journey of a thousand miles, and it must be taken one step at a time.

Lyndon B. Johnson. Speech, U. N. General Assembly, Dec. 17, 1963.

154. I didn't just screw Ho Chi Minh. I cut his pecker off.

(In the wake of the Tonkin Gulf incident, the United States had bombed and destroyed North Vietnamese naval installations.)

Lyndon B. Johnson. Remark to a reporter, Aug. 5, 1964.

155. Your daddy may go down in history as having started World War III.

Lyndon B. Johnson. Comment to daughter Luci. Quoted in *The Washington Post*, May 12, 1967.

156. For all I know, our navy was shooting at whales out there.

Lyndon B. Johnson. Remark after the Tonkin Gulf incident. Quoted in David Halberstam, *The Best and the Brightest*, 1969.

157. The Russians feared Ike *[Eisenhower, in Korea]*. They didn't fear me *[in Vietnam]*.

Lyndon B. Johnson. Quoted by Richard Nixon, *Time*, July 29, 1985.

158. It is thus that mutual cowardice keeps us in peace. Were one-half of mankind brave and one-half cowards, the brave would always be beating the cowards. Were all brave, they would leave a very uneasy life; all would be continually fighting; but being all cowards, we go on very well.

Samuel Johnson (1709-1784), British writer and lexicographer. Quoted in James Boswell, *The Life of Samuel Johnson*, Apr. 28, 1778.

159. Tell General Howard I know his heart. What he told me before I have in my heart. I am tired of fighting. Our chiefs are killed. Looking Glass is dead. Toohoolhoolzote is dead. The old men are all dead. It is the young men who say yes and no. He who led the young men is dead. It is cold and we have no blankets. The little children are freezing to death. My people, some of them, have run away to the hills, and have no blankets; no food; no one knows where they are, perhaps freezing to death. I want to have time to look for my children and see how many I can find. Maybe I shall find them among the dead. Hear me, my chiefs. I am tired. My heart is sick and sad. From where the sun now stands, I will fight no more forever.

Joseph (c.1840-1904), Chief, Nez Percé Indians. Surrender speech to Gen. O. O. Howard, Oct. 1877.

160. In war the most successful armies are those in which each soldier has a clear conscience.

Flavius Josephus (37-105), Roman-Jewish general and historian. *Wars*, II.

161. Savage bears keep at peace with one another.

Decimus Junius Juvenal (c.60-c.140), Roman poet. *Satires*.

162. I do not want the peace which passeth understanding. I want the understanding which bringeth peace.

Helen Keller (1880-1968), American writer. *Let Us Have Faith*, 1940; alluding to *Philippians* 4:7.

163. Mankind must put an end to war or war will put an end to mankind.

John F. Kennedy (1917-1963), 35th President of the United States (D-MA). Speech to the U.N. General Assembly, Sept. 25, 1961.

164. The mere absence of war is not peace.

John F. Kennedy. Annual message to Congress, Jan. 14, 1963.

165. In the final analysis, it is their war. They are the ones who have to win it or lose it – the people of Vietnam.

John F. Kennedy. Sept. 1963.

166. I see this war *[Vietnam]* as an unjust, evil, and futile war. But if I had confronted the call to military service in a war against Hitler, I believe that I would have temporarily sacrificed my pacifism because Hitler was such an evil force in history.
Martin Luther King, Jr. (1929-1968), American clergyman and civil rights leader. Speech, Ebenezer Baptist Church, Atlanta, GA, Apr. 30, 1967.

167. We must come to see that peace is not merely a distant goal we seek, but the means by which we arrive at that goal. We must pursue peaceful ends through peaceful means.
Martin Luther King, Jr. Speech, Dec. 25, 1967.

168. Sophisticated modern weapons have not eliminated the uncertainty that puts war and warlike activities "in the province of chance" and makes war an extremely dangerous activity with results that are unpredictable and depend as much on "moral force" as on numbers and technology.
Jeane J. Kirkpatrick, U.S. Ambassador to the United Nations (R). *The Washington Post*, July 11, 1988.

169. I am a man of peace. God knows how I love peace. But I hope I shall never be such a coward as to mistake oppression for peace.
Lajos Kossuth (1802-1894), Hungarian patriot. 1880.

170. The right to control their own government according to constitutional forms is not one of the rights that the citizens of this country are called upon to surrender in time of war.
Robert M. La Follette (1855-1925), Governor of Wisconsin and U.S. Senator (R). Senate speech, Oct. 6, 1917.

171. I am against war, and because I am against war I went to war to fight against war.
Fiorello H. La Guardia (1882-1947), U.S. Congressman (R and Socialist) and Mayor of New York City (R and Fusion Party). Speech, Cooper Union, New York City, 1945.

172. Peace at any price.
Alphonse de Lamartine (1792-1869), French historian and politician. Quoted in Arthur Hugh Clough, *Poems and Prose Remains*, 1869.

173. Every nation prepares, through its government, to equip itself with the power to hurl death upon its fellow nations. No people seeks that power; it is governments that seek it.
Harold J. Laski (1893-1950), British political scientist. *The Nation*, Dec. 15, 1945.

174. It is well that war is so terrible – we should grow too fond of it.
Robert E. Lee (1807-1870), General-in-Chief, Confederate Army. Letter to Gen. James Longstreet, Dec. 13, 1862.

175. The bloody capitalists cannot conclude an honorable peace. They can conclude only a dishonorable peace, based upon a division of spoils.
V. I. Lenin (1870-1924), Premier of the U.S.S.R. In reference to the Versailles Treaty. *Letters from Afar*, No. 4, 1917.

176. Victory in war depends on the morale of the masses which are shedding their blood on the battlefield.
V. I. Lenin. 1921.

177. Free enterprise and the market economy mean war; socialism and planned economy mean peace. We must plan civilization or we must perish.
Pope Leo XIII (1810-1903). Encyclical, *Rerum Novarum*, May 15, 1891.

178. The last ray of hope for preserving the Union peaceably expired at the assault upon Fort Sumter.
Abraham Lincoln (1809-1865), 16th President of the United States (R-IL). 1st annual message to Congress, Dec. 3, 1861.

179. What would you do in my position? Would you drop the war where it is? Or would you prosecute it in the future with elder-stalk squirts charged with rose water? Would you deal lighter blows rather than heavier ones?... I shall do all I can to save the government, which is my sworn duty as well as my personal inclination.
Abraham Lincoln. Letter to Cuthbert Bullitt, July 28, 1862.

180. No one man shall hold the power to bring this oppression *[war]* upon us.
Abraham Lincoln. Quoted by Congressman Neil Abercrombie (D-HI) during the House debate on the Persian Gulf crisis, Jan. 10, 1991.

181. Woe to the vanquished. (*Vae victis.*)
Titus Livy (59 B.C.-A.D.17), Roman historian. *Annals*, V.

182. Believe me, Germany is unable to wage war.
David Lloyd George, 1st Earl of Dwyfor (1863-1945), Prime Minister of Great Britain (Liberal). In reference to German arms expenditures. Interview, *Le Petit Journal*, Aug. 1, 1934.

183. Wars are precipitated by motives which the statesmen responsible for them dare not publicly avow.
David Lloyd George. 1939.

184. This war *[World War II]*, like the next war, is the war to end all wars.
David Lloyd George. 1941.

185. The war of the giants is over. The quarrels of the pygmies have begun.
David Lloyd George. In reference to the Paris peace negotiations following World War I. Quoted on PBS, *Poland*, July 12, 1988.

186. War is no more inevitable than the plague is inevitable. War is no more a part of human nature than the burning of witches is a human act.
Meyer London (1871-1926), U.S. Congressman (Socialist-NY). Speech, Congress, Mar. 17, 1916.

187. We kind o' thought Christ went agin war an' pillage.
James Russell Lowell (1819-1891), U.S. Ambassador to Spain and Great Britain. *The Bigelow Papers*, No. 3, 1865.

188. James Madison, a second-time President, adopted a remedy for the wrongs of our seamen, infinitely more injurious to them than the evils which they suffered.... He ordered out the militia, in contempt of that very Constitution of which he was one of the principle framers.
John Lowell (1769-1840), American Federalist and pamphleteer. *Perpetual War, The Policy of Mr. Madison*, 1812.

189. I decline Christianity because it is Jewish, because it is international, and because, in cowardly fashion, it preaches Peace on Earth.
Erich von Ludendorff (1865-1937), General, German Army. *Belief in German God*.

190. I beg that the small steamers ... be spared if possible, or else sunk without a trace being left *[spurlos versenkt]*.
Karl von Luxburg, German Chargé d'Affaires at Buenos Aires. Message to Berlin, 1917.

191. There is no substitute for victory.
Douglas MacArthur (1880-1964), General, U.S. Army, and Supreme Commander, U.N. forces in Korea. Farewell speech to Congress, April 19, 1951.

192. The progress and survival of civilization *[are]* dependent upon ... the realization ... of the utter futility of force as an arbiter.
Douglas MacArthur. 1956.

193. War is no damn football game.
Douglas MacArthur. Commencement address, U.S. Military Academy at West Point, NY, May 12, 1962.

194. It is not armaments that cause war, but war that causes armaments.
Salvador de Madariaga y Roho (1886-1978), Spanish writer, diplomat, and statesman. *Morning Without Noon*.

195. "War is the continuation of politics." In this sense war is politics and war itself is political action.... It can therefore be said that politics is war without bloodshed while war is politics with bloodshed.
Mao Tse-tung (1893-1976), Chairman, Communist Party of China. *On Protracted War*, May 1938.

196. We are advocates of the abolition of war, we do not want war; but war can only be abolished through war, and in order to get rid of the gun it is necessary to take up the gun.
Mao Tse-tung. *Problems of War and Strategy*, Nov. 6, 1938.

197. Wars are bred by poverty and oppression. Continued peace is possible only in a relatively free and prosperous world.
George C. Marshall (1880-1959), General, U.S. Army, U.S. Secretary of State, U.S. Secretary of Defense, U.S. Ambassador to China, and Nobel Laureate in Peace. 1956.

198. Resolved that the present war ... was unconstitutionally commenced by the order of the President ... and that it is now waged by a powerful nation against a weak neighbor ... at immense cost of treasure and life.... That such a war of conquest, so hateful in its objects, so wanton, unjust, and unconstitutional in its origin and character, must be regarded as a war against freedom, against humanity, against justice.
Massachusetts State Legislature. Resolution against the Mexican War, Apr. 26, 1847.

199. All they that take up the sword shall perish by the sword.
New Testament, *Matthew* 26:52.

200. It would win for us a proud title – we would become the first aggressors for peace.
Francis P. Matthews (1887-1952), U.S. Secretary of the Navy (D). Argument for a preemptive war against the U.S.S.R. Quoted in *The Nation*, Sept. 9, 1950.

201. I am not – as I am sure I will be charged – for peace at any price, but for an honorable, rational, and political solution to this *[Vietnam]* war.

Eugene J. McCarthy, U.S. Congressman and U.S. Senator (D-WI). Press conference, Nov. 30, 1967.

202. We seem bent on saving the Vietnamese from Ho Chi Minh, even if we have to kill them and demolish their country to do it.
George S. McGovern, U.S. Congressman and U.S. Senator (D-SD). Senate speech, Apr. 25, 1967.

203. It is not possible to teach an entire generation to bomb and destroy others in an undeclared, unjustified war abroad without paying the price in the derangement of our own society.
George S. McGovern. In reference to the Vietnam War. Presidential campaign speech, 1971.

204. I have been through one war. I have seen the dead piled up, and I do not want to see another.
William McKinley (1843-1901), 25th President of the United States (R-OH). Feb. 1898.

205. We shall never war except for peace.
William McKinley. Speech, El Paso, TX, May 6, 1901.

206. I found nothing but progress and hope for the future.
Robert S. McNamara, U.S. Secretary of Defense (D). Comment after finishing an inspection tour of Vietnam. Quoted in *The New York Times*, May 12, 1962.

207. Bless the doves – we need more of them.
Robert S. McNamara. Toast. Quoted in David Halberstam, *The Best and the Brightest*, 1969.

208. Some day we may be able to forgive the Arabs for killing our children, but we will never forgive them for making us kill some of theirs.
Golda Meir (1898-1978), Prime Minister of Israel (Labour). Comment after the Six-Day War, July 1967.

209. It is true we have won all our wars, but we have paid for them. We don't want victories anymore.
Golda Meir. Quoted in *Life*, Oct. 3, 1969.

210. There's no difference between one's killing and making decisions that will send others to kill. It's exactly the same thing, or even worse.
Golda Meir. Interview, 1974.

211. Who overcomes by force hath overcome but half his foe.
John Milton (1608-1674), English poet, writer, and diplomat. *Paradise Lost*, I, 1648.

212. Peace hath her victories no less renowned than war.
John Milton. *Sonnet to Lord General Cromwell*, May 1652.

213. Every war is a national misfortune.
Helmuth von Moltke (1800-1891), General, German Army. 1880.

214. In the wars of the European Powers in matters relating to themselves we have never taken any part, nor does it comport with our policy to do so.
James Monroe (1758-1831), 5th President of the United States (Democratic Republican-VA). Annual message to Congress, Dec. 2, 1823.

215. War hath no fury like a noncombatant.
Charles E. Montague (1867-1928), British writer. *Disenchantment*, 1922.

216. It makes no difference who says that our objective is peace, even if he be the President of the United States. Our actions speak louder than words, and our actions in Asia today are the actions of warmaking.
Wayne L. Morse (1900-1974), U.S. Senator (R and Ind.-OR). Aug. 5, 1964.

217. You must understand that Americans are a warrior nation.
Daniel P. Moynihan, Chief American Delegate to the United Nations and U.S. Senator (D-NY). Speech to Arab leaders, Sept. 1990.

218. There is a time for all things – a time to preach, and a time to fight, and now is the time to fight.
John Peter Muhlenberg (1746-1807), clergyman; Major General, Continental Army; U.S. Congressman, and U.S. Senator (PA). A call to arms to his Woodstock, VA, parish, 1775; alluding to *Ecclesiastes* 3:1.

219. Needed: A Department of Peace
Karl E. Mundt (1900-1974), U.S. Congressman and U.S. Senator (R-SD). Title of Senate speech, 1945.

220. By God, you can't fight a war unless the people support it.
Edmund S. Muskie, U.S. Secretary of State and U.S. Senator (D-ME). Quoted in *Time 1968 Review*, Sept. 17, 1988.

221. War alone brings up to its highest tension all human energy, and puts the stamp of nobility upon the peoples who have the courage to meet it.
Benito Mussolini (1883-1945), dictator of Italy (Fascist). Speech to party members, quoted in *The New York Times*, Jan. 11, 1935.

222. If they want peace, nations should avoid the pin pricks that precede cannon shots.

Napoléon I (1769-1821), military leader and Emperor of France. Remark to Czar Alexander I, June 22, 1807.

223. Every one is growing tired of war; there is no longer any enthusiasm. The sacred fire is extinct.
Napoléon I. Remark after the Battle of Champ Aubert, Feb. 10, 1814.

224. In war all that is useful is legitimate.
Napoléon I. *Maxims*.

225. Without peace, all other dreams vanish and are reduced to ashes.
Jawaharlal Nehru (1889-1964), 1st Prime Minister of India. Address to the United Nations, Aug. 28, 1954.

226. The only alternative to coexistence is codestruction.
Jawaharlal Nehru. *Ibid*.

227. Perhaps my dynamite plants will put an end to war sooner than your *[pacifist]* congresses. On the day two armies corps can annihilate each other in one second, all civilized nations will recoil from war in horror.
Alfred Bernhard Nobel (1833-1896), Swedish munitions manufacturer and philanthropist. Speech, International Pacifist Congress, Switzerland, 1892.

228. I would like to say to this war god, You shall not coin into gold the lifeblood of thy brethren..... I feel we are about to put the dollar sign upon the American flag.
George W. Norris (1861-1944), U.S. Congressman and U.S. Senator (R and Independent Republican-NE). Opposition to U.S. entry into World War I, believing that American arms manufacturers were promoting the war for profit. Senate speech, Apr. 24, 1917.

229. *[We are declaring war on Germany]* because we want to preserve the commercial right of American citizens to deliver munitions of war to belligerent nations.... I feel that we are committing a sin against humanity and against our countrymen.
George W. Norris. *Ibid*.

230. Democratic open societies have to conduct war differently from closed societies.
Eleanor Holmes Norton, Delegate to U.S. Congress (D-DC) and Chair, Equal Employment Opportunity Commission (D). PBS, Special on the Persian Gulf War, Jan. 16, 1991.

231. Shall your brethren go to war, and you sit here?
Old Testament, *Numbers* 32:6.

232. There is altogether too much truth to the assertion that war and preparedness for war are nothing more than games, games for profit.
Gerald Nye (1892-1971), U.S. Senator (R-ND). Quoted in Green, *The Enemy Forgotten*, 1956.

233. War is not an instinct but an invention.
José Ortega y Gasset (1883-1955), Spanish philosopher and statesman. Epilogue, *The Revolt of the Masses*, 1930.

234. The quickest way of ending a war is to lose it.
George Orwell (Eric Blair) (1903-1950), British writer. *Shooting an Elephant*, 1950.

235. War involves in its progress such a train of unforeseen and unsupposed circumstances that no human wisdom can calculate the end. It has but one thing certain, and that is to increase taxes.
Thomas Paine (1737-1809), American political philosopher. *Prospects on the Rubicon*.

236. What do you care about those goddamned bolshies *[Russians]*? We're going to have to fight them sooner or later. Why not now while our army is still intact and we can kick the Red Army back into Russia?
George S. Patton (1885-1945), General, U.S. Army. Remark to President Truman, 1945.

237. The grim fact is that we prepare for war like precocious giants and for peace like retarded pygmies.
Lester B. Pearson (1897-1972), Prime Minister of Canada (Liberal) and Nobel Laureate in Peace. Nobel acceptance speech, Oslo, Norway, Dec. 10, 1957.

238. One of the advantages of winning a war is that you can make the rules afterward.
Richard Perle, U.S. Assistant Secretary of State (R). Interview, CNN, *Newsmaker Sunday*, Mar. 31, 1991.

239. First commit the nation, then commit the troops. Don't send men off to die if a country's not committed.
H. Ross Perot, American businessman. *U.S. News & World Report*, June 20, 1988.

240. I believe in moral suasion. The age of bullets is over.
Wendell Phillips (1811-1884), American orator and reformer. Quoted in Richard Hofstadter, *The American Political Tradition*, 1948.

241. Mexico has invaded our Territory and shed American blood upon American soil.
(In 1846 Mexican troops fired on an American patrol in the disputed area between Texas and Mexico.)

James K. Polk (1795-1849), 11th President of the United States (D-TN). Request to the Congress for a war resolution, May 11, 1846.

242. The *[Mexican]* war will continue to be prosecuted with vigor as the best means of securing peace.
James K. Polk. 2nd annual message to Congress, Dec. 8, 1846.

243. Seek peace, and pursue it.
Old Testament, *Psalms* 34:14.

244. Pray for the peace of Jerusalem.
Old Testament, *Psalms* 122:6.

245. Behold! How good and pleasant it is for brethren to dwell together in unity.
Old Testament, *Psalms* 133:1.

246. We shall have no peace worth anything till we gain it by the sword.
Israel Putnam (1718-1790), General, Continental Army, and leader, Connecticut Sons of Liberty. 1775.

247. For war one side is enough. For peace it takes both sides.
Yitzhak Rabin, Defense Minister, Israel (Labour). Interview, PBS, *MacNeil-Lehrer News Hour*, Feb. 8, 1989.

248. The surest way to prevent war is not to fear it.
John Randolph (1773-1833), U.S. Senator (VA) and U.S. Minister to Russia. Speech, House of Representatives, Mar. 5, 1806.

249. I want to stand by my country, but I cannot vote for war. I vote no.
Jeanette Rankin (1880-1973), U.S. Congresswoman (R-MT). Congressional debate, Apr. 6, 1917.

250. You can no more win a war than you can win an earthquake.
Jeanette Rankin. Campaign speech, 1943.

251. Peace is not the absence of conflict, but the ability to cope with conflict by peaceful means.
Ronald Reagan, 40th President of the United States (R). Commencement address, Eureka College, Eureka, IL, May 9, 1982.

252. People don't start wars, governments do.
Ronald Reagan. Quoted in *Time*, Mar. 18, 1985.

253. Nations do not mistrust each other because they are armed; they are armed because they mistrust each other.
Ronald Reagan. Speech, U.N. General Assembly, New York City, Sept. 22, 1986.

254. *[My goal is]* the extension of British rule throughout the world ... the ultimate recovery of the United States of America as an integral part of the British Empire ... and finally, the foundation of so great a power as to hereafter render wars impossible and promote the best interests of humanity.
Cecil Rhodes (1853-1902), Prime Minister of Cape Colony, South Africa, industrialist, and philanthropist. *Last Will and Testament*, 1877; this section was deleted from the final version.

255. No nation ought to be allowed to enter into a war until it's paid for the last one.
Will Rogers (1879-1935), American humorist. Quoted on PBS, *Will Rogers U.S.A.*, Oct. 3, 1988.

256. Follow after the things that make for peace.
New Testament, *Romans* 14:19.

257. It isn't enough to talk about peace. One must believe in it. And it isn't enough to believe in it. One must work at it.
Anna Eleanor Roosevelt (1884-1962), First Lady and U.S. Delegate to the United Nations. Radio message, Voice of America, Nov. 11, 1951.

258. Every war brings after it a period of materialism and conservatism.
Franklin D. Roosevelt (1882-1945), 32nd President of the United States (D-NY). Letter to Willard Saulsbury, Dec. 9, 1924.

259. I have seen war. I have seen war on land and sea. I have seen blood running from the wounded. I have seen men coughing out their gassed lungs. I have seen the dead in the mud. I have seen the cities destroyed. I have seen two hundred limping, exhausted men come out of the line – the survivors of a regiment of one thousand that went forward forty-eight hours before. I have seen children starving. I have seen the agony of mothers and wives. I hate war.
Franklin D. Roosevelt. Presidential campaign speech, Chatauqua, NY, Aug. 14, 1936.

260. There is a vast difference between keeping out of war and pretending that this war is none of our business.
Franklin D. Roosevelt. Jan. 3, 1940.

261. Yesterday, Dec. 7, 1941 – a date that will live in infamy – the United States of America was suddenly and deliberately attacked by naval and air forces of the Empire of Japan.
Franklin D. Roosevelt. Message to Congress asking for a declaration of war, Dec. 8, 1941.

262. We are going to win the war, and we are going to win the peace that follows.
Franklin D. Roosevelt. Radio address to the nation, Dec. 9, 1941.

263. Peace, like war, can succeed only where there is a will to enforce it, and where there is available power to enforce it.
Franklin D. Roosevelt. Speech, Foreign Policy Association, New York City, 1944.

264. More than an end to war, we want an end to the beginnings of all wars.
Franklin D. Roosevelt. Radio address scheduled for broadcast on Apr. 13, 1945, one day after his death.

265. This country needs a war.
Theodore Roosevelt (1858-1919), 26th President of the United States (R-NY). Letter to Sen. Henry Cabot Lodge, 1895.

266. We do not admire the man of timid peace.
Theodore Roosevelt. Speech, Chicago, IL, Apr. 10, 1899.

267. A splendid little war.
Theodore Roosevelt. Description of the Spanish-American War, 1900.

268. We fight in honorable fashion for the good of mankind fearless of the future, unheeding of our individual fate, with unflinching hearts and undimmed eyes. We stand at Armageddon, and we battle for the Lord.
Theodore Roosevelt. Presidential campaign speech, Progressive Party rally, Chicago, IL, June 17, 1912.

269. A pacifist is as surely a traitor to his country and to humanity as is the most brutal wrongdoer.
Theodore Roosevelt. Speech, Pittsburgh, PA, July 27, 1917.

270. The right of conquest has no foundation other than the right of the strongest.
Jean-Jacques Rousseau (1712-1778), French philosopher. *The Social Contract*, 1762.

271. No nation ever yet enjoyed a protracted and triumphant peace without receiving in its own bosom ineradicable seeds of future decline.
John Ruskin (1819-1900), British art historian. *Modern Painters*, IV, 1856.

272. War, in our scientific age, means, sooner or later, universal death.
Bertrand Russell, 3rd Earl Russell of Kingston (1872-1970), British philosopher and reformer. *Unpopular Essays*, 1950.

273. The only thing that will redeem mankind is cooperation.
Bertrand Russell. Recalled on his death.

274. Every pacifist in this country that goes about prattling of peace, every Congressman that introduces a peace resolution, every Senator that is playing the German game, is doing far more harm to the United States, to the cause of democracy, to the ideals of this country, than a million German soldiers on the battle line can do.
Charles Edward Russell (1860-1941), American newspaper editor and writer. Quoted in *The New York Times*, Aug 12, 1917.

275. If peace cannot be maintained with honor, it is no longer peace.
John Russell, 1st Earl of Kingston (1792-1878), Prime Minister of Great Britain (Whig). Speech at Greenoch, Scotland, Sept. 1853.

276. When the bells of peace ring, there will be no hands to beat the drums of war. Even if they existed, they would be stilled.
Anwar Sadat (1918-1981), President of Egypt. Speech to Israel's Knesset (parliament), Nov. 20, 1977.

277. If America cannot win a war in a week, it begins negotiating with itself.
William Safire, American political columnist and White House speech writer (R). *The New York Times*, Aug. 10, 1990.

278. So far as war has any biological effect, it is rather to kill off the fittest than to preserve them.
Herbert L. Samuel, 1st Viscount Samuel (1870-1963), Home Secretary, Great Britain, and 1st High Commissioner to Palestine (Liberal). *Belief and Action*, 1937.

279. Sometime they'll give a war and nobody will come.
Carl Sandburg (1878-1967), American poet and political biographer. *The People, Yes*, 1936.

280. When the rich wage war, it is the poor who die.
Jean-Paul Sartre (1905-1980), French philosopher. *The Devil and the Good Lord*, 1951.

281. Men are more the Sinews of War than Money.
George Savile, 1st Marquess of Halifax (1633-1695), Lord Privy Seal of England. *Moral Thoughts and Reflections*, 1750.

282. A Prince used to War getteth a military Logic that is not very well suited to the Civil Administration.

George Savile. *Political Thoughts and Reflections*, 1750.

283. All wars are popular for the first thirty days.

Arthur M. Schlesinger, Jr., American historian and presidential advisor (D). Attributed.

284. What deters war is the completeness and integrity of the U.S. deterrent.

James R. Schlesinger, U.S. Secretary of Defense (R), U.S. Secretary of Energy, and Director, Central Intelligence Agency. *Time*, Aug. 1, 1988.

285. It doesn't take a hero to order men into battle.

Norman Schwartzkopf, General, U.S. Army, and Commander, Desert Storm Allied Forces. Interview, ABC, *20/20*, Mar. 15, 1991.

286. Sagacity, boldness, and prudence, qualities so highly necessary to success in war.

Walter Scott (1771-1832), Scottish writer. *Rob Roy*, 1817.

287. We are mad, not only individually, but nationally. We check manslaughter and isolated murders; but what of war, and the much vaunted crime of slaughtering whole peoples?

Lucius Annaeus Seneca (The Younger) (4 B.C.-A.D.65), Roman statesman, dramatist, and philosopher. *Epistolae Morales*.

288. Few die well that die in battle.

William Shakespeare (1564-1616), English writer. *King Henry V*, IV, i.

289. Still, in thy right hand, carry gentle peace.

William Shakespeare. *King Henry VIII*, III, iii.

290. Wars are not made by politics, but by politicians.

Fulton J. Sheen (1895-1979), American Roman Catholic archbishop and television personality. *The Way to Happiness*, 1954.

291. I am sick and tired of war. Its glory is all moonshine. It is only those who have never fired a shot nor heard the shrieks and groans of the wounded who cry aloud for blood, more vengeance, more desolation. War is hell!

William Tecumseh Sherman (1820-1891), General, U.S. Army. Commencement address, Michigan Military Academy, June 19, 1879.

292. I rise to announce my candidacy for President of the United States. I am running with the understanding that I will resign after twenty-four hours in the White House.... What I propose to do in my day as President is to call home our fifteen thousand troops in South Vietnam and cancel our part of that ill-fated, unnecessary, and un-American campaign.

Eugene Siler (1900-1987), U.S. Congressman (R-KY). House debate, June 8, 1964.

293. The fact that we have not already been plunged into nuclear war is only due to the patience and restraint of Mr. Khruschev.

Sidney Silverman, Member of Parliament, Great Britain (Socialist). 1962.

294. War leads to a vicious circle of hatred, oppression, subversive movements, false propaganda, rearmament and new wars.

Declaration, Society of Friends (Quakers), 1952.

295. We have contingency plans for war, but none for peace.

Theodore Sorensen, presidential assistant and speech writer (D). Interview, NBC, *Today*, Nov. 1989.

296. We wanted no land. We committed no economic wrongs. We suppressed no civil liberties.... America is on the level and on the square.

Francis J. Spellman (1889-1967), American Roman Catholic cardinal and military vicar, U.S. Armed Forces. In reference to American World War II military activity. Quoted in Lawrence Wittner, *Rebels Against War*, 1969.

297. War, you have become the foundation of all human virtues.... You cleanse the world; peace litters it with corruption.

Yates Sterling (1873-1942), Admiral, U.S. Navy. Speech, Daughters of the American Revolution Convention, New York City, 1941.

298. War isn't politics.... It is indeed the only human activity that is rottener than politics.

Rex Stout (1886-1975), American writer. *The President Vanishes*, 1934.

299. Victory is the main object in war. If this is long delayed, weapons are blunted and morale is depressed. For there has never been a protracted war from which a country has benefitted.

Sun-tzu (c.400 B.C.), Chinese writer of the Age of Warring States. *The Art of War*.

300. War, that mad game the world so loves to play.

Jonathan Swift (1667-1745), Irish clergyman and satirist. *Ode to Sir William Temple*, 1699.

301. Where they make it a desert, they call it peace. (*Ubi solitudinem faciunt, pacem appellant*.)

Cornelius Tacitus (c.55-c.117), Roman historian. *Life of Agricola*, XXX.

302. This Korean War is a Truman war.

Robert A. Taft (1889-1953), U.S. Senator (R-OH). Speech, Milwaukee, WI, June 9, 1951.

303. Sacredness of human life! The world has never believed it! It has been with life that we settled our quarrels, won wives, gold, and land, defended ideas, imposed religions. We have held that a death toll was a necessary part of every human achievement, whether sport, war or industry.

Ida M. Tarbell (1857-1944), American writer. *New Ideals in Business*, 1916.

304. It is not the purpose of war to annihilate those who provoke it, but to cause them to mend their ways.

Maxwell D. Taylor (1901-1987), General, U.S. Army, U.S. Ambassador to South Vietnam, and Chairman, Joint Chiefs of Staff. Quoted in David Halberstam, *The Best and the Brightest*, 1969.

305. My life has been devoted to arms, yet I look upon war at all times, and under all circumstances, as a national calamity, to be avoided if compatible with national honor.

Zachary Taylor (1784-1850), 12th President of the United States (Whig-KY). Quoted in Paul F. Boller, Jr., *Presidential Anecdotes*, 1981.

306. War is a matter not so much of arms as of expenditure.

Thucydides (c.460-c.400 B.C.), Greek historian. *History of the Peloponnesian War*, II.

307. No protracted war can fail to endanger the freedom of a democratic country.

Alexis de Tocqueville (1805-1859), French writer. *Democracy in America*, 1835.

308. The attack upon *[South]* Korea *[across the 38th Parallel]* makes it plain beyond all doubt that Communism has passed beyond the use of subversion to conquer independent nations and will now use armed invasion and war.

Harry S Truman (1884-1972), 33rd President of the United States (D-MO). Speech authorizing naval and air units to support South Korea, June 27, 1950.

309. O Lord, our Father, our young patriots, idols of our heart, go forth to battle – be Thou near them! With them, in spirit, we also go forth from the sweet peace of our beloved firesides to smite the foe. O Lord our God, help us to tear their soldiers to bloody shreds with our shells; help us to cover their smiling fields with the pale forms of their patriot dead; help us to drown the thunder of the guns with the shrieks of their wounded, writhing in pain; help us to lay waste their humble homes with a hurricane of fire; help us to wring the hearts of their unoffending widows with unavailing grief; help us to turn them out roofless with their little children to wander unfriended the wastes of their desolated land in rags and hunger and thirst, sports of the sun flames of summer and the icy winds of winter, broken in spirit, worn with travail, imploring Thee for the refuge of the grave and denied it – for our sakes who adore Thee, Lord, blast their hopes, blight their lives, protract their bitter pilgrimage, make heavy their steps, water their way with their tears, stain the white snow with the blood of their wounded feet! We ask it, in the spirit of love, of Him who is the Source of Love, and who is the ever-faithful refuge and friend of all that are sore beset and seek His aid with humble and contrite hearts. Amen.

Mark Twain (Samuel Langhorne Clemens) (1835-1910), American writer. *The War Prayer*. Written during the Spanish-American War and published posthumously in *Europe and Elsewhere*, 1923.

310. War is not so onerous as slavery.

Marquis de Vauvenargues (1715-1747), French soldier and moralist. *Réflexions et Maximes*. Quoted by Georges Clemenceau, *In the Evening of My Thought*, 1929.

311. We are not interested in the possibilities of defeat. They do not exist.

Victoria (1819-1901), Queen of Great Britain and Ireland and Empress of India. Remark to Prime Minister Arthur J. Balfour, 1901.

312. To hold a pen is to be at war. (*Que plume a, guerre a.*)

Voltaire (François-Marie Arouet) (1694-1778), French historian and dramatist. Letter to Mme. d'Argental, Oct. 4, 1748.

313. I have been there when the bodies have been put in the body bags, and when you've seen that, you really know what war is about.

Vernon A. Walters, General, U.S. Army, and U.S. Ambassador to the United Nations. PBS, *MacNeil-Lehrer News Hour*, Aug. 1988.

314. During World War II, even during the most desperate battles, both sides refrained from using chemical weapons. The Iran-Iraq war ended that restraint and set a dangerous precedent for future wars. These weapons are thought to offer a cheap and readily obtainable means of redressing the military balance against more powerful foes.

William H. Webster, Director, Central Intelligence Agency. Quoted in *The New York Times*, Oct. 30, 1988.

315. If we are going to put lives at risk, we do that far better as one nation than as one man.

Lowell P. Weicker, Jr., U.S. Congressman (R-CT), U.S. Senator, and Governor of Connecticut (Ind.). Argument against the War Powers Act. Senate debate, Oct. 20, 1987.

316. Next to a battle lost, the greatest misery is a battle gained.

Arthur Wellesley, 1st Duke of Wellington (1769-1852), British Chief General at Waterloo, Ambassador to France, and Prime Minister of Great Britain (Tory). Quoted in Frances Shelly, *Diary*, 1874.

317. By setting the United States on fire we will not help put out the fire in Europe.

Burton K. Wheeler (1882-1975), U.S. Senator (D-MT). Argument against American involvement in the European conflict of World War II, 1940.

318. War is the devil's joke on humanity.

William Allen White (1868-1944), American writer and newspaper editor. *Autobiography*, 1946.

319. Peace hath higher tests of manhood
Than battle ever knew.

John Greenleaf Whittier (1807-1892), American poet and reformer. *The Hero*, 1853.

320. As long as war is regarded as wicked, it will always have its fascination. When it is looked upon as vulgar, it will cease to be popular.

Oscar Wilde (1854-1900), Irish writer. *The Critic as Artist*, 1890.

321. I will not be rushed into war, no matter if every last Congressman stands up on his hind legs and calls me a coward.

Woodrow Wilson (1856-1924), 28th President of the United States (D-NJ). Remark to Joseph P. Tumulty, 1916.

322. You have laid upon me this double obligation: "We are relying upon you, Mr. President, to keep us out of war, but we are relying upon you, Mr. President, to keep the honor of the nation unstained."

Woodrow Wilson. Speech, Cleveland, OH, Jan. 29, 1916.

323. I am the friend of peace and mean to preserve it for America as long as I am able.... War can only come by the willful acts and aggressions of others.

Woodrow Wilson. Speech, Congress, Feb. 26, 1916.

324. I can't keep the country out of war.

Woodrow Wilson. Statement to U.S. Secretary of the Navy Josephus Daniels after a German submarine arrived in Newport, RI, harbor and destroyed nine British merchant vessels, Oct. 1916.

325. Property can be paid for; the lives of peaceful and innocent people cannot be. The present German submarine warfare against commerce is a warfare against mankind.

Woodrow Wilson. War message to Congress, Apr. 2, 1917.

326. My message today was a message of death for our young men. How strange it seems to applaud that.

Woodrow Wilson. Remark to Joseph P. Tumulty about the reaction to his congressional address asking for a declaration of war against Germany, Apr. 2, 1917.

Chapter 99

Welfare

1. Bread for the needy, clothing for the naked, and houses for the homeless.
   Slogan and chant of twenty thousand unemployed protesters, Chicago, IL, 1873.

2. No man can live well, or indeed live at all, unless he be provided with necessaries.
   Aristotle (384-322 B.C.), Greek philosopher and teacher. *Politics*.

3. The good of man must be the goal of the science of politics.
   Aristotle. *Nicomachean Ethics*, I.

4. We're creating an attitude that disaster relief is an entitlement program like Medicare or Social Security.
   William C. Bailey, spokesman, U.S. Department of Agriculture. Quoted in *The New York Times*, July 24, 1988.

5. Our whole way of life is dedicated to the removal of risk. Cradle to grave we are supported, insulated, and isolated from the risks of life – and if we fall, our government stands ready with Band-aids of every size.
   Shirley Temple Black, U.S. Chief of Protocol and U.S. Ambassador to Czechoslovakia (R). Speech, Kiwanis International Convention, June 1967.

6. And having looked to government for bread, on the very first scarcity they will turn and bite the hand that fed them.
   Edmund Burke (1729-1797), British statesman. *Reflections on the Revolution in France*, 1790.

7. Most women are only a husband away from welfare.
   Virginia Anne Carabillo, Vice President, National Organization of Women. Speech, Long Beach, CA, Nov. 24, 1974.

8. The end to be achieved *[by public welfare]* is the quality of men and women.
   Benjamin N. Cardozo (1870-1938), U.S. Supreme Court Justice. *Adler* v. *Deegan*, 1919 (NY).

9. Congress may spend money in aid of the "general welfare."
   Benjamin N. Cardozo. *Helvering* v. *Davis*, 1936.

10. Though the people support the government, the government should not support the people.
    Grover Cleveland (1837-1908), 22nd and 24th President of the United States (D-NY). Veto message of the Texas Seed Bill, Feb. 16, 1887.

11. Man becomes great exactly in the degree in which he works for the welfare of his fellow men.
    Mohandas K. Gandhi (1869-1948), Indian political and spiritual leader. *Ethical Religion*.

12. Am I my brother's keeper?
    Old Testament, *Genesis* 4:9.

13. Welfare is hated by those who administer it, mistrusted by those who pay for it, and held in contempt by those who receive it.
    Peter C. Goldmark, Jr., Budget Director, New York State. Quoted in *The New York Times*, May 24, 1977.

14. If you ask, "Am I my brother's keeper?" The answer is, "You are."
    William Randolph Hearst (1863-1951), U.S. Congressman (D-NY); founder, Independence League Party; journalist; and publisher. Dec. 1929.

15. The character of a people may be ruined by charity.
    Theodor Herzl (1860-1904), Austrian journalist and political Zionist. *Diaries*, June 2, 1895.

16. A people can be helped only by itself; and if it cannot do that then it cannot be helped.
    Theodor Herzl. Opening address, 1st Zionist Congress, Basle, Switzerland, Aug. 29, 1897.

17. The impersonal hand of government can never replace the helping hand of a neighbor.
    Hubert H. Humphrey (1911-1978), Vice President of the United States and U.S. Senator (D-MN). Feb. 10, 1965.

18. If we can spend the money to put a man on the moon, we ought to be able to find the funds to put a man on his feet.
Hubert H. Humphrey. Address, Job Corps awards ceremony, 1966.

19. The people who wrote the constitution ... didn't say life, liberty, and welfare or life, liberty, and food stamps.
Howard Jarvis, American tax reformer. Interview, NBC, *Meet the Press*, June 18, 1978.

20. There are eight rungs in charity. The highest is when you help a man to help himself.
Moses Maimonides (1135-1204), Egyptian physician and philosopher. *Mishneh Torah*, "Gifts to the Poor," 10:7.

21. To pity distress is but human; to relieve it is God-like.
Horace Mann (1796-1859), American educator, founder, and 1st President, Antioch College, Yellow Springs, OH. *Lectures on Education*, 1845.

22. From each according to his ability, to each according to his needs.
Karl Marx (1818-1883), German economist and Socialist. *Critique of the Gotha Program*, 1875.

23. I'm a bleeding heart. I see lots of things to bleed about.
Karl A. Menninger (1893-1990), American physician and educator. Quoted in *Life*, Fall 1990.

24. A third of all the children born today will be on welfare.
Daniel P. Moynihan, Chief American Delegate to the United Nations and U.S. Senator (D-NY). Quoted on *ABC News*, Jan. 15, 1989.

25. Welfare became a term of opprobrium – a contentious, often vindictive area of political conflict in which liberals and conservatives clashed and children were lost sight of.
Daniel P. Moynihan. *The Washington Post*, Nov. 25, 1990.

26. If we take the route of the permanent handout, the American character will itself be impoverished.
Richard M. Nixon, 37th President of the United States (R-CA). Comment on welfare reform. Speech, Aug. 8, 1969.

27. The people who work for a living don't need government.
Robert Novak, American political columnist. ABC, *Money Politics*, Apr. 15, 1990.

28. Charity separates the rich from the poor. Aid raises the needy and sets him on the same level as the rich.
Eva Perón (1919-1952), First Lady of Argentina. Speech, American Congress of Industrial Medicine, Dec. 5, 1949.

29. They *[welfare cheaters]* are no more evil than industrialists using high-powered accountants to avoid taxes.
Philip, Duke of Edinburgh, Prince Consort of Elizabeth II. Interview, BBC, *The Jimmy Young Program*, 1981.

30. In California, with some realistic rules about determining eligibility, we reduced the *[welfare]* rolls by more than three hundred thousand people in three years.
Ronald Reagan, 40th President of the United States (R-CA). Quoted in *U.S. News & World Report*, May 31, 1976.

31. Society is under obligation to provide for the support of all its members either by procuring work for them or by assuring the means of existence for those who are not in condition to work.
Maximilien-François-Marie de Robespierre (1758-1794), French revolutionist. *Déclaration des Droits de l'homme*, Apr. 24, 1793.

32. One curious thing is that I have always seen life personally; that is, my interest or sympathy or indignation is not aroused by an abstract cause but by the plight of a single person whom I have seen with my own eyes. Out of my response to an individual develops an awareness of a problem to the community, then to the country, and finally to the world.
Anna Eleanor Roosevelt (1884-1962), First Lady and U.S. Delegate to the United Nations. *Autobiography*, 1961.

33. One of these duties of the State is that of caring for those of the citizens who find themselves the victims of such adverse circumstances as to make them unable to obtain even the necessities of mere existence.... To those unfortunate citizens aid must be extended by government, not as a matter of charity, but as a matter of social duty.
Franklin D. Roosevelt (1882-1945), 32nd President of the United States (D-NY). Address, New York State Legislature, Aug. 1931.

34. Now this is a pension program. It isn't welfare, is it?
Franklin D. Roosevelt. Remark while signing the Social Security bill into law, 1935.

35. Both egoism and altruism are necessary to welfare. Both are moral motives. Right living is the balance between them.

Herbert L. Samuel, 1st Viscount Samuel (1870-1963), Home Secretary, Great Britain, and 1st High Commissioner to Palestine (Liberal). *Belief and Action,* 1937.

36. Compassion is not measured by how many people are on food stamps.

Patricia R. Schroeder, U.S. Congresswoman (D-CO). PBS, *Firing Line,* Oct. 9, 1988.

37. Nobody who has wealth to distribute ever omits himself.

Leon Trotsky (1879-1940), Russian revolutionary theorist. Attributed.

38. Children and dogs are as necessary to the welfare of this country as Wall Street and the railroads.

Harry S Truman (1884-1972), 33rd President of the United States (D-MO). Speech, National Conference on Family Life, May 6, 1948.

39. All communities are apt to look to government for far too much. Even in our own country ... we are prone to do so, especially at periods of distress. But this ought not to be.

Martin Van Buren (1782-1862), 8th President of the United States (D-NY). Message, special session of Congress on the Panic of 1837, Sept. 4, 1837.

40. Work saves us from three great evils: boredom, vice and need.

Voltaire (François-Marie Arouet) (1694-1778), French historian and dramatist. *Candide,* 1759.

41. Ours is become a nation too great to offend the least, too mighty to be unjust to the weakest, too lofty and noble to be ungenerous to the poorest and lowliest.

Stephen S. Wise (1874-1949), American rabbi. Speech, July 4, 1905.

Author Index

Index references are to chapter and quotation numbers, not to page numbers. Thus, **61:215** refers to quotation number 215 of Chapter 61.

A

B

C

D

E

F

H

I

J

K

L

M

N

Q

R

S

T

U

V

W

X

Y

Z

Anonymous

Concept Index

Index references are to chapter and quotation numbers, not to page numbers. Thus, **61:215** refers to quotation number 215 of Chapter 61.

A

B

C

D

F

G

H

I

J

M

N

O

P

Q

R

S

T

U

V

W

Z